THE Good Food Guide 1998

WHICH? BOOKS

Which? Books is the book publishing arm of Consumers' Association, which was set up in 1957 to improve the standards of goods and services available to the public. Everything Which? publishes aims to help consumers, by giving them the independent information they need to make informed decisions. These publications, known throughout Britain for their quality, integrity and impartiality, have been held in high regard for four decades.

Independence does not come cheap: the guides carry no advertising, and no restaurant or hotel can buy an entry in our guides, or treat our inspectors to free meals or accommodation. This policy, and our practice of rigorously re-researching our guides for each edition, helps us to provide our readers with information of a standard and quality that cannot be surpassed.

THE
Good Food Guide 1998

Edited by Jim Ainsworth

CONSUMERS' ASSOCIATION

Which? Books are commissioned and researched by Consumers' Association and published by Which? Ltd, 2 Marylebone Road, London NW1 4DF

Distributed by The Penguin Group: Penguin Books Ltd, 27 Wrights Lane, London W8 5TZ

British Library Cataloguing in Publication Data
A catalogue record for this book is available from the British Library

ISBN 0 85202 663 3

Photoset by Tradespools Ltd, Frome, Somerset
Printed in England by Clays Ltd, St Ives plc

Cover photograph by ACE Photo Agency/Peter O'Keefe
Cover design by Paul Saunders
Typographic design by Tim Higgins

Contents

To all readers

The Good Food Guide is your guide. It is independent, takes no free meals, inducements or advertising, and reflects the experience of thousands of consumers in restaurants throughout the land. It is not a self-appointed arbiter of hide-bound gastronomic taste. It reports on real experiences by real people in search of nourishment, pleasure or celebration.

As a purchaser of this *Guide*, you are part of a huge network of correspondents, and you are a member of the Good Food Club. Please help other readers by recounting your own experiences to us.

There is a form at the back of this book (just before the maps); you can ask for more report forms from the *Guide* office; the address is FREEPOST, so you do not have to use a stamp. Or email your report to: *guidereports@which.co.uk*. Every letter or email received is one more brick in the edifice of next year's *Guide*.

The *Guide* online

If you have access to the Internet, you can find *The Good Food Guide* online at the Which? Online web site (http://www.which.net). Every entry in the *Guide*, including those in the Round-up sections, can be accessed via your computer. In addition, the online version has a searchable map: just click on the area you wish to visit, where you will see any recommended establishments in the vicinity, and then you can go straight to their full entries. The online version also has a text-search tool, so if you are looking for restaurants where, for example, mussels and chips are mentioned in the narrative, you can find them in seconds. For a free CD which gives you more details about Which? Online and how to be connected to the Internet, phone 0345 300 190 (quoting JOGF 97).

Telephone update service

Readers with a touch-tone telephone can use a 24-hour information service giving details of restaurant sales, closures, chef changes and so on, since this edition of the *Guide* was published. This service for the 1998 edition will be available from 1 December 1997 to 1 May 1998. Telephone (0171) 830 7575 to hear the latest information, or to leave a message.

How to use the *Guide*

FINDING A RESTAURANT

If you are seeking a restaurant in a particular area: *First go to the maps* at the back of the book. Localities where *Good Food Guide* restaurants can be found are indicated on the maps (the London maps give the name of the restaurant). Once you know the locality (or, for London, the restaurant name), go to the relevant section of the book to find the entry for the restaurant. The *Guide*'s main entries are divided into eight sections: London, England, Scotland, Wales, Channel Islands, Isle of Man, Northern Ireland, and Republic of Ireland. In the London section, restaurants are listed alphabetically by name; in all other sections, they are listed by locality (usually the name of the town or village).

In addition to the main entries are the Round-ups (a range of restaurants, cafés, bistros and pubs that are worth a visit but do not merit a full entry): those for London can be found just after the London main-entry section, and those for everywhere else are towards the back of the book just after the Republic of Ireland main-entry section.

If you know the name of the restaurant: *Go to the index* at the back of the book, which lists both main and Round-up entries.

If you are seeking award-winning restaurants, those offering a particular cuisine, etc.: *Make use of the lists* starting on page 12. They will tell you the Top-Rated Restaurants, Restaurants with Outstanding Wine Cellars, Restaurants of the Year, New Entries in the *Guide*, Closures (since the last edition), London Restaurants by Cuisine, London Party Bookings, and Budget Eating (including this year for the first time restaurants with exceptionally good-value lunches). There is also a list of restaurants that include a service charge on their bill but have not confirmed that they close credit card slips.

HOW TO READ A GUIDE *ENTRY*

A sample entry is set out overleaf. At the top of the entry you will find the restaurant's name, map number, address, telephone and fax numbers, any symbols that may apply to the establishment, the mark awarded by the Editor for cooking, and the cost range for a three-course meal. (Full explanations of symbols, the cooking mark and the cost range follow the sample entry.) The middle part of the entry describes food, wines, atmosphere and so on, while the final section gives a wealth of additional information (explained in greater detail on pages 10-11).

LOCALITY County map 4

▲ *Restaurant Name* 🍷 🍾 £ [£] **NEW ENTRY**

Address COOKING **6**

TEL: (01234) 111111 FAX: (01234) 222222 COST £15 to £100

This is where you will find information about the restaurant – cuisine, service, décor, wine list, and any other points of interest not covered by the details at the foot of the entry. Each entry in the *Guide* has been re-researched from scratch, and is based on information taken from readers' reports received over the past year, confirmed where necessary by anonymous inspection. In every case, readers and inspectors have been prepared to endorse the quality of the cooking.

Restaurants that receive a wine award (see explanation of 'glass' and 'bottle' symbols below) conclude with a CELLARMAN'S CHOICE. These wines are usually more expensive than the house wines, but are recommended by the restaurant as particularly suitable for the kind of food it serves.

CHEFS: John and Mary Smith PROPRIETOR: Mary Smith OPEN: Mon to Fri L 12 to 2, Mon to Sat D 7 to 10 CLOSED: 25 and 26 Dec, Easter, 2 weeks July, bank hols MEALS: alc (main courses £9 to £15). Set D £16 (2 courses) to £20. Cover £1.50. Light L available. BYO £5 SERVICE: not inc, card slips closed; 10% for parties of 6 or more CARDS: Amex, Delta, Diners, MasterCard, Switch, Visa DETAILS: 50 seats. 15 seats outside. Private parties: 25 main room, 15 private room. Car park. Vegetarian meals. Children's helpings. No children under 7. Jacket and tie. No smoking in dining-room. Wheelchair access (also WC). No music. Air-conditioned ACCOMMODATION: 5 rooms, all with bath/shower. TV. Phone. Air-conditioned. B&B £35 to £80. Deposit: £20. Rooms for disabled. Children welcome. Baby facilities. Dogs welcome. Afternoon teas. Garden. Swimming-pool. (*The Which? Hotel Guide*)

Explanation of symbols

▲ accommodation is available.

🍷 the wine list is well above average.

🍾 the restaurant has a truly outstanding wine cellar.

the chef has changed since last year's entry, and the Editor has judged that the change is of sufficient interest to merit the reader's attention. See also explanation of NEW CHEF on page 9.

smoking is banned either throughout the whole restaurant, or at least in one separate dining-room. The symbol is not given if the restaurant has only a no-smoking area, although this information is given in the details at the end of the entry. An establishment that does not allow smoking in the dining-room may allow it elsewhere, such as in a bar or lounge. If you are a smoker, it is always worth telephoning in advance to check.

£ it is possible to have a three-course meal, including coffee, half a bottle of house wine and service, for £25 or less per person, at *any* time the restaurant is open, i.e. at dinner as well as lunch. It may be possible to spend considerably more than this, but by choosing carefully you should find £25 or less achievable.

£ it is possible to have a two-course lunch, including a glass of house wine, coffee and service, for £12 or less per person, *in addition* to fulfilling the criteria for three-course budget meals described just above.

NEW ENTRY appears after the restaurant's name if the establishment was not a main entry in last year's *Guide*, although it may have been a Round-up or appeared in previous editions.

Cooking mark

This year the *Guide* has a new rating system. Marks are given out of 10, rather than out of 5 as previously. The marks are for cooking only, as perceived by the *Guide* and its readers. They signify the following:

1–2 COMPETENT COOKING Cafés, pubs, bistros and restaurants which offer sound, basic, competent cooking. Those scoring 2 use better ingredients, take fewer short-cuts, please more reporters, and make good neighbourhood restaurants.

3–4 COMPETENT TO GOOD COOKING These restaurants use fine ingredients and cook them appropriately, although some inconsistencies may be noted. They please reporters most of the time. Those scoring 4 show greater skill in handling materials, and are worthy of special note in the locality.

5–6 GOOD TO VERY GOOD COOKING These restaurants use high-quality ingredients, achieve consistently good results, and are enthusiastically reported. Those scoring 6 show a degree of flair, and are among the best in the region.

7–8 VERY GOOD TO EXCELLENT COOKING A high level of ambition and achievement means that the finest ingredients are consistently treated with skill and imagination. Those scoring 8 are worth a special effort to visit.

9–10 THE BEST These are the top restaurants in the country. They are few in number, and can be expensive, but are highly individual and display impressive artistry. Those scoring 10 are the A-team, and can comfortably stand comparison with the stiffest international competition.

NEW CHEF is indicated instead of a cooking mark if there was a change of chef as we were going to press, too late for inspection. (See also the explanation of [symbol] on page 8.)

Cost

The price range given is based on the cost of a three-course meal (lunch and/or dinner) for one person, including coffee, house wine, service and cover charge where applicable, according to information supplied by the restaurant. The lower figure is the least you are likely to pay, from either à la carte or set-price menus, and may apply only to lunch. The higher figure indicates a probable maximum cost, sometimes based on a set-price meal of more than three courses, if that is what is offered. This figure is inflated by 20 per cent to reflect that some people may order more expensive wine, extra drinks and some higher-priced 'special' dishes, and that price rises may come into effect during the life-time of this edition of the *Guide*. It may still be possible to exceed this top figure in some restaurants.

Meals

At the bottom of entries information on the types of meals offered is given, with any variations for lunch (L) and dinner (D), and details of availability. An à la carte menu is signified by the letters *alc*. This is followed by a range of prices for main courses, rounded up to the nearest 50p. *Set L* denotes a set-price lunch; *Set D* means set-price dinner. Set meals usually consist of three courses, but can include many more. If a set meal has fewer than three courses, this is stated. If there is a cover charge, this is also indicated. *BYO* signifies that you may bring your own bottle of wine, and the corkage charge (if any) is given.

Service

Net prices means that prices of food and wine are inclusive of service charge, and this is indicated clearly on the menu and bill; *not inc*, that service is not included and is left to the discretion of the customer; *10%*, that a fixed service charge of 10 per cent is automatically added to the bill; *10% (optional)*, that 10 per cent is added to the bill along with the word 'optional' or similar qualifier; and *none*, that no service charge is made or expected and that any money offered is refused. *Card slips closed* indicates that the total on the slips of credit cards is closed when handed over for signature.

Other details

Information is also given on *seating*, *seating outside* and *private parties*. We say *car park* if the restaurant provides free parking facilities for patrons;

vegetarian meals only if menus list at least one vegetarian option as a starter and one as a main course (if this is not noted, a restaurant may still be able to offer vegetarian options with prior notice – it is worth phoning to check); *children welcome* if there are no particular restrictions on children, and *children's helpings* if smaller portions are available at a reduced price; *jacket and tie* if it is compulsory for men to wear a jacket and tie to the restaurant; *wheelchair access* if the proprietor has confirmed that the entrance is at least 80cm wide and passages at least 120cm wide in accordance with the Royal Association for Disability and Rehabilitation (RADAR) recommendations, and *also WC* if the proprietor has assured us that toilet facilities are suitable for disabled people (*no WC* means these are not available or the proprietor is not sure). *Music* indicates that live or recorded music is played in the dining-room at least some of the time; *no music* that it never is.

Accommodation

For establishments offering overnight accommodation, the number of rooms, along with facilities provided in the rooms (e.g. bath/shower, TV, phone, air-conditioning), is set out. Prices are given usually for bed and breakfast (*B&B*). *D,B&B* indicates that the price also includes dinner. The first figure given is the lowest price for one person in a single room, or single occupancy of a double, the second is the most expensive price for two people in a double room or suite. *Rooms for disabled* means the establishment has stated that its accommodation is suitable for wheelchair-users. Restrictions for children and dogs, and facilities for guests with babies, are noted. *Afternoon tea* means the hotel offers teas to non-residents. *The Which? Hotel Guide* means the establishment is also listed in the 1998 edition of our sister guide to over 1,000 hotels in Britain.

The top-rated restaurants

(See inside front cover for explanation of new marking system.)

Mark **10** for cooking

London
Chez Nico at
Ninety Park Lane, W1
La Tante Claire, SW3

Scotland
Altnaharrie Inn, Ullapool

Mark **9** for cooking

London
Aubergine, SW10

England
Gidleigh Park, Chagford
Waterside Inn, Bray

Mark **8** for cooking

London
The Capital, SW3

England
Box Tree, Ilkley
Castle Hotel, Taunton
Chester Grosvenor Hotel, Arkle, Chester
Cliveden, Waldo's, Taplow
Croque-en-Bouche, Malvern Wells
Fat Duck, Bray
Fischer's Baslow Hall, Baslow
Gordleton Mill Hotel, Provence, Lymington
Hambleton Hall, Hambleton
Lettonie, Bristol
Le Manoir aux Quat' Saisons, Great Milton
Merchant House, Ludlow
21 Queen Street, Newcastle upon Tyne
Winteringham Fields, Winteringham

Scotland
La Potinière, Gullane

Wales
Walnut Tree Inn, Llandewi Skirrid

Restaurants with outstanding wine cellars

marked in the text with a 🍷

London
Au Jardin des Gourmets, W1
Bibendum, SW3
Clarke's, W8
Fifth Floor, SW1
Leith's, W11
Odette's, NW1
Le Pont de la Tour, SE1
Ransome's Dock, SW11
RSJ, SE1
Tate Gallery Restaurant, SW1

England
Adlard's, Norwich
Angel Inn, Hetton
Bowlish House, Shepton Mallet
Buckland Manor, Buckland
La Cachette, Elland
Carved Angel, Dartmouth
Cherwell Boathouse, Oxford
Chewton Glen, Marryat Restaurant, New Milton
Cobwebs, Leck
Corse Lawn House, Corse Lawn
Croque-en-Bouche, Malvern Wells
The Crown, Southwold
Epworth Tap, Epworth
Evesham Hotel, Evesham
French Partridge, Horton
Gidleigh Park, Chagford
Gravetye Manor, East Grinstead
Hambleton Hall, Hambleton
Harveys, Bristol
Hotel du Vin & Bistro, Winchester
Le Manoir aux Quat'Saisons, Great Milton
Michael's Nook, Grasmere
Old Beams, Waterhouses
Old Manor House, Romsey
Old Vicarage, Ridgeway
Old Vicarage, Witherslack
Pheasant Inn, Keyston
Pheasants, Ross-on-Wye
Porthole Eating House, Bowness-on-Windemere
Priory Hotel, Wareham
Read's, Faversham
Röser's, Hastings
Seafood Restaurant, Padstow
Sharrow Bay, Ullswater
Sir Charles Napier, Chinnor
Sous le Nez en Ville, Leeds
Summer Lodge, Evershot
Le Talbooth, Dedham
Three Horseshoes, Madingley
Village Restaurant, Ramsbottom
Waterford House, Middleham
White Hart, Great Yeldham
White Horse Inn, Chilgrove
White House, Williton
White Moss House, Grasmere

Scotland
Airds Hotel, Port Appin
Altnaharrie Inn, Ullapool
Braeval, Aberfoyle
Cellar, Anstruther
Champany Inn, Linlithgow
Clifton House, Nairn
The Cross, Kingussie
Inverlochy Castle, Fort William
Kinnaird, Dunkeld
Knipoch Hotel, Oban
Peat Inn, Peat Inn
La Potinière, Gullane
Summer Isles Hotel, Achiltibuie
Ubiquitous Chip, Glasgow
Valvona & Crolla Caffè Bar, Edinburgh

Wales
Fairyhill, Reynoldston
Hotel Portmeirion, Portmeirion
Old Rectory, Llansanffraid Glan Conwy
Penhelig Arms Hotel, Aberdovey
Plas Bodegroes, Pwllheli
Walnut Tree Inn, Llandewi Skirrid

Republic of Ireland
Arbutus Lodge, Cork
Le Coq Hardi, Dublin
King Sitric, Howth
Park Hotel, Kenmare
Sheen Falls Lodge, La Cascade, Kenmare
Newport House, Newport

Restaurants of the year

This award does not necessarily go to the restaurants with the highest mark for cooking, but rather to ones which have shown particular merit or achievement during the year, whether as all-rounders or in some particular field. It may go to an old favourite or to a new entry, but in either case the places listed below are worth visiting in their own right, and have enhanced the eating-out experience in some way.

London
Café Japan, NW11
Connaught, W1
Momo, W1
Moro, EC1

England
Blackpool, September Brasserie
Bowness-on-Windermere, Linthwaite House
Brighton, One Paston Place
Carlton, Foresters Arms
Cambridge, Midsummer House
Cumnor, Bear & Ragged Staff
East Grinstead, Gravetye Manor
Emsworth, 36 on the Quay
Evershot, Summer Lodge
Hetton, Angel Inn
Ilkley, Box Tree
Kenilworth, Simpson's
King's Cliffe, King's Cliffe House
Leceister, Heath's
Lifton, Arundell Arms
Long Melford, Scutcher's Bistro
Looe, Trawlers
Melmerby, Village Bakery
Newcastle, Leela's
Paxford, Churchill Arms
Stanton, Leaping Hare Cafe
Swanage, Galley
Taunton, Castle Hotel
Windermere, Miller Howe
Winteringham, Winteringham Fields

Scotland
Aboyne, White Cottage
Bowmore, Harbour Inn
Cupar, Ostlers Close
Edinburgh, Winter Glen
Glasgow, Ubiquitous Chip
Linlithgow, Champany Inn

Wales
Capel Garmon, Tan-y-Foel
Pwllgloyw, Seland Newydd
Talyllyn, Minffordd Hotel
Whitebrook, Crown at Whitebrook

Republic of Ireland
Blacklion, MacNean Bistro

The *Guide's* longest-serving restaurants

The *Guide* has seen many restaurants come and go. Some, however, have stayed the course with tenacity. (Qualification for this list is that the restaurant has been in each edition of the *Guide* subsequent to its first entry.)

Connaught, W1	45 years
Gay Hussar, W1	41 years
Porth Tocyn Hotel, Abersoch	41 years
Gravetye Manor, East Grinstead	37 years
Sharrow Bay, Ullswater	37 years
Dundas Arms, Kintbury	35 years
French Partridge, Horton	33 years
Walnut Tree Inn, Llandewi Skirrid	33 years
Black Bull Inn, Moulton	31 years
Chez Moi, W11	29 years
Rothay Manor, Ambleside	29 years
Sundial, Herstmonceux	29 years
Le Gavroche, W1	28 years
Summer Isles Hotel, Achiltibuie	28 years
The Capital, SW3	27 years
Miller Howe, Windermere	27 years
Cringletie House, Peebles	26 years
Old Fire Engine House, Ely	26 years
Ubiquitous Chip, Glasgow	26 years
Peat Inn, Peat Inn	25 years
Plumber Manor, Sturminster Newton	25 years
Druidstone, Broad Haven	25 years
Waterside Inn, Bray	25 years
White Moss House, Grasmere	25 years
Carved Angel, Dartmouth	24 years
Isle of Eriska, Eriska	24 years
Old Woolhouse, Northleach	23 years
Airds, Port Appin	22 years
La Potinière, Gullane	22 years
Stane Street Hollow, Pulborough	22 years
Blostin's, Shepton Mallet	21 years
Farlam Hall, Brampton	21 years

New entries

These restaurants are new to the *Guide* this year, although some may have appeared in previous years, or in the Round-ups last year.

London

Agadir, W2
Anonimato, W11
Assaggi, W2
Balzac Bistro, W12
Bank, WC2
Belair House, SE21
Bistrot Soho, W1
Bluebird, SW3
Byron's, NW3
Café Spice Namaste, E1
Cambio de Tercio, SW5
Chavot, SW3
Chelsea Hotel, Chelsea Restaurant, SW1
Chutney Mary, SW10
La Ciboulette, SW3
Cicada, EC1
City Rhodes, EC4
Cow Dining Room, W2
Crescent, W1
Delfina, SE1
Gabriel, W1
Helter Skelter, SW9
Hempel, I-Thai, W2
Istanbul Iskembecisi, N16
Justin de Blank, W1
Lola's, N1
Misato, W1
Momo, W1
Moro, EC1
MPW, E14
Nobu, W1
Novelli W8, W8
Oxo Tower, SE1
Putney Bridge, SW15
Quo Vadis, W1
Redmond's, SW14
755 Fulham Road, SW6
Sotheby's Café, W1
The Square, W1
Stephen Bull St Martin's Lane, WC2
Sushi-Say, NW2
White Onion, N1
Yo! Sushi, W1
Zujuma's, SW19

England

Amersham, Gilbey's
Ardington, Boars Head
Ashburton, Holne Chase
Bakewell, Renaissance
Bath, Moody Goose
Blakeney, White Horse Hotel
Broxton, Frogg Manor
Burpham, George and Dragon
Cambridge, Midsummer House
Canterbury, Canterbury Hotel, La Bonne Cuisine
Caunton, Caunton Beck
Clanfield, Clanfield Tavern
Dartmouth, Aragua
Dartmouth, Cutter's Bunch
Emsworth, 36 on the Quay
Farnborough, Chapter One
Ferrensby, General Tarleton
Foulsham, The Gamp
Grange in Borrowdale, Borrowdale Gates
Hampton Hill, Monsieur Max
Harome, Star Inn
Horndon on the Hill, Bell Inn
Hovingham, Worsley Arms, The Restaurant
Ipswich, Scott's Brasserie
Leeds, Fourth Floor
Leeds, Salvo's
Leicester, Heath's
Looe, Trawlers
Manchester, Colony
Manchester, Mash and Air
Manchester, Simply Heathcotes
Middleham, Waterford House
Newcastle upon Tyne, Metropolitan
Oxford, Lemon Tree
Oxford, White House
Paxford, Churchill Arms
Portloe, Tregain
St Ives, Hunters
St Martin's, St Martin's Hotel
Scarborough, Lanterna
Shepton Mallet, Charlton House Hotel
Snape, Crown Inn
Southall, Lahore Karahi & Tandoori
South Molton, Whitechapel Manor
Ware, Riverside Cafe
Wembley, Sakonis
Winsford, Savery's at Karslake House

Scotland

Aberdeen, Q Brasserie
Aboyne, White Cottage
Archiestown, Archiestown Hotel
Bowmore, Harbour Inn
Edinburgh, Fishers Bistro
Edinburgh, Haldanes
Edinburgh, Skippers
Edinburgh, Winter Glen
Glasgow, Splash
Spean Bridge, Old Pines
Stonehaven, Tolbooth
Turriff, Fife Arms

Wales

Bassaleg, Junction 28
Hay-on-Wye, Nino's
Llanarmon Dyffryn Ceiriog, West Arms
Llandeilo, Cawdor Arms Hotel
Llyswen, Griffin Inn
Pembroke, Left Bank
Pwllgloyw, Seland Newydd

Northern Ireland

Belfast, Deane's

Republic of Ireland

Blacklion, MacNean Bistro
Dublin, The Clarence, Tea Room
Kinvara, Merriman

Closures

Whatever happended to that restaurant? Those listed below have closed since the last edition of the *Guide*, though one or two may still be open under new owners or have re-opened under a different name.

London

All Saints, W11
B Square, SW11
Chiaroscuro, WC1
Exxo, W1
Le Mesurier, EC1
Tabac, W10
La Truffe Noire, SE1
Waltons, SW3

England

Brimfield, Roebuck, Poppies
Cheltenham, Staithes
Darlington, Victor's
Frampton on Severn, Saverys
Holdenby, Lynton House
Northampton, Le Sous-Sol
Powburn, Breamish House
Oxford, 15 North Parade
Stonham, Mr Underhill's
Dorking, Partners West Street
North Cheam, Partners Brasserie
Stratford-upon-Avon, Liaison
Semington, Highfield House

Scotland

Auchencairn, Collin House
Edinburgh, Rendezvous
Kinloch Rannoch, Cuilmore Cottage

Wales

Brechfa, Tŷ Mawr
Freystrop, Jemima's
Llanwrda, Seguendo di Stagioni

Northern Ireland

Helen's Bay, Deanes on the Square

Republic of Ireland

Cork, Clifford's

London restaurants by cuisine

Boundaries between some national cuisines – British, French and Italian particularly – are not as marked as they used to be. Therefore, the restaurants listed below are classified by the predominant influence, although there may be some crossover.

American
Bradleys, NW3
Christopher's, WC2
Montana, SW6

Belgian
Belgo Noord, NW1

British
Alfred, WC2
Butlers Wharf Chop House, SE1
City Rhodes, EC4
Connaught, W1
Dorchester, Grill Room, W1
English Garden, SW3
French House Dining Room, W1
Greenhouse, W1
Quality Chop House, EC1
Rules, WC2
St John, EC1
The Savoy, Grill Room, WC2
Tate Gallery Restaurant, SW1
Wilsons, W14
Wiltons, SW1

Chinese
Cheng-Du, NW1
Dorchester, Oriental, W1
Fung Shing, WC2
Golden Dragon, W1
Mandarin Kitchen, W2
Mr Kong, WC2
Poons, WC2
Royal China, W2
Vegetarian Cottage, NW3
Zen Central, W1

Fish
Brady's, SW18
Café Fish, SW1
Livebait, SE1
Lobster Pot, SE11
Lou Pescadou, SW5
Le Suquet, SW3
Two Brothers, N3
Upper Street Fish Shop, N1

French
Alexandra, SW20
Les Associés, N8
Aubergine, SW10
Au Jardin des Gourmets, W1
Balzac Bistro, W12
Brasserie St Quentin, SW3
Chavot, SW3
Chez Nico at Ninety Park Lane, W1
La Ciboulette, SW3
Criterion Brasserie, W1
La Dordogne, W4
L'Estaminet, WC2
Le Gavroche, W1
Inter-Continental Hotel, Le Soufflé, W1
Interlude, W1
Le Meridien, Oak Room Marco Pierre White, W1
Mon Plaisir, WC2
L'Oranger, SW1
Le P'tit Normand, SW18
Pied-à-Terre, W1
Les Saveurs, W1
755 Fulham Road, SW6
La Tante Claire, SW3
Village Bistro, N6

Greek
Daphne, NW1
Kalamaras, W2

Hungarian
Gay Hussar, W1

Indian/Pakistani
Café Spice Namaste, E1
Chutney Mary, SW10
Great Nepalese, NW1
Lahore Kebab House, E1
Mirch Masala, SW16
Ragam, W1
Salloos, SW1
Tamarind, W1
Zujuma's, SW19

Indian vegetarian
Kastoori, SW17
Rani, N3
Rasa, N16
Sabras, NW10
Sree Krishna, SW17

Indonesian/ Straits
Gourmet Garden, NW4
Melati, W1
Singapore Garden, NW6

Italian
Alba, EC1
Al San Vincenzo, W2
Assaggi, W2
Bertorelli's, WC1 and W1
Billboard Cafe, NW6
Cantina del Ponte, SE1
Como Lario, SW1
Daphne's, SW3
Del Buongustaio, SW15
Green Olive, W9
Halkin Hotel, SW1
L'Incontro, SW1
Neal Street Restaurant, WC2
Olivo, SW1
Orsino, W11
Orso, WC2
Osteria Antica Bologna, SW11
Osteria Basilico, W11
Red Pepper, W9
Riva, SW13
River Café, W6
Zafferano, SW1

Japanese
Café Japan, NW11
Inaho, W2
Matsuri, SW1
Misato, W1
Mitsukoshi, SW1
Miyama, W1
Moshi Moshi Sushi, EC2 and EC4
Nobu, W1
Saga, W1

Suntory, SW1
Sushi-Say, NW2
Tatsuso, EC2
Tokyo Diner, WC2
Wagamama, WC1
Yo! Sushi, W1

Korean

Bu San, N7

Mauritian

Chez Liline, N4

North African/ Middle Eastern

Adams Café, W12
Agadir, W2
Al Bustan, SW1
Al Hamra, W1
Istanbul Iskembecisi, N16
Iznik, N5
Laurent, NW2
Momo, W1

Spanish

Cambio de Tercio, SW5
Moro, EC1

Thai

Bahn Thai, W1
Blue Elephant, SW6
Mantanah, SE25
Sri Siam, W1
Thai Bistro, W4
Thai Garden, E2
Thailand, SE14

London party bookings for 25 or more in private rooms

Agadir, W2
Alba, EC1
Alexandra, SW20
Atlantic Bar and Grill, W1
Bahn Thai, W1
Balzac Bistro, W12
Bertorelli's (Charlotte Street), W1
Café du Jardin, WC2
Café Nico, W1
Cambio de Tercio, SW5
Chelsea Hotel, Chelsea Restaurant, SW1
Chinon, W14
Christopher's, WC2
Chutney Mary, SW10
Cicada, EC1
Claridge's, W1
Crescent, W1
Delfina, SE1
La Dordogne, W4
L'Escargot, W1
Fire Station, SE1
First Floor, W11
Fung Shing, WC2
Gabriel, W1
Golden Dragon, W1
Green Olive, W9
Halkin Hotel, SW1
Hempel, I-Thai, W2
Hilaire, SW7
L'Incontro, SW1
Ivy, WC2
Justin de Blank, W1
Kalamaras, W2
Lanesborough, SW1
Lansdowne, NW1
Launceston Place, W8
Leith's, W11
Lou Pescadou, SW5
Maison Novelli, EC1
Melati, W1
Mr Kong, WC2
Mitsukoshi, SW1
Mon Plaisir, WC2
MPW, E14
Noughts 'n' Crosses, W5
Orsino, W11
Quaglino's, SW1
RSJ, SE1
Rules, WC2
The Savoy, River Restaurant, WC2
755 Fulham Road, SW6
Singapore Garden, NW6
Snows on the Green, W6
Soho Soho, W1
Sree Krishna, SW17
Sri Siam, W1
33, SW1
Village Bistro, N6

Budget eating I

At the restaurants listed below, it is possible to have a **two-course lunch** (at all lunch sessions), including a glass of house wine, coffee and service, for £12 or less per person. In addition, a **three-course meal** at such establishments – including a half-bottle of house wine, service and coffee – is available at all meal sessions for less than £25 (although some meal options may cost more than this).

London

Anglesea Arms, W6
Bu-San, N7
Daphne, NW1
Istanbul Iskembecisi, N16
Kastoori, SW17
Lahore Kebab House, E1
Mirch Masala, SW16
Misato, W1
Mr Kong, WC2
Moshi Moshi Sushi, E2 and EC4
Ragam, W1
Rani, N3
Rasa, N16
Sree Krishna, SW17
Thai Garden, E2
Tokyo Diner, WC2
Upper Street Fish Shop, N1
Wagamama, WC1

England

Durham, Bistro 21
Huddersfield, Bradley's
Liskeard, Bacchus Bistro
Liverpool, Far East
Liversedge, Healds Hall Hotel
Manchester, Koreana
Manchester, Pearl City
Mawgan, Yard Bistro
Newcastle upon Tyne, Metropolitan
Paxford, Churchill Arms
Shelf, Bentley's
Southall, Brilliant
Southall, Lahore Karahi & Tandoori
Sudbury, Red Onion Bistro
Thornton Cleveleys, Didier's
Wembley, Sakonis
Winchester, Wykeham Arms
Windermere, Miller Howe Café

Scotland

Auchmithie, But 'n' Ben
Bowmore, Harbour Inn
Edinburgh, Kalpna
Edinburgh, Siam Erawan
Glasgow, Café Gandolfi
Kinlochmoidart, Kinacarra
Milngavie, Gingerhill
Stein, Lochbay

Wales

Cardiff, La Brasserie
Cardiff, Champers
Creigiau, Caesar's Arms
Llanfihangel nant Melan, Red Lion Inn
Newport, Cnapan
Rosebush, Tate's at Tafarn Newydd
Swansea, La Braseria
Trefriw, Chandler's

Northern Ireland

Belfast, La Belle Epoque

Republic of Ireland

Cork, Crawford Gallery Café

Budget eating II

£

At the restaurants below, it is possible to have a **three-course meal**, including coffee, half a bottle of house wine and service, for £25 or less per person, at any time the restaurant is open, i.e. at dinner as well as lunch. It may be possible to spend considerably more than this, but by choosing carefully you should find £25 or less achievable.

London

Adams Café, W12
Agadir, W2
Andrew Edmunds, W1
Balzac Bistro, W12
Belgo Noord, NW1
Billboard Cafe, NW6
Brackenbury, W6
Brady's, SW18
Café Japan, NW11
Cheng-Du, NW1
Chez Liline, N4
Chiswick, W4
Crescent, W1
Cucina, NW3
Del Buongustaio, SW15
Eagle, EC1
Fire Station, SE1
Golden Dragon, W1
Gourmet Garden, NW4
Great Nepalese, NW1
Helter Skelter, SW9
Inaho, W2
Iznik, N5
Justin de Blank, W1
Kalamaras, W2
Lansdowne, NW1
Laurent, NW2
Mandarin Kitchen, W2
Mantanah, SE25

Moro, EC1
Osteria Antica Bologna, SW11
Osteria Basilico, W11
Poons, WC2
Red Pepper, W9
RSJ, SE1
Sabras, NW10
Thailand, SE14
Two Brothers, N3
Vegetarian Cottage, NW3

England

Aldeburgh, Lighthouse
Aldeburgh, Regatta
Ambleside, Glass House
Amersham, Gilbey's
Barton-upon-Humber, Elio's
Bath, No. 5 Bistro
Beckingham, Black Swan
Birmingham, Chung Ying
Birmingham, Maharaja
Birtle, Normandie
Blakeney, White Horse Hotel
Bristol, Melbournes
Bristol, Muset
Buckland, Lamb Inn
Burnham Market, Fishes'
Bury St Edmunds, Mortimer's
Carlton, Foresters Arms
Cartmel, Aynsome Manor
Castle Cary, Bond's
Caunton, Caunton Beck
Clanfield, Clanfield Tavern
Cockermouth, Quince & Medlar
Colchester, Warehouse Brasserie
Corscombe, Fox Inn
Crosthwaite, Punch Bowl
Cumnor, Bear & Ragged Staff
Darlington, Cottage Thai
Denmead, Barnard's
Diss, Weaver's Wine Bar & Eating House
East Witton, Blue Lion
Elland, La Cachette
Epworth, Epworth Tap
Exeter, St Olave's Court Hotel
Folkestone, Paul's
Foulsham, The Gamp
Great Yeldham, White Hart
Harrogate, La Bergerie
Harrogate, Grundy's
Haworth, Weaver's
Huddersfield, Café Pacific
Ipswich, Mortimer's on the Quay
Ipswich, Scott's Brasserie
Knutsford, Belle Epoque Brasserie
Leamington Spa, Lansdowne
Leeds, Leodis
Leeds, Salvo's
Leeds, Sous le Nez en Ville
Leicester, Heath's
Lidgate, Star Inn
Lincoln, Wig & Mitre
Looe, Trawlers
Manchester, Chiang Rai
Manchester, Colony
Manchester, Kosmos Taverna
Manchester, Lime Tree
Manchester, Little Yang Sing
Manchester, Tai Pan
Manchester, That Café
Masham, Floodlite
Melmerby, Village Bakery
Nayland, White Hart
Oxford, Al-Shami
Plumtree, Perkins
Ponteland, Café 21
Portloe, Tregain
Richmond, Chez Lindsay
Rye, Landgate Bistro
Sale, Hanni's
Saxton, Plough Inn
Scarborough, Lanterna
Snape, Crown Inn
Staithes, Endeavour
Stanton, Leaping Hare Café
Stoke Holy Cross, Wildebeest Arms
Stokesley, Chapters
Tadcaster, Singers
Trusham, Cridford Inn
West Bay, Riverside
Whitby, Magpie Café
Winkleigh, Pophams
Yarm, D. P. Chadwick's

Scotland

Archiestown, Archiestown Hotel
Cairndow, Loch Fyne Oyster Bar
Canonbie, Riverside Inn
Edinburgh, Fishers Bistro
Edinburgh, Shore
Edinburgh, Silvio's
Edinburgh, Valvona & Crolla Caffè Bar
Glasgow, Mitchells
Glasgow, Mitchells West End
Glasgow, La Parmigiana
Glasgow, Splash
Kylesku, Kylesku Hotel
Perth, Let's Eat

Wales

Broad Haven, Druidstone
Cardiff, Armless Dragon
Cardiff, Le Monde
Crickhowell, Nantyffin Cider Mill Inn
Forden, Edderton Hall
Hay-on-Wye, Nino's
Llyswen, Griffin Inn
Mathry, Ann FitzGerald's Farmhouse Kitchen
Rossett, Churtons

Isle of Man

Douglas, L'Expérience

Northern Ireland

Belfast, Strand
Portrush, Ramore

Credit card checklist

The *Guide* asks restaurants to indicate whether or not service is included in their prices, and this information appears in the details below each entry. They are also asked whether or not they close credit card slips. The following restaurants, which include a charge for service in the total bill, either leave the credit card slip open, or have failed to confirm to the *Guide* that they close it. This list may help to save you paying twice for service.

London

Alexandra, SW20
Atelier, W1
Balzac Bistro, W12
Blue Print Café, SE1
Butlers Wharf Chop House, SE1
Cantina del Ponte, SE1
Cheng-du, NW1
La Dordogne, W4
Le Gavroche, W1
Langan's Brasserie, W1
Magno's, WC2
Matsuri, SW1
Mezzo, W1
Mr Kong, WC2
Mitsukoshi, SW1
Miyama, W1
Osteria Basilico, W11
Oxo Tower, SE1
Le Pont de la Tour, SE1
Quaglino's, SW1
Royal China, W2
Saga, W1
Soho Soho, W1
Tamarind, W1
La Tante Claire, SW3

England

Bishopstrow House, Warminster
Croque-en-Bouche, Malvern Wells
Harveys, Bristol
Little Yang Sing, Manchester
Lords of the Manor, Upper Slaughter
Pearl City, Manchester
Pheasants, Ross-on-Wye
Tai Pan, Manchester
Waterside, Bray
Yang Sing, Manchester

Republic of Ireland

Dunworley Cottage, Clonakilty
Ernie's, Dublin
Les Frère Jacques, Dublin
Kapriol, Dublin
Patrick Guilbaud, Dublin
Thorntons, Dublin

Introduction

I rang to book a table in a large London restaurant recently. I wanted to eat on a Friday evening. 'Certainly, sir, what time?' Momentarily fazed by the unexpected choice, I ventured, 'Around 8 o'clock.' 'Certainly, sir. May I take a telephone number?' 'What time do you want the table back?' I asked quickly, suspecting a trap. 'The table is yours for the evening, sir.'

When I arrived my reservation was recognised, I was addressed by name (the one I had booked under), and the staff spoke understandable English. They even knew what was in the dishes. My risotto was cooked to order, the rice perfectly done. There was hardly any truffle oil at all in most of our dishes, and the only cappuccino was coffee. The lamb was pink, the sea bass fresh, and the two came with different sauces. Nobody used a mobile phone. There wasn't a smoker to be seen. Service was included in the price and the credit card slip was closed. The restaurant was called ...

... And then I woke up. It doesn't happen in real life, does it? Bits of it might happen, but getting the whole lot to work at one go is a never-ending quest. For example, properly made risotto takes time and care, which inevitably costs money. Yet hundreds, perhaps thousands, of restaurants continue to try to serve it on the cheap. I have personally eaten dozens of poor examples over the past year: dry ones, greasy ones, stodgy ones, tasteless ones, underdone ones, overcooked ones, made-with-the-wrong-rice ones .... It is so easy for a lazy kitchen to make up a batch, keep it warm, and dole it out when there's an order. And of course that doesn't just go for risotto. Almost any dish in a modern brasserie can be plated and left to keep warm. The chef lines them up, and if your order arrives immediately you get a fresh one; if not, you might get a plate that has been standing around too long.

This helps to explain why we get conflicting reports about the detail in some restaurants: your pink, just-cooked, crisp-skinned duck breast is my grey and tough one. Your sauce is fine, mine has congealed or separated. And we could well have been lunching in the same restaurant on the same day! Well-run kitchens, on the other hand, work within their limitations, offering only dishes they can produce comfortably and accurately. They may not have 18 starters and 15 main courses on the menu, but they cook a more limited range to order.

Then there's the truffle oil. And the cappuccinos. And the new national sport: finding 1,001 uses for black pudding. When will they ever end? And what will the craze be next year? Can't be chicken Kiev or baked Alaska: they're already back. Whatever it is, there's a few bob in it for the man or woman who gets there first. Could it perhaps be beef?

Giving the customers what they want

If there is a silver lining to the various animal health issues over the past couple of years, it is that more restaurants are choosing their supplies with greater care, typically turning to closed herds of grass-fed beef, free-range poultry and organic vegetables. It is a pity that it has taken a crisis to provide the momentum, but only when enough customers (trade or private) insist on humane methods of rearing and proper animal husbandry – by perhaps seeking out properly run small-scale producers of real food – will catastrophes of the kind we have witnessed (BSE in British beef, salmonella in chickens, and so on) begin to decline.

But the restaurant industry in the '90s is nothing if not resourceful and responsive. The resurgence of vigour and excellence that the *Guide* identified last year, and which was taken up by countless newspapers and magazines, continues unabated. There is a lot going on, much of it exciting. Japanese restaurants, for example, seem to have undergone a sea-change, partly by bringing mechanical novelty (automated sushi and drinks trolleys, for example) to bear, and partly by opening up to a wider clientele. They now provide more fun for more people than they have ever done (for a list of Japanese and other London restaurants by cuisine, see page 18). Other cultures are making more of an impact too, not least Indian and Middle Eastern: sometimes in a relatively 'pure' form, but more commonly as ideas and materials for jackdaw British chefs to raid in their restless search for something new.

While we might be excited by the ingenuity and vitality of modern cooking, some reporters have wondered whether there is a danger that it may all merge into a rather anonymous mess: perhaps London is becoming one big restaurant with cloned branches dotted all over the place.

The dilemma is that, on the one hand, we seem to want our food to be constantly re-invented. We soon get tired of yesterday's dishes, and are prepared to descend like flies on any chef who gives a new twist, however small, to the repertoire: deep-fried foie gras with fig and blue cheese risotto? Book me a table! On the other hand, we want individual and distinctive styles. Are we asking too much?

Either way, it seems to be metropolitan chefs, often serving multi-purpose food in multi-purpose outlets, who have established what amounts to a new British tradition. Where once the restaurant initiative came from a couple who holidayed in France, cooked from

Elizabeth David, and opened a country restaurant in order to share the thrills of pink lamb, fresh vegetables and decent wine, now it is the townie chefs who capture for their generation the buzz and excitement of eating out.

The consequences for country restaurants are mixed. They have to suffer the perennial rural problem of couples who only show up to celebrate three anniversaries a year – his, hers and theirs – and who eat out only at weekends. But more and more of them (even country-house restaurants) are waking up to the importance of casual eating, closing off stuffy half-empty dining-rooms that serve fussy and expensive food, and opening bistros that get packed on Tuesday evenings: unheard of before. London is so competitive on price nowadays, and country-house hotels often so expensive, that customers are no longer prepared to tolerate the difference. Even with the easing of recessionary times, native Brits with an eye for a fair deal are easily tempted by a cheaper weekend across the Channel. In addition, foreign tourists certainly find the UK expensive. Unless they change, some posh country-house dinosaurs may soon find themselves extinct.

Business or pressure?

As the standard of food generally improves, reporters increasingly turn their attention to how they feel in a restaurant. They like to be treated well: not surprisingly, given the amount of money that can change hands. From the minute they pick up the phone to book a table, to the arrival of the bill with its obligatory 'optional' service charge, they are sizing up the service.

Among their experiences from this year's files is the strange daytime-only booking procedure at one West End restaurant. A receptionist then spends much of the evening on the phone explaining to callers why she cannot take bookings during the evening, which of course takes far longer than it would to accept the booking in the first place, and doesn't do anything for customer relations. It is a refined form of madness.

Another central London restaurant provides this gem: 'The waiter brought my main course as soon as I put my knife and fork down from the starter. I told him that I was there for a relaxing supper, and he could bring it to me a bit later. He told me that I had had my 20 minutes: if I didn't want it then I would have to wait one and a half hours! I told him I would rather do this, and did.' Now is that crazy or what? Both restaurants, incidentally, are in the *Guide*. It is devoutly to be wished that service is the next area to be improved. Perhaps the rate of restaurant expansion has something to do with the problem. As more mega-restaurants open, pressure on the supply of both kitchen and waiting staff increases, attracting many with no previous experience or training. But that in turn may hardly be surprising: waiting staff at one well-known and prestigious London restaurant (again in the *Guide*) are paid as little as £1 an hour, plus a share of the 'optional' service charge. If and when a minimum wage is introduced, prices at some restaurants are obviously set to rise dramatically – unless of course the owners (some of them millionaires) intend to absorb the costs themselves . . . .

What's the score?

The *Guide*'s new 10-point scoring system for assessing the standard of cooking is summarised inside the front cover, but a few words of explanation for the change may be in order. Scoring began with the 1985 *Guide*, which rated restaurants on a 20-point scale; this changed to a 5-point scale in 1990. Further changes were resisted because it was reasoned that readers had got used to the system and were comfortable with it, despite its extension with asterisks. Originally intended to indicate 'a fine example within its numeric classification', the asterisk came to be thought of as something of a half-mark. Attempts to tidy the whole thing up by doing away with the proliferation of asterisks, however, failed; they obviously served a purpose. The present change is simply designed to rationalise rather than radically alter how cooking marks are awarded. For a brief history of the scoring system, and a more detailed explanation of how the new 10-point scale works, see box on page 28.

An anticipated consequence of the scoring change is that the *Guide* will get a large postbag from disgruntled chefs and proprietors complaining that they had the same cooking mark as so-and-so last year, and now their rival is one point ahead of them. What do we think we are playing at? May I ask them, before they put pen to paper, to re-read the box. I am the first to admit that scoring restaurants on any kind of scale is an inexact science. Readers have different experiences, and chefs have off-days as well as days off. A good number of the chefs and proprietors who write to the *Guide* want to know why their cooking mark is not at least one point higher than it is. They know they can cook better than their mark suggests.

I do not disagree. But I believe they are assessing their optimum performance, while readers and reporters experience the actual, sustained performance of a chef over weeks and months, and thus often see more clearly and honestly than the chef him- or herself. So please, chefs, before you complain about your score, ask yourselves why there should be a discrepancy between what you perceive and what others see. Maybe you will be honest enough to recognise that not every single dish that comes out of your kitchen is the best that you could possibly do. Yet you ask all customers to pay the same, regardless.

It's your vote that counts

If it is any consolation, even inspectors disagree with each other from time to time. Some readers suggest very strongly that a given restaurant should on no account appear in the following edition of the *Guide*, and are then shocked to discover that it is a main entry once again. 'Why did we bother writing?' I can hear them asking. What they do not know is that we also received a report from somebody who was equally adamant that the restaurant should score top marks. The editor's job is to try to find a compromise between the sometimes extreme views that a restaurant evokes.

It may therefore seem to some readers that their voice is being ignored. I can assure you that it is not. Every form, every letter, every last electronic scrap of e-mail is logged, read, digested, and put in the file alongside all the other correspondence, and used to compile the entry for the next edition. But wherever there are conflicting or contradictory opinions, a compromise is inevitable.

It is here that inspectors come in handy. They are not Consumers' Association staff. We don't pay them anything, beyond reimbursing the cost of an inspection meal. In that sense they are well-informed amateurs: people who eat out for pleasure, and whose judgement we trust. They are a mixed bunch, which is part of their strength. One inspector started with Raymond Postgate, creator of the *Guide*, back in the 1950s, others are in their 20s and 30s, a couple have run their own restaurants, some travel the world and are familiar with foreign cuisines on their home turf, some have written books and are specialists in a particular field. All, however, are completely independent, accepting no hospitality, free meals or favours from any restaurant. Their views can never invalidate those of our readers, but they do give an opinion based on their knowledge and experience, especially when readers' reports have given us conflicting opinions or too little detail to go on.

But your view, whatever it is, counts. Without it, we might have given restaurant X a higher mark, so you have helped restore the balance, helped to warn others what to expect. Conversely, your letter may have been the one to tip the scales and persuade us that restaurant Y should remain in the *Guide* after all. Or you may have alerted us to a potential new entry.

So please, if our assessment does not correspond exactly with your opinion, do not give up. Instead, write to us more often. The more you write, the more likely it is that we will reflect your views.

Thank you for helping to make the 1998 *Guide* what it is. Please help us to make the 1999 edition even better.

Settling scores old and new

A word or two of explanation about the new scoring system for cooking this year:

The five categories used to classify restaurants have remained more or less unchanged since the *Guide* began to give cooking marks in the mid-1980s. They were the basis of the original, truncated 20-point scale which, by beginning at 8 or 9 and finishing somewhere around 17, addressed the entire population of possible restaurants, both actual and theoretical, whether in the *Guide* or not.

The new scale, by contrast, uses the full range from 1 to 10, because it deals only with a subset of that population, i.e. only those restaurants that actually appear in the *Guide*. This means that a score of 1 is not to be confused with the 1/10 that some of us may have found scribbled above 'See me!' on our English or maths homework. A score of 1 in this system means that the restaurant is already highly selected, already among the best in the country, since the *Guide* rates fewer than 1,000 restaurants out of the many tens of thousands in Britain.

This standard for scoring was also in effect the basis of the 5-point scale introduced in 1990, although its inherent restrictions did not allow readers to make some of the distinctions they felt were necessary. The use of asterisks introduced some flexibility, and also re-established one of the characteristics of the 20-point scale, namely the use of two levels or points per category. The new system simply brings all these strands together and rationalises them, now representing each of these points by a whole number.

There is a short-term problem to confront. Under the old system there were five numbers and four asterisks; in other words, it was a 9-point scale. One consequence of the change is that new scores are a little less bunched up than they were; the scale has stretched slightly. This 'stretching' means that old scores do not translate directly into a 10-point scale, and comparisons of scores by, for example, doubling an old 2* to get 5 in the new system does not work. An old 2* could just as easily convert to a new 4, which represents the top half of the second band. Only when we all forget the old system and work exclusively with the new one will it seem entirely coherent.

On the water front

Susy Atkins, co-editor of *The Which? Wine Guide*, urges restaurants to offer more information on the water they serve, and more choice

Here is a short test. Question one: what is the difference between the following two groups of branded bottled water? Group A: Perrier, Evian and Highland Spring; Group B: Ty Nant, Ashbourne and Strathmore Mineral Water. Question two: what exactly is contained in those fancy frosted-glass bottles (etched with the restaurant's logo) that have started to appear in front of diners in place of branded waters? You are probably stumped on both counts. If so, you are in good company, because when it comes to ordering water in restaurants most of us are all at sea.

Branded waters

In answer to question one, the branded waters in Group A are classed by the European Union (EU) as natural mineral water, while those in Group B are categorised as spring water. The standards required to earn the former classification are pretty tough. First, the source has to be officially registered with the EU. It must be a single natural site, sealed off and protected from the various mucky agricultural and recreational activities that might pollute it. Then, under an EU directive, the water is monitored by the local authority for a two-year probationary period to prove it is of consistent quality and composition, and that any natural bacteria found in it are benign. If it is given the go-ahead, it may be filtered and carbonated before bottling, but otherwise it must be left totally untreated. And once the water is in the bottle, its natural mineral content must be clearly labelled.

Spring water, by contrast, though of course not literally bog-standard, *is* subject to far fewer restrictions than natural mineral water. It may have been drawn from any number of sources; it may have been purified to destroy bacteria (perhaps by being treated with ultra-violet light), blended with other spring water and filtered; and its composition does not need to be listed on the label.

Does this mean that spring water is inferior to natural mineral water? Not necessarily. Like spring water, natural mineral water is not required to contain a minimum level of any one mineral, and some brands of spring water taste just as good as many natural mineral waters. But these are clearly two different creatures, and few restaurants take the trouble to point this out. And once the water is on the table, the fact that some natural mineral waters have the word 'spring' in their brand names – while some spring waters use the word 'mineral' on their labels – only adds to the confusion.

Filtered tap water

And then there are those frosted bottles etched with the restaurant's logo. A recent addition to the deluge of waters on offer, these in most cases contain tap water, taken directly from the mains, which has then been passed through a small industrial unit that cleans, filters and treats it with UV rays. Makers of these in-house filtration systems claim that the industrial unit removes the chlorine often found in tap water, along with any herbicides and pesticides that might lurk in the system, and 'bugs' such as cryptosporidium, which caused the outbreak of illness in north-west London and Hertfordshire in early 1997.

The end result is decanted into reusable bottles with flashy flip-tops. It's a process the manufacturers claim is ecologically sound – bottles are recycled, and the in-house system cuts down on energy-wasting deliveries – but the water doesn't arrive at your table for free. Prices for filtered tap water vary from restaurant to restaurant, averaging around £1 for a half-litre. Many consumers are unaware that what they are paying for is not mineral water. Although at least one manufacturer of the filter systems emphasises that the restaurants his company supplies are instructed to describe the product as 'table water' when selling it to customers, most restaurants don't call it anything at all. And even consumers in the know can find it grating to pay extra for what is only filtered tap water.

Unmuddying the waters?

'Restaurants have a key role to play in educating consumers about water,' agrees Wenche Marshall Foster, chairwoman of the Natural Mineral Water Association (NMWA), a group of producers which was set up in the late '80s and began promoting its products to the public in 1996. 'Restaurateurs obviously can't tell customers which water to buy,' she says, 'but they can make more effort to explain the differences between natural mineral water, spring water and tap water; and they certainly shouldn't be deluding anyone.'

Quite right. There ought to be much more information about water on the drinks list. Indeed, in most restaurants bottled water is not listed at all and consumers do not know what they have ordered until it is set on the table before them. Even more disconcertingly, the cost often remains a mystery until the bill arrives.

In place of this off-hand attitude towards bottled waters, it would be helpful if restaurants started treating them a little more like wine. In an ideal world, the drinks list would offer a choice: for example, at least two brands of water, one each of natural mineral water and spring water, with a brief explanation of the difference, and a word on the origins of each. The list should explain which brands are carbonated or still, or available either way, and prices should be listed.

While full tasting notes might be taking things a bit far, simple observations, such as the fact that one bottled water has, for example, a salty taste, another an earthy flavour, would be useful. Just as with wine, the bottle should arrive at the table unopened and clearly labelled as the brand ordered. If it is a natural mineral water, that phrase will appear on the label, and UK brands will display the logo of the NMWA.

Then again, no one should ever be made to feel awkward about ordering ordinary tap water. Customers should have the option at *all* restaurants of ordering tap water, and it should arrive free of charge, and in a refillable jug. If the bottled water they are paying for is simply filtered tap water, that too should be made perfectly clear, preferably on the drinks list, or at the very least by a quick word from the waiter.

Prices that baffle

The mark-ups on some branded waters can be enormous: bottles which sell for 60–70p in supermarkets cost as much as £5 in some restaurants. There is also the nefarious practice (among some) of quietly supplying new bottles that have not been ordered, but of course charging full whack for them – which can be quite a surprise when the bill arrives.

Some restaurants try to blame inflated charges – whether on food, wine or water – on the need to recoup high overheads. There may be an argument for that in some cases, but there is no justification for keeping customers in the dark about what they are getting for their money. After all, it wasn't so long ago that many diners were baffled by wine lists, yet today we expect to be offered a reasonable choice of styles on a list, along with information on producers and vintages.

Perhaps at some time in the future we will be able to choose from a selection of several different waters when we dine out, even plumping for different brands on different occasions, according to the cost, flavour or the subtle variations in bubbliness. Unrealistic? Not at all: we just need more information to start filtering through.

Getting back to basics

Mary Ann Gilchrist, chef/proprietor of Carlton House in Llanwrtyd Wells, muses on the pitfalls chefs face if they try too hard to impress

Well, it happened. After two years in *The Good Food Guide*, my rating slipped a notch in the 1997 edition. This set me wondering, 'Where have I gone wrong?' I have put a lot of thought into the matter and analysed my cooking over the last year. Perhaps I had lost my way to some degree.

Maybe it was because I forgot my own basic food principles and got carried away with out-of-season ingredients – tasteless imported strawberries, farmed partridge in June, imported asparagus and other exotica chosen to impress the eye and the *Guide* rather than the tastebuds. Regional specialities and seasonal produce lost out in favour of presentation. I had reaped the whirlwind of my own ambition.

I am sure that I am not the only chef to have fallen prey to ego. I recently met a young colleague who, in the course of conversation, said, 'I cook for me!' But our aim, surely, is to feed customers who will pay for their own eating enjoyment and, in the process, keep us solvent. If not, we are, as a profession, at risk of losing the plot. We must ask ourselves why we cook for a living. I know why *I* do it. I love to cook, I love to entertain and it is a privilege bestowed on me by my customers that I get paid by them for doing something that has given me great pleasure for many years.

A matter of taste

It is crucially important to remember that food should taste of what it is. If you take a chicken, stuff it with one thing, roll it in something else, coat it in an unrelated sauce and garnish it with an unsuitable accompaniment you end up with a culinary disaster. Many skills may have been involved in its creation, but if it has no identifiable coherence the final dish will fail to impress.

Locally reared free-range corn-fed chickens taste like chickens did when I was young. Don't muck them about – let the flavour of the chicken speak for itself. The bones from that chicken will make beautiful stock to enhance the flavour of the sauce for any chicken dish. Occasionally I do a desperately simple recipe. I lightly sauté the breast of chicken in a little butter, then transfer the chicken to a hot oven and roast for 10 minutes while I deglaze the pan with a little of the chicken stock, reduce, add a dollop of fresh double cream and a little salt and pepper. Any juices from the roasted suprême are added back and it is then served with creamy, buttery parsley champ and a few runner beans from my gardener's allotment. It is heaven. It is packed with flavour, and – guess what? – it tastes like chicken.

Forget tasteless baby sweetcorn. Look to your own vegetable plot if you are lucky enough to have one. Alternatively, talk to allotment owners, market gardeners and smallholders. I get marvellous free-range eggs and corn-fed free-range chickens from a local chap with a smallholding. Idwil – my next-door neighbour's handyman, aged 86 – grows cabbages the size of small footballs, but so tender and sweet that they need only the briefest of cooking with a drop of stock and a knob of farm butter, finished with a little salt and a grind of black pepper. He also provides me with superb tomatoes: with a drizzle of virgin olive oil and a sprinkling of home-grown chives, salt and pepper, they are a dish fit for the most discerning palate.

Locally caught wild trout from another friend are so fresh that when they hit the pan they curl up. There is a small farm just north of us that produces some of the best goat's cheese that I have ever tasted. A small butcher in Carmarthen sells a raw ham to rival that of Parma. A farm at Bwlch produces venison properly hung for at least three weeks to allow the flavour to develop. In season the local wild mushrooms are superb with spinach and complement Welsh Black beef perfectly.

Go local

As for local or regional specialities, I have had to review my attitude to laverbread, that muddy-looking seaweed so peculiar to Wales. I was recently asked to devise a couple of recipes for an article on the stuff. Bravely I overcame my own prejudices and put together two ideas: roast monkfish wrapped in Carmarthen ham served in a laverbread and wholegrain mustard sauce, and roast cannon of Welsh lamb in an oatmeal and laverbread crust finished with a light lamb *jus*. I was forced to admit that they were good, and both dishes received great acclaim when we served them in the restaurant.

It is my belief that modern British cooking needs to be rooted first and foremost in British ingredients. I am not suggesting that we ignore the more exotic items from abroad which we British use to such effect, but that we should look first at the marvellous array of seasonal local produce. English asparagus is only with us for six weeks; use it during its short season, then forget it till next year. British strawberries are superb, bursting with flavour and sometimes even available into October. And don't ignore the comforting root vegetables of winter. Deep-fried julienne of parsnip goes perfectly with the rich, gamey meats that Britain is justly famous for.

What I have learnt from my 'demotion' in the *Guide* is the importance of getting back to basics. No longer will I be tempted to contrive dishes for the critics; now I know to be ingredient-led, not fashion-fed.

A gladiator amongst chickens . . .

Readers send *The Good Food Guide* their comments in a variety of styles, some short and to the point, others missing no detail however trivial. Sometimes the reports are merely factual, at other times full of the personal angst or joy that the meal has occasioned. In general, readers get most worked up when they feel they have been insulted in some way: by being asked to wait too long, or eat something they wouldn't give to their dog. Some of the most heartfelt comments, therefore, are forged in the heat of passion, making them among the most apposite and revealing that we receive.

For reasons that soon become obvious when reading them, these 'fillers' have appeared necessarily shorn of their context, scattered throughout the book at the bottom of any page with an odd space to fill. This has enabled the comments to see the light of day and enrich the *Guide*, without causing embarrassment to any particular individual or restaurant. We felt readers might enjoy reading some of our favourites.

Evidence on the plate

'[It was] a meal that spanned the culinary range from A to B, as Dorothy Parker might have said.' (London, 1997)

'The pigeon had been around a long time. Its pâté was a dry tasteless heap of a meat-like substance served on what I understand is called "a bed of lettuce". The bed had been slept in for some time.' (Scotland, 1994)

'The only memorable moment in the meal came as I approached the bottom of a pallid minestrone and was at last able to utter the immortal line, "Waiter, there's a fly in my soup."' (Derbyshire, 1992)

'The braised thigh I was given came from a chicken which had been working out intensively, so bulging it was almost spherical. The sort of chicken you would not wish to meet in a vest and Lycra shorts down the gym. A gladiator amongst chickens.' (Hampshire, 1997)

'When I asked the waitress if she could recommend the cheeses, she said, "If I were you I'd stick to the sweets."' (Wiltshire, 1995)

'Four round, bright red pieces of meat the size and shape and colour of red rubber doorstops – they even had a hole in the middle to screw them to the floor. No screws supplied, though.' (West Midlands, 1993)

'The "aromatic duck" was so dried up and inedible that one would think twice before using it in a stock at home. I told the waitress that we were not prepared to eat it; the manageress came out and, after much arguing, we put £12 on the table (very generous for what we had consumed) and said we were leaving. The manageress then locked us in and called the police. After ten minutes the policemen came in and, with much good humour, took all our names and told the woman she could take us to court if she wanted to.' (Gloucestershire, 1991)

'We asked the waitress what the gâteau was. She said, "I don't know. It looks like choux pastry and cold custard, and looks revolting."' (Cumbria, 1992)

'On finding a live worm in my fish the chef commented as follows on the back of the bill: "As is commonly known, Nematodes are often found in perfectly healthy fish. There is nothing unhealthy or unhygienic about this occurrence but it is regretted."' (London, 1991)

'Weakish Cona coffee was supposed to be accompanied by "Plaisirs de Danse". These never appeared, which was just as well because by this juncture nothing short of the chef's balls on a silver platter would have pleased my wife.' (Manchester, 1987)

'The pear soufflé looked like ET's stomach – sort of brown and wrinkled and rather dry. It tasted alien too, as if it wanted to go home.' (Dorset, 1984)

'I was picking over this huge plate of shellfish with a needle when one of the clams suddenly opened up and grabbed hold of the needle. It was still alive. I dropped the needle and it waved back at me. I thought about its brothers and sisters inside my stomach. . . .' (St Malo, 1984)

'The next table asked, "What is tiramisù?" "It's white and kind of sloshy," explained the waitress.' (Sussex, 1995)

'The menu said that the vegetables were fresh. They probably were once. Two days in the restaurant, three days at market and two days getting to it. They had expired somewhere along the M1.' (Lincolnshire, 1985)

'The choice of sweets was enormous. I felt like a mosquito at a nudist camp and didn't know where to start.' (London, 1987)

'The "pool" of brown sauce was said to be three-pepper. Asked head waiter if "three" meant green, red and yellow. He said "Yes, but if you mix them all up that's what you get – brown."' (Hampshire, 1990)

'The pistachio nuts would have needed the dexterity, determination and incisors of a squirrel to break into.' (London, 1996)

'There was a strange crunchy deep-fried wun-tun thing perched on top. I had noticed several other diners bite this, look at it in bewilderment and then put in on their side plates. I tasted it and did the same. When I asked the head waiter why it was there, he said that people were always asking that and he would have a word with the chef Monday morning.' (London, 1996)

'In between first and second courses we were offered, gratis, a strange choice: apple sorbet or salad leaves with melon and yoghurt. Took both, tried both, left both.' (Dorset, 1991)

The human element

'Service is crushingly formal, and the topping-up of water is solemnly methodical and slow, each twirl of the wrist accompanied by a deferential inclination of the head, eliciting a mumbled "Thank you" from each recipient. After about three rounds of this you resolve to go to a Greek plate-smashing restaurant next time.' (Lancashire, 1997)

'The service was excellent and also very friendly; we followed dinner the second night with a game of croquet with the waiter.' (Scotland, 1993)

'We arrived at 8pm. Just before 9 o'clock a plate of amuse-gueules arrived. By this time we were ravenous, and the two offerings hardly touched the sides. The couple beyond us were clearly feeling even hungrier (they had been there longer) as they started to devour each other.' (Warwickshire, 1997)

'Whenever I asked the waiter anything he didn't know, he went and found out the answer from the kitchen, and dropped it at my feet like a happy dog with a stick.' (the West Country, 1997)

'There was a lot of service. I could see people enjoying a quiet threesome – husband, wife and waiter.' (London, 1989)

'[There were] more signs of life in the spaniel which wandered in and out of the kitchen than in most of the staff.' (Wales, 1993)

'When I arrived at my seat a large cat sat there. No attempt was made to remove same. It seemed churlish to sit on it, so I prodded it. The cat gave me a dirty look and proceeded with its more intimate toilet. I suggested to the young lady that perhaps, rather than examining it with a fatuous expression on her face, she could actually remove it. Which she did, saying "Come with Mummy to the kitchen." It didn't inspire confidence.' (Hampshire, 1985)

'The service was cheerful and not fast enough to cause gut-gallop: the kind that has three courses following each other at a fast canter and you need only one falter in the passage towards the stomach and there is a pile up which can crease you up for days.' (Scotland, 1984)

'Service was pathetically slow, full of misplaced preciosity that involves placing your plate before you as if it were the Ark of the Covenant, turning it through half a centimetre to get the angle just so, and then murmuring in mortal sorrow, "The tart," as if the sous-chef had just run off with the sommelier.' (London, 1997)

'The wine waiter was totally charming and was one of those men who really have to be flirted with. Anything else would have been rude. I duly obliged.' (London, 1996)

'The staff had decided that table 11 was to be ours, and there then followed a short discussion between them as to which table actually was number 11, and who was looking after it.' (Essex, 1995)

'From my personal experience, the following establishment should be included in the *Guide*, but only if its staff agree to attend charm school.' (London, 1987)

'The wine was decanted upon my asking, but could have done without the sneering and incredulous "DECANTED!" from the head waiter.' (Surrey, 1997)

'Like policemen, chefs seem to be getting younger these days as I get older. They also seem, like supermodels, to be increasingly thin, pale and frail. The poor guy looked whacked. He had only had one day off in the last three months and had the pallor of the kitchen. Bet he wishes he was a junior doctor.' (Somerset, 1997)

'We arrived to find the establishment apologetically understaffed because a new waitress had knocked herself unconscious opening a bottle of champagne.' (Gloucestershire, 1994)

'Every time we saw the chef he had his hand on someone's bottom.' (Nottinghamshire, 1995)

'[The waiter] sported a hilarious tie: plastic, part translucent, part luminescent, ending in a bikini-clad female reclining on a beach of real sand. I inquired whether he used it as an egg timer.' (Hereford & Worcester, 1997)

'The maître d' here is definitely an undertaker with an evening job.' (London, 1994)

'Our glasses were refilled after almost every sip. This was hardly relaxing, so I asked if I could pour it myself. The wine waiter said he would prefer it if we asked him. The head waiter then explained that there might be writers of guidebooks in the restaurant and they would receive a bad impression.' (Hampshire, 1993)

From where I sit . . .

'There may not be Muzak but the air-conditioning – welcome as it was – sounded like the mating cry of a hovercraft.' (Kent, 1997)

'The waitress is gaunt and unsmiling. We are given a table overlooking the church cemetery, and I mentally try to guess from which grave our funereal hostess may have recently risen. We are not offered pre-lunch drinks, but then no one ever is when they visit that inn – you know, the one in Transylvania where our hero stops to ask the way to Dracula's castle.' (Suffolk, 1997)

'The restaurant is split-level – no, I can't describe it more than that – it's got a tented ceiling and pine tables, etc. A notice taped to the till instructed us to "chant Hare Krishna and be happy" – I didn't and I wasn't.' (Yorkshire, 1994)

'The response to our preference for a no-smoking area was to put a handwritten sign on our table, saying: "Please, no smoking at this table."' (Yorkshire, 1997)

'My husband had another pudding, about which he had asked that the bill be adjusted, but it was not charged and when he queried this he was told, "[The proprietor] admires anyone who has more than one pudding".' (Shropshire, 1997)

'If you get upset by young stockbrokers complaining about how bad things are while drinking their third glass of champagne, perhaps best not to go here.' (London, 1992)

'The information which you provide in the *Guide* does not mention the £1.50 cover charge, nor the 15 per cent service charge. You do suggest that dinner may cost an arm and a leg. The arrival of the bill nearly resulted in paraplegia.' (London, 1986)

'Absolute bliss – and I was with my mother in law.' (Lincoln, 1984)

'The next table had an intriguing mix of people, including one who looked like the Dalai Lama. He launched into a plate of foie gras in a most un-Buddhist fashion and was a joy to watch. If he was the Dalai Lama, I'm converting to Buddhism next week. He was also the only man in the restaurant who was not required to wear a tie, which my husband thought most unfair.' (London, 1996)

'To finish: peach soufflés. I was not intending to have a second soufflé but one of my party passed out and I ate her pudding.' (Channel Islands, 1994)

'The tables were crammed together but fortunately my neighbour resembled Gina Lollobrigida's daughter.' (London, 1992)

Vintage chart

In order to retain earlier vintages of note, some later, lesser vintages have been omitted.

SYMBOLS:

△ = immature
● = mature
▽ = drink up
□ = wines unlikely to be found in Britain, or undeclared vintages for port and champagne, which come from regions where only certain years are 'declared' or marketed as vintage wines.
★ = vintages not yet 'declared' or marketed (port, champagne)

All figures and symbols apply to the best wines of each vintage in each region.

Vintages have been rated on a 1 to 20 point scale (20 being the best).

	1	2	3	4	5	6	7	8	9	10	11
1996	18△	16△	16△	14△	15△	15△	15△	16△	16△	15△	14△
1995	17△	17△	15△	14△	16△	17△	15△	15●	16△	17△	16△
1994	14△	13△	15●	12△	13△	15△	17△	13●	16△	15△	13△
1993	11△	12△	12●	8△	14△	14△	13△	13●	13●	14△	13△
1992	12△	12△	13●	8△	15△	15△	14△	14●	18△	16△	15△
1991	14△	12△	13●	12△	14△	14△	13△	12▽	14●	16△	13●
1990	17△	18△	14●	19△	19△	19●	19△	19●	19△	18△	18●
1989	19△	19△	17●	19●	17●	19●	20△	18●	18●	16△	18●
1988	18△	19△	16●	18△	18△	15●	16△	17●	19●	18△	17●
1987	14●	13●	15●	10●	13●	15●	8●	12▽	12●	14●	11▽
1986	19△	18△	14●	17△	14●	18●	16●	18▽	16●	15●	16●
1985	18●	18●	18●	15●	19●	16●	18●	16▽	17●	18●	19●
1984	13●	10●	12●	13●	11▽	12▽	8▽	10▽	12▽	14●	13●
1983	18△	17●	18●	18△	14▽	17●	16●	14▽	18●	19●	17●
1982	19●	19●	16●	14●	13▽	15▽	13●	13▽	13▽	16●	15●
1981	16●	15●	15●	13●	11▽	8▽	16●	17▽	16▽	13▽	12▽
1980	11▽	10▽	11▽	12●	13▽	11▽	13●	12▽	8▽	14▽	14▽
1979	16●	18●	17●	14●	14▽	16▽	14●	14▽	10▽	15●	14●
1978	17●	17●	17●	12●	18●	17●	15●	18▽	12▽	19●	18●
1977	9▽	9▽	7▽	6▽	7▽	10▽	5▽	8▽	7▽	8▽	7▽
1976	16▽	14▽	16▽	17●	14▽	14▽	18●	16▽	18▽	18●	14▽
1975	16●	17●	17▽	18●	4▽	6▽	16●	15▽	14▽	10▽	9▽
1971	15▽	16▽	18●	16●	18●	17▽	16●	18▽	19●	17●	17▽
1970	18●	17●	16●	14●	13▽	13▽	16▽	16▽	11▽	16▽	18▽
1969	11▽	9▽	8▽	13▽	16▽	17▽	18●	16▽	13▽	18●	17▽
1967	12▽	12▽	11▽	17●	13▽	14▽	13▽	12▽	17▽	16▽	18▽
1966	17●	18●	16▽	14▽	13▽	14▽	15●	18▽	16▽	17●	18▽
1964	14▽	16▽	11▽	6▽	14▽	14▽	18●	14▽	15▽	17▽	16▽
1963	5▽	5▽	3▽	□	11▽	14▽	□	□	8▽	7▽	8▽
1962	14▽	15▽	16▽	17●	16▽	18▽	15●	14▽	14▽	17▽	16▽
1961	20●	20●	18▽	16▽	14▽	16▽	14●	16▽	18▽	20●	19●

1 = Red Bordeaux: Médoc & Graves
2 = Red Bordeaux: St-Emilion & Pomerol
3 = Dry white Bordeaux
4 = Sweet white Bordeaux: Sauternes & Barsac
5 = Red burgundy
6 = White burgundy
7 = Loire (sweet)
8 = Loire (dry)
9 = Alsace
10 = Northern Rhône
11 = Southern Rhône
12 = Midi
13 = Champagne
14 = Rioja
15 = Vintage port
16 = Red Portuguese
17 = Barolo & Barbaresco
18 = Tuscany
19 = Mosel–Saar–Ruwer
20 = Rhinelands
21 = Australia (red wines)
22 = New Zealand (white wines)
23 = California (red wines)

12	13	14	15	16	17	18	19	20	21	22	23	
14△	★	16△	★	16△	14△	16△	13△	16△	17△	17●	15△	**1996**
17△	★	16△	★	16△	17△	16△	17△	18△	15△	13●	17△	**1995**
16△	★	17△	18△	16△	14△	13△	15△	15△	15△	19●	17△	**1994**
13△	★	14△	□	13△	17△	14△	19△	14△	13△	14●	15△	**1993**
15△	★	16●	19△	16●	14△	13△	18●	17●	16△	15●	19△	**1992**
16△	15△	16●	18△	16●	13△	14△	13●	14●	18△	18●	19△	**1991**
19●	17△	18●	□	17●	18△	20△	20●	20△	17●	15●	18△	**1990**
18●	16●	18●	□	17●	18△	13●	19●	18●	10●	19●	14●	**1989**
18●	19△	17●	□	11▽	17△	19△	17●	17●	16●	14●	15●	**1988**
14▽	□	16●	17△	15●	14●	14●	6▽	7▽	18●	16▽	12●	**1987**
16●	15●	17●	□	9▽	15●	17●	11▽	13▽	19●	18▽	14●	**1986**
18●	19●	19●	19●	19●	20●	19●	15▽	15▽	17●	□	19●	**1985**
13▽	□	13●	□	14▽	8▽	9▽	3▽	5▽	18●	□	13●	**1984**
18●	16●	15●	18△	18●	13▽	15▽	16▽	14▽	14●	□	12▽	**1983**
17▽	17●	16●	13●	15▽	19●	17●	7▽	8▽	19●	□	15●	**1982**
17▽	16●	17●	□	10▽	13▽	14▽	8▽	10▽	13▽	□	14▽	**1981**
15▽	10▽	16▽	16●	16●	11▽	13▽	3▽	4▽	18●	□	17●	**1980**
□	17●	14▽	□	14▽	14▽	17▽	11▽	12▽	16●	□	14▽	**1979**
□	12▽	19●	□	15▽	18●	16▽	9▽	9▽	18●	□	16●	**1978**
□	□	6▽	20△	16▽	11▽	16▽	5▽	8▽	14▽	□	12▽	**1977**
□	18●	13▽	□	12▽	14▽	13▽	19●	17●	17●	□	14▽	**1976**
□	14▽	15▽	13▽	13▽	12▽	17▽	17●	18●	19●	□	14▽	**1975**
□	17▽	9▽	□	9▽	18▽	18▽	20●	19●	20●	□	14▽	**1971**
□	16▽	19●	18●	17▽	17▽	16▽	12▽	11▽	14▽	□	17●	**1970**
□	14▽	12▽	□	9▽	14▽	14▽	16▽	13▽	□	□	16▽	**1969**
□	13▽	12▽	16▽	14▽	16▽	18▽	17●	17●	15▽	□	14▽	**1967**
□	16▽	15▽	18●	19▽	15▽	16▽	16▽	16▽	19●	□	16▽	**1966**
□	17▽	20●	□	□	19▽	18▽	17▽	15▽	□	□	16▽	**1964**
□	□	12▽	20●	16▽	□	□	12▽	12▽	17▽	□	16▽	**1963**
□	15▽	13▽	□	□	13▽	16▽	14▽	16▽	18●	□	13▽	**1962**
□	16▽	10▽	□	□	18▽	15▽	10▽	12▽	□	□	15▽	**1961**

London

Abingdon map 13

54 Abingdon Road, W8 6AP COOKING 3
TEL: (0171) 937 3339 FAX: (0171) 795 6388 COST £22–£43

This is a 'pleasant, airy place for a casual summer evening's dining', and the road has little traffic so outside tables are an asset. The uncluttered dining-room is decorated in cool pastel shades, and simplicity is the watchword of Brian Baker's cooking. Salad starters get the thumbs-up from reporters: green beans and potted shrimps 'worked splendidly', and goats' cheese and wild mushrooms came with a well-judged vinaigrette. There may also be grilled squid with anchovy dressing, or a chicken liver tart with balsamic dressing, while main courses might typically include grilled calf's liver with French beans, olives and shallots, and steamed breast of chicken with a yoghurt and mint dressing. For dessert, vanilla crème brûlée has proved a successful choice. Set lunches are reckoned to be great value, and service is 'down-to-earth and unintrusive'. The wine list is short but adequate and includes a white zinfandel and an organic cabernet, both from California. House French is £9.25.

CHEFS: Brian Baker and Laurent Lemangen PROPRIETOR: My Kinda Town plc OPEN: all week 12 to 2.30 (12.30 to 3 Sun), 6.30 to 11 (10.30 Sun) CLOSED: 25 and 26 Dec, 1 Jan MEALS: alc Mon to Sat L, all week D (main courses £8.50 to £14). Set L Mon to Sat £9.95 (2 courses), Set L Sun £13.50 SERVICE: 12.5% (optional), card slips closed CARDS: Amex, Delta, MasterCard, Switch, Visa DETAILS: 52 seats. 20 seats outside. Private parties: 24 main room. Vegetarian meals. Children's helpings. No cigars/pipes in dining-room. Wheelchair access (no WC). Music. Air-conditioned

Adams Café £ map 12

77 Askew Road, W12 9AH COOKING 3
TEL/FAX: (0181) 743 0572 COST £21–£34

This forerunner of today's Maghrebian boom first appeared in the 1992 *Guide*. Despite its location on a street of numerous take-aways, it is more than the modest name suggests. Its white walls, tiled dado, copper and brass ornaments, tourist posters and oilcloth-covered tables typify a family-run restaurant. Service is amiable, knowledgeable and helpful, and Tunisian and Moroccan specialities have a home-cooked taste. Starters might be doigts de Fatma (beef-filled 'spring rolls'), or Tunisian brik (a parcel of filo pastry filled with egg, tuna and herbs or seafood). For main courses there are fish and meat grills with rice and vegetables, and Moroccan tagines which bring dignity and rich herby-spicy flavours to that much-maligned word, stew. The usual couscous dishes with chicken, lamb or merguez are offered, and the 'royal' version includes all these ingredients. To finish, baklava pastries are a revelation to those accustomed to mass-produced Hellenic travesties, and mint tea, with or without pine-nuts, is even better than Arabic coffee with cardamom. Gris de Balouene, a Moroccan rosé wine, makes an ideal accompaniment to this sort of cooking. Tunisian Boukha (fig eau-de-vie) and Thibarine (date liqueur) are more of an acquired taste. French house wines start at £7.50.

CHEF: Abdel Boukraa PROPRIETORS: Abdel and Frances Boukraa OPEN: all week D only 7 to 11 CLOSED: 1 week Christmas and New Year MEALS: alc (main courses £7 to £11). BYO £1.20 SERVICE: not inc CARDS: Amex, Delta, Diners, MasterCard, Switch, Visa DETAILS: 60 seats. Private parties: 36 main room, 24 private room. Vegetarian meals. Children welcome. Wheelchair access (no WC). Music

Agadir £

NEW ENTRY map 13

84 Westbourne Grove, W2 5RT — COOKING 3
TEL: (0171) 792 2207 — COST £19–£32

Hanging carpets, bellows and non-existent arches outlined in fragments of mirror decorate the walls of this unassuming Moroccan eating-house done out in bright green and red. Crowded tables with ethnic cloths and paper napkins, and pleasant if sometimes overworked service, define it as a family-run place. Briouat (filo rolls filled with herby meat) pleased an inspector, and maakouda (mashed potato fried with egg in parsley and spices) is like an ethereally light latke.

Tangia marrakchia, a tagine of tender lamb with green olives and preserved lemon, is well matched by dry and fluffy couscous to absorb the rich, tangy sauce. 'Foul foul' is doubly misnamed because it is not beans, as in the eastern Mediterranean, but iced ratatouille with 'wonderful spicy flavours'. In addition to couscous and tagines (including fish), there are a few kebabs. Home-made Moroccan pastries are more subtle, less sweet than their Eastern cousins. Mint tea in a traditional pot comes with gilt-decorated tumblers. The short wine list features around half a dozen Moroccan bottles. House French is £8.50.

CHEF/PROPRIETOR: Mustafa Lagnatha OPEN: all week D only 6 to 12 MEALS: alc (main courses £5.50 to £10) SERVICE: 10%, card slips closed CARDS: Amex, Delta, MasterCard, Switch, Visa DETAILS: 55 seats. Private parties: 80 main room, 80 private room. Vegetarian meals. Children welcome. Wheelchair access (no WC). Music. Air-conditioned

Alastair Little

map 15

49 Frith Street, W1V 5TE — COOKING 5
TEL: (0171) 734 5183 — COST £36–£49

Alastair Little's original Soho restaurant was one of the places that, in the late 1980s, led the move to a more straightforward and direct style of cooking than London was then by and large being treated to. The décor is challengingly spare, menus are written in plain English, and the food can be alarmingly simple. The kitchen guard has changed – Juliet Peston has moved to Lola's, Alastair Little divides his time between here and Alastair Little Lancaster Road (see entries,

London), and his new deputy here is Jonathan Ricketts – but the ideals have not been lost.

Pizzetta bianca is a stalwart of the menus, a frisbee of light dough drenched with olive oil, paved with potato slices and heaped up with rocket leaves. Starchy assemblages of haricots and chickpeas are much favoured: for example, 'farro' (a tomato and bean stew) with an 'excellent' confit of duck, the skin of the meat singed and salted. Roast salt cod with chickpeas is given a Chinese twist in the form of five-spiced seafood stock and pak choi. Energetic salting is a feature of the cooking, even the ciabatta acquiring a toasted salt crust that revs up the appetite. Chic Mediterranean ways yield to more traditional British ones at dessert stage, in a very sweet strawberry pavlova, and a 'triumphant' gooseberry crumble that is 'not too heavy, not too sweetened'. The frequently changing short wine list has representatives from around the world, and starts with house French at £13.

CHEFS: Alastair Little and Jonathan Ricketts PROPRIETORS: Alastair Little, Mercedes Andre-Vega and Kirsten Pedersen OPEN: Mon to Fri L 12 to 3, Mon to Sat D 6 to 11 MEALS: Set L £15 (2 courses) to £25, Set D £30 SERVICE: not inc CARDS: Amex, Delta, MasterCard, Switch, Visa DETAILS: 55 seats. Private parties: 8 main room, 20 private room. Vegetarian meals. Children's helpings. Wheelchair access (no WC). No music. Air-conditioned

Alastair Little Lancaster Road map 12

136A Lancaster Road, W11 1QU COOKING 3
TEL: (0171) 243 2220 COST £27–£44

'A terrific local restaurant, with all the friendliness and personality you expect,' writes an enthusiast. Everything is white, from canopy to walls to tablecloths, and although 'nobody eats at Mr Little's restaurants for comfort', the place is bright and relaxed; be prepared for chatty neighbours. Toby Gush left just as the *Guide* went to press, leaving Alastair Little as executive chef both here and in Frith Street (see entry above). Clearly he cannot cook everywhere at once, but was expected to take a turn in the Lancaster Road kitchen, along with a deputy to be appointed. The Lancaster Road style is typically straightforward – wild garlic omelette with chips and salad for instance – but is not above turning out lambs' sweetbreads with pink fir-apple potatoes, or grilled fillet of sea bass (notably fresh and well timed) with tabbouleh.

The menu changes slightly at every meal-time, but the focus is generally on effective treatment of unshowy ingredients: skate wing served with purple sprouting broccoli and anchovies, perhaps, with ricotta fritters or passion-fruit ice-cream to follow. It is the package that appeals, from simple food at realistic prices, to cheerful, helpful service, and a varied spread of modern wines starting at £12.

CHEF: Alastair Little PROPRIETORS: Alastair Little, Kirsten Pedersen and Mercedes André-Vega OPEN: Mon to Sat 12.30 to 2.30 (3 Sat), 7 to 11 CLOSED: bank hols MEALS: alc L (main courses £7.50 to £10). Set D £25 SERVICE: not inc; 12.5% for parties of 6 or more CARDS: Amex, MasterCard, Switch, Visa DETAILS: 42 seats. 8 seats outside. Private parties: 10 main room. Vegetarian meals. Children's helpings. Wheelchair access (no WC). No music

Alba

map 13

107 Whitecross Street, EC1Y 8JH
TEL: (0171) 588 1798

COOKING 2
COST £23–£45

Should City folk or theatre-goers on their way to the Barbican – or anyone else for that matter – desire a spot of gutsy Piedmont cooking, this is the place to come. Unadorned simplicity is the mode, as shown in a starter of three thin slices of grilled aubergine topped with puréed tomato and melted mozzarella. Pasta dishes might include braised rabbit ravioli, or penne with peas and pancetta. A main-course salad of large warm-water prawns 'grilled to perfection' is given a kick with olive oil, garlic and chilli, while meatier appetites might go for grilled venison steak with red cabbage and polenta. Side vegetables seem worth the surcharge for a good selection softened in butter, and bitter chocolate mousse with blueberries and 'a pond of cream' made a good close to one reporter's meal. Service is usually 'very correct and efficient' but has shown signs of inexperience. A useful spread of Piedmontese grape varieties heads up the Italian wine list, but prices feel a touch uncomfortable throughout. House Chardonnay is £9.90, while the red is a Dolcetto at £10.90.

CHEF: Armando Liboi PROPRIETOR: Rudi Venerandi OPEN: Mon to Fri 12 to 3, 6 to 11 CLOSED: 25 Dec to 3 Jan, bank hols MEALS: alc (main courses £9 to £15). Set D £9.90 (2 courses) to £16.90, Set pre-theatre D (6 to 7.30pm) £9.95 SERVICE: 12.5%, card slips closed CARDS: Amex, Delta, Diners, MasterCard, Switch, Visa DETAILS: 55 seats. Private parties: 70 main room, 30 private room. Vegetarian meals. Children's helpings. Wheelchair access (no WC). Music. Air-conditioned

Al Bustan

map 14

27 Motcomb Street, SW1X 8JU
TEL: (0171) 235 8277 and 1668
FAX: (0171) 235 1668

COOKING 2
COST £26–£46

'Care and authenticity' set Al Bustan 'streets ahead of the Middle Eastern norm in Britain', writes one who knows his falafel. The restaurant name means 'garden' in Arabic, and the interior suitably enough is done out in pastel shades and trellises of greenery. As befits the Belgravia setting, service is formal, deferential and smooth; it also has heart. 'Meze, meze, meze!' enthused a correspondent who marvelled at the 'extraordinary flavours from frequently uncooked fresh vegetables and salads'. The range of cold and hot Lebanese morsels covers everything from creamy hummus and moussaka bizeit 'redolent of cinnamon' to lahem bil agine (a kind of savoury tart), excellent kibbeh filled with minced lamb and pine kernels, and gamey makanek (mini-sausages). Main courses centre on gargantuan mixed grills and big doses of animal protein in other forms, both raw and cooked. Incidentals such as two kinds of freshly made bread, pickled turnips, first-rate pastries and Turkish coffee all hit the button. France dominates the short wine list, although a handful of Lebanese bottles is also offered. House wine is £12.

CHEF: Inam Atalla PROPRIETOR: Mr and Mrs R. Atalla OPEN: all week 12 to 11 CLOSED: 24 Dec to 5 Jan MEALS: alc (main courses £9 to £10.50). Set L £13, Set D £18. Cover £2 SERVICE: not inc CARDS: Amex, Diners, MasterCard, Visa DETAILS: 65 seats. 25 seats outside. Private parties: 20 main room, 8 to 20 private rooms. Vegetarian meals. Children's helpings. Music. Air-conditioned

Alexandra

map 12

507 Kingston Road, SW20 8SF — COOKING 1
TEL: (0181) 542 4838 FAX: (0181) 947 3805 — COST £14–£31

Eric Lecras's pink and cream French restaurant, named after his daughter, is a strongly personal venture geared to neighbourhood trade at outer London prices. This year's postbag has indicated one or two ups and downs in both food and service, but extra staff have been drafted in to address the problem. Starters have included a classical home-made terrine of foie gras, and a very creamy seafood one. A simple dish of roast pork was accomplished, and sauces continue to garner praise. Desserts might include 'very good' tarte Tatin with apricot coulis, or a simple but refreshing raspberry sorbet. Wines are mostly French and nearly all under £20, starting at £8.90 for the house Louis Alexandre.

CHEF/PROPRIETOR: Eric Lecras OPEN: Sun to Fri L 12 to 1.30, all week D 7 to 9.30 CLOSED: 26 Dec MEALS: Set L Sun to Fri £6.95 to £16.95, Set D Sun to Thur £6.95, Set D Fri and Sat £16.95 SERVICE: 12.5% (optional) CARDS: MasterCard, Visa DETAILS: 60 seats. 15 seats outside. Private parties: 36 main room, 36 private room. Vegetarian meals. Children welcome. No cigars/pipes in dining-room. Music

Alfred

map 15

245 Shaftesbury Avenue, WC2H 8EH — NEW CHEF
TEL: (0171) 240 2566 FAX: (0171) 497 0672 — COST £25–£49

Yellow Formica-topped tables, paper napkins and basic cutlery lend Alfred something of a post-modern French-bistro air: an odd backdrop, perhaps, for a very unmodern collection of British dishes. Patrick Smith, Alfred's third chef of 1997, arrived too late for us to receive any feedback on performance, but the style is set to continue with Glamorgan patties, braised duck with pan haggerty, wild boar sausages, and bread-and-butter diplomat pudding with vanilla sauce. Fourteen English and Scottish beers, plus Guinness, head up the drinks list, and there is a good choice of whiskies as well as a decent assortment of wines that include several from England. Prices start at £11.90.

CHEF: Patrick Smith PROPRIETOR: Fred Taylor OPEN: Mon to Fri L 12 to 3.30, Mon to Sat D 6 to 11.30 CLOSED: 24 Dec to 3 Jan, bank hols MEALS: alc (main courses £9 to £16). Set L and D 6 to 7.30 and 10 to 11.30 £12.95 (2 courses) to £15.90 SERVICE: not inc CARDS: Amex, Delta, Diners, MasterCard, Switch, Visa DETAILS: 58 seats. 38 seats outside. Private parties: 20 main room, 20 private room. Vegetarian meals. Children's helpings. Wheelchair access (no WC). No music. Air-conditioned

'The restaurant was entirely as I had expected it to be, which was a bit soul destroying. I am an optimist and like to be proved wrong.' (On eating in the West Country)

Al Hamra

map 15

31–33 Shepherd Market, W1Y 7HR — COOKING 6
TEL: (0171) 493 1954 FAX: (0171) 493 1044 — COST £32–£58

After six months' closure, Al Hamra reopened in July 1997 and was immediately packed, customers warmly welcomed by friendly waiters. The square corner dining-room has windows on three sides, and a large mirror on the fourth so it does not feel too crowded even though tables are close together, and some privacy is provided by movable troughs of plants between tables. Despite the very low ceiling (the tall waiters risk developing a permanent stoop), the new air-conditioning is efficient, so smokers, even at the next table, are no problem. Family parties make enough happy noise to render loud background music virtually inaudible. The few tables outside benefit from infra-red heating.

To eat here, writes an inspector, 'is to understand how Lebanese food got its high reputation'. To the intense spice and herb flavours of Middle Eastern food, French influence adds an extra dimension to create dishes such as Samakeh harra (baked trout with hot spicy sauce) with 'a fine flavour, not overwhelmed by the creamy tomato and onion sauce'. An entirely satisfying meal could be had by sticking to hot and cold meze: moutabal baba ghanoush (grilled aubergine paste with sesame extract, olive oil and lemon juice) was 'just about as good as it can be', felt a reporter. Other successes have included foul moukala (broad beans in garlic, coriander and olive oil), haliwat (sweetbreads in a 'wonderfully flavoured' lemon-based sauce), and fatayer (little pastries filled with spinach, onion, pomegranate and pine-nuts). For dessert there is no need to look beyond the pastries filled with honey, nuts and fruits. Ayran, a sour milk drink, goes well with the food. The wine list – mainly French with a few Lebanese offerings – is expensive, but there are useful New World bottles. House wines are £12.75.

CHEFS: Mahir Abboud and Ahmed Batah PROPRIETORS: Riad Nabulsi and Hassan Fansa OPEN: all week 11.30 to 11.30 CLOSED: 25 Dec, 1 Jan MEALS: alc (main courses £11 to £15). Set L and D £20 to £25. Cover £2.50 SERVICE: not inc CARDS: Amex, Diners, MasterCard, Visa DETAILS: 75 seats. 16 seats outside. Private parties: 80 main room. Vegetarian meals. Children welcome. Wheelchair access (no WC). Music. Air-conditioned

Al San Vincenzo

map 13

30 Connaught Street, W2 2AF — COOKING 4
TEL: (0171) 262 9623 — COST £32–£57

'Do not expect formal service,' write the owners, and indeed it would be hard to imagine the logistics of silver-serving vegetables or flourishing dome lids in such a tiny space. Few, surveying this small Bayswater room when it was part of a private house, could have envisaged a restaurant here, and yet it works precisely because the tone of the approach is tailored to suit. Vincenzo Borgonzolo's cookery is in keeping too: a rough-edged country style with no superfluous frills, but delivering artichokes poached with chicken, pine-nuts and Parmesan, or pork chops marinated in chillies and oil, grilled and served with zucchini. Sea bass is doused with olive oil and herbs and simply baked, or there may be deep-fried eels with radicchio di Treviso.

One reporter had a mixed experience, starting with 'delicious . . . very light' fritto misto that brought together sweetbreads, zucchini and artichokes, followed by a disappointing leg of lamb with peas, but finished on a high note with 'richly alcoholised' panettone bread-and-butter pudding. Another found more consistency in an 'excellent' pairing of Parma ham and mango, a breaded spinach-stuffed chicken breast, and 'interesting' unpasteurised Italian cheeses. If the cheeses don't tempt, try a glass of vin santo with biscotti, or chocolate semifreddo. The wine list takes a short canter through some of the more diverting Italian localities: Greco di Tufo or Aglianico del Vulture make refreshing changes from Soave and Chianti. House wines from Piedmont are £11.

CHEF: Vincenzo Borgonzolo PROPRIETORS: Elaine and Vincenzo Borgonzolo OPEN: Mon to Fri L 12.30 to 2, Mon to Sat D 7 to 10 CLOSED: 25 and 26 Dec MEALS: alc (main courses £12 to £21) SERVICE: not inc CARDS: Delta, MasterCard, Visa DETAILS: 24 seats. No children under 12. No cigars/pipes in dining-room. Music

Andrew Edmunds £ — map 15

46 Lexington Street, W1R 3LH — NEW CHEF
TEL: (0171) 437 5708 — COST £20–£32

Lexington Street, a modest Soho thoroughfare in every sense, houses some equally unassuming café-restaurants in its little historic houses. At Andrew Edmunds comfort may not be a strong point, but that would not deter one reporter from returning for 'homely cooking' of fine-quality ingredients. Paul Croal left as the *Guide* went to press, and his deputy of three years took over. Typical of the tersely expressed style might be frisée, shredded duck, apple and pecans; or lamb chump chop with tabbouleh, green beans and aubergine caviare. The restaurant is handy for pre-theatre dinners. House wine is £9.

CHEF: Rebecca St John Cooper PROPRIETOR: Andrew Edmunds OPEN: all week 12.30 (1 Sat) to 3, 6 to 10.45 (10.30 Sun) CLOSED: 24 to 31 Dec, 4 days Easter MEALS: alc (main courses £6.50 to £8.50) SERVICE: not inc CARDS: Amex, Delta, MasterCard, Switch, Visa DETAILS: 56 seats. 4 seats outside. Private parties: 28 main room. Vegetarian meals. No music. Air-conditioned

Anglesea Arms £ — map 12

35 Wingate Road, W6 0UR — COOKING 3
TEL: (0181) 749 1291 FAX: (0181) 749 1254 — COST £14–£34

This is how London pubs used to be: plain, wood-dominated interiors, no burbling video games to rend the air, but loads of smoke and noise from punters enjoying themselves. On the other hand, the catering in days of old would not have run to griddled squid with mango, ginger and coriander, or chargrilled baby leeks with wild kale in sauce maltaise. There is an infectious air of experimentation about the blackboard menus, and low prices help entice the curious to try, for example, 'trio of wild sea trout – Japanese style', or salted ox tongue accompanied by a mix of white beans and mustard fruits. Poignant flavours increase the impact of dishes, so sweet-and-sour cherries, spring greens and celeriac come with a breast of duck, and dessert sorbets are composed of tart apple and rhubarb. Value is paramount throughout: a glass of cava is included in the price for crème brûlée and glazed peaches. Staff work hard and are 'helpful and cheerful'. Wines on the short list are thoughtfully selected. House Italian is £8.75.

CHEF: Dan Evans PROPRIETORS: Dan and Fiona Evans OPEN: all week L 12.30 to 2.45 (1 to 3.30 Sun), all week D 7.30 to 10.45 CLOSED: 24 to 30 Dec MEALS: alc (main courses £5 to £10). Set L £7 SERVICE: not inc CARDS: Delta, Mastercard, Switch, Visa DETAILS: 80 seats; 24 outside. Vegetarian meals. Children's helpings. No cigars/pipes in dining-room. Wheelchair access (no WC).

Anonimato

NEW ENTRY map 13

12 All Saints Road, W11 1HH COOKING 3
TEL: (0171) 243 2808 COST £24–£43

The saints have gone marching out: that is, the previous inhabitant of this upper Notting Hill site, All Saints, is no more. In its place is Anonimato, with its warm saffron and rust colours, curved bar and sloping glass ceiling. Chef and co-owner Nilton Campos, previously having done good things for several years at nearby First Floor, produces mostly Mediterranean and Pacific dishes and goes in for some intriguing combinations. 'Perfectly cooked' seared scallops with rocket are well complemented by a slightly sharp sauce of roast beet tapénade, while goats' cheese comes on a stack of sweet potato, aubergine and red pepper. Very rare roast rack of lamb served with pancetta, Puy lentils and a rosemary *jus* would have benefited from arriving on a warmed plate, but a main course of smoked tomato and leek salsa, shiitake mushroom and slightly gamey seared kangaroo fillet was felt by an inspector to work like a dream. Desserts may run from fresh and fruity satsuma and strawberry sorbet to light and spongy steamed chocolate and banana pudding. Service is both professional and friendly. The short wine list features bottles from around the globe, with some obscure producers. House wine is £10.

CHEF: Nilton Campos PROPRIETORS: Nilton Campos and Simon Reader OPEN: Sat and Sun L 12 to 4, Mon to Sat D 7 to 11 CLOSED: 24 to 26 Dec, bank hols MEALS: alc (main courses L £7 to £9.50, D £9 to £13) SERVICE: 12.5% (optional), card slips closed CARDS: Delta, MasterCard, Switch, Visa DETAILS: 50 seats. Private parties: 50 main room. Vegetarian meals. Children welcome. No cigars/pipes in dining-room. Music

Assaggi

NEW ENTRY map 13

The Chepstow, 39 Chepstow Place, W2 4TS COOKING 3
TEL: (0171) 792 5501 COST £27–£59

The first-floor room over the Chepstow pub (enter round the side) is a conversion with a difference. Strong, vivid colours from 'rust' to 'passion-fruit', and wooden floors and tables, announce that this is going to be cheerful and casual, but stylish with it. The menu is deeply Italian (you may need to ask for an explanation of *surbir d'Agnoli* or *coriandoli*, for example), and suitable for 'small tastes' (*assaggi*) of pasta and salads, as well as more substantial veal chop, or fillet of beef with wild mushrooms and truffle oil. Meats and fish are generally grilled or pan-fried, simplicity and freshness are apparent – in seafood or vegetable salads dressed at table with olive oil and balsamic vinegar – and if the food appears frugal, that is due more to its humble rustic origins than any mean-spiritedness. Nevertheless, prices can seem high. Bread is either focaccia or *carta di musica*, an impressively wafer-thin Sardinian speciality, and a short but decent list of Italian wines starting at £9.75 includes six by the glass.

CHEF: Nino Sassu PROPRIETORS: Nino Sassu and Pietro Fraccari OPEN: Tue to Sun L 12.30 to 2.30 (1 to 5 Sun), Tue to Sat D 7.30 to 11 CLOSED: Christmas MEALS: alc (main courses £8 to £19) SERVICE: not inc, card slips closed CARDS: Amex, MasterCard, Switch, Visa DETAILS: 35 seats. Vegetarian meals. Children's helpings. No cigars in dining-room. No music

Les Associés

map 12

172 Park Road, N8 8JT — COOKING 3
TEL: (0181) 348 8944 — COST £17–£44

Sitting opposite Crouch End swimming-baths, Les Associés is a cosy, neighbourly sort of place with close-together tables, a regular clientele and – despite the florid wording on the menus ('la soupe de poissons et sa garniture traditionelle', for example) – unfussy food. A decorative feuilleté of asparagus is a typical starter, while main courses might include glazed pork casserole with armagnac-steeped prunes, and rabbit with rosemary and thyme; at inspection, both of these married their ingredients successfully. There is some creative dash, too: 'meltingly tender' scallops on Mediterranean vegetables with a thyme and red pepper sauce, say, or the catch of the day cooked in paper with a slice of fresh duck liver. Desserts include 'rich and crisp' tarte Tatin, 'good' nougat glacé, and 'classic' creme brûlée. 'Dinner at Les Associés is an exercise in relaxation and patience,' wrote one visitor, adding, 'chef refuses to be rushed.' The short wine list is all French, with enough regional wines to contain the prices. House wine is £9.80.

CHEF: Marc Spindler PROPRIETOR: Dominique Chéhère OPEN: Tue to Sun 12 to 2, 7.30 to 10 (11 Sat) CLOSED: 10 days Sept, 10 days Jan MEALS: alc (main courses £9.50 to £15). Set L Tue to Fri £10.50, Set L Sun £12.50 SERVICE: not inc, card slips closed CARDS: MasterCard, Switch, Visa DETAILS: 38 seats. 6 seats outside. Private parties: 40 main room. Children's helpings. No children under 6. No cigars/pipes in dining-room. Wheelchair access (no WC). Music

Atelier

map 15

41 Beak Street, W1R 3LE — COOKING 5
TEL: (0171) 287 2057 FAX: (0171) 287 1767 — COST £27–£52

'What excellent value this place is,' began one report on Canaletto's former studio. Large abstract pictures and blank canvas screens make the 'painterly' link without overdoing things, but the real artistry is in the kitchen, where Stephen Bulmer has been joined by a sous-chef and a 'dedicated' pastry-chef. Menus are still sensibly limited, the early-evening deal is a good one, and 'much more sophisticated cooking occurs here than at the endless Modern British chargrill 'n' coriander clones'. Main courses can be elaborate and interesting, yet stop short of being fussy: pot-roast lamb, for example, comes with a lamb sausage, poached monkfish has a crab and ginger dumpling for company, and accurately grilled red snapper, served on a rosemary-flavoured croûton covered with tapénade, arrives with a small squid stuffed with tomato and pepper.

Be prepared for visual puns, perhaps in the form of a giant field mushroom, upended, stuffed with spinach, gratinated, and placed on a 'stalk' of mashed potato so that the whole thing looks like an even more giant mushroom the right way up; or a 'stunning' dessert consisting of a coffee-cup and saucer made from dark chocolate, filled with coffee cream and topped with cocoa to look like a cappuccino. A short wine list benefits from intelligent sourcing in its search for value, starts with southern hemisphere house wine at £13.25 and offers nine wines by the glass.

CHEF: Stephen Bulmer PROPRIETOR: JSB Restaurants Ltd OPEN: Mon to Fri L 12 to 2.30, Mon to Sat D 6 to 10.45 CLOSED: 1 week Dec/Jan (but open 31 Dec), 1 week Easter, 2 weeks Aug MEALS: alc (main courses £14.50 to £16). Set L and D £16.50 (2 courses) to £19.50, Set D 6 to 8 £12.50 (2 courses) to £15.50 SERVICE: 12.5% (optional) CARDS: Amex, Delta, Diners, MasterCard, Switch, Visa DETAILS: 50 seats. Private parties: 50 main room, 16 private room. Vegetarian meals. Children's helpings. Wheelchair access (no WC). No music

Atlantic Bar and Grill 🍷 

map 15

20 Glasshouse Street, W1R 5RQ — COOKING 4
TEL: (0171) 734 4888 FAX: (0171) 734 3609 — COST £33–£73

The Atlantic is a gawper's idea of heaven. Non-reservees must wait at the rope outside and try to talk themselves in, while a pre-booked youthful crowd of 'the wealthy, beautiful and self-conscious' sweeps in and packs the place to bursting. Everybody expects to see somebody, and if you don't, the vast underground space, done in oceanic blues with electric art installations, will make an impression anyway.

Stephen Terry, who also lists himself as chef at the sister restaurant Coast (see entry, London), is helped here by Darren Roberts. The style of food may have become a little more conservative, but is none the worse for that. Leek and blue cheese tart, crab spring rolls with hot-and-sour sauce, and whole grilled lobster with mushy peas and chips are the name of the game these days. At inspection, crab spring rolls came with a crunchy garnish and spicy dipping sauce, and a black lacquer tray of sashimi 'would have done credit to any Japanese restaurant': oriental items are clearly the smart option. A plate of mixed 'Atlantic cookies and brownies' failed to impress a transatlantic diner, although the 'hugely rich and satisfying' boozed-up chocolate cake was another matter. Service is 'impeccable' and 'stylish', if 'a bit faceless', but attention to detail is impressive.

A few French classics have helped to expand the wine list, but it still crosses the Atlantic – and Pacific – and nets some first-class producers. Mark-ups, inevitably, can be on the steep side, but there is a reasonable choice under £20. The house selection starts at £11.50 and offers 21 wines by the small or large glass. CELLARMAN'S CHOICE: Champagne Louis Roederer Brut nv, £28.50; St-Aubin Premier Cru 1993, Dom. Larue, £25.

CHEFS: Stephen Terry and Darren Roberts PROPRIETOR: Oliver Peyton OPEN: Mon to Fri L 12 to 3, all week D 6 to 12 (10.30 Sun) CLOSED: bank hols MEALS: alc (main courses £8 to £21.50). Set L £14.90 (2 courses). Cover £1 SERVICE: not inc; 12.5% for parties of 6 or more CARDS: Amex, Delta, MasterCard, Switch, Visa DETAILS: 180 seats. Private parties: 250 main room, 70 private room. Vegetarian meals. Children welcome. Wheelchair access (also WC). Music. Air-conditioned

Aubergine 🍷

map 14

11 Park Walk, SW10 0AJ — COOKING 9
TEL: (0171) 352 3449 FAX: (0171) 351 1770 — COST £39–£87

Is it only five years since Gordon Ramsay opened Aubergine in genteel and affluent Chelsea? It will be in 1998, although the amount of press coverage he attracts makes it feel like much longer. Modestly sized, but colourful and cheering thanks to distressed yellow walls and bright landscape paintings, the restaurant is hugely popular: 'we got in quite easily by booking about two months in advance'. The à la carte is a journey through luxury ingredients – lobster, foie gras, scallops, langoustines – some of them integrated into Ramsay's signature pasta formats of tortellini, ravioli and the like. Nothing is straightforward, as dishes undergo a multitude of layering, wrapping, frothing and stuffing before finally being plated. Despite the fuss, 'some of it pretentious', the food is resoundingly confident.

The impact of forthright flavours kicks in from the word 'go', perhaps with an appetiser of vichyssoise soup, and then the fireworks begin. Foie gras cooked three ways is 'theatrical': a small terrine, a half-cooked disc in a small ramekin of slightly underwhelming Earl Grey jelly, and a fiercely seared nugget sitting on a bed of stewed fig (the combination of charred surface, rich liver, and sweet fruit proving 'mind-blowing' for one reporter). Attractive presentation goes hand in hand, as in generously filled ravioli of lobster and langoustine, with 'savoury back-up' from fennel purée and rosemary *jus* 'artistically drilled in circles around the plate'.

Given the complexity of some dishes, consistency – even on a single plate – can be difficult to control. But among the highlights of an inspection lunch was a pot au feu of Bresse pigeon: two 'magnificent, juicy, soft' breasts poached in court bouillon, served with ceps and 'a garden full of vegetables'. Any shortcomings at this meal were 'easily and mightily outweighed by the superb technique, timing and panache'. Some reporters amuse themselves trying to guess the delicate flavours of the trio of crème brûlées, but chocolate is undisputed king among desserts, whether in the form of a 'stunning' sorbet dropped into an apricot souffle at the last minute, or a 'deep, intensive dollop' of dark chocolate ice-cream sandwiched between crisp nut-studded tuiles. A couple of reporters have remarked on the small quantities delivered by the 'menu prestige', but it is a seven-course tasting menu after all, and it does provide a good sampling of the kitchen's output.

Service is helpful, enthusiastic and attentive, 'accents are straight from "Allo Allo"', and the sommelier is praised for his knowledge and tact. Wines make all the right noises, mostly in French. Aristocratic claret and burgundy head up the lengthy list, but lesser regions are also featured and the New World makes a few notable contributions. Prices are high, like the quality, but some wines under £20 can be found, including the house French at £15. CELLARMAN'S CHOICE: Alsace Geisburg Riesling 1992, André Kientzler, £35; Châteauneuf-du-Pape, Ch. de La Nerthe 1991, £35.

CHEF/PROPRIETOR: Gordon Ramsay OPEN: Mon to Fri L 12.15 to 2.30, Mon to Sat D 7 to 10.30 CLOSED: 2 weeks Christmas, 1st 2 weeks Aug MEALS: Set L £24 to £45, Set D £45 to £55. BYO Corkage £15 SERVICE: not inc CARDS: Amex, Delta, Diners, MasterCard, Switch, Visa DETAILS: 45 seats. Vegetarian meals. Children welcome. No cigars/pipes in dining room. No music. Air-conditioned

Au Jardin des Gourmets 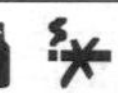 map 15

5 Greek Street, W1V 6NA COOKING 5
TEL: (0171) 437 1816 FAX: (0171) 437 0043 COST £30–£60

Describing itself as 'London's oldest French restaurant', the Jardin occupies a smart first-floor spot in the heart of Soho. The Russian company that owns it keeps it supplied with Oscietra caviare – 25g and a glass of champagne for £24 – but otherwise Vincent Hiss concentrates on a generous *carte* that might include roast scallops with braised chicory and lime, duck breast with lentil purée, and tarte au citron or pain perdu. He also throws in a few luxuries, including foie gras and morels, alongside roast rump of lamb, saddle of rabbit, and baked cod.

What seems to exercise reporters much of the time is the cost, especially the *carte*. 'Very well presented, well cooked, but only as good as food half the price' was one view. Someone else, happening upon 'excellent beef and lamb' but 'tough duck' at the same meal, objected to a £2 a head cover charge at dinner, although anybody who is grateful for small mercies might note that the service charge has come down from 15% to 12.5%. Service is generally good.

The wine list is a veritable Garden of Eden for French wine buffs, although the small number of choice wines from other countries may tempt them to stray. Château-bottled clarets date all the way back to 1949, and the impressive burgundies include a 1947 Corton from Joseph Drouhin. Fifty wines are priced under £20. House wines begin with Duboeuf at £9.75. CELLARMAN'S CHOICE: Côtes de Provence, Ch. Miraval 1993, £15.50; St-Emilion, Ch. Montalbert 1989, £27.50.

CHEF: Vincent Hiss PROPRIETOR: Novoport Group Ltd OPEN: Mon to Fri L 12 to 2.30, Mon to Sat D 6 to 11.15 CLOSED: bank hols MEALS: alc (main courses £14.50 to £19.50). Set L and D £16.50 (2 courses). Cover £2 D SERVICE: 12.5%, card slips closed CARDS: Amex, Delta, Diners, MasterCard, Switch, Visa DETAILS: 50 seats. Private parties: 55 main room, 8 and 14 private rooms. Vegetarian meals. Children's helpings. No smoking in 1 dining-room. Wheelchair access (no WC). No music. Air-conditioned

Avenue  map 15

7–9 St James's Street, SW1A 1EE COOKING 5
TEL: (0171) 321 2111 FAX: (0171) 321 2500 COST £32–£59

Sitting between a hatter's and a bootmaker's, the Avenue gives the impression of rather enjoying the incongruity of its location. A sweeping picture window flanked by classical columns sets the tone. Inside, a wall of TV screens plays anything from pop videos to fashion shows, while bright lights and a white-tiled floor make a bold backdrop for the ultra-modern cooking, which is served up with tremendous confidence.

The sad death of head chef Enda Flanagan at the end of 1996 must have a been a great shock for the team and Dean Carr is now in charge of the kitchen. A creamy risotto, further enriched with Gruyère, and topped with deep-fried leeks for textural contrast, made a satisfying start to an inspection dinner. Interesting combinations might include sea bass crusted with a strong provençale herb mixture, timed to retain moistness and accompanied by broad beans and spinach, or calf's liver roasted and partnered with black pudding, peppered beetroot and a sauce of bitter orange. Flaky salmon fish-cakes with buttered vegetables scored highly with one reporter, and chips are commended once more: 'some of the best I have had all year'. Desserts take in honey and oat parfait with lemon sauce, baked vanilla cheesecake with blueberry compote, and an artfully crafted assiette of chocolate that includes a fine dark chocolate tart. Service is both good-humoured and properly attentive.

Wines on the main list are arranged by varietal or style and achieve a good balance between traditional and modern. A shorter list, 'Christie's at the Avenue', features a regularly changing selection of fine wines – mainly classed growth clarets – supplied by the auction house and carrying 'a very small mark-up'. Twenty-seven wines are offered by the glass from £3.25, while house wines from Argentina and France are £12.50. CELLARMAN'S CHOICE: Bourgogne Chardonnay 1994, Paul Pernot, £18.50; Châteauneuf-du-Pape, Cuvée de Sommeliers 1990, Mestre, £26.50.

CHEF: Dean Carr PROPRIETOR: Moving Image Restaurants plc OPEN: Mon to Sat 12 to 3, 5.45 to 12 (12.30 Fri and Sat), Sun 12 to 3.30, 7 to 10 CLOSED: 3 days Christmas MEALS: alc (main courses £13 to £16). Set L £16.50 (2 courses) to £19.50, Set pre- and post-theatre D £13.50 (2 courses) to £15.50 SERVICE: 12.5% (optional), card slips closed CARDS: Amex, Diners, MasterCard, Switch, Visa DETAILS: 180 seats. Private parties: 10 main room. Vegetarian meals. Children welcome. Wheelchair access (also WC). Music. Air-conditioned

Bahn Thai 🍷 ✱

map 15

21A Frith Street, W1V 5TS — COOKING 4

TEL: (0171) 437 8504 FAX: (0171) 439 0340 — COST £28–£60

'Bahn Thai is still attempting to serve the most authentic home-cooked Thai food that we are able,' says owner Philip Harris, although there have been a few changes. The whole restaurant is now non-smoking, the ground-floor bistro has been abandoned and one menu (all 26 pages of it) is served throughout. Despite some simplification, it still takes 'an age to look through', even for those knowledgeable about Thai food, though an inspector found the content a 'delight for its breadth and daring'. Guidance notes encourage novices to ask for advice.

A vegetarian reporter particularly admired a 'hot, salty, sour' som tam papaya salad with small salty shrimps, and pad pak boong (stir-fried Thai 'water lily' stems with yellow beans, chilli, garlic and oyster sauce), a popular dish in Bangkok but rarely seen on menus in the UK. Also commended have been a generous portion of pad Thai noodles containing big juicy prawns, and a green vegetable curry, although it included broccoli – 'which you don't get in

Thailand' – alongside the more usual aubergines, Thai basil and Chinese mushrooms in a fresh-tasting curry sauce.

A pleasant touch is that the 12.5 per cent service charge really is optional: a perforated slip on the bill includes an invitation to detach it if you prefer not to pay it. The Thai food served here is a long way from the now ubiquitous high street versions, and priced accordingly, but interesting set menus – 'vegetarians', 'carnivores', 'general omnivores' and 'mainly seafood' – keep costs within limits and become cheaper as numbers of diners get larger. While some people might prefer Singha Thai beer or chrysanthemum tea as an accompaniment to the food, it would be a shame to overlook the list of appealing wines offered at very attractive prices. House French in three colours is £7.95. CELLARMAN'S CHOICE: Auffray Chardonnay 1995, Maipo Valley, Chile, £13.95; Brown Brothers Tarrango 1996, Victoria, Australia, £11.50.

CHEF: Penn Squires PROPRIETOR: Philip Harris OPEN: all week 12 to 2.45 (12.30 to 2.30 Sun), 6 to 11.15 (10.30 Sun) CLOSED: Christmas, Easter, bank hols MEALS: alc (main courses £7.50 to £20). Set L and D £18.50 to £25.50 (minimum 2). Light L and pre- and post-theatre D available SERVICE: 12.5% (optional), card slips closed CARDS: Amex, Delta, Diners, MasterCard, Switch, Visa DETAILS: 120 seats. Private parties: 50 main room, 20 to 50 private rooms. Vegetarian meals. Children welcome. No smoking in dining-room. Wheelchair access (no WC). Air-conditioned

Balzac Bistro £

NEW ENTRY map 12

4 Wood Lane, W12 7DT COOKING **2**
TEL: (0181) 743 6787 FAX: (0181) 997 1378 COST £18–£39

The ashtrays still bear London's old '01' telephone number prefix, and there are gingham cloths on the tables and recorded Piaf, but, with its polished granite floor and walls, potted palms and large mirrors and windows, Balzac Bistro bears little resemblance to the Franglais bistros of yesteryear. 'It's like going into a restaurant in any town in provincial France,' observed a visitor. The cooking is straightforward bistro-style, with stews and steaks as well as straight-up dishes of avocado with prawns in orange dressing, or grilled Dover sole. Reporters have endorsed baby squid in garlic, 'utterly classic' fish soup, and tomatoey rabbit chasseur. A good way to finish might be a neo-bistro banoffi mango pie, or crème brûlée with raspberries. Service is pleasant, prompt and confident, and the value of the set menus is hard to beat. The almost entirely French wine list is short but sweet, with low mark-ups, some sound white burgundies and several classy clarets. House wine from Duboeuf is £8.60.

CHEF: F. Ver PROPRIETOR: P. Tarelli OPEN: Mon to Fri L 12 to 2.30, Mon to Sat D 7 to 11 CLOSED: Christmas, bank hols MEALS: alc (main courses £8 to £13.50). Set L and D £10 to £13.90. Cover £1 SERVICE: 10% CARDS: Amex, Delta, Diners, MasterCard, Switch, Visa DETAILS: 80 seats. Private parties: 60 main room, 20 and 60 private rooms. Vegetarian meals. Children welcome. No pipes in dining-room. Music. Air-conditioned

£ *indicates that it is possible to have a three-course meal, including coffee, a half-bottle of house wine and service, at any time the restaurant is open (i.e. at dinner as well as at lunch, unless a place is open only for dinner), for £25 or less per person.*

Bank

NEW ENTRY map 13

1 Kingsway, WC2B 6XF — COOKING 5
TEL: (0171) 379 9797 FAX: (0171) 379 9014 — COST £23–£75

Bank was launched, with the customary snowstorm of newspaper reviews, just as the last edition of the *Guide* was published. After a much-lamented five-year gap in the record (his previous restaurant, L'Arlequin, last appeared in the 1993 *Guide*), Christian Delteil has emerged in a different guise. He now takes more of an overseer's role, caters for vastly more customers, and has replaced his impeccably classical haute cuisine with what he calls 'liberated French' cooking. The location midway between West End and City is canny, and the décor is something else. A busy bar leads past the open kitchen into a room with hundreds of shards of glass suspended from the ceiling ('watch out if there's an earthquake'), and a 'seaside caff' mural. A varied menu caters for business breakfasters, pre-theatre-goers and afternoon Saturday shoppers, as well as lunchers and diners.

If 'comfort food with oriental twists' appeals, then this could be for you: terrine of foie gras with fig jam maybe, or wok-fried lobster with Thai spices and noodles. It is not, perhaps, the place to expect chicken Kiev, but here it is all the same, 'nicely crispy, very tasty', alongside baked fish and chips ('very fresh cod'), artichoke risotto, and sausage and mash with onion sauce. One problem with this kind of food, where stocks and reductions often take a back seat, is that it can feel like flavour surfing. The word 'bland' has been used more than once, and cooking times have not always been as accurate as they might. But for every niggle there is a corresponding endorsement: for fresh and 'accurately grilled' mackerel, properly done vegetables, and desserts from nougat glacé and treacle pudding to 'bowl-scrapingly good' apple Tatin slice.

Perhaps the biggest surprise of all for reporters is that, in contrast to many other large London restaurants which also levy a 12.5% charge, service comes out with flying colours, variously described as on the ball, friendly and engaging, brisk, and generally 'excellent, from greeting to paying the bill'. Wines are grouped by style, and anyone with a £20 budget will be looking under 'lively fruity', certainly not 'round smooth', which only begins at £34.50. House French is £10.50.

CHEFS: Christian Delteil and Tim Hughes PROPRIETORS: Eric Garnier, Jeremy Ormerod, Ron Truss, Tony Allen and Christian Delteil OPEN: all week 12 to 3, 5.30 to 11.30 (10.30 Sun) MEALS: alc (main courses £8.50 to £26). Set L Sat £9.95 (2 courses) to £12.95. Set L and pre-theatre D (5.30 to 7pm) all week £12.90 (2 courses) to £16.50 SERVICE: 12.5%, card slips closed CARDS: Amex, Delta, Diners, MasterCard, Switch, Visa DETAILS: 200 seats. Vegetarian meals. Children welcome. Wheelchair access (also WC). Air-conditioned

Belair House

NEW ENTRY map 12

Gallery Road, SE21 7AB — COOKING 5
TEL: (0181) 299 9788 FAX: (0181) 693 3230 — COST £31–£58

On a rise overlooking Belair Park, the Adam-designed mansion, dating from 1785, was in poor shape until Gary and Jayne Cady restored it, opening their restaurant and bar in April 1997. The dining-room divides into a large vibrant-yellow room and a smaller, more soberly designed one, and the bar, which has the best view of the park, functions as an all-day brasserie.

Chef Nigel Davies combines individual components cleverly in dishes of, for instance, 'rich and well-flavoured' shellfish macaroni with tomato, fennel and chives, or seared scallops with spinach tagliolini in sauces of yellow pepper and deep-flavoured squid ink. Venison – 'the best I have ever tasted' – comes with a robust mix of dauphinois, red cabbage, green beans and peas, while halibut might be cooked in a soft green crust of thyme and served with a rich red wine *jus* made from veal stock. Reporters have praised lemon tart with crème fraîche, and passion-fruit tart with red grapefruit sorbet. Nouvelle-sized portions can make prices feel high, and while service is described as 'perfectly efficient and solicitous', there can be 'not enough of it' at busy times. A worldly wine list has some decent offerings under £20 a bottle and a few fine ones over £40. House wines start at £9.50.

CHEF: Nigel Howard Davies PROPRIETORS: Gary and Jayne Cady OPEN: Tue to Sun L 12 to 2.30, Tue to Sun D 7 to 10.30 MEALS: alc (main courses £11.50 to £19.50). Set L £19.95. Bar food available SERVICE: 12.5% (optional), card slips closed CARDS: Amex, Delta, MasterCard, Switch, Visa DETAILS: 100 seats. 50 seats outside. Car park. Vegetarian meals. Children's helpings. No cigars in dining-room. Wheelchair access (also WC). Music

Belgo Noord £ map 13

72 Chalk Farm Road, NW1 8AN COOKING **2**
TEL: (0171) 267 0718 FAX: (0171) 267 7508 COST **£24–£49**

Belgo is now practically synonymous with mussels and frites. The unique design of this, the original Belgo (see also Belgo Centraal in London Round-ups), is one of its strengths. It is an echoey bierkeller with a monastic refectory theme – staff are dressed as monks – plus design-conscious touches, including pickaxe handles on tables and chairs. Fat, succulent mussels come in pots with variously flavoured broths (marinière, beer and bacon, coconut cream and lemon grass, for instance), or open-faced with a variety of fillings (ham with chicory and cheese, and garlic butter with herbs). The list of Belgian specialities is ambitiously long but full of interest: for example, pan-fried soft-shell crab, wild boar sausages, and baked cod with a white beer and oyster cream. Puddings include deep-fried milk chocolate ice-cream coated in coconut served on caramel sauce. A two-sittings policy in the evenings may make things seem rushed. The list of beers supports Belgium's claim as the world's most interesting beer-producing country, and helpful descriptions inspire experimentation. Wines take second place, but the choice is sound. French house wine is £8.95.

CHEF: Richard Coates PROPRIETORS: André Plisnier and Denis Blais OPEN: Mon to Fri 12 to 3, 6 to 11.30, Sat 12 to 11.30, Sun 12 to 10.30 CLOSED: D 24 Dec, and 25 Dec MEALS: alc (main courses £7 to £22). Set L £5 (1 course) to £12.95 (2 courses), Set D Mon to Fri 6 to 7.30 £10 (1 course), Set D £12.95 (2 courses), all inc beer SERVICE: 15% (optional), card slips closed CARDS: Amex, Delta, Diners, MasterCard, Switch, Visa DETAILS: 140 seats. Private parties: 35 main room. Vegetarian meals. Children welcome. Wheelchair access (also WC). No music. Air-conditioned

Bertorelli's 🍷 map 15

44A Floral Street, WC2E 9DA
TEL: (0171) 836 3969 FAX: (0171) 836 1868
19–23 Charlotte Street, W1P 1HP COOKING 1
TEL: (0171) 636 4174 FAX: (0171) 631 0216 COST £25–£59

Bertorelli's is in two places: a branch on Charlotte Street, where the crowds tend to be 'gay young things and eccentric show-offs', and a more relaxed one in Covent Garden opposite the stage door of the Opera House with a more informal café next door. Reports suggest that top form is reached when Maddalena Bonino is on site (she alternates between the two), when the menu of old Italian faithfuls and trendier things is rendered with confidence. Salad combinations such as baby spinach, avocado, mushrooms, croûtons, bacon and Pecorino should fire up the appetite, while a pasta dish of broccoli and toasted almonds in a four-cheese sauce artfully manages to avoid both mozzarella and Parmesan. The side-order of deep-fried zucchini with wine vinegar is eulogised by more than one reporter, while desserts such as cappuccino cha-cha (coffee and vanilla ice-creams with a swirl of cream and smashed amaretti biscuits) prove quite compulsive. It's as well as to leave room for those, as earlier courses come in gargantuan portions. Tireless and charming service is praised at both addresses. The all-Italian wine list – champagnes excepted – offers a wide range of respected names, quite a few of them at reasonable prices. Table wines from Verona start the ball rolling at £9.50 a bottle. CELLARMAN'S CHOICE: Chardonnay 1996, Cantina Mezza Corona, £13.50; Regaleali Rosso 1994, Sicily, £16.

CHEF: Maddalena Bonino PROPRIETOR: Groupe Chez Gérard OPEN: Floral Street Mon to Sat 12 to 3, 5.30 to 11.30; Charlotte Street Mon to Fri L 12 to 3, Mon to Sat D 6 to 11 CLOSED: Floral Street 25 Dec, L bank hols; Charlotte Street 25 and 26 Dec, bank hols MEALS: alc (main courses £7.50 to £16). Cover £1.50 SERVICE: 12.5% (optional), card slips closed CARDS: Amex, Delta, Diners, MasterCard, Switch, Visa DETAILS: 85 seats (Floral Street), 53 seats (Charlotte Street). Private parties: 36 main room (Floral Street), 18 and 40 seats private rooms (Charlotte Street). Vegetarian meals. Children welcome. No-smoking area. No pipes/cigars in dining-room. Wheelchair access (no WC). Music. Air-conditioned

Bibendum 🍾 map 14

Michelin House, 81 Fulham Road, SW3 6RD COOKING 6
TEL: (0171) 581 5817 FAX: (0171) 823 7925 COST £41–£83

A decade old in November 1997, Bibendum still ranks (along with Pont de la Tour, see entry) as one of the top Conran restaurants. Dining-rooms do not come much more attractive, and this one is 'sunny and elegant' even in January, with the rubber-tyred Michelin theme extending from stained glass windows to ashtrays and carafes. It manages the difficult art of being both relaxed and formal, thanks partly to 'affable well trained staff' who are 'pleasant, discreet and professional'.

The à la carte's generosity is difficult to resist, given its 18 or so first courses, but the set-price lunch has a lot to recommend it too, not least on account of similar dishes for less money. The food is interesting without appearing contrived. Some staples are hardly ever off the menu – fish soup, Bresse chicken with tarragon, deep-fried lemon sole with chips and tartare sauce – but the appeal lies in relative simplicity, combined with a traditional and often hearty streak that might take in oeufs en meurette, properly made risotto, or 'pinkly undercooked' lamb kidneys, with an 'intense' topping of ceps with onions and garlic.

Offal and fish are both strong suits, the latter producing 'refined, well-executed and terrific combinations' such as ravioli of salt cod with a creamy chive sauce. 'Sound judgement' is typical from start to finish, including a 'fine wobbly' Rivesaltes and peach jelly, served with blueberry ice-cream. Venerable wines from Bordeaux and Burgundy form the backbone of a majestic wine list, while the Rhône and Italy make some impressive contributions. The plethora of grand names and equally grand prices can be intimidating, but there are good-quality, pocket-friendly bins in the house selection, starting at £10.95. Fans of old cognac, armagnac or calvados should not overlook the spirits section. CELLARMAN'S CHOICE: Rully, Les St-Jacques 1994, Dom. Aubert de Villaine, £32.50; Bandol, Mas de la Rouvière 1991, £24.50.

The Oyster Bar downstairs has been expanded and is 'nearer than anywhere I know to providing the perfect light lunch'. It is informal and unpretentious, yet impeccable, with no compromise on quality, and deals largely in cold seafood and salads, offering 'a kind of perfection within a limited range'. Good raw materials, immediacy of flavour, 'brisk but friendly and efficient service', and reasonable prices all help.

CHEFS: Matthew Harris and Athene O'Neill PROPRIETORS: Sir Terence Conran, Paul Hamlyn, Simon Hopkinson and Graham Williams OPEN: all week 12.30 to 2.30 (3 Sat and Sun), 7 to 11.30 CLOSED: 24 to 26 Dec MEALS: alc D (main courses £13.50 to £23). Set L £28 SERVICE: 12.5% (optional), card slips closed CARDS: Amex, Delta, Diners, MasterCard, Switch, Visa DETAILS: 72 seats. Private parties: 80 main room. Vegetarian meals. Children's helpings. No pipes in dining-room. Wheelchair access (no WC). No music. Air-conditioned

Billboard Cafe £

map 13

280 West End Lane, NW6 1LJ — COOKING 1
TEL: (0171) 431 4188 — COST £20–£44

Simple Italian fare is on the bill at the Billboard. It is a pleasant, wooden-floored triangular space, open to the great outdoors when the sun shines on West Hampstead, with a nice patch of green and trees for shade. There are leafy salads aplenty to begin, and pasta dressed simply with sage and butter, or more elaborately with artichokes, pancetta and porcini in a light cream sauce. A reporter who ate chargrilled marinated calamari, rolled and stuffed breast of chicken, and ice-cream to finish had sampled the sort of cooking the Café does best. Other puddings to tempt may include carrot cake with lemon cream sauce, or tiramisù. Service tries hard to please, and the wines do likewise, with one or two Australians popping up among the Italians. House wines start at £7.95 for basic Trebbiano and Sangiovese.

CHEF/PROPRIETOR: M.T. Nateghi OPEN: Sat 12 to 11.30, Sun 12 to 10.30, Mon to Fri D 6.30 to 11.30 CLOSED: 25 and 26 Dec MEALS: alc (main courses £5.50 to £13.50). Set L and D £12.50 SERVICE: 10%, card slips closed CARDS: Amex, Delta, MasterCard, Switch, Visa DETAILS: 50 seats. 8 seats outside. Private parties: 50 main room. Vegetarian meals. Children's helpings. No-smoking area. Wheelchair access (no WC). Music. Air-conditioned

Bistrot Soho

NEW ENTRY map 15

64 Frith Street, W1V 5TA COOKING 4
TEL: (0171) 734 4545 FAX: (0171) 287 1027 COST £26–£54

Here is an address that has seen some changes in the last few years. It opened as Bistrot Bruno when Bruno Loubet left the Four Seasons. Next door became Café Bruno, which came over all North African, rematerialising as Bruno Levantine. The two merged as Bruno Soho, then Loubet disappeared altogether and it is now known as Bistrot Soho, but a few African accents remain, at least for the time being.

The new chef is James Kirby, ex-Fables (see entry), and while there is still couscous royale made with lamb shoulder, chicken and merguez, the menu has taken on a rustic French complexion. Hence, jambon persillade, tomate farcie, and grilled onglet with shallots, the latter a success at inspection, served with a portion of rich, well-puréed mashed potato. Also 'simple but effective' were a first-course bowl of mixed lamb's offal (kidney, tongue and sweetbreads) with asparagus and broad beans, and pan-fried skate wing dressed with ginger, garlic and soy. Aromatic desserts might include petit pot de crème au jasmin, an apple poached in fruit tea ('a much gentler effect than the more customary wine liquor'), or raspberry tart with basil sorbet. Staff are 'smiling and willing enough'. North African and Lebanese bottles feature amid the more mainstream wines. Choice is wide, prices start at £10.50, and there is plenty available by the glass.

CHEF: James Kirby PROPRIETORS: Pierre and Kathleen Condou OPEN: Mon to Fri L 12 to 2.30, Mon to Sat D 6 to 11.30 CLOSED: 25 and 26 Dec, 1 Jan MEALS: alc D (main courses £8.50 to £17). Set L £14.50 (2 courses) to £16.50. Cover £1.25 SERVICE: not inc CARDS: Amex, Delta, Diners, MasterCard, Switch, Visa DETAILS: 90 seats. Private parties: 90 main room. Vegetarian meals. Children welcome. No cigars/pipes in dining-room. Wheelchair access (no WC). Music. Air-conditioned

Bluebird

NEW ENTRY map 14

350 King's Road, SW3 5UU COOKING 4
TEL: (0171) 559 1000 FAX: (0171) 559 1111 COST £25–£73

Not a man to do things by halves, Sir Terence Conran has crammed into this multi-purpose gastrodome (opened in May 1997) a foodmarket, traiteur, wine merchant, café, kitchenware shop, private dining club, and, of course, a restaurant. The Bluebird Garage was built in 1923, and its conversion owes something to the spirit of Malcolm Campbell. A dark green limestone floor, white-painted girders, kite-like artwork dangling from the ceiling, and a large skylight make it a 'memorable' and 'uplifting' dining-room, and one observer found the bright open spaces 'more relaxing than the underground caverns of Mezzo and Quaglino's' (see entries, London). Everything, from mineral water to ashtrays, house wine and glasses, is an ambassador for the Bluebird image.

The kitchen cruises though the modern British repertoire, enlivened by the presence of a wood-fired oven that has produced 'an inspired dish' of rabbit with broad beans, black olives and artichokes, and 'stunningly good' squab with a 'delicate smokiness', served with creamy gratin dauphinoise. A seafood display tempted one reporter to a plate of 'magnificent' langoustines cooked in their shells and served with a little tub of mayonnaise, while another enjoyed grilled squid with a juicy salsa. It doesn't take a very sensitive seismometer to pick up on the latest trends: fish-cakes spiked with a few mild green chillies and served with aïoli, lamb and lemon salad with parsley and sheep's yoghurt, and duck and crab sausages (which come with a dipping sauce) that were 'meaty, flavourful and decidedly unusual'. Desserts are less good. The sharp modern wine list is full of interest. House French is £11.75.

CHEF: Michael Moore PROPRIETOR: Sir Terence Conran OPEN: all week 12 to 3.30 (11 to 4.30 Sat and Sun), 6 to 11.30 (10.30 Sun) MEALS: alc (main courses Mon to Fri £8.50 to £26.50, Sat and Sun £7.50 to £12.50). Set L and pre-theatre D (6 to 7pm) Mon to Fri £11.50 (2 courses) to £14.50, Set L Sun £15 SERVICE: 12.5% (optional), card slips closed CARDS: Amex, Diners, MasterCard, Switch, Visa DETAILS: 240 seats. Private parties: 20 main room, 20 private room. Vegetarian meals. Children welcome. Wheelchair access (also WC). Music. Air-conditioned

Blue Elephant

map 12

4–6 Fulham Broadway, SW6 1AA — COOKING **2**

TEL: (0171) 385 6595 FAX: (0171) 386 7665 — COST £32–£64

Stepping off Fulham Broadway into this justly celebrated Thai restaurant really is a case of entering another world. Staff in national dress conduct you into what, to one reporter, felt like a 'tropical rainforest'. Trailing plants hang from somewhere high above, a 'stream' divides the room into separate dining-areas, and some of the tables are in a kind of open-sided bamboo hut. One half-expects to hear the screech of a macaque as the cocktails are brought. The cooking is equally ceremonial in style, the vegetable garnishes carved into flowers, the hors d'oeuvre arriving on little cake-stands. Chilli-hot chicken salad, prawns with vermicelli, and fish-cakes with a sweet-and-sour dipping sauce all showed up well one evening. Seafood is the focus, to the extent that meat dishes can seem a little dull by comparison. The elephant symbols on the menu denote the degree of spice heat in each dish: some may be found searingly ferocious to those unused to Thai cooking. Fresh fruits or ice-creams are how meals end. Service has been thought a bit stifling, notably with regard to the topping-up of wine, but the philosophy is to oblige at all costs. An enterprisingly wide-ranging wine list has some energetic mark-ups. House French is £10.50.

CHEF: Rungsan Mulijan PROPRIETOR: Blue Elephant International plc OPEN: Sun to Fri L 12 to 2.30, all week D 7 to 12.30 CLOSED: 24 to 27 Dec MEALS: alc (main courses £7.50 to £17). Set L and D £29 to £34. Cover £1.50. BYO £10 SERVICE: not inc CARDS: Amex, Diners, MasterCard, Visa DETAILS: 250 seats. Private parties: 250 main room. Vegetarian meals. Children welcome. Wheelchair access (also WC). Music. Air-conditioned

Blue Print Café

map 13

Design Museum, Butlers Wharf, SE1 2YE — COOKING **4**

TEL: (0171) 378 7031 FAX: (0171) 357 8810 — COST £31–£53

The clean-lined Blue Print Café, above the Design Museum, has plenty of buzz plus one of the best views of the Thames, to be enjoyed in all seasons now that its balcony has been glassed in. The kitchen is open, waiters smartly uniformed, and the food 'trendy'.

Mediterranean influences come across in 'light, vivid, appetising' tagliatelle with asparagus, new potatoes, broad beans and pancetta, or a 'sensational' confit of new season's garlic with tapénade and goats' cheese. 'Absolutely *à point,*' wrote a visitor about John Dory with creamy mashed potatoes surrounded by a yellow-ochre sauce tasting lightly of crab and firmly of saffron. The kitchen handles chicken well, too, perhaps baked and accompanied by capers, shallots, ceps, anchovy and garlic. Desserts might include an original rhubarb, amaretti, mascarpone and pistachio trifle, or ginger and praline parfait with chocolate sauce. Coffee, bread and unobtrusive and helpful staff have all come in for praise. The short wine list is up to date in both vintages and range, and dessert wines are well chosen. Prices start at £12.95.

CHEF: Jeremy Lee PROPRIETOR: Conran Restaurants OPEN: all week L 12 to 3 (3.30 Sun), Mon to Sat D 6.30 to 11 MEALS: alc (main courses £9.50 to £14.50) SERVICE: 12.5% (optional) CARDS: Amex, Delta, Diners, MasterCard, Switch, Visa DETAILS: 120 seats. Vegetarian meals. Children welcome. Wheelchair access (also WC). No music

Boyd's 

map 13

135 Kensington Church St, W8 7LP — COOKING 4
TEL: (0171) 727 5452 FAX: (0171) 221 0615 — COST £26–£57

Boyd Gilmour left in January 1997 to pursue his first love – music – with the Royal Opera. The name remains, as does the conservatory-style dining-room with its plants, simple furniture and intimate atmosphere, while Maria Zarari, Gilmour's former sous-chef, continues his style of cooking. A contemporary menu puts the emphasis on lightness, helped along by a good selection of fish, including scallop salad, halibut ceviche, or perhaps grilled monkfish wrapped in Parma ham with pesto. Chargrilling is a favoured technique, applied successfully to sea bass in a champagne velouté, as well as to vegetables and to chicken with a tarragon sauce. Richer fare comes in the form of black pudding with apple and cider sauce, and sauté calf's liver and sweetbreads with a foie gras sauce. 'Well made, with just the right textures and flavours,' was one judgement on prune and armagnac ice-cream, and the crème brûlée is good too.

The wine list has changed yet again, slimming down to around 80 items plus a varying selection of bin-ends, and taking the more user-friendly form of arrangement by style with short explanatory notes. The split between Old and New Worlds is more balanced, and although far fewer bottles are available under £20, the choice of house wines, starting at £11.50 a bottle (£3 a glass), is still reasonable. CELLARMAN'S CHOICE: Pinot Blanc d'Alsace 1995, Dom. Bott-Geyl, £17.95; Paracombe Cabernet 1994, Adelaide Hills, S. Australia, £19.50.

CHEFS: Maria Zarari and A. Afonso PROPRIETOR: Maria Zarari OPEN: Mon to Sat 12.30 to 2.30, 7 to 10.45 CLOSED: Christmas, Easter, bank hols MEALS: alc (main courses £12.50 to £17.50). Set L £12.50 (2 courses) to £15 SERVICE: not inc CARDS: Amex, Delta, MasterCard, Switch, Visa DETAILS: 40 seats. Private parties: 40 main room, 10 private room. Vegetarian meals. No children under 5. No-smoking area. Wheelchair access (no WC). No music. Air-conditioned

Brackenbury £

map 12

129–131 Brackenbury Road, W6 0BQ — COOKING 4
TEL: (0181) 748 0107 FAX: (0181) 741 0905 — COST £20–£36

'What a fine place this is, and especially, what stunning value!' exclaimed a seasoned reporter. Since the present owners took over in 1997 there has been a subtle but distinct shift of orientation in the cooking, with a softer focus and slightly more obvious refinement now characterising the food, although the emphasis is still on assembling strong, direct flavours. An inspection starter of artichoke hearts with asparagus, peas, white onions and a goose egg that came with a Pecorino dip impressed for its 'simple execution, every ingredient cooked just right'. Duck gizzards, a Gascon speciality, turn up in a warm salad with new potatoes, French beans, bacon and a poached egg. Lobster tagliatelle in its own bisque with asparagus and spinach is 'simple yet effective', while a more complex dish of lamb fillets with a 'ratatouille' of diced white beans, red pepper, courgette and a forthright pesto also works well 'maximising the flavours and textures'.

Puddings are variable: pear Tatin, and apricot sorbet failed to inspire one reporter, but well-balanced apple and redcurrant crumble with good vanilla ice-cream earned praise from another. An intelligently thought-out list of international wines consists almost entirely of sub-£20 offerings. Prices open at £8.95 for Vins de Pays d'Oc. As the *Guide* went to press the new regime was still settling in and may revise opening times, so phone in advance to avoid disappointment.

CHEF: Marsha Chang Hong PROPRIETORS: Nick Smallwood and Simon Slater OPEN: Tue to Fri and Sun L 12.30 to 2.45, Mon to Sat D 7 to 10.45 CLOSED: Christmas, most bank hols MEALS: alc (main courses L £4.50 to £9, D £4.50 to £25). BYO £5 SERVICE: not inc CARDS: Amex, Delta, MasterCard, Switch, Visa DETAILS: 55 seats. 15 seats outside. Private parties: 8 main room. Vegetarian meals. Children's helpings. No cigars/pipes in dining-room. No music

Bradleys

map 13

25 Winchester Road, NW3 3NR — COOKING 5
TEL: (0171) 722 3457 FAX: (0171) 431 4776 — COST £22–£42

Bradleys owes its calm and collected demeanour to its backstreet location, creamy yellow and burgundy colour scheme, and indirect lighting. The space is cleverly broken up with a raised area, a bar, a descending spiral staircase and pillars. New chef M. Mouzaoui, who arrived in early 1997, is joined by Simon Bradley himself. The *carte* remains East meets West Coast America, is more fishy than meaty and doesn't change all that often, although it has grown more daring.

A first course mille-feuille of Gorgonzola, roasted peaches and Bayonne ham contains good ingredients and avoids overpowering the senses. More conventional pan-fried monkfish with Mediterranean vegetables, sauce vierge and deep-fried capers ('a revelation') bursts with flavour. Other main courses have included roasted Barbary duck with chicory, and rack of lamb with a sage and onion gratin, and desserts might take in raspberry créme brûlée with Grand Marnier, or apricot maple cheesecake. Service is deft and accommodating. It would be hard to find a more Eurosceptic wine list, the only Old World contingent being a pair of champagnes. Nearly half the bottles cost more than £20, although house Chilean is £9.95.

CHEFS: Simon Bradley and M. Mouzaoui PROPRIETORS: Mr and Mrs Simon Bradley OPEN: Sun to Fri L 12 to 3, all week D 6 to 11 CLOSED: 25 and 26 Dec, 1 Jan MEALS: alc D (main courses £10 to £14). Set L £12 (2 courses) to £15 SERVICE: not inc; 12% for parties of 5 or more CARDS: Amex, Delta, MasterCard, Switch, Visa DETAILS: 65 seats. Private parties: 70 main room. Vegetarian meals. Children's helpings. No cigars/pipes in dining-room. Wheelchair access (no WC). Music. Air-conditioned

Brady's £

map 12

513 Old York Road, SW18 1TF — COOKING 1
TEL: (0181) 877 9599 — COST £15–£22

'Basic bistro which happens to sell fish & chips,' is Luke and Amelia Brady's way of describing their small Wandsworth operation. It is open only in the evenings and grills more fish than it fries, although good-quality battered cod, haddock and plaice come with 'good' chips. The blackboard menu lists starters such as cod's roe pâté, and anchovies and rollmops, as well as grilled bream, tuna, sardines, marlin and so on, according to availablility. No mention of the 'optional' service charge is made until you get the bill. Chilean house wine is £6.95.

CHEF: Luke Brady PROPRIETORS: Luke and Amelia Brady OPEN: Mon to Sat D only 7 to 10.30 (10.45 Thu and Fri) CLOSED: Christmas, Easter, bank hols MEALS: alc (main courses £4 to £7) SERVICE: 10% (optional) CARDS: none DETAILS: 36 seats. Children's helpings. Music

Brasserie St Quentin

map 14

243 Brompton Road, SW3 2EP — COOKING 3
TEL: (0171) 589 8005 FAX: (0171) 584 6064 — COST £25–£54

'Very Paris' is how one reporter described the style and mood of the place, with its mirrored walls, unhurried pace and professional, courteous staff who are there 'at a glance' if needed. Ownership passed to Groupe Chez Gérard in March 1997, but Nigel Davis remains in the kitchen and the food continues much as before. The menu is written in French, with concise English translations, and is bourgeois Gallic in tone. People are generally more than happy with the kitchen's endeavours: witness fish soup, brochette of scallops and bacon, 'excellent' chicken stuffed with foie gras, and fillet of beef with béarnaise sauce. Highest praise is reserved for desserts: lemon tart receives plaudits, as does an impeccable chocolate pavé, and prune and armagnac mousse. The wine list is 100 per cent French, which can be a boon or a drawback depending on your viewpoint. House wine is £9.90. Under the same ownership is Grill St Quentin, 3 Yeoman's Row, London SW3; Tel (0171) 581 8377. Reports please.

CHEF: Nigel Davis PROPRIETOR: Groupe Chez Gérard OPEN: all week 12 to 3 (3.30 Sun), 6.30 to 11.30 (11 Sun) MEALS: alc (main courses £7 to £19). Set L £11 (2 courses), Set D 6.30 to 7.30 £11 (2 courses) SERVICE: 12.5% (optional), card slips closed CARDS: Amex, Delta, Diners, MasterCard, Switch, Visa DETAILS: 75 seats. Private parties: 20 main room, 20 private room. Vegetarian meals. Children welcome. No cigars in dining-room. No music. Air-conditioned

Bu-San [£]

map 13

43 Holloway Road, N7 8JP — COOKING 1
TEL: (0171) 607 8264 — COST £21–£60

Korean restaurants (and, it is said, potential wives) are judged by their kim-chee (pickled cabbage) and other pickled vegetables which come as appetisers, side dishes or ingredients in main courses, and Bu-San's version 'with lots of garlic and chilli' won the approval of an inspector. Spinach in sesame, fried courgette and garlic with salt and sesame, and radish in soy and chilli are also 'very good and clean-tasting', while fried nori is 'compulsively crunchable and lickable'. The Korean repertoire takes in 'spicy and light' fried or raw meat and fish – sizzling squid in chilli sauce, yuk hoe (Korean 'steak tartare' mixed with sliced pear and sesame seeds), or sunomono (raw prawns in rice wine), for example – and dishes are 'beautifully presented'. They don't take it seriously when Europeans ask for lots of chilli, but service in this simple family-run place is 'charming and good natured'. House wines are £8.90.

CHEF: Young Hyung Lee PROPRIETORS: Young Hyung and Kim Lee OPEN: Mon to Fri L 12 to 2.30, Mon to Sat D 6 to 11 CLOSED: 25 and 26 Dec, 1 and 2 Jan MEALS: alc (main courses £6.50 to £30). Set L (1 course) £4.20 to £6.60, Set D (all minimum 2) £14.75 to £19 SERVICE: 10%, card slips closed CARDS: Switch, Visa DETAILS: 46 seats. Private parties: 46 main room. Vegetarian meals. Children's helpings. Wheelchair access (also WC). Music. Air-conditioned

Butlers Wharf Chop House 🍷

map 13

36E Shad Thames, Butlers Wharf, SE1 2YE — COOKING 3
TEL: (0171) 403 3403 FAX: (0171) 403 3414 — COST £36–£79

Arriving from the north, take a left from Tower Bridge, follow the line of the river till Shad Thames, and the Chop House is the first restaurant you come across. The big beige interior has none-too-comfy chairs, shelving piled with crockery, and tables of heavily knotted wood. It is all designed to make you feel at home, as is Henrik Iversen's cooking, which is basically heritage British with a few twists. Chicken soup with parsley, asparagus with hollandaise, and smoked eel with beetroot, horseradish and crispy bacon could all be taken from Dorothy Hartley. On the other hand, a terrine of rabbit with French beans and hazelnuts is decidedly Continental. Breast of pheasant cooked in Kentish wine with chestnuts has been judged 'beautiful, moist and tender', but the real plaudits are reserved for steak and kidney pudding, 'evoking memories of Mother's puddings in the past'.

Finish with strawberry shortbread, Cambridge burnt cream, or rhubarb and custard tart. A carefully chosen wine list keeps quality high at all price levels, while supplying plenty of interesting bins from the New World and Italy alongside the expected French classics. Ten house wines start at £13.95 a bottle, £3.50 a glass; six clarets are offered by the 75cl jug from £17.95.

CHEF: Henrik Iversen PROPRIETORS: Sir Terence Conran and Joel Kissin OPEN: Sun to Fri L 12 to 3, Mon to Sat D 6 to 11 MEALS: alc D (main courses £11.50 to £21). Set L £18.75 (2 courses) to £22.75 SERVICE: 12.5% (optional) CARDS: Amex, Diners, MasterCard, Switch, Visa DETAILS: 115 seats. 44 seats outside. Private parties: 30 main room. Vegetarian meals. Children welcome. Wheelchair access (also WC). No music

Byron's

NEW ENTRY map 13

3A Downshire Hill, NW3 1NR — COOKING 3
TEL/FAX: (0171) 435 3544 — COST £23–£61

Here is one of those addresses that have seen restaurants come and go over the years. If the new venture fares better than its predecessors, it may well be because Jonathon Coxon, previously of the now-defunct Waltons in Chelsea, is at the stoves. The lively menu might offer aubergine and mackerel terrine with pesto, calf's liver with sweet potato purée, or sea bass dressed with lemon and vanilla. Seared tuna at an inspection meal was 'a stunningly good piece of fish, perfectly cooked to highlight its solid yet tender texture and intense flavour', accompanied by a mixture of charred peppers and purple onions. Lamb shank was braised to 'appropriately sticky tenderness', and came on a richly meaty stock reduction and a mound of 'crushed and cluttered' potatoes. Standard French desserts may be supplemented by mint parfait with Mexican chocolate sauce, or pecan brownie with ice-cream. 'Pleasant and efficient' service lightens the mood. Wines are commendably cosmopolitan in range, but prices have been kept in check. House vins de pays are £11.95.

CHEF: Jonathon Coxon PROPRIETOR: Dalgreave (Byron's) Ltd OPEN: all week 12.30 to 2.30 (3.30 Sun), 7 to 11 (10 Sun) CLOSED: 25 and 26 Dec MEALS: alc (main courses L £6 to £16.50, D £10 to £16.50). BYO £11.95 SERVICE: 12.5% (optional), card slips closed CARDS: Amex, Delta, MasterCard, Switch, Visa DETAILS: 45 seats. 10 seats outside. Private parties: 40 main room. Vegetarian meals. Children's helpings. No children under 8 at D. No smoking in 1 dining-room. Wheelchair access (no WC). Music. Air-conditioned

Café dell'Ugo

map 13

56–58 Tooley Street, SE1 2SZ — NEW CHEF
TEL: (0171) 407 6001 FAX: (0171) 357 8806 — COST £23–£45

Smack in the middle of a Thames-side development housing the London Dungeon and several wine bars, Café dell'Ugo occupies a large railway arch. Downstairs is a cavernous bar with ample standing room; upstairs is the main restaurant, with square tables in neat rows and simple bentwood chairs. The menu has typically been in Antony Worrall-Thompson mould, with bold Mediterranean flavours to the fore, but he is no longer a director of Simpsons of Cornhill, and new chef Andrew Farquimarson arrived to replace David Massey just as the *Guide* went to press, so we are not quite sure what to expect. Around ten house wines are sold by the glass from a lively modern list. House wine is £8.95. Reports please.

CHEF: Andrew Farquimarson PROPRIETOR: Simpsons of Cornhill plc OPEN: Mon to Fri L 12 to 3, Mon to Sat D 6 to 11 CLOSED: bank hols MEALS: alc (main courses £8.50 to £13). Set D £12 (2 courses) to £15 SERVICE: not inc CARDS: Amex, Delta, Diners, MasterCard, Switch, Visa DETAILS: 85 seats. Private parties: 95 main room. Vegetarian meals. Children welcome. Music

'The separate elements swam around in a watery and tasteless nage lacking in nageness, not speaking to each other, like two goldfish in a bowl who had had a tiff over the ants' eggs.' (On eating in the West Country)

Café du Jardin

map 15

28 Wellington Street, WC2E 7BD
TEL: (0171) 836 8769 and 8760 COOKING 5
FAX: (0171) 836 4123 COST £21–£48

The *jardin* the café is in is Covent, making this prime-site street-corner restaurant a sure bet for theatre patrons as well as casual walk-ins on a West End night out. It all looks modishly monochrome on entering, halogen lamps in the ceiling bouncing light off the sparkling glassware. Steven Nash was appointed to run the kitchen in January 1997, and the lengthy menu offers fairly complicated modern European food. Super-fresh, rapidly seared tuna with dried tomatoes, black olives, new potatoes, French beans and egg is really a deconstructed salade niçoise, but its dazzling flavours make it stand out. Crabmeat and asparagus deep-fried in tempura batter and served on a green onion and chilli risotto shine as a result of the kitchen's wise understanding of contrasting textures and tastes.

Main courses raise the stakes further with grilled swordfish on cardamom-scented polenta with gazpacho dressing, but the simplicity of calf's liver with sauté potatoes and caramelised onions in a red wine sauce is also satisfying. A dish of tart summer berries in a tuile tulip with sweet cream and a raspberry coulis impressed for its balance, while the pairing of sticky toffee pudding – not with the usual butterscotch but with a fromage frais sorbet – shows that the kitchen has a lively streak. Service is fully up to the press of business. Wines offer a wide range of grape varieties and styles from four continents and provide good drinking at all price levels. House French is £9.50 a bottle, £2.95 for a 250ml glass.

CHEF: Steven Nash PROPRIETORS: Robert Seigler and Tony Howorth OPEN: Mon to Sat 12 to 3, 5.30 to 12, Sun noon to 11 CLOSED: 25 and 26 Dec MEALS: alc (main courses £9 to £13). Set L and D 5.30 to 7 and 10 to 12 £9.95 (2 courses) to £13.50 SERVICE: 15% (optional), card slips closed CARDS: Amex, Delta, Diners, MasterCard, Switch, Visa DETAILS: 110 seats. 20 seats outside. Private parties: 55 main room, 60 private room. Vegetarian meals. Children welcome. Wheelchair access (no WC). Music. Air-conditioned

Café Fish

map 15

39 Panton Street, SW1Y 4EA COOKING 2
TEL: (0171) 930 3999 FAX: (0171) 839 4880 COST £30–£56

Think 'café' as well as 'fish', for the frenetic pace of service and turnover is part of the appeal of this corporate fish restaurant off Haymarket. It represents a more imaginative option for pre- and post-theatre eating than much else in the vicinity. 'I ate here four times last year,' recalls a reporter, 'and each time was impressed by the freshness of the fish and the overall service.' The range extends from oysters with shallot vinegar, through skate wing in peppercorns and cognac, to monkfish baked with lardons and mushrooms. Plain grilled fish is always good, though, whether sardines to start, or whole Dover sole as a main, and the mixed seafood platters are generous to a fault. Fine French cheeses offer an alternative to the likes of truffe au chocolat. The cover charge buys you not just baguette, but appetising fish pâté to smear on it. Wines are listed by grape variety, offer an impressively broad-minded selection and are naturally mainly white. Prices start at £8.95.

CHEF: Andrew Magson PROPRIETOR: Groupe Chez Gérard OPEN: Mon to Fri L 12 to 3, Mon to Sat D 5.45 to 11.30 CLOSED: bank hols L MEALS: alc (main courses £9.50 to £17.50). Bar meals available. Cover £1.50 SERVICE: 12.5% (optional), card slips closed CARDS: Amex, Diners, MasterCard, Switch, Visa DETAILS: 89 seats. Vegetarian meals. Children welcome. No cigars/pipes in dining-room. No-smoking area. Music. Air-conditioned

Café Japan £

GOOD VALUE 1998 JAPANESE

map 13

626 Finchley Road, NW11 7RR — COOKING 5
TEL: (0181) 455 6854 — COST £20–£40

If this 'casual Japanese restaurant' (their own description) can produce food that 'compares with the finest Japanese in London' (an inspector's comment) at modest prices, why can't others? One answer, perhaps, is the 'basic' décor: oilcloth-covered tables, a one-sized tumbler that does for wine, water and coffee, and – for interest no doubt – a small pot-plant standing on the counter in a white plastic pot labelled 'Salmon Eggs'. There have been changes since last year: tempura, not a strong point, has been dropped and, sadly but understandably, the Friday-night offer of all the sushi you can eat for £15 is also gone. Prices have increased: some are now as much as half what you might pay for smaller portions in the West End. 'Super de luxe assorted sushi', for example, includes tuna, salmon, scallop, turbot, sweet shrimp, slamon roe and sea urchin for a mere £12.

Yakitori (skewers of grilled meat, seafood or vegetable) are superbly seasoned and 'not spoiled by sweet teriyaki sauce', and cost less than £2 per skewer; or choose any six for £8.50. Don't miss the Japanese mushroom version with 'tender, strong-flavoured' shiitake, and beef rolled with Japanese leaves which demonstrates the magical effect of shiso on the flavour of beef, and explains its English name, beefsteak plant. The specialities are sushi and teriyaki: at inspection, nori-wrapped awabi sushi, from the handwritten list of daily specials, showed Japanese presentation at its finest, the plate decorated with a calligraphic character painted in dark, slightly sweet sauce that enhanced the delicate flavour of the shellfish. Other successes include sunomono, comprising mildly vinegared sea-eel fillets, mackerel, octopus, squid and seaweed; al dente boiled mooli and yellow tail; and a whole 'nicely browned' grilled squid. Wine is £7.90, or drink hot or cold saké.

CHEF: Mr K. Konnai PROPRIETOR: Mr H. Matsuda OPEN: Mon to Sat D only 5.30 to 10.30 CLOSED: bank hols MEALS: alc (main courses £3.50 to £9). Set D £8 to £15. BYO £3 SERVICE: not inc CARDS: Delta, MasterCard, Switch, Visa DETAILS: 37 seats. Private parties: 37 main room. Vegetarian meals. Children welcome. Music. Air-conditioned

▲ *Café Nico* $✱

map 15

Grosvenor House, Park Lane, W1A 3AA — COOKING 3
TEL: (0171) 495 2275 FAX: (0171) 493 3341 — COST £47–£56

A taste of the Nico experience at Grosvenor House may be had at the Café, an informal eating-area that makes the most of its panoramic view of Park Lane and Hyde Park beyond. Andy Lee tacks faithfully to the master's course by giving a gleaming polish to what are essentially fairly earthy dishes. Tomato soup with basil, duck terrine with onion marmalade, or smoked salmon pancake with chive cream are the kinds of things you might encounter in a good country pub, but here are given the sort of lustre that the prices and surroundings deserve. Venison sausage braised in red wine, smoked haddock with spinach, and poached maize-fed guinea-fowl with lentils indicate the thrust of main courses. For dessert, expect bread-and-butter pudding, or something lighter such as crème caramel, or raspberry jelly with chocolate sorbet. Soups, salads and sandwiches are available on an all-day menu. In this context, it might feel rather extravagant to spend £275 on 1978 Lafite, although there is nothing under £20 a bottle, anyway, other than house Bordeaux at £19.50.

CHEF: Andy Lee PROPRIETOR: Grosvenor House OPEN: all week 12 to 3, 6 to 11 MEALS: Set L and D £24.50 (2 courses) to £29.50. Light all-day menu available. BYO £10 SERVICE: 10%, card slips closed CARDS: Amex, Delta, Diners, MasterCard, Switch, Visa DETAILS: 110 seats. Private parties: 100 private room. Vegetarian meals. Children's helpings. No smoking in 1 dining-room. Music. Air-conditioned ACCOMMODATION: 675 rooms, all with bath/shower. TV. Phone. Air-conditioned. D,B&B £210 to £285. Rooms for disabled. Children welcome. Afternoon teas. Swimming-pool

Café Spice Namaste

NEW ENTRY map 13

16 Prescot Street, E1 8AZ — COOKING 5

TEL: (0171) 488 9242 FAX: (0171) 488 9339 — COST £24–£45

Hard labour it may be to find (persist through the one-way system), but converted Victorian courthouses don't come brighter than this one. Vibrant purple, turquoise and maroon walls, drapes in Indian national colours, and naive paintings arranged in geometrical patterns all provide a contrasting background to the blue suits of City customers. Mrs Todiwala, wife of chef and co-owner Cyrus, runs front-of-house 'with efficiency and charm', although when others take over it may be less perfect. Her guidance through the long and largely unfamiliar menu can be invaluable. Goa is Cyrus Todiwala's principal inspiration but he also draws on all the main areas of India, plus some lesser-known. There are a few Thai dishes too.

Home-made chutneys are 'the real thing', according to a visitor who went on to relish tandoori grilled breast of Barbary duck. Other tandooris include galinha cafreal ('the Goanese version of a classic Portuguese grill'), and a minced lamb kebab created for the Nizam of Hyderabad. An inspector also praised Goan seafood pilau with octopus, tomato, prawns and spring onions, accompanied by a prawn curry, and kharu gos, a Parsee dish of 'dissolvingly tender lamb'.

Weekly specials reflect Cyrus Todiwala's explorations of the markets and might include haunch of kangaroo, marinated, skewered and grilled in the tandoor; or a vegetarian dish of corn 'boiled then sautéed' in yoghurt and tomatoes. Interesting desserts include lagan nu pudding, a baked custard 'like a dense crème caramel' flavoured with nutmeg, cardamom and rose extract. Decent house wines, priced £9.75, and 30 others are well chosen to match the food. As the *Guide* went to press a second branch was due to open at 247 Lavender Hill, London SW11; Tel: (0171) 738 1717.

All entries, including Round-ups, are fully indexed at the back of the Guide.

CHEF: Cyrus Todiwala PROPRIETORS: Cyrus Todiwala and Michael Gottlieb OPEN: Mon to Fri L 12 to 3, Mon to Sat D 6.15 to 10.30 (6.30 to 10 Sat) CLOSED: 1 week Christmas, bank hol Mons MEALS: alc (main courses £8 to £14.50) SERVICE: not inc; 10% for parties of 10 or more CARDS: Amex, Delta, Diners, MasterCard, Switch, Visa DETAILS: 110 seats. Private parties: 90 main room. Vegetarian meals. Children's helpings. No music. Air-conditioned

Cambio de Tercio 🍷 NEW ENTRY map 14

163 Old Brompton Road, SW5 0LJ COOKING 2
TEL/FAX: (0171) 244 8970 COST £27–£49

The name of this lively Kensington restaurant refers to the three stages of a bullfight and the décor takes up the theme with blood-red colours and a wall displaying a matador's gear. That, plus an informal atmosphere and loud music, is the unlikely backdrop for fine Spanish wines, first-class service and some good Spanish cooking. The chef hails from the Basque region, the source of most of the dishes on the menu. Simple and satisfying griddled calamares with garlic and parsley is one of a page of dishes that can be eaten as starters or tapas. Segovian-style suckling pig is a speciality, and another is bacalao à la vizcaina (dried cod with a piquant sun-dried red pepper sauce).

Less strictly Spanish, and less successful in an inspector's view, was tuna with sauté onions and capers, and vegetables could be improved. Desserts, mainly plain, stay largely in Spain: cheesecake with fruit coulis, and 'very good' sweet and milky almond sponge, for instance. With the exception of two champagnes, wines are Spanish through and through but still manage to offer plenty of variety at all price levels, from the single varietals of Viñas del Vero in Somontano, to the traditional Riojas from Muga, up to the revered Vega Sicilia Unicos from Ribera del Duero. House wines start at £10.50.

CHEFS: Inigo Ruiz de Alegria and Oier Biritxinaga PROPRIETORS: Abel Lusa and David Rivero OPEN: all week 12 to 2.30, 7 to 11.30 (11 Sun) CLOSED: 24 Dec to 2 Jan MEALS: alc (main courses £7.50 to £15) SERVICE: not inc; 12.5% for parties of 7 or more CARDS: Amex, Delta, MasterCard, Switch, Visa DETAILS: 55 seats. 10 seats outside. Private parties: 120 main room, 18 and 50 private rooms. Children welcome. Wheelchair access (no WC). Music

Canteen map 12

Unit G4, Harbour Yard, Chelsea Harbour, SW10 0XD COOKING 6
TEL: (0171) 351 7330 FAX: (0171) 351 6189 COST £32–£73

The playing-card symbols that adorn the interior and the menus here allude to the fact that a 'canteen' was once a gambling-den, according to the management. This one is essentially a brasserie, set in the cavernous post-modernist pavilion that is the Chelsea Harbour development. Marco Pierre White was formerly a partner here, and the menus still reflect his influence in both their scope and culinary style. This is not the English demotic mode of somewhere like Langan's (despite the involvement of Michael Caine in both), but a fairly refined classical French idiom with light Mediterreanean overtones.

Tim Powell, who saw the kitchen through Marco's departure, has now himself moved on to play a part in the gastronomic scene of the new Hong Kong. Sous-chef David Ali has moved up to take his place. A first course of ballottine of foie gras, duck rillettes, grape chutney and brioche had 'fine balance, excellent ingredients and was a real pleasure to eat', according to our inspector. Risotti have always been lavishly praised too, and David Ali has proved himself just as capable in that department, producing a pale green asparagus and salmon version given 'an extra dimension' by an intense seafood sauce. The muscular treatment of fish lives on in a sauté of tender monk with peas and bacon in a cream chive sauce, enhanced by a creamy ball of champ. Rabbit saltimbocca, or grilled pork loin with choucroûte and an apple and thyme *jus*, may be among meat alternatives.

Desserts, too, have rated highly: 'faultless' chocolate soufflé with chocolate sauce and pistachio ice-cream, and 'spot-on' tarte Tatin on a 'classy' caramel sauce. Coffee comes with first-rate petits fours. Service is usually, but not always, 'exemplary'. The wine list is now weighted more in favour of France, with a page of classed-growth clarets as the centrepiece. As a result, the New World selection now looks somewhat unimaginative. House Vin de Pays d'Oc is £14.

CHEF: David Ali PROPRIETORS: Michael Caine and Claudio Pulze OPEN: Sun to Fri L 12 to 3, Mon to Sat D 6.30 to 11 (12 Fri and Sat) CLOSED: Christmas, bank hols MEALS: alc (main courses £13). Set L £15.50 (2 courses) to £19.50, Set D £28. Cover £1 SERVICE: not inc; 12.5% for parties of 6 or more CARDS: Amex, MasterCard, Switch, Visa DETAILS: 120 seats. Private parties: 80 main room. Vegetarian meals. Children welcome. No cigars/pipes in dining-room. Wheelchair access (also women's WC). Music. Air-conditioned

Cantina del Ponte map 13

36C Shad Thames, Butlers Wharf, SE1 2YE COOKING 1
TEL: (0171) 403 5403 FAX: (0171) 403 0267 COST £28–£48

The Cantina is perhaps the least showy of the Conran places at Butlers Wharf. Bare wooden tabletops and a quarry-tiled floor set the tone, and an interesting mural depicts a bustling marketplace. A fairly approximate version of Mediterranean cooking is going on here under Mark O'Brien. The food is more snack-like than full-dress dinner: Piedmont pepper with mozzarella was 'light and fresh', the cheese well marinated, and a chargrilled veal escalope with a 'very tasty stock reduction' successful for one reporter. The simplicity of fried hake on roasted red peppers and olives was also appreciated, and bananas in hot toffee sauce with rum and raisin ice-cream has worked well. Service is sometimes 'poor and unattentive', sometimes 'delightful, welcoming and eager to please'. The compact but largely Italian wine list allows room for exploration. Prices open at £11.95.

CHEF: Mark O'Brien PROPRIETOR: Sir Terence Conran OPEN: all week L 12 to 3, Mon to Sat D 6 to 11 (and Sun D 6 to 10 May to Aug) MEALS: alc (main courses £8 to £13.50) SERVICE: 12.5% (optional) CARDS: Amex, Delta, Diners, MasterCard, Switch, Visa DETAILS: 98 seats. 41 seats outside. Vegetarian meals. Children welcome. Wheelchair access (also WC). No music

London Round-ups listing additional restaurants that may be worth a visit can be found after the main London section.

▲ *The Capital* 🍷

map 14

22 Basil Street, SW3 1AT — COOKING 8
TEL: (0171) 589 5171 FAX: (0171) 225 0011 — COST £37–£105

The Capital does as much as it can to make eating in a posh Knightsbridge hotel a pleasurable experience. It is 'one of London's most understated hotels', with a comfortable dining-room decorated in restful shades of apricot and beige. 'It is the warmth of this intimate restaurant that wins my vote,' confessed one. Philip Britten runs a 'classy and confident kitchen', and the menus read as if he is on the go 24 hours a day. Dishes demand a lot of time and skill to put together, and when you consider their number and variety the job seems all the more daunting. The two set-price dinner menus (of seven and nine courses) offer smaller versions of dishes from the *carte* and are a good way to sample the range. If only they were called something other than Temptation and Seduction.

For one reporter the more expensive of the two started off with muted flavours and 'built up in a crescendo' to a high point of lobster and morel soup served with a dill risotto. Another's meal began with two 'concentrated yet wonderfully light' jellied consommés (one of langoustine, the other of ceps and celeriac), progressed to a rich risotto of foie gras, a 'super combination' of red mullet on olive pasta with grilled peppers, and spiced fillet of lamb with basil and tomato couscous. Contrasting flavours and textures 'leave you highly satisfied but not too full'. 'Faultless' rhubarb crumble and 'delicate' apricot soufflé have shared the pudding plaudits with blueberry and apple pie served with 'lots of old-fashioned custard'.

There are four kinds of bread, and service is such that 'a raised eyebrow is sufficient to bring the bread lady to the table'. The three-course lunch menu offers five choices at each stage, and provided 'as good a lunch as I can remember' for one reporter. Coffee at an extra £5 'is worth it for the stunning petits fours'.

Staff are 'delightful, always welcoming and very knowledgeable', and both the sommelier and maître d' are mentioned in dispatches, the former for steering people 'away from price-laden extravagance to cheaper but delicious drinking'. Even so, very few bottles cost less than £20, but as the list majors in good vintage claret and burgundy, that is to be expected. The New World takes a minor but none the less worthwhile part. House wines from the Loire are £14.50 a bottle (£4 a glass).

CHEF: Philip Britten PROPRIETOR: David Levin OPEN: all week 12 to 2.30, 7 to 11.15 (10.30 Sun) CLOSED: D 25 Dec MEALS: alc (main courses £23.50 to £25.50). Set L £25, Set D £55 to £75 SERVICE: none, card slips closed CARDS: Amex, Delta, Diners, MasterCard, Switch, Visa DETAILS: 44 seats. Private parties: 8 main room, 10 and 22 private rooms. Car park. Children welcome. Jacket and tie. No cigars/pipes in dining-room. No music. Air-conditioned ACCOMMODATION: 48 rooms, all with bath/shower. TV. Phone. Air-conditioned. Room only £196 to £243. Deposit: 1 night's stay. Children welcome. Baby facilities. Dogs welcome. Afternoon teas (*The Which? Hotel Guide*)

Dining-rooms where music, either live or recorded, is never played are signalled by No music *in the details at the end of an entry.*

Le Caprice

map 15

Arlington House, Arlington Street, SW1A 1RT — COOKING 5
TEL: (0171) 629 2239 FAX: (0171) 493 9040 — COST £35–£69

'Chic, smart, cool', and 'as slick as Brian Ferry's hair', Le Caprice has been attracting luminaries and showbusiness people for more than a decade and a half. 'Style style style' is everywhere, from David Bailey prints on the walls to smartly attired staff in black and white.

The name of the place cannot refer to the menu, which rarely strays from the realm of the modern brasserie. Cooking is skilful, and even though Kevin Gratton has replaced Tim Hughes as head chef, consistency has been maintained in, for example, a pair of 'brilliant' starters of sauté foie gras in a Sauternes *jus*, and 'perfectly cooked' grilled scallops with spinach and crispy bacon. Other reporters have endorsed risotto nero, roasted fillet of sea bass served on a bed of runner beans, and confit of goose with Savoy cabbage, prunes and calvados. Vanilla-flavoured cappuccino brûlée, and a light and dark chocolate mouse are enjoyable ways to finish.

There is praise, too, for unobtrusive but attentive service that 'makes you feel important', but Le Caprice's popularity means you may have to book well in advance. A manageable list of quality wines exploits France, Italy and Spain, as well as California and the southern hemisphere, and has something for most pockets. Around a dozen wines by the glass start at £3.25.

CHEFS: Mark Hix and Kevin Gratton PROPRIETORS: Christopher Corbin and Jeremy King OPEN: all week 12 to 3, 5.30 to 12 (Sun L 12 to 3.30) CLOSED: 24 Dec D, 25 and 26 Dec, 1 Jan MEALS: alc (main courses £9 to £20). Cover £1.50 SERVICE: not inc CARDS: Amex, Delta, Diners, MasterCard, Switch, Visa DETAILS: 70 seats. Private parties: 8 main room. Vegetarian meals. Children welcome. Music. Air-conditioned

Charco's

map 14

1 Bray Place, SW3 3LL — COOKING 2
TEL: (0171) 584 0765 FAX: (0171) 351 0365 — COST £26–£45

Hidden in a narrow back street parallel to the King's Road, Charco's is both wine bar and restaurant. The clientele personify the area's opulence, but they are a canny lot because – unusually for this district – prices, particularly for the short set-price lunch menus, are pretty keen. Artichoke and truffle soup followed by grilled tuna with stir-fried vegetables would set anyone up for an afternoon's spending spree in Chelsea. One who began an evening with a tartlet of sun-dried tomatoes, olives and Parmesan thought it 'a light meal in itself'. A main-course of baked monkfish with garlic, herbs and baby vegetables offers fresh and well-timed fish, while dessert may be a half-set butterscotch mousse accompanied by slices of vanilla-flavoured poached pear. This is a well-run place where 'people are made to feel welcome'. A huge and commendable selection of wines by the glass prefaces a predominantly French list. Bottle prices open at around £8.25.

CHEF: Chris Wellington PROPRIETOR: Pillarcrest Ltd OPEN: Mon to Sat 12 to 2.30 (3 Sat), 6.30 to 10.30 CLOSED: bank hols MEALS: alc (main courses £10.50 to £12.50). Set L £9.50 (2 courses) SERVICE: not inc CARDS: Amex, Delta, MasterCard, Switch, Visa DETAILS: 55 seats. 8 seats outside. Private parties: 35 main room. Vegetarian meals. Children welcome. Music. Air-conditioned

Chavot NEW ENTRY map 14

257–259 Fulham Road, SW3 6HY COOKING 6
TEL: (0171) 351 7823 FAX: (0171) 376 4971 COST £29–£68

Thanks to Eric Chavot's move across town, last year's Interlude de Chavot has now split in two, with Interlude at the old address (see entry, London) and Chavot at what used to be called Fulham Road. The neighbourhood is genteel, unashamedly expensive and 'very Chelsea', and little has been done to the dining-room since Stephen Bull left: it retains the dark fabrics, animal motifs, and atmospheric, grainy photographs of London. The food's heart is in the south of France, among olive oil, red mullet, sauce provençale and niçoise garnish, although it borrows from elsewhere as the need arises.

Typically accurate timing gets the best out of roast scallops (with mustard oil and horseradish potatoes), and pan-fried cod fillet – 'bright, white, glistening, translucent' – although the accompanying ratatouille and bouillabaisse 'appeared to cancel each other out'. At its most exciting, the kitchen can produce two 'plump, juicy' quail legs roasted to a gentle shade of pink, accompanied by crostini with a liver-enriched topping, a 'masterfully executed' tian of crab, and a quivering foie gras tarte Tatin that was 'unctuous and almost ambrosial'.

Among desserts, rhubarb soufflé, 'light and cakey at the same time, got a firm thumbs-up', and lemon tart is well reported, but this department rather let the side down at inspection. Staff are diligent, knowledgeable and unpretentious: this is 'French service at its best'. Wines are mostly French too, and of good pedigree, though a few high mark-ups have even plugged some of the traditional New World bolt-holes. Over 15 wines (including dessert) are available by the glass, starting at £3.50.

CHEF: Eric Crouillere-Chavot PROPRIETORS: Robert Seigler, Tony Howorth and Eric Crouillère-Chavot OPEN: Mon to Fri L 12 to 2.30, Mon to Sat D 7 to 11 CLOSED: 1 week Christmas MEALS: alc (main courses £16 to £20). Set L £15.50 (2 courses) to £18.50 SERVICE: not inc CARDS: Amex, Delta, Diners, MasterCard, Switch, Visa DETAILS: 80 seats. Private parties: 6 main room, 15 private room. Vegetarian meals. Children welcome. No pipes in dining-room. Wheelchair access (no WC). No music. Air-conditioned

▲ *Chelsea Hotel, Chelsea Restaurant* NEW ENTRY map 14

17 Sloane Street, SW1X 9NU COOKING 4
TEL: (0171) 201 6330 FAX: (0171) 235 3705 COST £31–£51

The borderline between food and fashion is becoming less distinct by the week, and Bruno Loubet's new venture in a large Knightsbridge hotel aims to blur it further. The £2 million refurbishment was only partially complete as the *Guide* went to press (the rest is due in 1998), but the atrium restaurant is already up and running, making abundant use of chrome, glass and wood. It is pitched as a lunchtime pit-stop for ladies who shop in Knightsbridge, which may explain why our inspector, who falls into none of these categories, felt the chairs might be 'from the Torquemada school of modern design' with matching tables. 'It is as though the furniture selection has been made by elves.'

The ladies will be provided with a 'fashion library' in which they can check up on 'the latest developments in all the major fashion houses', as well as a light 'jardinier' menu and a seasonal *carte*. Adam Gray perms all sorts of ingredients, and among successes have been a well-balanced crab and sweetcorn risotto, and cannelloni filled with puréed mackerel. Some readers may wish to renew their acquaintance with Bruno's 'signature dish' (listed as such on the menu) from L'Odéon: a line of scallops alternating with slices of black pudding, all on a bed of mashed potato with a little smear of garlic cream and parsley purée.

Finish with a hot chocolate fondant 'full of rich flavour with a moist centre', or an apricot sorbet surrounded by raspberries, with 'a flamboyant splash of champagne being applied by the waiter'. A very smart up-to-the-minute list of around 60 wines offers four reds and four whites by the glass from £2.75.

CHEFS: Bruno Loubet and Adam Gray PROPRIETOR: B&B (Chelsea) Ltd OPEN: all week L 12 to 2.15 (4 Sun), Mon to Sat D 7 to 10.45 MEALS: alc (main courses £12 to £17.50). Set L Mon to Sat £16.50 (2 courses) to £22.50, Set D £22.50. Bar food available SERVICE: not inc CARDS: Amex, Diners, MasterCard, Switch, Visa DETAILS: 80 seats. Private parties: 24 main room, 30 and 80 private rooms. Vegetarian meals. Children welcome. No pipes in dining-room. Wheelchair access (no WC). Music. Air-conditioned ACCOMMODATION: 224 rooms, all with bath/shower. TV. Phone. Air-conditioned. Room only £149 to £229.25. Rooms for disabled. Children welcome. Baby facilities. Dogs welcome in bedrooms only. Afternoon teas

Cheng-Du £ map 13

9 Parkway, NW1 7PG COOKING 3
TEL/FAX: (0171) 485 8058 COST £22–£52

An 'atmosphere of calm' pervades the predominantly green and white room with soft overhead lighting and decorations placed according to feng shui principles. Tables are well-spaced, red roses add a note of romance, Taiwanese waiters are attentive and smiling, and quiet jazz for once justifies the description 'background music'.

Cheng-Du is the capital of Szechuan province, and the emphasis is on Szechuan and Peking cooking, although there are Cantonese and Straits dishes too. Happily, everything is MSG-free even if its absence occasionally results in a touch of blandness in chicken stock-based soups. High points of one meal included 'soft plump' Szechuanese beef shui mai dumplings, prawns in black-bean sauce, and ho fun noodles with beef. Best of all was drunken fish which, on enquiry, turned out to be monkfish – and, as students of kung fu movies know, a drunken monk can be the most ferocious fighter of all. But red bean pancakes will bring the meal to a peaceful conclusion. House wine is £8.90.

CHEF: Fook Deng PROPRIETOR: Gingerflower Ltd OPEN: all week 12 to 2.30 (3 Sun), 6.30 to 11.30 CLOSED: 24 to 26 Dec MEALS: alc (main courses £5 to £18). Set D £19.50 SERVICE: 12.5% CARDS: Amex, Delta, MasterCard, Switch, Visa DETAILS: 80 seats. Private parties: 80 main room. Vegetarian meals. Children welcome. Wheelchair access (no WC). Music

Chez Bruce 🍷 map 12

2 Bellevue Road, SW17 7EG COOKING 4
TEL: (0181) 672 0114 FAX: (0181) 767 6648 COST £28–£43

Chez Bruce sits in a parade of shops fronting Wandsworth Common, and its textured draped ceiling, false windows and curious architectural drawings give the eye something to do when not scrutinising the set-price menu. Bruce Poole has his finger on the pulse of ideas in circulation about southern European and Middle Eastern food, producing a salad version of imam bayaldi, and, closer to home, deep-fried sardines with tartare sauce. A starter of goats' cheese and tomato tart with basil and 'decent' puff-pastry kicked off one reporter's meal well, and led on to 'superbly cooked' roast John Dory served with mashed potato, truffle oil and spinach. Also endorsed by reporters have been roast cod ('with an excellent crust I can never seem to perfect at home'), and pinkly cooked rump of lamb accompanied by savoury couscous, 'wonderfully aromatic' merguez sausage and an anchovy butter sauce.

Good cheeses from a catholic selection are the alternative to textbook French desserts, which have included a competent croustade aux pommes, St-Emilion au chocolat and, more divertingly, a gâteau basque with plums and lemon-curd ice-cream. Staff contribute to a sense of conviviality, although the verdict at inspection was 'friendly, but not totally together'. Wine selections are almost Desert-Island-Disc-like in their desirability, offering a good range of styles and varieties at all price levels, culminating with the 'super second' Château Cos d'Estournel from 1985. House French is £10.95 a bottle, £2.25 a glass.

CHEFS: Bruce Poole and Olivier Couillaud PROPRIETOR: Bruce Poole OPEN: all week L 12 to 2 (12.30 to 3 Sun), Mon to Sat D 7 to 10.30 CLOSED: 1 week Christmas, bank hols MEALS: Set L £17.50, Set D £24.50. BYO £10 SERVICE: 12.5% (optional), card slips closed CARDS: Amex, Delta, Diners, MasterCard, Switch, Visa DETAILS: 70 seats. Private parties: 8 main room, 20 private room. Vegetarian meals. Children welcome but no very young children at D. Wheelchair access (no WC). No music. Air-conditioned

Chez Liline £ map 12

101 Stroud Green Road, N4 3PX
TEL: (0171) 263 6550 and 272 9719 COOKING 3
FAX: (0171) 263 9767 COST £20–£41

The charm of the family who own this north London restaurant (and the fishmonger's shop next door) more than compensates for any lack of elegance in the décor. To judge by an inspector's leisurely lunch in the almost empty room, the slow arrival of the food is due to its being cooked to order. Of the starters, vindaye de poisson, probably a Gallicised vindaloo, was a rather solid textured red snapper in a powerful mustard and turmeric sauce. It was a complete contrast to the pure French-style feuilleté d'homard containing a 'delicately sauced' half-lobster with spinach. Plateau sètoise was another half-lobster plus salmon, prawns and scallop that came in a 'deep-flavoured sauce that owed more to Mauritius than Provence'. The achard (pickled vegetables) may have been authentic, but lacked the palate-searing flavour of Indian and Malaysian versions, although the Basmati rice would have done credit to any Indian cook.

The good impression of Mauritian cuisine was reinforced by 'beautifully crusty' baguette, a correct crème caramel, and good coffee. French house wine is £9.25.

CHEFS: Mario Ho Wing Cheong and Pascal Doudrich PROPRIETOR: Mario Ho Wing Cheong OPEN: Mon to Sat 12.30 to 2.30, 6.30 to 10 CLOSED: bank hols MEALS: alc (main courses £8.25 to £13.75). Set L and D £10 (2 courses) to £18.75 SERVICE: not inc CARDS: Amex, Delta, MasterCard, Switch, Visa DETAILS: 44 seats. Private parties: 26 main room. Vegetarian meals. Children's helpings. No cigars/pipes in dining-room. Music

Chezmax

map 13

168 Ifield Road, SW10 9AF NEW CHEF
TEL: (0171) 835 0874 FAX: (0181) 947 4461 COST £21–£60

Since the departure of Max Renzland, chefs have come and gone at a rate that makes it difficult for an annual publication to keep up. Last year's newcomer Gilles Chirat left, then Nigel Horton left just as the *Guide* was going to press, and Gary Pavitt arrived, having worked previously at Charco's and Stephen Bull Blandford Street (see entries). Renzland's bourgeois-French cooking has been the inspiration for the style throughout, typically producing a ballottine of foie gras, navarin d'agneau, and crêpe soufflé Grand Marnier, although whether this will continue remains to be seen. France also dominates the rather ordinary wine list, and mark-ups are high. Reports on the new regime, please.

CHEF: Gary Pavitt PROPRIETORS: Graham Thomson and Steven Smith OPEN: Tue to Fri L 12.30 to 2.30, Tue to Sat D 6.30 to 11 CLOSED: Christmas, 2 weeks in August, bank hols MEALS: Set L £10 (2 courses), Set Menu Vite £10 (12 to 2, 6.30 to 7.30), Set D £24.50. BYO £7.50 SERVICE: 12.5% (optional), card slips closed CARDS: Amex, Delta, MasterCard, Switch, Visa DETAILS: 56 seats. Private parties: 40 main room, 16 private room. Children's helpings. No cigars/pipes in dining-room before 11pm. Music

Chez Moi

map 12

1 Addison Avenue, W11 4QS COOKING 6
TEL: (0171) 603 8267 FAX: (0171) 603 3898 COST £24–£51

Richard Walton wears his three decades here lightly, and although he is unafraid to try out the new – just look at the red, black and purple colour scheme and the tiger-skin drapes – consistency is beyond question. Chicken liver pâté is unfashionably light ('almost a mousse') but unfailingly achieves great intensity of flavour. Set-price lunches are hugely popular, and thought to represent exemplary value. They might include 'gently spiced and beautifully cooked' couscous with tomato and a sliced langoustine to start, then perhaps salmon and cod fish-cake with spinach and a watercress sauce, or confit of duck, plus a choice of puddings from the full menu.

Evening dishes that have impressed include a tartlet of quail's eggs and smoked salmon, herb-crusted lamb with boulangère potatoes and shredded cabbage and bacon, as well as 'beautifully rare and tender' venison with a sauce Périgueux and a parsnip gâteau. Traditional British sponge puddings are usually recommended, as is the warm lemon tart that comes with well-made crème anglaise, and crêpes have pleased too, not least the one filled with cream cheese, sultanas and maple syrup. Service 'hits the right blend of formality and relaxation, *le patron* presiding with a benign and personal welcome.' As one would expect, the wine list nails its colours unambiguously to the French mast, Burgundy and Bordeaux as ever the favoured regions, with a few New Worlders just for the look of the thing. Halves are well supplied, and prices open at £9.75 for southern hemisphere house wines.

CHEF: Richard Walton PROPRIETORS: Richard Walton and Colin Smith OPEN: Mon to Fri L 12.30 to 2, Mon to Sat D 7 to 11 CLOSED: bank hols MEALS: alc (main courses £12.50 to £17). Set L £15 SERVICE: not inc CARDS: Amex, Delta, Diners, MasterCard, Switch, Visa DETAILS: 45 seats. Private parties: 16 main room. Vegetarian meals. Children's helpings. No babies. No pipes in dining-room. Wheelchair access (no WC). No music. Air-conditioned

Chez Nico at Ninety Park Lane

map 15

Grosvenor House, 90 Park Lane, W1A 3AA — COOKING 10
TEL: (0171) 409 1290 FAX: (0171) 355 4877 — COST £46–£106

Nico Ladenis began his restaurant career in Dulwich 25 years ago and, apart from an awkwardly timed move one year, has appeared in every edition of the *Guide* since. Single-mindedness, and a fiery determination to produce the best, have landed him an enviable record. It is easy to slacken off once you get to the top, but Nico still runs a tight ship and wows the customers. 'Faultless, the best meal of my life,' concluded one. The room is 'gracious' for a big West End hotel, with a generous and uncluttered use of space, and one first-time visitor, noting that not everybody dresses up, was surprised at how down-to-earth the whole thing seemed.

The food is 'no frills, no smart tricks, just the best', although inevitably anything considered the best can raise expectations alarmingly. But this food is not designed to be flashy or innovative, or to break new ground with knock-me-down flavour combinations. Rather it aims to excel within neo-classical French boundaries. The menu may not change radically, but a few variations keep the whole thing moving along. It is also written in English, which is considered a plus and, although it is sad to see bills falling into line with everywhere else and adding a service charge, at least the credit card totals are filled in. Options include a ten-course 'gastronomic' menu at £75, considered good value in view of the luxury ingredients, balance and variety of flavours and exceptional craftsmanship.

The set lunch is three courses, on one occasion goats' cheese ravioli, crisp-skinned salmon on basil mash with chive velouté, and a 'pretty damned good' chocolate tart that was 'rich and dense'. 'You won't beat this', maintained one reporter, 'and I doubt if there is much better value at the price'. Immediacy of flavour has shown itself in, for example, foie gras (with bitter-sweet caramelised orange) that tasted 'as if taken from the duck or goose that morning'. 'Forget any other chicken,' wrote one who ate a breast of corn-fed bird on a bed of leeks in a cream sauce, while another's herb-crusted saddle of lamb was 'simply the finest piece of meat I have ever eaten', accompanied by vegetables that 'delivered all the flavours and textures of Provence in one small compass'. Risotto is 'light in texture, intense in flavour', and the kitchen 'really does know how not to overcook fish'.

The glazed lemon tart with raspberry coulis remains exemplary, although chocolate 'Negus' runs it a close second, and coffee includes a magnificent collection of petits fours. Waiters are 'attentive and expert but don't fawn', although one reporter who was brought a fresh glass when he changed from Perrier to Badoit wondered if this might be going a bit far. Wines are very good, mostly French, and very expensive, though ten under £30 are singled out for attention, and three dry wines are available by the glass.

CHEFS: Nico Ladenis and Paul Rhodes PROPRIETORS: Nico and Dinah Jane Ladenis OPEN: Mon to Fri L 12 to 2, Mon to Sat D 7 to 11 CLOSED: 10 days Christmas, 4 days Easter, bank hol Mons MEALS: Set L £33, Set D £51 (2 courses) to £75 SERVICE: 12.5% (optional), card slips closed CARDS: Amex, MasterCard, Visa DETAILS: 65 seats. Private parties: 20 private room. No children under 5. No pipes in dining-room. Wheelchair access (no WC). No music. Air-conditioned

Chinon

map 12

23 Richmond Way, W14 0AS — COOKING 5
TEL: (0171) 602 5968 FAX: (0171) 602 4082 — COST £25–£52

The dining-room in this Shepherd's Bush restaurant is 'very pretty' with gentle yellow walls, and spotlit trees seen through the back window at night. The music may be loud, but an agreeable ambience pervades, and service from Barbara Deane generally pleases. The set dinner is still £15 and offers two choices per course, although we are unable to confirm this since the restaurant has chosen not to furnish the *Guide* with any details. On one occasion the set meal offered a warm salad of rabbit, spaghetti with squid and tomato sauce, and a vanilla bavarois served with a pastry basket containing apricot sorbet.

Jonathon Hayes often returns to old favourites, much to the delight of regulars. Shellfish and seasonal game are typical, the latter coming in for special praise. 'Where else in London – or the UK – can you get a superb young partridge, beautifully cooked and presented for £12.50?' There may also be saddle of hare with creamed lentils, venison fillet, or a chunky breast and crisp, herb-crusted leg of mallard served with parsnip purée in a pastry box, surrounded by dabs of a rich red-wine sauce. No matter how simple the dish – a warm bacon and onion tart, for example, garnished with spinach and tomato – Hayes applies a combination of skill, good materials and sound judgement.

Desserts are enthusiastically received too, for example a 'brilliant' chocolate mousse with a brandy-snap basket containing blackcurrant sorbet, with a white chocolate sauce. Wine mark-ups are high, and 12.5% 'optional' service is added to the bill, but the result is still 'excellent value'. House vin de pays is probably £10.50.

CHEF: Jonathon Hayes PROPRIETORS: Barbara Deane and Jonathon Hayes OPEN: Mon to Sat D 7 to 10.45 CLOSED: 25 Dec MEALS: alc (main courses £9 to £15). Set D £15. SERVICE: 12.5% (optional) CARDS: Amex, Delta, MasterCard, Switch, Visa DETAILS: 60 seats. 6 seats outside. Private parties: 30 main room, 30 private room. No children under 10. No cigars/pipes in dining-room. Music. Air-conditioned

'My glass was greasy and smeary, but the proprietor took an old rag from his belt and buffed it until it was shiny, so they couldn't have been more obliging.'
(On eating in Co Durham)

Chiswick ❢ £

map 12

131 Chiswick High Road, W4 2ED — COOKING 3

TEL: (0181) 994 6887 — COST £22–£52

A party of 11 lunching one Monday at the Robinsons' spare, but inviting Chiswick eatery emerged almost universally satisfied, having tested the menu to its limits. The range is indeed impressively broad, encompassing the kinds of foursquare flavours and full-on seasonings that characterise the most confident modern cooking. When Ian Bates left for the Bluebird (see entry), Mark Broadbent competently assumed the chef's mantle in May 1997. By June he was turning out grilled sea bass on a bed of spinach, deep-fried infant John Dory ('the batter a delight') with tartare sauce, and a well-crafted rabbit and foie gras terrine with onion marmalade. Spot-on gooseberry fool delicately laced with elderflower may be a better bet than heavy summer pudding.

The frequently changing wine list caters for all tastes, whether it be Sauzet's Puligny-Montrachet or Dancing Goat White Mourvèdre from California. For those who are less certain of their taste, the proprietors say you can try any wine on the list for free. House French is £9.50. CELLARMAN'S CHOICE: Weingut Johannishof Riesling 1989, Germany, £16.95; Leeuwin Estate Prelude Cabernet Sauvignon 1992, Margaret River, W. Australia, £24.30.

CHEF: Mark Broadbent PROPRIETORS: Adam and Kate Robinson OPEN: Sun to Fri L 12.30 to 2.45, Mon to Sat D 7 to 11.30 CLOSED: 3 days Christmas MEALS: alc (main courses L £7.50 to £12.50, D £7.50 to £16). Set L £9.50 (2 courses), Set D 7pm to 8pm £9.50 (2 courses). BYO £7.50 SERVICE: not inc CARDS: Amex, Delta, MasterCard, Switch, Visa DETAILS: 70 seats 15 seats outside. Private parties: 8 main room. Vegetarian meals. Children's helpings. Wheelchair access (also WC). No music. Air-conditioned

Christopher's

map 15

18 Wellington Street, WC2E 7DD — COOKING 1

TEL: (0171) 240 4222 FAX: (0171) 240 3357 — COST £30–£69

Christopher Gilmour's American bar-grill takes up three floors of a large Victorian pile near Waterloo Bridge. A dramatic stone stairway leading up to the restaurant, along with soaring opera music, heightens the sense of the dramatic. A relaunch in 1997 followed refurbishment and a few alterations to the menu, but American cooking past and present is still the menu's basic drift. Expect to find grilled chicken Caesar salad, Maryland crab-cake, and sweetcorn and crab soup, and a brunch menu at weekends offering eggs Benedict, and 'cowboy breakfast roll'. A 'wilder' dish of pan-fried foie gras with prosciutto, raisin French toast and veal maple glaze was more successful than its reporter had anticipated. Desserts might take in pecan tartlet with bourbon ice-cream, baked New York cheesecake, or strawberries with balsamic vinegar and mascarpone. The two-course pre- and post-theatre menu is a bargain. There are some good but pricey Californian and Washington State wines among the New World offerings, and some prestigious burgundies among the Old. House wines starts at £13.

CHEF: Adrian Searing PROPRIETOR: Christopher Gilmour OPEN: all week L 12 to 3, Mon to Sat D 6 to 11.30 CLOSED: bank hols MEALS: alc (main courses £9.50 to £21, brunch menu Sat and Sun L). Set pre- and post-theatre D £15. Cover 50p (optional) SERVICE: 12.5% (optional), card slips closed CARDS: Amex, Diners, MasterCard, Switch, Visa DETAILS: 160 seats. Private parties: 110 main room, 60 private room. Vegetarian meals. Children's helpings. Music. Air-conditioned

Chutney Mary

NEW ENTRY map 12

535 King's Road, SW10 0SZ COOKING 1
TEL: (0171) 351 3113 FAX: (0171) 351 7694 COST £35–£59

This metaphor for the colonial history of India is as luxuriously comfortable as was life at the zenith of the Raj, with a profusion of vast potted plants gracing the downstairs dining-room and conservatory. The backbone of the menu is regional dishes plus a handful of Anglo-Indian specialities, among them scallop kedgeree. An inspector enjoyed starters of crab-cake with coriander and a good mint chutney, and clear-tasting papri chat (crisp biscuits topped with lentil dumplings). Also commended have been brill curry, and good-quality Chettinad chicken (a spicy stir-fry). Rice and vegetable side-dishes are well reported, nan and paratha are freshly made, and there could be 'excellent' home-made chocolate kulfi to finish. Service is impeccable. Forty-plus wines have been chosen to match the food and are grouped by style with a guide to which types of dishes they are most suited to. House Vin de Pays d'Oc is £11.25, while Cobra, Tiger and Elephant beers start at £2.75 a bottle and lassi is £3.10 a glass.

CHEF: Hardev Singh Bhatty PROPRIETORS: Ranjit Mathrani and Namita Panjabi OPEN: Mon to Sat 12.30 to 2.30, 7 to 11.15, Sun 12.30 to 3, 7 to 10.15 CLOSED: 25 Dec MEALS: alc (main courses £9 to £15.50). Set L Mon to Sat £12.50, Set L Sun £15, Set D £31.50 (minimum 2). Cover £1.50 SERVICE: 12.5% (optional), card slips closed CARDS: Amex, Delta, Diners, MasterCard, Switch, Visa DETAILS: 135 seats. Private parties: 120 main room, 50 private room. Vegetarian meals. Children welcome. Music. Air-conditioned

La Ciboulette

NEW ENTRY map 14

138A King's Road, SW3 4XB COOKING 1
TEL: (0171) 823 7444 FAX: (0171) 823 7457 COST £23–£53

Daniel Gobet's new French restaurant is in a seriously expensive part of Chelsea but fears of scary prices are soon dispelled. La Ciboulette is a simply designed, low-ceilinged basement made 'warm and pleasant' with large vases of fresh flowers, a few pictures and emerald-green chair cushions. Previously head chef at Mon Plaisir and the Green Olive (see entries, London), Daniel Gobet sustains interest by taking a modern look at Provence in dishes of roasted scallops with basil and olive oil, potato and fois gras terrine, or baked sea bass on a tian provençale. Desserts did not past muster at inspection, but native cheeses, staff and wines 'add to the Frenchness of it all'. The carefully chosen list taps lesser-known as well as popular vineyards, and those wishing to pay under £20 should look south, starting with house vins de pays at £10.95.

CHEF/PROPRIETOR: Daniel Gobet OPEN: all week L 12 to 2.30, Mon to Sat D 6.30 to 10.45 CLOSED: bank hols MEALS: alc (main courses £10 to £16). Set L £8.50 (1 course) to £13.50, Set D £16.50 (2 courses) to £18.50 SERVICE: 12.5%, card slips closed CARDS: Delta, MasterCard, Switch, Visa DETAILS: 38 seats. Private parties: 34 main room. Vegetarian meals. Children's helpings. No children under 8. No pipes in dining-room. Music. Air-conditioned

Cicada

NEW ENTRY map 13

132–136 St John Street, EC1U 4JT
TEL: (0171) 608 1550 FAX: (0171) 608 1551

COOKING 3
COST £24–£41

Currently sprouting restaurants as if to the West End manner born, St John Street now boasts Cicada, a modern bar and restaurant doing Far Eastern cooking with several twists. No ceremonials are observed – cutlery, including chopsticks, is thrown into a pot on the table and topped up after each course – and while the noise level rises and the cigarette smoke thickens, staff remain 'perfectly unflustered'. Cafeteria style seating emphasises the tone of an oriental snack bar. Seared tuna sashimi is flash-cooked outside, the rest properly raw, and comes with pickled cabbage, wasabi, sweet soy and a hunk of lime. Grilled tiger prawns with spiced papaya and mango offered 'lively, light and refreshing' flavours at inspection, but the most arresting dish was a whole wok fried crab that arrived dismembered in a mixture of chilli paste and rice wine with a pick, crackers and a finger-bowl: 'the most fun dish I have eaten in a long time'.

Side-orders include Burmese cucumber salad, sweet ginger noodles, and also, disconcertingly, chips. A version of crème brûlée with chocolate and lemon grass very nearly comes off, and wacko ice-cream varieties include star-anise as well as lemon grass and pepper. Wines make a good stab at matching the food with sharp, aromatic flavours, but prices are on the high side. However, four of the six house wines are £9.50.

CHEF: Graham Harris PROPRIETOR: William Ricker OPEN: Mon to Sat 12.30 (6 Sat) to 11 CLOSED: Christmas MEALS: alc (main courses £7 to £10). Set L and D (before 7pm) £7 (2 courses) SERVICE: 12.5% (optional), card slips closed CARDS: Amex, Diners, MasterCard, Switch, Visa DETAILS: 70 seats. 30 seats outside. Private parties: 50 private room. Vegetarian meals. Children welcome. Wheelchair access (also WC). Music

City Rhodes

NEW ENTRY map 13

1 New Street Square, EC4A 3BF
TEL: (0171) 583 1313 FAX: (0171) 353 1662

COOKING 6
COST £37–£73

In common with a number of other canny restaurateurs, Gary Rhodes opted for a location within striking distance of the City, yet not of it, in order to make the most of both lunch-time and evening trade. His immediate catchment area includes financial and legal communities, but his name guarantees interest from almost any quarter. The first floor dining-room is friendly, modern and light, with 'hardly any mobile phones, and an air of decorum'. Rhodes is one chef who not only cooks British food but has come to define it, so that when he puts escalope of salmon with black treacle on the menu we don't ask if it might be Caribbean, we just automatically assume it is British, and if it wasn't before, it is now.

The same with 'pigeon trotter', a boned pig's foot filled with a mix of pork and slightly gamey pigeon, in a 'delightfully sticky' sauce, with mashed potatoes and a small mound of red onions. Steak with 'kidney pie' also fits the British bill, but this is not tub-thumping food, and there is plenty more besides: bouillabaisse with snails, for example, roast foie gras on a potato cake, and spinach-filled tortellini on a bed of fried tomatoes with a creamy sauce poured over. Fish terrines have come of age, the one here made from layers of skate and potato, and the obligatory roast cod appears with obligatory risotto (of green pea).

Skill, invention, and 'a bit of personality in the food' are what set the place apart. Around eight varied items per course offer good choice, which might include 'jaffa cake' pudding, baked fig tart, or warm banana pudding oozing thick, rich chocolate. Around a dozen wines make it under the £20 barrier on a 40-strong modern list. House wines are Argentinian white (£11.75) and red (£10.95) at £2.95 a glass.

CHEFS: Gary Rhodes and Wayne Tapsfield PROPRIETOR: Gardner Merchant OPEN: Mon to Fri 12 to 2.30, 6 to 9 CLOSED: bank hols MEALS: alc (main courses £13.50 to £23.50) SERVICE: 12.5%, card slips closed CARDS: Amex, Delta, Diners, MasterCard, Switch, Visa DETAILS: 98 seats. Private parties: 10 main room, 12 private room. Vegetarian meals. No cigars in dining-room. No music. Air-conditioned

▲ *Claridge's*

map 15

Brook Street, W1A 2JQ — COOKING 3

TEL: (0171) 629 8860 FAX: (0171) 499 2210 — COST £38–£101

Usurped monarchs and ousted prime ministers have sought refuge in Claridge's since the late-Victorian era, when its new interiors were the last word in fashionable design. Although its hallways are sufficiently proportioned to permit crinolined ladies to pass each other without getting into a twiddle, the aloofness one might fear from such a place is largely absent.

Under the aegis of John Williams, the cooking has kept to the haute cuisine principles expected by patrons, but has not shied away from undertaking a few more modern turns, such as grilled suprême of salmon with artichoke and coriander salad. The *carte* offers lobster Thermidor at £38, and if you're mad for lobster, you can have it as a salad or in a bisque to start. Otherwise, consider gratinated scallops with Sauternes and lemon, before proceeding to grey-legged partridge with morel and truffle risotto. Desserts are thoroughly French: russet apple parfait with calvados caramel sauce rather than the expected spotted dick. The very traditional wine list is well-suited to its surroundings, but does tend to play safe, providing little opportunity outside the French classic regions for real wine enthusiasts. Mark-ups are about standard for the West End, and French house wines are £17.50.

CHEF: John Williams PROPRIETOR: Savoy Group plc OPEN: all week 12.30 to 3, 7 to 11 MEALS: alc (main courses £23 to £38). Set L £29 to £36, Set D Sun to Fri £38 to £40, Set D Sat £45 SERVICE: net prices, card slips closed CARDS: Amex, Delta, Diners, MasterCard, Switch, Visa DETAILS: 120 seats. Private parties: 9 main room, 20 to 250 private rooms. Vegetarian meals. Children's helpings. Jacket and tie. Wheelchair access (also WC). Music. Air-conditioned ACCOMMODATION: 197 rooms, all with bath/shower. TV. Phone. Air-conditioned. Room only £245 to £350. Rooms for disabled. Children welcome. Baby facilities. Afternoon teas

Clarke's

map 13

124 Kensington Church St, W8 4BH — COOKING 6
TEL: (0171) 221 9225 FAX: (0171) 229 4564 — COST £34–£53

On two floors, with an adjoining shop selling breads, cheese and other goodies, this is a comfortable, elegant restaurant. It tempers simplicity and restraint with just enough glamour not to feel saintly, and a view into the calm and orderly kitchen downstairs 'proves that screaming doesn't have to be the norm behind the scenes'. Lunch now has a slightly different format, with each course priced individually, and, although three courses add up to a little more than last year, this does allow more flexibility.

Meals are well balanced and satisfying, as they need to be particularly in the evening when there is no choice, and each dish is treated as an integrated whole. A typical four-course dinner might begin with goats'-cheese crostini with a bitter-leaf salad and marinated artichokes, followed by roast fillet of sea bass with a red wine sauce, cheese, then a pear baked in marsala and spices, served with chilled zabaglione. These are all decked out with the right sort of trimmings, and cheeses 'in perfect condition' have included rich Cashel Blue and nutty, mature Spenwood, served with oatmeal biscuits.

Lightness of style and treatment (mostly chargrilling and roasting) are hallmarks, and the naked simplicity of dishes works thanks to confident technique and accurate timing. Meals begin with bread – anything from raisin to soft brown to milk bread, all in huge, inch thick slices – and often finish on a light note such as lemon-curd 'puff' with raspberries, or peach and rum sorbet with vanilla ice-cream. Service is warm, attentive, friendly and courteous.

California dominates the short but well-chosen wine list, which includes some intriguing bins not readily available elsewhere; film buffs might like to try the three from Francis Coppola's estate, all at £34. For those who like to end a meal with fruit, there are four eaux de vie from Bonny Doon at £4.50 a glass. A small selection of wines by the glass is priced between £2.50 and £7.25. CELLARMAN'S CHOICE: Chalone Vineyard Pinot Blanc 1993, California, £29; Etude Rosé 1995, Carneros, California, £23.50.

CHEFS: Sally Clarke and Elizabeth Payne PROPRIETOR: Sally Clarke OPEN: Mon to Fri 12.30 to 2, 7 to 10 CLOSED: 10 days Christmas, 4 days Easter, 2 weeks Aug MEALS: alc L (main courses £14); Set D £40. BYO £10 SERVICE: net prices, card slips closed CARDS: Amex, MasterCard, Switch, Visa DETAILS: 90 seats. Private parties: 12 main room. Children welcome. No smoking in 1 dining-room. No cigars/pipes in dining room. Wheelchair access (no WC). No music. Air-conditioned

Coast

map 15

26B Albemarle Street, W1X 3FA — COOKING 6
TEL: (0171) 495 5999 FAX: (0171) 495 2999 — COST £38–£68

Here is one of the era-defining London restaurants of the 1990s, under the same ownership as the similarly trend-conscious Atlantic Bar and Grill (see entry) and soon to be followed by Mash II in W1. It is a resounding space with vast glass frontage so that passers-by can watch you eat (it was once a car showroom), and is loaded with PR and designed with unforgiving minimalism.

Stephen Terry, now joined by Martin Bradley from the Atlantic, turns in a vanguard metropolitan performance by, for example, perching foie gras on a tarragon waffle and anointing it with maple syrup, or partnering duck breast with Asian greens, Thai red curry and a 'poppadum mille-feuille of pineapple rice'. 'The menu is much gutsier and more vigorously executed these days,' writes one who has charted its progress since the opening. Reporters have commended fried pea risotto primavera ('very spring-like, very pretty'), and a 'pithiviers' of slow-roasted vegetables with goats' cheese dressed in parsley oil and balsamic.

Puddings mix and match the culinary references in a 'cannelloni' of rhubarb and ginger ice-cream, or Cashel Blue pannacotta with a poached pear and port. Service is as 'brisk and unfussy' as the surroundings. Wines are predominantly French, seasoned with some Italian and Spanish contributions and a sprinkling of fashionable bottles from the New World. Prices can be high, but there is good choice under £20. A cosmopolitan collection of house wines starts at £13. CELLARMAN'S CHOICE: St Mary's Riesling 1995, Coonawarra, S. Australia, £20; Gigondas 1989, Pascal Frères, £23.

CHEFS: Stephen Terry and Martin Bradley PROPRIETOR: Oliver Peyton OPEN: all week 12 to 2.30, 6 to 11.30 (10.30 Sun); Sat and Sun brunch 12 to 3.30 CLOSED: bank hols MEALS: alc (main courses £11 to £19.50) SERVICE: not inc; 12½% for parties of 6 or more CARDS: Amex, Delta, MasterCard, Switch, Visa DETAILS: 150 seats. Private parties: 8 main room. Vegetarian meals. Children welcome. Wheelchair access (no WC). Music. Air-conditioned

The Collection

map 14

264 Brompton Road, SW3 2AS — COOKING **2**
TEL: (0171) 225 1212 FAX: (0171) 225 1050 — COST £31–£63

'It seemed appropriate to make a dinner reservation here for the end of London Fashion Week,' wrote one who began her 'entertaining evening' at the 'long, long bar' of this impressive warehouse conversion, before going upstairs to eat. The oriental seam is successfully mined in, for example, chargrilled baby squid with wasabi, lime and mint, or crispy duck on yaki soba noodles with plum sauce, and the Mediterranean comes through in pumpkin ravioli with sage and Parmesan. Artichoke, fennel and samphire support the naturally forthright flavour of halibut, happily accompanied by a salsa of black olives and rosemary. Although a cranberry tart did not please one reporter at dessert stage, an interesting alternative might be spring rolls filled with banana and chocolate. Devil's Lair, Madfish Bay and Bonny Doon are among the more high-profile names on the tiny wine list, and a big plus is that virtually everything comes by the glass. House Argentinean is £11.50.

CHEFS: Christian Benians and Cass Titcombe PROPRIETOR: Mogens Tholstrup OPEN: Mon to Sat 12 to 3, 7 to 11.30 CLOSED: 25 Dec, bank hols MEALS: alc (main courses £12.50 to £21) SERVICE: 15% (optional) CARDS: Amex, Delta, Diners, MasterCard, Switch, Visa DETAILS: 230 seats. Private parties: 300 main room. Vegetarian meals. Children welcome. Wheelchair access (also WC). Music. Air-conditioned

Como Lario

map 14

22 Holbein Place, SW1W 8NL — COOKING 2
TEL: (0171) 730 2954 FAX: (0171) 244 8387 — COST £27–£46

The bright white interior – a hard-contoured space that forgoes the softening influence of carpets and curtains but does display pictures by Koo Stark – may be a shock to the system of those in search of an intimate tête-à-tête. Once attuned to the pitch, however, visitors may find plenty in the gutsy Italian cooking to divert them. Begin with a warm salad of bresaola with leeks and endive, or opt for the dramatic cuttlefish-ink risotto. The correspondent who lunched on calamaretti with sweet peppers was impressed by its generosity, and main courses such as lamb cutlets with anchovy sauce, and roasted quails with pomegranate, indicate a willingness to depart from the formulaic. Prices are fleshed out by extra tariffs for vegetables as well as a cover charge. Wines are a very sound up-to-date Italian selection, although the list keeps mum on vintages. House wines from Sicily are £9.50.

CHEF: Giancarlo Moeri PROPRIETORS: Guido Campigotto and Giancarlo Moeri OPEN: Mon to Sat 12.30 to 2.45, 6.30 to 11.30 CLOSED: Christmas, Easter, bank hols MEALS: alc (main courses £8 to £14). Cover £1.50 SERVICE: not inc CARDS: Amex, Delta, MasterCard, Switch, Visa DETAILS: 81 seats. Private parties: 14 main room, 14 private room. Vegetarian meals. Children's helpings. No pipes in dining-room. Wheelchair access (no WC). Music. Air conditioned

▲ *Connaught*

45 YEARS 1998 IN THE GUIDE

map 15

Carlos Place, W1Y 6AL — COOKING 6
TEL: (0171) 499 7070 FAX: (0171) 495 3262 — COST £47–£133

The Connaught was one hundred years old in 1997, and has spent very nearly half that time in the *Guide*. It hasn't missed an edition in 45 years, and for the last 23 of them Michel Bourdin has been maître chef des cuisines. Do not be surprised, therefore, if the menu offered in both Restaurant and Grill Room looks like a tablet of stone. Other dining-rooms may be more celestial, other chefs more daring, but when all others have surrendered to Mediterranean fashions, the Connaught will still be doing bangers and mash and calling it 'trio de saucisses maison pomme purée Cadurcienne'.

The food still shines in the ways it always has. A slice of hot turbot pâté with a piece of lobster flesh set in the centre 'tasted wonderfully of very fresh fish', and came with creamy pink sauce pudeur. Croustade of quail's eggs garnished with scrambled eggs and truffles never seems to disappoint, and was for one 'a stunning experience of taste, technical mastery and visual display'. Carré d'agneau forestière is highly praised, the meat full of springtime savour, crumbed and garlicky, and served with sauté potatoes and mushrooms. Not the least thrill is the ritual theatre with which food is delivered: rack of lamb presented for approval, withdrawn for carving and plating, watercress garnish arranged, juices poured over, and the dish served. A slice of summer-berry mille-feuille from the dessert trolley with 'splendidly unctuous' vanilla cream is good enough to make one forgive its means of transport, and cheeses, too, are spot-on. Wines, as one might expect, are expensive, although one reporter spoke highly of the house wine served by the 75cl carafe, £18 for white, £25 for red.

CHEF: Michel Bourdin PROPRIETOR: Savoy Group plc OPEN: restaurant all week 12.30 to 2.30, 6.30 to 10.45; Grill Room Sun to Fri 12.30 to 2, 6 to 10.45 MEALS: alc (main courses £12 to £40). Set L Mon to Sat £25, Set L Sun £30, Set D £35 (Grill Room) to £55 (restaurant) SERVICE: 15%, card slips closed CARDS: Amex, Diners, MasterCard, Switch, Visa DETAILS: 75 seats restaurant. 35 seats Grill Room. Private parties: 12 and 22 private rooms. Car park. Vegetarian meals. Children welcome. Jacket and tie. Wheelchair access (also men's WC). No music. Air-conditioned ACCOMMODATION: 90 rooms, all with bath/shower. TV. Phone. Air-conditioned. Rooms for disabled. Children welcome. Baby facilities. Afternoon teas (*The Which? Hotel Guide*)

Cookhouse

map 12

56 Lower Richmond Road, SW15 1JT — COOKING 4
TEL: (0181) 785 2300 — COST £26–£35

The Cookhouse is a small blue-painted room, with a screened kitchen in one corner, seating just 28 people and open only for dinner five nights a week. The 'Modern British' menu offers four starters and four mains, and the modern side of Tim Jefferson's cooking appears in Thai duck soup, braised lamb shank with sweet roasted aubergine and coconut rice, and mahi-mahi with black fettucine, peppers, lime and chilli oil. On the same menu, which changes monthly, traditional British tastes are represented by pot-roasted pigeon with root vegetables and mash, chicken and smoked bacon sausage, and a winter fruit crumble with clotted cream. The choice of four desserts is supplemented by a cheese selection that might include white Stilton or Jarlsberg with date chutney. The restaurant has opted for the simplicity of the longest and best of wine lists: choose a bottle from your own cellar or in the high street, and bring it along. Corkage is included in the £1.75 cover charge.

CHEF: Tim Jefferson PROPRIETORS: Tim Jefferson and Amanda Griffiths OPEN: Tue to Sat D 7 to 11 CLOSED: 2 weeks Aug, 1 week Christmas MEALS: alc (main courses £12 to £13). Unlicensed but £1.75 cover charge includes corkage SERVICE: not inc CARDS: Delta, MasterCard, Switch, Visa DETAILS: 28 seats. Private parties: 32 main room. Vegetarian meals. Children welcome. No cigars/pipes in dining-room. Wheelchair access (no WC). Music. Air-conditioned

Cow Dining Room

NEW ENTRY map 13

89 Westbourne Park Road, W2 5QH — COOKING 3
TEL: (0171) 221 0021 — COST £25–£40

Most born-again pubs are multi-purpose affairs obliging eaters and drinkers to share bench space and oxygen, but not the Cow. The pub part belongs to Tom Conran (son of Sir Terence), and since late 1996 Francesca Melman, previously at the River Café and Alistair Little Lancaster Road (see entries, London), has been leasing the upstairs dining-room. A pleasant room it is too, with large windows, tables covered in checked cloths, and off-white walls bedecked with cow-themed photos and food prints. The cooking is modern, with pick 'n' mix Mediterranean, Italian, British and Far Eastern flavours. Starters of borscht, or 'accomplished' chicken and foie gras terrine with onion confit and toasted brioche, might be followed by braised belly of pork with bok choy and soy sauce, or skate with red onions, fried capers and sauté potatoes. Vegetarians get the short straw, but one might expect as much given the name. Sunday lunch can be a traditional roast rib of beef with Yorkshire pudding, or salt cod poached in chickpea, mussel and chorizo broth. Desserts are unlikely to win new invention awards, but almond and raspberry tart with crème fraîche has been 'excellent'. Service is 'very amicable and mostly efficient'. The wine list is mainly European, with a baker's dozen of white and the same of red. House French is £9.50.

CHEF/PROPRIETOR: Francesca Melman OPEN: Sun L 12.30 to 4, Mon to Sat D 7 to 11.30 CLOSED: 2 weeks Christmas, some bank hols MEALS: alc (main courses £8.50 to £12) SERVICE: 12.5% (optional), card slips closed CARDS: Delta, Diners, MasterCard, Switch, Visa DETAILS: 35 seats. Children welcome. No cigars/pipes in dining-room. No music

▲ *Crescent* ✱ £ NEW ENTRY map 15

Montcalm Hotel, Great Cumberland Place, W1A 2LF COOKING 5
TEL: (0171) 402 4288 FAX: (0171) 724 9180 COST £20–£24

The Montcalm Hotel was refurbished a couple of years ago, with the Crescent restaurant as a suitably opulent centrepiece. The location – in a quiet curving terrace a short distance from Marble Arch – has been artfully echoed inside, where oval pillars divide the space, and curves and arches predominate. Dramatic use of colour includes a spring-green garden mural thrown into relief by slate-pale walls.

Jonathan Nicholson brings his experience at Congham Hall (see entry, Grimston) to bear on spiced mussel chowder with 'juicily sea-fresh' shellfish in a light froth of cream, and sauté peppered skate wing 'seared fiercely to give a caramelised coating, leaving the long strands of meat beautifully succulent'. Black-leg chicken has been another good main course, the leg and breast firm and full of flavour, the accompanying sage risotto and pancetta playing their supporting roles well. Lamb shank is cooked in the provençale idiom with olives, tomato and aubergine and scented with rosemary. Side-orders are pretty down-to-earth: big chips, and cheesy leeks, for example. Puddings, such as chocolate tart with orange custard, are as unrestrained as can be, and the cheese selection is garnished originally with stewed gooseberries set in jelly and spiced apple chutney. Impeccably correct service lifts the front-of-house operation into the top rank. A half-bottle of wine is included in the set price; otherwise there is a short list which makes all the right contemporary noises, although there isn't much below £20. House Californian is £16.

CHEF: Jonathan Nicholson PROPRIETOR: Montcalm Hotel OPEN: Mon to Fri L 12.30 to 2.30, Mon to Sat D 6.30 to 10.30 MEALS: Set L and D £15 (2 courses) to £18 SERVICE: not inc CARDS: Amex, Delta, Diners, MasterCard, Switch, Visa DETAILS: 58 seats. Private parties: 76 main room, 20 to 60 private rooms. Vegetarian meals. Children's helpings. No children under 12. No smoking in 1 dining-room. Music. Air-conditioned ACCOMMODATION: 120 rooms, all with bath/shower. TV. Phone. Room only £150 to £245. Rooms for disabled. Children welcome. Baby facilities. Afternoon teas

✱ *indicates that smoking is either banned altogether or that a dining-room is maintained for non-smokers. The symbol does not apply to restaurants that simply have no-smoking areas.*

Criterion Brasserie

map 15

224 Piccadilly, W1V 9LB — COOKING 6
TEL: (0171) 930 0488 FAX: (0171) 930 8380 — COST £28–£51

Extravagant decoration in the form of 'stunning' gold mosaics, tall potted palms and magnificent mirrors make this upmarket West End brasserie a 'pleasing and soothing sanctuary from the "circus" outside'. It operates a generous *carte* with soups, pasta, salads, and around ten fish and ten meat main courses (fewer at lunch), and has both classical French and traditional British roots, with other ideas tacked on. Few restaurants this size manage to knock up a proper risotto, yet both the 'fashionably slushy' saffron, and squid-ink black (with 'all the required elements of stickiness, texture and colour') are skilfully carried off.

Among fish, high-quality grilled sea bream with artichoke has been well-timed and 'exceptionally good and light', while crab-crusted turbot has come with a 'splendid' crab coulis. Or there may be a comforting old favourite such as smoked haddock with sliced new potatoes and poached egg. In line with the essentially simple nature of the food, there is much grilling and roasting ('superb' rump of lamb) as well as the confit treatment: of duck with flageolet beans drizzled with cep *jus*, or of rabbit with truffle oil and thyme *jus*.

Desserts maintain the momentum with pear tarte Tatin and runny cream, crème brûlée with a pleasingly crunchy top, and 'excellent' lemon tart with fine pastry. If service were on a par with the food, this would be a cracking place, but reporters have been put off by the two-hour 'slot' for a table, by the proximity of neighbouring tables ('a cigar on one side, two fags on the other'), and by unnecessary hauteur from staff. The tempting selection of first-rate, on-the-ball wines from around the world is a bit pricey for a brasserie. House Vin de Pays d'Oc is £13 (£3.50 a glass).

CHEF: Peter Raffel PROPRIETOR: Marco Pierre White OPEN: all week 12 to 2.30 (4 Sun), 6 to 12 (10.30 Sun) MEALS: alc (main courses £11.50 to £15). Set L Mon to Sat £14.95 (2 courses) to £17.95. BYO £12.50 SERVICE: 12.5% (optional), card slips closed CARDS: Amex, Delta, MasterCard, Switch, Visa DETAILS: 150 seats. Private parties: 200 main room. Vegetarian meals. Children welcome. Wheelchair access (no WC). Music

Crowthers

map 12

481 Upper Richmond Road West, SW14 7PU — COOKING 4
TEL: (0181) 876 6372 — COST £28–£39

'An old favourite of ours,' insist reporters from Richmond who clearly support their popular local restaurant, now with a new colour scheme of dark burgandy and sunny yellow. Philip and Shirley Crowther have been in residence since 1982 and they thrive on a combination of personal hospitality, and a fixed-price menu that delivers mainly French cooking with occasional forays into the less-easily pigeonholed modern gastro-world. Dishes such as Mediterranean fish soup with rouille, best end of lamb with provençale herb crust and a piquant shallot sauce, and pan-fried wing of skate with black butter represent the classical side of things. Seared scallops with spiced rice and a curry dressing, and grilled marinated monkfish with crisp curly kale and toasted sesame seeds strike more vigorous contemporary notes. Puddings are a sound selection, ranging from praline parfait with warm chocolate sauce to sticky toffee pudding. Around 40 wines provide keenly priced, affordable drinking. House wine is £9.50.

CHEF: Philip Crowther PROPRIETORS: Philip and Shirley Crowther OPEN: Tue to Fri L 12 to 2, Tue to Sat D 7 to 10 CLOSED: 1 week Christmas, 2 weeks Aug MEALS: Set L £14.75 (2 courses) to £18.50, Set D £18.50 (2 courses) to £23 SERVICE: not inc CARDS: MasterCard, Visa DETAILS: 32 seats. Private parties: 35 main room. Children's helpings. Wheelchair access (no WC). No music. Air-conditioned

Cucina £

map 13

45A South End Road, NW3 2QB — COOKING 4
TEL: (0171) 435 7814 FAX: (0171) 435 7815 — COST £23–£48

'My best Hampstead restaurant meal for many years' might not seem the highest accolade, given the competition, but reports continue to commend this style-conscious restaurant by Hampstead Heath. The bright décor has been called cheerful and comfortable, although the latter applies more to the booths than the designer chairs. With both chefs having strong ties with Australia, the cooking could be called Mediterranean Pacific, with soy sauce as strong a player as balsamic vinegar. Assimilations include rice-paper spring rolls with rock shrimps, peanuts and sweet-and-sour sauce ('as good as they sounded'), and chargrilled monkfish with wasabi beurre blanc and wild garlic leaves.

There are mainstream items, too, such as chargrilled rib of beef with french fries, and 'not oversweetened' rhubarb fool. Set lunches are an 'outstanding bargain', and service is pleasant. The short wine list gives only essential information, but there is plenty of interest. House vin de pays is £10.95

CHEFS: A. Poole and S. Baker PROPRIETORS: V. Mascarenhas, A. Poole and S. Baker OPEN: all week L 12 to 2.30, Mon to Sat D 7 to 10.30 (11 Fri and Sat) CLOSED: 3 days Christmas MEALS: alc (main courses £9 to £15). Set L Mon to Sat £10 (2 courses) to £13.95, Set L Sun £12.95 (2 courses) to £15.95, Set D £15.95 SERVICE: not inc CARDS: Amex, Delta, MasterCard, Switch, Visa DETAILS: 96 seats. Vegetarian meals. Children welcome. No cigars/pipes in dining-room. Music. Air-conditioned

Daphne [£]

map 13

83 Bayham Street, NW1 0AG — COOKING 2
TEL: (0171) 267 7322 FAX: (0171) 482 3964 — COST £15–£34

There's something affably unassuming about Panikos and Anna Lymbouri's popular little Greek-Cypriot restaurant. The atmosphere is 'down home', service has all the warmth and friendliness you could wish for, and the food plots a course between authentic gutsiness and refinement. Ingredients are procured from the big London markets, and menus are increasingly tilted towards fish and vegetarian dishes. Daily specials help to give the place its identity: two recent additions are 'gavros' (fresh fried anchovies) and 'anginares a la polita' (artichokes cooked with fennel, new potatoes, carrots, spring onions, lemon and olive oil). Otherwise you might find 'tsipoura' (chargrilled gilt-head bream), skewers of marinated monkfish, and 'pourekakia' (croquettes of Feta cheese encased in slices of aubergine). The main menu majors in all the classic favourites: avgolemono soup, tarama, beef stifado, sheftalia, not to mention a full quota of mezes. A clutch of Greek-Cypriot wines set it all off admirably. House wine is £10.25.

CHEF: Lambros Georgiou PROPRIETORS: Panikos and Anna Lymbouri OPEN: Mon to Sat L 12 to 2.30, all week D 6 to 11.30 CLOSED: 25 and 26 Dec, 1 Jan MEALS: alc (main courses £6.50 to £10.50). Set L £5.75 (2 courses) SERVICE: not inc CARDS: MasterCard, Switch, Visa DETAILS: 85 seats. 30 seats outside. Private parties: 30 main room. Vegetarian meals. Children's helpings. Music

Daphne's

map 14

112 Draycott Avenue, SW3 3AE
TEL: (0171) 589 4257 and 584 6883 — COOKING 1
FAX: (0171) 581 2232 — COST £26–£71

This is the original of the Tholstrup twins: Chelsea restaurants round the corner from each other catering to a smart regular clientele. Daphne's steers a safer culinary course than The Collection (see entry), offering salads, pastas and risotti in the authentic Italian, as opposed to Cal-Ital, manner. Daphne's knows its customers well and shocks to the system are not what is required. Tortellini of lobster, samphire and fennel, or chargrilled artichokes with olive oil, lemon and parsley indicate the palette of flavours that is drawn on, while herb-crusted rack of lamb, and costoletta milanese are there for meat-eaters. Pudding choice is not over-exciting but polenta and lemon cake with stewed plums might entice the adventurous. The fairly extensive wine list puts Italy first, followed by France and the New World in equal depth. Prices are not low, but house Italian is £11.50.

CHEF: Chris Benians PROPRIETOR: Mogens Tholstrup OPEN: all week 12 to 3, 7 to 11.30 (10.25 Sun) CLOSED: Christmas MEALS: alc (main courses L £6.50 to £16, D £8.50 to £21.50). BYO £10 SERVICE: 15% (optional), card slips closed CARDS: Amex, Delta, Diners, MasterCard, Switch, Visa DETAILS: 118 seats. Vegetarian meals. Children welcome Sun only. Wheelchair access (no WC). No music. Air-conditioned

Del Buongustaio 🍷 £

map 12

283 Putney Bridge Road, SW15 2PT — COOKING 2
TEL: (0181) 780 9361 FAX: (0181) 789 9659 — COST £21–£44

This animated osteria features both old-style cooking from all over Italy and classics from the north, and although the cramped and smoky interior can sometimes feel rather like a '70s pub, the food continues to please. The menu features plenty of variety, from sturdy peasant stews, panzanella (salad beefed up by bread), and rough-cut pasta, to more 'refined' offerings such as wind-cured bresaola with fresh artichokes and Parmesan shavings. From the good-value set-lunch menu, bruschetta di mare with a 'ragù' of six different kinds of fish was 'well cooked with some style'. At inspection, a dish of spinach rolls with nutmeg, Parmesan and carrot pudding with goats'-cheese sauce (and yes, that is all one dish) proved to be a successful but 'unusual combination of textures and tastes'. Boned duck might come with a pâté-like filling of many ingredients, including chicken livers, black truffles and mushrooms. Grilled tuna with oregano sauce and an artichoke and potato 'torta' reminded one reporter of Italian holidays. Almond tart, or perhaps a selection of home-made ice-creams, would be a good way to round off a meal. Enthusiastic and helpful staff usually cope well with numbers. A selection of house wine starts with two Italian bottles at £8.80.

CHEFS: Aurelio Spagnuolo and Antonio Strillozzi PROPRIETORS: Rochelle Porteus and Aurelio Spagnuolo OPEN: Sun to Fri L 12 to 3, all week D 6.30 to 11.15 (10.15 Sun) CLOSED: 10 days Christmas MEALS: alc (main courses £7 to £11.50). Set L £9.50 (two courses), Set D £22.50. Cover 90p SERVICE: not inc, card slips closed; 10% (optional) for parties of 5 or more CARDS: Amex, MasterCard, Visa DETAILS: 60 seats. Private parties: 60 main room. Vegetarian meals. Children's helpings. No cigars/pipes in dining-room. Wheelchair access (no WC). Music. Air-conditioned

Delfina

NEW ENTRY map 13

50 Bermondsey Street, SE1 3UD COOKING 4
TEL: (0171) 357 0244 FAX: (0171) 357 9157 COST £30–£45

The juxtaposition of art and food has come a long way since the hanging of watercolours by local artists on restaurant walls. Here is a contemporary gallery with accommodation for artists, the front turning into a café/restaurant at lunch-times. Almost hidden beneath London Bridge station, it occupies a large, white-pillared space that exudes a relaxed ambience.

Eddie Bleackley, who has cooked at posh hotels as well as Bertorelli's (see entry), joined the team at the end of 1996, bringing a lustrous brand of modern European food with him. Andalucian tapas are a straightforward but appetising collection of items such as chorizo, Serrano ham, deep-fried anchovies and squid. An 'original and successful' main course at inspection was seared scallops under a wigwam of crisp ink pasta in a 'light, creamy, subtly fishy' sauce containing salmon roe. Moroccan and Chinese splashes lend colour to the canvas, and although slow-cooked belly of pork with Thai beans has failed to impress, the sense of timing is such that most dishes work well. Puddings can be memorable. An unabashedly intense passion-fruit parfait sauced with peach and strawberry was both 'fresh-tasting and satisfying', or there may be baked figs with honey and port, or zabaglione ice-cream with amaretti. Full-strength espresso ends things on a high. The short wine list is imaginative and genuinely varied, with enough under £20 to suit lunchtime requirements. House Spanish is £10.75.

CHEF: Eddie Bleackley PROPRIETORS: Stephen Congdon and Digby Squires OPEN: Mon to Fri L only 12 to 3 (snacks available from 10am) CLOSED: 25 Dec, 1 Jan, bank hols MEALS: alc (main courses £9 to £13) SERVICE: 12.5% (optional), card slips closed CARDS: Amex, Delta, Diners, MasterCard, Switch, Visa DETAILS: 80 seats. Private parties: 45 private room. Vegetarian meals. Children's helpings. Wheelchair access (also WC). Music

dell'Ugo

map 15

56 Frith Street, W1V 5TA COOKING 1
TEL: (0171) 734 8300 FAX: (0171) 734 8784 COST £28–£49

The menus of the ground-floor café, first-floor 'bistro' and second-floor restaurant overlap. 'Eclectic' is the keyword with the usual emphasis on pasta and salads for the health-conscious, and meat dishes outnumbered by seafood and vegetarian. Despite garnishes which contribute a word on the menu or a colour on the plate, but do not add flavour, reporters have enjoyed pasta and the simpler meat dishes such as carefully cooked rib of beef and calf's liver. Desserts are variable too, but a light rice pudding with rhubarb and lemon has pleased. The short wine list kicks off with house French and Italian at £8.95.

CHEF: Matthew Fanthorpe PROPRIETOR: Simpsons of Cornhill plc OPEN: Mon to Fri L 12 to 3, Mon to Sat D 5.30 to 12; café all week 10am to 11pm CLOSED: bank hols MEALS: alc (main courses £8.50 to £13) SERVICE: 12.5% (optional), card slips closed CARDS: Amex, Delta, Diners, MasterCard, Switch, Visa DETAILS: 180 seats. 16 seats outside. Private parties: 55 main room, 9 to 16 private rooms. Vegetarian meals. Children welcome. Music. Air-conditioned

▲ *Dorchester, Grill Room* 🍷 map 15

Park Lane, W1A 2HJ COOKING 4
TEL: (0171) 317 6336 FAX: (0171) 317 6464 COST £37–£115

Traditional English food in lavish surroundings is the draw, a combination that appeals particularly to businessmen and overseas visitors. The room, modelled on a Spanish palace, makes a bold statement with its gold-encrusted ceiling, wall tapestries, dark wood tables and red leather chairs, and although service is black-tie formal the dress code is casual. This is the place to come to for nursery favourites of shepherd's pie, deep-fried cod in batter, rice pudding or trifle, as well as lunchtime specials: boiled leg of lamb with caper sauce on Thursday, braised beef with Guinness on Saturday. Trolleys abound for carving meat, displaying breads, puddings and so on.

Fresh ingredients make an impact, in the form of plump scallops 'perfectly cooked and very sweet', fillet of beef with mushrooms and artichokes, or fillets of Dover sole with prawns. Main courses come in generous portions, sauces are rich and well executed, and recommended desserts have included 'immaculately creamy' orange crème brûlée, and chocolate mousse on a walnut sponge base. Bread is a choice from eight to ten different loaves, sliced to order, and there are fifteen waters to choose from at a cost of £4 per litre. If money is no object, then the wine list is a good one (although it would be helpful to be told, for example, which varietal from Cloudy Bay is being offered). Bottles under £20 do exist, including house Vins Pays d'Oc at £18.50, but be prepared to spend around £30 if you want some choice. Outside classical France, Italy and California impress the most. Sixteen wines by the glass start at £5. CELLARMAN'S CHOICE: Arneis Blangé 1995, Ceretto, Piemonte, £37; Chorey-lès-Beaune 1993, Dom. Tollot-Beaut, £33.

CHEF: Willi Elsener PROPRIETOR: The Audley Group Ltd OPEN: all week 12.30 to 2.30, 6 to 11 (7 to 10.30 Sun and bank hols) MEALS: alc (main courses £17.50 to £48). Set L £28, Set D £37. BYO £15 SERVICE: net prices, card slips closed CARDS: Amex, Delta, Diners, MasterCard, Switch, Visa DETAILS: 81 seats. Private parties: 14 main room. Vegetarian meals. Children's helpings. Wheelchair access (also WC). No music. Air-conditioned ACCOMMODATION: 244 rooms, all with bath/shower. TV. Phone. Air-conditioned. Room only £282 to £352.50. Rooms for disabled. Children welcome. Baby facilities. Afternoon teas

'The dining-room is what I always think of as mother-in-law colours: a cool, relaxed pale sage green. Not my favourite colour.' (On eating in the West Country)

▲ *Dorchester, Oriental* 🍷 map 15

Park Lane, W1A 2HJ COOKING 4
TEL: (0171) 317 6328 FAX: (0171) 409 0114 COST £38–£138

Reports agree on the luxury of the room with ornate Chinese furniture, antique vases, rich silk robes, wonderfully soft carpets, and elegant tableware. The thrust of the cooking is Cantonese, although it seems a long way from Chinatown and closer to the big Hong Kong hotels; indeed, shark's fin and abalone are imported directly from there. The most successful dish at inspection was braised, peeled aubergine hotpot with chicken and salted fish, which was 'tremendous, smoky and succulent' and full of 'thick batons of aubergine drenched in a shrimp paste sauce'. Roast Peking duck – 'livery and juicy with crisp skin' – is carved at table and assembled into pancakes by the waiter, so that 'we were unable to stuff in extra bits of duck'. Although warm ground almond cream was not a successful dessert, other choices include chilled mango pudding, or (for £11) an assortment of 'tasters' (crispy lotus-bean tarts, red-bean-paste puffs, shredded coconut buns, sorbets and ice-creams).

There is general approval of the absence of MSG, although one reporter felt this meant flavours could sometimes be bland, and another was bemused by the appearance of a signature carved carrot in almost every dish. No one disagrees that the Oriental is very expensive: 'for the price, we could have died of dim-sum torture four or five times.' Service varies from 'disconnected' to 'friendly' and 'polished'. Wines are the same as in the Grill Room: for details and CELLARMAN'S CHOICE, see entry above.

CHEFS: Willi Elsener and Simon Yung PROPRIETOR: The Audley Group Ltd OPEN: Mon to Fri L 12 to 2.30, Mon to Sat D 7 to 11 CLOSED: Aug MEALS: alc (main courses £15.50 to £47). Set L £25 to £28, Set D £37 to £82. BYO £15 SERVICE: net prices, card slips closed CARDS: Amex, Delta, Diners, MasterCard, Switch, Visa DETAILS: 51 seats. Private parties: 16 main room, 7 to 16 private rooms. Vegetarian meals. Wheelchair access (also WC). No music. Air-conditioned ACCOMMODATION: See entry above for details

La Dordogne map 12

5 Devonshire Road, W4 2EU COOKING 3
TEL: (0181) 747 1836 FAX: (0181) 994 9144 COST £27–£49

In the days before we took a pride in British cooking, a typically romantic middle-class aspiration was to holiday in the Dordogne and eat foie gras and truffles until the money ran out. Any restaurant that captured the Périgord feel (this place 'transports you across the Channel as soon as you enter') was on to a winner. Even now, a qualification for working here is that you must be French. In the dozen years of its existence, La Dordogne's food has spread beyond the orbit of Sarlat to embrace a predominantly fishy repertoire of scallops with a ginger sauce, fish soup with the usual trimmings ('a richly flavoursome delight'), oysters from Ireland and Brittany, and lobster four ways. Main-course meats go down better than the vegetables, and French desserts – apple tart, crème brûlée – are well received. The cover charge pays for a glass of kir and bread and butter. Wines are French, with a short but proud showing from the south-west. House Bergerac opens the bidding at £9.50.

CHEF: Jean-Philippe Charrondière PROPRIETOR: La Dordogne Ltd OPEN: Mon to Fri L 12 to 2.30, all week D 7 to 11 CLOSED: bank hols MEALS: alc (main courses £9.50 to £12.50). Cover £1 SERVICE: 10% CARDS: Amex, Delta, Diners, MasterCard, Switch, Visa DETAILS: 80 seats. 20 seats outside. Private parties: 30 main room, 20 and 32 private rooms. Vegetarian meals. Children's helpings. Wheelchair access (also WC). Music

Eagle £

map 13

159 Farringdon Road, EC1R 3AL — COOKING 2
TEL: (0171) 837 1353 — COST £19–£31

Get there early. 'The '90s equivalent of a pie and pint' is always busy. It was once upon a time the pioneer of food pubs and hasn't changed much over the years. 'Spontaneous, often slightly crude, rustic, but packed with loud Mediterranean-inspired flavours' is how one reporter sized up the food, and much of the cooking is done on the chargrill behind the bar. Squid with potato, green bean and radicchio salad was bursting with flavour, and Italian sausages with sweet red onions and rocket were 'huge, filling, and just what we wanted to get us through election night'. It is not the place for a three-course meal – dessert is limited to Portuguese custard tart – but prices are very reasonable. One self-confessed 'old fogey' thought the music too loud but found the service zippy and efficient. There are beers on tap or bottled, and a compact blackboard list of mostly Italian and New World wines starting at £8.50, nearly all available by the glass.

CHEF: David Eyre PROPRIETORS: Michael Belben and David Eyre OPEN: Mon to Sat 12.30 to 2.30 (3.30 Sat), 6.30 to 10.30 CLOSED: 2 weeks Christmas, Easter, bank hols MEALS: alc (main courses £6.50 to £10) SERVICE: not inc CARDS: none DETAILS: 55 seats. 24 seats outside. Children welcome. Music

English Garden

map 14

10 Lincoln Street, SW3 2TS — COOKING 3
TEL: (0171) 584 7272 FAX: (0171) 581 2848 — COST £26–£59

It may sound like a tranquil rural retreat, but the English Garden is within shouting distance of the King's Road. Notwithstanding that, Roger Wren has persevered to create the feel of a genteel private house, and the cooking has an identifiable patriotic allegiance at its core. A spring luncher who ate asparagus salad, followed by roast duck with puréed parsnips, and a bowl of raspberries and ice-cream to finish, emerged a satisfied customer. There may also be a starter of caramelised red onion and Cheddar 'cheesecake', and main-course roast partridge with beetroot and juniper berries. Apricot and date sponge pudding, or blackberry and apple charlotte with apple custard, is a typical way to finish. Service is attentive and welcoming. The wine list focuses on France, with illustrious clarets and burgundies to the fore. Prices reflect that classicism. House Bordeaux is £11.

CHEF: Brian Turner PROPRIETOR: Roger Wren OPEN: all week 12.30 to 2.30 (2 Sun), 7.30 to 11.30 (7 to 10 Sun) CLOSED: 25 and 26 Dec MEALS: alc (main courses £9 to £17.50). Set L £16.70. Cover £3 SERVICE: not inc CARDS: Amex, Diners, MasterCard, Switch, Visa DETAILS: 70 seats. Private parties: 20 main room, 10 and 20 private rooms. Vegetarian meals. Children's helpings. Music. Air-conditioned

L'Escargot

map 15

48 Greek Street, W1V 5LQ
TEL: (0171) 437 6828 and 2679 — COOKING 6
FAX: (0171) 437 0790 — COST £47–£67

While the ground-floor brasserie produces Caesar salad, and roast lamb chump with dauphinoise and madeira, the upstairs dining-room is a bit posher: with cream-coloured star-flecked walls and bilingual menus. Refurbishment as the *Guide* went to press promised new upholstery upstairs and down, plus permanent exhibitions of twentieth-century art. The snail's new team (Billy Reid and David Hawksworth arrived just before last year's edition went to press, too late then for an assessment of the cooking) are setting a cracking pace. A bobby-dazzler of a starter one night delivered roasted scallops with aubergine caviare and truffle-oiled leaves, the plate vividly slashed like a Steadman cartoon with pepper sauces in traffic-light colours.

Real caviare garnishes a tian of crab and avocado served with tomato coulis, while an inspector's main course of pinkly roasted, moist squab was eloquently supported by caramelised sweet garlic and baby onions, earthy morels and cabbage. Desserts don't quite reach the same creative heights, although creme brûlée with mandarins was 'very good indeed', and lemony lemon tart 'stood alone, not needing anything with it'. Staff ensure everything runs smoothly. The classical wine list offers something for most tastes at a price. If things are a bit tight, best not go for the '49 Yquem at £1,490 a bottle, but consider the interesting and varied group of house wines, starting at £13.

CHEFS: Billy Reid and David Hawksworth PROPRIETOR: Jimmy Lahoud OPEN: Mon to Fri L 12.15 to 2.15, Mon to Sat D 6 to 11 CLOSED: 25 Dec, bank hols; brasserie Aug MEALS: dining-room Set L £25 (2 courses) to £30, Set D £32 (2 courses) to £38; brasserie Set L £14.50 (2 courses) to £17.50, Set D £18.45 (2 courses) to £23.45 SERVICE: dining room 15% (optional); brasserie 12.5% (optional), card slips closed CARDS: Amex, Delta, Diners, MasterCard, Switch, Visa DETAILS: 100 seats. Private parties: 20 main room, 10, 60 private rooms. Vegetarian meals. Children welcome. No cigars/pipes in dining-room. Wheelchair access (also men's WC). Music. Air-conditioned

L'Estaminet

map 15

14 Garrick Street, WC2E 9BJ — COOKING 1
TEL: (0171) 379 1432 FAX: (0171) 278 6847 — COST £18

One correspondent who knows the language reminds us that 'estaminet' means 'a rather humble eating-place in French'; most people seem to have a good time here, and everything is *comme il faut*. Pre-theatre menus remain a popular draw; otherwise go for the *carte* or the *plats du jour*, the latter 'read out of a notebook' by waiters who are generally attentive and cheery. The cooking is deep-rooted bourgeois, with fish and chips, and bangers and mash tossed in for good measure. A salad of marinated herrings is a favourite way to begin, and the kitchen knows how to cook asparagus. Other dishes of note might include grilled halibut, fillet of brill garnished with red peppers, and 'superb' honey-glazed duck. A mighty chariot of more than 20 ripe French cheeses is wheeled out before a second vehicle loaded with puddings comes along. House wine is £9.

CHEF: Philippe Tamet PROPRIETOR: Christian Bellone OPEN: Mon to Sat 12 to 2.30 (2 Sat), 5.45 to 11 CLOSED: 25 and 26 Dec, Easter, bank hols MEALS: alc (main courses £9.50 to £15.50). Set D 5.45 to 7.30 £9.99 SERVICE: 12.5%, card slips closed CARDS: Amex, MasterCard, Switch, Visa DETAILS: 50 seats. Private parties: 10 main room, 20 private room. Vegetarian meals. Children welcome. No pipes in dining-room. Music

Euphorium

map 13

203 Upper Street, N1 1RQ
TEL: (0171) 704 6909 FAX: (0171) 226 0241

COOKING 2
COST £26–£51

Keeping to lower-case letters on its sign, menu and wine list is one way in which Euphorium stands out from the many other trendy eateries along Islington's Upper Street. The design of the now-expanded restaurant, part of which is a bar, is as style-conscious as a 'huge red panel with strange wiggling shimmering forms' can make it, the clientele is typically young and laid back, and the atmosphere can crackle. Owner Marwan Badran has lost and gained several chefs in the past year, but the house style provides a common thread, with some original, often justified pairings of unusual ingredients. Among the more workable have been a 'star' rack of lamb with an aromatic butter-bean and rosemary purée, some crispy sweetbreads tossed in polenta crumbs and served with tabbouleh, and a broth of scallops with seaweed, ginger and glass noodles. The search for novelty has rendered some dishes less successful, but pavlova of rambutan, kiwi- and passion-fruit, and a date, almond and chocolate pudding have had the thumbs-up. Half of the 25 or so wines are under £20, and the list favours the New World, Italy and the lesser regions of France. House wine is £9.50.

CHEF: Peter Arrowsmith PROPRIETOR: Marwan Badran OPEN: all week L 12.30 to 2.30, Mon to Sat D 6 to 10.30 CLOSED: Christmas, bank hols MEALS: alc D (main courses £9.50 to £18.50). Set L £12 (2 courses) to £17.50 SERVICE: 12.5% (optional), card slips closed CARDS: Amex, Delta, MasterCard, Switch, Visa DETAILS: 50 seats. Private parties: 12 main room, 16 private room. Vegetarian meals. Children's helpings. Wheelchair access (no WC). No music. Air-conditioned

Fables

map 12

839 Fulham Road, SW6 5HQ
TEL: (0171) 371 5445 FAX: (0171) 371 5545

COOKING 4
COST £35–£52

Black-and-white illustrations of the La Fontaine fables cover two long walls of this narrow, pine-floored restaurant in Parsons Green. Although Matthew Bird took over the cooking in the spring of 1997, the gently contemporary style continues in, for example, five-spiced tuna, seared and dressed in ginger, spring onion and soy, and confit of duck leg with a shallot tartlet and mixed leaves. Whatever the main course, it will be served in a soup-plate, whether it be a fillet of turbot on fondant potato, or roast saddle of rabbit with a fine spinach and bacon stuffing in a rich wine-based sauce. Desserts, for one pair of reporters, were the highlight of the meal: caramelised banana tart with toffee ice-cream, and cassonade (a crystallised sugar-cane extract, scented with cardamom and partnered with a blood orange sorbet). Service has veered from having 'no idea of manners or organisational skills' to 'willing, friendly, professional'. The wine list has expanded a little, but is still unexpectedly Francocentric, with only cursory New World sections. Prices start at £12.50. The same partnership also owns The Parson's Nose, 803 Fulham Road, SW6; Tel: (0171) 731 7811.

CHEF: Matthew Bird PROPRIETOR: Falcon Group OPEN: Tue to Sat D only 7 to 11 MEALS: alc (main courses £13.50 to £16) SERVICE: 12.5% CARDS: Amex, Delta, Diners, MasterCard, Switch, Visa DETAILS: 46 seats. Private parties: 46 main room, 22 private room. Vegetarian meals. Children welcome. No cigars/pipes in dining-room. Wheelchair access (also WC). Music. Air-conditioned

Fifth Floor

map 14

Harvey Nichols, 109–125 Knightsbridge, SW1X 7RJ — COOKING 5
TEL: (0171) 235 5250 FAX: (0171) 823 2207 — COST £35–£82

Those in a hurry to eat should take the lift straight to the Fifth Floor, which is devoted entirely to eating and drinking: there is a serious deli, a bright babbly café with huddled tables and, shielded from the shopfloor view, the main restaurant. A round-windowed architrave at one end and an exciting Harlem Renaissance painting at the other frame the eating space, and window tables offer a bird's-eye view of Knightsbridge goings-on.

Henry Harris cooks confident modern food, keeping flavours fresh and clear. Half-a-dozen oysters are served with spicy sausages, while a steamed whole crab is done in a kind of chowder with clams, and acorn fed black pig ham comes with capers and quince cheese. An inspection meal started with morels on a piece of toast that was soaked with their 'rich, sweet, thick juices', the whole covered with a piece of half-melted cheese. Fish is a strong main course contender, whether Indian-spiced monkfish with cucumber and mint salad, or a chargrilled wild salmon 'sandwich' wrapped in Lebanese bread and served with battered onion fritters. Meat-eaters might prefer grilled veal chop with Roquefort butter, or poached ox tongue with parsley mash, leeks, and a relish of beetroot and horseradish. The pudding menu comes with a wine suggestion for each dish, Quady's Elysium Black Muscat, for instance, to accompany cherry parfait with a compote of cherries and shortbread. Service is cool but remarkably efficient and prompt.

The ace collection of wines is more than a match for the food, with good competition for France, albeit in smaller numbers, from Italy, Spain and the New World. As quality is high across the board, so is value; this is a list for all pockets, with some absolute gems at all price levels. House French is £11.95. CELLARMAN'S CHOICE: Stormy Cape 1996, South Africa £12.50; Gulbenzu 1993, Navarra £15. The Foundation (to be found below ground level) offers an alternative venue, but an equally contemporary menu.

CHEF: Henry Harris PROPRIETOR: Harvey Nichols & Co Ltd OPEN: all week L 12 to 3 (3.30 Sun), Mon to Sat D 6.30 to 11.30 CLOSED: 25 and 26 Dec MEALS: alc D (main courses £10 to £30). Set L (2 courses) £18.50 to £22.50 SERVICE: 12.5% (optional), card slips closed CARDS: Amex, Delta, Diners, MasterCard, Switch, Visa DETAILS: 110 seats. Private parties: 120 main room. Vegetarian meals. Children welcome. No pipes in dining-room. Wheelchair access (also WC). No music. Air-conditioned

Fire Station £

map 13

150 Waterloo Road, SE1 8SB — COOKING 1
TEL: (0171) 620 2226 FAX: (0171) 633 9161 — COST £19–£36

This up-to-date noisy eatery is handy for the Old Vic and for trains from Waterloo, and an easygoing crowd packs both the bar at the front, and the eating-area at the back. Tables and chairs seem straight from the junk shop, and the menu is chalked on a board at one end, so you may need to crane round to see what's on offer. What meets the eye is Welsh lamb tagine with couscous and baba-ghanoush, salad of chargrilled squid with green mango and garlic crisps, and twice-cooked belly-pork with chickpeas and chilli jam. Then, when it all seems to be getting hectically eclectic, there's Caesar salad with avocado, or venison sausages and parsnip rösti. Service is prone to drift when the place is heaving. Wines by the glass add to the flexibility of the whole operation; house wine by the bottle is £8.45.

CHEF: Paul Bloxham PROPRIETOR: Regent Inns plc OPEN: all week L 12.30 to 2.30 (3.30 Sun), Mon to Sat D 6 to 11 CLOSED: 25 Dec, some bank hols MEALS: alc (main courses £5 to £11.50). Set pre-theatre D Mon to Sat (6 to 7pm) £9.95 (2 courses). BYO £5 SERVICE: not inc; 10% for parties of 5 or more CARDS: Amex, Delta, Diners, MasterCard, Switch, Visa DETAILS: 85 seats. Private parties: 90 main room, 90 private room. Vegetarian meals. Children welcome. Wheelchair access (also WC). Music. Air-conditioned

First Floor

map 13

186 Portobello Road, W11 1LA — COOKING 6
TEL: (0171) 243 0072 FAX: (0171) 221 9440 — COST £23–£58

You want stars, you got 'em at this trendsetting Portobello pub conversion. Take your pick from Liam Gallagher, Sinéad O'Connor, Björk and Helena Bonham-Carter, but fingers-crossed they're not all there on the same night. It's an airy, cool space with singular décor and an absence of restaurant attitude.

The cooking is more idiosyncratic than ever since the arrival of Michael Smith in early 1997. Indian, Thai, Chinese, Moroccan and Caribbean bells are rung – and more besides – and much of it works like a dream. An inspection starter of headily scented gingered rice noodle salad came with sour pickled baby turnips, mango juice, apple purée and, laid across the top, a blackened rice paper bag of sweet grelot onions. Surprisingly, with so many flavours in the mouth at once, the overall effect was a triumph of co-ordination, as was a black pudding burger topped with a sliver of intense jellied crab meat, accompanied by a thin trickle of tomato chilli jam.

These are Force 10 flavours, and, inevitably, combinations occasionally go a little awry. A main-course fillet of smoked haddock in Indian-spiced batter with a watercress purée might have been better without its stuffing of anchovies, capers and Parmesan: part of a chef's skill is knowing when to leave well alone. Black liquorice custard in a syrup of rosemary with balamic roasted peaches was a bold try, but outshone by an 'inspired and clever' crème brûlée filled with rhubarb and star-anise with a bang-on gingerbread ice-cream. After the excitement of all those unusual dishes the wine list seems surprisingly ordinary, although it does contain the odd vinous superstar. Bins are arranged by style and a good number come in below £20. House wines start at £9.95 a bottle, £3 a glass. Breakfast and all-day brunch are available too,

CHEF: Michael Smith PROPRIETOR: Grosvenor Inns OPEN: all week 11 (12 Sun) to 4, 7.30 to 11 (11.30 Sat, 10 Sun) CLOSED: 25 and 26 Dec MEALS: alc (main courses L £9, D £10.50 to £18.50). Set L £10.50 (2 courses), Set D £30 SERVICE: 12.5%, card slips closed CARDS: Amex, Delta, Diners, MasterCard, Switch, Visa DETAILS: 120 seats. Private parties: 75 main room, 28 and 45 private rooms. Vegetarian meals. Children welcome. No cigars/pipes in dining-room. Music

▲ *Four Seasons* 🍷 map 15

Hamilton Place, Park Lane, W1A 1AZ COOKING 6
TEL: (0171) 499 0888 FAX: (0171) 493 6629 COST £34–£76

Whichever way you shake it, this still feels like a big hotel dining-room, replete with pillars, mirrors and floral displays, and service is both professional and friendly. Given the name, it should come as no surprise that menus change quarterly. Shaun Whatling's approach is well suited to the circumstances, dealing largely in mainstream materials, but he takes a sideways glance at some of them. Smoked breast and confit leg of duck might come with cinnamon sauce, or lamb cutlets with a goats'-cheese soufflé. Seafood is plentiful, and results show that the kitchen not only buys well but also treats what it buys with care. Among the more unusual ideas in spring were 'tiers' of blini and marinated trout with oyster cream, and a pairing of roast fillet of zander with pistachio and rosemary.

A few dishes claiming to be 'nutritionally balanced and lower in calories, cholesterol, sodium and fat' are highlighted on the menu, and might include roast fillets of Dover sole with herb tortellini, or roast fillet and braised leg of rabbit with baby vegetables. Desserts are not always so virtuous, although fruit is a popular component, as in spiced pear tarte Tatin with almond ice-cream, or cherry and chocolate tart with pistachio ice-cream.

Wines are high in quality, and very little is under £20. France dominates the list, with impressive selections of vintage clarets and burgundies. The cosmopolitan collection of 11 house wines begins at £15 a bottle, £3.80 a glass. CELLARMAN'S CHOICE: Chablis premier cru 'Vaillons' 1994, William Fèvre, £40; Cape Mentelle Zinfandel 1994, Margaret River, W. Australia, £26.

CHEF: Shaun Whatling PROPRIETOR: Four Seasons, Regent Hotels and Resorts OPEN: all week 12.30 to 3, 7 to 10.30 MEALS: alc (main courses £22.50 to £29). Set L £21 (2 courses) to £26, Set D £48 SERVICE: net prices, card slips closed CARDS: Amex, Delta, Diners, MasterCard, Visa DETAILS: 55 seats. Private parties: 12 main room. Car park. Vegetarian meals. Children welcome. No pipes in dining-room. Wheelchair access (also WC). Music. Air-conditioned ACCOMMODATION: 227 rooms, all with bath/shower. TV. Phone. Air-conditioned. Room only £282 to £347. Rooms for disabled. Children welcome. Baby facilities. Small dogs welcome. Afternoon teas. Garden

'I decided to be novel and bold and daring and order three starters and no main course. Had I asked for a lightly steamed copy of The Big Issue, *I could not have met with more incomprehension.'* (On eating in Somerset)

French House Dining Room

map 15

49 Dean Street, W1V 5HL — COOKING 4

TEL: (0171) 437 2477 FAX: (0171) 287 9109 — COST £26–£47

The first-floor setting, quieter than the busy pub below, may be 'bereft of any concessions to luxury', but a table by the window offers a ringside seat for Soho watchers, and service is amiable. As in its sister restaurant St John (see entry, London), there is an appealing puritanism about the food, which, despite confit, onglet, aïoli and brioche tart, considers itself defiantly British. Fussiness is out, dishes are unadorned, descriptions are spare, and ingredients are not expensive, judging by a starter of chickpeas, spinach, olives and mint, or a main course of baked egg, celeriac and chanterelles. Cuts of meat might include ox-tongue (with sausage and mash), while roast rabbit, smoked eel or steamed hake (with Swiss chard) bring welcome variety to the spectrum of flavours. The menu changes daily, and might end with a sticky treacle and date pudding or a 'wibbly-wobbly jelly' tasting like apple-flavoured Turkish Delight. Portions are generous. Thirty-plus French wines (and one from New Zealand) are intelligently chosen and fairly priced, starting at £9.50.

CHEF: Margot Clayton PROPRIETORS: Margot Clayton and Melanie Arnold OPEN: Mon to Sat 12.30 to 3.15, 6 to 11.15 CLOSED: 25 Dec to 1 Jan, bank hols MEALS: alc (main courses £7.50 to £15) SERVICE: not inc; 12.5% on parties of 5 or more CARDS: Amex, Delta, Diners, MasterCard, Switch, Visa DETAILS: 30 seats. Private parties: 30 main room. Vegetarian meals. Children welcome. No music

Fung Shing

map 15

15 Lisle Street, WC2H 7BE — COOKING 4

TEL: (0171) 437 1539 FAX: (0171) 734 0284 — COST £25–£61

In the frenetic hustle and bustle of Lisle Street with its profusion of Chinese restaurants and supermarkets, Fung Shing is in a class of its own. The dark blue exterior looks European, and inside there's a touch of quality and luxury, the extension at the back on to a mezzanine floor reminding one visitor of a 'French dining-room'. On its day the kitchen delivers some of the best Cantonese cooking in London, especially among the more classical dishes on the chef's special menu; as one expert pleaded, 'be bold and you could be in heaven'. Try the braised suckling pig and see.

Other high points have included deep-fried soft-shell crabs garnished with ultra-fresh chillies, peppercorns, spring onions and deep-fried garlic; roast whole crispy pigeon complete with its 'tiny head'; and shredded eel with coriander. From the more approachable reaches of the menu reporters have also sent in rave reviews for steamed scallops ('so gloriously undercooked they could hardly be separated from their shells'), sizzling chicken with ginger and spring onion, crab with black-bean sauce, and crispy belly-pork. To finish, delicate tapioca with yam and coconut milk is the pick of a modest selection of desserts. Tsing Tao beer and tea are alternatives to the up-market wine list. House wine is £10.

CHEF: T.X. Ly PROPRIETOR: Forum Restaurant Ltd OPEN: all week 12 to 11.15 CLOSED: 24 to 25 Dec MEALS: alc (main courses £7 to £55). Set L £15 (2 courses), Set D £15 to £28 (all min 2). BYO £3 SERVICE: 10%, card slips closed CARDS: Amex, Diners, MasterCard, Switch, Visa DETAILS: 115 seats. Private parties: 40 main room, 25 and 40 private rooms. Vegetarian meals. Children welcome. Music. Air-conditioned

Gabriel

NEW ENTRY map 15

9 Golden Square, W1R 3AF — COOKING 5
TEL: (0171) 439 2424 FAX: (0171) 439 2585 — COST £27–£48

Renaissance Italy provided inspiration for the décor of this newcomer to Golden Square: a mere 100 yards from Piccadilly Circus and close to Soho. Light boxes illuminate images from Orvieto cathedral in the ruddy-brown downstairs bar, and from the baptistry doors of Florence cathedral in the white and blue dining-room. A dark blue room behind offers privacy for parties. The food does not reflect Italy so much as 'the progressive attitude that has characterised London in the 1990s'. There may be less chargrilling than is customary, but this is a professional 'on-the-ball' kitchen with enough confidence to tackle more complex matters: for example, a small pear-shaped tarte Tatin filled with minced rabbit, topped with a thin slice of pear, that produces a lively interplay of sweet-sharp flavours and firm-soft textures.

Ideas are bright and sometimes unusual: an intriguing cabbage-wrapped ball of foie gras and apricot to accompany 'eight-spiced' guinea-fowl, for instance, or a puff pastry tart of ceps and bacon to go with roast monkfish. Some flavourings and seasonings can be shy, and the components of a dish – good in themselves – might not be always perfectly balanced, but there is much to tantalise and fascinate: fig and apple tart with blue cheese, for example. Chocolate, coconut and pistachio appear to be favourite components among desserts. Service might be more informed, but is willing enough. Wines are classy, with more over £20 than under. Prices start at £13, with around 10 available by the glass.

CHEF: Jamie Kimm PROPRIETOR: Jonathan Putsman OPEN: Mon to Fri L 12 to 3, Mon to Sat D 6 to 11 CLOSED: bank hols MEALS: alc (main courses £8 to £14). Set L £10 (2 courses) to £12.50, Set D £14 (2 courses) to £16 SERVICE: 12.5% (optional) CARDS: Amex, Delta, MasterCard, Switch, Visa DETAILS: 100 seats. 14 seats outside. Private parties: 40 main room, 35 private rooms. Vegetarian meals. Children welcome. Wheelchair access (no WC). Music. Air-conditioned

Le Gavroche 🍷

map 15

43 Upper Brook Street, W1Y 1PF
TEL: (0171) 408 0881 and 499 1826 — COOKING 7
FAX: (0171) 491 4387 and 409 0939 — COST £49–£136

The discreetly lit basement restaurant, decorated in bottle greens and plaids, with 'the unlikely juxtaposition of pictures by Chagall and photos of the Queen Mum', is 'a venerable institution resembling a gentlemen's bar on a luxury ship's lower deck'. Foreign and business customers tend to predominate. Old-fashioned gentility persists in offering ladies menus without prices, service from mostly young French staff is knowledgeable and attentive without being too intrusive, and they even manage the dome-removing ceremonies without too much formality.

The menu claims 'to reflect the imaginative and personal style of the chef, Michel Roux junior'. Half a dozen dishes pay homage to his father Albert (soufflé Suissesse and omelette Rothschild for example), and the *carte* is supplemented by two no-choice meals: at £60 (for three courses) and £85 (for seven), the last to be taken by the whole table. How imaginative and personal some of the items are is open to question, given a dish of asparagus with Parmesan and truffle oil, or crème brûlée, but the common thread seems to be a penchant for luxuries, coupled with impeccably classical techniques.

Shellfish appears among first courses, perhaps in the form of morsels of lobster arranged around a strongly flavoured sweet-and-sour confit of shallots, while fish and meat share main-course billing. 'There are certain presentations that only seem normal in a French restaurant,' observed an inspector, watching the deep red cooking liquid from his Bresse pigeon 'burst dramatically from its pig's bladder envelope when stabbed by the Gavroche's equivalent of Dr Kildare'. Desserts can be very sweet, but also first-class: 'regimentally precise' rows of blueberries, fraises des bois and raspberries are inserted between layers of crisp, sweetened pastry and served with a fromage blanc ice-cream and a slightly tart apricot coulis.

Unlimited free water for those who order wine, and inclusive service charge, are on the plus side, although prices are very high, and credit card slips are left open for more service. With over 60 champagnes and 18 vintages of Château Latour, the well-heeled – or those with corporate expense accounts – are spoiled for choice when it comes to wine. France's finest fill the list, apart from one page devoted mainly to Germany, Italy and California and a solitary English bottle from Devon. There are as many wines reaching four figures as there are under £20. Nine are available by the glass from £4. CELLARMAN'S CHOICE: Chablis St-Martin 'Cuvée Albert Roux' 1994, Dom. Laroche, £34; Pomerol, Ch. La Croix des Moines 1990, £32.

CHEF: Michel Roux PROPRIETOR: Le Gavroche Ltd OPEN: Mon to Fri 12 to 2, 7 to 11 CLOSED: Christmas to New Year, bank hols MEALS: alc (main courses £26.50 to £36.50). Set L £39 (inc half-bottle wine) to £85, Set D £60 to £85 SERVICE: net prices CARDS: Amex, Delta, Diners, MasterCard, Switch, Visa DETAILS: 60 seats. Private parties: 80 main room, 20 private room. Children welcome. Jacket and tie. No cigars/pipes in dining-room. Music. Air-conditioned

Gay Hussar map 15

2 Greek Street, W1V 6NB COOKING 3
TEL: (0171) 437 0973 FAX: (0171) 437 4631 COST £25–£52

Anybody who knew this veteran Hungarian warrior 20 or 30 years ago would instantly recognise him today. After the 41 years it has spent in the *Guide*, about the only thing to have changed is the meaning of 'gay'. You are greeted with 'politeness and reverence' by DJ'd waiters, although one couple 'felt like old friends almost by the time we sat down'. The *déjà mangé* food revels in slices of pressed boar's head, goose and pork pâté, and cold pike with beetroot sauce and cucumber salad. Calling a stuffed cabbage 'Transylvanian', and listing something as an 'Old Bosnian Dish', adds an adventurous dimension to essentially traditional food: smoked sausage, wild cherry soup, dumplings, and of course goulash. Pancakes (both savoury and sweet) are a feature, including chicken and veal, perhaps, or one filled with sweet cheese. Large chunks of brown bread are served, and portions are generous. The wine list is as short as it can get and still be called a list, although a 'Connoisseurs' version is available on request. House Hungarian is £10.

CHEF: Laszlo Holecz PROPRIETOR: Restaurant Partnership plc OPEN: Mon to Sat 12.15 to 2.30, 5.30 to 10.45 CLOSED: bank hols MEALS: alc (main courses £10.50 to £16.50). Set L £16 SERVICE: 12.5% (optional), card slips closed CARDS: Amex, Diners, MasterCard, Switch, Visa DETAILS: 70 seats. Private parties: 12 main room, 12 and 24 private rooms. Vegetarian meals. Children's helpings. Wheelchair access (no WC). No music. Air-conditioned

Golden Dragon £

map 15

28–29 Gerrard Street, W1V 7LP
TEL: (0171) 734 1073 and 2763 — COOKING 3
FAX: (0171) 734 1073 — COST £22–£54

Gerrard Street's current 'golden boy' shows no sign of losing its edge or popularity. Dining-rooms on two floors get packed lunch-time and evening, but service remains polite and the kitchen manages to keep pace with the influx. Daytime dim-sum (noon to 5) are still some of the classiest in Soho, thanks to tip-top ingredients and spot-on timing. Notable successes of late have included 'fantastically crisp' Vietnamese spring rolls, 'slippy white' cheung-fung stuffed with big prawns and char siu pork, chicken buns, and 'wonderful' egg custard tarts. The chef also brings into the limelight more esoteric offerings such as snails in curry sauce, black sesame-seed dumplings, minced prawns on sugar-cane and Japanese grilled siu mai; additional items are written tantalisingly in Chinese. The full menu is a fiery collection of barbecued dishes (including pigeon, veal and suckling pig), good roast meats, hotpots, rice and noodle specialities, plus Peking duck, stewed beef flank, spicy squid with garlic and chilli, and much more besides. Drink tea, Sun Lik or Tsing Tao beer, or something from the good-value wine list. House wine is £8.50. Next door is the Golden Dragon's sister restaurant, Royal Dragon.

CHEF: Yuk Cheung Man PROPRIETORS: Charlie Tsui and Lawrance Cheng OPEN: all week 12 (11 Sun) to 11.30 CLOSED: 25 Dec MEALS: alc (main courses £5 to £16). Set D £10 (min 2) to £20 (min 5) SERVICE: 10% CARDS: Amex, Delta, Diners, MasterCard, Switch, Visa DETAILS: 300 seats. Private parties: 180 main room, 30 private room. Children welcome. No music. Air-conditioned

Gourmet Garden £

map 12

59 Watford Way, NW4 3AX — COOKING 2
TEL: (0181) 202 9639 — COST £20–£44

The setting is an inauspicious terrace in a row of shops not far from Hendon tube station on the roaring Watford Way. Within, however, all is civilised and tranquil: tables are well spaced, and service is friendly and efficient. The menu has its share of mainstream Chinese dishes, such as Peking prawns and crispy aromatic duck, but the really interesting stuff is the range of Malaysian and Singaporean dishes, which are some of the most convincing outside central

London. Expect laksa soup, kweh pi tee (crispy pastry cups with various fillings), beef rendang, and hokkien fried noodles. Even more ambitious is the list of chef's recommendations, bringing into play such things as pork ribs in preserved red bean curd, fried mussels with sambal, and a hotpot of braised ikan-bilis (dried fish) with chicken and aubergine. Desserts are fun-loving offerings such as grass jelly drink, coconut crêpes, and chendol (green jelly strips with palm sugar syrup and coconut milk). Drink jasmine tea or Tiger beer. House wine is £7.50.

CHEF: Kia Lian Tan PROPRIETORS: Mr and Mrs Kia Lian Tan OPEN: Wed to Mon 12 to 2.30, 6 to 11.15 (10.45 Sun and bank hols) CLOSED: 25 Dec MEALS: alc (main courses £5 to £10.50). Set L and D £10.80 to £14.80 (all minimum 2) SERVICE: not inc CARDS: Amex, Delta, MasterCard, Switch, Visa DETAILS: 70 seats. Private parties: 70 main room. Vegetarian meals. Children welcome. No-smoking area. Music. Air-conditioned

Granita

map 13

127 Upper Street, N1 1QP — COOKING **4**
TEL: (0171) 226 3222 FAX: (0171) 226 4833 — COST £22–£41

'Islington has become a lively, exciting area in the last three years,' according to the owners, and Granita has played a part in its rejuvenation. The guiding principle is a bare-bones simplicity, from uncluttered wooden tables to a sensibly short menu written in matter-of-fact language. 'Two purées (chickpea, aubergine), tabbouleh, greens, flat bread', reads one item; 'chump of lamb, marinated, chargrilled, lentil purée, roasted parsnip, grilled red onion', reads another. The set lunch is considered good value, and the lack of fuss in both food and service is part of the appeal.

Simple chargrilling may be the mainstay, but accurate timing and well-chosen accompaniments give dishes a lift: lime and cucumber relish with Thai fish-cakes, or roasted tomato and cumin chutney with swordfish. One reporter's grilled calf's liver was 'relieved from being a cliché by creamy celeriac thyme gratin and grilled fennel'. Lightness is not a defining characteristic of desserts, although 'true flavours', whether in tarts, intense chocolate affairs or sorbets, are. The short list of young and mostly fruit-filled wines from around the world is reasonably priced. House French is £9.50.

CHEF: Ahmed Kharshoum PROPRIETORS: Vikki Leffman and Ahmed Kharshoum OPEN: Wed to Sun L 12.30 to 2.30, Tue to Sun D 6.30 to 10.30 (10 Sun) CLOSED: 10 days Christmas, 5 days Easter, 2 weeks Aug MEALS: alc (main courses £8 to £13). Set L £11.95 (2 courses) to £13.95 SERVICE: not inc CARDS: MasterCard, Visa DETAILS: 70 seats. Vegetarian meals. Children welcome. No cigars/pipes in dining-room. Wheelchair access (no WC). No music. Air-conditioned

Great Nepalese £

map 13

48 Eversholt Street, NW1 1DA — COOKING **2**
TEL: (0171) 388 6737 and 5935 — COST £17–£33

This must rate as one of the most amiable and good-humoured Eastern restaurants in the capital: the fact that it is virtually across the road from Euston Station is a bonus to many. Commuters in the know mix happily with Camden locals, students, tourists, and all comers are treated with consummate pleasantness and courtesy by Gopal Manandhar, his sons and relatives. The room is brightened up with Gurkha mementoes, photographs and prints, and a happy crowd devours some of the most persuasive Nepalese cooking in town. Herbs, spices, pulses and vegetables are used with real zing, and favourites from the special sections of the menu continue to include masco bara (black lentil pancakes), mamocha (steamed dumplings), and bhutuwa chicken laced with ginger and green herbs. Side dishes and accompaniments are in a different league from those of most similar establishments: try the black dhal or aloo kerauko achar (an extraordinary cold dish of potatoes and peas with ground sesame seeds). Nepalese Iceberg lager goes down a treat, and it's worth signing off with a shot of Coronation rum. House wine is £6.95.

CHEF: Masvic Miah PROPRIETOR: Gopal Manandhar OPEN: all week 12 to 2.30, 6 to 11.30 (11.15 Sun) CLOSED: 25 and 26 Dec MEALS: alc (main courses £4.50 to £9.50). Set L and D £11.75 (2 courses) SERVICE: 10% CARDS: Amex, Delta, Diners, MasterCard, Visa DETAILS: 48 seats. Private parties: 32 main room. Vegetarian meals. Children's helpings. Wheelchair access (no WC). Music

Greenhouse

map 15

27A Hays Mews, W1X 7RJ
TEL: (0171) 499 3331 and 3314
FAX: (0171) 499 5368

COOKING 7
COST £31–£60

Anywhere that can contrive to feel off the beaten track in Mayfair is on to a good thing. The entrance is from a back street, dimly lit at night, and despite the green trellising, whirring propellers and layers of napery the place feels 'just a little institutional'. But it is certainly comfortable, and staff are plentiful. Another change of chef heralds a more wide-ranging and adventurous menu than before, and although the strains of 'Rule, Britannia!' are fainter than they were in Gary Rhodes's day, fans have not deserted it. And why should they, with a line-up that includes salt-beef with pickled cabbage and salsa verde, and roast pumpkin risotto with deep-fried onion rings? There is much here that soothes and comforts, although the cooking also shows more bravado than before, judging by an 'inspired' combination of poached calf's tongue (with 'something of the flavour of old-fashioned corned beef') topped with a beetroot purée sharpened with horseradish. Another offal success was an inspector's 'preposterously plentiful plateful' of lamb sweetbreads with a buttery sauce and toasted brioche.

Technique is highly assured: surfaces are crisp where they should be, and textures soft in the right places, all a consequence of accurate timing. Puddings are none the worse for being as traditional as 'sloppy' bread-and-butter, while raspberry and chocolate tart is helped by good short pastry and a rich truffley filling. Service is generally entertaining and polished, although on a couple of occasions it seemed to have lost its shine by the time the bill arrived. The 20-bottle wine list has an eye for quality and starts at £12.

CHEF: Graham Grafton PROPRIETORS: David and Margaret Levin OPEN: Mon to Fri L 12 to 2.30, Sun L 12.30 to 3, all week D 6.30 to 11 (10.30 Sun) CLOSED: Christmas, bank hols MEALS: alc (main courses £11 to £18.50). Set L Sun £19.50. Cover £1 SERVICE: not inc CARDS: Amex, Diners, MasterCard, Switch, Visa DETAILS: 90 seats. Private parties: 10 main room. Vegetarian meals. Children welcome. No pipes in dining-room. No music. Air-conditioned

Green Olive

map 13

5 Warwick Place, W9 2PX — COOKING 4
TEL: (0171) 289 2469 FAX: (0171) 289 4178 — COST £22–£46

The Olive's décor is stylishly rustic, its bare brick walls hung with bright paintings, and the small lower-ground floor endowed with a little conservatory. The place still gets noisy when full. The short, set menu now focuses on northern Italian (having abandoned its original French persona), offering two, three or four courses, one of which is pasta: perhaps black tagliolini with scallops. It changes at most twice a month, is bolstered by a few daily blackboard specials, and stress is placed on lightness and freshness of ingredients.

Crab and scallop salad is a 'flavoursome' starter, and good judgement shows in tender, well-sauced veal medallions with asparagus and artichokes, and in stuffed calamari with tomato and olive sauce. 'Feather-light and very moreish' was the pronouncement on coffee pannacotta with chocolate sauce. Service is solicitous. Wines are mostly Italian, well chosen to give a breadth of styles, and descriptions are clear. House Sicilian red and Sardinian white are £9.50. Bijan Behzadi's vegetable empire includes the nearby Red Pepper, and the White Onion which opened in Islington in mid-1997 (see entries).

CHEF: Sandro Medda PROPRIETOR: Bijan Behzadi OPEN: Sun L 12.30 to 3, all week D 7 to 10.45 CLOSED: 25 and 26 Dec, Good Friday, bank hol Mons MEALS: Set L £12 (2 courses) to £16, Set D £18 (2 courses) to £24 SERVICE: not inc CARDS: Amex, Delta, MasterCard, Switch, Visa DETAILS: 55 seats. Private parties: 55 main room, 25 private room. Children's helpings. No cigars/pipes in dining-room. Wheelchair access (no WC). Music. Air-conditioned

Gresslin's

map 13

13 Heath Street, NW3 6TP — COOKING 5
TEL: (0171) 794 8386 FAX: (0171) 433 3282 — COST £19–£44

The Gresslins' narrow, bare-tabled dining-room, still a relative newcomer on the Hampstead dining scene, has become something of a local magnet. Anton Mosimann-trained Michael Gresslin cooks the kind of innovative modern food that London loves, essentially Mediterranean in orientation but with artful Asian twists here and there. A soup involving haricot beans, black mushrooms and a goats'-cheese wun-tun represents a number of different cultures in one crowded bowl, while a roast escalope of salmon with Puy lentils and a herb salad is less promiscuous. Grilled grouper fillet on a bed of fennel and tomato garnished with tapénade wowed one diner, the flavours 'marvellously balanced between sharp and gentle'. The oriental influence shows up again in roasted gingered duck with Chinese greens, black beans and a sauce of jasmine tea. Mosimann's shadow falls lightly across the dessert list of mixed sorbets on multicoloured coulis, orange terrine, and 'dazzlingly good' bread-and-butter pudding with the 'creamiest, wobbliest custard imaginable'. Service is friendly but unobtrusive. Red wines, which include a Montecillo Rioja and a fine Merlot from Chile's Valdivieso, are distinctly more inspired than the whites. House wines from France and Chile are £9.95.

CHEF: Michael Gresslin PROPRIETORS: Mr and Mrs Michael Gresslin OPEN: Tue to Sun L 12.30 to 2.45, Mon to Sat D 7 to 10.45 CLOSED: bank hols MEALS: alc (main courses L £9 to £12.50, D £9.50 to £13). Set L Tue to Sat £7.95 (2 courses) to £10.95 SERVICE: 12.5% (optional), card slips closed CARDS: MasterCard, Switch, Visa DETAILS: 56 seats. Private parties: 16 main room, 16 private room. Vegetarian meals. Children's helpings. No-smoking area. Music. Air-conditioned

▲ *Halcyon Hotel*

map 13

129 Holland Park Avenue, W11 3UT — COOKING 4
TEL: (0171) 221 5411 FAX: (0171) 229 8516 — COST £43–£65

The neighbourhood boasts some beautiful and historic houses, and the hotel itself is a listed building. A basement dining-room that doesn't feel as if it's in a basement impresses with a degree of comfort and elbow-room. Martin Hadden's food aims for a broadly Franco-Italian approach in calves' sweetbreads with morels and Parma ham, or braised shin of veal, but occasionally spills over into quasi-oriental mode with salmon teriyaki, or scallops sandwiched between layers of flaky pastry with spring onion, ginger and sesame seeds. 'Good ingredients, not too fussy' was one judgement of the style.

Although slicks of sauce painted on to the plate may look 'pictorially elaborate', all the right textures and flavours are there: for example in a pink-fleshed crisp-skinned duck breast, and noisettes of pig's trotter with 'a nice gelatinous feel' served with truffle oil and boiled potatoes. There is plenty to excite the palate on a menu that might include warm artichoke heart and chicken liver salad, or breast of chicken stuffed with foie gras served with a celeriac purée. Ice-creams partner some of the desserts – vanilla with banana pancake, or pistachio with chocolate tart – and the warm apple tart is a good one. Service has been described as 'willing more than able'. The wine list favours the French classics but also nods in the direction of the New World's finer (and pricier) offerings. Only 11 wines are priced under £20, including the three house French.

CHEF: Martin Hadden PROPRIETOR: Halycon Hotel Corporation Ltd OPEN: Sun to Fri L 12 to 2.30 (3 Sun), all week D 7 to 10.30 (11 Fri and Sat) CLOSED: Christmas, bank hols MEALS: alc (main courses £19), Set L £23 (2 courses) to £31, Set D £29 (2 courses) SERVICE: not inc; 15% for parties and residents CARDS: Amex, Delta, Diners, MasterCard, Switch, Visa DETAILS: 50 seats. 25 seats outside. Private parties: 50 main room, 12 private room. Vegetarian meals. Children welcome. No pipes in dining-room. Music. Air-conditioned ACCOMMODATION: 43 rooms, all with bath/shower. TV. Phone. Air-conditioned. Room only £165 to £600. Rooms for disabled. Lift. Children welcome. Baby facilities. Afternoon teas. Garden. Swimming-pool

▲ *Halkin Hotel*

map 14

5–6 Halkin Street, SW1X 7DJ — COOKING 5
TEL: (0171) 333 1000 FAX: (0171) 333 1100 — COST £32–£73

'Discreet elegance' is the Halkin's stock-in-trade, perceptible from the moment the glass doors slide silently open. The restaurant is done in delicate ochre with a pale puce granite floor and arched windows overlooking a shrubbery. Stefano Cavallini cooks Italian-inspired modern food with a feather-light touch. Where others have gone for earthy roots, strong herbs and plenty of starch, he favours lighter textures and discreet seasonings.

A main course of sole at a summer inspection was grilled on the bone then filleted, garnished with shaved bottarga, tiny fresh girolles and wilted spinach. Its mixture of 'sea and soil savours' showed admirable judgment, as did cannon of lamb topped with pesto and Parmesan, accompanied by a tartlet of courgette, tomato, onion and sweetbreads, everything accurately timed despite the complexity of the dish. At dessert, tiramisù is served with two coffee sauces, one pale, the other dark, the whole 'richly flavoured without being heavy'. Alternatively, Italian cheeses are usually a thoughtful and well-kept selection. Service is impeccable, but it is hard to ignore the Belgravia prices, especially when looking at the wine list. The Italian choices are inspired indeed, but those wanting to try Angelo Gaja's benchmark Piedmont Chardonnay had better be ready with £125. The house selection starts at £17.50.

CHEF: Stefano Cavallini PROPRIETOR: Christina Ong OPEN: Mon to Fri L 12.30 to 2.30, Mon to Sat D 7.30 to 11 CLOSED: 25 Dec, bank hols MEALS: alc (main courses £21 to £25). Set L £18 (2 courses) SERVICE: net prices, card slips closed CARDS: Amex, Delta, Diners, MasterCard, Switch, Visa DETAILS: 45 seats. Private parties: 60 main room, 30 private room. Vegetarian meals. Children welcome. Wheelchair access (also WC). Music. Air-conditioned ACCOMMODATION: 41 rooms, all with bath/shower. TV. Phone. Air-conditioned. Room only £240 to £525. Children welcome. Afternoon teas *(The Which? Hotel Guide)*

Helter Skelter £

NEW ENTRY map 12

50 Atlantic Road, SW9 8JN — COOKING 3
TEL: (0171) 274 8600 — COST £21–£36

Good eating came to the heart of Brixton Market with the opening of the Swerdlows' pleasingly laid-back restaurant opposite the railway arches. It may not be the loveliest location in London, but an inspector called on a packed and lively Saturday night and was impressed by the crossover Italian-Thai cooking on offer: fish-cakes with chilli dip were not as crisp as they might have been but the flavours were very satisfying, while the green chicken curry was both generous and carefully constructed. A more European main course was an unambiguous triumph: a roasted duck breast partnered by creamy mashed potato with plenty of leek, sweet-and-sour red cabbage, and a 'sweetly rich and concentrated' red wine *jus* flavoured with garlic and thyme. In addition to the main menu, daily-changing blackboard specials might feature penne with porcini and white truffle oil. A short slate of puddings includes baked blueberry cheesecake – 'certainly the best cheesecake I have had all year' – with tart blackberry coulis. Vegetables and salads are charged extra, but prices are by no means high in the first place. The wine list was in transition at the time of writing; house French is £8.95.

CHEFS: John Swerdlow and Patrice Buée PROPRIETORS: John and Natasha Swerdlow OPEN: Mon to Sat D 7 to 11 (11.30 Fri and Sat) MEALS: alc (main courses £5 to £10.50) SERVICE: 10% (optional), card slips closed CARDS: Delta, MasterCard, Switch, Visa DETAILS: 75 seats. Private parties: 45 main room. Vegetarian meals. Music

If a restaurant is new to the Guide *this year (did not appear as a main entry in the last edition),* NEW ENTRY *appears opposite its name.*

▲ *Hempel, I-Thai*

NEW ENTRY map 13

31–35 Craven Hill Gardens, W2 3EA — COOKING 3
TEL: (0171) 298 9000 FAX: (0171) 402 4666 — COST £41–£104

No signs announce the entrance to Anouska Hempel's latest designed-to-the-hilt hotel, just a standing doorman. The lobby is a pristine white wilderness, a bowl of white orchids the only adornment. 'It creates a calm, almost Zen-like effect,' said one who knows, before trotting down frosted glass stairs to the equally monochrome basement restaurant. There, he sat under a papyrus thatch, picked up 'the largest napkin I have ever seen', and declared 'This is a must-see hotel'. In contemporary fashion, two culinary cultures (Italian and Thai) have been grafted on to each other under the predictable title I-Thai.

At its best the food can be quite fascinating: a soup of chicken, coconut and foie gras with Thai basil that managed to be 'sweet, sour, spicy and rich all at the same time'. Presentation is highly original, as in the baked scallops with oriental vegetables in tamarind sauce that came in one half of a glass container, with a filo parcel of lime-seasoned rice occupying the other compartment. Four pieces of lamb cut from the rack came with a tiny spot of star-anise sauce and more lime rice. That main course was £24, which rather begs the question . . . . Add to that a 15% service impost, and it is clear that Zen-like tranquillity has its price. Desserts include blueberries wrapped in pandan leaves with blueberry and coconut sauces, but also gingered-up tiramisù to make the I-Thai point. Coolly efficient service reinforces the tone. The wine list is predominantly French, which seems a cop-out, while Italians are limited to a mere five. Mark-ups are high: try £39 (plus 15%) for Sancerre. House wines are £18.

CHEFS: Michael Hruschka and Ian Pengelley PROPRIETOR: Anouska Hempel Management OPEN: all week 12 to 2.45, 6.30 to 10.45 MEALS: alc (main courses L £11 to £17.50, D £21 to £26.50) SERVICE: 15% (optional), card slips closed CARDS: Amex, Delta, Diners, MasterCard, Switch, Visa DETAILS: 84 seats. 30 seats outside. Private parties: 200 main room, 12 to 200 private rooms. Vegetarian meals. Children welcome. Wheelchair access (also WC). Music. Air-conditioned ACCOMMODATION: 48 rooms, all with bath/shower. TV. Phone. Room only £215 to £255. Rooms for disabled. Children welcome. Baby facilities. Garden *(The Which? Hotel Guide)*

Hilaire 🍷

map 14

68 Old Brompton Road, SW7 3LQ — COOKING 7
TEL: (0171) 584 8993 FAX: (0171) 581 2949 — COST £35–£56

'We cannot praise Hilaire enough!' wrote one couple who rank it their favourite restaurant in London. The converted shop scores well on 'French provincial' atmosphere, with tongue-and-groove wood-panelled walls, and closely set tables on the ground floor (there's a bit more space in the basement). Bryan Webb has cooked here for over a decade, and if you like good food without the hype, he is your man. Leeks and salt-cured Welsh duck may betray his roots, but the food is in fine modern-classical vein. Early and late supper deals (a sort of evening version of lunch) are good, and the format is now a set-price menu with particularly generous choice at dinner.

Crab – a favourite ingredient – might come simply dressed, or with tagliatelle, or as an impressively made cake with a thin coating and creamy filling. Luxuries are well handled, as in a hefty slice of 'smooth, sweet and elegant' parfait of foie gras and chicken livers, while fish options have turned up 'moist and very fresh' grilled sea bass with a sharp laverbread beurre blanc. Webb rings the changes with other materials, adding interest as he goes: a salad of smoked eel, shin of veal served 'osso buco'-style, and calves' kidneys cooked pink and served in a deep-flavoured creamy stock-based sauce. Desserts might include a trio of chocolates or rich crème brûlée but don't get quite such an enthusiastic press. Service from English-speaking French waiters is 'assiduous and kind'.

Wines are grouped by style and helpfully annotated; France predominates but some classy examples from the New World help to extend the range of flavours. There is a good spread of half-bottles, and 18 wines are offered by the glass. House wines begin at £12.50. CELLARMAN'S CHOICE: Menetou-Salon, Clos des Blanchais 1995, Dom. Henry Pellé, £24; Ironstone Cabernet Shiraz 1994, Margaret River, W. Australia, £16.

CHEF: Bryan Webb PROPRIETORS: Bryan Webb and Dick Pyle OPEN: Mon to Fri L 12.15 to 2.30, Mon to Sat D 6.30 to 11.30 CLOSED: bank hols MEALS: Set L £18.50 (2 courses) to £23, Set supper 6.30 to 7.30 and 10 to 11.30 £18.50 (2 courses) to £24, Set D £28.50 (2 courses) to £34. BYO £12.50 SERVICE: not inc CARDS: Amex, Delta, MasterCard, Switch, Visa DETAILS: 60 seats. Private parties: 50 main room, 30 and 50 private rooms. Children's helpings. No cigars/pipes in dining-room. No music. Air-conditioned

Inaho £

map 13

4 Hereford Road, W2 4AA — COOKING 2
TEL: (0171) 221 8495 — COST £21–£44

'Hand-roll' sushi are now served every night of the week in this tiny Japanese restaurant housed in a rustically decorated front room. The range isn't vast, but you can expect to find ikura (salmon roe) and ume-shiso (pickled plum with basil) alongside sea eel, tuna and even avocado. The homespun décor is also reflected in the unpretentious style of the food: it may not be mould-breaking stuff, but ingredients are of a high standard, and the kitchen knows what it is doing. Appetisers such as yakitori or ingen-goma (French beans with sesame seeds) precede soups, sashimi, tempura and teriyaki; there's also a useful selection of soba and udon noodle dishes. Pickles are home-made, and there are seasonal fruits or green tea ice-cream to finish. Set lunches are fair value. Drink saké, Japanese beer or choose something from the short European wine list. House wine is £7.

CHEF: S. Otsuka PROPRIETOR: H. Nakamura OPEN: Mon to Fri L 12.30 to 2.30, Mon to Sat D 7 to 11 CLOSED: 2 weeks Christmas and New Year, 1 week Aug MEALS: alc (main courses £6.50 to £12). Set L £8 to £10, Set D £20 to £22 SERVICE: 10% CARDS: MasterCard, Visa DETAILS: 20 seats. Vegetarian meals. No children under 10. No cigars/pipes in dining-room. Music

L'Incontro

map 14

87 Pimlico Road, SW1W 8PH
TEL: (0171) 730 6327 and 3663 — COOKING 3
FAX: (0171) 730 5062 — COST £37–£82

Occupying a corner in a row of smart antique shops, L'Incontro has something of the feel of an exclusive club. Inside, all is white and bright, with mirrors and handsome monochrome photographs on the wall. The content of the menu – which is subdivided into antipasti, pasta, fish and meat – is neo-Italian, focusing on one style (Venetian) and keeping flavour combinations simple. Balsamic vinegar is about as newfangled as ingredients get, and, although lobster, langoustine and crab do their bit to lend class, it is the more humble offerings that shine: bean and pasta soup, for example, or veal kidneys in white wine and parsley sauce. Escalope of grouper with leek sauce has been a weekly speciality, and salmon with dill has appeared on the set-lunch menu. To finish, there might be chocolate délices or bavarois. Prices of wines on the all-Italian list are high: house wines are £18.50.

CHEFS: Danilo Minuzzo and H. de Carvalho PROPRIETOR: I. Santin OPEN: Mon to Fri L 12.30 to 2.30, all week D 7 to 11.30 (10.30 Sun) CLOSED: 25 and 26 Dec, some bank hols MEALS: alc (main courses £16 to £27.50). Set L £17.50 (2 courses) to £21.50. Cover £1.50 SERVICE: not inc CARDS: Amex, Delta, Diners, MasterCard, Switch, Visa DETAILS: 65 seats. Private parties: 65 main room, 35 private room. Vegetarian meals. Children's helpings. No pipes in dining-room. Wheelchair access (no WC). Music. Air-conditioned

▲ *Inter-Continental, Le Soufflé* 🍷 map 14

1 Hamilton Place, W1V 0QY COOKING 5
TEL: (0171) 318 8577 FAX: (0171) 491 0926 COST £39–£89

The Inter-Continental is one of those hotels that wears all its charm on the inside. Refracted light from chandeliers falls on polished marble floors, the air conditioning works, a pianist plays a white piano, and the green and mimosa-yellow dining-room beckons. Peter Kromberg's is one of the lengthier tenures among London hotel chefs, but he is not set in aspic. His self-confessed approach is 'progressive, innovative, but very much based in classical cuisine', with commendable restraint when it comes to dairy fats.

The expensive *carte* deals in all the luxuries one might expect, from hearty grilled ribeye of Buccleuch beef with béarnaise, to a rather lighter lobster marinated in olive oil, dressed to impress with oysters, anchovies, lemon juice and burnet leaves. You cannot, of course, go far without bumping into a soufflé, be it a savoury one – asparagus with glazed morels – or a sweet one made from simple seasonal fruit, or a humdinger made from Grand Marnier with an orange-flavoured chocolate centre.

The fixed-price 'Choix du Chef' menu at £47 offers a taste of the Kromberg style, with alternative options in most courses, and reporters have generally commended the service, which is correct without being nannying. The page of sommelier's suggestions from the foothills of the wine list acts as a gentle and useful introduction, then it is on to rare vintages of claret and seriously good burgndy at some very steep prices. House French is £16. CELLARMAN'S CHOICE: St-Véran 1995, Louis Latour, £23; Graves, Ch. du Seuil 1991, £28.

CHEF: Peter Kromberg PROPRIETOR: Intercontinental Hotels Group OPEN: Tue to Fri and Sun L 12.30 to 3 (3.30 Sun), Tue to Sat D 7 to 10.30 (11.15 Sat) CLOSED: 2 weeks after Christmas, L Aug, bank hols MEALS: alc (main courses £21 to £32). Set L Tue to Fri £24.50 (2 courses) to £32.50, Set L Sun £28, Set D £41.50 to £47 SERVICE: not inc CARDS: Amex, Delta, Diners, MasterCard, Switch, Visa DETAILS: 80 seats. Vegetarian meals. Children welcome. No pipes in dining room. No-smoking area. Music. Air-conditioned ACCOMMODATION: 460 rooms, all with bath/shower. TV. Phone. Air-conditioned. Room only £220 to £330. Rooms for disabled. Children welcome. Guide dogs only. Afternoon teas

Interlude

map 15

5 Charlotte Street, W1P 1HD
TEL: (0171) 637 0222 FAX: (0171) 637 0224

COOKING 6
COST £36–£84

Last year's Interlude de Chavot has separated neatly into two. Eric of that ilk departed to cook at Chavot (see entry, London), while Anand Sastry, whom some readers may remember from his days at Argyll and L'Esprit de l'Escalier, took over Interlude early in 1997. Considered more sober-looking than its neighbours, Interlude was ready for the decorative makeover promised by the time the *Guide* appears. Sastry cooks his own version of modern French food, and the appeal of the labour-intensive kitchen is immediately apparent in for example a clear, cold, tomato juice appetiser that appears to be sieved, filtered, fined, perhaps even distilled to extract such an intense flavour.

Choice typically involves liver and shellfish among first courses – a parfait of chicken livers and foie gras served with fig chutney, or a terrine of lobster and scallops – but might also take in a pithiviers of quail and truffles, or roast goats' cheese and provençale vegetables. Workmanship can be fine and detailed, as in a pretty arrangement of five ingredients in separate mounds, among them salmon tartare, langoustine salad, and a thinly sliced marinated scallop draped around pungent pickled carrot. Whether such elements do, or should, interact with each other, is perhaps a matter for debate, but it is clear that Sastry pays attention to colour and visual artistry, and enjoy puns. A trimmed loin of lamb, rolled in couscous and wrapped in spinach, then sliced and placed on a green pea purée, looked for all the world like a meaty version of sushi on wasabi.

'Desserts have always been Anand Sastry's strength' writes one who has followed his career. Demonstrations might include a 'divinely rich' dark chocolate tart with pistachio sauce, or 'intensely flavoured' banana mousseline with spikes of thin caramel wafer. A pre-dessert and generous petits-fours add to the indulgence. Sharper service would be welcome, as would a few more wines under £20 on the high-quality predominantly French list. House vin de pays Merlot and Chardonnay are £14.

CHEF: Anand Sastry PROPRIETORS: Charles Ullmann and Anand Sastry OPEN: Mon to Fri L 12 to 2.30, Mon to Sat D 7 to 11 MEALS: alc (main courses £18 to £21). Set L £17.50 (2 courses) to £22.50, Set D £55 SERVICE: 12.5% (optional), card slips closed CARDS: Amex, Diners, MasterCard, Switch, Visa DETAILS: 71 seats. Private parties: 16 main room, 16 private room. Vegetarian meals. No children under 12. No smoking in 1 dining-room. No pipes in dining-room. Wheelchair access (no WC). No music. Air-conditioned

Istanbul Iskembecisi £

NEW ENTRY map 12

9 Stoke Newington Road, N16 8BH
TEL: (0171) 254 7291

COOKING 3
COST £16–£24

It is far from easy to find a good iskembe at 4am in London, but here it is part of the resaurant's name and may even be its 'signature dish'. An inspector (eating at a more European 9.30pm) found that a bowl of the delicate broth filled with finely chopped tripe 'came exuberantly alive' with the judicious addition of salt, vinegar, lemon juice, pepper and dried chilli. This is also about the time the pace hots up, since its late hours are as authentically Turkish as the pink walls adorned with white plastic stucco and friezes. Upholstery is in assorted geometrical kelim patterns, all lit by chandeliers and wall lights.

Outstanding meze include garlicky ispanak salatesi (spinach in yogurt and olive oil) and muska borek (light, crisp pastries filled with feta and spinach). Shish kebab is not served on a skewer, but the lean and tender chunks of lamb, which take well to a touch of added sumac, are served with impressive herb-flecked rice. Be prepared for a little unevenness in the kitchen's output (that, too, is authentic), especially among vegetable dishes, and for good bread and Turkish coffee. An appealing change to the usual pastries is provided by warm armut tatlisi, a pear cooked in syrup with nuts, cream and chocolate sauce. The short list starts with house wine at £6.50, or drink Efes beer.

PROPRIETORS: Ali Demir and Ahmet Boyraz OPEN: all week 11am to 5am MEALS: alc (main courses £5.50 to £9) SERVICE: not inc, card slips closed CARDS: Amex, MasterCard, Switch, Visa DETAILS: 85 seats. Private parties: 85 main room. Car park. Vegetarian meals. Children's helpings. Music. Air-conditioned

Ivy

map 15

1–5 West Street, WC2H 9NE — COOKING 4
TEL: (0171) 836 4751 FAX: (0171) 240 9333 — COST £25–£74

Plumb in the middle of West End theatreland, within shouting distance of *The Mousetrap*, the Ivy is geared to cater for those bolting down a dressed Cornish crab with celeriac rémoulade before the show, as well as those hot-footing it, ravenous, from the curtain-calls. The tempo is hectic, the atmosphere starry, the décor remarkably elegant for the area, and a top-hatted doorman keeps spectators at bay. Those prescient enough to have booked well ahead may be regaled with leek and trompette tart with truffle oil, full of garlicky pungency, or roasted sea bass with lentils and pumpkin. 'Something for everyone' might be a fair description of the menu, and it is indeed possible to follow Sevruga caviare or sauté foie gras with shepherd's pie, kedgeree, or even curried chicken masala. International standards abound, from Caesar salad to potted shrimps, from eggs Benedict to baked Alaska. Coffee is 'fresh, aromatic and satisfying'. Staff wheel about like excitable seagulls, but can be stopped in their tracks by an extra-curricular request. A jug of tap water was an insurmountable problem at one meal: 'we have no jugs,' pleaded the waiter. The wine list holds the attention for just long enough – there is plenty to choose by the glass – but the £20 bottle barrier is soon breached. French vins de pays is £9.50.

CHEFS: Mark Hix and Des McDonald PROPRIETORS: Jeremy King and Christopher Corbin OPEN: all week 12 to 3 (3.30 Sun), 5.30 to 12 CLOSED: D 24 Dec, 25 and 26 Dec, 1 Jan MEALS: alc (main courses £7 to £22). Set L Sat and Sun £14.50. Cover £1.50 SERVICE: not inc CARDS: Amex, Delta, Diners, MasterCard, Switch, Visa DETAILS: 100 seats. Private parties: 6 main room, 60 private room. Vegetarian meals. Children welcome. No music. Air-conditioned

Iznik £

map 13

19 Highbury Park, N5 1QJ — COOKING 2
TEL: (0171) 354 5697 — COST £18–£27

This 'marvellous place makes my visits to Highbury (when Leeds play there) all the more enjoyable,' writes a supporter. He is backed up by a more local correspondent, who praises the 'quietly attentive, smiling, gentle service' in this friendliest of restaurants. The black and white tiled floor, black and gold tablecloths, and hanging lamps and ornaments contribute to a charming ambience matched by classical Ottoman food which maintains high standards. Even a 'rampant carnivore', as the Leeds fan describes himself, will find the wide range of vegetarian dishes more than satisfying. Dishes to please meat-eaters include kiymali börek (little filo pies filled with delicately spiced minced lamb), and kuzu firin (baked lamb). The Oners remind us that the bill is presented in a Turkish soap-box along with another holding complimentary Turkish Delight. House wines, from Turkey, are £7.95.

CHEF: Saim Berik PROPRIETORS: Adem and Pirlanta Oner OPEN: all week 10 to 3.30, 6.30 to 11 CLOSED: 25 to 28 Dec MEALS: alc (main courses £6.50 to £9.50) SERVICE: 10% CARDS: none DETAILS: 70 seats. Private parties: 70 main room. Vegetarian meals. Children welcome. Wheelchair access (no WC). Music

Joe's

map 14

126 Draycott Avenue, SW3 3AH — COOKING 1
TEL: (0171) 225 2217 — COST £27–£58

It's cool, it's trendy and it's owned by the Joseph fashion group. If you want to rub shoulders with the stars, then this is the place to be. Black and white pictures of fashion from a slightly older generation hang on the walls, most of the clientele wear black, and as the lights go down the music is turned up. The menu offers fashionable London café food, which means chargrilling, salsas, polenta and Parmesan in abundance. Seared scallops with wilted spinach and herb dressing is a typical starter, while pan-fried calf's liver with grain-mustard mash figures among the main courses. There's also a familiar clutch of salads, risottos and pastas, plus desserts ranging from pear and almond tart to prune and armagnac mousse with sabayon. A modest list of around 30 wines includes half a dozen by the glass. House French is £10.75.

CHEF: David Hodgins PROPRIETOR: Joseph Ettedgui OPEN: all week L 12 to 3 (4 Sat), Mon to Sat D 7 to 11 CLOSED: 2 days Christmas MEALS: alc (main courses £7 to £15.50). Cover £1. Minimum £12 SERVICE: 15% (optional), card slips closed CARDS: Amex, Delta, Diners, MasterCard, Switch, Visa DETAILS: 80 seats. Vegetarian meals. Children's helpings. Wheelchair access (no WC). Music. Air-conditioned

Justin de Blank £

NEW ENTRY map 15

120–122 Marylebone Lane, W1M 5FZ — COOKING 4
TEL: (0171) 486 5250 FAX: (0171) 935 4046 — COST £20–£34

Justin de Blank has been involved in everything from delicatessen and high-class cafeteria to pub, bakery and restaurant-with-rooms over the last quarter-century. April 1997 saw the opening of his latest venture, a light, airy and casually chic restaurant serving up big portions of good, cheap, unpretentious food. Early reports suggest that, 'despite his 70 years, he has hit the ground running'.

The *carte* is an appetising selection of around four starters and seven main courses, some items also available in the bar. Typically, expect to start with chilled or hot spicy red pepper soup, or rollmop herrings with dill potato salad, followed by sausages with red wine sauce and mash, or 'fish of the day': perhaps baked sea trout with roasted aubergines, new potatoes and a beurre blanc. Dishes that impressed at inspection included a generous wedge from a deep provençale vegetable tart, with 'wonderfully short and crunchy pastry and a wobbly egg filling', plus corn-fed chicken with 'divine' golden-brown chips, and lamb noisettes with mixed vegetables. Desserts are not quite as successful, although bread-and-butter pudding was 'decent'. Service by 'serious and charming' young staff, and the convenient opening hours – bar meals are served from 11 in the morning until 11 at night – have been approved. Wines, starting with own-label house French at £8.75, come from Adnams.

CHEFS: Julie Anderson and Paul Dodds PROPRIETOR: Justin de Blank Co Ltd OPEN: Mon to Fri 12 to 3, 5.30 to 10 CLOSED: Christmas, bank hols MEALS: alc (main courses £7 to £11.50). Bar food available. BYO £5 SERVICE: not inc CARDS: Amex, Delta, MasterCard, Switch, Visa DETAILS: 100 seats. 15 seats outside. Private parties: 100 main room, 40 and 60 private rooms. Vegetarian meals. Children welcome. Music

Kalamaras £

map 13

76–78 Inverness Mews, W2 3JQ — COOKING 2
TEL: (0171) 727 9122 FAX: (0171) 221 9411 — COST £22–£41

The décor and furnishings may not be to everyone's taste, but there's no denying the lively buzz of this old-stager among London's Greek restaurants. The kitchen deals in authentic, earthy flavours with a strong showing of meze providing the best choice. Look for things like horta (wild greens served with lemon juice), bamies (okra with leeks and tomatoes), kavouropites (filo pastries filled with crab), and fried salt cod with garlic sauce dip. Main courses include a few grills and kebabs although the tilt is towards long-cooked dishes and casseroles, such as young lamb with spinach and lemon juice, veal stifado, and rolled mincemeat with aromatic herbs and tomatoes. Sticky sweets round things off. A few French wines provide alternatives to Cambas, Demestica and Retsinas. House wine is £9.50. A sister restaurant, Micro Kalamaras, is nearby at 66 Inverness Mews; this is unlicensed but you can BYO.

CHEF: Karim Aziz PROPRIETOR: F.J. Ridha OPEN: Mon to Fri L 12.30 to 2.30, all week D 5.30 to 12 MEALS: alc (main courses £7.50 to £12.50). Set L £14 to £16, Set D £16. Cover 75p SERVICE: 10%, card slips closed CARDS: Amex, Diners, MasterCard, Visa DETAILS: 90 seats. Private parties: 30 main room, 30 private room. Vegetarian meals. Children's helpings. Wheelchair access (no WC). Music. Air-conditioned

Kastoori £

map 12

188 Upper Tooting Road, SW17 7EJ — COOKING 2
TEL: (0181) 767 7027 — COST £14–£26

'It was a delight to encounter authentic Indian cooking at very fair prices,' concluded one reporter. Kastoori's vegetarian food is distinguished by 'clear and distinct spicing' throughout the wide-ranging menu of unusual 'curries, main dishes and Thanki family specials'. The Indian origin of the family, and their stay in Uganda, is reflected in such dishes as chilli banana – made with plantains – and in special tomato curry: 'a dish so simple you'd never be able to repeat it at home'. Sunday special thali includes oro (roasted aubergine curry), and kadhi (yoghurt soup): 'an explosion of spicy flavour'. Rotlo (millet loaf) had the 'density of a brick', but bhatura, 'a fresh, puffed-up balloon of spiced bread', is a recommended staple. Shrikhand (a spiced curd-cheese-based dessert) has struck a mainly positive chord with reporters. Service is sometimes pressed, but none the less competent and friendly. Over 20 wines are accurately described, and only champagne is over £16. House wine is £7.25.

CHEF: Manoj Thanki PROPRIETOR: Dinesh Thanki OPEN: Wed to Sun L 12.30 to 2.30, all week D 6 to 10.30 CLOSED: 25 Dec, 1 week mid-Jan MEALS: alc (main courses £3 to £5) SERVICE: not inc, card slips closed CARDS: MasterCard, Visa DETAILS: 84 seats. Private parties: 20 main room. Vegetarian meals. Children welcome. Wheelchair access (no WC). No music. Air-conditioned

Kensington Place 🍷 map 13

201–207 Kensington Church Street, W8 7LX — COOKING **6**
TEL: (0171) 727 3184 FAX: (0171) 229 2025 — COST £24–£62

A decade on, Rowley Leigh's seminal restaurant still seems propelled by a sense of purpose. Once considered rowdy and noisy, it has been overtaken by more cavernous, echoing dining-rooms elsewhere, and now seems merely busy. Space is tight – you wouldn't come here for candlelit privacy – but if the surroundings don't shout 'comfort', the food often does, in the form of artichoke heart with poached egg, chanterelles and hollandaise, or potato salad with truffles.

Set lunches and evening specials use the market to ring changes, but the kitchen has a way of making even perennial favourites seem fresh and interesting, whether it be the ultra-British cod with parsley sauce, or the classic, wobbly, egg-custardy chicken and goats'-cheese mousse with mashed black olives on top and 'sticky red jam' around the outside. Though the style may no longer be considered innovative, the food still has a common-sense feel about it, from cockle chowder to venison stew, and the spicing (harissa with lamb and couscous, garlicky salsa verde with strips of sole and Puy lentils) is tried and tested rather than exotic. Traditional desserts are the norm, from steamed chocolate pudding with custard to 'impeccable' lemon tart.

The wine list offers a good choice of styles and flavours from both Old and New Worlds, with some just crying out to be explored further, such as the Redwood Valley Sauvignon Blanc from Nelson or the Madfish Bay Semillon from Western Australia. House wines start at £10.50 (£3.25 a glass). CELLARMAN'S CHOICE: Steenberg Sauvignon Blanc 1994, Constantia, South Africa, £15; Mulderbosch Faithful Hound 1994, Stellenbosch, South Africa £21.

CHEF: Rowley Leigh PROPRIETORS: Nick Smallwood and Simon Slater OPEN: all week 12 to 3 (3.30 Sat and Sun), 6.30 to 11.45 (10.15 Sun) CLOSED: Christmas, 1 Jan MEALS: alc (main courses £10 to £16.50). Set L £14.50. BYO £5, champagne £10 SERVICE: not inc CARDS: Amex, Delta, MasterCard, Switch, Visa DETAILS: 140 seats. Private parties: 25 main room. Vegetarian meals. Children's helpings. Music. Air-conditioned

🍾 denotes an outstanding wine cellar; 🍷 denotes a good wine list, worth travelling for.

Lahore Kebab House £

map 13

2 Umberston Street, E1 1PY — COOKING 1

TEL: (0171) 488 2551 and 481 9737 — COST £12–£19

The appeal of this fast-moving, bustling café is primarily the food, then the price, certainly not the décor. Look for the garish black and red sign in a side street off Commercial Road, and don't expect frills, kid-glove treatment or elaborate cooking. The menu, listed on a board behind the counter, doesn't amount to much more than lamb and chicken versions of tikka, curry and karahi, plus tarka dhal, biryani, sag aloo, and on Fridays paya (lamb's trotters), but the food is 'proof, if ever it were needed, that appearances can be deceptive'. Accurate charcoal grilling makes the best of ingredients, spicing is impressive, and 'simple and well-made' curries have 'a good depth of flavour', the lamb version flecked with coriander leaves and spiked with whole peppercorns. 'The bill had the same intangible qualities as the waiter's order pad', which is to say they were both verbal, but at these prices it is hardly worth wasting paper. Lahore is unlicensed, but customers are welcome to bring their own wine.

CHEF: M. Din PROPRIETOR: M. Siddique OPEN: all week 12 to 12 MEALS: alc (main courses £2 to £4.40) BYO (no corkage) SERVICE: not inc CARDS: none DETAILS: 100 seats. Private parties: 60 main room. Wheelchair access (no WC). Music. Air-conditioned

▲ *Landmark London, Winter Garden*

map 13

222 Marylebone Road, NW1 6JQ — COOKING 3

TEL: (0171) 631 8000 FAX: (0171) 631 8088 — COST £35–£59

The Landmark stands in front of Marylebone station, and was the headquarters of British Rail when such a body existed. In 1993 it reopened as a corporate hotel, its centrepiece an eight-storey atrium where gigantic palm trees are lit from below and Palm Court-type music tinkles for hour after hour. In the Winter Garden restaurant, the cooking has never settled into one obvious mode. Piedmontese food had its day, then Ken Hom turned up and gave the menus an oriental spin. Now there are garganelli arrabbiata, cod and chips with mushy peas, and amaretto creme brûlee with almond tuiles alongside each other on the menu.

The touch these days is as light as a feather, and cream and butter are elbowed aside to make way for balsamic and olive oil. Shellfish consommé with crab and ginger wun-tuns might be followed by pesto-crusted sea bass with chargrilled vegetables and saffron oil, as East meets West in style. Desserts such as sticky toffee pudding, amaretto crème brûlée, and hot apple strudel provide a little more in the way of richness. Wines are not cheap. House red and white are both £17.50, and ten wines by the glass start at £4.25.

CHEF: George Heise PROPRIETOR: Landmark Corporation OPEN: all week 11am to midnight MEALS: alc (main courses £12 to £19). Set L and D £16.50 (2 courses) to £21 SERVICE: net prices, card slips closed CARDS: Amex, Delta, Diners, MasterCard, Switch, Visa DETAILS: 105 seats. Vegetarian meals. Children welcome. No-smoking area. Wheelchair access (also WC). Music. Air-conditioned ACCOMMODATION: 304 rooms, all with bath/shower. TV. Phone. Air-conditioned. Room only £225 to £1220. Rooms for disabled. Children welcome. Baby facilities. Afternoon teas. Swimming-pool

▲ *Lanesborough, The Conservatory* map 14

1 Lanesborough Place, SW1X 7TA COOKING 4
TEL: (0171) 259 5599 FAX: (0171) 259 5606 COST £32–£80

Fronds tumble from monster vases, Grecian heads on the wall throw out water, and a pianist plays into the night. The vaulted glass roof is not the only thing that goes over the top, as Paul Gayler's cooking does its best to match the surroundings. He was doing East-meets-West long before others, and has refined the style to a harmonious and successful pitch. A tiny tortilla of spinach, mushroom and mozzarella was surrounded by mango and sweet red pepper strips to make a delicately 'sweet and luscious' first course. Chicken and shiitake soup is an equally light way to start, before going on perhaps to chargrilled Dover sole with scallion mash and caper oil, or barbecued rack of lamb with tabbouleh, chilli and mint.

Combinations are usually very successful, and buttressed by genuine intensity of flavour. That holds true through to desserts, when a nest of meringue filled with praline ice-cream and liberally strewn with raspberries comes with a coulis of the fruits to lend force. Mandarin parfait with warm chocolate sauce or toffeed banana 'indulgence' are among the other possibilities. 'Relaxed and unobtrusive' service makes a change in a grand hotel. An interesting selection of house wines is offered by the glass from £4.50, and by the bottle from £16.50. The rest of the list is fine but punishingly expensive.

CHEF: Paul Gayler PROPRIETOR: Rosewood Hotels OPEN: all week 12 to 2.30, 6.30 to 12 MEALS: alc (main courses £12.50 to £26.50). Set L £19.50 (2 courses) to £23.50, Set D £29.50. SERVICE: net prices, card slips closed CARDS: Amex, Delta, Diners, MasterCard, Visa DETAILS: 120 seats. Private parties: 40 main room, 12 to 100 private rooms. Vegetarian meals. Children's helpings. No cigars/pipes in dining room. Wheelchair access (also WC). Music. Air-conditioned ACCOMMODATION: 95 rooms, all with bath/shower. TV. Phone. Air-conditioned. Room only £228 to £335. Rooms for disabled. Children welcome. Baby facilities.Afternoon teas

Langan's Brasserie map 15

Stratton Street, W1X 5FD COOKING 2
TEL: (0171) 491 8822 FAX: (0171) 493 8309 COST £30–£51

'A pleasant restaurant for grown-ups,' in the words of one reader, Langan's marches on, oblivious to culinary fashion. If it seems on the ball, that may be because the brasserie food it has championed has come full circle. Start, say, with oeufs pochés au haddock fumé, go on to carré d'agneau rôti aux herbes de Provence (perhaps with a side-order of mushy peas), and finish with vacherin Montmorency. The extremely long menu may also include avocado salad with prawns, bangers and mash with white onion sauce, and apple and blackcurrant crumble. Whichever takes your fancy, everything is done with aplomb, and sleek black cars that disgorge famous people to fascinated gawps from within are for many an added attraction. A surprisingly brief slate of wines appears on the right-hand side of the menu and is mainly French with the odd Antipodean interloper. Own-label Duboeuf house wines are £9.50.

CHEFS: Roy Smith and Dennis Mynott PROPRIETORS: Richard Shepherd and Michael Caine OPEN: Mon to Fri 12.45 to 11.45, Sat 8 to 12.45 CLOSED: Christmas, bank hols MEALS: alc (main courses £11.50 to £14.50). Cover £1 SERVICE: 12.5% (optional) CARDS: Amex, Delta, Diners, MasterCard, Switch, Visa DETAILS: 300 seats. Private parties: 12 main room. Vegetarian meals. Children's helpings. Wheelchair access (no WC). Music. Air-conditioned

Lansdowne £

map 13

90 Gloucester Avenue, NW1 8HX — COOKING 2
TEL: (0171) 483 0409 — COST £20–£32

One of the earlier exponents of London's new-wave pub boom, the Lansdowne remains true to type. Its ill-matched assortment of wooden tables and chairs, colourful artwork on the walls and resident cats reinforce the homely feel. The laid-back atmosphere and simple, hearty food attract a youthful North London crowd and things quickly reach fever pitch, even on midweek nights. Once you've managed to bag a table, make your way to the bar and order from the blackboard menu: this is the usual romp around the Mediterranean, done here with proper regard for freshness and a certain amount of flair. Typical dishes are goat's-cheese salad with rocket and grilled peppers, pork chops with Greek salad, or neck of lamb with lemon rind, olives and rice, while desserts include plum and almond tart, coffee granita and crème Catalan. A small choice of wines supplements the draught beers and cider; house French is £8.

CHEF/PROPRIETOR: Amanda Pritchett OPEN: Tue to Sun L 12.30 to 2.30 (1 to 2.00 Sun), all week D 7 to 10 CLOSED: 25 and 26 Dec, 1 Jan MEALS: alc Tue to Sat L, all week D (main courses £6.50 to £10.50). Set L Sun £15 SERVICE: not inc, card slips closed CARDS: Delta, MasterCard, Switch, Visa DETAILS: 100 seats. 30 seats outside. Private parties: 40 main room, 30 private room. Vegetarian meals. No music

Launceston Place 🍷

map 14

1A Launceston Place, W8 5RL — COOKING 4
TEL: (0171) 937 6912 FAX: (0171) 938 2412 — COST £27–£55

The villagey street in one of the more exclusive parts of Kensington comes about as close to a rural feel as London gets, and the small, warmly furnished rooms convey a sense of eating in someone's home: quite a contrast to the fashionably cavernous scale of things. It is much more restrained than its bolder sister (see Kensington Place, London), a relaxing place to come for good food without the fireworks. There is no shortage of cosmopolitan interest, though, from the ginger and coriander that spice up warm oysters with black beans, to the beetroot and sour cream that come with calf's liver. Risotto may incorporate peas and mint, or mussels and saffron, and other Italian input has varied from salads (of rocket, sun-dried tomato and Parmesan, for example) to gnocchi.

Materials might include lamb kidneys (devilled), rabbit leg (stewed with grain mustard), and chump of lamb (with artichoke purée) as well as roast cod (in a potato crust), and scallops (in a tomato and fennel butter sauce). Desserts – a highlight for more than one reporter – have ranged from predictable tiramisù to a more unusual dish of poached rhubarb with deep-fried scones and clotted cream. 'I hate scones, but this deep-fried variation was quite a revelation.'

Service has varied from 'cool and formal' to 'a happy balance of friendly helpfulness and total efficiency'. The wine list may only run to two pages but it neatly demonstrates that size isn't everything by providing an impressive range of styles and flavours at reasonable prices. House Chardonnay is £10.50, house claret £11.50.

CHEF: Derek Francis PROPRIETORS: Nick Smallwood and Simon Slater OPEN: Sun to Fri L 12.30 to 2.30 (3 Sun), Mon to Sat D 7 to 11.30 CLOSED: bank hols MEALS: alc (main courses £13.50 to £16.50). Set L and D 7 to 8 Mon to Fri £14.50 (2 courses) to £17.50, Set L Sun £17.50 SERVICE: not inc CARDS: Amex, Delta, MasterCard, Switch, Visa DETAILS: 85 seats. Private parties: 85 main room, 12 and 30 private rooms. Vegetarian meals. Children's helpings. No pipes in dining-room. Wheelchair access (no WC). No music. Air-conditioned

Laurent £

map 13

428 Finchley Road, NW2 2HY — COOKING 1
TEL: (0171) 794 3603 — COST £18–£29

'It's really easy to order here,' admits one correspondent: '"I'll have the starter, the standard couscous and extra merguez, please, some water, and mint tea to finish."' Laurent Farrugia has been in the business of providing honest North African food since 1983. His modest front room, with its oilcloths and Artex plasterwork, may not be the most auspicious in town, but the food makes amends: it manages to be 'light, zingy and nourishing all at once', and it's served in vast quantities. If you bring your own saucepan (as many locals seem to do) you can even order a take-away. The 'starter' is brique à l'oeuf (fried egg in filo pastry), couscous comes five ways, and proceedings are rounded off by sorbets, ice-creams and crêpes suzette. One reporter was delighted to find individual bottles of Perrier at the knock-down price of 50p; otherwise order one of the gutsy Moroccan wines. House wine is £8.20.

CHEF/PROPRIETOR: Laurent Farrugia OPEN: Mon to Sat 12 to 2, 6 to 11 CLOSED: first 3 weeks Aug, bank hols MEALS: alc (main courses £7 to £10.50) SERVICE: not inc CARDS: Amex, Delta, MasterCard, Visa DETAILS: 36 seats. Vegetarian meals. Children's helpings. No cigars/pipes in dining-room. Wheelchair access (no WC). No music

Leith's

map 13

92 Kensington Park Road, W11 2PN — COOKING 6
TEL: (0171) 229 4481 FAX: (0171) 221 1246 — COST £35–£77

Leith's has never looked less than immaculately trim, set in a genteel Victorian terrace in one of the leafier sectors of W11. The 'warmly inviting' dining-room is a discreetly lit place with cream walls and comfy chairs upholstered in cobalt blue. Over the seven years he has been cooking here, Alex Floyd's capabilities have kept pace with events. Although some fashionable reference points may be incorporated, nothing detracts from the classical techniques that are brought to bear on them.

Scallops are roasted and served with lemon couscous, artichoke crisps and a lightly curried butter sauce in a first course from the spring menu. Even bolder flavours are mobilised for a brandade of smoked haddock and cod with leeks, anchovy mayonnaise and a poached egg. Meaty treatments of fish main courses have always been one of the kitchen's touchstones; setting a fillet of salmon in oxtail consommé with wild mushrooms and lentils is indicative. One reader was struck by the way accompaniments of sweetbread and chicken dumplings, and roast vegetables, did not over-ride the flavour of a piece of accurately cooked beef fillet. Roasting has also been successfully applied to a dessert of mango and passion-fruit that was accompanied by white chocolate parfait. Another commended dessert was crème brûlée with rhubarb and mascarpone. Staff are 'talkative, and even humorous', as well as 'efficient'.

Wine enthusiasts will enjoy perusing the highly selective list, with its original collection of exciting, rare and exclusive bins from around the world, while the short, introductory guidelines to each region might help the uninitiated. Quality is the watchword, and mark-ups can be high, but a few wines under £20 are offered, starting with half a dozen house suggestions from £15.50, and a weekly-changing selection by the glass furthers the cause. CELLARMAN'S CHOICE: Alsace, Chasselas Vieilles Vignes 1994, Dom. Schoffit, £22.50; Crozes-Hermitage 1994, Dom. Alain Graillot, £27.50.

CHEF: Alex Floyd PROPRIETOR: Leith's School of Food & Wine OPEN: Tue to Fri L 12.15 to 2.15, Mon to Sat D 7 to 11.30 CLOSED: 2 weeks Christmas, 2 weeks Aug MEALS: alc (main courses £19.50 to £26). Set L £16.50 (2 courses) to £19.50, Set D £27.50 (2 courses) to £35 SERVICE: 12.5% (optional), card slips closed CARDS: Amex, Diners, MasterCard, Switch, Visa DETAILS: 75 seats. Private parties: 36 main room, 8 and 36 private rooms. Vegetarian meals. No children under 7. No-smoking area. No music. Air-conditioned

Livebait

map 13

43 The Cut, SE1 8LF — COOKING 2

TEL: (0171) 928 7211 FAX: (0171) 928 2299 — COST £32–£49

The expanding Groupe Chez Gérard, which bought Livebait in February 1997, has wisely left well alone. Theodore Kyriakou's lively cooking style continues in this single tiled room with its view of the kitchen. Fish is the business, and supplies are fresh, although the constantly fizzing change and invention may put a strain on the kitchen. One reporter ordered 'what sounded the most innovative first course in London', but found the carpaccio of smoked marlin served with African crevette, mussel blinis, salmon caviare and a glass of vodka a shade ambitious. Roast cod has been given a resourceful, if challenging, crust of baked banana, chilli and almond, and served with okra gumbo and bok choi. Whatever else, this food is not boring. Not everything aims to be outlandish, though, and there is scope for traditional eating with 'Cornish bouillabaisse', oysters, a shellfish platter, or bowls of cockles, winkles and whelks. 'Bread is worth a mention,' and the intelligent, well-priced wine list offers a good selection by the glass. House Muscadet is £9.95 (£2.85 a glass).

CHEF: Theodore Kyriakou PROPRIETOR: Groupe Chez Gérard OPEN: Mon to Sat 12 to 3, 5.30 to 11.30 CLOSED: bank hols MEALS: alc (main courses £11 to £17). Set D 5.30 to 7 £11 (2 courses SERVICE: not inc CARDS: Delta, MasterCard, Switch, Visa DETAILS: 76 seats. Private parties: 8 main room. Children welcome. No cigars/pipes in dining-room. Wheelchair access (also WC). No music

Lobster Pot

map 13

3 Kennington Lane, SE11 4RG — COOKING 1
TEL: (0171) 582 5556 FAX: (0171) 582 9751 — COST £22–£83

In keeping with its name and starting with the pavement lobster pots, the restaurant is decorated throughout with reminders of the sea. It has been described by reporters as anything from 'eccentric' to 'wacky', and the narrow room is overlooked by a 20-foot-long fish tank. Recordings of seagulls and sea shanties add to the 'surreal' feeling. Staff, dressed in Breton gear, do their best within the limitations of cramped tables and the small kitchen's ability to produce the food as quickly as required. Recommended dishes have been 'thick and shellfishy' soup, followed by 'delicately flavoured, well-presented' barracuda with sauce créole. Traditional puddings might include a pancake filled with crème pâtissière on a red fruit coulis, profiteroles or tarte Tatin. The short wine list is entirely French and starts with house red and white at £10.50.

CHEF: Hervé Régent PROPRIETORS: Hervé and Nathalie Régent OPEN: Tue to Sat 12 to 2.30, 7 to 10.45 CLOSED: 24 Dec to early Jan MEALS: alc (main courses £14.50 to £29.50). Set L £15.50 to £22.50, Set D £22.50 SERVICE: net prices, card slips closed CARDS: Amex, Delta, Diners, MasterCard, Switch, Visa DETAILS: 24 seats. Private parties: 30 main room, 14 private room. Vegetarian meals. Children's helpings (no babies). No cigars/pipes in dining-room. Wheelchair access (no WC). Music. Air-conditioned

Lola's

NEW ENTRY map 13

The Mall Building,
359 Upper Street, N1 0PD — COOKING 4
TEL: (0171) 359 1932 FAX: (0171) 359 2209 — COST £25–£43

Lola's hides away on the first floor of an Islington antiques mall, flooded with natural light during the day, with a large semi-circular window at one end and buttery yellow furnishings and napery. Juliet Peston arrived last year, after her long stint at Alastair Little's Frith Street restaurant (see entry), and that same feeling of directness and honesty – from the unreconstructed Mediterranean food to the handwritten menus – has been retained for an Islington clientele that would expect nothing less.

Chilled pea soup with tzatziki, a white-based pizza piled with grilled peppers or maybe even a simple collection of modern hors d'oeuvre might all start a meal off. The last may be a plate of vertically split roast green garlic, tomatoes, goats' cheese, grainy tapénade and a wedge of socca, a type of niçoise pancake made from chickpea flour: 'the sort of dish you can pick and fiddle with placidly,' said one who picked and fiddled. Seafood harira is a generous bowl of squid, scallops, crab and prawns, given body and meatiness with brown lentils and flavoured with coriander, cumin and parsley, while calf's liver and bacon is done with split-pea croquettes and a mustard sauce.

Finish with electrifying hot chocolate mousse cake served with an espresso granita, or a great version of pain perdu with crisply fried egg-soaked bread, caramelised apple wedges and 'richly creamy' ice-cream. Service is efficient and reliable. The short wine list offers a good range of varietals and styles from around the world, including a couple of second-growth clarets. House French is £9.50.

CHEF: Juliet Peston PROPRIETORS: Morfudd Richards and Carol George OPEN: all week L 12 to 2.30 (3 Sat and Sun), Mon to Sat D 6.30 to 11 CLOSED: bank hols MEALS: alc (main courses £10 to £14). Set L Mon to Fri £12 (2 courses) to £16.50 SERVICE: not inc CARDS: Amex, Delta, Diners, MasterCard, Switch, Visa DETAILS: 80 seats. Vegetarian meals. Children's helpings. Music. Air-conditioned

Lou Pescadou

map 13

241 Old Brompton Road, SW5 9HP — COOKING 2
TEL: (0171) 370 1057 FAX: (0171) 244 7545 — COST £19–£47

'Provençale is the key word,' say the owners, and the kitsch nautical décor emphasises the seafood theme: soupe de poisson, plateau de fruits de mer, roast sea bream with garlic, and grilled whole sea bass are all typical of the simple, no-nonsense approach. Oysters, squid (fried or à la chinoise), mussels (marinière, provençale, or à la crème), or whelks with thyme might begin the show, depending on the season and the catch. Main courses have included pan-fried salmon with mustard sauce, escabèche of tuna, and daily specials of, for example, stuffed mussels, cuttlefish cooked in its ink, and game such as wild boar in beer, or guinea-fowl with grapes. For dessert, expect crème brûlée, or fondant au chocolat. The wine list is short and French; house selections are £10.50.

CHEF: Laurent David PROPRIETORS: Daniel Chobert and Laurent David OPEN: all week 12 to 3, 7 to 12 CLOSED: 1 week Christmas MEALS: alc (main courses £5.50 to £13.50). Set L Mon to Fri £9. Cover £1 SERVICE: 15% (optional), card slips closed CARDS: Amex, Delta, Diners, MasterCard, Switch, Visa DETAILS: 70 seats. 22 seats outside. Private parties: 80 main room 40 private room. Vegetarian meals. Children's helpings. No music. Air-conditioned

Magno's

map 15

65A Long Acre, WC2E 9JH — COOKING 2
TEL: (0171) 836 6077 FAX: (0171) 379 6184 — COST £27–£50

Under new ownership since the last *Guide*, but with no change of chef, Magno's continues its course as a lively Covent Garden brasserie. Wine and theatre are the decorative motifs, and opening hours are tailored to suit curtain times at the large number of theatres within a 15-minute walk. Gilbert Rousset's Franco-Italian style takes in a terrine of Toulouse sausage and duck confit, tortellini with asparagus, and properly done crème brûlée. The set menu is a shortened version of the à la carte, choice on the latter is generous, and there is room for unusual ideas such as roast vegetable and fruit strudel with a chilli relish. Given the casual nature of early and late dining, even a dish of smoked salmon with poached egg on a muffin with hollandaise sauce doesn't seem out of place. Pastry-work is good, whether savoury – puff with leeks and a mustard cream sauce – or sweet, as in a light tart of raspberry and white chocolate. Service can be stretched when things get busy, and prices can be high on the largely French wine list, but house wine is £10.95.

CHEF: Gilbert Rousset PROPRIETORS: S. Caltagirone and F. Falcone OPEN: Mon to Sat 12 to 2.30, 5.30 to 11.30, Sun 12.30 to 3.30, 6 to 10 CLOSED: 1 week Christmas MEALS: alc (main courses £10 to £15.50). Set L and D £13.95 (2 courses) to £16.95, Set D 5.30 to 7.15 £10.95 (2 courses) SERVICE: 12.5% CARDS: Amex, Delta, Diners, MasterCard, Switch, Visa DETAILS: 65 seats. Children welcome. No cigars/pipes in dining-room. Wheelchair access (no WC). Music. Air-conditioned

Maison Novelli

map 13

29 Clerkenwell Green, EC1R 0DU — COOKING **6**
TEL: (0171) 251 6606 FAX: (0171) 490 1083 — COST £26–£88

Judging by the suits, this corner site in upwardly mobile Clerkenwell Green seems to have revived the business lunch, although it is far enough from the City to stay alive in the evening. A modestly proportioned first-floor restaurant has plain purply-blue walls, modern prints and potted plants, but plans are under way to extend it to the ground floor, currently occupied by the brasserie, which will eventually move next door.

Novelli's version of modern haute cuisine comes as 'a refreshing change for those weary of the Mediterranean diet and fusion food'. The *carte* seems ambitiously long for a small kitchen, but is carefully constructed to combine last-minute cooking with items prepared at leisure: a slice of cassoulet terrine, for example, with sausages, gizzard and foie gras in cross-section. Offal and charcuterie are two of the strengths, culminating in the 'magnificent' pig's trotter which changes daily. 'My version was stuffed with girolles and all manner of dark squidgy things gelatinous'; it came with finely puréed potatoes, and a glossy sauce 'with a reflection like polished shoes'.

Innovation is a characteristic – in a dish of poached turbot, for example, served in a coconut milk sauce with an 'interesting dollop' of mashed cauliflower flavoured with almonds – and flavours are carefully considered. 'Juicy, sweet' warm langoustines piled into a salady tower with beetroot oil and coral powder proved 'a stunner' for one reporter.

Desserts have included pineapple Tatin with coconut ice-cream, and a 'fountain' of mixed red fruits served with a 'cream horn' made from brandy-snap and filled with vanilla ice-cream. Service is attentive, and 'slightly formal, but nice with it', though the 'suggested gratuity' of 15% is considered excessive. Wines offer a bit more choice from the New World than is customary in French restaurants, but a concentration of high-quality French classics remains the backbone. House wine is £13.85.

CHEFS: Jean-Christophe Novelli and Richard Guest PROPRIETOR: Jean-Christophe Novelli OPEN: Mon to Fri L 12 to 3.30, Mon to Sat D 6.30 to 11.15 (12 Fri and Sat); brasserie all day Mon to Sat MEALS: alc (main courses £13.50 to £22). Set D £55 (minimum 2) SERVICE: 15% (optional), card slips closed CARDS: Amex, Delta, Diners, MasterCard, Visa DETAILS: 50 seats (restaurant), 50 seats (brasserie). 25 seats outside. Private parties: 50 main room, 50 private room. Vegetarian meals. Children's helpings. No cigars/pipes in dining-rooms. Music

Restaurateurs justifiably resent no-shows. If you quote a credit card number when booking, you may be liable for the restaurant's lost profit margin if you don't turn up. Always phone to cancel.

Mandarin Kitchen £

map 13

14–16 Queensway, W2 3RX
TEL: (0171) 727 9012

COOKING 4
COST £23–£76

A large window painted with marine images hints at the 'dazzlingly fresh, superbly cooked seafood' that brings crowds from miles around to this quirky place. It can be noisy and smoky, tables are close, and service has ranged from 'haphazard' to 'quite polite'. The long menu takes in most of the Cantonese repertoire, but the speciality is lobster: 'we use only the finest Scottish wild lobsters, simply because they are probably the best in the world', the restaurant tells us. It might be baked and served with soft noodles and lots of ginger and spring onion: 'a fine example of this popular dish', according to an inspector.

Other successes have included 'well-executed' deep-fried crispy soft-shell crabs with good batter, thick fillets of roast eel 'cooked just right' with garlic and chilli, and the oddly named 'crystal king prawn with an unexpected taste' (stir-fried prawns with yellow-bean paste and chilli). Mustard greens quickly stir-fried with ginger and garlic, and lotus-leaf-wrapped rice mixed with Chinese liver sausage, mushrooms and prawns make good accompaniments. House wines are £8.50.

CHEF: K.W. Man PROPRIETOR: Helen Cheung OPEN: all week 12 to 11.30 CLOSED: 24 to 26 Dec MEALS: alc (main courses £6 to £24). Set D £9.90 (minimum 2) SERVICE: not inc CARDS: Amex, Diners, MasterCard, Switch, Visa DETAILS: 120 seats. Private parties: 120 main room. Vegetarian meals. Children welcome. Music. Air-conditioned

Mantanah £

map 12

2 Orton Building, Portland Road, SE25 4UD
TEL: (0181) 771 1148 FAX: (0181) 771 2341

COOKING 4
COST £19–£38

'I would love to have Mantanah as my local restaurant,' writes one reporter. Its bright 'Thai blue' frontage stands out in this rather unprepossessing area, and within the small, fairly plain dining-room what caught the eye of one reporter were an embroidered sequinned picture of elephants, and a watermelon carved into a water lily. The owners are Ken and Tym Yeoh: she cooks, he runs front-of-house, assisted by 'gracious' staff. Better-than-average set menus are an easy option, but less fun than choosing from the long à la carte, which includes a section of north-eastern Thailand specialities and some 30 vegetarian choices. There is praise for mainstream dishes such as pork and beef satay ('subtle and vividly spiced at the same time'), and for more unusual stir-fried water lily with black-bean sauce.

Pay due attention to the word 'hot' in the section headed 'Yum Yum (Thai Hot Salad)'. It refers to the chilli content, and an inspector thought his yum neua (hot-and-sour chargrilled beef salad) called for a health warning. Look out too for curiously named dishes such as 'Adams Rib' (spare ribs in chilli paste with green peppercorns and sweet basil), and 'Cinderella's Best Friend' (deep-fried shredded pumpkin in coconut batter). There are no chocolates in 'Black Magic' but baby aubergine slices with red chilli and bright green Thai basil. Only on desserts are opinions divided. While one reporter enjoyed 'refreshing' hot bananas in light sugar syrup with strands of fresh coconut, another was unimpressed by his 'black jelly'. House wine is £7.50.

CHEF: Tym Srisawatt-Yeoh PROPRIETORS: Mr and Mrs K.S. Yeoh OPEN: Tue to Sun D only 6.30 to 11 CLOSED: 25 and 26 Dec, 1 Jan MEALS: alc (main courses £5.50 to £7). Set D £13.50 to £20 SERVICE: not inc, card slips closed CARDS: Amex, Delta, MasterCard, Switch, Visa DETAILS: 40 seats. Private parties: 40 main room. Vegetarian meals. Children's helpings. No cigars/pipes in dining-room. Wheelchair access (no WC). Music. Air-conditioned

Matsuri

map 15

15 Bury Street, SW1Y 6AL — COOKING 4
TEL: (0171) 839 1101 FAX: (0171) 930 7010 — COST £24–£106

Standing right next to the Conran glitz of Quaglino's (see entry) in one of the most moneyed quarters of Mayfair, this is a Japanese restaurant with class. The frontage may not look much, but the interior breathes lightness and simplicity with an attractive modern accent. Several dining-areas are run by ultra-smart staff, the men in black jackets, the ladies in kimonos. Matsuri (the name means 'festivals') concentrates its culinary efforts on two seminal traditions: the formal artistry of sushi and sashimi, and the up-front theatricality and entertainment of teppanyaki. Lunch is the most affordable deal, with lacquered bento boxes containing all manner of delights; there are set-menus and even one-dish meals ranging from triangular grilled rice balls to okonomi-yaki (a kind of Japanese pizza).

The full teppan experience in the evening requires a substantially greater outlay. To start, there is chicken yakitori, deep-fried soft shell crab, dobin mushi (clear soup served in a special pot), or chawan-mushi (a steamed egg custard); otherwise consider some sashimi or tempura. Holding centre stage are grills: fillet steak, turbot, abalone, lobster, saddle of lamb, and duck. The trinity of steamed rice, miso soup and pickles signals that the show is drawing to a close, and the final touch is provided by green-tea ice-cream, assorted fruits or lemon sorbet. A few fairly priced New World wines are the most affordable options on the wine list. House wines start at £16.50.

CHEF: Kanehiro Takase PROPRIETOR: JRK UK Ltd OPEN: Mon to Sat 12 to 2.30, 6 to 10 CLOSED: bank hols MEALS: alc (main courses L £5.50 to £20, D £12 to £29). Set L £10 (2 courses) to £40, Set D £25 to £55 SERVICE: 12.5% (optional) CARDS: Amex, Diners, MasterCard, Visa DETAILS: 133 seats. Private parties: 18 main room, 8 private room. Vegetarian meals. Children welcome. Wheelchair access (also WC). Music. Air-conditioned

Melati

map 15

21 Great Windmill Street, W1V 7PH
TEL: (0171) 734 6964 and 437 2745 — COOKING 1
FAX: (0171) 434 4196 — COST £23–£48

Deep in the throbbing heartland of strip-club Soho, this ethnic hot-spot continues to deliver no-nonsense food with undiluted flavours. It remains one of the few addresses in London where Indonesian and Malaysian cooking comes with a convincingly sure touch, and the long menu of more than 130 dishes aims to please carnivores and vegetarians alike. Recommendations have mentioned kari kambling (mutton curry on the bone), tahu telor (a crisp omelette filled with pieces of bean curd), and prawn fritters in sweet-and-sour sauce. Accompaniments also get the thumbs-up: gado-gado salad with peanut sauce, achar (pickled vegetables), and 'perfectly cooked' coconut rice have been mentioned. Service is brisk and efficient. House wine is £8.45, with jasmine tea and Tiger beer among the alternatives.

CHEF: Sjamsir Alamsjah PROPRIETORS: Margaret Ong and Sjamsir Alamsjah OPEN: all week 12 to 11.30 (12.30 Fri and Sat) CLOSED: 25 Dec MEALS: alc (main courses £6 to £7.50). Set L and D £16.50 to £22.50 (minimum 2; inc wine). BYO £1 per person SERVICE: not inc, card slips closed CARDS: Amex, Diners, MasterCard, Visa DETAILS: 120 seats. Private parties: 30 main room, 40 private room. Vegetarian meals. Children welcome. Wheelchair access (no WC). Music. Air-conditioned

▲ *Le Meridien, Oak Room Marco Pierre White* map 15

21 Piccadilly, W1V 0BH NEW CHEF
TEL: (0171) 734 8000 FAX: (0171) 437 3574 COST £55–£190

Buy-outs, sell-offs and other changes at Forte and Granada have had consequences for a number of London restaurants, perhaps the most significant of which is that Marco Pierre White has moved from The Restaurant at Hyde Park Hotel. The Oak Room is the first of seven such high profile restaurants planned in Forte hotels. Despite best efforts, the old address never quite captured the hearts of reporters, although it rarely mattered since the food invariably triumphed. The Oak Room with its limed oak, large mirrors, gilt mouldings, and half a dozen chandeliers is a much more spacious and appropriate setting for what one reporter considered 'clearly one of the finest and most talented chefs in England, and indeed the world'. Marco would have scored ten in our new rating system had he remained where he was, and since he is transferring lock, stock and barrel, the new premises hold out an exciting prospect.

On his menus, shellfish and foie gras between them typically claim a substantial number of first courses – mille-feuille of crab, oysters en gelée, terrine of foie gras with Sauternes jelly – while main courses might combine an array of fish from John Dory with lentils to skate with winkles, and include some hearty meat dishes: truffled calf's sweetbreads, or braised pig's trotter. An inspector, who had eaten Bresse pigeon several times during a tour of France's top restaurants, declared none better than the one he ate at The Restaurant. New dishes are introduced to the repertoire, but many old favourites are perfected until there is nothing else that can be done to improve them. An example is the Pyramide dessert, one that goes all the way back to Marco's days at Harveys in Wandsworth; it may be an 'odd-sounding combination' of nougat glacé, passion-fruit sorbet, grapefruit, and wafer-thin caramel walls, but it is 'a truly original creation'. Assuming the wine list remains the same, expect hefty prices: 'even Bill Gates would look twice.' There are some stunning bottles, but mark-ups are around four times the retail price. The details below may be subject to change by the new team; it is advisable to check.

CHEF: Marco Pierre White PROPRIETOR: Granada Group plc OPEN: Mon to Fri L 12 to 2.30, Mon to at D 7 to 10.30 MEALS: Set L £29.50, Set D £75 SERVICE: not inc CARDS: Amex, Delta, Diners, MasterCard, Visa DETAILS: 65 seats. Vegetarian meals. Children welcome. Vegetarian meals. Wheelchair access (also WC). Air-conditioned ACCOMMODATION: 266 rooms, all with bath/shower. TV. Phone. Air-conditioned. Room only £255 to £295. Children welcome. Baby facilities. Afternoon teas. Swimming-pool

Mezzo

map 15

100 Wardour Street, W1 3LE
TEL: (0171) 314 4000 FAX: (0171) 314 4040

COOKING 4
COST £25–£69

The straggling queues hoping to be squeezed into the ground-floor Mezzonine eatery signal the magnet this branch of the Conran empire has quickly become. They come for the likes of red mullet with aubergine and anchovies, peppered rib of beef with mustard, tom yum soup with wok-fried prawns, and caramelised pork hock with scallops, ginger and rock sugar. In the basement is the main Mezzo, where booking seems essential, a self-consciously theatrical space where the kitchen can be seen through a plate glass screen. Here the culinary boundaries grow wider still, to embrace a pickled pork and crab spring roll with cucumber water, caviare and shellfish in profusion, fried brill with pea purée, bacon and thyme, and chocolate marquise with a lump of honeycomb.

'I was fully prepared to hate this place,' one reporter confides, 'but I didn't hear any mobile phones, I didn't feel unfashionable, and the service was very pleasant.' She had red onion tart with rocket and tomato salad, followed by chicken breast with sauté wild mushrooms and confesses it was all 'pretty good'. Wines come from almost everywhere except Germany and Eastern Europe, prices are mostly acceptable and there is a good selection by the glass. House Vins de Pays d'Oc are £11.75.

CHEF: John Torode PROPRIETORS: Sir Terence Conran and Joel Kissin OPEN: all week 12 (12.30 Sun) to 3, 6 to 12 (2.30am Thur to Sat, 11 Sun); Mezzo closed Sat L CLOSED: 25 and 26 Dec MEALS: Mezzo alc (main courses £10.50 to £16.50). Set L £16.50 (2 courses) to £19.50, Set pre-theatre D (6 to 7pm) £14. Cover £5 after 10.30 Thur to Sat; Mezzonine alc (main courses £7.50 to £11.50). Set D (5.30 to 7pm) £7 (2 courses) SERVICE: 12.5% (optional) CARDS: Amex, Diners, MasterCard, Switch, Visa DETAILS: 350 seats (Mezzo), 300 seats (Mezzonine). Private parties: 350 main room. Vegetarian meals. Children welcome. Wheelchair access (also WC). Music. Air-conditioned

Mirch Masala £

map 12

1416 London Road, SW16 4BZ
TEL: (0181) 679 1828 and 765 1070

COOKING 1
COST £12–£30

Genuine Indian eating-houses are springing up in many parts of the capital, and Mirch Masala is one of the best of its kind south of the river. The place is vigorously supported by local Asian families, the atmosphere is convivial, and conversation is loud. Meals begin authentically with a dish of chopped onions with a chilli dip ('mirch' means 'green chillies' in Hindi). Karahi specialities cooked in iron woks are the kitchen's stock-in-trade, and vegetarians do particularly well: ingredients extend to mogo (cassava), karela (bitter gourd), butter-beans and corn. In contrast, piscophiles should note the presence of tilapia and pomfret on the menu. Even simple things like karahi gosht are a notch above the norm, and breads are splendid: potent garlic nan has been well received. Side-dishes feature not only pickles, fried ginger and so on, but also 'ice' at 50p a portion. Unlicensed, but you can bring your own or settle for lassi.

CHEF/PROPRIETOR: Raza Ali OPEN: Tue to Sun and bank hol Mon 12 to 12 MEALS: alc (main courses £2.50 to £8). Unlicensed, BYO (no corkage) SERVICE: not inc, card slips closed CARDS: Delta, MasterCard, Switch, Visa DETAILS: 70 seats. Vegetarian meals. Children's helpings. Wheelchair access (also WC). Music. Air-conditioned

Misato £

NEW ENTRY map 15

11 Wardour Street, W1V 3HE COOKING 2
TEL: (0171) 734 0808 COST £19–£39

As no bookings are taken, value-conscious Europeans and mainly young oriental people queue outside for a table at this noisy café; non-smokers aim for tables at the front. The décor is minimalist, and service is pleasant but, on one occasion, erratic. This is more than Japanese fast food, although dishes such as teriyaki hamburger, and basic fried pork in spicy breadcrumbs, are on the menu. Noodle soups come in portions from large to enormous, and well-executed sashimi and sushi include tuna, mackerel, prawn and white fish. Bento boxes, all around £8, comprise fried chicken, omelette, tofu, pickles and rice, plus a main ingredient such as accurately grilled salted salmon. Saké and plum wine are sold by the glass, and there's Kirin beer. House wines are £10.

CHEF: Yukimobu Kato PROPRIETOR: Yumi Miura OPEN: all week 12 to 2.45, 6 to 10.30 CLOSED: 24 and 25 Dec, 1 Jan MEALS: alc (main courses £4.50 to £12). Set L £5 to £6.80 (all 2 courses), Set D £7.80 to £8.40 (all 2 courses) SERVICE: not inc CARDS: none DETAILS: 40 seats. Vegetarian meals. Children welcome. No-smoking area. Music

Mr Kong £

map 15

21 Lisle Street, WC2H 7BA COOKING 4
TEL: (0171) 437 7341 and 9679 COST £20–£37

Distinguished, mainly Cantonese cooking continues to draw appreciative customers to this Chinatown restaurant: sometimes a few too many, for they are tightly crammed in, and you may find yourself next to a noisy party. While manager Edwin Chau is helpful, service otherwise is more efficient than congenial. A satisfied reporter, who preferred not to explore the more exotic areas of the menu, praised crispy aromatic duck, special fried rice, sizzling fillet steak with black peppers and garlicky sauce fiery from chillies (the last dish 'a class act'). Those with a more adventurous spirit are encouraged; 'We try to guide non-Chinese customers to eat as Chinese people do,' the restaurant claims, 'and we love to discuss the menu with them to make it more interesting.'

Pot dishes are seemingly designed to challenge Westerners with their emphasis on fish head and duck's web, but set meals are more soothing. Interest for all is maintained with over 170 dishes on the main menu and 48 more on the 'chef special' which offers items like 'dragon wistlers' (leaves and shoots of mange-tout with dried scallops), and salted quail. House wines are £7, or drink saké or Tsing Tao beer.

The Guide *always appreciates hearing about changes of chef or owner.*

CHEFS: K. Kong and Y.W. Lo PROPRIETORS: K. Kong, Y.W. Lo, M.T. Lee, K.C. Tang and C.Y. Chan OPEN: all week noon to 1.45am MEALS: alc (main courses £5.50 to £11). Set L £8.80 to £11 (all 2 courses), Set D £16 to £22 (all minimum 4). BYO £3 SERVICE: 10% CARDS: Amex, Diners, MasterCard, Visa DETAILS: 115 seats. Private parties: 40 main room, 30 private room. Vegetarian meals. Children welcome. Music. Air-conditioned

Mitsukoshi

map 15

Dorland House, 14–20 Regent Street, SW1Y 4PH COOKING **6**
TEL: (0171) 930 0317 FAX: (0171) 837 1167 COST £30–£98

Sited in the basement of the London outpost of Tokyo's answer to Harrods, the restaurant is appropriately grand. For discretion, wooden screens separate the widely spaced tables, while huge flower arrangements in elegant vases are enclosed in a glass case and a sandy floor evokes the raked sand of temples. Japanese music plays softly, and deferential waiters in tails, and waitresses in kimonos, serve. Everything is in place for a no-expense-spared Japanese meal, whether it is a set dinner with a specified main dish or one where not even the centrepiece is chosen by the customer, the menu stating only that a course is boiled vegetables or grilled fish. These menus culminate in the ten-course kaiseki, to be ordered in advance and served only in private rooms. Bento, too, are set meals, served in lacquered wooden boxes holding varied ceramic dishes containing perhaps tempura, grilled fish, omelette and fish-cake, vinegared salad, simmered vegetables and sashimi. Soup, rice, pickles and a tiny fruit dessert are included.

The short *carte* is supplemented by dishes of the day on a separate sheet, which includes stimulating specialities, one a salad of sea-urchin on slivers of slithery yam. Kuruma ebi onigariyaki (charcoal-grilled giant prawns on a pine leaf) were so enjoyable that an inspector 'ate the shell and all'. Agedashi dofu (deep-fried tofu in broth) has been declared 'perfect' and 'bland, as it should be'. Highest praise comes for the quality of the 'unbelievably luscious, oily and rich' fish in omakase temaki zushi, which are leave-it-up-to-the-chef hand-rolled sushi of raw salmon, raw tuna and crunchy fish roe, accompanied by well-flavoured rice and 'a lot of wasabi – not for faint-hearted foreigners'. Such Japanese haute cuisine does not come cheap, but sticking to saké, at £6 a bottle, should limit the damage. Prices on the wine list start at £15.

CHEF: Jiro Shimada PROPRIETOR: Izumi Kudo OPEN: Mon to Sat 12 to 2, 6 to 9.30 CLOSED: 25 and 26 Dec, 1 Jan, Good Friday, Easter Mon MEALS: alc (main courses £12 to £27). Set L £15 to £50, Set D £30 to £60. Cover £1.50 SERVICE: 15% (optional) CARDS: Amex, Diners, MasterCard, Visa DETAILS: 91 seats. Private parties: 80 main room, 4 to 30 private rooms. Vegetarian meals. No children under 5. Music. Air-conditioned

Miyama

map 15

38 Clarges Street, W1Y 7PJ COOKING **4**
TEL: (0171) 499 2443 FAX: (0171) 493 1573 COST £27–£65

The striking modern Japanese décor incorporates three-dimensional pictures, and there is a small teppanyaki bar downstairs. Dishes prepared at the table (sukiyaki and the like) are still offered, but, here as elsewhere, are now rarely seen. The rest of the standard repertoire – tempura, sushi, sashimi, noodles in soup, fried and grilled meat – are on the menu with a short 'Japanese menu' of small seasonal items. Amuse-gueules can be as perfectly simple as plain spinach with sesame seeds.

At the other extreme of the richness scale – indeed, shooting off its end – is unagi kabayaki (grilled eel), with a subtle faintly sweet glaze making it look like a celestial kipper fillet. The same delicacy (which is not the *mot juste* for this glorious flesh) becomes una-ju when on rice in an elegant papier-mâché box. Green tea ice-cream is a good way to finish. Service can sometimes be brusque. House wine is £10.

CHEF: Mr F. Miyama PROPRIETORS: Mr F. Miyama and Mr T. Miura OPEN: Mon to Fri L 12 to 2.30, all week D 6 to 10.30 CLOSED: 25 Dec, 1 Jan MEALS: alc (main courses £10 to £26). Set L £12 to £18, Set D £34 to £42. BYO £10 SERVICE: 15% CARDS: Amex, Delta, Diners, MasterCard, Switch, Visa DETAILS: 66 seats. Private parties: 32 main room, 4 to 10 private rooms. Vegetarian meals. Children welcome. Wheelchair access (no WC). Music. Air-conditioned

Momo

NEW ENTRY map 15

25 Heddon Street, W1R 7LG
TEL: (0171) 434 4040
FAX: (0171) 287 0404

COOKING 5
COST £25–£45

Since opening in early 1997 Momo has attracted a fashionable crowd and much media hype, but its success is deserved for it is 'a magical place: once inside, it is difficult to imagine you are in the heart of London'. The décor 'really invokes all the flavours of the Middle East and North Africa', with carved wooden screens and shutters, sculpted plaster columns, rugs on the stone and wood floor and low tables lit by candles in metal lanterns. Waiters are 'young, full of energy and very good'.

Start with tabbouleh, harira (lentil, chick-pea, tomato and lemon soup), or briouat (paper thin pastries) filled with chicken and saffron, prawns and mushrooms, or goats' cheese, mint and potato. For main course, tagines arrive piping hot in their elegant earthenware pots and may contain lamb with artichoke hearts and peas, or quail with dates and onions. Couscous comes in six parts: 'light, fluffy' couscous; a chunk of roasted lamb shoulder, merguez, or chicken brochette; a deep pot of carrot and turnip in a fine vegetable broth; and little pots of harissa, warm raisins, and chick-peas. Or there may be sauté squid with rice and coriander, grilled lamb's offal, or pastilla, a traditional pastry pie: at inspection the pigeon version was subtly spiced and the crisp pastry dusted with powdered sugar. To finish there are Berber pancakes with honey and almonds, orange salad with cinnamon and orange blossom water, or subtly flavoured and not too sweet patisseries Maghrebines. As a change from coffee, try mint tea, poured in the traditional manner from a great height. The short wine list is mostly French but also includes a handful of reds and rosés from the Maghreb and Lebanon, as well as Chilean Chardonnay and Pinot Noir. Prices start at £13.50.

CHEF: Abdullah Elrgrachi PROPRIETOR: Mourad Mazouz OPEN: Mon to Fri L 12.30 to 1.45, Mon to Sat D 7 to 11.15 MEALS: alc (main courses £10.50 to £15.50). Set L £12.50 (2 courses) to £15.50 SERVICE: 12.5% (optional), card slips closed CARDS: Amex, Delta, Diners, MasterCard, Switch, Visa DETAILS: 90 seats. Vegetarian meals. Children welcome L. Wheelchair access (also WC). Music. Air-conditioned

Monkeys

map 13

1 Cale Street, Chelsea Green, SW3 3QT — COOKING 4
TEL: (0171) 352 4711 — COST £30–£50

The name might suggest a bopping wine bar, but eating at Monkeys can feel more like joining a genteel dinner party. The Benhams' Anglo-French restaurant has a prime Chelsea address and – shelves of monkey-related ephemera notwithstanding – a sophisticated feel. Tom Benham's repertoire keeps to form, with classical French dishes (chateaubriand with béarnaise sauce) as well as classical English ones (home-potted shrimps, grilled Dover sole). More style-conscious offerings include calves' kidneys with grain mustard, and roast saddle of hare forestière. Caprice comes in the form of mille-feuille of salmon and chives, say, or fish cassoulet. Among mainstream desserts have been chocolate mousse, and treacle or lemon tart. Wines are mostly from France, with classical regions best represented. The house selection starts at £15.

CHEF: Tom Benham PROPRIETORS: Tom and Brigitte Benham OPEN: Mon to Sat L 12.30 to 2.30, Sun L 1 to 3, Mon to Sat D 7.30 to 11 CLOSED: 1 week Christmas, 1 week Easter, 3 weeks Aug MEALS: Set L Mon to Sat £15 (2 courses) to £20, Set L Sun £20, Set D £20 (2 courses) to £30 SERVICE: not inc CARDS: Delta, MasterCard, Switch, Visa DETAILS: 40 seats. Children's helpings. No pipes in dining-room. No music. Air-conditioned

Mon Plaisir

map 15

21 Monmouth Street, WC2H 9DD — NEW CHEF
TEL: (0171) 836 7243 FAX: (0171) 240 4774 — COST £21–£58

'I have been eating here for over 40 years and today it is as good as ever,' writes a veteran devotee of this seminal Covent Garden bistro. That was before new chef Frédéric Meurlay arrived from the Kensington branch, so at least the style should remain the same. The setting is authentically Gallic – including a map of the Chemins de Fer de France – and the menu offers old favourites of coq au vin, carré d'agneau and steak frites. The cheeseboard is one of the ripest in the capital, and there is tarte Tatin to finish. House wines are £9.20 (white) and £8.95 (red).

CHEF: Frédéric Meurlay PROPRIETOR: Alain Lhermitte OPEN: Mon to Fri L 12 to 2.15, Mon to Sat D 5.50 to 11.15 CLOSED: 9 days Christmas, 4 days Easter, bank hols MEALS: alc (main courses £8.50 to £16). Set L £14.95, Set D 5.50 to 7.15 £10.95 (2 courses) to £13.95, Set D £19.95 (minimum 2). BYO £6 SERVICE: 12.5% (optional), card slips closed CARDS: Amex, Delta, Diners, MasterCard, Switch, Visa DETAILS: 96 seats. Private parties: 28 private room. Vegetarian meals. Children welcome. No cigars/pipes in dining-room. Wheelchair access (no WC). Music. Air-conditioned

NEW CHEF *is shown instead of a cooking mark where a change of chef occurred too late for a new assessment of the cooking.*

Montana

map 12

125–127 Dawes Road, SW6 7EA — COOKING 2

TEL: (0171) 385 9500 FAX: (0171) 386 0337 — COST £25–£47

South-west USA is the geographical orientation of the food on offer at this lively restaurant situated opposite Fulham Baptist Church. Revivalism is not exactly the name of the game, though; rather, the Creole and Cajun influences are used in contemporary fashion as springboards for some daring gastronomic turns. Mussels are steamed, seasoned with Seville orange and accompanied by chorizo and roasted garlic, and Navajo rabbit comes with a fig quesadilla and sweet potato. Vivid flavourings with fish are enjoyed, as in trout given a blue-corn crust and stuffed with crab and green chilli. Pecan waffles with peach ice-cream and bourbon sauce is as ethnically specific as one could ask for, and the same nuts and liquor also go into the inevitable crème brûlée. Non-European wines shine out brightly from the round-the-world list, and house South African white and Vin de Pays d'Oc red are both £12.

CHEF: Daniel McDowell PROPRIETORS: Kevin Finch and Drew Barwick OPEN: Fri to Sun L 12 to 3.30, all week D 7 to 11 (11.30 Fri and Sat) CLOSED: 25 and 26 Dec, 1 Jan MEALS: alc (main courses L £5 to £10, D £10 to £13) SERVICE: 12.5% (optional), card slips closed CARDS: Amex, Delta, MasterCard, Switch, Visa DETAILS: 80 seats. Private parties: 80 main room. Vegetarian meals. Children welcome. Wheelchair access (no WC). Music. Air-conditioned

Moro £

LONDON 1998 NEWCOMER — NEW ENTRY — map 13

34–36 Exmouth Market, EC1R 4QE

TEL: (0171) 833 8336 — COOKING 5

FAX: (0171) 833 9338 — COST £24–£38

'This is an extraordinary place,' began our inspector's report. In a Victorian street in Clerkenwell, a short walk from Sadler's Wells, it boasts an open-plan kitchen, and a bare dining-room with a hard floor whose only feature is a pair of large angled mirrors on the wall. You can probably hear the noise already. Tables, chairs and place settings are as simple as can be, and snacks can either be eaten at the zinc bar or taken as starters at table. In a linguistic coupling which epitomises the cooking, they are called 'meze-raciones', Arabic and Spanish for large portions of tapas. The chefs have come from the River Café (see entry, London) and their inspiration is the culinary legacy of the Moorish occupation of Spain from the eighth to the fifteenth centuries. If that sounds like a dry subject for 'Mastermind', fear not.There some unusual ideas, and some vibrant flavours, as in a crab brik with cumin, coriander and harissa which, in a gastro-visual pun, eschewed the usual triangular shape for that of a brick.

In essence, this meeting of Hispanic and Arabic cultures is designed to put a different spin on the Mediterranean theme, and assembles materials from any country with a bit of shoreline. A charcoal grill and a wood-fired oven (turning out sourdough bread 'with an amazing crust') are essential bits of kit, and weekly-changing menus have already got to grips with mojama (Spanish wind-dried tuna), a near-paella of rice and pork topped with wilted spinach, and a dish reminiscent of the medieval Jewish-Arabic cooking still preserved in Andalusia: Sevillian spinach with pine-nuts, raisins and salted anchovies. To finish, there may be yoghurt with pistachio nuts and three sorts of honey, a 'very crunchy' quince, almond and oloroso tart, or a 'decadent' Malaga raisin ice-cream made with dark, sherryish Pedro Ximenez. A short wine list featuring Spain, Italy and France begins at £9.50. Our inspector dutifully tasted Turkish turnip juice from the 'softs' list, and considers its subsequent removal from that list a confirmation of the restaurant's good taste.

CHEFS: Jake Hodges, Mr and Mrs Sam Clark PROPRIETORS: Jake Hodges, Mr and Mrs Sam Clark and Mark Sainsbury OPEN: Mon to Fri 12.30 to 2.30, 7 to 10.30 CLOSED: 1 week Christmas, bank hols MEALS: alc (main courses £8.50 to £12.50) SERVICE: not inc CARDS: Delta, MasterCard, Switch, Visa DETAILS: 75 seats. 8 seats outside. Vegetarian meals. Children welcome. Wheelchair access (also WC). Music. Air-conditioned

Moshi Moshi Sushi  map 13

Unit 24, Liverpool Street Station, EC2M 7QH
TEL/FAX: (0171) 247 3227
7–8 Limeburner Lane, EC4M 7HY COOKING **2**
TEL: (0171) 248 1808 COST £13–£30

'Healthy fast food' is what Moshi Moshi Sushi peddles, but, as one correspondent pointed out, 'if you don't want to eat raw fish, then you either starve or leave'. For first-timers, the novelty of the sushi experience begins – in the case of the branch at Liverpool Street Station at least – with the location itself: perched on a high walk overlooking the tracks and the trains. You can sit at a table above the concourse or at the bar, where dishes pass before your eyes on a conveyor belt. This carries the more common specialities; others, such as abalone, Californian temaki or belly of tuna, have to be ordered from one of the cooks. Items are priced by the colour of the plate on which they are arranged; the bill is simply a question of adding up the crockery. Ebi (shrimp), tai (red snapper) and sake (salmon) have been enjoyed of late; to start there is miso soup, and to finish green-tea ice-cream served 'theatre-interval style in tubs with a plastic spoon'. The value for money is undeniable. Iced lemon tea, saké or Japanese lager are appropriate tipples. House Australian is £8.60.

CHEFS: Enrico Venson and Mr Hong PROPRIETOR: Caroline Bennet OPEN: Mon to Fri 11.30 to 9 CLOSED: 24 Dec D to New Year, bank hols MEALS: alc (plate prices £1 to £2.50). Geta (1-plate meals) £4.20 to £9 SERVICE: not inc, card slips closed CARDS: Delta, MasterCard, Switch, Visa DETAILS: 70 seats (Liverpool Street). Private parties: 100 main room (Liverpool Street). Vegetarian meals. Children welcome. No smoking in dining-room. Wheelchair access (also WC) at Limeburner Lane branch only. Music. Air-conditioned

MPW NEW ENTRY map 12

Second Floor, Cabot Place East,
Canary Wharf, E14 4QT COOKING **4**
TEL: (0171) 513 0513 FAX: (0171) 513 0551 COST £29–£52

Anybody who aims to keep a tally of Marco Pierre White's new restaurant openings will soon need more than just their fingers. This spanking new one – opened in July 1997 – aims to serve brasserie food in a chic modern setting. Reach it by Docklands Light Railway to Canary Wharf, and the restaurant is a couple of flights above the platform: crescent-shaped, mirrored and coloured mostly yellow and green. With a menu reminiscent of the Criterion, and under the direction of Garry Hollihead, who used to cook at L'Escargot (see entry), among other places, MPW aims for generally simple dishes, and turns them out with a degree of skill.

There is plenty of choice, although perhaps few surprises, on a *carte* that takes in gravlax, jellied terrine of ham and parsley, fish-cake topped with a poached egg on a bed of spinach, and grilled ribeye of beef. 'It is so long since I saw chicken Kiev on a menu I couldn't resist it,' confessed our inspector, pleased to see this one arrive with a small copper pan containing girolles and more garlic, although he was surprised to see a risotto arrive in next to no time. Lemon tart and chocolate truffle cake are among the puds, as is a more refreshing vanilla cream with red fruits. Crusty bread is good; the walnut and raisin version served with cheese is even better. In a span of some 60 bottles the wine list offers sensible choice below £20 and much of interest above it. House vin de pays is £10.

CHEF: Garry Hollihead PROPRIETORS: Marco Pierre White, Jimmy Lahoud and Garry Hollihead OPEN: Mon to Fri 12 to 2.30, 5.30 to 9 CLOSED: 25 Dec MEALS: alc (main courses £8.50 to £14.50) SERVICE: 12.5% (optional), card slips closed CARDS: Amex, Delta, MasterCard, Switch, Visa DETAILS: 200 seats. 40 seats outside. Private parties: 20 main room, 30 private room. Car park. Vegetarian meals. Children welcome. Wheelchair access (also WC). Music. Air-conditioned

Museum Street Café map 15

47 Museum Street, WC1A 1LY COOKING 5
TEL/FAX: (0171) 405 3211 COST £24–£38

Gail Koerber and Mark Nathan run their small, understated and 'civilised' restaurant near the British Museum with quiet commitment to the ideal of not messing around too much with ingredients. A little gentle innovation is about the extent of their interference, and the result is a short, modern, 'satisfying' but not conspicuously trendy menu that changes every week. 'A deft hand, and respect for the simple flavours and textures of lightly cooked food', marks out the accomplishment. Meals might begin with a salad (using organic Appledore produce) or a soup of perhaps spinach and Parmesan, or of Jersualem artichoke and garlic. To follow, tuna might be briefly seared and served with Thai spices, and the chargrill works to good effect on leg of lamb and corn-fed chicken.

It is not elaborate cooking, but it is well timed, well balanced, and not shy of bold flavours when they are called for, as in a roasted fennel, red onion and tomato sauce to accompany goats'-cheese ravioli. Bread, salads, dressings and vegetables are well up to standard. 'They do seem to have a way of grilling vegetables that few others can imitate,' and are commended for incorporating them in the main course: steamed kale and creamed celeriac, for example, with boned quail and porcini mushroom butter served on Puy lentils. Desserts use good chocolate, and cheese (from Neal's Yard) comes with nut bread, oatcakes and parsley biscuits. Efficient, friendly, 'fuss-free' service and a busy but relaxing atmosphere add to the appeal, and new banquette seating is designed to increase the comfort level.

The carefully selected list offers a varied group of wines, from a flowery Californian to a robust red from the Douro, which are keenly priced for London. Eight are by the glass, including three dessert wines. House French is £9. CELLARMAN'S CHOICE: Au Bon Climat Chardonnay 1995, Santa Barbara County, California, £22; Ridge Vineyards Lytton Springs 1994, Napa Valley, California, £25.

CHEFS/PROPRIETORS: Gail Koerber and Mark Nathan OPEN: Mon to Fri 12.30 to 2.15, 6.30 to 9.30 CLOSED: 1 week Christmas, 1 week August, Easter, bank hols MEALS: Set L £13 (2 courses) to £16, Set D £18 (2 courses) to £22. BYO £5 SERVICE: not inc CARDS: Amex, Delta, MasterCard, Switch, Visa DETAILS: 37 seats. Private parties: 8 main room. Vegetarian meals. Children welcome. No smoking in dining-room. Wheelchair access (also WC). No music

Neal Street Restaurant

map 15

26 Neal Street, WC2H 9PS — COOKING 4

TEL: (0171) 836 8368 FAX: (0171) 240 3964 — COST £46–£79

Neal Street, for those who haven't made the pilgrimage, is a genteel cobbled thoroughfare not far from Seven Dials. Antonio Carluccio's presence in these parts is keenly felt in both shop and restaurant, his range of goods extending from cookery books to decorative walking-sticks. A fabulous Eduardo Paolozzi wood-carving dominates the restaurant, though even that was overshadowed one week by a vast puffball mushroom at the centre of the fungi display.

Wild mushrooms and truffles are what the menu is built around. They form the base for soups and salads, and lend their meatiness and aromatic lustre to pasta dishes. The outstanding dish at inspection, however, was an open black raviolo of scallops, prawns, clams, mussels and sea bass, gently fired up with chilli and all held together with a restrained cream sauce. A fried fillet of turbot comes, as much does, with 'an abundance of very fine olive oil', and meat dishes lean towards the robust: roast Tuscan squab with broad beans and speck, or grilled entrecôte with freshly grated horseradish. If there are grumbles, they tend to derive from the pricing, as in a charge of £4 for a portion of new potatoes. Desserts might include a very gingery pannacotta with rhubarb sauce, and a trio (rhubarb, pineapple and orange) of sorbets. Service, reporters tell us, could be more attentive, especially in view of the 15% charged for it. The entirely Italian wine list is a standard selection and starts at £15.50.

CHEF: Nick Melmoth-Coombs PROPRIETOR: Antonio Carluccio OPEN: Mon to Sat 12.30 to 2.30, 6 to 11 CLOSED: 1 week Christmas, bank hols MEALS: alc (main courses £14 to £20) SERVICE: 15% (optional), card slips closed CARDS: Amex, Delta, Diners, MasterCard, Switch, Visa DETAILS: 65 seats. Private parties: 24 main room, 24 private room. Vegetarian meals. Children welcome. No pipes in dining-room. Wheelchair access (no WC). No music. Air-conditioned

Nico Central

map 15

35 Great Portland Street, W1N 5DD — COOKING 5

TEL: (0171) 436 8846 FAX: (0171) 436 3455 — COST £33–£43

The L-shaped premises to the north of Oxford Street were once Nico Ladenis's principal haunt, although the food these days is less formal, more in the mould of a sophisticated brasserie. Tables are pretty much cheek-by-jowl, and the décor doesn't uplift, but the maestro is still consulted over the cooking, to the extent that, as one reporter put it, 'it can only be described as Nico food'.

The robustness and intensity of flavour that comes with the territory is evinced in a starter of spatchcocked devilled quail with a salad of large dark mushrooms and al dente French beans. Mushrooms feature prominently among first courses: in a risotto of ceps with Parmesan for instance. Fish cookery is bang-on, as was shown by a fillet of 'very fresh and perfectly cooked' brill that sat on a bed of buttery, peppery noodles. Duck confit is the real thing, deepened by a rich madeira sauce (though, again, heavily peppered) and helped along with braised cabbage and carrot. Tarte Tatin is well-rendered, whether made with apples or pears, the pastry 'so thin it had almost disappeared' and the surface properly caramelised. Alternatively you may opt for nougat glacé and raspberry coulis, or a delicate parfait of orange and whisky. Fast-paced, efficient service could do with a bit more 'warmth and interest'. New World bottles inveigle themselves into a wine list that is predominantly French. Prices are stiffish, but there is just enough under £20 to make do. House French is £13.

CHEF: André Garrett PROPRIETOR: Restaurant Partnership plc OPEN: Mon to Fri L, Mon to Sat D 12 to 2, 7 to 11 CLOSED: Christmas, bank hols MEALS: Set L £21 (2 courses) to £25, Set D £27 SERVICE: net prices, card slips closed CARDS: Amex, Delta, Diners, MasterCard, Switch, Visa DETAILS: 55 seats. Private parties: 9 main room, 12 private room. Vegetarian meals. No children under 10. No cigars/pipes in dining-room. Wheelchair access (no WC). No music. Air-conditioned

Nicole's

map 15

158 New Bond Street, W1Y 9PA — COOKING 4

TEL: (0171) 499 8408 FAX: (0171) 409 0381 — COST £39–£58

The restaurant arm of Nicole Farhi's posh frock shop is 'very metropolitan and yet faintly Establishment'. There are few soft surfaces, but the elegance of the table settings and the impeccably courteous service have made this a magnet for a certain kind of West End customer. Two reporters who lunched in summer came away much struck by the fine judgement evident in Annie Wayte's simple but well-crafted dishes. A salad of roasted vegetables that brought together ratatouille ingredients with artichoke, rocket and a hunk of mozzarella was a winner. Fish is a strong suit, as in 'sparklingly fresh' chargrilled halibut with wild mushrooms, wild rice and a garnish of deep-fried leek, and 'stunningly attractive, excellent' sea bass. Relishes and chutneys are a favoured way of adorning a main course, while desserts such as fruit salad – 'the most enormous plate of completely wonderful fruit pieces' – with almond madeleine, or plum wholemeal crumble and custard, tend towards a fairly liberal definition of lightness. The range of breads receives widespread commendation. Old and New Worlds contribute evenly to an imaginative wine list, the greater part of its offerings available by the glass. House Sauvignon and Merlot are £10.75.

CHEF: Annie Wayte PROPRIETOR: Stephen Marks OPEN: Mon to Sat 12 to 3.30 (4 Sat), 6.30 to 11 CLOSED: 25 and 26 Dec, bank hols MEALS: alc (main courses £13.50 to £17). Cover £1 SERVICE: 12.5% (optional), card slips closed CARDS: Amex, Delta, Diners, MasterCard, Switch, Visa DETAILS: 68 seats. Private parties: 100 main room. Vegetarian meals. Children welcome. No smoking in 1 dining-room. Music. Air-conditioned

Nobu

NEW ENTRY map 15

Metropolitan Hotel, 19 Old Park Lane, W1Y 4LB COOKING 5
TEL: (0171) 447 4747 FAX: (0171) 447 4749 COST £33–£80

Is it a restaurant? Is it a fashion statement? Is it expensive? Yes, yes, yes. London is periodically treated to an exotic chef enveloped in a whirlwind of publicity and a maelstrom of money, bringing a wonderful new kind of cooking to lucky Mayfair or Belgravia. This year, Nobuyuki Matsuhisa has combined his Japanese background, South American travels, USA experience (restaurants in Los Angeles and New York) and glamorous international backing to bring about one of the hottest openings of the year. Bare wooden floors and table-tops, large etchy glass partitions, and eager staff in Issey Miyake uniforms 'like a cross between Greek national dress and a choirboy's surplice' take the minimalist route about as far as it ought to go.

The set menu from £50 a head relieves decision-making and is about what reporters seem to spend anyway. Most important, fish is notably fresh, and treatments vary from 'new-style' sashimi (small, sweet shrimp in a warm dressing of soy and oil) to Chinese-style sea bass with black-bean sauce. The food is light and accessible, chilli warmth often taking the place of wasabi heat, and limes provide much of the sharpness in dressings. Nasu miso (aubergine with a sweet caramelly dressing) is first-rate, tempura is the least successful department, and sushi are both unusual and good: try eel, or excellent crunchy soft-shell crab. Desserts are of mixed parentage – grilled nashi pear with ginger ice-cream, or chocolate cake in a bento box with green-tea ice-cream – and wines are a fusion of Old and New Worlds, mostly of good pedigree and with prices to match. House French is £13.50, or you could try one of four types of saké, starting at £5 a glass.

CHEFS: Nobuyuki Matsuhisa and Mark Edwards PROPRIETORS: Nobuyuki Matsuhisa, Robert De Niro, and Como Holdings OPEN: Mon to Fri L 12 to 2.15, Mon to Sat D 6 to 10.30 MEALS: alc (main courses £4.50 to £27.50). Set L and D from £50 SERVICE: 12.5% (optional), card slips closed CARDS: Amex, Delta, Diners, MasterCard, Switch, Visa DETAILS: 150 seats. Vegetarian meals. Children welcome. No cigars/pipes in dining-room. Wheelchair access (also WC). No music. Air-conditioned

Noughts 'n' Crosses

map 12

77 The Grove, W5 5LL COOKING 3
TEL: (0181) 840 7568 FAX: (0181) 840 1905 COST £26–£39

Noughts 'n' Crosses 'delivers what it promises – good-quality food and attentive service in a pleasant ambience'. Its location, in a residential street behind the Ealing Broadway Centre, helps confirm its image as a neighbourhood restaurant. Its appearance – three bright, plant-filled rooms, including a conservatory overlooking a floodlit patio garden – is more cosmopolitan. So is chef and co-owner Anthony Ma, who came from Hong Kong around 20 years ago.

He mingles classical French techniques with modern European/Asian flavours, the European contingent best represented by Italy: spinach gnocchi with walnut sauce, for instance, and garganelli pasta with sun-dried tomato, aubergine and olive tapénade. Soups range from inventive celeriac and cardamom to classic Mediterranean fish with rouille. Main courses might include red snapper with spring onion and black-bean sauce, or grilled chicken marinated with lime juice, mustard and herbs and served with tamarind and coconut cream sauce. An even more creative choice may be wild duck baked with juniper berries and allspice and accompanied by brandy and cranberry sauce. For desserts the Franglais – and indulgent – menu offers the likes of bread-and-butter pudding with apple and raisins wrapped in filo, and rhubarb and banana gratin with sabayon sauce. The wine list has plenty of interest, mark-ups are kind, and there are around half a dozen half-bottles. Country French house wine is £10.60.

CHEF: Anthony Ma PROPRIETORS: Jörgen Kunath and Anthony Ma OPEN: Sun L 12 to 2, Tue to Sat D 7 to 10 CLOSED: 26 Dec to 6 Jan, Aug MEALS: Set L Sun £13 (2 courses) to £16.70, Set D £16.90 (2 courses) to £21.50 SERVICE: not inc; 10% for parties of 7 or more CARDS: Amex, Delta, MasterCard, Switch, Visa DETAILS: 55 seats. 10 seats outside. Private parties: 25 main room, 25 private room. Vegetarian meals. Children's helpings. No-smoking area. Wheelchair access (no WC). Music

Novelli W8

NEW ENTRY map 13

122–4 Palace Gardens, W8 4RT COOKING 5
TEL: (0171) 229 4024 FAX: (0171) 243 1826 COST £24–£49

Jean-Christophe Novelli seems to have swapped his chef's knives for an executive briefcase, since he is now more of an entrepreneur, with two restaurants to run and other projects planned. But he sees things with a chef's eye, which is good news. So far he has kept away from glitzy Mayfair and multi-million pound deals, and opted for a more modest approach. The re-made Ark has been decorated in blue and purple, reminiscent of Maison Novelli (see entry, London), and although space is at a premium (all right then, it's cramped) staff cope easily enough. 'Why bowls of chips and salad do not more regularly get accidentally jogged into someone's lap is an intriguing mystery'. The payoff for customers is realistic prices.

With 18 starters and 16 main courses the menu is approaching Cantonese proportions. Once upon a time, 34 dishes might have sounded excessive for a smallish restaurant, but this menu benefits from a busy kitchen, some overlap with Maison Novelli (cassoulet terrine for example), a high turnover, and a good selection of charcuterie, which is one of Novelli's strengths. Among the offerings might be a rustic, home-smoked stuffed goose neck, or ham hock cervelas, and the signature dish: a pig's trotter cooked according to the chef's fancy. Contemporary flourishes include generous use of truffle oil and coriander leaf, and a tendency to froth, but results are sound, including an 'intensely flavoured and luxuriously velvety' cappuccino pea soup with foie gras, grilled scallops (two only, and for a supplement) lightly cooked and served with broad beans, and a salad of black pudding and poached egg.

Desserts look pretty: langue de chat biscuits made into a boat, complete with sail and tiny paddle, variously carrying an ice-cream or tiramisù 'cargo', or 'an amusing retro-'70s dish' of ice-cream 'cornets' made out of brandy-snaps surrounded by red fruits. Bread and butter is charged extra. Forty-plus wines are about right for the circumstances, starting with house vin de pays at £11.50.

CHEF: Nick Wilson PROPRIETOR: Jean-Christophe Novelli OPEN: all week 12 to 3, 6 to 11 (12 Fri and Sat) MEALS: alc (main courses £10.50 to £9.50). Set L £12.50 (2 courses) to £14.50 SERVICE: 12.5% (optional), card slips closed CARDS: Amex, Delta, Diners, MasterCard, Switch, Visa DETAILS: 60 seats. 15 seats outside. Private parties: 10 main room. Vegetarian meals. Children welcome. Wheelchair access (no WC). Music

L'Odéon 🍷

map 15

65 Regent Street, W1R 7HH — COOKING 4
TEL: (0171) 287 1400 FAX: (0171) 287 1300 — COST £27–£63

L'Odéon enjoys a dramatic site opposite the Café Royal, and the long, curving, bright room seems to stretch away forever. It can be pretty hectic when tables fill up, but the feeling of being plumb in the centre of the capital is what many people relish. Bruno Loubet is no longer involved, though shades of his style are preserved in Anthony Demetre's cooking.

Beetroot is still a favoured ingredient, used in a starter with red onions and a rocket and Parmesan salad, perhaps, or dressed with walnut vinaigrette to accompany calf's liver with onion salsa. Main courses might include pork knuckle on crushed root vegetables sauced with red wine, prunes and cinnamon, or neck end of lamb with merguez sausage and moussaka. One reporter who enjoyed goats'-cheese risotto with tarragon oil felt that the kitchen 'delivers all the essential ingredients of passion, simplicity, creativity and pride in the art of cooking'. Dessert might be banana and pineapple fritters with piña colada ice-cream. The two-page wine list travels to the four corners of the vinous world, collecting some 80 bins which are arranged by grape variety and style. A separate fine wine list offers superior clarets and burgundies at reasonably fair prices. House French starts at £12.50.

CHEF: Anthony Demetre PROPRIETORS: Pierre and Cathy Condou OPEN: Sun to Fri L 12 (11.30 Sun) to 3 (3.45 Sun), Mon to Sat D 5.30 to 11.30 CLOSED: 25 and 26 Dec, 1 Jan, bank hols MEALS: alc D (main courses £13.50 to £17.50). Set L Mon to Fri £21, Set L and D (5.30 to 7pm) £13 (2 courses) to £16. Cover £1.50 SERVICE: not inc; 12.5% for parties of 6 or more CARDS: Amex, Delta, Diners, MasterCard, Switch, Visa DETAILS: 200 seats. Private parties: 30 main room, 20 private room. Vegetarian meals. Children's helpings. No-smoking area L only. Wheelchair access (also WC). Music. Air-conditioned

Odette's 

map 13

130 Regents Park Road, NW1 8XL
TEL: (0171) 586 5486 and 8766 — COOKING 5
FAX: (0171) 586 0508 — COST £20–£61

In 1998 Odette's chalks up 20 years in this Primrose Hill parade of shops, and enters its third decade with new chef David Kennedy from Terence Laybourne's 21 Queen Street (see entry, Newcastle). This is more than just 'a neighbourhood restaurant for the well-heeled', and appeals for its all-round sympathetic approach to eating and drinking, with a wine bar downstairs serving most un-wine-bar-like food (escabèche of mackerel, spätzli with zucchini, grilled chilli quail, mango tart) and a justly celebrated no-choice three-course lunch in the restaurant for £10: for example, warm salad of poached salmon with asparagus and Jersey Royals, followed by navarin of lamb, and lemon curd parfait with strawberries.

A plant-filled garden room at the back is light and sunny, the green dining-room has a collection of gilt-framed mirrors, large and small, and its doors open on to the pavement in warm weather. Foie gras and ham knuckle terrine with pease pudding is one dish that bears the Laybourne thumbprint, on a broadly modern European menu that otherwise begins with fish and vegetables: fresh crab tartlet with coriander, or broad-bean risotto with roasted scallops.

Main courses might set old-fashioned fillet steak 'Rossini' alongside honey-roasted duck with pasta, and have also produced monkfish and mussel casserole in a 'good soupy sauce' with lots of herbs. Pastry and desserts (which remain the responsibilty of Antony Stott) are impressive, and have included chocolate espresso tart made with a good-quality dark chocolate, and a glazed goats'-curd tart with passion-fruit. The wine list impresses with its willingness to offer lots of good drinking under £20 as well as plenty of prestigious bins above. Simply arranged by style then price, concisely annotated and offering 30 wines by the glass, it constitutes a great introduction to the world of wine. Ten house recommendations start at £10.95. CELLARMAN'S CHOICE: Marsannay 1995, Alain Guyard, £25.40; Coteaux du Languedoc, Pic St-Loup Grand Cuvée 1994, Dom. de l'Hortus, £22.50.

CHEF: David Kennedy PROPRIETOR: Simone Green OPEN: all week L 12.30 to 2.30 (Sat and Sun wine bar only), Mon to Sat D 7 to 11 CLOSED: 10 days Christmas, bank hols MEALS: alc (main courses £9 to £15). Set L £10. BYO £5 SERVICE: not inc CARDS: Amex, Delta, Diners, MasterCard, Switch, Visa DETAILS: 50 seats. 10 seats outside. Private parties: 30 main room, 8 private room. Vegetarian meals. Children's helpings. No cigars/pipes in dining-room. Wheelchair access (no WC). No music

Olivo

map 13

21 Eccleston Street, SW1W 9LX — COOKING 2
TEL: (0171) 730 2505 FAX: (0171) 824 8190 — COST £26–£47

With its striking mustard and navy colour scheme and a dedication to advancing the sum of London's knowledge of Sardinian cuisine, Olivo is evidently seeking to lift itself free from the decidedly non-Mediterranean environs of Victoria. A soup of clams and couscous is one sort of Sardinian speciality, smoked pork neck with crusty bread another. Bottarga, the pungent roe of grey mullet dried and grated over a bowl of spaghetti, is a taste worth acquiring. An inspection meal went swimmingly, not least for the emphatic simplicity with which regional Italian cooking often scores even if it did extend the boundaries of Sardinia a little: stuffed baby squid with roasted tomatoes, fried calf's liver with balsamic vinegar and spinach, and a slice of chocolate and almond tart. Good coffee, and marinated olives for munching with the bread add class. The wine list takes the whole of Italy as its canvas, the selections pleasing but prices a little on the high side. House Sardinian is £9.50. A second branch, Oliveto, is at 49 Elizabeth Street, SW1; Tel: (0171) 730 0074.

The Guide *always appreciates hearing about changes of chef or owner.*

CHEFS: Marco Mellis and Giuseppe Sanna PROPRIETORS: Mauro Sanna and Jean-Louis Journade OPEN: Mon to Fri L 12 to 2.30, all week D 7 to 11 CLOSED: Christmas, bank hols MEALS: alc D (main courses £10.50 to £12.50). Set L £14 (2 courses) to £16 SERVICE: not inc CARDS: Amex, Delta, MasterCard, Switch, Visa DETAILS: 45 seats. Vegetarian meals. Children welcome. No cigars/pipes in dining-room. No music. Air-conditioned

192 🍷

map 13

192 Kensington Park Road, W11 2ES — COOKING 5
TEL: (0171) 229 0482 FAX: (0171) 229 0033 — COST £20–£47

The Groucho Club has taken over this stylish, bustling venue close to Notting Hill, but 'no major changes are planned' and continuity is ensured while Albert Clark remains at the stoves. He turns up few surprises, but fulfils expectations with ingredients sensitively treated.

The menu changes twice daily and incorporates starters of various salads – pear, rocket and pecorino, for example, or confit duck with beetroot and poached egg – plus wild garlic soup, or carpaccio with capers and Parmesan. Home-made pasta makes a regular appearance, maybe tagliatelle with courgettes, button mushrooms, tomato and pesto, or spinach and ricotta ravioli with a sage butter sauce. Main courses might be a simple affair of calf's liver with potato gratin, or a more complex sea bass with lentils and a crab and coriander sauce.

Successes at dessert stage have included a version of tarte Tatin, and a delicate pear mille-feuille with chocolate sauce. Staff are 'welcoming and efficient'. The wine list appeals for its sensible scope, high quality, and impressive number of good bottles under £20 (apart from a handful of 'grand' reds and whites) as well as nearly 50 by the large or small glass. CELLARMAN'S CHOICE: Chablis 1995, Dom. de la Genilottes, £19; Haut-Médoc 1986, Ch. Moulin de Bourg, £18.50.

CHEF: Albert Clark PROPRIETOR: The Groucho Club plc OPEN: all week 12.30 to 3, 7 to 11.30 (11pm Sunday) CLOSED: 25 and 26 Dec, Easter Mon, May and Aug bank hols MEALS: alc (main courses £8.50 to £13). Set L Mon to Sat £9.50 (2 courses), Set L Sun £12.50 SERVICE: not inc CARDS: Amex, Delta, Diners, MasterCard, Switch, Visa DETAILS: 105 seats. 16 seats outside. Private parties: 8 main room, 20 private room. Vegetarian meals. Children welcome. No cigars/pipes in dining-room. No-smoking area. Wheelchair access (no WC). No music

L'Oranger 🍷

map 15

5 St James's Street, SW1A 1EF — COOKING 6
TEL: (0171) 839 3774 FAX: (0171) 839 4330 — COST £33–£60

Any resemblance between the food here and at Aubergine (see entry, London) is quite intentional, since Gordon Ramsay is one of the owners. As empires go it is a small one, but there is no doubting its success. A long wooden bar funnels everybody through to the smart dining-room where mirrored walls, an atrium roof and a view on to a small courtyard make the most of a narrow space. Panelled walls and crisp linen reinforce the air of comfort that is expected of a St James's address, and professional service is of the correct but benign French school. The food is French too, decidedly modern, and although supplements for some items were considered 'an irritation' by one reporter, choice is generous.

A small but effective repertoire of good ideas is reworked over a range of dishes, and the kitchen deals in strong, clear flavours, from a cream of onion and port soup to a jellied terrine of ham hock and parsley, surrounded by slicks of gazpacho swirled in fruity olive oil. Fish figures prominently, often with an upbeat dressing: tapénade vinaigrette with mackerel salad, or bouillabaisse sauce with cod fillet. Beef shank, braised rabbit and roast pigeon are among the more interesting meats, and Marcus Wareing often goes in for layered presentation, as in a tower of spinach, potato galette and slices of pink roast lamb scattered with chopped black olives.

Desserts revolve around classical ideas such as dark chocolate mousse with raspberry sorbet, prune and armagnac tart, or strawberry sablé with a fromage frais sorbet. There are no appetisers or petits fours, but bread, butter and coffee are good. The predominantly French wine list features some of the top names from Bordeaux and Burgundy, with a few well-known producers from Italy, Spain and the New World. An interesting range of whites and reds 'of the moment' has sections under £17, £22 and £25. House French starts at £16 (£4.50 a glass). CELLARMAN'S CHOICE: Sancerre 'Les Caillottes' 1995, J.M. Roger, £26; Monthélie sur la Velle premier cru 1991, Eric Boigelot, £32.

CHEF: Marcus Wareing PROPRIETORS: Gordon Ramsay and Claudio Pulzo OPEN: Mon to Sat L 12 to 3, all week D 6 to 11.15 (10.45 Mon to Wed) CLOSED: 1 week Christmas MEALS: Set L £16 (2 courses) to £19.50, Set D £22 (2 courses) to £27 SERVICE: not inc CARDS: Amex, Delta, Diners, MasterCard, Switch, Visa DETAILS: 64 seats. 25 seats outside. Private parties: 6 main room, 20 private room. Vegetarian meals. Children welcome. No cigars/pipes while food is served. Wheelchair access (no WC). No music. Air-conditioned

Orsino 🍷

map 12

119 Portland Road, W11 4LN — COOKING 2

TEL: (0171) 221 3299 FAX: (0171) 229 9414 — COST £25–£51

The younger sibling of Covent Garden's Orso (see entry below) occupies a corner site away from the tourist crowds in Holland Park. Monochrome photos on walls that evoke Tuscan villas and vividly coloured tablecloths set the scene for lively flavours of modern Italian cooking. Garlic featured prominently in a lunch enjoyed by one reporter, from the white bean and olive oil dip offered with bread, to the aubergine and roasted tomato salad under a layer of gratinated mozzarella, to the potato and lentil accompaniments with roast saddle of lamb. Vegetarian options abound among first courses, while mains go for intensity of flavour, as in the saucing of red snapper with roast peppers and butter, or the partnering of trattoria-style veal escalopes in marsala with artichoke.

Desserts, too, aim for vibrancy: apricot and chocolate tart, for example, or passion-fruit mousse with a raspberry sauce. Service can be a touch laid-back, but the strength of the coffee should at least keep diners awake. The wine list consists of around 50 exciting Italians from some of the country's best producers, with four champagnes supplying the only foreign note. About half the bottles are under £20, and litre-sized carafes of the Umbrian house wines are £10.50.

🍾 denotes an outstanding wine cellar; 🍷 denotes a good wine list, worth travelling for.

CHEF: Anne Kettle PROPRIETOR: Orsino Restaurants Ltd OPEN: all week 12 to 11 CLOSED: 24 and 25 Dec MEALS: alc (main courses £7.50 to £14.50). Set L (until 6.30pm) £11.50 (2 courses) to £15.50 SERVICE: not inc CARDS: Amex, Delta, MasterCard, Switch, Visa DETAILS: 100 seats. Private parties: 8 main room, 34 private room. Vegetarian meals. Children welcome. No-smoking area. No music. Air-conditioned

Orso 🍷

map 15

27 Wellington Street, WC2E 7DA — COOKING **2**
TEL: (0171) 240 5269 FAX: (0171) 497 2148 — COST £21–£46

'It is always pleasant to find a restaurant which welcomes you after the theatre at 11pm,' remarked one correspondent. Orso has been serving the needs of theatregoers (both before and after the show) for some 12 years, and for many it remains a faithful and reliable old friend. The kitchen has been trading in Italian regional cooking for longer than most in the capital, and continues to come up with the goods. Creatively topped pizzas are a fixture, but reports have also applauded 'wonderful' risottos (perhaps with rock shrimps, rocket and saffron), saddle of hare with Gorgonzola polenta, and grilled lamb fillet with tomatoes, black olives and white beans. Side-dishes of braised 'black' cabbage have also been praised. Ice-creams, such as cinnamon and chocolate with hazelnuts, are a good way to finish; otherwise consider the quartet of Italian cheeses. The wine list is similar to that at Orsino (see entry above): resolutely Italian with a good selection under £20, and the same Umbrian house wines at £10.50 a litre.

CHEF: Martin Wilson PROPRIETOR: Orso Restaurants Ltd OPEN: all week 12 to 12 CLOSED: 24 and 25 Dec MEALS: alc (main courses £10.50 to £12.50). Set L Sat and Sun £11.50 (2 courses) to £13.50 SERVICE: not inc CARDS: Amex, Delta, MasterCard, Switch, Visa DETAILS: 100 seats. Vegetarian meals. Children welcome. No-smoking area. No music. Air-conditioned

Osteria Antica Bologna 🍷 £

map 12

23 Northcote Road, SW11 1NG — COOKING **3**
TEL: (0171) 978 4771 FAX: (0171) 789 9659 — COST £22–£39

'Over the last two years, Aurelio Spagnuolo has become fascinated with the cooking of Ancient Rome,' the restaurant tells us, although this does not yet extend to orgies. This intimate, low-beamed Italian place not far from Clapham Junction is appreciated for its affectingly informal approach, crammed-together tables and good value, especially at lunch-times. The generosity of the cooking ranges from filling soups that take in celery, potato, spicy sausage and egg, or fresh calamari sauté with garlic and asparagus and served with potato salad, to meatballs of lamb, capers, tarragon and Parmesan cooked in red wine and partnered by aubergine and olive salad. Ice-creams are a speciality, as is tiramisù, or you may finish with a baked peach. Service is plentiful and pleasant, and ready with advice when needed.

While Aurelio hasn't managed to unearth any amphorae of Falernum to fuel his fascination with Ancient Rome, the *lista dei vini* does contain a variety of appealing, modern Italian wines, succinctly described to aid matching with the food. Sicilian house wines are £7.90 for a 75cl jug, £2.95 a glass. CELLARMAN'S

CHOICE: Biancolella dell'Isola d'Ischia 1994, D'Ambra, £14.90; Montefalco Rosso 1991, Caprai, £15.90.

CHEFS: Aurelio Spagnuolo and Victor Cabreras PROPRIETORS: Aurelio Spagnuolo and Rochelle Porteous OPEN: Mon to Fri 12 to 3, 6 to 11 (11.30 Fri), Sat, Sun and bank hols 11am to 11.30pm (10.30 Sun) CLOSED: 10 days Christmas and New Year MEALS: alc (main courses £6.50 to £11). Set L Mon to Sat £7.50 (2 courses), Set L Sun £14.50. Cover 70p SERVICE: not inc; 10% for groups of 5 or more CARDS: Amex, MasterCard, Switch, Visa DETAILS: 75 seats. 15 seats outside. Private parties: 30 main room. Vegetarian meals. Children's helpings. No cigars/pipes in dining-room. Wheelchair access (no WC). Music. Air-conditioned

Osteria Basilico £

map 13

29 Kensington Park Road, W11 2EU — COOKING 1
TEL: (0171) 727 9957 and 9372 — COST £19–£38

'Nobody comes here for a culinary expedition into the regional dishes of Italy,' advises an experienced reporter. This is classic trattoria food and very popular with a young and enthusiastic Portobello clientele who cram it to bursting seven days a week. A starter of bresaola with mozzarella and rocket was successful for its 'simplicity coupled with good ingredients', while a poussin roasted with olive oil was 'golden brown with a lovely crisp skin, tender, perfectly cooked', and accompanied by good roast potatoes, chopped tomatoes and a rosemary *jus*. Pannacotta with chocolate sauce is properly smooth and not over-sweet, or there is zabaglione and most of the other stalwart Italian desserts. Service is tirelessly good-humoured, despite the hectic pace. 'Only Italian waiters can be this good under pressure,' volunteered one reporter, and the varied and reasonably priced wine list gives similar cause for national pride. House carafes are £7.90 for 75cl.

CHEF: Alex Palano PROPRIETOR: T. Levantesi OPEN: all week 12.30 to 3 (4 Sat), 6.30 to 11 (10.30 Sun) CLOSED: 25 Dec and 1 Jan MEALS: alc (main courses £5.50 to £10). BYO £7 SERVICE: 12.5% (optional) CARDS: Delta, MasterCard, Switch, Visa DETAILS: 80 seats. 15 seats outside. Private parties: 20 main room. Vegetarian meals. Children welcome. No cigars/pipes in dining-room. Music. Air conditioned

Oxo Tower 🍷

NEW ENTRY map 13

Oxo Tower Wharf, Barge House Street,
Southbank, SE1 9PH — COOKING 5
TEL: (0171) 803 3888 FAX: (0171) 803 3838 — COST £37–£69

A lift decants everybody on the eighth floor, and the reward for having found the inconspicuous entrance is a 'cinemascope' view across the Thames to St Paul's and Westminster, equally impressive day or night. Raked and louvred ceilings direct the eye over the long, narrow viewing terrace, floors are blond wood, and both restaurant and brasserie feel spacious and light. Each has its own kitchen and menu, and the restaurant is the one to which the cooking mark refers. It is the calmer of the two, softened by blue lighting from mid-evening, with comfortable leather chairs and lots of elbow room.

The kitchen cooks a well-constructed modern European menu with occasional input from the Far East, a style to which many London restaurants now subscribe: warm oysters with curry butter and spring onions, seared scallops with olive oil mash and squid ink sauce, or roast rack of lamb served with cumin-infused imam bayaldi and minted yoghurt. Luxuries include a caviare starter and a first-rate terrine of foie gras, and a hearty dimension is evident in open ravioli of pink chicken livers with a dark glossy sauce. Even fish tends towards meaty sea bass and turbot, served respectively with a red wine sauce and a risotto.

Fig and almond tart with fennel ice-cream is one way to finish, or there is an Oxo chocolate dessert consisting of milk chocolate ice-cream, chocolate brandy-snaps and a small tower of chocolate cake. Service is sharp, professional and 'altogether excellent'. The predominantly French wine list covers a similar range to that of its sister restaurant (see Fifth Floor, London), but is a more manageable size. Quality is the first consideration, and prices follow accordingly. A 40-strong house collection simplifies choice even more. CELLARMAN'S CHOICE: Pacherenc du Vic Bilh, Ch. Bouscassé 1994, Brumont, £18.50; Viña Bajoz Crianza 1991, Toro, £17.50. A less-formal 'everyday' restaurant called Bistrot 2 Riverside was due to open on the same site shortly after the *Guide* went to press.

CHEF: Simon Arkless PROPRIETOR: Harvey Nichols & Co Ltd OPEN: Restaurant all week L 12 to 3 (3.30 Sun), D 6 to 11.30 (Sun 6.30 to 10.30); brasserie all week 11 to 11.30 (10.30 Sun) MEALS: alc (main courses brasserie £9.50 to £14.50, restaurant £10 to £19). Set L restaurant £23.85; brasserie pre-theatre D 5.30 to 7.30 £15.50 SERVICE: 12.5% (optional) CARDS: Amex, Diners, MasterCard, Switch, Visa DETAILS: 175 seats. 60 seats outside. Private parties: 140 main room. Vegetarian meals. Children welcome. Wheelchair access (also WC). No music. Air-conditioned

Le Palais du Jardin

map 15

136 Long Acre, WC2E 9AD — COOKING **2**
TEL: (0171) 379 5353 FAX: (0171) 379 1846 — COST £29–£46

'Very smart and swish, but noisy and rather hectic' is how one reporter summed up this Covent Garden brasserie. Opening times make it suitable for both early- and late-evening meals, and the Anglo-French menu does a good line in fish and shellfish, from deep-fried softshell crab to fish-cakes. A platter of seafood contains lobster, oysters, mussels and crab, although one reporter with a Continental version in mind would have liked even more variety: 'where oh where were the winkles, whelks and little brown shrimps?' Other choices include seafood sausage, pasta dishes, a few vegetarian options, and meat dishes ranging from duck with cabbage and smoked bacon to beef fillet with sauce béarnaise. Ice-cream comes in four flavours (liquorice, saffron, pistachio and coconut), and cheeses are French 'farmhouse'. Service has been described as slow, jostling and 'less than reasonable', and seems to be stretched by the press of numbers. A short list of French wines is well balanced for style and price. House wine is £9.

If you have access to the Internet, you can find The Good Food Guide *online at the Which? Online web site (http://www.which.net).*

CHEFS: Winston Matthews and Paul Morris PROPRIETOR: Le Palais du Jardin Ltd OPEN: all week 12 to 3.30, 5.30 to 12 (11 Sun), oyster bar all week 12 to 12 (11 Sun) CLOSED: 25 and 26 Dec MEALS: alc (main courses £9.50 to £23.50) SERVICE: 12.5% (optional), card slips closed CARDS: Amex, Delta, Diners, MasterCard, Switch, Visa DETAILS: 350 seats. 20 seats outside. Private parties: 350 main room. Vegetarian meals. Children's helpings. Wheelchair access (no WC). Music. Air-conditioned

People's Palace

map 13

Royal Festival Hall, SE1 8XX COOKING 2
TEL: (0171) 928 9999 FAX: (0171) 928 2355 COST £24–£47

The room is big, the view bigger, and the Festival Hall location couldn't be handier for South Bank activities. 'I wasn't going to a concert but they had me in and out in an hour.' Stephen Carter's bold, brazen Yorkshire approach throws together a starter of black pudding and foie gras with a fried egg, and roast cod served with a lobster, shredded pork and white bean cassoulet: can't accuse him of not trying. The set two-course meal generally offers a meat, a fish and a vegetable option for main course and is considered a bargain providing you don't find the choices 'bizarre' or restricting. Vegetables are charged extra, 'the risotto changes every day', and although dishes appear modish enough – grilled calf's liver on a bed of mashed celeriac and Gorgonzola with a heavily reduced meat stock, perhaps – they may be subject to 'rather patchy performance'. A short, modern wine list is businesslike rather than inspired, and wine service can be 'pushy'. House wine is £10.50.

CHEF: Stephen Carter PROPRIETOR: David Levin OPEN: all week 12 to 3, 5.30 to 11 CLOSED: 25 Dec MEALS: alc (main courses £9.50 to £15). Set L £10.50 (2 courses) to £14.50, Set D 5.30 to 6.30 £10.50 (2 courses) to £14.50 SERVICE: not inc CARDS: Amex, Delta, Diners, MasterCard, Switch, Visa DETAILS: 200 seats. Private parties: 240 main room. Vegetarian meals. Children's helpings. No-smoking area. Wheelchair access (also WC). Music. Air-conditioned

Le P'tit Normand

map 12

185 Merton Road, SW18 5EF COOKING 2
TEL: (0181) 871 0233 COST £16–£37

The small, busy, cramped restaurant can be noisy and vibrant. Even Inspector Clouseau could work out what the red and white check tablecloths, dangling copper pots and Edith Piaf tapes add up to. All the Gallic props resemble a stage set, and 'you almost expect a French maid, scantily clad, with a feather duster, to be tripping about saying "Ooh, la, la!"' A printed menu lists a few staples – onion soup, snails, black pudding with apples – but most people order from the blackboard. Either way, Normandy is not the sole source of inspiration, given moules alsacienne, boeuf bourguignon and confit de canard. But no matter. Crab crêpe, fillet of lamb en croûte, and rabbit 'forestière' get the thumbs-up. A selection of 15 to 20 French cheeses might be followed by tarte Tatin, crème brûlée or nougat glacé. Service is informal but efficient – indeed, so efficient that you might need to nail your bread to the table. Begin with a kir (they make a good one) and finish with a vintage calvados. In between is a short list of French wines beginning with house red and white at £8.95.

CHEF/PROPRIETOR: Philippe Herrard OPEN: Sun to Fri L 12 to 2, all week D 7 to 10.30 (11 Fri and Sat) MEALS: alc (main courses £9 to £10). Set L Mon to Fri £5 (2 courses), Set L Sun £11.95 SERVICE: 12.5% (optional), card slips closed CARDS: Amex, Delta, Diners, MasterCard, Switch, Visa DETAILS: 34 seats. Private parties: 20 main room, 20 private room. Vegetarian meals. Children's helpings. No pipes in dining-room. Wheelchair access (no WC). Music. Air-conditioned

Pied-à-Terre

map 15

34 Charlotte Street, W1P 1HJ — COOKING 7

TEL: (0171) 636 1178 FAX: (0171) 916 1171 — COST £38–£91

The unassuming frontage, probably the most discreet in Charlotte Street, is not designed to attract passing trade. This is a 'destination restaurant' for those in search of carefully crafted modern French food from a talented young English chef. Although the frosted-glass front is the only window in the place, the 'somewhat spartan but comfortable' dining-room is brightened up with works by Jim Dine, including a portrait of Chairman Mao and Lyndon Johnson. Meals begin with good black olives and flavoured bread, followed perhaps by a coffee cup of foie gras mousse with pea soup.

The kitchen goes in for a lot of froth, and dispenses truffle oil with a generous hand. First courses rely to a large extent on foie gras and shellfish, with variety in the form of braised snails, or a dish of roasted sweetbreads and braised oxtail with ceps. Tom Aikens enjoys serving an item five different ways on the same plate, producing a kind of essay in foie gras, or a look-what-I-can-do with bananas. The assiette of foie gras, for example, includes a warm mousse – perhaps the 'ultimate nursery food' on account of its comforting creaminess – as well as a slice of foie gras in a lime and ginger jelly.

A massive amount of fine and painstaking workmanship goes into the cooking, with 'lots of energy, lots of ideas', and technical accomplishments are impressive. Braised pig's head and tongue with steamed trotter, for example, is neatly reduced to five little piles with cheek and tongue disposed between them, the trotter surmounted by a deep-fried brain that was crisp outside and creamy inside. 'I reckon this is about as far as you can take a pig's head.' Whether or not these particular dishes hang together is a matter for debate. This is food made to be admired, waiting for gasps from the audience, as much as it is intended for sheer sensuous enjoyment. More than one reporter has wondered whether 'something simpler, less costly and more *sympa*' might be in order.

After a pre-dessert crème brûlée might come caramelised apple and almond filo, banana five ways or chocolate six: fondant, ice-cream, tart, mousse, parfait and Negus. Then comes a generous array of petits-fours; no one need get up from the table feeling hungry. Wine waiter Bruno Asselin comes in for praise for his attentive service and knowledgeable advice on the mostly French collection of superior bins. An impressive selection of dessert wines, including four Canadian Icewines, rounds things off nicely. House vin de pays is £15.

Restaurateurs justifiably resent no-shows. If you quote a credit card number when booking, you may be liable for the restaurant's lost profit margin if you don't turn up. Always phone to cancel.

CHEF: Tom Aikens PROPRIETORS: David Moore and Tom Aikens OPEN: Mon to Fri L 12.15 to 2.15, Mon to Sat D 7.15 to 10.45 CLOSED: 2 weeks Christmas, 1 Jan, bank hols MEALS: Set L £23 to £39.50, Set D £29.50 to £46 (tasting menu to be taken by the whole table and not available after 10pm) SERVICE: 12.5% (optional), card slips closed CARDS: Amex, Delta, Diners, MasterCard, Switch, Visa DETAILS: 40 seats. Private parties: 40 main room, 12 private room. Vegetarian meals. Children welcome. Wheelchair access (no WC). Music. Air-conditioned

Le Pont de la Tour

map 13

36D Shad Thames, Butlers Wharf, SE1 2YE — COOKING 6
TEL: (0171) 403 8403 FAX: (0171) 403 0267 — COST £38–£77

Of all the Conran restaurants on the Thames waterfront, this is the one that makes the most impact. The ground floor of an old warehouse has been turned into a 'smart, attractive, well-designed' dining-room, the pale yellow walls hung with black-framed cartoons and drawings. A busy brigade of waiters dashes to and fro, reinforcing the fact that it is intended to be 'a serious eating-machine'. Those lucky enough to get a window table have a fine view of Tower Bridge.

David Burke is one of the better practitioners of the Mediterranean arts working within the Conran empire, offering 'imaginative salad combinations and classic French country dishes, with a lot of chic ingredients'. At inspection, that translated into first courses of brandade of cod with roast peppers, French beans and tapénade, and a 'terrific' crêpe Parmentier made with potato flour and piled with soured cream, smoked salmon and a sprinkling of caviare. Fish dishes tend to keep things straightforward, so that Dover sole is simply grilled and served with chips and spinach, while scallops are parsleyed and accompanied by grilled tomatoes and thyme. A plump pigeon, on the other hand, might be roasted, sauced with a rich gravy made with morels and truffles, and partnered with gratin dauphinois. Desserts offer a broad choice, including a sensuous prune and armagnac soufflé, with armagnac cream poured into a hole in the top at table. Otherwise, there might be chocolate terrine with coffee crème anglaise, or apple tart with caramel ice cream.

There are enough stars on the magnificent wine list to fill a galaxy. Vintage champagnes, first-class clarets and mature burgundies form a fine French constellation, while California and Australia make some heavenly contributions. If you can't afford the astronomical sums such bottles inevitably attract, the sommelier's recommendations at more down-to-earth prices come in very handy. House Vin de Pays d'Oc is £11.95.

CHEF: David Burke PROPRIETORS: Sir Terence Conran, Joel Kissin and David Burke OPEN: Sun to Fri L 12 (12.30 Sun) to 3, all week D 6 to 11.30 (11 Sun) MEALS: alc Sun L, all week D (main courses L £11.50 to £14.50, £16 to £23.50). Set L Mon to Fri £27.50 SERVICE: 12.5% (optional) CARDS: Amex, Delta, Diners, MasterCard, Switch, Visa DETAILS: 100 seats. 65 seats outside. Private parties: 20 private room. Vegetarian meals. Children welcome. Wheelchair access (also WC). Music

Several sharp operators have tried to extort money from restaurateurs on the promise of an entry in a guidebook that has never appeared. The Good Food Guide *makes no charge for inclusion.*

Poons £ map 15

4 Leicester Street, WC2H 7BL COOKING 1
TEL: (0171) 437 1528 FAX: (0181) 458 0968 COST £13–£45

This branch of the Poons empire continues to pull in the crowds, many of whom are tourists attracted by the near-legendary family name. The menu majors in the famous wind-dried ducks, sausages and bacon, plus casseroles, rice hotpots and different kinds of noodles, including Japanese udon and Shanghai-style wheat versions. Otherwise look for more esoteric offerings such as shredded chicken with jellyfish, fried quail's eggs in crabmeat sauce, or steamed duck with pickled plums. The star turn for one reporter, however, was a 'brilliant' dish of 'absolutely fresh, sweet prawns with a simple, perfectly seasoned sauce covered with shreds of ginger and spring onion'. Jasmine tea and Tsing Tao beer suit the food, or there is house wine at £7.30.

CHEF: Yuan Jin He PROPRIETOR: W.N. Poon OPEN: all week 12 to 11.30 CLOSED: 24 to 27 Dec MEALS: alc (main courses £4 to £13.50). Set L and D (minimum 2) £7 to £17 SERVICE: not inc CARDS: Amex, MasterCard, Switch, Visa DETAILS: 120 seats. Private parties: 70 main room, 24 private room. Vegetarian meals. Children welcome. Air-conditioned

Putney Bridge 🍷 **NEW ENTRY** map 12

The Embankment, SW15 1LB COOKING 5
TEL: (0181) 780 1811 FAX: (0181) 780 1211 COST £28–£53

It looks better from the towpath – or better still, a boat on the river – than from the main road. Proximity to water, with rowing clubs just up the road, and lights from the real Putney Bridge reflecting off the Thames at night, give the place a dose of glamour and a sense of vitality. It is made from glass, blond wood and steel, but then which self-respecting modern building isn't? Casual drinkers and restaurant customers alike tend to congregate at the long downstairs bar, while the two-tier arrangement in the comfortable and airy first-floor dining-room means that just about everybody gets a view.

Despite links with St John and the French House Dining Room (see entries, London), the food here is quite different. Paul Hughes was sous-chef to Fergus Henderson, but has foresaken the frugality that gives St John its character. Here is a pan-European approach with a degree of generosity and richness: in a fatty pork terrine (called a 'double confit'), or an 'intensely saffrony' and creamy risotto with a blob of salty black tapénade on top. Materials are sound, spectacularly so in the case of one reporter's crab mayonnaise – a dish of 'simple excellence' – and although the balance of flavours in a dish might tip over occasionally, timing is generally accurate, with 'everything pink and/or moist where it should have been'. Interesting fishy ideas might surface in the form of sliced beetroot with smoked eel, roast hake with chorizo and chickpeas, or salmon kedgeree with lime pickle.

Desserts have included passion-fruit tart with a blob of chocolate sorbet, and goat's-milk cheesecake with sour cherries. Service is organised and responsive, and wines are cleverly chosen, with over 150 bins tailored to meet most pockets and palates, and grouped by varietal or style on the well-structured list. Old World wines mingle with New, and prices start at a friendly £9.95. A generous number are offered by the glass, including some fine sherries, madeiras and ports. CELLARMAN'S CHOICE: Ninth Island Chardonnay 1996, Tasmania, £22; St-Emilion, Ch. Grand Lartigue 1993, £24.

CHEF: Paul Hughes PROPRIETOR: Trevor Gulliver OPEN: all week 12 (12.30 Sun) to 3, 6 to 11 (Sun 7 to 10.30) MEALS: alc (main courses £9 to £16.50). Set L £13.50 (2 courses) to £17 SERVICE: not inc; 12.5% for parties of 6 or more CARDS: Delta, MasterCard, Switch, Visa DETAILS: 152 seats. Private parties: 165 main room. Vegetarian meals. Children's helpings Sun only. Wheelchair access (also WC). Music. Air-conditioned

Quaglino's

map 15

16 Bury Street, SW1Y 6AL — COOKING 5
TEL: (0171) 930 6767 FAX: (0171) 839 2866 — COST £25–£85

Despite the sweeping staircase, this doesn't feel like a basement, thanks to enormous painted pillars, huge flower arrangements and the 'altar' of shellfish, but thanks mostly to the computerised artificial skylight which is programmed to emulate the sky as it changes from day to night, from winter to summer. After five years, Quaglino's 'has shaken down into what it was really always meant to be', according to one observer: 'mass catering (at a price) for those who want to see rabbit in mustard on the menu when they order their steaks'. Crustaceans are a big draw, with rock oysters, crab mayonnaise, and a seafood platter (£55 for two people, or £84 with lobster), and salt-cod fritters have gone down well.

If the food is going anywhere, it seems to be edging further east, producing rare tuna in a crust of wasabi and soy, or scallops with ginger, bamboo shoots and coriander. But that is not at the expense of more traditional standbys such as calf's liver and bacon with matchstick chips, or a variation on the cassoulet theme using hunks of lamb and various sausages. Puddings appear to be the weak link, but the overall impression is one of 'workmanlike' food which, given the press of custom and the potential for disaster when cooking on this scale, indicates a kitchen in capable hands. Service is variable. Wine mark-ups are on the high side, but there is much of interest and plenty of variety. In the absence of half-bottles, a dozen or so wines are served by the glass, and house Vin de Pays d'Oc is £11.75 a bottle.

CHEF: Paul Wilson PROPRIETOR: Conran Restaurants OPEN: all week 12 to 3, 5.30 to 11.30 (12.30 Fri and Sat, 10.30 Sun) MEALS: alc (main courses £10.50 to £29). Set L £14.50 to £19.50, Set D 5.30 to 6.30 £14.50 to £19.50 SERVICE: 12.5% (optional) CARDS: Amex, Diners, MasterCard, Visa DETAILS: 267 seats. Private parties: 40 main room, 10 private room. Vegetarian meals. Children welcome. No cigars/pipes in dining-room. Music. Air-conditioned

Quality Chop House

map 13

94 Farringdon Road, EC1R 3EA — COOKING 3
TEL: (0171) 837 5093 — COST £24–£46

'We are hoping to expand this year into the next building,' writes Charles Fontaine, 'to incorporate an oyster and champagne bar.' Otherwise this Victorian dining-room in 'gentrified Clerkenwell' continues as before. Behind the etched glass frontage lies a good stab at a period feel and eight high-backed wooden booths with 'bone-crunching' bench seats. 'Robust, no-nonsense grub' is the style, from scrambled eggs with smoked salmon to Toulouse sausage with mash and onion gravy, from corned beef hash with fried egg to grilled T-bone steak. The sense of simple honesty has timeless appeal, even if the food sometimes makes up in enthusiasm for what it may lack in subtlety. An off-duty inspector enjoyed a rustic dish of plump snails in garlic butter, a fish-cake with a good ratio of salmon to potato – 'fine ingredients, good cooking, and decent sorrel sauce' – and a 'quite light' bread-and-butter pudding. Service is friendly, and a short, sensible wine list (starting at £10) is backed up by a few good beers.

CHEF/PROPRIETOR: Charles Fontaine OPEN: Sun to Fri L 12 to 3 (4 Sun), all week D 6.30 (7 Sun) to 11.30 CLOSED: 10 days Christmas MEALS: alc (main courses £6 to £14) SERVICE: not inc CARDS: none DETAILS: 40 seats. Vegetarian meals. No cigars/pipes in dining room. Wheelchair access (no WC). No music. Air-conditioned

Quincy's

map 13

675 Finchley Road, NW2 2JP COOKING 3
TEL: (0171) 794 8499 COST £31–£38

It would seem more in keeping to come across Quincy's in a French provincial village than on one of north London's major arterial roads. Flowers trail from the window-boxes and, inside, half-curtained windows, wicker lampshades and floral cushions create an atmosphere of unpretentious domesticity. When a 'strongly flavoured' version of fish soup with rouille and croûtons arrives, the impression is complete.

David Philpott delivers three-course set dinners that might take in precision-cooked salmon steak with stir-fried vegetables, or a robust serving of roast lamb with 'richly aromatic' saffron mash. Salmis of pigeon with foie gras and sweet potato fondant suggests a confidence with luxury ingredients too. Puddings might offer crumbly chocolate brownie with vanilla ice-cream and a warm, buttery fudge sauce, or fresh fruits with a tuile biscuit and a sharply flavoured sorbet. Front-of-house, led by David Wardle, dispenses plenty of care and attention. There is scarcely a dull wine on the list, and prices are beyond reproach. House Duboeuf is £9.

CHEF: David Philpott PROPRIETOR: David Wardle OPEN: Tue to Sat D only 7 to 11 CLOSED: Christmas MEALS: Set D £24 SERVICE: not inc CARDS: Amex, Delta, MasterCard, Switch, Visa DETAILS: 30 seats. Vegetarian meals. Children welcome. Music. Air-conditioned

Quo Vadis 🍷

NEW ENTRY map 15

26 Dean Street, W1A 6LL COOKING 6
TEL: 437 9585/4809 FAX: (0171) 4349972 COST £31–£61

Marco Pierre White is the nearest thing to Midas in the catering business. One touch, and a traditional old-school Italian restaurant is turned into gastronomic gold. When it opened, an amazing number of newspaper columnists, who had previously kept quiet about it, suddenly remembered having eaten at the old Leoni's and were able to talk knowledgeably about the changes, although not even Roy Hattersley can claim to remember it from when Karl Marx lived here. It may be advisable to visit the upstairs Damien Hirst-filled bar after eating rather than before, on account of its skeletons, bovine heads in glass cases, and gleaming surgical instruments. The ground-floor dining-room is bright and white, with attractive stained-glass windows, colourful flower arrangements, and a huge model of a DNA molecule. Some of the exhibits move.

The long, classic brasserie *carte* has 'something for everyone', including a caviare starter at £250 that may well be the single most expensive dish in the *Guide*. Some items might be familiar to those who have eaten at other Marco Pierre White restaurants: a bright green ball of stuffed cabbage on a pool of scarlet tomato sauce, or crisp scallops with deep-fried calamares and dabs of squid ink sauce. Suckling pig is spit-roasted to produce 'super crackling' and served with apple sauce. Fine ingredients can be taken for granted, and timing appears to be 'spot-on' for just about everything, including that unforgiving divider of sheep from goats, risotto: a 'creamy interpretation' of wild mushroom, and a 'divine' saffron version.

The roll-call of successes includes a light caramelised apple tart with vanilla ice-cream, classic lemon tart, and biscuit glacé nougatine with raspberry sauce. Service from a two-tier brigade is professional, charming, and all eyes. Lovers of first-class Australian wines should note that the cellar is stocked with six vintages of Wynns Coonawarra Estate John Riddoch Cabernet Sauvignon, seven of Leeuwin Estate Art Series Chardonnay and eight of Penfolds Grange. North America makes some equally fine contributions, but this doesn't signal the decline of the Old World: some top-quality burgundies and clarets make their presence felt. Expect West End price tags, and look to South America and French country wines for bins under £20. House wines start at £13. CELLARMAN'S CHOICE: Rioja 1993, Misela de Murrieta, £20; Salice Salentino 1994, £16.50.

CHEFS: Jeremy Hollingsworth and Tim Payne PROPRIETORS: Marco Pierre White, Jimmy Lahoud, Jonathan Kennedy, Matthew Freud OPEN: Mon to Fri L 12 to 3, all week D 6 to 12 (Sun 10.30) CLOSED: 25 and 26 Dec, 1 Jan MEALS: alc (main courses £11.50 to £14.50). Set L £13.05 (2 courses) SERVICE: 12.5% (optional), card slips closed CARDS: Amex, Delta, Diners, MasterCard, Switch, Visa DETAILS: 120 seats. Private parties: 20 main room, 20 private rooms. Vegetarian meals. Children welcome. No cigars/pipes in dining room. Wheelchair access (no WC). No music. Air-conditioned

Ragam £

map 15

57 Cleveland Street, W1P 5PQ
TEL: (0171) 636 9098

COOKING 1
COST £17–£34

The speciality here is the vegetarian food of Kerala, dishes such as masala dosai – a rice and lentil flour pancake 'like a huge roll of parchment' stuffed with onion and potato – served with coconut sambal and vegetable curry, but the fiercely hot 'exotic' starter 'chilly chicken' receives as much praise. The rest of the menu is that of a conventional non-vegetarian curry-house. One reporter found tables a bit cramped, while another praised the 'restful décor in rusty pink'. Prices are modest, and wines start at £8 (£1.50 a glass).

CHEF: G.K.C. Nair PROPRIETOR: J. Dharmaseelan OPEN: all week 12 to 2.45, 6 to 11.15 (11 Sun and bank hols, 12 Fri) CLOSED: 25 and 26 Dec MEALS: alc (main courses £5 to £7) SERVICE: 10%, card slips closed CARDS: Amex, Diners, MasterCard, Visa DETAILS: 36 seats. Private parties: 20 main room, 20 private room. Vegetarian meals. Children welcome. No cigars/pipes in dining-room. Wheelchair access (also WC). Music. Air-conditioned

Rani £

map 12

7 Long Lane, N3 2PR
COOKING 2

TEL: (0181) 349 4386 FAX: (0181) 349 4386
COST £20–£28

A short walk from Finchley Central tube station, Rani looks every bit the traditional Indian restaurant, occupying two adjoining rooms of a converted shop, and serving vegetarian Gujurati dishes off paper tablecloths. The user-friendly menu explains everything carefully (there is even a braille version) and indicates which dishes contain sugar, dairy products, wheat or nuts, an exemplary practice for anyone with an allergy. Apart from set meals, thalis and a children's menu, it offers a few bhajias, and samosa or aloo tiki to start, followed perhaps by banana methi, or akhaa ringal (with aubergine). Chutneys are good, and fenugreek is widely used (even in some of the bread), although spicing seems to have adapted to Western tastes and tends not to be too bold. Indeed, those familiar with the real thing might murmur about Rani 'not being Asian enough'. If that is the case, perhaps avoid Marine ices in favour of shrikand (yogurt flavoured with saffron and cardamom) or carrot halva. Drink lassi or one of the dozen decent wines costing between £8.50 and £13.50. Another branch is at 3 Hill Street, Richmond; Tel: (0181) 332 2322.

CHEF: Sheila Pattni PROPRIETOR: Jyotindra Pattni OPEN: Sun L 12.15 to 2.30, all week D 6 to 10 (10.45 Fri and Sat) CLOSED: 25 Dec, 1 Jan MEALS: alc (main courses £5 to £8). Set L and D £5.90 (1 course) to £9.95 (2 courses; min 2). BYO £4 SERVICE: 10% (optional), card slips closed CARDS: Amex, Delta, MasterCard, Switch, Visa DETAILS: 90 seats. Private parties: 50 main room, 23 private room. Vegetarian meals. Children's helpings. No smoking in 1 dining-room. No cigars/pipes in dining-room. Wheelchair access (no WC). Music

Ransome's Dock

map 12

35–37 Parkgate Road, SW11 4NP

TEL: (0171) 223 1611 and 924 2462
COOKING 4

FAX: (0171) 924 2614
COST £26–£51

'The setting is great, and we liked the décor and atmosphere,' summed up one reporter of Martin Lam's waterside spot just south of the river. The version of modern British food on offer has few exotic Asian flourishes, taking its lead more from the traditional European repertoire. Duck cassoulet, and Elizabeth David's spinach and ricotta gnocchi with sage butter may not be ground-breakingly modern, but the ensemble of dishes makes for satisfying eating. The two-course set lunch might run to warm smoked salmon tart followed by home-made pork and veal sausage, while the *carte* (which changes around ten times a year) has produced French onion soup, and calf's liver with olive oil mash.

Meat comes from a Cirencester farm specialising in traditional breeds reared organically, ducks are Trelough, and seasonal produce is a strength. Among desserts of New York cheesecake and organic Devon ice-creams, the prune and armagnac soufflé with a jug of cream sauce has been judged 'well worth the wait'. Sunday brunch is typically indulgent. Service is usually friendly, intelligent and well paced. Drinks include water from an artesian well, a few beers, and a Bayeux cider. The excitingly diverse wine list begins with some tempting Almacenista sherries and ends with a mouthwatering choice of dessert wines. In between, bins are grouped by style, ranging from an aromatic

Bernkasteler Badstube Kabinett Riesling to a 'very big red' Tim Adams Shiraz. There is also a 'big bottle section' of magnums and jeroboams for large parties. House wines are from £11.95. CELLARMAN'S CHOICE: Cloudy Bay Sauvignon Blanc 1997, Marlborough, New Zealand, £19.50; Crozes-Hermitage 1995, Alain Graillot, £22.50.

CHEF: Martin Lam PROPRIETORS: Martin and Vanessa Lam OPEN: all week 12 to 11 (12 Sat, 3.30 Sun) CLOSED: Christmas, summer bank hols MEALS: alc (main courses £8.50 to £16.50). Set L Mon to Fri £11.50 (2 courses). Brunch menu L Sat and Sun. BYO £5.50 SERVICE: not inc CARDS: Amex, Delta, Diners, MasterCard, Switch, Visa DETAILS: 60 seats. 25 seats outside. Private parties: 14 main room. Car park (D and weekends only). Vegetarian meals. Children's helpings. No pipes in dining-room. Wheelchair access (also WC). Music. Air-conditioned

Rasa £ map 12

55 Stoke Newington Church Street, N16 0AR COOKING 3
TEL: (0171) 249 0344 FAX: (0171) 249 8748 COST £15–£25

Redecorated in pinks and yellows, with a floor done out in white terracotta tiles, Rasa impresses for its 'endearing charm, cool civility and cultural awareness'. The style is that of Kerala, a cuisine dominated by flavours of coconut milk, tamarind, cardamom, ginger and chillies, and featuring bananas, mangoes and nuts. Bhel pooris, samosas and 'soft and spongey' dosais strike a comfortingly recognisable note, yet there is plenty of interest, including a wide variety of vegetable curries which might include one of green papaya and split peas. There is also a poppadum dipped in a spiced rice flour batter, and fried, 'for extra crunch' as the menu puts it. Ingredients are good, flavours are finely tuned, and 'the kitchen knows what it's about'. Part of the appeal is that 'you are continually surprised with new flavours and ideas; it is not all over in the first couple of mouthfuls'. Service from Mr and Mrs Padmabhan is courteous and helpful.

CHEF: Sivadas Sreedahran PROPRIETOR: Rasa Ltd OPEN: all week 12 to 2.30, 6 to 11 (12 Fri and Sat) CLOSED: 25 and 26 Dec MEALS: alc (main courses £5 to £7). Set L £10, Set D £15 SERVICE: not inc CARDS: Amex, Delta, MasterCard, Visa DETAILS: 45 seats. Private parties: 25 main room. Vegetarian meals. Children welcome. No smoking in dining-room. Wheelchair access (also WC). Music. Air-conditioned

Redmond's NEW ENTRY map 12

170 Upper Richmond Road West, SW14 8AW COOKING 5
TEL: (0181) 878 1922 FAX: (0181) 878 1133 COST £25–£43

Redmond and Pippa Hayward, once a Cheltenham fixture, have now decamped to the capital. In May 1997 they opened what they call a 'local' restaurant in a former tool importer's emporium in East Sheen. It is a chintz-free zone that lets daylight stream in through tall picture windows on to the large, vivid, abstract pictures that hang on plain yellow walls. The food is vivid too, making use of chillies, tapénade, ginger and mustard to sharpen things up, and grafting a few Far Eastern ideas on to a European base.

It may seem rather a mix and match approach, given a flavoured couscous and squid ink sauce to partner roast cod and scallops, or a tempura of sardine fillets with tomato and chilli salsa, but results are convincing, as an inspector found in a thin oriental broth of spider crab, clams and mussels, aromatised with lime leaves and coriander. Lightness characterised the early dishes, maybe because they were summery ones, one of the heartiest being calf's liver with thyme risotto.

Mango and lime parfait with a polenta biscuit offers a refreshing mix of flavours, as well as a hint of the kitchen's openness to novelty. Raspberry soufflé is sharpened with lemon-grass ice cream, and even mandatory crème brûlée is pepped up with lemon. Wine prices are kept on a tighter leash than East Sheen may be accustomed to, and the choices are impeccably up-tempo, from Jurançon sec and Cape Mentelle to Filliatreau's Saumur-Champigny. Prices open at £9.50.

CHEF: Redmond Hayward PROPRIETORS: Redmond and Pippa Hayward OPEN: Mon to Fri and Sun L 12 to 2.30 (3 Sun), Mon to Sat D 7 to 10.30 CLOSED: 3 days Christmas, bank hols MEALS: Set L £12.50 (1 main course or 2 starters), Set L and D £17.50 (2 courses) to £25 SERVICE: not inc CARDS: Delta, MasterCard, Switch, Visa DETAILS: 50 seats. Private parties: 50 main room. Children's helpings. No cigars/pipes in dining-room. Wheelchair access (no WC). No music

Red Pepper £

map 13

8 Formosa Street, W9 1EE — COOKING 3
TEL: (0171) 266 2708 — COST £24–£40

A diminutive Italian restaurant in a back street of Maida Vale, the Red Pepper can get hectically busy. When it does, the noise level may increase and service become frenetic, but the smile doesn't fade and regulars keep coming back. Pizzas cooked in a wood-fired oven form the centrepiece of the menu and offer variations of smoked chicken and Gorgonzola, or leek, ham and Parmesan. A warm salad of octopus and potato is carefully assembled and obviously fresh, while a main course of sauté turbot with stir-fried cabbage and fennel was for one reporter 'the most refined dish of the meal, the ingredients combining well together'. At dessert stage, tiramisù is commended for avoiding over-sweetness, while egg custard with lemon sorbet has been described as 'surprisingly refreshing'. The Italian wine list keeps prices within reason and also hauls in some of the lesser-known southern regions. House wines are £9.

CHEF: Paola Zancca PROPRIETORS: Bijan Behzadi OPEN: Sat and Sun L 12.30 to 2.30 (3.30 Sun), all week D 6.30 to 10.45 (10.30 Sun) MEALS: alc (main courses £6 to £12) SERVICE: not inc; 12.5% for parties of 5 or more CARDS: Delta, MasterCard, Switch, Visa DETAILS: 48 seats. 20 seats outside. Private parties: 25 main room. Vegetarian meals. Children's helpings. No cigars in dining-room. Wheelchair access (no WC). Music. Air-conditioned

Riva

map 12

169 Church Road, SW13 9HR — COOKING 3
TEL: (0181) 748 0434 — COST £26–£47

Riva flies the flag for an unshowy approach to Italian food. Although it shuns ostentation, it looks smart enough, with caramel-coloured walls, fresh flowers, lights strung out across the room, and mirrors to make it all feel bigger. The appeal lies in its simplicity, allied to an awareness of the seasons and a modest resourcefulness that 'seems to make meals out of more or less nothing'. This is the Italian way, and an approach that cooks invariably find satisfying. It may amount to no more than a rustic cardoon soup with chunks of roasted pumpkin, or a tripartite plate of artichoke with fonduta, fennel gratinata, and asparagus with a poached egg, but each dish combines a variety of tastes and textures.

Grilled calf's liver might come with a generous quantity of porcini mushrooms, and 'really juicy' best end of lamb with vegetable fritters on a bed of spinach, but there are plenty of non-meat options, including pasta and risotto dishes, and fish, from grilled squid to sea bass. Sweet milk gnocchi with honey butter sauce makes a pleasant diversion from zuppa inglese and apple strudel, and a blueberry and prune pancake with cinnamon ice-cream was judged 'a slightly unusual and very successful dish'. Flavours tend to the understated, dishes may not correspond exactly with the menu description, and prices may seem high, but the food is applauded for its integrity and variety. Thirty-plus wines from northern and central Italy are full of interest, starting with house Tokai and Merlot at £9.75.

CHEF: Francesco Zanchetta PROPRIETOR: Andrea Riva OPEN: Sun to Fri L 12 to 2.30, all week D 7 to 11 (11.30 Fri and Sat, 9.30 Sun) CLOSED: Christmas, Easter, last 2 weeks Aug, bank hols MEALS: alc (main courses £7 to £13.50) SERVICE: 10%, card slips closed CARDS: Amex, Delta, MasterCard, Switch, Visa DETAILS: 50 seats. 8 seats outside. Private parties: 40 main room. Vegetarian meals. Children's helpings. No cigars/pipes in dining-room. Wheelchair access (no WC). Music. Air-conditioned

River Café 🍷

map 12

Thames Wharf Studios, Rainville Road, W6 9HA — COOKING 6
TEL: (0171) 381 8824 FAX: (0171) 381 6217 — COST £40–£67

Bright, simple food using good ingredients, plus a couple of books (there is now a second River Café cookbook) and a generous peppering of publicity have all helped to transform this out-of-the-way riverfront place, lost amid warehouse conversions, into one of London's most talked-about addresses. People really do travel the distance to eat here, and although it is fair to say that not all readers see the point of the River Café's food, most do enjoy the sense of uncluttered cool, the river view, and the serious contemporary Italian style of cooking. Such is the excellence of the primary materials that they can be served with the apparent minimum of preparation and yet still produce a memorable impression, as in a starter of penne with cavolo nero, extra virgin olive oil, garlic and Parmesan.

The wood-fired oven (best not to sit too near it on a warm evening) is used for many dishes, including a slice of turbot accompanied by braised spinach and black olives. The food looks easy to replicate, but looks can be deceptive. The lightness of tone is helped by a preponderance of fish and vegetables, and by good use of herbs and spices: chilli and mint for seared wild salmon accompanied by zucchini fritters, for instance. This is also a rocket-propelled kitchen – it seems to use the leaves in everything – but the impact of all the salads, oils, capers and the rest is an appealing directness of flavour.

Pannacotta is the real thing, 'unctuously rich and creamy', with an enlivening splash of grappa, while vin santo is used to make an ice-cream. Alternatively, try the frangipane tart. Moans and groans tend to focus on prices. Staff talk with authority about the food, 'although none of them look as though they are eating lots of it'. The wine list is a roll-call of some of Italy's finest – Conterno, Jermann,

Ornellaia, Pieropan, Quintarelli to name but a few – and dessert wines are particularly enticing, if grappa doesn't appeal. Plans are afoot to expand the list with many more older wines. Prices start at £9.50.

CHEFS: Rose Gray, Ruth Rogers and Theo Randall PROPRIETORS: Richard and Ruth Rogers and Rose Gray OPEN: all week L 12.30 (1 Sun) to 3, Mon to Sat D 7.30 to 9.30 CLOSED: 1 week Christmas to New Year, Easter, bank Hols MEALS: alc (main courses £16 to £24) SERVICE: 12.5%, card slips closed CARDS: Amex, Delta, MasterCard, Switch, Visa DETAILS: 100 seats. 35 seats outside. Private parties: 8 main room. Car park. Vegetarian meals. Children's helpings. No cigars/pipes in dining-room. Wheelchair access (also WC). No music

Royal China

map 13

13 Queensway, W2 4QJ — COOKING 1
TEL/FAX: (0171) 221 2535 — COST £29–£74

Views on this popular Chinatown restaurant are mixed: dim-sum are 'wonderful . . . still divine' according to an inspector; another found them disappointing overall but praised cheung fung and char siu. The menu runs through the provincial repertoire with an emphasis on Cantonese and features luxury ingredients such as lobster and abalone. Reporters have enjoyed 'wonderfully tasty and slithery' udon noodles with seafood, squid with black-bean sauce, bok choi with garlic and chives, and a 'beautifully baveuse' oyster omelette with chives containing half a dozen 'very plump' oysters. Décor is in the 'Hong Kong kitsch' mode, some finding the opulent black and gold theme over the top, and comments on service range from 'very pleasant and quite smooth' to 'neglectful'. The wine list is a thoughtful selection, starting with house French at £8.50. There is another branch at 40 Baker Street, W1; Tel: (0171) 487 3123.

CHEF: Simon Man PROPRIETOR: Pearl Investments Ltd OPEN: all week 12 to 11 (11.30 Fri and Sat, 10.30 Sun) CLOSED: 23 to 25 Dec MEALS: alc (main courses £5.50 to £45). Set L and D £22 to £28 (all minimum 2) SERVICE: 12.5% CARDS: Amex, Delta, Diners, MasterCard, Switch, Visa DETAILS: 200 seats. Private parties: 160 main room, 20 private room. Vegetarian meals. Children welcome. Music. Air-conditioned

▲ *Royal Garden Hotel, The Tenth*

map 13

2–24 Kensington High Street, W8 4PT — COOKING 6
TEL: (0171) 361 1910 FAX: (0171) 361 1921 — COST £31–£60

The views over Kensington Gardens and Hyde Park are impressive in daylight, although at night you may see nothing more than your own reflection in the windows. The '1970s disco' décor draws mixed responses: 'I was half-expecting John Travolta to come out and dance with the ever-changing colourful lights.' No matter, for the food is the real draw. Paul Farr's approach is contemporary, with Far Eastern flavourings playing an important role alongside European ones. Thus one might, if so inclined, begin with coconut and lime broth with lemon grass, coriander and prawn dumpling, and proceed to bangers and mash with onion gravy.

Ingredients are prime and fresh, a quality that shows to particularly good effect in fish: tartare of thinly sliced raw scallop and tuna, grilled sea bream with confit potatoes, or a crab and saffron pudding soufflé with watercress butter sauce. Confident execution (rack of lamb with 'beautiful texture and flavour'), careful balancing and interesting ideas (duck tortellini with chilli jam) all add to the pleasure, while desserts exploit a degree of skill: for example, a pear of 'just the correct ripeness' with dark chocolate wrapped in thin pastry, served with almond ice-cream and liquid honey. Although each member of staff might appear to come from a different country, service is 'friendly and competent'. Unusually for a large London hotel, the wine list is modern and brief, with some affordable and drinkable bottles. House Vin de Pays d'Oc is £12.50.

CHEF: Paul Farr PROPRIETOR: Goodwood Group of Hotels OPEN: Mon to Fri L 12 to 2.30, Mon to Sat D 5.30 to 11.30 CLOSED: 26 to 30 Dec, bank hols MEALS: alc (main courses £10.50 to £19.50). Set L £15.95 (2 courses) to £19.95 SERVICE: not inc, card slips closed CARDS: Amex, Diners, MasterCard, Switch, Visa DETAILS: 80 seats. Private parties: 100 main room. Vegetarian meals. Children welcome. No-smoking area. Wheelchair access (also WC). Music. Air-conditioned ACCOMMODATION: 401 rooms, all with bath/shower. TV. Phone. Air-conditioned. Room only £145 to £250. Rooms for disabled. Children welcome. Baby facilities. Afternoon teas

RSJ £ map 13

13A Coin Street, SE1 8YQ COOKING 4
TEL: (0171) 928 4554 COST £23–£41

RSJ shows no sign of sagging despite the growing weight of competition vying for the South Bank theatre- and concert goers' business. It is 'a refuge from pretension as well as from the bleak concrete environment,' writes a reader from Hampshire who was glad to be seated in the 'intimate' first-floor dining-room. Reporters cite the list of Loire wines and the outstanding value of the set-price menus as chief attractions, but the Anglo-French food, now in the hands of Peter Lloyd, has also won good notices. It 'tends to taste clearly and cleanly of what it is meant to'. Tagliatelle with caramelised scallops, asparagus, baby fennel and vanilla *jus* shows the kitchen's skill at handling a potentially fussy mix. It has also produced 'superb' mussel and saffron soup, and 'rare, as ordered' roast rump of lamb with provençale vegetables and basil mash. A new pastry chef has 'added a new dimension to desserts', including dark chocolate and confit orange terrine, and lemon-curd crème brûlée. Service can be 'frenetic but cheerful' at busy times, but most people find it to their liking.

Nigel Wilkinson does offer a few perfectly good wines from outside the Loire, but to take him up on it would seem to miss the point. Chenin Blanc may not appeal to everyone but when it is handled by Joly in Savennières or Huet in Vouvray, or made into the wonderfully long-lived sweet wines of Coteaux du Layon, Bonnezeaux and Quarts de Chaume, it is bound to win friends. And where else would one be invited to choose between seven Muscadets? House wines from Anjou are £9.95. CELLARMAN'S CHOICE: Quincy, Dom. des Ballandors 1995, £14.95; Saumur Champigny, Ch. de Villeneuve 1995, Chevalier, £15.95.

Card slips closed *in the details at the end of an entry indicates that the total on the slips of credit cards is closed when handed over for signature.*

CHEF: Peter Lloyd PROPRIETOR: Nigel Wilkinson OPEN: Mon to Fri L 12 to 2.15, Mon to Sat D 5.45 to 11 CLOSED: 3 days Christmas, bank hols exc Good Friday D MEALS: alc (main courses £11 to £14). Set L and D £14.95 (2 courses) to £15.95 SERVICE: 10% (optional), card slips closed CARDS: Amex, Delta, Diners, MasterCard, Switch, Visa DETAILS: 90 seats. 15 seats outside. Private parties: 10 main room, 20 and 30 private rooms. Vegetarian meals. Children welcome. No cigars/pipes in dining-room. Music. Air-conditioned

Rules

map 15

35 Maiden Lane, WC2E 7LB — COOKING **4**
TEL: (0171) 836 5314 FAX: (0171) 497 1081 — COST £35–£56

While the rest of London prepares for the Millennium, Rules – claiming to be the city's oldest restaurant – celebrates its bicentenary in 1998. Although long-aproned French waiters may lend the place the air of a Parisian brasserie, do not be deceived: this is a traditional British restaurant. Seasonal game (most of the customers will probably know the dates of each season) is the jewel in the crown, supplemented by freshwater fish, Aberdeen Angus steak and kidney pudding with oysters, and treacle sponge and custard.

Following the death of previous head chef Rory Kennedy, the kitchen has made an enviable acquisition in David Chambers, formerly of the Hilton, although the old Rules style continues unabashed. Braised lamb shank at an inspection dinner came with 'herby mash and a deep unctuous gravy', and griddled fallow deer with pork sausage and junipered cabbage was also highly impressive. The fancier puddings may turn out to be richer than bargained for: Sauternes-laced crème caramel with armagnac prunes that had the texture of whipped double cream. Wines may look startlingly modern, in that they are predominantly from the New World, but in Rules' terms, they count as 'wines from the former colonies' (including Bordeaux). House French is £10.95.

CHEF: David Chambers PROPRIETOR: John Mayhew OPEN: all week 12 to 11.30 CLOSED: 5 days Christmas MEALS: alc (main courses £14 to £16), Set L Sat and Sun £15.95 (2 courses), Set pre-theatre D Mon to Fri £15.95 (2 courses) SERVICE: not inc CARDS: Amex, Delta, Diners, MasterCard, Switch, Visa DETAILS: 130 seats. Private parties: 6 main room, 16 to 40 private rooms. Vegetarian meals. Children welcome. Wheelchair access (no WC). No music. Air-conditioned

Sabras £

map 12

263 Willesden High Road, NW10 2RX — COOKING **4**
TEL: (0181) 459 0340 — COST £18–£36

'Consistently the best Gujarati food in London,' writes a reporter of this family-run vegetarian eating-house in deepest Willesden. The unsophisticated décor includes pictures of Indian celebrities, framed newspaper cuttings and award certificates on the walls, and fresh flowers on each of the seven Formica-topped tables. Start with fine crispy poppadums, home-made chutneys (there are seven to choose from) and pickles, including zingingly pungent lime, and proceed to one of the farsan snacks: banana methi pakoda (fenugreek leaves and banana fried with gram flour), or – since the menu is not limited to the dishes of Gujarat – a South Indian dosai pancake.

Alternatively opt for North Indian mater paneer of cottage cheese and peas with 'distinct and harmonious spices' in creamy tomato-laced sauce. Farsan patra (rolled yam leaves intricately stuffed, steamed and fried), rarely seen on restaurant menus, manages to retain the distinctive tastes of all its components. Rice, bread and raita have all been praised, but an inspector's highest tribute was reserved for sev puri: puffed up little biscuits, 'light as air', filled with spiced potatoes and chutneys, producing 'a veritable explosion of spicy tastes and contrasting textures'. To finish, there are shrikand and kulfi. The choice of beers is tempting, and sweet lassi is described as 'one of the best I have had anywhere'. The short wine list kicks off with house Australian at £9.95.

CHEFS/PROPRIETORS: Hemant and Nalinee Desai OPEN: Tue to Sun D only 6.30 to 10.30 MEALS: alc (main courses £4 to £6.50). Set D 6.30 to 8pm £10 to £15 SERVICE: 10% CARDS: none DETAILS: 32 seats. Private parties: 32 main room. Vegetarian meals. Children welcome. Wheelchair access (no WC). Music

Saga map 15

43–44 South Molton Street, W1V 1HB NEW CHEF
TEL: (0171) 408 2236 FAX: (0171) 629 6507 COST £31–£89

This not-quite-authentic Japanese farmhouse amid the fashion boutiques of a pedestrianised street reminded one reporter of an Alpine ski lodge: dated in design, but comfortable. As the *Guide* went to press, Mr Kai replaced Mr Kikuchi as chef, but the menu has typically offered a whole page of sushi, and recommended dishes have included beef teriyaki and prawn tempura. Green tea and Kirin beer are among the drink options, there's a good selection of sake, and house wine (from a short list) is £12.90. Reports please.

CHEF: Mr Kai PROPRIETOR: Mr K. Hashimoto OPEN: Mon to Sat L 12.30 to 2.30, all week D 6.30 to 10 (6 to 9.30 Sun) CLOSED: 25 Dec, 1 Jan MEALS: alc (main courses £6.50 to £22). Set L £9 to £25, Set D £35 to £55. Cover £1. Minimum £7.50 SERVICE: not inc L, 15% D CARDS: Amex, Delta, Diners, MasterCard, Switch, Visa DETAILS: 100 seats. Private parties: 30 main room, 6 to 12 private rooms. Vegetarian meals. No cigars/pipes in dining-room. Music. Air-conditioned

Saint map 15

8 Great Newport Street, WC2H 7JA COOKING 4
TEL: (0171) 240 1551 FAX: (0171) 240 0829 COST £33–£42

This 'ultra-modern, very cool and stylish' basement dining-room, with blue corduroy banquettes, and pink and turquoise lights glowing over the bar, is 'a perfectly pleasant place to pose', one reporter found. Come early for food, though, as the place can fill up with music, smoke and people dancing as restaurant-style gives way to club-mode.

The stylish cooking of Australian Neale White shows a great deal of Eastern influence, particularly Thai, which means delivery of dishes such as kangaroo with dumplings and vegetable noodles, tempura of organic vegetables, or pan-roasted monkfish, seared scallops and red wine *jus*. Behind the fashion lies a lightness of touch, and an inspector praised chargrilled asparagus with a perfectly timed soft-poached egg and deep-fried capers, followed by 'Asian-rubbed' pink durrard (a fish, though it 'sounds like a form of massage') with brinjal (aubergine) spiced up with coriander and chilli. The meal finished with a refreshing dessert of lime sorbet with galangal. The short, something-for-everyone wine list shows a New World bias but ends with a clutch of champagnes. House wine is £10.50.

CHEF: Neale White PROPRIETORS: Eric Yu and Connie O'Donovan OPEN: Mon to Sat D only 7 to 1 CLOSED: 25 and 26 Dec, 1 Jan MEALS: Set D £17.50 (2 courses) to £21.50. Bar menu available SERVICE: Mon to Thu not inc, Fri and Sat 12.5%; 12.5% for parties of 6 or more CARDS: Amex, Delta, Diners, MasterCard, Switch, Visa DETAILS: 60 seats. Private parties: 70 main room. Vegetarian meals. No children. No pipes in dining-room. Wheelchair access (also WC). Music. Air-conditioned

St John

map 13

26 St John Street, EC1M 4AY
TEL: (0171) 251 0848 and 4998 — COOKING 5
FAX: (0171) 251 4090 — COST £28–£49

Clerkenwell and its environs have fought their way on to the map in recent years, but for one experienced reporter, even with all the choice, this is still 'the one I like best'. The plain white converted smokehouse is about as spartan and functional as a restaurant can get. The whole idea is no-frills, whether in décor, food or service. 'I simply love the "back-to-basics" style of British cooking in friendly and unstuffy surroundings.' At first sight this is 'not the place for vegetarians or the squeamish', according to one who cited dried salted pig's liver, and tripe and onions, in evidence. But in addition to duck hearts on toast, and bloodcake with fried egg, there might be pigeon with chard, skate with black butter, or baked tomato with cheese crottin.

The logo is a pig, and so well bred it might appear in *Debrett*: smoked Gloucester Old Spot with chutney, or roast Tamworth with rape that was 'far superior to the norm' with 'brilliant crackling'. 'They try hard, and succeed part of the time,' reckoned one reporter. Roast bone marrow with parsley salad continues to draw plaudits 'and you get to use every implement on the table to finish this dish'. Bread is good, and desserts are as straightforward as rhubarb fool or stuffed baked apple. Decent, up-to-date and inexpensive wines offer relatively few half-bottles but plenty by the glass. Prices start at £10 a bottle.

CHEF: Fergus Henderson PROPRIETORS: Fergus Henderson, Jon Spiteri and Trevor Gulliver OPEN: Mon to Fri L 12 to 3, Mon to Sat D 6 to 11.30 CLOSED: 25 Dec and 1 Jan MEALS: alc (main courses £8 to £15) SERVICE: not inc; 12.5% (optional) for parties of 6 or more CARDS: Amex, Delta, Diners, MasterCard, Switch, Visa DETAILS: 100 seats. Private parties: 130 main room, 22 private room. Vegetarian meals. Children's helpings. No music

Salloos

map 14

62–64 Kinnerton Street, SW1X 8ER — COOKING 4
TEL: (0171) 235 4444 FAX: (0171) 259 5703 — COST £27–£62

'The cooking is fine enough to convert a conservative French gastronome' ran one report about this upper-crust Pakistani restaurant. Both Muhammad Salahuddin (aka Salloo) and his head chef have been here since the place opened in 1977, which no doubt helps to explain its consistency. The mood inside is pleasantly intimate, with attractive oriental paintings, a warm colour scheme and well-chosen fabrics adding a touch of luxury. There's a subtlety and elegance about the cooking which set the place apart from most of its rivals, and the kitchen takes its cue from the traditions of home cooking. Among the specialities, look for tender and superbly flavoured tandoori lamb chops, gurda masala (chopped lambs' kidneys 'in special hot spices'), and chicken karahi. Dhals and assorted vegetable dishes are out of the top drawer, as is the 'aromatic' rice cooked in stock, and crisp, light and fluffy nan bread. To finish, try carrot halva, which is served warm and decorated with silver leaf. If there are quibbles, they have to do with the high prices and what has been dubbed 'pushy' service. Not surprisingly, wine doesn't come cheap either, but there are some affordable Corney & Barrow selections to keep the bill in check. House wine is £12.50.

CHEF: Abdul Aziz PROPRIETOR: Muhammad Salahuddin OPEN: Mon to Sat 12 to 2.30, 7 to 11.15 CLOSED: 25 and 26 Dec MEALS: alc (main courses £11 to £17). Set L £16, Set D £25. Cover £1.50 SERVICE: 12.5% (optional), card slips closed CARDS: Amex, Delta, Diners, MasterCard, Switch, Visa DETAILS: 65 seats. Private parties: 65 main room. Vegetarian meals. No children under 8. No cigars/pipes in dining-room. No music. Air-conditioned

Les Saveurs

map 15

37A Curzon Street, W1Y 7AF — COOKING 6

TEL: (0171) 491 8919 FAX: (0171) 491 3658 — COST £38–£68

At one point Les Saveurs must have felt like a ping-pong ball as it was batted back and forth between the empires of Sir Rocco Forte and Marco Pierre White, even if that was sometimes only on paper. The latest we have is that Marco is in possession of the ball: a corporate 1980s basement dining-room, with blond wood panelling, lots of mirrors, green cushioned chairs, deep pile carpet and vast amounts of elbow room. Mark Wishart, who has worked for Marco, brings a typical mix of classical and contemporary ideas to the generous and luxury-strewn *carte*. First and main courses offer around nine or ten choices each, and some of the dishes may be familiar to MPW-watchers, including perhaps parfait of foie gras and chicken livers, or oysters en gelée with watercress.

Fish is one of the strengths, judging by an impeccable fillet of sea bass stuffed with a soft mushroom paste, served with a mix of tomatoes and potatoes with tarragon and olive oil. A dollop of béarnaise mousseline 'was scooped out from a silver container on to my plate by the waiter', and the dish had 'all the right flavours and a good sense of balance'. Wishart is helped by 'outstanding' ingredients, including a Bresse pigeon cooked rare, and is obviously a safe pair of hands, since he can also turn out an unusual ragoût of langoustines and pig's trotter with an excellent mustard beurre blanc.

The excitement here has less to do with innovation, and more to do with a sound grasp of technique, as in a mango soufflé with passion-fruit sauce: 'fine texture, perfect delivery, good flavours'. Service is young, male, French and could be improved, although our inspector may have caught it before it fully settled down. The massive wine list features many aristocratic bottles and high prices. Among the few wines below £30 are house red and white at £19.

See inside the front cover for an explanation of the symbols used at the tops of entries.

CHEF: Mark Wishart PROPRIETOR: Marco Pierre White OPEN: Mon to Fri L 12 to 2.30, Mon to Sat D 7 to 11 CLOSED: bank hols MEALS: Set L £21.50 to £38, Set D £38 SERVICE: not inc CARDS: Amex, Delta, MasterCard, Switch, Visa DETAILS: 60 seats. Private parties: 12 private room. Children's helpings. No pipes in dining-room. No music. Air-conditioned

▲ *The Savoy, Grill Room* map 15

The Strand, WC2R 0EU NEW CHEF
TEL: (0171) 836 4343 FAX: (0171) 240 6040 COST £48–£87

More 'seventies posh' than starched Edwardian, the Grill Room exudes 'a relaxed patrician hum' of contentment: if they wrap the Melba toast in a napkin, and give the butter a refreshing shallow bath in its little dish, imagine what they can do for you. As the *Guide* went to press, Simon Scott arrived from the Ritz to replace David Sharland, although it is unlikely that the weight of tradition will be much disturbed. This is the place to come for regular weekly offerings from the trolley – Lancashire hotpot Monday lunch, beef Wellington Tuesday dinner – as well as an Anglo-Italian *carte* that might take in omelette Arnold Bennett, risotto of langoustines, or roast woodpigeon. Formal service means that it can take three waiters to serve coffee, but they are cheerful and chatty. The wine list, shared with the River Restaurant (see entry below), concentrates on high-quality clarets and burgundies at equally high prices, but anyone with around £30 to spend will find plenty to entertain. Ten house wines start at £17.95.

Simon Scott also takes charge of Upstairs, a small, narrow room overlooking the entrance that deals in informal and speedy eating without the full-dress majesty of the other dining-rooms: tuna tartare on wasabi and avocado purée perhaps, or tempura of monkfish. Prices on the short wine list are high, with ten good wines offered by the glass from £4.95. Reports on both venues please.

CHEF: Simon Scott PROPRIETOR: Savoy Group plc OPEN: Mon to Fri L 12.30 to 2.30, Mon to Sat D 6 to 11.15 CLOSED: Aug, bank hols MEALS: alc (main courses £13 to £23). Set D (6 to 7pm) £27.95 (2 courses) to £29.75 SERVICE: not inc, card slips closed CARDS: Amex, Delta, Diners, MasterCard, Switch, Visa DETAILS: 100 seats. Private parties: 20 main room. Vegetarian meals. Children welcome. Jacket and tie. No pipes in dining-room. Wheelchair access (also WC). Music. Air-conditioned ACCOMMODATION: 202 rooms, all with bath/shower. TV. Phone. Air-conditioned. Room only £210 to £750. Rooms for disabled. Children welcome. Baby facilities by arrangement. Afternoon teas. Swimming-pool (*The Which? Hotel Guide*)

▲ *The Savoy, River Restaurant* map 15

The Strand, WC2R 0EU COOKING 4
TEL: (0171) 836 4343 FAX: (0171) 240 6040 COST £45–£123

At the back of the Savoy, on the opposite side to the Strand, the River Restaurant enjoys a wide-angled view of the Thames and the Embankment Gardens. It is a distinctly more palatial space than the Grill Room (see entry above), and evening patrons can dance themselves dizzy to the old-fangled band that plays every night bar Sunday. This is definitely old school, with a dessert trolley to prove it.

Anton Edelmann's menus have, however, made a good stab at keeping up with the world outside. There may be apple and onion rings with the calf's liver, and chateaubriand with béarnaise at £54 for two, but there is also scallop ravioli, asparagus risotto, and turbot in wasabi butter sauce with summer truffles. First courses and fish seem to hold most interest – lobster salad with a light curry dressing, or spinach and haddock soufflé with quail's eggs – although few other places would serve pig's trotter as a starter (here filled with smoked ham and sage). That said, scant portions can cause sulks at these prices. French cheeses are a better bet than most of the sweet things. The wine list is shared with the Grill Room (see entry above).

CHEF: Anton Edelmann PROPRIETOR: Savoy Group plc OPEN: all week 12.30 to 2.30, 7 to 11.30 (10.30 Sun) MEALS: Set L Mon to Fri £28.75 (2 courses) to £35, Set L Sat and Sun £22.50 (2 courses) to £28, Set D Sun to Thur £31.50 (2 courses) to £80, Set D Fri and Sat £33.50 to £42.50 SERVICE: net prices, card slips closed CARDS: Amex, Delta, Diners, MasterCard, Switch, Visa DETAILS: 160 seats. Private parties: 50 main room, 6 to 60 private rooms. Vegetarian meals. Children's helpings. Jacket and tie. No pipes in dining-room. Wheelchair access (also WC). Music. Air-conditioned ACCOMMODATION: See entry above for details

Searcy's at the Barbican map 13

Level 2, Barbican Centre, Silk Street, EC2Y 8DS COOKING 5
TEL: (0171) 588 3008 FAX: (0171) 382 7247 COST £30–£62

The L shaped room, looking out over artificial lakes to St Giles Church, has a new livery, with plenty of light maplewood and brushed steel in evidence, and some screening to break up the space. For one reporter 'it made the normally drab Barbican almost interesting'. Searcy's purpose is obviously to feed concert and theatre-goers, but it does much more than that. The set-price menu, for example, with a choice of three items per course, is designed for speed and aimed at pre-performance diners, but as fast food goes this is encouraging stuff: brandade of salt-cod with a poached egg, breast and ballottine of chicken with salted belly-pork and salsa verde, and lemon bavarois with blackberry compote.

Richard Corrigan has been joined by Tom Illic from Stepping Stone (see entry, London), and the ideas come thick and fast: goats' cheese and potato terrine, steamed foie gras with split-peas and ham hock, red mullet with truffled turnip purée, and a typically earthy dish of pork fillet, crubeens, black pudding and pig's cheek served with turnip sauerkraut. Among fish, mackerel seems a favourite, perhaps served with wilted cabbage and smoked bacon butter. Poultry and game are well handled, including pink-roasted squab pigeon with buttered leeks and Serrano ham, although ups and downs in standards have disappointed some reporters. Desserts, for example, might be improved, and more experienced service would be welcome. Fifty-plus wines are chosen carefully (try the Australian reds), and some are served by the glass and by just-short-of-a-half-litre pot. Prices start at £9.95.

CHEFS: Richard Corrigan and Tom Illic PROPRIETOR: Searcy Tansley OPEN: Sun to Fri L 12 to 2.45, all week D 5 to 10.30 (7 Sun) CLOSED: 25 Dec MEALS: alc (main courses £15 to £19.50). Set L and D £17.50 (2 courses) to £20.50 SERVICE: not inc CARDS: Amex, Delta, Diners, MasterCard, Switch, Visa DETAILS: 130 seats. Private parties: 130 main room. Vegetarian meals. Children's helpings. No-smoking area. Wheelchair access (also WC). Music. Air-conditioned

See inside the front cover for an explanation of the symbols used at the tops of entries.

755 Fulham Road

NEW ENTRY map 12

755 Fulham Road, SW6 5UU COOKING **6**
TEL: (0171) 371 0755 FAX: (0171) 371 0695 COST £23–£57

The address-as-name is reminiscent of those modern paintings simply labelled 'Untitled', and the striking interior of Alan and Georgina Thompson's new restaurant at the far end of Fulham Road features a long blue wave on one wall, banquette seating, and handsome table settings. Anything that is not blue is yellow. Modern French is the kitchen's style – Alan Thompson once worked at Turner's (see entry, London) – and it might take in a mille-feuille of snails with wild mushrooms and Puy lentils, ravioli of langoustines with broad-bean casserole, or rillettes of smoked haddock with soft poached quail's eggs.

Thompson's training shows in a dish of 'fresh, meaty' seared scallops sandwiched between wafers of deep-fried aubergine, accompanied by a delicate salt cod brandade. Another successful vertical construction began with a heap of rocket, on which was perched an unwieldy-looking but crisp Yorkshire pudding, in turn supporting a slab of griddled foie gras. A combination of textural contrasts and a powerful madeira gravy helped to make it 'one of those dishes I'll remember for years'. Fish constitutes a generous proportion of what's on offer, including smoked whiting (with asparagus, poached egg and hollandaise), and there might be a game dish such as roast venison with wild mushrooms and garlic potato purée.

Desserts tend to work such familiar themes as pear Tatin or summer pudding, and the version of death by chocolate is a platter containing five artfully crafted weapons with which to carry out the fatal deed. As to service, 'relaxed professionalism would best describe the overall feeling'. Wines are divided about equally between Old and New Worlds, the majority pegged commendably below £20. House French is £9.50.

CHEF: Alan Thompson PROPRIETORS: Alan and Georgina Thompson OPEN: Tue to Sun L 12.30 (12 Sun) to 2.30 (4 Sun), Mon to Sat D 7 to 11 CLOSED: 2 weeks Aug, 5 days Christmas, 3 days Easter, bank hols MEALS: alc (main courses £11.50 to £17.50), Set L £10 (2 courses) to £14, Set D £18 (2 courses) to £22 SERVICE: not inc CARDS: Amex, Delta, MasterCard, Switch, Visa DETAILS: 60 seats. Private parties: 35 main room, 35 private room. Vegetarian meals. Children's helpings and Sun L children's menu. Wheelchair access (no WC). Air-conditioned

Shaw's 🍷

map 14

119 Old Brompton Road, SW7 3RN COOKING **2**
TEL: (0171) 373 7774/4472 FAX: (0171) 370 5102 COST £31–£58

Shaw's is smart enough to do South Kensington proud, full of luxuriously heavy soft furnishings and 'an atmosphere of wealth that doesn't just hang in the curtains'. Clientele look moneyed, but a couple who fancied themselves a trifle underdressed in the event were treated with the utmost courtesy. Gerald and Frances Atkins moved to the Yorke Arms at Ramsgill (see Round-up entry) at the beginning of 1997, and the new chef is Jean-Pierre Venuto. The relaxed, modern feel of the menus preserves continuity with the earlier era. A light, clear vegetable consommé, infused with lovage, was 'quietly delicious', while sea bass with crisp-fried saffron noodles and a sauce of puréed asparagus also demonstrated a sensitive touch. More complex was a tower of courgette slices and French beans that accompanied cannelloni, and beef fillet served on spaghetti squash with artichoke chips. Desserts use bold flavours to good effect, as in mango and passion-fruit coulis with white chocolate mousse, or a fluffy liquorice-flavoured sponge that supported a praline bavarois. Tasting notes are a feature of the well-chosen wine list, which offers a good range of quality bins at reasonable prices. House French is £14.50. CELLARMAN'S CHOICE: St-Aubin 1994, Gérard Thomas, £23.50; Haut-Médoc, Ch. Tour du Haut-Moulin 1989, £21.95.

CHEF: Jean-Pierre Venuto PROPRIETORS: Sir Neil and Lady Shaw, David Banks and Torunn Fieldhouse OPEN: Mon to Fri L 12 to 2, Mon to Sat D 7 to 10 CLOSED: 1 week Christmas, 1 week Easter, 2 weeks August MEALS: Set L £15 (2 courses) to £18.50, Set D £29.95 (2 courses) to £32.95. Pre- and post-theatre D £15 (2 courses) to £18.50 Mon to Sat 5.30 to 7pm and 10 to 11pm SERVICE: not inc CARDS: Amex, Delta, Diners, MasterCard, Switch, Visa DETAILS: 45 seats. 10 seats outside. Private parties: 40 main room. Vegetarian meals. Children welcome. Wheelchair access (no WC). No music. Air-conditioned

Simply Nico

map 13

48A Rochester Row, SW1P 1JU — COOKING 4

TEL: (0171) 630 8061 FAX: (0171) 828 8541 — COST £34–£53

'Reasonable value for serious brasserie food prepared with quality ingredients,' noted one visitor, 'in an area where it would probably be easy to take advantage of expense-account diners.' And the House of Commons is not far away. On-the-ball service (included in the price) from well-trained and obliging staff compensates to some extent for the closely set tables in this sunny yellow room, and the rich and hearty food has a modern European feel with a classical tilt.

The comfortable, safe and well-tried style goes in for tomato and basil risotto, grilled lamb leg steak with ratatouille, and terrine of prune and armagnac ice-cream with plum sauce. Presentation is appealingly simple, with no fussy garnishes to distract attention from good-quality materials, although the food can be rich. The kitchen is undoubtedly skilled – first-rate pastry, satisfying boudin blanc, crisp-skinned duck – but an inspector came away with the impression that more 'edge' might be welcome. Fifty-plus varied and mostly youthful wines suit the circumstances and maintain a sense of proportion. Wines by the glass start at £4.

CHEF: Richard Hugill PROPRIETOR: Restaurant Partnership plc OPEN: Mon to Fri L 12 to 2, Mon to Sat D 7 to 11 CLOSED: 2 weeks Christmas, bank hols MEALS: Set L £22 (2 courses) to £25, Set D £27 SERVICE: net prices, card slips closed CARDS: Amex, Delta, Diners, MasterCard, Switch, Visa DETAILS: 45 seats. Vegetarian meals. Children welcome. No cigars/pipes in dining-room. No music. Air-conditioned

Singapore Garden

map 13

83–83A Fairfax Road, NW6 4DY — COOKING 2

TEL: (0171) 328 5314 FAX: (0171) 624 0656 — COST £27–£53

A cherry blossom tree stands at the front window of this 'truly consistent local restaurant', and the dining-room emphasises the garden theme with exotic plants and floral displays, green colour schemes and prints on the walls. The atmosphere is immediately relaxing, and the mood is helped along by an all-female team dressed in colourful blouses. An interesting range of Chinese dishes appears on the menu, but the strength of the kitchen is its dedication to authentic Singaporean and Straits cooking. 'The laksa soup is a must', as are 'Mrs Lim's chilli mussels', and steamboat is 'a delightful way to spend a couple of hours eating too much and ending up with great, refreshing soup'. From the list of specials, reporters have commended deep-fried chiew yim soft-shell crabs, 'wonderfully gelatinous' teochew braised pig's trotters ('rustic and lip-sticking all the way'), and kang kong blachan (Chinese hollow-stalk spinach with a fiery prawn-paste sauce). To finish, try sago pudding with 'gorgeous' palm sugar and coconut milk. Drink Tiger beer or something from the 'much-improved' wine list. House wine is £10.25. Singapore Garden II is at 154–156 Gloucester Place, London NW1 6DT; Tel: (0171) 723 8233.

CHEF: Mrs S.K. Lim PROPRIETORS: the Lim family OPEN: all week 12 to 2.45, 6 to 10.45 (11.15 Fri and Sat) CLOSED: 1 week Christmas MEALS: alc (main courses £5.50 to £20). Set L £5.95 (2 courses) to £8, Set D £17.50 (minimum 2) to £30 (minimum 4) SERVICE: 12.5% (optional), card slips closed CARDS: Amex, Delta, Diners, MasterCard, Switch, Visa DETAILS: 100 seats. 10 seats outside. Private parties: 50 main room, 50 private room. Vegetarian meals. Children welcome. No cigars in dining-room. Music. Air-conditioned

Snows on the Green map 12

166 Shepherd's Bush Road, W6 7PB COOKING 3
TEL: (0171) 603 2142 FAX: (0171) 602 7553 COST £26–£42

Sebastian Snow, having sold his Battersea establishment, is concentrating on keeping Hammersmith and Shepherd's Bush locals happy, and to this end has expanded into the next-door premises. The restaurant has always had a sunny disposition, with lavender on the walls and pictures evoking summers in the South of France. The food, which appeared to lose some of its vibrancy last year, appears to be perking up. Dishes inspired by Provence and Italy are the stars on the *carte*, including squid ink risotto, and roast lamb chump with Piedmontese peppers and anchovy sauce.

There is a modern British contingent, too, with smoked salmon, beetroot and horseradish, 'an informal assembly of hearty ingredients' that worked well. Spicy celeriac pancake couscous with mango and lime salsa is a dish to satisfy fusion-fanciers. Robust stews and soups in winter make sensible use of available produce: tender venison casserole, for instance, served with gnocchi-style dumplings for mopping up the rich juices. 'Superb' blood-orange tart had a moist, orange-flecked filling 'rather like a rich and eggy Bakewell tart'. 'Pleasant, knowledgeable staff' look after things well. Around 40 mostly French and New World wines have been carefully chosen. House French is £9.50.

CHEFS: Sebastian Snow and Mathew Read PROPRIETOR: Sebastian Snow OPEN: Sun to Fri L, Mon to Sat D 12 to 3, 6 to 11 CLOSED: 24 to 30 Dec MEALS: alc (main courses £9.50 to £12). Set L £12.50 (2 courses) to £15.50 SERVICE: not inc CARDS: Amex, Delta, Diners, MasterCard, Switch, Visa DETAILS: 75 seats. Private parties: 75 main room, 30 private room. Vegetarian meals. Children's helpings. No cigars/pipes in dining room. Wheelchair access (no WC). Music. Air-conditioned

The Guide *always appreciates hearing about changes of chef or owner.*

Soho Soho

map 15

11–13 Frith Street, W1V 5TS — NEW CHEF

TEL: (0171) 494 3491 FAX: (0171) 437 3091 — COST £26–£56

Smack in the middle of Soho, and part of the Chez Gérard group, which also owns Livebait (see entry), this two-floored restaurant has traditionally taken its inspiration from Provence. The ground-floor rotisserie is a permanent hive of activity, with live music contributing to the air of letting-it-all-hang-out, while the first floor offers a calmer persepective on street life and a more considered menu. Just as the *Guide* went to press, however, Laurent Lebeau left to take up a position at Chez Gérard, 64 Bishopsgate Street, London EC2, Tel: (0171) 588 1200, and Stephan Baille took over. We welcome reports. Wines from France, Italy and Spain, meanwhile, echo the Mediterranean thrust of the food, and prices start at £9.95 on the first floor, £8.95 downstairs.

CHEF: Stephan Baille PROPRIETOR: Groupe Chez Gérard OPEN: restaurant Mon to Fri L 12 to 2.45, Mon to Sat D 6 to 11.45; rotisserie all week 12 noon to 12.45am (10.30pm Sun) CLOSED: 25 Dec MEALS: alc (main courses rotisserie £6.50 to £13, restaurant £8.50 to £14.50). Set D restaurant 6 to 7.30pm and 10.15 to 11.30pm £12.50 to £15.50. Cover (restaurant only) £1.50 SERVICE: 12.5% (optional) CARDS: Amex, Delta, Diners, MasterCard, Switch, Visa DETAILS: 62 seats. Private parties: 30 main room, 60 private room. Car park. Vegetarian meals. Children welcome. No cigars/pipes in dining room. Music. Air-conditioned

Sonny's

map 12

94 Church Road, SW13 0DQ — COOKING 5

TEL: (0181) 748 0393 FAX: (0181) 748 2698 — COST £23–£44

The long, cream room has stark, functional tables and no carpet, but is saved from minimalist overkill by, among other things, Roman busts, prints of Mickey Mouse, and an outline of a man made entirely of hair. Now in the hands of Leigh Diggins, the cooking remains suitably unpretentious, but has shed some of its more exotic elements. Just as the menus and wine list come from recycled paper, so classic European dishes are revisited, but with a special twist. Duck confit comes with loganberry vinaigrette, and tarte Tatin might be made with peaches.

Roast sea bass with peas, baby artichokes, dandelion leaves and lemon oil shows how well the kitchen handles intricate combinations, while strawberry and champagne jelly, with lots of chopped fruit suspended in it and strawberry coulis and cream swirled around, is a simple idea that spawns complex flavours. Vegetables tend to be al dente, and service has been judged 'absolutely perfect'. The short wine list has a trio of reds from the American north-west but only one claret – at £50. House wines are £9.50.

CHEF: Leigh Diggins PROPRIETOR: Rebecca Mascarenhas OPEN: all week L 12.30 to 2.30, Mon to Sat D 7.30 to 11 CLOSED: Christmas, bank hols MEALS: alc (main courses £8.50 to £13). Set L £12 (2 courses) SERVICE: not inc CARDS: Amex, Delta, MasterCard, Switch, Visa DETAILS: 100 seats. Private parties: 24 private room. Vegetarian meals. Children's helpings. No cigars/pipes in dining-room. Wheelchair access (no WC). No music. Air-conditioned

indicates that there has been a change of chef since last year's Guide, *and the Editor has judged that the change is of sufficient interest to merit the reader's attention.*

Sotheby's Café ⚘

NEW ENTRY map 15

34 New Bond Street, W1A 2AA COOKING 3
TEL: (0171) 408 5077 COST £25–£35

Sited in one of the world's swankiest shopping streets, this is 'about as upmarket as cafés come', though it is little more than a recess off the main hallway: 'a bit like eating in a railway carriage, albeit on the Orient Express'. They don't hold up plates of food and ask 'What am I bid?' nor is there any need to worry about raising a hand to attract a waiter and ending up with a Gaugin: service is prompt from 'courteous and extremely chic staff'. The short *carte* relies more on good shopping than complex cooking, and high-quality materials are allowed to shine: in a generous helping of asparagus with fragrant herb butter, for instance, or in sweet potato pancakes with sour cream, watercress, red onions and toasted pine-nuts.

Lobster club sandwich, a regular fixture, is a dainty version: the brioche 'light and well textured', the lobster 'sweet and succulent'. Well-kept cheeses are served with cakes, or there may be indulgent desserts such as blackcurrant and almond tart with clotted cream. The wine list, a short but canny selection chosen by Master of Wine Serena Sutcliffe, head of Sotheby's wine department, opens the bidding at £9.95 and keeps mostly under £20.

CHEF: Caroline Crumby PROPRIETOR: Sotheby's OPEN: Mon to Fri L only 12 to 2.30 CLOSED: Christmas, last 2 weeks Aug MEALS: alc (main courses £9.50 to £14) SERVICE: net prices, card slips closed CARDS: Amex, Delta, MasterCard, Switch, Visa DETAILS: 40 seats. Private parties: 40 main room. Vegetarian meals. No smoking in dining-room. Wheelchair access (also WC). No music. Air-conditioned

The Square 🍷

NEW ENTRY map 15

6–10 Bruton Street, W1X 7AG COOKING 7
TEL: (0171) 495 7100 FAX: (0171) 495 7150 COST £39–£70

This appears as a new entry only because it was about to move premises as the last edition of the *Guide* was being prepared. In February 1997 it swapped St James's for Mayfair, exchanging Christie's and Fortnum's for new neighbours Sotheby's and Cartier. Once through the glass doors 'the feeling of total design engulfs you in a bold sweep', from parquet floor through orange and 'brown-as-the-new-black' colours, to the enormous, striking, abstract canvasses by Deborah Lanyon that dominate the space and give it vibrancy.

These expensive decorative trimmings are echoed in the enticing, symmetrical (eight choices per course) menu full of luxury items: roasted or terrined foie gras, langoustines, and calves' sweetbreads, all brought into fashionable congruence with raviolis, lasagnes, confits, sausages, mousselines and caramelised vegetables. Cappuccinos are taken for granted, although not always carried off with the necessary verve and attack. Cannelloni of lobster with shellfish cappuccino, however, was a 'glorious combination of textures and positive flavours' for one reporter; and in case there is any doubt about its luxury status, a spoonful of Sevruga caviare puts your mind at rest.

When the kitchen's sights are focused it can come up with some very fine cooking, from a 'robust and filling' dish of roast Bresse pigeon with ravioli of foie gras, to a large rectangular fillet of roast sea bass resting on vivid red puddles of pungent tomato concasse, together with morels, spinach, shallots, garlic, and a swirly tower of tagliatelle. Although there were a few lapses at inspection, there is undeniable skill in the kitchen, not least in a light, foamy, well-risen praline soufflé with Grand Marnier, and in the 'great' breads and first rate petits fours.

Service is disciplined and professional, and if things are done 'with stylised charm' there is also a degree of personal attention. The lengthy wine list boasts a fine collection of vintage clarets, and positively shows off when it comes to burgundies (well, we call 16 Puligny-Montrachets showing off). This even extends to the New World, which provides four vintages of Henschke's Hill of Grace Shiraz. For lower prices look to regional France. More dry wines by the glass would help, but half-bottles are in good supply, and a sommelier's selection of eight French wines opens at £18.50. CELLARMAN'S CHOICE: Meursault 'Les Narvaux' 1994, Olivier Leflaive, £45; Moulin-à-Vent Roche Grés 1995, Dom. du Vissoux, £24.50.

CHEF: Philip Howard PROPRIETORS: Nigel Platts-Martin and Philip Howard OPEN: Mon to Fri L 12 to 3, all week D 7 to 11 (10 Sun) CLOSED: 25 and 26 Dec MEALS: alc (main courses £13.50 to £16.50). Set D £39. BYO £15 SERVICE: 12.5% (optional), card slips closed CARDS: Amex, Delta, Diners, MasterCard, Switch, Visa DETAILS: 80 seats. Private parties: 80 main room, 18 private room. Vegetarian meals. Children's helpings. Smart dress preferred. No cigars/pipes in dining-room. Wheelchair access (also WC). No music. Air-conditioned

Sree Krishna £

map 12

192–194 Tooting High Street, SW17 0SF — COOKING 1
TEL: (0181) 672 4250 and 6903 — COST £13–£34

'Kerala tiffin', 'home-made specialities' and 'exotic Cochin specialities' are some of the menu headings at this South Indian, mainly vegetarian restaurant. Variations on dosai (thin lentil and rice-flour pancakes) remain popular, while steamed and fried dumplings made from lentils, semolina and rice flour make appetising starters or satisfying snacks. Meat and prawn curries tend to be ordinary, but 'chilly chicken', and chicken doplaza have been praised, and the Keralan specialities, among them masala dosai and uthappam, are consistently reliable. Service is generally friendly and efficient. House wines, from Italy, are £7 a bottle, £1.60 a glass, and, for those wanting something more authentic, there's lassi and Cobra beer.

CHEF: Terab Ali PROPRIETORS: T. Haridas and family OPEN: all week 12 to 3, 6 to 11 (12 Fri and Sat) CLOSED: 25 and 26 Dec MEALS: alc (main courses £2 to £6.50). BYO £1.50 SERVICE: 10%, card slips closed CARDS: Amex, Diners, MasterCard, Visa DETAILS: 120 seats. Private parties: 60 main room, 60 private room. Vegetarian meals. Children welcome. No smoking in dining-room. Wheelchair access (also WC). Music. Air-conditioned

Sri Siam

map 15

16 Old Compton Street, W1V 5PE — COOKING 3
TEL: (0171) 434 3544 FAX: (0171) 287 1311 — COST £20–£49

Consistency remains a strength of this Thai restaurant in gastronomically saturated Soho. The dining-room has a touch of contemporary elegance with its stencilled designs, tapestries and ethnic artefacts, and the kitchen works to a menu of around 60 dishes bolstered by an enterprising contingent of vegetarian options ranging from clear cucumber soup to stir-fried pumpkin with garlic. The plate of half a dozen hors d'oeuvre is a perennial favourite with carnivorous customers, and the popular special fried rice is served in a hollowed-out pineapple. Other dishes worth noting are moo takrai (spicy pork balls on a skewer of lemon grass), neua prig sod sai (fresh chilli peppers filled with minced beef and topped with yellow bean sauce), and crab claws cooked in a claypot with herbs and vermicelli, not to mention curries and salads. Set lunches and dinners are good value and a useful sampler of the full repertoire. Drink tea, Singha Thai beer or something from the modern wine list. House wine is £8.95. There is a second branch at 85 London Wall, EC2; Tel: (0171) 628 5772.

CHEF: W. Rodpradith PROPRIETOR: Oriental Restaurant Group Ltd OPEN: Mon to Sat L 12 to 3, all week D 6 to 11.15 (10.30 Sun) CLOSED: 24 to 26 Dec, 1 Jan MEALS: alc (main courses £6.50 to £9.50). Set L £11.50, Set D £16.80 SERVICE: 12.5% (optional), card slips closed CARDS: Amex, Diners, MasterCard, Switch, Visa DETAILS: 150 seats. Private parties: 100 main room, 20 and 35 private rooms. Vegetarian meals. Children welcome. Wheelchair access (no WC). Music. Air-conditioned

▲ *Stafford* — map 15

St James's Place, SW1A 1NG — COOKING **3**
TEL: (0171) 493 0111 FAX: (0171) 493 7121 — COST £31–£80

The Stafford is geared to the top end of the business and tourist trade, marking out its Englishness partly with appearance – sporting memorabilia in the bar make a fascinating backdrop – and partly with food. It follows the customary old-fashioned route of many London hotels, offering a daily lunchtime dish from the trolley: Lancashire hotpot on Mondays, fish pie on Fridays. The 'Classics' *carte* also deals in caviare, smoked salmon, grilled Aberdeen Angus steak, and treacle tart with clotted cream, all of which may seem oddly institutional to those who remember Chris Oakes's style at his former restaurant in Stroud.

By its side, however, is a more contemporary streak featuring shellfish risotto with truffle oil, or deep-fried skate wing with pickled samphire. This 'New' menu, clearly in a different mould, gives the kitchen some more interesting material to work with, perhaps in the form of a salad of sliced pigeon breast and black pudding. New desserts, such as prune and armagnac ice-cream on Grand Marnier-flavoured orange segments, appear to have the edge over Classics. The monumental wine list of classical proportions and venerable vintages has an eye for quality, but is not a bargain-hunter's paradise. House French is £15.50.

CHEFS: Chris Oakes and Peter Williams PROPRIETOR: The Stafford Hotel OPEN: Sun to Fri L 12.30 to 2.15, all week D 6.30 to 10.15 MEALS: alc (main courses £17.50 to £28). Set L £20.50 (2 courses) to £23.50, Set D £20.95 (2 courses) to £26.25 SERVICE: net prices, card slips closed CARDS: Amex, Diners, MasterCard, Switch, Visa DETAILS: 50 seats. Private parties: 44 main room. Vegetarian meals. Children welcome. Jacket and tie. No pipes in dining-room. Wheelchair access (also WC). Music. Air-conditioned ACCOMMODATION: 80 rooms, all with bath/shower. TV. Phone. Air-conditioned. Room only £190 to £375. Rooms for disabled. Children welcome. Baby facilities. Afternoon teas

Stephen Bull 🍷

map 15

5–7 Blandford Street, W1H 3AA — COOKING 6
TEL: (0171) 486 9696 FAX: (0171) 490 3128 — COST £33–£51

The neat, smart restaurant just off Marylebone High Street looks 'minimalish rather than minimalist', with wooden floors, black chairs against white cloths, and pale washes of colour on the walls. Mercy Fenton left at the end of 1996 and John Hardwick took over, but the style remains in Stephen Bull mould – contemporary, gently innovative, and predominantly European – with a choice of seven items per course. There are riches, including a rather classical terrine of foie gras layered with artichoke and served with onion compote, but there is also an attractive lightness about much of the food, and sensible use of good-quality but less-mainstream materials such as hake, or 'moist, tender, tasty' boned saddle of rabbit on a green ragoût of broad beans, peas and Savoy cabbage.

This is not arty food, but it is skilled, and impresses for its sound grasp of principles: for example, a terrine of mackerel, potato and lentils (dubbed 'fish, chips and peas') taking advantage of the affinity between starchy vegetable and oily fish, or an exemplary glistening pig's trotter at inspection that was admirably cooked, enough to soften the gelatinous bits, yet not so much as to dry it out. There is an absence of showy gestures, and even truffle oil is used in an appropriate context: to aromatise an otherwise rustic dish of gnocchi with 'crushed' butter-beans and pieces of chicken.

Desserts are a high point, judging by an intriguing hot rhubarb fondant (a sort of free-standing crumble) served with mascarpone sorbet, and a dish called chocolate 'devastation': scoops of ice-cream made with high-quality dark chocolate, with thin planks of brittle chocolate laid on top, surrounded by raspberries in a coulis. Bread is good. Eighty-plus wines are carefully chosen, the great majority over £20, half-bottles are fair, and around ten wines are available by the glass. House Sauvignon de Touraine is £14, red Languedoc £15.50.

CHEF: John Hardwick PROPRIETOR: Stephen Bull OPEN: Mon to Fri L 12.15 to 2.30, Mon to Sat D 6.30 to 10.30 CLOSED: 10 days Christmas, bank hols MEALS: alc (main courses £10 to £15). BYO £5 SERVICE: not inc, card slips closed CARDS: Amex, MasterCard, Switch, Visa DETAILS: 55 seats. Private parties: 15 main room. Vegetarian meals. Children's helpings. No cigars/pipes in dining-room. Wheelchair access (no WC). No music. Air-conditioned

Stephen Bull St Martin's Lane 🍷

NEW ENTRY map 15

12 Upper St Martin's Lane, WC2H 9DL — COOKING 5
TEL: (0171) 379 7811 FAX: (0171) 490 3128 — COST £29–£48

'Another Stephen Bull, another stark interior,' began one reporter, eyeing the long narrow space and plain white walls relieved by huge back-lit mustard-coloured (or 'toasted beige' if you prefer) padded banquette upholstery. After selling Fulham Road, Stephen Bull opened this new venture in May 1997. More informal than the Blandford Street original, and less of a bistro than the one in St John Street (see previous and following entries), it reverts to a more typical Bull style of food, the kind that appeals for its simplicity and clarity. Materials are modest, and a degree of ingenuity produces interesting ideas such as a tarte flambée with Ticklemore goats' cheese, or celery soup containing walnut and garlic tortellini. In addition to the *carte,* it makes a bid for pre-theatre custom with a short versatile menu served until 7pm.

Innovation is apparent in, for example, a version of Scotch egg in which a just-cooked quail's egg is surrounded by a light mix of white crab meat with a thin, crisp crust. It comes with a bowl of mayonnaise with dark crab meat stirred in, plus a little mustard, the whole thing paying careful attention to flavours and textures, and 'expertly done'. Other successes have included a feuilleté of lamb sweetbreads, a warm summer salad with 'jewel-bright peas and broad beans', and a slow-baked shoulder of lamb with field mushrooms. The 'utter simplicity' of the style is captured in a rum junket served with cinnamon shortbread biscuits. Service is friendly, courteous and professional: 'it's a long time since I have seen the balance struck as well as here.'

The latest addition to the Stephen Bull stable of wine lists is helpfully arranged by style, from 'light, dry, refreshingly fruity whites' through to 'rich complex reds' with 'oak and power', and gives concise tasting notes for each bin. Prices are reasonable too. A 'quick list' of 26 assorted bins starts at £10.75 a bottle, with 19 offered by the glass from £2.50. CELLARMAN'S CHOICE: Sauvignon de Touraine 1996, Alain Marcadet, £14.25; Pic-St-Loup 1995, Dom. de l'Hortus Classique, £15.95.

CHEF: John Bentham PROPRIETOR: Stephen Bull OPEN: Mon to Fri L 12 to 2.30, Mon to Sat D 5.45 to 11.30 CLOSED: 1 week Christmas, bank hols MEALS: alc (main courses £10 to £15), pre-theatre alc 5.45 to 7pm SERVICE: not inc, card slips closed CARDS: Amex, MasterCard, Switch, Visa DETAILS: 70 seats. Private parties: 60 main room. Vegetarian meals. Children's helpings. No pipes/cigars in dining-room. Wheelchair access (no WC). No music. Air-conditioned

Stephen Bull Smithfield map 13

71 St John Street, EC1M 4AN COOKING 3
TEL: (0171) 490 1750 FAX: (0171) 490 3127 COST £30–£45

The Smithfield district suddenly has more good restaurants than you could shake a breadstick at, a trend celebrated – whether deliberately or not – in the renaming of Stephen Bull's Bistro. One reporter noted a 'West Coast feel' in the sparsely decorated interior with its bare wooden floor, black tables and staff in T-shirt and jeans. Space is at a premium, but the air of cheerful hubbub confirms its popularity, and a seafood bar offers oysters, sushi, and soused mackerel. Otherwise there may be Emmental tart with roasted garlic and chives, crépinette of braised oxtail with red wine *jus,* and egg noodles with Jerusalem artichoke, butternut squash and ginger. Crisp-skinned duck breast with white beans, cabbage and deep-fried onions was a good composition for one reporter, though shy on seasoning. Alcohol often turns up in desserts: calvados parfait, for example, or grapefruit and caramel sabayon with a grappa sorbet.

Over half the 80-plus bins cost less than £20, and modern styles of winemaking are well to the fore with contributions from Catena's Argentinian operation, and Viñas del Vero's Spanish barrel-fermented Chardonnay, although traditionalists will still find some good burgundies and clarets. House wines start at £11.50. CELLARMAN'S CHOICE: Bergerac, Ch. Tour des Gendres 1995, £14.50; Côtes de Bourg, Ch. Montaigut 1990, £18.50.

CHEF: Danny Lewis PROPRIETOR: Stephen Bull OPEN: Mon to Fri L 12 to 2.15, Mon to Sat D 6.30 to 10.30 CLOSED: 1 week Christmas, bank hols MEALS: alc (main courses £9.50 to £11.50). BYO £4 SERVICE: not inc, card slips closed CARDS: Amex, MasterCard, Switch, Visa DETAILS: 120 seats. Private parties: 60 main room. Vegetarian meals. Children's helpings. No smoking in 1 dining-room. Wheelchair access (no WC). Music. Air-conditioned

Stepping Stone

map 12

123 Queenstown Road, SW8 3RH COOKING 3
TEL: (0171) 622 0555 FAX: (0171) 622 4230 COST £24–£41

Linen, metal, sharp halogen lighting and a lively atmosphere proclaim the restaurant's modern credentials, an impression strongly backed up by the menu. Peter Harrison moved in from Sonny's (see entry, London), and continues to produce an appealing mix of dishes from seared blue fin tuna to red-blooded calf's liver with mash, lentils and mustard sauce. Seasons might appear to collide now and then, and some combinations may need working on, but materials are good, and the policy is to use meats 'only from traceable sources'. Desserts proved a high point for one visitor who enjoyed coffee mousse with chocolate sauce, and there may also be steamed marmalade pudding, or peach and Sauternes jelly with shortbread and cream. A lively bunch of up-to-date wines at very fair prices is just the ticket, backed up by a few beers and weekly-changing recommendations. House wine starts at £8.75.

CHEF: Peter Harrison PROPRIETORS: Gary and Emer Levy OPEN: Sun to Fri L 12 to 2.30, Mon to Sat D 7 to 11 (10.30 Mon) CLOSED: 24 to 30 Dec, bank hols MEALS: alc (main courses £8.50 to £13). Set L Mon to Fri (2 courses) £10.50, Set L Sun (2 courses) £11.75. BYO £5 per person SERVICE: not inc CARDS: Amex, Delta, Diners, MasterCard, Visa DETAILS: 55 seats. Private parties: 55 main room. Children's helpings. No smoking in 1 dining-room. Wheelchair access (no WC). No music. Air-conditioned

Sugar Club

map 13

33A All Saints Road, W11 1HE COOKING 4
TEL: (0171) 221 3844 FAX: (0171) 229 2759 COST £23–£50

This may be London's answer to Sydney's vibrant cooking, and Peter Gordon's grasp of the complexities of the world larder, and his attempts to juggle contrasting flavours, make for some arresting food. After choosing where to eat – ground floor or non-smoking basement – many reporters have their work cut out deciphering the trendy food vocabulary. What would you make of mujjol, or a dish containing cecina, lomo and garrotxa, for example? The whole thing buzzes with exciting ideas – lobster and tamarind broth with crabmeat, coriander and squid ink noodles, for example – although some dishes have a job living up to the promise of their thrilling descriptions.

Nevertheless there is much to dazzle, intrigue or simply enjoy: grilled kangaroo, roast ham knuckle, or grilled squid with sweet piquillo peppers, parsnip crisps and smoked paprika oil. The kitchen's ability to grill, roast and pan-fry accurately is evident, and some flavour combinations are handled extremely well: for example, scallops with a sweet and mildly hot chilli jam and bitter rocket leaves. Shortcomings are probably due more to the variable quality of ingredients than to any inconsistency in the cooking. Mustard is a favourite condiment, working to good effect in the mash, and desserts are more mainstream, in the mould of rhubarb and peach tart, or buttermilk bavarois. Competent antipodean service delivers wine from a short but enthusiastic round-the-world list that starts with house Italian at £10.50.

CHEF: Peter Gordon PROPRIETORS: Vivienne Hayman and Ashley Sumner OPEN: all week 12.30 to 2.30, 6.30 to 11 CLOSED: during Notting Hill Carnival MEALS: alc (main courses £10 to £16). Set L £11.50 (2 courses) to £14.50 SERVICE: not inc CARDS: Amex, Delta, MasterCard, Switch, Visa DETAILS: 70 seats. 25 seats outside. Vegetarian meals. No children under 7. No smoking in 1 dining-room. Wheelchair access (no WC). No music

Suntory map 15

72–73 St James's Street, SW1A 1PH COOKING **6**
TEL: (0171) 409 0201 FAX: (0171) 499 0208 COST £27–£139

The London branch of this international chain of archetypal Japanese restaurants fulfils, at an appropriate price, the highest expectations, with added elements of surprise and contrast. The teppan room and the formal restaurant share a sophisticated rustic décor, enlivened with fine pottery and modern works of art. Formality reigns, with suave, generally helpful waiting staff wearing tails or kimono, irrespective of their ethnic origins. On the tables, which have central gas fittings for cooking sukiyaki and the like, are white paper mats and napkins, which, although they seem out of place in an otherwise de luxe environment, at least help to relieve the room's overall brown tone

The à la carte choice covers most of the Japanese classics, from appetisers such as yakitori and Scotch smoked salmon, via broiled dishes (including lobster and foie gras), and tempura, to sukiyaki, and shabu-shabu. Alternatively, there is a wide range of set menus to choose from. Special nigiri sushi was the highlight of a set menu for one reporter, although sashimi in the wateishoku lunch included disappointingly hard-edged pieces of seared tuna instead of succulent raw fish. Another pinnacle has been dobin-mushi soup served in the traditional tiny flattened teapot with a minute cup: this 'exquisitely delicate yet deep-flavoured' consommé includes a slice of fish-cake, chicken, prawn, wakame seaweed and shiitake mushroom. Even more pleasing was a simple 'braised dish', or nimono, of mixed vegetables, among them yam, pumpkin and aubergine. A 'small appetiser' of a medium-sized savoury-sweet plum comes in a cocktail glass of iced, pale red plum wine with a sprig of mint, giving a whole new meaning to 'liquid lunch'. A long list of expensive wines are mostly French, but there are also bottles of saké priced up to £95. House wine is £17.

CHEF: N. Hoshino PROPRIETOR: Suntory Ltd OPEN: Mon to Sat 12 to 2, 6 to 10 CLOSED: Christmas, bank hols MEALS: alc (main courses £26 to £45). Set L £15 to £38, Set D £49.80 to £73 SERVICE: net prices, card slips closed CARDS: Amex, Delta, Diners, MasterCard, Switch, Visa DETAILS: 120 seats. Private parties: 100 main room. Vegetarian meals. Children's helpings. No children under 7. Wheelchair access (no WC). No music. Air-conditioned

Net prices *in the details at the end of an entry indicates that the prices given on a menu and on a bill are inclusive of VAT and service charge, and that this practice is clearly stated on menu and bill.*

Le Suquet

map 14

104 Draycott Avenue, SW3 3AE — COOKING 3

TEL: (0171) 581 1785 FAX: (0171) 225 0838 — COST £21–£76

The competition in this wealthy, busy part of London is fierce, but Le Suquet continues to pack them in, especially those willing to pay fairly stiff prices for spankingly fresh fish. Tables are crammed together in the nautically themed dining-room, though French windows allow diners to spill out on to the busy street in warm weather. Mussels, scallops and clams are dished up in an assortment of styles, from marinière to Madras, while langoustines, lobster and oysters are served plain. The huge plateau de fruits de mer is a popular choice, as are 'fresh and glistening' turbot and Dover sole. Desserts, in an inspector's view, tend to be not much more than an afterthought. Service is impersonal but efficient, and the short wine list is exclusively French, with house wine at £10.50.

CHEF: Phillipe Moron PROPRIETOR: Pierre Martin OPEN: Mon to Fri 12 to 2.30, 7 to 11.30, Sat and Sun 12 to 11.30 MEALS: alc (main courses £10 to £30). Set L £12. Cover £1 SERVICE: 15% (optional), card slips closed CARDS: Amex, Diners, MasterCard, Switch, Visa DETAILS: 70 seats. 8 seats outside. Private parties: 16 private room. Children welcome. Music. Air-conditioned

Sushi-Say

NEW ENTRY map 12

33B Walm Lane, NW2 5SH — COOKING 3

TEL: (0181) 459 7512 FAX: (0181) 459 2971 — COST £21–£53

This architecturally odd restaurant might once have been a covered walkway to the church situated behind it, which would account for the long, narrow room's low ceiling, linked by diagonal slopes to the walls. The conventional brown and white Japanese rustic décor includes *objets de petit vertu* such as calendars, prints and plastic good-luck cats on the walls. In typical Japanese style, set dinners are a feature, and are much less expensive than in the West End or City. It is best to choose those incorporating the restaurant's specialities, sashimi and sushi.

Superlative-quality fish is skilfully prepared at the counter by sushi chef-patron Katsuharu Shimizu, who has been working in the Tokyo style for over 30 years. Among seaweed-rolled sushi note 'sour plum paste with herb', a term which does scant justice to what an inspector describes as the 'amazing shiso or perilla or beefsteak plant, a herb combining mint, basil and oregano flavours in one leaf straight from the Garden of Eden'. One page of the long menu lists sushi bar à la carte starters including engawa ponzu (cold sliced 'turbot wing' marinated in a citrussy sauce to 'a wonderful firm, chewy, but not tough texture'). Also in this section are sunomono (vinegared seafoods) and a variety of squid, tuna, and herring preparations with unusual sauces. The happy and relaxed ambience is mainly because the service by Mrs. Shimizu and young waitresses is 'exceptionally gracious'. 'Semi-frozen saké', in a tumbler with lots of crushed ice, goes well with Japanese food in warm weather; otherwise house French wine is £8.

See inside the front cover for an explanation of the symbols used at the tops of entries.

CHEF: Mr K. Shimizu PROPRIETORS: Mr and Mrs K. Shimizu OPEN: Tue to Sun D 6 to 10.30 CLOSED: 1 week Christmas, 1 week Aug, Tues after bank hols MEALS: alc (main courses £7.50 to £17.50). Set D £14.50 to £25.50 SERVICE: not inc CARDS: MasterCard, Switch, Visa DETAILS: 36 seats. Private parties: 20 main room, 6 private room. Vegetarian meals. Children welcome. Wheelchair access (also WC). No music. Air-conditioned

Tamarind

map 15

20 Queen Street, W1X 7PS — COOKING 3
TEL: (0171) 629 3561 FAX: (0171) 499 5034 — COST £28–£55

Delhi meets Mayfair at Tamarind. Forget flock wallpaper and vindaloo, this is a very different experience. The décor is as chic as can be, with sandy golden colour schemes, impressive gilded columns, sinuous wrought-iron chairs and a 'distressed tree' to catch the eye as you enter the swish basement dining-room. The cooking is a world away from Southall or Sparkhill; northern India provides the backbone, although influences are pulled in from near and far. Items such as machchi sofiyani (monkfish marinated in saffron and yoghurt) feature, but there is much more besides. Whet the appetite with jhinga khyber (prawns in ginger, sunflower and carom seeds), or hara kebab (chickpeas, lentil, spinach and potato cakes), before tackling inventive kebabs, tandooris or classic curries such as rogan josh and dum ka gosht korma (both lamb dishes). Flavours and rich, intense spicing shine through. Reporters have waxed ecstatic about vegetables as well as pilau rice, but the entire repertoire impresses. Cobra beer is a suitable tipple; otherwise delve into the wine list, which promises sound drinking from around the globe. House wine from Chile is £13.50.

CHEF: Atul Kochhar PROPRIETOR: Indian Cuisine Ltd OPEN: Sun to Fri L 12 to 3, all week D 6 to 11.30 CLOSED: 25 and 26 Dec MEALS: alc (main courses £10 to £16). Set L and pre- and post-theatre D £16.50. BYO £5 SERVICE: 12.5% (optional) CARDS: Amex, Delta, Diners, MasterCard, Visa DETAILS: 100 seats. Vegetarian meals. Children's helpings. Wheelchair access (no WC). Music. Air-conditioned

La Tante Claire 🍷

map 14

68 Royal Hospital Road, SW3 4HP — COOKING 10
TEL: (0171) 352 6045 FAX: (0171) 352 3257 — COST £34–£91

The appeal is immediate: a welcoming, 'light and lovely' room with big windows, lots of space, immaculate linen, and an unpretentious feel. Pierre Koffmann has long been a leading exponent of 'modern classical' French cooking, and reporters typically enjoy the clarity and precision of his food. Significantly, he is a hands-on chef who prefers to stay in the kitchen rather than glad-hand the customers, and has combined impeccable haute cuisine standards with inspiration from his native south-west France. Among the renowned dishes are pig's trotter stuffed with morels ('a wonderfully rich, sticky dish of deep flavours') served with pommes mousseline, and a 'stunning' croustade of caramelised apples with delicate buttered filo pastry.

Truffles and foie gras appear here with more justification than on most menus, because of the regional slant, and while the pairing of luxuries with humbler ingredients is a fashion statement for some, here it is an integral part of the cuisine: in a first course of foie gras with duck gizzard, for example. Materials are of the highest quality, and even when combinations are not typically Gascon they work just as well; for example, in a gamey fillet of venison with two sauces: a demi-glace, and one combining raspberry vinegar and bitter chocolate. What counts here is that complementary flavours combine into a satisfying whole.

As a counterpoint to the food's earthy dimension, seafood can produce feather-light fritters of langoustine and asparagus on sweet tomato confit, and perfectly griddled scallops on a colourful trio of sauces of 'immense sophistication'. Visual impact is enticing without becoming a separate issue, as in a dish of lobster pieces arranged over a bed of spinach, with a Madiran wine sauce: 'brilliant execution and superb ingredients'.

As for the set lunch, 'why go anywhere else at this price?' asked one reporter, noting that the figure includes appetiser, coffee with petits fours, service and unlimited mineral water, as well as three courses. The choice is effectively two items per course, and has always been considered one of London's great bargains, although inspection meals suggest that it may not always be in the same class as the 'staggeringly wonderful' à la carte. Tante Claire can be compared favourably with the very best in Koffmann's native France. Service has varied too, but at its best is smooth and professional 'without a hint of stuffiness'.

The entirely French wine list (fortifieds excepted) opens with two dozen modestly priced bins from lesser-known areas, helpfully listed by their dominant grape variety, before moving on to serious stuff from the classic regions. But even here, mark-ups are considerably more sympathetic than in any comparable London restaurant. Half bottles are generous and the sommelier conscientious. CELLARMAN'S CHOICE: Vin de Pays de l'Ardeche, Dom. de Terriers Viognier 1994, £23; Vins de Pays d'Oc, Les Montilles 1993, Dom. du Bosquet-Canet, £18.40.

CHEF/PROPRIETOR: Pierre Koffmann OPEN: Mon to Fri 12.30 to 2, 7 to 11 CLOSED: Christmas, Easter, Aug MEALS: alc (main courses £24.50 to £28). Set L £27 SERVICE: net prices CARDS: Amex, Diners, MasterCard, Visa DETAILS: 48 seats. Private parties: 48 main room. Children welcome. Jacket at D. No pipes in dining-room. Wheelchair access (also WC). No music. Air-conditioned

Tate Gallery Restaurant

map 13

Millbank, SW1P 4RG — COOKING 2

TEL: (0171) 887 8825 FAX: (0171) 887 8902 — COST £29–£49

The restaurant in the basement of the Tate has its confirmed supporters, among both wine-lovers with an eye for a bargain and devotees of English heritage cooking. The latter tendency brings on to the menu such Grade I listed treasures as potted prawns, fish-cakes, braised beef with carrots and dumplings, and 'Mrs Beeton's Oxfordshire sausages' with mash. There is the occasional Continental excursion in the shape of tagliatelle with tomato and coriander sauce, or pigeon terrine in port gelée, but it is clear where the kitchen's heart is. Lemon jelly, rice pudding, and apple tart with clotted cream await you at the finishing line. 'Very friendly, jolly' service helps to make this an appealing lunchtime venue.

The wine list opens with a new quarterly personal selection by art critic and wine lover David Sylvester. Claret and burgundy enthusiasts are well served, both by the range of excellent producers and (for London) good value. Fourteen wines by the glass start at £3, rising to around £7.50 for three prestige wines; an impressive 29 are available by the half-bottle. House wines start at £11.95. CELLARMAN'S CHOICE: Puligny-Montrachet Les Folatières 1989, Louis Latour, £29.50; St Hallett Old Block Shiraz 1993, Barossa Valley, S.Australia, £22.50.

CHEF: Shaun Rowlands PROPRIETOR: Trustees of the Tate Gallery OPEN: Mon to Sat L only 12 to 3 CLOSED: 24 to 26 Dec, 1 Jan MEALS: alc (main courses £9.50 to £15). Set L £14.95 SERVICE: not inc, card slips closed CARDS: Amex, MasterCard, Switch, Visa DETAILS: 100 seats. Private parties: 10 main room. Vegetarian meals. Children welcome. No-smoking area. Wheelchair access (also WC). No music

Tatsuso

map 13

32 Broadgate Circle, EC2M 2QS — COOKING 4
TEL: (0171) 638 5863 FAX: (0171) 638 5864 — COST £32–£112

Japanese business entertaining is the raison d'être of this restaurant, as much in the ground-floor teppan room as in the main basement restaurant. There are private tatami rooms and a small sushi bar too. The décor is 'olde worlde' Japanese with silk paintings and painted gold screen on the walls, and tables are separated by slatted wooden screens for additional privacy. The feeling of luxury is sustained by 'exquisite fan-shaped chopstick rests' and by fine porcelain saké flasks and cups.

The long à la carte menu lists the standard repertoire, including sashimi, sushi and dishes cooked at table like sukiyaki, as well as a more unusual section of tofu dishes, and delicacies such as deep-fried turbot fins, or sea tangle between herring roe wafers. An inspector started with seven different zensai hors d'oeuvres 'exquisitely presented' on a bamboo leaf on a lacquered tray, and enjoyed 'rich and oily' kani misoae (crab meat with miso dressing). Sashimi and tempura were disappointing at a busy lunch-time, but a simple dish of braised aubergine and taro was properly done, and accurately cooked salmon teriyaki was delicately sauced. There is also a wide choice of set menus. The wine list includes some magnificent, though not cheap, bottles, but starts with house Chardonnay and Pinot Noir at £14, and the fully annotated saké list adds a new dimension to matching Japanese food and drink.

CHEFS: Nobuyuki Yamanaka, Miroyuri Saotome and Hikaru Maehara PROPRIETOR: Terutoshi Fujii OPEN: Mon to Fri 11.30 to 2.30, 6 to 9.45 CLOSED: Christmas, bank hols MEALS: alc (main courses £10 to £20). Set L and D £21 to £75. Teppanyaki menu available SERVICE: 13%, card slips closed CARDS: Amex, Delta, Diners, MasterCard, Switch, Visa DETAILS: 125 seats. Private parties: 8 main room, 4 and 8 private rooms. Vegetarian meals. Children welcome. No music. Air-conditioned

Thai Bistro

map 12

99 Chiswick High Road, W4 2ED — COOKING 1
TEL: (0181) 995 5774 — COST £18–£33

The picture window beckons with blue hanging chains and lights: 'just the kind of tasteful ornament you might encounter in Bangkok.' Bench seating and paper napkins indicate just how informal the small dining-room is, and the draw is straightforward 'no nonsense food' from an unusually varied menu. As well as offering tom ka gai soup, pork toasts, spring rolls and red curries, it also strays into specialities from one of the four major regions: green papaya salad, or fried fish with ginger and mushrooms from the north-east, for example. Vegetarians are well catered for with lots of beancurd dishes as well as fried curried aubergine or sweet and sour vegetables. Service is friendly and keeps its charm even when busy. There is a short, functional wine list, but it is 'best to stick to beer'.

CHEF/PROPRIETOR: Vatcharin Bhumichitr OPEN: Mon, Wed and Fri to Sun L 12 to 3, all week D 6 to 11 CLOSED: bank hols MEALS: alc (main courses £3.50 to £7) SERVICE: not inc CARDS: MasterCard, Visa DETAILS: 60 seats. 20 seats outside. Private parties: 12 main room. Vegetarian meals. Children welcome. No music

Thai Garden  map 12

249 Globe Road, E2 0JD COOKING 3
TEL: (0181) 981 5748 COST £22–£37

Situated in a pretty, gentrified corner of Bow, the main feature of this pleasant little restaurant's décor is striking colour photographs of seafood and vegetables, which is appropriate, as its main business is to serve Thai food enthusiasts who eschew meat. The longish menu is divided into vegetarian and seafood sections: the former includes starters such as hot and sour vermicelli salad with mushrooms, nuts and raisins, followed by fried aubergine with chilli and basil in a black-bean sauce, or chinese mushrooms in red wine sauce. The latter might offer marinated prawns in satay sauce with pickles, hot and sour mixed seafood salad with lemon grass and lime juice, and main courses of fried pomfret with cucumber, pineapple, peppers, tomatoes and onions in a sweet-and-sour sauce, and prawns, crab claws and fish balls with vermicelli and mixed vegetables. There are also vegetarian and seafood set-price menus. As in so many Thai family restaurants, charming service and ambience are among its greatest assets. House wine is £7.50.

CHEF: Napathorn Duff PROPRIETORS: Suthinee and Jack Hutton OPEN: Mon to Fri L 12 to 2.45, all week D 6 to 10.45 CLOSED: bank hols MEALS: alc (main courses £4 to £7). Set L £7.50 (2 courses), Set D £7.50 (2 courses, available 6 to 7.30pm) to £21 SERVICE: 10%, card slips closed CARDS: Delta, MasterCard, Visa DETAILS: 32 seats. Private parties: 20 main room, 14 private room. Vegetarian meals. Children welcome. No smoking in 1 dining-room. Wheelchair access (no WC). Music

Thailand £ map 12

15 Lewisham Way, SE14 6PP COOKING 5
TEL: (0181) 691 4040 COST £19–£41

'I am going to Bangkok next week, but doubt whether I will find much better food there,' commented one much-travelled correspondent. The location is hardly glamorous, and the interior may seem unassuming, but the kitchen 'consistently turns out the best Thai food in London'. Three dishes tell their own story: magnificent tom yum goong (a bench-mark soup of real complexity), a classic version of green prawn curry, and 'lap' – minced pork marinated with spices, scooped up with strips of lettuce and eaten with balls of spicy rice. There's no mystique about the menu, no need to hide behind esoteric language and descriptions: accuracy and the results on the plate speak for themselves.

Chef/proprietor Mrs Gong Cambungoet Herman hails from the village of Ban Kwao, and much of her culinary inspiration is from north-east Thailand as well as Laos. Her clearly annotated 90-dish menu takes in Thai sausages, fish-cakes with green beans, and a mixture of crabmeat and chicken steamed in cabbage leaves among starters, then moves on to pounded catfish with chillies, garlic, fish sauce and lime juice, stir-fried beef with spring onions in oyster sauce, and hot-and-sour bamboo shoots. To finish, look for sweet variations on the theme of sticky rice. A handful of carefully chosen wines is an alternative to Tiger beer, and the restaurant is proud of its range of malt whiskies. House wine is £8.50.

CHEF/PROPRIETOR: Mrs G. Cambungoet Herman OPEN: Tue to Sat D only 6 to 10.30 MEALS: alc (main courses £5.50 to £11). Set D £20 SERVICE: not inc, card slips closed CARDS: MasterCard, Visa DETAILS: 25 seats. Private parties: 25 main room. Vegetarian meals. No music. Air-conditioned

33

map 15

33 St James's Street, SW1A 1HD — COOKING 4

TEL: (0171) 930 4272 FAX: (0171) 930 7618 — COST £37–£69

Competition in and around St James's Street is strong, and restaurants need to live up to a wide range of expectations. They have to be smart, too, and 33's glass frontage and rag-rolled mustard-yellow walls are certainly that. Tables are well spaced, the large foodie paintings appear sombre, and there is lots and lots of service. Kristian Smith-Wallace came up from sous-chef and has taken an ambitious stance with a busy modern menu that promises much, from seared foie gras to ostrich salad, from scallops glazed under a curry Sauternes sauce to a meaty and sticky braised pig's cheek. Some dishes attract a supplement.

High-quality materials get the show off to a cracking start, including an inspector's small piece of 'brilliantly fresh' red snapper that was 'moist, perfectly timed, a triumph', although it came, not altogether appropriately, with potatoes topped with cheese and diced ham. Saucing strives for subtlety: for example, a barely detectable infusion of smoked lemon peel to enhance the snapper, or a likewise ginger hollandaise to accompany smoked haddock risotto topped with a perfectly poached egg. Pastry chef Lisa Speddings turns out a generous array of desserts, from hot mango soufflé, through iced aniseed parfait to yellow plum tart. Wines are enterprising, with fair choice by the glass, but prices are high. House white (Saumur) is £15, red (Bordeaux) is £20.

CHEF: Kristian Smith-Wallace PROPRIETOR: Vincenzo Defeo OPEN: Mon to Fri L 12 to 2.30, Mon to Sat D 6 to 11.30 (12 Fri and Sat) CLOSED: Christmas, bank hols MEALS: Set L £16.95 (2 courses) to £21.90, Set D £22.95 (2 courses) to £28.45. Cover £1. BYO £5 SERVICE: 12.5% (optional), card slips closed CARDS: Amex, Diners, MasterCard, Switch, Visa DETAILS: 75 seats. Private parties: 90 main room, 35 private room. Vegetarian meals. Children's helpings. No smoking in 1 dining-room. Wheelchair access (no WC). Music. Air-conditioned

Tokyo Diner [£]

map 15

2 Newport Place, WC2H 7JJ — COOKING 2
TEL: (0171) 287 8777 FAX: (0171) 434 1415 — COST £14–£23

Bonsai stools and tables, bonsai prices, but not bonsai portions feature in Richard Hills's bright Tokyo-style low-priced eating-house. Satisfying bento boxes comprise rice, glass noodle salad, salmon sashimi salad, and a 'main' item such as tofu steak, or salmon teriyaki. Basic Japanese-style 'fast food' curries, 'donburi' rice with seasoned egg plus meat or vegetable toppings, or soup noodles, all arrive at the table quickly. Modest but adequate sushi and sashimi take a little longer, but you have all day, from noon to midnight, to eat here. Tea is free, and there's a cheer for the menu's last line: 'Japanese style: we do not take tips.' Banzai! Drink hot or cold saké, or house wine at £6.90 (£1.80 a glass).

CHEF: Takuro Fujiama PROPRIETOR: Richard Hills OPEN: all week 12 to 12 MEALS: alc (main courses £6 to £13). Set L Mon to Fri £5.90 SERVICE: none, card slips closed CARDS: MasterCard, Switch, Visa DETAILS: 75 seats. Vegetarian meals. Children welcome. No smoking in 1 dining-room. Wheelchair access (no WC). Music. Air-conditioned

Turner's

map 14

87–89 Walton Street, SW3 2HP — COOKING 7
TEL: 0171-584 6711 FAX: 0171 584 4441 — COST £27–£64

As ever, the *Guide* is inundated with readers' reports on Turner's, and nobody ever seems to have a less than splendid time. The lemon-coloured room is cool and tasteful, the seating comfortable, and the 'T' motif discreet. Such is our familiarity with Brian Turner's vernacular mode, as evidenced by appearances on TV shows such as 'Ready Steady Cook', it seems difficult to recall that his background is in grand-hotel cooking, or that his restaurant, now into its second decade, was a product of the high tide of London nouvelle cuisine. The cooking is based on honest classical principles, using admirable materials, executed with a degree of flair, and with an ability to produce flavours that combine strength and finesse.

One great asset of this restaurant has been its willingness to let some remarkably good-value fixed-price deals bolster the serious dinner menu. This, together with the unpretentious cooking, is what has kept it popular for years. Among many dishes that effortlessly proclaim the kitchen's class has been a consommé of crab, 'aromatic, savoury, the colour of old sherry', full of deep-driven shellfish flavour, texture coming from shreds of thinly sliced spinach pancake added at the last moment. Technique shows to dazzlingly good effect in a dish of sliced saddle of rabbit stuffed with spicy sausage and white beans on a mixed leaf salad: in effect, high class charcuterie. Offal is accorded star prominence in calves' and lambs' kidneys seared to just pink and served with creamed potatoes, caramelised baby onions and garlic. John Dory, meanwhile, is still nervelessly topped with a mousse of foie gras.

It is easy to get carried away by opting for the platter of mixed desserts, which is worth every penny of the asking price, or there may be Grand Marnier parfait with spiced strawberries. The French-led wine list is full of classic delights, including a run of Chablis from William Fèvre, which tends to push up the base price. Having said that, there is certainly no shortage of choice under £20. House Bordeaux is £13.50.

CHEF: Charles Curran PROPRIETOR: Brian Turner OPEN: Sun to Fri L 12.30 to 2.30, all week D 7.30 to 11 (6.30 to 8.30 Sun) CLOSED: 1 week Christmas, bank hols MEALS: Set L Mon to Fri £12.50 (2 courses) to £38.75, Set L Sun £21.50 to £38.75, Set D £26.50 to £38.75 SERVICE: not inc CARDS: Amex, Delta, Diners, MasterCard, Switch, Visa DETAILS: 54 seats. Private parties: 52 main room, 8 private room. Children's helpings L and early D. Wheelchair access (no WC). Music. Air-conditioned

Two Brothers £ map 12

297–303 Regents Park Road, N3 1DP COOKING 3
TEL: (0181) 346 0469 FAX: (0181) 343 1978 COST £18–£37

Leon and Tony Manzi are too modest to call it anything more than an up-market chippie, but in some ways Two Brothers is more like a bourgeois seafood restaurant in a Paris suburb. The pleasant, open room is decorated with posters, menus and large colour photographs. Service is relaxed and friendly yet efficient.

Fish and chips is at the heart of the menu, but as well as the usual cod and haddock, there might be rock eel, wing or middle of skate, halibut steak and Dover sole. This alone would justify the description 'up-market', but, perhaps more importantly, all the fish is cooked to order, in matzo meal on request, and chips are consistently crisp. Sophistication creeps in with rock oysters, sardines with herbs and garlic, and Arbroath smokies in cream sauce, but jellied eels, and home-made white fish soup are there too. No bookings are taken, but cosmopolitan north Londoners happily queue for tables. The short, carefully chosen wine list includes house white at £9.20 from the brothers' own vines in the Côtes de Duras.

CHEFS/PROPRIETORS: Leon and Tony Manzi OPEN: Tue to Sat 12 to 2.30, 5.30 to 10.15 CLOSED: last 2 weeks Aug, bank hols (exc Good Friday) and days following MEALS: alc (main courses £7 to £14). BYO £5 SERVICE: not inc, card slips closed CARDS: Amex, Delta, MasterCard, Switch, Visa DETAILS: 90 seats. Children's helpings. No-smoking area. Music. Air-conditioned

Union Café map 15

96 Marylebone Lane, W1M 5FP COOKING 3
TEL: (0171) 486 4860 COST £26–£51

This is the essence of a modern café. A high ceiling, big windows and white walls combine to give it a bright, smart, bare and spacious feel, the simple, clean effect enhanced by a brushed-steel counter and plain wooden floors and tables. Other things in its favour include informality and a simple menu, which suits casual lunches and light evening meals down to the ground. What stood out for one reporter were the 'wonderfully fresh flavours from obviously top-class ingredients'. The short, conservative *carte* generally offers soups, salads, perhaps smoked salmon, or a crisp tomato and anchovy pizza that was 'freshness encapsulated' for its reporter.

Lightness is a feature, as in bruschetta topped with black olives and a 'gazpacho-style' mix of tomato and onion. Simple roasting and chargrilling are at the heart of more substantial items, such as monkfish fillets with coriander-spiked lentils, or chump of lamb with imam bayaldi. Nutty, crumbly brown bread is praised, as are sorbets such as 'sharp and refreshing' Victoria plum, and the espresso is particularly good. Service is friendly without being intrusive. The biggest cloud on the horizon appears to be that reporters can feel they have paid something closer to restaurant prices by the time the bill arrives. Soft drinks include fruit 'smoothies', and the tiny wine list offers Dancing Goat, Faithful Hound and Nine Popes, plus South African house wine at £10.50.

CHEFS/PROPRIETORS: Caroline Brett and Sam Russell OPEN: Mon to Sat 9.30 to 12, 12.30 to 3.30, 6.30 to 10.30 CLOSED: 2 weeks Christmas, bank hols MEALS: alc (main courses £9 to £13). Minimum £12.50 L and D SERVICE: 12.5% (optional), card slips closed CARDS: Delta, MasterCard, Switch, Visa DETAILS: 70 seats. Private parties: 80 main room. Vegetarian meals. Children welcome. No-smoking area. Wheelchair access (no WC). No music

Upper Street Fish Shop £

map 13

324 Upper Street, N1 2XQ — COOKING 1
TEL/FAX: (0171) 359 1401 — COST £10–£27

The Conways' simple, cheerfully dated fish-and-chip restaurant is in a prime position to have seen food trends flourish and fade on Upper Street. Its own contribution to Islington eating is fresh fish, such as plaice, skate and haddock, cooked in exemplary crisp, dry batter with options of mushy peas and pickled onions on the side. Every table is furnished with tartare sauce and ketchup. Value can be superb: how about four fat green-lipped mussels deep-fried on a skewer for £2? Chips are normally good: best if you 'strike lucky and get them straight out of the fryer'. Puddings, such as rhubarb crumble and treacle tart, come with plenty of cream or custard. There is no licence but no corkage either; the easiest thing is to pop across the road to Oddbins and see what's in the fridge.

CHEF: Stewart Gamble PROPRIETORS: Alan and Olga Conway OPEN: Tue to Sat L 12 to 2.15 (3 Sat), Mon to Sat D 5.30 to 10.15 CLOSED: Christmas, bank hols MEALS: alc (main courses £4.50 to £10). Unlicensed. BYO (no corkage) SERVICE: not inc CARDS: none DETAILS: 50 seats. Children's helpings. Wheelchair access (no WC). No music. Air-conditioned

Vegetarian Cottage £

map 13

91 Haverstock Hill, NW3 4RL — COOKING 1
TEL: (0171) 586 1257 — COST £15–£32

As its name suggests, this commendable neighbourhood restaurant majors in the vegetarian strands of Chinese cuisine. In a quite smart, modish setting of white walls, black-framed prints and high-backed wooden chairs, a mainly local crowd enjoys crispy sliced yam rolls, braised Chinese mushrooms with black moss, and Szechuan-style aubergines. Bean curd and gluten appear in many guises: the former might be deep-fried with salt and chilli or steamed with soy; the latter could be fashioned into balls with sweet-and-sour sauce or stir-fried with chilli and black-bean sauce. As an alternative, the menu includes a handful of seafood dishes ranging from steamed scallops with garlic to baked lobster with ginger and spring onions. Rounding things off are toffee apples, walnut pudding and pancakes with red-bean paste. Australian house wine is £8.80.

CHEF: C.K. Wong PROPRIETOR: S.W. Chu OPEN: Sun L 12 to 3.30, all week D 6 to 11.15 CLOSED: 25 and 26 Dec MEALS: alc (main courses £4.60 to £15.50). Set L £8.50, Set D £12.50 to £13.50 SERVICE: not inc, card slips closed CARDS: Delta, MasterCard, Switch, Visa DETAILS: 48 seats. Vegetarian meals. Children welcome. No smoking in 1 dining-room. Music. Air-conditioned

Village Bistro

map 12

38 Highgate High Street, N6 5JG
TEL: (0181) 340 5165 and 0257 — COOKING 1
FAX: (0181) 347 5584 — COST £26–£44

The menu is largely 'bistro French', but now its language is English: even for French onion soup, and peppered sirloin steak. Invading exotic ingredients include guacamole, ginger and coriander. Execution may vary, but chicken liver parfait at a seasoned reporter's set lunch was 'divinely light and smooth', and vegetable garnishes have been praised. Fried halibut was a major disappointment at the same meal, but assurance returned with a dessert of lemon parfait with passion-fuit and red-fruit sauce. Other desserts might include crème brulée, chocolate truffle, cheesecake or a selection of sorbets. 'Relaxed' service has sometimes seem disconnected but is generally 'courteous'. The modestly priced short wine list starts with house French at £9.95.

CHEF: Nicholas Rochford PROPRIETOR: Darela Ltd OPEN: all week 12 to 3, 6 to 11 CLOSED: Christmas MEALS: alc (main courses £9 to £13). Set L £13.50 (2 courses). BYO £5 SERVICE: not inc CARDS: Amex, Delta, MasterCard, Switch, Visa DETAILS: 50 seats. Private parties: 35 main room, 20 and 35 private rooms. Vegetarian meals. Children's helpings. No cigars/pipes in dining-room. Music. Air-conditioned

Vong

map 14

Berkeley Hotel, Wilton Place, SW1X 7RL — COOKING 5
TEL: (0171) 235 1010 FAX: (0171) 235 1011 — COST £32–£73

'This is probably the only restaurant in a hotel that does not look or feel like one,' reckoned a well-travelled visitor. It gets a large dose of glamour from its customers, who make the cool, brightly lit décor seem like a stage set. Jean-Georges Vongerichten's day-to-day control has passed seamlessly to Daniel del Vecchio, who turns out the French-Thai crossover food with skill. Although the idea is hardly revolutionary, dishes are innovative, and the repertoire includes many that don't appear anywhere else. Lightness is a characteristic, fresh flavours are to the fore, and fish has a lot to do with it: crab spring roll with a tamarind dipping sauce, perhaps, or sea bass in a sweet-and-sour mushroom broth.

'Refined' is a word that recurs to describe the style, whether in chicken and foie gras dumplings with a truffle dipping sauce, or plump and 'beautifully cooked' squab pigeon breasts on an egg noodle basket with glazed pearl onions. Whether or not the two cultures interact significantly, as they do in foie gras with ginger and mango, hardly seems to matter. The food has a vitality that sets it apart, and this runs through to desserts of roast Asian pear with sableuse cake and liquorice ice-cream, and warm Valrhona chocolate cake, 'simply the best dish, ever so light, with long chocolate flavours'. A vegetarian menu and a £45 tasting menu are also available. Wines are at Knightsbridge prices, but there is decent drinking at under £25, with house red £13.50, house white £14.95.

CHEF: Daniel del Vecchio PROPRIETOR: Savoy Group plc OPEN: Mon to Sat L 12 to 2.30, all week D 6 to 11.30 (10 Sun) CLOSED: Christmas MEALS: alc (main courses £11.50 to £27). Set L £20, Set pre-theatre D (6 to 7pm) £17.50 SERVICE: 12.5% (optional), card slips closed CARDS: Amex, Delta, Diners, MasterCard, Switch, Visa DETAILS: 140 seats. Vegetarian meals. Children's helpings. Wheelchair access (also WC). Music. Air-conditioned

Wagamama £ — map 15

4A Streatham Street, WC1A 1JB — COOKING 1
TEL: (0171) 323 9223 FAX: (0171) 323 9224 — COST £15–£28

Wagamama runs on vitality. Based on the ramen shops that have been part of Japanese life for more than 200 years, it offers noodles for the '90s in a setting of utilitarian benches and 'mobile drinks monitors', as the menu describes them. The queues are endless, and the noise can be deafening, which isn't surprising, because the management claims to serve 'around 1,200 meals per day'. The menu focuses on ramen noodles in soup, pan-fried soba and udon noodles with all kinds of toppings, and ultra-thin somen noodles with a spicy sauce. 'Positive eating' continues with various side-dishes, which are also eaten as starters: gyoza (hand-made dumplings) and ebi katsu (deep-fried king prawns with lime and a chilli dip) are typical. Drinks emphasise the healthy, energising theme: carbonated ginseng, spiced tomato juice, calpico, and free green tea, not to mention organic wines, with prices starting at £8.50. A second branch, at 10A Lexington Street, W1R 3HS, operates on identical lines.

PROPRIETOR: A. Yau OPEN: all week 12 to 11 (12.30 to 10 Sun) CLOSED: Christmas MEALS: alc (main courses £4.50 to £7). Set L and D £7.50 to £9 (2 courses) SERVICE: not inc CARDS: MasterCard, Switch, Visa DETAILS: 112 seats. Vegetarian meals. Children welcome. No smoking in dining-room. No music. Air-conditioned

White Onion NEW ENTRY — map 13

297 Upper Street, N1 2TU — COOKING 3
TEL: (0171) 359 3533 — COST £23–£47

Bijan Behzadi, owner of the Green Olive and the Red Pepper (see entries), has sprouted another vegetable, although, given the colour scheme, 'Purple Aubergine' might have suited it better. The large, high-ceilinged, minimally decorated dining-room conveys a sense of confidence, which extends to the food: a French/Mediterranean menu as modern as they come, full of grilling and 'guess-me' items such as potato ravioli niçoise (served with lamb). Clear winners have included an unusual and highly successful foie gras, mozzarella and rocket salad, 'beautiful' risotto with a crown of jewel-bright peppers, and delicate crab ravioli with a tang of lemon grass. Desserts are less adventurous: apple tart, summer pudding, or a fig tart that was outshone by its accompanying cinnamon ice-cream. Chairs are unlikely to enamour even those with good backs, and service has been described as 'patchy'. Prices, especially for the set-lunch menu, are extremely competitive for this neck of the woods. Fifty wines centre on France, and there are three dessert wines including a rare Moscato Passito. House wines start at £9.50.

CHEF: Eric Guignard PROPRIETOR: Bijan Behzadi OPEN: Wed to Sun L 12 to 2.30 (3.30 Sun), Mon to Sat D 6.30 to 10.30 (11 Fri and Sat) MEALS: alc Sat and Sun L, Mon to Sat D (main courses L £6.50 to £8, D £9 to £12.50). Set L Wed to Fri £10.50 (2 courses) to £13.50, Set D (available before 8.30pm) £13.50 SERVICE: not inc CARDS: Amex, Delta, MasterCard, Switch, Visa DETAILS: 65 seats. Private parties: 30 main room. Vegetarian meals. Children's helpings. No cigars/pipes in dining-room. Music. Air-conditioned

Wilsons

map 12

236 Blythe Road, W14 0HJ COOKING 1
TEL: (0171) 603 7267 FAX: (0171) 602 9018 COST £27–£41

Bob Wilson's set-up is just about classifiable as a Scottish restaurant thanks to Finnan haddock pudding, haggis, Atholl Brose and, when he is in residence, an occasional skirl on the bagpipes. The Highland repertoire is also buttressed with salmon fish-cakes with parsley sauce, and grilled venison steak with tarragon butter. On the other hand, there may be king prawns with an 'appropriately fiery' Thai dressing of chilli and lime, or a well-constructed mound of sauté calf's liver with spinach and red onions, approvingly described as 'superior home cooking'. Vegetables are charged extra. Puddings, which may include a calorific lemon and lime posset with a piece of shortbread, seem to hit the target. Informal and good-humoured service ('both waiters were dressed as if they were in the middle of doing the decorating') is generally appreciated. Wines are a rather cursory French-led bunch, with house vins de pays at £8.95.

CHEF: Robert Hilton PROPRIETORS: Robert Hilton and Bob Wilson OPEN: Sun to Fri L 12.30 to 2.30, Mon to Sat D 7.30 to 10 MEALS: alc (main courses £8 to £11.50) SERVICE: 12.5% (optional), card slips closed CARDS: Amex, Delta, MasterCard, Switch, Visa DETAILS: 44 seats. Private parties: 44 main room. Vegetarian meals. Children's helpings. Wheelchair access (no WC). Music. Air-conditioned

Wiltons

map 15

55 Jermyn Street, SW1Y 6LX COOKING 4
TEL: (0171) 629 9955 FAX: (0171) 495 6233 COST £32–£75

St James's is London at its most dignified, and Wiltons salutes the Edwardian era with polished brass, etched glass, heavy velvet curtains and mock gas lamps, plus a multitude of fishing prints. It is 'the place to go if you are looking for a fish restaurant with a cosy, Establishment atmosphere and don't mind how much it costs'. The food takes up the old-fashioned theme too, majoring in simply treated seafood 'of the highest quality': potted shrimps, dressed crab, Native oysters, or lobster four ways. Plaice, turbot and halibut may be poached or grilled, and a more elaborate dish occasionally thrown in for good measure, perhaps lemon sole stuffed with pike and spinach mousse, in a champagne butter sauce.

Alternatively, start with asparagus (presented with melted butter and hollandaise in silver jugs), and move on to sirloin steak, mixed grill or lamb's kidneys, or else game in season. A choice of four savouries provides competition for sherry trifle, or simple fresh fruit in season. Bread comes already buttered.

One couple felt like millionaires, but then the long-serving staff are probably used to those. A page of champagnes heads up the wine list, which continues with mostly classy French wines at St James's prices. House wines start at £13.50.

CHEF: Ross Hayden PROPRIETORS: Rupert, Richard and James Hambro OPEN: Sun to Fri 12 to 2.30, 6 to 10.30 CLOSED: Easter and Christmas MEALS: alc (main courses £9.50 to £26). Set L Sun £19.75 SERVICE: not inc CARDS: Amex, Diners, MasterCard, Switch, Visa DETAILS: 100 seats. Private parties: 18 main room. No children under 12. Jacket and tie. Wheelchair access (no WC). No music. Air-conditioned

Yo! Sushi £✱

NEW ENTRY map 15

52 Poland Street, W1V 3DF COOKING 1
TEL: (0171) 287 0443 FAX: (0171) 287 2324 COST £13–£27

'More fun than anywhere else in town to eat,' reckoned one visitor, and the contrast with formal Japanese eating could not be greater. This is the place to graze on accessible, relatively inexpensive sushi, served up in a manner reminiscent of Charlie Chaplin's *Modern Times*: made by automatic sushi machines, and delivered on a conveyor belt (it claims to be the world's longest at 60 metres), with the added attraction of robot drinks trolleys offering cold beer and warm saké. Water is piped to auto dispensers on the counter. Plates are colour-coded according to price, and might carry tuna, sole, prawn, salmon roe, scallop or squid. An expert's advice is to stick to salmon off the conveyor belt, and order what you fancy to be made fresh (hand-rolled): attract a waiter's attention, and he will shout 'Yo!' to attract the chef's attention. Expect 'fusion' sushi and some vegetarian novelties.

CHEF: Nacer Arab PROPRIETOR: Simon Woodroffe OPEN: all week 12 to 12 CLOSED: 25 Dec MEALS: alc (main courses £1.50 to £3.50) SERVICE: none, card slips closed CARDS: Amex, Delta, Diners, MasterCard, Switch, Visa DETAILS: 120 seats. Vegetarian meals. Children welcome. No smoking in dining-room. Wheelchair access (no WC). Music. Air-conditioned

Zafferano

map 14

15 Lowndes Street, SW1X 9EY COOKING 6
TEL: (0171) 235 5800 FAX: (0171) 235 1971 COST £29–£54

'I would say this is some of the very best Italian food in London,' volunteered one experienced reporter. It is served to a 'well-heeled crowd' (what else in Belgravia?) in two street-side rooms, the first cream with colourful curtains, the second more 'rustic' with bare red brick walls and wooden floors. It may not have the drama of a wood-fired oven or a kitchen on view, but it doesn't half get the essentials right. In true Italian fashion, simplicity is the keynote, from beef carpaccio with truffle oil to gnocchi with smoked cheese. The menu's generous length is helped by a few cold starters, including 'utterly straightforward' chargrilled aubergine, courgette and fennel with shreds of basil, or good quality buffalo mozzarella with a slice of aubergine and dressed salad leaves.

Three things stand out above all else. First, 'fresh and impeccably cooked pasta', including linguine with clams, or ravioli filled with pheasant and black truffle. Second, fish comes in for unqualified praise. It varies from monk with walnuts and capers to cod with lentils, from John Dory with potatoes and olives to simply cooked salmon served with nothing more than cooking juice and spinach. Third, desserts are well done, maybe figs in a red wine and cinnamon sauce, rhubarb tart with frozen yoghurt, or chocolate and almond tart with amaretto ice cream. Even those that sound mundane – tiramisù and rum baba for instance – are impressively done. Bread comes with a saucer of olive oil, service has generally been pleasant and attentive, and the Italian regions are well represented on the wine list, particularly Tuscany, Piedmont and Veneto. There is just enough to provide interest under £20, and house red and white are £10.70.

CHEF/PROPRIETOR: Giorgio Locatelli OPEN: Mon to Sat 12 to 2.30, 7 to 11 CLOSED: 2 weeks in Dec, 2 weeks in Aug, bank hols. MEALS: Set L £16.50 (2 courses) to £19.50, Set D £21.50 (2 courses) to £28.50 SERVICE: not inc CARDS: Amex, Delta, MasterCard, Switch, Visa DETAILS: 55 seats. Vegetarian meals. Children welcome. Smart dress preferred. Wheelchair access (no WC). Music. Air-conditioned

Zen Central

map 15

20 Queen Street, W1X 7PJ
TEL: (0171) 629 8089 and 8103
FAX: (0171) 493 6181

COOKING **6**
COST £44–£90

The simple luxuries at this flagship of a chain of Chinese restaurants include quietly efficient air-conditioning, subtle lighting, widely spaced tables, and a deep-pile carpet that makes the room less noisy than 1990s minimalism normally allows. The kitchen uses fine (and often rare) ingredients (and eschews MSG) in correspondingly fine dishes, so expect to see abalone, shark's fin, suckling pig, and 'superbly fresh' sauté scallops. But making clichés exciting is an even more severe test of culinary skills. This kitchen passes with honours in fried seaweed with added pine-kernels, and in crispy aromatic Szechuan duck with perfect, thin pancakes that do not break up when wrapped around the filling; and for once there are enough pancakes to match the generously sized duck. Despite minor disappointments at an inspecton meal, the cooking engenders enough confidence to suggest that a no-holds-barred banquet, 'leaving the choice mainly to the chef' would be worth considering.

The menu is not dauntingly long, but caters for demanding palates with crispy chicken with ham and nuts, lobster baked with tangerine peel and garlic, and shredded pork with mixed vegetables, alongside earthier delights such as chicken and pig's trotter marinated in rice wine and served with jellyfish. Western traditionalists will appreciate being able to finish with good ice-creams and refreshing sorbets, but there's also more exotic honey-melon tapioca pudding. Service is generally pleasant and helpful. The predominantly French wine list is geared towards the well-heeled, with even the house wines costing £15 a bottle, £4 a glass.

CHEF: Ming Kong Kwan PROPRIETOR: Tealeaf Ltd OPEN: all week 12.15 to 2.30, 6.30 to 11.30 (10.45 Sun) CLOSED: 24 and 25 Dec MEALS: alc (main courses £10.50 to £24). Set L £28, Set D £38 to £45. Cover £1 SERVICE: 15% (optional), card slips closed CARDS: Amex, Delta, Diners, MasterCard, Switch, Visa DETAILS: 90 seats. Private parties: 80 main room, 20 private room. Vegetarian meals. Children welcome. No cigars in dining-room. Music. Air-conditioned

Zujuma's

NEW ENTRY map 12

58A Wimbledon Hill Road, SW19 7PA COOKING 3
TEL: (0181) 879 0916 FAX: (0181) 944 0861 COST £19–£36

Zujuma's is a joint venture between Zuju Shareef and the Whitbread group. Their declared aim is not to be 'an Indian restaurant' but a modern, informal place serving food 'from India . . . and beyond'. The striking modern décor uses a harmonious range of terracotta, yellow ochre and dusty green, with antique artefacts vying for visual attention with spice-filled glass tubes. Relaxed service is by pleasant young people knowledgeable about the menu.

Zuju Shareef was brought up in Hyderabad, where the cooking styles of many Indian regions interact. Her menu is almost entirely new even to *cognoscenti*, and incorporates some Middle Eastern overtones in the form of fez-un-jun (chicken in a walnut and pomegranate sauce). 'Portion control' is oxymoronic: some dishes are impertinently small, others insultingly large. Among the more successful dishes might be ground lamb patties served on a wok-like skillet, 'slices of chicken breast lightly tossed in ginger and peppers', and 'lentils in a tamarind sauce with cumin and curry leaves'. Breads and rice (the lemon version with mustard and cumin is good) are included with every dish. More interesting desserts than usual have included a superb ice-cream made with Kisan mangoes, and mitha (poached guavas with cream). A final surprise is proper filter coffee. Decent wines from £9.75 include six by the glass.

CHEF: Zuju Shareef PROPRIETOR: Zujuma's Restaurants Ltd OPEN: all week 12 to 3, 6 to 10.30 (Sun 10) CLOSED: 25 and 26 Dec, 1 Jan MEALS: alc (main courses £6.50 to £9). Set L £6.95 to £11.95 SERVICE: not inc CARDS: Amex, Delta, MasterCard, Switch, Visa DETAILS: 60 seats. Vegetarian meals. Children welcome. No-smoking area. Wheelchair access (no WC). Music. Air-conditioned

London Round-ups

Eating out in London is largely a question of picking the location that offers the right kind of food for the occasion. To assist *Guide* readers, the Round-up section provides details of a range of restaurants, bistros and cafés that are well worth a visit, but do not merit a full entry. Each is included for a specific reason: you may find lunchtime bolt-holes for shoppers, good hotel dining-rooms, chippies, Cantonese soup kitchens, up-and-coming brasseries, even a new star or two in the making. Entries are based on readers' recommendations, often backed up by inspectors' reports. In some cases we have put an establishment in the Round-ups rather than in the main-entry section because there are changes in the air or because there has been a dearth of votes in its favour. Reports on these places are especially welcome, as they enable us to extend our overall coverage of good food in the capital. This year, weekend closures and unusual opening times are given in the entries

Akasaka NW11
10A Golders Green Road map 12
(0181) 455 0676
Simple and homely Japanese restaurant that is 'low in subtlety and prices'. Hand-rolled sushi are the stars – fresh tuna with seaweed and a 'Californian' version with crab-sticks and avocado have been praised. Otherwise go for noodles (perhaps with tempura prawns in a light soup), agedofui (deep-fried bean curd), and mixed seaweed salad. Japanese residents and locals appreciate service from the lady of the house. Closed Sat L and Sun.

Albero and Grana SW3
Chelsea Cloisters, map 13
89 Sloane Avenue
(0171) 225 1048
Up-beat Chelsea venue patronised by 'a fashionable and very hip Eurocrowd'. The décor assaults the eyeballs with its vibrant colours and the pounding music comes straight from clubland. Tapas draws good reports and the bread is genuine ciabatta. The dining-room at the back offers Spanish regional dishes. Choose one of the better Torres wines if you are looking for reliably good drinking. Closed Sun L.

Apprentice SE1
31 Shad Thames map 13
(0171) 234 0254
Billed as the Butlers Wharf Chef School and a training ground for chefs working out their appenticeships prior to getting down to business. The mood is amiable, staff can be forgiven a few 'jitters' and the chefs bustle around. A fixed menu shows lots of 'Conranesque' overtones and the food is backed up by a fine choice of drinks. Reporters have particularly liked deep-fried goats' cheese, grape salad and beetroot vinaigrette, also saddle of rabbit with couscous and roast tomato salad, although the highlight is reckoned to be desserts such as lemon tart, and bread-and-butter pudding with peanut praline. Closed Sat and Sun.

L'Arte W1
126 Cleveland Street map 15
(0171) 813 1011
Philip Owens moved here in 1996 from the basement of the Arts Theatre near Leicester Square and his restaurant is now a firmly established part of the Fitzrovia scene. Black-and-white tiles and wooden tables are as rustic as the food. Robust Italian cooking might include

warm fennel salad, grilled swordfish, or Tuscan mixed meat stew. Desserts such as plum compote with rosemary and mascarpone have been praised. Closed Sat L and Sun.

Back to Basics W1
21A Foley Street map 15
(0171) 436 2181
Admirable little place specialising in fresh fish of all kinds, from cod and mackerel to more exotic items such as red emperor, sea bream, mahi-mahi and marlin. Start with fish soup, moules marinière, or avocado and bacon salad with raspberry and mint dressing, and finish with bread-and-butter pudding or chocolate tart. Simple bistro-style décor, friendly service by Polish girls. Closed Sat and Sun.

Belgo Centraal WC2
50 Earlham Street map 15
(0171) 813 2233
Much the same as its Chalk Farm sibling, Belgo Noord (see main entry), but bigger and noisier. Take the lift to the basement dining-room and sit at long communal benches for big portions of mussels, frites and Belgian beer served by waiters dressed as monks.

Beotys WC2
79 St Martin's Lane map 15
(0171) 836 8768/8548
'A wonderfully reassuring restaurant' and perfect if you want some relief from the relentless modernism of more fashionable addresses. For over half a century this bastion of the London scene has been delivering Continental cooking of the old school. Greece dominates the menu, although the Mediterranean and England also have their say. The presence of a full vegetarian menu impressed one couple who enjoyed mushrooms in tomato and garlic sauce, Spanish omelette, and vegetable risotto, plus strawberries to finish. Beguiling waiters have seen it all, but they still offer a little box of Turkish delights to take away. Closed Sun.

Bistrot 190 SW7
190 Queen's Gate map 14
(0171) 581 5666
Convenient for the Albert Hall, but don't expect quick service or much peace and quiet. Traditional French onion soup with rouille and croûtons, calf's liver cooked pink with mashed potato and leeks, and gnocchi with scallops have all been praised.

Blenheim NW8
21 Loudoun Road map 13
(0171) 625 1222
This tastefully converted pub was taken over by the Café Med group shortly before we went to press, but most of the staff seem set to stay on. Currently the pub still trades as the Blenheim. Menus promise dishes such as mixed mushroom risotto, marinated corn-fed chicken with lemon and basil, and prune and armagnac crème brûlée.

Bombay Brasserie SW7
Courtfield Close map 14
(0171) 370 4040/373 0971
Once a jewel in the crown among London's Indian restaurants and renowned for its luxurious Raj décor complete with huge potted palms, chandeliers and a live pianist. A useful venue if you want to embark on a gastronomic tour of the Subcontinent. Bombay roadside snacks, Goan fish dishes, tandooris from the north-west Frontier and more make up the pricey menu. Lunch is a ten-dish buffet.

Books for Cooks W11
4 Blenheim Crescent map 13
(0171) 221 1992
Not so much a restaurant, more a 'test kitchen' for recipes gleaned from the shelves of cookbooks on sale in the shop. The menu, naturally, changes daily, but there's always a soup followed by two mains (one of which is likely to be vegetarian) plus some sweet things to finish. Rock-bottom prices. Open 9.30am to 6pm and closed Sun.

Le Braconnier SW14
467 Upper Richmond Road map 12
(0181) 878 2853
Modest neighbourhood French restaurant that survives in a street peppered with eating places of every complexion. Outside it looks bright and welcoming, inside continues the theme of jolliness. Starters and desserts have been singled out from the menu: lobster terrine with lobster sauce, a tartlet of spicy prawns and spinach, chocolate mousse, and 'glace de bastide' for example. Main courses can be uneven, although lamb cutlets on ratatouille has been well received. Closed Saturday and Sunday lunch-times.

Brook W6
320 Goldhawk Road map 12
(0181) 741 1994
Another graduate from the bare-boarded school of 'gastropub' conversions. This one is high-ceilinged, airy and relaxed, with a blackboard menu that changes from day to day. Reporters have sung the praises of pan-fried chicken breast with wild garlic mash, braised lamb shank, and 'superb' poached haddock with poached egg and a creamy leek sauce. Wines on the short, inexpensive list offer a fair choice.

Le Cadre N8
10 Priory Road map 12
(0181) 348 0606
This 'cheap and cheerful' North London bistro celebrated ten years in 1997. Expect 'classic French with a modern touch': red mullet and orange soup, medallions of pork with leeks and a Noilly Prat and mustard sauce, and 'French bread-and-butter pudding' with pears and cognac. Closed Sat L and Sun.

Café du Marché EC1
22 Charterhouse Square map 15
(0171) 608 1609
'Excellent' French restaurant hidden away down an alley off Charterhouse Square. The décor is defined by much polished wood and the regularly changing menu impresses with its creativity and consistency. Typical dishes might include roast duck with orange and bacon, or veal kidneys with cider, followed by black cherry tart. Decent French, Spanish and New World wines. Live jazz in the evenings. Closed Sat L and Sun.

Chapel NW1
48 Chapel Street map 13
(0171) 402 9220
A pair of reporters who dropped into this born-again watering-hole around Chrtistmas time found it to be much better than the usual pub grub. They dined splendidly on hot game salad with sultanas, a terrine of crab and smoked salmon, 'perfectly pink' fillet of venison with red wine and juniper *jus*, and 'fresh-from-the-sea' sole with rich langoustine and scallop sauce. To finish, there was a hedonistic dark chocolate mousse. Reasonably priced wines.

Chez Gérard W1
8 Charlotte Street map 15
(0171) 636 4975
'Continues to produce steaks cooked as specified (so long as you specify rare, I suspect) and the best frites in the capital,' commented a reporter. The décor is reminscent of a railway carriage, but what matters is the food and the value for money. Details such as breads, salads, and desserts of petit pot au chocolate and nougat glacé are on target. Service is 'splendidly Gallic', the wine is highly palatable. Part of a mini-chain including branches at 31 Dover Street, W1, tel. (0171) 499 8171, and 119–120 Chancery Lane, WC2, tel. (0171) 405 0290, and a newly-opened branch at 64 Bishopsgate, EC2, tel. (0171) 588 1200 where Laurent Lebeau (ex-Soho Soho, see main entry) is cooking. More reports please.

Christoph's SW10
7 Park Walk map 14
(0171) 349 8866
'Pleasant, enjoyable' neighbourhood spot next door to the auspicious Aubergine

(see main entry). Bread is good, salads are seasonal and cheese of the day is worth ordering. Otherwise, the menu promises rillettes of rabbit, rack of lamb, Catalan stew, and some cracking sweets including 'superb' lemon and raspberry brûlée, and nougat parfait with citrus sauce. Wines are praiseworthy and young 'smiley' staff are eager to please.

Chuen Cheng Ku W1
17 Wardour Street map 15
(0171) 734 3281 and 3509
A famous totem-pole marks the entrance to this venerable Chinatown warhorse that operates on several levels. Dim-sum are wheeled around on heated trolleys from 11am to 6pm, although reports have homed in on the main menu, which sticks to its Cantonese roots while drifting occasionally into northern territory. Prawn dumplings, whole crab in chilli and black bean sauce, barbecued pork, and Cantonese roast duck have been endorsed. Service copes amicably with pre- and post-theatre orders.

Chung's W1
22 Wardour Street map 15
(0171) 287 3886
If fish lips, pig's intestines and duck's tongues sound appealing, then this is where to go: it has 'one of the most extensive listings of Chinese exotica ever to be seen in Soho,' writes an aficionado. Although the menu lists its share of Westernised dishes, it pays to take the plunge and go for the special menu, which features a page of hotpots as well as seafood aplenty; note deep-fried duck stuffed with taro and served with mushroom sauce. Staff are 'unusually helpful'. More reports please.

Clerkenwell Restaurant & Bar EC1
73 Clerkenwell Road map 13
(0171) 831 7595
Vibrant restaurant with zany metallic artwork on the walls, grey tiles on the floors and a menu that goes the whole way with modern Italian renditions. One reporter thought the roast cod with aubergines and a tomato and caper salsa was 'terrific', but the repertoire also embraces tagliatelle verde with scallops and pepper oil, grilled bluefin tuna with peperonata, oregano and black olives. The house dessert is a Sicilian speciality: cannoli' with ricotta, candied orange, Vermouth rosso and honey sauce.

Condotti W1
4 Mill Street map 14
(0171) 499 1308
West End shoppers home in on this ultra-reliable independent pizza place down Mayfair way. What it offers is a fistful of flavours and toppings, plus a supporting cast of garlic bread, Mediterranean salads, ice-creams and cheesecake. To drink, go for one of the gutsy Italian wines or Peroni beer, and don't miss the cappuccino.

Cork & Bottle WC2
44–46 Cranbourn Street map 15
(0171) 734 7807
Still rated as one of the most successful wine bars in London, even though there are plenty of new kids on the block these days. What attracts is the gregarious atmosphere, the perfectly appropriate choice of food and, of course, Don Hewitson's predominantly Antipodean wine list. The Hanover Square Wine Bar & Grill, 25 Hanover Square, Wl, tel. (0171) 408 0935, is also out of the same stable.

Diwana Bhel Poori NW1
121 Drummond Street map 13
(0171) 387 5556
The pick of the bunch among Drummond Street's Indian vegetarian restaurants: 'as consistent as can be,' notes a regular. Stay with snacks for the best results – bhel pooris, aloo papri chat, and sev puris are 'truly excellent', while very fine 'fat' samosas are filled to bursting with spiced vegetables and served with a chilli-laced tomato sauce. Don't miss the lassi, which has few rivals in the capital.

Ebla W6
262–264 King Street map 12
(0181) 741 1177
Sound Lebanese cooking in a coolly decorated room with abstract blue patterns on the walls and an oriental carpet on the floor. Spicing is distinctive, flavours are true and familar dishes are often given an unexpected twist. Wagon-wheel-shaped falafel with tahini dip, crunchy fried kibbeh, delicate cold aubergine dip, and 'punchily spiced lamb kawarma' (diced with pine-nuts) have showed the kitchen in a good light. Drink Lebanese beer or Middle Eastern wine.

Efes Kebab House W1
80 Great Titchfield Street map 15
(0171) 636 1953
Opened in 1973 and still one of the most cherished Turkish restaurants in town. Vegetarians and carnivores are equally well catered for, especially with the line-up of around 20 hot and cold meze, ranging from spinach with yoghurt and garlic to chicken with walnut sauce. Main dishes are built around man-sized quantities of protein in the shape of grills and kebabs. Finish with one of the gooey pastries from the trolley. Efes beer is an alternative to the short list of gutsy Turkish wines. Closed Sun. Efes II is at 175–177 Great Portland Street, NW1, tel. (0171) 436 0600.

Enoteca Turi SW15
28 Putney High Street map 12
(0181) 785 4449
The name means roughly 'wine place or wine library' and the fruit of the grape is given equal billing alongside food in Guiseppe Turi's Putney restaurant. Contemporary realisations of Italian regional dishes are the kitchen's stock-in-trade, and the menu promises specialities such as marinated fillet of trout with fruit mustard, wild boar with sausage and almond stuffing, or breast of chicken with oven-dried tomato, tarragon and porcini. Finish with grilled nectarines and pannacotta, or fresh raspberries with mascarpone cream and Neapolitan shortbread.

L'Escargot Doré W8
2–4 Thackeray Street map 13
(0171) 937 8508
'A little treasure in Kensington', much favoured by locals as well as others from further afield. The menu is dyed-in-the-wool 'Français' with helpful English translations. What the kitchen delivers is classic stuff with a few modern twists: scallops with lime and coriander sauce, and saddle of wild venison wrapped in three peppers share the billing with snails in garlic butter, breast of chicken with tarragon sauce, and hot apple tart with caramel sauce. Closed Sat L and Sun.

Formula Veneta SW10
14 Hollywood Road map 14
(0171) 352 7612
Really friendly Italian place where the kitchen comes up with some out-of-the-ordinary offerings such as refreshing zucchini and radicchio soup, as well as a good clutch of pasta dishes: ravioli stuffed with ricotta and basil with a home-made pesto sauce brought smiles to one reporter. Start with 'fabulous' bread dotted with coarse sea salt and finish with cappuccino and biscotti. Not expensive. Closed Sun.

Frederick's N1
Camden Passage map 13
(0171) 359 2888
Much used by the rich and famous, whether they be glitzy film heroes, media folk or new stars in the political firmament. Chef Andrew Jeffs cooks to a menu that makes all the correct culinary noises: crispy duck is served with spiced aubergine salad, baked plaice comes with champ, pea cream and crispy bacon, while pan-fried veal chop is accompanied by Parmesan, asparagus and artichoke gnocchi. Desserts such as lime parfait with Amaretti biscuits and lemon confit are equally in tune. Closed Sun.

Gate W6
Temple Lodge, map 12
51 Queen Caroline Street
(0181) 748 6932
Enterprising vegetarian cooking in a secluded spot on the edge of the Hammersmith roundabout. The restaurant is a high-ceilinged room with mustard walls and old church chairs, and the menu is overtly ambitious. Ingredients tumble onto the plate in colourful clutter: risotto fritters with Dolcelatte, lamb's lettuce and yellow pepper coulis; Thai spring rolls with coconut and chilli dipping sauce; and sesame-crusted teriyaki aubergines with shiitake mushrooms and noodles. Balls of melon in port with mint and a ginger sorbet makes a refreshing finale. Closed Sat L and Sun.

Geales W8
2 Farmer Street map 13
(0171) 727 7969
A celebrity fish-and-chip restaurant on the corner of a pretty London street, much frequented by famous faces who know a good piece of haddock when they see one. Start with deep-fried clams, finish with apple crumble and sip a glass of champagne if you're feeling flush. Open Tue to Sat.

Gecko NW1
7–9 Pratt Street map 15
(0171) 424 0203
'Fresh, fun and fusion' is one reporter's summing up of this modernist, red and purple addition to the Camden scene. The kitchen deals in 'Pan-Asian' dishes with influences from most parts of the Far East. Singapore contributes potato fritters with sweet-and-sour chutney, Thailand provides spiced fish-cakes with sesame and soya sauce, while from Malaysia there is bah mee goreng (fried pork noodles topped with shredded omelette). Also note other assemblages such as chargrilled tuna on kintobi noodles with paw-paw salsa. Willing youthful service.

Gopal's of Soho W1
12 Bateman St map 15
(0171) 434 1621/0840
The first of a trio of swish Indian venues opened by N.S. Pittal (known to all as 'Gopal'). As in many new-breed establishments, the menu covers a lot of territory, taking in specialities from all parts of the Subcontinent. Mutton xacutti is a Goan dish cooked with coconut, vinegar and 'rare spices'; in addition, expect mangalorean crab, murgh tikka makhani, and a good showing of vegetables and breads.

Le Gothique SW18
Royal Victoria Patriotic Building map 12
(0181) 870 6567
Difficult to find at the rear of a large block of flats and situated on the first floor of an amazing Gothic building. French-style à la carte menu might offer moules provençale, followed by boned quail stuffed with port-soaked raisins, or tiger prawns and red snapper with a lemon butter sauce. Closed Sat L and Sun, and also note that the rear car park closes at midnight.

Greek Valley NW8
130 Boundary Road map 13
(0171) 624 3217
Peter and Effie Bosnic's Greek-Cypriot taverna has been given a 'new modern look' of late, with tiled floors and contemporary prints on the walls. The cooking remains true to its roots with plentiful hot and cold meze accompanied by Greek bread or pitta, then dishes along the lines of kleftiko, beef stifado with savoury rice, various kebabs and grills such as kotopoulo (baby chicken sprinkled with oregano). Drink one of the affordable Greek wines. Only open for dinner Monday to Saturday.

Green Cottage NW3
9 New College Parade, map 13
Finchley Road
(0171) 722 5305 and 7892
'Long may Green Cottage survive,' declared one reporter. The surroundings

may be utilitarian, but the cooking is good and honest in this reliable neighbourhood restaurant. Some dishes are on a par with the best in Soho Chinatown: squid baked with salt and chilli is reckoned to be 'outstanding'. Open all day.

La Grignote NW3
77 Heath Street map 13
(0171) 433 3455
Small French Hampstead favourite with friendly service offering excellent grilled sea bass with mange-tout, and smoked haddock with poached egg on a bed of spinach. Good wine list, but not cheap for food or wine. Closed Sun.

Jindivick N1
201 Liverpool Road map 13
(0171) 607 7710
Antipodean pub conversion, 'slightly off the Islington beaten track', offering 'Pacific Rim' and 'Mediterranean Rim' (i.e. including Maghrebian) cooking. Aboriginal decoration is bright and cheerful, so are the staff. Approved dishes include lamb with an onion, feta and olive salsa, and duck with red cabbage. 'Good food, good value, excellent for children.' More reports please. Closed Sun D.

Lavender SW11
171 Lavender Hill map 12
(0171) 652 7502
'Laid-back but friendly' is the attitude and that suits the 'trendy' clientele and sparseness of the room – wooden floors and assorted tables and chairs. The menu is chalked on blackboards and changes thoughout the day. Starters might include smoked haddock daube with herb tagliatelle, followed by chargrilled marinated chicken and finishing with pannacotta or lemon posset.

Lemonia NW1
89 Regents Park Road map 12
(0171) 586 7454
'Big, bustling, brasserie-type place' offering ample portions of genuine Greek food. Admirable meze include deep-fried squid, smoked pork loin with toasted goats' cheese, and artichokes with broad beans, as well as hummus, tabbouleh and the like. Main courses tend to be hefty chunks of chargrilled protein or slow-cooked casseroles. Splendid value, brisk professional service. Closed Sat L and Sun D.

London Hilton, Windows Rooftop Restaurant W1
22 Park Lane map 15
(0171) 493 8000
The Windows has an impressive view and chef Jacques Rolancy an impressive pedigree. He has been awarded the 'Meilleur Ouvrier de France en Cuisine', a high accolade indeed. We are disappointed by the lack of reports. The cuisine is described as 'bourgeoise légère' and produces a tartare of lobster and asparagus, pan-fried fillet of beef with a bacon potato cake, and a croustillant of fruits with an apricot sorbet. Closed Sat L and Sun D.

Mandalay W2
444 Edgware Road map 13
(0171) 258 3696
'A treasure of a place' is one reporter's description of this cheerful Burmese café run by two enthusiastic extrovert brothers. Assorted fritters with a trio of dips are perennial favourites, mixed vegetables are ultra-fresh and rice is 'divinely coconutty'. The menu also takes in lamb with tamarind, sweet-and-sour king prawns with pineapple, and chicken with lemon grass. Drink Tiger beer or Burmese tea. Closed Sun.

Manzi's WC2
1–2 Leicester Street map 15
(0171) 734 0224
'After cricket or rugby matches I find this a good place to eat before catching a train home,' writes a Midlander: perhaps he is unware that this, the oldest of old-stagers among London's fish restaurants, also has accommodation. The Manzi family set up the place more than 60 years ago and it

seems to tick over, oblivious to fashion or local ethnic competition. Go for the grilled fish with chips or salad, although crab cocktail and scallops with bacon have also been praised. Staff know the ropes. Closed Sun L.

Marquis W1
121A Mount Street map 15
(0171) 499 1256
Radically revamped Mount Street oldie with a cool, stylish and modern interior with serene colour schemes and eye-catching light fittings. Densely flavoured fish soup, and an 'immaculate' foie gras terrine have found favour with reporters, while other dishes on the menu might include spinach and ricotta tortellini, or roasted monkfish tail in a red wine sauce. Closed Sat L and Sun.

Mezzanine SE1
National Theatre, map 13
Upper Ground
(0171) 928 3531
'We enjoyed the food more than the play,' noted one critical couple. The format is flexible, menus are well thought out and service is confident but relaxed. Timing is crucial if you have to be fed and watered before curtain-up, but this place succeeds brilliantly. Praiseworthy offerings have included wholewheat pancakes with spinach and ricotta, salmon fish-cakes, and asparagus risotto, not to mention excellent rice-pudding brûlée. Closed Sun.

New World W1
1 Gerrard Place map 15
(0171) 434 2508
Along with Chueng Cheng Ku (see Round-up entry) this vast amphitheatre of a place is the best-known Soho venue for 'trolley-based' dim-sum. Hundreds pack the three floors where there is oodles of space for the waitresses to wheel around their wares. Go early for the best and freshest selection of steamed dumplings, crispy morsels, slithery chueng fung, roasted meats and more besides.

Oceana W1
Jason Court, map 15
76 Wigmore Street
(0171) 224 2992
This light and airy basement restaurant off Wigmore Street has seen a few good chefs come and go. Pierre Khodja is now at the stoves, having moved from Bistrot Soho (see main entry, London), and early menus have included a foie gras and duck plate with toasted brioche, and cured salmon with lobster mash potato and truffle oil. Reports please. Closed Sat L and Sun.

Parson's Nose SW6
803 Fulham Road map 12
(0171) 731 7811
An offspring of nearby Fables (see main entry) serving contemporary rustic food in an uncluttered 'farmhouse' setting. The food is served in deep earthenware dishes and the menu moves into the realms of corn-fed chicken with split peas, button onions and bacon; pot-roast monkfish with ceps; and pear tarte Tatin. Cocktails are dispensed in the front bar area and there are some decent wines.

Patisserie Valerie W1
R.I.B.A., 66 Portland Place map 15
(0171) 580 5533
The first Patisserie Valerie opened in Soho in 1926 and now there are a number of branches scattered around the centre of the capital, including this outlet in the Royal Institute of British Architects. The formula is straight and true: great cakes and pastries, incomparable coffee, plus light lunches along the lines of marinated chicken salad, or hand-made pasta stuffed with goats' cheese and red peppers served with asparagus sauce.

Phoenix SW15
162 Lower Richmond Road map 12
(0181) 780 3131
Gargantuan white parasols mark the entrance to this stylish venue run by Rebecca Mascarenhas, owner of Sonny's (see main entries in London and Nottingham). The décor is as cool and

'90s designerish as they come, and the menu reads like a shopping list for the world market: caper berries, wasabi, lemon grass, sweet potatoes and cornbread all have their say. Recommendations have included crab and cod spring rolls with pickled vegetables, chargrilled rib of beef with 'rustic fries', and Kahlua and chocolate mascarpone cake.

Pierre Victoire SW1
9 William Street map 14
(0171) 823 1414
The empire has expanded from Edinburgh, conquered the south and is now consolidating. Still very popular and excellent value – particularly for its amazingly cheap lunches – it has proved a successful formula. Recommended starters have included broccoli and yoghurt soup, and steamed mussels in cider, followed by beef casserole with red peppers, or cod meunière. Finish with tarte Tatin or banoffi pie.

Pizzeria Castello SE1
20 Walworth Road map 13
(0171) 703 2556
'Totally reliable pizzas and pastas,' noted one devotee of this jolly place near the Elephant & Castle. Toppings and sauces are spot-on and blackboard specials are worth exploring (black tagliolini with clams and prawns has been 'absolutely superb'). Start with funghi trifolati and don't miss out on the excellent garlic bread. Value for money extends to the largely Italian wine list. Closed Sat L and Sun.

Poetry Café WC2
22 Betterton Street map 15
(0171) 240 5081
Subsidised by the Poetry Society – which has its HQ upstairs – and dedicated to the art of literary contemplation, the Café is fuelled by up-to-the-minute food. Sit at one of the tables endowed by well-known publishers and sample the likes of Thai fish soup, gravlax of tuna, accurately cooked guinea-fowl, and 'unbelievably tender' chargrilled lamb steak with spiced couscous. Sweets are not a particularly strong point, but the wine list is a corker in terms of value. Closed Sat L and Sun.

Polygon Bar & Grill SW4
4 The Polygon, map 12
Clapham Old Town
(0171) 622 1199
The location may seem 'slightly dilapidated', but the interior is pure 'blond wood' Conran, with blue and orange colours defining the tone, and a clientele of 20-somethings attuned to the loudness of '90s dance Muzak. What is offered is 'London eclectic' – which means lots of tangy warm salads, chargrilling at every turn and some seductively comforting puddings. Good intentions show in white gazpacho soup, juniper-marinated venison leg with apricot sambal, and rhubarb fool with pecan biscuits. Service is casual, cool and polite.

Poons WC2
27 Lisle Street map 15
(0171) 437 4549
The original 'Little Poons', now with a smart new frontage, more seats and stylish décor. Near-legendary wind-dried foods (duck, sausages, liver and so on) still appear on the revamped menu alongside Cantonese dim-sum, crispy belly pork, and soya chicken. Specialities include stir-fried eel with chillies and black mushrooms, deep-fried aubergines, and lamb and tofu hotpot. Presentation appeals to Western customers and service is ever-helpful.

Porte des Indes W1
32 Bryanston Street map 13
(0171) 224 0055
Marble stairways, cascades of water falling the whole height of the building and heavy vegetation set the tone in this exotic domed ballroom. The effect is 'amazing'. Indo-French cuisine is what the menu promises and flavours are convincingly varied. Starters might feature crab Malabar, and a salad of many

things including banana-flower, chicken and tamarind. Among main dishes, crevettes Assadh (prawns in coconut curry with mangos) and magret de canard Pulivar ('dark and mysterious' duck) in a rich sauce have been singled out. Service is full of smiles. Closed Sat L.

Randall & Aubin W1
16 Brewer Street map 15
(0171) 287 4447
Fun venue in a one-time butcher's and grocery store deep in X-certificate Soho. White tiled walls, wooden floors and marble-topped tables set the tone and the dining-room is dominated by a rotisserie and a counter display of crustacea. Go for the baguettes, soups, salads and seafood rather than a full three-course meal. Mixed crostini and Mediterranean prawn salad with great home-made mayo have been much enjoyed. Wines by the glass. No bookings. Closed Sun D.

Rebato's SW8
169 South Lambeth Road map 12
(0171) 735 6388 and 582 8089
'The suckling pig . . . transported us to Majorca,' enthused a couple who revelled in the happy atmosphere of this old-stager among south London restaurants. In the dining-room, Continental favourites include 'terrific' cuttlefish, grilled sardines, lamb cutlets, and liver and bacon. Alternatively park yourself in the tapas bar at the front, nibble some genuine Spanish tapas and wash it all down with a bottle or two of Torres. Closed Sat L and Sun.

Ritz Hotel W1
Piccadilly map 15
(0171) 493 8181
Maître chef des Cuisines (that's what they call the head chef at the Ritz) David Nicholls is off to the Hyde Park Hotel, and Giles Thompson has been recruited from Danesfield House in Medmenham, Buckinghamshire, to fill his shoes. Expect classical French cuisine with some modern influences. The dining-room always impresses and service has been described as 'excellent'. Reports please.

Rive Gauche SE1
61 The Cut map 13
(0171) 928 8645
Intimate little restaurant ideally placed for the Old Vic, Young Vic and 'everything on the South Bank'. The kitchen delivers consistently good French cooking along the lines of poached egg on spinach with a 'wonderful' tarragon sauce, steamed sole stuffed with prawns, thick-cut pork chop with prunes and a 'golden brown' armagnac sauce, followed by dark chocolate truffle mousse. Friendly, prompt service. Closed Sat L, Sun.

Satay House W2
13 Sale Place map 13
(0171) 723 6763
Genuine 'Muslim Malay home-cooking' is the order of the day in this popular restaurant close to Paddington Station. Satays are a must, along with kambing (traditional lamb soup), squid with soy and chillies, mee goreng, and murtabak (stuffed Malaysian pancake), which is reckoned to be 'as good as anything back in the East'. Drink iced tea or Tiger beer.

Sofra WC2
36 Tavistock Street map 15
(0171) 240 3972
Sunday opening and incredible value for money – not to mention occasional live guitar music – are the attractions at this branch of a mini-chain of cut-price Turkish eateries. Menus are flexible and meze stand out: zingy fresh salads, hummus topped with toasted nuts, herby tabbouleh, savoury aubergines, grilled halloumi cheese and more have been recommended. Lentil soup, braised lamb hock with potatoes, and a dessert of stuffed apricots sprinkled with pitachios have also earned praise, as have bread and the house red wine.

Spread Eagle SE10
2 Stockwell Street map 12
(0181) 853 2333
Victorian comedian Dan Leno once lived at this centuries-old coaching-inn much

favoured by today's thespians and visitors to the nearby Greenwich Theatre. For the last 30 years, Dick Moy has been providing a constantly changing repertoire of Anglo-French dishes with the emphasis on value for money. Reports have singled out home-cured duck breast on a salad of young spinach, fillet of pork with buttered lentils, medallions of lamb béarnaise, and crème Catalan. Closed Sun D.

Sun and Doves SE5
61 Coldharbour Lane map 12
(0171) 733 1525
Somewhat rough and ready décor, but there is decent food to be had at this Victorian pub conversion near King's College Hospital. A fan of chips and jelly was delighted to see both on the menu – albeit the latter was orange and elderflower with sliced fig and coconut to accompany. Elsewhere the menu zooms around taking in apple, celery and beetroot soup, bruschetta with mixed mushrooms, roast lamb, and Welsh rarebit along the way. Good-value wines.

Thistells SE22
65 Lordship Lane map 12
(0181) 299 1921
A short bar menu of snacks with a Middle Eastern bias is one crowd-pleasing feature of this quirkily decorated one-time grocer's shop. Sami Youssef also offers 'working lunches', celebratory blow-outs and a standard repertoire that takes in duck cassoulet, horura (main-course bean soup), and best-end of lamb with tarragon sauce, plus sweets like banoffi pie.

Toffs NW10
38 Muswell Hill Broadway map 12
(0181) 883 8656
'The best chippie I have tried in London,' writes a devotee of the genre. The 'always excellent' haddock is fried to order in crisp, grease-free batter, chips are 'competent' and the home-made tartare sauce is splendid. As for the gherkins, they are as good as anywhere. Closed Sun.

Vasco & Piero's Pavilion W1
15 Poland Street map 15
(0171) 437 8774
'Still the restaurant we visit most frequently,' noted a couple who have been eating at this favoured Italian for the best part of 20 years. The best deal is undoubtedly the fixed-price evening menu: 'seriously good' marinated salmon with pink grapefruit, grilled polenta with asparagus and Parmesan, then lamb cutlets with rosemary and garlic or linguine with monkfish and squid. Desserts such as piedmontese cake with chocolate sauce also hit the button. Worthwhile Italian wines, too.

Villandry Dining Room W1
170 Great Portland Street map 15
(0171) 631 3131
As we went to press the Carrarinis moved their restaurant and deli to larger premises in Great Portland Street. The deli and lunches continue, but they now open for dinner as well. The vibrant atmosphere should survive the move, as should the daily-changing menus offering goujons of sole with chips, chicken and lemon grass curry, or imam bayaldi with spiced yoghurt. Reports please.

Vincent's SW15
147 Upper Richmond Road map 12
(0181) 780 3553
Named after the painter of sunflowers and suitably emblazoned with colourful prints, Vincent's pleases the denizens of Putney with its relaxed atmosphere and commendable bistro-style food. Caesar salad, Cornish crab mousse, various pastas and apple pie are the sort of dishes to expect. The wine list features some interesting and unusual offerings. Closed Sun.

The Vine NW5
86 Highgate Road map 13
(0171) 209 0038
Yet another born-again pub-turned-

restaurant, but useful in an area bereft of decent neighbourhood eating places. Original decorative touches blend well with the pub décor and the atmosphere really buzzes. The handwritten daily menu tries to offer a bit more than Mediterranean/Pacific Rim clichés: falafel dribbled with thin hummus, Moroccan shank of lamb with couscous, jerk chicken, and tilapia with mango and paw-paw salsa suggest some imagination in the kitchen. Czech lager is on tap, wines are basic.

Wodka W8
12 St Albans Grove map 14
(0171) 937 6513
Much-liked Kensington venue famous for its range of around 30 mind-blowing flavoured vodkas and its menu of down-to-earth Polish food. 'Excellent' leek and potato soup, roast duck with red cabbage, and salt beef with carrots and broccoli have been among successes. Staff are young and professional, and on some nights you may find the pleasant Polish proprietor at the stove.

Yoshino W1
3 Piccadilly Place map 15
(0171) 287 6622
'You don't have to be Japanese to eat here but it helps,' noted a reporter, adding that the place serves 'good fish, good sushi and is somewhere to bear in mind as a bolt-hole off Piccadilly'. Everyone is made welcome in the thriving dining-room which is done out in bare, minimalist style. Prices are fair, appetisers really do wake up the palate and hot saké served in charming celadon flasks rounds things off.

England

ABBERLEY Hereford & Worcester map 5

▲ *Elms*

Abberley WR6 6AT
TEL: (01299) 896666 FAX: (01299) 896804
on A443, between Worcester and Tenbury Wells, 2m W of Great Witley

COOKING 2
COST £23–£49

This early-eighteenth-century house in the Teme Valley has huge rooms, high ceilings, and enough antiques and carved wood to give a convincing period feel. Botanical prints, a favourite device of the owners, decorate the dining-room, and the Frichots maintain an active and welcome front-of-house presence. Three-course meals offer a balanced choice of dishes – typically fish, red meat or fowl for main course – and tend to have a mainstream European tilt: hence a tortellini of crab, or guinea-fowl with mushrooms and madeira. The more-expensive dinner menu, although not significantly different in scope, might offer terrine of foie gras, scallops with herb risotto, or squab pigeon with Savoy cabbage and truffle *jus*. Desserts cover traditional territory from lemon tart to chocolate marquise. Service is the human side of formal. The predominantly French wine list also includes some interesting bottles from the New World. The house selection starts at £10.50.

CHEF: Andrew Palmer PROPRIETORS: Marcel and Corinna Frichot OPEN: all week 12 to 2, 7.30 to 9 MEALS: Set L Mon to Sat £10 (2 courses) to £12.50, Set L Sun £15.95, Set D £22.50 to £29.50 SERVICE: not inc, card slips closed CARDS: Amex, Delta, Diners, MasterCard, Switch, Visa DETAILS: 80 seats. 20 seats outside. Private parties: 80 main room, 30 and 50 private rooms. Car park. Children's helpings. No smoking in dining-room. Wheelchair access (also men's WC). No music ACCOMMODATION: 16 rooms, all with bath/shower. TV. Phone. B&B £75 to £135. Children welcome. Afternoon teas. Garden (*The Which? Hotel Guide*)

ALDEBURGH Suffolk map 6

Lighthouse £

77 High Street, Aldeburgh IP15 5AU
TEL/FAX: (01728) 453377

COOKING 2
COST £17–£31

'Nice place, nice people' neatly sums up the feel of this converted high-street shop. The kitchen has moved upstairs, making way for a pleasant new ground-floor room that looks out to the walled garden. The cooking brings in Japanese and Thai as well as Mediterranean flavours, ingredients are from local sources and cooking techniques are generally simple. Notably fresh Cromer crab, or Thai beef salad, might be among the starters, and main courses of fish are well reported: cod in beer batter, skate with black butter, and Dover sole with herb butter, for instance. Meat dishes appear to be less successful, although grilled lamb has been singled out as 'cooked to perfection'. Bread-and-butter pudding, or chocolate and brandy pot, could round things off. Service is informal and friendly. The wine list runs to some fifty sensibly priced bottles, with eight house wines starting at £8.50.

CHEFS: Sara Fox, Guy Welsh and Gavin Battle PROPRIETORS: Sara Fox and Peter Hill OPEN: all week 12 to 2.30, 7 to 10 CLOSED: Sun D and Mon L in winter, 2 weeks Jan, 1 week Oct MEALS: alc L (main courses £5.50 to £9). Set D £13.50 (2 courses) to £15.75 SERVICE: not inc, card slips closed CARDS: Delta, MasterCard, Switch, Visa DETAILS: 90 seats. 20 seats outside. Private parties: 50 main room, 25 private room. Children's helpings. No smoking in 1 dining-room. Wheelchair access (no WC). No music. Air-conditioned

Regatta £

171–173 High Street, Aldeburgh IP15 5AN — COOKING 3
TEL/FAX: (01728) 452011 — COST £21–£35

Aldeburgh thrives on visitors, a fact reflected in Regatta's seasonal opening times. Always 'relaxed and casual', its mood varies from a 'cheerful holiday atmosphere' to a more leisurely feel in winter when the Mabeys might have time to sit and chat. They have sold the Sudbury brasserie and the branch in Ipswich, but have other projects to occupy them, leaving Nigel Ramsbottom to provide the continuity here. Locally caught seafood is at the heart of the operation, from plain shellfish to roast cod on garlic-flavoured butter-beans, or grilled skate wing with black olives and capers.

There is much else besides, including Tuscan bread salad, spicy lamb meatballs, game in season, and sirloin steak with 'exquisite' chips. Somewhat unusually for a seaside fish restaurant, desserts are taken seriously, producing a string of endorsements for chocolate truffle pudding with coffee cream sauce, 'light' almond cake with apricot sauce, and banana and raisin strudel with cinnamon ice-cream. Around thirty wines begin with house French at £7.95.

CHEFS: Nigel Ramsbottom and Robert Mabey PROPRIETORS: Robert and Johanna Mabey OPEN: all week 12 to 2, 7 to 10 (phone to check Oct to Apr) MEALS: alc (main courses £7 to £12) SERVICE: not inc CARDS: Amex, Diners, Visa DETAILS: 90 seats. Private parties: 30 main room. Children's helpings. No smoking in 1 dining-room. No music

ALTRINCHAM Greater Manchester — map 8

Juniper

21 The Downs, Altrincham WA14 2QD — COOKING 7
TEL: (0161) 929 4008 FAX: (0161) 929 4009 — COST £24–£48

Paul Kitching is propelled by a sense of purpose, and 'his determination to serve black pudding and pearl barley risotto in an environment like Altrincham is either very brave or very foolhardy'. This is Cheshire stockbroker belt, after all, but the gamble seems to be paying off, and Juniper is now considered an established success. The cool and comfortable dining-room, with a swish downstairs bar for drinks before and after a meal, is variously described as 'after Mackintosh' and 'Tuscan' in theme, and the food likewise adopts an individual approach.

'For me, fish is an eternal inspiration,' writes Kitching, who sometimes devotes as much as 60 per cent of the menu to it. His speciality – fish soup – is not really a soup at all, but tiny pieces of grilled fish (perhaps four varieties), with diamonds of root vegetables, and a frothy white mussel stock thickened with cream, topped with herbs and olive oil. Game features in winter, although sadly 'south Manchester just doesn't seem to eat a great deal of offal'.

Cooking technique revolves around fast grilling and roasting. Even a 'ragoût' (like the fish 'soup') is not a slow-cooked dish but put together at the last minute, and meat tends to come as pink 'nuggets': of lamb with a strewing of vegetables, or duck with morels. Depth of flavour is supplied by first-rate materials, properly reduced stocks and, in the case of a fillet of hare on puff pastry, a purée of the liver. Careful treatment of texture adds to the appeal.

Desserts have included a 'bizarre but fabulous' ravioli of apricot with caramelised bananas, but soufflés draw most superlatives: 'ridiculously light' rice-pudding soufflé with vanilla ice-cream, 'intense' and locally famous passion-fruit soufflé, or an unlikely Christmas pudding soufflé that 'captured the essence of Christmas pud'. Some prices have escalated since last year, but 'slick and professional' service keeps glasses topped up unobtrusively and delivers 'an endless supply' of bread produced in-house. The wine list may be 'frustratingly haphazard', but what there is demonstrates careful selection. Prices start at £12.50.

CHEFS: Paul Kitching and Alan Hill PROPRIETORS: Peter and Nora Miles OPEN: Tue to Fri L 12 to 2, Mon to Sat D 7 to 9.30 (10 Fri and Sat) MEALS: alc (main courses £6 to £12 L, £16 D). Set L £14.95, Set D £25 SERVICE: not inc, card slips closed CARDS: Amex, Delta, MasterCard, Switch, Visa DETAILS: 50 seats. Private parties: 40 main room, 14 private room. Children's helpings. No cigars/pipes in dining-room. Music. Air-conditioned

---

ALVECHURCH Hereford & Worcester map 5

The Mill

Radford Road, Alvechurch B48 7LD — COOKING **4**
TEL: (0121) 447 7005 FAX: (0121) 447 8001 — COST £16–£41

This redbrick mill on the outskirts of Birmingham makes a diverting setting for a restaurant with its old beams, decorative cog wheel, and light yellow and blue colour scheme. Carl Timms cooks in essentially a straightforward French classical style, with the occasional pyrotechnical trick thrown in – for example, the poached egg inserted into a thin envelope of baked salmon – just to show it can be done. That was a first course from the spring menu, sauced with a white wine sabayon with plenty of chives to add savoury depth. Main courses such as monkfish with leeks on saffron sauce, or minted rack of lamb with ratatouille won't shock, and the canonical tournedos with shallots, mushrooms and red wine sauce is particularly well rendered. Inventiveness is let rip at dessert stage, with fruit flavours mobilised to the maximum, dried apples and raspberries accompanying nougatine ice-cream, and ginger-syruped kiwi adorning a wobbling lime mousse.

Wines for the main list are supplied by Tanners of Shrewsbury and these, combined with those on the fine wine list and the bin-ends, add up to around 300 bins of mostly very good quality. Prices are more than fair, with plenty of bottles under £15 and even quite a few under £10, and there are some real bargains to be found among the mature clarets. House wines start at £8.25. CELLARMAN'S CHOICE: Klein Constantia Sauvignon Blanc, Constantia, South Africa, £13.50; Juliénas 1995, Joubert, £14.25.

CHEF: Carl Timms PROPRIETORS: Geoffrey, Vivienne and Stefan McKernon OPEN: Sun L 12.30 to 2 (booking essential), Tue to Sat D 7 to 9 (9.30 Sat) CLOSED: first week Jan, 3 days Christmas, first two weeks Aug MEALS: alc D (main courses £9.50 to £15). Set L Sun £14.75, Set D Tue to Thu £14 (2 courses) to £16 SERVICE: not inc CARDS: Amex, MasterCard, Visa DETAILS: 32 seats. Private parties: 36 main room. Car park. Vegetarian meals. No small children at D. Children's helpings Sun L. No smoking in dining-room. Music

AMBERLEY West Sussex map 3

▲ *Amberley Castle, Queen's Room*

Amberley BN18 9ND
TEL: (01798) 831992 FAX: (01798) 831998 COOKING 3
on B2139, between Storrington and Bury Hill COST £29–£73

For a good dose of history with your dinner, look no further than this mellow twelfth-century fortress, now a comfortable hotel. The moat may have been converted into a croquet lawn, but drawbridge, portcullis, gate towers and curtain wall are intact. Previous guests Elizabeth I and Charles II would doubtless still feel at home in the splendid barrel-vaulted dining-room, and even the modern-British menu would not entirely flummox them: timeless kitchen-garden ingredients such as wild nettles, sorrel and lemon balm all have their place.

Dishes can be elaborate, and the kitchen's anxiety to try new combinations means that the balancing of flavours may take a back seat – or so thought one visitor who ate tempura of squid and shellfish with cabbage and a ginger-infused red wine sauce – but another's rare and 'juicy' duck breast was well accompanied by a barley risotto with bacon and sage. Desserts are where the real talent surfaces, in a tower of rich, dark chocolate mousse with prunes and cognac, or a blackcurrant délice served with a sticky sauce of ripe, mixed berries. Service has varied from 'unhelpful' to 'impeccable'. Mark-ups are high on the extensive wine list, which kicks off with Australian house wine at £16.50.

CHEF: Sam Mahoney PROPRIETORS: Martin and Joy Cummings OPEN: all week 12 to 2, 7 to 9.30 MEALS: alc (main courses £16 to £23). Set L £18.10, Set D £27.50 to £45 SERVICE: not inc CARDS: Amex, Diners, MasterCard, Switch, Visa DETAILS: 48 seats. Private parties: 48 main room, 12 and 48 private rooms. Car park. Vegetarian meals. Children's helpings. No children under 12. Jacket and tie. No smoking in dining-room. Music ACCOMMODATION: 15 rooms, all with bath/shower. TV. Phone. B&B £130 to £300. Deposit: 50%. No children under 12. Afternoon teas. Garden

AMBLESIDE Cumbria map 8

Glass House £

Rydal Road, Ambleside LA22 9AN COOKING 3
TEL: (01539) 432137 FAX: (01539) 431139 COST £19–£40

'The Glass House is to food what Habitat is to furniture,' commented one correspondent. In other words, it has a 'young, modern and lively feel to it'. Customers wear denims, folk music plays in the background, and 'efficient and chirpy' service matches the mood. Glassmaker Adrian Sankey's sixteenth-century mill conversion, next door to the National Trust 'House on the Bridge', is an impressive piece of restoration. Light lunches and snacks please the daytrippers, but the kitchen rolls up its sleeves for more serious business in the evening. Boned skate wing stuffed with anchovy paste on a bed of stir-fried peppers and cabbage, all topped with spinach, was 'colourful, unusual and very tasty', found one couple. The repertoire includes equally up-beat dishes such as pot-roast best end of lamb with minted couscous, and pan-fried courgette and risotto cake with tapénade crostini.

As for desserts, there might be hot orange and Grand Marnier pudding 'so light and tangy that it could have hopped off the plate', or spiced marinated pears in Beaujolais. Cappuccino comes in cups 'large enough to swim in'; there are also some intriguing bottled beers as well as a racy list of around 20 wines. House wine is £9.95.

CHEF: Stuart Birkett PROPRIETOR: Adrian Sankey OPEN: Tue to Sun 12 to 2.45, 6.30 to 9.45 CLOSED: 25 to 27 Dec MEALS: alc (main courses L £4.50 to £6, D £8.50 to £14). Set L £7.50 (2 courses) SERVICE: not inc, card slips closed CARDS: Delta, MasterCard, Switch, Visa DETAILS: 75 seats. 25 seats outside. Private parties: 60 main room. Car park. Vegetarian meals. Children's helpings. No smoking in dining-room. Music

▲ *Rothay Manor*

Rothay Bridge, Ambleside LA22 0EH
TEL: (01539) 433605 FAX: (01539) 433607 COOKING 2
off A593 to Coniston, ¼m W of Ambleside COST £22–£48

Although only a quarter of a mile from the centre of Ambleside, Rothay Manor has the bypass and one-way system to thank for making it seem farther. It is a Regency building with style, and a dining-room that sparkles with silver and glass. Unusually for the Lake District, there is no synchronised eating of identical dishes at dinner. Instead, a short choice with the option of two, three or five courses might bring a savoury ham and mushroom pancake, French onion soup, and poached halibut with chervil sauce, followed by profiteroles filled with coffee cream. This is old-fashioned country-house cooking, untouched by exotic flourishes; vegetarians might be offered herb and nut loaf alongside lentil and cheese bake or a multi-veg crumble. Lunch is a cold buffet of cooked meats and salad, supplemented by a few hot dishes such as beef bourguignon or chicken with tarragon. Service is pleasant, friendly and efficient under the watchful eye of one of the Nixon brothers.

Bordeaux and Burgundy are the wine list's strong suits, with Australia and Germany showing a good hand. The joker in the pack is the sparkling medium-sweet Italian red Recioto della Valpolicella 1990 from Bertani, which, at £26.70, might tempt those with a gambling streak. Four house wines are £11.50. CELLARMAN'S CHOICE: Alamos Ridge Chardonnay 1994, Argentina, £13.60; Cono Sur Pinot Noir 1996, Rapel Valley, Chile, £12.50

CHEFS: Jane Binns and Colette Nixon PROPRIETORS: Nigel and Stephen Nixon OPEN: all week 12.30 to 2 (12.45 to 1.30 Sun), 7.45 to 9 CLOSED: Jan MEALS: alc L Mon to Sat (main courses £8). Set L Sun £16, Set L Mon to Sat £13.50, Set D £24 (2 courses) to £30. BYO (no corkage) SERVICE: not inc, card slips closed CARDS: Amex, Diners, MasterCard, Switch, Visa DETAILS: 75 seats. 20 seats outside. Private parties: 12 main room, 34 private room. Car park. Vegetarian meals. Children's helpings. No smoking in dining-room. Wheelchair access (also WC). No music. Air-conditioned ACCOMMODATION: 18 rooms, all with bath/shower. TV. Phone. B&B £76 to £166. Deposit: £60. Rooms for disabled. Children welcome. Baby facilities. Guide dogs only. Afternoon teas. Garden (*The Which? Hotel Guide*)

AMERSHAM Buckinghamshire map 3

Gilbey's 🍷 £

NEW ENTRY

1 Market Square, Old Amersham HP7 0DF COOKING 2
TEL: (01494) 727242 FAX: (01494) 431243 COST £19–£41

Wines are appealingly charged at shop prices in this 400-year-old listed building (once the grammar school) next to the church. Inside, it is full of old beams, but light, airy and hung with modern paintings. The food is a mixture of trad and trendy: French onion soup, 'excellent aubergine and tomato tart', or salmon and herb fish-cakes with a 'light and piquant' Thai sauce. Pan-fried fillet of black bream comes with chargrilled polenta, Parma ham and green olive tapénade, while carefully cooked calf's liver and bacon is served with good herby mash. For dessert there is lemon tart ('always a winner') or pink grapefruit gratin. Service is friendly if sometimes lacking direction. The wine list is unashamedly French, but there is one English wine: the Gilbeys' own Pheasants Ridge, from their vineyard in Hambledon. Prices are even lower on takeaway bottles if you join their Wine Club. House country French is £5.25. CELLARMAN'S CHOICE: Muscadet, Ch. de la Ragotière 1995, £7.70; St-Emilion, Ch. Pavie-Decesse 1992, £16.35. The family also owns the Eton Wine Bar.

CHEF: Stephen Spooner PROPRIETORS: Michael and Linda Gilbey, and William and Caroline Gilbey OPEN: all week 12.30 to 2.30, 7 to 10 (11 Sat) CLOSED: 23 to 26 Dec MEALS: alc Mon to Sat L, all week D (main courses £7 to £14). Set L Sun £8.95 (2 courses) to £12.50, Set D Sun £8.95 (2 courses) SERVICE: 10% (optional), card slips closed CARDS: Amex, Delta, Diners, MasterCard, Switch, Visa DETAILS: 50 seats. 24 seats outside. Private parties: 20 main room, 10 private room. Vegetarian meals. Children's helpings. No cigars/pipes in dining-room. Wheelchair access (also WC). Music

Kings Arms

30 High Street, Old Amersham HP7 0DU COOKING 3
TEL: (01494) 726333 FAX: (01494) 433480 COST £21–£45

One may expect half-timbering and mullioned windows at a former coaching-inn on Old Amersham's main street, and the King's Arms does not disappoint. Most of the reports received this year are from satisfied customers, pleased to praise a certain consistency that seems to have eluded the kitchen in the past. Gary Munday's cooking aims at the tried-and-tested rather than new-fangled complexity, and delivers the likes of split pea soup with smoked ham, and tomato and basil tart dressed with olive oil and balsamic vinegar. Prawns, mussels and crab in a langouste sauce are 'well-timed and full of sweet sea flavour', and chicken ballottine with truffle oil can be 'hauntingly sexy'. Meals might end with Bakewell tart and custard, or the more highfalutin chocolate and passion-fruit parfait. At its best, 'the place is buzzing with professional attitude'. The wine list is much stronger in France than anywhere else, although house wines, at £8.75, are from Chile.

CHEF: Gary Munday PROPRIETOR: John Jennison OPEN: Tue to Sun L 12 to 2, Tue to Sat D 7 to 9.30 CLOSED: 26 to 31 Dec MEALS: alc (main courses £13 to £17). Set L Tue to Sat £9.50 (2 courses) to £12.50, Set L Sun £15, Set D Tue to Fri £17, Set D Sat £26. BYO £5 SERVICE: not inc CARDS: Amex, Delta, Diners, MasterCard, Switch, Visa DETAILS: 30 seats. Private parties: 50 main room, 12 to 50 private rooms. Car park. Vegetarian meals. Children welcome. No cigars/pipes in dining-room. Wheelchair access (no WC). No music

APPLETHWAITE Cumbria map 10

▲ *Underscar Manor*

Applethwaite CA12 4PH
TEL: (017687) 75000 FAX: (017687) 74904 COOKING 6
off A66, ½m N of Keswick COST £28–£64

The nineteenth century Italianate house benefits from the typical Victorian eye for a good spot: overlooking Derwent Water, with Skiddaw as a backdrop and Scafell Pike in the distance. It is 'aloof from the tripperish mess far below', and if we doled out gongs for views it would get one. The hotel is sumptuously ('perhaps fussily') furnished, very comfortable and, although a family affair with a small team, takes itself seriously: dress code for diners, professional but friendly service, and 'great attention to detail'.

'Confident, classical cooking' is how one experienced observer rated the style. Menus may not change that often, but Robert Thornton works hard at his dishes, especially main courses, turning up anything from chargrilled ostrich fillet with polenta to a roast breast of corn-fed guinea-fowl filled with Swiss cheese and sage, wrapped in Parma ham, and served on a bed of lentils with pumpkin and braised leek. Luxuries are given an airing, as in a hot gâteau of lobster and langoustine with lobster butter sauce, for instance, and while the kitchen has a foot in the European camp – saddle of local venison with a Savoy cabbage parcel of wild mushrooms and pearl barley risotto – it also sparks interest with flashes of Thai spicing, or maybe a Chinese aromatic crispy duck.

Desserts have included mint chocolate gâteau with crème de menthe sauce and Ovaltine ice cream, as well as hot raspberry soufflé in a pastry tart with chocolate sauce. Residents have a free choice from the full à la carte menu, 'a refreshing change from the usual restrictions', and one considered the deal 'fairly expensive, but on the whole good value'. France forms the backbone of the wine list, prices are generally fair, and Derek Harrison is usually on hand for advice. House wines start at around £14.50.

CHEF: Robert Thornton PROPRIETORS: Pauline and Derek Harrison, and Gordon Evans OPEN: all week 12 to 1, 7 to 8.30 (9 Sat) MEALS: alc (main courses £17.50 to £19.50). Set L £18.50, Set D £29.50 SERVICE: not inc, card slips closed CARDS: Amex, MasterCard, Switch, Visa DETAILS: 60 seats. 16 seats outside. Private parties: 40 main room, 20 and 40 private rooms. Car park. Vegetarian meals. No children under 12. Jacket and tie. No smoking in dining-room. Music ACCOMMODATION: 11 rooms, all with bath/shower. TV. Phone. D,B&B £85 to £250. No children under 12. Garden (*The Which? Hotel Guide*)

ARDINGTON Oxfordshire map 2

Boars Head NEW ENTRY

Church Street, Ardington OX12 8QA COOKING 4
TEL: (01235) 833254 COST £28–£40

Duncan and Elizabeth Basterfield's country pub scores highly thanks to first-class ingredients, good ideas and sharp technical skills. The blackboard menu lists seven or eight choices at each course. Starters and snacks might include simple ploughman's or soup, or something a shade more inventive such as home-marinated salmon 'bursting with flavour', served with crisp, young asparagus and a creamy horseradish sauce. Main courses have produced honeyed duck on celeriac purée, a 'hotpot' of scallops and asparagus with basil, and a tower of sauté vegetables in a pool of Cumberland sauce, with a sliced roast pigeon breast on top, that 'looked very attractive and smelled wonderful'. 'Beautiful, wobbly, clear-tasting' coconut mousse with roasted bananas and mango sorbet has made a successful dessert. One reporter who wasn't keen on the loud music was won over by the food and warm welcome. Beers include Fuller's London Pride and Morland Original, and most of the dozen or so wines are from the southern hemisphere. House Rioja is £9, Chilean sauvignon £9.95.

CHEF: Duncan Basterfield PROPRIETORS: Duncan and Elizabeth Basterfield OPEN: Tue to Sun L 12 to 2, Tue to Sat D 7 to 9 CLOSED: 25 and 26 Dec MEALS: alc (main courses £12 to £14) SERVICE: not inc, card slips closed CARDS: Amex, Delta, MasterCard, Switch, Visa DETAILS: 34 seats. 10 seats outside. Private parties: 30 main room. Car park. Vegetarian meals. Children's helpings. Wheelchair access (also WC). Music

ARNCLIFFE North Yorkshire map 8

▲ *Amerdale House* £✗

Arncliffe, Littondale BD23 5QE COOKING 4
TEL/FAX: (01756) 770250 COST £37–£44

Nigel and Paula Crapper's handsome Victorian manor is set in one of the remotest parts of the Yorkshire Dales in wonderful hiking country, but the warm, personal style, elegant furnishings and four-course dinners make it more than just a handy base for walkers. 'I believe that quality ingredients should be cooked simply and only be complemented and not swamped by any sauce or garnish,' writes Nigel Crapper.

This philosophy comes through in his cooking, several reports making special mention of the simple but 'wonderful' sauces: a subtle curry version with griddled breast of chicken, for instance, or a concentrated gravy with loin of lamb and apricots. An inspection meal began with chicken livers with bacon in a 'superb, and I mean superb,' wine and stock sauce. The second (often fish) course, the only stage with no choice, might simply be smoked salmon, or chargrilled tuna on a bed of fine ratatouille. Lightly steamed sea bass with herbs, or roast tenderloin of pork on spinach with a Meaux mustard sauce might follow, then a 'creamy, thick-textured' lemon and raspberry posset. The bar runs to more than 20 malt whiskies, and there's a solid list of wines from France, Spain, Germany and the New World, a fair number below £10, and plenty of half-bottles. House wines start at £10.95.

CHEF: Nigel Crapper PROPRIETORS: Paula and Nigel Crapper OPEN: all week D only 7 to 8.30 CLOSED: mid-Nov to mid-Mar MEALS: Set D £27 SERVICE: not inc, card slips closed CARDS: MasterCard, Switch, Visa DETAILS: 24 seats. Private parties: 14 main room. Car park. Children's helpings. No smoking in dining-room. No music ACCOMMODATION: 11 rooms, all with bath/shower. TV. D,B&B £64.50 to £119. Children welcome. Baby facilities. Garden (*The Which? Hotel Guide*)

ASENBY North Yorkshire map 9

▲ *Crab & Lobster*

Dishforth Road, Asenby YO7 3QL
TEL: (01845) 577286 FAX: (01845) 577109 COOKING 2
off A168, between A19 and A1 COST £23–£53

The thatched low-beamed pub off the A1 makes a handy stop on a long journey. Every item that can be collected has been, and lurks somewhere among the Bohemian junk in the bar. Not many items have been missed off the menu either. Informal meals can be ordered at the counter and eaten there: roll up for fish soup, Thai fish-cakes, oysters, or crab risotto, followed perhaps by 'posh' fish & chips, fish pie or lobster thermidor. A bookable dining-room with waitress service trades up to warm smoked salmon and asparagus salad with rocket and coriander dressing, before chargrilled tuna, scallops and king prawns with sauce vierge. There is no shortage of meat dishes either, and puddings might run to warm chocolate tart or iced banana parfait. Wines offer good choice below £20 beginning with house Chilean at £9.50.

CHEF: Michael Pickard PROPRIETORS: David and Jackie Barnard OPEN: all week L 12 to 2.30, Mon to Sat D 7 to 10 CLOSED: 25 Dec MEALS: alc (main courses £10.50 to £21). Set L £11.95 (2 courses) to £13.95 SERVICE: not inc, card slips closed CARDS: Amex, Delta, MasterCard, Switch, Visa DETAILS: 140 seats. 80 seats outside. Private parties: 70 main room, 12 and 22 private rooms. Car park. Vegetarian meals. Children welcome. No smoking in dining-room. Music ACCOMMODATION: 5 rooms, all with bath/shower. TV. Phone. B&B £45 to £60. Rooms for disabled. Children welcome. Dogs welcome. Garden

'The alternative to the main course did not appear on the menu. It purported to be a rare fish, specially flown in from the Loire, that did not even have a name in English. It had both the taste and texture of cotton wool and its price, when the bill appeared, was extortionate. It turned out to be shad, rare on the table only because most fishermen throw it back.' (On eating in Scotland)

ASHBOURNE Derbyshire map 8

▲ *Callow Hall* 🍷 🚭

Mappleton Road, Ashbourne DE6 2AA
TEL: (01335) 343403 FAX: (01335) 343624
¾m NW of Ashbourne, turn left off A515 at crossroads with Bowling Green pub on left, Mappleton Road first on right

COOKING 4
COST £23–£55

This regal grey-stone Victorian hall overlooking the vale of the river Dove is one of the Peak District's more alluring country hotels. The Spencers have run it for 15 years, bringing a human touch to the business that isn't always forthcoming in such places. There are two dining-rooms, one decorated with red William Morris wallpaper, the other in calm peach. The format is a daily-changing fixed-price menu supplemented by an extensive *carte* with fish illustrations in the manner of an angler's textbook. The *Dicentrarchus labrax* (sea bass) is grilled and comes with red peppers, leeks and a Noilly Prat sauce. Meat courses follow classic French lines: veal escalope with Dijon mustard and asparagus, for example, or roast guinea-fowl wrapped in smoked bacon with morels and a madeira sauce. Rich desserts, such as chocolate and orange mousse in a Grand Marnier and chocolate sauce, are heavily garnished but good.

Wines have been carefully chosen, with a fine French range and a particularly good choice of styles from around the world. However, the layout of the list is confusing: although the bins are grouped by region/country, there is no logical order within each category, either by price, vintage or even grape variety. Six house wines are £9.75 a bottle (£2.75 a glass). CELLARMAN'S CHOICE: Down St-Mary Dry White 1995, Devon, £12.95; Merlot 1994, Valentino Paladin, Veneto, £12.95.

CHEFS: David and Anthony Spencer PROPRIETORS: David, Dorothy and Anthony Spencer OPEN: Sun L 12 to 1.30, Mon to Sat D 7.15 to 9 CLOSED: 25 and 26 Dec, 1 Jan MEALS: alc (main courses £14.50 to £19). Set L Sun £15.50, Set D £33 SERVICE: not inc CARDS: Amex, Delta, Diners, MasterCard, Switch, Visa DETAILS: 60 seats. Private parties: 35 main room, 20 and 35 private rooms. Car park. Vegetarian meals. Children's helpings. No smoking in dining-room. Wheelchair access (also WC). No music ACCOMMODATION: 16 rooms, all with bath/shower. TV. Phone. B&B £70 to £130. Rooms for disabled. Children welcome. Baby facilities. Dogs welcome in bedrooms only by prior arrangement. Garden. Fishing (*The Which? Hotel Guide*)

ASHBURTON Devon map 1

▲ *Holne Chase* 🍷 🚭 NEW ENTRY

Ashburton TQ13 7NS
2m N of Ashburton on road to Two Bridges
TEL: (01364) 631471 FAX: (01364) 631453

COOKING 3
COST £28–£46

Once the hunting-lodge of Buckfast Abbey, this white-painted hotel, with its neatly barbered lawns and massing troops of azaleas and rhododendrons, stands in the heart of Dartmoor. The nearby river makes for spectacular views, and summer visitors may catch a glimpse of deer. Alternatively, the resident basset hound may be amusement enough.

The dining-room drill is as formal as it comes, with plates arriving on silver trays to be borne to table by further attendants. Wayne Pearson, ex-Well House (see entry, St Keyne), has been head chef since February 1997 and is sufficiently experienced to cope with offering an inclusively priced *'carte'* to underpin the daily-changing set-price menus. A first course of smoked haddock with a Welsh rarebit topping has offered good fish and nice judgement of flavours. Salmon on a compote of onion and anchovy comes accurately cooked and well supported by its accompaniments, and loin of lamb on vigorously vinegared red cabbage has also impressed. A chocolate tart with tender pastry and forthright filling makes a successful dessert, home-made ice-creams are perfectly sound, and petits fours excellent.

Businesslike wine service reflects the traditional nature of the list, which has very few bins from the New World. A small collection of Vega Sicilia Unicos and some magnums of a few fine, old clarets should raise the pulse of wine buffs with money to spend; those who are strapped for cash may find consolation in the range of Beaujolais *crus*. Seven house wines from France and Australia start at £10.25. CELLARMAN'S CHOICE: Gewurztraminer d'Alsace Cuvée Réservée 1993, Henri Fuchs, £17.90. Brouilly, Ch. des Tours 1995, £18.50.

CHEF: Wayne Pearson PROPRIETORS: Philippa and Sebastian Hughes OPEN: all week 12 to 2, 7.15 to 9 MEALS: Set L £20, Set D £25 to £29 SERVICE: not inc, card slips closed CARDS: Amex, Delta, Diners, MasterCard, Switch, Visa DETAILS: 60 seats. 30 seats outside. Private parties: 75 main room, 10 private room. Car park. No children under 10 at D. No smoking in dining-room. Wheelchair access (also WC). No music ACCOMMODATION: 18 rooms, all with bath/shower. TV. Phone. B&B £60 to £150. Deposit: £50. Rooms for disabled. Children welcome. Baby facilities. Dogs welcome in bedrooms only. Afternoon teas. Garden. Fishing (*The Which? Hotel Guide*)

ASTON CLINTON Buckinghamshire map 3

▲ *Bell Inn*

Aston Clinton HP22 5HP
TEL: (01296) 630252 FAX: (01296) 631250
on A41, between Tring and Aylesbury

NEW CHEF

COST £30–£62

The inn is a mellow red-brick building beside a main road that runs through a pastoral Buckinghamshire village, with a flag-floored bar and classical jardinière murals in the dining-room. Michael Harris, owner since the mid-'60s, is one of the pioneers of British country-house eating, and has seen many chefs come and go. One went as the *Guide* was going to press, and Colin Woodward arrived to take over the kitchens too late for us to receive any feedback. The house style has typically embraced a broadly European approach, with local duck naturally playing a starring role as the centrepiece of a fixed-price meal for two. French classics are the mainstay of the extensive wine list, but it also winkles out a couple of kosher wines for interest, and has a good dessert section. Mark-ups can be high, but three pages of house recommendations starting at £12.95 simplify selection. CELLARMAN'S CHOICE: Rully, Dom. Joseph Drouhin 1995, £30.50; Rioja Reserva, Marques de Riscal 1992, £25.

CHEF: Colin Woodward PROPRIETOR: Michael Harris OPEN: all week 12.30 to 1.45, 7.30 to 9.30 MEALS: alc Mon to Sat L, all week D (main courses £12.50 to £21). Set L Mon to Sat £12 (2 courses) to £15, Set L Sun £9.75, Set L and D (Duck Menu) £39 (minimum 2). BYO £10 SERVICE: not inc CARDS: Amex, Delta, MasterCard, Switch, Visa DETAILS: 90 seats. 48 seats outside. Private parties: 100 main room, 10 and 20 private rooms. Car park. Vegetarian meals. Children's helpings. No smoking in dining-room. Wheelchair access (also WC). Music ACCOMMODATION: 20 rooms, all with bath/shower. TV. Phone. Room only £55 to £120. Rooms for disabled. Children welcome. Baby facilities. Afternoon teas. Garden

---

AYLESBURY Buckinghamshire map 3

▲ *Hartwell House*

Oxford Road, Aylesbury HP17 8NL
TEL: (01296) 747444 FAX: (01296) 747450 COOKING 4
on A418, 2m from Aylesbury towards Oxford COST £33–£67

'Like a squat French château set in a classically English park' is how one reporter described this 'absolutely stunning' part-Jacobean, part-Georgian stone mansion, which was home for a time to Louis XVIII. 'It oozes class and, bolshie as we are, we could immediately see the point about wearing a tie'. One couple, lunching alone, enjoyed 'the not disagreeable sensation of having a stately home for the day with the staff thrown in'. The staff are, by the way, attentive and discreet.

Although the food may not quite match the regal setting of the huge, yellow-painted, high-ceilinged, French-windowed dining-room, it does aim high: boudin of Cornish crab, warm wood pigeon salad, or breast of chicken served with a truffle and foie gras risotto. Roger Barstow (previously at Billesley Manor) might give his dishes a boost with, say, chilli dressing (for tiger prawn tempura) or home-made piccalilli for a pressed ham and lentil terrine. Seafood has appeared in the form of a dark, intense shellfish consommé with crab ravioli, and 'impeccably fresh' roast halibut with a thick, crispy green herb crust. Desserts vary from warm pear and banana brioche pudding to simpler glazed berries with raspberry sorbet, or lemon meringue pie.

The imaginative wine list comprises high-quality bins from mainly France and the New World, but you may have to steel yourself when it comes to the stately prices: a bottle of Cloudy Bay Sauvignon 1996 will set you back £41.50, for example. A glass of the very good house champagne from Barancourt may help to steady your nerves, but it does cost £7. Some affordable wines can be found, however, starting with house French at £12.90. CELLARMAN'S CHOICE: Goldwater Chardonnay 1993, Marlborough, New Zealand, £26.50; Gigondas 1989, Pascal Frères, £24.50.

CHEF: Roger Barstow PROPRIETOR: Historic House Hotels Ltd OPEN: all week 12.30 to 1.50, 7.30 to 9.45 MEALS: Set L £20 (2 courses) to £26.50, Set D £42 SERVICE: net prices, card slips closed CARDS: Amex, Delta, MasterCard, Switch, Visa DETAILS: 80 seats. 20 seats outside. Private parties: 60 main room, 18 to 60 private rooms. Car park. Vegetarian meals. No children under 8. Jacket and tie. No smoking in dining-room. Wheelchair access (also WC). Music ACCOMMODATION: 46 rooms, all with bath/shower. TV. Phone. Room only £110 to £260. Rooms for disabled. No children under 8. Dogs welcome in bedrooms only. Afternoon teas. Garden. Swimming-pool. Fishing (*The Which? Hotel Guide*)

BAKEWELL Derbyshire map 8

Renaissance

NEW ENTRY

Bath Street, Bakewell DE45 1BX COOKING 4
TEL: (01629) 812687 COST £27–£44

The stone-faced, beamed house in a one-way street near the centre of this old market town has had a chequered restaurant history, its present French owners arriving in 1994. The interior is not exactly Peak District, but more farmhouse in the Auvergne, with a well-tended walled garden at the back, and smart table-settings. Eric Piedaniel's culinary style is classical French with the subtlest of modern embellishments.

A first course of baked avocado interleaved, mille-feuille-fashion, with crabmeat and sauced with a deep-gold mousseline scattered with chive snippets is a well-conceived, sensitively timed dish. Sliced quail and foie gras go into a 'pithiviers' of crisp flaky pastry surrounded by a trickle of sweet rhubarb sauce. Simpler and perhaps better is a main course of poached chicken breast served on a sauce based on olive oil and torn basil leaves, the inventive vegetables including carrot mousse and a hollowed courgette filled with onion marmalade. Between starter and main may come an apple and calvados sorbet. The signature dessert, an elaborate gâteau of caramel and chocolate mousses in chocolate and vanilla sponge with a white chocolate sauce, is as rich as it sounds, while iced Benedictine soufflé makes a lighter, if 'gloriously alcoholic', alternative. Service is relaxed and friendly. Wines are a largely French and rather conservative selection with one or two names missing: if we're going to spend £95.75 on Bienvenues-Bâtard-Montrachet, we may as well know who made it. House wines are £9.80.

CHEF: Eric Piedaniel PROPRIETORS: E. and C. Piedaniel, and D. Beraud OPEN: Tue to Sun L 12 to 2, Tue to Sat D 7 to 10 CLOSED: first 2 weeks Jan, first 2 weeks Aug MEALS: Set L and D £17.95 CARDS: Delta, MasterCard, Switch, Visa DETAILS: 45 seats. Private parties: 60 main room, 25 private room. Vegetarian meals. Children's helpings. No smoking in dining-room. Wheelchair access (also WC). Music

BARNARD CASTLE Co Durham map 10

Blagraves House

The Bank, Barnard Castle DL12 8PN COOKING 4
TEL: (01833) 637668 COST £21–£38

Kenneth and Elizabeth Marley have been here a decade: a mere flicker in the eventful history of this fifteenth-century house, perhaps, but not to be sniffed at. The past is easy to conjure up, thanks to the 'aged dignity' of beams and large open fireplaces, and it's worth studying the original crested strapwork ceiling on the first floor. The Marleys' hard work and creative flair are also easy to admire. Their monthly-changing *carte*, supplemented by a set-price menu, features substantial gamey terrines – with pistachio nuts and lavender jelly, perhaps – and meat pies, while beef Wellington is something of a signature dish.

Counterbalancing these are mousses – perhaps of smoked haddock with a yoghurt dressing – and steamed or grilled fish: sea bass on a julienne of vegetables with a light oyster sauce, for example. Vegetables (considered 'rather mundane' by one visitor) are treated simply. Home-made ice-creams – Turkish Delight, say, or coffee and brandy – have been recommended, or there may be a tart of plain chocolate. 'Having found Blagraves, we do not now consider treating ourselves or friends anywhere else,' comment one couple. The well-rounded wine list tops 50 bottles, with house French at £8.50.

CHEFS/PROPRIETORS: Kenneth and Elizabeth Marley OPEN: Tue to Sat D only 7 to 9.30 MEALS: alc (main courses £9 to £14). Set D Tue to Fri £13.50 SERVICE: not inc, card slips closed CARDS: Delta, MasterCard, Switch, Visa DETAILS: 26 seats. Private parties: 24 main room, 40 private room. Vegetarian meals. No children under 7. No smoking in dining-room. Music

BARNET Hertfordshire map 3

Mims

63 East Barnet Road, Barnet EN4 8RN COOKING **6**
TEL/FAX: (0181) 449 2974 COST £23–£35

If judged solely on appearances, it's a mystery that Mims has survived all this time. Set in an unprepossessing shopping parade, it looks 'more like a computer shop than a restaurant' although the old emerald colour scheme has been replaced by a snazzy yellow, black and gold theme with faux-marble tables and lots of modern prints. The sharp, contemporary food is as good as ever, making it 'an extraordinary find' for one reporter, and the overriding opinion is that it provides stupendous value for money. Be in no doubt: this is an original.

Terse menu descriptions conceal surprisingly complex dishes. An inspector who ate 'braised lamb's tongue, noodles, curry broth' found it an 'extraordinarily bold' Middle Eastern-style soup with tomatoes, spinach, mushrooms and coriander, while crab sausage, served on a heap of deep-fried rice noodles, was delicately flavoured and lightly textured. Main courses, such as spicy lamb-burger with sweetbreads, or seared scallops with mashed potatoes and asparagus, maintain the punchy flavours, although Ali Al-Sersy is equally at home with simple but 'perfectly cooked' calf's liver. Well-received puddings have included pear and almond tart, blueberry sorbet, and a 'brilliant and original' mille-feuille of banana and coconut. The steady stream of praise for the food is tempered by complaints about muddled service and long waits between courses. House wine is £9.50, and few bottles on the short list hit the £20 mark.

CHEF: A. Al-Sersy PROPRIETORS: A. Al-Sersy and P. Azarfar OPEN: Tue to Fri and Sun L 12 to 2.30, Tue to Sun D 6.30 to 10.30 CLOSED: 1 week Christmas, 1 week Sept MEALS: Set L £9.50 (2 courses) to £13.50, Set D £15 (2 courses) to £19 SERVICE: not inc CARDS: MasterCard, Visa DETAILS: 45 seats. Private parties: 70 main room. No children under 7. No cigars in dining-room. Wheelchair access (also WC). Music

Prices quoted in the Guide *are based on information supplied by restaurateurs. The prices quoted at the top of each entry represent a range, from the lowest meal price to the highest; the latter is inflated by 20 per cent to take account of likely price rises during the year of the* Guide.

BARNSLEY South Yorkshire map 9

Armstrongs 

102 Dodworth Road, Barnsley S70 6HL COOKING 4
TEL: (01226) 240113 and 244990 COST £24–£32

Despite its location – on the main road through the busy Barnsley suburb of Dodworth – this grandly spacious Victorian villa manages to retain a sense of tranquillity amid the high ceilings and stained-glass windows. Admire the beautiful walnut piano while reading the menu in the comfortable bar, but be prepared for Frank Sinatra (on tape) rather than live Chopin. Simon Shaw has left the kitchen for the Fourth Floor restaurant at Harvey Nichols (see entry, Leeds), and owner Nick Pound has once again taken charge of the stoves.

His time away doesn't seem to have blunted his skills, and his commitment to high-quality materials is readily discernible even in such detail as the tiny tartlets of Szechuan-spiced vegetables served as an appetiser. It also shows in soft and delicately flavoured goats'-cheese mousseline with a melting centre, served with chargrilled vegetables and a balsamic dressing; and 'perfectly cooked' king scallops in a creamy saffron sauce. Dauphinoise potatoes have stood out among vegetables, served perhaps with pink rack of lamb in a rosemary gravy. For dessert, a clafoutis of raspberry, pear and peach with vanilla custard and amaretto biscuits was considered well worth the 20-minute wait at inspection. Wines cover a good range of styles and are helpfully grouped by region and/or varietal. Quality is mostly high and New World bins are particularly praiseworthy. Prices are reasonable, with house selections starting at £9.95.

CHEF: Nick Pound PROPRIETORS: Nick Pound and Deborah Swift OPEN: Tue to Fri L 12 to 2, Tue to Sat D 7 to 10 CLOSED: 2 weeks summer MEALS: alc D (main courses £9.50 to £16.50). Set L £7.50 (2 courses) to £14.50, Set D Tue to Fri £15 SERVICE: not inc CARDS: Amex, Delta, MasterCard, Switch, Visa DETAILS: 55 seats. Private parties: 30 main room. Car park. Vegetarian meals. Children's helpings. Wheelchair access (no WC). Music

BARNSTAPLE Devon map 1

▲ *Lynwood House* £*

Bishop's Tawton Road, Barnstaple EX32 9EF
TEL: (01271) 43695, changing to 343695
FAX: (01271) 79340, changing to 379340 COOKING 3
1m S of town centre, before A377 roundabout COST £30–£47

The Roberts family has been running this seafood restaurant-cum-hotel for 28 years and the Victorian yellow-brick house feels comfortably lived-in. Their menu eschews modern influences to concentrate on the soothing and creamy school of fish cookery. Thus salmon is poached in white wine and served with cream and dill, lemon sole mousse is accompanied by a rich lobster sauce, and scallops are simply wrapped in bacon and grilled. The style may not exactly be cutting-edge, but dishes are lighter and less rich than one might expect. Cooking techniques are sound, supported by a commendable emphasis on fresh ingredients: local fish whenever possible, and vegetables supplied by three local organic farms.

Non-fish choices might include warm salad of quail, followed by roast duck with apple sauce, while vegetarians are catered for with savoury pancakes, or stuffed baked avocado. Most puddings continue the creamy theme, with crème caramel, and Belgian milk chocolate truffle mousse. 'Soft and delicious' lemon sorbet with Russian vodka offers a more refreshing finale. A lighter menu concentrates on soups, salads and sautés. The wine list is wide-ranging both in price and geography, with house wine at £9.05.

CHEFS: Ruth and Matthew Roberts PROPRIETORS: John, Ruth and Matthew Roberts OPEN: Mon to Sat 12 to 2, 7 to 9.30 MEALS: alc (main courses £13.50 to £14.50). Light L and D available SERVICE: card slips closed CARDS: Amex, Delta, Diners, MasterCard, Switch, Visa DETAILS: 50 seats. Private parties: 50 main room, 20 private room. Car park. Vegetarian meals. Children's helpings. No smoking in dining-room. Wheelchair access (also WC). No music ACCOMMODATION: 5 rooms, all with bath/shower. TV. Phone. B&B £47.50 to £67.50. Children welcome. No dogs in public rooms

BARTON-UPON-HUMBER North Lincolnshire map 9

▲ *Elio's* £

11 Market Place, Barton-upon-Humber DN18 5DA COOKING 1
TEL: (01652) 635147 COST £16–£44

'It may be old-fashioned but good things never die,' says Elio Grossi of his long-running ristorante in a corner of Barton's market-square next to Lloyds Bank. Fresh fish is the star attraction, the day's dishes chalked on a blackboard, the choices by no means confined to the obvious: baked conger eel turned up in January, for instance. One reader enjoyed a generously packed seafood risotto and then a piece of halibut in piquant agrodolce sauce. Meatballs on beans and rice come with a spicy sauce; otherwise most trattoria favourites seem to be here, including tournedos Rossini. Desserts won't have you writing home but are confined to the likes of cassata and zabaglione. Everything may be extremely simple but, as a reporter comments, 'there is nothing to touch it in the locality'. House wines from the Veneto are £9.25 a litre. A Tuscan-style extension has been added along with a patio for al fresco lunches and pre-dinner drinks.

CHEFS: Elio Grossi, Nick Lyon and Louise Kuyath PROPRIETOR: Elio Grossi OPEN: Tue to Fri L 12 to 2, Mon to Sat D 6.30 to 10.30 CLOSED: 25 and 26 Dec, 2 weeks Aug, bank hols MEALS: alc (main courses £6.50 to £16.50). Set L £8.95, Set D 6.30 to 7.30 £10 SERVICE: not inc; 10% on parties of 6 or more CARDS: Amex, Delta, Diners, MasterCard, Switch, Visa DETAILS: 60 seats. 16 seats outside. Private parties: 60 main room, 6 and 20 private rooms. Car park. Vegetarian meals. Children's helpings. No smoking in 1 dining-room. Wheelchair access (no WC). Music ACCOMMODATION: 2 rooms, both with bath/shower. TV. B&B £25 to £45. Garden

'The view was wonderful, but I could have enjoyed that by standing outside with a salt beef sandwich and a mug of Bovril.' (On eating in London)

The Guide *relies on feedback from its readers. Especially welcome are reports on new restaurants appearing in the book for the first time. All letters to the* Guide *are acknowledged.*

BARWICK Somerset map 2

▲ *Little Barwick House* 🍷 $✱

Barwick BA22 9TD
TEL: (01935) 423902 FAX: (01935) 420908 COOKING 5
off A37, take second left opposite Red House pub COST £32–£38

The white-painted three-storey Georgian dower house, barely a couple of miles outside Yeovil, is called Little, presumably, to distinguish it from the huge pile a few hundred yards away in Barwick Park. Indeed nothing is on a very big scale here: it is a family home and feels all the warmer and more idiosyncratic for its lack of overt refinement, a point appreciated by diners who can enjoy the food without having to dress up for it. Appetisers appear with drinks in the comfortable lounge, followed by a pastry 'bonne bouche' at table in the red-painted dining-room.

Veronica Colley's menu offers a fair choice from a short repertoire that rolls gently along, some items hardly changing at all, others making use of seasonal produce, fish from Lyme Bay, and much local game and vegetables. Pigeon breast with leeks in a thin tartlet is at the simple end of the spectrum, while roast guinea-fowl with Thai spices and coconut milk indicates a willingness to experiment. Overall, there is perhaps a feel of good dinner-party cooking, for example in one reporter's meal of spinach and cream cheese pancake, gamey partridge with an orange *jus*, and a Catalan crème brûlée flavoured with fennel.

Some 70 wines from around the world combine drinkability with value, most being priced under £20. A new collection of ten house wines from France, Germany, Spain and South Africa, all at £10.90, adds to the appeal. CELLARMAN'S CHOICE: Sancerre 1995, Dom. Serge Laporte, £16.90; Tulbagh Winery Merlot 1995, Swartland, South Africa, £10.90.

CHEF: Veronica Colley PROPRIETORS: Christopher and Veronica Colley OPEN: Mon to Sat (and Sun by reservation only) D only 7 to 9 (9.30 Sat) CLOSED: Christmas, New Year MEALS: Set D £19.90 (2 courses) to £24.90 SERVICE: net prices, card slips closed CARDS: Amex, MasterCard, Switch, Visa DETAILS: 40 seats. Private parties: 40 main room, 16 private room. Car park. Vegetarian meals. Children's helpings. No smoking in dining-room. No music. Air-conditioned ACCOMMODATION: 6 rooms, all with bath/shower. TV. Phone. Air-conditioned. B&B £52 to £84. Deposit: £20. Children welcome. Dogs welcome. Garden (*The Which? Hotel Guide*)

BASLOW Derbyshire map 9

▲ *Fischer's Baslow Hall* 🍷 $✱

Calver Road, Baslow DE45 1RR COOKING 8
TEL: (01246) 583259 FAX: (01246) 583818 COST £30–£63

In 1998 the Fischers celebrate a decade at this mellow Derbyshire-stone hall, built in 1907 but looking older. Antiques, Victorian furniture and heavy fabrics set the tone, though the dining-room's high ceiling and fresh warm colours give it an airy feel. The 'hint of formality' in approach is a consequence of carefully managing the food's context. Large tables are dressed in white linen, wine glasses are as 'correct as soldiers on parade', hot and cold nibbles with drinks are followed by more at table, butter is the finest, and main courses arrive under domes. Menus, in big enough print for even middle-aged eyes, can read like the manifest on Noah's Ark: beef, venison, duckling, lamb, rabbit, pigeon, calf's liver and pig's trotter in spring, for example.

Max Fischer follows the seasons rigorously, and his classical background determines the style. First-rate ingredients are worked on until they are just right, novelties and gimmicks are eschewed, although 'big machismo dishes' with strong flavours (and perhaps a bit of oriental spicing) are right up his street. So, at least, an inspector found with a 'substantial and intensely flavoured' dish of rabbit saddle in a silky tarragon sauce and braised leg in a red wine sauce. Technical accomplishment is not in doubt – in a risotto with plump scallops cooked to 'well-judged opalescence', for instance – but the skills don't just impress, they delight: as when sweetbreads are cooked with a surface crust in order to emphasise the soft texture within.

Artistic presentation applies throughout, but really comes into its own with pastry chef Luke Dalton's desserts. Here, 'themes' take priority over flavour contrasts, although the workmanship again ensures that complexity is built in. An assiette of rhubarb desserts (a 'harbinger of spring') came as doll's house portions of crème brûlée, sorbet, jelly and strudel pastry, while a crème brûlée with orange also managed to combine warm and cold, smooth and crisp, delicate and intense. At peak times things can begin to unravel ('We felt like profit fodder' was the view of one reporter), but this marks a rare lapse in an otherwise smooth-running operation. Café Max offers a less-formal approach. The wine list concentrates on quality rather than bargains, but there are also some wines under £20 well worth drinking. House French starts at £11. CELLARMAN'S CHOICE: Poggio alle Gazze 1995, Tenuta dell'Ornellaia, £21; Madfish Bay Shiraz 1995, W. Australia, £16.65.

CHEF: Max Fischer PROPRIETORS: Max and Susan Fischer OPEN: Sun to Fri L 12 to 1.30, Mon to Sat D 7 to 9.30 (Sun D residents only) CLOSED: 25 and 26 Dec MEALS: Set L Mon to Fri £18 (2 courses) to £22, Set L Sun £21.50, Set D £42. Café menu Mon to Fri L and D, and Sat L SERVICE: not inc CARDS: Amex, Delta, Diners, MasterCard, Switch, Visa DETAILS: 76 seats. Private parties: 40 main room, 12 and 24 private rooms. Car park. Children's helpings. No children under 12 at D. No smoking in dining-room. Wheelchair access (also WC). No music ACCOMMODATION: 6 rooms, all with bath/shower. TV. Phone. B&B £75 to £130. Deposit: £50. Children welcome. Baby facilities. Afternoon teas. Garden (*The Which? Hotel Guide*)

BATH Bath & N.E. Somerset map 2

▲ *Bath Spa Hotel, Vellore Restaurant*

Sydney Road, Bath BA2 6JF COOKING **2**
TEL: (01225) 444424 FAX: (01225) 444006 COST £29–£79

This is a huge hotel with a small bar, a ballroom for a dining-room, and a kitchen that is happy to borrow ideas from just about anywhere. Mafia salad may be a starter you can't refuse, house-smoked beef fillet is partnered by sweet potato, and Jamaican banana tart comes with toffee sauce and rum and raisin ice-cream. It may be one of the last bastions of pepper-grinding in the *Guide*, but raw materials and timing are good, and the 'menu without meat' offers a generous choice including a cross-cultural nan bread pizza, and a Thai-spiced, coconut-flavoured curry. Home-made pasta features on most menus, and the alfresco

Colonnade opens for lunches of cod and chips with mushy peas, and hot chocolate fondue with fruit and marshmallows for dipping. Staff are arranged in strict hierarchical order, the better to carry out their particular tasks. Wines cover a lot of territory, and there are some first-rate bottles, but prices are high: anywhere that can't put on a house wine for less than £18.50 just isn't trying. Water is £3.25 for 70 centilitres.

CHEF: Jonathan Fraser PROPRIETOR: Forte Hotels OPEN: Sun L 12.30 to 2, all week D 6 to 10 MEALS: alc D (main courses £19.50 to £25), Set L Sun £16.95, Set D £35. BYO £10 SERVICE: not inc CARDS: Amex, Delta, Diners, MasterCard, Switch, Visa DETAILS: 100 seats. Private parties: 180 main room, 8 to 140 private rooms. Car park. Vegetarian meals. Children's helpings. No smoking in dining-room. Wheelchair access (also WC). Music. Air-conditioned ACCOMMODATION: 98 rooms, all with bath/shower. TV. Phone. B&B £79 to £218. Rooms for disabled. Children welcome. Baby facilities. Dogs welcome. Afternoon teas. Garden. Swimming-pool

Clos du Roy

1 Seven Dials, Saw Close, Bath BA1 1EN — COOKING 3
TEL: (01225) 444450 FAX: (01225) 404044 — COST £22–£41

As elegant as you'd expect in a perfectly proportioned city such as Bath, this almost semi-circular restaurant has numerous balconied windows overlooking the busy square below – excellent entertainment for people-watchers. Philippe Roy no longer cooks here but has entrusted his kitchens to David Olliverin, who continues to produce modern French food with a provençale accent. The menu promises some bold flavour marriages, although it is the classic combinations that win the most praise: a beautifully gauged starter of salmon marinated with dill and lime, 'superb' lamb cutlets with gratin dauphinoise and a light thyme *jus*, and 'luscious' sea bass fillet with tapénade. Puddings can be a little lacklustre, although one party was delighted by excellent tarte Tatin. Estimates of the service vary from 'wonderfully attentive' to 'rather offhand'. The wine list is helpfully arranged by style, and prices rarely stray over £20. House wine is £9.95.

CHEF: David Olliverin PROPRIETOR: Philippe Roy OPEN: all week 12 to 2, 6 to 10.30 MEALS: alc (main courses £14). Set L and D 6 to 7 and post-theatre £9.95 (2 courses) to £12.95, Set D £16.50 (2 courses) to £19.50 SERVICE: not inc, card slips closed; 10% for parties of 8 or more CARDS: Amex, Delta, Diners, MasterCard, Visa DETAILS: 85 seats. Private parties: 100 main room. Vegetarian meals. No children under 8. Wheelchair access (no WC). Music

Hole in the Wall

16 George Street, Bath BA1 2EN — COOKING 4
TEL/FAX: (01225) 425242 — COST £21–£38

Non-smokers get the more colourful of the two dining-rooms, just below street level, in Bath's best-known restaurant where Eric Lepine has moved into the kitchen from Toxique (see entry, Melksham). The menu's interest derives partly from its increased length – a dozen à la carte main courses – which has produced a huge blini ('a sort of James the Giant Crumpet') served with muscly, dense smoked salmon, and soups from bouillabaisse to one of small sweet scallops with lentils and coriander. A struggle between East and West in the fish department (grilled tuna with warm potato salad and an orange, ginger and chilli dressing) suggests that the simpler and more confident meat dishes may be the best option.

Some of the experimentation might seem at odds with the previous high seriousness of the Hole in the Wall's output (an inspector considered the food 'fussier' and 'less intense' than before), but there is much to enjoy, not least the terrines: one of spring lamb with kidney and sweetbread 'delicately and perfectly cooked', wrapped round with an eggy mousse, or a 'robust, countrified' one of foie gras and duck livers, served with onion marmalade. The Anglo-French theme continues througlr puddings of rhubarb parfait and tarte Tatin. Indications are that service has, if anything, become even more efficient and friendly. The small but perfectly formed wine list manages to encompass some exciting wines from the major regions at a range of prices to suit most pockets. Twenty-two wines are available by the glass from £2.50 to £5.50, including one champagne and four desserts, while house French is £9.50 a bottle.

CHEF: Eric Lepine PROPRIETORS: Mr and Mrs C. Chown OPEN: all week L 12 to 2, Mon to Sat D 6 to 10.30 MEALS: alc (main courses L £5.50 to £6.50, D £12). Set L Sun £13.50 SERVICE: not inc CARDS: Amex, MasterCard, Switch, Visa DETAILS: 70 seats. Private parties: 16 main room. Vegetarian meals. Children's helpings. No smoking in 1 dining-room. No music. Air-conditioned

Moody Goose — NEW ENTRY

7A Kingsmead Square, Bath BA1 2AB — COOKING 4
TEL: (01225) 466688 — COST £24–£49

The basement (a wine bar in its time) has been cleaned up, pared back to reveal some attractive arches, and painted magnolia. A huge free-standing ceramic goose takes pride of place in the dining-room. Is it moody? 'I would say it looks a bit cross,' reckoned one visitor, who also noted goose prints on the walls, though nothing goosey on the menu. Stephen Shore's new venture, opened at the end of 1996, could be seen as 'an English version of a French restaurant' in its espousal of moules marinière, or terrine of duck confit, although he goes beyond that to a ravioli of Cornish crab with lemon grass and basil, and hot apple fritters.

Shore has a track record on the country-house circuit, having worked most recently at Mallory Court (see entry, Bishop's Tachbrook). He is not the first – and will probably not be the last – to desert this rarified world in favour of a more modest operation under his own steam, and the change shows in the less-expensive ingredients chosen and (in the absence of a large brigade) less ambitious dishes: oxtail, terrine of ham hock and black pudding, or smoked haddock croquettes, although there has also been roast leg of rabbit together with the saddle wrapped in chicken mousseline, served with a reduced red wine sauce and rösti potatoes. Finish, perhaps, with glazed lemon tart, or the Moody Goose gâteau with cherries. Around 50 wines soon escalate in price, though six house wines start at £10.50 and stay below £20.

CHEFS: Stephen Shore and Andy Blackburn PROPRIETORS: Stephen and Victoria Shore OPEN: Mon to Sat 12 to 2.30, 6 to 10 (10.30 Sat) CLOSED: 26 Dec, last week Feb, first week Mar, bank hol Mons MEALS: alc (main courses L £7.50 to £9, D £12 to £17.50). Set L £10 (2 courses), pre-theatre D £10 (2 courses) to £13.50 SERVICE: not inc CARDS: Delta, Diners, MasterCard, Switch, Visa DETAILS: 30 seats. 16 seats outside. Private parties: 20 main room, 8 private room. Vegetarian meals. Children's helpings. No children under 8. No smoking in 1 dining-room. Music

No. 5 Bistro £

5 Argyle Street, Bath BA2 4BA COOKING 1
TEL: (01225) 444499 FAX: (01225) 318668 COST £20–£43

It helps to pick your day at this good-value bistro near Pulteney Bridge with its wooden floor, plants and colourful prints. Monday and Tuesday are for BYO with no corkage charge, Wednesday is for fish: baked red snapper with salsa, for example. Otherwise there is a choice of simple one-plate lunches such as grilled sardines or lamb rissoles, and an evening *carte* (plus a list of daily specials) that might take in Thai-style fish soup, chargrilled poussin with tarragon and mustard sauce, and plum pudding with brandy sauce. A clutch of good bottled beers complements the short, lively wine list. House French is £8.50.

CHEFS: Stephen Smith, Paul Hearne and Sarah Grantins PROPRIETORS: Charles Home and Stephen Smith OPEN: Tue to Sat L 12 to 2.30, Mon to Sat D 6.30 to 10 (10.30 Fri, 11 Sat) CLOSED: 24 to 28 Dec MEALS: alc (main courses L £6 to £10, D £9.50 to £15). BYO Mon and Tue D (no corkage) SERVICE: not inc CARDS: Amex, Delta, Diners, MasterCard, Switch, Visa DETAILS: 35 seats. Private parties: 12 main room. Vegetarian meals. Children's helpings. Music

▲ *Queensberry Hotel, Olive Tree*

Russel Street, Bath BA1 2QF COOKING 5
TEL: (01225) 447928 FAX: (01225) 446065 COST £23–£50

Just far enough away from the bustling throngs in the heart of Bath, the Queensberry is a smart, sophisticated hotel on a human scale. Down the steps to the left of the hotel's entrance, the Olive Tree inhabits one of those basement rooms that manages to seem improbably light and airy at all times. The white-tiled floor and good lighting help, and pleasant gastronomic watercolours enliven the wall space. Stephen Ross was always one of the more enthusiastic practitioners of the Mediterranean arts, and his current kitchen team shares that predilection, serving up provençale fish soup with rouille, and saffron risotto with grilled courgettes and Parmesan. In different mood, calf's liver with onions and a madeira gravy was well judged at inspection, as were the 'plump, rich, tasty' smoked haddock fish cakes that preceded it. Gratin dauphinoise is served as an article of faith and is rendered as well as anywhere. Desserts such as chocolate tart with vanilla ice-cream, or prune and armagnac parfait in an Earl Grey syrup, have impressed. Service is 'efficient'.

The wine list has grown in size again, introducing Germany, Spain and South Africa for the first time. The New World section is particularly appealing, with wines from Chile and Argentina offering great value-for-money, but Joseph Drouhin's 1985 Chassagne-Montrachet at £39 a magnum must be hard to resist.

House wines are £12.50 a bottle and a tasty half-dozen are available by the glass at £2.50. CELLARMAN'S CHOICE: Costières de Nîmes Viognier, Ch. Belle Coste 1995, £16.75; Qupé Syrah 1993, California, £25.50.

CHEFS: Mathew Prowse and Gary Rosser PROPRIETORS: Stephen and Penny Ross OPEN: Mon to Sat L 12 to 2, all week D 7 to 10 (9 Sun) CLOSED: 1 week Christmas MEALS: alc (main courses £10.50 to £16). Set L £10.50 (2 courses) to £12.50, Set D Mon to Sat £19 SERVICE: not inc, card slips closed; 10% on parties of 10 or more CARDS: MasterCard, Switch, Visa DETAILS: 50 seats. Private parties: 35 main room. Vegetarian meals. Children's helpings. No smoking in dining-room. Wheelchair access (also WC). Music. Air-conditioned ACCOMMODATION: 22 rooms, all with bath/shower. TV. Phone. B&B £89 to £175. Rooms for disabled. Children welcome. Baby facilities. Afternoon teas. Garden (*The Which? Hotel Guide*)

▲ *Royal Crescent, Pimpernel's*

16 Royal Crescent, Bath BA1 2LS — COOKING **6**
TEL: (01225) 739955 FAX: (01225) 339401 — COST £57–£69

Shortly after the 1997 edition of the *Guide* appeared, the Royal Crescent Hotel was bought by the owners of Cliveden (see entry, Taplow). They embarked on a £2.5 million refit, beginning with the Mansion House – the centrepiece of John Wood's famous 500-foot curve of Georgian houses – and as the *Guide* went to press the new main dining-room, called Pimpernel's and smartly kitted out with striped walls and bright red chairs, opened to replace the Dower House.

Although Steven Blake still plays a role, Stephen Midgley, who has worked at Gidleigh Park and Harveys in Bristol, has been recruited to run the new kitchen. The format is a set-price dinner only, with around five choices per course, in a style that combines Anglo-French ideas with some Far Eastern flavours. Among the crossover ideas might be baked foie gras with mango chutney, or squab pigeon with lime sauce and ginger dressing, as well as more straightforward sauté of scallops with crab beignets, or roast duckling and confit. Mango, papaya and coconut feature among desserts, alongside banana soufflé and Valrhona bitter chocolate mousse. A new wine lists starts with house wine at £15.50. Reports please. The informal Grill Room opens all week for lunch and dinner.

CHEFS: Stephen Midgley and Steven Blake PROPRIETOR: Cliveden plc OPEN: Tue to Sat D only 7 to 9.30 MEALS: Set D £42 SERVICE: not inc, card slips closed CARDS: Delta, Diners, MasterCard, Switch, Visa DETAILS: 60 seats. 15 seats outside. Private parties: 20 main room, Car park. Children's helpings. No smoking in dining-room. Wheelchair access (also WC). Music. Air-conditioned ACCOMMODATION: 42 rooms, all with bath/shower. TV. Phone. Room only £160 to £260. Children welcome. Baby facilities. Dogs welcome. Afternoon teas. Garden. Swimming-pool (*The Which? Hotel Guide*)

The 1998 Guide *will be published before Christmas 1997. Reports on meals are most welcome at any time of the year, but are particularly valuable in the spring (no later than June). Send them to* The Good Food Guide, *FREEPOST, 2 Marylebone Road, London NW1 1YN. Or email your report to guidereports@which.co.uk.*

Woods

9–13 Alfred Street, Bath BA1 2QX COOKING **2**
TEL: (01225) 314812 FAX: (01225) 443146 COST £22–£42

This thriving city-centre brasserie had a face-lift early in 1997, and a sense of chic has been restored to the dining-room. Antony Edwards has left but the remainder of the kitchen team is still in place, and the menus continue in their innovative way to set a cracking pace. Cod fillet, for instance, is crusted with cashews, leeks and caraway seeds and served on a roasted red pepper sauce, while a brace of quail are given a beetroot glaze and accompanied by vegetable crisps. Moreover, the kitchen is capable of turning out a mean roast beef and Yorkshire pudding for Sunday lunch, and offers imaginative vegetarian dishes too. The pudding list is headed 'Cholesterol Corner' but not everything on it will clog the arteries – iced guava parfait with a fresh fruit coulis shouldn't be too risky. Special-offer weekday lunches at £6 for two courses are irresistible value. The mainly French wine list contains some good bargains, starting with house red and white at £9, and there is plenty available by the glass from £1.85.

CHEFS: Leigh Davidson and David Price PROPRIETORS: David and Claude Price OPEN: all week L 12 to 3, Mon to Sat D 6 to 11 CLOSED: 24 to 26 Dec MEALS: alc (main courses £10.50 to £13.50). Set L Mon to Fri £6 (2 courses), Set L Sat £7 (2 courses), Set L Sun £7 (1 course) to £14, Set D Mon to Fri £11.25 (2 courses) to £15.50, Set D Sat £19.95 SERVICE: not inc CARDS: MasterCard, Visa DETAILS: 120 seats. 12 seats outside. Private parties: 70 main room, 40 private room. Vegetarian meals. Children's helpings. No cigars/pipes in dining-room. Wheelchair access (also WC). Music

BEAMINSTER Dorset map 2

▲ *Bridge House*

3 Prout Bridge, Beaminster DT8 3AY COOKING **3**
TEL: (01308) 862200 FAX: (01308) 863700 COST £22–£41

Once a favourite of Thomas Hardy, Beaminster is now a centre for golfers and visitors to National Trust gardens and properties. Among its attractions is Bridge House, just down the hill from the market square, occupying a thirteenth-century clergy house. Flagstone floors, oak beams and open fireplaces are the setting for Jacky Rae's country cooking, and little changes from one year to the next: 'same staff, same style, same owners, same chef,' confirms Peter Pinkster.

Dinner is the main business, at a set price with a few supplements for sirloin steak or grilled lemon sole. A traditional streak accounts for much of the repertoire, including braised shoulder of lamb with garlic and rosemary, tenderloin of pork with apricots, and breast of chicken with blue cheese sauce, but there may also be warm onion tart, or red mullet fillets on a chive sauce. Strudel has appeared as a vegetarian main course with mushrooms and walnuts, and as a dessert filled with banana and chocolate, while local cheeses offer something Hardy never did: an alternative ending. Prices are kept within reason on the modest but appealing wine list, starting with six house wines at £9.50.

CHEF: Jacky Rae PROPRIETOR: Peter Pinkster OPEN: all week 12 to 2, 7 to 9 MEALS: Set L £12.50 (2 courses) to £14.50, Set D £19.45. Light L available. BYO £8.50 SERVICE: not inc, card slips closed CARDS: Amex, Delta, Diners, MasterCard, Switch, Visa DETAILS: 36 seats. 12 seats outside. Private parties: 48 main room, 16 private room. Car park. Vegetarian meals. Children's helpings. No smoking in dining-room. No music ACCOMMODATION: 14 rooms, all with bath/shower. TV. Phone. B&B £55 to £102. Deposit: £25. Children welcome. Baby facilities. Dogs welcome in bedrooms only and not left unattended. Afternoon teas. Garden (*The Which? Hotel Guide*)

BECKINGHAM Lincolnshire map 6

Black Swan £

Hillside, Beckingham LN5 0RQ
TEL: (01636) 626474 COOKING 4
off A17 to Sleaford, 6m E of Newark-on-Trent COST £20–£41

Beckingham is a little difficult to find, and the Black Swan has managed to camouflage itself well once you get there, but if at a loss, ask: passers-by evidently assume as soon as you've wound down the car window that the Indans' country retreat is where you're headed. Once settled in one of the enveloping sofas, you'll be glad you persevered. Anton Indans's style is a model of classical restraint that does not, however, stint on flavour. One luncher reported that 'my taste-buds got very excited' by a bowl of curried celery and parsnip soup, and the coarse-textured lamb and mint sausages that followed satisfied too. Menus have also featured a kebab of red mullet and monkfish bedded on spinach and sauced with Noilly Prat, and duck magret glazed with marmalade and served with an apple and mango compote.

Fancy desserts are the order of the day; be prepared for mocha mousse with fruit pavlova and butterscotch sauce. White-gloved service maintains an atmosphere of seemly civility. Regulars report that it is essential to book ahead for lunch. The wine list deals routinely in big French names, with around ten from the rest of the world, but prices are moderate. House French is £8.40.

CHEF: Anton Indans PROPRIETORS: Anton and Alison Indans OPEN: Tue to Sun L 12 to 2, Tue to Sat D 7 to 9.30 CLOSED: 1 week Jan, 2 weeks Aug MEALS: alc D (main courses £9.50 to £14.50). Set L Tue to Sat £10.95 (2 courses), Set L Sun £13.95. BYO £3 SERVICE: not inc CARDS: Delta, MasterCard, Switch, Visa (5% surcharge) DETAILS: 35 seats. 12 seats outside. Private parties: 28 main room, 12 and 28 private rooms. Car park. Vegetarian meals. Children's helpings Sun L. No smoking in dining-room. Wheelchair access (also WC). Music

BIRCH VALE Derbyshire map 8

▲ *Waltzing Weasel*

New Mills Road, Birch Vale SK12 5BT
TEL/FAX: (01663) 743402 COOKING 3
on A6015, ½m W of Hayfield COST £20–£38

The Weasel waltzes in the shadow of Kinder Scout amid charming, rough-hewn Derbyshire countryside. It is a traditional inn that weaves its magic by remaining small enough to offer friendly service, and cooking that successfully combines classicism with originality. Ingredient-sourcing is clearly conscientious, the provenance of supplies proudly indicated on the menus: gravad lax, for example, uses top-drawer fish from Loch Fyne, and seafood platter brings together crayfish, anchovies, prawns and salmon. There may be Cheddar and spinach soufflé, and accurately timed duckling, 'meaty and succulent with crispy skin'. Bread-and-butter pudding, treacle tart, and fruit crumble are ways to finish. A simpler menu operates in the rustic bar, where shrimps on toast, dressed crab salad, or chicken curry are the mode. The wine list is enterprising and keenly priced, although the French and Italian bottles look more enticing than the non-European offerings. House French is £8.95.

CHEF: George Benham PROPRIETOR: Michael Atkinson OPEN: all week 12 to 2, 7 to 9 MEALS: alc L (main courses £7 to £12.50). Set D £21.50 (2 courses) to £24.50 SERVICE: not inc, card slips closed CARDS: Amex, Delta, MasterCard, Switch, Visa DETAILS: 30 seats. 12 seats outside. Private parties: 36 main room. Car park. Vegetarian meals. Children welcome. Wheelchair access (no WC). Music. Air-conditioned ACCOMMODATION: 8 rooms, all with bath/shower. TV. Phone. Air-conditioned. B&B £45 to £95. Deposit: £20. Children welcome. Dogs welcome. Garden (*The Which? Hotel Guide*)

BIRDLIP Gloucestershire map 2

▲ *Kingshead House* 🍷

Birdlip GL4 8JH
TEL: (01452) 862299
on B4070 towards Stroud, ½m off A417 between Gloucester and Cirencester

COOKING 4
COST £25–£47

Judy and Warren Knock have been in the restaurant game a good few years, and they run both the dining-room and the single guest-room of this old Cotswold house, complete with inglenooks and worn flagged floors, with appreciable attention to detail. Judy Knock grows her own herbs outside the kitchen window and uses them to good effect in the nibbles and amuse-gueules that form an essential part of the catering. A vivid pairing of duck and chicken, both 'seriously smoked', served with an onion and beetroot confit, found favour with one visitor, or there may be salmon fillet braised in red wine and served on a red bean purée, or something more obviously classical, such as medallions of beef fillet with garlicky red wine sauce and a mixture of mushrooms. Rich desserts, perhaps dark chocolate mousse with a Cointreau sauce, are the alternative to a selection of quality British and French cheeses. Service, commented one reporter, 'was hardly noticed, so it must have been excellent'.

'Value for money' could be the motto for the good-quality wine list, where most bottles come in under £20, although you could splash out on Krug champagne at £85 if so inclined. Half-bottles are numerous and house wines start at £10.50 (£2 a glass). Wine lovers might enquire about the occasional tasting evenings. CELLARMAN'S CHOICE: Tokay-Pinot Gris d'Alsace Furstentum 1992, Albert Mann, £19.50; St-Joseph 1987, Bérard, £17.50.

▲ *means accommodation is available.*

CHEF: Judy Knock PROPRIETORS: Judy and Warren Knock OPEN: Tue to Fri and Sun L 12.15 to 1.45, Tue to Sat D 7.30 to 9.45 CLOSED: 25 and 26 Dec, 1 to 3 Jan MEALS: alc (main courses L £8 to £11.50, D £14.50 to £17). Set L Sun £16.50 SERVICE: not inc; 10% for parties of 6 or more CARDS: Amex, Diners, MasterCard, Visa DETAILS: 34 seats. 10 seats outside. Private parties: 34 main room. Car park. Vegetarian meals. Children's helpings. Wheelchair access (no WC). Music ACCOMMODATION: 1 room, with bath/shower. TV. B&B £38 to £65. Deposit: £20. Children welcome. Dogs by arrangement. Garden

BIRKENHEAD Merseyside map 8

Beadles

15 Rosemount, Oxton, Birkenhead L43 5SG COOKING 3
TEL: (0151) 653 9010 COST £27–£35

'Beadles is more like a club than a restaurant,' writes a regular visitor to this long-stayer, twenty-one years old in 1998. 'We always know a few people there whenever we go. What will Birkenhead do for a good restaurant when Roy and Bea retire?' Perish the thought. Two decades have failed to dim Bea Gott's passion for culinary adventure, and she seems able to carry her supporters with her whenever a new direction is embarked on. A warm smoked salmon salad dressed with blended smoked salmon, anchovy oil and tomato purée won converts at a December dinner, while a month earlier seared tuna steaks with lime salsa and caper dressing had done the business. There is no kid-glove treatment for the fancier cuts of meat, so beef fillet is sharpened with cranberries and horseradish. Finish with hot cardamom bananas or a meringue with forest fruit ice-cream and chocolate sauce. The rough-and-ready furnishings and calor-gas heating do not in the least detract from the Beadles experience for its devotees. A broad-minded selection of wines at extravagantly fair prices suits the food well. House red and white are £8.

CHEF: Bea Gott PROPRIETORS: Roy and Bea Gott OPEN: Wed to Sat D only 7.30 to 9 CLOSED: 2 weeks Feb MEALS: alc (main courses £10.50 to £11.50) SERVICE: not inc; 10% for parties of 6 or more CARDS: Delta, MasterCard, Switch, Visa DETAILS: 32 seats. Private parties: 28 main room. No children under 7. No smoking before coffee. Wheelchair access (no WC). Music

BIRMINGHAM West Midlands map 5

Chung Ying £

16–18 Wrottesley Street, Birmingham B5 4RT
TEL: (0121) 622 5669 and 622 1693 COOKING 1
FAX: (0121) 666 7051 COST £22–£44

For years this redoubtable Cantonese dragon has set the standard for generosity and big flavours in Birmingham's Chinatown. It now has competitors around the Arcadian complex but is holding fast. The menu is a monster, running to more than three hundred dishes, mostly in the die-hard tradition of big soups, casseroles, roast meats, rice and noodles, backed up by sizzlers and specials such as steamed pork pie with salted egg, fried fish-cake with mange-tout, and fried frog's leg with bitter melon. Otherwise go conventional with crispy aromatic duck, baked crab with ginger and spring onions, or stir-fried aubergines with black-bean sauce. Some fifty high-class dim-sum form the main entertainment between noon and 6pm. Drink jasmine tea and Tsing Tao beer, or dip into the wine list. House wine is £10 a litre. A related restaurant, Chung Ying Garden, is at 17 Thorp Street; Tel: (0121) 666 6622.

CHEF/PROPRIETOR: Siu Chung Wong OPEN: all week noon to 11.30 (10.30 Sun) CLOSED: 25 Dec MEALS: alc (main courses £5.50 to £17). Set D £12.50 to £19 (all minimum 2) SERVICE: not inc CARDS: Amex, Delta, Diners, MasterCard, Switch, Visa DETAILS: 250 seats. Private parties: 120 main room, 120 private room. Vegetarian meals. Children welcome. Wheelchair access (no WC). Music. Air-conditioned

Leftbank

79 Broad Street, Birmingham B15 1QA COOKING 2
TEL/FAX: (0121) 643 4464 COST £24–£47

The word 'Bank' is carved in stone above the doorway of this solid three-storey building, but otherwise little remains of its former incarnation beyond a few metal grills and a large vault door. Bill Marmion cooks in modern brasserie mould, producing tortellini of lobster with lentils and smoked bacon, smoked haddock with poached egg, and tomato tart with mozzarella and a tapénade dressing. Some dishes may involve a loose interpretation of classical terms, seasoning may be variable, and black pudding may crop up in unlikely places – for example on top of a 'cassoulet' of duck with black-eyed beans – but ingredients are good and main items are well handled, including plump 'vigorously seared' scallops for one reporter. Finish perhaps with pear and cinnamon turnover, iced nougat parfait, or a selection of cheeses served with bramble chutney. House wine is £9.90.

CHEF: Bill Marmion PROPRIETOR: Caroline Benbrook OPEN: Mon to Fri L 12 to 2, Mon to Sat D 7 to 10 (10.30 weekends) CLOSED: 2 weeks Christmas, bank hols MEALS: alc D (main courses £10 to £15.50). Set L £12 (2 courses) to £14.50 SERVICE: not inc CARDS: Amex, Delta, Diners, MasterCard, Switch, Visa DETAILS: 80 seats. Private parties: 60 main room, 16 private room. Vegetarian meals. No children under 12. No children after 8pm. Wheelchair access (also WC). Music. Air-conditioned

Maharaja £

23–25 Hurst Street, Birmingham B5 4AS COOKING 2
TEL: (0121) 622 2641 FAX: (0121) 622 4021 COST £21–£32

More than 25 years old and still firing on all cylinders: no wonder the modest little Maharaja is one of the most reliable venues for Indian food in Birmingham. The kitchen has been in the same hands since 1982 and the cooking has an assured touch. It is also unmoved by fashion: balti houses go their own way, and what you get here is sound Punjabi and Mughlai cooking based emphatically on decent raw materials and fresh, razor-sharp spicing. The menu treads a familiar path through seekh kebab, chicken korma, bhuna gosht and keema peas, backed up by a dhal of the day and specials such as chicken samarkand, shahi murgh and bara kebab. Breads and rice are reckoned to be 'excellent'. Staff are as courteous and charming as you could hope for: 'the badinage with what were obviously regular customers showed how far ideas about good "service" have developed over the last 20 years,' observed one reporter. Lassi and Kingfisher beer suit the food, and there are two dozen wines to choose from. House wine is £7.15.

CHEF: Bhupinder Waraich PROPRIETOR: N.S. Batt OPEN: Mon to Sat 12 to 2, 6 to 11 CLOSED: bank hols MEALS: alc (main courses £6 to £8). Set L and D £11.80 SERVICE: 10%, card slips closed CARDS: Amex, Diners, MasterCard, Switch, Visa DETAILS: 62 seats. Private parties: 30 main room. Vegetarian meals. Children welcome. Wheelchair access (also WC). Music. Air-conditioned

BIRTLE Greater Manchester map 8

▲ *Normandie* 🍷 £

Elbut Lane, Birtle BL9 6UT
TEL: (0161) 764 3869 and 1170
FAX: (0161) 764 4866 COOKING **6**
off B6222, 3m NE of Bury COST £20–£47

A steep, winding lane leads to this assortment of buildings, perched on a Pennine foothill overlooking Greater Manchester, where a 'prompt and friendly' greeting awaits. One reporter found the service in the vivid blue and yellow dining-room 'more relaxed and less pompous than it used to be, and still as attentive as ever'. Paul Bellingham's food adopts a contemporary approach and focuses on clear, unambiguous flavours such as leek cannelloni filled with goats' cheese, or fillet of red bream with pesto mashed potatoes. The repertoire may be a familiar one, embracing caramelised onion tart, or a warm bacon and black pudding salad with poached egg ('rather like having breakfast with lettuce beneath'), but confirms the message that this is food to comfort, with fillets, parcels, sausages and dumplings adding to the sense of contentment.

Fish appears to be as successful as anything, producing endorsements for smoked haddock soup with vegetable ravioli, and salmon fish-cakes with a crisp crust and lemon butter sauce, which also came with an impressive accompaniment of shredded vegetables. Portions can be generous, but those with room for dessert have enjoyed armagnac parfait with prunes, 'light' toffee pudding, and caramelised pear with chocolate sauce. Set-price meals, though more limited in scope than the *carte*, are considered good value.

The wine list has seen a few departures and new arrivals over the last year but continues to provide variety and good-quality drinking at all price levels. Although the balance is tipped in favour of the Old World, some New World gems add weight to the list. House Vin de Pays des Côtes du Tarn is £9.95. CELLARMAN'S CHOICE: Montgras Chardonnay 1995, Chile, £13.75; Bourgogne Rouge 1993, Dom. Robert Chevillon, £28.50.

CHEF: Paul Bellingham PROPRIETORS: Gillian and Max Moussa OPEN: Mon to Fri L 12 to 2, Mon to Sat D 7 to 9.30 CLOSED: 26 Dec to 9 Jan, 1 week Easter, bank hols exc 25 Dec MEALS: alc (main courses £10 to £20). Set L £12.50, Set D £15 SERVICE: none, card slips closed CARDS: Amex, Delta, Diners, MasterCard, Switch, Visa DETAILS: 50 seats. Car park. Vegetarian meals. Children welcome. No cigars/pipes in dining-room. Wheelchair access (also WC). Music ACCOMMODATION: 23 rooms, all with bath/shower. TV. Phone. B&B £49 to £79. Rooms for disabled. Children welcome. Baby facilities. Afternoon teas. Garden

BISHOP'S TACHBROOK Warwickshire map 5

▲ *Mallory Court*

Harbury Lane, Bishops Tachbrook CV33 9QB
TEL: (01926) 330214 FAX: (01926) 451714 NEW CHEF
off B4087, 2m S of Leamington Spa COST £41–£80

Formal gardens surround the creeper-covered house, comfort is given priority in the bright, floral, scatter-cushioned lounge, and the demure but expansive dining-room is wood-panelled. The setting betokens a degree of care and luxury, which have typically been echoed in the food. Stephen Shore left last year, and Allan Holland took a more active role in the kitchen for a while, but then Trevor Blyth (whose CV includes stints at Cliveden in Taplow, Le Manoir aux Quat' Saisons in Great Milton, and Alfred in London – see entries) was appointed just as the *Guide* went to press. Mallory Court has typically adopted a refined, modern-classical approach to cooking, with something of a French bias, although this may broaden under the new regime. An early menu included smoked salmon and scrambled eggs, grilled minute steak with chips, and lemon tart. We welcome reports. France, California and Australia figure prominently on the wine list, with some excellent producers making an appearance, but mark-ups are on the hefty side. Nine house wines start at £14.25.

CHEF: Trevor Blyth PROPRIETORS: Allan Holland and Jeremy Mort OPEN: all week 12.30 to 2, 7 to 9.45 CLOSED: 1 to 9 Jan MEALS: alc (main courses £21 to £25). Set L £18.50 (2 courses) to £26, Set D £30. BYO £12.50 SERVICE: none, card slips closed CARDS: Amex, Delta, Diners, MasterCard, Switch, Visa DETAILS: 50 seats. 25 seats outside. Private parties: 25 main room. Car park. No children under 9. No smoking in dining-room. Wheelchair access (no WC). No music ACCOMMODATION: 10 rooms, all with bath/shower. TV. Phone. B&B £120 to £225. No children under 9. Afternoon teas. Garden. Swimming-pool

BLACKPOOL Lancashire map 8

September Brasserie

LANCASHIRE 1998 LIVE WIRE

13–17 Queen Street, Blackpool FY1 1PU COOKING 4
TEL: (01253) 23282 FAX: (01253) 299455 COST £20–£41

The ground floor is a hairdresser's, with the brasserie above: a light, airy room with the kitchen in full view and an atmosphere that bustles. The location, in a street near the sea-front, may be candy-floss Blackpool, but the cooking is a world away from holiday-resort clichés. The short menu fizzes with modern invention, ingredients are pure metropolitan 1990s and global to boot, and dishes are forever taking unexpected turns. Turkey soup is enlivened with pimento oil, poached halibut comes with ink spätzli and wasabi vinaigrette, and 'free-range bison' is cooked bourguignon-style and accompanied by buckwheat pilaff. Less extravagant ideas are also done with flair: fish-cakes with well-flavoured tomato concassée, and succulent lamb couscous with harissa have both been enjoyed by reporters. Desserts seem more down to earth as in lemon and lime tart, rhubarb crumble or a 'gorgeous' white Belgian chocolate mousse. Wines are mostly sourced from Bibendum and Pagendam Pratt, with prices starting at around £11.

CHEF: Michael Golowicz PROPRIETORS: Michael Golowicz and Pat Wood OPEN: Tue to Sat 12 to 1.45, 7 to 9.30 CLOSED: 1 week winter, 2 weeks summer MEALS: alc (main courses £6 to £14). Set D £16.95. BYO £6 SERVICE: not inc, card slips closed CARDS: Amex, Diners, MasterCard, Visa DETAILS: 40 seats. Private parties: 30 main room. Vegetarian meals. Children's helpings. Music

BLAKENEY Norfolk map 6

▲ *White Horse Hotel* £ **NEW ENTRY**

4 High Street, Blakeney NR25 7AL COOKING 2
TEL: (01263) 740574 COST £21–£37

Of the handful of hotels in Blakeney, the White Horse lays claim to being the oldest. In the seventeenth century it was a coaching-inn, and the split-level dining-room occupies what were the stables. With some cobblestoned walls and a conservatory entrance, it is a relaxing place with no second sittings to make you feel hurried. Starters may include a thoughtfully composed salad of king prawns, fennel and tomato in a creamy herbed dressing, the shellfish themselves offering plenty of flavour. Main courses might take in grey mullet with soy, ginger and garlic, or chargrilled lamb chops on ratatouille, and the vegetarian option can be a cut above the norm: chillied bean stew with a cooling dollop of avocado and soured cream salsa on top, for example. Chocolate and walnut tart with 'great, very rich short pastry' and a scoop of mocha ice-cream makes an impressive dessert. Wines are a fairly conservative bunch, despite being sourced from Adnams, but prices are demonstrably fair. House French country wines are £7.50.

CHEF: Christopher Hyde PROPRIETORS: Daniel Rees and Sue Catt OPEN: Tue to Sat and bank hol Sun D only 7 to 9 (9.30 Sat and during July and Aug) CLOSED: 24 and 26 Dec D MEALS: alc (main courses £7.50 to £13.50). Bar food available SERVICE: not inc, card slips closed; 10% for parties of 10 or more CARDS: Amex, Delta, MasterCard, Switch, Visa DETAILS: 32 seats. Private parties: 30 main room. Car park. Vegetarian meals. No children under 8. No-smoking area. Wheelchair access (no WC). Music ACCOMMODATION: 10 rooms, all with bath/shower. TV. Phone. B&B £30 to £70. Deposit: £20. Children welcome. Baby facilities. Garden (*The Which? Hotel Guide*)

'The plate was strewn with bits of superfluous red and green lettuce. It looked like an overturned shopping trolley in Tesco.' (On eating in the West Country)

The Guide *office can quickly spot when a restaurateur is encouraging customers to write recommending inclusion – and sadly, several restaurants have been doing this in 1997. Such reports do not further a restaurant's cause. Please tell us if a restaurateur invites you to write to the* Guide.

Restaurateurs justifiably resent no-shows. If you quote a credit card number when booking, you may be liable for the restaurant's lost profit margin if you don't turn up. Always phone to cancel.

All details are as accurate as possible at the time of going to press, but chefs and owners often change, and it is wise to check by telephone before making a special journey. Many readers have been disappointed when set-price bargain meals are no longer available. Ask when booking.

BOLLINGTON Cheshire map 8

Mauro's

88 Palmerston Street, Bollington SK10 5PW COOKING **2**
TEL: (01625) 573898 COST £22–£44

'Mauro's is back on form,' noted a correspondent after a meal on Christmas Eve. Compared with the brave new world of Italian regionality, its version of trattoria cooking may seem almost quaint, but the kitchen clearly knows what it's at. Home-made pasta appears in several different guises, and the potato gnocchi with tomato sauce, mozzarella and basil comes highly recommended. Fresh fish – at least five different varieties – is also worth considering: simply cooked lemon sole with lime and dill has been praised. Otherwise expect all sorts of antipasti, breast of chicken with a sauce of citrus fruit and dry Martini, saltimbocca, and fillet steak with dolcelatte. Desserts are from the ubiquitous trolley, but there are some unusual offerings such as 'excellent-looking' zucchini cake alongside 'real' tiramisù and fresh fruit. The list of around 60 wines is, by and large, an oenophile's tour round the Italian regions with stopovers at some of the best producers in the land. House wine is £9.

CHEF/PROPRIETOR: Vincenzo Mauro OPEN: Mon to Fri L (and first Sun in month Oct to Apr) 12.30 to 2, Mon to Sat D 7 to 10 CLOSED: 25 and 26 Dec MEALS: alc (main courses £9 to £17). Set L Sun £14.95 SERVICE: not inc; 10% for parties of 6 or more CARDS: Amex, Delta, MasterCard, Switch, Visa DETAILS: 65 seats. Private parties: 65 main room, 65 private room. Vegetarian meals. Children's helpings. Wheelchair access (also WC). Music

BOLTON ABBEY North Yorkshire map 9

▲ *Devonshire Arms, Burlington Restaurant* 🍷✱

Bolton Abbey BD23 6AE
TEL: (01756) 710441 FAX: (01756) 710564 COOKING **5**
at junction of A59 and B6160, 5m NW of Ilkley COST £28–£58

The eighteenth-century converted coaching-inn, which forms part of the Duke of Devonshire's estate, is decorated with antiques from the family's other home, Chatsworth House. Although the flagstoned bar still functions as a pub, the hotel and restaurant have other ambitions. The feel is sedate and unhurried (there are leisure facilities too, just to be on the safe side), and Andrew Nicholson's food manages simultaneously to comfort and intrigue. He has the advantage of rabbit, pheasant, grouse and roe deer from the estate, as well as herbs, fruit and vegetables from the garden, and puts his materials through a modern mill.

Dinner is the centre of attention, where pheasant may be given a brown ale sauce, and where a few luxuries creep in: a terrine of corn-fed chicken and foie gras with sauce gribiche, or halibut served with leek and lobster in a tarragon and chervil dressing. Sauces tend to be light affairs derived from cooking juices: made from poultry to accompany grilled skate with polenta chips and lentils, for example, or spiced with ginger and soy for Gressingham duck breast. Non-meat options might include tomato and courgette tart with a black olive dressing, and desserts run to flambé pineapple with mango sorbet, and lemon mousse with kataif wafers. Staff have varied from 'charming and friendly' to 'incomprehensible and undertrained', and the predominantly French wine list, while good, is rather pricey. House French is £13.95.

CHEF: Andrew Nicholson PROPRIETORS: Duke and Duchess of Devonshire OPEN: all week 12.30 to 2, 6.45 to 10 (9.30 Sun) MEALS: Set L £18.50, Set D £37 SERVICE: not inc, card slips closed CARDS: Amex, Delta, Diners, MasterCard, Switch, Visa DETAILS: 75 seats. Private parties: 120 main room, 12 to 120 private rooms. Car park. Vegetarian meals. Children's helpings. No children under 12 at D. No smoking in dining-room. Wheelchair access (also WC). No music ACCOMMODATION: 41 rooms, all with bath/shower. TV. Phone. B&B £130 to £160. Rooms for disabled. Children welcome. Baby facilities. Dogs welcome. Afternoon teas. Garden. Swimming-pool. Fishing

BOUGHTON LEES Kent map 3

▲ *Eastwell Manor*

Eastwell Park, Boughton Lees TN25 4HR
TEL: (01233) 219955 FAX: (01233) 213017 COOKING **5**
on A251, 3m N of Ashford COST £28–£62

The manor, dating from 1069, was conceived on a grand scale, with 62 acres of garden and another 3,000 of estate. Walls are creeper-covered outside, richly wood-panelled inside. 'I know that some people don't want the formal setting and service,' wrote one reporter, 'but some jolly well do.' Eastwell rises to special occasions, with white-gloved service from 'a team of observant people', and a menu that takes its sourcing seriously. Game birds are from the estate, vegetables, fruits and salads come either from the manor's own kitchen garden or from Appledore Salads, and scallops are from Rye Bay, very likely roasted and served with parsnip purée and a light dressing of mustard oil.

Some of Ian Mansfield's ideas have a distinctly individual complexion – shredded crab and salt-cod with caviare, avocado and curry oil, for instance – while others have more to offer than one might think. A warm salad of endive sprinkled with clementine segments, crumbled Roquefort, and toasted pine-nuts turns out to be full of interest and 'greater than the sum of its parts' for its reporter. An earthy dimension to the food is not unusual, as in braised lamb shank, squab pigeon with beetroot, or in a starter of thin slices of large Desirée potatoes interleaved with wild mushrooms and surrounded by an intense gravy. English cheeses share the board with some French and Spanish, and desserts typically include a chilled component: iced hazelnut nougat with orange and passion-fruit, or warm apple tart with prune and armagnac ice-cream. Mark-ups are steep on the predominantly French wine list, which opens with around ten house wines under £15.

CHEF: Ian Mansfield PROPRIETOR: T.F. Parrett OPEN: all week 12.30 to 2, 7.30 to 9.45 MEALS: alc (main courses £16.50 to £20.50). Set L £19.50, Set D £28.50 SERVICE: not inc, card slips closed CARDS: Amex, Delta, Diners, MasterCard, Switch, Visa DETAILS: 68 seats. Private parties: 68 main room, 30 and 68 private rooms. Car park. Vegetarian meals. Children's helpings. No smoking in dining-room. Wheelchair access (also WC). Music ACCOMMODATION: 23 rooms, all with bath/shower. TV. Phone. D,B&B £85 to £300. Rooms for disabled. Children welcome. Dogs welcome. Afternoon teas. Garden

BOWNESS-ON-WINDERMERE Cumbria map 8

▲ *Linthwaite House* 🍷 £✱

CUMBRIAN 1998 CHEESE

Crook Road, Bowness-on-Windermere LA23 3JA COOKING 5
TEL: (01539) 488600 FAX: (01539) 488601 COST £25–£47

High on a hill near Windermere golf course, with verandahs overlooking the lake, Linthwaite provides ample lounges with an abundance of comfortable chairs and settees, log fires and old sea trunks adapted as drinks tables. The feel is 'welcoming and relaxing', and the menu offers individually priced courses for those who don't want to eat all four at a set price. Ian Bravey makes good use of Cumbrian provender, serving up Flookburgh shrimps, Cartmel venison, or Lakeland lamb layered with spinach and tomato, served on a redcurrant and mint *jus*. Local trout and Scottish salmon have been generous in quantity, moist and not overpowered by saucing.

Some flavours have a traditional orientation – carrot and orange soup, Scottish beef with mustard – but there may also be a puff pastry case of stir-fried vegetables with a ginger and soy sauce. One thing not to miss is the cheese selection, which mixes lesser-known British examples (unpasteurised smoked Cobble from north Lancashire, perhaps) with Cotherstone, Bonchester and Cashel Blue, plus local Boile, a soft goats' cheese marinated in olive oil. Gin and tonic sorbet or Welsh rarebit may precede the main course, and meals might end with crème brûlée, bavarois or steamed chocolate chip sponge. Service is 'excellent'. A good selection of round-the-world wines is arranged by style. A short list of vintage clarets starts at £32, half bottles (or half-carafes) are generous, and a few are also served by the glass at £3. House wine is from Argentina and France, from £14.25 a bottle.

CHEF: Ian Bravey PROPRIETOR: Mike Bevans OPEN: Sun L 12.30 to 1.30, all week D 7.15 to 8.45 MEALS: alc (main courses £16). Set L Sun £15.95, Set D £32. Bar L available Mon to Sat SERVICE: net prices, card slips closed CARDS: Amex, Delta, MasterCard, Switch, Visa DETAILS: 40 seats. 18 seats outside. Private parties: 8 main room, 18 private room. Car park. Vegetarian meals. Children's helpings. No children under 7 at D. No smoking in dining-room. Wheelchair access (also women's WC). Music ACCOMMODATION: 18 rooms, all with bath/shower. TV. Phone. D,B&B £59 to £254. Deposit: £80. Rooms for disabled. Children welcome. Baby facilities. Afternoon teas. Garden. Fishing (*The Which? Hotel Guide*)

Porthole Eating House 🍾

3 Ash Street, Bowness-on-Windermere LA23 3EB NEW CHEF
TEL: (01539) 442793 FAX: (01539) 488675 COST £20–£51

'Our twenty-fifth season at the Porthole,' the Bertons proudly announced in 1997. Their seventeenth-century cottage in one of Bowness's oldest thoroughfares has traditionally majored in old-fashioned French and Italian cooking along the lines of veal escalope with mushrooms in marsala and cream, and raspberry pavlova. Mike Metcalfe, who cooked these and scores of other dishes for nigh on 20 years, left in 1997, and Andy Fairchild arrived from Scotland too late for the *Guide* to receive any feedback on his performance.

The cellar of over 350 bins has been carefully built up over the years and contains some great and rare bottles. Italy, naturally, is well represented, and there is a superb spread of Germans alongside the more usual French classics as well as some wonderful offerings from the New World. Despite the grand names, plenty of good-value drinking is to be had under £20, starting with house Italian at £10.

CHEF: Andy Fairchild PROPRIETORS: Judy and Gianni Berton OPEN: Mon, Wed to Fri and Sun L 12 to 3, Wed to Mon D 6.30 to 11 CLOSED: Christmas to end Feb MEALS: alc (main courses £7 to £15) SERVICE: not inc, card slips closed CARDS: Amex, Delta, Diners, MasterCard, Switch, Visa DETAILS: 40 seats. 40 seats outside. Private parties: 40 main room, 40 private room. Vegetarian meals. Children's helpings. Music

---

BRAITHWAITE Cumbria map 10

▲ *Ivy House*

Braithwaite CA12 5SY
TEL: (01768) 778338 FAX: (01768) 778113 COOKING 3
just off B5292 Keswick to Braithwaite road COST £28–£33

The setting is undiluted Lake District, and reporters praise the unwavering enthusiasm of the Shills in their approach to running this comfortable small hotel with its galleried dining-room. Wendy Shill cooks a fixed-price four-course menu, the second a choice of soup or sorbet in the Cumbrian manner. Ideas include starters of peach with herbed cream cheese coated with curried mayonnaise, or carrot and apricot pâté with apricot chutney, but there are more mainstream options too. Fish might run to lemon sole meunière, or halibut mornay, while Gressingham duck breast may be sauced with either black cherries or orange, and rack of lamb with redcurrants and thyme. Aberdeen Angus sirloin comes, reassuringly enough, with Yorkshire pudding and horseradish. After dessert – sharply flavoured lemon tart with lemon curd ice-cream, or sticky toffee pudding, perhaps – coffee and mints are served in the very Red Lounge.

A short, well-rounded wine list offers an exciting collection of bottles, mostly under £20. Bibendum supplies the Mature Margaux, which is, in fact, Château Brane-Cantenac 1977: great value at £19.95, but bear in mind that it will need to be decanted. Argentinean house wines from Nicolas Catena's Libertad range are £9.50 a bottle, £1.95 per glass. CELLARMAN'S CHOICE: Simon Hackett Chardonnay 1995, Barossa Valley, S. Australia, £14.50; Simon Hackett Cabernet Sauvignon 1994, McLaren Vale, S. Australia, £14.95.

CHEF: Wendy Shill PROPRIETORS: Nick and Wendy Shill OPEN: all week D only 7.30 for 8 CLOSED: Jan MEALS: Set D £19.95 SERVICE: not inc CARDS: Amex, Delta, Diners, MasterCard, Switch, Visa DETAILS: 30 seats. Car park. Vegetarian meals. Children welcome. No smoking in dining-room. Music ACCOMMODATION: 12 rooms, all with bath/shower. TV. Phone. D,B&B £48 to £114. Deposit: £40. Children welcome. Baby facilities. Dogs welcome by arrangement. Afternoon teas. Garden (*The Which? Hotel Guide*)

'"How would you like your liver?" my guest was asked. "Rare or well done?" "Medium," she replied. "No, I think you misheard me. You can have it either rare or well done."'
(On eating in London)

BRAMPTON Cumbria map 10

▲ *Farlam Hall*

Brampton CA8 2NG
TEL: (01697) 746234 FAX: (01697) 746683 COOKING 3
on A689, 2½m SE of Brampton (not at Farlam village) COST £40–£48

Roaring fires, deep leather sofas, antique furniture and acres of chintz: this grand country house leaves guests in no doubt as to its Victorian credentials. Impeccably old-fashioned service contributes to the 'Upstairs Downstairs' feel, and the small but impressive dining-room is 'terribly proper', with immaculate starched table-linen and sparklingly clean crockery, glasses and silver.

Dinner is a four-course fixed-price affair spanning a short choice of well-judged combinations: perhaps a pea and mint or broccoli and hazelnut soup to start, followed by Gressingham duckling with plums, ginger and red wine, or local beef with a wild mushroom and port sauce. An inspector found the food almost secondary to the splendours of the setting and service, but was nevertheless impressed by 'Morning Salad', a tribute to the great English breakfast, with poached quail's egg, chipolatas, bacon and cherry tomatoes on salad leaves with fresh, earthy flavour; a well textured lemon sole came off the bone easily, and accurate timing was also evident in calf's liver with mashed potatoes, good crisp bacon and fried onions. A somewhat uninspired choice of desserts is supplemented by a perfectly adequate selection of English cheeses. The reasonably priced wine list is French-led, with house wine at £12.75.

CHEF: Barry Quinion PROPRIETORS: the Quinion and Stevenson families OPEN: all week D only 8 to 8.30 CLOSED: 26 to 30 Dec MEALS: Set D £29.50 SERVICE: not inc, card slips closed CARDS: Amex, MasterCard, Switch, Visa DETAILS: 40 seats. Private parties: 40 main room. Car park. No children under 5. No cigars/pipes in dining-room. No music ACCOMMODATION: 12 rooms, all with bath/shower. TV. Phone. D,B&B £110 to £240. No children under 5. Dogs welcome. Afternoon teas. Garden (*The Which? Hotel Guide*)

BRAY Berkshire map 3

Fat Duck

1 High Street, Bray SL6 2AQ COOKING 8
TEL: (01628) 580333 FAX: (01628) 776188 COST £43–£71

Reporters wonder what Bray has done to deserve two restaurants as fine as these (see Waterside Inn, below). 'The talent of the chef is prodigious, the tastes stunning, creativity outstanding, value for money excellent,' summed up one enthusiast. A 'sleek, snazzy interior' of metal and dried teasels chimes well with the casual but animated atmosphere. The idea – not to fall into the trap of making fine dining a formal activity – is helped by smart Riedel glasses, bare tables, and hand-made hunting knives to cut the meat. Not that the meat is tough, but these touches do add to the sense of an individual at work, and Heston Blumenthal's approach is one of the most distinctively personal in Britain today. A reworking of traditional French techniques is at the heart of it, producing a rich, smooth parfait of foie gras with fig compote, and an 'intriguing and unusual' crème brûlée of jasmine tea and orange flower water. But there is more to it than this.

Many dishes take days to make, as when a pork chop is wreathed in salt and herbs, garnished with an andouillette mixed with caramelised onions and mustard, and served with a sauce made from pig's ears.

'I liked his bold innovation,' concluded one reporter, and he could say that again. Here is how Blumenthal tackles one unlikely-sounding first course, a feuillantine of crab with salmon, seaweed, foie gras and oyster vinaigrette: a crab stock is reduced to a syrup, which is then used to make very thin biscuits, which are then interleaved with the salmon (marinated in coriander and green peppercorns), foie gras (with chives and balsamic vinegar), and crystallised seaweed (made by brushing with egg white and sugar, and drying in the oven). 'A superb piece of engineering,' reckoned one reporter. Oysters are puréed with olive oil and lemon juice to make the vinaigrette, and bring the whole thing to life.

Is all this just restless activity and innovation for the sake of novelty? Far from it. The effects can be vivid and galvanising. For one reporter, butternut squash soup 'reached the outer limits of perfection', a feat matched by potatoes 'puréed to silkiness with a taste of truffle oil'. For another, the 'excellent sense of seasoning, flavours and textures' came together in roast chicken with a mixture of parsley and squid ink stuffed under its skin, and rump of lamb with braised potatoes and mashed aubergines, 'the whole combination spot on'. Service is warm, very knowledgeable, and copes well under pressure. The wine list has increased to over 150 bottles, showing particular expansion in the French classics, and is now more complementary to the high-quality cuisine. A new collection of half-bottles and wines by the glass was being put together as we went to press. House French starts at £14.50.

CHEF: Heston Blumenthal PROPRIETORS: Heston and Susanna Blumenthal OPEN: Tue to Sun L 12 to 2 (3 Sun), Tue to Sat D 7 to 9.30 (10 Fri and Sat) CLOSED: 2 weeks Christmas MEALS: alc (main courses £15.50 to £23.50). Set L £16.50 (2 courses) to £32.50. BYO £15 SERVICE: not inc CARDS: Amex, Delta, MasterCard, Switch, Visa DETAILS: 50 seats. 20 seats outside. Private parties: 50 main room. Vegetarian meals. Children's helpings. No smoking area. Wheelchair access (no WC). Music

▲ *Waterside Inn* 🍷

Ferry Road, Bray SL6 2AT
TEL: (01628) 620691 FAX: (01628) 784710 — COOKING **9**
off A308 Maidenhead to Windsor road — COST £62–£164

It would be hard to improve on the stylish and characterful setting on a quiet stretch of the Thames. Nobody seems to linger in the lounge or bar, at least during fine weather when the dining-room's wide glass doors are flung open. Drinks are taken under the weeping willow or in the tiny pagoda on the river bank. Over a quarter of a century on, the dining-room is not in the least bit dated. Banquettes line the octagonal walls, and mirrors reflect the green, rust and deep stone colours, although the combination of closely set tables and lack of segregation of smokers does not please everybody.

This is a shrine to classical French cooking that leaves nothing to chance, and general adulation can be taken as read. Indeed, one reporter felt it more closely resembled art than food, so meticulous is the workmanship. The emphasis remains on the highest-quality luxury ingredients, from a terrine of lightly smoked foie gras with quince confit via lobster medallions to warm oysters with truffle and caviare. Options are sufficiently broad to take in relatively simple scrambled eggs with caviare, tricky-to-make pike quenelles or chicken and truffle sausage, and more substantial veal medallions served with cep duxelles, grilled kidney and a pithivier of sweetbreads. Alternatives to the à la carte either trade a lower price for less choice (the winter dinner menu for example), or offer smaller samples of dishes from the *carte* in the form of a five-course *menu exceptionnel.*

Outstanding saucing contributes much to success, for example a velvety smooth pistachio and sauternes version that came with sole fillets around a timbale of carrot mousse and courgette, or a light but intensely flavoured tomato and black olive *jus* with pink milk-fed lamb. Integral vegetables are generally sculpted, turned or scooped into balls. Technique triumphs throughout, not least among desserts, where traditional mirabelle soufflé might share the spotlight with a walnut pithiviers and Drambuie sauce, or a variation on floating islands incorporating dates and a coffee sauce. High-quality unpasteurised French and English cheeses are kept in excellent condition. Attentive service is 'formal and professional in the best French tradition'.

Meals like this do not come cheap – 'It would be churlish to expect otherwise' – but the practice of including service while leaving the credit card slip open, begging for more, is rather out of place. Wines don't come cheap either. While the quality is beyond doubt, you may find yourself querying mark-ups that are high even by industry standards. With the exception of vintage ports and madeiras, the list is as classically French as the cooking and the selection of *vins doux* is particularly impressive. CELLARMAN'S CHOICE: St-Romain 1994, Dom. Chartron et Trébuchet, £35; Margaux, Ch. Palmer 1991, £68.

CHEFS: Michel Roux and Mark Dodson PROPRIETOR: Michel Roux OPEN: Wed to Sun L 12 to 2 (2.30 Sat and Sun), Tue to Sun D 7 to 10 CLOSED: Sun D mid-Oct to late Apr, 5 weeks from 26 Dec MEALS: alc (main courses £24 to £37). Set L £30.50 to £69.50, Set D £52.50 (winter only) to £69.50 SERVICE: net prices CARDS: Amex, Delta, Diners, MasterCard, Switch, Visa DETAILS: 75 seats. Private parties: 80 main room, 8 private room. Car park. Vegetarian meals. No children under 12. No cigars in dining-room. Wheelchair access (no WC). Music ACCOMMODATION: 9 rooms, all with bath/shower. TV. Phone. B&B £140 to £220. Deposit: £100. No children under 12

BRIGHTON East Sussex map 3

Black Chapati

12 Circus Parade, New England Road,
Brighton BN1 4GW COOKING 4
TEL: (01273) 699011 COST £25–£35

'People either love it or loathe it. We think it's great,' summed up one couple. Behind the black fascia – the place can actually look closed from even a few paces away – is a 'seriously eccentric' restaurant, now into its second decade. Expectations are important here. Go prepared for something ordinary and you may well be struck by the original and intelligent approach, and by a stream of unusual flavours.

The menu may be limited to four or five items per course, and descriptions may not correspond exactly with international convention, but the food is certainly varied. As to style, India is the epicentre, but there are Chinese spices in the potted duck, and steamed mussels might come with lemon grass and udon noodles. Sound technique holds everything together: for example, roast duck leg with a mildly salty but crackly crisp skin, or moist, firm haddock fillets, fried golden brown and 'judged to a nicety', served with a ginger and tamarind sauce. 'A sudden worldwide shortage of coriander leaf would bring the kitchen juddering to a halt.'

Desserts tend to be more European – poached pear, 'full of ripe flavour', with a buttery shortbread biscuit and cinnamon ice-cream, for instance – and at their best are done with 'absolute correctness'. No frills, no nibbles and no bread helps to keep costs down, and service is 'unflustered'. French cider 'works wonderfully' with the complex flavours, which is a good job in view of the perfunctory wine list. House wines are £9.50.

CHEFS/PROPRIETORS: Stephen Funnell and Lauren Alker OPEN: Tue to Sat D only 7 to 10.30 CLOSED: 2 weeks Christmas, 2 weeks July MEALS: alc (main courses £9.50 to £12) SERVICE: 10%, card slips closed CARDS: Amex, Delta, MasterCard, Switch, Visa DETAILS: 30 seats. Private parties: 12 main room. Vegetarian meals. Children welcome. Wheelchair access (no WC). Music

EAST SUSSEX 1998 ACHIEVER

One Paston Place

1 Paston Place, Brighton BN2 1HA COOKING **5**
TEL: (01273) 606933 FAX: (01273) 675686 COST £26–£51

This is 'the restaurant that Brighton always deserved', in one reporter's view, and a steady period under the Emmersons' ownership has made a big difference. 'Perhaps the change has been gradual,' our informant admits, 'but the cooking here now outclasses anything they did before.' 'It has gone from strength to strength,' confirmed another, 'and never compromised excellence for quick economy.' The setting is a single room with a light and breezy Parisian feel, and 'endlessly cheery and unflappable' service from Nicole Emmerson, while Mark's food takes inspiration mostly from the southern half of France: lentil soup comes with smoked bacon and saucisson de Lyon, there may be an assiette landaise, and black bream or sea bass might well be served bouillabaisse-style.

What strikes the observer is the food's clear identity. Typical might be a dish of three components, each with something to say: noisettes of venison, for example, served with spiced pineapple chutney, and lemon and coriander pasta; or roast cod served with salt cod brandade and parsley *jus*. There is enough on each plate to maintain interest, but not so much that it muddies the picture. Add 'exemplary saucing', and vegetables tailored to each dish (Jerusalem artichoke mash with canon of lamb, or ratte potatoes and fennel for the bouillabaissse-style fish) and here you see a kitchen on top form.

Desserts are 'extraordinarily fine', according to one who noted 'flavours of utmost clarity within dishes of some complexity', while another simply enjoyed his roast pineapple with coconut ice-cream. The mostly French wines make an effort to stay under £20, with short excursions into grander bottles and the New World. House Chardonnay and Syrah are £9.50.

See inside the front cover for an explanation of the symbols used at the tops of entries.

CHEF: Mark Emmerson PROPRIETORS: Mark and Nicole Emmerson OPEN: Tue to Sat 12.30 to 2, 7.30 to 10 CLOSED: first 2 weeks Jan, first two weeks Aug MEALS: alc (main courses £14.50 to £17.50). Set L £14.50 (2 courses) to £16.50 SERVICE: 10%, card slips closed CARDS: Amex, Delta, Diners, MasterCard, Switch, Visa DETAILS: 45 seats. Children welcome at L. No children under 5 at D. No cigars/pipes in dining-room. Wheelchair access (not WC). Music. Air-conditioned

Whytes

33 Western Street, Brighton BN1 2PG COOKING 3
TEL: (01273) 776618 COST £29–£37

Ian Whyte reckons that his cooking, once essentially Anglo-French, is 'becoming more eclectic' as the compact but comfortable restaurant he runs with his wife Jane – in a terrace on the cusp of Brighton and Hove – enters its ninth year of operations. There are no surprises on the menu, but that is not to say it is dull. Serrano ham with peppered pear, rocket and Parmesan makes a provocative starter, salmon fish-cakes with ketchup a homelier one. French overtones are most noticeable in meat main courses that may take in pheasant with calvados, apples and cream, or medallions of beef fillet with Dijon mustard and rosemary sauce. An inventive vegetarian dish is always offered. The unashamedly rich puddings are recited with gusto by Jane Whyte, who runs an altogether welcoming front-of-house. Why the owners don't once and for all set about tidying up the short wine list as to producer names and vintages remains a mystery. Prices open at £8.55.

CHEF: Ian Whyte PROPRIETORS: Ian and Jane Whyte OPEN: Tue to Sat D only 7 to 9.30, Sun L and Mon D by arrangement CLOSED: 2 weeks end Feb MEALS: Set D £16.45 (2 courses) to £20.50 SERVICE: not inc CARDS: Amex, MasterCard, Visa DETAILS: 36 seats. Private parties: 30 main room, 16 private room. Vegetarian meals. Music

BRISTOL Bristol map 2

Bell's Diner

1 York Road, Montpelier, Bristol BS6 5QB
TEL: (0117) 924 0357 FAX: (0117) 924 4280
take Picton Street off Cheltenham Road (A38) – runs into York Road NEW CHEF
COST £24–£35

Things are changing at the Diner. The owners, due to open a 150-seat restaurant near the docks towards the end of 1997 – to be called the River Station – are leasing out the old premises in York Road, and Chris Wicks was about to take on the cooking just as the *Guide* went to press. Mr Wicks used to work here, and it is anticipated that he will continue cooking in a similar contemporary vein, offering three-course set-price meals. If he keeps the wine list, too, it will offer a short but varied selection mostly at under £20. Reports, please.

NEW CHEF *is shown instead of a cooking mark where a change of chef occurred too late for a new assessment of the cooking.*

CHEF: Chris Wicks PROPRIETORS: Peter Taylor, Shirley-Anne Bell and Mark Hall OPEN: Mon to Fri and Sun L 12 to 2.30, Mon to Sat D 7 to 10.30 CLOSED: 1 week Christmas, 1 week Easter, 1 week Aug MEALS: Set L Mon to Fri £7.50 (2 courses) to £10.50, Set L Sun £8 (2 courses) to £11, Set D £12 (2 courses) to £15 SERVICE: not inc, card slips closed; 10% for parties of 8 or more CARDS: MasterCard, Switch, Visa DETAILS: 50 seats. Private parties: 28 main room. Vegetarian meals. Children's helpings. No smoking in dining-room. Music

Glass Boat

Welsh Back, Bristol BS1 4SB — COOKING 4
TEL: (0117) 929 0704 FAX: (0117) 929 7338 — COST £24–£43

Everyone mentions the setting. This 'terribly pretty' floating restaurant is moored by Bristol Bridge and some 'handsome' warehouses, a short walk from the city's galleries, theatres and churches. Chef Michel Lemoine worked in London alongside Alastair Little and Simon Hopkinson before moving out west, and recent reports suggest that his cooking is gaining in confidence as the months pass. He describes his style as 'modern French classical . . . with Italian and Asian influences'. In practice, this might mean a salad of duck ham with griddled baby sweetcorn, candied tomatoes and hazelnut oil dressing, or grilled seafood with aïoli and a Thai dipping sauce. Alternatively, it might also produce saucisson de Lyon en brioche with madeira sauce, or rib of beef with red wine and shallots.

Good-value lunch and dinner menus are peppered with robust offerings such as rabbit rillettes with horseradish and cucumber relish, and steamed game and kidney pudding on a bed of creamed potato and celeriac. Desserts continue the East-West mix in the shape of cranberry brûlée with kumquat compote, and coconut and lime bavarois, while 'old-fashioned' bread-and-butter pudding seems immune to tampering. Service is skilled and attentive without becoming obtrusive. A particularly strong showing of burgundies is a feature of the well-spread, contemporary wine list. House wine is £9.50.

CHEF: Michel Lemoine PROPRIETOR: Arne Ringner OPEN: Mon to Fri L 12 to 2, Mon to Sat 6 to 10.45 CLOSED: 24 Dec to 8 Jan MEALS: alc (main courses £13 to £16). Set L £10.95 (2 courses), Set D £17.50. BYO £5 SERVICE: not inc CARDS: Amex, Delta, MasterCard, Switch, Visa DETAILS: 130 seats. 12 seats outside. Private parties: 100 main room, 40 private room. Vegetarian meals. Children welcome. Wheelchair access (no WC). Music. Air-conditioned

Harveys

12 Denmark Street, Bristol BS1 5DQ — COOKING 4
TEL: (0117) 927 5034 FAX: (0117) 927 5003 — COST £24–£58

The cellars are medieval, and everything about the décor will serve as a reminder (if the name itself doesn't) that wine has been Harveys' business for generations. This is where they used to bottle the famous sherry when it was still shipped over in cask. Giant barrels and antique glassware (some of it the famous Bristol blue) form the backdrop for Daniel Galmiche's cooking, which is fairly elevated French with modern embellishments. A smoked salmon paupiette, for example, comes with sevruga caviare and a herb salad, while turbot is given a veal stock and mustard *jus*. Flavours of the main components did not stand up all that well at inspection, but accompaniments are mostly well rendered, as in a mix of sage leaves, garlic and honey for pork loin medallion. Spiced crème brûlée with a slice of caramelised pear cake makes an imaginative dessert. If dissatisfaction were to focus on any one aspect, it would probably be the small scale of dishes.

On the other hand, the quality of wines on offer would silence even the harshest critics. Nineteen vintages of Ch Latour dating back to 1934 are yours for the asking – at a price – alongside many other bins from the list's predominant strength, the classical French regions. The choice from elsewhere is perfectly sound, and there is plenty of good drinking to be had under £20, starting with house wines at £12. It would surely be a wasted opportunity not to preface a meal with a glass of one of Harvey's fine old sherries. CELLARMAN'S CHOICE: Reynolds Yarraman Chardonnay 1992, Hunter Valley, New South Wales, £26; Pauillac, Les Forts de Latour 1986, £40.

CHEF: Daniel Galmiche PROPRIETORS: John Harvey and Sons OPEN: Mon to Fri L 12 to 1.45, Mon to Sat D 7 to 10.45 CLOSED: bank hols MEALS: alc (main courses £18 to £21). Set L £12.95 (2 courses) to £15.95, Set D £39.95 SERVICE: net prices CARDS: Amex, Delta, Diners, MasterCard, Switch, Visa DETAILS: 120 seats. Private parties: 80 main room, 40 private room. Vegetarian meals. No children under 8. No smoking in 1 dining-room. Music. Air-conditioned

Howards

1A–2A Avon Crescent, Hotwells, Bristol BS1 6XQ — COOKING 2
TEL: (0117) 926 2921 FAX: (0117) 925 5585 — COST £21–£40

The staff at this three-storey restaurant on a corner near the Clifton Suspension Bridge in Georgian Bristol 'are chosen for being interesting and intelligent people as well as for their ability in catering'. So says the owner, who clearly enjoys a good conversation. Whether you are there to be fed or philosophised at, the relaxed bistro atmosphere of the place is good at winning converts. Seared smoked salmon on a potato-cake with a poached egg is a trend-conscious way of starting a meal, as is a warm salad of scallops and Jerusalem artichokes with hazelnut vinaigrette. Main-course meat dishes impressed one pair of reporters who ate duck breast with redcurrants and rosemary, and venison with a whisky and pink peppercorn sauce. France accounts for the bulk of the wine list, but there is a smattering of good New World bottles and the varied, and interesting 'fine wines' are worth a peep. House French is £7.95.

CHEF: David Short PROPRIETOR: Christopher J. Howard OPEN: Mon to Fri L 12 to 2.30, Mon to Sat D 7 to 11 CLOSED: 25 to 27 Dec MEALS: alc (main courses £9 to £14.50). Set L £13.50, Set D Mon to Fri £15 SERVICE: not inc; 10% for parties of 8 or more CARDS: Amex, Delta, Diners, MasterCard, Visa DETAILS: 65 seats. Private parties: 28 main room, 12 and 28 private rooms. No children under 12. Wheelchair access (no WC). Music

Hunt's

26 Broad Street, Bristol BS1 2HG — COOKING 5
TEL/FAX: (0117) 926 5580 — COST £23–£46

Old mahogany shop fittings remain from the tea and coffee merchant's this once was, and eighteenth-century hand-coloured engravings hang on the walls. One reporter who ate here five years ago returned to find that 'virtually nothing has changed'. OK, the décor might look five years older, but this is still a comfortable place in which to eat, and Andrew Hunt still offers high-quality bourgeois cooking of staples such as venison in a cream and gherkin sauce, or guinea-fowl with apples and calvados. The Anglo-French style may hold few surprises, but the kitchen handles standards of the repertoire well, from fish soup – a thick brown broth with croûtons and a vivid orange rouille of purée red pepper – to breast of Trelough duck with plums.

Within the menu's short compass there is an opportunity to move from rich tagliatelle with a mustard and parsley cream to a crisp-skinned fillet of salmon with pungent soy and ginger. Unctuous gratin dauphinoise is probably the pick of the accompanying vegetables, but an inspector felt that the kitchen's greatest skills seem to be reserved for dessert, judging by an individually baked Normandy apple tart in a honey and butter sauce, and a 'beautifully dense' iced lemon parfait with oatmeal meringue and a cranberry coulis. Meals begin with fat black olives, and cheese and cumin pastries, and end with decent espresso. Wines from a predominantly French list are 'impeccably served', with half a dozen house wines (£9.75 to £16.25) also available by the glass.

CHEF: Andrew Hunt PROPRIETORS: Anne and Andrew Hunt OPEN: Tue to Fri L 12 to 2, Tue to Sat D 7 to 10 CLOSED: 24 Dec to 3 Jan, 1 week Easter, 1 week Aug bank hol MEALS: alc (main courses £14 to £16). Set L £11.95 (2 courses) to £13.95 SERVICE: not inc, card slips closed CARDS: Amex, Delta, MasterCard, Switch, Visa DETAILS: 40 seats. Private parties: 26 main room. Vegetarian meals. Children's helpings. Wheelchair access (no WC). Music

Lettonie 🍷

9 Druid Hill, Stoke Bishop, Bristol BS9 1EW — COOKING **8**
TEL: (0117) 968 6456 FAX: (0117) 968 6943 — COST £33–£66

Martin and Siân Blunos are, as ever, contemplating a move to premises more in keeping with their aspirations and achievements. The present site, next to a laundrette in a row of shops, gives no clue as to the culinary pyrotechnics on offer. Step into a small, dark room decorated with landscape paintings of Martin Blunos's native Latvia, where a warm welcome from Siân Blunos sets the tone. Service from French waiters is deft and accomplished, with a marked absence of pretence, and the whole operation runs smoothly, with no fuss, no hassle; meals are eaten in a 'quietly pleasant and enjoyable' atmosphere.

The fireworks come with Lettonie's best-known starter, a 'showy and spectacular' combination of scrambled duck egg with a spoonful of sevruga caviar, and vodka two ways: iced and flaming. The taste of the runny egg is 'delicious in a decadent sort of way'. Another first course, bortsch, is deconstructed and reassembled into a beetroot terrine, served with little yeast buns filled with shredded beef, and a bowl of soured cream. It is clear that the kitchen takes an imaginative approach, but what keeps it all within bounds is the level of skill, and the practised accomplishment that has accurately reproduced these and dishes like them time and again.

'Precision of cooking and lightness of touch were confidently displayed throughout the meal' for one visitor, who found it all 'quite breathtaking'. Another, impressed by the textural contrast between nettle fritters and roast cod, wondered if the 'exquisite presentation' might be getting the upper hand on occasion. But there is no doubt that when all the elements come together, as in a simple noisette of lamb with potato and mint croquettes in a tasty *jus*, this is very fine cooking.

Desserts are introduced by a visual pun – a 'boiled egg' made from vanilla cream with mango yolk, plus a shortbread 'soldier', 'salt' (sugar) and 'pepper' (chocolate) – and might proceed to hot pistachio and chocolate tart, strongly flavoured apple and vanilla parfait, or a savoury of goats'-cheese tortellini with ratatouille. Ancillary details are 'immaculate', from the deep-fried parsnip crisps at the beginning, via 'brilliant crusty breads', to petits-fours that are 'a real treat'. Wines are almost entirely French and are not cheap, although a few bins under £20 are scattered throughout the list, and the eight attractive house wines are mostly below £15. There is also a fair number of reasonably priced half-bottles. CELLARMAN'S CHOICE: Meursault 1993, J-P. Fichet, £41; Mercurey premier cru, 'Les Velay' 1993, Dom. de la Monette, Granger, £28.95.

CHEF: Martin Blunos PROPRIETORS: Siân and Martin Blunos OPEN: Tue to Sat 12.30 to 2, 7 to 9 CLOSED: 2 weeks Aug, 25 Dec, bank hols MEALS: Set L £19.95 to £36.50, Set D £25 (not available Fri and Sat) to £36.50 SERVICE: not inc CARDS: Amex, Diners, MasterCard, Switch, Visa DETAILS: 24 seats. Private parties: 24 main room. Children welcome. Music

Markwicks 🍷

43 Corn Street, Bristol BS1 1HT — COOKING 6
TEL/FAX: (0117) 926 2658 — COST £36–£53

Marble steps lead down to this imposing basement of a former bank. Bright, colourful paintings in the dining-room share wall space with English country cottages and decorative Georgian urns, while impeccably starched white linen tablecloths and napkins set the tone for the classy food that is to come. Set-price dinners get the thumbs-up, though the *carte* offers more choice, with a prominent role for fish: turbot baked in cider, 'outstanding' salmon and haddock tart, or dressed Cornish crab with a salad of rocket, asparagus and avocado. Stephen Markwick rarely strays outside Europe for ideas, and keeps his feet firmly on the ground with mussel and saffron soup, grilled goats' cheese with tapénade, and fillet steak 'au poivre'.

Vegetarian options (there are usually four or five) can be taken as either a first or main course, and luxuries, though few, are handled well. A salad arrives before the main course: perhaps Trelough duck with Puy lentils in Sauternes sauce, or 'mildly flavoured' rack of lamb with a herb crust, served with leeks and Cumbrian air-dried ham in a sherry vinegar sauce. Salting generally may be strong for some tastes. Desserts, especially those with a 20-minute wait, intrigue: pear, pineapple and black pepper tart perhaps, or a cappuccino soufflé with cinnamon ice-cream.

The wine list opens with a group of house wines selected by the Markwicks as being excellent examples of their region/appellation at reasonable prices (from £10 a bottle). The same could be said of the rest of the list: prices remain fair and the producers reliable. CELLARMAN'S CHOICE: Pacherenc du Vic-Bilh, Ch. Bouscassé 1995, Brumont, £16.60; St Hallett Old Block Shiraz 1993, Barossa Valley, S. Australia, £22.50.

CHEF: Stephen Markwick PROPRIETORS: Stephen and Judy Markwick OPEN: Tue to Fri L 12 to 2, Tue to Sat D 7 to 10 CLOSED: 1 week Christmas, 1 week Easter, 2 weeks Aug MEALS: alc (main courses £14.50 to £17.50). Set L £12.50 (2 courses) to £15, Set D £21.50 SERVICE: not inc, card slips closed CARDS: Amex, MasterCard, Switch, Visa DETAILS: 50 seats. Private parties: 30 main room, 6 and 20 private rooms. Vegetarian meals. Children's helpings. No music

Melbournes £

74 Park Street, Bristol BS1 5JX — COOKING **2**
TEL: (0117) 922 6996 — COST £17–£29

Close to the university, Melbournes draws the crowds like moths to a flame. The brightness emanates from appropriately Aussie prints, an easygoing style, and appealing set prices combined with fair choice. Laminated menus list the more enduring items – chicken liver parfait, plain grilled sirloin steak, key lime pie – while a blackboard chips in with today's soup, the market's fish, and any seasonal opportunities. A broad brush is applied, producing ramekins of smoked haddock with cheese sauce, or brochette of duck marinated in soy and Chinese spices, while non-meat dishes appear as cameos: spinach and ricotta gnocchi with tomato and basil, or goats' cheese baked in filo with capers and peppercorns. 'All our puddings are home-made,' writes Tony Wilshaw of chocolate cheesecake, and pineapple tart with coconut ice-cream. Around 50 wines are well chosen and sensibly priced. There is no corkage charge for BYO, and house Australian is £7.75. A sister restaurant, Redcliffs, is at Redcliff Quay, 125 Redcliff Street; tel (0117) 987 2270.

CHEFS: R. Smith and Stephane Müller PROPRIETORS: A.P. Wilshaw and N.J. Hennessy OPEN: Tue to Fri and Sun L 12 to 2 (3 Sun), Mon to Sat D 7 to 10.30 CLOSED: 24 Dec to 31 Dec MEALS: Set L £8.50 (2 courses) to £10.50, Set D £14.50 (2 courses) to £16.50. BYO (no corkage) SERVICE: 10%, card slips closed CARDS: Amex, Delta, Diners, MasterCard, Switch, Visa DETAILS: 100 seats. Private parties: 50 main room. Vegetarian meals. Children's helpings. No cigars/pipes in dining-room. Wheelchair access (no WC). Music

Muset £

16 Clifton Road, Clifton, Bristol BS8 1AF — COOKING **2**
TEL: (0117) 973 2920 FAX: (0117) 904 3254 — COST £24–£36

Muset is a popular brasserie-style operation occupying corner premises in smart Clifton. It seems to be chock-a-block most evenings, the crowds attracted by the level-headed menu pricing and BYO wine policy, although there is a charge for bread and an 'optional' one for service. The cooking has maintained a competitively fashionable edge through a decade with David Wheadon at the helm. Roast tuna comes with Parmesan and rocket pesto, duck breast with a compote of rhubarb, and chicken breast with bacon, garlic and nettle cheese. More traditional dishes take in, for example, salmon fillet with asparagus and hollandaise. Forest fruit brûlée is a typical dessert, or there may be cappuccino charlotte with a coffee and Tia Maria sauce. The wine list on offer for those who missed the off-licence spans a broad stylistic range from Luneau's Muscadet sur lie to the monumental Cabernet Sauvignon from California's Renaissance Vineyards. House French is £8.25.

CHEFS: David Wheadon and Ian Taylor PROPRIETORS: Adrian and Carol Portlock, and David Wheadon OPEN: all week D only 7 to 10.30 MEALS: Set D £14.95 (2 courses) to £15.95. BYO (no corkage) SERVICE: 10% (optional), card slips closed CARDS: Amex, Delta, Diners, MasterCard, Switch, Visa DETAILS: 150 seats. Private parties: 40 main room, 25 and 10 private rooms. Vegetarian meals. Children welcome. Wheelchair access (no WC). Music. Air-conditioned

Rocinantes 🍷

85 Whiteladies Road, Bristol BS8 2NT COOKING 3
TEL: (0117) 973 4482 FAX: (0117) 974 3913 COST £22–£40

'Consistently good and reliable, high-quality Spanish food' and equally exciting wines and beers attract hordes of lively eaters and drinkers to this tapas bar-restaurant. Even the terrace, which seats only 35, can be 'jammed with several hundred noisy people'. One reporter would have wished for a less-smoky atmosphere, given that this is such a 'green' establishment, proud of using organic meat and vegetables, wild fish from boats not working in over-trawled waters, diver-caught shellfish; and avoiding microwave ovens and aluminium cookware. Service is 'pleasant and professional', although it can be slow at busy times.

The menu is mainly Spanish with a few dishes from Italy, Greece, France, 'modern Britain', even 'Grandfather's England'. The old gentleman might be a bit flummoxed, though, to find a 'mixed grill' comprising wild boar sausage and lamb steak with coleslaw. Spanish-style charcuterie is approved, as are seared scallops with pea purée and olive oil, wild mushroom tart, veal escalope, and best end of lamb. If the frozen margaritas and jugs of sangria don't claim your attention, there is a wide-ranging collection of attractive wines at reasonable prices, with over 20 available by the glass from £2. House Spanish is £8.95.

CHEFS: Barny Haughton PROPRIETORS: Barny Haughton and Mathew Pruen OPEN: all week 12 to 3, 6 to 11 (10.30 Sun) CLOSED: 24 to 30 Dec MEALS: alc (main courses £8.50 to £16). Set L Mon to Fri 12 to 3 £9.50. Tapas and bar menu available all day SERVICE: not inc; 10% for parties of 5 or more CARDS: Amex, Delta, Diners, MasterCard, Switch, Visa DETAILS: 60 seats. 35 seats outside. Private parties: 50 main room, 30 private room. Vegetarian meals. Children welcome. Wheelchair access (no WC). Music

BROADHEMBURY Devon map 2

Drewe Arms

Broadhembury EX14 0NF
TEL/FAX: (01404) 841267 COOKING 3
off A373, between Cullompton and Honiton COST £30–£40

Although only 15 minutes from the M5, this quiet, thatched village, with no through road, feels like another world. The Drewe Arms is next to the church and is best described as a pub with a dining-room: boundaries between eating and drinking areas are blurred, even for those who are sober. The kitchen's main business is fish, and a set menu and à la carte are chalked on boards in different rooms, which makes ordering 'a bit confusing'. Between them, however, they cover a range that takes in red mullet, plaice, turbot, monk, sea bass, and a whole or half lobster. Open sandwiches, and gravlax with a tot of aquavit, hint at a Scandinavian background. Freshness is the key to success, and one reporter enjoyed the best langoustines and Dover sole he had ever eaten. A good spread of white wines stays mostly under £20, and five house wines at £9.50 are also available in two glass sizes.

CHEFS/PROPRIETORS: Kerstin and Nigel Burge OPEN: all week L 12 to 2, Mon to Sat D 7 to 10 CLOSED: 25 Dec MEALS: alc (main courses £14). Set L and D £19.50 (2 courses) to £22.50. BYO minimum £4 SERVICE: not inc CARDS: none DETAILS: 40 seats. 40 seats outside. Private parties: 22 main room. Car park. Vegetarian meals. Children's helpings. No smoking in dining-room. Wheelchair access (also WC). No music

BROADWAY Hereford & Worcester map 5

▲ *Dormy House* 🍷

Willersey Hill, Broadway WR12 7LF
TEL: (01386) 852711 FAX: (01386) 858636 COOKING **4**
just off A44, 1m NW of Broadway COST £26–£63

The hotel's seventeenth-century farmhouse origins are now mostly obscured by modern trappings, facilities and extensions, the better to attract weddings and weekenders as well as conference delegates. One dining-room evokes the past with stone and dark wood; the main one, smoke-free, is a spacious and plush conservatory. Staff look formal in their black and white uniforms but are not stuffy, and the pace is unrushed. In the French way, a set-price menu and a four-course gourmet menu are offered as well as the *carte*.

A broad range of ingredients and some novel combinations produce dishes of greater interest than are typical of a modern conference hotel: timbale of turbot and Cornish scallops with a coriander and green lentil sauce, say, or roast pigeon with deep-fried sage, pine-kernels and madeira sauce. Among highlights of an inspection meal were a simple cream of broccoli and almond soup, and duck with stir-fried vegetables and a nicely zippy sauce of soy, honey and sherry. Iced brown-bread ice-cream with strawberry and Cointreau sauce makes an admirable finish, or there might be a chocolate soufflé with armagnac and raisin ice-cream.

The wine list features a lively series of introductions to each major region with a helpful note accompanying each bin. The wines themselves are predominantly French, with an interesting trio from Switzerland, some good German Rieslings and a few useful bottles from the New World. Ten French house wines start at £9.95. CELLARMAN'S CHOICE: Côtes du Rhône Blanc 1993, Dom. de l'Oratoire, £14.80; Ochoa Tempranillo 1993, Navarra, £16.85.

All entries in the Guide *are re-researched and rewritten every year, not least because restaurant standards fluctuate. Don't rely on an out-of-date* Guide.

Dining-rooms where music, either live or recorded, is never played are signalled by No music *in the details at the end of an entry.*

CHEFS: Alan Cutler and Colin Seymour PROPRIETOR: Jorgen Philip-Sorensen OPEN: Sun to Fri L 12.30 to 2, all week D 7 to 9.30 (9 Sun) CLOSED: 25 and 26 Dec MEALS: alc (main courses L Mon to Fri £8 to £9, D £15 to £21). Set L Sun £18.50, Set D £28.50 to £34. BYO £8 SERVICE: not inc CARDS: Amex, Delta, Diners, MasterCard, Switch, Visa DETAILS: 80 seats. Private parties: 40 main room, 8 and 14 private rooms. Car park. Vegetarian meals. Children's helpings before 7.30. No smoking in 1 dining-room. Music ACCOMMODATION: 49 rooms, all with bath/shower. TV. Phone. B&B £65 to £157. Rooms for disabled. Children welcome. Baby facilities. Dogs welcome in bedrooms only. Afternoon teas. Garden (*The Which? Hotel Guide*)

▲ *Lygon Arms*

High Street, Broadway WR12 7DU — COOKING 6
TEL: (01386) 852255 FAX: (01386) 858611 — COST £37–£72

The picture-postcard frontage of this archetypal Cotswold inn is familiar to tourists around the world. Immaculately maintained, it plays the role of senior historical ambassador with well-practised grace, helped by wobbly floors, oak panelling, ancient armour and weaponry, and a barrel-vaulted dining-room ceiling. It also boasts every mod con you could imagine, and then some. Likewise, Roger Narbett's food satisfies those in search of the traditional British grail: English lamb cutlets, Scottish sirloin steak, or black pudding with bubble and squeak. But these repertory standards are eclipsed by an enthusiastically modern range of dishes that really mean business.

There seems to be a lot going on in some of them, but it is all well controlled, and an inspector praised the 'deft handling of ingredients' as well as 'some impressive combinations'. Chinese spices are used to season Cornish turbot, mango chutney is partnered with rack of Cotswold lamb, and sea bream is served with a risotto of crab and asparagus. Arrangements are pretty – a triangular terrine of fish and shellfish with carefully composed saladings and puddles of pink sauce – and techniques accomplished: confit of duck leg, for instance, is a proper one with moist, dense meat, served with well flavoured leek and potato gâteau. Desserts might include a soufflé, a tart such as pear and almond, and perhaps a chocolate marquise with Grand Marnier syrup. A sophisticated, international wine list is weighted towards the higher-quality bins and this is reflected in the rather high prices. France dominates, but the New World makes its presence felt with some sound offerings. House French is £14 and eight wines are available by the glass from Australia, Italy and France, starting at £2.75.

CHEF: Roger Narbett PROPRIETOR: Savoy Group plc OPEN: all week 12.30 to 2, 7.30 to 9.15 (9.30 Sat) MEALS: alc (main courses £18.50 to £23.50). Set L £23.25, Set D £36. BYO £10 SERVICE: not inc, card slips closed CARDS: Amex, Delta, Diners, MasterCard, Switch, Visa DETAILS: 120 seats. 40 seats outside. Private parties: 95 main room, 12 to 95 private rooms. Car park. Vegetarian meals. Children's helpings. Wheelchair access (also WC). Music ACCOMMODATION: 65 rooms, all with bath/shower. TV. Phone. B&B £98 to £225. Rooms for disabled. Children welcome. Baby facilities. Dogs welcome. Afternoon teas. Garden. Swimming-pool (*The Which? Hotel Guide*)

'The diners at the next table turned down a complimentary Kir as "foreign", and then ordered French beer.' (On eating in Suffolk)

BROCKENHURST Hampshire map 2

Le Poussin

The Courtyard, Brookley Road,
Brockenhurst SO42 7RB COOKING **6**
TEL: (01590) 623063 FAX: (01590) 622912 COST £32–£60

The restaurant does its best to be invisible – there is no sign down the red brick alley until you reach the door – and it can be 'whispery and serious' inside. The welcome is warm from a 'very sensible and reassuring' Caroline Aitken, and the rest of the service appears 'textbook' and efficient. There is, however, a feeling that the food has become 'unspectacular' in its impact. When reporters compare recent meals with ones they have eaten here in the past, the balance is firmly in favour of yesteryear. Menus rely on a 'well-worn formula' of ballottines and terrines, fine sausages, and twice-baked cheese soufflé, with an emphasis on puréeing and processing. Soft textures are the norm.

There is much that appeals on a menu of rabbit saddle with morels, dived scallops with leek purée, and hot passion-fruit soufflé. Alex Aitken thrives on truffles and wild mushrooms (perhaps giving autumnal menus the edge), and the food's comfort factor is high. At inspection both timing and seasoning required some adjustment, but 'perfectly cooked duck' with crispy skin showed the kitchen's mettle, and 'vegetables were a high point'. While the wine list won't win any prizes for presentation, the content is fine, with a good range of wines from respected producers. Lovers of the luscious should note the request to allow time for chilling, as mature sweeties from Bordeaux and Germany are a highlight. House wines start at £11, with eight wines offered by the glass at £2.50. CELLARMAN'S CHOICE: La Fortuna Sauvignon Blanc, Lontué Valley, Chile £11; Vacqueyras 1990, Pascal, £17.50.

CHEF: Alex Aitken PROPRIETORS: the Aitken family OPEN: Wed to Sun 12 to 1.30, 7 to 9 MEALS: Set L £15 (2 courses), Set D £22.50 (2 courses) to £45 CARDS: MasterCard, Switch, Visa DETAILS: 24 seats. 8 seats outside. Private parties: 24 main room. Car park. Vegetarian meals. Children welcome. No smoking in dining-room. Wheelchair access (also WC). Music

BROMSGROVE Hereford & Worcester map 5

▲ *Grafton Manor*

Grafton Lane, Bromsgrove B61 7HA
TEL: (01527) 579007 FAX: (01527) 575221 COOKING **3**
off B4091, 1½m SW of Bromsgrove COST £30–£57

Grafton is essentially a fine Elizabethan manor house that was largely rebuilt during the eighteenth century. It maintains a grand atmosphere with intricately carved ceilings, embossed fabrics, antique furnishings, and open fireplaces. The Morrises have run it for nigh on twenty years, and in that time chef Simon has developed his passion for India and its food. He rushes off there every January, and on his return cooks up a two-week Indian Food Festival full of interesting crossover ideas: English ham marinated in tandoori paste and served with mushy peas, or Lancashire hotpot cooked in coconut milk with cardamom and cinnamon.

During the rest of the year European influences may be easier to discern: in the form of carpaccio of tuna, goats' cheese in filo, or battered and deep-fried halibut. Dishes from the three- and four-course menus can be mixed, allowing fair choice, and they buzz along with the help of tapénade (for chicken terrine) or honey and chive dressing (for baked pork fillet). The garden is stocked with useful salad ingredients, herbs, vegetables, and some unusual fruit trees such as quince, medlar and Warwickshire drooper plum. Desserts might include whisky steamed pudding or iced banana parfait. The wine list was being updated as the *Guide* went to press; house French starts at £10.95.

CHEF: Simon Morris PROPRIETORS: the Morris family OPEN: Sun to Fri L 12.30 to 1.30, all week D 7.30 to 9.30 MEALS: Set L Mon to Fri £20.50, Set L Sun £18.50, Set D £25.95 to £31.50 SERVICE: not inc, card slips closed CARDS: Amex, Delta, Diners, MasterCard, Switch, Visa DETAILS: 60 seats. Private parties: 50 main room, 50 private room. Car park. Vegetarian meals. Children's helpings. No smoking in dining-room. Wheelchair access (also WC). No music ACCOMMODATION: 9 rooms, all with bath/shower. TV. Phone. B&B £85 to £150. Rooms for disabled. Children welcome. Baby facilities. Dogs welcome in kennels only. Afternoon teas. Garden. Fishing (*The Which? Hotel Guide*)

BROXTON Cheshire map 7

▲ *Froggy Manor* NEW ENTRY

Nantwich Road, Fullers Moor, Broxton CH3 9JH COOKING 3
TEL: (01829) 782629 FAX: (01829) 782238 COST £23–£61

The white-painted Georgian house sits amid nine acres and lots of frogs. John Sykes milks his mild eccentricity and the froggy theme for all they are worth, having assembled over a hundred amphibians in various guises, materials and attitudes. This appears to be a one-man operation with a little help from waiting staff: hence the two hours' notice required for lunch and the obligatory pause over aperitifs while the food is prepared. The one place frogs do not appear is on the menu, which goes in instead for wide-ranging Poona prawn vol-au-vent, goats' cheese in filo pastry, and Mongolian-style chicken. Saucing is effective (lemon and ginger sweet-and-sour sauce for roast breast of duck, for example), vegetarian and vegan dishes are offered, and beef fillet is served six different ways, all at a supplement.

Desserts are recited and have included crumbles, assorted ice-creams and sorbets, and 'light and creamy' bread-and-butter pudding. Canned music is a choice between Al Bowley, and Al Bowley accompanied by John Sykes: 'he presented us with the menu, told us how good it all was, and departed humming.' Midweek custom is encouraged by a Wednesday dinner tag of £12.95, wines from the short list are left on the table for self-service, and house South African is £10.

CHEF/PROPRIETOR: John Sykes OPEN: all week 12 to 0 (booking essential), 7 to 11.30 CLOSED: 1 Jan MEALS: alc (main courses £14.50 to £22.50). Set L £16, Set D Wed £12.95, all week £25.95 SERVICE: not inc, card slips closed CARDS: Amex, Delta, Diners, MasterCard, Switch, Visa DETAILS: 55 seats. Private parties: 55 main room. Car park. Vegetarian meals. Children's helpings. No-smoking area. Music ACCOMMODATION: 6 rooms, all with bath/shower. TV. Phone. Room only £50 to £120. Children welcome. Dogs welcome. Afternoon teas. Garden (*The Which? Hotel Guide*)

BRUTON Somerset map 2

Truffles

95 High Street, Bruton BA10 0AR COOKING 4
TEL/FAX: (01749) 812255 COST £22–£41

Truffles inhabits the diminutive front room of an old weaver's cottage, a handful of tables and a tiny panelled bar the bare concessions to catering. Ornamental plants and window boxes brighten things up, and candles are lit at dinner. Martin Bottrill's cooking is shot through with a vein of restless creativity, and he is unafraid to put smoked chicken and mango together in a filo parcel and then dress it with cassis, or to add pistachios to wild mushrooms in a sauce for saddle of rabbit. Not all ideas may please, but at one meal a main course of marinated salmon crusted with Dijon mustard and dill, and sauced with a thin chive hollandaise, offered an appealing medley of textures and well-timed fish. Grilled kangaroo medallions in a sauce of blue gum honey and rosemary might induce gulps of apprehension in some, but it worked well for its reporter.

Lemon tart with raspberry coulis does the business at dessert stage, or there may be coffee mousse with dates in a coconut crème anglaise. Bread is described as 'outstanding'. In comparison with the cooking, the wine list looks rather old-fangled and humdrum, but there are a few good growers, and prices are not silly. House French starts at £9.50.

CHEF: Martin Bottrill PROPRIETORS: Martin and Denise Bottrill OPEN: Sun L 12 to 2, Tue to Sat D 7 to 9.30 (weekday L by arrangement) CLOSED: last 2 weeks Jan MEALS: Set L Sun £13.50, Set D £21.95 SERVICE: not inc, card slips closed CARDS: MasterCard, Visa DETAILS: 20 seats. Private parties: 24 main room. No children under 5. No smoking while others eat. Wheelchair access (no WC). No music

BUCKLAND Gloucestershire map 5

▲ *Buckland Manor* 🍷 £✱

Buckland WR12 7LY
TEL: (01386) 852626 FAX: (01386) 853557 COOKING 4
off B4632, 2m SW of Broadway COST £33–£73

Many visitors are wooed by the setting – stunning grounds in a classic Cotswold village – and by the thirteenth-century mellow stone manor-house itself. The accoutrements of gracious living are in place – large, dignified portraits, polished floors, dark wood panelling and rich fabrics – and the *carte* is mindful of the mostly well-to-do international clientele. There might be oak-smoked salmon with capers and toasted brioche to start, perhaps followed by braised lamb shank with olive mash and winter root vegetables. Innovation is evident in the likes of pan-fried John Dory on a red onion compote with chicken and tarragon flavoured *jus,* while among the 'dreamy puddings' may be gratin of figs with armagnac sabayon and citrus sorbet. 'Perfectly cooked and intelligently garnished' vegetables, many grown in the hotel's gardens, are individually matched to main courses. One reporter found it all 'well worth the journey from London, even though I had to dress up to go there'. Service is very formal but 'pleasant, efficient and helpful'.

Over 500 bottles feature on the wine list, every one of them annotated. The French collection is impressive, California is a delight, and there's an intriguing Swiss quartet at the end. Some of the mark-ups are a bit high but the 28 house and French country wines offer good drinking from £11.50 and are all available by the glass. CELLARMAN'S CHOICE: Henschke Eden Valley Sauvignon/Semillon 1995, Adelaide Hills, S. Australia, £25.50; Frog's Leap Zinfandel 1993, Napa Valley, California, £24.30.

CHEF: Martyn Pearn PROPRIETORS: Roy and Daphne Vaughan OPEN: all week 12 to 1.45, 7 to 9 MEALS: alc (main courses £18 to £24.50). Set L Mon to Sat £27.50, Set L Sun £23.50 to £25.50 SERVICE: not inc CARDS: Amex, Delta, Diners, MasterCard, Switch, Visa DETAILS: 38 seats. 20 seats outside. Private parties: 38 main room. Car park. No children under 8. Jacket and tie. No smoking in dining-room. Wheelchair access (no WC). No music ACCOMMODATION: 13 rooms, all with bath/shower. TV. Phone. B&B £168 to £325. Rooms for disabled. No children under 12. Afternoon teas. Garden. Swimming-pool (*The Which? Hotel Guide*)

BUCKLAND Oxfordshire map 2

▲ *Lamb Inn* £

Lamb Lane, Buckland SN7 8QN COOKING 1
TEL: (01367) 870484 FAX: (01367) 810475 COST £20–£42

The setting is a 200-year-old building on the very edge of the Cotswolds, with glorious views across the Thames flood plain. Paul Barnard is nothing if not industrious, providing an outside catering service, and staging barbecues on Sunday evenings in summer as well as cooking admirable '90s pub food. One menu is served throughout. The repertoire is seasonal and regularly changing, although fish shows up most of the year. What is on offer is a blend of Anglo-French dishes, with occasional forays into the Mediterranean and the Far East. From this side of the Channel come salmon and prawn kedgeree, rack of lamb with mint and sorrel sauce, junket and steamed syrup sponge; from further afield you might find peperonata soufflé, poached fillet of brill with a creamy prawn, avocado and vermouth sauce, and apple, pear and calvados pancakes. More than half of the 70 wines on the list hail from France, but there are some decent offerings from the New World for those who prefer something less traditional. Eighteen wines are available as half-bottles and sixteen are offered by the glass. The five house wines are good value at £8.95 a bottle or £1.65 per glass. CELLARMAN'S CHOICE: Sauvignon de Touraine 1995, Vinival l'Ouchetcau £8.95; Mitchelton Chinamans Bridge Merlot 1993, Victoria, Australia, £15.95.

CHEF/PROPRIETOR: Paul Barnard OPEN: all week 12 to 2 (2.30 Sun), 6.30 to 9.30 CLOSED: 24 to 26 Dec MEALS: alc (main courses £6 to £15). Set L Sun £16.95 SERVICE: not inc, card slips closed CARDS: Amex, Delta, MasterCard, Switch, Visa DETAILS: 90 seats. 50 seats outside. Private parties: 60 main room, 18 private room. Car park. Vegetarian meals. Children's helpings. No smoking in dining-room. Music ACCOMMODATION: 4 rooms, all with bath/shower. TV. Phone. B&B £35 to £50. Deposit: £10. Children welcome. Afternoon teas. Garden

'The crab mayonnaise was well-balanced, although at £10.50 it worked out at £1.50 a mouthful.' (On eating in London)

BURNHAM MARKET Norfolk map 6

Fishes' £

Market Place, Burnham Market PE31 8HE COOKING 3
TEL: (01328) 738588 FAX: (01328) 730534 COST £19–£44

Misanthropes who wish to avoid the crowds should come to Fishes' out of season, since crowds there will surely be in summer, poring over books, admiring the morning glories on the windowsills and awaiting the fishy delights of Gillian Cape's simple but proficient cooking. Grilled sole, writes one reporter, was 'plainly and perfectly done' and accompanied by a salad of tomato, black olives and spring onions. Scallops and prawns cooked au gratin are similarly hard to fault. Starters may include highly praised crab soup or potted shrimps, and puddings offer sticky toffee or tiramisù. Bread and coffee flow freely, and service on the whole is 'cheerfully forthcoming'. Wines are as unpretentious as the food, a run of Chablis from the excellent La Chablisienne co-operative an encouraging indicator, and there's even some local apple wine. House wines are £8.50.

CHEFS: Gillian Cape and Paula Ayres PROPRIETOR: Gillian Cape OPEN: Tue to Sun L 12 to 2, Tue to Sat D 6.45 to 9.30 (9 Tue to Thur in winter) CLOSED: 23 to 27 Dec, 3 weeks Jan MEALS: alc (main courses £7.50 to £13). Set L Tue to Fri £9.40 (2 courses) to £11.95, Set L Sat and Sun £10.95 (2 courses) to £13.50. BYO £5 SERVICE: not inc, card slips closed CARDS: Amex, Delta, Diners, MasterCard, Switch, Visa DETAILS: 42 seats. Private parties: 14 main room. Children's helpings. No children under 5 after 8.30. Wheelchair access (no WC). No music

BURPHAM West Sussex map 3

George and Dragon NEW ENTRY

Burpham BN18 9RR
TEL: (01903) 883131 FAX: (01903) 883341
2½m up single track, no-through road signposted COOKING 3
Warningcamp off A27, 1m E of Arundel COST £23–£33

Set in the heart of a well-groomed village with views across the Arun valley to Arundel Castle and the South Downs, the George and Dragon is a characterful country pub. The core of the building is old and venerable, but many extensions and modifications have made the whole a 'harmonious jumble' of styles. The fairly formal eating-area, with bay windows looking over the village, is smart and trim. Pub food of sound English pedigree is offered in the bar, but the dining-room is more ambitious.

Lemon-scented scallops with vegetable spaghetti and chervil beurre blanc is 'excellent in every way', while fillet of hake with a walnut and breadcrumb crust and a tomato and basil sauce successfully brings together contrasting flavours. Scotch beef fillet topped with Stilton and bacon in a pastry lattice satisfied a correspondent who worried that it sounded fussy. The kitchen's enthusiasm for pastrywork brings desserts of apple strudel bursting with sultanas, and pithiviers with marzipan and cream. One reporter felt he would be proud to show this place off to an overseas visitor as the sort of thing that England does so well. A few decent wines from around the world back up the house wines at £9.75.

CHEFS: Kate Holle, David Futcher and Gary Scutt PROPRIETOR: Grosvenor Inns OPEN: Sun L 12.15 to 1.45, Mon to Sat D 7.15 to 9.30 CLOSED: 25 Dec, bar food only bank hols MEALS: Set L £15.95, Set D £16.50 (2 courses) to £19.50. Bar meals available all week L and D SERVICE: 10%, card slips closed CARDS: Amex, Delta, MasterCard, Switch, Visa DETAILS: 36 seats. Private parties: 36 main room. Car park. Vegetarian meals. No children under 8. No pipes in dining-room. Wheelchair access (also WC). Music

---

BURY ST EDMUNDS Suffolk map 6

Mortimer's 🍷 ⚘ £

31 Churchgate Street, Bury St Edmunds IP33 1RG COOKING 2
TEL: (01284) 760623 FAX: (01284) 761611 COST £21–£46

This stalwart among East Anglian seafood restaurants has been going strong since its inception in 1984 and has recently undergone complete redecoration. Two newly acquired oenophilic paintings by Ralph Steadman also remind customers that wine is treated seriously. The menu is 100 per cent fish – apart from soup and puds – and the repertoire varies daily, depending on the market. Starters are tried and tested favourites such as crab pâté, scrambled egg with smoked salmon, Loch Fyne oysters, and seafood gratin, although centrepiece dishes occasionally drift off into more adventurous territory. Chargrilled tuna, and whole sea bream provençale share the stage with fillet of cod with prawn and dill butter, sea bass meunière, and lemon sole with watercress sauce. Desserts range from apple and almond pudding to chocolate pots spiked with rum. Alsace makes its presence felt in the bottles of potent beer on offer as well as eleven white wines, two reds and a sparkler, all from good producers. The largely white selection suits the seafood menu. House wines are £8.50 (£1.75 per glass). CELLARMAN'S CHOICE: Alsace Riesling 1992, Hugel, £18.95; Rioja Viña Real 1991, CVNE, £11.90.

CHEFS: Kenneth Ambler and Justin Adams-Newton PROPRIETORS: Kenneth Ambler and Michael Gooding OPEN: Mon to Fri L 12 to 2, Mon to Sat D 6.30 to 9 (6.15 Mon) CLOSED: 24 Dec to 5 Jan, 2 weeks Aug, bank hol Mons and Tues MEALS: alc (main courses £8 to £19). BYO £4 SERVICE: not inc CARDS: Amex, Delta, Diners, MasterCard, Switch, Visa DETAILS: 76 seats. Private parties: 12 main room, 16 private room. Children's helpings. No smoking in 1 dining-room. Wheelchair access (also women's WC). No music

---

CALSTOCK Cornwall map 1

▲ *Danescombe Valley Hotel* 🍷 ⚘

Lower Kelly, Calstock PL18 9RY
TEL: (01822) 832414 FAX: (01822) 832446 COOKING 4
1m W of Calstock on riverside road COST £39–£46

'A place after our own hearts,' declared a reporter, charmed by this balconied Victorian villa tucked away on a bend in the River Tamar on the Devon/Cornwall border. A hotel since 1860, it has the intimate and informal atmosphere of a restaurant-with-rooms, and 'plenty of character'. Anna Smith is no longer in charge of the kitchen but her subtly Italian-influenced style has been adopted by three new chefs, who take it in turns to produce the no-choice four-course dinner menu. Dishes are simple, based on excellent raw materials, and, at their best, skilfully rendered.

The Italian bias is most evident in starters of asparagus risotto, or semolina gnocchi with funghi, while main courses are more in the British country-house tradition: lamb with a mustard and herb crust, or saddle of roe deer with port sauce. Tarts and ice-creams are the most likely offerings for dessert, or perhaps something unashamedly sticky such as date and coffee pudding with hazelnut caramel. A generous selection of well-kept unpasteurised West Country cheeses, served before dessert, is a permanent fixture on the menu. Service is 'friendly'.

The wine list (arranged by grape variety) reflects Martin Smith's interest in Italian wines, and his enthusiastic tasting notes are a useful and informative guide for those who are unfamiliar with the likes of Arneis, Erbaluce or Marzemino. Generous prices encourage an adventurous choice although the more familiar wines are just as tempting. House wines and wines by the glass vary 'according to whim'.

CHEFS: Chris Dew, Melissa Haywood and Jill Urwin PROPRIETORS: Martin and Anna Smith OPEN: all week D only 7.30 for 8 (1 sitting) MEALS: Set D £30 SERVICE: net prices, card slips closed CARDS: Amex, Diners, MasterCard, Switch, Visa DETAILS: 12 seats. Car park. No children under 12. No smoking in dining-room. No music ACCOMMODATION: 5 rooms, all with bath/shower. D,B&B £102.50 to £185. Deposit: £50. No children under 12. Garden (*The Which? Hotel Guide*)

CAMBRIDGE Cambridgeshire map 6

Midsummer House

Midsummer Common, Cambridge CB4 1HA COOKING 6
TEL: (01223) 369299 FAX: (01223) 302667 COST £36–£58

'Something exciting is happening in Cambridge,' enthused one reporter. Anton Escalera, who has worked in Barcelona as well as round Britain, seems to have taken the city by storm. The house faces the common, and revels in a strong sense of colour and design. Meals are eaten in the canary-yellow conservatory with its Iberian vases and 'riotously bright' paintings of seafood, and bold plates make the most of the food's sometimes striking colours.

The kitchen has the confidence to keep menus short and combinations relatively simple, yet still go for strong flavours. A lunchtime inspection, for example, produced a vibrantly coloured slab of guinea-fowl and sweetbread terrine with Mediterranean vegetables, served with sweet pepper oil, followed by pan-fried red mullet arranged in a characteristic criss-cross stack, accompanied by artichoke and fennel purée.

Meats are organic, and vegetables are given prominence, sometimes in the form of purées or chopped raw vegetables to serve as a counterpoint to meat and fish, as in a dish of lamb cutlets 'each with a little cap of delicate Stilton soufflé', surrounded by grated turnip 'confit' which kept the sauce in place. Not every item works equally well, but the balance comes out easily in favour of successful ones. Desserts typically arrive as towers too: for example, scoops of apple confit and apple sorbet, one on top of the other inside an apple shell. Different breads and flavoured butters add interest, meals begin with an appetiser – cold soup tasting 'intensely of freshly picked peas' at a summer meal – and end with 'excellent' petits-fours. Wines are predominantly French and of high quality, but there is precious little under £20 outside the house selection, which starts at £11.95.

CHEF: Anton Escalera PROPRIETORS: Anton Escalera and Russell Morgan OPEN: Tue to Fri and Sun L 12 to 2.15, Tue to Sat D 7 to 10.15 CLOSED: 26 and 31 Dec MEALS: Set L £19 (2 courses) to £26, Set D £29 (2 courses) to £36, Menu Dégustation Tue to Fri D £45. BYO £8.50 SERVICE: not inc CARDS: Amex, Delta, Diners, MasterCard, Switch, Visa DETAILS: 35 seats. Private parties: 30 main room, 10 and 15 private rooms. Vegetarian meals. Children's helpings. No smoking in dining-room. Wheelchair access (no WC). No music

22 Chesterton Road 🍷

22 Chesterton Road, Cambridge CB4 3AX — COOKING 4
TEL: (01223) 351880 FAX: (01223) 323814 — COST £32–£53

Candle-lit dinners are the form in this Victorian house near the River Cam, where Ian Reinhardt's cooking aims to strike a balance between traditional and modern. To allow for different appetites, the deal is three courses (plus an intermediate mixed leaf salad) for a set price, with the option to add on a fish and/or cheese course at a supplement. The attempt to please all palates seems to work well. Among the more traditional items might be green pea and ham soup, roast pork fillet with sage and onions, and steamed date and fig pudding, but be prepared also for mussel tart with a black bean and coriander dressing, or steamed cod with soured lime cream. Black pudding seems to be a favourite ingredient, perhaps appearing in an 'intriguing' warm salad of rabbit, or on a brochette with mullet and monkfish. The kitchen's capable handling of materials – pink roasted pigeon breast, or 'thin and crisp' pastrywork, for example – is backed up by a wide-ranging wine list that combines variety and quality with good value for money. A new feature is the seasonal selection of eight to ten interesting or even outstanding wines of limited availability. The house quartet at £9.25 and £11.25 covers France, Hungary, Australia and Chile. CELLARMAN'S CHOICE: Vin de Pays d'Oc Viognier, Dom. des Salices 1995, J & F. Lurton, £13.95; Cono Sur Pinot Noir Reserve Selection 1994, Rapel Valley, Chile, £14.95.

CHEF: Ian Reinhardt PROPRIETORS: David Carter and Louise Crompton OPEN: Tue to Sat D only 7 to 9.45 (L by arrangement for parties of 10 or more) CLOSED: 25 Dec to 2 Jan MEALS: Set D £22.50 SERVICE: not inc CARDS: Amex, Delta, MasterCard, Switch, Visa DETAILS: 40 seats. Private parties: 34 main room, 12 private room. Vegetarian meals. No children under 10. No smoking until after main course. Music. Air-conditioned

'The loos now have attendants, and a boy in immaculate white jacket runs the taps as you're buttoning up, and shows you how to use the soap dispenser in case you've just dropped in from Mars. As you lather up he prepares a bouquet of tissues, points invitingly to the array of moisturisers, exfoliants, essential oils, emery boards and all the perfumes of Araby, and also – in passing – the silver salver bristling with pound coins to which you add your own thankful tribute.' (On eating in London)

CAMPSEA ASHE Suffolk map 6

▲ *Old Rectory*

Campsea Ashe IP13 0PU
TEL/FAX: (01728) 746524 COOKING 2
on B1078, 1½m E of A12 COST £26–£31

The converted rectory, a commodious house next to the church, in a huge garden of trees and shrubs, has a 'comfortable, antiquey' feel. Stewart Bassett is 'a most genial man', and a 'house-party atmosphere' generally prevails. In winter, meals are taken in one of the two log-fired dining-rooms; in summer, the conservatory opens up and diners look out on to the garden. There is no choice on the three-course menu (except for vegetarian and dietary requirements, which are dealt with in advance) and a certain richness is typical of the food, as in a chicken breast topped with a mixture of cream, cheese, butter, shallots, crunched-up bacon and herbs.

Good judgement ensures that the end result is not too heavy, though, and one summer visitor enjoyed a small whole Dover sole with anchovy butter, roast rack of lamb with baby roast potatoes and 'unadulterated' courgettes, and strawberry tartlet with crisp pastry, judging it 'one of Mr Bassett's best'. The choice of wines also demonstrates acumen, with a wide range of quality bins on offer at reasonable prices. Selections from the Rhône, Alsace and Bordeaux deserve particular praise while wine buffs may well give thanks for the eight vintages of Ch. Musar dating back to 1961. House French is £9.50 a bottle, £2.25 a glass. CELLARMAN'S CHOICE: St-Aubin premier cru 1994, Gérard Thomas, £17.75; Ch. Musar 1989, Gaston Hochar, Lebanon, £14.50.

CHEF/PROPRIETOR: Stewart Bassett OPEN: Mon to Sat D only 7.30 to 8.30 CLOSED: 1 week Christmas MEALS: Set D £18.70 SERVICE: not inc CARDS: Amex, Diners, MasterCard, Visa DETAILS: 45 seats. Private parties: 36 main room, 8 to 36 private rooms. Car park. Children's helpings. No smoking in dining-room. Music ACCOMMODATION: 11 rooms, all with bath/shower. B&B £30 to £65. Deposit: £15. Children welcome. Dogs welcome. Garden (*The Which? Hotel Guide*)

CANTERBURY Kent map 3

▲ *Canterbury Hotel, La Bonne Cuisine* NEW ENTRY

71 New Dover Road, Canterbury CT1 3DZ COOKING 5
TEL: (01227) 450551 FAX: (01227) 780145 COST £21–£41

Mark the address carefully for there are several hotels on this stretch of New Dover Road. This one is an elegant red-brick Georgian building set back from the road, with a flight of steep steps leading up to the front door. Inside is 'all patterns and twirls', and the dining-room is strongly yellow with a huge chandelier.

Jean-Luc Jouvente cooks an unabashed classical style of French haute cuisine for a clientele that readily appreciates it. Visual impact is at a premium: a generous plate of tiny ravioli filled with spinach have been served with a pink, creamy essence of langoustines flecked with black poppy seeds. A main course of 'exceptionally lean and blood-red' duck breast might come with a mint infusion and a bundle of French beans tied up with bacon. When imagination is let loose, dishes can be complex – chicken breast stuffed with langoustines and served with a light curry sauce, or spiced John Dory with smoked salmon on a bed of leeks and olives – but the technique is usually there to back it up. Desserts might include tarte Tatin with vanilla ice-cream, or crème brûlée with walnuts and honey. Service is as French as the cooking; it may help to speak slowly. A new wine list was being prepared as the *Guide* went to press.

CHEF: Jean-Luc Jouvente PROPRIETORS: Mr and Mrs Bevan OPEN: all week 12 to 2, 7 to 10 (9 Sun) MEALS: alc (main courses £8.50 to £13.50). Set L (2 courses) £10.50, Set D £14.50 SERVICE: not inc, card slips closed CARDS: Amex, Delta, Diners, MasterCard, Switch, Visa DETAILS: 65 seats. Private parties: 24 main room, 15 and 24 private rooms. Car park. Vegetarian meals. Children's helpings. No children under 12. Music ACCOMMODATION: 26 rooms, all with bath/shower. TV. Phone. B&B £45 to £68. Deposit: £45. Rooms for disabled. Children welcome. Baby facilities. Dogs welcome by arrangement in bedrooms only. Afternoon teas. Garden

---

CARLTON North Yorkshire map 9

▲ *Foresters Arms* £

Carlton, nr Leyburn DL8 4BB
TEL: (01969) 640272 FAX: (01969) 640272
off A684, 5m SW of Leyburn

COOKING 2
COST £23–£49

Built in 1640, with beamed ceilings, flagged floors and a log fire, the Foresters Arms combines its twin roles as pub and more formal restaurant in a way that makes everybody happy. Choice is huge, from black pudding with Dijon dressing, or ham and eggs, to leek and blue cheese strudel, and pot-roast shoulder of lamb. Main-course meats might be roasted or chargrilled, but ambition of a different sort is evident in an 'opulent' ragoût of wild mushrooms and foie gras between layers of filo pastry. Fish (listed on a blackboard) is a strong point and might include baked crab and asparagus gâteau, or cod wrapped in potato slices, but Barrie Higginbotham also goes in for bolder flavours: smoked haddock dumpling with a curry sabayon, or lemon sole with lime and salsa. If 20 minutes is too long to wait for raspberry soufflé, consider bitter chocolate terrine, or steamed syrup sponge. Well-chosen wines under £20 are supplemented by a short but still fairly priced 'reserve' list of flashier bottles. The house selection starts at £9.60.

CHEF/PROPRIETOR: B.K. Higginbotham OPEN: Tue to Sun L 12 to 2, Tue to Sat D 7 to 9.30 (9 bar) MEALS: alc (main courses £9 to £15.50). Light L available Tue to Sat; blackboard main courses from £8 Sun SERVICE: not inc, card slips closed CARDS: Delta, MasterCard, Switch, Visa DETAILS: 60 seats. 24 seats outside. Private parties: 36 main room, 15 private room. Car park. Vegetarian meals. Children's helpings. No smoking in 1 dining-room. Music. Air-conditioned ACCOMMODATION: 3 rooms, all with bath/shower. TV. B&B £30 to £60. Deposit: £20. Children welcome. Baby facilities. Dogs welcome (*The Which? Hotel Guide*)

The text of entries is based on unsolicited reports sent in by readers, backed up by inspections conducted anonymously. The factual details under the text are from questionnaires the Guide *sends to all restaurants that feature in the book.*

CARTMEL Cumbria map 8

▲ *Aynsome Manor* £

Cartmel LA11 6HH
TEL: (01539) 536653 FAX: (01539) 536016
off A590, ½m N of village

COOKING 2
COST £17–£33

'Well worth the time taken to find it,' reckoned one reporter of this family-run business on the Cartmel peninsula. It is a peaceful sixteenth-century manor-house with good views, notable antiques and a Victorian dining-room. The Varleys' format departs from the Lakeland norm in that dinner is a choice of three to five courses, and one who dined off bobotie, pheasant, and a banana and Tia Maria meringue returned for more two days later, considering it all good value for money. Local resources include game birds and venison from Holker Hall and shrimps from Flookburgh, alcohol is a favourite saucing ingredient, and the menu varies by the day, perhaps including Polish barley and vegetable soup, smoked haddock and asparagus roulade, or guinea-fowl with a mushroom and marsala sauce. Staff are helpful and attentive. A new wine list was being compiled as the *Guide* went to press; house wines from Italy and Australia are £10.50 a litre.

CHEFS: Victor Sharratt and Christopher Miller PROPRIETORS: Anthony and Margaret Varley OPEN: Sun L 1 (1 sitting), Mon to Sat D 7 to 8.30 (residents only Sun D) CLOSED: 2 to 27 Jan MEALS: Set L Sun £11.95, Set D £15.50 to £19.50 SERVICE: not inc, card slips closed CARDS: Amex, Delta, MasterCard, Switch, Visa DETAILS: 28 seats. Private parties: 32 main room. Car park. Children's helpings. No children under 5 at D. No smoking in dining-room. No music ACCOMMODATION: 12 rooms, all with bath/shower. TV. Phone. D,B&B £52 to £106. Children welcome. Baby facilities. Dogs welcome in bedrooms only. Afternoon teas. Garden (*The Which? Hotel Guide*)

▲ *Uplands*

Haggs Lane, Cartmel LA11 6HD
TEL: (015395) 36248 FAX: (015395) 36848
2½m SW of A590, 1m up road opposite Pig and Whistle

COOKING 5
COST £21–£41

The spacious lounge and dining-room of this mustard-coloured house are due for a refit over the winter of 1997–8, but the views across Morecambe Bay are sure to stay, and Diana Peter's 'wide smile and friendly approach' is a fixture. The food is unlikely to change either. 'We tend to stick to our tried-and-tested methods and recipes and ways of doing things,' write the Peters, which seemed 'rather dated' to one visitor but pleases the many regulars: 'never a disappointing meal after some four to five visits a year since it opened.'

Lunch is three courses, dinner four, and local resources include game (from Holker Hall), smoked duck breast, and Morecambe Bay shrimps, which might be served in a ripe Galia melon with mayonnaise. Soup is a generous self-service tureen – Jerusalem artichoke, perhaps, or a full-bodied mushroom and apple – accompanied by a whole cut-it-yourself loaf of bread per table. 'Fat, sweet, fresh and firm' sea bass, precisely timed, shows what the kitchen can do, although the relevance of five busy vegetables (the same for both fish and meat) divides reporters.

Pastry-work has produced an impressive tartlet of feta and Emmental with onion, and desserts might include chocolate and Grand Marnier mousse, or strawberry shortbread. Service is gently paced and well mannered, and the southern hemisphere is strongly represented on the sensibly priced wine list, which opens with house Australian red and French white at £8.50.

CHEF: Tom Peter PROPRIETORS: Tom and Diana Peter, and John Tovey OPEN: Thur to Sun L 12.30 for 1 (1 sitting), Tue to Sun D 7.30 for 8 (1 sitting) CLOSED: 1 Jan to 1 Mar MEALS: Set L £15, Set D £26.50. BYO £3.50 SERVICE: not inc, card slips closed CARDS: Amex, MasterCard, Visa DETAILS: 28 seats. Private parties: 18 main room. Car park. Vegetarian meals. Children welcome. No children under 8 at D. No smoking in dining-room. Music ACCOMMODATION: 5 rooms, all with bath/shower. TV. Phone. D,B&B £59 to £138. No children under 8. Dogs welcome in bedrooms only. Garden (*The Which? Hotel Guide*)

CASTLE CARY Somerset map 2

▲ *Bond's* £

Ansford, Castle Cary BA7 7JP
TEL/FAX: (01963) 350464 COOKING 2
on A371, 400yds past station towards Wincanton COST £21–£39

The rough-stone house is creeper covered, with a log fire in the lounge, and a light, fresh feel to the dining-room. Two set-price menus are offered, one changing monthly, the less expensive no-choice one daily, which builds in enough flexibility for most requirements. Soups often contain a fishy element – crab in partan bree, or prawns and bacon in cream of butter-bean – while main-course fish has ranged from poached gurnard (in a cream and dill sauce) to herb-crusted fillets of salmon or tuna. Beef fillet is a regular on the monthly menu, which has also produced venison and rabbit pie, and a boned baby chicken stuffed with pistachios and served with apricot sauce. Yvonne Bond takes great pride in her vegetables, including perhaps a hollowed-out courgette filled with sweet potato purée, and bread is good. 'Pleasant' and 'unobtrusive' is Kevin Bond's front-of-house style and, in order to overcome what he considers a national shortage of good half-bottles, his fairly priced and manageable wine list includes seven house wines (from £8.50), all available either by the glass or payable according to the quantity consumed.

CHEF: Yvonne Bond PROPRIETORS: Kevin and Yvonne Bond OPEN: all week D only 7 to 9.30 (7.30 Sun and Mon) CLOSED: 1 week Christmas MEALS: Set D £13.50 to £21.50. Light L available SERVICE: not inc, card slips closed CARDS: MasterCard, Visa DETAILS: 20 seats. 8 seats outside. Private parties: 14 main room. Car park. Vegetarian meals. Children's helpings. No smoking in dining-room. No music ACCOMMODATION: 7 rooms, all with bath/shower. TV. Phone. B&B £38 to £80. Deposit: £10. Babies and children over 8 welcome. Afternoon teas. Garden

Card slips closed *in the details at the end of an entry indicates that the total on the slips of credit cards is closed when handed over for signature.*

CASTLE COMBE Wiltshire map 2

▲ *Manor House Hotel*

Castle Combe SN14 7HR
TEL: (01249) 782206 FAX: (01249) 782159 COOKING 5
on B4039, 3m NW of junction with A420 COST £31–£94

Given that this is 'one of the prettiest villages in England', and on the edge of the Cotswolds, visitors are to be expected. The fifteenth-century stone-built mullion-windowed Manor House not only shields itself from the crowds with 26 acres of gardens and an 18-hole golf course, it has also bagged a private stretch of the Bybrook, the village trout stream. The effect, together with lawns, fountains and huge trees, is 'old England at its best'. Considered 'ancient yet smart, fussy yet functional', the house is 'a joy to relax in'. Staff are dressed (or perhaps 'overdressed') in frock coats, and this is one of a dwindling band of places where crêpes Suzette are 'flamed at your table', but the 'sheer pampering' is welcomed.

Mark Taylor is not one to stop at a culinary border and ask for directions. He delves into the world of crab risotto, venison sausage, garlic chips, langoustine wun-tuns, and (possibly a first) a soufflé of cheese and banana with which one couple began their lunch. Main courses marshal prime ingredients and treat them well, as in a smoked fillet of Scottish beef that comes with foie gras and pea purée. 'The set meal was reasonable value,' reckoned one who shunned the *carte*'s luxuries and higher prices. This is not a place for low rollers, nor indeed faint appetites, though one couple who lunched felt their meal had 'all the attributes and intricacies of dinner', since it included a mini-soup appetiser, plenty of choice, and coffee with petits-fours.

A list of fine British cheeses (helpfully annotated) provides an alternative to desserts such as passion-fruit soufflé with caramel and pecan ice-cream. The weighty, international wine list is designed for a wealthy international clientele, but ten-plus house wines stay below £20.

CHEF: Mark Taylor PROPRIETOR: Manor House Hotel (Castle Combe) Ltd OPEN: all week 12 to 2, 7 to 10 MEALS: alc D (main courses £22.50 to £27). Set L £16.95 (2 courses) to £18.95, Set D £35 SERVICE: not inc, card slips closed CARDS: Amex, Diners, MasterCard, Switch, Visa DETAILS: 105 seats. Private parties: 105 main room, 12 to 30 private rooms. Car park. Children's helpings. Jacket and tie. No smoking in dining-room. Wheelchair access (also WC). Music ACCOMMODATION: 45 rooms, all with bath/shower. TV. Phone. Room only £115 to £350. Rooms for disabled. Children welcome. Baby facilities. Afternoon teas. Garden. Swimming-pool. Fishing (*The Which? Hotel Guide*)

CAUNTON Nottinghamshire map 5

Caunton Beck £ NEW ENTRY

Caunton NG23 6AB COOKING 2
TEL: (01636) 636793 FAX: (01636) 636828 COST £20–£41

The early-nineteenth-century inn, with mustard-washed walls and Elizabethan timbers, is a country version of the Wig & Mitre (see entry, Lincoln). The Michael and Valerie Hope stamp is clearly seen in the perpetual-motion approach to innkeeping in which food and drink are administered all over the premises and throughout the week, from nine in the morning to ten at night. Fine ingredients and modern ideas are clear in 'simple yet effective' grilled goats' cheese on a garlic croûton with grapes and pine-nuts. Mussel and saffron soup is full of good flavours, and might be followed by slices of woodpigeon breast pan-fried to a 'succulent pinkness' and served with a wild mushroom sauce. Among a standard range of desserts might be banoffi pie, or lemon tart. Young staff are relaxed and friendly. The succinctly annotated wine list is arranged by style and offers a wide variety of flavours, from reliable producers. Four house wines, hailing from Burgundy, Germany and South Africa, are £10 a bottle, £2.50 a glass, and there are plenty of halves.

CHEFS: Paul Vidic, Jamie Matts and Adrian Graves PROPRIETORS: Michael and Valerie Hope, and Paul Vidic OPEN: all week 9am to 10pm MEALS: alc (main courses £6 to £15) SERVICE: not inc, card slips closed CARDS: Amex, Delta, Diners, MasterCard, Switch, Visa DETAILS: 120 seats. 40 seats outside. Private parties: 30 main room, 30 private room. Car park. Vegetarian meals. Children's helpings. Wheelchair access (also WC). No music

CHAGFORD Devon map 1

▲ *Gidleigh Park*

Chagford TQ13 8HH
TEL: (01647) 432367 FAX: (01647) 432574
from Chagford Square turn right at Lloyds Bank into Mill Street, take right fork after 150 yards, follow lane for 1½m

COOKING 9
COST £43–£85

After 20 years at Gidleigh, Paul Henderson collects his bus pass at the end of 1998, though what use it will be in the winding Devon lanes around Chagford is hard to imagine. The brick-built, tall-chimneyed, black and white house reassures with the gentle smell of woodsmoke, and the menu comforts with roast rabbit and tarragon hollandaise, pheasant with black pudding and lentils, and saddle of lamb with tongue and sweetbreads. Michael Caines may not be the world's most adventurous chef, but he does go to a lot of trouble to construct dishes carefully, and takes luxuries in his stride, slicing seasonal white truffle on to tagliatelle with a rosemary cream sauce, for example.

Soups 'really are in a class of their own', be it a delicate froth of white haricot beans or one with Jerusalem artichoke and truffle, which achieved 'a rich satin-like texture with a tremendous density of flavour'. Where fish is concerned, reporters typically resort to the word 'stunning' to describe both the raw material and its precise timing. Everything impresses, from 'very fine' langoustine ravioli and 'just stiffened' scallops with a truffle-infused salad, to pieces of pan-fried red mullet on a bed of finely chopped Mediterranean vegetables. Meat dishes can be rich, and portions generous. The kitchen also treats game seriously, including 'precisely cooked, plump' roast partridge, hung long enough to be pleasantly gamey, with a 'clear and gloriously rich' sauce.

One senior reporter wondered whether some of the dishes may be too intricate for their own good, while another was struck by a few 'touches of carelessness which are infuriating given the level of brilliance regularly on display'. Desserts are certainly a *tour de force*, from a 'glorious' prune and armagnac soufflé, to a hot apple tart with pastry so delicate 'the fruit seems to be balanced on thin air', by way of a pistachio parfait in a filo parcel tied with chocolate string, resting beside an unctuous, oozing chocolate pudding. Local cheeses might include a blue goat's.

Amuse gueules, bread, and all other peripheral items 'are granted the same care as the main ingredients', and water (like service) is included in the price. The sheer quality and variety of the wines on the 520-strong list will bring joy to an oenophile's heart, and the very reasonable mark-up system means the bank manager's won't sink. French and Italian classics and American varietals are a continuing strength, with extra vigour provided by the new range of eight 'outstanding' sherries, six in handy half-bottles, which you are urged to try with your meal. CELLARMAN'S CHOICE: Qupé Viognier/Chardonnay 'Bien Nacido' 1995, Santa Barbara, California, £26; Niebaum-Coppola Rubicon Cabernet Sauvignon 1982, Napa Valley, California, £45.

CHEF: Michael Caines PROPRIETORS: Kay and Paul Henderson OPEN: all week 12.30 to 2, 7 to 9 MEALS: Set L Mon to Thu £27, Set L Fri to Sun £32, Set D £55. BYO £10. Light L available SERVICE: net prices, card slips closed CARDS: Delta, Diners, MasterCard, Switch, Visa DETAILS: 35 seats. Private parties: 30 main room. Car park. Children welcome. No smoking in dining-room. Wheelchair access (no WC). No music ACCOMMODATION: 14 rooms, all with bath/shower. TV. Phone. D,B&B £210 to £415. Children welcome. Baby facilities. Dogs welcome in bedrooms only. Afternoon teas. Garden. Fishing

CHEESDEN Greater Manchester map 8

Nutters

Edenfield Road, Cheesden, nr Rochdale OL12 7TY COOKING **6**
TEL/FAX: (01706) 50167 COST £26–£48

Perched high on the moors above Rossendale, where winter comes early and to be half-buried in a snowdrift is nothing remarkable, the Nutters' converted pub is old-Lancashire through and through. It capitalises on its uncompromising setting and warm welcome, and aims high. If you are expecting just a pie and a pint, expect again. Andrew Nutter has bagged himself an occasional stint on daytime TV, and his mission to entertain encompasses the restaurant too. Creamy cauliflower soup, for instance, comes with a knob of Roquefort and a stream of white truffle oil, while wing of skate is coated in potato, dipped in ginger beer batter, and given a creamy 'salt & vinegar' flavoured sauce.

Demonstrably good raw materials have produced properly gamey pheasant served with a juniper-scented reduction, and medallions of pork with caramelised apples and a coulis of sweet red peppers, while desserts keep up the cracking pace. Black cherry parfait with 'chewy pineapple flowers' might tempt the adventurous away from bread-and-butter pudding or lemon tart. A 'surprise' six-course menu (available only for the whole table) gives an opportunity to sample some of the Nutter specialities. France is the focus of the wine list, the choices good in Bordeaux, a touch pedestrian in Burgundy, but with a welcome smattering of antipodeans and Chileans. House wines start at £10.50.

All entries, including Round-ups, are fully indexed at the back of the Guide.

CHEF: Andrew Nutter PROPRIETORS: Rodney, Jean and Andrew Nutter OPEN: Wed to Mon 12 to 2, 7 (6.45 Sat) to 9.30 CLOSED: first 2 weeks Aug MEALS: alc (main courses £9.50 to £16). Set L Sun £19.95, Set Gourmet Menu D £29.50 SERVICE: not inc CARDS: Amex, Delta, MasterCard, Switch, Visa DETAILS: 52 seats. Private parties: 56 main room. Car park. Vegetarian meals. Children's helpings. No smoking in dining-room. Wheelchair access (also WC). Music

---

CHELTENHAM Gloucestershire map 5

Le Champignon Sauvage 🍷

24–26 Suffolk Road, Cheltenham GL50 2AQ COOKING 7
TEL/FAX: (01242) 573449 COST £28–£59

As the *Guide* went to press, the Everitt-Matthiases were celebrating their tenth anniversary here with more refurbishment, adding new flooring, seating and lighting to the colourful art-filled dining-room. The set-price menu format has been extended slightly to offer a less-expensive weekday alternative at dinner, but the classically based contemporary style of food continues. This is a kitchen that aims to get the balance right between the main component of a dish and its accompaniments, adding just enough to create interest yet keeping the focus clear, as in a spiced fillet of cod with bacon and lentil salsa, or chump of lamb with black olive polenta and roasted fennel. 'Well-defined flavours but not overpowering' is how one reporter described this clarity of purpose in a first-course pork dumpling served on sweet potato purée with a bay leaf sauce.

The menu turns slowly through the seasons (though the larder may not always be perfectly synchronised) and there is a sense of proportion, a balance between lightness and earthiness. An eye for modest invention, meanwhile, has produced duck confit sausage with a pickled apple tart and foie gras sauce, and desserts such as lemon crème brûlée with pistachio madeleines, or a rich bitter chocolate mousse studded with prunes. In case anyone doubts the seriousness of intent, dinner might begin with a pre-meal cup of haricot bean and lentil cappuccino sprinkled with cep powder, and there is a pre-dessert offering as well as a pre-cheese nibble of cheese beignet: no one should go hungry. Or, indeed, thirsty, for the broad sweep of flavours, styles and prices among the wines should ensure that there is something for most palates and pockets. Quality throughout the well-annotated list is constant, whether you choose an Alsace Gewurztraminer from Albert Mann or a New Zealand Pinot Noir from Jane Hunt. House French wines from Charles Vienot are £9.95. CELLARMAN'S CHOICE: Mâcon-Uchizy 1994, Dom. Talmard, £13.50, Coudoulet de Beaucastel 1992, Perrin, £15.95.

CHEF: David Everitt-Matthias PROPRIETORS: David and Helen Everitt-Matthias OPEN: Mon to Fri L 12.30 to 1.30, Mon to Sat D 7.30 to 9.15 CLOSED: 10 days Christmas, 2 weeks summer, bank hols MEALS: Set L £15.50 (2 courses) to £18.50, Set D Mon to Fri £15.50 (2 courses) to £19.95, Set D Mon to Sat £25 (2 courses) to £37 SERVICE: not inc CARDS: Amex, Diners, MasterCard, Switch, Visa DETAILS: 28 seats. Private parties: 22 main room. Children welcome. Wheelchair access (also WC). No music. Air-conditioned

81 Restaurant

81 The Promenade, Cheltenham GL50 1PJ COOKING 6
TEL: (01242) 222466 FAX: (01242) 222474 COST £29–£54

New owners have taken over Cheltenham's finest Regency terrace, overlooking the Promenade, which was formerly home to the Epicurean. Menus and décor may be new, but chef Jason Lynas and the three-storey format remain. It is considered smart thinking these days to offer several eating and drinking options, and 81 does that with a basement bar, ground-floor bistro and first-floor restaurant, the last elegant and cool, with heavily swagged curtains, and silver plates on crisp white tablecloths. The restaurant's preoccupation is with modern Anglo-French cooking along the lines of parsley soup with shellfish, and glazed pig's trotter with crisp belly-pork.

Some of the food is quite rich, including a perfectly timed fillet of beef served with dauphinois potatoes and shallot tarte Tatin, and creams figure prominently: poached oysters with scrambled egg and chive cream, for instance, or poached guinea-fowl stuffed with tarragon and foie gras cream. Something to modify this richness, such as an apple and walnut dressing for a terrine of duck and foie gras, is thus especially welcome. The kitchen gilds the lily with a pre-starter – a coffee-cup of white haricot bean soup, perhaps – and a pre-dessert of crème caramel topped with sultanas.

Ingredients are prime, and even if a summer berry trifle with strawberries and raspberries appears in March, the kitchen can certainly handle with confidence and skill such classic items as a glazed lemon tart. Service is attentive and helpful. Around half of the 40-plus wines on the list – a mixture of New World and classic French – are below £20. The bistro goes in for less-formal, less-expensive food such as grilled goats' cheese on provençale vegetables, or salad of black pudding with poached egg.

CHEF: Jason Lynas PROPRIETORS: Nicola Stone and Fiorentino Izzo OPEN: Tue to Sun L 12 to 2.30, Tue to Sat D 7 to 9.30 (10 Fri and Sat) CLOSED: 26 to 30 Dec, bank hols MEALS: alc (main courses £15 to £17). Set L £15 (2 courses) to £18 SERVICE: not inc CARDS: Amex, Delta, MasterCard, Switch, Visa DETAILS: 20 seats. 8 seats outside. Private parties: 40 main room, 12 private room. Vegetarian meals. Children welcome. No smoking in dining-room. Music

Mayflower

32–34 Clarence Street, Cheltenham GL50 3NX
TEL: (01242) 522426 and 511580 COOKING 1
FAX: (01242) 251667 COST £14–£60

'Still going after 15 years; same family, same style and attitude,' writes Chun Kong. A reporter echoes the sentiment: 'still very consistent and one of our all-time favourites.' Decorated in 'Regency-oriental' style, it touches base – on a long menu – with everything from Szechuan and Peking duck to Cantonese shredded beef, garlic chilli squid, and sizzling lamb. It may not go in for the more esoteric Chinatown dishes, but it has included specials of wok-cooked Dover sole, lobster with ginger and spring onions, and rice in lotus leaves. Among the banquets and set meals is a seafood feast (for four people), and special nights have drawn the crowds with prices of ten years ago. The modestly priced but well-chosen wine list is a bonus, with house vin de pays at £8.95.

CHEFS: Mrs M.M. Kong and Mr C.F. Kong PROPRIETORS: the Kong family OPEN: Mon to Sat L 12 to 1.45, all week D 6 to 10.30 CLOSED: 24 to 26 Dec MEALS: alc (main courses £5.50 to £10). Set L £6.75, Set D £17 (minimum 2) to £19 (minimum 4) SERVICE: not inc CARDS: Amex, Delta, Diners, MasterCard, Switch, Visa DETAILS: 120 seats. Private parties: 80 main room, 40 private room. Vegetarian meals. Children welcome. Music. Air-conditioned

CHESTER Cheshire map 7

▲ *Chester Grosvenor Hotel, Arkle*

Eastgate Street, Chester CH1 1LT COOKING **8**
TEL: (01244) 324024 FAX: (01244) 313246 COST £37–£85

Approach from the car park, and it feels like entering an 'aristocratic bunker', with luxury goods on display in glass cases along the way, a darkish 'library' for aperitifs and coffee, and a dining-room with a huge artificial skylight, inevitable horsy prints, and large, extravagantly spaced tables. It is like eating in a posh, private club. 'If your calorific requirements are not large, you could make do with the nibbles and appetisers,' volunteered a reporter who felt somewhat overwhelmed by the bounteous olives, nuts, and assorted canapés, roulade of salmon amuse-bouche, sorbet before the main course, the 'appetiser' before dessert, and a two-tier cakestand of petits fours (most involving chocolate), not to mention bread (a dozen large loaves on a carving trolley) and butter.

The food is well practised, controlled, leaving little to chance, and 'there wasn't a dull dish on the menu', according to our inspector. Daily fish specials add variety, and the style embraces colourful presentation, richness, and 'some incredibly skilful cooking'. Parfaits, purées and sauces impress, and 'brilliant flavour combinations' have included scallops with a 'smooth, silky and intense' carrot purée and a moat of creamy vanilla sauce, and a parfait of wild duck with hot smoked breast and a salad of finely diced chestnuts. Truffles abound, buried in an oxtail and chicken sausage maybe, or in the cream sauce for a fillet of turbot.

'Those who insist on five portions of fruit and veg each day had better look elsewhere,' commented one reporter, although plum and date pudding with a compote of spiced plums fits the bill, as does a 'terribly clever' soufflé of marinated apricots encased in a pastry tart, served with concentrated butterscotch sauce and a mild apricot ice-cream. The food is served with much style and panache. Chairs are pulled back, napkins draped, domes lifted, and 'one is topped up, but not without a glance requesting permission to do so'. Food in the Brasserie is less formal and less expensive.

Wines are a serious collection of mostly mature bottles at some very serious prices. A trawl through the list will net a few under £20, but the biggest catch is a 1921 Ch. d'Yquem at £3,500. House wines start at £11.50. CELLARMAN'S CHOICE: Bordeaux, Notre Dame de Landiras 1993, P.Vinding-Diers, £22; Pipers Brook Pellion Pinot Noir 1995, Tasmania, £34.

The Guide *always appreciates hearing about changes of chef or owner.*

CHEFS: Paul Reed and Richard Cotteral PROPRIETOR: Grosvenor Estate Holdings OPEN: Tue to Sun L 12 to 2.30, Mon to Sat D 7 to 9.30 CLOSED: 25 to 30 Dec MEALS: Set L £22.50, Set D £38 (2 courses) to £45 SERVICE: not inc CARDS: Amex, Diners, MasterCard, Visa DETAILS: 40 seats. 40 seats outside. Private parties: 18 to 220 private rooms. Car park. Vegetarian meals. Children's helpings. No smoking in dining-room. Wheelchair access (also WC). Music. Air-conditioned ACCOMMODATION: 86 rooms, all with bath/shower. TV. Phone. Air-conditioned. Room only £120 to £200. Deposit: 100%. Rooms for disabled. Children welcome. Baby facilities. Guide dogs only. Afternoon teas

CHILGROVE West Sussex map 3

White Horse Inn

Chilgrove PO18 9HX
TEL: (01243) 535219 FAX: (01243) 535301 COOKING **2**
on B2141, between Chichester and Petersfield COST £30–£41

The wooded South Downs rise steeply around the low flint building opposite the village green, while inside, wine bottles (some full, some empty) signal the main attraction. 'The menu is not cutting-edge,' felt one reporter, but that is part of its 'old-fashioned charm'. Soups have included rich, dark, watercress and spinach, and reporters have also enjoyed salmon and crab roulade, 'moist, firm and fresh' halibut, and game sausage on coarsely chopped leeks. Indeed, game figures prominently, with hare, pheasant, grouse, teal, woodcock and partridge all appearing in season.

That the wine outshines the food is not in doubt. One correspondent came here for a birthday treat because he 'wanted to spend it with a good friend – Barry Phillips's wine list'. The man himself is 'omnipresent, cheerful, opinionated, a true enthusiast', and more than willing to act as a guide to his massive collection of fine wines from around the world, although the constantly changing mixed bag of house wines, available by the bottle, half-bottle and glass, provides a helpful introduction. A photographic memory for merchants' prices might come in handy for there are some bargains to be found among the hundreds of mature clarets (including 20-odd vintages of Ch. Mouton Rothschild for instance), but it might take a while to spot them. CELLARMAN'S CHOICE: Wairau River Sauvignon Blanc 1996, Marlborough, New Zealand, £16.50; Bandol, Ch. de Pibarnon 1990, £27.50. Neil Rusbridger also owns nearby Forge Cottage, which offers B&B accommodation.

CHEF: Neil Rusbridger PROPRIETORS: Barry Phillips and Neil Rusbridger OPEN: Tue to Sat 12 to 2, 7 to 9.30 (10.30 during festival season) CLOSED: 1 week Oct, 1 week Feb MEALS: Set L £16.50 (2 courses) to £19.50, Set D £19.50 to £23.50. Bar meals available SERVICE: 10%, card slips closed CARDS: Delta, Diners, MasterCard, Switch, Visa DETAILS: 70 seats. 12 seats outside. Private parties: 32 main room, 12 private room. Car park. Vegetarian meals. No smoking in 1 dining-room. Wheelchair access (no WC). No music. Air-conditioned

'I could not manage the rest of the petits fours after biting into the first chocolate and watching the repulsive green slime sinisterly ooze out over my fingers, reminiscent of a scene from Alien 3.*'* (On eating in Essex)

CHINNOR Oxfordshire map 2

Sir Charles Napier

Sprigg's Alley, nr Chinnor OX9 4BX
TEL: (01494) 483011 FAX: (01494) 485434
off B4009; at Chinnor roundabout, take Sprigg's Alley turn, continue straight up hill

COOKING **4**
COST £33–£49

The brick and flint house is in a clearing, up among the beechwoods on Bledlow Ridge, a couple of miles out of Chinnor. Statues and sculptures on the lawn give way to squat buddhas and gorillas inside where candle-holding arms stick spookily out of walls (candles *à bras*, one visitor called them). The food is just as lively, thanks to a seasonal slant that makes use of local mushrooms, fruits and game, and the kitchen's zest for spicing: coriander (in crab-cakes), cumin (with saddle of lamb) or lime, ginger and soy (with duck).

The rolling *carte* of around ten items per savoury course appears equally at home with simple steamed whole crab with basil oil, more classical osso buco, or a contemporary goats'-cheese and red pepper tart which was the star dish at inspection. Desserts are well handled too, including a very light version of crème brûlée, and a superior hot chocolate pot. There have been niggles about both food and service, but none about the wine list, which continues to roam the world for exciting new finds from little-known wineries, while maintaining a core of high-quality bins from more famous producers. Ardent tasting notes and very fair prices add to the delights in store. Australian house white and French house red are both £10.75. CELLARMAN'S CHOICE: Paracombe Sauvignon Blanc 1995, Piccadilly, S. Australia, £18.95; Frankland Estate Isolation Ridge Shiraz 1994, Great Southern, W. Australia, £16.25.

CHEFS: Batiste Tolu and David Jones PROPRIETOR: Julie Griffiths OPEN: Tue to Sun L 12 to 2.30 (3.30 Sun), Tue to Sat D 7 to 10 CLOSED: 26 and 27 Dec MEALS: alc (main courses £11.50 to £15.50). Set L Tue to Fri £13.50 (2 courses), Set D Tue to Fri £14.50 (2 courses). BYO £5.50 SERVICE: 12.5% (optional), card slips closed CARDS: Amex, Delta, MasterCard, Switch, Visa DETAILS: 80 seats. 80 seats outside. Private parties: 45 main room, 30 and 45 private rooms. Car park. Vegetarian meals. Children's helpings. No children under 7 at D. No-smoking area. Wheelchair access (no WC). Music

CHOBHAM Surrey map 3

Quails

1 Bagshot Road, Chobham GU24 8BP
TEL/FAX: (01276) 858491

COOKING **2**
COST £24–£48

Quails is a local favourite, although it also draws a following from further afield. This is a modest place with a 'friendly but professional atmosphere', and those who have found the plain wooden chairs a shade uncomfortable will be pleased to learn that upholstered seats were on order as the *Guide* went to press. The set-price weekday lunches offer great value with gratinated cider and onion soup, grilled mackerel with red pepper sauce, and walnut tart, while the monthly-changing *carte* takes a more global view of things. France still has its say with cannon of lamb with provençale vegetables and rosemary-scented *jus*, but also expect filo parcels of monkfish and sushi ginger on braised pak choi, or crispy duck with bean shoots, lime and saké. Service copes efficiently even under pressure, and the wine list offers a fair spread of styles and prices. House French is £9.75.

CHEF: Christopher Wale PROPRIETORS: the Wale family OPEN: Tue to Fri and Sun L 12.30 to 2, Tue to Sat D 7 to 10 CLOSED: 26 Dec, 1 Jan MEALS: alc (main courses £13 to £14.50). Set L Tue to Fri £11.95 (2 courses) to £14.95, Set L Sun £15.95, Set D Tue to Fri £16.95 (2 courses) to £19.95 (each inc wine) SERVICE: not inc; 10% for parties of 6 or more CARDS: Amex, Delta, Diners, MasterCard, Switch, Visa DETAILS: 40 seats. Private parties: 40 main room. Car park. Vegetarian meals. Children welcome. Wheelchair access (no WC). Music. Air-conditioned

CHRISTCHURCH Dorset map 2

Splinters

12 Church Street, Christchurch BH23 1BW COOKING 3
TEL/FAX: (01202) 483454 COST £28–£57

Splinters occupies a Grade II listed building hard by Christchurch's eleventh-century priory and backs on to the castle. This is 'Olde Englande at its best'. Enter through the bar into one of several small dining-rooms, where tablecloths, candles and large menus await. The strength lies in 'reliable food and service', and Eamonn Redden's repertoire is 'varied and interesting', with a modern tilt and plenty of choice: from wild boar with New Forest mushrooms to fish of the day, and duck with peppered pineapple slices.

Some dishes try rather hard to impress given the context – poached quails' eggs popped into a creamy spinach soup for example – but there is obvious skill in a 'fresh, good-looking and simple' crumpet topped with goats' cheese and asparagus, or in pan-fried salmon fillets with a creamy sauce. A pastry chef from Chewton Glen (see entry, New Milton) has taken charge of the puddings, which might include a 'chocolate special' arranged in dark and white chessboard squares, or 'abundant' summer pudding with clotted cream. Sensible prices add to the appeal of the wine list, which kicks off with house French at £11.80.

CHEF: Eamonn Redden PROPRIETORS: Timothy Lloyd and Robert Wilson OPEN: all week 12 to 2.30, 7 to 10.30 MEALS: Set L £13.95 (2 courses) to £15.95, Set D £21.95 (2 courses) to £24.95 SERVICE: not inc CARDS: Amex, Delta, Diners, MasterCard, Switch, Visa DETAILS: 42 seats. Private parties: 22 main room, 8 to 22 private rooms. Vegetarian meals. Children welcome. No smoking in dining-room. Music

CLANFIELD Oxfordshire map 2

Clanfield Tavern £

NEW ENTRY

Brampton Road, Clanfield OX18 2RG
TEL: (01367) 810223 COOKING 1
on A4095 Witney to Farringdon road COST £20–£39

Built in 1610, the pub is one of two in this pretty, creeper-clad village of warm stone. One look at the dramatic conservatory, though, tells you it has aspirations beyond beer and ploughman's: banners hang from the canopy, Italian tiles cover the floor, and brightly coloured fabrics are thrown on to wrought-iron chairs, making it feel 'inviting and theatrical'. The food tries to keep everybody happy with old-fashioned deep-fried Brie parcels, grilled steaks and a home-made burger, but a blackboard of specials, hoiked over to the table for inspection, is where the real interest lies. From it might come prawn beignets in sweet-and-sour sauce, haunch of venison, or a fricassee of monkfish and halibut in a velouté sauce surrounding a timbale of 'perfectly cooked' rice. 'Honest and direct' treatment is what sets the food apart. To finish, 'unexpectedly successful' butterscotch and toffee ice-cream wrapped in a filo parcel and deep-fried was dubbed 'the '90s version of baked Alaska' by one visitor. Twenty-plus wines are commendably priced, starting at £8.50 (£1.95 a glass).

CHEF: Andron Ingle PROPRIETOR: Keith Gill OPEN: all week 11.30 to 2, 6 (7 Sun) to 10 MEALS: alc (main courses £7 to £13.50) SERVICE: not inc CARDS: Delta, Diners, MasterCard, Switch, Visa DETAILS: 130 seats. 50 seats outside. Private parties: 70 main room, 18 and 70 private rooms. Car park. Vegetarian meals. Children's helpings. No smoking in 1 dining-room. Wheelchair access (also WC). No music

CLAYGATE Surrey map 3

Le Petit Pierrot

4 The Parade, Claygate KT10 0NU COOKING 2
TEL: (01372) 465105 FAX: (01372) 467642 COST £26–£44

'Very much in the style of a French provincial restaurant in a parade of shops' accurately sums up Jean-Pierre and Annie Brichot's much-loved little establishment. She looks after front-of-house in true Gallic fashion with hugs and lots of 'kisses in the air'; it is all very good-natured and polite. The cooking remains excellent value for money, particularly if you look in for lunch. Expect the likes of baked-to-order tomato and aubergine tart with pesto, pan-fried fillet of Scotch beef with grapes and a red wine sauce, and roast rack of lamb with a green peppercorn crust. Desserts fly the tricolour with gâteau Saint-Honoré, oeufs à la neige and so forth, while the wine list 'demonstrates cultural faithfulness' with a good spread from the French regions. House wine is £9.75.

CHEF: Jean-Pierre Brichot PROPRIETORS: Jean-Pierre and Annie Brichot OPEN: Mon to Fri L 12.15 to 2.15, Mon to Sat D 7.15 to 9.30 CLOSED: 1 week Christmas, bank hols MEALS: Set L £10.75 (2 courses) to £18.75, Set D £21.75 SERVICE: not inc CARDS: Amex, Diners, MasterCard, Visa DETAILS: 32 seats. Private parties: 32 main room. No children under 8. No cigars/pipes in dining-room. Wheelchair access (no WC). Music. Air-conditioned

CLITHEROE Lancashire map 8

Auctioneer

New Market Street, Clitheroe BB7 2JW COOKING 4
TEL/FAX: (01200) 427153 COST £17–£40

A couple who ate in the verandah room at the Van Heumens' popular Lancashire restaurant on a bleak midwinter's day found it as comforting as they could have wished. Henk Van Heumen still specialises in finding new and untried cuisines (untried, at least, in Clitheroe) with which to regale his loyal supporters, so spring lamb samosas with peach chutney have enhanced the repertoire this year, as have cassoulet and osso buco Milanese. The mainstream menus have produced good things too, such as prawn and crabmeat timbale, and a crisp-crusted individual Bowland game pie that brought together duck, hare, guinea-fowl and venison in an impressive stock. Chocolate praline flan, and Amaretto cheesecake made with mascarpone provide alternatives to the farmhouse cheese selection that usually includes exemplary Lancashire. Service is both capable and friendly, and Henk himself has been known to emerge from the kitchen for an end-of-sitting chat. The brisk international wine list offers a breadth of choice at reasonable prices, opening with a slate of French, Italian and American house wines at £11.

CHEF: Henk Van Heumen PROPRIETORS: Henk and Frances Van Heumen OPEN: Tue to Sun 12 to 1.30, 7 to 9 (9.30 Sat) MEALS: alc L Tue to Sat (main courses £7.50 to £11). Set L Tue to Sat £7.95 (2 courses) to £9.95, Set L Sun £13.75, Set D £18.75 (2 courses, not available Sat) to £21.75 SERVICE: not inc CARDS: Amex, Delta, MasterCard, Switch, Visa DETAILS: 48 seats. Private parties: 24 main room, 24 private rooms. Vegetarian meals. Children's helpings. No smoking in 1 dining-room. Music

COCKERMOUTH Cumbria map 10

Quince & Medlar £

13 Castlegate, Cockermouth CA13 9EU — COOKING 1
TEL: (01900) 823579 — COST £21–£27

'Two old fruits inspired the name of this restaurant,' write the owners, conscious of the Georgian origins of their listed building near Cockermouth Castle. The vegetarian ethic is pursued with commendable zeal, attracting some far-flung custom: a 250-mile round trip for one reporter who felt it well worth the effort. While many others look to simple chargrilled Italian vegetables for inspiration, the Le Vois concentrate on a busier style: perhaps globe artichokes cooked in white wine and cream, bound with eggs and cheese, then baked in a bulgar wheat crust, and served with watercress sauce and a selection of fresh vegetables. They ring the changes with cheese gnocchi, buckwheat pancakes, or a nostalgic 'nutty nest' with madeira sauce, finishing perhaps with butterscotch tart, baked honey cream flan, or bread-and-butter pudding. A few organic wines feature among the three dozen simple and fairly priced bottles from around the world. House wine is £6.80.

CHEFS/PROPRIETORS: Colin and Louisa Le Voi OPEN: Tue to Sun D only 7 to 9.30 CLOSED: 1 week Nov, 24 to 26 Dec, 2 weeks mid-Jan, Sun winter MEALS: alc (main courses £8 to £9) SERVICE: not inc, card slips closed CARDS: MasterCard, Visa DETAILS: 26 seats. Private parties: 14 main room. Vegetarian meals. No children under 6. No smoking in dining-room. Music

All details are as accurate as possible at the time of going to press, but chefs and owners often change, and it is wise to check by telephone before making a special journey. Many readers have been disappointed when set-price bargain meals are no longer available. Ask when booking.

COLCHESTER Essex map 3

Warehouse Brasserie £

12 Chapel Street North, Colchester CO2 7AT COOKING 3
TEL: (01206) 765656 FAX: (01206) 560048 COST £19–£37

'A sense of happy energy' defines the mood in this unadorned yet vibrant brasserie in an anonymous Colchester side street. Another asset is the clear value for money. In a setting of primary colours, mirrors, and dining areas on different levels, people come to chat and eat. Service is on the ball: 'if it copes with a party of ten, it passes; this passed with credit,' noted one reporter, adding that the efficient staff were overseen by a front-of-house French lady of great 'charm and calm'. The owners now have 'three brilliant new suppliers' who provide organic vegetables and herbs as well as organic beef and lamb from rare breeds. Subtle sauces, excellent vegetables and touches of ambition are what impress, and the kitchen shows its mettle with home-made wild mushroom ravioli, navarin of lamb, fillet of sea bass stuffed with spring onions and ginger, and venison sausages with bubble and squeak. Desserts, such as rhubarb crumble tartlet and white chocolate and strawberry marquise, are in similar vein. The wine list is a global slate organised by style; wines of the month are worth considering. House wine is £8.95.

CHEFS: Anthony Brooks, Mark Burley, Cheryl Hilham and Paul James PROPRIETORS: Anthony Brooks and Mel Burley OPEN: all week L 12 to 2, Mon to Sat D 7 to 10, pre- and post-theatre D by arrangement CLOSED: Christmas, bank hols MEALS: alc (main courses £7 to £12). Set L £8.95 (2 courses) to £10.95 SERVICE: not inc, card slips closed CARDS: Amex, Delta, Diners, MasterCard, Switch, Visa DETAILS: 80 seats. Private parties: 110 main room. Vegetarian meals. Children's helpings. No smoking in 1 dining-room. Wheelchair access (also WC). No music. Air-conditioned

COOKHAM Berkshire map 3

Alfonso's

19–21 Station Hill Parade, Cookham SL6 9BR COOKING 3
TEL: (01628) 525775 COST £28–£42

Everyone agrees the Baenas are out to please, and the general consensus is that they succeed. Their small restaurant in an unpromising parade of shops is comfortable and fastidiously furnished. The 'modern English, classic French' cooking often relies on the Mediterranean, pairing meats and fish with Puy lentils, herbed olive oil, pesto, salsa verde, black olives, oven-dried tomatoes and the like. It might dip into the Far East, as in chicken with lemon grass, ginger, soya and sesame, or indulge in a flight of fancy: leeks 'fragranced with truffle dressing', perhaps, or a casserole of scallops and prawns in a chamomile cream. A good tart of Mediterranean vegetables, and poached salmon in red wine sauce – 'a real gourmet choice' – have been cited as successful dishes. One reporter, who complimented the presentation of dishes, singled out a 'dreamy' nougat in chocolate sauce as a good example of the mostly calorific desserts. Another appreciated being greeted like a long-lost friend. Just under fifty wines are strong on Spain, the owners' country of origin. House French is £8.95.

CHEF: Richard Manzano PROPRIETORS: Mr and Mrs Alfonso Baena OPEN: Mon to Fri L 12.30 to 2, Mon to Sat D 7 to 10 CLOSED: 2 weeks Aug, bank hols MEALS: Set L £7.50 (2 courses) to £19.50, Set D £19.50 SERVICE: not inc CARDS: Amex, Delta, Diners, MasterCard, Visa DETAILS: 34 seats. Private parties: 34 main room. Car park. Children's helpings. Wheelchair access (no WC). Music. Air-conditioned

COPPULL MOOR Lancashire map 8

Coppull Moor

311 Preston Road, Coppull Moor PR7 5DU COOKING **1**
TEL: (01257) 792222 FAX: (01257) 793666 COST **£25–£42**

Expansion continues at this roadside halt on the A49 – last year it was the kitchen, in 1998 it will probably be the lounge – all in the service of elaborate five- and six-course dinners. The menu talks up the dishes and leaves little to the imagination, as in 'a ravioli of oak-smoked fish and sweet braised leeks served with aromatic steamed mussels and accompanied by a white wine and chive sauce with a garnish of buttered asparagus tips', for example. In essence, though, combinations generally run along familiar lines – lamb with rosemary and garlic, or pork with apple sauce – and the six vegetables have included mashed carrots with coriander, and beetroot glazed with sherry. Main courses and desserts typically offer a choice of five items, the latter perhaps including rhubarb and apple crumble, or rice-pudding with nutmeg and Cointreau. Bottled water is free, and any of the 80-plus wines on the list can be ordered by the glass, a gesture unmatched anywhere in the *Guide*. Prices start at £12.

CHEF/PROPRIETOR: Barry J. Rea OPEN: Sun brunch 11.30 for 12 (1 sitting), Tue to Sun D 8 for 8.30 (1 sitting) MEALS: Set brunch Sun £18.50, Set D £26.50 to £28.50 SERVICE: none, card slips closed CARD: Amex DETAILS: 26 seats. Private parties: 14 main room, 12 and 14 private rooms. Car park. Vegetarian meals. No children under 14. No smoking in dining-room. Wheelchair access (no WC). Music

CORSCOMBE Dorset map 2

Fox Inn £

Corscombe DT2 0NS
TEL/FAX: (01935) 891330 COOKING **2**
off A356, 6m SE of Crewkerne COST **£18–£37**

As quiet rural surroundings go, these are hard to beat: 'woods, fields, bird-song, a stream, that's it.' The stone-built, flower-bedecked thatched inn has no fruit machines and 'nothing plastic' (except credit cards this year). Instead it has a slate-topped bar, copper pans and much blue gingham. 'It will always be a pub,' writes owner Martyn Lee, who appears genuinely friendly and chatty, and the menu deals appropriately in such staples as half a pint of prawns, and sirloin steaks. But that is only half the story. A blackboard offers more ambitious items: warm salad of pigeon breast, perhaps, grilled turbot in chanterelle sauce, or braised local rabbit with mustard. Materials are good, and seafood (from West Bay) gets varied treatment, from Cajun crab to Kerala-style fish curry, to just-cooked scallops with stir-fried vegetables and a rich winey sauce. Puddings are in 'British comfort' mould (banoffi pie, clotted cream in meringues), and the place is well staffed. Choose a real ale, or a wine from the short, sensibly priced list. House wines are £9.

CHEFS: Will Longman and Richard Hartley PROPRIETOR: Martyn Lee OPEN: all week 12 to 2, 7 to 9 (9.30 Fri and Sat) CLOSED: 25 Dec D MEALS: alc (main courses £4.50 to £13). BYO £5 SERVICE: not inc, card slips closed CARDS: MasterCard, Switch, Visa DETAILS: 65 seats. 35 seats outside. Private parties: 20 main room, 20 private room. Car park. Vegetarian meals. Children welcome. Wheelchair access (no WC). No music

CORSE LAWN Gloucestershire map 2

▲ *Corse Lawn House* 

Corse Lawn GL19 4LZ
TEL: (01452) 780771 FAX: (01452) 780840 COOKING **5**
on B4211, 5m SW of Tewkesbury COST £27–£59

'We sat outside by the duck pond watching the semi-wildlife,' began one summer report, touching on the pastoral appeal of this roadside halt. The Hines celebrate 20 years at Corse Lawn in 1998, and their enthusiasm appears to be undimmed. They are refurbishing the 250-year-old building 'as fast as the pennies allow', and still maintain a high standard of cooking whatever the day or time: 'reliability such as this is to be treasured,' noted one observer.

The active kitchen team continues to collect nettles, sorrel and chives to make into soup, to smoke their own mackerel, and to pursue their own version of modern Anglo-French food: hot crab sausage, mille-feuille of wild mushrooms and oxtail crépinettes with red wine and mashed potato. The repertoire moves along gently, combining old favourites with new lines such as Thai fish-cakes with coriander and seaweed, or spiced pork with lime leaves.

Vegetables have been described as 'hit and miss', but desserts are a strong point: crème brûlée perhaps, or blackberry tart with elderberry ice-cream. Service is 'efficient and polite', although a couple who stayed a week would have preferred a more personal touch, given that the place is family-run. Prices can seem high, but the Bistro (set with gingham cloths, French café style) runs on main courses of less than £10. The wine list offers an impressive selection of French golden oldies plus some New World gems, and the generous collection of half-bottles includes some dry sherries from Lustau. House vins de pays are £9.95 a bottle (£2.20 a glass). CELLARMAN'S CHOICE: Mâcon-Cruzille la Croix 1992, Guillot-Broux £13.50; Bordeaux Supérieur, Ch. de Reignac 1990, £19.80.

CHEFS: Baba Hine and Tim Earley PROPRIETORS: the Hine family OPEN: all week 12 to 2, 7 to 10 MEALS: alc (main courses £16 to £20). Set L Mon to Sat £14.95 (2 courses) to £16.95, Set L Sun £17.95, Set D £24.50. Bistro food available SERVICE: not inc, card slips closed CARDS: Amex, Delta, Diners, MasterCard, Visa DETAILS: 50 seats. 40 seats outside. Private parties: 80 main room, 18 and 36 private rooms. Car park. Vegetarian meals. Children's helpings. No smoking in dining-room. Wheelchair access (also WC). No music ACCOMMODATION: 19 rooms, all with bath/shower. TV. Phone. B&B £75 to £100. Rooms for disabled. Children welcome. Baby facilities. No dogs in public rooms. Afternoon teas. Garden. Swimming-pool (*The Which? Hotel Guide*)

CROSTHWAITE Cumbria map 8

▲ *Punch Bowl* £

Crosthwaite LA8 8HR COOKING 4
TEL: (01539) 568237 FAX: (01539) 568875 COST £18–£32

'Immensely popular and rightly so' sums up the view of this sixteenth-century coaching-inn that sits at the upper end of the pretty Lyth Valley. The informal, no-trimmings atmosphere is very like that of a pub, but by minimising the bar, having a reception desk and providing waitress service it clearly aspires to restaurant status. With Steven Doherty's competent and even adventurous cooking, it meets its aims, and most reports mention remarkable value for money.

A well-balanced tomato and basil soup found favour with an inspector, as did roasted tuna steak with sesame seeds. There have been favourable comments, too, about gravlax with blinis and cucumber relish, 'excellent and proper' French onion soup, lamb fillet in a light curry sauce, and braised oxtail with red wine gravy and herb dumplings. Desserts might include apple feuilleté with 'a welcoming taste of calvados in the almond cream', or 'real' tarte Tatin. Service is 'no-frills' and 'friendly'. The 20-strong wine list is as gently priced as the food, with house French at £12 a litre.

CHEFS: Steven Doherty and Duncan Collinge PROPRIETORS: Steven and Marjorie Doherty, Alan Bell and Lionel Yates OPEN: all week 12 to 2, 6 to 9 CLOSED: 25 Dec MEALS: alc Mon to Sat (main courses £7 to £9). Set L and D Sun £9.25 (2 courses) to £11.25. BYO (no corkage) SERVICE: not inc, card slips closed CARDS: Delta, MasterCard, Switch, Visa DETAILS: 80 seats. 20 seats outside. Private parties: 20 main room. Car park. Children's helpings. No smoking in 1 dining-room. No music. Air-conditioned ACCOMMODATION: 3 rooms, all with bath/shower. TV. B&B £35 to £50. Deposit: £10. Children welcome

CRUDWELL Wiltshire map 2

▲ *Crudwell Court*

Crudwell, nr Malmesbury SN16 9EP
TEL: (01666) 577194 FAX: (01666) 577853 COOKING 3
on A429, 3m N of Malmesbury COST £19–£46

'On a cold, windy, rainy November Sunday it was nice to sit by the fire in the lounge,' wrote one visitor, who was left to imagine what the three acres of walled garden might look like in spring and summer. The seventeenth-century Cotswold rectory is a relaxing place, attracting reporters for its value, especially at lunch-time. The food – 'good without being original', according to one – adopts a straightforwardly traditional approach in chicken breast with orange and kumquat sauce, or salmon 'cooked so it was still juicy' in a chervil and white wine sauce.

Although some items, such as soft herring roes in a creamy tarragon sauce, or pork with mustard sauce, appear pretty regularly, menus maintain a good balance of fish, meat, game and vegetable options, and the country-style repertoire might run from leek and potato soup to roast saddle of rabbit to rose-water ice-cream. A regular endorses guinea-fowl and lambs' liver, another praises the cheese and biscuits, which are left on the table for people to help themselves. Wines reflect the great diversity now available to drinkers. Diners are urged to experiment with some of the New World varietals, though the Old World classics make a strong case for immutability. Australian and French house wines are £9.75 a bottle (£2.75 for a large glass), while the Joly Brut house champagne is a tempting £23.50 a bottle (£4.25 a flute). CELLARMAN'S CHOICE: Crozes-Hermitage, Mule Blanche 1993, Paul Jaboulet, £14.25; Fleurie 1994, André Colonge et Fils, £17.

CHEF: Chris Amor PROPRIETOR: Nick Bristow OPEN: all week 12 to 2, 7.30 to 9.30 MEALS: Set L Mon to Sat £7.50 (2 courses) to £10.45, Set L Sun £11.50, Set D £19.50 SERVICE: not inc, card slips closed CARDS: Amex, Delta, Diners, MasterCard, Switch, Visa DETAILS: 90 seats. Private parties: 50 main room, 30 private room. Car park. Vegetarian meals. Children's helpings. No smoking in dining-room. Wheelchair access (also WC). Music ACCOMMODATION: 15 rooms, all with bath/shower. TV. Phone. B&B £45 to £114. Children welcome. Baby facilities. Dogs welcome in bedrooms only. Afternoon teas. Garden. Swimming-pool (*The Which? Hotel Guide*)

CUMNOR Oxfordshire map 2

OXFORDSHIRE 1998 FISH

Bear & Ragged Staff £

Appleton Road, Cumnor OX2 9QH COOKING 2
TEL: (01865) 862329 FAX: (01865) 865366 COST £24–£48

The setting is a quintessential English country pub in a well-heeled village complete with a duck pond, and inside is all you might expect, right down to the oak beams, open fireplaces and flagstones in the bar. Bruce Buchan has made a name for himself with vibrant modern fish cookery and his short menu is in tune with the times: fried Cornish squid is served with aïoli and sun-dried tomatoes, fillet of salmon comes with pike soufflé and crayfish sauce, while whole roast baby sea bass is cooked with lardons and chickpeas. Lovers of meat and game will not be disappointed either: saddle of hare with its sweet-and-sour confit, and fillet of beef with onion and Gruyère tart are typical. Puddings have been ecstatically received of late – the assiette of chocolate desserts is a feature, otherwise you might find bread-and-butter pudding, or poached vanilla pear with almond ice-cream. The dependable wine list always includes up to ten house selections by the glass, including a 'sensational' Chilean Merlot. Prices start at £9.50.

CHEF: Bruce Buchan PROPRIETORS: Bruce and Kay Buchan OPEN: all week 12 to 2.15, 7 to 10 MEALS: alc (main courses £8 to £15.50). Set L Mon to Sat £14.95, Set L Sun £8.95 (1 course) to £14.95. BYO £3.50 SERVICE: card slips closed CARDS: Amex, Delta, Diners, MasterCard, Switch, Visa DETAILS: 60 seats. Private parties: 45 main room. Car park. Vegetarian meals. Children's helpings. No smoking in 1 dining-room. Wheelchair access (also WC). Music

£ *indicates that it is possible to have a three-course meal, including coffee, a half-bottle of house wine and service, at any time the restaurant is open (i.e. at dinner as well as at lunch, unless a place is open only for dinner), for £25 or less per person.*

DARLINGTON Co Durham map 10

Cottage Thai £

94–96 Parkgate, Darlington DL1 3RX COOKING 1
TEL: (01325) 361717 COST £12–£39

The charming modesty of small family-run Thai restaurants shows here in the ethnic décor and ambience, including Kan Tok seating at low tables. The menu of around 75 dishes is short by Thai standards, and an enthusiasm for duck is obvious from the 'chef's specials': three out of five are variations on roast duck. Salads, another Thai speciality, include larb (finely chopped chicken and pork in a hotly spiced dressing), and yum woon sen (or jelly vermicelli, which sounds even better under its alternative name, 'glass noodles'), which comes with minced pork and prawns. House French is £7.95, or perhaps choose Thai Singha Beer.

CHEF/PROPRIETOR: Malinee Burachati OPEN: Mon and Wed to Sat L 12 to 1.45, Mon to Sat D 6.30 to 10.15 CLOSED: first 2 weeks Aug MEALS: alc (main courses £6 to £9). Set L £6.25 (2 courses), Set D £14.95 SERVICE: not inc CARDS: Amex, Delta, MasterCard, Switch, Visa DETAILS: 50 seats. Private parties: 50 main room. Vegetarian meals. Children's helpings. Wheelchair access (also WC)

DARTMOUTH Devon map 1

Aragua 🍷 NEW ENTRY

St Saviours Square, Dartmouth TQ6 9DH COOKING 2
TEL/FAX: (01803) 832224 COST £23–£48

The 'Hispanic splash of primary colours' works well in a spacious Victorian auction room with cast iron pillars and iron chairs at well-spaced tables. This harmony echoes that of the rarely ruffled Anglo-Venezuelan family who cook and serve there. 'They are very nice people who have created a different and refreshing Latin American environment.' Acknowledged influences on their cooking include Africa and Spain, as one might expect, but also the USA, Italy and England. Only the proximity of Venezuela to Russia can explain the stone-ground cornmeal pancake with crème fraîche and smoked salmon (caviare an optional extra), a dish which is the one constant on the frequently changed short menus. Set lunches offer two choices per course, the à la carte four or five. One reporter thought the cooking could do with a bit more oomph, although he exempted rice with shredded coconut and chilli from the charge of under-seasoning.

The small but perfectly formed wine list includes a baker's dozen of fine wines from Latin America, ably supported by some choice bins from Spain, France, California and Australia. Four house wines change on a weekly basis and may include, for example, a crisp Galician white at £8.50 to complement the coastal flavours of the food. CELLARMAN'S CHOICE: Mont Gras Sauvignon Blanc 1995, Colchagua, Chile, £13.50; Bodega y Cavas de Weinert Malbec 1991, Mendoza, Argentina, £15.

CHEFS: Franz and Elizabeth Conde PROPRIETORS: Patricia Thomas, and Franz and Elizabeth Conde OPEN: Fri to Sun L 12 to 2, Wed to Sat D 7 to 9 (9.30 summer); open Mon and Tues D summer CLOSED: last 2 weeks Oct, last 2 weeks March MEALS: alc (main courses L £5.50 to £12.50, D £11 to £16.50). Set L (2 courses) £13.50 SERVICE: net prices, card slips closed CARDS: Delta, Diners, MasterCard, Switch, Visa DETAILS: 29 seats. Private parties: 29 main room. Car park. Children's helpings. No smoking while others eat. Music

Billy Budd's

7 Foss Street, Dartmouth TQ6 9DW — COOKING 1
TEL/FAX: (01803) 834842 — COST £16–£39

Pedestrianised Foss Street in the heart of Dartmouth dates back seven centuries, though this one-roomed bistro is more recent. 'Jolly' and 'unpretentious' sum up the feel of pine tables, paper napkins and 'happy and willing service'. At its best, Keith Belt's cooking is enticing. Camembert fritters are alive and well, served with mango chutney, and the coarse-textured terrine of pork and chicken comes with 'an excellent onion confiture'. Breezy lunchtime specials – a giant banger with mash and vegetables perhaps – eke out the soups, baked potatoes and omelettes, but dinner is when they bring on the fillet steak, piled high with mushrooms, or roast duck with plum and cherry sauce. Fish is a strength – a Brixham fish casserole maybe – and blackboard puddings have included a creamy chocolate and Cointreau pot, and bread-and-butter pudding that was judged 'the genuine article'. Two dozen varied and fairly priced wines begin with simple house Australian at £9.50.

CHEF: Keith Belt PROPRIETORS: Keith and Lynne Belt OPEN: Tue to Sat 12 to 2, 7.00 to 10 CLOSED: 1 week Nov, 4 weeks Jan to Feb MEALS: alc (main courses L £3.50 to £6, D £10 to £14) SERVICE: not inc, card slips closed CARDS: MasterCard, Switch, Visa DETAILS: 35 seats. Private parties: 20 main room. Vegetarian meals. Children's helpings. No cigars/pipes in dining-room. Wheelchair access (no WC). Music

Carved Angel

2 South Embankment, Dartmouth TQ6 9BH — COOKING 7
TEL: (01803) 832465 FAX: (01803) 835141 — COST £38–£63

The ship's figurehead presides benignly over this light, bright dining-room, its large window framed by the distinctive Tudor frontage. There may be bustle in the open-plan kitchen, and out front by the harbour, but the room itself is made for 'instant relaxation'. Reporters are, as ever, divided. Some wonder if it is resting on its laurels, while others treasure it. 'I don't want it ever to change.' If there is a rule of thumb, it is that long-standing reporters are most willing to forgive a few foibles.

The package can appear stark. There is no ostentatious lounge full of comfortable sofas, service may be distant rather than warm, ingredients and dishes can be remarkably normal, even humble – brawn with toast, rather than foie gras with brioche – and you may have to pour your own wine. All this simply indicates that attention is focused where it should be: raw materials are of good quality, techniques are sound, and tastes and textures are properly considered.

Despite some contemporary 'crossover' dishes (such as smoked haddock wun-tun with guacamole and coriander mayonnaise), the kitchen's heart is in the French provinces, in a mixed fish and vegetable bourride with aïoli, for example. It also has a clear-cut idea of what a dish is all about. Salmon in puff pastry with ginger and sultanas is not exactly modern, but the fish is accurately cooked, the pastry is 'perfectly made', and the elements are well balanced: so it works.

It is worth remembering that the set-price meal includes mineral water, coffee with petits-fours, and service, while the *carte* offers a generous choice that has included 'wonderful' chicken livers in madeira sauce, goujons of skate with a 'brilliant' dressing of cucumber, yogurt and dill, or a densely flavoured lobster soup with lime and coconut, served with thin lobster sesame toasts. Among desserts that have pleased are iced nougatine with strawberry sauce, pineapple fritters with kirsch ice-cream, and a rich, eggy quince brûlée. Meals begin with good olives and cheese straws, and end with 'excellent home-made petits-fours'.

Wines are a well-chosen collection of high-quality French bins supported by some superb offerings from the New World, Italy and Spain. Their appeal is enhanced by reasonable prices (and some bargain bin-ends) plus a selection of sherries, madeiras, ports and Rutherglen Liqueur Muscats available by the glass between £3.75 and £7. Half a dozen house wines are £15 a bottle, £3 a glass. CELLARMAN'S CHOICE: Wairau River Chardonnay 1992, Marlborough, New Zealand, £24; Vacqueyras 1992, Dom. Le Sang de Cailloux, S. Ferigoule et F. Aymard, £16.

CHEFS: Nick Coiley and Joyce Molyneux PROPRIETORS: Joyce Molyneux, Nick Coiley, Meriel Matthews and Zoë Wynne OPEN: Tue to Sun L 12.30 to 2.30, Tue to Sat D 7 to 9.30 CLOSED: 5 days Christmas, 6 weeks from 1 Jan MEALS: alc L (main courses £18 to £26). Set L Tue to Sat £15 (2 courses) to £30, Set L Sun £38, Set D £28 (1 course) to £48. BYO £2.50 SERVICE: net prices, card slips closed CARDS: Delta, MasterCard, Switch, Visa (2% surcharge for MasterCard and Visa) DETAILS: 50 seats. Private parties: 40 main room, 16 and 18 private rooms. Vegetarian meals. Children's helpings. No smoking in dining-room. No music

Cutter's Bunch

NEW ENTRY

33 Lower Street, Dartmouth TQ6 9AN — COOKING 2

TEL: (01803) 832882 — COST £27–£44

Nick and Jo Crosley's small bistro, directly behind the Yacht Club, is immensely jolly, with local artists' paintings, photos of boats, and varnished blond-wood tables set with basic crockery and cutlery. Nick Crosley's repertoire is more elaborate, reflecting flavours experienced on his travels. There might be Thai seafood pot, duck Jamaican-style, Moroccan-style baby chicken, or prawn sambal with Malaysian flat bread. Those with less adventurous palates might opt for rack of lamb with mint béarnaise, or plain fillet steak. Cooking skills as well as wanderlust were evident in duck confit with Thai accents. Other good dishes have included 'fresh, tender and firm' sea bass roasted in balsamic vinegar with asparagus, and lobster given a lift by a light calvados cream sauce. Desserts might be 'ambrosial' sticky toffee pudding or chocolate hazelnut meringue cake. Service is 'effective and intelligent'. The wine list is short and worldly, but mostly omits producers and years, which makes choosing difficult. House wines start at £9.85.

CHEF: Nick Crosley PROPRIETORS: Nick and Jo Crosley OPEN: Thu to Mon (and Tue July and Aug) D only 7 to 10 CLOSED: 25 and 26 Dec MEALS: alc (main courses £12.50 to £18). BYO £5 SERVICE: not inc, card slips closed CARDS: MasterCard, Switch, Visa DETAILS: 28 seats. Private parties: 30 main room. Children's helpings. No pipes in dining room. No cigars while others eat. Music

DEDDINGTON Oxfordshire map 5

Dexter's

Market Place, Deddington OX15 0SE COOKING 4
TEL: (01869) 338813 COST £22–£51

Fourteen sessions a week is a lot for any catering operation, but represents a particularly determined effort in a place the size of Deddington. Situated just outside Banbury, Dexter's is the ambitious vision of its eponymous owner-chef whose cooking style is as varied as the jumble of furniture in the 'friendly-custard-yellow' dining-room.

Red mullet is grilled and served in a salad dressed with lime and coriander, while fillet of sea bass is given the popular oriental treatment of noodles, spring onions and soy. 'Quite unpretentious, well prepared and stylishly presented' was one reporter's description of a meal of field mushrooms on pesto-flavoured toast, followed by braised duck legs with parsleyed mash and red wine sauce. As to the more obviously English desserts, bread-and-butter pudding has been found 'a touch on the solid side', but a gently citric lemon tart was deemed 'beautifully judged'. While it can feel a little cramped at busy sittings, Dexter's is none the less 'competently and charmingly run'. Fairly priced wines extend from Italian Verdicchio to Barossa Shiraz, with house Argentinian at £9.50.

CHEF/PROPRIETOR: Jamie Dexter Harrison OPEN: all week 12 to 2.15 (2.30 Sun), 7 to 9.15 (10 Sat) MEALS: alc Mon to Sat L, all week D (main courses L £7 to £8.50, D £9 to £16.50). Set L Mon to Sat £10.50 (2 courses) to £14, Set L Sun £13.50, Set D all week £16.95 (2 courses) to £19.95 SERVICE: not inc, card slips closed; 10% for parties of 8 or more CARDS: Delta, MasterCard, Switch, Visa DETAILS: 34 seats. Private parties: 45 main room. Vegetarian meals. Children's helpings. No cigars/pipes in dining-room. Wheelchair access (no WC). Music

DEDHAM Essex map 6

▲ *Fountain House* 🍷 £✗

Dedham Hall, Brook Street, Dedham CO7 6AD COOKING 1
TEL: (01206) 323027 FAX: (01206) 323293 COST £25–£32

'This could be nowhere else in the world but England,' mused a reporter after driving up one April evening, daffodils everywhere, to this enchantingly situated restaurant/guesthouse in six acres of Constable country. Simplicity and straightforward cooking is the house style and the kitchen offers an uncontroversial fixed-price dinner menu that could kick off with heaps of fresh asparagus with lemon butter, stuffed mushrooms, or smoked salmon rolls with prawns. Main courses such as Normandy pork fillet, pan-fried chicken livers with bacon, or baked salmon with parsley butter come with a large dish of fresh unadorned vegetables, while the extensive sweet menu promises such things as strawberry vacherin. Wines are cleverly chosen and helpfully grouped by variety/style. Pricing is reasonable, the range of half-bottles generous and the bin-ends are very tempting. Nine house wines – all French – start at £8.50. CELLARMAN'S CHOICE: Alan Scott Sauvignon Blanc 1996, Marlborough, New Zealand, £17; Bourgogne Rouge 1994, Dom. Mongeard Mugneret, £17.50.

CHEF: Wendy Sarton PROPRIETORS: James and Wendy Sarton OPEN: 12 to 1.45, 7 to 9.30 CLOSED: 25 Dec, Easter Sun MEALS: Set L £17.50, Set D £19.50 SERVICE: not inc, card slips closed CARDS: Delta, MasterCard, Switch, Visa DETAILS: 45 seats. Private parties: 50 main room. Car park. Vegetarian meals. Children's helpings. No smoking in dining-room. Wheelchair access (also women's WC). Music ACCOMMODATION: 6 rooms, all with bath/shower. TV. B&B £35 to £60. Children welcome. Baby facilities. Garden

▲ *Le Talbooth*

Gun Hill, Dedham CO7 6HP
TEL: (01206) 323150 FAX: (01206) 322309 COOKING 4
on B1029, off A12, 6m NE of Colchester COST £28–£69

Impressions get off to a good start, with a picture-postcard setting of manicured gardens, a half-timbered building with leaded lights, and views over the river, all backed up by sympathetic modernisation inside. The combination of a *carte* and a weekly-changing fixed-price menu for both lunch and dinner is worthy of note, and certainly gives the kitchen lots to do. You might well come across kedgeree, air-cured bresaola, potted shrimps, or sage-smoked duck with pease pudding to begin, with hot banana soufflé or baked Alaska to finish. In between might be 'creamy, buttery scallops' or 'gently gamey, succulent venison', and a rotating daily lunchtime roast: honey-roast ham on Mondays, beef Thursdays and turkey Fridays. Some praise Le Talbooth to the skies, while for others the combination of inconsistent cooking, long waits and high prices has led to some steamy correspondence.

Many of the wines on the list are sourced from award-winning wine merchants Lay & Wheeler, and quality is high. French bins tend to be expensive, but when you look at the pedigree of the Burgundy growers and Bordeaux châteaux you can see why, and you won't find any mongrels in the New World section either. The seven house wines are good value, starting at £11.50. CELLARMAN'S CHOICE: Quincy 1995, Jean-Michel Sorbe, £18.95; Optima L'Ormarins 1991, Franschhoek, South Africa, £19.50.

CHEF: Terry Barber PROPRIETORS: Gerald, Diana and Paul Milsom OPEN: all week 12 to 2, 7 to 9.30 CLOSED: Sun D in winter MEALS: alc (main courses £14 to £22.50). Set L Mon to Sat £16.50 (2 courses) to £19, Set L Sun £23.50, Set D £21 (2 courses) to £24 SERVICE: 10%, card slips closed CARDS: Amex, Delta, Diners, MasterCard, Switch, Visa DETAILS: 75 seats. 50 seats outside. Private parties: 85 main room, 35 private room. Car park. Vegetarian meals. Children's helpings. No children under 10. No smoking while others eat. Music ACCOMMODATION: 10 rooms, all with bath/shower. TV. Phone. B&B £85 to £140. Rooms for disabled. Children welcome. Garden (*The Which? Hotel Guide*)

Not inc *in the details at the end of an entry indicates that no service charge is made and any tipping is at the discretion of the customer.*

DENMEAD Hampshire map 2

Barnard's £

Hambleden Road, Denmead PO7 6NU
TEL/FAX: (01705) 257788 COOKING 2
on B2150, 2m NW of Waterlooville COST £17–£45

The unprepossessing canopied exterior and bare brick walls indicate that aesthetic appeal is not the draw here, but friendly service and David Barnard's competent classical cooking seem to ensure a regular flow of returnees. A twice-baked Swiss cheese soufflé, done to firmness and rolled in ground almonds, sits on salad leaves dressed in hazelnut vinaigrette to make a starter full of apposite flavours. Main courses favour traditional treatments such as red wine and mushrooms with fillet steak, or king prawn kebab in a Chinese marinade served with rice. The fish dish of the day at inspection was an appealingly rare – as requested – tuna steak with a creamy mustard sauce. Desserts, too, mobilise a lot of cream, whether whipped up to top marsala trifle, or served with good lemon-flavoured bread-and-butter pudding. The useful wine list does well by the southern hemisphere and keeps its prices on a reassuringly tight rein. House French is £9.

CHEF: David Barnard PROPRIETORS: David and Sandie Barnard OPEN: Tue to Fri L 12 to 1.45, Tue to Sat D 7 to 9.45 CLOSED: 1 week Christmas MEALS: alc (main courses £13.50 to £17). Set L £8.50 (2 courses) to £10, Set D £15 (2 courses) to £17.50. BYO £4 SERVICE: not inc, card slips closed CARDS: Amex, Delta, Diners, MasterCard, Switch, Visa DETAILS: 40 seats. 12 seats outside. Private parties: 34 main room, 20 and 34 private rooms. Car park. Vegetarian meals. Children's helpings. No smoking in dining-room. Music

DERBY Derbyshire map 5

Darleys

Darley Abbey Mills, Darley Abbey, Derby DE22 1DZ
TEL: (01332) 364987 FAX: (01332) 541356 COOKING 2
off A6, 2m N of Derby city centre COST £21–£48

Occupying a commanding position on a bend of the River Derwent, this single-storey former mill canteen was getting ready for a total refurbishment just as the *Guide* was going to Press. There may be 'nothing to shock the unwary' on the monthly-changing menu, but it does have ideas of its own, and ambition is kept largely within the kitchen's grasp, even if the *carte* is a generous length. It might begin with pork and apricot sausage, or smoked haddock and mussel bourride, and progress to sauté calf's liver with egg and bacon rösti, or braised partridge with brown bread mash. You need to ask to find what the chef's hot pudding and home-made desserts are. Wines favour the classic regions of France, indeed they don't stray outside Europe, but are well chosen and start at £10.

CHEFS: David Gillan and Caroline Oliver PROPRIETOR: David Pinchbeck OPEN: all week L 12 to 2 (2.30 weekends), Mon to Sat D 7 to 10 (10.30 weekends) CLOSED: bank hols MEALS: alc (main courses £10 to £18). Set L £13.50 SERVICE: not inc CARDS: Amex, Delta, Diners, MasterCard, Switch, Visa DETAILS: 80 seats. Private parties: 80 main room. Car park. Vegetarian meals. Children's helpings. No smoking in dining-room. Wheelchair access (no WC). Music. Air-conditioned

DINTON Buckinghamshire map 3

La Chouette

Westlington Green, Dinton HP17 8UW
TEL/FAX: (01296) 747422 COOKING **5**
off A418, 4m SW of Aylesbury COST £19–£59

'This restaurant is not a clone of anything,' observed one reporter, identifying its individuality straightaway. This derives from Frédéric Desmette's passion, and from his single-handed approach to menus, cooking and often service as well. If this limits the options, or involves an element of surprise – the £10 one-hour lunch is three unspecified dishes – then so be it. He operates in a former pub with regulation wooden floor, beams and low ceiling, decorated with another of his passions: 'owls every which way', from candles to paintings to photographs.

Seafood is a mainstay – scallops with chicory, lobster with leek – and he keeps things simple: sea bass with sorrel sauce, duck breast with girolles, or fillet of brill of 'excellent quality and well timed' served with morels in spring. Some might quarrel with girolles on toast at £15, but good value is the norm. 'I consider his cooking skilful,' wrote one who finished a meal with a pancake of wafer-thin apple slices flamed in calvados. When he is busy and doing everything himself, M. Desmette can become 'visibly harassed', but otherwise he is convivial and full of good humour. The French wine list (with one characterful interloper from Italy) doesn't compromise on quality, though prices tend to be high. House Cabernet Sauvignon and Chardonnay are £10.

CHEF/PROPRIETOR: Frédéric Desmette OPEN: Mon to Fri L 12 to 2, Mon to Sat D 7 to 9 MEALS: alc (main courses £10 to £15). Set L £10 to £36, Set D £26.50 to £36. BYO by arrangement SERVICE: 12.5%, card slips closed CARDS: Amex, Delta, MasterCard, Visa DETAILS: 35 seats. 12 seats outside. Private parties: 45 main room. Car park. Children's helpings. No cigars/pipes in dining-room. Music

DISS Norfolk map 6

▲ *Salisbury House*

84 Victoria Road, Diss IP22 3JG COOKING **3**
TEL/FAX: (01379) 644738 COST £21–£49

The Victorian building on the edge of Diss feels like 'an intimate country house', and covers a wide range of dishes between its restaurant and more relaxed bistro. The owners cook and oversee front of house, delivering 'friendly and informal' service and monthly-changing menus. The dining-room's set-price meal offers anything from three to five courses, along the lines of one reporter's mozzarella and tomato tart, roulade of sole with a chive sauce, and breast of pheasant with rösti and a top notch ginger sauce, followed by chocolate pudding. Some dishes in the bistro overlap, but they also take in jaunty ideas such as avocado deep-fried in beer batter, pork and chestnut sausages, or black cherry pancake. Wines are attractively varied in style and price, beginning with house Chardonnay and Syrah at £7.95.

CHEF: Barry Davies PROPRIETORS: Barry and Sue Davies OPEN: bistro and restaurant Tue to Fri L 12.15 to 1.45, Tue to Sat D 7.15 to 9.15 (booking essential for restaurant) CLOSED: 1 week Christmas, 2 weeks Summer MEALS: bistro alc (main courses £5.50 to £8.50); restaurant Set L and D £24.95 to £32.50. BYO £5 SERVICE: not inc CARDS: MasterCard, Visa DETAILS: 36 seats. 10 seats outside. Private parties: 20 main room, 20 private room. Car park. Vegetarian meals. Children's helpings. No smoking in dining-room. Wheelchair access (also WC). Music ACCOMMODATION: 3 rooms, all with bath/shower. TV. B&B £39 to £70. Deposit: £10. Rooms for disabled. Children welcome. Garden (*The Which? Hotel Guide*)

Weaver's Wine Bar & Eating House £

Market Hill, Diss IP22 3JZ — COOKING 2
TEL: (01379) 642411 — COST £19–£35

'Even though it is a round trip for us of over 220 miles, we shall go back,' write one pair of experienced reporters of the Bavins' thoroughly welcoming wine bar in the centre of this unmolested Norfolk market town. The resourceful service provided by 'a gem of a waitress' added to their enjoyment. There is an option for set-price eating as well as a *carte*, and a pleasing sense of creativity runs through both. Mussels tossed in garlic butter with white wine and cream are familiar enough, but more novel are collops of venison on a chestnut tartlet in a sauce of ginger wine. Simple lunchtime dishes, such as steak and kidney pie and brown-bread ice-cream, also receive enthusiastic notices. The pudding list tries to work its magic on those susceptible to adjectives: 'hot squidgy upside down chocolate sponge set in a pool of creamy semolina' will press all the right buttons for some. An enterprising and fairly priced wine list parades its New World offerings first. House Vins de Pays d'Oc are £9.75.

CHEF: William Bavin PROPRIETORS: William and Wilma Bavin OPEN: Tue to Fri L 12 to 1.30, Mon to Sat D 7 to 9 (9.30 Sat) CLOSED: 2 weeks Christmas, last 2 weeks Aug MEALS: alc D (main courses £9 to £13). Set L £7.95 (2 courses) to £10.75, Set D Mon to Fri £12 SERVICE: not inc, card slips closed CARDS: Delta, Diners, MasterCard, Switch, Visa DETAILS: 80 seats. Private parties: 50 main room, 50 private room. Vegetarian meals. Children's helpings. No smoking L, before 9.30 D; no cigars. Wheelchair access (no WC). Music

DORRINGTON Shropshire — map 5

▲ *Country Friends*

Dorrington SY5 7JD
TEL: (01743) 718707 — COOKING 6
on A49, 5m S of Shrewsbury — COST £35–£46

Dark earthy tones and plush settees made one reporter describe the cosy lounge at Country Friends as womb-like, but it's hardly a womb with a view, unless the A49 should inspire. The dining-room, at least, looks on to a garden with a rockery, but there's far more to divert attention in the output from the

Whittakers' industrious and imaginative kitchen. Much is made on the premises or in the close vicinity. Shropshire brown flour goes into the moist-crumbed loaves, as does a speckling of laverbread on occasion, while unapologetically salty butter is a local farmhouse product.

The culinary style is balanced carefully between the country-house idiom of Dover sole turban with spring onions and saffron sauce, and gutsier modern combinations such as thick slices of venison with a sauce of damsons and home-made damson gin. Vegetables, served separately, have also impressed and might include deep-fried breaded cauliflower, sauerkraut, and spinach mousse. Lemon tart comes as a kind of upside-down flan accompanied by a puddle of satisfyingly sharp cassis sauce. The wine list is not vast but the choices are thoughtful and prices reasonable. House wines are £10.50.

CHEF: Charles Whittaker PROPRIETORS: Charles and Pauline Whittaker OPEN: Tue to Sat 12 to 2, 7 to 9 (9.30 Sat) CLOSED: 2 weeks early July MEALS: Set L and D £23 (2 courses) to £29.50. Light L available SERVICE: not inc CARDS: Delta, MasterCard, Switch, Visa DETAILS: 45 seats. Private parties: 45 main room. Car park. Vegetarian meals. Children welcome. No smoking while others eat. Wheelchair access (no WC). No music ACCOMMODATION: 3 rooms, 1 with bath/shower. D,B&B £65 to £102. Children welcome. Garden

DREWSTEIGNTON Devon map 1

▲ *Hunts Tor* ✱

Drewsteignton EX6 6QW COOKING **3**
TEL: (01647) 281228 COST £30–£40

A nineteenth-century house with some sixteenth-century remnants, Hunts Tor is 'an honest, well-run, ambitious enterprise', presided over by 'highly dedicated amateurs'. Sober décor and small numbers (the dining-room seats only eight) make an evening feel halfway towards a dinner party. Some dishes might reinforce that impression too, while a degree of regimentation demands that dinner is served 'bang on time' (no chance for a late aperitif, as one couple found), meals need to be booked at least 24 hours in advance (no reprieve for one last-minute B&B booking), and all members of a party eat the same dishes.

A summer meal that began with Dorset air-dried ham, served with pesto-dressed chargrilled peppers and aubergines, was followed by strips of sole in a Noilly Prat sauce, strewn with sorrel from the garden, which supplies a range of salad leaves, herbs and soft fruits. 'We have just discovered a new source of excellent free-range pork,' writes Sue Harrison, who typically serves the roast fillet with mustard and tarragon. To finish, there might be 'absolutely fine' crème brûlée, or pear sablé with butterscotch sauce. Around 45 wines are carefully chosen with an eye to economy. Prices start at £10.80, though there are no wines by the glass and only three half-bottles.

CHEF: Sue Harrison PROPRIETORS: Sue and Chris Harrison OPEN: all week D only 7.30 (1 sitting; 24 hours' notice essential) CLOSED: end Oct to early Mar MEALS: Set D £20 to £23 SERVICE: not inc CARDS: none DETAILS: 8 seats. Private parties: 8 main room. Car park. No children under 10. No smoking in dining-room. Music ACCOMMODATION: 3 rooms, all with bath/shower. TV. B&B £40 to £70. Deposit: £10. Children welcome. Dogs welcome in bedrooms only

DRYBROOK **Gloucestershire** map 5

Cider Press

The Cross, Drybrook GL17 9EB
TEL: (01594) 544472

COOKING 4
COST £24–£40

The press may be long gone, but cider is still available at this rustic little restaurant on the northern edge of the Forest of Dean. Herbs are grown in the small garden, meat is free-range, but fish – wild rather than farmed – is the main business of the menu, cooked simply to highlight its quality. A lightness of touch is evident in sea bass with a Thai-style stuffing, and turbot poached with dry vermouth and fennel. Meat choices might include roast lamb with smoked aubergine and tomato ragoût, and chicken stuffed with pesto. Puddings are satisfyingly rich, although many diners succumb to the temptations of the cheeseboard – a generous selection of mainly English and Welsh varieties. The pace is leisurely, although service may buckle a little under pressure. All dishes are cooked to order, so be prepared for a wait between courses. There are plenty of bargains on the short wine list and an unusually large choice of organic wines. House wine is £8.75.

CHEF: Christopher Stephen Challener PROPRIETOR: Bernadette Fitzpatrick OPEN: Wed to Sat D only 7 to 11; L and Sun and Mon D by arrangement CLOSED: first 2 weeks Jan MEALS: alc (main courses £10.50 to £15) SERVICE: not inc CARDS: Delta, MasterCard, Visa DETAILS: 24 seats. 8 seats outside. Private parties: 28 main room. Vegetarian meals by arrangement. Children's helpings. No smoking in dining-room. Wheelchair access (also WC). Music

DURHAM **Co Durham** map 10

Bistro 21 [£]

Aykley Heads House, Aykley Heads,
Durham DH1 5PS
TEL: (0191) 384 4354 FAX: (0191) 384 1149

COOKING 4
COST £16–£39

'Durham is such a lovely city it deserves a good restaurant' was one visitor's view, and Bistro 21 certainly does the place proud. The restored seventeenth-century farmhouse with sandy ochrous walls and blue paintwork could easily double for a Mediterranean villa. Inside, a glassed walkway leads to a relaxed dining-room in light wood and pale colours. The Laybourne style (see 21 Queen Street, Newcastle, and Café 21, Ponteland) is simple and robust: deep-fried plaice with chips and tartare sauce, braised ham knuckle with lentils, or a big chunk of baked hare with carrots and mashed parsnip, for example.

Quite a few dishes manage perfectly well without meat, including a thick lentil broth with a powerful flavour of roasted cumin seeds that impressed for its 'rustic edge but carefully considered flavour'. Puddings can be as rich as chocolate truffle cake, and nutmeg ice-cream brings a strong presence to plain custard tart. Service combines professionalism with informality, and wines are dispensed intelligently, with details comprehensively checked; if you order by the glass (of which there are eight), a measure is poured then decanted into a larger glass. The list itself is a modern, varied and appealing selection of around 50 wines, beginning with House Duboeuf at £9.50. CELLARMAN'S CHOICE: Alsace Pinot Blanc 1994, Hugel et Fils, £15.80; Bandol 'Moulin des Costes' 1992, Dom. Bunan, £18.80.

CHEF: Adrian Watson PROPRIETORS: Terence and Susan Laybourne OPEN: Tue to Sat 12 to 2.30, 6 to 10.30 CLOSED: bank hols MEALS: alc (main courses L £3 to £12.50, D £7.50 to £12.50). Set L £11 (2 courses) to £13.50 SERVICE: not inc CARDS: Amex, Delta, Diners, MasterCard, Switch, Visa DETAILS: 100 seats. 24 seats outside. Private parties: 60 main room, 10 to 20 private rooms. Car park. Vegetarian meals. Children welcome. No cigars/pipes in dining-room. Wheelchair access (also WC). Music

EAST BOLDON Tyne & Wear map 10

Forsters

2 St Bedes, Station Road, East Boldon NE36 0LE
TEL: (0191) 519 0929
just off A184 Newcastle to Sunderland road, 3m NW of Sutherland

COOKING 3
COST £23–£42

Light wood, a dark carpet and a bar in the corner give this square suburban room a spruce and modern feel. Barry Forster's aim is not to dazzle with invention and brio, but to work a traditional seam of Anglo-French cooking with quiet proficiency, turning out Cheddar cheese soufflé, steak au poivre with cream, brandy and green peppercorns, and a nightcap Ovaltine ice-cream. Changing partnerships vary the repertoire: this week chargrilled chicken breast may come with Savoy cabbage, bacon and mushrooms, next time with grilled king prawns and a Thai-style curry sauce. Skills are apparent in timing and technique: for example, an accurately poached egg and accomplished tarragon-infused béarnaise sauce to accompany smoked salmon on a toasted muffin. Vegetarians need to order 48 hours in advance from a selection that takes in curried parsnip soup, mushroom risotto, pasta with pesto, blue cheese soufflé, or a variation on Caesar salad. Some 30 wines are modestly priced, starting with Duboeuf house red and white at £8.15.

CHEF: Barry Forster PROPRIETORS: Barry and Sue Forster OPEN: Tue to Sat D only 7 to 9.30 CLOSED: 1 week Sept, 10 days Christmas to New Year, 2 weeks June, bank hols MEALS: alc (main courses £13 to £14). Set D Tue to Fri £17. BYO £5 SERVICE: not inc CARDS: Amex, Diners, MasterCard, Visa DETAILS: 30 seats. Private parties: 30 main room. Car park. Children's helpings. No children under 7. No cigars/pipes in dining-room. Music

EASTBOURNE East Sussex map 3

▲ *Grand Hotel, Mirabelle*

Jevington Gardens, Eastbourne BN21 4EQ
TEL: (01323) 410771 FAX: (01323) 412233

COOKING 7
COST £26–£58

Hiding behind foliage on the seafront, the Grand is as white as meringue and awash with gentility. The Mirabelle restaurant, accessed from its own pillared portal on a side street to the right, occupies a relentlessly beige dining-room, with baby grand piano and lavishly ruched curtaining. It tries not to be too formal but somehow can't quite help it. Mark Jones has been head chef here since 1994, and his cooking style aims to marry genuine creativity with the expected trappings of corporate eating. It has been refined to an appreciable and heartening degree, using the full panoply of set-price menus and a *carte* for high rollers.

An inspection dish of smoked quail with roasted shallots and couscous was a fine balancing act, the earthiness of the grains supporting the unrestrained pungency of the meat with great panache. Sauté scallops perhaps needed something more demanding than a tangle of underseasoned ink tagliatelle to bring them into focus, but the shellfish themselves were top-notch and beautifully timed. One pair of reporters, who broke off from Christmas shopping to lunch here, were reinvigorated by a 'superb' fried skate wing on fennel and lime, and braised lamb shank with garlic mash: they thought the food 'novel and successful'. Standing out among desserts have been apple and pear charlotte with unabashedly creamy brown bread ice-cream, and a caramel bavarois with poached fruits in a rose-water sabayon. Trimmings include a sorbet before the main course, a little cup of soup to set you off, and inventive canapés, all extending the sense of value. The wine list doesn't seem to have stretched anybody's imagination. Presentation is messy, and mark-ups soon press. House French is £10.75.

CHEFS: Keith Mitchell and Mark Jones PROPRIETOR: De Vere Hotels OPEN: Tue to Sat 12.30 to 2, 7 to 10 CLOSED: first 2 weeks Jan, first 2 weeks Aug MEALS: alc (main courses £16.50 to £22.50). Set L £15.50 (2 courses) to £18.50, Set D £25 to £31 SERVICE: not inc, card slips closed CARDS: Amex, Diners, MasterCard, Visa DETAILS: 48 seats. 30 seats outside. Private parties: 48 main room, 10 to 400 private rooms. Car park. Vegetarian meals. Children's helpings. No cigars/pipes in dining-room. Music. Air-conditioned ACCOMMODATION: 164 rooms, all with bath/shower. TV. Phone. B&B £110 to £270. Rooms for disabled. Children welcome. Baby facilities. Dogs welcome in bedrooms only. Afternoon teas. Garden. Swimming-pool

---

EAST GRINSTEAD West Sussex map 3

DAY OUT 1998 FROM LONDON

▲ *Gravetye Manor*

Vowels Lane, East Grinstead RH19 4LJ
TEL: (01342) 810567 FAX: (01342) 810080
off B2028, 2m SW of East Grinstead

COOKING 7
COST £37–£93

In 1998 Peter Herbert and his family clock up 40 years at Gravetye, which means they have run this Elizabethan manor house for one-tenth of its life. William Robinson's natural English garden is the pride of the estate, although the 1,000-acre forest in which it stands is also pretty impressive. Inside, oak panelling, log fires and period furniture add to the solid, ancient feel. One reporter who had not visited for 30 years, and found 'the old place looking even more beautiful than I remembered', was pleased by the seemingly timeless excellence of the food, drink and service. A London reader who hopped on a train to Gatwick for a day out was well rewarded by a few hours in this 'magical refuge' for the city dweller.

Mark Raffan takes a thoughtful and refined approach to Franco-British cooking, serving appealing combinations of warm artichoke heart with foie gras, roast Hebridean scallops with crab-cakes, or roast calves' kidneys with a rich steak pudding. The one-acre kitchen garden supplies seasonal fruit and vegetables, game (from pigeon to local venison) is a strong suit, and salmon and venison are smoked on the premises. But this is not just industry for its own sake. Dishes are intelligently put together, flavours extend to Thai-spiced fish soup with squid ink noodles, and the gamut of dishes runs from a delicately textured pike sausage to heartier grilled calf's liver and bacon on an 'organised heap' ('galette' on the menu) of cabbage, served with a mushroom sauce. The level of skill also enables the kitchen to turn out a prune and armagnac soufflé that was 'worth every second of the 20-minute wait'. Opposition to government takes many forms; here it consists of adding VAT at 17.5 per cent to the prices quoted, as if to say 'don't blame us'. Even so, the value is considered good.

Wines merit attention for the range of classic vintages alone, but the number also offered in magnums and half-bottles makes it particularly praiseworthy. Although France dominates, fans of German whites will find much to tempt them, and Australia and New Zealand deserve an honourable mention. Please note that, again, VAT must be added to the prices. House French is £15.50. CELLARMAN'S CHOICE: Vouvray, Château Gaudrelle 1995, Monmousseau, £19; Cornas 1983, Paul Jaboulet Aîné, £26.

CHEF: Mark Raffan PROPRIETORS: Peter Herbert and family OPEN: all week 12.30 to 1.45, 7.30 to 9.30 (9.45 Sat, 8.45 Sun) CLOSED: D 25 Dec exc for residents MEALS: alc (main courses £17 to £26). Set L £24, Set D £30; all prices exclusive of VAT SERVICE: net prices, card slips closed CARDS: MasterCard, Switch, Visa DETAILS: 55 seats. Private parties: 8 main room, 16 private room. Car park. Vegetarian meals. Children's helpings. No children under 7. No smoking in dining-room. Wheelchair access (no WC). No music ACCOMMODATION: 18 rooms, all with bath/shower. TV. Phone. Room only £105 to £215; all prices exclusive of VAT. No children under 7 exc babies in arms. Baby facilities. Garden. Fishing (*The Which? Hotel Guide*)

EAST WITTON North Yorkshire map 8

▲ *Blue Lion* £

East Witton DL8 4SN
TEL: (01969) 624273 FAX: (01969) 624189
on A6108 Ripon to Leyburn road, 2m SE of Middleham

COOKING **2**
COST £25–£46

Originally a coaching-inn serving the needs of travellers on their way through Wensleydale, the Blue Lion now puts on a very different show. It's nothing if not ambitious, calling into play starters such as pressed terrine of sea bass with a coriander, saffron and mussel nage, and main courses of roasted woodpigeon with provençale peas, pancetta ham and a Beaujolais *jus*. Vegetarians have a good choice – spinach and mascarpone tart, for example – and meat-eaters who like their food simpler can opt for fish, chicken or steaks from the chargrill. In addition, items from the extensive bar menu, such as 'excellent' calf's liver on olive oil mash with bacon, are available in the dining-room for a supplement. The offer of eight 'very decent' wines by the glass, including dessert wines, is appreciated, and the keenly priced list is peppered with serious names. House wine is £8.95.

▲ *means accommodation is available.*

CHEF: Chris Clarke PROPRIETOR: Paul Klein OPEN: all week 12 to 2.15, 7 to 9.30 MEALS: alc (main courses £11 to £14.50). Bar meals available L and D all week SERVICE: not inc CARDS: Delta, MasterCard, Switch, Visa DETAILS: 80 seats. 30 seats outside. Private parties: 40 main room, 16 private room. Car park. Vegetarian meals. Children's helpings. No music ACCOMMODATION: 12 rooms, all with bath/shower. TV. Phone. B&B £45 to £75. Children welcome. Baby facilities. Dogs welcome. Afternoon teas. Garden (*The Which? Hotel Guide*)

EDENBRIDGE Kent map 3

Honours Mill

87 High Street, Edenbridge TN8 5AU COOKING **5**
TEL: (01732) 866757 COST £23–£50

Tucked away at the end of Edenbridge High Street, this beautifully converted water mill provides an elegant setting for some polished cooking. The format is a set-price menu with limited choice, although the weekday dinner version includes half a bottle of house wine. There is no stinting on luxury items: foie gras appears frequently, perhaps as a terrine, in a sauce for duck, or a stuffing for chicken. Less rich alternatives might include warm terrine of red mullet with a saffron sauce to start, followed by fricassee of rabbit with sherry, shallots and artichokes. High points of an inspection meal included a prettily interwoven sole and salmon terrine, the flavour of the fish underlined by a white butter sauce speckled with pink lumpfish roe, and succulent Scotch beef rib with a rich but refined madeira sauce. Desserts, however, disappointed on this occasion, although extras such as vegetables, bread and petits fours were more than up to scratch. Service for one reporter was cool though 'willing'. Mark-ups on the predominantly French wine list tend to be high, although it's good to see a separate list offering an exceptional choice of half-bottles. House wine is £10.15.

CHEF: Martin Radmall PROPRIETORS: Neville, Duncan and Giles Goodhew OPEN: Tue to Fri and Sun L 12.15 to 2, Tue to Sat D 7.15 to 10 CLOSED: 2 weeks Christmas MEALS: Set L Tue to Fri £15.50 to £32.75, Set L Sun £23.50, Set D Tue to Fri £26 (inc wine), Set D Tue to Sat £32.75 SERVICE: not inc CARDS: Delta, MasterCard, Switch, Visa DETAILS: 38 seats. Private parties: 40 main room. Children welcome. Children's helpings Sun L. No music

ELLAND West Yorkshire map 8

La Cachette  £

7–10 Town Hall Buildings, Elland HX5 0EU COOKING **2**
TEL: (01422) 378833 FAX: (01422) 377899 COST £18–£43

The owners reckon they pack in a broad spectrum of customers from ladies who lunch to corporate groups on an evening jolly. The result is happy bustle within what looks like the biggest Victorian pile in this small town outside Leeds. It is owned by the same partnership as Sous le Nez en Ville (see entry, Leeds), and aims for the same impeccably fashion-conscious style of cooking. A piece of roasted rabbit sits on a tian of haggis and swede in a red wine *jus* for starters, while mains might take in sauté calf's liver with onion rings, beetroot and crème fraîche. Vegetables must be added on to the total charge, but note the value of the daily Menu du Soir, which may run from fish-cake with lobster sauce through smoked pork steak to apple and sultana crumble with custard.

The exemplary wine list spreads its favours between Old and New Worlds and finds them equally rewarding. Quality impresses at all price levels; indeed, plenty of interesting drinking is to be had under £15. Ten house wines starting at £8.50 a bottle, £1.60 a glass, include a manzanilla sherry from Hidalgo. CELLARMAN'S CHOICE: Mâcon-Charnay Vieilles Vignes 1994, Manciat Poncet, £14.75; Seville Estate Pinot Noir, 1990, Yarra, Victoria, £15.75.

CHEF: E. Poli PROPRIETOR: C&O Partnership OPEN: Mon to Sat 12 to 2.30, 6 to 10 (11 Fri and Sat) CLOSED: 26 Dec, L bank hols MEALS: alc (main courses £7 to £12). Set D £10.95 to £13.95 (inc wine). BYO £5 SERVICE: not inc, card slips closed CARDS: Amex, Delta, MasterCard, Switch, Visa DETAILS: 140 seats. Private parties: 60 main room, 14 to 50 private rooms. Vegetarian meals. No children after 7.30pm. Wheelchair access (no WC). Music. Air-conditioned

ELY Cambridgeshire map 6

Old Fire Engine House

25 St Mary's Street, Ely CB7 4ER COOKING **2**
TEL: (01353) 662582 FAX: (01353) 666966 COST £27–£42

Informality is the name of the game at this brick-built former farmhouse by Ely cathedral: it could hardly be otherwise when you have to walk through part of the kitchen to reach the dining-room. The cooking aims for heartiness and flavour rather than clever presentation. Seconds of main courses are cheerily offered, making people feel genuinely at home. A summer lunch that began with chilled cucumber soup, and wild Norfolk samphire, served like asparagus with a trickle of melted butter, was a fond memory for one reporter. Another pair who enjoyed smoked salmon mousse, lemon sole and plum crumble were particularly grateful to be able to leave their car in the car park while they went for a wander round the cathedral. The solicitude derives from the fact that, as a regular attests, the place is run by 'grown-ups, not young things hired by the hour'. A mature mind is also clearly behind the wine list as it contains some fine bins – mainly from France – and enthusiastic tasting notes provide a helpful guide for the novice. House wines from Concha y Toro are good value at £8. CELLARMAN'S CHOICE: Sauvignon de St-Bris 1995, Tabit, £13.80; Côtes-du-Rhône 1993, Guigal, £13.50.

CHEF: Terri Kindred PROPRIETORS: Ann Ford and Michael Jarman OPEN: all week L 12.30 to 2, Mon to Sat D 7.30 to 9 CLOSED: 24 Dec to 6 Jan, bank hols MEALS: alc (main courses £12 to £14). BYO £3.50 SERVICE: not inc CARDS: Delta, MasterCard, Switch, Visa DETAILS: 55 seats. 20 seats outside. Private parties: 36 main room, 8 to 22 private rooms. Car park. Vegetarian meals. Children's helpings. No smoking in 1 dining-room. No music

'We had a Pouilly Fumé Chateau de Tracey 1995 because of the silly name, and then realised that we had ordered this before because of the silly name. It was lovely.'
(On eating in the West Country)

EMSWORTH Hampshire map 2

Spencers

36 North Street, Emsworth PO10 7DG COOKING 4
TEL/FAX: (01243) 372744 COST £32–£48

The building started off in 1850 as two cottages and, as part of a growing trend, is divided into two eating-areas: a first-floor Victorian-style restaurant lit by gas-lamps, and a casual ground-floor brasserie in more modern vein. A la carte lunches and dinners are served in the brasserie, along the lines of marinated herring fillets, steak frites, duck confit, and hot banana tart, while the non-smoking restaurant now does only dinner, at a set price. Here Denis Spencer dips into a cosmopolitan bag and brings out fried halloumi cheese salad, crab and spring onion in filo, and breast of duck with butter-beans.

Fish is the kitchen's first love, not surprisingly given the location, and daily offerings might run to grilled plaice with roast peppers, salmon and crab cakes, or sauté haddock with Puy lentils. Simple meaty alternatives generally include grills of sirloin steak, or lamb cutlets, while desserts have been as ambitious as pear in a puff pastry lattice with butterscotch sauce, and hot chocolate gâteau with an oozing centre. Around 30 sensibly chosen and fairly priced wines begin with house Australian at £9.95.

CHEF: Denis Spencer PROPRIETORS: Denis and Lesley Spencer OPEN: Tue to Sat D only 7 to 10.30 CLOSED: 25 and 26 Dec MEALS: Set D Tue to Fri £18.50 (2 courses) to £24.50, Set D Sat £22 to £24.50 SERVICE: not inc CARDS: Amex, Delta, Diners, MasterCard, Switch, Visa DETAILS: 34 seats. Private parties: 24 main room, 10 private room. Vegetarian meals. No smoking in dining-room. Music. Air-conditioned

36 on the Quay

SOUTH COAST 1998 STAR

NEW ENTRY

47 South Street, Emsworth PO10 7EG COOKING 5
TEL: (01243) 375592 FAX: (01243) 375593 COST £31–£59

After four years at Harveys in Bristol (see entry), Ramon Farthing has moved to take charge of this smaller, pastel-coloured restaurant overlooking Emsworth Bay and its yachts. Dating from the eighteenth century, the former smugglers' inn is 'a happy place to be', with a warm welcome and service from Karen Farthing and her team. The food can be elaborate, and a six-course menu with a generous adjective count is designed to show off some of the high-wire cooking. Eating from the three-course menu, an inspector enjoyed woodpigeon breasts that were 'very rare, very gamey, chewy enough to be interesting and tender enough to be decadent'. They came with goose liver, wine-soaked plums, and bacon and cabbage tortellini, the whole dish indicating a seriously labour-intensive kitchen.

The question inevitably arises as to whether or not elaborate dishes are worth the effort. In that example, our inspector felt, it was, although not so in every case. There is both a richness to the food – 'I would hate to see this guy's butter bill' – and a seemingly high salt content, but Farthing has a good eye for design on the plate, which makes the most of, for example, herby rabbit sausage divided into four piles, sitting on creamed celeriac and potato. Desserts might include a hot soufflé, and more riches in the form of chocolate tart, or rhubarb cream inside a praline biscuit with a vanilla sauce and sorbet. England dominates the cheeseboard, and France the wine list, which features a serious collection of bins from that country's top producers and includes some fine old burgundies and mature clarets. High quality is reflected in the prices, with very little available under £20, but there is the odd bargain and the bin-end list is well worth a look. House French is £13. CELLARMAN'S CHOICE: Limoux Chardonnay 1995, Les Caves du Sieur d'Arques, £20.50; Côtes du Luberon, Ch. Val Joanis Les Griottes 1992, £21.50.

CHEF: Ramon Farthing PROPRIETORS: Ramon and Karen Farthing OPEN: Tue to Fri L 12 to 2, Mon to Sat D 7 to 10 CLOSED: 4 days Christmas to New Year, 2 weeks mid-Jan, 1 week Oct, bank hols MEALS: Set L £16 (2 courses) to £19, Set D £29.95 to £36.50 SERVICE: not inc CARDS: Amex, Delta, Diners, MasterCard, Switch, Visa DETAILS: 35 seats. Private parties: 28 main room, 10 private room. Car park. Vegetarian meals. Children's helpings. No smoking in dining-room. Wheelchair access (no WC). Music. Air-conditioned

EPWORTH North Lincolnshire map 9

Epworth Tap £

9–11 Market Place, Epworth DN9 1EU
TEL: (01427) 873333 FAX: (01427) 875020 COOKING 4
3m S of M180 junction 2 COST £23–£39

Wine is taken seriously in this converted pub, with its beams, flagstones, polished wood tables and pew-like banquettes, but a reporter who remarked, 'Oh, what a find,' was referring as much to the food and the buzzy atmosphere. Helen Wynne's cooking 'makes no attempt to show off, but delivers round, satisfying dishes' rooted in Elizabeth David territory. Those chalked up on the blackboard have included beef in beer with roasted pumpkin, parsnip and potato, and loin of pork stuffed with prunes. Although there have been mild criticisms (an 'uninspired' hot asparagus salad for example), seasoning and timing are accurate and good ingredients are clearly a high priority, as shown in a thick, golden-brown crab bisque tasting of 'shellfish and the sea'.

Many of the wines are remarkably good value, particularly some of the older vintages of claret and the mature burgundies, while Loire enthusiasts will be delighted by the range of dry to *moelleux* and *pétillant* Vouvrays from Huet dating back to 1962. Expert advice is given, and tasting and pouring are performed without pretentiousness by quiet and efficient staff headed by John Wynne. House wines start at £9.50 a bottle, £1.65 a glass. CELLARMAN'S CHOICE: Henschke Tilly's Vineyard 1995, Eden Valley, S. Australia, £15; Châteauneuf-du-Pape 'Clos de Pape' 1993, Avril, £22.

CHEF/PROPRIETOR: Helen Wynne OPEN: Thu to Sat D only 7.30 to 9.30 MEALS: alc Thu and Fri (main courses £8.50 to £13.50). Set D Sat £18.50 to £21. BYO £5 SERVICE: not inc, card slips closed CARDS: Delta, MasterCard, Switch, Visa DETAILS: 50 seats. Private parties: 24 main room, 24 private room. Children's helpings. No children under 8. No smoking in 1 dining-room. Music

denotes an outstanding wine cellar; *denotes a good wine list, worth travelling for.*

ERPINGHAM Norfolk map 6

▲ *Ark*

The Street, Erpingham NR11 7QB
TEL: (01263) 761535 COOKING **4**
on A140 Cromer road, 4m N of Aylsham COST £20–£42

There is a timeless quality about this rambling Norfolk flint and brick house, reached via a narrow hedged lane. A stone-flagged hall leads to a small lounge where pre-dinner drinks can be taken, and fresh flowers adorn tables in the dining-room with its garden views. Mike and Sheila Kidd are as committed as ever: he is a genial host, she an intelligent self-taught cook inspired by Elizabeth David and trips to Italy, France and Australia. Vegetable plots take up a lot of the garden and might yield, for instance, a supply of rocket, to accompany Puy lentils with pungent goats' cheese and 'balsamised' onions.

Crab-cakes with capsicum sauce has been praised, as have lamb with walnut stuffing and 'startlingly tasty' *jus*, and salmon with tomatoes and basil (so fresh and soft it 'squeaked on the teeth'). The flexible set-price dinner menu offers British and French farmhouse cheeses from Neal's Yard either as a fourth course, or as an alternative to desserts, of gooseberry crumble, or tangy cherry and loganberry compote with home-made vanilla ice-cream. Sunday lunch is a straightforward three-course menu. A dozen attractive house wines priced between £8 and £9 make a great start to a list which tours most of the major regions and offers great-value drinking wherever it alights. Half-bottles are generous too. CELLARMAN'S CHOICE: Mulderbosch Sauvignon Blanc 1996, Stellenbosch, South Africa, £15.50; St-Emilion, Ch. Gravet 1990, £16.50.

CHEF: Sheila Kidd PROPRIETORS: Mike and Sheila Kidd OPEN: Sun L 12.30 to 2, Tue to Sat D 7 to 9.30 CLOSED: 25 Dec MEALS: Set L £14.25, Set D £19.75 (2 courses) to £26 SERVICE: not inc CARDS: none DETAILS: 30 seats. 10 seats outside. Private parties: 36 main room, 8 and 16 private rooms. Car park. Vegetarian meals. Children's helpings. No smoking in dining-room. No music ACCOMMODATION: 3 rooms, all with bath/shower. TV. D,B&B £65 to £125. Deposit: £25. Rooms for disabled. Children welcome. Baby facilities. Dogs welcome. Garden

EVERSHOT Dorset map 2

DORSET 1998 LUNCH

▲ *Summer Lodge*

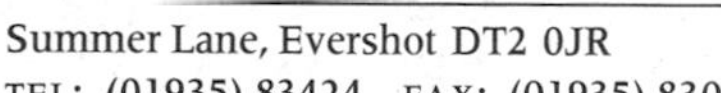

Summer Lane, Evershot DT2 0JR COOKING **6**
TEL: (01935) 83424 FAX: (01935) 83005 COST £19–£71

'One of our very favourite places,' summed up a regular visitor to this comfortable stone-built house. Peace and calm are among its attributes, a certain amount of cosseting goes on, afternoon teas are 'outstanding', and breakfasts are a real bonus. Tim Ford's dependable hand on the tiller is appreciated – 'long may he stay' – and his self-styled 'country-house cooking' is appealing: consider pan-fried calves' sweetbreads with baby broad beans in spring, or pink-roasted squab pigeon with a ravioli of wild mushrooms. The à la carte rather outshines the set-price menu, but lunches (with three choices per course from Monday to Saturday, more on Sunday) are an absolute steal.

Local supplies figure prominently: free-range, organic Gressingham duck, Dorset lamb, venison from Melbury Park and so on. Fish (much of it from West Bay) and shellfish are offered as a first, intermediate or main course and priced accordingly: perhaps a gâteau of Cornish crab layered with buckwheat pancakes and served with a shellfish sauce, or a sole boudin with white truffle in a chive sauce. Soup is 'nearly always good', and the tureen is available for second helpings. This is one of an increasing number of restaurants making the most of the renaissance in British cheesemaking, a particularly strong force in the West Country. Desserts might well include a trio – lemon meringue, syllabub and sorbet, for example – alongside hot rhubarb soufflé or iced banana parfait. The wine list is topped by a page of sherries and tailed by a grand range of Hine and Delamain cognacs, all available by the glass. In between is a mouthwatering selection of fine wines from all over. If cost is an issue – for high-quality wines rarely come cheap – a list of a dozen starting at £11.75 represents good value, or you could take a patriotic look at the quartet of English whites. Half-bottles are plentiful.

CHEFS: Tim Ford and Philippe Edmond PROPRIETORS: Margaret and Nigel Corbett OPEN: all week 12.30 to 2, 7.30 to 9 MEALS: alc (main courses £10 to £28.50). Set L Mon to Sat £11.75, Set L Sun £18.50, Set D £32.50. BYO £5.95 SERVICE: not inc, card slips closed CARDS: Amex, Delta, Diners, MasterCard, Switch, Visa DETAILS: 50 seats. 20 seats outside. Private parties: 50 main room, 20 private room. Car park. Vegetarian meals. Children's helpings. No smoking in dining-room. Wheelchair access (also WC). No music ACCOMMODATION: 17 rooms, all with bath/shower. TV. Phone. B&B £115 to £215. Rooms for disabled. Children welcome. Baby facilities. Dogs welcome in bedrooms only. Afternoon teas. Garden. Swimming-pool (*The Which? Hotel Guide*)

EVESHAM Hereford & Worcester map 5

▲ *Evesham Hotel* 

Coopers Lane, off Waterside, Evesham WR11 6DA COOKING **2**
TEL: (01386) 765566 FAX: (01386) 765443 COST £18–£41

The Georgian hotel (originally a Tudor farmhouse) has been in the family since 1975, and its vitality derives largely from John Jenkinson's spirited and iconoclastic approach: in a refreshing change from the norm, he doesn't appear to have taken himself seriously in all that time. Be prepared for the menu's cascade of puns and asides as it explains away tobasmo tart or phoenix salad. Generosity is the chef's middle name when it comes to planning the weekly-changing menus: any fewer than ten main courses and you have been short-changed. There may be potted crab, or wild mushroom tart to begin, and wild boar cutlets with a maple syrup and cream sauce to follow. Vegetarians are not excluded from the largesse, and typically have some seven dishes to choose from.

The kitchen makes use of locally shot venison, organically reared meat, the short asparagus season in the Vale of Evesham, and its own garden for herbs and autumnal mulberries. To finish, interesting cheeses vie for attention with apple enchilada, or malted chocolate ice-cream. Among current Jenkinson campaigns are one against users of mobile phones and one against smokers. As he reasonably points out on the menu, 'the smell of burning tobacco does not enhance the flavour of food', and trade has not suffered as a consequence of the ban. Another campaign, which mysteriously proved less successful, was to interest customers in a range of wines by the glass. Perhaps their lack of enthusiasm was down to the good value of the whole bottles, which have a maximum mark-up of £10. The wines are a delightful and intriguing bunch from everywhere except France and Germany (*that* campaign dates back to 1977). If you've always wanted to try a Swedish Chenin Blanc, a Chinese Chardonnay or a cashew nut wine from Belize – yes, really – then this is the place to head for. And there are some very fine wines to be found alongside the fun bins, with the likes of Heggies, Grange and Ridge setting the standard. Chilean house wines from Concha y Toro are £9.60. CELLARMAN'S CHOICE: Wolf Blass President's Selection Chardonnay 1995, Barossa Valley, S. Australia, £20.50; Boschendal Grand Reserve Cabernet/Merlot 1993, Paarl, South Africa, £17.20.

CHEF: Ian Mann PROPRIETORS: the Jenkinson family OPEN: all week 12.30 to 2, 7 to 9.30 CLOSED: 25 and 26 Dec MEALS: alc (main courses £7 to £16.50) SERVICE: net prices, card slips closed CARDS: Amex, Delta, Diners, MasterCard, Switch, Visa DETAILS: 55 seats. Private parties: 10 main room, 12 private room. Car park. Vegetarian meals. Children's helpings. No smoking in dining-room. No music ACCOMMODATION: 40 rooms, all with bath/shower. TV. Phone. B&B £58 to £88. Children welcome. Baby facilities. Dogs welcome in bedrooms only. Afternoon teas. Garden. Swimming-pool (*The Which? Hotel Guide*)

EXETER Devon map 1

Lamb's

15 Lower North Street, Exeter EX4 3ET COOKING 2
TEL: (01392) 254269 FAX: (01392) 431145 COST £28–£49

The restaurant occupies two floors of this five-storeyed, eighteenth-century listed town house, close to both the cathedral and the Victorian Iron Bridge. One of the dining-rooms opens out into a courtyard, bounded on one side by the old Roman city wall, which gives a rarely matched feeling of continuity to the premises. The Aldridges have been here since 1991, and in early 1997 Alison Aldridge – on the departure of Carolyn Seath – took charge of the stoves.

The food owes much to local produce: fish arrives daily from Brixham or Plymouth, meat includes 'welfare-friendly' veal, and the garden yields herbs in summer. A lot of time goes into baking, curing, smoking chicken or fish, and dreaming up what to cook next, since ideas seem to come thick and fast: smoked salmon tart, seared scallops with coriander, honey-glazed duck with spiced plums, or black-bean and spinach sausage, while desserts range from cider syllabub to steamed ginger pudding. Half-bottles are a feature of the varied, interesting and clued-up wine list, which starts with eight house wines all at £10 (£2 a glass).

CHEF: Alison Aldridge PROPRIETORS: Ian and Alison Aldridge OPEN: Tue to Fri L 12 to 2, Tue to Sat D 7 to 10 (booking essential) CLOSED: last week Aug, first week Sept MEALS: alc (main courses £10.50 to £17). Set L £15 (2 courses) to £19, Set D Tue to Thur £15 (2 courses) to £19, Set D Fri and Sat £20. BYO £5 SERVICE: not inc CARDS: Amex, Delta, MasterCard, Switch, Visa DETAILS: 42 seats. 8 seats outside. Private parties: 26 main room, 26 private room. Vegetarian meals. Children's helpings. No smoking in 1 dining-room. Wheelchair access (no WC). Music

▲ *St Olaves Court Hotel* £

Mary Arches Street, Exeter EX4 3AZ — COOKING 5
TEL: (01392) 217736 FAX: (01392) 413054 — COST £24–£52

This Georgian house within a walled garden in the city centre has been externally spruced up since the last edition of the *Guide*. Victorian prints in the dining-room remain, as does the predominantly turquoise colour scheme. A reshuffle in the kitchens has seen John Winstanley promoted to head chef, and although the food is still elaborate there is a feeling that the technique to back it up is solidly grounded.

A 'lasagne' of salmon and smoked salmon, layered with nori and garnished with rings of squid in their own ink, contained 'all sorts of interesting and varied tastes and textures'. Fish cooking generally is bold and original, as in a pairing of halibut with stewed rhubarb, while meat preparations are more traditional. Rack of lamb comes with devilled kidneys (described as 'pretty innocent as to satanic content') but a feuilleté of rabbit with morels and subtle grain-mustard sauce was 'a wow', the earthiness of the morels combining well with chopped smoked ham. Tuile baskets of ice-cream, not to mention spun-sugar cages, tend to figure heavily on dessert plates, but the central elements are up to scratch. A lemon tart in agreeably crisp pastry with a raspberry coulis went down well, as did crêpes of apple and pear with a citrus-flavoured cider sauce. Enjoyable petits fours accompany coffee, and 'eminently cheerful' service adds to a sense of occasion. Eight wines by the glass head up a thoughtfully selected list, the prices mostly realistic. House French is £10.50.

CHEF: John Winstanley PROPRIETORS: Raymond and Ute Wyatt OPEN: Mon to Fri L 12 to 2, all week D 6.30 to 9.30 MEALS: alc (main courses L £11.50, D £14.50 to £18.50). Set L and D £11.50 (2 courses) to £14.50. BYO £6 SERVICE: not inc, card slips closed CARDS: Amex, Delta, Diners, MasterCard, Switch, Visa DETAILS: 65 seats. 20 seats outside. Private parties: 45 main room, 8 and 16 private rooms. Car park. Vegetarian meals. Children's helpings. No smoking in dining-room. No music ACCOMMODATION: 15 rooms, all with bath/shower. TV. Phone. B&B £53 to £93. Rooms for disabled. Children welcome. Baby facilities. Dogs welcome in bedrooms only. Afternoon teas. Garden

---

FARNBOROUGH Kent — map 3

Chapter One — NEW ENTRY

New Fantail Building, Farnborough Common,
Locksbottom, Farnborough BR6 8NF — COOKING 3
TEL: (01689) 854848 FAX: (01689) 858439 — COST £25–£49

The long-standing New Fantail has been turned into a swish cosmopolitan restaurant and brasserie with 'newly smart austere décor' and a kitchen team under John Wood, who used to work at the Dorchester (see entry, London). The menu is written staccato fashion – 'saffron herb risotto, vegetable beignet' is one starter – and warns that dishes may arrive tepid, just in case anybody has missed the point that this is a modern brasserie trying to make its mark outside central London. Most reporters register a word of gratitude for the attempt, though they also note the big-city prices that come with it.

Dishes see-saw from traditional sole véronique to brave-sounding haddock bourguignon, but the bulk of the repertoire is a modish collection of favourite brasserie ideas, from salad of trotters with black pudding and sauce gribiche, to hare civet, braised rump of lamb, and grilled calf's liver. Fruit typically features among desserts: for example red cherry soufflé, or pear Belle Hèléne. Excellent service is efficient without being fussy. The wine list, divided into 'French' and 'Rest of the World', offers some classy and expensive bottles, but a selection of house wines starts at £10. A Chapter Two is planned in Blackheath.

CHEF: John Wood PROPRIETOR: Selective Restaurant Group OPEN: all week 12 to 2.30 (3.30 Sun), 6.30 to 11 (11.30 Fri and Sat, 9.30 Sun) MEALS: alc D (main courses £13.50 to £16.50). Set L Mon to Sat 19.50, Set L Sun £16 SERVICE: 10% (optional), card slips closed CARDS: Amex, Delta, Diners, MasterCard, Switch, Visa DETAILS: 120 seats. Private parties: 12 main room, 60 private room. Car park. Vegetarian meals. Children's helpings. No cigars/pipes in dining-room. Music. Air-conditioned

---

FAVERSHAM Kent map 3

Read's

Painter's Forstal, Faversham ME13 0EE
TEL: (01795) 535344 FAX: (01795) 591200 COOKING 7
on Eastling road, 2m S of Faversham COST £29–£60

Given the unpromising exterior – likened by reporters both to a 1960s primary school and the HQ of International Rescue – it's a pleasant surprise to find that, inside, Read's is light, airy and spacious, with comfortable sofas in the bar, well-spaced tables in the dining-room, and a neat terraced garden overlooking the beautiful Belmont Valley. For anyone who is really smitten, the premises are approved for civil marriages. Diners who just want to enjoy sophisticated and impressively fine-tuned English cooking have probably come to the right place.

Pride in the carefully sourced ingredients is much in evidence on the menu, which specifies Lunesdale duckling, Whitstable codling, and Kentish herbs. David Pitchford's skill in the kitchen is more than a match for his raw materials. Starters of duck liver parfait with toasted brioche, and smoked salmon layered with smoked salmon mousse (no less than 14 layers) win praise for their rich, well-balanced flavours. Main courses are characterised by good timing – of sauté breast of farmyard chicken with home-dried tomato risotto – and intensely flavoured sauces: spiked with peppercorns, perhaps, for Aberdeen Angus beef served with crispy onions, Cumbrian air-dried ham and field mushrooms. Puddings cater for the unashamedly greedy, who can choose the 'Chocoholics Anonymous', consisting of five small but 'incredible' chocolate treats, or the oddly named 'The Image', six miniatures of puddings from the menu. Service is well-paced and unobtrusive.

The outstanding list of over 250 wines is helpfully prefaced by an international selection of 40 bottles, all priced under £20, for those who don't feel up to choosing from – or can't quite afford – the fine wines in the main section. Fans of rich nutty dessert wines should seize the opportunity to try Scholtz Hermanos Solera 1885 Málaga, which sadly is no longer being produced. CELLARMAN'S CHOICE: Sancerre 1994, Comte Lafond, £18; Cape Mentelle Cabernet Sauvignon 1992, Margaret River, W. Australia, £18.

CHEF: David Pitchford PROPRIETORS: David and Rona Pitchford OPEN: Tue to Sat 12 to 2, 7 to 10 CLOSED: bank hols MEALS: Set L £17.50, Set D £20 (Tue to Fri) to £36 SERVICE: not inc, card slips closed CARDS: Amex, Diners, MasterCard, Switch, Visa DETAILS: 40 seats. 12 seats outside. Private parties: 60 main room, 20 private room. Car park. Vegetarian meals. Children's helpings. No pipes/cigars in dining-room. Wheelchair access (no WC). Music

FELSTED Essex map 3

Rumbles Cottage

Braintree Road, Felsted CM6 3DJ
TEL: (01371) 820996 COOKING 1
on B1417, between A130 and A120 COST £21–£39

This unassuming, white-painted sixteenth-century cottage in a prosperous-looking village is 'a bit Tardis-like once you are inside, with many more tables than you'd think'. The food is something of a curiosity. Joy Hadley grows many of her own vegetables and adopts an experimental approach. 'Ingredients were fine, and execution was not without skill,' conceded one visitor, but results divide reporters. 'Bizarre' and 'weird' was the view of one who ate smoked chicken breast stuffed with banana, enclosed in puff pastry and served with banana chutney; and this wasn't even on the adventurous Guinea Pig menu, reserved for trying out new ideas. Another couple expressed their gratitude for being introduced to 'so many new dishes we liked' over several visits. Among the options might be egg and aubergine curry, deep-fried king prawns, and (in spring) a layered dessert of rhubarb purée, ginger sponge and custard. Cheeses are a speciality, and 40 affordable wines begin with house French at £9.75.

CHEF/PROPRIETOR: E. Joy Hadley OPEN: Sun L 12 to 2, Tue to Sat D 7 to 9 CLOSED: 2 weeks Feb MEALS: alc (main courses £11 to £13). Set L Sun £13, Set D £13 SERVICE: not inc, card slips closed CARDS: MasterCard, Visa DETAILS: 50 seats. Private parties: 22 main room, 8 and 22 private rooms. Vegetarian meals. Children's helpings. No smoking in 1 dining-room. Wheelchair access (no WC). Music

FERRENSBY North Yorkshire map 9

▲ *General Tarleton* **NEW ENTRY**

Borough Bridge Road, Ferrensby HG5 0QB COOKING 5
TEL: (01423) 340284 FAX: (01423) 340288 COST £20–£39

Those who know the Angel Inn (see entry, Hetton) will welcome Denis Watkins's latest venture: a 250-year-old inn close to Harrogate and the A1, with nooks, crannies, beams and open log fires. As the *Guide* goes to press, extensive refurbishment is being carried out, but the operation is already up and running, with a kitchen under the supervision of Jamie O'Connor, who worked at the Angel a while back. A house manager is also installed, so the team is in place to provide the kind of food that put Hetton on the map: an AWT open sandwich, rustic fish soup, and little money-bags of seafood in filo pastry with a lightly creamy lobster sauce.

Both menus and wine list are being updated, but before refurbishment got under way our inspector enjoyed a busy warm salad incorporating confit of duck, chorizo, lardons and croûtons, followed by pot-roast shoulder of lamb with olive mash and salsa verde, and accurately grilled sea bream served with pesto-flavoured crushed potatoes and roasted plum tomatoes tasting of garlic and olive oil: 'a wonderful dish.' Equally successful were sticky toffee pudding, and warm chocolate mousse with mango sorbet. House Vin de Pays d'Oc is £9.45. Reports, please.

CHEF: James O'Connor PROPRIETORS: Denis Watkins and John Topham OPEN: Sun L 12 to 2, Mon to Sat D 7 to 9.30 MEALS: alc (main courses £6.50 to £11). Set D £25. Bar meals available all week L and D. BYO £7 SERVICE: not inc CARDS: MasterCard, Switch, Visa DETAILS: 102 seats. Private parties: 34 main room. Car park. Vegetarian meals. Children welcome. No smoking in dining-room. Wheelchair access (also WC). No music ACCOMMODATION: 15 rooms, all with bath/shower. TV. Phone. B&B £47.50 to £62.50. Rooms for disabled. Children welcome. Baby facilities. Dogs welcome in bedrooms only. Afternoon teas. Garden

FOLKESTONE Kent map 3

Paul's £

2A Bouverie Road West, Folkestone CT20 2RX COOKING 1
TEL: (01303) 259697 FAX: (01303) 226647 COST £24–£31

For well over 20 years Paul and Penny Hagger have served their wide-ranging food to an appreciative audience, many of them local. The relaxed atmosphere helps, as do the fair prices: consider the weekday lunchtime buffet at £4.95. Ten or more items per course sounds an uncommonly generous choice, but we are told that high turnover helps to keep it that way. Nor is the kitchen shy of industry, turning out slices of wild boar sausage with apple and spring onions baked in a tomato and red wine sauce, or rack of lamb stuffed with pâté, wrapped in bacon, roasted, and served with a mustard and onion sauce. There may also be locally landed fish, game such as braised teal, or perhaps ostrich fillet in a creamy sauce with pink peppercorns and madeira. Vegetarians have a choice, too, and sweets are from the trolley. A round-the-world wine list stays mostly under £20, but there are some tempting clarets at around £35. House French is £8.65.

CHEFS: Darren Byer, and Paul and Penny Hagger PROPRIETORS: Paul and Penny Hagger OPEN: all week 12 to 2.30, 7 to 9.30 CLOSED: few days after Christmas MEALS: alc (main courses £10 to £11). Buffet L Mon to Sat £4.95 (1 course), Set L Sun £10.95 BYO £6 SERVICE: not inc CARDS: Delta, Diners, MasterCard, Switch, Visa DETAILS: 120 seats. 40 seats outside. Private parties: 100 main room, 40 private room. Vegetarian meals. Children's helpings. Wheelchair access (also WC). No music

FOULSHAM Norfolk map 6

The Gamp £

NEW ENTRY

Claypit Lane, Foulsham NR20 5RW COOKING 2
TEL: (01362) 684114 COST £16–£31

In Dickens's *Martin Chuzzlewit*, Mrs Gamp always carried a faded cotton brolly. In deepest Norfolk, the Bushes' country restaurant is named after her because at the beginning of the century the landlord is said to have used an umbrella as a repair to his tenant's leaky roof. The roof is now pristine, and so are the comfortable and spacious pair of dining-rooms, garden room and bar. The aims are clear and laudable: to provide unfussy meals with a lightness of touch, often using local materials. Such intentions show to advantage in fennel-dominated vegetable soup, and loin of pork with apple and dry cider, a dish that had 'nicely concentrated flavours'. Vegetables are multifarious and embellished just enough to please: a mustardy cheese sauce on cauliflower, crisp breadcrumbs on sauté potatoes. Rump steak, perhaps with pepper and brandy sauce, is, the menu explains, 'cut from a well-hung rump'. Desserts might include light vanilla ice-cream in meringue with intense raspberry sauce, or indulgent warm chocolate and orange fudge cake. Service is amiable, although there may be gaps between courses. Forty wines provide reasonable drinking at affordable prices, although it would be helpful if the list included vintages. House French is £7.95.

CHEFS: Andy Bush and Simon Nobbs PROPRIETORS: Daphne and Andy Bush OPEN: Wed to Sun L 12 to 1.45, Tue to Sat D 7 to 9.30 CLOSED: first 2 weeks Jan MEALS: alc (main courses £10 to £13). Set L £10.95, Set D Tue to Fri £11.50 SERVICE: net prices, card slips closed CARDS: Delta, MasterCard, Switch, Visa DETAILS: 40 seats. 6 seats outside. Private parties: 40 main room, 20 private room. Car park. Vegetarian meals. Children's helpings. No smoking in 1 dining-room. Wheelchair access (also WC). No music

FOWEY Cornwall map 1

Food for Thought

Town Quay, Fowey PL23 1AT COOKING **4**
TEL: (01726) 832221 FAX: (01726) 832060 COST £26–£49

Martin and Caroline Billingsley's small seaside restaurant, in the former Customs House, has been going for nigh on 20 years, so it is perhaps unsurprising that 'the cooking has a calm confidence'. Fish and shellfish make up the bulk of the menu, treated with respect and without flamboyance: delicate crab ravioli with lobster sauce and lumpfish caviar, or a 'mouthwatering' platter of red mullet, salmon, sea bass, scallops and monkfish in a buttery cream sauce. Martin Billingsley takes equal care in handling meat: 'very tender and delicious' rack of lamb with a herb crust and well-reduced sauce, for instance. A dash of Cointreau and a glob of clotted cream add interest to bread-and-butter pudding; a more gutsy caramel sauce would have done the same to a 'smooth, bouncy, light' crème caramel. A reporter was expecting a more personal touch in the service, but the long, divided dining-room is charming and intimate, with beams, exposed shale walls and plenty of greenery. The wine list is simple and French-based. House wine starts at £7.50.

CHEF: Martin Billingsley PROPRIETORS: Martin and Caroline Billingsley OPEN: Mon to Sat D only 7 to 8.30 CLOSED: Christmas to mid-Mar MEALS: alc (main courses £14 to £17). Set D £18.95 SERVICE: not inc CARDS: MasterCard, Switch, Visa DETAILS: 38 seats. Private parties: 50 main room. Children welcome. No music

See inside the front cover for an explanation of the symbols used at the tops of entries.

FRESSINGFIELD Suffolk map 6

Fox and Goose

Fressingfield IP21 5PB
TEL: (01379) 586247 FAX: (01379) 586688 COOKING 3
on B1116, 3½m S of Harleston COST £25–£54

The building dates from the sixteenth century and has just the right amount of wear and tear to feel convincing. Apart from the fact that the old sign – of a goose holding a fox in its beak – has been swapped for one showing the animals side by side, visitors might not realise that anything has changed. They still charge for black olives and warm tapénade bread in the bar, and although Ruth Watson has departed for a career in food journalism, Max Dougal remains at the stoves under the new ownership, cooking in broadly similar vein as before.

At the heart is a varied repertoire, equally at home with Peking-style crispy duck pancakes as with curried crab-cake and courgette pickles, taking in griddled ciabatta with tomatoes and melted mozzarella along the way. 'Ingredients are good and carefully cooked,' reckoned an inspector, who enjoyed a dish of lambs' liver, bacon, black pudding and mash, and a 'perfectly executed' vanilla crème brûlée. There may be niggles (a tendency to oversalt, and improvable bread and coffee) but the combination of set meals, bar snacks, à la carte, vegetarian and children's menus adds up to a generously flexible arrangement.

Wines have been greatly reduced in number, and although the loss of the older vintages of Bordeaux, Burgundy and Alsace – and all the vintage ports – will be mourned by many, the new list still has plenty to offer in the way of quality wines from top producers. French classics still take pride of place, supported by some astute selections from the New World. House wines start at £13.50. CELLARMAN'S CHOICE: Corbans Chardonnay 1995, Gisborne, New Zealand, £13; Valpolicella Ripasso 'Campo Fiorin' 1991, Masi, £18.

CHEF: Maxwell Dougal PROPRIETORS: Tim and Pauline O'Leary OPEN: Wed to Sun 12 to 2, 7 to 9.30 CLOSED: Sun D in winter (exc bookings), 25 to 27 Dec, first week Jan MEALS: alc (main courses £9.50 to £15). Set L Wed to Sat £10.50 (2 courses) to £13.95, Set D Wed to Fri £17.50 SERVICE: not inc CARDS: Delta, MasterCard, Switch, Visa DETAILS: 48 seats. 16 seats outside. Private parties: 30 main room, 22 private room. Car park. Vegetarian meals. Children's helpings. No cigars in dining-room. No music

FROME Somerset map 2

▲ *Crofts*

21 Fromefield, Frome BA11 2HE COOKING 3
TEL: (01373) 472149 COST £18–£29

The paintings, drawings and sculptures in Margaret Graham's country-style restaurant reflect her artistic interests, and the tall, neat, white, beamed house is considered a 'well-meaning, decent sort of place' that is 'homely, modest, domestic and everyday'. By contemporary measures the approach is hardly innovative, but neither is it dull. Instead, a short menu offers straightforward dishes of game tart, stuffed quail in pastry, casserole of pork with gin and juniper, and braised oxtail. The word 'amateur' is much misused, but applies here in the best sense, indicating that there is no artifice, no sleight of hand, just a clear perception of what is right. Baking skills are a strong point, and a senior inspector considered the bread some of 'the best I have had for a long time'. Modest wines at fair prices complete the deal, starting with house French at £8.50.

CHEF/PROPRIETOR: Margaret Graham OPEN: Sun L 12 to 2, Wed to Sat D 7 to 9.45 CLOSED: 23 Dec to 2 Jan MEALS: Set L Sun £10.50, Set D £15.95 SERVICE: not inc, card slips closed CARDS: MasterCard, Visa DETAILS: 30 seats. Private parties: 22 main room. Vegetarian meals. Children's helpings. No smoking in dining-room. Music ACCOMMODATION: 1 room, with bath/shower. TV. B&B £25 to £45. Deposit: £10

GATESHEAD Tyne & Wear map 10

▲ *Eslington Villa Hotel*

8 Station Road, Low Fell, Gateshead NE9 6DR
TEL: (0191) 487 6017 FAX: (0191) 420 0667 COOKING 3
on A6127, 2m S of Newcastle city centre COST £21–£49

The garden at the back of this Edwardian villa slopes down towards the railway line, but the trains are not intrusive. This is the suburban side of Gateshead. A dark dining-room and bright conservatory are the setting for a wide-ranging repertoire that takes in both the exotic – king prawn tempura with a chilli ginger sauce, or wild boar sausage with olive oil mash – and more mundane items, such as sirloin steak with garlic butter. Some dishes can work exceptionally well – for example, a single large lobster raviolo ('properly and expertly made') with a herb-flecked shellfish cream sauce – although vegetables have been 'uninspiring'. Puddings might include iced peach parfait, blueberry and mascarpone brûlée, or a 'rich, viscous' milk chocolate honey-pot mousse. Service is well paced and good humoured, and the carefully chosen wines are sensibly priced, beginning with house red and white at £8.95.

CHEF: Ian Lowrey PROPRIETORS: Nick and Melanie Tulip OPEN: Sun to Fri L 12 to 1.45, Mon to Sat D 7 to 9.45 MEALS: alc (main courses £16.50 to £18). Set L £9.95 (2 courses) to £14.95, Set D Mon to Fri £16.95 (2 courses) to £20.95 SERVICE: not inc CARDS: Amex, Delta, MasterCard, Switch, Visa DETAILS: 55 seats. Private parties: 40 main room, 18 private room. Car park. Vegetarian meals. Children's helpings. No smoking in dining-room. Wheelchair access (no WC). Music ACCOMMODATION: 12 rooms, all with bath/shower. TV. Phone. B&B £40 to £65. Rooms for disabled. Children welcome. Baby facilities. Garden (*The Which? Hotel Guide*)

GILLINGHAM Dorset map 2

▲ *Stock Hill*

Stock Hill, Gillingham SP8 5NR
TEL: (01747) 823626 FAX: (01747) 825628 COOKING 5
off B3081, 1½m W of Gillingham COST £30–£49

A narrow drive flanked by mature beech trees leads to the door of this late-Victorian mansion set in 11 acres, with a lake where guests may fish for brown trout. The interior is ornately furnished in idiosyncratic style, described by one reporter as 'a little bit of Middle Europe on the edge of Dorset'. The dining-room is a restful place of high-backed chairs and swagged curtains, where the Hausers offer 'excellent and friendly service'. 'We left feeling thoroughly spoilt,' wrote a satisfied couple.

Peter Hauser's cooking draws on his Austrian background – most evident in the painstakingly crafted desserts, such as chocolate-necked meringue swans – and there's little point in counting the calories. 'Classical cooking of meats and expertly sauced fish' are the mainstays of the rest of the menu, perhaps taking in saddle of venison on red cabbage and sultanas served with chestnut purée, or sea bream with mustard seed sauce. Although wiener schnitzel regularly appears, there is a willingness to dabble in other cultures: rabbit casseroled with ginger, coconut milk and lemon grass and served with polenta, for example, or a dessert of Alsace apple flan with coriander syrup. France is the first love of the wine list, the New World and other European selections being more perfunctory. There is a handful of Austrian wines too, and house French is £13.50.

CHEFS: Peter Hauser and Lorna Connor PROPRIETORS: Peter and Nita Hauser OPEN: Tue to Fri and Sun L 12.30 to 1.45 (1.30 Sun), all week D 7.30 to 8.45 (8.30 Sun) MEALS: Set L £20, Set D £30 SERVICE: not inc, card slips closed CARDS: Amex, Diners, MasterCard, Switch, Visa DETAILS: 34 seats. Private parties: 22 main room, 12 private room. Car park. Children's helpings. No children under 7. No smoking in dining-room. Wheelchair access (no WC) No music ACCOMMODATION: 10 rooms, all with bath/shower. TV. Phone. D,B&B £105 to £280. Deposit: £60. No children under 7. Afternoon teas. Garden. Fishing (*The Which? Hotel Guide*)

GOLCAR West Yorkshire map 8

Weavers Shed

Knowl Road, Golcar HD7 4AN
TEL/FAX: (01484) 654284
on B6111, 2m W of Huddersfield from A62

COOKING 4
COST £21–£52

The Shed may be adorned with menus by Nico, Marco and their ilk, but there isn't a trace of misplaced grandeur about the place. It was once a working mill and the beams and bare flagstone floor bear witness to its past. There is no pretension in the service either, thanks in part to the warmth and experience of Shirley Bramald, who runs front-of-house. The kitchen team under Ian McGunnigle works hard, chopping herbs to go with seared salmon, making a 'cottage pie' of duck confit with a honeyed and spiced breast of the bird, or roasting pineapple and boiling mango syrup to accompany a vanilla and coconut rice pudding. Pre-dinner drinks come, to the delight of one pair, with 'some very small but beautifully cooked pigeon pies'.

There are plenty of original ideas and novel presentations, but the focus is on sound culinary principles and traditional cooking methods. Steak and mushrooms arrives as three medallions of beef fillet surrounded by sauté wild fungi in a creamy reduction of madeira perfumed with sage. A reporter praised sticky toffee pudding that lived up to its name, or there may be iced cappuccino mousse with chocolate coulis. Wines are a bright and enticing international bunch, although many of the mark-ups will take a bit of swallowing. House wines from Duboeuf in France or de Martino in Chile are £10.95.

CHEFS: Ian McGunnigle, Robert Jones and Stephen Jackson PROPRIETOR: Stephen Jackson OPEN: Tue to Fri L 12 to 2, Tue to Sat D 7 to 10 CLOSED: first 2 weeks Jan, 2 weeks July/Aug MEALS: alc (main courses £12 to £16). Set L £12.95 SERVICE: not inc CARDS: Amex, Delta, MasterCard, Switch, Visa DETAILS: 65 seats. Private parties: 40 main room, 25 private room. Car park. Vegetarian meals. Children's helpings. No cigars/pipes in dining-room. Wheelchair access (also women's WC). Music

GORING Oxfordshire map 2

Leatherne Bottel

Goring RG8 0HS
TEL: (01491) 872667 FAX: (01491) 875308 COOKING **5**
on B4009 out of Goring, 5m S of Wallingford COST £35–£57

As riverside locations go, this one takes some beating. Perhaps the best time to visit is on a warm summer's day – bag a spot just feet from the river for an aperitif – although a blazing fire in winter is equally welcoming. The dining-room is stylish, skilfully set with exposed brickwork, cream-washed stone, boldly rag-rolled walls, and an abundance of fresh flowers, not to mention striking photographs of Turkish life and tasteful drawings of nudes. The menu is refreshingly innovative, and its attempts to create a complex mix of flavours generally work. Soup of the day sounds innocent enough, but the one at inspection was made from Japanese miso stock, roasted red pepper, spring onion, ginger and coriander, and served with brioche croûtons: it was 'bold, spicy and enjoyable'.

This is typical of the lively output, which incorporates most spices known to man. Seared tuna might be cooked with crushed pepper and ground galangal, and served with wasabi, sesame prawn toasts, chickweed and mustard leaves, while other dishes make use of lemon oil, roast garlic, harissa, horseradish chips and edible flowers. Fish is undercooked because 'Keith believes it should be cooked that way', portions are generous, and desserts have included terrine of chocolate with raspberry and coffee. Bread is often mentioned in despatches, and one reporter wondered why, in view of its excellence, frequent attempts were made throughout the meal to remove it. The place is powered by 'visible self-confidence and exuberance', the downside of which is 'arrogance', and although service has been 'attentive' and 'friendly', a couple of reporters have been less than satisfied by their treatment. Around three dozen wines soon hit the £20 barrier, and of the two half-bottles available, one is a 'bizarre' Château Pétrus at £125. House French is £12.50.

CHEF/PROPRIETOR: Keith Read OPEN: all week L 12 to 2 (3.30 Sun), Mon to Sat D 7 to 9.30 CLOSED: 25 Dec MEALS: alc (main courses £10.50 to £18.50) SERVICE: not inc, card slips closed CARDS: Amex, MasterCard, Visa DETAILS: 55 seats. 75 seats outside. Private parties: 20 main room, 20 private room. Car park. Vegetarian meals. No music. Air-conditioned

£ *indicates that it is possible to have a three-course meal, including coffee, a half-bottle of house wine and service, at any time the restaurant is open (i.e. at dinner as well as at lunch, unless a place is open only for dinner), for £25 or less per person.*

GRANGE IN BORROWDALE Cumbria map 10

▲ *Borrowdale Gates Hotel* 🍷

NEW ENTRY

Grange in Borrowdale CA12 5UQ
TEL: (01768) 777204 FAX: (01768) 777254
off B5289, about 3m S of Keswick, ¼m N of Grange

COOKING **4**
COST **£18–£52**

The Victorian house is set in the heart of walking country, with marvellous views from its picture windows. Its most recent extension uses Borrowdale stone and Buttermere slate, and refurbishment has brought modern comforts and furnishings. Michael Heathcote's broad-ranging repertoire touches on aubergine piedmontese, oriental spring roll, and ceviche of salmon and monkfish, but local resources figure prominently in the form of Cumbrian pork, Mansergh Hall lamb, Morecambe Bay shrimps and Waberthwaite ham, which might be used in a terrine, or combined with leeks in a strudel.

A contemporary British strand to the cooking has produced fillet of haddock with beetroot, and a warm salad of duckling with chorizo, and a lunching inspector enjoyed a meal of Devon crabmeat with avocado, calf's liver cooked 'nicely pink, as requested', and 'a good homely pudding' of rhubarb crumble. Non-sweet eaters can choose three out of seven or eight cheeses, daily-changing menus help to keep up residents' interests, and service from uniformed staff is 'good without being oppressive'.

Wines are a praiseworthy collection from the world's main regions, and most manage to stay under £20. Half-bottles are generous in number and French house wines (at £11.50) are from Georges Blanc.

CELLARMAN'S CHOICE: Pouilly Fumé, Dom. des Berthiers 1995, Jean Claude Dagueneau, £18.75; Gigondas 1994, Dom. Santa Duc, £19.75.

CHEF: Michael Heathcote PROPRIETORS: Terence and Christine Parkinson OPEN: all week 12.15 to 1.30, 7 to 8.45 CLOSED: Jan MEALS: alc L (main courses £4 to £7). Set L Sun £13.75, Set D £24.75 SERVICE: not inc CARDS: Amex, Delta, MasterCard, Switch, Visa DETAILS: 60 seats. 15 seats outside. Private parties: 60 main room. Car park. Children's helpings. No children under 5 at D. No smoking in dining-room. Wheelchair access (no WC). No music ACCOMMODATION: 28 rooms, all with bath/shower. TV. Phone. D,B&B £57 to £145. Deposit: £25. Rooms for disabled. Children welcome. Baby facilities. Afternoon teas. Garden (*The Which? Hotel Guide*)

GRASMERE Cumbria map 8

▲ *Michael's Nook*

Grasmere LA22 9RP
TEL: (01539) 435496 FAX: (01539) 435645

COOKING **7**
COST **£41–£71**

The Nook, named after a character in one of Wordsworth's lyric poems, excites great affection in those who visit. 'Mark Treasure displays a great deal of culinary imagination and has terrific potential,' wrote one reporter. 'That, coupled with a most friendly environment and a lovely setting, ensured that this evening will remain high in our memory.' The setting is the Grasmere Vale, the house a simple early-Victorian edifice of grey Lakeland stone, its interior replete with mahogany, fine plasterwork, barometers, grandfather clocks and copper warming-pans. The effect is elegant without being grandiose.

Reg Gifford has always had a talent for picking thoroughbred chefs, and Mark Treasure's cooking is immensely refined, yet achieves many of its triumphs through deceptively simple means: smoked salmon omelette as a starter, for example, or a plate of baby vegetables done on the griddle and made aromatically sumptuous with truffle. After the first course comes a choice of soup – langoustine and celery with ginger, perhaps – and then the main business. A reporter thought 'the blend of flavours worked perfectly' in pavé of salmon with Jerusalem artichokes, morels and leeks. Another who signed up for the six-course gourmet menu enjoyed a fillet of Scotch beef with foie gras arranged in a tower that also included potato and tomato and was headily infused with rosemary. Skilful desserts – a consummate strawberry mille-feuille with a refreshing strawberry sorbet, for example – precede a selection of British cheeses. Service has been praised as 'very accurate and very friendly'.

The wines delight with their broad sweep of flavours from all over the globe. Prices are fair throughout; even though they almost reach a lofty four figures among the grand vintage clarets, there are a few single-figure bottles and plenty of choice at all levels. Half-a-dozen house wines from France and Australia start at £10.50. CELLARMAN'S CHOICE: Oak Knoll Chardonnay 1992, Williamette Valley, Oregon, £17.25; Meerlust Rubicon 1989, Stellenbosch, South Africa, £19.75.

CHEF: Mark Treasure PROPRIETORS: Mr and Mrs R.S.E. Gifford OPEN: all week 12.30 to 1, 7.30 to 8.15 (8.30pm Fri and Sat) MEALS: Set L £31.50, Set D £41.50 to £48.50 SERVICE: not inc CARDS: Amex, Delta, Diners, MasterCard, Switch, Visa DETAILS: 50 seats. Private parties: 40 main room, 40 private room. Car park. No children under 7. Jacket and tie. No smoking in dining-room. Wheelchair access (also WC). No music ACCOMMODATION: 14 rooms, all with bath/shower. TV. Phone. D,B&B £130 to £260. Deposit: £50. Children welcome by arrangement

▲ *White Moss House*

Rydal Water, Grasmere LA22 9SE
TEL: (015394) 35295 FAX: (015394) 35516 COOKING **6**
on A591, at N end of Rydal Water COST £35–£43

The Wordsworth card is not overplayed. The fact is that two of the poet's homes, Dove Cottage and Rydal Mount, are less than a mile away, and White Moss was bought for his son Willie. It was built in 1730 between Grasmere and Rydal Water, at the foot of what Wainwright has dubbed 'the motorists' route' (on account of the car park) up the Terrace to Loughrigg, one of the Lake District's easiest and most rewarding short climbs. For resident walkers, Sue and Peter Dixon provide excellent breakfasts and packed lunches, which add enormously to the appeal. At dinner they maintain the format which has kept them in business here for 17 years. Everybody sits down at 8 o'clock for five courses (no choice before dessert), and dishes cover territory familiar to regulars, some of whom make an annual pilgrimage.

'Soups here are always a treat,' writes one who enjoys the 'thick, grainy consistency' of, as it may be, fennel with apple and asparagus, or courgette and chervil. Second-course fish might appear as a trio of warm Wastwater trout, Coniston char and River Eden smoked salmon, indicating that local materials are central to the operation. Roast rack of Herdwick spring lamb is a regular item, 'crisp and tasty' mallard might be served with sage and onion stuffing, and sauces benefit from a dash of merlot, pinot noir or perhaps port. Huntsman's pudding – like a Christmas pudding but not nearly as heavy – is a likely dessert, and there is a good selection of British cheeses, from which 'you choose one from the list, rather than get a variety'.

The impressive collection of wines is logically divided into the classic French regions, each section accompanied by a group of similar varietals from elsewhere. The range of vintages within France is quite stunning, particularly the mature burgundies, and prices are sufficiently low to justify a spending spree. Half-bottles are liberally scattered throughout. CELLARMAN'S CHOICE: Mâcon Chardonnay 1995, Dom. Talmard, £13.95; Savigny-lès-Beaune 1993, Camus-Bruchon, £15.95.

CHEFS: Peter Dixon and Colin Percival PROPRIETORS: Sue and Peter Dixon OPEN: Mon to Sat D only 8 (1 sitting) CLOSED: Dec to Feb MEALS: Set D £27.50 SERVICE: not inc, card slips closed CARDS: MasterCard, Switch, Visa DETAILS: 18 seats. Private parties: 10 main room. Car park. Children's helpings. No smoking in dining-room. Wheelchair access (no WC). No music ACCOMMODATION: 8 rooms, all with bath/shower TV. Phone. D,B&B £118 to £178. Children welcome. Garden. Fishing (*The Which? Hotel Guide*)

GREAT GONERBY Lincolnshire map 6

Harry's Place ★

17 High Street, Great Gonerby NG31 8JS
TEL: (01476) 561780 COOKING 7
on B1174, 2m NW of Grantham COST £45–£80

The single, dark pink, comfortable room in a Georgian-fronted house might feel like someone's home, but there is 'none of the awkward silence and hushed conversations common in small restaurants'. This is due at least in part to Caroline Hallam, who is notably welcoming and friendly, and to the sense of purpose that defines the restaurant. There is 'total dedication' to the business in hand from both Hallams, no doubt helped by the small numbers: it seats ten at most. The menu is short, too – a choice of two items per course – the sources indicating a serious search for quality materials: Filey sea trout, Yorkshire grouse, Lincolnshire salt-marsh teal, or a stack of 'brilliant' plump Orkney scallops, perfectly timed, served with a bright orange sauce of mango, lime, ginger and basil.

The cooking is distinguished by its simplicity and directness, and the force and freshness of flavours show in a 'tangy' tomato soup with pistou, for example, or a rich and creamy terrine of Filey crab with horseradish and dill mayonnaise. One who had not visited for a while felt that the food was becoming 'more refined, lighter in touch, but with even more depth to the flavours', which certainly make an impact. Trimmed loin of Devon lamb – 'deep red inside, caramelised outside, and very tender' – has come with a 'classic' madeira sauce, rich and glossy, with a 'pronounced but not overpowering' flavour of rosemary, while 'fabulous' monkfish has been lightly sauté and served with a pool containing olive oil, lemon juice, Pernod and herbs: 'I will remember that sauce for a long time.' It is the combination of lightness and intensity that excites, the latter helped by copious use of powerfully fresh herbs.

Desserts display the same sureness of touch and sense of balance, ranging from hot plum soufflé, via strawberry shortbread, to 'rich but very light' caramel mousse brûlée with raspberry sauce. The deal may seem expensive, but reporters consider it good value for money, despite there being only a couple of wines at under £20 on the short list, and no house wine. Water, however, is free.

CHEF: Harry Hallam PROPRIETORS: Harry and Caroline Hallam OPEN: Tue to Sat 12.30 to 2, 7 to 9.30 CLOSED: 25 and 26 Dec, bank hols MEALS: alc (main courses £18.50 to £27.50) SERVICE: not inc CARDS: Delta, MasterCard, Visa DETAILS: 10 seats. Private parties: 10 main room. Car park. Children's helpings. No children under 5. No smoking in dining-room. Wheelchair access (no WC). No music

GREAT MILTON Oxfordshire map 2

▲ *Le Manoir aux Quat' Saisons*

Church Road, Great Milton OX44 7PD
TEL: (01844) 278881 FAX: (01844) 278847 COOKING **8**
off A329, 1m from M40 J7 COST £48–£119

The manor-house, dating from the fifteenth century, is a splendid building, with tall chimneys and a quiet, calming lawn at the back. In fine weather it is well worth sitting outside among the statuary, wandering into the neat vegetable garden, or even neater Japanese garden. This is a place for reflection. The enterprise concerns itself not just with fine food, but also with notions of equilibrium and harmony which go beyond edible details to a wider concern with a healthy body and mind. Raymond Blanc's success over the last 14 years here owes much to his own exacting standards and his vigorous, dynamic approach to food and cooking. This success, not surprisingly, brings expansion, and as the *Guide* goes to press the kitchen is due to be extended and a cookery school built.

Former head chef Clive Fretwell, who contributed much to the Manoir's success, has moved to Manchester, where he plans to open a brasserie and bar early in 1998, and in his place comes Jonathan Wright, ex-premier sous-chef here, to head up the team. In many ways the food carries on as before, laying great emphasis on garden freshness, on seafood hors d'oeuvres such as langoustines and squid with Thai spices, and on a high degree of impeccable workmanship. Although the dish may hark back a decade or two, a pair of courgette flowers filled with crab mousse (one dark meat, one claw meat) still has the capacity to impress.

Oriental flavourings figure prominently – a lime-leaf-scented *jus* with turbot and shellfish, or lemon grass in a langoustine bisque – but a strong European emphasis remains in the ravioli incorporated into a dish of veal and wild mushrooms, or the kromeski of foie gras that partners roasted squab pigeon. At inspection, however, some of the promised flavours did not come through with the pristine clarity they should, and some dishes seemed to consist of independent flavours having little to do with each other, rather flouting the maxim that every item on a plate should be there for a good reason. This is more a question of judgement than technique, for there is no doubting the skill that produced a dessert of roasted Williams pear in a puff pastry case that was rated 'wonderfully light, gently buttery, the very best'.

Service (some of it still at the training stage) and wines are both largely French: the sommelier will taste your chosen wine himself before inviting you to do so. The prices are as high as you might fear but the list is as outstanding you could wish for. If you were hoping to spend around £30 on a bottle, then south-west France and Alsace would be a good place to start your search, but if money is no object you will already be leafing through the excellent burgundies and clarets. CELLARMAN'S CHOICE: Jurançon Sec 'Cuvée Marie' 1994, Charles Hours, £32; Alsace, Pinot Noir Herrenweg Turckheim 1992, Zind-Humbrecht, £41.50.

CHEFS: Raymond Blanc and Jonathan Wright PROPRIETOR: Raymond Blanc OPEN: all week 12.15 to 2.15, 7.15 to 10.15 MEALS: alc (main courses £29 to £33). Set L Mon (exc bank hols) to Sat £32, Set D £69 SERVICE: not inc CARDS: Amex, Delta, Diners, MasterCard, Switch, Visa DETAILS: 95 seats. Private parties: 8 main room, 46 private room. Car park. Vegetarian meals. Children's helpings. No smoking in 1 dining-room. Wheelchair access (also WC). No music. Air-conditioned ACCOMMODATION: 19 rooms, all with bath/shower. TV. Phone. Room only £195 to £425 (double rooms). Deposit: £150. Rooms for disabled. Children welcome. Baby facilities. Dogs welcome. Afternoon teas. Garden. Swimming-pool (*The Which? Hotel Guide*)

GREAT MISSENDEN Buckinghamshire map 3

La Petite Auberge

107 High Street, Great Missenden HP16 0BB COOKING 2
TEL: (01494) 865370 COST £33–£48

The Martels are clearly happy in their tiny cottage at one end of the high street, and are well supported, having appeared in eight editions of the *Guide*. The cooking is somewhat more refined than the bistro ambience may suggest. Freshly made terrine of foie gras, cabbage parcels filled with prawns and garnished with beluga caviare, and veal sweetbreads sauced with calvados are the style. Raw materials are carefully sourced: one reporter praised the forthright gaminess of the grouse he ate and was equally impressed with caramelised lemon tart. Other dessert stalwarts include chocolate mousse, and crème brûlée. The front-of-house manages to radiate genuine friendliness without obtruding. A short French wine list caters for most pockets, starting with Muscadet de Sèvre-et-Maine at £9.50.

CHEF: Hubert Martel PROPRIETORS: Mr and Mrs Hubert Martel OPEN: Mon to Sat D only 7.30 to 10.30 CLOSED: 2 weeks Christmas MEALS: alc (main courses £14 to £16) SERVICE: not inc CARDS: Diners, MasterCard, Visa DETAILS: 30 seats. Private parties: 35 main room. Children welcome. Wheelchair access (also WC). Music

The Guide *office can quickly spot when a restaurateur is encouraging customers to write recommending inclusion – and sadly, several restaurants have been doing this in 1997. Such reports do not further a restaurant's cause. Please tell us if a restaurateur invites you to write to the* Guide.

GREAT YELDHAM Essex map 3

White Hart £

Poole Street, Great Yeldham CO9 4HJ COOKING **2**
TEL: (01787) 237250 FAX: (01787) 238044 COST £19–£47

The White Hart is neither a pub nor a restaurant, declare the owners, and guests may eat what they like where they like. The snack menu might offer chicken liver pâté with plum chutney and brioche, and beer-battered lemon sole and chips, while the grander *carte* takes in pork tenderloin with an apple and spinach tart and potato dauphinois. One reader enjoyed a main course of six pigeon breasts on a potato galette with puréed parsnip, but doubted whether he really needed the quantity offered. Desserts have included pineapple polenta cake with crème fraîche, and rice pudding with a brochette of exotic fruits and coconut ice-cream. Service has been widely praised: 'From the moment of our arrival to our departure, the attention from young and enthusiastic staff was excellent.'

The wine list has been compiled by Master of Wine John Hoskins, and is every bit as good as you might expect. Some 100 characterful wines from around the world are grouped by style and accompanied by succinct tasting notes. Mark-ups decrease as you get higher up the price scale, but there is good drinking to be had at all levels, starting with 16 house wines at £9.45 a bottle (£1.80 a glass). CELLARMAN'S CHOICE: Condrieu 'La Bonnette' 1994, Rostaing, £30; Chianti Rufina Riserva 1990, Selvapiana, £25.

CHEF: Roger Jones PROPRIETOR: Huntsbridge Ltd OPEN: all week 12 to 2, 6.30 to 10 (9.30 Sun) CLOSED: D 25 and 26 Dec and 1 Jan MEALS: alc (main courses £4.50 to £15.50). Set L Mon to Sat £7.50 (2 courses) to £10.50 SERVICE: not inc, card slips closed CARDS: Amex, Delta, Diners, MasterCard, Switch, Visa DETAILS: 120 seats. 30 seats outside. Private parties: 80 main room, 24 private room. Car park. Vegetarian meals. Children's helpings. No smoking in 1 dining-room. No smoking in dining-room. Wheelchair access (no WC). Music

GRIMSTON Norfolk map 6

▲ *Congham Hall*

Lynn Road, Grimston PE32 1AH
TEL: (01485) 600250 FAX: (01485) 601191 COOKING **3**
off A148 or B1153, 7m E of King's Lynn COST £25–£51

Forty acres of tranquil parkland surround this Georgian house near Sandringham. The door is opened as you arrive, and although service can be formal, the flexibility of being able to perch anywhere to eat anything from soup or a sandwich to a four-course meal at lunch-time is welcomed. Dinner is in the Orangery, a light room with flowers overlooking the lawn, and Stephanie Moon's repertoire takes account of local produce and seasons: King's Lynn brown shrimps with Parmesan, or a spring dish of poached asparagus with scoops of fresh, soft goats' cheese.

Since the herb garden is stocked with over 600 varieties, it would be surprising if a few of them didn't make it into the kitchen, and indeed they crop up in parsley *jus*, bayleaf sauce and the like. Interesting ideas abound, from lemon verbena sweetcorn fritters that come with a confit of chicken terrine, to sablé of pineapple with pistachio ice-cream and snow eggs, or vanilla mascarpone with praline squares and raspberry coulis. High wine mark-ups don't do anybody any favours; try to make one of the half-bottles go a long way, or drink one of the house wines at £12.75 (£2.20 a glass).

CHEF: Stephanie Moon PROPRIETORS: Trevor and Christine Forecast OPEN: Sun to Fri L 12.30 to 2, all week D 7.30 to 9.30 MEALS: alc L Mon to Fri (main courses £7.50 to £16). Set L Sun £17.50, Set D £25 (2 courses) to £32. BYO £10 SERVICE: not inc, card slips closed CARDS: Amex, Delta, Diners, MasterCard, Switch, Visa DETAILS: 50 seats. 50 seats outside. Private parties: 50 main room, 20 private room. Car park. Vegetarian meals. No children under 12. Jacket and tie. No smoking in dining-room. Wheelchair access (also WC). No music ACCOMMODATION: 14 rooms, all with bath/shower. TV. Phone. B&B £74 to £198. No children under 12. Dogs in kennels. Afternoon teas. Garden. Swimming-pool (*The Which? Hotel Guide*)

HALIFAX West Yorkshire map 9

Design House

Dean Clough, Halifax HX3 5AX — COOKING 4
TEL: (01422) 383242 FAX: (01422) 322732 — COST £19–£46

Clean lines, curves, wood and chrome mark out the modern interior of this old carpet mill which, ever since it opened in 1994, has had a clear purpose and message. It aims to make good food widely available, and achieves it with the help of sound ingredients, sensitive cooking, and a fair pricing policy. Those in search of value may find the set-price lunch a good place to begin; chicken and pearl barley broth, Scarborough woof, vanilla sponge with stewed summer fruits, and coffee for £12.95 isn't bad going.

Realistic prices are helped by the choice of materials – rabbit salad, perhaps, or creamed Whitby cod – and variety infuses the menus, which jump from salsify and wood mushrooms with a truffle-scented broth, to woodpigeon breast with red wine risotto, to roast leg of pork with five-spice and chilli noodles. Behind all the cooking is a degree of skill that can knock up a chocolate and almond pithiviers to order, and service that does all the right things. Wines are an eclectic bunch, arranged by style and finishing with a mouthwatering selection for dessert. Mark-ups are low, with a half-dozen sold by the glass at £2. Even so, you may be tempted to try a bottle or two of the speciality beers instead. CELLARMAN'S CHOICE: Meursault 1993, Louis Latour, £23.50; St-Emilion, Ch. Rocheyron 1990, £19.50.

CHEF: David Watson PROPRIETOR: John Leach OPEN: Mon to Fri L 12 to 2, Mon to Sat D 6.30 to 10 CLOSED: 25 and 26 Dec, 1 Jan MEALS: alc (main courses £7.50 to £14.50). Set L £9.95 (2 courses) to £12.95 SERVICE: not inc CARDS: Amex, Delta, MasterCard, Switch, Visa DETAILS: 70 seats. 12 seats outside. Private parties: 50 main room. Car park. Vegetarian meals. Children's helpings. No cigars/pipes in dining-room. Music. Air-conditioned

'Making a decent sponge or biscuit base is surely not beyond the talents of this kitchen (or even my kitchen), so it is all the harder to understand the significant lapses here. Still, this problem is easily rectified (with a P45 to whoever made this sponge).'
(On eating in London)

HAMBLETON Rutland map 6

▲ *Hambleton Hall*

Hambleton LE15 8TH
TEL: (01572) 756991 FAX: (01572) 724721 COOKING **8**
off A606, 3m SE of Oakham COST £43–£100

Well off the main road in a cul-de-sac village, Hambleton has a hideaway quality about it. Although less grand or imposing than many of its type, it does have fine views across the countryside and a glimpse of Rutland Water from the terrace. The scale, though, is appealingly human, with a comfortable bar, a fine display of flowers in the lounge, and 'helpful, friendly and professional' service that contributes to the relaxed atmosphere. Behind the scenes, Aaron Patterson has joined the board of directors and now works from a larger and completely rebuilt kitchen, adding to the sense of stability.

The food takes a broadly seasonal approach with its annual cycle of two à la cartes, one for spring and summer, one for autumn and winter. The style is modern, European, highly wrought, generous in scope (ten or more main courses) and luxury-strewn. On the autumn menu, white truffles might turn up in the broth of white haricot beans which accompanies a ravioli of wild mushrooms; foie gras with endive and lentils may be followed by roast lobster served with basil-flavoured tortellini. The set menu, by offering no choice, is quite a contrast and would be easy to ignore in favour of the *carte* were it not for the large price differential. However, the set menus can deliver a high degree of satisfaction, as one couple discovered at a summer lunch that began with an appetiser of Mediterranean vegetables, followed by an assiette of fish, then breast of chicken with morels, and a passion-fruit soufflé that is a match for any.

The cooking does not attempt to surprise, but sticks to the familiar territory of red wine sauce for meats, grain-mustard sauce for rabbit, and ratatouille with a rosemary and tapénade juice for loin of lamb, all of which give a coherence and identity to the style. It is worth casting an eye over desserts at the beginning, since some – pear tarte Tatin with caramel ice-cream, for example – might involve a 20-minute wait. A huge list of wines from around the globe manages to keep quality high on every page. France is given the full works, and there is an impressive collection from California. An introductory group of 30 'wines of the moment' set in price bands from £15 and upwards helps to simplify selection. CELLARMAN'S CHOICE: Spottswoode Vineyard Sauvignon Blanc 1995, Napa Valley, California, £28; Il Podere dell Olivos Barbera 1995, Santa Barbara, California, £23.

CHEF: Aaron Patterson PROPRIETORS: Tim and Stefa Hart OPEN: all week 12 to 1.30, 7 to 9.30 MEALS: alc (main courses £24.50 to £30). Set L £14.50 (2 courses), Set D £35 SERVICE: net prices, card slips closed CARDS: Amex, Delta, Diners, MasterCard, Switch, Visa DETAILS: 60 seats. Private parties: 40 main room, 15 to 60 private rooms. Car park. Vegetarian meals. Children's helpings. No cigars/pipes in dining-room. Wheelchair access (also WC). No music ACCOMMODATION: 15 rooms, all with bath/shower. TV. Phone. B&B £115 to £285. Rooms for disabled. Children welcome. Baby facilities. Afternoon teas. Garden. Swimming-pool (*The Which? Hotel Guide*)

'When asked, the manager did not know the name of the chef.' (On eating in London)

HAMPTON HILL Greater London map 3

Monsieur Max

NEW ENTRY

133 High Street, Hampton Hill TW12 1NJ COOKING 4
TEL/FAX: (0181) 979 5546 COST £33–£46

The Renzland twins have long been favourites of *Guide* reporters, and when Marc died suddenly in late 1995 many expressed their sadness. Since then, Max has moved the short distance from Hampton Wick to less-cramped premises, taking his contemporary version of French bourgeois cooking with him. He has also brought his customary list of priorities, in which décor is not usually at the top. But reporters are happy to brave the rag-rolled walls, stained glass, bare wooden floor, tables that might have come from a sewing machine factory and battered looking chairs, in search of the high-quality ingredients and attention to detail that are Renzland hallmarks.

Some early reports were mixed, but since Alex Bentley and sous-chef Morgan Meunier joined in April 1997 an inspector enjoyed 'the epitome of honest cooking' in a simple soup with its 'mixture of the peasant (celeriac) and the grand (truffle)'. A sense of balance prevails in that main items take centre stage. Slices of fanned pink duck breast are given just enough green peppercorn sauce, and a generous slab of carefully timed salmon fillet comes with fennel, champ and a rich shellfish and chive sauce. Desserts have included a smooth, creamy chocolate pot ('beyond reproach'), and fine-textured crème brûlée with a crisp top 'that would not have been out of place at a much grander restaurant'. Two dozen wines start with house French at £8.50.

CHEF: Alex Bentley PROPRIETOR: Max Renzland OPEN: Sun to Fri L 12 to 2.30 (3.30 Sun), all week D 7 to 10.30 (11 Fri and Sat) CLOSED: 25 Dec MEALS: Set L Mon to Fri £11 (2 courses) to £14, Set L Sun £23, Set D £23. BYO £5 SERVICE: 12.5% (optional), card slips closed CARDS: Amex, Delta, MasterCard, Switch, Visa DETAILS: 95 seats. 8 seats outside. Private parties: 95 main room. Vegetarian meals. Children's helpings. Wheelchair access (no WC). No music. Air-conditioned

HAMPTON WICK Greater London map 3

Dijonnais

35 High Street, Hampton Wick KT1 4DA COOKING 3
TEL: (0181) 977 4895 COST £26–£49

Everything about the décor should prepare you for the fact that this is a bistro français of the old school, right down to the checked undercloths and seats, and framed posters on the walls. As the name suggests, the owner is Burgundian and that means you will get a proper Kir. The set-price menus are sensibly brief, usually offering a choice from two or three starters and main courses. Sliced and fanned avocado accompanied by hot spiced crabmeat made an elegant starter at one dinner, and was not let down by what followed: escalopes of tender lamb with a well-executed tarragon sauce. Other nights have seen monkfish with a light curry sauce, wild duck with cassis, and beef braised in ginger and lemon. The *carte* gives a broader choice, from perhaps frogs' legs in mustard sauce, to Dover sole in saffron butter, or rack of lamb in a parsley crust. Crème brûlée accompanied by a little pot of Grand Marnier sorbet and brandy-snaps was an 'absolutely first-class' rendition, or there may be a simple fruit compote with crème Chantilly. The approach is commended by a regular as 'delightfully welcoming but unfussy'. The short and rather pricey wine list is, not surprisingly, entirely French. House wines are around £9.50.

CHEFS: Lionel Jolivet and Jerome Aurejac PROPRIETORS: Lionel and Jan Jolivet OPEN: Mon to Fri L 12 to 2.30, Mon to Sat D 6 to 10 CLOSED: Easter, bank hols MEALS: alc (main courses £9.50 to £16.50). Set L £11 (2 courses), Set D £18.95 SERVICE: not inc, card slips closed CARDS: Amex, Delta, Diners, MasterCard, Switch, Visa DETAILS: 30 seats. 4 seats outside. Private parties: 25 main room. Children's helpings. No music

HAROME North Yorkshire map 9

Star Inn NEW ENTRY

Harome YO6 5JE
TEL: (01439) 770397 COOKING 3
off A170, 3m SE of Helmsley COST £20–£56

The village comes complete with duck pond and cricket team, and the fourteenth-century inn has a thatched roof, stable-door entrance, beams and crooked walls, but 'typical old-fashioned pub' would be a misleading description. Since taking it over in mid-1996, Andrew and Jacquie Pern have spruced up the Star and started serving some classy, untypical pub food. She looks after front of house while he cooks 'revamped' British dishes of steak and kidney suet pudding, 'posh' rabbit pie, or breast of duck with black pudding risotto. Fish comes from Whitby and Bridlington (turbot with noodles and chive sauce, perhaps), herbs are from the garden and game in season is a speciality. Creamy sauces are a feature too. Portions are big, and one visitor was nearly defeated by the calorific dessert selection of lemon tart, bread-and-butter pudding, chocolate gâteau with chocolate sauce and much more. 'I wish it were in my village,' said another reporter who enjoyed the busy and pleasant atmosphere. Wine prices aren't greedy, the list is strong on Burgundy and the New World, and there is a decent choice of half-bottles. 'Speciality selected wines' start at £8.50.

CHEF: Andrew Pern PROPRIETORS: Andrew and Jacquie Pern OPEN: all week L 12 to 2 (6 Sun), Tue to Sat D 6.45 to 9.30 CLOSED: 2 weeks Jan MEALS: alc (main courses £6 to £20) SERVICE: not inc CARDS: none DETAILS: 55 seats. 30 seats outside. Private parties: 35 main room. Car park. Vegetarian meals. Children's helpings. Wheelchair access (no WC). Music

HARROGATE North Yorkshire map 8

La Bergerie £ *

11–13 Mount Parade, Harrogate HG1 1BX COOKING 2
TEL: (01423) 500089 COST £19–£38

'Unsophisticated' is how the Girons describe the setting, and reporters would not disagree, although the place is scheduled for redecoration. Judging from the pictures as well as the menu, the centre of gravity would appear to be south-west France and the Pyrenees, although 'gravity' may not be the word to describe the restaurant in full flow. The culinary mood is cheerfully traditional, carried along on a wave of alcohol, cream, herbs and garlic. Jacques Giron produces 'wonderfully thick' French onion soup, venison with cider, salmon with sorrel, and 'excellent' cassoulet. The set-price menu looks a bargain, offering duck and armagnac terrine in a truffle sauce served with 'doorstep-thick wedges of toasted French bread', lamb with a 'provençale garnish', and apple tart. An appropriately French wine list starts with house Duboeuf at £8.50.

CHEF: Jacques Giron PROPRIETORS: Jacques and Juliet Giron OPEN: Mon to Sat D only 7 to 11; L by arrangement CLOSED: 25 and 26 Dec MEALS: alc (main courses £8 to £13.50). Set D £11.50. BYO £2.50 SERVICE: not inc CARDS: MasterCard, Visa DETAILS: 50 seats. 12 seats outside. Private parties: 25 main room, 15 private room. Children's helpings. No smoking in 1 dining-room. Wheelchair access (also WC). Music

The Bistro

1 Montpellier Mews, Harrogate HG1 2TG COOKING 3
TEL: (01423) 530708 FAX: (01423) 567000 COST £26–£43

The kitchen guard has changed again at the Bistro, Darren Prideaux arriving in late-summer 1996. Despite a change of ownership not long before that, a degree of consistency has been maintained. 'It seems to flourish, thrive and achieve,' noted an inspector. Set among antique shops in a quiet little mews, the only drawback to this rather formally run place is its feeling of cramming a quart into a pint pot. Don't expect to exchange incriminating confidences here, for tables are cheek by jowl.

The menu deals in fashionable fare, with pork knuckle, shiitake mushrooms and baby onions amalgamated into a balsamically dressed terrine, and roasted scallops appearing with wasabi mayonnaise, deep-fried celery leaves and lime oil. Cod comes with fried basil and a vanilla dressing, and Chinese-spiced duck breast with beetroot crisps and honey sauce: 'perfectly prepared, crispy skin and richly flavoured'. Good, sharp flavours sustain a dessert of lime tart with passion-fruit coulis. A curiosity of presentation is that sauces are used sparingly throughout. The predominantly French collection of wines offers sound drinking at very reasonable prices, with most bins priced under £20. House vins de pays are £9.25 a bottle, £1.75 a glass.

CHEF: Darren Prideaux PROPRIETOR: Maurizio Capurro OPEN: Tue to Sat 12 to 2, 7 to 10 CLOSED: 2 weeks Christmas, first 2 weeks Aug MEALS: alc (main courses £10.50 to £14.50). Set L £7.95 (2 courses) SERVICE: not inc CARDS: Delta, MasterCard, Switch, Visa DETAILS: 32 seats. 12 seats outside. Private parties: 30 main room. Vegetarian meals. Children welcome. No cigars/pipes in dining-room. Music

Drum and Monkey

5 Montpellier Gardens, Harrogate HG1 2TF COOKING 4
TEL: (01423) 502650 FAX: (01423) 522469 COST £17–£42

This Victorian pub conversion has been packing them in for nearly 20 years now in its guise as an unpretentious seafood restaurant. It is intimate to the extent that you may have to live with others' cigarette fumes, though regulars don't seem to mind. Shellfish and crustacean salads are the main business at lunch, while the evening menu gets all gussied up with salmon and watercress mousse, medallions of mixed seafood with sauce béarnaise, and hake in prawns and brandy. At inspection, thick and peppery lobster bisque impressed, as did fillet of whiting stuffed with brown and white crab meat, sauced with an eggy hollandaise studded with button mushrooms. Treacle tart with a touch of stem ginger and accompanied by good vanilla ice-cream seems to be the star of the pudding show. Service is efficient and down-to-earth. The short, reasonably priced wine list starts with house Duboeuf at £7.25.

CHEFS: Keith Penny and Tina Nuttall PROPRIETOR: William Fuller OPEN: Mon to Sat 12 to 2.30, 6.45 to 10.15 CLOSED: D 24 Dec to 2 Jan MEALS: alc (main courses L £5 to £14, D £7 to £16.50). BYO £3 SERVICE: not inc CARDS: Delta, MasterCard, Switch, Visa DETAILS: 50 seats. Private parties: 10 main room. Vegetarian meals. Children's helpings. No music

Grundy's £

21 Cheltenham Crescent, Harrogate HG1 1DH — COOKING 1
TEL: (01423) 502610 FAX: (01423) 502617 — COST £21–£38

Harrogate seems to have a restaurant round every corner, in every row of shops, most of them buoyed along by the comings and goings of the conference trade. In 1998 Val and Chris Grundy celebrate a decade in their modest but smart terraced dining-room, where the repertoire stays the same to please the locals. Old-fashioned deep-fried Brie with a cranberry and orange relish shares the billing with chickpea and coriander cakes, or mushrooms baked with brandy, cream and cheese. Highlights have included apple, celery and tomato soup, and a 'substantial' fillet of grilled sea bass with rice wine vinaigrette. Puddings vary from a creamy, fluffy strawberry mousse to a weightier treacle sponge, and service has been pleasantly friendly and efficient. Around forty fairly priced wines and ten half-bottles suit the circumstances, beginning with house French and South African at £8.95.

CHEF: Val Grundy PROPRIETORS: Val and Chris Grundy OPEN: Mon to Sat D only 6.30 to 10; L by arrangement CLOSED: 2 weeks Jan/Feb, 2 weeks July/Aug, bank hols MEALS: alc (main courses £9.50 to £14). Set D £11.50 (2 courses) to £13.50 SERVICE: 10% (optional), card slips closed CARDS: Amex, Delta, MasterCard, Switch, Visa DETAILS: 40 seats. Private parties: 32 main room. Vegetarian meals. Children's helpings. No pipes in dining-room. Music

HARWICH Essex — map 6

▲ *The Pier at Harwich* 🍷

The Quay, Harwich CO12 3HH — COOKING 2
TEL: (01255) 241212 FAX: (01255) 551922 — COST £23–£59

'I went for a weekend of sea breeze,' wrote a correspondent, who took advantage of the accommodation at this popular venue overlooking the nautical junketings along the Stour and Orwell estuaries. On the ground floor is the Ha'penny Pier, a family restaurant geared up for fish and chips, lasagne and salads; upstairs is the smarter dining-room. Fish is – not surprisingly – the main attraction: 'as good as any I have come across – in Britain or France,' noted a reporter. Lobsters are kept in sea-water tanks; most of the rest is delivered daily from the quayside. Platters of mixed 'fruits de mer' have been 'incredibly fresh', and when the kitchen sets about cooking, the results are equally praiseworthy: an 'outstanding' piece of roast sea bass served on a heap of red cabbage and apple with a puddle of calvados cream sauce. Desserts such as Atholl brose, and chocolate and rum torte have also been happily received. Service is full of enthusiasm and goodwill.

Lay & Wheeler from nearby Colchester supplies a sound bunch of wines, offering plenty of variety from around the world at decent prices. House wines kick off with a Chardonnay and a Merlot from Moldova at £9.95. CELLARMAN'S CHOICE: Whitestone Chardonnay 1995, Stellenbosch, South Africa, £13.95; Mezzo Corona Cabernet Sauvignon nv, Trentino, £13.50.

CHEF: Chris Oakley PROPRIETOR: The Pier at Harwich Ltd OPEN: all week 12 to 2, 6 to 9.30 CLOSED: D 25 and 26 Dec MEALS: alc (main courses £11.50 to £25). Set L £10.50 (2 courses) to £14, Set D £14.50 (2 courses) to £18 SERVICE: 10%, card slips closed CARDS: Amex, Delta, Diners, MasterCard, Switch, Visa DETAILS: 80 seats. Private parties: 90 main room, 40 private room. Car park. Vegetarian meals. Children's helpings. Music ACCOMMODATION: 6 rooms, all with bath/shower. TV. Phone. B&B £50 to £80. Children welcome. Baby facilities (*The Which? Hotel Guide*)

HASLEMERE Surrey map 3

Fleur de Sel

23–27 Lower Street, Haslemere GU27 2NY COOKING 6
TEL: (01428) 651462 FAX: (01428) 661568 COST £23–£56

A trio of seventeenth-century terraced cottages perched high above the main road through Haslemere have been knocked through to create the Perrauds' classically French restaurant. The windows are camouflaged with opaque net curtains, and tables are set with the crispest napery. The tone throughout, enhanced by Madame Perraud and the French waitresses, is one of attentive civility.

Michel Perraud mixes 'very French cooking' with modern ideas in a style that one reporter found 'a little too nouvelle'. An inspection meal opened with a tiny crab-cake adorned with fresh mango chutney and accompanied by mixed leaves: a nice enough combination, though served very cold. Better was a dish of scallops and langoustines with black pasta, and beurre blanc dotted with tomato, and more than one report speaks highly of a main course that brings together a selection of different fish – maybe sea bass, sea bream and salmon – in a creamy sauce. Red meats such as duck and lamb are cooked pink (although perhaps 'an English pink rather than a French one'), and the timing certainly suited a tasty magret that came with a spot-on honey and ginger sauce. Vegetables appear on the main plates but in fairly scant quantities. M. Perraud adds kirsch-marinated cherries to his crème brûlée and also offers the fashionable selection (or rather 'farandole') of desserts at a supplement to the fixed-menu price. Pineapple parfait and peppered strawberry gratin show a willingness to break with the standard repertoire. Wines are mostly classical French at prices that will test most budgets to the full, with only three bins under £15. There is a good representation of half-bottles, though, and the southern French house wines are £11.

CHEF: Michel Perraud PROPRIETORS: Michel and Bernadette Perraud OPEN: Tue to Fri and Sun L 12 to 2, Tue to Sat D 7 to 10 CLOSED: 2 weeks summer MEALS: Set L and D all week £21 (2 courses) to £26, Set L Tue to Fri from £9.50 (2 courses), Set L Sun and Set D Tue to Thur from £12.50 (2 courses) SERVICE: 12.5% (optional), card slips closed CARDS: Amex, Delta, MasterCard, Switch, Visa DETAILS: 50 seats. Private parties: 50 main room. Vegetarian meals. Children welcome. No cigars in dining-room. Wheelchair access (no WC)

HASTINGS East Sussex map 3

Röser's

64 Eversfield Place, St Leonards on Sea,
Hastings TN37 6DB COOKING 7
TEL/FAX: (01424) 712218 COST £27–£66

Over the years, readers may have noticed Röser's moving about a bit. It used to be in St Leonard's, but has now settled down comfortably in Hastings. Last year it was 100 metres east of the pier, this year it is to the west of it. In all this, it should be said that the restaurant itself has not moved an inch. We hope the new co-ordinates will be sufficient to pinpoint one of the best restaurants on the north coast, sorry south coast. It occupies an unassuming terraced Victorian house and operates on a domestic scale, yet the room is generously proportioned and tables are well-spaced. There are no frills, however, in either décor or cooking, save for an appetiser of cappuccino soup to start things off.

Gerald Röser's style is defined less by his choice of ingredients (though he seeks out the best quality) than by his skill in turning them into carefully balanced dishes, each with a distinct identity: smoke-roasted salmon with a gewurztraminer sauce, for example, or pork and coriander sausages with red cabbage. He collects mushrooms, and smokes and cures meat and fish, turning them into pickled wild mushroom salad to serve with roast wood pigeon breast, perhaps, or into port-cured and smoked wild boar ham. Desserts may explore a limited repertoire, but are supremely well-executed and might include chocolate mousse, apple mille-feuille, or lime mousse with bitter orange sauce. Jenny Röser writes that they have been 'experimenting with bread this year', and are particularly proud of the saffron and sourdough varieties.

One thing which definitely hasn't changed direction at Röser's is the quality of the wines. The vast majority come from just across the Channel, including dozens of classed clarets and fine old burgundies, plus some very tempting Rhônes. If you fancy a change, head south to Spain or nip across to Italy for a good spread of sound bins. Five house wines, all French, start at £10.95. CELLARMAN'S CHOICE: Alsace, Tokay-Pinot Gris 'Cuvée Caroline' 1995, Dom. Schoffit, £22.95; Bandol 1990, Dom. de la Noblesse, £18.95.

CHEF: Gerald Röser PROPRIETORS: Gerald and Jenny Röser OPEN: Tue to Fri L 12 to 2, Tue to Sat D 7 to 10 (booking essential) CLOSED: first 2 weeks Jan, last 2 weeks Jun MEALS: alc (main courses £13 to £22). Set L £18.95, Set D Tue to Fri £21.95 SERVICE: net prices, card slips closed CARDS: Amex, Delta, Diners, MasterCard, Switch, Visa DETAILS: 30 seats. Private parties: 16 main room, 30 private room. Vegetarian meals. Children welcome. No cigars/pipes in dining-room. Wheelchair access (no WC). No music

HAWORTH West Yorkshire map 8

▲ *Weaver's* £

15 West Lane, Haworth BD22 8DU — COOKING 2
TEL: (01535) 643822 FAX: (01535) 644832 — COST £21–£42

Colin and Jane Rushworth have occupied these old weavers' cottages at the top of the main cobbled street close to the parsonage for 20 years. Spindles, old adverts and bric-à-brac clutter the bar, while the dining-room is 'a little posher'. The simple provincial cooking style seems to have found its own strengths, and the repertoire doesn't change much, weighing into cheese fritters with a will, and serving parsnip and cashew-nut loaf alongside more ambitious fillet and belly of pork with crackling, herb stuffing and a cider and apple sauce. Shoulder of Yorkshire lamb is slowly cooked and served with onion mash, while a hotpot enterprisingly combines rabbit, pigeon and lamb with sliced potatoes. Puddings offer the comfort of hot chocolate, sticky toffee, or 'nannie's surprise', and early diners get a good deal from a more limited menu. Well-selected and reasonably priced wines are the backbone of a list that begins with 18 recommendations under £14.

CHEFS/PROPRIETORS: Colin and Jane Rushworth OPEN: Tue to Sat D only 6.45 to 9.15 CLOSED: 2 weeks Christmas, 2 weeks June MEALS: alc (main courses £8 to £16). Set D Tue to Thur 6.45 to 7.45 and Fri 6.45 to 7.15 £10.95 (2 courses) to £12.95. BYO £3 SERVICE: not inc CARDS: Amex, Delta, Diners, MasterCard, Switch, Visa DETAILS: 60 seats. Private parties: 16 main room, 16 private room. Vegetarian meals. Children's helpings. No smoking in dining-room. Music. Air-conditioned ACCOMMODATION: 4 rooms, all with bath/shower. TV. Phone. B&B £49.50 to £69.50. Children welcome (*The Which? Hotel Guide*)

HAYDON BRIDGE Northumberland map 10

General Havelock Inn

Radcliffe Road, Haydon Bridge NE47 6ER — COOKING 1
TEL: (01434) 684376 — COST £18–£38

Warm hospitality from the Clydes is a feature of this dark green pub on the main road near the centre of Haydon Bridge. The dining-room, decorated with ancient agricultural implements and military paraphernalia, is a converted barn at the back, overlooking the South Tyne river, and makes a restful stop for motorists Sunday lunch is three courses, dinner four, the extra one being a creamy soup such as leek, or onion and Stilton. A *carte* is available Wednesday to Saturday lunch-times. The homely style, well practised over 18 years, might offer devilled crab, or a thick chunk of coarse terrine made with ham and duck liver, followed by roast duck with Cumberland sauce, or fresh-tasting plaice with lemon butter. Finish with sticky toffee pudding, or poached pear with butterscotch sauce, and drink either Tetley bitter or one of the under-£20 wines. House wine is £8.25.

CHEF: Angela Clyde PROPRIETORS: Ian and Angela Clyde OPEN: Wed to Sun L 12 to 1.30, Wed to Sat D 7.30 to 8.45 MEALS: alc L Wed to Sat (main courses £6 to £6.50). Set L Sun £12.25, Set D £20 SERVICE: not inc CARDS: none DETAILS: 28 seats. 8 seats outside. Private parties: 28 main room. Car park. Vegetarian meals. Children's helpings. Wheelchair access (also WC). Music

HAYFIELD Derbyshire map 9

▲ *Bridge End*

7 Church Street, Hayfield SK12 5JE COOKING **4**
TEL: (01663) 747321 FAX: (01663) 742121 COST £25–£44

'Comfortably the same', Barbara Tier's unfussy and rustic restaurant-with-rooms can be found near the attractive centre of this village on the fringes of the Peak District. Meals are served only five evenings a week: one reason, perhaps, why Joanne Winch appears to have lost no enthusiasm for her craft. She continues to sidestep the mundane and conventional, matching dill and raisin butter with salmon in puff pastry, for instance, and apples, marjoram and orange with guinea-fowl. Olives, canapés and home-made breads were auspicious precursors for one party who reported 'some first-class cooking' in goats' cheese tart with fromage frais, monkfish in a herby cream sauce, and sticky date sponge pudding with brandy and pecan sauce. An innovation called 'The Unabridged' allows ditherers to sample a selection of desserts. Coffee is strong and comes with home-made chocolates. Wines, listed with helpful descriptions but not necessarily vintages, are divided between France and the New World, with a few representatives from Germany, Italy and Spain. House wines are £9.50 and £10.95.

CHEF: Joanne Winch PROPRIETOR: Barbara Tier OPEN: Tue to Sat D only 7.30 to 10 CLOSED: first week Jan MEALS: alc (main courses £10 to £15.50) SERVICE: not inc CARDS: Amex, Diners, MasterCard, Visa DETAILS: 50 seats. Private parties: 36 main room, 20 private room. Vegetarian meals. Children's helpings. No smoking before coffee. Music ACCOMMODATION: 4 rooms, all with bath/shower. TV. Phone. B&B £30 to £45. Deposit: £20. Children welcome. Baby facilities. Dogs welcome (*The Which? Hotel Guide*)

HERSTMONCEUX East Sussex map 3

Sundial £✱

Gardner Street, Herstmonceux BN27 4LA COOKING **5**
TEL: (01323) 832217 COST £31–£76

Styling itself a French auberge, the Sundial attracts a well-to-do crowd, amiably looked after by the 'civilised and welcoming' Bertolis. Fish is the strength, although the long menu also takes in interesting meat dishes such as lambs' kidneys combined with pigeon breast in a mustard sauce. Perhaps not surprisingly, given a proprietor with the name of Giuseppe Bertoli, there is some Italian input too – pig's trotter with polenta, for example, osso buco, or langoustines with risotto – but provincial French dishes of snails with garlic and pastis, or bouillabaisse with rouille, are at the heart of things. Fish demands last-minute preparation, and gets it.

The style may not move much with the times, but there is no arguing with the quality and care in cooking. Judgement is sound, even down to the balancing acidity in a dish of oxtail in port sauce, while an apparently standard-sounding pan-fried escalope of veal with tomato sauce and cheese has appealed for being 'so simple, so beautifully executed'. Game dishes of pigeon and jugged hare have been endorsed, but desserts do not have the same impact. In sum, the *carte* may cost 'serious money' but delivers 'serious food' in return. The long, conventional wine list, which generally aims for the upper end of the market, has picked up some classic claret over the years but shows little interest in the modern wine world. House Valpolicella and Soave are £12.25.

CHEF: Giuseppe Bertoli PROPRIETORS: Giuseppe and Laure Bertoli OPEN: Tue to Sun L 12 to 2 (2.30 Sun), Tue to Sat D 7 to 9.30 CLOSED: 25 Dec to 20 Jan, 10 Aug to first week Sept MEALS: alc (main courses £17.50 to £27.50). Set L Tue to Sat £19.50, Set L Sun £22.50, Set D £26.50 to £39.50 SERVICE: 10%, card slips closed CARDS: Amex, Delta, Diners, MasterCard, Switch, Visa DETAILS: 50 seats. 25 seats outside. Private parties: 65 main room, 23 private room. Car park. Vegetarian meals. Children's helpings. No smoking in dining-room. Wheelchair access (also WC). Music

HETTON North Yorkshire map 8

NORTH YORKS 1998 STAR

Angel Inn

Hetton BD23 6LT
TEL: (01756) 730263 FAX: (01756) 730363 COOKING 5
off B6265, 5m N of Skipton COST £26–£43

'Would that more pubs were like it,' began one reporter, happy to drive for two hours across the Pennines to get there. The good news for motorists on arrival is that there is now a new car park. 'Even though the décor is basic,' added another, 'the overall package is outstanding.' Several dishes are common to both the good-value bar/brasserie and the smarter restaurant dining-room, among them the long-standing 'money-bags of fishy bits' enclosed in filo pastry and served with a shellfish sauce, which is now being challenged for supremacy by a rich, marbled terrine of ham shank and foie gras served with Cumberland sauce. A table queuing system in the bar/brasserie has helped to reduce the scramble, and a regular reports that items on the printed menu are just as interesting and reliable (a key word for reporters) as the daily blackboard specials.

The kitchen is perfectly at home with a range of seafood, from 'startlingly fresh crab' sandwiched between layers of tuile-like pastry, to plaice – 'a mountain of excellent fillets of this underrated fish' – served skate-style with butter and capers. Slow-cooked dishes are also a forte, including a herby shoulder of Lothersdale lamb, which is first dry-marinated in sea salt, rosemary and garlic, then served with olive and thyme mash and a drizzle of pesto. Jaffa-cake pudding appears to play to the gallery, sticky toffee is a regular, Hetton mess is rather like Eton mess, and warm chargrilled peach is served on toasted brioche with vanilla ice-cream. Yorkshire Dales and Lancashire farmhouse cheeses are well kept.

The reasonably priced wine list opens with a selection of estate-bottled Italians, then moves on to a fine choice of burgundies and claret. An impressive 42 half-bottles include eight sticky dessert wines to challenge the sticky toffee pudding. House wines are from £9.50 and there is even an Angel Inn own-label champagne at £19.80. CELLARMAN'S CHOICE: Pouilly Fumé 1996, Dom. de Berthier, Jean-Claude Dagueneau, £16.95; Beaune premier cru 'Les Bressandes' 1989, Dom. Albert Morot, £23.75. Denis Watkins and John Topham also own the General Tarleton in Ferrensby (see entry).

CHEF: John Topham PROPRIETORS: Denis and Juliet Watkins, and John Topham OPEN: restaurant Sun L 12 to 2, Mon to Sat D 7 to 9.30; bar/brasserie all week 12 to 2, 6 to 9.30 CLOSED: 1 week Jan MEALS: restaurant Set L Sun £18.95, Set D £27.85; bar/brasserie alc (main courses £5.50 to £14.50) SERVICE: not inc, card slips closed CARDS: Amex, MasterCard, Switch, Visa DETAILS: restaurant 50 seats; bar/brasserie 60 seats. 40 seats outside. Private parties: 40 main room. Car park. Vegetarian meals. Children's helpings exc Sun L. No smoking in 1 dining-room. Wheelchair access (also WC). No music. Air-conditioned

HINTLESHAM Suffolk map 6

▲ *Hintlesham Hall* 🍷

Hintlesham IP8 3NS
TEL: (01473) 652268 FAX: (01473) 652463 COOKING 5
on A1071, 4½m W of Ipswich COST £28–£71

A 'grand but not intimidating' house, Hintlesham aims for comfort with lots of rooms, sumptuous sofas and expensively upholstered chairs. Relaxation is helped by a walk in the herb garden, coffee on the terrace, and knowledgeable and pleasant service from friendly and attentive staff. It is a 'fabulously well-run hotel' with a busy kitchen that typically deals in a dozen dishes per course at dinner when the set-price and à la carte menus are both in operation. There may be a few luxuries – sauté foie gras with pools of buttery Sauternes sauce – but the food generally strikes a balance between the reassurance of prime ingredients and the excitement of unusual partnerships.

Soups, for example, are enlivened with an addition of something appropriate: a 'little bomb' of pungent tapénade in a red pepper soup, small quenelles of salt-cod in fish chowder, or a clear chicken broth with diced tomato flesh, 'the sharpness of lemon grass giving everything zip'. The kitchen has delivered moist pork loin, a 'superior version' of rack of lamb with roasted Mediterranean vegetables and tapénade sauce, and breast of Gressingham duck with a 'mildly gamey flavour' and crispy skin, served with caramelised nectarines. Dishes may not always deliver the expected flavour combinations and textural contrasts, however.

For one reporter desserts were the star turn, and the choice might include iced prune and armagnac parfait, and mango soufflé with a papaya and pistachio sorbet. The 'stuffy dress code for men' can take the shine off things, but value is good. The wine list impresses with its intelligent selection of fine and interesting bins from around the world. Prices are about what you might expect from a country-house cellar which features clarets dating back to 1945, but there is good-value drinking to be found at all price levels, with excellent house recommendations starting at £12.50. An extensive collection of half-bottles adds to the appeal. CELLARMAN'S CHOICE: Quincy 1995, Mardon et Fils, £19.90; Graves, Ch. D'Arricaud 1988, £23.85.

'Rooms don't have numbers, but names of flowers. "I'm Bluebell," I said, returning from a walk and trying not to sound like a fairy.' (On eating in Scotland)

CHEF: Alan Ford PROPRIETOR: David Allan OPEN: Sun to Fri L 12 to 1.45, all week D 7 to 9.30 MEALS: alc (main courses £16.50 to £23). Set L £19.50, Set D Sun to Thur £25 SERVICE: net prices, card slips closed CARDS: Amex, Diners, MasterCard, Switch, Visa DETAILS: 120 seats. Private parties: 81 main room, 14 to 81 private rooms. Car park. Vegetarian meals. No children under 9. Jacket and tie. No smoking in dining-room. Wheelchair access (also WC). No music ACCOMMODATION: 33 rooms, all with bath/shower. TV. Phone. B&B £89 to £300. Children welcome. Baby facilities. Dogs by arrangement. Garden. Swimming-pool. Fishing (*The Which? Hotel Guide*)

HINTON CHARTERHOUSE Bath & N.E. Somerset map 2

▲ *Homewood Park*

Hinton Charterhouse BA3 6BB
TEL: (01225) 723731 FAX: (01225) 723820 COOKING 7
off A36, 6m SE of Bath COST £35–£85

Although within the orbit of Bath, this ivy-covered grey-stone Georgian building exerts its own pull. Bay windows look out over the grounds and surrounding countryside, the bar is 'cosy and jolly', and Gary Jones now has a new kitchen in which to put together his often demanding dishes. The monthly-changing à la carte dinner menu is condensed into a seven-course tasting version at £50 for anybody who wants to sample a range of them, supplemented by a couple of extra daily items per course. As one reporter noted, choice is difficult because everything looks good, from foie gras with potato confit and lentils, through poached fillet of Cornish turbot with a saffron and garlic bouillon, to chocolate and banana 'moon' with white chocolate sorbet.

This is sharp, well-focused cooking in which the components of a dish work together to give it a distinct identity. The approach may seem elaborate at times, but technique does not appear to be an end in itself, which is reassuring. At the lighter end of the spectrum, a civet of fish is spiked with lemon grass and served with scallop and coriander ravioli, while a contrasting braised pig's trotter might be served with sweetbreads and black pudding. Gary Jones has 'a laudable passion for quality', notable in the materials, and an 'ability to blend flavours with no disparate notes'. The effect is helped along by slicks of balsamic or sherry vinegar dressings, a herb-flavoured *jus* such as tomato and basil for chump of lamb, or rosemary for roast breast of chicken served with spiced pease pudding.

Though perhaps less liable to change, desserts are just as interesting, and have included mille-feuille of rhubarb with vanilla custard, mulled winter fruits with cinnamon and clove ice-cream, and tiramisù with espresso sauce and chocolate spaghetti. French wines tend to come from less-well-known producers, while those from the New World may be more familiar. Either way, prices are on the high side. House French is £14.50.

'Their blurb talks about nostalgic charm in an informal but elegant setting. I would say that it is somewhere between a poorly stocked antique shop and the village hall on jumble sale day.' (On eating in West Yorkshire)

CHEF: Gary Jones PROPRIETORS: the Gueuning and Fentum families OPEN: all week 12 to 1.30, 7 to 9.30 MEALS: alc (main courses £16 to £27). Set L £21, Set D £50 SERVICE: not inc CARDS: Amex, Delta, Diners, MasterCard, Switch, Visa DETAILS: 60 seats. Private parties: 40 main room. Car park. Vegetarian meals. Children's helpings. No smoking in dining-room. Wheelchair access (also WC). No music ACCOMMODATION: 19 rooms, all with bath/shower. TV. Phone. B&B £98 to £195. Rooms for disabled. Children welcome. Baby facilities. Afternoon teas. Garden. Swimming-pool (*The Which? Hotel Guide*)

HOLT Norfolk map 6

Yetman's

37 Norwich Road, Holt NR25 6SA COOKING 3
TEL: (01263) 713320 COST £38–£49

This is a very personal enterprise, in a low-ceilinged cottage with a light, fresh air about it. Like many couples who run a restaurant simply because they want to, Alison and Peter Yetman open in the evenings only (apart from Sunday lunch), presumably to give themselves a life outside the confines of a kitchen. They serve a bright-sounding daily-changing menu in which favourite dishes recur, and the natural curiosity that entertains Louisiana crab-cakes, or hot gougère of local asparagus also concerns itself with organic meat and bio-dynamic vegetables. Roasting and chargrilling are typically applied to noisettes of local spring lamb, or apple-fed Hereford duck, and peppers seem to be a favourite ingredient: red and yellow ones might be served with the duck, and roasted red ones are wrapped in sauté aubergine and served with creamed goats' cheese as a first course. Desserts have a bias towards fruit – rhubarb fool, or wild strawberry crème brûlée – and a glass of damson gin or raspberry vodka may tempt the intrepid.

Although wines are served without fuss, a great deal of care has gone into their selection, high quality combining with value for money on every page of the enthusiastically annotated list. Sauvignon Blanc is still the Yetmans' favourite grape, and there are some excellent New World examples. CELLARMAN'S CHOICE: Mulderbosch Vineyards Sauvignon Blanc 1996, Stellenbosch, South Africa, £15.50; Parker Cabernet Sauvignon 1989, Coonawarra, S. Australia, £22.75.

CHEF: Alison Yetman PROPRIETORS: Alison and Peter Yetman OPEN: Sun L 12.30 to 1.30, Wed to Sun D and Mon D in summer 7.30 to 9 MEALS: Set L and D £21.75 (2 courses) to £28 SERVICE: not inc, card slips closed CARDS: Amex, Delta, MasterCard, Switch, Visa DETAILS: 32 seats. Private parties: 18 main room, 12 private room. Vegetarian meals. Children welcome. No smoking in dining-room. Wheelchair access (no WC). No music

HONLEY West Yorkshire map 8

Mustard & Punch

6 Westgate, Honley HD7 2AA COOKING 4
TEL: (01484) 662066 COST £25–£40

A change of ownership and kitchen management in autumn 1996 came just too late for us to register a cooking mark in the 1997 *Guide*, but as Messrs Dunn and

Wood have settled in, the verdict seems to be steady as she goes. The interior, an extended exercise in the quirkiest of taste, hasn't changed; it is the proprietors who cheerfully describe it as 'cluttered'. The basement ceiling is festooned with hats and baskets, while *Punch* cartoons and mustard jars liven up the ground floor.

As an evening progresses, the lighting is dimmed, as if to emphasise the culinary dramatics taking place. Rillettes of duck confit and red chilli with pear compote and dried tomatoes is a starter for the adventurous, and more mainstream dishes, such as moules marinière and a soufflé of farmhouse Wensleydale, are well reported. A piece of beef fillet may gain little from its garnish of melted goats' cheese, but the brûlée dessert with banana pulp and brandy whisked into it is an undisputed winner. Breads and coffee are good, and service is uniformly obliging. The wine list has been streamlined since last year but still contains some interesting bottles at reasonable prices, and the Louis Latour Puligny-Montrachet 1994 is good value at £29.95. Chilean house wine is £9.50.

CHEFS: Christopher Dunn and Andrew Wood PROPRIETORS: Anna Young and Dorota Pencak OPEN: Tue to Fri L 12 to 2, Tue to Sat D 7 to 10 CLOSED: 25 Dec, bank hols MEALS: alc (main courses £9.50 to £14.50). Set L £5 to £10 (2 courses) SERVICE: not inc CARDS: Delta, MasterCard, Switch, Visa DETAILS: 50 seats. Private parties: 35 main room. Vegetarian meals. Children's helpings. No cigars/pipes in dining room. Music

HORNCASTLE Lincolnshire map 9

Magpies

73–75 East Street, Horncastle LN9 6AA COOKING 4
TEL: (01507) 527004 FAX: (01507) 524064 COST £25–£51

The Lee family's 'beautifully appointed' restaurant, just south of the Wolds, has featured on Lincolnshire's gastronomic scene for many years. It is a long, low building on the main coastal road, with naive art depicting cows, pigs, chicken and sheep. The real ones are carefully chosen: locally reared beef comes with parsley purée, and loin of lamb with pea purée. Careful cooking rather than novelty is the forte, producing a dish of salmon on a bed of spinach with a tarragon cream sauce, and an assiette of seafood that combined tuna and roast scallops. The good-value three-course lunch went down well with one reporter, who praised spinach tagliolini, and baked red mullet. Dinner is also three courses, though cheese may be taken as an extra. Service is usually 'friendly, informal and attentive' but can show signs of pressure on busy nights.

The ever-expanding wine list now tops 220 bins and the good news is that quality has not been sacrificed for the sake of quantity. Highlights include seven vintages of Ch. de Beaucastel in a particularly good Rhône section, and some fine reds from Australia. Half bottles are numerous and there are plenty of interesting bins under £20. CELLARMAN'S CHOICE: Mâcon-Chaintré 'Vieilles Vignes' 1995, Dom. Valette, £17; Casa Lapostolle Merlot 'Cuvée Alexandre' 1994, Chile, £20.

CHEFS: Matthew and Simon Lee PROPRIETORS: the Lee family OPEN: Wed to Fri L by arrangement, Tue to Sat D 7.15 to 10 CLOSED: 2 weeks Jan, 2 weeks Oct MEALS: Set L £10 to £12, Set D £25 SERVICE: not inc CARDS: MasterCard, Visa DETAILS: 40 seats. Private parties: 40 main room, 8 private room. Children welcome. No smoking in dining-room. Music

HORNDON ON THE HILL Essex map 3

▲ *Bell Inn* **NEW ENTRY**

High Road, Horndon on the Hill SS17 8LD COOKING **2**
TEL: (01375) 673154 FAX: (01375) 361611 COST **£25–£38**

Although dating from the fifteenth century, this former coaching-inn with its beams, flagstone floors and vaulted ceilings has a restaurant with a modern approach to food. An aubergine and goats'-cheese gâteau, for example, consists of a central tower of ratatouille topped with cheese and surrounded by a zigzagged drizzle of dressing. Main courses are similarly inventive: halibut steak in a herb crust with clams, and pigeon breast with haggis and rösti. Desserts might take in fresh fruit tart, or poached peaches in saffron and star-anise jelly with amaretto anglaise, a prettily presented and satisfying grown-up version of fruit jelly with custard. As the village's main watering-hole, the Bell is often packed, but 'pleasant, willing' young staff deal well under pressure. Around half of the hundred bottles on the fairly priced wine list come from France. House Australian is £9.

CHEF: Sean Kelly PROPRIETORS: J.S.B. and C.M. Vereker OPEN: Sun to Fri L 12 to 1.45, all week D 7 to 9.45 CLOSED: 25 and 26 Dec MEALS: alc (main courses £10 to £12.50) SERVICE: not inc, card slips closed CARDS: Amex, Delta, MasterCard, Switch, Visa DETAILS: 80 seats. 36 seats outside. Private parties: 10 main room, 26 and 36 private rooms. Car park. Vegetarian meals. Children's helpings. No-smoking area. No music ACCOMMODATION: 14 rooms, all with bath/shower. TV. Phone. Room only £45 to £70. Deposit: £25. Rooms for disabled. Children welcome. Baby facilities. Dogs welcome (*The Which? Hotel Guide*)

HORTON Northamptonshire map 5

French Partridge

Horton NN7 2AP
TEL: (01604) 870033 FAX: (01604) 870032 COOKING **6**
on B526, 6m SE of Northampton COST **£36–£43**

Thirty-five years is a long stretch in the restaurant business, and in all that time there doesn't seem to have been so much as a wobble in this kitchen's output. Perhaps it is because there are no managers, executive chefs or other devolved titles: all responsibility rests with the family. David and Mary Partridge are still going strong, son Justin is number two in the kitchen, his wife Helen serves, and there is simply no reason for the enterprise to veer from its well-charted course. Although there is no accommodation, the food has the feel of an English country house, with all the traditional French links that implies: onion soup, home-made terrines, oeufs à la neige, prunes in armagnac, and so on.

Nobody succeeds for this length of time without adapting to change, and the Partridges embrace variety with a will, happy to serve cod ceviche, braised shoulder of lamb with couscous, and Moroccan-style meatballs in a tomato sauce with cumin, allspice and mint. They also produce that rarity, a good chicken Kiev. There is no hint of pretension, and part of the appeal is that the mercifully modest and realistic aims are consistently achieved. It all hangs together because of the well-balanced four-course format, rightly considered a bargain, which might end with a savoury such as mushrooms on toast for anyone who is not tempted by caramelised apple tart, strawberry parfait, or peaches in marsala.

Good value extends to the wines too, which cheerfully combine high quality with reasonably low prices. Germany and the Rhône strike gold on a list which has also found some New World gems. Brief tasting notes introduce the grape varieties and styles, but Mary Partridge will gladly lend advice when it is needed. CELLARMAN'S CHOICE: Cloudy Bay, Pelorus 1991, Marlborough, New Zealand, £19; Irouléguy 1992, Dom. Ilarria, £16.

CHEFS: David and Justin Partridge PROPRIETORS: David and Mary Partridge OPEN: Tue to Sat D only 7.30 to 9 CLOSED: 2 weeks Christmas, 2 weeks Easter, 3 weeks mid-July to Aug MEALS: Set D £26 SERVICE: net prices CARDS: none DETAILS: 50 seats. Private parties: 20 main room. Car park. Children welcome. No smoking in dining-room. Wheelchair access (no WC). No music

HOVINGHAM North Yorkshire map 9

▲ *Worsley Arms, The Restaurant* **NEW ENTRY**

Hovingham YO6 4LA COOKING 2
TEL: (01653) 628234 FAX: (01653) 628130 COST £19–£49

Hovingham, in the wealthy heart of North Yorkshire, is the seat of the Worsley clan and birthplace of the Duchess of Kent. The Worsley Arms, which dates from 1841, has the rather formal air of a country gent's retreat, with copies of *Country Life* and the *Daily Telegraph* in the lounges. Like many pubs, it has a more informal bar bistro as a counterpoint to the dining-room proper. The latter's sensibly short menu turns up some interesting items, such as cream of snow pea and coriander soup with roast langoustines, or a pressed terrine of haricot beans, duck confit and home-smoked ham. Fish makes a strong impact, in one case a 'magnificent' piece of turbot, 'incredibly firm, wonderfully flavoured' – though perhaps it was misplaced in a broth of ham hock – and local game has included pot roast Hovingham pheasant. Vegetarians get a fair deal, and desserts run to lemon-flavoured crème brûlée in a pastry case, and raspberries set in elderflower jelly. Staff are uniformed, polite and proper – 'we were looked after very well' – and a global spread of 60 wines is offered, starting with house French at £11.

CHEF: Andrew Jones PROPRIETOR: A. E. Rodger OPEN: Sun L 12 to 2, all week D 7 to 9.30 MEALS: alc D (main courses £13.50 to £17). Set L £16. Set D £23.50. Bistro menu available all week L and D. BYO £5 SERVICE: not inc, card slips closed CARDS: Amex, Delta, Diners, MasterCard, Switch, Visa DETAILS: 60 seats. 20 seats outside. Private parties: 60 main room, 10 and 30 private rooms. Car park. Vegetarian meals. Children's helpings. No smoking in dining-room. Wheelchair access (no WC). Music ACCOMMODATION: 18 rooms, all with bath/shower. TV. Phone. B&B £60 to £90. Deposit: £30. Rooms for disabled. Children welcome. Baby facilities. No dogs in public areas. Afternoon teas. Garden (*The Which? Hotel Guide*)

HUDDERSFIELD West Yorkshire map 9

Bradley's £

84 Fitzwilliam Street, Huddersfield HD1 5BB COOKING 2
TEL: (01484) 516773 FAX: (01484) 538386 COST £12–£41

Although Andrew Bradley's busy, congenial bistro in a warehouse conversion is about half a mile from the centre of town, reporters head there for its exceptional value for money and cheery atmosphere. The set three-course lunch has actually plunged in price since the last edition of the *Guide*: a fiver will easily pay for, say, salmon mousse, escalope of pork with lovage sauce, and iced rum and vanilla parfait. An equally affordable deal is the early-bird menu, particularly as the price includes half a bottle of house wine. The *carte* also promises sound brasserie-style dishes along the lines of lamb and mint sausage with blackeye beans and shallot sauce, and chargrilled breast of chicken with beetroot, pear and curly endive, as well as steaks and grills. The wine list offers a good range of around 50 bins with prices in keeping with the food. House wine is £8.95.

CHEF: Jonathan Nichols PROPRIETORS: Andrew Bradley and Jonathan Nichols OPEN: Mon to Fri L 12 to 2, Mon to Sat D 6 to 10 (10.30 Fri and Sat) CLOSED: bank hols MEALS: alc (main courses £8 to £15). Set L £4.90, Set D (inc wine) 6 to 7.30 (9 Mon, 7 Sat) £12.95 SERVICE: not inc CARDS: Delta, MasterCard, Switch, Visa DETAILS: 75 seats. Private parties: 75 main room. Car park (D only). Vegetarian meals. Children's helpings. No cigars/pipes in dining-room. Wheelchair access (also WC). Music. Air-conditioned

Café Pacific £

3 Viaduct Street, Huddersfield HD1 5DL COOKING 3
TEL: (01484) 559055 FAX: (01484) 559155 COST £19–£30

This conversion of a railway arch into an open-plan café with a slate floor and blond-wood furniture is 'welcoming and comfortable, but no money has been wasted on spurious opulence'. Last year's Pennine Newcomer is still on track, offering some exciting cooking at come-hither prices, and dishes on two big blackboards embrace a united nations of flavours headed by Italy and the Pacific Rim. Moist tuna kebabs with Mediterranean vegetables and a sesame and soy sauce, and a cake of potato and celeriac with spicy tomato salsa are two starters that have been praised. Commended main courses include cod in a light curry sauce with saffron and bacon, 'moist, delicately pink' salmon Wellington with well-made tarragon sauce, and oxtail with parsley dumplings in thick, meaty gravy. For dessert, try fig frangipane tart, or steamed sponge pudding stuffed with nuts served with butterscotch sauce. The wine list of 30-plus bottles is biased towards the New World, with house wines opening at £8.50.

CHEF/PROPRIETOR: Scott Hessel OPEN: Tue to Sat 12 to 2.30, 6 to 10 (later Fri and Sat) CLOSED: 25 Dec MEALS: alc (main courses L £4 to £6, D £6 to £9.50) SERVICE: not inc; 10% on parties for 7 or more CARDS: Delta, MasterCard, Switch, Visa DETAILS: 55 seats. Private parties: 70 main room. Vegetarian meals. Children welcome. Wheelchair access (no WC). Music

See inside the front cover for an explanation of the symbols used at the tops of entries.

▲ *Lodge Hotel* 🍷

48 Birkby Lodge Road, Birkby,
Huddersfield HD2 2BG — COOKING 3
TEL: (01484) 431001 FAX: (01484) 421590 — COST £21–£41

'Despite being a hotel, it still retains the air of a family home,' reckoned one visitor to this stone-built creeper-covered Victorian building a few miles from Huddersfield. Drapes abound, and bold colours make a splash in the dining-room, where refurbishment has brought some of the art nouveau features to life. A soup (maybe French onion, or tomato and celeriac) converts the basic three-course format into four, and there is usually something to tempt the adventurous. A starter of linguine with sweet-and-sour chicken and mango indicates the kitchen's predilection for fruit and meat partnerships.

Seasoning and timing are well managed, and skills are evident in, for example, ravioli of lobster and crab in a clear seafood broth. Main courses concentrate more on meat than fish, ranging from osso buco (correctly served with risotto milanese and gremolata) to roast squab pigeon with wild mushrooms, to saddle of spring lamb. Puddings tend to console, offering steamed raspberry roly-poly with 'proper custard', or warm chocolate soufflé with chocolate sauce and mocha cream. 'Mr Birley is a cheerful, knowledgeable front-of-house man', and wines play their part in keeping interest high and prices reasonable. Plenty of exciting bottles feature on the list, which manages to cover most of the points on the wine compass. House wines start at £10.95. CELLARMAN'S CHOICE: Rias Baixas Alabariño 1994, Pazo de Barrantes, £21.95; Grant Burge Black Monster Old Vine Shiraz 1993, Barossa Valley, S. Australia, £18.50.

CHEFS: Garry and Kevin Birley, and Richard Hanson PROPRIETORS: Garry and Kevin Birley OPEN: Mon to Fri L 12 to 1.45, Mon to Sat D 7.30 to 9.45 CLOSED: 3 days after Christmas MEALS: Set L £13.95, Set D £23.95 SERVICE: not inc, card slips closed CARDS: Amex, Delta, MasterCard, Visa DETAILS: 100 seats. 20 seats outside. Private parties: 62 main room, 10 to 24 private rooms. Car park. Vegetarian meals. Children's helpings. No toddlers at D. No smoking in dining-room. Wheelchair access (also WC). Music ACCOMMODATION: 11 rooms, all with bath/shower. TV. Phone. B&B £60 to £80. Children welcome. Baby facilities. Dogs welcome. Garden

---

HUNSTRETE Bath & N.E. Somerset — map 2

▲ *Hunstrete House*

Hunstrete, Chelwood BS18 4NS
TEL: (01761) 490490 FAX: (01761) 490732 — COOKING 6
off A368, 4m S of Keynsham — COST £34–£84

The 92-acre deer park makes a fine setting, and if the low grey building is no beauty, it is commanding and has pretty climbers growing up its façade. From the white and pink dining-room with its decorative friezes and fine marble fireplace, diners can look out on to the pleasant paved courtyard with its weeping pear trees. The Fentums, who also jointly own Homewood Park (see entry, Hinton Charterhouse), took over in March 1997, and with them has come Clive Dixon, who made a considerable splash at Lords of the Manor hotel (see entry, Upper Slaughter). His style is Anglo-French though not constrained by either discipline, and he is fond of earthy flavours such as lentils and offal, including his favourite, foie gras.

Although served on large plates, dishes are not weighed down by fussy presentation. Some ideas are 'dead simple', but none the worse for that. Seared tuna niçoise, for instance, comes with first-class vegetables and fresh anchovies to produce 'resounding flavours'. A more complex dish of Trelough duckling, on the other hand, impressed an inspector for its pink flesh, crisp skin, unlikely but successful sauce of honey and vanilla, and accompanying tian of potatoes and shredded leg confit. Pain perdu made from brioche with poached figs in a spiced red wine sauce, served with cinnamon ice-cream, was a 'perfect' dessert for one reporter. You can spend – and eat – a lot by going for the Menu Dégustation of eight courses, less by choosing carefully from the *carte*, and even less with the daily-changing Market Menu. The wine list harbours some quality bins, mainly from the classical French regions but with some useful New World contributions too, and this is reflected in the prices, with few bottles coming in under £20. House French is £14.95.

CHEF: Clive Dixon PROPRIETORS: Mr and Mrs Haydn Fentum OPEN: all week 12.15 to 2, 7.15 to 9.45 (10 Fri and Sat) MEALS: alc (main courses £20 to £25) Set L £19.95, Market Menu £33, Menu Dégustation £55 (whole table only) SERVICE: not inc CARDS: Amex, Delta, Diners, MasterCard, Switch, Visa DETAILS: 80 seats. 30 seats outside. Private parties: 50 main room, 18 and 48 private rooms. Car park. Vegetarian meals. Children's helpings. No smoking in dining-room. Wheelchair access (also women's WC). No music. Air-conditioned ACCOMMODATION: 23 rooms, all with bath/shower. TV. Phone. D,B&B £95 to £250. Children welcome. Dogs welcome by arrangement. Afternoon teas. Garden. Swimming-pool. Fishing (*The Which? Hotel Guide*)

HURSTBOURNE TARRANT Hampshire map 2

▲ *Esseborne Manor* 🍷

Hurstbourne Tarrant SP11 0ER
TEL: (01264) 736444 FAX: (01264) 736725 COOKING 5
on A343, 1½m N of Hurstbourne Tarrant COST £28–£55

This cream-painted house of irregular shape has 'a real country feel about it', and is one reporter's ideal of what a hotel restaurant should be. A pinkish dining-room with flowers and Wedgwood china is the setting for Nick Watson's technically accomplished cooking. He might turn out a first course of sliced pink pigeon breast in a filo basket, among leaves of buttered spinach on a rich madeira sauce, or one of red mullet fillets with deep-fried leeks and a sauce of tomato, basil and ginger. The food is lively, colour and presentation are well thought out, saucing is interesting without being experimental, and dishes are carefully balanced so as to be complex but not too elaborate, as in a main course of monkfish in a chive butter sauce accompanied by a duxelles of red peppers in a nest of smooth mash, plus a little bundle of okra tied up with chive: 'best monkfish in many a moon' for its reporter.

The style may strike a traditional note, but there is a marked confidence in the cooking, not least in desserts such as poached pears in raspberry and cinnamon coulis, or a sablé of strawberries in vanilla cream. Service is courteous to a fault, although perhaps a little too eager to please when it comes to pouring wine. The wine list continues to favour France, with three-quarters of the bottles hailing from there. In the New World section, Australia just has the edge over New Zealand and California, and newcomers Chile and South Africa make an appearance with one Sauvignon each. Pricing is fair, and five house wines start at £13.50 a bottle, £3 a glass.

CHEF: Nick Watson PROPRIETOR: Ian Hamilton OPEN: all week 12 to 2.30, 7 to 9.30 MEALS: alc (main courses £13 to £21). Set L and D Sun to Thur £13 (2 courses) to £17 SERVICE: not inc, card slips closed CARDS: Amex, Delta, Diners, MasterCard, Switch, Visa DETAILS: 40 seats. 20 seats outside. Private parties: 45 main room. Car park. Vegetarian meals. No children under 7. No cigars/pipes in dining-room. Wheelchair access (also women's WC). Music ACCOMMODATION: 14 rooms, all with bath/shower. TV. Phone. B&B £88 to £160. Rooms for disabled. No children under 7. Dogs welcome. Afternoon teas. Garden (*The Which? Hotel Guide*)

HUXHAM Devon map 1

▲ *Barton Cross*

Huxham, Stoke Canon EX5 4EJ
TEL: (01392) 841245 FAX: (01392) 841942 COOKING 2
off A396 at Stoke Canon, signposted Huxham COST £32–£44

Located in countryside close to the village of Stoke Canon, the hotel comprises three seventeenth-century thatched cottages with modern extensions. Tables are set in the gallery as well as on the ground floor of the beamed restaurant, and a log fire adds cheer in winter. Everything from canapés and bread to puddings and petits fours is made in-house, and the menu moves with the seasons. In warm weather you are likely to find Brixham fish – in a red wine ragoût, perhaps – while in winter there may be venison with root vegetables and black pudding. Strongly flavoured gazpacho of langoustines with scallops, or a terrine of pheasant, duck and venison might be among the starters, and rack of lamb ('tender, pink and full of flavour') or 'excellent, very fresh, firm' turbot with a beer butter sauce among main courses. Desserts run to rhubarb parfait, or perhaps chocolate sponge pudding. Portions tend to be large, and service is friendly. The long wine list is well set out, with house wines (from £9.25) to the fore, plenty of half-bottles and affordable prices.

CHEF: Paul George Bending PROPRIETORS: B.A. and G.A. Hamilton OPEN: Mon to Sat D only 6.45 to 9.45 MEALS: alc (main courses £12.50 to £16.50). Set D £18.50 (2 courses) to £22.50 SERVICE: not inc, card slips closed CARDS: Amex, Delta, MasterCard, Switch, Visa DETAILS: 45 seats. Private parties: 40 main room, 12 private room. Car park. Vegetarian meals. Children's helpings. No smoking in dining-room. Wheelchair access (also WC). Music ACCOMMODATION: 7 rooms, all with bath/shower. TV. Phone. B&B £63.50 to £85. Rooms for disabled. Children welcome. Baby facilities. Dogs welcome. Afternoon teas. Garden

'Never have I seen a wine waiter play out one bottle of wine for so long between five people. It was masterly. So masterly, I wanted to watch him do it all over again, so ordered another bottle.' (On eating in London)

HYTHE Hampshire map 2

Boathouse Brasserie

29 Shamrock Way, Hythe Marina Village,
Hythe SO45 6DY COOKING **5**
TEL: (01703) 845594 FAX: (01703) 846017 COST £22–£45

Yachts of all descriptions bob about in the marina where this bright and cheery brasserie is situated. 'Pleasant, restrained and tasteful' is how one reporter summed up the appeal of the place, the eating-area raised a little above the space reserved for those who are only drinking. Mismatched tables and chairs add to the informality, and pictorial decorations have a relentlessly nautical air about them, so you might feel you have acquired your sea-legs by the end of the meal.

Chef Ian McAndrew has cooked in Ireland and across southern England, as well as being a cookery writer. His first collection of recipes was devoted to fish, and it comes as no surprise to find sea creatures on the menus here. Sole is made into a terrine with leeks on (as the menu puts it) 'a bed of frizzy', sea bass is accompanied by poached oysters in a light oyster cream, while salmon fillet is given the Chinese treatment with braised pak choi and a soy and ginger sauce. Substantial meat dishes take in venison with celeriac, parsnip purée and wild mushrooms, and braised pork belly with haricot beans and grain mustard. If you want more vegetables, they must be paid for, but the cosmopolitan choice includes potatoes in the Indian or lyonnaise manner and Polish-style cauliflower. Puddings may favour homely rhubarb crumble, or pile on the style for chocolate marquise with pear sorbet. The wine list takes a quick spin round France, Italy and Australia. Prices are mostly agreeable, starting with house selections at £9.

CHEF: Ian McAndrew PROPRIETOR: Leisure Great Britain (Oakley) Ltd OPEN: Tue to Sun L 12 to 2.30, Tue to Sat D 7 to 10 CLOSED: 2 weeks early Jan MEALS: alc (main courses L £7.50 to £9, D £10.50 to £14). Set L Tue to Fri £10.50 (2 courses). BYO £5 SERVICE: not inc CARDS: Delta, MasterCard, Switch, Visa DETAILS: 50 seats. 25 seats outside. Private parties: 40 main room, 12 private room. Children welcome. Wheelchair access (also WC). Music. Air-conditioned

ILKLEY West Yorkshire map 8

Box Tree 🍷 $✱

WEST YORKS 1998 INDIVIDUAL

37 Church Street, Ilkley LS29 0QS COOKING **8**
TEL: (01943) 608484 FAX: (01943) 607186 COST £38–£72

'The Box Tree really is on top form,' reckoned one of several visitors who came away full of praise for the talented Thierry LePrêtre-Granet. Much-needed redecoration to the pretty eighteenth-century farmhouse beside the A65 has produced some striking gold, deep red and cream colours in the bar, although the dining-room's high-backed chairs are genuine antiques 'last upholstered 50 years ago'. Well-spaced tables are immaculately set, and napkins are unfurled on to knees, in readiness for some of the best cooking in the north of England.

Menus read simply, a first indication that the skill here lies not so much in gastronomic somersaults, as in poised, well-executed and subtle renditions, very much against the busy, innovative trend. As one reporter put it, 'The Box

Tree is one of those places where what arrives on the plate is much more exciting than what one reads on the page,' a view prompted by 'tender gamey' pigeon in a rich sticky stock, with 'a happy pairing of cabbage', all done with 'perfect seasoning and timing'. Despite the traditional tilt of ideas, the food has a zest and lightness to it. At an inspection meal, freshness and 'spot-on' timing combined to produce a winning first course of scallops with a lightly curry-flavoured chutney and lemon sauce.

The set-price lunch is considered good value, but dinner is not much dearer, and choice might take in a starter of snails with garlic purée, sea bass with a tarragon cream sauce, or noisettes of fat-free lamb in a thin rosemary *jus* 'packed with flavour'. Finely diced vegetables are typically woven into main courses. A 13-year-old regular visitor writes: 'I am a vegetarian and all my meals have been exquisite,' citing in evidence a vegetable risotto topped with a quail's egg, and a lattice of mushrooms in pastry with asparagus tips and carrots. Desserts are first-rate too, including perhaps a compote of cherries surrounding a kirsch parfait, topped with a chocolate sorbet, and a 'heavenly' hot prune and armagnac soufflé with a jug of hot vanilla sauce.

'We were called "sir" and "madam" but the service was not at all pompous,' and meals progress at a natural pace from appetisers of cherry tomatoes and tapénade right through to an amazing choice of coffees with good petits-fours. The wine list is well worth a few minutes' consideration for it has a splendid collection of first-class bottles, not only from France but also Italy and Australia. Prices reflect the grandeur of the wines, but lower levels are not neglected: a house selection starts at £12 and 20 wines are available by the glass from £3. CELLARMAN'S CHOICE: Champagne Pommery Brut Royale nv, £29.95; Barolo 1991, Nicolello, £10.35.

CHEF: Thierry LePrêtre-Granet PROPRIETOR: The Box Tree Restaurant (Ilkley) Ltd OPEN: Tue to Sun 12 to 2.30, 7 to 9.30 CLOSED: 25 Dec to 1 Jan, last 2 weeks Jan MEALS: alc (main courses £16 to £20). Set L £22.50, Set D £29.50 SERVICE: not inc, card slips closed CARDS: Amex, MasterCard, Visa DETAILS: 50 seats. Private parties: 26 main room, 16 private room. Vegetarian meals. No children under 5. No smoking in dining-room. Wheelchair access (no WC). No music

IPSWICH Suffolk map 6

Mortimer's on the Quay £

Wherry Quay, Ipswich IP4 1AS
TEL: (01473) 230225 FAX: (01284) 761611

COOKING **2**
COST £21–£48

The forte of this ten-year-old restaurant by the quay – and its older sister in Bury St Edmunds (see entry) – is plainly cooked, exceedingly fresh fish. The menu changes daily, depending on the fish market's offerings, and there are a few blackboard dishes. One winter special, a kebab of monkfish and giant prawns, was 'leaping out of the sea, gently chargrilled and good value at £5.25'. Halibut florentine and breadcrumbed and pan-fried plaice with first-rate tartare sauce are also considered winners, although less-simple dishes such as red mullet with both mushrooms and dill butter can be less successful. The well-chosen, mostly French wine list includes some prestigious producers. House wines start at £8.50.

CHEF: Kenneth Ambler PROPRIETORS: Kenneth Ambler and Michael Gooding OPEN: Mon to Fri L 12 to 2, Mon to Sat D 6.30 to 9 (8.15 Mon) CLOSED: 24 Dec to 5 Jan, 2 weeks Aug, bank hol Mon and Tue MEALS: alc (main courses £8 to £19) SERVICE: not inc CARDS: Amex, Delta, Diners, MasterCard, Switch, Visa DETAILS: 60 seats. Private parties: 12 main room, 22 private room. Children's helpings. No smoking in 1 dining-room. Wheelchair access (no WC). No music

Scott's Brasserie £

NEW ENTRY

4A Orwell Place, Ipswich IP4 1BB — COOKING **3**
TEL: (01473) 230254 FAX: (01473) 218851 — COST £22–£27

'It really is a place where you can be comfortable, feel cosseted and, above all, enjoy good food,' concluded one reporter. At the front is a small snack bar, and up some stairs to the back is a dining-room with copper pan lids and pictures (for sale) on the walls. Linen napkins tied with ribbons are unfurled and placed on the lap by waiters in brocaded waistcoats: they look after you well here.

To mix a metaphor, Scott Davidson goes about his task in a freewheeling way without going overboard. An inspector praised Bermuda fish chowder laced with rum and 'sherry peppers', and 'moist, flavoursome' roast pork tenderloin filled with apple and Stilton mousse, served with a marsala sauce. A specials board might offer fillet of trout wrapped round baby asparagus with a lemon and hazelnut sauce, and indulgent desserts have included steamed ginger pudding with 'a superb lime and vanilla sauce that lifted the dish into [the] memorable category'. France is the focus of the list of around 30 wines. House wines start at £9.25 (£2.25 a glass).

CHEF: Scott Davidson PROPRIETORS: Scott Davidson and Charles Lewis OPEN: Mon to Fri L 12 to 2.30, Tue to Sat D 6.30 (7 Sat) to 10 CLOSED: bank hols MEALS: Set L and D £13.95 (2 courses) to £11.95, Set D £16.95 SERVICE: not inc, card slips closed CARDS: Amex, Delta, MasterCard, Switch, Visa DETAILS: 75 seats. Private parties: 35 main room, 30 private room. Vegetarian meals. Children's helpings. No pipes in dining-room. Wheelchair access (no WC). Music

IXWORTH Suffolk — map 6

Theobalds

68 High Street, Ixworth IP31 2HJ — COOKING **4**
TEL/FAX: (01359) 231707 — COST £29–£39

'I sometimes wish,' confided one perverse reporter, 'that there was a good restaurant in the area that was not housed in an interesting old building with exposed beams, and did not have a small lounge where one took a pre-meal drink in a luxurious armchair while perusing the menu.' Well, tough, because Theobalds is all of that. Aren't some people ungrateful? The house was built in 1650, Simon and Geraldine Theobald arrived 331 years later, and have been here ever since, serving up lots of ideas, many with a strong provincial feel: pigeon breasts wrapped in bacon, for example, or noisettes of hare with a red wine and gooseberry jelly sauce.

Menu choice is varied and generous, and the format has altered slightly since last year: each dish on the *carte* is now priced individually. One reporter enjoyed a 'really superb' twice-baked soufflé made from Red Leicester cheese, which he considered ideal for the job on account of its mild taste and vivid colour, and was pleased to see that vegetables are 'treated with respect'. Many sauces contain herbs or alcohol – tarragon with breast of cornfed chicken, or sherry with roast best end of lamb, for instance – and desserts can be rich: chocolate marquise with coffee-bean sauce, or hazelnut praline ice-cream in chocolate sauce.

Wines are straightforwardly listed by colour and price, and helpful notes accompany the specially recommended ones. Over 30 half-bottles seems more than reasonable, and quality throughout is high. House wines start at £12.50. CELLARMAN'S CHOICE: Gewurztraminer d'Alsace grand cru 1991, Dom. Eugene Meyer, £32.65; Crozes-Hermitage 1995, Dom. du Colombier, £22.35.

CHEF: Simon Theobald PROPRIETORS: Simon and Geraldine Theobald OPEN: Tue to Fri and Sun L 12.15 to 1.30, Tue to Sat D 7.15 to 9.15 CLOSED: 2 weeks Aug MEALS: alc (main courses L £8.50, D £10 to £17). Set L £12.50 (2 courses), Set L Sun £16.95. BYO £5 SERVICE: not inc CARDS: Delta, MasterCard, Switch, Visa DETAILS: 36 seats. 10 seats outside. Private parties: 36 main room. Vegetarian meals. Children's helpings. No smoking in dining-room. No music

JEVINGTON East Sussex map 3

Hungry Monk $*

Jevington BN26 5QF
TEL/FAX: (01323) 482178 COOKING 3
off A22, between Polegate and Friston COST £33–£45

It doesn't seem possible that banoffi pie is a mere 27 years old, but it must be because it was invented at the Hungry Monk three years after it opened its doors in 1968. The house is strong on creature comforts, with much of the space given over to sofas and log fires, while the menu, with around seven dishes per course, is unusual in including in the price a post-prandial glass of port rather than a cup of coffee. The Mackenzies long ago found a formula that worked and, by sticking to it, have attracted a loyal following. And if that means soothing customers with tried-and-tested ideas rather than challenging them with novelty, so be it.

Here you might find smoked haddock chowder, potted prawns, and rack of lamb with roast garlic. Not all combinations work equally well, but among successes have been sweet onion tarte Tatin balanced by bitter rocket leaves, a thick and well-flavoured leek and coriander soup with chorizo, and roast, stuffed rabbit with a bacon sauce and celeriac purée. If banoffi doesn't appeal, consider bread-and-butter pudding with plum compote, Sussex pond, or hot chocolate tart with caramelised oranges. A classical French tilt to the wine list is balanced by some affordable New World wines. Half-bottles are generous, and house wines start at £9.

CHEF: Claire Burgess PROPRIETORS: Nigel and Sue Mackenzie OPEN: Sun L 12 to 2.15, all week D 7 to 10.15 CLOSED: 24 to 26 Dec, bank hols MEALS: Set L and D £23.50. BYO £5, champagne £8 SERVICE: not inc, card slips closed; 12.5% for parties of 8 or more CARD: Amex DETAILS: 41 seats. 10 seats outside. Private parties: 41 main room, 4 to 16 private rooms. Car park. Vegetarian meals. Children's helpings. No children under 3. No smoking in dining-room. Music. Air-conditioned

KELSALE Suffolk map 6

Hedgehogs $*

Kelsale IP17 2RF
TEL: (01728) 604444 FAX: (01728) 604499 COOKING 3
on A12, 1m N of Saxmundham COST £17–£30

A 400-year-old thatched house on the A12 is the setting for Stephen and Desmond Yare's restaurant on two floors, indicated on approach by hedgehog-shaped signs along the road. Oak beams and inglenook fireplaces are the order of the day within, and the rooms retain their original floors of Suffolk brick, imparting a welcome lack of pretension to the ambience. Anglo-French is the culinary idiom, a style that allows duck liver and smoked chicken salad to sit comfortably alongside a pork cassoulet terrine dressed with piccalilli. Fish has impressed – red mullet with peppers, and a well-timed skate wing served with tomato and olive salsa instead of the more usual black butter – as has pheasant breast with white beans and ceps, though desserts have come in for some criticism. Bread has been commended and service is chatty and charming. A brisk international wine selection kicks off with house French and German at £7.50.

CHEFS/PROPRIETORS: Stephen and Desmond Yare OPEN: Tue to Sun L 12 to 2.30 (3.30 Sun), Tue to Sat D 7 to 10.30 MEALS: Set L Tue to Sat £9.95, Set L Sun £13.95, Set D £13.95 (2 courses) to £16.95. BYO £3 SERVICE: not inc, card slips closed CARDS: Amex, Delta, MasterCard, Switch, Visa DETAILS: 66 seats. 20 seats outside. Private parties: 26 main room, 20 private room. Car park. Vegetarian meals. Children's helpings. No smoking in 1 dining-room. Wheelchair access (also WC). Music

KENILWORTH Warwickshire map 5

Restaurant Bosquet 🍷

97A Warwick Road, Kenilworth CV8 1HP COOKING 5
TEL: (01926) 852463 COST £33–£47

'This is the sort of place one would be pleased to have stumbled across on a country road in France,' reckoned one visitor, and its appeal is no less strong for being within the orbit of Coventry. This is a family home as well as a restaurant, and the dining-room has the feel of a converted suburban living-room. South-west France provides inspiration for quite a few of Bernard Lignier's dishes, so it is no surprise to find foie gras and truffles among the provender. Crayfish appears regularly among starters – combined with artichoke and aïoli in a salad, for example, or in a soup with wild mushrooms – alongside duck foie gras with spicy figs, tomato and bean soup with smoked duck breast, or a gratin of asparagus and gnocchi.

Despite an occasional gesture to fashion – maybe duck with ginger and lime sauce perfumed with mango tea – main courses tend to rely on a more traditional approach: saddle of lamb with rosemary and garlic, or breast of guinea-fowl served with a pâté made from the leg meat and black pudding in a madeira sauce. Fish varies according to the market, and one reporter enjoyed 'a huge tranche of jolly nice salmon', served with a creamy shellfish sauce. As to desserts, 'go for anything in pastry', recommended one, while another judged them 'the highlight of the meal'. Cooking counts most, but the 'pleasant and attentive service' from Jane Lignier 'should not be underestimated in the success'. The wine list continues the Gallic theme and introduces some interesting bins from south-west France alongside the expected classed growth clarets and renowned Rhônes, Loires and burgundies. House wines start at £11.50. CELLARMAN'S CHOICE: Jurançon Sec, 'Cuvée Marie' 1996, Charles Hours, £18; Gamay de Touraine 1996, Marionnet, £11.50.

CHEF: Bernard Lignier PROPRIETORS: Bernard and Jane Lignier OPEN: Tue to Fri L 12 to 1.15, Tue to Sat D 7 to 9.15 CLOSED: 1 week Christmas, 3 weeks Aug MEALS: alc (main courses £15). Set L £22, Set D Tue to Fri £22. BYO £5 SERVICE: not inc CARDS: Amex, Delta, MasterCard, Switch, Visa DETAILS: 26 seats. Private parties: 30 main room. Children welcome. Wheelchair access (no WC). No music

Simpson's

101–103 Warwick Road, Kenilworth CV8 1HP — COOKING 3
TEL: (01926) 864567 FAX: (01926) 864510 — COST £24–£44

A bistro atmosphere prevails, tables are close together, and the place can get busy, but there is no denying the serious focus on food. Brick walls are decorated with menus from other restaurants, brought along by staff who previously worked there, which might also help to explain the kitchen's debt to a wide variety of influences. It is perfectly possible, for example, to begin with seared foie gras, and proceed to kleftiko with lentil sauce, followed by caramel crème brûlée with banana sandwich, although of course you don't have to. Nevertheless, the playfulness is appealing, and an individual approach is developing, judging by roast woodpigeon with mushy peas, and confit of belly-pork with black pudding mash. Fortunately, an eye for presentation keeps everything on the plate looking tidy, including integral vegetables. Lemon and blueberry sponge, snow eggs, and apple fritters with apricot parfait might be among desserts. Service is cheery, unobtrusive and plentiful, and wines combine interest and good value across a wide range of countries and prices, beginning with house French at £9.95.

CHEFS: Andreas Antona and Andrew Waters PROPRIETORS: Andreas and Alison Antona OPEN: Mon to Fri L 12.30 to 2, Mon to Sat D 7 to 10 CLOSED: 24 Dec to 3 Jan MEALS: Set L £10 (2 courses) to £15, Set D £19.50 (2 courses) to £23.50 SERVICE: not inc; 10% for parties of 8 or more CARDS: Amex, Delta, Diners, MasterCard, Switch, Visa DETAILS: 80 seats. Private parties: 70 main room, 70 private room. Car park. Vegetarian meals. Children's helpings. No smoking in 1 dining-room. Music. Air-conditioned

'Of course there are two sides to the smoking debate, but when a whole table of . . . diners chain-smoked throughout the meal (not just between courses, but actually puffing away between mouthfuls), including cigars, then I think this goes a little too far. A cloud of smoke drifted across quite an expanse of the room, like a battle scene from a war movie.'
(On eating in London)

KESWICK Cumbria map 10

▲ *Swinside Lodge*

Grange Road, Newlands, Keswick CA12 5UE
TEL/FAX: (017687) 72948
off A66 Penrith to Cockermouth road; turn left at Portinscale and follow Grange road for 2m

COOKING 4
COST £28–£37

Where else in England, mused one reporter, can you park your car and walk 14 miles through unparalleled mountain scenery in a 'perfect horseshoe' to come back to a meal that 'satisfies the appetite in such an elegant yet friendly setting'? This quiet, small country hotel near Derwent Water has no licence, but diners are welcome to bring their own wine and are treated to complimentary sherry before dinner (of four courses, with cheese an optional fifth), which starts at 7.30 and takes place by candlelight. Choice comes only at dessert, so it is best to phone ahead to discuss any special needs, and consider what wine to bring.

There may be an element of 'safety first' about dishes that have to please everybody, but their impact is still strong. A spring meal kicked off with pasta with oyster mushrooms and a creamy herb sauce, proceeded to intensely flavoured pea and mint soup, then to roast loin of lamb (cooked to 'pink perfection') with a shallot tartlet, and ended with 'excellent' lemon tart. Other reporters have praised roasted red pepper soufflé, watercress and leek soup, trout stuffed with spinach and prawns, and hot chocolate soufflé with chocolate ice-cream. 'No rushing and yet no lack of attention' describes the service.

CHEF: Christopher Astley PROPRIETOR: Graham Taylor OPEN: all week D only 7.30 (1 sitting) CLOSED: Dec and Jan MEALS: Set D £25. Unlicensed, BYO (no corkage) SERVICE: not inc CARDS: none DETAILS: 18 seats. Private parties: 18 main room. Car park. No children under 10. No smoking in dining-room. No music ACCOMMODATION: 7 rooms, all with bath/shower. TV. D,B&B £72 to £160. Deposit: £50. No children under 10. Afternoon teas. Garden (*The Which? Hotel Guide*)

KEYSTON Cambridgeshire map 6

Pheasant Inn

Keyston PE18 0RE
TEL: (01832) 710241 FAX: (01832) 710340
on B663, 1m S of junction with A14

COOKING 2
COST £22–£44

Log fires brighten up the winter in this thatched pub/restaurant in a charming village a stone's throw from the A14. The format, shared with others in the mini-chain (see Three Horseshoes, Madingley, and White Hart, Great Yeldham), suits both casual callers and more serious (non-smoking) eaters who want to book a table. Everybody chooses from the same menu and pays the same prices. Martin Lee's lively food puts down modern markers, from twice-baked goats'-cheese soufflé to saffron risotto, from sauté lambs' kidneys with braised lentils to chocolate tart or polenta cake with crème fraîche.

Choice is generous, with a fair balance of fish and vegetable dishes (roast fillet of brill with braised fennel and herb dressing, perhaps) among more red-blooded options such as wild boar sausages with mashed potato. Value for money is praised, service is relaxed, with staff 'there when you need them', and 'you are left on your own to look after your wine', which is considered a plus. The wines themselves are a fine bunch from around the world, arranged by style for ease of choice. At £15, Charles Melton's 'Rose of Virginia' Australian red served cold would make a refreshing change. House wines start at £9.45, 12 of which are also offered by the glass at very reasonable prices (£1.80 to £2.40). CELLARMAN'S CHOICE: Moa Ridge Sauvignon Blanc 1996, Marlborough, New Zealand, £12.95; Chianti Rufina 1994, Selvapiana, £14.50.

CHEF: Martin Lee PROPRIETOR: Huntsbridge Ltd OPEN: all week 12 to 2, 6 (7 Sun) to 10 CLOSED: D 25 Dec MEALS: alc (main courses £7 to £14). BYO £5 SERVICE: not inc, card slips closed CARDS: Amex, Delta, Diners, MasterCard, Switch, Visa DETAILS: 94 seats. 28 seats outside. Private parties: 25 main room. Car park. Vegetarian meals. Children's helpings. No smoking in 1 dining-room. Wheelchair access (no WC). No music

KING'S CLIFFE Northamptonshire map 6

King's Cliffe House

31 West Street, King's Cliffe PE8 6XB COOKING 4
TEL: (01780) 470172 COST £23–£39

Spanning a period from Georgian to Victorian, the large house in the centre of the village overlooks a quiet garden at the back. Stained-oak floorboards, tiled corridors, and contemporary paintings provide an individual setting for this small but serious operation. Andrew Wilshaw is a welcoming and knowledgeable host, and since all the efforts of this two-strong team are concentrated into a mere four openings a week, they have time to source materials well, and to produce a varied weekly-changing *carte*. Seasons are properly observed, bringing asparagus in April and May, and strawberries from June to August. Organic produce and rare breeds of pork and lamb are sought out. Local suppliers might show up with a few wild mushrooms, mulberries, quinces or vine leaves, and their own herb garden, vegetable patch and orchard make a contribution too.

Despite the resolute Englishness of all this, some dishes can be surprisingly exotic. A soup of Cromer crab is infused with lemon grass, ginger and coconut, and a Sicilian-style vegetable stew is served with grilled polenta. That still leaves room for local asparagus with sorrel hollandaise, or loin of Soay lamb with creamed onions, rosemary and deep-fried garlic. 'Constantly appealing and never disappointing' was one reporter's view of the style, which might also take in almond and lemon tart, or vin santo ice-cream. The wine list has expanded since last year to become a cheerful collection at impressively low prices – there aren't many restaurants that sell Cloudy Bay Sauvignon 1996 at £18.75. House wines, three French and one Australian, start at £9.95 a bottle, £2 a glass, and a good choice of half-bottles is offered. CELLARMAN'S CHOICE: Entre-Deux-Mers, Ch. de Castelneau 1994, £16.50; Warwick Farm Estate Pinotage 1995, Stellenbosch, South Africa, £17.

CHEFS/PROPRIETORS: Emma Jessop and Andrew Wilshaw OPEN: Wed to Sat D only 7 to 9 CLOSED: 25 and 26 Dec, 1 Jan, 2 weeks spring, 2 weeks autumn MEALS: alc (main courses £9 to £14) SERVICE: net prices CARDS: none DETAILS: 20 seats. Private parties: 20 main room. Car park. Vegetarian meals. Children's helpings. No smoking in dining-room. No music

KING'S LYNN Norfolk map 6

Riverside

27 King Street, King's Lynn PE30 1HA COOKING 1
TEL: (01553) 773134 COST £19–£46

The 500-year-old building, made of brick and ships' timbers, is through a courtyard off King Street near the Tuesday Market, very handy for the Corn Exchange. It makes a point of serving early and late suppers for concert-goers (opening at 6pm by arrangement), and sports a fine-weather terrace with parasols overlooking the Great Ouse. The setting is a winner, the style unchanging, and the kitchen team has a catholic range of tastes to cater for, from National Trust visitors and the arts community to shoppers and tourists. It comes up with Norfolk mussels, Arbroath smokies and grilled cheese, and a beefy line in brandy-flamed fillet or sirloin steaks, as well as one-course lunches of turkey and mushroom vol-au-vent, or fisherman's pie. Finish, perhaps, with strawberry mille-feuille, or triple chocolate bavarois. Over half the 60-plus wines stay below £20 and half-bottles are generous for the context. House French and German wines are £8.25.

CHEFS: Dennis Taylor and Pat Isbill PROPRIETORS: Michael and Sylvia Savage OPEN: Mon to Sat 12 to 2, 7 (6 by arrangement) to 10 MEALS: alc (main courses L £6 to £15, D £14 to £17.50) SERVICE: not inc, card slips closed CARDS: Delta, MasterCard, Switch, Visa DETAILS: 60 seats. 50 seats outside. Private parties: 85 main room. Car park. Vegetarian meals. Children's helpings. Music

Rococo 🍷

11 Saturday Market Place, King's Lynn PE30 5DQ COOKING 4
TEL: (01553) 771483 COST £24–£54

The Andersons' seventeenth-century cottage stands across from the massive St Margaret's Church in the old part of town. The dining-room is comfortable, light and airy, with plenty of well-selected pictures to entertain the eye. Nick Anderson's aims are to produce good, modern British dishes using as much local produce as possible. He tries to keep things light, as borne out by an 'excellent' seafood ragoût with salmon, cod, sea bass and scallops in their own *jus*. Pigeon on mashed potatoes with Puy lentils was deemed by a reporter the 'best-executed' version of the dish she'd encountered in a while. Pasta with 'the best pesto I've had', and chocolate marquise with memorable gin and lavender ice-cream, made an 'outstanding' start and finish to lunch for one reporter. Delays between courses have been noted by some, but the welcome by Anne Anderson and her 'young and good' staff get full marks.

Wines are a globe-trotting collection, offering a good range of prices while keeping quality at a high level. Rococo's list opens with a 'personal choice' of 16 wines of varied styles and varietals including, rather appropriately, the Baroque grape which is unique to Tursan. House wines start at £11.95. CELLARMAN'S CHOICE: Tursan, Baron de Bachen 1991, Michel Guerrard, £24.50; Hollick Whilga Shiraz-Cabernet 1993, Coonawarra, S. Australia, £18.95.

CHEFS: Nick Anderson and Tim Sandford PROPRIETORS: Nick and Anne Anderson OPEN: Tue to Sat L 12 to 1.30, Mon to Sat D 7 to 10 CLOSED: 1 week Christmas MEALS: Set L £9.95 (2 courses) to £13.50, Set D £22.50 (2 courses) to £37.50. Light L available. BYO £2.50 SERVICE: not inc, card slips closed CARDS: Amex, Delta, Diners, MasterCard, Switch, Visa DETAILS: 40 seats. Private parties: 40 main room. Vegetarian meals. Children's helpings. No smoking while others eat. Wheelchair access (also WC). Music

KINGTON Hereford & Worcester map 5

▲ *Penrhos Court*

Kington HR5 3LH
TEL: (01544) 230720 FAX: (01544) 230754 COOKING 2
on A44, 1m E of Kington COST £33–£40

'One of Britain's most idiosyncratic restaurants – and long may they flourish,' summed up one reporter. Daphne Lambert and Martin Griffiths have been nominated for a Millennium Marque award in recognition of their conservation of the 'glorious' cluster of medieval and Elizabethan buildings that constitute the business. They are also the proud owners of the world's first Organic Restaurant Certificate, issued by the Soil Association. Healthy eating, in the broadest possible sense, is their preoccupation, and organic produce is marshalled to service a menu that they call 'rural Italian in flavour'.

The description may not fit Dover sole or mango sorbet like a glove, but it certainly captures the honesty and integrity of purpose. Fish, poultry, pasta, beans, grains and vegetables are the mainstays of four-course dinners that might begin with white bean soup with rosemary and garlic, followed by chicory tarte Tatin, and then spinach and ricotta cannelloni. Finish, perhaps, with French apple tart, or date and walnut pudding. A few organic wines pepper the list, alongside some fine clarets and nine house wines at around £12.

CHEF: Daphne Lambert PROPRIETORS: Martin Griffiths and Daphne Lambert OPEN: all week D only 7.30 to 9 MEALS: Set D £25 SERVICE: not inc CARDS: Amex, MasterCard, Visa DETAILS: 50 seats. 20 seats outside. Private parties: 80 main room, 12 private room. Car park. Vegetarian meals. Children's helpings. No smoking in dining-room. Wheelchair access (also WC). Music ACCOMMODATION: 15 rooms, all with bath/shower. TV. Phone. B&B £45 to £92.50. Children welcome. Baby facilities. Garden

KINTBURY Berkshire map 2

▲ *Dundas Arms*

53 Station Road, Kintbury RG17 9UT
TEL: (01488) 658263 FAX: (01488) 658568 COOKING 1
1m S of A4, between Newbury and Hungerford COST £20–£49

Picnic tables overlook the canal, and there is lots to watch in summer. This is basically a pub with a restaurant attached, and while bar meals might offer scampi and chips, or steak and kidney pie, the dining-room aims a bit higher, with large flat mushrooms on Italian bread, grilled scallops with peppers, and first-rate home-cured gravlax, followed perhaps by simply cooked monkfish or rack of lamb. Puddings are not a high point, but the wines offer much by way of consolation. Claret lovers can choose from nearly 60 bins, ranging from a humble Bordeaux Supérieur at £15 to a grand Ch. Latour 1966 at £300, and burgundies are an equally fine bunch. The selection of New World wines is short but sound. CELLARMAN'S CHOICE: Au Bon Climat Chardonnay 1993, Santa Barbara, California, £24; Devil's Lair Pinot Noir 1994, Margaret River, W. Australia, £23.

CHEFS: David Dalzell-Piper, Sue Bright and Stuart Hall PROPRIETORS: D.A. and W.E. Dalzell-Piper OPEN: Mon to Sat L 12 to 2, Tue to Sat D 7 to 9 CLOSED: Christmas and New Year MEALS: alc (main courses £5 to £16) SERVICE: not inc CARDS: Amex, Delta, MasterCard, Switch, Visa DETAILS: 50 seats. 50 seats outside. Private parties: 22 main room. Car park. Vegetarian meals. No smoking in 1 dining-room. No music ACCOMMODATION: 5 rooms, all with bath/shower. TV. Phone. B&B £55 to £70. Children welcome (*The Which? Hotel Guide*)

KIRKHAM Lancashire map 8

Cromwellian

16 Poulton Street, Kirkham PR4 2AB COOKING **4**
TEL/FAX: (01772) 685680 COST £23–£37

A relaxing, unpretentious environment and modest prices are part of the appeal of this small restaurant. It hides in a row of shops on the main street, its tiny front room filled with three tables, and the domesticity immediately becomes apparent. 'Mr Fawcett greeted us warmly, and Mrs Fawcett popped out of the kitchen with a plate of warm canapés.' Since last year the à la carte menu has gone, and the naming of dishes has been abandoned; no more Pot Luck or Lamb Bhorgini ('even I was ashamed of that,' jokes Peter Fawcett). In has come a three-course set-price menu with supplements for fillet steak and cheese (a generous assortment in good condition), plus a blackboard for daily extras.

If you hanker after an old-fashioned nut roast, this is the place to come. If not, don't worry. There may be creamy risotto of smoked haddock with al dente grains and masses of flaked, undyed fish, or chicken (a leg and boneless breast) with Puy lentils, garlic and bacon lardons. Seasoning may be on the cautious side, but timing is spot-on, and desserts have included Canary Pudding (well, perhaps not all the names have gone) and an 'elegant' version of rhubarb brown betty deriving a welcome uplift from cinnamon. Some of the details – bread and canapés, for instance – are worthy of more ambitious places. The revamped wine list opens with a personal selection of six wines priced between £9 and £12.50 a bottle, or £2.50 to £3 a glass. The burgundies and clarets have been slimmed down, but some interesting bins and decent half-bottles can still be found.

CHEF: Josie Fawcett PROPRIETORS: Peter and Josie Fawcett OPEN: Tue to Sat D only 7 to 9 CLOSED: 1 week Sept, 2 weeks June MEALS: Set D £15 SERVICE: not inc, card slips closed CARDS: Amex, Delta, Diners, MasterCard, Switch, Visa DETAILS: 28 seats. Private parties: 10 main room, 10 private room. Vegetarian meals. Children welcome. Music

£ *indicates that it is possible to have a three-course meal, including coffee, a half-bottle of house wine and service, at any time the restaurant is open (i.e. at dinner as well as at lunch, unless a place is open only for dinner), for £25 or less per person.*

KNUTSFORD Cheshire map 8

▲ *Belle Epoque Brasserie* £

60 King Street, Knutsford WA16 6DT — COOKING 2
TEL: (01565) 633060 FAX: (01565) 634150 — COST £16–£40

Somehow the modern brasserie approach seems quite at home amid the flamboyant art nouveau décor, and it is encouraging to see this kind of food, normally the preserve of cities, thriving in a smaller town. Tables are lavishly set with tall vases filled with lilies, napery and glassware reinforce the upmarket tone, and reporters generally feel well looked after. 'Welcome and service were friendly, attentive and prompt,' was one summing up.

A generous *carte* is supplemented with a good-value three-course lunch, and David Mooney plates up an appealing selection of modern British standbys, including sausage and mash, haddock and chips with mushy peas, braised lamb shank, and Bury black pudding with onion rings. Fish – grilled tuna or cod – is fresh, flavours are straightforward and direct, and prices are fair for both food and wine: a round-the-world list offers plenty of variety from Cinsault and Grenache to Colombard and Riesling. Bottles start at £9.95, and there is a decent choice by the glass.

CHEF: David Mooney PROPRIETORS: Keith and Nerys Mooney OPEN: Mon to Fri L 12 to 2, Mon to Sat D 7 to 10.30 CLOSED: Christmas, bank hols MEALS: alc (main courses £8.50 to £14.50). Set L £9.95 SERVICE: not inc, card slips closed CARDS: Amex, Delta, Diners, MasterCard, Switch, Visa DETAILS: 80 seats. 30 seats outside. Private parties: 18 to 80 private rooms. Children's helpings. No smoking in 1 dining-room. Wheelchair access (no WC). Music ACCOMMODATION: 7 rooms, all with bath/shower. TV. Phone. B&B £40 to £50. No children under 12. Garden (*The Which? Hotel Guide*)

LANGAR Nottinghamshire map 5

▲ *Langar Hall*

Langar NG13 9HG
TEL: (01949) 860559 FAX: (01949) 861045 — COOKING 4
between A46 and A52, 4m S of Bingham — COST £24–£65

The house, at the end of a long drive near the church, is built of warm stone and is 'a super place for a relaxing weekend'. Its stone-flagged floors are part-covered in carpets, and it has 'a vaguely Regency air about it'. Greek columns in the dining-room, together with an ornate fireplace and old brown prints, are probably what prompted the words 'faded' and 'grandeur' to spring to one reporter's mind. The place's character is enormously strengthened by Imogen Skirving, who, 'occasionally singing to herself', oversees the ordering in a 'likeable and gently eccentric fashion'.

The food tends to combine simple English country dishes – asparagus with lemon butter, or lettuce and sorrel soup – with more Mediterranean ideas of grilled tuna with pesto dressing, or risotto with sun-dried tomato and black olives. Not all flavours have the impact they might, but fresh ingredients and accurate timing (especially of fish) impressed an inspector who ate 'plump, meaty' scallops with their coral, served with a chilli and butter dressing, and roast John Dory fillets ('moist and flaky') with a rustic sauce vierge. Chargrilled fillet of lamb with rosemary and garlic, and sirloin of beef with chips and salad have also been enjoyed. Desserts are less exciting. The house's own purified, carbonated water comes free, and wines make a serious attempt to combine quality with value, starting with half a dozen house wines at around £12.

CHEFS: Toby Garratt and Nick Aiello PROPRIETOR: Imogen Skirving OPEN: all week L 12.30 to 2, Mon to Sat D 7 to 9.30 (9.45 Fri and Sat; Sun D residents only) CLOSED: 25 to 27 Dec MEALS: alc (main courses £8.50 to £20). Set L Mon to Sat £10 (2 courses) to £15, Set L Sun £17.50, Set D Mon to Thur £15, Set D Fri and Sat £25 SERVICE: not inc, card slips closed CARDS: Amex, Diners, MasterCard, Visa DETAILS: 50 seats. 10 seats outside. Private parties: 46 main room, 8 and 22 private rooms. Car park. Vegetarian meals. Children's helpings. No smoking in 1 dining-room. Wheelchair access (also WC). Music ACCOMMODATION: 10 rooms, all with bath/shower. TV. Phone. B&B £60 to £135. Rooms for disabled. Children welcome. Dogs by arrangement. Afternoon teas. Garden. Fishing (*The Which? Hotel Guide*)

LANGHO Lancashire map 8

▲ *Northcote Manor*

Northcote Road, Langho BB6 8BE
TEL: (01254) 240555 FAX: (01254) 246568 COOKING **6**
on A59, 8½m E of M6 J31 COST £23–£68

Comfort has been given a high priority at this red-brick manor-house in the Ribble Valley. Luxurious drapes, magnificent chandeliers, and well-spaced tables with crisp cloths all make for serious expectations. Comparisons with Heathcote's (see entry, Longridge) are almost inevitable, given the springtime 'back-to-back' deal which includes dinner at both restaurants and two nights' accommodation at Northcote. A little more variety in main courses would not go amiss, but the flexibility of mixing and matching dishes on the set-price lunch menu with those on the à la carte menu is welcome, and the three-course set lunch is considered particularly good value, since it comes out at less than the cost of a main course on the *carte*.

The food provides a meeting point for traditional and contemporary ideas, ranging from bouillabaisse to a creamy, frothy artichoke soup with truffle, from plain fillet steak to woodpigeon breast with a pearl barley risotto sweetened with beetroot juice. Nigel Haworth's entries for the 1,001 Things To Do With A Black Pudding competition include serving it with buttered pink trout ('an unusual and tasty combination of flavours and textures'), with pork confit, and infiltrating it on to 'a plate of tiny Lancashire delicacies' alongside brawn, tripe, Morecambe Bay shrimps and Fleetwood smoked salmon. Any suggestion that he might be going too far in his quest for wacky combinations is dispelled by the results. Apple crumble soufflé with Lancashire cheese ice-cream was considered 'a most impressive sweet' by our inspector.

Wines are well chosen (the fistful of Germans is something of a rarity these days) but mark-ups can be high. Those with over £20 to spend fare much better than those expecting change from it, but house Vin de Pays d'Oc is £12.50. CELLARMAN'S CHOICE: Altenbourg Riesling d'Alsace 1993, Dom. A. Mann, £23.85; Pata Negra Gran Reserva Valdepeñas 1983, Abastecedores, £17.65.

CHEF: Nigel Haworth PROPRIETORS: Craig Bancroft and Nigel Haworth OPEN: all week 12 to 1.30 (2 Sun), 7 to 9.30 (10 Sat, 9 Sun) CLOSED: 1 and 2 Jan MEALS: alc (main courses £17 to £21.50). Set L £15, Set D £37 SERVICE: 10% (optional), card slips closed CARDS: Amex, Delta, Diners, MasterCard, Switch, Visa DETAILS: 80 seats. Private parties: 100 main room, 40 private room. Car park. Vegetarian meals. Children's helpings. No smoking in dining-room. Wheelchair access (also WC). Music ACCOMMODATION: 14 rooms, all with bath/shower. TV. Phone. B&B £80 to £120. Rooms for disabled. Children welcome. Afternoon teas. Garden (*The Which? Hotel Guide*)

LANGLEY MARSH Somerset map 2

▲ *Langley House Hotel*

Langley Marsh, Wiveliscombe TA4 2UF
TEL: (01984) 623318 FAX: (01984) 624573 COOKING 5
½m N of Wiveliscombe COST £35–£49

'One of the nicest smaller country houses around', Langley House is an old building with Georgian additions and the well-kept feel of a 'gracious home'. Dinner is at 8pm: a set price, with no choice before dessert, although Peter Wilson writes that alternatives are always available, so it is best to check when booking.

Meals typically begin with a fruity first course (such as a pear marinated in oil, with a herb savoury), followed by fish (sea bass with leeks and a thyme beurre blanc). A summer visitor's experience conveys the appeal, beginning with an attractively presented avocado and orange salad dressed with olive oil, lemon juice and fresh herbs from the kitchen garden. Smoked salmon soufflé (half a dozen mouthfuls of 'creamy smoked salmon flavour') was followed by two pieces of 'meltingly tender' mustard-crusted beef fillet, cooked as the kitchen deems best unless requested otherwise, and surrounded by a dark, glossy, madeira-style sauce. Vegetables are plainly cooked and unadorned.

Desserts vary from terrine of dark and white chocolates, via bread-and-butter pudding, to a simple but effective galette of strawberries, consisting of 'a little stack of crisp pâte sucrée biscuits' layered with crème Chantilly and fragrant fruit from the garden. Bread is 'almost' home-made, in that it comes from the baker up the road. Mature claret and burgundy are still the wine list's main selling points, but the New World contributes some impressive bins too. Choice under £20 is very restricted, although a quartet of French house wines starting at £11.50 lends some assistance. Wine service is all it should be: both knowledgeable and helpful. CELLARMAN'S CHOICE: St-Romain 1994, Dom. Olivier Leflaive, £28.50; Stag's Leap Clos du Val Cabernet Sauvignon 1988, Vichon, California, £26.50.

CHEF: Peter Wilson PROPRIETORS: Peter and Anne Wilson OPEN: all week D only 7.30 to 8.30 MEALS: Set D £26 to £29.85. BYO £8.50 SERVICE: not inc, card slips closed CARDS: Amex, MasterCard, Visa DETAILS: 18 seats. Private parties. 10 private room. Car park. Vegetarian meals. Children's helpings. No smoking in dining-room. Wheelchair access (no WC). No music ACCOMMODATION: 8 rooms, all with bath/shower. TV. Phone. B&B £68.50 to £118.50. Children welcome. Baby facilities. Dogs welcome in bedrooms only. Afternoon teas. Garden (*The Which? Hotel Guide*)

LAVENHAM Suffolk map 6

▲ *Great House*

Market Place, Lavenham CO10 9QZ
TEL: (01787) 247431 FAX: (01787) 248007

COOKING **2**
COST £22–£55

The house stands on a corner of the market square in this medieval wool town, as it has done for around six centuries. 'After 11 years, the Crépys should be thinking of refurbishing,' ventured one who lunched in the summer. No sooner said than done. Come winter, carpets were ripped out, exposing the floorboards, and a new colour scheme was jazzed up with bright pictures. A traditional French hand still guides the cooking, adding cream, butter and alcohol to sauces, but there are plenty of other ideas, including lunchtime snacks of marinated salmon with spicy tomato salsa, and warm spinach mousseline with a poached egg and black olive sauce.

More elaborate dinners might play the French hand with a warm terrine made from confit of cockerel and duck gizzard, followed perhaps by slow-cooked shank of lamb, or skate with black butter and capers. The cooking 'may not scale the culinary heights', and there is a feeling among reporters that some ingredients might benefit from more careful sourcing, but Francophile regulars are happy with the package. Both service and wines are predominantly French, the latter assembled into a balanced list combining good quality and fair value. A handful of house wines starts at £9.50.

CHEF: Régis Crépy PROPRIETORS: Régis and Martine Crépy OPEN: Tue to Sun L 12 to 2.30, Tue to Sat D 7 to 9.30 (10 Sat) CLOSED: 3 weeks Jan MEALS: alc (main courses L £6.50 to £9, D £14 to £18). Set L Tue to Sat £9.95 (2 courses) to £12.95, Set L Sun £16.95, Set D Tue to Fri £16.95. BYO £5 to £9 SERVICE: not inc CARDS: Amex, Delta, MasterCard, Switch, Visa DETAILS: 45 seats. 30 seats outside. Private parties: 60 main room. Children's helpings. Music ACCOMMODATION: 4 rooms, all with bath/shower. TV. Phone. B&B £50 to £88. Deposit: £25. Children welcome. Baby facilities. Dogs welcome. Garden

LEAMINGTON SPA Warwickshire map 5

▲ *Lansdowne* £

87 Clarendon Street, Leamington Spa CV32 4PF
TEL: (01926) 450505 FAX: (01926) 421313

COOKING **1**
COST £25–£35

Leamington is full of white-stuccoed Regency town houses, and the Lansdowne's corner site joins together two rows of them. Lucinda Robinson is happiest in pursuit of the traditional, sourcing her materials from all around Britain – Aberdeen Angus beef, Cornish lamb, Scottish salmon, Norfolk duck breast – and often applying the simplest of treatments: garlic butter for steaks (or jumbo prawns), for instance. Occasionally she might branch out by wrapping pieces of Brie in streaky bacon and pan-frying them, but this is hardly the place for novelty, more the spot for a brochette of salmon and monkfish, rhubarb brown betty with a rich egg custard, and a short list of wines that takes £20 as its ceiling. House Duboeuf is £8.95.

CHEF: Lucinda Robinson PROPRIETORS: David and Gillian Allen OPEN: Mon to Sat D only 6.30 to 9.30 (residents only Sun D) CLOSED: 25 and 31 Dec MEALS: Set D £14.95 (2 courses) to £17.95 SERVICE: not inc, card slips closed CARDS: Delta, MasterCard, Visa DETAILS: 24 seats. Private parties: 20 main room. Car park. Vegetarian meals. Children's helpings. No smoking in dining-room. Wheelchair access (also WC). Music ACCOMMODATION: 14 rooms, all with bath/shower. TV. Phone. B&B £29.95 to £63.90. Deposit: £20. No children under 5 (*The Which? Hotel Guide*)

Les Plantagenêts

15 Dormer Place, Leamington Spa CV32 5AA — COOKING 3
TEL: (01926) 451792 FAX: (01926) 435171 — COST £15–£32

A good-value lunch of warm cheese salad, sole meunière, followed by a welcome cheeseboard prompted one devotee to write: 'Here is a splendid example of what a small provincial restaurant should be.' Bourgeois French describes Rémy Loth's small restaurant in a terraced Regency house. The menu's layout is certainly French, the set dinner menu costing not much more than the price of a main course on the *carte*. Basic skills and ingredients are *comme il faut*, pavé de boeuf and fricassee de poulet are long-standing favourites on the menu, and approval has come for well-executed flambé lambs' kidneys, and a gigot of spring lamb and rosemary with good game chips. Desserts might include passion-fruit bavarois, crème brûlée or meringue with fruit. There have been niggles about the bread and extremely al dente vegetables, and the limited English of the staff can sometimes cause problems. French house wines are £10.50.

CHEF/PROPRIETOR: Rémy Loth OPEN: Mon to Fri L 12 to 2.30, Mon to Sat D 7 to 10 CLOSED: Christmas, bank hols MEALS: alc D (main courses £13.50 to £16). Set L £6.95 (2 courses) to £8.95, Set D £18.50 SERVICE: not inc CARDS: Amex, MasterCard, Visa DETAILS: 40 seats. Private parties: 45 main room. Children's helpings. No smoking in 1 dining-room. Music. Air-conditioned

LECK Lancashire — map 8

▲ *Cobwebs*

Leck, Cowan Bridge LA6 2HZ
TEL/FAX: (015242) 72141
2m SE of Kirkby Lonsdale on A65, turn left at Cowan Bridge — COOKING 6
COST £38–£46

This attractive, personally run small hotel is a double-fronted Victorian house, in remote countryside between the Lake District and the Yorkshire Dales. Paul Kelly greets guests and settles them in with a drink in one of the two parlours, and Yvonne brings and describes dainty warm canapés. At eight you are escorted into the dining-room, a built-on verandah where soft classical music plays. The set menu stretches to four courses, with a choice only of starters.

Winning dishes have included mushroom and pigeon soup 'with bags of flavour', and salmon prepared four ways: poached, smoked, gravad lax, and diced with cucumber. A main course of chicken pinwheeled with asparagus and Parma ham had the unusual but effective addition of strawberries in accompanying Parmesan risotto. Chocolate typically features among desserts: in a cold soufflé with lemon, or as a flan with orange segments. Good northern cheeses follow, then diners proceed back to the parlour for coffee.

Paul advises on wines, but take the opportunity to browse through the list and marvel at old vintages from first-class producers. Of particular note are the Marqués de Murrieta Castello Ygay Riojas, Hugel and Zind-Humbrecht whites from Alsace, and Moss Wood wines from Australia's Margaret River region. Prices are fair, although the frequent appearance of the POA tag remains an irritant. Bonny Doon's Bloody Good White and Red are the aptly named house wines, costing £14 and £13 respectively. CELLARMAN'S CHOICE: Wairau River Sauvignon Blanc 1994, Marlborough, New Zealand, £16; Buckleys Grenache 1994, Barossa Valley, S. Australia, £16.

CHEF: Yvonne Thompson PROPRIETORS: Paul Kelly and Yvonne Thompson OPEN: Wed to Sat D only 7.30 for 8 (1 sitting) CLOSED: Jan to Feb MEALS: Set D £28. BYO (no corkage) SERVICE: not inc, card slips closed CARDS: MasterCard, Visa DETAILS: 25 seats. Private parties: 50 main room. Car park. No children under 12. No smoking in dining-room. Music ACCOMMODATION: 5 rooms, all with bath/shower. TV. Phone. B&B £45 to £60. Deposit: £20. No children under 12. Afternoon teas. Garden (*The Which? Hotel Guide*)

LEDBURY Hereford & Worcester map 5

▲ *Hope End*

Hope End, Ledbury HR8 1JQ
TEL: (01531) 633613 FAX: (01531) 636366 COOKING 5
2m N of Ledbury, just beyond Wellington Heath COST £34–£46

Exotic additions to this Georgian house – pools and Greek temples among them – combine with the location (in a hollow) and mature sheltering trees to create 'a feeling of total exclusion from the world'. Gardens and grounds are not manicured, but the eighteenth-century walled vegetable garden is more ordered and provides some of the material that gives Patricia Hegarty's cooking its edge. The house's décor dates back a decade or two with its pine tables and vinyl-upholstered chairs.

It is 'a very English place' that runs on its own terms, offering three-course dinners that can be turned into four with cheese. The choice of only three items at each stage (which includes a vegetarian option) might be considered restricted for the price, although an appealing seasonal slant produces asparagus pancakes in spring, lovage and potato soup in summer, and roast loin of free-range pork with cider gravy in autumn. Other dishes – best end of lamb with kidneys and a fruit jelly – might appear at any time, while the Hegartys' own vegetables, herbs and fruit, might translate into a supply of stored winter pears or bottled nectarines, quite apart from the fresh seasonal highlights. At its best, the food has 'originality and class'.

The wine list is full of appealing bins. A half-bottle of good house champagne (from Tanners) at £12 would be a pleasant enough way to start the evening, but the main attraction is the collection of excellent clarets dating back to 1970. In addition, generously priced offerings from Australia and New Zealand help provide plenty of good drinking at all levels. House burgundy, red and white, is £8.

CHEF: Patricia Hegarty PROPRIETORS: John and Patricia Hegarty OPEN: all week D only 7.30 to 8.30 CLOSED: mid-Dec to early Feb MEALS: Set D £30 SERVICE: none, card slips closed CARDS: Delta, MasterCard, Switch, Visa DETAILS: 24 seats. Private parties: 6 main room. Car park. Vegetarian meals. No children under 12. No smoking in dining-room. No music ACCOMMODATION: 8 rooms, all with bath/shower. Phone. B&B £87 to £144. Deposit: £60. No children under 12. Garden (*The Which? Hotel Guide*)

LEEDS West Yorkshire map 8

Brasserie Forty Four

44 The Calls, Leeds LS2 7EW COOKING 5
TEL: (0113) 234 3232 FAX: (0113) 234 3332 COST £21–£42

A converted corn mill in Leeds city centre houses this 'extremely pleasant' brasserie and its more formal sister, Pool Court (see entry). White-painted brick walls and a polished wood floor are the simple setting for cooking that takes inspiration from the Far and Near East as well as the Mediterranean. You might find Chinese duck with pancakes and plum sauce, Turkish spiced aubergines, or lemon garlic chicken with Thai-spiced vegetables. From closer to home comes grilled stuffed pig's trotter with Puy lentils, and 'perfectly cooked' pan-fried calf's liver on polenta cake with truffle. Strictly European desserts might include chocolate cheesecake with Baileys ice-cream sauce, or 'light as a feather' apple turnover. An inspector could not fault treacle tart with lemon and cream, and commended the coffee and the fact that second cups were free.

Good-value set-price meals are offered to lunchers and early- and late-night diners, although this policy can make for crowds. One lunchtime visitor complained about being unceremoniously whisked through proceedings, though another reporter described service as 'efficient and unobtrusive'. The mixed-bag of wines starts at £9.90 and there is a daily-changing wine on offer by the glass.

CHEF: Jeff Baker PROPRIETOR: Michael Gill OPEN: Mon to Fri L 12 to 2, Mon to Sat D 6.30 to 10.30 (11 Fri and Sat) CLOSED: bank hols MEALS: alc (main courses £7.50 to £12.50). Set L £5 (1 course) to £11.95, Set D (before 8.15pm Mon to Sat and after 10.15pm Fri and Sat only) £8.75 (2 courses) to £11.95 SERVICE: not inc; 10% for parties of 10 or more CARDS: Amex, Delta, Diners, MasterCard, Switch, Visa DETAILS: 110 seats. Private parties: 52 main room, 52 private room. Vegetarian meals. Children's helpings. No cigars/pipes in dining-room. Music. Air-conditioned

Fourth Floor NEW ENTRY

Harvey Nichols, 107–111 Briggate, Leeds LS1 6AZ COOKING 2
TEL: (0113) 204 8000 FAX: (0113) 204 8080 COST £26–£47

The move to open a branch of this posh Knightsbridge store in a down-to-earth northern city certainly required substance as well as style. The fourth-floor café-bar has a rooftop view and a balcony terrace for fine days, a parquet floor, plenty of stainless steel and some modern art. The café approach is evident in the food's straightforward appeal and lack of clever tricks: sole meunière, or chargrilled ribeye steak with fried onions and horseradish ketchup.

Its sensibly limited ambition may produce few surprises, but there are some attractive-sounding combinations, a good mix of light and more substantial dishes, and plain and fancy flavours, ranging from a 'simple and impressive' green salad with Parmesan shavings to Thai fish-cakes with lime and coriander salsa. The menu maintains a consistent style but changes daily, delivering 'full-flavoured' Mediterranean fish soup, satay of squid with lightly battered tempura king prawns distinguished by 'excellent-quality ingredients and fresh flavours', and braised lamb shank with sweet potato and onion sauce. Finish, perhaps with lemon tart or sticky toffee pudding. A short list of well-chosen wines under £20 is supplemented by some French classics, many in three figures. House French is £11.95.

CHEF: Simon Shaw PROPRIETOR: Harvey Nichols & Co Ltd OPEN: Mon to Sat L 12 to 3, Thu to Sat D 7 to 10.30 CLOSED: 25 and 26 Dec MEALS: alc Mon to Sat L and Thur to Fri D (main courses £9 to £14). Set D £12.50 (2 courses) to £15.95 SERVICE: not inc CARDS: Amex, Delta, Diners, Mastercard, Switch, Visa DETAILS: 95 seats. 45 seats outside. Private parties: 150 main room. Vegetarian meals. Children's helpings. No-smoking area. Wheelchair access (also WC). Music. Air-conditioned

Leodis 🍷 £

Victoria Mill, Sovereign Street, Leeds LS1 4BJ — COOKING 4
TEL: (0113) 242 1010 FAX: (0113) 243 0432 — COST £23–£42

Since opening in 1992, Leodis has established a useful reputation as a must-go Leeds brasserie. Part of the canal-side redevelopment, it is a converted warehouse with a majestic vaulted ceiling and cast-iron columns. Etched glass partitions divide up the eating-area sensitively, and staff work flat out to keep things running smoothly. The fixed-price option may incorporate cabbage, potato and Gruyère soup, followed by spring rolls with chilli salsa, or beef and beer casserole. Otherwise, an à la carte offers the likes of smoked chicken and goats'-cheese salad with roast garlic dressing, and grilled halibut with scampi and spinach tortellini. An inspector praised an accurately cooked seafood medley, a 'huge quantity' that took in king prawns, scallops, monkfish, salmon (fresh and smoked) and an oyster, served with hollandaise and pesto sauces. Chump of lamb in two thick pieces comes on a well-made dauphinois of celeriac and a reduced stock sauce. Black Forest gâteau is a brave dessert to offer these days, but it is properly made and reminded a reporter how good it can be. Chocolate and mint parfait, or a richly creamy bavarois of mandarins may be other ways to finish.

The truly international list rounds up wines from Canada, Israel, Lebanon and Tasmania as well as the usual suspects. Rather than grouped by country, grape or style, wines are simply divided into sparkling, white and red, and listed in order of price; those over £20 are placed in the 'expensive' section. However, helpful tasting notes are provided for all. Six house wines are £10.75 a bottle, £2.65 a glass. CELLARMAN'S CHOICE: Bisquertt Chardonnay 1995, Colchagua Valley, Chile, £13.45; Savigny-lès-Beaune 1994, Louis Latour, £17.25.

CHEF: Steven Kendell PROPRIETORS: Martin Spalding and Steven Kendell OPEN: Mon to Fri L 12 to 2, Mon to Sat D 6 to 10 (11 Fri and Sat) CLOSED: 25 and 26 Dec, L bank hols MEALS: alc (main courses £7 to £15). Set L and D £13.95 (not available after 7.30 Sat) SERVICE: not inc CARDS: Amex, Delta, Diners, MasterCard, Switch, Visa DETAILS: 180 seats. 40 seats outside. Private parties: 180 main room. Vegetarian meals. Children's helpings. Wheelchair access (no WC). Music. Air-conditioned

Pool Court at 42

42 The Calls, Leeds LS2 7EW — COOKING 7
TEL: (0113) 2444242 FAX: (0113) 2343332 — COST £30–£63

The clean, smart, light, modern room overlooking the canal and Tetley's brewery is more restful than the adjoining Brasserie Forty Four (see entry, above) although, as one reporter observed as he went in search of the gent's toilet, 'its customers seemed to be having more fun than we were'. If they are, they are unlikely to be eating quite so well, even though both places share the same chef and kitchen. Pool Court's calm owes something to its cool colours – dark blue, beige and grey – relieved by some eye-catching metal and fabric, and the food owes much to Jeff Baker's assured classical style of cooking.

It is, as one observer put it, 'a welcome haven from the experimentation and innovation found elsewhere'. When roast scallops are served with wasabi, lime and coriander, that Far Eastern touch is very much an exception to the rule. More typical is a grilled 'boudin' of fresh and smoked salmon with lentils, or a 'brilliant' terrine of foie gras with a Sauternes-soaked prune and a drizzle of Sauternes sauce.

The relative simplicity and directness of the food exposes the quality of the buying and the kitchen's considerable skills. It is this, rather than brash spicing or whizz-bang flavour combinations, that creates the excitement. For one visitor, a sauce accompanying chargrilled fillet of beef with 'truly excellent' wild mushroom risotto was 'a reminder of how good sauces used to taste before chefs decided to reduce them to a sticky glue'. Another's beef fillet, on a bed of trompette mushrooms, came with a small oxtail pie, as good a foil as anyone could ask for.

A tripartite assiette of chocolate is a well-reported dessert, but competition is strong from sherry trifle (with poached apricots), and baked lemon and lime custard pot. The 'Classics' menu arranges dishes from the main menu into a just about cost-effective four courses, topped and tailed with an 'amuse bouche' and coffee with chocolate truffles. Service is slightly formal, value for money is considered good, and wines combine interest and quality at a fair range of prices. There is no house wine, but a short selection by the glass (£3.85) changes daily.

CHEF: Jeff Baker PROPRIETORS: Michael and Hanni Gill OPEN: Mon to Fri L 12 to 2, Mon to Sat D 7 to 10 (10.30 Fri and Sat) CLOSED: bank hols MEALS: Set L £12.50 (2 courses) to £17, Set L and D £24.50 (2 courses) to £39.50 SERVICE: 10%, card slips closed CARDS: Amex, Delta, Diners, MasterCard, Switch, Visa DETAILS: 38 seats. 20 seats outside. Private parties: 38 main room. Vegetarian meals. Children's helpings. No babies. No cigars/pipes in dining-room. Wheelchair access (also WC). Music. Air-conditioned

Rascasse

Canal Wharf, Water Lane, Leeds LS11 5BB COOKING **2**
TEL: (0113) 244 6611 FAX: (0113) 244 0736 COST £25–£56

The converted grain store, stone-built in 1815 on the terminal basin of the Leeds–Liverpool Canal, has been sympathetically restored. A grand staircase sweeps up to the bar, while stainless steel, glass, contrasting woods and a watery view induce a feeling of calm in the spacious dining-room. Expect to see sharp business suits at lunch-time and smartly dressed folk in the evening, as Leeds lives up to its confident role as a prosperous city. 'We describe the cooking as Anglo-French with strong Mediterranean influences,' writes Nigel Jolliffe. So would scores of restaurants in the *Guide*, but Simon Gueller is among the more convincing exponents of the style, offering potato and smoked haddock soup alongside goats'-cheese ravioli with confit tomatoes and pesto, and making fish a forte: roast sea bass, or seared scallops with celeriac and truffle.

The *carte* is generous in scope, covering papillotes of squab pigeon with essence of ceps as well as braised lamb shank with saffron risotto, and delivers portions that are 'not for the faint-hearted'. A 'Fastrack' lunch menu (also available early evening) might begin with a lightly frothy velouté soup (of white haricot beans, maybe, or asparagus), or a niçoise salad made with 'beautifully fresh, just-pink tuna', followed by calf's liver with spinach, or grilled smoked haddock. Impressive desserts have included 'light and airy' chocolate fondant with an 'indulgent' filling, and first-rate lemon tart with thin, crisp pastry. The room is 'full of waiting staff, all smiles', although in the event service can be 'distant', and communication could be improved. France dominates the wine list, which makes a good stab at mixing quality bottles with affordable ones. Around eight wines (starred on the list) are available by the glass.

CHEF: Simon Gueller PROPRIETORS: Simon Gueller and Nigel Jolliffe OPEN: Mon to Fri L 12 to 2, Mon to Sat D 6.30 to 10 (10.30 Fri and Sat) CLOSED: 1 week after Christmas, bank hol Mons MEALS: alc (main courses £10.50 to £17.50). Set L £13.50 (2 courses) to £17, Set D Mon to Fri 6.30 to 7.30 £13.50 (2 courses) to £17 SERVICE: not inc CARDS: Amex, Delta, Diners, MasterCard, Switch, Visa DETAILS: 100 seats. 25 seats outside. Private parties: 50 main room. Car park. Children welcome. No cigars/pipes in dining-room. Wheelchair access (also WC). Music. Air-conditioned

Salvo's £

NEW ENTRY

115 Otley Road, Headingley, Leeds LS6 3PX COOKING **2**
TEL: (0113) 275 5017 COST £19–£37

A cheery band of staff welcomes everyone and makes Salvo's feel like 'a family affair', according to one reporter, which isn't surprising because this long-standing Italian restaurant has been run by the Dammone family for two decades now. Set in the cricketing suburb of Headingley, it offers a no-frills approach to pizza and pasta cookery, but with a few contemporary flourishes too. Langoustine tart with five plump tails in a Cheddary sauce on a shortcrust pastry base prompted one reporter to declare, 'I would order it again.' English tradition is used to inventive effect in a chargrilled chicken breast served with two sauces – one of Stilton and one of port – and garnished with grapes. Most main dishes come with potatoes, vegetables and a salad, so the extra charges beloved of many restaurants may be side-stepped. Good tiramisù and cakey chocolate mousse served with a marzipan basket of fruits wait to indulge sweet-lovers. The wine list leads with Italians, but has some decent southern hemisphere offerings too. House wines from Umani Ronchi are £8.95.

CHEFS: Michael Leggiero and Pam Nelson PROPRIETORS: the Dammone family OPEN: Mon to Sat 12 to 2, 6 to 10.45 (5.30 to 11 Fri and Sat) CLOSED: 24 to 26 Dec, 31 Dec, 1 Jan, some bank hol Mons MEALS: alc (main courses £5.50 to £13) SERVICE: not inc CARDS: Amex, Delta, MasterCard, Switch, Visa DETAILS: 65 seats. Private parties: 15 main room. Vegetarian meals. Children's helpings. No cigars/pipes in dining-room. Wheelchair access (no WC). Music. Air-conditioned

Sous le Nez en Ville £

The Basement, Quebec House, Quebec Street,
Leeds LS1 2HA — COOKING 4
TEL: (0113) 244 0108 FAX: (0113) 245 0240 — COST £20–£46

As the name announces, this ever-popular city brasserie is under your nose: in the 'quite starkly furnished, but bright and smart' basement of Quebec House, that is. Two areas are divided by a bar: one acts as a wine bar, serving lighter food such as sandwiches and tapas, while the other provides the full restaurant menu. The main business of Andrew Carter's kitchen is fish: from fish soup with rouille and Gruyère to seared king scallops with garlic and thyme lentils and a mint and coriander dressing. More elaborate treatment might involve stuffing a fillet of salmon with mousseline of curried sole, and serving it with a version of raita. Meat options might include noisettes of pork with apple and sage brioche and a *jus* of roasted tomatoes. Vegetarian dishes can be inventive – one brings together a gâteau of spinach and hazelnuts, goats' cheese, couscous and a ragoût of field mushrooms – while side-orders of vegetables are charged extra.

Blueberry and almond tart with crème anglaise is a good way to finish, or perhaps opt for three chocolate mousses with a honey sauce. 'Service is affable, being neither too distant nor too familiar', while wines combine lots of old friends with some newer acquaintances. Good-quality drinking is to be had at all price levels, aided by an impressive number of bins below £20. The Old World may still be in the ascendant but there are quite a few rising New World stars too. House wines start at £8.95 a bottle, £1.65 a glass. CELLARMAN'S CHOICE: Bourgogne Blanc 1995, Yves Davenay, £17.50; Savigny-lès-Beaune 'Serpentières' 1992, Maurice Ecard, £27.50.

CHEF: Andrew Carter PROPRIETOR: C.R.C.R. Partnership OPEN: Mon to Sat 12 to 2.30, 6 to 10 (11 Fri and Sat) CLOSED: 24 and 25 Dec, 1 Jan, bank hols MEALS: alc (main courses £7 to £14.50). Set D 6 to 7.30 (7 Sat) £14.95 (inc wine). BYO £5 SERVICE: not inc, card slips closed CARDS: Amex, Delta, Diners, MasterCard, Switch, Visa DETAILS: 86 seats. Private parties: 80 main room, 20 private room. Vegetarian meals. Children welcome before 7.30. Music. Air-conditioned

'A note on the menu requests guests not to smoke during meals. When I asked the maître d'hôtel why a smoker was not being asked to extinguish her cigarette, he said that he never enforces the rule since "smokers don't like it".' (On eating in London)

LEICESTER Leicestershire map 5

MIDLANDS 1998 FISH

Heath's £ NEW ENTRY

169 Evington Road, Leicester LE2 1QL COOKING 2
TEL/FAX: (0116) 273 3343 COST £20–£43

John Heath gets his supplies for both shop and restaurant direct from the coast on twice-weekly visits. Décor is not its strongest point – 'all nets, mock crabs and half a trawler' – but a calm, unfussy atmosphere prevails, and the freshness is a revelation, from impeccable oysters and Brancaster mussels to 'one of the freshest crabs I have ever tasted'. Menus combine to produce a good variety of dishes, ranging from simple dressed Scarborough crab or charcoal-grilled sardines, to traditional deep-fried haddock in either batter or crumbs with tartare sauce.

Some items are jazzed up with nothing more than a dash of citrus (orange vinaigrette with chargrilled smoked salmon, for instance), but the kitchen manages to combine interest with generally simple treatments, producing roast cod with a Tuscan bean cassoulet, and sea bass in a Thai sauce. At least one man would 'kill for their chips'. Desserts include Belgian ices and peach Melba. Friendly, relaxed service 'couldn't have been nicer', and the short list of mostly white wines is sensibly priced. House wine is £8.95, or £2.25 for a large glass.

CHEF: Tim Warry PROPRIETOR: John Heath OPEN: Tue to Sun L 12 to 1.45, Tue to Sat D 6 to 10 MEALS: alc Tue to Sat (main courses £9 to £17). Set L Tue to Sat £9.95 (2 courses) to £11.95, Set L Sun £11.95 (2 courses) to £13.95, Set D Tue to Fri £9.95 (2 courses) to £11.95, Set early-bird D £7.95. BYO £2.50 SERVICE: not inc CARDS: Delta, MasterCard, Switch, Visa DETAILS: 60 seats. Private parties: 20 main room, 20 private room. Vegetarian meals. Children's helpings. No smoking in 1 dining-room. Wheelchair access (no WC). Music

LIDGATE Suffolk map 6

Star Inn £

The Street, Lidgate CB8 9PP
TEL: (01638) 500275 COOKING 1
on B1063, 6m SE of Newmarket COST £24–£38

The setting is a quintessentially English, five-centuries-old country pub, where games of 'ring the bull' and bar billiards are played, and real ales are dispensed. But this isn't the place to come if you're hoping for steak and kidney pie. Chef/landlady Maria-Teresa Axon looks to Spain and the Med for her culinary inspiration, and delivers forthright flavours with generosity and plenty of gusto. Mediterranean fish soup, paella valenciana, and lamb steaks in blackcurrant sauce are perennial favourites, but the 'carta' is always evolving. Recent additions to the list have included carpaccio of venison, wild boar, and albondigas (Spanish meatballs). Staff are a cosmopolitan, cheery bunch from down under, which ensures that the mood remains lively and chatty. A few riojas show up on the short, eclectic wine list. House wine is £10.

CHEF/PROPRIETOR: Maria-Teresa Axon OPEN: all week L 12.30 to 2.30, Mon to Sat D 7.30 to 10 CLOSED: 24 and 25 Dec MEALS: alc (main courses £7.50 to £12.50). Set L Mon to Sat £7.50 (2 courses), Set L Sun £12.50 SERVICE: not inc, card slips closed; 10% for parties of 10 or more CARDS: Amex, Delta, Diners, MasterCard, Switch, Visa DETAILS: 50 seats. 25 seats outside. Private parties: 22 main room, 22 private room. Car park. Vegetarian meals. Children's helpings. Music

LIFTON Devon map 1

WEST COUNTRY 1998 CHARMER

▲ *Arundell Arms* 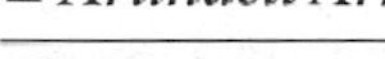

Lifton PL16 0AA
TEL: (01566) 784666 FAX: (01566) 784494 COOKING 5
just off A30, 3m E of Launceston COST £28–£56

The sixteenth-century inn at the heart of this tranquil village has been run for 38 years by Anne Voss-Bark, now an MBE for her services to tourism. Angling is central to its existence (it has 20 miles of river at its disposal), and framed fishing flies, tackle, drawings and photographs are much in evidence. Shooting parties might take centre stage in winter, but this remains an accessible and comfortable place for all and sundry to enjoy, with rugs on the slate floors, a smart bar and modern dining-room.

Part of its appeal lies in the accommodating menus, from snacks in the bar to a choice of two or three courses at both lunch and dinner. The range extends from artichoke soup, or roast cod, to fritters of sole, or Trelough duck with a red wine and bacon risotto, and a serious effort is made to secure local and organic supplies of meat and vegetables. Grilled St Enodoc asparagus, for example, may be served with Parmesan and chervil butter, but has only a short five-week season. South Devon lamb, meanwhile, might come marinated in honey and rosemary, served with a mint and saffron sauce. Devon cheeses offer an alternative to rhubarb and strawberry sherbert, or steamed ginger sponge, and around 10 wines by the glass (30 by the half-bottle) add to the cellar's appeal. Look outside France for change from £20. House wines start at £9.75.

CHEFS: Philip Burgess and Nick Shopland PROPRIETOR: Anne Voss-Bark OPEN: all week 12.30 to 2.30, 7.30 to 9.30 CLOSED: D 24 to 26 Dec MEALS: Set L £14.50 (2 courses) to £18, Set D £26 to £33. Bar meals available SERVICE: not inc CARDS: Amex, Diners, MasterCard, Switch, Visa DETAILS: 70 seats. Private parties: 80 main room, 30 private room. Car park. Vegetarian meals. Children's helpings. No smoking in dining-room. Wheelchair access (no WC). Music ACCOMMODATION: 28 rooms, all with bath/shower. TV. Phone. B&B £64 to £102. Children welcome. Baby facilities. Dogs welcome. Afternoon teas. Garden. Fishing (*The Which? Hotel Guide*)

LINCOLN Lincolnshire map 9

Jew's House

15 The Strait, Lincoln LN2 1JD COOKING 3
TEL: (01522) 524851 COST £22–£48

'The oldest house in Lincoln' – some of the stone is twelfth-century – is just off its steepest street. The feel is of 'a good local restaurant', smartened up with a new carpet and a lick of paint. Richard Gibbs's approach can best be summed up as follows: if ingredients work well together, why add other components just to make an unusual combination? This, together with his training in France, accounts for the kitchen's traditional stance: mussels served marinière-style or as a soup with saffron, grilled halibut with fennel, or fillet steak bordelaise, for example.

To complement braised rabbit in puff pastry, or pigeon and duck with madeira and smoked bacon, daily fish specials are posted up on a blackboard: scallops with tarragon and tomato cream sauce, perhaps, or dishes for two, such as bouillabaisse and paella. One reporter reckons the chef has a passion for sauces, citing wild mushrooms in puff pastry with 'masses of excellent cream sauce' as just one example. The French provincial appeal continues with desserts of Grand Marnier soufflé, and tarte Tatin with calvados, while Cantal, Reblochon, Livarot, and Coulommiers are part of 'a good selection of cheeses in good condition'. Service is from 'pleasant, efficient young ladies'. Wines are well chosen, fairly priced, and range from Tasmanian Pinot Noir to Bourgogne Aligoté, with a few special bottles sprinkled about. Half a dozen house wines start at £9.50; jugs of water are free.

CHEFS: Richard Gibbs and William Ginnelly PROPRIETORS: Richard and Sally Gibbs OPEN: Tue to Fri L 12 to 1.30, Tue to Sat D 7 to 9.15 CLOSED: bank hols MEALS: alc (main courses £11 to £16). Set L £10 (2 courses) to £12.95, Set D £21 SERVICE: not inc CARDS: Amex, Delta, Diners, MasterCard, Switch, Visa DETAILS: 28 seats. Private parties: 30 main room, 10 private room. Vegetarian meals. Children's helpings. No children under 5. No smoking in dining-room. Music

Wig & Mitre £

29 Steep Hill, Lincoln LN2 1LU
TEL: (01522) 535190 and 523705 — COOKING 4
FAX: (01522) 532402 — COST £20–£46

Valerie and Michael Hope have been at the helm of this fourteenth-century inn, in the upper part of medieval Lincoln, for two decades. Perhaps by way of celebration, they have expanded their empire as far as Caunton Beck (see entry, Caunton). 'No music noises, and above all there are no pretensions,' they say. No lack of options for diners, either. There is a proper restaurant upstairs as well as an informal ground floor, and food is 'in perpetual motion' all week from eight in the morning until eleven at night. Breakfast-lovers get two cracks at fry-ups: mid-afternoon as well as morning.

Positive verdicts cite cheese soufflé, salmon and crab fish-cakes, and pink duck breast served with creamed onion in a puff pastry shell. Citrus fruit and stem ginger cheesecake might be among the puddings, along with baked-custard tart with nutmeg ice-cream. Service is 'handled very competently'. The wine list is helpfully arranged by style with brief tasting notes and a multitude of flavours. Although there are few mature bins, producers are reliable and half-bottles helpful. A quartet of house wines are £10 a bottle, £2.50 a glass.

CHEFS: Paul Vidic, Peter Dodd, Mark Cheseldine and Gavin Aitkinhead PROPRIETORS: Michael and Valerie Hope OPEN: all week 8am to 11pm CLOSED: 25 Dec MEALS: alc (main courses £6 to £17) SERVICE: not inc, card slips closed CARDS: Amex, Delta, Diners, MasterCard, Switch, Visa DETAILS: 120 seats. 24 seats outside. Private parties. 60 main room, 45 private room. Vegetarian meals. Children's helpings. Wheelchair access (also WC). No music

---

LINTON West Yorkshire map 8

▲ *Wood Hall*

Trip Lane, Linton LS22 4JA
TEL: (01937) 587271 FAX: (01937) 584353
from Wetherby take A661 N for ½m, turn left to Sicklinghall and Linton, then left to Linton and Wood Hall, and turn right in Linton opposite Windmill pub

COOKING 3
COST £24–£47

This imposing pile is set in 100 acres of park and woodland, with the River Wharfe flowing through. The house, dating from 1750, has a neo-classical and rather formal air about it, while the dining-room conveys 'a faint feeling of chinoiserie'. During the past year Stephanie Moon left for Congham Hall (see entry, Grimston), and Philip Pomfret arrived in April 1997. The set-price format is flexible enough to allow for one- or two-course dinners, and the comfort-led, sometimes ambitious menu deals in chicken liver and truffle parfait, leek and Brie tart with poached egg and hollandaise, and roast woodpigeon with black pudding.

'Interesting accompaniments and sauces' are a feature, and the foundation of good ingredients shows through in home-smoked scallops 'almost raw on the inside but lovely and crisp on the outside' served with a 'natural' tomato broth, and in young, sweet, tender, honey-roast lamb, well trimmed, with 'as good a sauce as one could have wanted' made from juices and port. Blackberry soufflé, or crème brûlée with rhubarb, might be among desserts. Formally dressed staff are capable and confident, although there is a feeling that both food and staff are being careful not to put a foot wrong. 'It is all a bit proper,' summed up one visitor. A few French regional wines creep in under £20, but although quality is high, so are mark-ups. Four house wines from France and Argentina start the ball rolling at £11.95.

CHEF: Philip Pomfret PROPRIETOR: Arcadian International plc OPEN: Sun to Fri L 12 to 2.30, all week D 7 to 10 (9.30 Sun) MEALS: Set L £15.95, Set D £18 (1 course) to £29.95. Bar food available SERVICE: not inc CARDS: Amex, Delta, Diners, MasterCard, Switch, Visa DETAILS: 60 seats. 16 seats outside. Private parties: 6 main room, 14 to 80 private rooms. Car park. Vegetarian meals. Children's helpings. No smoking in dining-room. Wheelchair access (also WC). No music ACCOMMODATION: 43 rooms, all with bath/shower. TV. Phone. Room only £99 to £145. Rooms for disabled. Children welcome. Baby facilities. Dogs welcome. Afternoon teas. Garden. Swimming-pool. Fishing

---

indicates that there has been a change of chef since last year's Guide, *and the Editor has judged that the change is of sufficient interest to merit the reader's attention.*

LISKEARD Cornwall map 1

Bacchus Bistro 🍷 [£]

18 Pike Street, Liskeard PL14 3JE — COOKING 4
TEL: (01579) 347031 — COST £17–£33

In 'an otherwise gastronomically benighted area', the Bacchus Bistro, under the clock-tower in the centre of town, offers 'interesting and original food' in stylish and friendly surroundings. Michael Green has now opened the courtyard at the back to allow for alfresco dining during the summer months, thus adding to the allure. Innovative cooking takes in roasted goats' cheese with Mackeson stout and pineapple, a salad of red cabbage, peppered bacon and Roquefort, and Italian bean stew with Cornish kale. 'Sage-smoked pork fillet with caramelised shallots was a totally new taste sensation for me,' wrote one reporter. Lunchtime dishes, such as braised leg of rabbit stuffed with prunes and juniper, cost a fiver at most, which looks like excellent value for money.

Pudding may be crème brûlée or, for those seeking novelty, treacle oat tart with whisky butterscotch sauce. Service is friendly and lively. As you might expect, the wine list is full of Bacchic delights from around the world – including Cornwall – and is modestly priced (to make revelry affordable). Ten house wines start at £8.50. CELLARMAN'S CHOICE: Premières Côtes de Bordeaux, Château de Pic 1995, £16.65; Ochoa Tempranillo 1992, Navarra, £16.50.

CHEF/PROPRIETOR: Michael Green OPEN: Sun to Fri L 12 to 2.30, Mon to Sat D 7 to 10.30 MEALS: alc L (main courses £3.50 to £5). Set L Mon to Fri and D £12.95 (2 courses) to £15.95. Sun L 'jazz menu' SERVICE: not inc, card slips closed CARDS: Delta, MasterCard, Switch, Visa DETAILS: 54 seats. 20 seats outside. Private parties: 60 main room. Vegetarian meals. Children's helpings. Wheelchair access (also WC). Music

LITTLE SHELFORD Cambridgeshire map 6

Sycamore House 🍷

1 Church Street, Little Shelford CB2 5HG — COOKING 4
TEL: (01223) 843396 — COST £32–£38

The setting is a converted pub in an attractive Cambridgeshire village, although the up-lighting on the papered walls, the chintzy curtains and the neat napery immediately suggest comforting country restaurant. Michael and Susan Sharpe work to a well-tried formula: fixed-price four-course dinners with high-quality ingredients as the starting point. A typical menu might kick off with a soup (chilled spiced aubergine and mint, or celeriac and Parmesan, for example), crab-cakes with tarragon sauce, or perhaps a terrine. Next comes a palate-cleansing salad before main courses along the lines of crispy duck with soy sauce and spring onions, roast monkfish on a lentil and coriander sauce, or a risotto of broad bean, onion and saffron. Also be prepared for the unexpected in the shape of, say, lamb marinated in pomegranate and rice wine, or roast cod with horseradish Yorkshire pudding and shrimp gravy. Proceedings conclude with a choice of desserts such as apple fritters with plum sauce, a novel-sounding rhubarb and Muscat wine trifle, or baked egg-custard tart with nutmeg ice-cream; otherwise opt for the platter of cheeses.

The wine list has clearly been put together by an enthusiast, and an uncommonly generous one at that. Pricing throughout is extremely reasonable and even Scrooge would deem the bubblies a bargain. House French wines start at £8.95. CELLARMAN'S CHOICE: Ormond Estate Chardonnay 1994, Marlborough, New Zealand, £17; Rockford 'Basket Press' Shiraz 1994, Barossa Valley, S. Australia, £19.75

CHEF: Michael Sharpe PROPRIETORS: Michael and Susan Sharpe OPEN: Tue to Sat D only 7.30 to 9.30 (L by arrangement) CLOSED: Christmas MEALS: Set D £22.50. BYO £5 SERVICE: not inc, card slips closed CARDS: Delta, MasterCard, Visa DETAILS: 24 seats. Private parties: 24 main room. Car park. Vegetarian meals. No children under 12. No smoking in dining-room. No music

LITTLE WALSINGHAM Norfolk map 6

▲ *Old Bakehouse* $*

33 High Street, Little Walsingham NR22 6BZ
TEL/FAX: (01328) 820454 COOKING 1
on B1105, 4½m N of Fakenham COST £19–£42

Pilgrims have been beating a path to Little Walsingham since before the Norman Conquest, and the collection of medieval buildings indicates the importance of the village over the centuries. The Old Bakehouse is more recent, with a Georgian frontage, and brick ovens dating from 1550, but it lives on more than just heritage appeal. One reporter found it a pleasant change from all the 'country-house palaver' to which rural areas are prone, and enjoyed a 'reassuring' meal that took in dishes from both the à la carte and vegetarian menus. Curried nut roast is alive and well, but there may also be warm goats'-cheese salad, or courgette, aubergine and lentil pancakes, with plenty for meat-eaters in the form of beef in puff pastry, salad of chicken livers, or a steak, kidney and smoked oyster pie with herb dumplings. Puddings can sound filling – banoffi pie, sticky toffee, or rum chocolate marquise – and the largely French wine list starts with own-label house wine at £9.95.

CHEF: Chris Padley PROPRIETORS: Chris and Helen Padley OPEN: Sun L once a month 12.30 to 1.30, Wed to Sat D 7 to 8.30 (9 Sat) CLOSED: 2 weeks Nov, 3 weeks Jan to Feb MEALS: alc D (main courses £14.50 to £16). Set L Sun £12.50. BYO £5 SERVICE: not inc, card slips closed CARDS: Delta, MasterCard, Switch, Visa DETAILS: 40 seats. Private parties: 30 main room, 10 private room. Vegetarian meals. Children's helpings. No smoking in dining-room. Wheelchair access (no WC). Music ACCOMMODATION: 3 rooms, 1 with bath/shower. TV. B&B £37 to £43 (double room). Deposit: £5. Children welcome. Dogs by arrangement (*The Which? Hotel Guide*)

LIVERPOOL Merseyside map 8

Far East £

27–35 Berry Street, Liverpool L1 9DF COOKING 1
TEL: (0151) 709 3141 COST £14–£46

The restaurant, which occupies a first floor deep in the heart of the city's Chinatown, has been spruced up inside and out of late, and it draws the crowds. 'Sunday lunch-time sees the place packed out with both Chinese and English families' who've come for the dim-sum, which arrives on trolleys. From noon to 6 each day there's a choice of around 20, ranging from fried crabmeat balls, roast pork buns, and beef dumplings to chicken feet in black-bean sauce, duck's web with four meats, and turnip cakes. The sprawling menu is forthright Cantonese, with dishes of crispy shredded duck roll, steamed chicken with Chinese sausage, and fresh squid with pickled cabbage lining up alongside casseroles and abundant one-plate rice and noodle dishes. Tuesday and Thursday evenings bring a fixed-price 'gourmet' dinner in addition to the set meals, while a hot buffet is the added attraction on Monday, Wednesday and Friday nights. House wine is £8.

CHEF: C.K. Cheung PROPRIETOR: S.Y. Leung OPEN: all week 12 to 11.25 (12.45 Fri and Sat, 11 Sun) CLOSED: 25 and 26 Dec, Good Fri MEALS: alc (main courses £5 to £10.50). Set L £6 (2 courses) to £6.80, Set D £11 to £19 (min 6) SERVICE: not inc CARDS: Amex, Diners, MasterCard, Switch, Visa DETAILS: 180 seats. Private parties: 240 main room. Car park. Vegetarian meals. Children's helpings. Music. Air-conditioned

LIVERSEDGE West Yorkshire map 9

▲ *Healds Hall Hotel* [£]

Leeds Road, Liversedge WF15 6JA COOKING **2**
TEL: (01924) 409112 FAX: (01924) 401895 COST £15–£41

Built in 1764 and once famous for its connections with the Brontë family, this stone mansion is now a 'very likeable' hotel with relaxed staff and a leaning towards conferences and functions. On the food front, the kitchen produces its own breads, chutneys and marmalade, and an adventurous spirit is at work behind the scenes. A wide-ranging *carte* offers such things as oxtail and bacon faggots, and grilled sirloin steak with Dijon mustard and peppercorn sauce, but the most interesting stuff is on the weekly-changing set-price menu. Here you might find red pepper and mint soup, and organic ham salad as well as a goodly showing of fish: grilled fillet of black bream with a mussel and coriander broth, monkfish ravioli on a bed of scallops and asparagus, or grilled sea bass with tagliatelle and tomato sauce, for example. Desserts are overshadowed by the first-class cheese selection, which includes such names as Bonchester, Cotherstone and Cooleeney. Around 50 thoughtfully chosen wines show a bias towards the New World. House French is £8.25.

CHEF: Philip McVeagh PROPRIETORS: Thomas and Nora Harrington OPEN: Sun to Fri L 12 to 2, Mon to Sat D 6.30 to 9.30 CLOSED: 26 Dec, 1 Jan, bank hol Mons MEALS: alc (main courses L £2 to £12.50, D 7 to £15). Set L Mon to Fri £9.75, Set L Sun £10.50, Set D £16.95 SERVICE: not inc, card slips closed CARDS: Amex, Delta, Diners, MasterCard, Switch, Visa DETAILS: 50 seats. Private parties: 35 main room, 12 to 130 private rooms. Car park. Vegetarian meals. Children's helpings. No smoking in dining-room. Wheelchair access (also WC). Music ACCOMMODATION: 25 rooms, all with bath/shower. TV. Phone. B&B £35 to £75. Rooms for disabled. Children welcome. Baby facilities. Dogs welcome in bedrooms only. Afternoon teas. Garden

All entries, including Round-ups, are fully indexed at the back of the Guide.

LOCKINGTON East Riding of Yorkshire map 9

Rockingham Arms

52 Front Street, Lockington YO25 9SH COOKING 2
TEL: (01430) 810607 FAX: (01430) 810734 COST £34–£45

It is all change again at the Rockingham Arms, a pleasant country restaurant in a converted pub. David Barker is still front-of-house, and his fine professional control is still in evidence, but Adam Richardson now joins Susan Barker in the kitchen. Choose between two or three courses on the set dinner menu. The cooking remains modern English with some Far Eastern influences thrown in, and a reporter has noted 'one or two refinements creeping in'. Cod on seaweed with soy sauce, or goats'-cheese salad on tapénade crostini may precede main courses of 'lovely textured' lamb in a herb crust, or halibut topped with crispy duck breast, which may be followed by lime and lemon posset with raspberry sauce. David Barker 'knows his food and his customers' and his staff back him up well. Forty-odd wines, mostly from France and the New World, are fairly priced, starting at £9.95.

CHEFS: Adam Richardson and Susan Barker PROPRIETORS: David and Susan Barker OPEN: Tue to Sat D only 7 to 10.15 CLOSED: 2 weeks in summer, bank hols MEALS: Set D £21.95 (2 courses) to £25.95 SERVICE: not inc CARDS: Delta, MasterCard, Switch, Visa DETAILS: 60 seats. Car park. Vegetarian meals. Children welcome. Music

LONG MELFORD Suffolk map 6

Scutcher's Bistro

Westgate Street, Long Melford CO10 9DP COOKING 3
TEL: (01787) 310200 FAX: (01787) 310620 COST £22–£41

If Long Melford's antique shops induce a sense of nostalgia, the light, fresh interior of Scutcher's is sure to restore focus. It is a colourful place, all the way from its turquoise radiators to a roasted vegetable tart with tomato and mozzarella. Flavours are just as bright, taking in tempura tiger prawns with chilli dressing, or roast fillet of halibut with soured lime cream and a curry dressing. Fish, as well reported as anything, has also included chargrilled smoked salmon on cucumber spaghetti, and steamed sea bass with lemon butter sauce.

Options range from one-course snack lunches to the full monty with a centrepiece of pink beef fillet served with a caramelised shallot and red wine sauce. Vegetables come in generous portions but bread is charged extra. Dessert may include a simple cocktail of strawberries, raspberries and mango with a squeeze of lime, or banana fritters with rum fudge sauce and peanut brittle ice-cream. Service continues to please. The thoughtful selection of around 100 wines, ordered by grape variety for simplicity, manages to include most of the major wine regions. Prices are fair and there is a good spread of half-bottles. Ten house wines start at £8.50, £1.70 a glass. CELLARMAN'S CHOICE: Staton Hills Fumé Blanc 1994, Yakima Valley, Washington State, £13.40; Côtes du Rhône 1994, Guigal, £15.

CHEF/PROPRIETOR: Nicholas Barrett OPEN: Tue to Sat 12 to 2.30, 7 to 9.30 CLOSED: first 2 weeks Jan MEALS: alc (main courses £7.50 to £14) SERVICE: not inc CARDS: Amex, Delta, MasterCard, Switch, Visa DETAILS: 75 seats. 60 seats outside. Car park. Vegetarian meals. Children's helpings. No cigars/pipes in dining-room. Wheelchair access (also WC). Music

LONGRIDGE Lancashire map 8

Paul Heathcote's

104–106 Higher Road, Longridge PR3 3SY
TEL: (01772) 784969 FAX: (01772) 785713
from Preston, follow Town Centre signs, drive uphill though centre of Longridge, then turn left, following signs for Jeffery Hill

COOKING 7
COST £33–£83

The converted cottages with their 'bottle bottom' windows stand on a bend in the road leading out of Longridge: a modest setting for the kitchen's high achievement. Comfortable sofas and chairs, and a surprising number of spacious tables, are shoehorned into the small, interlinked rooms, creating 'a curious mixture of semi-detached gentility and smartly serious restaurant'. Paul Heathcote has developed a style of cooking that brings together his Lancashire roots, manifest skills, and formative years in some of the country's top kitchens. Hence, for example, a penchant for black pudding, pig's trotter and ham hock, alongside lobster, foie gras and other luxuries, plus of course local Goosnargh duckling.

The lavish appeal is captured by a well-reported first course of two discs of foie gras terrine, glazed with aspic, placed on a mound of sharply dressed salad leaves; around them are pink chicken livers coated in black pepper ('the star in this collection of luxury items') sitting in a truffle-flecked sauce. An impressive lightness of touch is a characteristic too, as in a roasted lobster arranged on a shellfish stock, scattered with wilted lettuce and green vegetables: a dish of 'fresh colours and succulent lobster flesh'. Refinement rather than continual creativity is the kitchen's watchword.

Paul Heathcote has a lot to do keeping his eye on the brasserie (see entry, Preston) and Simply Heathcote's in Manchester (see entry), but if Longridge is not blessed with a comparable catchment area, it does attract custom with its 'tremendous value' lunch (only served two days a week) plus alternatives to the *carte* such as the 'signature menu' (a ten-course tasting meal for the whole table), and a 'gourmet' version listing five set courses at a not unreasonable £38 including coffee. Note, too, the maximum service charge of £15.

Meals are supported by good breads, and carefully sourced and well-kept British cheeses. A savoury, such as deep-fried Stilton fritters, provides a welcome alternative to bread-and-butter pudding, or a baked egg custard flavoured with rosewater and served with honey ice-cream. Service has varied (at the same meal) between 'excessive formality' and 'a relaxed charm'. The only disappointment on the wine list is that mark-ups do not allow much of interest below £20; a ceiling of £30 brings some decent bottles within range. Otherwise the quality is extremely high. Wines by the glass start at £3.25, and house wine is £14.50.

CHEFS: Paul Heathcote and Andrew Barnes PROPRIETOR: Paul Heathcote OPEN: Fri and Sun L 12 to 2, Tue to Sun D 7 to 9.30 MEALS: alc D Tue to Sat (main courses £18 to £22). Set L Fri and Sat £22.50, Set D Tue to Sun £38 to £55, Set D Sun £25 SERVICE: 10% (optional, maximum £15) card slips closed CARDS: Amex, Delta, Diners, MasterCard, Switch, Visa DETAILS: 60 seats. Private parties: 65 main room, 18 private room. Car park. Vegetarian meals. Children's helpings. No children under 10. No smoking in dining-room. Music

LOOE Cornwall map 1

Trawlers £

NEW ENTRY

Buller Quay, East Looe PL13 1AH COOKING 5
TEL: (01503) 263593 COST £21–£39

'An absolute find' was the verdict of an inspector sent to investigate Jean-Claude and Tessa Denat's seafood restaurant named in honour of the boats that bring in their raw materials. Set a course for the fish market on East Looe quay and stride on towards the water: 'we are almost in the river,' the proprietors advise. They have been open only since March 1996, and yet 'the food is as good as, if not better than, many a place with better views and flashier fitments', thought our reporter. That unbooked parties were having to be turned away in droves on a Wednesday evening is perhaps the soundest testimony of all to the truth of that.

A long menu is offered, which may be thought ambitious when it is mostly fresh fish and there are so few covers to accommodate, but the quality throughout is high. Fish soup has the deep savour of crustaceans in the stock and comes with a properly pungent rouille. Another starter of crab and mushroom thermidor served in a scallop shell impresses because of the fine balance of ingredients in the sauce. Meat-eaters and vegetarians are not neglected, but it is fish-lovers who are most obviously looked after: medallions of monkfish in a sauce of pastis and saffron have a real waft of the Mediterranean about them, and a selection of Cajun-blackened mixed fish and prawns also shows great judgement. Nor are puddings run of the mill: a variation on crème caramel apparently has its caramel syrup stirred into the custard before cooking and comes with two sauces, one powerfully infused with vanilla, the other of dark chocolate. Go easy on dessert, because coffee comes with plentiful petits fours. Service is 'deft and friendly', and wines are predominantly French and reasonably priced, although quite a few of the producers' names are missing. House burgundy is £7.95.

CHEF: Jean-Claude Denat PROPRIETORS: Jean-Claude and Tessa Denat OPEN: Tue to Sat D only 6.30 to 9 CLOSED: occasionally Nov to end Feb: phone to check MEALS: alc (main courses £9 to £14.50) SERVICE: not inc CARDS: Delta, MasterCard, Switch, Visa DETAILS: 24 seats. Private parties: 28 main room. Vegetarian meals. Children's helpings. Wheelchair access (no WC). No music

'The attentiveness of the staff did not always mean competence. A ruddy-faced young lad grandly put down a plate of petits fours in front of us, just after the first course had been removed. My wife whacked my hand as I quite innocently reached for a little creamy strawberry tartlet as a palate cleanser before my duck.'
(On eating in Suffolk)

LOWER BEEDING West Sussex map 3

Jeremy's at the Crabtree

Brighton Road, Lower Beeding RH13 6PT
TEL: (01403) 891257 FAX: (01403) 891606 COOKING 4
on A281, just S of village COST £25–£42

This cream-painted Georgian building is 'probably best thought of as a roadside restaurant and pub', although food dominates even more since the public bar was incorporated into the rest of the scheme. Jeremy Ashpool is in overall charge of the kitchen, but Norwegian Pia Waters has been here since the start in 1991, and the two are joined this year by Yves Nivesse. Their food is 'interesting, well cooked and presented', with meat and fish outshining vegetarian options in a regular's view. A breezy cascade of dishes gives a clue to the kitchen's orientation: vegetable tart with cep sauce, pork steaks fried in ginger, chilli and soy, or roast rib of beef with Yorkshire pudding and onion compote.

The strong fishy theme, meanwhile, runs from smoked haddock on spinach purée with poached egg to monkfish in coconut cream and chilli sauce, by way of marinated fish on polenta with roasted pepper dressing. Puddings, by contrast, are likely to be as simple as lemon tart, or chocolate and coffee cake. Good walnut bread adds to the pleasure. A bright list of around 50 wines looks mostly to the southern hemisphere for bottles under £20, but house French is £10. 'We hope,' writes the owner, 'to open a second Jeremy's in spring 1998.'

CHEFS: Jeremy Ashpool, Pia Waters and Yves Nivesse PROPRIETOR: Jeremy's Restaurants Ltd OPEN: all week L 12.30 to 2, Mon to Sat D 7.30 to 9.45 CLOSED: 25 Dec, D bank hols MEALS: alc L (main courses £9 to £11). Set L Mon to Sat £10.50 (2 courses), Set L Sun £16.95, Set D Mon to Wed £13.50 to £25, Set D Thur to Sat £25 SERVICE: not inc L Mon to Sat, 10% other times, card slips closed CARDS: Amex, Delta, MasterCard, Switch, Visa DETAILS: 45 seats. 15 seats outside. Private parties: 26 main room. Car park. Vegetarian meals. Children's helpings. No smoking in 1 dining-room. Wheelchair access (no WC). No music

▲ *South Lodge*

Brighton Road, Lower Beeding RH13 6PS
TEL: (01403) 891711 FAX: (01403) 891766 COOKING 3
on A281, 6m SE of Horsham COST £29–£76

The rambling stone building dating from 1833 is awash in dark oak panelling, ornate plasterwork and heavy chandeliers, but the staff do a good job of lightening the atmosphere, quickly bringing drinks, canapés and menus and proffering good milk bread. The kitchen has aspirations towards a light and distinctly modern Mediterranean style, applying some nifty footwork to, for example, a pressed terrine of duck flesh with wild mushrooms and Savoy cabbage, partnering it with chopped crab-apple jelly and little stacks of courgette fritters, or 'a sort of tandoori chicken with Thai flavours that came sandwiched between two thin discs of pasta'. Materials are good, dishes are impeccably presented – turbot coated with a lobster mousse, on a pale green sauce of watercress and orange – and vegetables from the Victorian kitchen garden are an integral part of the main course. The bill, though, is 'vastly out of line with the capacity of the kitchen'. Aristocratic wines constitute the bulk of the list, and prices seem directed towards the business clientele. House Vin de Pays d'Oc is £14.50.

CHEF: Timothy Neal PROPRIETOR: Laura Hotels Ltd OPEN: all week 12.30 to 2.30 (3 Sun), 7.30 (7 Sat) to 10 (10.30 Fri and Sat) MEALS: alc D (main courses £22 to £24.50). Set L £14.50 (2 courses) to £16.50, Set D £25 to £32. Bar food available SERVICE: not inc, card slips closed CARDS: Amex, Delta, Diners, MasterCard, Switch, Visa DETAILS: 40 seats. Private parties: 40 main room, 2 to 80 private rooms. Car park. Vegetarian meals. Children's helpings. Jacket and tie. No smoking in dining-room. Wheelchair access (also WC). No music ACCOMMODATION: 39 rooms, all with bath/shower. TV. Phone. Room only £120 to £295. Rooms for disabled. Children welcome. Afternoon teas. Garden

LOWER SLAUGHTER Gloucestershire map 5

▲ *Lower Slaughter Manor*

Lower Slaughter GL54 2HP
TEL: (01451) 820456 FAX: (01451) 822150 COOKING 6
off A429, at sign 'The Slaughters' COST £53–£92

'Delightful' is a word that recurs in reports on this seventeenth-century manor house. Mullioned windows, well-tended gardens, a croquet lawn and 'lovely old trees' contribute to the impression. It also has a formal air about it, with ornate plaster ceilings, and tends to be rather set in its ways: jacket and tie for men, desserts to be ordered at the start of the meal. The fixed-price dinner menu is where Alan Dann's energy is concentrated, with ample choice and variety. Lunch is a simpler affair, while the 'menu dégustation' picks out half a dozen stylish examples from the repertoire.

The food can be subtle, as in a starter of pressed crab and queen scallops, a dish that also points up the 'superb' quality of the seafood. But there is a boldness, too, in the tropical fruit chutney that comes with rillettes of duck, and a degree of luxury in the truffle sauce served with saddle of venison. The intricate detail of dishes might defy casual analysis, for there can be a lot going on, but the main components remain clearly in focus. 'Enormously clever and very decorative' is how one observer described the style, referring not least to the 'bits stuck out at angles' from the mounds that form main courses, and to the streaks of vegetable or fruit purées in bright, contrasting colours, often two per dish.

Unusually flavoured ice-creams are a feature of desserts – cardamom with a warm chocolate mousse perhaps, or green peppercorn with a tarte Tatin of mango – while cheese is served with beetroot chips. Extras arrive in one salvo after another at both the beginning and end of a meal, a generous gesture no doubt, although for purists their sheer numbers can detract from the essential clarity of a meal. High-quality wines from France and the New World dominate the list, but there are some silly prices. House white is £17.50, house red £18.50.

CHEF: Alan Dann PROPRIETORS: Roy and Daphne Vaughan OPEN: all week 12.15 to 2, 7.15 to 9.30 (10 Fri and Sat) MEALS: Set L Mon to Sat £19.95 to £57, Set L Sun £24.50 to £57, Set D £35.50 to £57 SERVICE: not inc CARDS: Amex, Diners, MasterCard, Switch, Visa DETAILS: 40 seats. Private parties: 40 main room, 18 private room. Car park. Vegetarian meals. No children under 10. Jacket and tie. No smoking in dining-room. No music ACCOMMODATION: 15 rooms, all with bath/shower. TV. Phone. B&B £120 to £335. No children under 10. Afternoon teas. Garden. Swimming-pool (*The Which? Hotel Guide*)

LOW LAITHE North Yorkshire map 9

Dusty Miller

Low Laithe, Summerbridge HG3 4BU
TEL: (01423) 780837 FAX: (01423) 780065 COOKING **6**
on B6165, 2m SE of Pateley Bridge COST £32–£51

Dusty Miller is one reporter's 'favourite restaurant for feel, atmosphere, views and certainly food'. The stone house looks out on Nidderdale, and although the dining-room is compact it has an easy grace, with candles and good linen and glassware on the tables. A 'wonderfully relaxed yet extremely professional' hostess, Elizabeth Dennison knows the menu and cooking methods backwards, and the dishes that come from husband Brian's kitchen are pleasingly free of showy contrivance.

The formula that makes seared tuna niçoise into a 'wonderful blend', for instance, is fine ingredients simply cooked and combined in perfect balance. Such is also the way with Nidderdale steak and kidney pie (made from lamb), which is slowly cooked and comes with a much-reduced, unthickened sauce and a crumbly and buttery puff pastry crust. A reporter gave nine out of ten to roast duckling with orange, again slowly cooked, taken off the bone and the meat wrapped in a parcel of crisp skin. The set-price 'Proprietors' Menu', an alternative to the short *carte*, gives other starters, no choice of main course, and the option of cheese instead of, say, passion-fruit bavarois or strawberries and cream. Mineral water is free. The short wine list is mostly French but not short on variety. House wines start at £9.90.

CHEF: Brian Dennison PROPRIETORS: Brian and Elizabeth Dennison OPEN: Tue to Sat D only 7 to 11 CLOSED: 25 and 26 Dec, 1 Jan MEALS: alc (main courses £17 to £18). Set D £24 SERVICE: not inc, card slips closed CARDS: Amex, MasterCard, Visa DETAILS: 44 seats. Private parties: 32 main room, 14 private room. Car park. Children's helpings. No children under 9. Wheelchair access (no WC). Music

LUDLOW Shropshire map 5

Merchant House $*

Lower Corve Street, Ludlow SY8 1DU COOKING **8**
TEL/FAX: (01584) 875438 COST £30–£41

The setting is two small rooms with six tables in a black and white Jacobean house, with ancient boards beneath your feet, plain polished tables, and simple, comfortable furniture. Shaun Hill lives up to expectations – 'no gimmicks, no fuss' – and cooks what he likes, following his nose rather than any particular school. Meals have begun with a generous bowl of 'full-flavoured' pheasant and chestnut soup, and properly timed risotto of artichoke and saffron served with slices of Parma ham, while richer first courses (served in 'sensibly small portions') have included calves' kidneys and sweetbreads with an olive potato cake, and postcard-sized slices of 'wonderfully spreadable' foie gras terrine.

Nothing superfluous is added to dishes, the marriage of flavours and textures is thoughtful, and the food looks appetising and attractive 'without being fiddled about'. Fish impresses for freshness, texture and sensitive treatment:

'firm and springy' grilled red mullet, or meaty turbot served with a mix of tomato, coriander and ginger that was 'part relish, part sauce and part vegetable'. Ingredients are first-rate, flavours are 'subtle yet distinct', and there is 'an admirable precision and consistency' about the cooking 'as if you are in the hands of a master who will not let you down'. Game – plentiful locally – is extremely well handled. Slices of rare roasted hare fillet have been casually draped over a purée of celeriac and potato (vegetables are integral to main courses), while deep pink saddle of venison ('I didn't know venison could taste like this,' confessed an experienced reporter) has come with a small heap of sauté goats'-cheese gnocchi that 'tasted wonderful'.

Dishes may appear simple and unfussy, but they embody considerable skill and sound judgement, not least among desserts of 'flawless' plum and almond tart, and 'exemplary' raspberry crème brûlée with a golden topping that 'shattered satisfactorily with a light tap'. Service from Anja Hill and one assistant is variously attentive, efficient and informative, and the excellent value owes much to the fact that the price, which includes appetising nibbles, bread 'to die for', and service, has barely changed in three years. Wines are an appealing mix of sensible everyday drinking and special bottles. 'I don't list anything I do not like or would not drink,' writes Hill, who has an eye for quality. House Italian is £12.50.

CHEF: Shaun Hill PROPRIETORS: Shaun and Anja Hill OPEN: Fri and Sat L 12.30 to 2, Tue to Sat D 7 to 9 CLOSED: 1 week Christmas, 1 week spring MEALS: Set L and D £26 SERVICE: net prices, card slips closed CARDS: Amex, Delta, MasterCard, Visa DETAILS: 24 seats. Private parties: 10 main room. No smoking in dining-room. Wheelchair access (no WC). No music

---

LYDGATE Greater Manchester map 8

▲ *White Hart*

51 Stockport Road, Lydgate OL4 4JJ
TEL: (01457) 872566 FAX: (01457) 875190 COOKING 4
on A6050, 3m E of Oldham COST £20–£40

As food increasingly takes priority in this refurbished 200-year-old building, its role as a local pub diminishes, but 'a lively atmosphere and consistently good food' draw reporters back for more. The stone-walled, log-fired brasserie turns out a populist spread of grilled local sausage with mash and onion gravy, cod fish-cakes with tartare sauce, and hot banana muffin with chocolate sauce, while the more formal first-floor dining-room extends to lemon sole with risotto cake, or roast breast of Goosnargh duckling with choucroute. John Rudden has an inventive streak and an eye for some unusual ingredients and combinations. These are not outlandish, but they do stoke up interest and curiosity: a langoustine and pearl barley broth, for example, or risotto of lambs' fries with woodpigeon.

You don't have to be a vegetarian to consider a main-course option of tomato and feta tart, or broccoli mousse with roasted tomatoes and basil oil. Desserts have been described as 'consistently ordinary', which may increase the appeal of a savoury alternative such as grilled sardines with tomato dressing. Service has veered unsteadily from 'good' to 'haphazard' to worse. The wine list continues to draw inspiration from around the world: those in a mood to celebrate might like to try the Californian sparkling rosé from Schramsberg, which, at £23.50, is a good-value alternative to champagne. House French is £9. CELLARMAN'S CHOICE: Gewurztraminer d'Alsace 1994, Les Vignerons de Pfaffenheim, £16.50; Languedoc-Roussillon, Ch. De la Liquière 1993, Faugères, £14.50.

CHEF: John Rudden PROPRIETORS: Charles Brierley and John Rudden OPEN: restaurant Sun L 12 to 2.30, Tue to Sat D 7 to 10; brasserie all week 12 to 2.30, 6 to 9 MEALS: restaurant Set L Sun £16, Set D £23; brasserie alc (main courses £6.50 to £13.50). BYO £10 SERVICE: not inc, card slips closed CARDS: Amex, Delta, MasterCard, Switch, Visa DETAILS: restaurant 56 seats, brasserie 44 seats. 24 seats outside. Private parties: 24 main room. Car park. Vegetarian meals. Children's helpings. No smoking in dining-room. Wheelchair access (also WC). Music ACCOMMODATION: 5 rooms, all with bath/shower. TV. Phone. B&B £50 to £75. Deposit: £25. Children welcome. Baby facilities. Afternoon teas. Garden

LYMINGTON Hampshire map 2

▲ *Gordleton Mill Hotel, Provence*

Silver Street, Hordle, Lymington SO41 6DJ COOKING **8**
TEL: (01590) 682219 FAX: (01590) 683073 COST £35–£79

'If you like elaborately and wittily turned out food, made from high-class ingredients and cooked with talent and skill, this is surely one of the best places to find it,' summed up an inspector. The garden of the seventeenth-century mill is 'a willow pattern plate come to life', and takes romantic advantage of the millstream and old orchard, while 'posh French' is the tone of the spacious, comfortable and well-lit interior. Toby Hill's food is definitely in the 'ooh aah' category – 'theatrical, done to be admired for looks as much as taste' – and includes a six-course tasting menu at dinner, as well as a generous *carte*.

The style is modern and classical, light yet powerfully flavoured, and some items pay homage to fellow chefs: an unctuous terrine of smoked ham hock and foie gras (a favourite of 21 Queen Street – see entry, Newcastle), or a 'very clever café minute', consisting of a cup and saucer made from chocolate, filled with coffee mousse, with a biscuit 'spoon' and chocolate truffle 'sugar lumps', made famous some years ago by Raymond Blanc (see Le Manoir aux Quat' Saisons, Great Milton).

Dishes tend to come as a centrally placed cylindrical tower made up of layers: foie gras, langoustine, fennel and potato galette, for example, described as a 'mille-feuille' yet with not a flake of pastry in sight. And most have a moat of *jus* or coulis, on which garnishes are set out like a clock face: perhaps 'juicy, sweet, warm scallops' and teaspoon-sized blobs of tomato sorbet, arranged alternately around a 'pompom' of ornamental edible greenery. Spears of chive, feathers of chervil, and spun sugar spirals are thrown around for good measure, yet the food stays on the right side of the abyss and doesn't become overblown.

Two small minus points: the main-course centrepiece may not be large, and integral vegetables, though 'brilliantly incorporated', tend to be minimal. On the other hand, materials are tiptop, not least fish such as pan-fried sea bass – 'a marvellous hunk of freshness' – with sauce antiboise, and 'a splendid array of cheeses', mostly French but including British Elmhurst, Tornegus and Exmoor Jersey Blue. Earnest, discreet service is good-humoured. French classics dominate the hefty wine list, with some famous names from the New World adding their support, but although the quality is high, prices are even higher. Anyone tempted to round off a meal with a half-bottle of Brown Brothers Orange Muscat & Flora at £24.50 may well get a touch of indigestion when they consider that it could be bought for little more than a quarter of that from a reputable wine merchant. Even house vins de pays are £17 a bottle (£3.50 a glass). CELLARMAN'S CHOICE: Chablis 'Les Mignottes' 1994, Jean Durup, £23.50; Chorey-lès-Beaune 1992, Joseph Drouhin, £27.

CHEF: Toby Hill PROPRIETOR: William Stone OPEN: Tue to Sun L 12 to 2, Tue to Sat D 7 to 9.30 (10 Sat) CLOSED: first 2 weeks Nov MEALS: alc (main courses L £17.50 to £24, D £19.50 to £24). Set L Tue to Sat £19.50, Set D £45. BYO £12 SERVICE: not inc CARDS: Amex, Delta, Diners, MasterCard, Switch, Visa DETAILS: 45 seats. 14 seats outside. Private parties: 55 main room, 16 private room. Car park. Vegetarian meals. Children's helpings. No children under 7. No smoking in dining-room. Wheelchair access (also WC). Music. Air-conditioned ACCOMMODATION: 7 rooms, all with bath/shower. TV. Phone. B&B £97 to £136. Deposit: 25%. No children under 7. Dogs welcome in kennels only. Afternoon teas. Garden. Fishing (*The Which? Hotel Guide*)

LYMPSTONE Devon map 1

▲ *River House*

The Strand, Lympstone EX8 5EY COOKING 1
TEL: (01395) 265147 COST £44–£57

'Don't go to the River House if you want to impress a business customer,' advises one reporter; 'go to relax.' This isn't difficult, given the casual furnishings and the wonderful view across the river to Powderham Castle ('try not to go when it's foggy'). The standard repertoire moves slowly, relying on cheese or wine for some of its effect: red pepper and onion marmalade tart with melted Brie, for example, or chicken with Noilly Prat, tarragon and mushrooms. There is support for home-made pasta with flaked white crabmeat and a covering of cheese sauce, less enthusiasm for Moroccan lamb, but vegetables are a high point, on account of being 'well (i.e. under) cooked'. To finish, 'superb' chocolate roulade is a crisp light sponge rolled around a creamy chocolate filling. Wines are varied, well chosen and fairly priced, with nine available by the glass. House wines start at £9.95.

CHEF: Shirley Wilkes PROPRIETOR: Michael Wilkes OPEN: Tue to Sat 12 to 1.30, 7 to 9.30 (10.30 Sat) CLOSED: 25 to 27 Dec, 1 and 2 Jan, bank hols MEALS: Set L and D £28.95 (2 courses) to £33. Light L available Tue to Sat SERVICE: not inc CARDS: Amex, Delta, MasterCard, Visa DETAILS: 40 seats. Private parties: 40 main room, 14 private room. Car park. Vegetarian meals. No children under 6. No smoking in dining-room. Wheelchair access (no WC). No music ACCOMMODATION: 3 rooms, all with bath/shower. TV. B&B £44 to £96. No children under 6

indicates that smoking is either banned altogether or that a dining-room is maintained for non-smokers. The symbol does not apply to restaurants that simply have no-smoking areas.

MADINGLEY Cambridgeshire map 6

Three Horseshoes

High Street, Madingley CB3 8AB COOKING **2**
TEL: (01954) 210221 FAX: (01954) 212043 COST £22–£49

This thatched pub in a small village just outside Cambridge is a sister to the Pheasant and the White Hart (see entries, Keyston and Great Yeldham) and thrives on informality and a thoroughly modern menu. The format is an appealing one, with the same food available in both bar and bookable dining-room. While Sunday brunch might bring comforting eggs Benedict and corned beef hash, Richard Stokes has obviously been on his travels and serves up a busy menu of bright-sounding dishes, from pigeon crostini to 'tagine-style' brill with couscous. Simple roasting or grilling of chicken, salmon, or venison may be the foundation, but all sorts of condiments – from coriander pesto and mustard butter to lemon confit and truffle oil – keep the tone upbeat. This is a hearty version of Mediterranean food, and rich puddings are the norm, from panettone bread-and-butter to chocolate nemesis.

With an intriguing range of around 100 good-quality bottles at fair prices, the wine list is particularly strong in the New World and Burgundy. Bins are grouped by style, and each has a short but helpful tasting note; six tempting dessert wines priced between £1.85 and £2.85 per glass can be found on the pudding menu. House wines start at £9.45 and 12 are sold by the glass. CELLARMAN'S CHOICE: Lawsons Dry Hills Gewurztraminer 1995, Marlborough, New Zealand, £17.50; Bearboat Pinot Noir 1994, Russian River Valley, California, £28.50

CHEF: Richard Stokes PROPRIETOR: Huntsbridge Ltd OPEN: all week L 12 to 2, Mon to Sat D 6.30 to 10 MEALS: alc (main courses £7 to £15.50) SERVICE: not inc CARDS: Amex, Delta, Diners, MasterCard, Switch, Visa DETAILS: 90 seats. 35 seats outside. Private parties: 65 main room. Car park. Vegetarian meals. Children's helpings. No smoking while others eat. Wheelchair access (no WC). No music

MAENPORTH Cornwall map 1

Pennypots

Maenporth TR11 5HN COOKING **6**
TEL/FAX: (01326) 250251 COST £36–£48

In among the holiday homes that dominate the beach, Pennypots looks out through large french windows to Falmouth Bay and beyond, and has a balcony for summer eating. Inside are comfortable cane chairs, paper flowers, deep-pile carpeting, and a sense that everything is efficiently run. But 'we deliberately don't fuss around our guests', writes Jane Viner, who prefers to let them get on with the business of relaxing. Kevin Viner's approach to food is direct, simple and sometimes strongly flavoured, as in finely sliced chargrilled scallop, with shredded courgette and leek, in a powerful sweet, sour and hot sauce. Positive flavouring among starters can be a difficult act for main courses to follow, but first-rate materials, especially fish, work in their favour. Helford oysters have a journey of three miles, Newlyn fish market is twenty miles away, and 'fresh and tasty' red mullet and turbot have proved its value.

Non-fishy successes have included foie gras served with pasta, and loin of lamb, well crusted with rock salt and coarse pepper, served with sweetbreads, tiny asparagus tips and plump garlic cloves. Professionalism shows through in everything from bread rolls, petits fours and appetisers (perhaps creamy shellfish soup, or sweet-tasting green pea soup) to such standards of the repertoire as bread-and-butter pudding: 'by far the best of its genre' that our inspector tasted in a sweep through the south-west. Eye-catching presentation is a feature of desserts, including raspberry shortbread decked out with small mounds of fruit, cream, ice-cream, coulis and lots more. Wines are varied in style, and there is much from both France and the southern hemisphere below £20. Twenty-odd half-bottles are helpful, and house French is £8.95.

CHEF: Kevin Viner PROPRIETORS: Jane and Kevin Viner OPEN: Tue to Sat D only 7 to 9.30 CLOSED: 4 weeks winter MEALS: Set D £22 (2 courses) to £26.50. BYO £3 SERVICE: not inc, card slips closed CARDS: Amex, Delta, Diners, MasterCard, Switch, Visa DETAILS: 40 seats. Private parties: 40 main room. Car park. Vegetarian meals. Children's helpings. No smoking in dining-room before 10pm. Wheelchair access (also WC). No music. Air-conditioned

MAIDEN NEWTON Dorset map 2

Le Petit Canard

Dorchester Road, Maiden Newton DT2 0BE
TEL: (01300) 320536 COOKING 5
off A37, 7m N of Dorchester COST £34–£43

Fairy lights strung across cream-painted beams, plus tall candles on the well-spaced tables provide the illumination in this small cottagey restaurant in the heart of Dorset. Geoff Chapman's repertoire is worldly, drawing on the Pacific Rim for stir-fried venison and 'Chinese' vegetables in black-bean and chilli orange oil, or kangaroo fillet with chilli roasted onions. He often gives classical themes an interesting variation, as in a rack of lamb with a rosemary swede flan and pepper béarnaise. Reporters have praised seared scallops with crispy bacon and Asian sesame dressing, and warm breast of woodpigeon with truffle-dressed new potatoes, as well as 'excellent vegetables'.

There is no sign of imagination fatigue at dessert stage, where tiramisù is turned into a chocolate and raspberry torte, and rhubarb tartlet is 'Sauternes roasted' and accompanied by 'not too hot' black-pepper ice-cream. Alternatively, you might finish with West Country farmhouse cheeses. 'Efficient, pleasant' service is provided by Lin Chapman and helpers, and it is Lin who has tracked down some fascinating bins from the New World – Stellars Jay sparkler from Canada's Sumac Ridge, for example – while continuing to provide some mature burgundies for Old World fans. Prices are very fair. CELLARMAN'S CHOICE: Church Road Chardonnay 1994, Hawkes Bay, New Zealand, £15.95; Henry Pelham, Baco Noir 1995, Ontario, Canada, £14.95.

CHEF: Geoff Chapman PROPRIETORS: Lin and Geoff Chapman OPEN: Tue to Sat D only 7 to 8.45 CLOSED: first week Jan, 1 week June MEALS: Set D £23.50 SERVICE: not inc CARDS: MasterCard, Visa DETAILS: 30 seats. Private parties: 34 main room. Vegetarian meals. No children under 7. No smoking in dining-room. Music

MALMESBURY Wiltshire map 2

▲ *Old Bell Hotel* 

Abbey Row, Malmesbury SN16 0AG COOKING 5
TEL: (01666) 822344 FAX: (01666) 825145 COST £21–£38

The Old Bell was built in 1220 to house visitors to the nearby abbey's renowned library, so its life as a hostelry goes back a long way. Today's guests can see the past in warren-like passages, carved window surrounds and canopied fireplace, but furnishings are more in tune with the Edwardian era, when the hotel was enlarged. Hospitality is also old-style: children are welcomed warmly, and courtesy and charm make the staff, in the view of one reporter, 'absolute sweeties'. The dining-room, in a high-ceilinged extension, has something of a stately air about it, with oil portraits on pale walls and crisp linen on large tables.

New chef David Richards has settled in well, producing technically accomplished meals from first-rate raw materials. Praise has come for a salad of pan-fried Cornish scallop and lobster with a shellfish vinaigrette, and for 'three ways with duck': foie gras terrine, liver parfait and duck ham. Pan-fried beef fillet with 'beautiful texture' has been served with glazed artichoke in a perfectly judged red wine *jus*, while, for one reporter, pear and almond tart on a toffee sauce was 'alone worth coming to the Bell for'. Wines are grouped by grape variety, starting at £11.75 per bottle, £2 per glass.

CHEF: David Richards PROPRIETORS: Nicholas Dickinson and Nigel Chapman OPEN: all week 12.30 to 2, 7.30 to 9.30 MEALS: Set L Mon to Sat £15, Set L Sun £16, Set D £18.50 to £26 SERVICE: none, card slips closed CARDS: Amex, Delta, Diners, MasterCard, Switch, Visa DETAILS: 80 seats. 20 seats outside. Private parties: 80 main room, 14 to 24 private rooms. Car park. Vegetarian meals. Children's helpings. No smoking in dining-room. Wheelchair access (no WC). Music ACCOMMODATION: 31 rooms, all with bath/shower. TV. Phone. B&B £60 to £160. Children welcome. Baby facilities. Dogs welcome in bedrooms only. Afternoon teas. Garden (*The Which? Hotel Guide*)

MALVERN WELLS Hereford & Worcester map 5

Croque-en-Bouche 

221 Wells Road, Malvern Wells WR14 4HF
TEL/FAX: (01684) 565612 COOKING 8
on A449, 2m S of Great Malvern COST £31–£43

Robin and Marion Jones, who celebrate 20 years at Croque-en-Bouche in 1998, offer 'one of the best restaurant deals in Britain'. Restricted opening – three mealtimes a week – is partly due to the fact that the wine business occupies an increasing amount of Robin Jones's time. The setting is a former shop, decorated in shades of apricot, with a long garden sloping down the hill at the back. Everything is 'simply and elegantly ordered' and a relaxed atmosphere prevails, 'as long as you arrive on time'.

The style is an individual one. There is no main course as such, rather a fish course and meat course (with a choice of three items at each), and among the constants might be a 'Japanese selection' of three or four items, a croustade filled with shellfish or mushrooms, and probably a choice between lamb, game and poultry. Soup is a help-yourself tureen left on the table: for example, a green purée of lettuce with pea and spring onion that was 'the essence of summer' for our inspector.

Fish is a highlight, and often colourful: maybe a fillet of white halibut covered with black olive tapénade, on a bed of peperonata, red peppers and onions, surrounded by a circle of rocket leaves and a trickle of pesto. Simple grilling, of venison or boar (with Mediterranean vegetables perhaps), has 'added excitement to what were already superb raw materials'. Gratin dauphinois is an unchanging accompaniment to meat, followed by a salad from the garden. Cheeses in prime condition are firmly British and served from a trolley: Bonchester, maybe, goats' cheese in oil, or Stinking Bishop.

Cantucci biscuits with a glass of vin santo is a regular dessert, and the geraniums that grow in pots near the entrance might be used to make a fragrant lemon geranium ice-cream to accompany a wedge of 'intensely flavoured' glazed passion-fruit and mascarpone tart. Incidentals, from appetisers through bread and butter to petits-fours, are out of the top drawer. Gently paced service is 'never anything but impeccable'.

Copies of the wine list with its conversational notes are available in advance – there are hundreds of marvellous wines to choose from – although Robin Jones will happily offer advice if you prefer. Great value for money is another strong point, and diners pour for themselves. House wines start at £12. CELLARMAN'S CHOICE: Kumeu River Chardonnay 1995, Auckland, New Zealand, £16.30, St Hallett Old Block Shiraz 1993, Barossa Valley, S. Australia, £19.50.

CHEF: Marion Jones PROPRIETORS: Robin and Marion Jones OPEN: Thu to Sat D only 7.30 to 9 CLOSED: Christmas to New Year, 1 week May, 1 week July, 1 week Sept MEALS: Set D Thu £23 to £27, Set D Fri and Sat £33 to £36 SERVICE: net prices CARDS: Delta, MasterCard, Visa DETAILS: 22 seats. Private parties: 6 main room, 6 private room. Children welcome. No smoking in dining-room. Wheelchair access (no WC). No music

Planters

191–193 Wells Road, Malvern Wells WR14 9HE
TEL: (01684) 575065 COOKING 3
on A449, 3m S of Great Malvern COST £27–£41

Malvern Wells may not be the first place you would think of looking for South-east Asian food, but here it is in the shape of Sandra Pegg's relaxing small restaurant next to the post office. Indonesian dishes are the specialities, but there are Thai, Singaporean and Indian influences on the menu too. A la carte eating is supplemented by an appealing fixed-price feast that takes in prawn cracker, satays, hot-and-sour chicken soup, deep-fried fish in red ginger sauce, green chicken curry, vegetable dishes and coconut rice, a choice of dessert and coffee. Otherwise, there may be sweet-and-sour duck breast, king prawns stir-fried with chilli, lamb cooked in yoghurt and spices, and nasi goreng.

A good-value deal on weekdays is a main course with vegetables and rice for under £10 and, if supplemented with a starter, pudding is thrown in too. Wines are a truly international selection that do the food proud: southern hemisphere Sauvignons and good demi-sec Vouvray are just what is required. House wines from the South of France are £7.95.

CHEF: Chandra de Alwis PROPRIETOR: Sandra Pegg OPEN: Tue to Sat (and bank hol Mons) D only 7 to 9 CLOSED: 25 and 26 Dec, 1 Jan MEALS: alc (main courses £8 to £8.50). Set D Tue to Fri £9.50 (1 course) to £21.50 (minimum 2), Set D Sat £15.50 to £21.50 (both minimum 2) SERVICE: not inc, card slips closed CARDS: Delta, MasterCard, Switch, Visa DETAILS: 40 seats. Private parties: 40 main room. Vegetarian meals. Children welcome. No cigars/pipes in dining-room. Wheelchair access (no WC). No music

MANCHESTER Greater Manchester map 8

Chiang Rai £

16 Princess Street, Manchester M1 4NB COOKING 3
TEL: (0161) 237 9511 COST £23–£35

In the basement below the same owner's Colony (see entry, below) is this spacious, white-painted Thai restaurant with décor 'well above the local norm'. Service is pleasant and helpful. Set meals, especially those for four or more people, are more adventurous than usual, and the à la carte menu, although quite short, is varied. It includes a section of northern Thai starters which can also be served as side dishes with the main course. Among them are classic chilli-hot laab and somtum salads, and si ooah (fried sausage). Sauces, dips and vegetables have impressed: for example a sour dip with poached mussels, and chopped vegetables with a sweet vinegar dressing to accompany trout fish-cakes. 'Fiercely hot' green chicken curry, bursting with flavours from lime leaves, coconut milk and tiny aubergines was 'the best version I've had of this dish'. A separate page of the menu is devoted to a wide range of vegetarian dishes, such as mushroom satay, and sweetcorn cakes with cucumber pickle. Of the 20 wines listed only pink champagne ventures over £20, and house wines are £8.95. Another branch of Chiang Rai can be found at 762–766 Wilmslow Road, Didsbury; Tel: (0161) 448 2277.

CHEF: Suppaporn Klintaworn PROPRIETOR: Andy Parkhouse OPEN: Mon to Sat L 12 to 2.30, all week D 6 to 11 CLOSED: bank hols MEALS: alc (main courses £5 to £9). Set L £5 to £9 (all 2 courses), Set D £19.50 to £22 SERVICE: 10%, card slips closed CARDS: Amex, Delta, Diners, MasterCard, Switch, Visa DETAILS: 90 seats. Private parties: 90 main room, 60 private room. Vegetarian meals. Children's helpings. Music

Colony £ **NEW ENTRY**

16 Princess Street, Manchester M1 4NB COOKING 1
TEL: (0161) 236 4516 COST £19–£28

Sharing ownership, roof and wine list with Chiang Rai (see entry, above), this cool-looking, converted ground-floor warehouse has white walls, exposed brickwork and cast-iron pillars. Service is 'youthful, pleasant and knowledgeable', and taped jazz adds to the lively ambience. The cooking is 'modern oriental with a European twist', say the owners. Among a dozen starters and main dishes, Burmese 'fish bowl', Sri Lankan chicken curry with pineapple sambal, and Indonesian vegetables with sticky rice dumplings and pickled cabbage jostle with Chinese (Szechuan fried fish), Japanese (vegetable tempura) and Thai (coconut mussels with coriander). A reporter found sauces rather sweet but they did not diminish his enthusiasm for tempura-style crispy fried duck breast, or smoked salmon and halibut sushi. House wine is £8.95.

CHEF: Simon Hayward PROPRIETOR: Andy Parkhouse OPEN: Mon to Fri L 12 to 2.30, Mon to Sat D 5.30 to 10.30 CLOSED: bank hols MEALS: alc (main courses £5.50 to £7.50). Set L £6 to £8 (all 2 courses), Set D (5.30 to 7pm) £8 (2 courses) SERVICE: not inc, card slips closed; 10% for parties of 6 or more CARDS: Amex, Delta, MasterCard, Switch, Visa DETAILS: 70 seats. Private parties: 70 main room. Vegetarian meals. Children welcome. Music

Koreana £

Kings House, 40A King Street West,
Manchester M3 2WY COOKING 2
TEL: (0161) 832 4330 FAX: (0161) 832 2293 COST £14–£33

Fiery Korean flavours may be tamed to comply with local tastes, but a long-time supporter of this restaurant still enjoys dependable cooking here. Among the starters may be crab-cakes, deep-fried pork crackling, battered and fried fish, and chicken rolls. The substitution of well-marinated 'moist, juicy' pork for beef in bulgogi has been surprisingly successful, and cod fillets may come in a sauce of rice wine, garlic and soy. Kim-chee, absolutely essential to Korean food, is an optional extra, but three-course meals are created by choosing from among a dozen starters, three soups, and seventeen main courses, with rice cake among the puddings; even more stimulating are five-course banquets. Any lack of excitement in the ambience is offset by 'courteous and helpful' service and modest prices. House wines are £7.95.

CHEFS: H. Kim and H. Shin PROPRIETOR: Koreana Ltd OPEN: Mon to Fri L 12 to 2.30, Mon to Sat D 6.00 to 10.00 CLOSED: 25 to 30 Dec, L bank hols MEALS: Set L £5.50 to £7.30, Set D £13.50 to £19.50 (min 2) SERVICE: not inc, card slips closed; 10% for parties of 8 or more CARDS: Amex, Delta, Diners, MasterCard, Switch, Visa DETAILS: 60 seats. Private parties: 80 main room. Vegetarian meals. Children welcome. Music

Kosmos Taverna £

248 Wilmslow Road, Manchester M14 6LD COOKING 2
TEL: (0161) 225 9106 FAX: (0161) 256 4442 COST £15–£35

'The food is a lot fresher than the waiter's jokes,' writes a reporter who nevertheless felt his tip was fully justified. But the classic restaurateur's reply to the complaining customer – 'you want good food, or real Greek food?' – emphatically doesn't apply here. In this relaxed taverna where 'the atmospherics are played down', TV cook and chef-patronne Loulla Astin produces dishes that are authentically Greek. Mezethes, complete meals of more than ten items, come in meat, seafood or vegetarian versions. Chopped chicken livers with scrambled egg, and yemista (tomatoes and peppers stuffed with rice, pumpkin seeds and currants) are some of the less-usual dishes on the long *carte*. More conventional but also highly approved are imam bayaldi, chicken and lamb kebabs, and feta cheese salad with a well-judged oil and lemon juice dressing. Because other desserts had run out, a reporter enjoyed 'clearly home-made, clear and sharp' Greek yoghurt with honey and chopped nuts, and 'chunky, very short' Greek shortbread biscuits. Greece and Cyprus dominate the wine list, with house wines at £10.

CHEF: Loulla Astin PROPRIETORS: Stewart and Loulla Astin OPEN: Sun L 1 to 5, all week D 6 to 11.30 (12.30 Fri and Sat) CLOSED: 25 and 26 Dec, 1 Jan MEALS: alc (main courses £5.50 to £12.50). Set L Sun and Set D 6 to 7.30 £7.95, Set D £11 to £14 (min 2) SERVICE: not inc CARDS: Delta, MasterCard, Switch, Visa DETAILS: 94 seats. Private parties: 50 main room. Vegetarian meals. Children's helpings. No cigars/pipes in dining-room. Wheelchair access (no WC). Music. Air-conditioned

Lime Tree £

8 Lapwing Lane, West Didsbury,
Manchester M20 8WS — COOKING 2
TEL: (0161) 445 1217 — COST £19–£39

The Lime Tree is an informal and well-established restaurant on the edge of Didsbury. At weekends it can be lively to the point of noisy, but a reporter who celebrated his sixty-ninth birthday here writes, 'It's friendly noise, so no complaints.' Starters from the short but something-for-everyone menu range from mussels with pesto, through deep-fried tempura squid, to 'lightly textured' pâté. Chargrilled peppered chicken breast with mushrooms, or goats' cheese, asparagus and mushrooms in puff pastry, might be main-course options. The kitchen seems fond of duck, which has appeared three times on the same menu. For afters, there may be warm apple and hazelnut cake, or strawberry tart with Cointreau cream. Staff know their stuff and are 'attentive without being overbearing'. A pair of wines of the month kicks off a largely French list. Ten house wines start at £8.95.

CHEF: Jem O'Sullivan PROPRIETOR: Patrick Hannity OPEN: Tue to Fri and Sun L 12 to 2.30, all week D 6 to 10.30 CLOSED: 25 Dec, bank hol Mons MEALS: alc (main courses L £5.50 to £7, D £9.50 to £14). Set L Tue to Fri and D 6 to 7 £8.95 (2 courses) SERVICE: not inc; 10% for parties of 10 or more CARDS: Amex, Delta, MasterCard, Switch, Visa DETAILS: 80 seats. 30 seats outside. Private parties: 40 main room. Vegetarian meals. Children welcome. No-smoking area. Wheelchair access (no WC). Music

Little Yang Sing £

17 George Street, Manchester M1 4HE — COOKING 3
TEL: (0161) 228 7722 FAX: (0161) 237 9257 — COST £24–£45

An 'unhurried, open-all-day feel' attracts the crowds to this basement restaurant in the heart of Manchester's Chinatown. To celebrate its tenth anniversary, an extensive and 'trendy' refurbishment is planned, due for completion after the *Guide* goes to press. The dining-room might even, we understand, end up on the ground floor, looking like a wine bar. If all carries on as before, vegetarians will be well catered for: 'nothing could dim the sheer pleasure of having so many different and delicious things to eat at once!' exclaimed a thankful correspondent, who opted for a selection of 'terrific' dim-sum including coconut milk balls, spring rolls, spicy nut dumplings wrapped in a translucent rice noodle coating, and much more. A special daytime menu (with cut-price options for kids) is a major draw, as are the special banquets. Otherwise, the kitchen provides better-than-average Cantonese cooking in the shape of steamed scallops with garlic, stewed bean curd with shredded pork and Chinese mushrooms, and sliced duck with winter bamboo shoots and oyster sauce. Service is generally on the ball, although it may seem a touch 'severe'. Drink tea or Chinese beer. House wine is £9.95.

CHEF: Ting Chung Au PROPRIETOR: L.Y.S. Ltd OPEN: all week noon to 11.30 (11.45 Fri and Sat) CLOSED: 25 Dec MEALS: alc (main courses £6.50 to £10). Set L £9.50, Set D £15 to £30 (some minimum 2). BYO £3 SERVICE: 10% CARDS: Amex, MasterCard, Switch, Visa DETAILS: 90 seats. Private parties: 100 main room. Vegetarian meals. Children's menu daytime. Music. Air-conditioned

Mash and Air 🍷 **NEW ENTRY**

40 Chorlton Street, Manchester M1 3HW COOKING 5
TEL: (0161) 661 1111 FAX: (0161) 661 1112 COST £25–£56

Occupying four floors of a converted mill by the canal, this is the nearest thing to a gastrodrome north of the Thames. So far. It is the brainchild of Oliver Peyton (owner of Atlantic Bar and Grill, and Coast; see entries, London) – a man who takes innovation and novelty in his stride – and consists of a first-floor bar, the green-coloured Mash above (for light, informal eating), and the blue and white Air restaurant on the top floor. As distance from the ground increases, so do prices. Common to all floors is a micro-brewery (in which 'mashing' is part of the process), with porthole viewing for the curious, three brews to sample, and tours every Saturday lunch-time.

Informality is integral to Mash, where the food centres around wood-burning ovens producing pizzas with a variety of exotic toppings, plus salads and the like. The cooking mark of this entry, however, and all the details, refer to the 'bang up-to-date but comfortable' Air, with its clean, uncluttered curvy lines, and modern fusion cooking: tandoori salmon with scallop sandwich and pickled cucumber, perhaps, or tea-smoked quail with yellow wax beans. Jason Atherton seems to have had a galvanising effect on the city's eating habits. Meat plays a subordinate role, and the food is 'imaginative, full of flavour and well balanced', taking in 'juicy little scallops' on a mixture of girolles and white haricot beans, and 'perfectly crisp and ungreasy' spring roll of rabbit confit.

Among desserts, chocolate pudding has been 'a palpable hit', and although Thai ice-cream (made with coconut, lemon grass and galangal) might be something of a culinary inevitability, it works extremely well and comes with strips of tropical fruit. The bill arrives in an envelope jokily marked 'the damage'. The wine list at Air is essentially the same as its London cousins, albeit about 50 bins lighter. Old World favourites predominate, but a small collection of New World bottles makes an appealing contribution. Prices can be high, but the house selection starts at £11.50, and there are 20 wines by the glass ranging from £2.40 to £6 for champagne. And then there are the Mash brews at £2.40 a pint. CELLARMAN'S CHOICE: Bordeaux, Notre Dame de Landiras 1993, Dom. La Grave, £20.50; Châteauneuf-du-Pape, Dom. du Vieux Télégraphe 1990, £34.

CELLARMAN'S CHOICE: *Wines recommended by the restaurateur, normally more expensive than house wine.*

CHEF: Jason Atherton PROPRIETOR: Oliver Peyton OPEN: Mon to Fri L 12 to 3, Mon to Sat D 6 to 11 CLOSED: 25 Dec, bank hols MEALS: alc (main courses £9 to £15). Set L and Set D 6 to 7 £12.50 (2 courses) to £15.50 SERVICE: 10% (optional), card slips closed CARDS: Amex, Delta, MasterCard, Switch, Visa DETAILS: 130 seats. Private parties: 130 main room, 12 private room. Valet parking D. Vegetarian meals. Children welcome. Wheelchair access (also WC). Music. Air-conditioned

▲ *Moss Nook*

Ringway Road, Manchester M22 5WD
TEL: (0161) 437 4778 FAX: (0161) 498 8089 — COOKING 6
on B5166, 1m from Manchester Airport — COST £24–£62

The Harrisons' long-established south Manchester restaurant is only a mile from the airport. Pass the security guard in the car park and proceed to the crimson comfort of the dining-room, where dark woodwork and an antique clock lend gravitas to the scene, and lacy tablecloths keep things homely. Service, while correct, is pleasingly non-ceremonial.

The italic-scripted menus with their prices fully written out may sound a note of pretension, but the kitchen's judgement is sound. Lobster and asparagus salad served cold with raspberry vinaigrette (*twelve pounds ninety-five pence*) is the sort of dish that once had the power to startle, but which seasoned eaters-out now take in their stride. Fish main courses are recited; if you want more than one species, opt for a mixed grill with basmati rice and béarnaise, otherwise consider sauté scallops surrounding a portion of crisply fried cabbage, the assembly given point with a red pepper coulis. A wide choice of meats is offered, the prime cuts ranging from almond-crusted rack of lamb with red wine sauce to chicken breast stuffed with morels. A multi-course tasting menu of unannounced dishes is available for the adventurous. Imaginative cheese selections may tempt some away from the dessert menu. While the seriously aspirational may heave a sigh over 1985 Ch. Margaux on the wine list, there are some fine New World selections to be going on with. House wines start at £9.50.

CHEF: Kevin Lofthouse PROPRIETORS: Pauline and Derek Harrison OPEN: Tue to Fri L 12 to 1.30, Tue to Sat D 7 to 9.30 CLOSED: 2 weeks Christmas MEALS: alc (main courses £18 to £20). Set L £16.95, Set D £29.95 SERVICE: not inc, card slips closed CARDS: Amex, Diners, MasterCard, Visa DETAILS: 65 seats. 20 seats outside. Private parties: 55 main room. Car park. No children under 12. Jacket and tie. No music ACCOMMODATION: 1 room in cottage, with bath/shower. TV. Phone. D,B&B £85 to £140

Pearl City [£]

33 George Street, Manchester M1 4PH — COOKING 1
TEL: (0161) 228 7683 FAX: (0161) 237 9173 — COST £22–£50

The owners plan to turn this Chinatown restaurant into a 'major food complex' that will include 'different styles of cooking from the Far East'. Meanwhile, it offers a huge Cantonese menu featuring the usual stalwarts, from shark's fin to sweet-and-sour pork, fish, chicken or beef, as well as 'Szechuan dishes – spicy hot' and 'Szechuan chilli dishes – fairly hot'. A range of set menus includes a totally vegetarian one that might take in gluten 'chicken' (made with soya bean).

Dim-sum are always available: the Chinese equivalent of 'English breakfast all day'. French house wine is £7.90.

CHEF/PROPRIETOR: Tony Cheung OPEN: all week noon to 1.30am (3.30am Fri and Sat, 11.30pm Sun) MEALS: alc (main courses £6 to £30). Set L £4.90 (2 courses) to £9.50, Set D £15.50 to £19.50 (minimum 2 to 5) SERVICE: 10% CARDS: Amex, Delta, MasterCard, Switch, Visa DETAILS: 400 seats. Private parties: 160 main room, 240 private room. Vegetarian meals. Children welcome. Music. Air-conditioned

Simply Heathcotes

NEW ENTRY

Jackson Row, Deansgate, Manchester M2 5WD — COOKING 4
TEL: (0161) 835 3536 FAX: (0161) 835 3534 — COST £20–£59

In the Great British Brasserie Race, Manchester left the starting-blocks after Leeds, but thanks to Paul Heathcote and Oliver Peyton (see Mash and Air, above) it is coming up fast on the inside. Simply Heathcotes – in the former City Register Office near Deansgate – is founded on Heathcote's Brasserie (see entry, Preston), and Max Gnoyke's experience in getting that one up and running made him a natural choice to take on Manchester. Loud blocks of colour shout from the walls, ceilings are high, hard surfaces and bare wooden floors add to the echo, and moulded bucket chairs confirm that Philippe Starck is still the furniture designer of choice.

The kitchen deals in familiar modern brasserie staples – risotto of smoked haddock or wild mushrooms, salt-cod brandade with poached egg, chargrilled tuna – with a bias towards the north in the form of a salad of 'Lancashire cooked breakfast' with black pudding, and a leaning towards porky things: terrine of pig's cheek, braised pork shank, and raised pork pie. Capable handling of materials across the board has been evident in a range of dishes from 'cebiche' of salmon (with celeriac, mustardy mayonnaise and white crabmeat) to thickly sliced chump of lamb served with a polenta 'scone' and oily roasted vegetables. The *carte* changes quarterly, and the three-course lunch is considered 'superb value'.

'Cream of Manchester' (peanut shortbread with Boddingtons Bitter ice-cream) is more of 'a good joke' than a culinary breakthrough, possibly outstripped by hot banana and chocolate chip soufflé, or apple tart served with melting Lancashire cheese. 'Pleasant and professional' sums up the service, and 40-plus wines from around the world include ten by the glass. Prices start at £10.25.

CHEF: Max Gnoyke PROPRIETOR: Paul Heathcote OPEN: Mon to Sat 11.45 to 2.30, 6 to 11, Sun 12 to 9 CLOSED: 25 and 26 Dec, 1 Jan MEALS: alc (main courses £12 to £25). Set L £9.50 (2 courses) to £11.50, Set D Mon to Sat 6 to 7, Sun to 9 £17.50 SERVICE: not inc CARDS: Amex, MasterCard, Switch, Visa DETAILS: 160 seats. Private parties: 160 main room, 40 private room. Vegetarian meals. Children welcome. No cigars/pipes in dining-room. Wheelchair access (also WC). Music. Air-conditioned

If you have access to the Internet, you can find The Good Food Guide *online at the Which? Online web site (http://www.which.net).*

Tai Pan £

Brunswick House, 81–97 Upper Brook Street,
Manchester M13 9TX COOKING 1
TEL: (0161) 273 2798 FAX: (0161) 273 1578 COST £25–£39

'The biggest one-floor restaurant in Manchester,' claim the owners of this sprawling Chinese venue above an oriental cash-and-carry. Go up a spiral staircase, past the smart lobby, then into a dining-room decorated with screens and dragons. It is well supported by the Chinese community, who come for genuine Cantonese food with a few nods to Peking and Szechuan along the way. For light lunches and snacks there are over 80 dim-sum to choose from, while the 180-dish menu roams through aromatic crispy duck, deep-fried shredded beef with chilli and garlic, scallops with seasonal vegetables, plus a fair contingent of roast meats and noodle dishes. Vegetarians have plenty of choice, and there are also set banquets of various sorts. House French is £8.20.

CHEF: Garry Wan PROPRIETOR: K.K. Chan OPEN: all week 12 to 11.30 (9.30 Sun and bank hols) MEALS: alc (main courses £6.50 to £11.50). Set L Mon to Fri 12 to 2 £5.45 (2 courses), Set D £14 to £22 (all minimum 2) SERVICE: 10% CARDS: Amex, Delta, Diners, MasterCard, Switch, Visa DETAILS: 350 seats. Private parties: 300 main room, 100 private room. Car park. Vegetarian meals. Children welcome. Wheelchair access (also WC). Music. Air-conditioned

That Café £

1031–1033 Stockport Road, Levenshulme,
Manchester M19 2TB COOKING 2
TEL: (0161) 432 4672 COST £19–£38

Joseph Quinn converted his antique shop into a restaurant in the early 1980s, and although the 'more whimsical bric-à-brac' has been cleared away in a bout of redecoration over the past year, it is still very much a retreat from the minimalist look: 'always welcoming, always a pleasure to go.' Opening hours, however, are minimal, just five dinners a week plus Sunday lunch, which helps keep up standards. Dishes often incorporate fruit, as in chicken and mango salad, mackerel and gooseberry pie ('a winning combination'), roast duck with kumquats, or leek and apple strudel, one of the more than token choices for vegetarians. Turkey in hazelnut and Drambuie sauce made a pleasing variation on the Christmas roast. Desserts, such as chocolate torte, are 'always successful, with a lightness of touch', and service is 'efficient and helpful'. The wine list is short but broad in scope, with a trio of organic English fruit wines. House Australian is £8.95.

CHEF: Joseph Quinn PROPRIETORS: Joseph Quinn and Stephen King OPEN: Sun L 12 to 5, Tue to Sat D 6 to 10.30 (11 Sat) CLOSED: 3 days Christmas MEALS: alc D (main courses £9 to £14). Set L Sun £9.95 (2 courses) to £12.95, Set D Tue to Fri £14.95. BYO £3.50 SERVICE: not inc, card slips closed; 10% for parties of 8 or more CARDS: Amex, Delta, MasterCard, Switch, Visa DETAILS: 80 seats. Private parties: 55 main room, 35 private room. Vegetarian meals. Children's helpings. No-smoking area. Wheelchair access (no WC). Music

Yang Sing 🍷

34 Princess Street, Manchester M1 4JY — COOKING 6
TEL: (0161) 236 2200 FAX: (0161) 236 5934 — COST £26–£45

Manchester now rejoices in mega-restaurant openings, but this popular Chinese eating palace predates them by many years. It operates on two levels – a bustling basement and a more relaxed ground-floor dining-room (both of which were about to undergo major refurbishment as the *Guide* went to press) – and goes in for dim-sum in a big way. 'We usually have 60 to 70 dishes of the day which do not appear on the menu,' say the owners; 'please talk to our staff.' Examples are classic steamed sea bass, and less-classic ostrich in lemon grass sauce. Also changed daily are vegetarian dishes running from everyday spring roll, via crispy yam roll, to spicy 'three shreds' with seaweed.

Most reports concentrate on dim-sum. Happy surprises for those used to a standard list have included cheung-fun rice rolls filled with carp and prawns, and pig's intestines steamed with pickled vegetables, the latter with a 'fairly delicate combination of flavours'. Although some 'crossovers' – crabmeat balls with cheese, and vine leaves stuffed with chicken – have been less well received, they do show that the kitchen is prepared to experiment: even roast duck served off the bone is a welcome improvement on tradition. Alternatively, whole or half-ducks are braised with various garnishes. Reporters confirm the freshness of flavours in 'startlingly good' deep-fried cuttlefish balls with coriander, scallops and squid, and fried dumplings with wind-dried meats and Chinese greens. Service is usually, but not always, friendly and helpful.

Although jasmine tea is often the preferred accompaniment to Cantonese cuisine, it would be a shame not to make use of a wine list which offers some high-quality bins at very reasonable prices. France is the favoured country, with burgundy from the likes of Ramonet and some good mature clarets, but the few New World selections are very sound. Four food-friendly house wines are £9.95 a bottle, £1.90 a glass. CELLARMAN'S CHOICE: Bienvenues-Bâtard-Montrachet 1990, Joseph Drouhin, £55; Margaux, Ch. Lascombes 1990, £35.

CHEF: Harry Yeung PROPRIETOR: Yang Sing Restaurant Ltd OPEN: basement all week noon to 11.15, ground floor Mon to Sat 5 to 11 CLOSED: 25 Dec MEALS: alc (main courses £7 to £10). Set L £11.90, Set D £11.00 to £22 (all minimum 2) SERVICE: 10% CARDS: Amex, Delta, MasterCard, Switch, Visa DETAILS: 250 seats. Private parties: 30 to 220 private rooms. Vegetarian meals. Children welcome. Music. Air-conditioned

---

MARSDEN West Yorkshire — map 8

Olive Branch

Manchester Road, Marsden HD7 6LU
TEL: (01484) 844487 — COOKING 2
on A62, between Slaithwaite and Marsden — COST £24–£45

Bottles of herb-infused olive oil sit on scrubbed pine tables in the Listers' stone-built inn, but only the occasional whiff of the Mediterranean comes from the open kitchen. The name derives from the last century, when the inn was one of many on an old packhorse route through the Pennines. Unlike its rowdy competitors, it banned drinking and swearing on Sundays and so became a peaceful stopover. Raw materials are good, and the daily-changing menu, written on cards and blackboards, has some unusual combinations and permutations. An inspection meal found 'first-class' rillettes of crab and avocado with chilli oil as a starter, and main courses of sauté monkfish with sauce vierge, and roast fillet of sea bass with a strongly flavoured 'cappuccino' of vanilla. Puddings may include a classic lemon tart with 'very fine, thin' shortcrust pastry, and farmhouse cheeses are in good condition. Waitresses keep the mood relaxed and mostly know their stuff. The wine list is long, carefully annotated and considerately priced. House French is £9.95.

CHEF: John Lister PROPRIETORS: John and Ann Lister OPEN: Sun L 12 to 1.45, all week D 6.30 to 9.30 (4 to 9 Sun) CLOSED: 26 Dec, first week Jan, third week June MEALS: alc Sun L and Sun to Fri D (main courses £7.50 to £15). Set D Sat £16.50 (2 courses) to £19.50 SERVICE: not inc, card slips closed CARDS: Delta, MasterCard, Switch, Visa DETAILS: 65 seats. 8 seats outside. Private parties: 36 main room, 36 private room. Car park. Vegetarian meals. Wheelchair access (no WC). Music

MASHAM North Yorkshire map 9

Floodlite £

7 Silver Street, Masham HG4 4DX
TEL: (01765) 689000 COOKING **5**
off A6108, 9m NW of Ripon COST £16–£42

The name might conjure up visions of neon lights and fast food amid the tranquillity of the Yorkshire Dales, but instead Charles and Christine Flood's tiny converted shop offers heaps of bric-à-brac, candles and good honest cooking. The set three-course lunch is a bargain, while the *carte* shows a marked preference for game: perhaps hare pâté with blackcurrant sauce to start, followed by saddle of roe-deer with wild mushrooms, or wild boar with pimentos. Fish is not neglected either, from Dover sole with lemon to a more complex terrine of salmon and pike with dill mayonnaise.

Local ingredients are used where possible and treated simply yet skilfully. Flavours are intense but never overbearing. An inspector found his starter of king prawns and squid with ginger and garlic extremely well judged, with a subtle dressing of light soy, while rack of lamb with rosemary and garlic was 'the finest new spring lamb I have ever tasted'. Puddings may include a simple chocolate mousse with vanilla sauce, or something more sophisticated: perhaps Mr Flood's ever-popular apple and blackcurrant bread-and-butter pudding, or a classic lemon tart. An extensive wine list continues the fair pricing, with house French and Australian at £7.95.

CHEF: Charles Flood PROPRIETORS: Charles and Christine Flood OPEN: Fri to Sun L 12 to 2, Tue to Sat D 7 to 9.30 CLOSED: 2 weeks Jan/Feb MEALS: alc (main courses £9 to £16.50). Set L £10.50, Set D £12.50 (2 courses) to £15 SERVICE: not inc, card slips closed CARDS: Amex, MasterCard, Visa DETAILS: 38 seats. Private parties: 28 main room. Vegetarian meals. Children's helpings. Wheelchair access (no WC). Music

MAWGAN Cornwall map 1

Yard Bistro [£]

Trelowarren, Mawgan TR12 6AF
TEL: (01326) 221595 COOKING 1
off B3293, 3m SE of Helston COST £12–£35

'A neighbourhood bistro with sound, competent food at reasonable prices,' summed up a visitor to Trevor Bayfield's converted stable-block with its cheerful gingham cloths. Fish is the mainstay, starting with soup, pickled salmon, or lemon sole with red Thai spices, followed by steamed sea bass, or well-timed turbot in beurre noisette. Caramelised bread-and-butter pudding with moist eggy bread 'properly set' is a winning dessert, and a short list of mostly white wines stays comfortably below £20. House wines are around £8.

CHEF/PROPRIETOR: Trevor Bayfield OPEN: Tue to Sun L 12 to 2, Wed to Sat D 7 to 9 CLOSED: Christmas and New Year MEALS: alc (main courses L £3.50 to £5.50, D £10.50 to £13.50). Set L Sun £8 SERVICE: not inc, card slips closed CARDS: Delta, Diners, MasterCard, Switch, Visa DETAILS: 40 seats. 12 seats outside. Private parties: 40 main room, 40 private room. Car park. Vegetarian meals. Children's helpings. Wheelchair access (also WC). Music

MAWNAN SMITH Cornwall map 1

▲ *Nansidwell*

Mawnan Smith TR11 5HU
TEL: (01326) 250340 FAX: (01326) 250440
off A494 Helston road, take left fork at Red Lion COOKING 3
in village COST £23–£62

The mullion-windowed Edwardian Arts and Crafts house overlooks Falmouth Bay, close to the Helford Estuary. After a decade the Robertsons have redone the dining-room and added a chargrill to the kitchen, opening up the options for Tony Allcott's cooking: sirloin steak and turbot typically benefit from the new treatment. He is already a busy man – pickling, preserving, smoking and curing are all part of the kitchen's cycle of activity – and deals in seasonal game and year-round shellfish. Roast saddle of hare and rabbit might be served with goose liver and caramelised pear, and glazed Helford oysters have appeared as a first course with spinach, Emmental cheese and asparagus.

Menus are curiously presented. Supplements rarely go down well with reporters, yet here they are built in to the system: home-smoked peppered mackerel on the simpler standard menu, or a dish of home-smoked salmon with Dover sole and lobster roulade on the more complex and expensive one. The intricate style shows up in puddings too – iced pear and brandy soufflé with warm parcels of plum and pistachio, for example – and south-west cheeses feature on the board. Jamie Robertson, 'very much the patron', takes charge of ordering, and Berry Bros & Rudd bottlings feature on the wine list, although the short Spanish section offers more interest. House Spanish is £10.

CHEF: Anthony Allcott PROPRIETORS: Jamie and Felicity Robertson OPEN: all week 12.30 to 1.45, 7 to 9 CLOSED: Jan MEALS: Set L £15.75, Set D £27.50 SERVICE: not inc CARDS: Delta, MasterCard, Switch, Visa DETAILS: 40 seats. 10 seats outside. Private parties: 40 main room. Car park. Vegetarian meals. Children's helpings. No young children at D. No smoking in 1 dining-room. Wheelchair access (no WC). No music ACCOMMODATION: 12 rooms, all with bath/shower. TV. Phone. B&B £55 to £168. Deposit: £100. Rooms for disabled. Children welcome. Dogs welcome in bedrooms only. Garden

MELBOURN Cambridgeshire map 6

Pink Geranium

25 Station Road, Melbourn SG8 6DX
TEL: (01763) 260215 FAX: (01763) 262110 COOKING **6**
just off A10, 2m N of Royston COST £23–£74

Flower-beds, neatly trimmed lawn, and a fifteenth-century, very pink thatched cottage with chintzy sofas and armchairs in its beamed interior: this exceedingly English scene forms the backdrop for some very French cooking. Chef Steven Saunders might stray from the home range occasionally, cooking for TV cameras and writing cookery books, but he has a sound back-up team, now headed by Mark Jordan, who replaced Paul Murfitt shortly after last year's edition of the *Guide* went to press. Diners can go à la carte or take the two- or three-course set-price menu with four choices per course. If the ceiling is Olde-Worlde low, dishes are modern high-rise, their components stacked in towers surrounded by greenery and sauces. The effect is visually pleasing and, despite an inspector's minor reservations about sauces lacking oomph, flavours do not usually disappoint.

Scented oils turn up in first courses: beetroot oil with a 'little fussy but none the less delicious' crostini of woodpigeon with wild mushrooms and speck salad, for example. Steamed saddle of rabbit with whole garlic cloves is another dish that works, as does loin of mint-steamed lamb with rosemary and Parmentier potatoes. Desserts usually get the thumbs-up: chocolate and caramel charlotte, perhaps, or classic lemon tart. Sally Saunders oversees the front-of-house, and if most visitors compliment the warm reception and friendliness – to children as well – some have complained of long waits and inexperienced staff. The excellent, well-chosen wine list has the sensible policy of reducing mark-ups as wines become more expensive. House wines are remarkable value at £10.

CHEFS: Steven Saunders and Mark Jordan PROPRIETORS: Steven and Sally Saunders OPEN: Tue to Fri and Sun L 12 to 2, Tue to Sat D 7 to 9.30 MEALS: alc (main courses £16 to £27.50). Set L Tue to Fri £10 (2 courses) to £15, Set L Sun £20, Set D £20 (2 courses) to £25 SERVICE: not inc CARDS: Amex, Delta, MasterCard, Switch, Visa DETAILS: 65 seats. Private parties: 18 main room, 18 private room. Car park. Vegetarian meals. Children's helpings. No smoking in dining-room. Wheelchair access (also WC). No music

'The head waiter is very good. He has been there for years and pretends to remember you.' (On eating in London)

MELKSHAM Wiltshire map 2

▲ *Toxique*

187 Woodrow Road, Melksham SN12 7AY
TEL: (01225) 702129 FAX: (01225) 742773
take Calne Road at Melksham centre mini-roundabout; turn left into Forest Road and Toxique is on the left

COOKING 2
COST £28–£46

A stone farmhouse it may be, but this restaurant-with-rooms feels more cosmopolitan than rustic. It is done out in vibrant colours including midnight blue, with jazz Muzak to match, and among the unexpected decorative touches are pine cones dangling from the ceiling. Eric Lepine moved to Hole in the Wall (see entry, Bath) and Helen Bartlett has been joined by Phil Rimmer. A related enterprise, Toxique Fish, has opened in Bath, but the chef there changed just as the *Guide* went to press (see entry, Round-ups). Meanwhile, back at the stoves, intense and spicy flavours are the order of the day, along the lines of smoked duck salad with mango and chilli salsa, lamb with salted lemons, or 'seriously' hot-and-sour fish stew. Vegetarian options might include a cheesy ragoût of pasta with artichokes and spring onions, but the best dish at inspection was a breast of Trelough duckling served with good rösti and pleasantly spiced plums. Dessert was less impressive. The wine list, which includes a fair choice of half-bottles, centres on France, backed up by good quality from elsewhere. Four house wines start at £11.

CHEFS: Helen Bartlett and Phil Rimmer PROPRIETORS: Helen Bartlett and Peter Jewkes OPEN: Sun L 12 to 2, Wed to Sat D 7 to 10 MEALS: Set L £16.50 (2 courses) to £18.50, Set D £28 SERVICE: not inc, card slips closed CARDS: Amex, Delta, Diners, MasterCard, Switch, Visa DETAILS: 40 seats. Private parties: 24 main room. Car park. Vegetarian meals. Children's helpings. No smoking in dining-room. Music ACCOMMODATION: 5 rooms, all with bath/shower. D,B&B £95 to £150. Deposit: £50. Rooms for disabled. Children welcome. Garden (*The Which? Hotel Guide*)

MELMERBY Cumbria map 10

Village Bakery £

NORTH COUNTRY 1998 BREAD

Melmerby CA10 1HE
TEL: (01768) 881515 FAX: (01768) 881848
on A686, between Penrith and Alston

COOKING 1
COST £18–£27

Andrew Whitley's breakfast, lunch and tea house is an ecologically minded enterprise. Behind is a five-acre smallholding of organic fruits and vegetables, and there are free ranging pigs. In the converted stone barn, bread is baked in wood-fired brick ovens using traditional methods. Breakfast might be oak-smoked Inverawe kippers, croissants, or spicy buns, while the quality and copious quantity of the Baker's Lunch of North Country cheeses and organic breads 'remembered from childhood' impressed one visitor. 'More flavour than I have tasted for years,' wrote another of lamb and apricot casserole. Vegetable, soups (including chard and mushroom) are well made, Ullswater trout is grilled in garlic butter, and side salads are 'as fresh as spring and a delight to the eye'.

Desserts such as plum brûlée, and bread-and-butter pudding, are also well reported. Sit in the conservatory to avoid the hubbub of the shop and dining-room. Herefordshire perry and cider, traditionally brewed ales, and elderflower wine are the main interest on the short drinks list. House wines are £7.60 a bottle.

CHEFS: Katherine Wilkinson and Diane Richter PROPRIETOR: Andrew Whitley OPEN: all week L 12 to 3; breakfast 8.30 (9 Sun) to 11; snacks 3 to 5 (11 to 4.30 Sun) CLOSED: 25 and 26 Dec MEALS: alc (main courses £6 to £8). BYO (no corkage) SERVICE: not inc, card slips closed CARDS: Delta, Diners, MasterCard, Switch, Visa DETAILS: 42 seats. Private parties: 30 main room, 30 private room. Car park. Vegetarian meals. Children's helpings. No smoking in dining-room. Wheelchair access (no WC). Music

MIDDLEHAM North Yorkshire map 8

▲ *Waterford House*  NEW ENTRY

Kirkgate, Middleham DL8 4PG COOKING 3
TEL: (01969) 622090 FAX: (01969) 624020 COST £28–£46

On a hill overlooking the village square stands this Grade II listed stone-built house, furnished in early-century style with embroidered linens, swaths of lace and a grand piano. Everyl Madell is inclined to stick to tried-and-true culinary principles for the backbone of what she cooks, although there is the occasional foray into the way-out, such as sole baked with banana in a light cheese sauce. Fish stew incorporates undyed smoked haddock and mussels in a creamy broth, while rack of lamb (for two) is given a herb- and mustard-based breadcrumb crust and sauced with red wine and madeira. Fresh fruit makes the simplest of puddings, but there may be chocolate and almond torte, or tiramisù (the latter served at table from a large bowl) for those who want something richer. Full-throttle cafetière coffee is highly praised, as are the gargantuan breakfasts.

The wine list is a hefty tome that covers Burgundy and Bordeaux in great depth, has some fine German and Alsace whites, and specialises in mature Spanish reds, with four pages of Riojas dating back to 1934 and 11 vintages of Vega Sicilia Unico. New World gems include six vintages of Cloudy Bay Chardonnay. Sixty-seven low-priced house wines start at £9.50 a bottle, £2.50 for a 'glass' the size of a quarter-bottle, and the Madells will happily open any of the 900-plus bottles on the list, magnums excluded. CELLARMAN'S CHOICE: Sancerre Vieilles Vignes 1994, Dom. Hubert Brochard, £22.75; Corton 'Clos du Roi' Grand Cru 1983, Dom. Pierre Ponnelle, £31.50.

CHEF: Everyl Madell PROPRIETORS: Everyl and Brian Madell OPEN: all week 12.30 to 2.30, 7.30 to 10 MEALS: alc (main courses £14 to £16.50). Set L £17.50, Set D £19.50. BYO (no corkage) SERVICE: not inc, card slips closed CARDS: Delta, MasterCard, Switch, Visa DETAILS: 24 seats. Private parties: 20 main room. Car park. Children's helpings. No smoking in dining-room. No music ACCOMMODATION: 5 rooms, all with bath/shower. TV. Phone. B&B £45 to £85. Children welcome. Baby facilities. Dogs welcome in bedrooms only. Afternoon teas. Garden (*The Which? Hotel Guide*)

Report forms are at the back of the book; write a letter if you prefer; or email us at guidereports@which.co.uk.

MIDDLESBROUGH Middlesbrough map 10

Purple Onion

80 Corporation Road, Middlesbrough TS1 2RF COOKING **2**
TEL: (01642) 222250 FAX: (01642) 248088 COST £21–£46

In its original guise the Onion was an archetypal 1960s coffee-house and bistro with live music, the north-east's answer to the Cavern, perhaps. After a wilderness period, the 'Nouveau Onion' has been revived as a brasserie. It is 'a fun place' with 'a riot of weird and wonderful objects' including a zinc bar, *fin de siècle* mirrors and other bric-à-brac picked up from Paris flea markets. The food has been picked up from further afield – Tuscany and California particularly – producing hot and spicy San Francisco fish soup with aïoli and crostini, and chargrilled vegetables anointed with a holy trinity of extra-virgin olive oil, balsamic vinegar and basil.

It hits all the fashionable buttons with sour-dough bread, buffalo mozzarella (in a salad with tomatoes and 'torn basil', of course), wild mushroom risotto with truffle, and lots of chargrilling. But the essentials are taken seriously. Steaks are hung for a minimum of three and a half weeks, there is a generous range of vegetarian options, and a proper children's menu. Three dozen varied wines begin at £10.95, though the serious ones start a little higher.

CHEFS: Graham Benn and Massimo Cecere PROPRIETORS: John and Bruno McCoy OPEN: all week L 12 to 2.30 (4.30 Sun), Mon to Sat D 5 to 10.30 CLOSED: 25 Dec, 1 Jan MEALS: alc (main courses £7.50 to £15.50). Set L Sun £9.95 (2 courses) to £12.50 SERVICE: not inc, card slips closed CARDS: Delta, Diners, MasterCard, Switch, Visa DETAILS: 100 seats. Private parties: [illegible] main room. Vegetarian meals. Children's helpings. Wheelchair access (also WC). Music. Air-conditioned

MIDHURST West Sussex map 3

▲ *Angel Hotel, Cowdray Room* 

North Street, Midhurst GU29 9DN COOKING **4**
TEL: (01730) 812421 FAX: (01730) 813928 COST £32–£64

The splendid dereliction of Cowdray Castle can be seen across meadows from this old posting-inn set in Midhurst's main thoroughfare. The county set and media types use it and there are three different ambiences in which to eat: in elegant primrose-hued civility in the Cowdray Room, more informally in the brasserie (where some of the dishes are duplicated), or on the hop for a quick snack in the bar.

New boy Darren Tidd arrived in early 1997, and the modestly trendy idiom of the cooking has held steady. Wild mushroom risotto with scallops and Parmesan makes a substantial first course, the shellfish timed to retain tenderness and the rice appealingly creamy. Accompaniments are generally in the classical mould, so that cold poached salmon is dressed with a lemon mayonnaise and served with minted potatoes, while beef fillet comes with rösti and shallots. More adventurous pairings have included John Dory fillets with butter-beans and lentils, and roasted tamarillo with mascarpone cream. Cheesecake studded with pistachios and chunks of ginger with a sweet-sharp syrup of star-anise and vanilla has been an undisputed triumph. Service on one spring evening showed 'lots of goodwill but not a lot of English'. Wines are a wide-ranging collection, and succinct tasting notes are helpful, although some pretty high mark-ups are scattered around. House wines include Concha y Toro at £13.75.

CHEF: Darren Tidd PROPRIETORS: Nicholas Davies and Peter Crawford-Rolt OPEN: all week 12 to 2, 7.30 to 10 (10.30 Sat) MEALS: alc (main courses £16 to £19.50). Set L Sun £17.95. BYO £7.50 SERVICE: 12.5% (optional), card slips closed CARDS: Amex, Delta, Diners, MasterCard, Switch, Visa DETAILS: 50 seats. 20 seats outside. Private parties: 80 main room, 30 and 100 private rooms. Car park. Vegetarian meals. Children's helpings. Wheelchair access (no WC). No music ACCOMMODATION: 28 rooms, all with bath/shower. TV. Phone. B&B £75 to £145. Deposit: £50. Rooms for disabled. Children welcome. Afternoon teas. Garden (*The Which? Hotel Guide*)

Maxine's £*

Elizabeth House, Red Lion Street,
Midhurst GU29 9PB — COOKING 3
TEL: (01730) 816271 — COST £21–£38

A prime attraction of this 'really civilised' town-house restaurant, with its bric-à-brac, beams, red patterned carpet and spindle-backed chairs, is the value, especially the set-price menu available at both lunch and dinner except on Saturday nights. Solid cooking is the order of the day and it can occasionally produce surprises, as in a main course of sweetbreads combined with prawns in a white wine sauce. Sweetbreads are also teamed with kidneys, or there could be king prawns with coconut and chilli, or venison casserole ('all that a game casserole should be'). Crab-cakes in a tangy tomato and coriander sauce, and 'meltingly soft' twice-baked Gruyère soufflé have pleased, and desserts may include sticky toffee pudding, or vanilla ice-cream with piquant coffee sauce. Service is polite and helpful. The reasonably priced wine list has examples from around the world, and features 16 half-bottles. House French is £9.95.

CHEF: Robert de Jager PROPRIETORS: Robert and Marti de Jaeger OPEN: Wed to Sun L 12 to 1.30, Wed to Sat D 7 to 9.30 MEALS: alc (main courses £10 to £15). Set L £14.95, Set D Wed to Fri £14.95 SERVICE: net prices, card slips closed CARDS: Amex, Delta, MasterCard, Switch, Visa DETAILS: 24 seats. Private parties: 30 main room. Children's helpings. No smoking in dining-room. No music

MILFORD ON SEA Hampshire — map 2

Rocher's

69–71 High Street, Milford on Sea SO41 0QG
TEL: (01590) 642340 — COOKING 3
on B3058, 3m SW of Lymington — COST £21–£37

A homely, old-fashioned feel and a warm welcome for all have earned Rocher's a loyal local following: a Friday-night visitor found it full to capacity, though generously spaced tables prevent any feeling of overcrowding. The table d'hôte menu offers a good helping of culinary nostalgia, with dishes such as poached egg florentine, avocado vinaigrette and poire Belle-Hélène harking back to the

'70s. They are not necessarily the worse for that, however, and the evidence is that Alain Rocher sticks to what he knows and does it well.

The more ambitious (and more expensive) gastronomic menu has a backbone of classic dishes including terrine de coquille St-Jacques and sole meunière, with a few contemporary touches sneaked in, such as the sun-dried tomatoes and balsamic dressing that accompany a salmon escalope. Standards can at times vary, however: an inspection meal chosen from the gastronomic menu included a 'deservedly popular' feuilleté of spinach and shallot, and nicely cooked brill, but calf's liver with raspberry vinegar sauce was less successful. Service is attentive, if a little overstretched at times. The wine list, which has a varied choice of half-bottles, is predominantly French but also includes a selection from the New World. House wine is £9.50.

CHEF: Alain Rocher PROPRIETORS: Alain and Rebecca Rocher OPEN: Sun L 12.15 to 1.45, Wed to Sat D 7.15 to 9.45 (and Sun D bank hols) MEALS: Set L Sun £14.50, Set D Wed to Fri £13.95 (2 courses) to £17.50, Set Gastronomic D £19.95 (2 courses) to £23.50 SERVICE: not inc, card slips closed CARDS: Amex, Delta, Diners, MasterCard, Switch, Visa DETAILS: 26 seats. Private parties: 34 main room. No children under 7. No smoking while others eat. Wheelchair access (no WC). Music

MINSTER LOVELL Oxfordshire map 2

▲ *Lovells at Windrush Farm*

Old Minster Lovell OX8 5RN
TEL: (01993) 779802 FAX: (01993) 776212
off B4047, 3m NW of Witney, on S bank of River Windrush

COOKING 6
COST £35–£61

The large house on an 80-acre farm 'exudes hospitality from arrival to departure'. Scrunch up the gravel, enter a grandly refurbished stone barn, and be prepared to have the burden of umming, aahing, weighing and choosing relieved. At dinner there are almost too many courses to count; estimates vary from seven to nine, depending on whether pre-dinner mouthfuls and coffee are included. This feat is made possible by serving it all at a set time, offering no choice at any stage, and making a long, leisurely evening of the whole affair; we might almost be in the Lake District, or at a dinner party.

Meals in the light, cream-coloured dining-room typically begin with Welsh rarebit and rhubarb chutney, a sensible way of using up cheeseboard leftovers. If the prospect of what is to come seems daunting, fear not. Reporters come away 'beguiled and happy, and still want breakfast in the morning', thanks to Marcus Ashenford's sense of restraint. He builds up slowly through, perhaps, an onion tartlet topped with a sliver of foie gras, then on to tortellini of crab and tarragon sitting in a crab bisque, before fillet of brill with pesto, leeks and tomato. For main course (if such an idea makes sense in this context) there might be roast breast of wild mallard with a duck sausage, integral vegetables and a cassis sauce. The half-dozen items on the 'outstanding' cheeseboard come with a recommended eating order and are followed by a pre-dessert (poached pear with cinnamon ice-cream, perhaps) followed by the real thing: maybe a clementine and Grand Marnier mousse topped with chocolate sorbet and served with caramelised bananas and passion-fruit syrup. Service is friendly and knowledgeable.

The extensive wine list offers a good choice of French classics and an intelligent selection from other major regions. Quality is high and this is reflected in the pricing, with very little available for less than £20; look to the Loire or French country wines. On the plus side, you can have half of any bottle on the list at half-price plus 10%. CELLARMAN'S CHOICE: Mâcon-Viré, Dom. de Roally 1990, Henri Goyard, £23; Monthélie, Vignes Rondes 1995, Michel Dupont-Fahn, £28.

CHEF: Marcus F. Ashenford PROPRIETOR: Lovells Windrush Farm Ltd OPEN: Fri and Sun L 1 (1 sitting), Tue to Sat D 8 (1 sitting) CLOSED: Jan MEALS: Set L £23, Set D £37 SERVICE: not inc CARDS: Amex, Delta, Diners, MasterCard, Visa DETAILS: 18 seats. Private parties: 18 main room. Car park. Children welcome. No smoking in dining-room. Wheelchair access (no WC). No music ACCOMMODATION: 3 rooms, all with bath/shower. TV. D,B&B £95 to £175. Children welcome. Baby facilities. Dogs welcome. Garden. Fishing

---

MOLLINGTON Cheshire map 7

▲ *Crabwall Manor* 🍷

Parkgate Road, Mollington CH1 6NE
TEL/FAX: (01244) 851666 COOKING **5**
off A540, 3m N of Chester COST £44–£62

Arrive after dark for the total Crabwall experience, when crenellated ramparts and the tower are dramatically floodlit, and you are struck by the mad grandiosity of one sort of Victorian architectural vision. Inside is nowhere near as Gothic. Instead, relaxing country-house plush is the feel, with log fires, comfortable sofas and low tables. The dining-room looks out over a rugged bit of Cheshire; tables are smartly set and dressed with long, crisp cloths.

Michael Truelove has been in charge of the kitchen for a decade, and while that length of tenure may instil familiarity in some chefs, it is the springboard here for new ideas; and the menu reads well because they make sense. A mille-feuille of red mullet and braised cabbage is given a gazpacho sauce for a Mediterranean accent; truffles and morels add depth to a bowl of mushroom consommé. Cannelloni filled with scallops in a Sauternes sauce was thought a hugely accomplished starter by one reporter, and main courses might take in grilled sea bass on egg noodles with deep-fried leek tagliatelle, or braised shank of lamb with garlic mash. Classic tarte Tatin is a good rendition, or there may be coffee-flavoured crème brûlée topped with chocolate sabayon. Staff are adept and pleasant.

The huge wine list covers most of the major regions, and although it concentrates on France it offers plenty of choice at all price levels. For those who don't have the stamina for the main list, the 'Sommelier's Selection' of around 50 bins is arranged mostly by style, and chosen to complement the seasonal menus. French house wines start at £13. CELLARMAN'S CHOICE: Sancerre Vieilles Vignes 1995, Dom. Brochard, £21.50; Juliénas 'Les Fouillouses' 1995, Dom. M. Pelletier, £16.

CHEFS: Michael Truelove and Kevin Woods PROPRIETOR: Carl Lewis OPEN: all week 12 to 2, 7 to 9.30 MEALS: alc (main courses £22 to £24) SERVICE: not inc CARDS: Amex, Delta, Diners, MasterCard, Switch, Visa DETAILS: 100 seats. Private parties: 100 main room, 36 to 100 private rooms. Car park. Vegetarian meals. Children's helpings. No cigars/pipes in dining-room. Wheelchair access (also WC). Music. Air-conditioned ACCOMMODATION: 48 rooms, all with bath/shower. TV. Phone. Room only £72.50 to £200. Rooms for disabled. Children welcome. Baby facilities. Afternoon teas. Garden (*The Which? Hotel Guide*)

MONTACUTE Somerset map 2

▲ *Milk House*

The Borough, Montacute TA15 6XB COOKING 2
TEL: (01935) 823823 COST £29–£41

At 7.30pm precisely a light goes on over the old oak door of this listed fifteenth-century golden stone house, bolts are slid back, and a cordial welcome is followed by an aperitif beside the large open fire. One observer noted that the Duftons 'seemed to be running the place almost as a hobby', and indeed they are scaling down the operation, with fewer covers, longer seasonal closures, and still only four openings a week. The place is filled with polished antiques, and well-spaced dining-room tables are simply laid with lace mats, ready for Lee Dufton's three-course dinners. Fish, game and vegetables are given prominence: a ramekin of creamed smoked salmon, spiced onion tart, or braised guinea fowl with herbs (grown in the garden along with some fruit and vegetables). 'We don't use beef, we never have,' writes Mrs Dufton, but duck is a speciality, and wine and cream sauces are typical. Cheeses are from Somerset, Devon and Dorset, and desserts have included a 'generous' portion of hot rummed banana crumble with redcurrant jelly. Good organic wines feature on the sensibly priced list, among them house white and red from France at £11.80 and £12.80.

CHEF: Lee Dufton PROPRIETORS: Lee and Bill Dufton OPEN: Wed to Sat D only 7.30 to 8.30 (L by arrangement) CLOSED: Nov to March MEALS: alc (main courses £13). Set D £19.80. BYO £5 SERVICE: not inc CARDS: none DETAILS: 10 seats. 8 seats outside. Private parties: 24 main room. Vegetarian meals. Children's helpings. No smoking in 1 dining-room. Wheelchair access (no WC). No music ACCOMMODATION: 3 rooms, all with bath/shower. B&B £40 to £58. Deposit: £20. No children under 8. Garden (*The Which? Hotel Guide*)

MORETON-IN-MARSH Gloucestershire map 5

Annie's

3 Oxford Street, Moreton-in-Marsh GL56 0LA COOKING 2
TEL/FAX: (01608) 651981 COST £25–£52

Annie's wears its Cotswold livery well. Chintz curtains, family pictures and linen cloths are draped over a framework of flagstones, beams and exposed stone, producing an informal cottage-like atmosphere. A decade on, it attracts faithful support for a straightforward approach to country cooking. 'We go four or five times a year and the standard remains high,' confirms one reporter. Tomato and rosemary soup is well reported, seafood salad might incorporate scallops, prawns and squid, while oven-baked salmon with mustard sauce might be among the daily fish options. Juices from roasting or pan-frying are typically turned into a simple 'gravy' to accompany the Barbary duck, boneless pork chop, or fillet steak from which they were derived, perhaps with lime juice or balsamic vinegar for acidity, and cream for richness. There is nothing too complicated, which is all to the good, and desserts follow a well-ploughed furrow of treacle tart, chocolate brandy biscuit cake, and ratafia cake. A largely French wine list is headed by house Vins de Pays d'Oc at £12.50.

CHEF: David Ellis PROPRIETORS: Anne and David Ellis OPEN: Mon to Sat D 7 to 9.30 (10 Sat), Sun L by arrangement CLOSED: end Jan to early Feb MEALS: alc (main courses £15.50 to £22). SERVICE: net prices, card slips closed CARDS: Amex, Diners, MasterCard, Visa DETAILS: 30 seats. Private parties: 32 main room, 10 private room. Children's helpings. Music

Marsh Goose

High Street, Moreton-in-Marsh GL56 0AX — COOKING **6**
TEL: (01608) 652111 FAX: (01608) 652403 — COST £22–£58

Redecoration has brought freshness rather than a change of style to this Cotswold favourite. It is still divided into several eating areas, though the former private dining-room is now a demonstration kitchen where Sonya Kidney gives weekly lessons. As to the format, 'we have permanently replaced the supplements on the set menu by a small à la carte,' writes Leo Brooke-Little, 'though we still offer the same range on the set menu, which is written daily as before.' That is one of the kitchen's strengths, that it continually reviews its repertoire and progress, and is ever-inventive. Among the ideas might be hot beetroot in a creamy grain mustard sauce with parmesan fritters, lamb sweetbreads in an artichoke heart with spinach, or fillet of cod with rosemary risotto and nutmeg butter sauce.

More careful buying of meat has been prompted by a desire to ensure that animals are 'reared and killed in a humane manner', and also 'in response to the disturbing facts being brought to light about intensive farming and its dangers'. In this context Gloucester Old Spot pork has made an appearance, served with creamed onion. There is more praise for 'old-fashioned' vegetables such as parsnip fritters and creamed turnips than for boiled broccoli, while desserts offer as much variety as the other courses: apple and sultana strudel with coconut ice-cream, for example, or glazed rice pudding with rhubarb parfait. Although a little more warmth would not go amiss, reporters have complimented the quick, unobtrusive service from young staff, which leaves people free to pour their own wine. The list concentrates on small but highly regarded producers, and plans are afoot to expand the already improved collection of 24 half-bottles. Prices, however, remain on the high side, although Spanish house wines are still £9 a bottle. Sonya Kidney and Leo Brooke-Little also own the Churchill Arms in Paxford (see entry).

CHEFS: Sonya Kidney and Robert Stanforth PROPRIETORS: Sonya Kidney, Leo Brooke-Little and Gordon Campbell-Gray OPEN: Tue to Sun L 12.30 to 2.30, Tue to Sat D 7.30 to 9.30 CLOSED: 26 and 27 Dec, 1 to 3 Jan MEALS: alc L Tue to Sat (main courses £10 to £14), alc D (main courses £16 to £20). Set L Tue to Sat £13.50, Set L Sun £18, Set D £25. BYO £8 SERVICE:

not inc CARDS: Amex, Delta, Diners, MasterCard, Switch, Visa DETAILS: 60 seats. Private parties: 22 main room. Vegetarian meals. Children's helpings. No smoking in dining-room. Wheelchair access (also WC). No music

MORSTON Norfolk map 6

▲ *Morston Hall* 🍷

Morston NR25 7AA
TEL: (01263) 741041 FAX: (01263) 740419 COOKING 5
on A149, 2m W of Blakeney COST £23–£42

Set in 'one of England's most beautiful regions', according to a visitor, the Jacobean brick and flint house is comfortable, tranquil and well cared for. Annual mid-winter closure affords an opportunity for redecoration, and the pink lounge now sports attractive Fired Earth colours. In addition to quiet beaches and open skies, the location brings an abundance of seafood, samphire, wild mushrooms, venison from Holkham Hall, and fruits and game birds from Sandringham, all contributing to the seasonal cast of the menus. Galton Blackiston's set four-course deal (options are discussed when booking) changes daily, and although (or perhaps because) there is no choice apart from cheese or dessert, the balance is carefully considered.

Typical of the output might be a February dinner that began with sauté wild mushrooms served on a grilled apple boudin with mustard sabayon, followed by lobster and salmon spring roll on pan fried skate wing, with a dip of garlic, coriander and soy. Braised shank of lamb came with three vegetables (mashed potato, sage-flavoured cabbage, and glazed shallots), and dessert was a warm chocolate fondant with pistachio ice-cream. Cheese (usually a board of half a dozen) is served with home-made biscuits and quince cheese. A red and white wine of the month are served by the bottle or glass, and a further 11 are available by the glass, starting at £2. Indeed, prices throughout the wide-ranging, well-annotated list are keen, with plenty under £15, including a half-bottle of Brown Brothers 1995 Late Harvest Orange Muscat and Flora at £11. CELLARMAN'S CHOICE: Rothbury Estate Chardonnay 1994, Hunter Valley, Australia, £13.25; Lalande de Pomerol, Clos de Reges 1993, £14.25.

CHEF: Galton Blackiston PROPRIETORS: Galton and Tracy Blackiston, and Justin Fraser OPEN: Sun L 12.30 for 1 (1 sitting), all week D 7.30 for 8 (1 sitting) CLOSED: 1 Jan to Feb MEALS: Set L Sun £16, Set D £27. BYO £10 SERVICE: not inc, card slips closed CARDS: Amex, Delta, MasterCard, Switch, Visa DETAILS: 40 seats. Private parties: 40 main room. Car park. Children's helpings Sun L. No smoking in dining-room. Wheelchair access (also WC). No music ACCOMMODATION: 6 rooms, all with bath/shower. TV. Phone. D,B&B £80 to £180. Children welcome. Baby facilities. Dogs welcome in bedrooms only. Afternoon teas. Garden (*The Which? Hotel Guide*)

'We made our way to the main lobby, which was amazingly tacky, like Cecil B. De Mille meets B&Q. The bad taste was not quite bad enough to have the courage of its convictions.' (On eating in London)

MOULSFORD Oxfordshire map 2

▲ *Beetle & Wedge*

Ferry Lane, Moulsford OX10 9JF
TEL: (01491) 651381 FAX: (01491) 651376 COOKING 5
off A329, down Ferry Lane to river COST £37–£55

An Edwardian inn in a 'glorious setting' on a wide stretch of the Thames's upper reaches, the Beetle & Wedge offers diners at every table good views of the swans, rowing boats and other to-ings and fro-ings on the river. The main dining-room is a conservatory extension looking over an attractive garden that leads to the landing-stage, and the air of brightness and cheer makes for relaxed and convivial eating.

Richard Smith's cooking is much given to richness of one sort or another, so that Stilton soufflé might come with wild mushroom sauce, turbot fillet with scallop mousse and truffles, or brill with mussels and Oscietra caviare. Two huge scallops 'seared to a nutty roastedness' and scattered with lardons and early asparagus makes an impressive-looking first course, and a main dish of venison medallions with black cherries comes in a heavily reduced, caramelised and brandied sauce. To finish, well-flavoured Cointreau soufflé is accompanied by a pleasingly concentrated raspberry sauce decanted into it from a small copper saucepan. Another good dessert pairing is of coffee parfait with a serving of rum-spiked chocolate truffle cake. 'Well-trained' service takes things seriously. A separate à la carte menu is available in the Boat House restaurant, open all week for lunch and dinner.

Wines are predominantly French and high in quality, with prices to match. However, good bins under £20 can found, particularly on the page of Italians, and the 'dipstick' policy of allowing guests to drink half or more of a bottle and pay pro rata with a £1.25 supplement helps to keep costs down. Schlumberger's Alsace Gewurztraminers are particularly recommended. Five house wines are £12.95.

CHEFS: Richard Smith and Robert Taylor PROPRIETORS: Kate and Richard Smith OPEN: Tue to Sun L 12.30 to 2, Tue to Sat D 7.30 to 10 CLOSED: 25 Dec MEALS: Set L £27.50, Set D £35 SERVICE: not inc CARDS: Amex, Delta, Diners, MasterCard, Switch, Visa DETAILS: 30 seats. 50 seats outside. Private parties: 30 main room, 64 private room. Car park. Children's helpings. No smoking in 1 dining-room. Wheelchair access (also WC). No music ACCOMMODATION: 10 rooms, all with bath/shower. TV. Phone. B&B £80 to £125. Rooms for disabled. Children welcome. Baby facilities. Dogs by arrangement. Garden (*The Which? Hotel Guide*)

MOULTON North Yorkshire map 9

Black Bull Inn

Moulton DL10 6QJ
TEL: (01325) 377289 FAX: (01325) 377422 COOKING 4
1m SE of Scotch Corner, 1m from A1 COST £24–£58

The tiny hamlet of Moulton is home to one of England's truly singular village pubs. Through the main bar is the conservatory and behind that the Brighton Belle, an immaculately preserved 1932 Pullman railway carriage. For one couple, 'the whole atmosphere was wonderful', from the discreet lighting and lacy curtains to the functioning period loo.

Generosity is the watchword of Paul Grundy's cooking, as demonstrated at inspection by a seafood pancake thermidor containing salmon and white fish, plus lobster, mussels, prawns and scallops, all bound together in its well-made cheese, mustard and wine sauce. Skill is evident too in crab mousse with a light chive butter, and while seafood is obviously the strong point – there is a separate Fish Bar – meat is well handled too. Aberdeen Angus beef fillet comes Rossini-style on a croûton with foie gras, wild mushrooms and a forthright madeira sauce. Duck is done with blackcurrants, and lamb with a leek and potato crumble. Some of the food may be old-fashioned, but early occupants of the Brighton Belle were probably not offered mascarpone quenelles with their hot chocolate pudding. Other desserts might include apricot roly-poly with custard, or hazelnut marquise with butterscotch ice-cream.

A strong Burgundy section, with bins from Bonneau du Martray, Bernard Morey and La Chablisienne, is the highlight of a wine list which offers particularly good value for money. The New World adds diversity, but the scales lean heavily towards France. House wines start at £8.50. CELLARMAN'S CHOICE: Muscadet 'Cuvée LM' 1993, Louis Métaireau, £11.50, Buitenverwachting Grand Vin 'Cuvée Christine' 1992, Constantia, South Africa, £16.95.

CHEF: Paul Grundy PROPRIETORS: G.H., A.M.C. and S.C. Pagendam OPEN: Mon to Fri L 12 to 2, Mon to Sat D 6.45 to 10.15 CLOSED: 24 to 26 Dec MEALS: alc (main courses £14.50 to £20). Set L £14.95. BYO £5 SERVICE: not inc CARDS: Amex, Delta, Diners, MasterCard, Switch, Visa DETAILS: 100 seats. 20 seats outside. Private parties: 80 main room, 12 and 30 private rooms. Car park. Vegetarian meals. No children under 7. No music

NAILSWORTH Gloucestershire map 2

William's Bistro

3 Fountain Street, Nailsworth GL6 0BL COOKING 5
TEL: (01453) 835507 FAX: (01453) 835950 COST £26–£45

Cotton tablecloths have replaced plastic in this self-styled French bistro, but otherwise not much has changed. The green and pink dining-room is the 'sit-down' arm of an enterprise that includes an outside catering business and a delicatessen (William's Kitchen) specialising in fish. Seafood is the big attraction, from simple fish soup or moules marinière, through a chunk of monkfish with a herb crust and horseradish cream, to spider crabs, lobsters, oysters and – the crowning glory – a big platter of fruits de mer at £35. Other shellfish offerings might include crab-cakes with red pepper and chilli jelly, or a langoustine and crab risotto, showing that the kitchen is at home with diverse ways of dealing with what one reporter described as its 'brilliant raw materials'.

One visitor spent a great part of the evening marvelling 'at how good things could taste', whether mussels and octopus, lamb, or even cauliflower. The key perhaps lies in simple grilling, frying and steaming, and in timing all this to a nicety. Plates are unfussily arranged and look colourful, and saucing plays a supporting rather than a dominant role, which makes no end of a difference. A sweet balsamic sauce might accompany salmon or halibut, a red wine *jus* partners venison, and an orange and marmalade sauce comes with breast of duck. Puddings are more traditional in style and 'no match for the rest of the meal'. Wines (mostly French) rarely stray over £15, and house white (£8) is from Jersey and bottled in Gloucestershire.

CHEFS: Craig Schofield and Katie Beeston PROPRIETORS: William and Rae Beeston OPEN: Tue to Sat D only 7 to 9.30 CLOSED: Christmas, New Year, Good Fri, Tue after bank hols MEALS: alc (main courses £11 to £15.50) SERVICE: not inc, card slips closed CARDS: MasterCard, Switch, Visa DETAILS: 45 seats. Private parties: 45 main room. Children welcome. No music

NANTWICH Cheshire map 5

Churche's Mansion

150 Hospital Street, Nantwich CW5 5RY NEW CHEF
TEL: (01270) 625933 FAX: (01270) 627831 COST £28–£60

This Elizabethan merchant's house was built, so the brochure informs us, just as Drake was setting off to circumnavigate the world. Oak panelling and carvings abound, much of the wooden flooring is original, and there is a walled garden for summer eating, as well as two dining-rooms. Graham Tucker left just as the *Guide* went to press, and Micheal Lea, who has been in the kitchen since the present owners took over in 1992, has moved up to take charge of the kitchen. The pattern to date has included monthly-changing menus with generous choice, and a high degree of industry: from in-house smoking to some eleaborate presentation. Reports on the new regime, please. The enthusiastically annotated wine list has something for most palates and pockets, combining French classics with some juicy offerings from the New World. Half-bottles are plentiful and house wines start at £11.75. CELLARMAN'S CHOICE: Katnook Estate Chardonnay 1994, Coonawarra, S. Australia, £24; Mature Margaux nv, Lucien Lurton, £26.

CHEF: Michael Lea PROPRIETORS: Robin Latham and Amanda Simpson OPEN: Tue to Sun L 12 to 2.30, Tue to Sat D 7 to 9.30 CLOSED: last 2 weeks Jan MEALS: Set L £13.95 (2 courses) to £17.25, Set D £26.75. BYO £8 SERVICE: not inc, card slips closed CARDS: Delta, Diners, MasterCard, Switch, Visa DETAILS: 55 seats. 20 seats outside. Private parties: 48 main room, 48 and 24 private rooms. Car park. Vegetarian meals. Children's helpings. No children under 10. No smoking in dining-room. Music

NAYLAND Suffolk map 6

Martha's Vineyard

18 High Street, Nayland CO6 4JF
TEL: (01206) 262888 COOKING **6**
off A134, 5m N of Colchester COST £39–£36

'Perfect refinement, *à point* timing and fashionable presentation are not the point of this place,' reckoned one visitor. What matters is that it provides original food and good wines at a fair price in the colourful but informal surroundings of a cheerful dining-room in a picturesque building on Nayland's sleepy high street. Larkin Rogers and Christopher Warren bemoan the fact that, to some people, 'American cooking' can mean blackened this, Cajun that, or quite possibly lo-fat fudgy marshmallow brownie nut sundae. They (and we) are at pains to point out that their food is nothing like that. Local supplies (organic where possible) are the kitchen's foundation, while rare breeds of meat include Essex saddleback pigs, and Portland, Soay and Norfolk horned lamb.

The kitchen applies a mix of ingenuity and common sense, turning out sweetcorn soup with lime chipotle butter, or seared monkfish with warm flageolet beans, bacon and a garlic salad. Saucing is often what provides the unexpected twist: chicken breast now with bramble butter, now with bouillabaisse sauce, or a smoked Nantua sauce for fish-cakes. Fritters have proved popular: crisp-coated and 'splendidly pungent' anchovy ones, and cheese ones served with 'posh leaves' and an apple and raisin 'curry'. Brightness of tone and directness of purpose are among the defining characteristics of the food, and if that is American cooking then we are all for it. Fine bread-and-butter pudding, pear frangipane tart, and British farmhouse cheeses are ways to finish. Wines are sensibly priced and complement the cuisine nicely. The Oregon and Californian reds are a particularly intelligent collection and include some rare Cabernet Sauvignons from Martha's Vineyard – naturally. House wines start at £10.95. CELLARMAN'S CHOICE: Pacherenc Sec, Ch. Bouscassé 1995, Alain Brumont, £15.50; Madiran, Ch. Montus 1992, Alain Brumont, £19.75.

CHEFS: Larkin Rogers and Melissa Deckers PROPRIETORS: Christopher Warren and Larkin Rogers OPEN: Sun L 12.30 to 2, Thur to Sat D 7.30 to 9 (9.30 Sat) CLOSED: 2 weeks winter, 2 weeks summer MEALS: Set L and D £18.50 (2 courses) to £22. BYO £5 SERVICE: not inc, 10% for parties of 6 or more CARDS: MasterCard, Visa DETAILS: 41 seats. Private parties: 30 main room, 14 private room. Vegetarian meals. Children's helpings. No smoking in dining-room. Wheelchair access (no WC). No music

White Hart £

11 High Street, Nayland CO6 4JF COOKING 3
TEL: (01206) 263382 FAX: (01206) 263638 COST £21–£44

This timber-framed fifteenth-century coaching-house in Gainsborough and Constable country considers itself a pub rather than a restaurant, although the food may suggest otherwise. Mark Prescott was trained and is backed financially by (and his restaurant is showered in publicity about) Michel Roux of the Waterside Inn (see entry, Bray). His classical tutelage is evident in a menu (with blackboard supplements) that takes in Tuscan white-bean soup, pork terrine, and breast of chicken with chasseur sauce. He goes in for a degree of richness, for some heavily reduced sauces, and for much roasting and grilling: of cod, lobster, pork chop, and lamb cutlets. Desserts span a range from apple crumble with custard to nougat glacé by way of steamed orange and chocolate-chip pudding. One reporter clocked up ten 'satisfactory visits', with only a couple of disappointing ones, which sounds like a good track record. Apart from fine wines (how many pubs offer grand cru burgundy at £58?), the short, modern list aims for simple but characterful flavours from some excellent producers. House French starts at £9.25.

The Guide *always appreciates hearing about changes of chef or owner.*

CHEF: Mark Prescott PROPRIETORS: Mark Prescott and Michel Roux OPEN: all week 12 to 2.30 (4 Sun), 6.30 to 9.30 (10 Sat, 8.30 Sun) CLOSED: 26 Dec, 1 and 2 Jan MEALS: alc D (main courses £8 to £14). Set L £13.50 (2 courses) to £16. Bar food available. BYO £10 SERVICE: not inc CARDS: Amex, Diners, MasterCard, Switch, Visa DETAILS: 70 seats. 48 seats outside. Private parties: 70 main room, 48 private room. Car park. Vegetarian meals. Children's helpings. Wheelchair access (no WC). Music

NEAR SAWREY Cumbria map 8

▲ *Ees Wyke*

Near Sawrey LA22 0JZ
TEL/FAX: (015394) 36393 COOKING **2**
on B5286 from Hawkshead COST £27–£32

Set back from the road between Hawkshead and the ferry to Windermere, this small country house is run 'rather like a superior seaside boarding-house' in that overnighters get a good deal with the all-in price. The dining-room looks on to open countryside, and Mrs Williams runs front-of-house single-handedly, chats to guests 'and laughs a lot'. Five courses – not unusual in the Lakes – might begin with Flookburgh shrimps in hot spiced butter, or stuffed mushrooms in garlic sauce, then a no-choice item such as Stilton and walnut terrine, followed perhaps by roast rack of lamb. Desserts are recited, and have included baked lemon cheesecake, and tarte Tatin served with good ice-cream. Proceedings end with 'most agreeable' cheeses, and coffee with fudge. Around 40 wines are fairly priced, beginning with house French at £9.

CHEF: John Williams PROPRIETORS: Margaret and John Williams OPEN: all week D only 7 for 7.30 (1 sitting) CLOSED: Jan and Feb MEALS: Set D £20 non-residents SERVICE: not inc, card slips closed CARD: Amex DETAILS: 16 seats. Private parties: 16 main room. Car park. No children under 10. No smoking in dining-room. Wheelchair access (no WC). No music ACCOMMODATION: 8 rooms, all with bath/shower. TV. B&B £42 to £84. No children under 10. Dogs welcome in bedrooms only. Garden (*The Which? Hotel Guide*)

NEW ALRESFORD Hampshire map 2

▲ *Hunters*

32 Broad Street, New Alresford SO24 9AQ COOKING **1**
TEL/FAX: (01962) 732468 COST £22–£45

Steam rail enthusiasts will know the town for its Watercress Line; others might go shopping for antiques in the broad main street, and those who come to eat will find that the mood has lightened in this Georgian coaching-inn. Gone are the heavy drapes and dark wallpaper, replaced by a brasserie feel at lunch-time, with candles in the evening, and the prospect of al fresco dining in summer. Andrew Sherlock's menu has a lot to offer, from tomato tart to pork with couscous, from a generous bowl of plump mussels with good bread to a dish of smoked haddock with Welsh rarebit and a tangy mustard sauce. Youthful talent is evident, most notably at inspection in a pear tart with butterscotch ice-cream. Service is willing and friendly, and a functional wine list keeps prices commendably low. House wine from Reynier is £8.95.

CHEF: Andrew Sherlock PROPRIETOR: Martin Birmingham OPEN: all week L 12 to 2, Mon to Sat D 7 to 10 CLOSED: Sun L in summer, 1 week Christmas MEALS: alc (main courses L £6.50 to £8, D £10 to £16). Set D Mon to Fri £12.95 (2 courses) to £14.95 SERVICE: not inc; 10% for parties of 6 or more CARDS: Amex, Diners, MasterCard, Switch, Visa DETAILS: 30 seats. 20 seats outside. Private parties: 70 main room. Vegetarian meals. Children's helpings. No smoking during dining hours. Wheelchair access (also WC). Music ACCOMMODATION: 3 rooms, all with bath/shower. TV. B&B £32.50 to £47.50. Deposit: £10. Children welcome. Baby facilities. Garden

NEWCASTLE UPON TYNE Tyne & Wear map 10

Courtney's

5–7 Side, Quayside, Newcastle upon Tyne NE1 3JE COOKING **3**
TEL: (0191) 232 5537 FAX: (0191) 221 1745 COST £24–£42

On Newcastle's rejuvenated quayside area sits Michael and Kerensa Carr's pint-sized but enduringly popular restaurant. Some may feel a touch compressed in the surroundings; not so the reader who avowed that 'as there are only 30 seats, you feel personally served and looked after'. The short set-price lunch menu has three choices for starter and main, while the *carte* offers around eight main courses.

Expressive seasonings are favoured, whether it be cardamom in carrot soup, or garam masala in the sauce for yoghurt-coated chicken. Those Indian influences share the menu with Italian in aubergine salad with Parma ham and Parmesan, and with American for Maryland crab-cakes with avocado and basil salsa. Despite the eclecticism, most of the dishes have a familiar ring to them: no one will be shocked to see monkfish paired with king prawns and sauced with Noilly Prat, butter and chives, or loin of lamb crusted with garlic breadcrumbs and Dijon mustard. Pudding options have included pot au chocolat scented with orange, passion-fruit soufflé, and lemon tart with coconut ice-cream. The wine list is as cosmopolitan as the food requires, and the range of half-bottles is generous. Australian house wines are £10.

CHEF: Michael Carr PROPRIETORS: Michael and Kerensa Carr OPEN: Mon to Fri L 12 to 2, Mon to Sat D 7 to 10.30 CLOSED: 1 week Christmas, 2 weeks May, bank hols MEALS: alc (main courses £10.50 to £15). Set L £13 (2 courses) to £15 SERVICE: not inc, card slips closed CARDS: Amex, MasterCard, Switch, Visa DETAILS: 30 seats. Private parties: 30 main room. Vegetarian meals. Children welcome. No cigars/pipes in dining-room. Music. Air-conditioned

Fisherman's Lodge

Jesmond Dene, Newcastle upon Tyne NE7 7BQ COOKING **6**
TEL: (0191) 281 3281 FAX: (0191) 281 6410 COST £26–£73

The nineteenth-century Lodge, once the town residence of Lord Armstrong, is reached by a long drive that runs beside a gently flowing stream, where strolling families come for respite from the traffic and shops. It feels about as rural as it is possible to feel in a city, but there is nothing country-bumpkin-ish about the place. The bar is smart and modern, while a splash of black and gold livens up the pink-suffused dining-room. A professional air to the service confirms that this is a place of serious intent.

The kitchen's first love is fish and shellfish – from North Shields and the west coast of Scotland – which might appear in tempura form, or as deep-fried monkfish, baked oysters, or grilled halibut. Lobster comes grilled or in a salad, with a cheese sauce atop lemon sole, and with fillet steak in that old surf 'n' turf cliché, but overall the cooking is technically accomplished without being showy. Mushroom risotto with blewits and chanterelles pleased a lunching inspector, and the quality of meat has been evident in a sliced and fanned fillet of lamb: 'good flavour, great texture, very satisfying.' Vegetables are enterprising too.

Care in buying, skill in preparation, and restraint in presentation are hallmarks, and the largely classical desserts can be very fine. A warm shortcrust tart filled with crème pâtissière, artfully piled with raspberries and blackberries, with custard and vanilla ice-cream on the side, succeeded wonderfully despite, or perhaps because of, the three different kinds of cream. The set lunch is considered good value, and there are enough bottles under £20 (including Australian Chardonnay and Cabernet Shiraz) on the varied wine list to keep the final bill within reason.

CHEFS: Steven Jobson and Paul Amer PROPRIETORS: Franco and Pamela Cetoloni OPEN: Mon to Fri L 12 to 2, Mon to Sat D 7 to 11 CLOSED: bank hols MEALS: alc (main courses £18 to £28). Set L £17.80, Set D Mon to Fri £28.50 SERVICE: not inc CARDS: Amex, Delta, Diners, MasterCard, Switch, Visa DETAILS: 65 seats. 35 seats outside. Private parties: 14 main room, 14 and 43 private rooms. Car park. Vegetarian meals. Children's helpings. No children under 9 at D. No smoking in dining-room. Wheelchair access (also WC). Music

Leela's £✶

NORTH OF ENGLAND 1998 SOUTH INDIAN

20 Dean Street, Newcastle upon Tyne NE1 1PG — COOKING 3
TEL: (0191) 230 1261 FAX: (01661) 823916 — COST £17–£46

Leela Paul left her native home in Kerala 30 years ago, and since 1990 has sought to promote the healthy virtues of South Indian food to Geordies. The family atmosphere, soft colour schemes and obliging mood of her restaurant are much appreciated: 'we were greeted with a smile and invited to sit and relax on big floppy settees before the meal.' Leela's style is based on a clear, light approach: many dishes depend on overnight marinating, spices are freshly ground, cooking is done in vegetable oil rather than butter or ghee. The results can be impressive: 'like no other Indian I have tasted,' enthused one over the subtle complexity of flavours running through his meal. Packavadas (better known as vegetable pakoras) continue to top the list of favourite starters, although 'superb' paper dosas also get a look in. Among main dishes there has been applause for kerala meen (fillet of salmon baked in tomato and tamarind sauce) and batham kozhi (marinated breast of chicken slowly cooked in almonds, cream and herbs). Side dishes and vegetables are definitely worth exploring: kathricka (spiced aubergines in coconut milk) to name but one. The wine list also deserves more than a cursory glance. House wine is £9.95.

CHEF: Kuriakose Paul PROPRIETORS: Kuriakose and Leela Paul OPEN: Mon to Sat 12 to 2.30, 5.30 to 11.30 CLOSED: 2 weeks Jan MEALS: alc (main courses £8 to £13). Set L £9.95, Set D £18.95 SERVICE: not inc CARDS: Amex, Delta, Diners, MasterCard, Visa DETAILS: 45 seats. Private parties: 30 main room. Vegetarian meals. Children's helpings. No smoking in dining-room. Music

Metropolitan £ **NEW ENTRY**

35 Grey Street, Newcastle upon Tyne NE1 6EE — COOKING 3
TEL: (0191) 230 2306 FAX: (0191) 230 2307 — COST £18–£41

The former bank on what John Betjeman called England's finest street is the venue for this all-day brasserie done out in a mix of art deco, American and Terence Conran. The food is also an amalgamation, borrowing ideas from here, there and everywhere to produce, for example, starters of beef carpaccio with fennel and Parmesan, Thai-style seafood broth, or seared tuna with niçoise dressing. Good-quality ingredients and well-honed cooking skills shine through main courses of rump of lamb with potatoes crushed with garlic and cheese served with deep-fried basil, and cooked halibut garnished with prawns in beurre blanc. Other options run from perhaps Toulouse sausages to well-reported roast monkfish with spinach and Parma ham.

Imagination doesn't flag at dessert stage, with Newcastle Brown Ale ice-cream getting special mention, and iced tiramisù parfait with coffee sauce – which came with 'designer blobs' of 'excellent' amaretti biscuits – inspiring the adjective 'beautiful'. Service is amiable. Wines, a short, widespread mix selected by Lay & Wheeler, start at £8.95, with a dozen sold by the glass.

CHEFS: Nick Gardiner and Maggie Naylor PROPRIETORS: Sean Parkinson and Nick Gardiner OPEN: Mon to Sat 10.30 to 5, 6 to 11 CLOSED: Christmas, bank hols MEALS: alc (main courses L £4 to £7, D £6.50 to £15). Set L £7.95 (2 courses) to £10.95 SERVICE: 10% (optional), card slips closed CARDS: Amex, Delta, MasterCard, Switch, Visa DETAILS: 170 seats. Private parties: 32 private room. Vegetarian meals. Children's helpings. No-smoking area. Wheelchair access (also WC). Music. Air conditioned

21 Queen Street 🍷

19–21 Queen Street, Princes Wharf, Quayside,
Newcaste upon Tyne NE1 3UG — COOKING 8
TEL: (0191) 222 0755 FAX: (0191) 221 0761 — COST £28–£58

'This is outstanding in every way,' enthused one reporter of the 'civilised and calm restaurant' that has become a Newcastle landmark. Waterfront rejuvenation has not yet reached the section underneath the Eiffel-like Tyne Bridge, but the Laybournes have done their best to make up for it inside. Spare lines, bare wooden floors and starched tablecloths indicate a serious modern restaurant. But there is nothing austere about it; quite the contrary. A relaxed, colourful and informal atmosphere prevails, enjoyment level is high, and there is a complete lack of pretence. 'Sharp as a button' service is happily able to combine 'an air of professionalism with an informal approach'. Despite juggling with three balls at once (see Bistro 21, Durham, and Cafe 21, Ponteland), Terence Laybourne has not spread himself too thinly and still turns out the best food in the North-East.

Fine ingredients are put through a classical mill and emerge bright and smiling. His version of modern European cooking takes an individual turn when partnering ravioli of salmon with sauerkraut, or stuffing beef fillet with oxtail and giving it a Newcastle Brown Ale sauce. Among the 'signature' dishes, filo pastry and a good variety of tomato produce an impressive tart, and the combination of smooth rich foie gras with earthy ham hock makes a characterful terrine, which only a better accompanying pease pudding would improve.

Workmanship includes serving duck five ways (for a supplement) but dishes are never showy. A roast fillet of turbot, for example, comes with onion compote, spinach, 'stupendously good' mushrooms and a meaty *jus*, the whole dish 'a joy to eat because of the real honest flavours'.

The set lunch – on one occasion watercress soup, roast cod with capers, and pear and almond tart 'with exquisite pastry' – is 'incredibly good value'. Desserts are as good as anything else, from a parfait of gingerbread judged 'inspired and intriguing in equal measure', to chocolate in one of its many guises: as a warm, liquid-centred cake, a 'perfectly timed' soufflé with pistachio ice-cream, or (for another supplement) as an Extravaganza. The wine list favours France, but none the less offers a good range of styles at fair prices, helped by the addition of some reliable bins from the New World. The house selection of 21 wines starts at £12, and there are 26 half-bottles, including three dessert wines. CELLARMAN'S CHOICE: Vin de Pays de l'Ardèche, Viognier 1996, Georges Duboeuf, £14; Mount Langi Ghiran Shiraz 1994, Victoria, Australia, £18.90.

CHEF/PROPRIETOR: Terence Laybourne OPEN: Tue to Fri L 12 to 2, Tue to Sat D 7 to 10.45 CLOSED: bank hols MEALS: alc (main courses £16.50 to £21.50). Set L £14.50 (2 courses) to £17.50 SERVICE: not inc CARDS: Amex, Delta, Diners, MasterCard, Switch, Visa DETAILS: 70 seats. Private parties: 60 main room. Vegetarian meals. Children's helpings. No pipes in dining-room. Wheelchair access (no WC). Music

NEW MILTON Hampshire map 2

▲ *Chewton Glen, Marryat Restaurant* 

Christchurch Road, New Milton BH25 6QS
TEL: (01425) 275341 FAX: (01425) 272310
from A35 follow signs to Walkford and Highcliffe, take second turning on left after Walkford down Chewton Farm road

COOKING **6**
COST £35–£70

The brick-built, green-shuttered house is a 'lovely building in a pretty setting', on the edge of the New Forest, close to the sea. It offers sybaritic luxury for those who want it, or a health spa with all manner of 'treatments'. Typical of the Skans' approach is that every detail seems to have been thought of. Good service from lots of staff is part of the appeal, although 'one feels a bit processed', according to one reporter. 'Our processing went well, however,' beginning in the lounge with salted almonds and black olives, followed at table by a small salad incorporating foie gras pâté on toast.

Pierre Chevillard's three-course dinner menu is a long one – around a dozen first courses, for example, with supplements for foie gras and caviare – and it singles out dishes marked 'vegetarian or wellness choice' such as wild mushroom tortellini, or grilled Dover sole. The largely European flavour spectrum is supplemented with slightly more exotic notes among the fish: sea bass with bean sprouts, shiitakes, ginger and coriander, for example. Skill shows to good effect in a 'perfectly risen' double-baked Emmental soufflé at inspection that was 'light, yet not over-aerated', set on a pool of creamy golden 'fondue' sauce. Well-timed roast fillet of lamb has appeared 'with upmarket trimmings': rolled in a layer of 'red pepper confit', and sitting on a round of polenta in a 'magnificent' thinnish gravy.

Desserts (no wellness choice here) might take in a compote of raw strawberries and cooked rhubarb served in a 'bowl' made of crisp gingery pastry, with a 'spoon' of the same and a scoop of ginger ice-cream, or a trio of 'pungent' fruit sorbets (mango, banana and coconut) piled into a scooped-out pineapple and topped with meringue. Breads offer an 'amazing' selection. High-rolling corporate entertainers tend to bring along cigars, mobile phones and 'language we don't use at home'. The wine list now numbers over 500 items, including *grande marque* champagnes, mature burgundies and first-class clarets, and southern French wines get a look-in too. California and Australia make some impressive contributions, and there is a singular offering from the Ukraine of a 1929 Livadia Rosé Muscat. Despite many high prices, bottles under £20, even under £15, can be found. House wines are £15. CELLARMAN'S CHOICE: Montagny La Grande Roche 1994, Louis Latour, £25.50; St-Emilion, Ch. Beauséjour 1985, £49.50.

CHEF: Pierre Chevillard PROPRIETORS: Martin and Brigitte Skan OPEN: all week 12.30 to 1.45, 7.30 to 9.30 MEALS: Set L £18.50 to £23.50, Set D £45. BYO £10 SERVICE: not inc, card slips closed CARDS: Amex, Delta, Diners, MasterCard, Switch, Visa DETAILS: 120 seats. 30 seats outside. Private parties: 120 main room, 6 to 70 private rooms. Car park. Vegetarian meals. Children's helpings. No children under 7. Jacket and tie. No smoking in dining-room. Wheelchair access (also WC). No music. Air-conditioned ACCOMMODATION: 52 rooms, all with bath/shower. TV. Phone. D,B&B £323 to £563. Rooms for disabled. No children under 7. Afternoon teas. Garden. Swimming-pool

---

NEW POLZEATH Cornwall map 1

▲ *Cornish Cottage Hotel* 

New Polzeath PL27 6US
TEL: (01208) 862213 FAX: (01208) 862259
signposted off B3314 between Wadebridge and Port Isaac

COOKING 6
COST £24–£53

The setting is good, even by Cornish standards: on a remote headland north-east of Padstow with 'lovely views across the inlet and up the cove', where surfers and walkers abound. The décor is 'in a bit of a time warp, all Laura Ashley and frills' in one reporter's view, and although a mid-meal sorbet might suggest that the food is in the same mould, in fact it provides something of a contrast. The handover from Tim Rogers to his former sous-chef Martin Walker in early summer 1997 appears to have been seamless, and the modern classical style continues with pork and apple sausage, and tartare of mushrooms with a herb-strewn tomato and shallot salad.

A lightness of touch is evident in a 'clear, fragrant and subtle' smoked fish consommé with al dente tortellini of smoked salmon, while expert handling of fine ingredients, combined with accomplished saucing, has produced roast wing of 'amazingly fresh' skate with a velvety butter sauce pungent with capers. Vegetables are integral to main courses, and 'carrots roasted with cumin seeds deserve a separate mention', according to a reporter who found them especially appropriate for a well-timed duck breast in red wine sauce. Chocolate is hard to resist at dessert stage, at least it was for our inspectors, who enjoyed the long-standing assiette as well as a 'light, yet closely textured' steamed chocolate pudding that was an impressive example of the genre.

Aperitifs are taken in the conservatory, where the first nibbles arrive, and coffee and petits fours are served there afterwards, mini brandy snaps and chocolate-dipped strawberries among them. 'Oh, what charming service!' exclaimed one reporter, though another found it rude and unhelpful. Three dozen wines span a fair range of styles and prices, which start at £10, and three wines by the glass come in the large size.

CHEF: Martin Walker PROPRIETORS: Clive and Christine Mason OPEN: Sun L 12 to 1.30, all week D 7 to 9 CLOSED: Jan MEALS: alc (main courses £10.50 to £18.50). Set L Sun £16.50, Set D £28 SERVICE: not inc, card slips closed CARDS: Amex, Delta, Diners, MasterCard, Switch, Visa DETAILS: 32 seats. 16 seats outside. Private parties: 50 main room. Car park. Vegetarian meals. No children under 12. No smoking in dining-room. Wheelchair access (also WC). Music ACCOMMODATION: 12 rooms, all with bath/shower. TV. Phone. B&B £38 to £96. Deposit: £30. No children under 12. Baby facilities. Dogs welcome. Afternoon teas. Garden. Swimming-pool

NORTHLEACH Gloucestershire map 2

Old Woolhouse

Market Place, Northleach GL54 3EE COOKING **5**
TEL: (01451) 860366 COST **£52–£63**

'Nothing of any significance has changed,' writes one who visits from time to time, and that, as far as we are aware, goes for the food as well as décor. Mr and Mrs Astic choose not to furnish the *Guide* with menus or wine list – there is no written menu for their customers either – but the format is generally a four-course meal with a choice between two starters (fish is customary) and four main courses, then salad, cheese (usually St-Marcellin) and dessert. 'What impressed me was the gutsiness of this quietly accomplished, basically classical French cooking,' summarised an observer. In particular there are good reports of scallops and turbot, roast partridge in a game sauce, and at one meal a choice between chocolate gâteau or honey and nut ice-cream for dessert. Service is 'attentive, friendly and professional'. A wine list, 'handwritten on something strongly resembling parchment', includes champagne (without prices) and a few wines from Burgundy and Bordeaux. There is very little, if anything, under £30, and no house wine.

CHEFS/PROPRIETORS: Mr and Mrs Jacques Astic OPEN: Tue to Sat D only from 8.15; other times by arrangement CLOSED: 1 week Christmas MEALS: Set D £40 SERVICE: not inc CARDS: none DETAILS: 18 seats. Private parties: 18 main room. Children welcome. No music

Wickens 🍷 $✱

Market Place, Northleach GL54 3EJ COOKING **6**
TEL/FAX: (01451) 860421 COST **£33–£39**

Christopher and Joanna Wickens do not let up. Their modern-meets-classical English restaurant no longer does lunch and is open only five evenings a week, but there is no questioning the dedication. A top priority is to seek out traditional and unusual ingredients. This, and an enterprising way with English herbs, has produced a 'delicious and intriguing' Elizabethan pork casserole containing small pieces of Gloucester Old Spot, apricots, shallots, lemon balm and costmary. Among fish dishes, North Atlantic prawns with a very strong smoked garlic and lemon dip made an impact and shark may be one of four or five options on the set three-course menu.

Joanna Wickens's fondness for desserts is obvious in her excellent crème brûlée, and she takes a lot of care in selecting and describing cheeses. 'A remarkable capacity for remembering the little touches' runs to bringing good nibbles with drinks, providing jugs of water and escorting guests to the door at the end of the meal. It is a genteel and charming, if rather slow-paced, sort of place, and service is smooth and capable. Wines are a praiseworthy bunch, gathered mostly from the great and the good of the New World. France merely provides a couple of champagnes and a trio of dessert wines, which makes even more pleasing the fact that the dozen English estate wines are there by merit rather than just to add to the 'Englishness' of the place. House wines start at £8.95 per bottle or £2 for a small glass. CELLARMAN'S CHOICE: Haute-Cabrière Chardonnay/Pinot Noir 1996, Franschhoek, South Africa, £15.95; Chapel Down Epoch 1 1995, England, £13.75.

CHEFS/PROPRIETORS: Christopher and Joanna Wickens OPEN: Tue to Sat D only 7.20 to 9 MEALS: Set D £25 SERVICE: not inc, card slips closed CARDS: Delta, MasterCard, Switch, Visa DETAILS: 38 seats. Private parties. 22 main room. Vegetarian meals. Children welcome. No smoking in dining-room. Music

NORWICH Norfolk map 6

Adlard's

79 Upper St Giles Street, Norwich NR2 1AB COOKING 7
TEL: (01603) 633522 FAX: (01603) 617733 COST £28–£56

Adlard's singularly fails to display the usual indications of serious intent that many ambitious restaurants go in for. It is painted green, covered in artwork, adopts an informal approach, and that's about it: no decorative flourishes or waves of nibbles, amuse-gueules or presents from the chef, just a few cheese straws to accompany the menu. David Adlard scuttles in and out, doing almost everything except cooking, which is now in the hands of Aiden Byrne. Menus are flexible, offering set-price and à la carte options, and seem to favour rabbit, poultry and game birds as much as lamb and seafood. Saddle of rabbit has been stuffed with peas and basil, while pigeon sausage has come with lentils, beetroot, and Jerusalem artichoke mousse. At its best the food can be inspired, justifying the price.

Dishes make a strong visual impact – red mullet fillets on rounds of saffron-yellow potatoes, on top of watercress purée, for instance – and classic flavour combinations are carried out with assurance. Steamed pigeon, for example, partnered with foie gras and choucroute one lunch-time impressed its reporter with the interplay between sweet, livery richness and the tartness of pickled cabbage. A light touch and a fine sense of timing have made the most of scallops with garlic purée, and langoustines in a delicate buttery-milky shellfish broth. Straightforward roasting and steaming are applied with skill, and components of a dish are treated with care, although an inspector – presented with a fancy dish of banana parfait looking like 'a mock-up of an art deco airline terminal' – wondered whether such gratuitous elaboration was warranted.

The enthusiastically annotated wine list opens with two dozen 'bin beginnings' costing under £20, followed by three pages of half-bottles, before moving on to the extensive main section. The New World selection is exemplary and French classics are well represented; fans of Viognier are advised to head for the Rhône.The French house white and the Argentinian house red are both good value at £9.50 a bottle, £2.75 a glass. CELLARMAN'S CHOICE: Luigi Bosca Chardonnay 1994, Mendoza, Argentina, £15; Bourgogne Côte Chalonnaise, Clos de Liroy 1992, M. Sarrazin, £17.

CHEFS: Aiden Byrne and David Adlard PROPRIETOR: David Adlard OPEN: Tue to Sat L 12.30 to 1.45, Mon to Sat D 7.30 to 10.45 CLOSED: 1 week Christmas, bank hols MEALS: alc (main courses L £11, D £19). Set L £15 (2 courses) to £19, Set D £28 (2 courses) to £35. BYO £5 SERVICE: not inc CARDS: Amex, Delta, Diners, MasterCard, Switch, Visa DETAILS: 40 seats. Vegetarian meals. Children's helpings. No smoking until after main course. No music

Brasted's

8–10 St Andrews Hill, Norwich NR2 1AD COOKING 2
TEL: (01603) 625949 FAX: (01603) 766445 COST £24–£40

Brasted's occupies a corner spot in the ancient heart of Norwich, between the castle and cathedral. Striped fabric still covers the walls, though the distinctive tent-like swathes have gone from the ceiling, making the dining-room look a shade more conventional. Adrian Clarke – 'a good, reliable, "traditional" chef', in one reporter's view – serves up duck terrine with Cumberland sauce, twice-baked cheese soufflé, and pork tenderloin with mustard sauce. The day's fish is generally grilled, non-meat dishes (of which there may be half a dozen) have included goats'-cheese tart with good pastry, and some items can be taken either as a first or main course. 'No dud meals from six courses over two days' was one endorsement of the standard, helped by service from the 'ever jovial' John Brasted. This may not be the place to come for innovation, but it is the place for 'a comforting meal and a good bottle' from the globe-trotting list. House Coteaux du Tricastin red and Côtes de Duras white are £10.85.

CHEF: Adrian Clarke PROPRIETOR: John Brasted OPEN: Mon to Fri L 12 to 2, Mon to Sat D 7 to 9.30 CLOSED: Christmas, bank hols MEALS: alc (main courses £12.50 to £18) SERVICE: not inc, card slips closed CARDS: Amex, Delta, Diners, MasterCard, Switch, Visa DETAILS: 22 seats. Private parties: 24 main room. Vegetarian meals. No music

Marco's

17 Pottergate, Norwich NR2 1DS COOKING 2
TEL: (01603) 624044 COST £23–£46

In the old part of town, and feeling smaller inside than it looks from the wide Georgian frontage, Marco's puts on sophisticated livery to produce its own interpretation of Italian classics, some of them with a regional slant: a burrida of mixed fish from Genoa, for example. Bresaola is made from boar, and cheese figures in a few pasta dishes such as spaghetti with Gorgonzola sauce. Few restaurants these days combine meat and seafood in a single dish, but Marco pairs chicken with scallops, and beef with Parma ham and smoked salmon in a lemon sauce. One reporter who 'went all fishy' enjoyed his meal of pancake with a prawn filling, followed by monkfish in a red pepper sauce. Zabaglione shares the billing with sorbets, or perhaps a dish combining meringue, strawberries, ice-cream and chocolate sauce. An espresso machine adds to the appeal. Wines, broadly grouped by style, include some choice examples from top to toe. House Sicilian is £9.50.

CHEF/PROPRIETOR: Marco Vessalio OPEN: Tue to Sat 12 to 2, 7 to 10 CLOSED: Christmas, bank hols MEALS: alc (main courses £15 to £17). Set L £14 SERVICE: not inc CARDS: Amex, Diners, MasterCard, Visa DETAILS: 22 seats. Private parties: 20 main room. Vegetarian meals. Children's helpings. No smoking in dining-room. Wheelchair access (no WC). Music

NOTTINGHAM Nottinghamshire map 5

Sonny's

3 Carlton Street, Hockley, Nottingham NG1 1NL COOKING 3
TEL: (0115) 947 3041 FAX: (0115) 950 7776 COST £20–£43

Ten years on and the northern outpost of Sonny's in London (see entry) is still 'a thoroughly good neighbourhood restaurant'. Its longevity could be attributed to 'sheer competence', in the words of one reporter, plus the 'modern but not too intimidating' décor that pleases young as well as old, along with good service, generous portions and reasonable prices.

And then there's the food itself, which embraces the homespun in Barnsley chop, travels south-east for boudin blanc with wild mushroom risotto, and ventures to more distant parts with mussels in a Thai broth, or blackened sirloin steak with Cajun butter. 'Ace' home-made basil gnocchi come with roast peppers and cherry tomatoes, jerk spiced chicken is perfectly set off by cucumber with mint, and a young visitor made short work of chargrilled steak and chips. Lemon cardamon cake with grilled peaches makes a satisfying finish. France stars on the well-chosen list of around 45 wines. House Merlot and Sauvignon Blanc are £8.95.

CHEF: Graeme Watson PROPRIETOR: Rebecca Mascarenhas OPEN: all week 12 to 3 (2 Sun), 7 to 10.30 (11 Fri and Sat) CLOSED: bank hols MEALS: alc (main courses £9 to £13). Set L Mon to Fri £8.95 (2 courses) to £11.95, Set L Sun £13.95 SERVICE: not inc; 10% for parties of 6 or more CARDS: Amex, MasterCard, Switch, Visa DETAILS: 75 seats. 20 seats outside. Private parties: 70 main room. Vegetarian meals. Children's helpings. No cigars/pipes in dining-room. Wheelchair access (no WC). Music. Air-conditioned

OLD BURGHCLERE Hampshire map 2

Dew Pond 🍷 $✱

Old Burghclere RG20 9LH
TEL/FAX: (01635) 278408 COOKING 6
off old A34, 3m W of Kingsclere COST £37–£52

This pair of linked sixteenth-century cottages, once inhabited by cattle-drovers, now makes an invitingly domestic setting for the Marshalls' practised skills. You can survey two counties from the Winchester Room, while the Pond Room naturally overlooks water. Seasonality and regionality are the two best motivators for any country restaurant, and they certainly come top of Keith Marshall's agenda.

A winter menu featured saddle of local hare with flageolet beans and a cider reduction sauce, alongside honey-roast Gressingham duck served with assorted root vegetables in a pastry case on a sauce of Muscat wine. One reporter began dinner with a crab and avocado gâteau, before proceeding to saddle of venison in port which was 'perfectly cooked, succulent and pink in the middle'. Fish dishes could scarcely be described as delicate when monk is done 'au poivre' and served with garlic mash and a coriander and lemon butter, or tuna is seared and bedded on ratatouille with black olives, basil and tomato.

Tried-and-tested desserts are often given added impetus, as when sorbets are layered and frozen together to form a terrine adorned with seasonal fruits; kirsch finds its way into crème brûlée, and a rhubarb and cherry compote appears beside it. The staff cope well even when every seat is taken, and the atmosphere is 'warm and welcoming'. The updated and redesigned wine list places bins from forward-thinking producers in the New World alongside fine wines from the Old and presents them by style. Prices are suitably modest, and the pocket is further aided by the welcome presence of two dozen half-bottles. Four house wines are £11.95. CELLARMAN'S CHOICE: Cape Charlotte Dry Muscat 1996, S.E. Australia, £11.95; Frankland Estate Isolation Ridge Shiraz 1994, Frankland, W. Australia, £14.75.

CHEF: Keith Marshall PROPRIETORS: Keith and Julie Marshall OPEN: Tue to Sat D only 7 to 10 CLOSED: 2 weeks Jan, 2 weeks Aug MEALS: Set D £25 SERVICE: not inc CARDS: MasterCard, Switch, Visa DETAILS: 45 seats. 10 seats outside. Private parties: 20 main room, 20 private room. Car park. Vegetarian meals. No children under 5. No smoking in dining-room. Wheelchair access (also WC). No music

OSWESTRY Shropshire map 7

▲ *Sebastian*

45 Willow Street, Oswestry SY11 1AQ COOKING 3
TEL: (01691) 655444 FAX: (01691) 653452 COST £16–£55

The building is sixteenth-century with heavy beams and low ceilings, and the food, with its mid-meal sorbets, domed main courses, dainty portions and flamboyant ideas, is French. A typical set dinner might comprise a puff pastry case of mushroom duxelles topped with poached eggs in mustard cream sauce, sirloin steak with hollandaise and deep-fried onion rings, and strawberry vacherin.

Elaboration may be accorded a high priority, as in a not entirely successful salad of prawns, tuna and squid at inspection, though raw materials tend to be first-rate. Lamb fillet – 'good meat, very nicely timed' – might come with a herb crust, or garnished with a shallot and rice flan. Our inspector also thought that vegetables could be improved. Though formal and efficient, service can be slow, and the assiduous topping-up of wine glasses has not pleased everyone. The New World is represented by around ten wines on the otherwise exclusively French list. Prices are fair, with house wines at £9.75 a bottle and £2.10 a glass. Note that parking is for residents only.

CHEF: Mark Sebastian Fisher PROPRIETORS: Michelle Adrienne and Mark Sebastian Fisher OPEN: Tue to Sat D only 6.30 to 10 CLOSED: 25 and 26 Dec, 1 Jan MEALS: alc (main courses £12.50 to £22.50). Set D £17.95 SERVICE: not inc, card slips closed CARDS: Amex, Delta, MasterCard, Switch, Visa DETAILS: 40 seats. 25 seats outside. Private parties: 24 main room. Vegetarian meals. Children's helpings. No smoking in dining-room. Wheelchair access (no WC). Music ACCOMMODATION: 3 rooms, all with bath/shower. TV. Phone. Room only £30 to £38. Children welcome. Baby facilities. Garden

Walls

Welsh Walls, Oswestry SY11 1AW — COOKING 2
TEL: (01691) 670970 FAX: (01691) 653820 — COST £17–£55

One part of this Victorian school building on a quiet lane outside the town centre is a simple wine bar, the other a classier restaurant. Inside, the décor is both striking and welcoming. The wine bar trades generally on old favourites, while the dining-room offers what Geoff Hughes describes as 'simple invention'. Some ingredients come from his smallholding, and menus change daily. Roast duck is often accompanied by fruit and spice – smoked plum and ginger, for instance, or apple and peppercorns – and leeks might turn up in a mustard sauce with ostrich, or in a broth with mussels for pan-fried halibut. Children as well as adults can expect friendly treatment. The recently expanded list of around 70 mostly French and New World wines includes a page of wines of the week, 20-odd house recommendations and a dozen or so pricier 'classics'. House wines are £8.

CHEFS: Geoff Hughes and Simon Newberry PROPRIETORS: Geoff Hughes, Kate Bottoms and Ruth Williams OPEN: all week L 12 to 3, Mon to Sat D 6 to 10.30 CLOSED: 26 Dec, 1 Jan MEALS: alc (main courses L £4.50 to £14, D £7 to £24). Set L Sun £10 (1 course) to £14 SERVICE: not inc CARDS: Amex, MasterCard, Visa DETAILS: 205 seats. 30 seats outside. Private parties: 205 main room, 40 private room. Car park. Vegetarian meals. Children's helpings. Wheelchair access (also WC). Music

OXFORD Oxfordshire — map 2

▲ *Al-Shami* £

25 Walton Crescent, Oxford OX1 2JG — COOKING 2
TEL: (01865) 310066 FAX: (01865) 311241 — COST £21–£39

This 'oasis on a steamy hot day' lifted an inspector's spirits with its airiness and uncluttered simplicity, matched by courteous and unhurried service. A complete Lebanese meal can be chosen from the long list of hot and cold hors d'oeuvre. Moutabel (roasted aubergine) has a 'great smoky flavour', and spicy sujuq (Armenian sausages) are also approved, and an interesting combination is 'very fine, creamy hummus' with slices of 'fine-flavoured lamb'. Lamb figures among the main courses, too, in laham mashwi (cubes chargrilled with onions, tomatoes and mushrooms), while other Middle Eastern dishes run from kibbeh istanbuliyah – ground meat with crushed wheat and pine-kernels – to baked cod with hot sesame sauce. Ch. Musar features on the short wine list, with house Lebanese at £9.99.

CHEF: Mimo Mahfouz PROPRIETOR: A.C. & A. Ltd OPEN: all week noon to midnight MEALS: alc (main courses £6.50 to £12). Cover £1 SERVICE: not inc, card slips closed; 10% for parties of 6 or more CARDS: MasterCard, Switch, Visa DETAILS: 78 seats. Private parties: 48 main room, 30 private room. Vegetarian meals. Children welcome. Wheelchair access (also WC). Music ACCOMMODATION: 12 rooms, all with bath/shower. TV. Phone. B&B £35 to £45. Children welcome. Baby facilities

▲ *Bath Place*

4–5 Bath Place, Holywell Street, Oxford OX1 3SU — COOKING 3
TEL: (01865) 791812 FAX: (01865) 791834 — COST £28–£66

Down a little alleyway between New College and Hertford College, next to Oxford's oldest inn, this group of seventeenth-century cottages clusters around a tiny flagstoned courtyard. Medieval city walls are exposed at the back of the dining-room, and the Fawsitts have charted the building's history from its construction by Flemish weavers through to literary associations with Thomas Hardy and Dorothy L. Sayers. In the kitchen, meanwhile, Jeremy Blake O'Connor's penchant for game-cooking continues, although the menus have a broad sweep that takes in lobster raviolo, onion tartlet, grilled 'onglet' of Scottish beef, and floating islands.

Two entirely separate monthly-changing menus are offered at lunch-time, with no fewer than 28 different dishes between them. The kitchen's range is represented by John Dory with risotto, roast veal kidney with mustard sauce, and a warm chocolate tart served with pistachio ice-cream, chocolate sorbet, and hazelnut sauce. Note that some dishes attract a price supplement, and that incidentals – appetiser, bread and petits-fours among them – are charged extra. Wines are an intelligent selection, helpfully arranged by style with succinct tasting notes. Australia and France top the honours list, and pricing is fair. Four house wines are £11.95 a bottle, or £3 a glass. CELLARMAN'S CHOICE: Mitchells Dry Watervale Riesling 1995, Clare Valley, S. Australia, £16.95; Shottesbrook Merlot 1994, McLaren Vale, S. Australia, £18.50.

CHEF: Jeremy Blake O'Connor PROPRIETORS: Kathleen and Yolanda Fawsitt OPEN: Wed to Sun L 12 to 2 (12.30 to 2.30 Sun), Tue to Sat D 7 to 10 (10.30 Fri) CLOSED: last week Dec, first week Jan MEALS: Set L £14 (2 courses) to £23.50, Set D £23.50 (2 courses) to £29.50 SERVICE: not inc; 10% for parties of 5 or more CARDS: Amex, Delta, MasterCard, Switch, Visa DETAILS: 32 seats. 8 seats outside. Private parties: 35 main room. Vegetarian meals. Children's helpings. No smoking in dining-room. Wheelchair access (no WC). Music. Air-conditioned ACCOMMODATION: 12 rooms, all with bath/shower. TV. Phone. B&B £75 to £130. Deposit: £25. Children welcome. Baby facilities. Dogs by arrangement

Cherwell Boathouse

50 Bardwell Road, Oxford OX2 6SR — COOKING 3
TEL/FAX: (01865) 552746 — COST £23–£35

Hidden away down a narrow lane on a 'secret part of the river', this restaurant in a former boathouse comes complete with its own punts. One visitor, having heard about it for years, expected it to be rather grand and was surprised to be met with bare wooden tables and simple décor. Frills may be few, but the good value, especially of the set menus, compensates. Top marks at an inspection meal went to Tuscan fish soup with rouille ('piles of flavour, thick and unctuous'), and main courses of pork have come in for praise, both loin ('tender and tasty' in a creamy sauce) and fillet with a redcurrant and pistachio sauce. Alternatively there may be duck breast with lime sauce, or smoked cod with horseradish. Puddings are 'comfortable and homely': trifle ('all the right things'), or crusty and bitter chocolate nemesis. There are good words, too, for approachable but unobtrusive staff.

The wine list merits a 'blue' for its stunning collection of bottles assembled by London merchants Morris & Verdin. Specialities include a series of mature Meursaults from Domaine des Comtes Lafon and some fine Alsace whites from the eccentric young grower, André Ostertag, but selections from the New World are equally enticing. Prices at all levels are amazingly generous, beginning with 16 appealing house wines from £7.50 to £15. CELLARMAN'S CHOICE: Isabel Estate Sauvignon Blanc 1996, Marlborough, New Zealand, £15; Au Bon Climat Pinot Noir 1993, Santa Barbara, California, £20.

CHEFS: Gerard Crowley and Wayne Cullen PROPRIETOR: Anthony Verdin OPEN: Tue to Sun L 12 to 2, Tue to Sat D 6 to 10.30 CLOSED: 24 to 30 Dec MEALS: alc L (main courses £8 to £12). Set L £10 (2 courses) to £17.50, Set D £18.50 SERVICE: not inc; 10% for parties of 6 or more CARDS: Amex, Diners, MasterCard, Visa DETAILS: 60 seats. 24 seats outside. Private parties: 50 main room, 120 private room. Car park. Vegetarian meals. Children's helpings. No smoking before 2.15 L and 10.30 D. Wheelchair access (also WC). No music

Gee's

61A Banbury Road, Oxford OX2 6PE — COOKING 3
TEL: (01865) 553540 FAX: (01865) 310308 — COST £18–£43

This is a restaurant in a conservatory serving up-to-the-minute modern brasserie food to a knowledgeable and loyal clientele. The menus moved up a gear with the change of ownership a couple of years ago, and the mode is now roast polenta with aubergine, peppers and pesto, chargrilled squid with chillies, and roast cod with aïoli and butter-beans. 'Ample portions on deepish plates, free of designer flourishes,' was how one reporter approvingly summed it up. Chargrilled spatchcocked quails on pasta ribbons with a sauce of lemon, garlic and ginger won praise from another. Desserts are simple but effective, along the lines of chocolate mousse with orange segments or lemon tart with raspberry coulis. Solicitous service is praised by all, and a thoughtful wine list brings in some forthright flavours from Alsace and Australia to do the food justice. House wines are £9.95.

CHEF: Graham Corbett PROPRIETOR: Jeremy Mogford OPEN: Mon to Sat 12 to 2.30, 6 to 11, Sun 12 to 11 CLOSED: 25 and 26 Dec MEALS: alc (main courses £8.50 to £12.50). Set L Mon to Sat £9.75 SERVICE: not inc, card slips closed; 10% for parties of 7 or more CARDS: Amex, Delta, MasterCard, Switch, Visa DETAILS: 85 seats. Private parties: 90 main room. Vegetarian meals. Children's helpings. No cigars/pipes in dining-room. Wheelchair access (no WC). Music. Air-conditioned

All entries, including Round-ups, are fully indexed at the back of the Guide.

Lemon Tree

NEW ENTRY

268 Woodstock Road, Oxford OX2 7NW — COOKING 3
TEL: (01865) 311936 FAX: (01865) 311936 — COST £27–£46

Proprietor Clinton Pugh designed this restaurant and bar in north Oxford as an escapist's idea of the Mediterranean. The mustard frontage and blue-tiled roof make a bold initial impact, but don't quite prepare the first-timer for the spacious elegance of the interior with its Californian overtones. Part of the roof is glassed over, and there are alfresco tables, making this an ideal fine-weather venue. Staff in cream denim skirts and jeans are friendly and helpful.

Menus draw from the southern European repertoire: pastas and leafy salads, crostini, vichyssoise and summer fruits grilled with mascarpone are the order of the day. Goats'-cheese ravioli in a pimento sauce looks grand on a great white plate, and Thai-seasoned duck soup has a dark clear stock, morsels of crispy duck and shards of chilli and spring onion. Roasted fillet of sea bream comes with roast new potatoes and a sweet chilli dressing, while guinea-fowl is served with olive butter, mashed potatoes and garlic confit. Side orders include potatoes cooked in sea salt. 'Generous, comforting and gooey' treacle pudding with ice-cream seems to be the smart choice to finish. The wine selection is short and to the point, featuring big brash flavours ranging from New Zealand Sauvignon to Meursault. Prices start at £8.75.

CHEF: Paul Keeble PROPRIETOR: Clinton Pugh OPEN: all week 12 to 11 MEALS: alc (main courses £9 to £15) SERVICE: not inc, card slips closed; 10% (optional) for parties of 5 or more CARDS: Delta, MasterCard, Switch, Visa DETAILS: 90 seats. 50 seats outside. Private parties: 100 main room. Car park. Vegetarian meals. Children's helpings. Wheelchair access (also WC). Music

Old Parsonage Hotel, Parsonage Bar

1 Banbury Road, Oxford OX2 6NN — COOKING 1
TEL: (01865) 310210 FAX: (01865) 311262 — COST £30–£53

The seventeenth-century hotel, a short walk from the city centre (under the same ownership as Gee's, see entry above), is less of a restaurant, more 'an upmarket pub dining-room'. Prints, cartoons and paintings cover the walls (it was renovated in 1991), and the short and simple menu can be treated as a collection of bar snacks. Ground-breaking food it isn't, but lovers of tradition will be happy with dishes ranging from Middle Eastern falafel and hummus to old-fashioned tagliatelle with prawns and avocado in cream sauce, and baked Alaska. More substantial items might include roast cod with a lime hollandaise, rack of lamb with a herb crust, or grilled steak with french fries. The short, sharp list of three dozen wines includes a good showing of half-bottles and wines by the glass, starting at £2.95 (or £11 the bottle).

CHEF: Alison Watkins PROPRIETOR: Jeremy Mogford OPEN: all week 12 to 3, 6 to 11 CLOSED: 25 to 26 Dec MEALS: alc (main courses £9.50 to £17) SERVICE: not inc, card slips closed CARDS: Amex, Diners, MasterCard, Switch, Visa DETAILS: 37 seats. 30 seats outside. Car park. Vegetarian meals. Children welcome. No cigars/pipes in dining-room. Wheelchair access (no WC). Music. Air-conditioned ACCOMMODATION: 30 rooms, all with bath/shower. TV. Phone. B&B £120 to £205. Children welcome. Afternoon teas. Garden (*The Which? Hotel Guide*)

White House **NEW ENTRY**

2 Botley Road, Oxford OX2 0AB COOKING 2
TEL: (01865) 242823 FAX: (01865) 793331 COST £23–£39

As the *Guide* went to press, Whites in Turl Street was up for sale, and the plan was to move the restaurant and wine merchants to the village of Woodstock. Chef Christopher Lennox-Bland is now cooking here, at the owner's other new venture in a former pub near the railway station. A sign on the door of the single-storey building draws attention to the garden, and to the availability of all-day snacks, while the open-plan blue and yellow bar and restaurant take a breezy line in brasserie dishes culled from here, there and everywhere. Among the lively modern offerings might be chorizo and black pudding salad with mustard dressing, chicken Kiev, deep-fried haddock with mushy peas, or a rather more arresting pork belly in Guinness with garlic and coriander risotto. Some of this may be quite ambitious, but an inspection lunch produced a successful roast duck breast with a glossy crisp skin. Desserts might run to hazelnut marquise or strawberry tart. Brief jokey notes flesh out the short international wine list, which starts with house Vin de Pays du Gers at £8.95.

CHEF: Christopher Lennox-Bland PROPRIETOR: Whites Restaurant (Oxford) Ltd OPEN: all week 12 to 3, 6.30 to 9.30 MEALS: alc (main courses £6.50 to £10). Bar snack menu available SERVICE: not inc CARDS: Amex, Delta, Diners, MasterCard, Switch, Visa DETAILS: 60 seats. 60 seats outside. Private parties: 40 main room. Car park. Vegetarian meals. Children's helpings. No-smoking area. Wheelchair access (also WC). Music

PADSTOW Cornwall map 1

Bistro Margot Thomas

11 Duke Street, Padstow PL28 8AB COOKING 1
TEL: (01841) 533441 COST £31–£42

This modest bistro, a minute from the harbour, serves simple, straightforward dishes based around current themes: cheese and chive soufflé, roast lamb shank, and lemon tart. In a sure sign of the times, tables are equipped with a bottle of balsamic vinegar as well as salt and pepper. Home-cured gravad lax with a pungent dill sauce and a wedge of herby corn bread made a substantial starter at one meal, and fish is fresh and generally well handled, producing a 'firm and succulent' piece of cod on olive oil mash with sun-dried tomatoes, and monkfish in a herb crust. Eight accompanying vegetables have been considered 'superfluous but excellent', and desserts might include bread-and-butter pudding with calvados, or sticky toffee. Around 20 wines range from Italy to Uruguay at reasonable prices. House Sangiovese and Trebbiano are £7.95.

CHEFS: Elaine Meredith, Adrian Oliver and Adam Vout PROPRIETORS: Michael and Elaine Meredith OPEN: all week D only 7 to 9.30 CLOSED: 25 and 26 Dec, Jan MEALS: Set D £18.95 (2 courses) to £22.95 SERVICE: not inc, card slips closed CARDS: Delta, MasterCard, Visa DETAILS: 30 seats. Private parties: 30 main room. Children welcome. No smoking in dining-room. No music

▲ *Seafood Restaurant*

Riverside, Padstow PL28 8BY — COOKING 7
TEL: (01841) 532485 FAX: (01841) 533344 — COST £34–£85

Everybody wants to eat here, not surprisingly given the honest enthusiasm with which Rick Stein promotes the simple pleasures of eating fresh seafood. As a fishy messiah he is unequalled – satellite operations include nearby St Petroc's, a delicatessen and a café – and the unprejudiced visitor admires the calm and excellence of this long-established pioneer. The Seafood sits near the quayside where boats tie up, with a conservatory for aperitifs and herby olives, and a spacious, light, characterful dining-room with bright paintings, where constant custom makes for a warm and lively atmosphere.

The food is 'almost disarmingly simple' and generally free of distracting flourishes. It goes its own way, directed by ultra-fresh supplies and intelligent treatment. Exemplary flavours and textures are typical, as in 'only slightly cooked' roast cod, teasingly sprinkled with spices, on a bed of Puy lentils. 'Upbeat flavours might call on lime, lemon grass and particularly chilli (which some reports suggest is overused), but there is a classically simple dimension, too, in baked crab tart, or rocket risotto.

The fish and shellfish soup would be hard to better 'at the best French coastal restaurants', while fish broth combines firm, silvery sea bass, creamy white scallop, soft orange coral, pink crab claw meat, crisp bean sprouts and slithery angel hair pasta, all in a delicately flavoured stock. An inspector had 'nothing but praise for the raw materials', which have included a huge turbot steak with 'wonderfully sticky and moist' flesh, served with a thick, eggy, canary-yellow hollandaise. 'No fuss' is a recurring theme of reports, applied equally to food and the generally friendly and attentive service, although occasional disappointments are registered. 'Our young waiter explained that with the fixed sitting arrangements the chef likes to cook five or so dishes at once, and we were unlucky to be last served.'

Cheese comes ready-plated with no choice, while desserts have included 'properly made pavlova' with strawberries and an intense raspberry coulis, and passion-fruit tart. Professional but relaxed service applies across the board: 'we were glad to be left to our own devices as far as pouring wine was concerned'. The house selection, priced mostly under £20, that the Steins are 'currently particularly enthusiastic about' is an easy introduction to an impressive list which majors in whites – as you would expect – but also gives space to some classy reds. And it is good to see a few bins from winemakers who have been making waves in the wine world berthed alongside all the grand old names.

CHEF: Rick Stein PROPRIETORS: Mr and Mrs Rick Stein OPEN: Mon to Sat 12 to 1.30, 7 to 10 CLOSED: Christmas and New Year MEALS: alc (main courses L £14.50 to £17.50, D £20.50 to £33). Set L £23, Set D £33.50 SERVICE: not inc CARDS: Delta, MasterCard, Switch, Visa DETAILS: 70 seats. 14 seats outside. Children's helpings. No children under 5. Music. Air-conditioned ACCOMMODATION: 26 rooms, all with bath/shower. TV. Phone. B&B £33 to £125. Children welcome. Baby facilities. Dogs welcome. Garden (*The Which? Hotel Guide*)

PAINSWICK Gloucestershire map 2

Country Elephant

New Street, Painswick GL6 6XH — COOKING 4
TEL/FAX: (01452) 813564 — COST £21–£53

If you want to know how it's done, Robert Rees offers one-off cookery courses under the name 'A Day in the Life of a Chef' at this young but rapidly developing Cotswold restaurant on the Stroud to Cheltenham road. If that sounds like too much hard work, though, sit back and let him worry about the leek terrine with smoked salmon and Chablis vinaigrette, or the tart of confit of red onions and foie gras.

This is indeed an industrious kitchen. If it can be made on the premises, it is, right down to the filo pastry. Combinations can be very daring, as in a first-course casserole of snails, wild mushrooms and almonds cooked in Chartreuse, and only occasionally are they straight-down-the-line classical, such as breast of roast duck that comes with a confit of the leg, fondant potatoes and a port sauce. Fish dishes are allowed to join in the creative fun too: Thai-spiced rösti and saffron butter are the accompaniments for a grilled wing of skate. Rice-pudding is given a new spin by being served chilled with raspberries and a custard flavoured with rosemary, while mulled wine sauce adds depth to white and dark chocolate sorbets. 'Excellent, helpful service' was reported by one correspondent, and the globe-trotting wine list helps in its own way by offering nine listings by the glass. House wines from Australia and South Africa are £9.80 the bottle.

CHEF: Robert Rees PROPRIETOR: John Rees OPEN: Tue to Sat 12 to 2, 7 to 10, bank hol Suns 12 to 2 CLOSED: 1 week Christmas MEALS: alc (main courses £14 to £18). Set L Tue to Sat £10 (2 courses) to £13, Set L bank hol Sun £13 (2 courses) to £18, Set D Tue to Fri £13 (2 courses) to £18, Set D Sat £22 SERVICE: not inc CARDS: Amex, Delta, Diners, MasterCard, Switch, Visa DETAILS: 32 seats. 20 seats outside. Private parties: 32 main room. Children's helpings. No smoking in dining room. Wheelchair access (no WC). Music

PAULERSPURY Northamptonshire map 5

▲ *Vine House*

100 High Street, Paulerspury NN12 7NA
TEL: (01327) 811267 FAX: (01327) 811309 — COOKING 4
off A5, 2m SE of Towcester — COST £26–£41

The stylishly refurbished seventeenth-century limestone house is at the end of a quiet village just off the A5. Park at the back, walk through the garden and sit in the small bar for a glass of home made lemonade or ginger beer. There is just enough space, when the dining-room is full, for staff to manoeuvre themselves between tables, bearing rustic chunks of malty brown wholemeal bread and a small cup of introductory soup. Marcus Springett's three-course meals are varied and ever changing, relying on first-rate ingredients and a good grasp of technique.

: spring meal began with light, crisp-coated fish-cakes of salmon, potato ... abbage, served with a fresh tomato butter sauce, and went on to a boneless chicken breast, perfectly timed, sitting next to a potato cake wrapped in smoked bacon. The sauce it sat in – silky, stock-based, translucent and truffle-flecked – was considered 'an enormous improvement on what they have done before'. Part of the appeal is the restraint with which dishes are handled: for example, three sole fillets served with a delightfully mushroomy duxelles and a (rather unctuous) chive butter sauce. Vegetables are included in the price but served separately.

Puddings tend to be rich, and that is the point when, in an inspector's view, simplicity is abandoned and the elements of a dish don't quite hang together. Chilled rice pudding at one meal came in a brandy-snap basket with a scoop of brown-bread ice-cream, surrounded by warm bananas covered in runny honey and shards of strong ginger. The wine list has a short selection from the New World but is mainly focused on France. House wines are £9.95.

CHEF: Marcus Springett PROPRIETORS: Marcus and Julie Springett OPEN: Thu and Fri L 12.30 to 1.45, Mon to Sat D 7.30 to 9.45 CLOSED: 2 weeks from 24 Dec MEALS: Set L £16, Set D £23.50 SERVICE: not inc CARDS: MasterCard, Visa DETAILS: 45 seats. Private parties: 35 main room, 12 private room. Car park. Children welcome. No smoking in dining-room. No music ACCOMMODATION: 6 rooms, all with bath/shower. TV. Phone. B&B £39 to £66. Children welcome. Garden (*The Which? Hotel Guide*)

PAXFORD Gloucestershire map 5

GLOUCESTERSHIRE 1998 PUB

▲ *Churchill Arms* £

NEW ENTRY

Paxford, Chipping Norton GL55 6XH COOKING **5**
TEL: (01386) 593203 COST £19–£35

Sonya Kidney and Leo Brooke-Little (co-owners of the Marsh Goose, see entry, Moreton-in-Marsh) took over this pub with a colleague in the summer of 1997. It stands at the crossroads, diagonally opposite the church, in this 'very Cotswold' hamlet and is, they are careful to point out, 'a pub with food, not a restaurant with beer'. There is no obligation to eat, but there is a blackboard menu, orders are taken and payment made at the bar, cutlery is wrapped in paper napkins, and if you want anything you need to get up and ask for it, just like in a pub. Sonya Kidney oversees the food, helped by Rupert Staniforth, and although aspirations are modest the quality is undeniable.

The same 'brilliance and freshness of ideas' that works for the Marsh Goose also applies here. A dish of hot cheese fritters, for example, consists of five Cheddar balls with a light, thin, crisp coating, served with a creamy, tangy, grain mustard vinaigrette. There is a daily soup, a few sandwiches, perhaps a vegetable pancake, sauté lamb kidneys, or 'a wonderful pub dish' of tuna steak, smeared with a paste of green olives, onions and capers, lightly grilled and served on a colourful leafy salad. The range of dishes is sensibly limited, but few other pubs turn out anything remotely resembling, say, an intensely fruity raspberry terrine with an even better praline parfait in the centre, and a moat of white chocolate sauce. A rudimentary wine list (three reds and three whites initially) starting at £8.50 confirms the pub style. Beers include Hook Norton.

CHEF: Sonya Kidney PROPRIETORS: Leo Brooke-Little, Sonya Kidney and Jonathan Warhurst OPEN: all week 12 to 2, 7 to 9 (9.30 Sat) CLOSED: 25 Dec MEALS: alc (main courses £7 to £12). BYO £3.50 SERVICE: not inc CARDS: Delta, MasterCard, Switch, Visa DETAILS: 60 seats. 40 seats outside. Vegetarian meals. Children's helpings. No music ACCOMMODATION: 4 rooms, all with bath/shower. TV. Phone. B&B £40 to £60. Children welcome. Garden

PENZANCE Cornwall map 1

Harris's

46 New Street, Penzance TR18 2LZ COOKING **4**
TEL: (01736) 364408 FAX: (01736) 333273 COST £37–£62

The Harrises record a quarter-century of supporting the local economy this year, and are justly pleased that their restaurant has stood the test. To find out the reason for their longevity, first find the tiny narrow cobbled street off Penzance's main shopping area, and be prepared to be dazzled. The interior is in orange and shell pink, which 'gives a warm and cosy feel on a wet and windy night'. Whatever the weather, there are highlights in Roger Harris's cooking too. A June dinner produced king prawns in unrestrained garlic butter, an 'unusual and very refreshing' wild thyme sorbet, agreeably tender best end of lamb with redcurrants and rosemary, and 'wonderfully sticky and gooey' treacle tart. Locally caught fish and seafood are given star billing as Dover sole meunière, or John Dory poached with saffron, and game is allowed a fair shout as well: pheasant breast comes on a bed of celeriac with baby onions, bacon and mushrooms in a madeira sauce. Crème brûlée and properly textured apple strudel have also met with approval. Service is 'very correct', it is felt, but could do to loosen up a little. A quick round-up of Spain, Italy, Germany and the antipodes supports the otherwise French wine list. House wines start at £11.50.

CHEF: Roger Harris PROPRIETORS: Roger and Anne Harris OPEN: Tue to Sat L 12 to 2, Mon to Sat D 7 to 10 CLOSED: 25 and 26 Dec, 1 Jan, 4 weeks in winter MEALS: alc (main courses £15 to £25). Light L available SERVICE: 10%, card slips closed CARDS: Amex, Delta, MasterCard, Switch, Visa DETAILS: 40 seats. Private parties: 24 main room. Children welcome. Music

PLUMTREE Nottinghamshire map 5

Perkins £

Old Railway Station, Plumtree NG12 5NA
TEL: (0115) 937 3695 FAX: (0115) 937 6405 COOKING **2**
off A606, 2m S of Nottingham COST £21–£37

This old railway station was privatised long before the national network – the Perkinses have been here since 1982 – and the peaceful tree-lined track that runs past the conservatory feels more appropriate to Thomas the Tank Engine than Inter-City 125s. People mill about in the bar ordering drinks, collecting menus, trying to figure out what the blackboard specials are, and finding somewhere to sit. It feels casual, and service is both amiable and well organised.

Dishes recur, but the repertoire is a large one, taking in a multitude of salads, poached egg Bénédictine, soused fillet of trout, pot-roast chicken, brochette of pork fillet, and skate wing with black butter. Among recommendations have been seasonal English asparagus with a light, fluffy hollandaise; baked plaice; and chunks of boiled lamb in a parsley sauce with puff pastry. Puddings are recited, and might include cherry frangipane, or chocolate tart with locally made ice-cream. Good French country wines (from £8.95) head up the short list, and quality and value are keen throughout.

CHEF: Tony Perkins PROPRIETORS: Tony and Wendy Perkins OPEN: Tue to Sat 12 to 2.30, 6.30 to 9.30 CLOSED: 1 week Christmas, 2 weeks late Aug, bank hols MEALS: alc (main courses £7.50 to £11.50). BYO £5 SERVICE: not inc CARDS: Amex, Delta, Diners, MasterCard, Switch, Visa DETAILS: 73 seats. 24 seats outside. Private parties: 12 main room, 30 private room. Car park. Vegetarian meals. No children under 7 after 8. No smoking in 1 dining-room. Wheelchair access (no WC). No music. Air-conditioned

PLYMOUTH Devon map 1

Chez Nous 🍷

13 Frankfort Gate, Plymouth PL1 1QA COOKING **6**
TEL/FAX: (01752) 266793 COST £41–£49

'A little corner of France behind white wooden louvred shutters,' promise the Marchals. The shutters lend a stylish feel to the exterior and serve to 'keep out Plymouth reality' (the restaurant is in a post-Blitz shopping development in a town-centre square near the Western Approach car parks). Seventeen years have elapsed since Jacques Marchal decided to go it alone in the kitchen here, and a reporter who has followed his progress emphasises the fact that little changes from year to year, but then it does not need to, for the level of achievement is high.

In his 'supernaturally tidy' little galley at the back, M. Marchal reliably cooks up a storm. 'Simplicity with judgement and care' is the principle running through it all, which may mean perfectly timed scallops with a faultless stock and cream liaison aromatised with ginger, quail breasts on a mound of salad with a dressing enriched with cooking juices and sweetened with raisins soaked in alcohol, or a handsomely flavoured duck breast cooked pink, sliced and fanned out on brown lentils, in an uncluttered wine and stock sauce. Vegetables – perhaps Cornish new potatoes and young spinach – are served separately. Pavé au chocolat with vanilla crème anglaise is a well-reported dessert, and there may be grilled peppered pineapple, or almond gâteau with rose-petal ice-cream.

Wines continue the French theme: a few ports and 15 *vins d'autres pays* are permitted, but mature burgundies and clarets dating back to 1959 are the main attractions. House wines are £10.50. CELLARMAN'S CHOICE: Pouilly-Vinzelles 1995, Dom. Jean Mathias, £17.50; Chambolle Musigny, Clos du Village 1990, Dom. Antonin Guyon, £47.

CHEF: Jacques Marchal PROPRIETORS: Suzanne and Jacques Marchal OPEN: Tue to Sat 12.30 to 2, 7 to 10.30 CLOSED: first 3 weeks Feb, first 3 weeks Sept MEALS: Set L and D £29.50 SERVICE: not inc CARDS: Amex, Diners, MasterCard, Switch, Visa DETAILS: 28 seats. Private parties: 28 main room. Children welcome. Wheelchair access (no WC). Music. Air-conditioned

PONTELAND Northumberland map 10

Café 21 £

35 The Broadway, Darras Hall, Ponteland NE20 9PW COOKING 4
TEL: (01661) 820357 COST £21–£39

The setting – in a parade of shops serving a large housing estate way out of Newcastle – is not immediately endearing, but the mood lightens inside, helped by relaxed and good-humoured service. 'Its heart is in the right place,' reckoned one visitor, noting the paper cloths, blackboard menu and generous selection of brasserie-style dishes. It is owned by the Laybournes of 21 Queen Street (see entry, Newcastle upon Tyne), and some dishes are a chip off the old block – ham and foie gras with pease pudding, or braised oxtail in Newcastle Brown Ale, for instance – but the general tenor is modern with a French bias, ranging from fish soup with rouille and croûtons, via black pudding fritters, to duck confit with braised butter-beans.

Despite its café status, sound technique underpins the cooking, as in a twice-baked soufflé of Cheddar cheese and spinach, with a moat of cream, that was judged light, moist, 'really cheesy' and 'one of the best of its kind'. The intelligent approach has also produced accurately chargrilled pork cutlet served with a creamy, herby risotto and a stock-based tomato-flavoured gravy; something of a 'trencherman' dish maybe, but more importantly one of 'generosity and warmth'. It came with a small refreshing green salad that neatly paved the way for a rich chocolate and banana pudding with a runny inside and a scoop of Horlicks ice-cream. The set-price lunch is a bargain, and the wine list is short and sensibly priced, starting with house Duboeuf at £9.50 a bottle and £12 a litre.

CHEFS: Andrew Moore and Andrew Waugh PROPRIETORS: Terence and Susan Laybourne OPEN: Tue to Sat 12 to 2, 6 to 10.30 CLOSED: Christmas, bank hols MEALS: alc (main courses £8 to £12.50). Set L £12 (2 courses) to £14.50 SERVICE: not inc CARDS: Amex, Delta, Diners, MasterCard, Switch, Visa DETAILS: 40 seats. Private parties: 40 main room. Vegetarian meals. Children's helpings. No cigars/pipes in dining-room. Music

POOLE Dorset map 2

▲ *Mansion House, Benjamin's* 🍷 $

Thames Street, Poole BH15 1JN COOKING 4
TEL: (01202) 685666 FAX: (01202) 665709 COST £22–£54

The Mayor family of Poole founded the Newfoundland cod trade and built this house for themselves in 1779, just a short haul from the old quayside. Period décor throughout and an atmosphere of restrained civility are appreciated by local regulars and members of the house dining club. Gerry Godden cooks in the modern British idiom, bringing foreign influences to bear with a gentle touch: 'superbly flavoured and plentiful' Dorset mussels are cooked in white wine aromatised with Thai spices and coconut cream; ravioli are stuffed with Gorgonzola and accompanied by honeyed walnuts, leeks and salsa verde. The menu is particularly strong on local fish, which may include scallops in a saffron and orange nage, and there is always a catch of the day. Meat-eaters might opt for roast woodpigeon on creamed cabbage with wild mushrooms and thyme *jus*, while pudding-lovers might choose between iced gingerbread parfait with brandy snaps, and warm blackberry and apple torte with clotted cream. Service has been described as 'helpful' and 'extremely friendly'. A separate bistro, called JJ's, is open every day except Sunday lunch-time.

The carefully considered wine list is divided into two sections. The first contains good value wines from around the world, classified by style with helpful tasting notes, nearly half of which cost less than £15. The second section features French classics with no price limit. House wines start at £10.50. CELLARMAN'S CHOICE: Cloudy Bay Sauvignon Blanc 1996, Marlborough, New Zealand, £23.50; Penfolds Kalimna Bin 28 1994, Barossa Valley, S. Australia, £19.75.

CHEF: Gerry Godden PROPRIETOR: Robert Leonard OPEN: Sun to Fri L 12 to 2, Mon to Sat D 7 to 9.30 CLOSED: L bank hol Mons MEALS: Set L Mon to Fri £13.40, Set L Sun £15.80, Set D £18.35 (2 courses). Meal prices reduced by 15% for residents SERVICE: not inc CARDS: Amex, Delta, Diners, MasterCard, Switch, Visa DETAILS: 85 seats. Private parties: 100 main room, 14 to 40 private rooms. Car park. Vegetarian meals. Children's helpings. No children under 5. No smoking in 1 dining-room. No music. Air-conditioned ACCOMMODATION: 28 rooms, all with bath/shower. TV. Phone. B&B £52 to £115. Children welcome. Baby facilities. Dogs by arrangement. Afternoon teas (*The Which? Hotel Guide*)

PORTHLEVEN Cornwall map 1

▲ *Critchards*

The Harbourside, Porthleven TR13 9JA COOKING **2**
TEL: (01326) 562407 COST £28–£49

The converted 300-year-old mill overlooks Porthleven harbour, pictures of things 'fishy' plus a ship's figurehead bedeck the neat dining-room, and – surprise, surprise – fish is the main focus of the menu. The Critchards appear to scour the planet for inspiration, and some pairings of ingredients might seem curious: banana with John Dory, for instance, or Kaffir lime leaves with Helford mussels. Such combinations, however, have earned praise even from those who normally prefer their fish plainly grilled. Pan-fried Thai-style red gurnard is a combination that works well, using coconut milk, lemon grass and chilli, while sea bass with mint, vermouth and a cucumber yoghurt sauce is 'simple and quite effective'. Vegetarians will find a separate menu, bread now comes free, and service is pleasant but may not be prompt. The wine list of around 40 bottles features one from Cornwall's Lizard peninsula. House wines are £9.50.

CHEF: Jo Critchard PROPRIETORS: Steve and Jo Critchard OPEN: Mon to Sat D only 6.30 to 9.30 CLOSED: most of Jan MEALS: alc (main courses £12 to £29) SERVICE: not inc, card slips closed CARDS: MasterCard, Switch, Visa DETAILS: 44 seats. Private parties: 34 main room. Vegetarian meals. Children's helpings. No children under 6. No smoking in dining-room. Music ACCOMMODATION: 2 rooms, both with bath/shower. TV. B&B £22 to £50. Deposit: 25%. Children welcome

PORTLOE Cornwall map 1

▲ *Tregain* £ NEW ENTRY

Portloe TR2 5QU
TEL/FAX: (01872) 501252

COOKING 3
COST £17–£39

A working harbour it may be, but Portloe is an enchanting village that gets its share of visitors. Many will stop at Tregain, for although 'village tea-room' best describes the low, beamed cottage, it is more multi-purpose than that. As well as coffee, cakes, light lunches and cream teas, Clare Holdsworth offers dinner, souvenirs and bed and breakfast. She is even the village post office. Mainstays on the all-day menu are salads, fresh crab, baked potatoes and the like, with variously filled omelettes turning up on Sundays.

In the evening, tablecloths come out for starters of 'faultless' vegetable soup, and light and creamy crab-cakes. More unusual combinations may be found in main courses: well-reported neck of lamb with a summer fruit and grenadine sauce, and immense scallops with cashew-nuts and ginger. Fish is a strong point – sea bass with saffron and mustard seeds may feature on the blackboard – and crab soup is something of a signature dish. Cornish clotted cream accompanies desserts of perhaps treacle pudding, or a summer salad of red fruits. Home-made herb rolls are highly commended, presentation is of a high standard, and service is cheerful and knowledgeable. Three house wines on the short list are £7.95.

CHEF/PROPRIETOR: Clare Holdsworth OPEN: all week light L menu available all day, Mon to Sat D 7 to 8.30 CLOSED: late Oct to late Mar MEALS: alc (main courses L £4 to £10, D £9 to £14) SERVICE: not inc, card slips closed CARDS: MasterCard, Switch, Visa DETAILS: 22 seats. 10 seats outside. Private parties: 22 main room. Vegetarian meals. Children's helpings. No smoking in dining-room. Music ACCOMMODATION: 2 rooms. B&B £19 to £38. Deposit: £5. Children welcome. Baby facilities. Dogs welcome. Afternoon teas

'When two people decided to switch seats just before the first course arrived, the bewildering panoply of cutlery, glasses, napkins and plates were changed with immaculate panache and at ultra-high speed, like the man who can do Rubik's cube in 25 seconds without breaking into a sweat.' (On eating in London)

All details are as accurate as possible at the time of going to press, but chefs and owners often change, and it is wise to check by telephone before making a special journey. Many readers have been disappointed when set-price bargain meals are no longer available. Ask when booking.

£ *indicates that it is possible to have a three-course meal, including coffee, a half bottle of house wine and service, at any time the restaurant is open (i.e. at dinner as well as at lunch, unless a place is open only for dinner), for £25 or less per person.*

All entries in the Guide *are re-researched and rewritten every year, not least because restaurant standards fluctuate. Don't rely on an out-of-date* Guide.

POULTON-LE-FYLDE Lancashire map 8

▲ *River House*

Skippool Creek, Thornton-le-Fylde,
Poulton-le-Fylde FY5 5LF
TEL: (01253) 883497 FAX: (01253) 892083
from roundabout junction of A585 and B5412 follow signs to Skippool Creek

COOKING 1
COST £35–£56

'Beaten-up charm' was one reporter's view of the River House, a red-brick edifice overlooking the mudflats of a tidal estuary which may flood the road at high tide. Bill Scott has been in this line of business for 40 years, and his cooking harks back nostalgically to earlier times. Creamy, wobbling soufflé suissesse, baked seafood in a herbed cream sauce, and Dover sole fried in lashings of butter make 'a refreshing contrast to the Mediterranean diet', but if you really want to keep up with the Joneses, there's roast ostrich with béarnaise. Fish and seafood are estimably fresh, and vegetables arrive in profusion. One couple were greeted by a pair of amiable dogs who conducted them inside. Others, encountering the human members of the team, have felt a bit sergeant-majored. The 'pot luck' wine list is short on details of vintages and producers. House wines from California are £12.50.

CHEF: Bill Scott PROPRIETORS: the Scott family OPEN: Mon to Sat 12 to 2, 7.30 to 9.30 CLOSED: 25 and 26 Dec, 1 Jan MEALS: alc (main courses £16 to £20). Set L and D Mon to Fri £25 SERVICE: not inc CARDS: Amex, Delta, MasterCard, Switch, Visa DETAILS: 40 seats. Private parties: 40 main room, 14 private room. Car park. Children welcome ACCOMMODATION: 5 rooms, all with bath/shower. TV. Phone. B&B £50 to £80. Children welcome. Dogs welcome. Garden (*The Which? Hotel Guide*)

PRESTBURY Cheshire map 8

▲ *White House*

New Road, Prestbury SK10 4DG
TEL: (01625) 829376 FAX: (01625) 828627
on A538, 4m N of Macclesfield

COOKING 2
COST £24–£56

Set on a village street that is 'the stuff of chocolate boxes', the White House is a large, comfortable restaurant decked out with antique lace, Macclesfield silk and a profusion of artificial greenery. Set-price menus and an ambitious *carte* offer self-styled 'contemporary British' cuisine: which is to say, virtually anything but British. Instead, there is a global tour of ingredients and techniques, with tapénade and tempura, rice noodles and rösti, blinis and balsamic vinegar appearing in quick succession. Generous portions have included a 'monster' guinea-fowl sausage happily partnered with gingered parsnips, and fillet of sea bass with crispy courgette julienne. Desserts such as roast pecan pear in caramel come with 'particularly good' ice-creams (maybe brown-bread, or bourbon whisky) and sorbets (mango, for instance). Service can be somewhat rushed. The long wine list holds no surprises but offers plenty of decent, well-priced bottles from both the Old and New Worlds. House wine is £11.50 a litre.

CHEFS: Mark Cunniffe and Paul Burton PROPRIETORS: Ryland and Judith Wakeham OPEN: Tue to Sun L 12 to 2, Mon to Sat D 7 to 10 CLOSED: 25 Dec MEALS: alc (main courses £9.50 to £14). Set L £12.95, Set D Mon to Fri £16.95 SERVICE: not inc, card slips closed CARDS: Amex, Delta, Diners, MasterCard, Switch, Visa DETAILS: 75 seats. 12 seats outside. Private parties: 104 main room, 28 and 40 private rooms. Car park. Vegetarian meals. Children's helpings. No cigars/pipes in dining-room. Wheelchair access (no WC). Music ACCOMMODATION: 11 rooms, all with bath/shower. TV. Phone. Room only £65 to £110. Rooms for disabled. Children welcome. Baby facilities. Dogs welcome by arrangement. Garden (*The Which? Hotel Guide*)

PRESTON Lancashire map 8

Heathcote's Brasserie 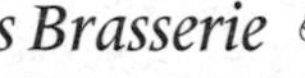

23 Winckley Square, Preston PR1 3JJ COOKING 4
TEL: (01772) 252732 FAX: (01772) 203433 COST £19–£50

Winckley Square and its environs form a pleasant enclave of red-brick Georgian and Victorian terraces in the centre of Preston, full of busy offices during the day and quiet streets in the evening. Lawrence Dodds took over the stoves at the beginning of 1997 as Max Gnoyke moved to Simply Heathcote's (see entry, Manchester). Reservations are now accepted, which should encourage custom from a wider catchment area. Although it calls itself a brasserie (there is also a seafood and rotisserie bar downstairs), the blond wood, frosted glass and bright mural combine to make it feel more like a modern restaurant, overseen by a team of efficient young staff.

There is much chargrilling and roasting (of monkfish and suckling pig, for example) and a commitment to updating some Lancashire dishes. How about a cold terrine of Lancashire hotpot, with chunks of potato, carrot, leek and two pink nuggets of lamb? Timing has been praised in grilled fillet of mackerel served in a salad with juicy shelled mussels, and in a 'pink' chicken breast and thigh, served with herb risotto and a piquant sauce bois boudran. Desserts may be 'less impressive than the rest of the meal', and bread is an optional chargeable extra, but worth the investment. The policy of serving all 23 varied wines by the glass is eminently sensible, and pricing – most are under £20 a bottle – is fair. House wine (£10.25) changes every three months.

CHEF: Lawrence Dodds PROPRIETOR: Paul Heathcote OPEN: Mon to Sat 12 to 2.15, 7 (6 Sat) to 10.30, Sun 12 to 9 CLOSED: 25 and 26 Dec, 1 Jan MEALS: alc (main courses £9 to £22). Set L £8.50 (2 courses) to £10.50 SERVICE: not inc, card slips closed CARDS: Amex, Delta, MasterCard, Switch, Visa DETAILS: 90 seats. Private parties: 90 main room, 60 private room. Vegetarian meals. Children's helpings. No cigars/pipes in dining-room. Wheelchair access (no WC). Music. Air-conditioned

indicates that there has been a change of chef since last year's Guide, *and the Editor has judged that the change is of sufficient interest to merit the reader's attention.*

'The only communication problem we noted was when I was delivered a plate of capers for breakfast when I thought I had ordered kippers.' (On eating in Scotland)

PULBOROUGH West Sussex map 3

Stane Street Hollow

Codmore Hill, Pulborough RH20 1BG
TEL: (01798) 872819 COOKING **2**
on A29, 1½m NE of Pulborough COST £27–£48

A Swiss chef running a largely French restaurant in an unimpeachably English setting is the deal here. The cottage of Bargate stone is set in a pretty garden, topiary is freshly clipped, and ducks swim on the pond. It is a family affair: René began his career in catering 40 years ago and has spent half of it here; Ann conducts the entire service – welcoming, serving drinks, taking orders, and delivering plates – single-handedly, and it is a lot for one pair of hands to do so the pace can be slow. The seasonal menu is in French with English translations, and in May delivered a warm asparagus mousse encased in paper-thin leek, and a trencherman pancake stuffed with prawn and asparagus and baked in cheese sauce. Meaty main courses have included crisply sauté lamb sweetbreads with chickpeas and spinach in a sticky stock reduction, and desserts have ranged from blackberry bombe through a selection of sorbets to a rich, dark chocolate 'truffe' with slices of orange.

The wine list opens appropriately enough with a couple of Swiss whites, followed by a predominantly French collection of attractive bins that gains extra appeal from some choice New World offerings. Three 'open' wines are available by the glass at £2.50. CELLARMAN'S CHOICE: Pinot Blanc d'Ardon 1994, Valais, Switzerland, £19; St-Emilion, Ch. Lapelletrie 1992, £17.50.

CHEF: René Kaiser PROPRIETORS: René and Ann Kaiser OPEN: Wed to Fri and Sun L 12.30 to 1.15, Wed to Sat D 7.15 to 9.15 CLOSED: 2 weeks late Oct, 24 Dec to 5 Jan, 2 weeks late May MEALS: alc (main courses £11 to £13). Set L £12.50 (2 courses) to £15.50 SERVICE: not inc, card slips closed CARDS: Delta, MasterCard, Switch, Visa DETAILS: 30 seats. Private parties: 22 main room, 14 and 22 private rooms. Car park. Vegetarian meals. Children's helpings. No smoking in dining-room. Wheelchair access (no WC). No music

RAMSBOTTOM Greater Manchester map 8

Village Restaurant

16–18 Market Place, Ramsbottom BL0 9HT
TEL: (01706) 825070 FAX: (01706) 822005 COOKING **5**
off A56/M66, 4m N of Bury COST £14–£40

This is a restaurant, a delicatessen and a wine business, all with a mission. It is not a large place. Church pews were never meant to be comfortable, but 'I would caution any of your readers with a waist much above 44 inches or inside leg much above 34 inches to think twice when trying to sit down'. However, that is not the mission. Careful sourcing is the prime consideration – vegetables and dairy products are organic, meat is 'bought from trusted local farmers' – and there is still no salt in the cooking, surely a challenge for any chef. Four-course dinners offer no choice before pudding, and revolve around meaty chargrills and braises. 'Superb' beef is served with homely gravy, and, in an act of unparalleled generosity in the restaurant trade, seconds and thirds are offered.

Concerning value, the three-course set-lunch deal is as reasonable as they come, the only small print being the additional £2 cover charge for those who don't drink, a sort of non-corkage. While two-course lunchtime 'quickies' can take under an hour, dinner expands to fill the entire evening: after a plate of something from the deli (smoked salmon, or pork terrine with orange, perhaps) comes a soup, such as nettle shoot or leek and potato, while 'wonderfully light' sticky toffee pudding seems to reign supreme among desserts.

The uncompromising dedication to virtuous materials may come close to sounding 'anoraky', but the fundamentals remain convincing. 'More a showcase of good food than sophisticated skills,' one called it, but the enterprise has honesty and integrity written all over it. A list of two dozen wines is presented at the table, but there are several hundred in the shop below. A corkage charge of £5 for ordinary wines, rising to £9 for fine wines – i.e. retailing at £15 or over – is added to the shop price. If you enjoy the wine and find yourself buying a case to take away, you won't be the first to do so. Alternatively, choose one or two of the 60 beers and ciders offered. House French is £9 a bottle, £2 a glass.

CHEF: Ros Hunter PROPRIETORS: Ros Hunter and Chris Johnson OPEN: Wed to Sat L 12 to 2.30, Sun L 1 to 1.30, Wed to Sat D 7.30 for 8 (1 sitting) MEALS: alc L Wed to Sat (main courses £4.50 to £12.50). Set L Mon to Sat £7, Set L Sun £19.50, Set D £19.50. BYO £9 SERVICE: not inc, card slips closed CARDS: Amex, Delta, Diners, MasterCard, Switch, Visa DETAILS: 40 seats. Private parties. 30 main room, 10 and 30 private rooms. Vegetarian meals. Children welcome. No smoking in dining-room. Music

REIGATE Surrey map 3

Dining Room *

59A High Street, Reigate RH2 9AE COOKING 6
TEL: (01737) 226650 COST £18–£62

'The Dining Room is getting better than ever,' reckoned one reporter. The stairs lead to a 'smart and comfortable' L-shaped room with rich red curtains and ornate Victorian fireplace. Anthony Tobin's cooking uses a wide palette of flavourings, many of them bold and spicy, and drawing on Italy, France and Thailand. Crisp-skinned confit of duck, for example, comes with mustard mash and pineapple chutney, while salmon marinated in ginger, served with beetroot and a yogurt dressing, has produced a 'perfectly balanced combination of strong flavours'.

Some trendy techniques have been noted, including an inclination to stack ingredients to gravity-defying heights – a 'dizzy tower' of spiced aubergine surmounted by wafer-thin caramelised tomato, for instance – and to froth up soup cappuccino-style. Simplicity brings good results, as in a fine fillet of seared beef 'cooked to a wonderful pink', and fish is very well handled: translucent, crisp-skinned scallops, red mullet soup with 'a glorious aroma', or roasted John Dory, perfectly timed to retain its 'delicate flavour and texture'.

Tarte Tatin is made with banana for a change, and accompanied by caramel sauce and vanilla ice-cream, while the food's visual impact extends to desserts such as a white chocolate mousse, set in a thin box of dark chocolate, raspberries on top, the whole thing covered in a lattice of plain chocolate. Assured and willing service by young staff comes in for praise, as does the value for money. A dozen fine wines supplement the short round-the-globe collection. House Vin de Pays d'Oc is £8.50.

CHEF: Anthony Tobin PROPRIETOR: Paul Montalto OPEN: Mon to Fri L 12 to 2, Mon to Sat D 7 to 10 CLOSED: 1 week Christmas, 1 week Easter, 2 weeks summer MEALS: alc (main courses £14 to £22). Set L £10, Set D £13.95 (2 courses) SERVICE: not inc CARDS: Amex, MasterCard, Switch, Visa DETAILS: 50 seats. Private parties: 45 main room. Vegetarian meals. Children welcome. No smoking in dining-room. Music. Air-conditioned

RICHMOND Surrey map 3

Burnt Chair 🍷

5 Duke Street, Richmond TW9 1HP COOKING 3
TEL: (0181) 940 9488 FAX: (0181) 255 8585 COST £28–£46

Weenson Oo, 'a real character', opened Burnt Chair in 1991 with the hope that guests would 'feel as though they were coming to a home from home'. The small restaurant, handy for Richmond Theatre, is suitably small, if echoey, and avoids an off-the-peg look with unmatching chairs, 'triffid' wall-lights, and a collection of brightly coloured glass bottles that look like props from *The Alchemist*. The cooking is done with flair and precision, and is as Asian and Mediterranean as it is Anglo-French: Mr Oo calls it 'modern international'. Starters might take in coriander and lemon grass vichyssoise, 'outstanding' brandade of cod, or black pudding with celeriac and apple purée. Praise has come in for a cold, lightly curried salmon brochette with cucumber raita, and a daube of 'wild' beef (from organic free-range Devon cows) served with frites. Marzipan plum flan with plum sorbet may be among the desserts, along with citrus cake with lemon ice and orange curd, which a reporter considered the high point of his meal.

Friendly service extends to the wines, and Mr Oo will gladly assist if you can't decide between all the appealing bins on his enthusiastically annotated list. Burgundy, a particular passion, receives strong competition from the rest of France and from some classy Americans. House vins de pays are £9.75. CELLARMAN'S CHOICE: Geyser Peak Sauvignon Blanc 1996, Sonoma, California, £20; St-Emilion, Ch. Gravet 1990, £19.50.

CHEFS: Gordon Gellatly and Weenson Oo PROPRIETOR: Weenson Oo OPEN: Mon to Sat D only 6 to 11 CLOSED: 1 week Christmas, 1 week summer, bank hols MEALS: alc (main courses £9.50 to £14). Set D 6 to 7.30 (7 Sat) £14 (2 courses). Cover £1 SERVICE: not inc CARDS: Delta, MasterCard, Switch, Visa DETAILS: 36 seats. Private parties: 36 main room. Vegetarian meals. Children's helpings. Music

Chez Lindsay £

12 Hill Rise, Richmond TW10 6UA COOKING 3
TEL: (0181) 948 7473 COST £18–£43

Lindsay Wotton's love of Breton cooking has switched Richmond on to the delights of galettes and crêpes, classically stuffed with variations of egg, cheese, ham, mushrooms, onions and tomato, or served plain with a cup of buttermilk. More adventurous galette fillings may be andouille, onion compote and mustard, for example, or 'Saisonnière' (asparagus, prawns and cantaloupe melon). It all takes place in a modestly appointed but cosy room near Richmond Bridge, and a Breton chef, Christian Chatelain, has now been recruited to the kitchen. Crêpes and galettes are available all day, but there is also a lunch and dinner menu of authentic Breton dishes such as oysters served hot with carrot mousseline and a cider cream sauce, mussels à la St-Malo in white wine and cream with shallots and thyme, or grilled lamb leg steak with haricots and tomato. Dessert pancakes incorporate honey and almonds, or perhaps chocolate sauce and banana, and may be either glâcé or flambé. Non-pancake alternatives may include a trio of sorbets, including an apple and calvados version, or ice-creams, with gin and lavender among the enticements. Breton cider is, of course, the recommended drink, served in traditional earthenware cups, but diehard oenophiles are not forgotten. A short and almost entirely French wine list kicks off with house burgundy at £8.90.

CHEFS: Lindsay Wotton and Christian Chatelain PROPRIETOR: Lindsay Wotton OPEN: all week 12 to 2.30, 6 to 11 (10 Sun, all week 11am to 11pm (10 Sun) for galette and crêpe menu) CLOSED: 25 Dec MEALS: alc (main courses £4.50 to £11.50). Set L and D £9.99 SERVICE: not inc CARDS: Delta, MasterCard, Switch, Visa DETAILS: 48 seats. Private parties: 50 main room, 36 private room. Vegetarian meals. Children's helpings. No cigars/pipes while others eat. Wheelchair access (no WC). Music

RIDGEWAY Derbyshire map 9

Old Vicarage

Ridgeway Moor, Ridgeway S12 3XW
TEL: (0114) 247 5814 FAX: (0114) 247 7079 COOKING 7
off A616, on B6054 nearly opposite village church COST £41–£62

The rather grand old vicarage may be only a short ride out of Sheffield, but a sense of the countryside prevails. Oil-paintings combine with light fabrics and colours to convey the feel of a 'comfortable, plush country house', and immaculate table-settings serve notice that intentions are serious. Menus may cover a limited range – in one case, for example, two of the four main courses were fish, one was vegetarian and one beef – but they turn up some bright-sounding flavours in the form of sardines marinated in chilli and lemon, or roast fillet of brill with a cumin and coriander crust served with mango salsa. The vegetarian option can be equally vivid, perhaps incorporating sweet potato in filo pastry on coconut and basil rice, accompanied by courgettes stuffed with walnuts, and a pineapple and chilli salad. 'I am a vegetarian and this is the best meal I have eaten,' ran one report.

Lest we convey the impression that Tessa Bramley's food is all about Thai spices and tropical fruit, it is worth noting the more traditional leanings apparent in calf's liver with braised red cabbage, or confit of Barbary duck on an apple salad with raspberry dressing. Local produce (game, for example) is a feature, and the kitchen garden makes its own seasonal contribution. All is pulled together by the kitchen's 'unforced skill', and one visitor noted 'an excellent match between ambition and achievement', although a couple of reporters felt that the old edge was missing. English and Irish cheeses are a strong point, and desserts sometimes play on a theme: a citrus trio of lemon tart, passion-fruit soufflé and lime sorbet, or a chocolate selection. Service has been dubbed professional, friendly and knowledgeable.

A short list of around 75 wines which have been carefully selected to complement the food will be presented, but do ask to see the full list if wine is your thing. High-quality bins abound, from lovely old burgundies to classed growth clarets dating back to 1945, and Alsace seems to be a bit of a passion too. Germany and Spain make some fine contributions, while the New World provides a few top producers. Prices can be high, but some good drinking can be found below £20, starting with house wines at £14. CELLARMAN'S CHOICE: St-Joseph Blanc, Clos de l'Arbalestrier 1987, Emile Florentin, £32; Tim Knappstein Cabernet-Merlot 1994, Clare Valley, S. Australia, £25.

CHEFS: Tessa Bramley, Nathan Smith and Andrew Gilbert PROPRIETORS: Tessa and Andrew Bramley OPEN: Tue to Fri and Sun L 12 to 2, Tue to Sat D 7 to 10 (booking essential L and D) CLOSED: 26 and 31 Dec, 1 Jan MEALS: Set L and D £28 to £38 SERVICE: not inc, card slips closed CARDS: Amex, Delta, Diners, MasterCard, Switch, Visa DETAILS: 50 seats. Private parties: 50 main room, 30 and 50 private rooms. Car park. Vegetarian meals. Children's helpings. No smoking in dining-room. Wheelchair access (also WC). Music

RIPLEY Surrey map 3

Michels'

13 High Street, Ripley GU23 6AQ
TEL: (01483) 224777 FAX: (01483) 222940 COOKING **5**
off A3, 4m SW of Cobham COST £32–£65

The Michels' restaurant occupies a brick-fronted Georgian house in leafiest Surrey, where generously sized tables, damask napkins and discreet lighting herald a formal approach. Prices, too, suggest that this is a place for special occasions. Although Erik Michel's cooking might well be considered avant-garde across the Channel, it is founded on familiar steamed sea bass, wild mushroom risotto and magret of duck, often with a classical accompaniment in the form of an oyster mousseline sauce for asparagus tips, or a madeira sauce for pork fillet. Where he departs from custom is in sometimes unusual combinations such as pan-fried calf's liver with sorrel and sweet potato.

Erik Michel has a sharp talent capable of delivering dishes of subtlety and complexity, having produced stuffed pumpkin on a Gruyère sauce for example, and salmon fillet on a bed of cabbage cooked in gewurztraminer and bacon. Each dish is conceived as a whole, so vegetables are an integral part of main courses. Dinner includes a plate of (improvable) Anglo-French cheeses before desserts of spiced-bread ice-cream with apple sauce, or warm rum baba. The Michels have addressed service problems by appointing extra staff. Some well-chosen New World bottles add interest to the weighty collection of French classics, and nine house wines start at £9.50.

CHEF: Erik Michel PROPRIETORS: Erik and Karen Michel OPEN: Tue to Fri and Sun L 12.30 to 1.30, Tue to Sat D 7.30 to 9 (7 to 9.30 Sat) CLOSED: early Jan, 2 weeks Aug MEALS: alc (main courses £16 to £22). Set L £21, Set D Tue to Fri £23 to £30 SERVICE: not inc CARDS: Amex, Delta, MasterCard, Switch, Visa DETAILS: 50 seats. Private parties: 12 private room. Car park. Children welcome. Music

RIPLEY North Yorkshire map 9

▲ *Boar's Head*

Ripley HG3 3AY COOKING 5
TEL: (01423) 771888 FAX: (01423) 771509 COST £24–£54

Sir William Ingilby's portrait hangs above the staircase at this old coaching-inn on the Harrogate to Ripon road. He rebuilt Ripley in the 1830s, but closed the Boar's Head upon discovering that his tenants and labourers were having rather too jovial a time there. The present generation of Ingilbys reopened it in 1990, complete with comfortable lounges and renovated guest rooms.

Chef Steven Chesnutt brings his own class to the enterprise, having worked previously at the Chester Grosvenor and Waterside Inn at Bray (see entries). Not surprisingly, refinement marks the cooking, but that doesn't preclude a few modern pyrotechnics as well. Try a 'tarte Tatin' of celeriac, beetroot and (of course) apple with a walnut and orange salad to start, followed perhaps by a piece of seared salmon, laid on a gribiche potato-cake and anointed with Italian parsley liqueur. Braised shank of Yorkshire lamb is accorded more classical treatment, served with mustardy mashed potato and a port and rosemary sauce. Desserts may include a simple assiette of champagne-glazed fruits, or what the menu describes as 'huge ginger tubes', stuffed with orange and mascarpone syllabub and served with berries steeped in red wine. Willing and knowledgeable service adds to the appeal. The long wine list is hearteningly inclusive and displays some canny buying in many areas. Prices on the whole are more than reasonable. A quartet of French house wines starts things off at £9.95.

CHEF: Steven Chesnutt PROPRIETOR: Sir Thomas Ingilby OPEN: all week 12 to 1.45, 7 to 9.30 MEALS: Set L Mon to Sat £13.50 (2 courses) to £17.50, Set L Sun £14.95, Set D £27.50 to £36. Bar food available SERVICE: not inc, card slips closed CARDS: Amex, Diners, MasterCard, Switch, Visa DETAILS: 45 seats. 60 seats outside. Private parties: 30 main room. Car park. Children's helpings. No children under 10. No smoking in 1 dining-room. Wheelchair access (also WC). Music ACCOMMODATION: 25 rooms, all with bath/shower. TV. Phone. B&B £85 to £110. Deposit: £50. Rooms for disabled. Children welcome. Baby facilities. Dogs welcome in bedrooms only. Afternoon teas. Garden. Fishing (*The Which? Hotel Guide*)

ROADE Northamptonshire map 5

Roade House

16 High Street, Roade NN7 2NW
TEL: (01604) 863372 COOKING 5
off A508, 4m S of Northampton COST £21–£40

After 15 years, changes are afoot. The Kewleys are building six bedrooms, expanding the kitchen, and aiming to become 'a small hotel rather than a restaurant-with-rooms', although food will still be the main focus of the operation. Some of this will have been completed by the time the *Guide* appears, and the knock-on effects include more staff to cope with the extra workload, among them an extra pair of hands in the kitchen. 'I become more instinctively conservative as time passes, and I am opposed to novelty purely for its own sake,' writes Chris Kewley, putting down a marker that the food looks set to continue in the same vein as before.

Meals revolve around straightforward but generally prime ingredients of fillet steak, halibut, calf's liver and pigeon breast, accompanied by a sauce in the tried-and-tested mould: wild mushroom with chicken, port and red wine for roast woodpigeon, and apple and calvados for duck. The pairings are fine, and timing is accurate, although results have not always matched the kitchen's best performance. Vegetables come as a selection rather than as part of a dish. Anything with poached egg – warm smoked salmon, or roast asparagus – is usually a good way to begin, and desserts tend to be filling: iced tiramisù parfait with coffee sauce, or sticky toffee pudding with butterscotch sauce. Europe and Australia account for most of the 60-odd wines, which are varied and fairly priced. House French is £10.

CHEFS: Chris Kewley and Steven Barnes PROPRIETORS: Chris and Susan Kewley OPEN: Tue to Fri and Sun L 12.30 to 1.45, Mon to Sat D 7 to 9.30 (10 Sat) CLOSED: bank hols MEALS: alc D (main courses £11 to £16). Set L £16. BYO £7 SERVICE: net prices, card slips closed CARDS: Amex, MasterCard, Switch, Visa DETAILS: 45 seats. Private parties: 50 main room. Car park. Children's helpings. No cigars/pipes in dining-room. Wheelchair access (also WC). Music

ROMALDKIRK Co Durham map 10

▲ *Rose & Crown*

Romaldkirk DL12 9EB
TEL: (01833) 650213 FAX: (01833) 650828 COOKING **2**
on B6277, 6m NW of Barnard Castle COST £18–£41

There is something disarmingly English about Romaldkirk, with its two greens, stocks, ancient church and historical water pumps. The Rose & Crown fits the place to a T. The building, which dates from 1733, is cherished and cared for by Christopher and Alison Davy, and their devotion shows in the polished woodwork and gleaming brass. An ever-growing band of local suppliers provides the best the region can offer, and daily four-course dinner menus are peppered with seasonal ideas: braised pheasant comes with black pudding and roasted shallots, while loin of venison is served on pan haggerty with madeira sauce. In spring there are Teesdale Fell lambs, and there's always roast rib of beef with Yorkshire pudding for Sunday lunch. Fish-lovers are treated to mussels with bacon and cider, or fillet of halibut with beurre blanc. Cheeses are from the North Country, and desserts range from queen of puddings to home-made Amaretto ice-cream. Bar meals are also highly commended. Nine wines are sold by the glass, and the full list is an enthusiastic trot from the New World into the Old. House wine is £9.50.

CHEFS: Christopher Davy and Dawn Stephenson PROPRIETORS: Christopher and Alison Davy OPEN: Sun L 12 to 1.30, Mon to Sat D 7.30 to 9 CLOSED: 24 to 26 Dec MEALS: Set L Sun £11.95, Set D £23. Bar food available all week L and D SERVICE: not inc, card slips closed CARDS: MasterCard, Switch, Visa DETAILS: 24 seats. Private parties: 30 main room. Car park. Children's helpings. No children under 6 at D. No smoking in dining-room. No music ACCOMMODATION: 12 rooms, all with bath/shower. TV. Phone. B&B £58 to £88. Deposit: £30. Rooms for disabled. Children welcome. Dogs welcome in bedrooms only. Afternoon teas (*The Which? Hotel Guide*)

ROMSEY Hampshire map 2

Old Manor House

21 Palmerston Street, Romsey SO51 8GF COOKING **6**
TEL: (01794) 517353 COST £28–£50

The beamed and gnarled Tudor house is easy to find in the centre of Romsey. Mauro Bregoli is an enthusiastic forager after wild mushrooms, and also a pork butcher of repute. First rear your pig (a local breed that incorporates a bit of wild boar in its make-up), then turn it into coppa, cotechino and prosciutto, and serve the first simply with extra virgin oil and black pepper, the second hot with lentils, and the last in a dish of 'buttery, silken' tagliatelle with peas. Carpaccio of foie gras was a novel and inspiring experience for one correspondent. It came on a bed of watercress and walnuts, the whole thing sprinkled with lemon juice and sea salt: 'there was very little of it and yet it was so satisfying'.

Set-price menus offer a choice of five starters and main courses, but the more adventurous may opt for the à la carte in order to try, for example, barbecued eel – 'three hulking fillets' accompanied by a ramekin dish of sharp salsa verde – or roe deer escalopes with red onion confit, spiced apricots and prunes. Vegetables, served separately, are good, though one reporter would have wished for larger portions. Crème brûlée is successfully flavoured with fennel and scattered with thyme, or there might be white-chocolate and mint délice, or lemon tart. Mixed reports of service show some people occasionally encountering the language barrier, but when Signora Bregoli is in charge, all is relaxed civility.

That the wine list boasts a very fine collection of Italian bins is hardly surprising, but the presence of so many top-class clarets (five vintages of Ch. Pétrus, seven of Ch. Latour) is an unexpected bonus for those with deep pockets. Fortunately, there is the odd bargain to be had as well. Sixteen house wines priced between £11.50 and £19.50 come in very handy too.

CHEF/PROPRIETOR: Mauro Bregoli OPEN: Tue to Sun L, Tue to Sat D 12 to 2, 7 to 9.30 CLOSED: 1 week Christmas, 1 Jan MEALS: alc (main courses £12.50 to £17.50). Set L £17.50, Set D £19.50 SERVICE: not inc, card slips closed CARDS: Amex, Delta, MasterCard, Switch, Visa DETAILS: 45 seats. Private parties: 40 main room, 20 private room. Car park. Vegetarian meals. Children welcome. No cigars/pipes in dining room. No music

ROSS-ON-WYE Hereford & Worcester map 5

Pheasants

52 Edde Cross Street, Ross-on-Wye HR9 7BZ COOKING **3**
TEL: (01989) 565751 COST £34–£41

Eileen Brunnarius's civilised restaurant and 'wine-lover's paradise' has celebrated its tenth birthday by making a few changes. Accommodation is no longer offered, and in place of the *carte* is a set, three-course menu with around five choices at each stage. 'Authentic British with European influences' is how Adrian Wells, ebullient front-of-house, describes Eileen's cooking. Starters of leeks provençale with tapénade-spread croûtons, and a simple dish of asparagus tips with salmon confit, have both been praised, and main-courses of beef fillet in rye whisky and green peppercorn sauce, and roast sea trout with cucumber spaghetti and dill hollandaise, have also pleased. To finish, look for 'quite delicious' bread-and-butter pudding, or apple charlotte with lemon, cloves and butterscotch sauce. Incidentals such as vegetables, nutty brown bread, and petits fours score highly too.

Enthusiasm for wines shines through in the highly individual list which opens with 24 bins chosen for their food-enhancing flavours, arranged by style and offered on a 'try before you buy basis'. The main list continues with a varied collection, mostly priced under £20. An exemplary 28 fine fortified wines are offered by the glass as 'starter partners', and there are 26 ports or pudding wines. CELLARMAN'S CHOICE: Bourgogne Hautes Côtes de Nuits 1994, Dom. Thévenot, £22.80; Rioja Alavesa 1993, Remelluri Reserva, £23.30.

CHEF/PROPRIETOR: Eileen Brunnarius OPEN: Tue to Sat D only 7 (6.30 May to Sept) to 9.30 CLOSED: 25 Dec to 2 Jan, 1 week early June, bank hols MEALS: Set D £25, plus Set D 6.30 to 7.30 May to Sept £18.50 (2 courses). BYO £5 SERVICE: net prices CARDS: Amex, Delta, Diners, MasterCard, Switch, Visa DETAILS: 22 seats. Private parties: 10 main room. Vegetarian meals. No children under 12. No smoking in dining-room. Wheelchair access (no WC). Music

ROWDE Wiltshire map 2

George & Dragon ✱

High Street, Rowde SN10 2PN COOKING **6**
TEL: (01380) 723053 FAX: (01380) 724738 COST £19–£47

If you notice an even sprightlier mood than normal in the George & Dragon, that is because Tim and Helen Withers are now the proud freeholders, masters of all they survey, and at liberty to buy their wines where they will. Those who have supported their cheery country pub/restaurant over the years will share their glee while continuing to enjoy the impeccable fish cookery that is the kitchen's forte. Mediterranean inspiration is never far away, so the fish soup comes with rouille, Gruyère and croûtons, the tuna comes as carpaccio with pickled cucumber, and hake is roasted with peppers and served with aïoli. 'The great thing about the food is the balance achieved between fish and sauce: light, almost frothy hollandaise with salmon fish-cakes, and a pleasantly sweet cider sauce with baked gurnard.' Vegetable accompaniments are full of imagination too: pink fir-apple potatoes, and 'lightly but tantalisingly spiced' stir-fried shredded cabbage, for example.

Puddings are designed to indulge, with the likes of marmalade sponge with whisky sauce and custard, brown sugar meringues and Jersey cream, or lemon curd tart. The sheer warmth with which it is all dispensed is what keeps this place high in people's affections. The new wine list is from Reid Wines of Bristol, and makes inroads into some of the world's more dynamic regions. Prices may ascend a little sharply for a pub/restaurant, but the quality is not in dispute. House wines are vin de pays varietals at £9.50.

CHEFS: Tim Withers, Hannah Seal and Kate Phillips PROPRIETORS: Tim and Helen Withers OPEN: Tue to Sat 12 to 2, 7 to 10 CLOSED: 2 weeks Christmas and New Year MEALS: alc (main courses £6 to £18). Set L £8.50 (2 courses) to £10 SERVICE: not inc, card slips closed CARDS: Delta, MasterCard, Switch, Visa DETAILS: 35 seats. 20 seats outside. Private parties: 12 main room. Car park. Vegetarian meals. Children's helpings. No smoking in dining-room. No music

RYE East Sussex map 3

Landgate Bistro £

5–6 Landgate, Rye TN31 7LH COOKING 5
TEL: (01797) 222829 COST £23–£37

'The food at the Landgate Bistro is head and shoulders above anywhere else in Rye,' commented a local reporter. Stripped-down and simple décor suits the bistro style, and service is 'willing enough in spirit' but 'don't expect any frills or flattery'. What you're there for is Toni Ferguson-Lees's accomplished cooking, a technique continually honed since 1980 and capable of scaling great heights. A correspondent who encountered an up-and-down performance praised a warm crab terrine that combined resonance and lightness, roast partridge with spiced red cabbage, and a dessert of 'perfectly cooked' quince compote with a 'nicely balanced' lemon mousse. Less successful were a first course of courgette with almond stuffing, and 'dry' potato gratin.

Desserts aim for simplicity, and may include mango sorbet, ginger mousse, or banana ice-cream scented with cardamom. The midweek fixed-price menus of three courses plus coffee are deemed good value. Wines are a cannily chosen and imaginative bunch, and seven are available by the glass. House wines from Mommessin are £8.40 a bottle.

CHEF: Toni Ferguson-Lees PROPRIETORS: Nick Parkin and Toni Ferguson-Lees OPEN: Tue to Sat D only 7 to 9.30 CLOSED: 1 week Christmas, 2 weeks autumn MEALS: alc (main courses £9 to £12). Set D Tue to Thurs £15.90. BYO £5 SERVICE: net prices, card slips closed CARDS: Amex, Delta, Diners, MasterCard, Switch, Visa DETAILS: 30 seats. Private parties: 30 main room. Children's helpings. No cigars/pipes in dining-room. Music

ST IVES Cornwall map 1

Hunters

NEW ENTRY

16 St Andrews Street, St Ives TR26 1AH COOKING 3
TEL: (01736) 797074 COST £22–£40

The Browns are veterans of superior pub catering, but have long been itching for a chance to run their own place and spread their wings a little. In spring of 1997, it came, and they are now installed in this little restaurant in a narrow street behind St Ia's church, decorated with stained-glass windows and vividly coloured plaster mouldings. Fish and shellfish are the mainstays, and the cooking keeps things refreshingly simple. Crab mornay uses the local catch, and timing of main-course fish dishes is bang-on, a large piece of succulent monkfish tail gaining piquancy from preserved ginger, while, at inspection, a piece of roast hake was similarly moist and given a prawn and white wine sauce. Vegetable selections are a cut above the norm, a dish of grated courgettes done in garlic and cream standing out. Peach chantilly in a brandy-snap adds a touch of fancy to the puddings, or there's splendidly rich treacle tart with good crisp pastry. The warm, chatty front-of-house approach makes for a thoroughly agreeable time, and note there is a 10 per cent discount for paying with cash. A very basic wine list offers everything except champagne for less than £16. House French is £6.95.

CHEF: Colin Brown PROPRIETORS: Mr and Mrs C.J. Brown OPEN: Sun L 12 to 2, Mon to Sat D 6.30 to 9.30 (later by arrangement) MEALS: alc (main courses £9 to £15) SERVICE: not inc CARDS: Delta, MasterCard, Switch, Visa DETAILS: 40 seats. No children under 11. No smoking in 1 dining-room. Music

Pig 'n' Fish

Norway Lane, St Ives TR26 1LZ — COOKING 4
TEL: (01736) 794204 — COST £29–£45

A disused fishing-shed on what some call the Cornish Riviera is home to the Sellars' piscatorial restaurant. More specifically, it's on the upper floor, a long, low-ceilinged room made bright with pleasing modern pictures. The menus these days suggest it might more accurately be called the Duck 'n' Fish, if either the starter of confit with new potatoes and cress, or the main course of Gressingham breast with chicory and balsamic, is anything to go by. Fishy offerings might include a ceviche of turbot with avocado, brill with leeks and a herbed butter sauce, or simple breaded plaice with tartare sauce. One reporter praised the way that even the more pungent accompaniments, such as the onions, garlic and lemon that came with hake, do not mask the fish itself, although some combinations – mashed swede with lemon sole, for example – may not be to everyone's taste. Not all desserts are equally successful, but a concoction called Lemon Delicious has met with approval. Service can be a little slow and silent but picks up considerably when Debby Sellars is in charge. A handwritten list of mainly white and French wines suits the food and starts with house Vin de Pays d'Oc at £9.50.

CHEF: Paul Sellars PROPRIETORS: Debby and Paul Sellars OPEN: Tue to Sat (and bank hol Mon) D only 7 to 9.30 (Nov to mid-Dec Fri and Sat only) CLOSED: mid-Dec to Mar MEALS: alc (main courses £11.50 to £16.50). Set D £19.50 SERVICE: not inc CARDS: MasterCard, Switch, Visa DETAILS: 30 seats. 20 seats outside. Private parties: 6 main room. Children's helpings. No children under 2. Music

ST KEYNE Cornwall — map 1

▲ *Well House*

St Keyne PL14 4RN
TEL: (01579) 342001 FAX: (01579) 343891
on B3254, 3m S of Liskeard; at end of village near church follow sign to St Keyne Well — NEW CHEF — COST £34–£47

The house, built at the turn of the century by a Victorian tea planter, is considered 'mildly eccentric' – which place of character isn't? – and its quiet location is valued by reporters who come to relax and get away from things. Nick Wainford is usually on hand to provide a welcome (often with the help of four spaniels), and rural views from the yellow-painted, pink-furnished dining-room contribute to its 'sunshine feeling'. After Wayne Pearson, who had cooked here since the end of 1993, departed for Holne Chase (see entry, Ashburton), a new chef was appointed. He left, so did another, and sous-chef Cameron Brown moved into the top job just as the *Guide* was going to press. The technically accomplished food has typically been contemporary without being showy, buttressed by quality wines at very fair prices, starting with house wine at £8.50. Reports please.

CHEF: Cameron Brown PROPRIETOR: Nick Wainford OPEN: all week 12.30 to 2, 7 to 9.15 MEALS: Set L and D £21.95 (2 courses) to £31.70 SERVICE: not inc, card slips closed CARDS: Amex, Delta, Diners, MasterCard, Switch, Visa DETAILS: 32 seats. 12 seats outside. Private parties: 30 main room. Car park. Vegetarian meals. No children under 8 at D. No cigars/pipes in dining room. Wheelchair access (also WC). No music ACCOMMODATION: 9 rooms, all with bath/shower. TV. Phone. B&B £70 to £145. Deposit: £50. Children welcome. Baby facilities. Well-behaved dogs welcome. Garden. Swimming-pool (*The Which? Hotel Guide*)

ST MARGARET'S AT CLIFFE Kent map 3

▲ *Wallett's Court*

West Cliffe, St Margaret's at Cliffe CT15 6EW
TEL: (01304) 852424 FAX: (01304) 853430
on B2058, off A258 Dover to Deal road, 3m NE of Dover

COOKING 3
COST £35–£51

When the Oakleys first gazed on the overgrown wreck that Wallett's Court was in the mid-1970s, it must have required more than the usual measure of what estate agents like to call 'vision' to see that it could become a fetchingly restored country-house hotel. Renovations continue, and an appreciative clientele – often stopping off before the Channel crossing – are grateful for the warmth and hospitality with which it is run. Jacobean huntsman's platter turns out to be a slab of 'moist and well-seasoned' wild boar terrine served with spiced pear chutney. Wild salmon may be a main-course option, perhaps accompanied by king prawns, or there might be baked rabbit with sage in 'good gravy' paired with bubble and squeak with smoked bacon. Desserts have included a version of Eton mess with raspberries, as well as chocolate and nut tart with crumbly short pastry and coffee ice-cream. Service gives the impression that it is still learning the ropes, but the enthusiasm is beyond reproach. France is the centre of gravity on the wine list, offerings from elsewhere being little more than cursory, but prices are mostly keen. House wines from France and Italy are £14.

CHEF: Christopher Oakley PROPRIETORS: the Oakley family OPEN: all week D only 7 to 9 CLOSED: 1 week Christmas MEALS: alc Mon to Fri (main courses £17 to £19.50). Set D Sun to Fri £23.50, Set D Sat £29.50. BYO £5 SERVICE: not inc CARDS: Amex, Delta, Diners, MasterCard, Switch, Visa DETAILS: 60 seats. Private parties: 35 main room, 30 private room. Car park. Children's helpings. No smoking in dining-room. Wheelchair access (no WC). Music ACCOMMODATION: 12 rooms, all with bath/shower. TV. Phone. B&B £50 to £85. Rooms for disabled. Children welcome. Baby facilities. Afternoon teas. Garden (*The Which? Hotel Guide*)

ST MARTIN'S Isles of Scilly

▲ *St Martin's Hotel*

NEW ENTRY

Lower Town, St Martin's TR25 0QW
TEL: (01720) 422092 FAX: (01720) 422298

COOKING 5
COST £46–£55

If you are washed up on St Martin's and need a place for the night, you won't have too far to look. This is the only hotel on the island. It is well disguised, too, being a collection of rough cast grey-stone cottages rather than one unified building, but reports have flowed in of heart-warming hospitality and good food. In the bay-fronted dining-room looking over the quay to the isles of Tean and Tresco, Patrick Pierre Tweedie's cooking shows something of his training at Le Gavroche (see entry, London): in terrine of foie gras with figs and hazelnuts, perhaps, or tender, pink roast pigeon on Puy lentils and salsify with an extravagantly rich sauce.

This is cooking in the grand manner, and lavish treatments are extended to fish dishes too: brill and lobster are sauté together and given a beurre blanc that incorporates champagne and keta caviare. More bubbly goes into a pear charlotte on an intense blackcurrant coulis. Other desserts include soufflés and symphonies – the latter of chocolate and nuts – or there are mature English and Continental cheeses served with olive and walnut bread. The bare bones of a good wine list are there, with one or two great burgundy growers and tempting Alsace wines from Sparr, but selections outside France are more mundane. House white is Sauvignon de St-Bris from Fèvre and the red a fine Navarra blend, both £13.50.

CHEF: Patrick Pierre Tweedie PROPRIETOR: Peter Sykes OPEN: all week D only 7 to 10 CLOSED: Nov to March MEALS: Set D £35. Bar L available SERVICE: not inc, card slips closed CARDS: Amex, Delta, Diners, MasterCard, Switch, Visa DETAILS: 60 seats. 50 seats outside. Private parties: 90 main room. No children under 12. No smoking in dining-room. Music ACCOMMODATION: 30 rooms, all with bath/shower. TV. Phone. D,B&B £95 to £350. Deposit: 20%. Children welcome. Baby facilities. Dogs welcome. Afternoon teas. Garden. Swimming-pool (*The Which? Hotel Guide*)

ST MICHAEL'S ON WYRE Lancashire map 8

Mallards

Garstang Road, St Michael's on Wyre PR3 0TE COOKING 1
TEL: (01995) 679661 COST £17–£33

The Steels have been running this small, comfortable restaurant in the former village smithy for a decade. Ann manages front-of-house with efficiency and care, and John works to a well-tried formula in the kitchen, offering a flexible menu of two to four courses at dinner. Sunday lunch is considered 'exceptional value for money'. The style is simple, straightforward and professionally turned out, offering home-made soups, a fish of the day, and meaty main courses of lamb steak with onion gravy, or sirloin steak with a creamy garlic and mushroom sauce. Black pudding appears in various guises – baked with leeks and cheese sauce, or stuffed into a breast of local chicken along with some apple, to be served with a creamy mustard sauce – while desserts offer few surprises. A good spread of sensibly chosen and reasonably priced wines begins with house French at £8.50.

CHEF: John Steel PROPRIETORS: Ann and John Steel OPEN: Sun L 12 to 2.30, Mon to Sat D 7 to 9 (9.30 Sat) CLOSED: 1 week Jan, 2 weeks July/Aug MEALS: Set L Sun £11.50, Set D £15.50 (2 courses) to £18.95 SERVICE: not inc, card slips closed CARDS: Delta, MasterCard, Switch, Visa DETAILS: 30 seats. Private parties: 36 main room. Car park. Children's helpings. No smoking while others eat. Music

SALE Greater Manchester map 8

Hanni's £

4 Brooklands Road, Sale M33 3SQ COOKING 1
TEL: (0161) 973 6606 FAX: (0161) 928 3901 COST £21–£39

Morocco eastwards to Iran, with excursions to Caucasia, India, Greece and Italy are the extent of the menu's coverage. Baba ganoush (grilled aubergine with tomato, onion, pepper, garlic and spices), moutabal (baked aubergine purée mixed with garlic, tahina and yoghurt), and hummus with fried aubergines could make a fascinating comparative tasting of aubergine meze. Main dishes include a variety of kebabs and couscous, plus salads, a few fish dishes – samak magli (fried halibut), for example – and a page of house specialities. Equally varied desserts range from halva, and fried halloumi cheese, to dates or figs. Finish with powerful Turkish coffee. What is offered might seem ambitious for a small family restaurant but standards are sustained; so are traditional Middle Eastern hospitality and courtesy. Good Middle Eastern producers are well represented on the wine list, and house French is £11.

CHEF: Mr Hoonanian PROPRIETOR: Hanni Al-Taraboulsy OPEN: Mon to Sat D only 6 to 10.30 (11 Fri and Sat) CLOSED: 25 and 26 Dec, last 2 weeks Aug MEALS: alc (main courses £8 to £12.50) SERVICE: not inc CARDS: Amex, Delta, MasterCard, Switch, Visa DETAILS: 50 seats. Private parties: 50 main room. Vegetarian meals. Children's helpings. Music. Air-conditioned

SANDGATE Kent map 3

▲ *Sandgate Hotel, La Terrasse*

Wellington Terrace, The Esplanade,
Sandgate CT20 3DY COOKING 7
TEL: (01303) 220444 FAX: (01303) 220496 COST £30–£59

English seaside landladies have been serving greasy bacon and fried eggs, powdered mash and frozen peas with truculent hostility for as long as anyone can remember. Then along comes a Frenchman pushing foie gras, lobster ravioli, and Valrhona chocolate puddings in a sea-front boarding-house a handy five minutes from Le Shuttle. It makes you weep: for all the seaside towns that don't have one of these. The Victorian house differs from the norm in having huge comfortable sofas, open fires, fresh flowers, paintings of Samuel Gicqueau's native Loire, and a terrace for fine weather. Zara Jackson is English, but as far removed from the curlered landlady as you could imagine, and service by the French brigade is 'simply excellent'.

Advantage is taken of local seafood supplies, with shellfish often dominating first courses – pan-fried langoustines with a croustillant of sesame seeds and balsamic vinegar, for instance – while the 'modern classical' approach shows to good effect in a main course of, say, sea bass covered in thin potato scales and served on braised cabbage with a red wine sauce. Although there may be fewer meat dishes, workmanship is still a significant component, as in a boned leg of guinea-fowl filled with a morel mousse, served with wild mushroom ravioli and spinach. Close ties with France produce cheeses from Philippe Olivier, black truffles to wrap in puff pastry alongside scallops in a butter sauce, and the wherewithal to make a ballottine of foie gras with Sauternes jelly. Canapés and petits fours sandwich the meal, breakfast is 'the best sort of Continental', and 'incredible value' was the judgement of one who ate midweek.

The French connection is emphasised on the wine list with only half-a-dozen other countries getting a look-in with one or two bottles. Nevertheless the list presents a wide range of styles, including some fine vintage clarets and burgundies, and – *quelle surprise* – a good selection from the Loire. House wines are £11.50 a bottle, £2.60 a glass. CELLARMAN'S CHOICE: Givry Clos des Vignes Rondes 1993, François Lumpp, £19.90; Chorey-lès Beaune 1993, Dom. Maillard, £22.

CHEF: Samuel Gicqueau PROPRIETORS: Samuel Gicqueau and Zara Jackson OPEN: Tue to Sun L 12 to 1.30, Tue to Sat D 7 to 9.30 CLOSED: mid-Jan to mid-Feb MEALS: alc (main courses £13.50 to £19.50). Set L and D Tue to Fri £18.50, Set L Sat and Sun £24.50, Set D Sat £24.50 SERVICE: not inc CARDS: Amex, Delta, Diners, MasterCard, Switch, Visa DETAILS: 26 seats. Private parties: 26 main room. Car park. Vegetarian meals. Children's helpings. No smoking in dining-room. Music ACCOMMODATION: 15 rooms, all with bath/shower. TV. Phone. B&B £39 to £67. Deposit: £20. Children welcome. Baby facilities. Afternoon teas

SANDIWAY Cheshire map 7

▲ *Nunsmere Hall*

Tarporley Road, Sandiway CW8 2ES
TEL: (01606) 889100 FAX: (01606) 889055 COOKING **6**
off A49, 4m SW of Northwich COST £27–£65

The site, on a wooded peninsula by a 60-acre lake in rural Cheshire, is enviable, and 'the gardens are a joy'. To call the hotel posh – as in port out, starboard home – is appropriate, given that it was built at the beginning of the century by a shipping magnate, Sir Aubrey Brocklebank. Nunsmere's persona as hotel began in the mid-1980s, and chef Simon Radley, who arrived in mid-1996, produces imaginative and cleverly constructed dishes that generally bring out the best in flavours and textures. A Savoy cabbage parcel of poached salmon, studded with crabmeat and surrounded by griddled scallops on a moat of sweet carrot sauce was the highlight of a meal for one reporter, and other first courses have included terrine of rabbit with foie gras and leeks. A main course of saddle of venison with shallot and juniper choucroute slightly disappointed at inspection, although the venison itself was judged well-hung and 'brilliant'.

Other main-course options might include plainly grilled sea bass with fennel dauphinois and tomato confit, or pot roast guinea-fowl with parsnips and mushrooms. Vegetarians get a separate menu, and 'well thought out to the last detail' describes a caramel trio of warm butterscotch pudding, soufflé glacé of praline and ginger, and caramel cream. Ingredients are outstanding throughout, canapés are 'interesting and impeccable', and vegetables – some grown on the premises – and freshly baked breads are well reported. Service by French staff gets top marks. The wine list is built around the classical French regions (don't miss the connoisseurs' selection at the end), with some interesting supporting bins from the New World. Most of the high-quality stuff is over £20, but there is a reasonable choice below, with house wines starting from £13.50.

CHEF: Simon Radley PROPRIETORS: Malcolm and Julie McHardy OPEN: Mon to Fri and Sun L 12 to 1.45, all week D 7 to 9.45 (9.15 Sun) MEALS: alc D Mon to Sat (main courses £16 to £21). Set L Mon to Fri £16.95 (2 courses) to £19.50, Set L Sun £19.50, Set D Sun £30 SERVICE: not inc, card slips closed CARDS: Amex, Delta, Diners, MasterCard, Switch, Visa DETAILS: 60 seats. 60 seats outside. Private parties: 70 main room, 42 private room. Car park. Vegetarian meals. Children's helpings for under-10s before 7. No smoking in dining-room. Wheelchair access (also WC). Music ACCOMMODATION: 32 rooms, all with bath/shower. TV. Phone. Room only £105 to £300. Rooms for disabled. Children welcome. Baby facilities. Afternoon teas. Garden (*The Which? Hotel Guide*)

SAWBRIDGEWORTH Hertfordshire map 3

Shoes 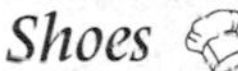

52 Bell Street, Sawbridgeworth CM21 9AN COOKING **2**
TEL: (01279) 722554 COST £20–£48

In the past hundred years, the building in which Shoes is housed has been, among other things, a coaching-inn, furniture shop, insurance brokers and even a shoe shop. The restaurant is light and airy, with bags of space and good-quality linen, crockery, glasses and cutlery. Mark Green, at the stoves since late 1996, continues in Allan Stephens's shoes by crossing British ideas with French. Set lunch and dinner menus, changed weekly, run in tandem with a *carte,* and there is a separate vegetarian list. The choice is sensibly short but eclectic enough to satisfy most tastes.

Timbale of crab and asparagus makes a commendable first course, or there may be chicken and foie gras sausage with balsamic *jus.* A main course of pan-fried fillet steak is glazed with blue cheese and served with garlic rösti, while grilled red sea bream – 'what the chef really does well' – is accompanied by a raspberry vinegar sauce and crisp celeriac. Puddings range from an 'excellent' apple and caramel crumble to more unusual deep-fried prunes stuffed with frangipane. 'Polite, friendly and unhurried service' is typical of comments, as is 'they kept taking the wine away and hiding it'. *Shoes News,* a quarterly newsletter, alerts regulars to special evenings, jazz nights, and Spanish or Italian dinners, for instance. The wine list offers plenty of choice at below £20, with house French £10.25.

CHEF: Mark Green PROPRIETORS: Lyndon Wootton, and Peter and Doreen Gowan OPEN: Tue to Fri L 12 to 2, Mon to Sat D 7 to 9.30 CLOSED: 2 weeks after Christmas, 2 weeks Aug, bank hol Mons MEALS: alc (main courses £11 to £15.50). Set L £8.50 (2 courses) to £11, Set D Mon to Thur £17 SERVICE: not inc CARDS: Delta, MasterCard, Switch, Visa DETAILS: 60 seats. Private parties: 40 main room. Vegetarian meals. Children's helpings. No-smoking area. Wheelchair access (also WC). Music. Air-conditioned

'We went on one of the warmest evenings of the year and our table was set next to a radiator which was on full heat. When we asked for it to be turned off we were told it could not be done as there was a central heating system installed and the "plumber had made an error".' (On eating in Scotland)

SAXTON North Yorkshire map 9

Plough Inn £

Headwell Lane, Saxton LS24 9PB
TEL: (01937) 557242 COOKING 3
off A162, between Tadcaster and Sherburn in Elmet COST £18–£39

Standing at a crossroads in a small village near Tadcaster, the Plough is a white-painted early-Victorian edifice that has been a pub since before the war. To one side of the narrow corridor as you enter is a pair of connected rooms done in deep pink that form the restaurant. Here the whole approach, including Simon Treanor's food, is as unstuffy as one could ask for. A filo parcel of mixed fish and prawns with diced and shredded vegetables on a good shellfish sauce delivered plenty of flavour for one enthusiastic reporter, while lamb shank was roasted and served on the bone with roasted roots, its sauce a vigorous reduction that 'packed a punch'. Although main-course dishes are already garnished, more vegetables come on a separate plate. Classic desserts such as lemon tart and sticky toffee pudding do the business, even if on one occasion the sauce with the latter 'had gone rather lumpy'. The imaginative wine list is reasonably priced and starts with house French from Languedoc at £8.25.

CHEF: Simon Treanor PROPRIETORS: Simon and Nicola Treanor OPEN: Tue to Sun L 12 to 2, Tue to Sat D 6.30 to 10 CLOSED: 3 days Christmas, 1 to 15 Jan MEALS: alc Tue to Sat (main courses £9 to £12.50). Set L Sun £11.95, Set D £29.50 SERVICE: not inc, card slips closed CARDS: Delta, MasterCard, Switch, Visa DETAILS: 55 seats. 16 seats outside. Private parties: 55 main room. Car park. Vegetarian meals. Children's helpings. No smoking in dining-room. Wheelchair access (also WC). Music

SCARBOROUGH North Yorkshire map 9

Lanterna £

NEW ENTRY

33 Queen Street, Scarborough YO11 1HQ COOKING 3
TEL/FAX: (01723) 363616 COST £21–£42

In a quiet byway off Scarborough's main thoroughfare, Lanterna is a charmingly run Italian restaurant specialising in impeccably seasonal cookery with seafood the star of the show. Simple table-settings and half-height curtains at the windows lend the place a homely air, and the ornamental centrepiece is an antique Italian vine-sprayer (in case you were wondering). Scallops – tiny queenies of exemplary freshness – are cooked in white wine and butter, and unfussily garnished with a clump of watercress. Pasta shows up well: ravioli filled with spinach and ricotta with a 'concentrated and tasty' tomato, basil and garlic sauce of great panache. Steak au poivre, too, is well executed, the beef properly hung and thickly cut, the crusting of cracked peppercorns generously applied, while autumn diners may be regaled with hare marinated in Barbera wine, cloves and bay leaves and served with fried polenta. Desserts include Italian standards such as tiramisù and zabaglione. Good filter coffee comes with mini-meringues and amaretti. A straightforward short list of Italian wines is supplemented by a few from France and Germany. House wines are £9.75.

CHEF: Giorgio Alessio PROPRIETORS: Giorgio and Rachel Alessio OPEN: Mon to Sat 12 to 2, 6 to 11 CLOSED: 25 and 26 Dec, 1 Jan, first 2 weeks Feb MEALS: alc (main courses £9.50 to £16.50). BYO £5 SERVICE: not inc, card slips closed CARDS: Delta, MasterCard, Switch, Visa DETAILS: 30 seats. Private parties: 35 main room. Vegetarian meals. Children's helpings. No children under 2. Wheelchair access (no WC). Music. Air-conditioned

SEAFORD East Sussex map 3

Quincy's

42 High Street, Seaford BN25 1PL COOKING 3
TEL: (01323) 895490 COST £32–£38

One of the few bright spots along this stretch of coast, Quincy's is a small, comfortable, cottagey conversion in the old part of town. The gas fire may be a coal lookalike, but the food is real enough. Everything is reassuringly straightforward – décor, food and service – and 'it has the easy self-confidence that comes from knowing one's craft (and one's limitations)'. The choice is six to eight items per course, and Ian Dowding obviously approaches things with an open mind, offering Moroccan artichoke and almond soup, for example, or cured salmon with lime and ginger salsa and anchovy ice-cream.

There is an earthy dimension to the food, too, in crispy breast of duck with roasted root vegetables, and fillet steak with melted Gruyère cheese is 'good of its type, if this is the sort of thing you like'. The food may have a dinner-party feel to it, but it has 'more flair – and better puds – than most of the dinner parties I go to'. Indeed, puddings are a highlight, not least the 'spectacularly risen' soufflés (caramel, with rum ice-cream, for example), treacle tart, and sticky toffee pudding. Service is extremely friendly. The well-priced wine list is strongest in the French classics, but there are some interesting bottles from elsewhere, including three from England's Breaky Bottom. The selection of half-bottles is particularly good, with many priced under £8. House French is from £8.95 a bottle. CELLARMAN'S CHOICE: Côtes du Rhône 1993, E. Guigal, £14.95; Redwood Zinfandel 1995, California, £12.95.

CHEF: Ian Dowding PROPRIETORS: Ian and Dawn Dowding OPEN: Sun L 12 to 2, Tue to Sat D 7 to 10 MEALS: Set L and D £18.95 (2 courses) to £22.45. BYO £5 SERVICE: not inc CARDS: Amex, MasterCard, Visa DETAILS: 28 seats. Private parties: 20 main room. Vegetarian meals. Children's helpings. No smoking in 1 dining-room. Music

SEATON BURN Tyne & Wear map 10

▲ *Horton Grange*

Seaton Burn NE13 6BU
TEL: (01661) 860686 FAX: (01661) 860308 COOKING 5
off A1, at Stannington, 3m N of Newcastle upon Tyne COST £43–£52

Straddling town and country, on the outskirts of Newcastle, Horton Grange offers 'nocturnal peace' as a bonus for those who stay. Menus are handed out in the lounge and bar amid a profusion of flexibly arranged chairs and sofas, with foliage and flowers from the garden. The appeal combines 'the charm and professionalism of the owners', who ensure that everything proceeds smoothly and pleasantly, with well-crafted food that doesn't take too many risks. The style is country-house, with four courses, remarkably generous choice, and a repertoire that involves a lot of work behind the scenes. First courses are predominantly cold, along the lines of pork and mushroom terrine with apricot chutney, and are followed by soup or sorbet.

Fruits appear in sauces and as part of savoury dishes – poached apricots with honey-roast duck breast, for instance – and if the general tenor of accompaniments is traditional (for example, juniper berries with venison), then it is an indication of the sensible planning that Steven Martin brings to his dishes. Balance and interest seem to be the keynotes, judging by a breast of herb-crumbed chicken served with spinach, mustard sauce and an onion and smoked bacon tartlet. Seafood, meanwhile, has included Orkney crab with smoked salmon, and a main course of Tweed salmon, steamed and served with noodles on a basil and tomato sauce. Desserts are impressively presented, and pastry-work is good. The short wine list omits vintages and begins with house Ochoa from Navarra at £10.90.

CHEF: Steven Martin PROPRIETORS: Andrew and Sue Shilton OPEN: Mon to Sat D only 7 to 8.30 CLOSED: 25 and 26 Dec MEALS: Set D £34. BYO £3.50 SERVICE: not inc, card slips closed CARDS: Amex, MasterCard, Switch, Visa DETAILS: 60 seats. Private parties: 60 main room. Car park. Vegetarian meals. No smoking in dining-room. Wheelchair access (also WC). Music ACCOMMODATION: 9 rooms, all with bath/shower. TV. Phone. B&B £59 to £90. Rooms for disabled. Garden. Fishing (*The Which? Hotel Guide*)

SHAFTESBURY Dorset map 2

La Fleur de Lys 🍷

25 Salisbury Street, Shaftesbury SP7 8EL COOKING **4**
TEL: (01747) 853717 COST **£32–£50**

Refurbishment in early 1997 may have opened out the dining-room (now done up with wood panelling, dark green and gold), but the aim, write the owners, is to maintain the feeling of intimacy and personal attention that have been lavished on their regulars over the past six years. Non-regulars should note that this restaurant doesn't exactly announce its presence to the world: find it above the stables behind a private house, at the end of a passageway that gives on to a secluded courtyard.

The cooking avoids making an unnecessary show of itself too. It looks good on the plate, but extraneous garnishes and garish combinations are out. Lunch may begin with a tossed salad of smoked chicken, apples, bacon, lentils and cos in grain-mustard dressings, and go on to salmon on a creamy sorrel sauce. Dinner can be either fixed price or à la carte, the range taking in smoked haddock soufflé wrapped in a fillet of lemon sole (a labour of love, that), or a riotously fruity duck breast dish that incorporates not just caramelised apples and kumquats but also a passion-fruit sauce into the bargain. Puddings may be as ground-breaking as pancakes filled with figs served with ice-cream made of halva, or as traditional as a dish of red berries with clotted cream. The wine list opens with a page of fine clarets dating back to 1976, moves on to a reliable collection from classical France, then ventures forth to newer regions with some appealing bins from South Africa, Australia and New Zealand. House wines, two French and two

South African, start at £11. CELLARMAN'S CHOICE: Stoneleigh Vineyard Riesling 1995, Marlborough, New Zealand, £15; Mont Gras Merlot 1994, Colchagua Valley, Chile, £15.

CHEFS: D. Shepherd and M. Preston PROPRIETORS: D. Shepherd, D.M. Griffin and M. Preston OPEN: Tue to Sun L 12 to 2.30, Mon to Sat D 7 to 10 CLOSED: Mon D Jan to Mar, occasionally Jan MEALS: alc (main courses £15 to £18). Set D Mon to Thur £19.95 (2 courses) to £23.50, Set D Fri and Sat £23.50. BYO £8 SERVICE: not inc CARDS: Amex, Delta, MasterCard, Visa DETAILS: 40 seats. Private parties: 35 main room, 12 private room. Vegetarian meals. Children's helpings. No smoking at D before 10. Music

SHEFFIELD South Yorkshire map 9

Rafters

220 Oakbrook Road, Nether Green, Sheffield S11 7ED COOKING **2**
TEL: (0114) 230 4819 COST £27–£36

Rafters makes the best of its location in a terrace of shops. The dining-room is a brick-walled hexagon with guess-what holding up the ceiling, and a pleasant informality about it. You might not feel 'exhilarated' by the food, reckoned one reporter, but 'you won't feel robbed' either, adding that the Bosworths 'can cook, prepare and present good ingredients in reasonable sauces'. Among these might be a tarragon *jus* for grilled fillet of beef, a basil and olive pesto with grilled salmon, and a coarse-grain mustard sauce to accompany a fennel-stuffed chicken breast. The menu is generous enough without being too ambitious, and keeps up the interest with a first-course Yorkshire pudding served with mustard mash and black pudding, and a robust-sounding main course of roast Cajun cod with creamed cabbage and a red wine sauce. One dish that never comes off the menu is baked apple bread-and-butter pudding covered in sticky toffee sauce. A modest wine list suits the circumstances, starting with house French at £8.90.

CHEFS/PROPRIETORS: Wayne and Jamie Bosworth OPEN: Mon and Wed to Sat D only 7 to 10 CLOSED: 25 Dec, 1 Jan, 2 weeks Aug MEALS: Set D £18.95. BYO £1.50 SERVICE: not inc, card slips closed CARD: Amex DETAILS: 40 seats. Private parties: 40 main room. Vegetarian meals. Children's helpings. No children under 6. Music

Smith's of Sheffield

34 Sandygate Road, Sheffield S10 5RY COOKING **3**
TEL: (0114) 266 6096 COST £30–£40

Head out of Sheffield in the general direction of Glossop to find Richard Smith's modest, wood-panelled restaurant in a shopping terrace on the outskirts. A tented ceiling adds an appealing touch of the bizarre. 'Multicultural transatlanticism' is what the cooking is about (Smith has cooked in the States), which means the menu has a modern kaleidoscope effect. One glance and it's New England cod chowder, the next it's monkfish with couscous, then mozzarella, aubergine, tomato and pesto tart. Some dishes are a kind of polyglot pile-up: breast of Gressingham duck, for example, appears with five-spiced greens, 'oriental duck gravy' and duck leg confit. For those not up to a gastronomic world tour, there's fillet of Aberdeen Angus with braised onions, chive-flecked potato purée and a red wine sauce. Yorkshire rhubarb sharpens up the crème brûlée, and mango sorbet and a pineapple salsa do the same for passion-fruit tart. The wine list zips around the world, pulling in some inspired choices as it goes. House wines from the Vallée de l'Aude are £9.

CHEF: Richard Smith PROPRIETORS: Richard and Victoria Smith, and John and Sallie Tetchner OPEN: Tue to Sat D only 6.30 to 10 CLOSED: last 2 weeks Aug MEALS: alc (main courses £12 to £15). BYO £2 SERVICE: not inc, card slips closed CARDS: Delta, MasterCard, Switch, Visa DETAILS: 45 seats. Private parties: 45 main room. Children welcome. No smoking in dining-room. Wheelchair access (no WC). Music

SHELF West Yorkshire map 8

Bentley's [£]

12 Wadehouse Road, Shelf HX3 7PB COOKING **2**
TEL: (01274) 690992 COST **£14–£34**

Bentley's Food and Wine Company, to give it its full name, occupies a converted two-up, two-down house on the main road between Halifax and Bradford. Paul and Pamela Bentley's grandparents are the source of some of the pictures and furniture that decorate the cellar restaurant, which itself musters original stone flags and fireplaces. The market dictates what the kitchen prepares, and dishes are likely to include simply prepared fish, which, says Pamela Bentley, 'is what we love to sell'. An inspector noted a love of salt as well, but most dishes are interesting and carefully constructed. Black pudding comes in a delicate batter, and ash-rolled goats' cheese with balsamic-dressed leaves is served 'bubbling and brown on the top'. The highlight of one reporter's evening was home-made chocolate ice-cream in a tuile basket with toffee sauce and strawberry coulis. Good coffee and petits fours, ungreedy prices to match generous portions, and cordial and helpful service also get mentioned. The well-annotated list of 50-plus wines includes good choices at below £15 and ends with a page of fine wines. House French is £8.95.

CHEFS: Paul Bentley and Anthony Bickers PROPRIETORS: Paul and Pamela Bentley OPEN: Tue to Fri and Sun L 12 to 2, Tue to Sat D 6.30 to 9.30 CLOSED: 24 to 31 Dec, 2 weeks Aug MEALS: alc (main courses £9 to £10.50). Set L £5.95 (2 courses) to £6.95 SERVICE: not inc, card slips closed CARDS: MasterCard, Switch, Visa DETAILS: 44 seats. Private parties: 24 main room. Children's helpings. No smoking in dining-room. Music

SHEPTON MALLET Somerset map 2

Blostin's

29 Waterloo Road, Shepton Mallet BA4 5HH COOKING **2**
TEL/FAX: (01749) 343648 COST **£26–£35**

Nick and Lynne Reed bought the two cottages next to their restaurant, allowing them to expand the kitchen and add a private dining-room. Now it is done, 'it looks like it has always been there'. Above-average raw materials are the foundation of a simple, rarely changing menu that mixes classic bistro and a few more recent ideas: fish soup with rouille and croûtons, fillet of beef in pastry with madeira sauce, and brioche-and-butter pudding. The kitchen has produced rack of spring lamb – 'good meat, nicely prepared' – roasted pink on the bone, with a rosemary sauce, and local flavours are explored in guinea-fowl with apples and Somerset cider brandy. Sorbets and ice-creams are home-made, steamed chocolate sponge might tempt lovers of traditional desserts, and service by Lynne Reed is 'alert, bright and friendly'. A well-priced short wine list is grouped by variety. House French is £7.95.

CHEF: Nick Reed PROPRIETORS: Nick and Lynne Reed OPEN: Tue to Sat D 7 to 9.30 (10 Sat) CLOSED: 2 weeks Jan, 2 weeks Jun MEALS: alc (main courses £11 to £13), Set D £13.95 to £15.95. BYO £4 SERVICE: not inc, card slips closed CARDS: Delta, MasterCard, Switch, Visa DETAILS: 50 seats. Private parties: 32 main room, 18 private room. Vegetarian meals. Children's helpings. No children under 6. No smoking in 1 dining-room. Wheelchair access (no WC). Music

▲ *Bowlish House*

Wells Road, Shepton Mallet BA4 5JD
TEL/FAX: (01749) 342022
on A371 to Wells, ¼m from town centre opposite Horseshoe Inn

COOKING 4
COST £25–£30

In 1998 the Morleys celebrate their first decade at this white Georgian house, on the outskirts of town. The place is full of character. Bob Morley welcomes guests in the seriously flagged entrance hall, floors creak convincingly, and the dining-room has had a makeover, with bright yellow walls and architectural prints. Half a dozen choices are offered per course, from a slowly evolving repertoire that runs from simple smoked chicken in filo pastry to North African flavourings of spiced chickpea falafel fritter, or a Thai-spiced sauce with halibut.

The cooking is sound, the food enjoyable, and Linda Morley ('she should be cherished') is focused on the main issue. She 'doesn't mess the food around', but takes a gentle country approach typified by daube of venison with red wine and herbs, for example. Soup is well reported, and the twice-cooked soufflé is a winner: made with smoked haddock perhaps, or korma chickpeas. Excitement is less important here than the accomplished style, which is capable of producing a clear, light, glossy, stock-based sauce for lamb cutlets that was 'a model of its kind'. Desserts tend to be creamy, and cheeses are now given greater prominence. 'In my ideal world,' writes Bob Morley, 'everybody would have a cheese course.'

Wines take in not only well-known names from France and Italy, but also small producers in less-fashionable regions. Prices are geared to encourage experimentation: for example, five English whites come in under £10. Four vintages of Ch. Musar are available, and twelve house wines offer good value at £9.45 (£1.95 per glass). CELLARMAN'S CHOICE: Gewurztraminer d'Alsace 1993, A Mann, £14.95; Rioja Reserva 1989, Viña Salsada, £15.95.

CHEF: Linda Morley PROPRIETORS: Bob and Linda Morley OPEN: L first Sun of month 1.30 (1 sitting), all week D 7 to 9.30 CLOSED: 1 week autumn, 1 week spring MEALS: Set L Sun £12.95, Set D £22.50 SERVICE: not inc, card slips closed CARDS: Amex, MasterCard, Visa DETAILS: 24 seats. Private parties: 36 main room. Car park. Vegetarian meals. Children welcome. No smoking while others eat. No music ACCOMMODATION: 3 rooms, all with bath/shower. TV. B&B £48. Children welcome. Baby facilities. Dogs welcome in bedrooms only. Garden (*The Which? Hotel Guide*)

▲ *Charlton House Hotel* **NEW ENTRY**

Charlton Road, Shepton Mallet BA4 4PE — COOKING 5
TEL: (01749) 342008 FAX: (01749) 346362 — COST £30–£70

Signposted from the main road, the Georgian house is owned by Roger Saul and his wife Monty, founders of the nearby Mulberry Company, known for its fabrics, furnishings and accessories. 'Welcome to the Mulberry World,' remarked one visitor, impressed by the meticulous care put into making everything look so casual. Luxury bedrooms include 'sumptuous bathrooms and working fireplaces', some with 'their own secret gardens'. As to service, 'everything is done to make you feel at home and not out of place'.

Trevor Brooks makes a welcome return to the *Guide* with his 'clever and confident' cooking; some readers may remember him from the Table (see entry, Torquay). He combines local produce with south-coast seafood, European ideas and global spicing. He is also good with vegetables, great at sauces, and a dab hand at pastry: pre-meal nibbles are a highlight. A summer set dinner (with a choice of two items per course) included a salad of artichokes with asparagus and peas, and fillet of Cornish turbot with broad beans and truffle sauce, while the *carte* has turned to more exciting crab-cake served with roasted tomato couscous, mango and onion salsa, and langoustine oil.

Despite the evident skills, a little more generosity, cohesion and joie de vivre would have been welcomed at inspection, but the meal produced 'sweet, juicy' scallops in a salad with new potatoes, and a main course of thin, chargrilled calf's liver on a bed of buttery spinach, with a reduction of veal *jus* and balsamic vinegar. Sugar and cream seem to be lavished on desserts, and a safe pair of hands delivers raspberry crème brûlée, and hot apple tartlet with armagnac ice-cream. Lunch is considered good value. The wine list can be relied on to furnish a sound bottle at a reasonable price. Helpfully divided by style, it presents a good cross-section of varietals from around the world. House wines start at £12.

CHEF: Trevor Brooks PROPRIETORS: Mr and Mrs R.J. Saul OPEN: all week 12.30 to 2, 7.30 to 9.30 MEALS: alc (main courses £18.50 to £21). Set L £18.50, Set D £29.50 SERVICE: not inc, card slips closed CARDS: Amex, Delta, Diners, MasterCard, Switch, Visa DETAILS: 75 seats. 20 seats outside. Private parties: 32 main room, 24 to 32 private rooms. Car park. Vegetarian meals. Children's helpings No children under 7 at D. No smoking in dining-room. Wheelchair access (also WC). Music ACCOMMODATION: 17 rooms, all with bath/shower. TV. Phone. B&B £85 to £285. Children welcome. Baby facilities. Dogs welcome in 1 bedroom only and not in public rooms. Afternoon teas. Garden. Swimming-pool. Fishing (*The Which? Hotel Guide*)

SHERE Surrey — map 3

Kinghams

Gomshall Lane, Shere GU5 9HE
TEL: (01483) 202168 — COOKING 3
just off A25 Dorking to Guildford road — COST £26–£45

A well-tended garden surrounds this beamed and low-ceilinged seventeenth-century cottage. Tables are set under the apple tree in fine weather, while inside they are packed closely together, which either adds to the charm or detracts from it, depending on your point of view. 'Good, simple produce, well cooked' was one verdict on the food. It doesn't aim to dazzle, but steers a steady course through roast pigeon breast on glazed apple rings, sauté calf's liver, and chargrilled rib steak. Daily fish specials chalked on a board have included mussels with white wine and cream, and Dover sole with coriander butter, and there might be caramelised mango tart or 'gooey chocolate pudding' to finish. Service is cheerful rather than polished, but this is not a place to stand on ceremony, just 'good news for a neighbourhood where unpretentiousness is at a premium'. Around two dozen varied wines at under £20 constitute the core of the list, helped by a handful of smarter bottles, half-bottles, good fizz, and Chilean house wine at £9.50.

CHEF/PROPRIETOR: Paul Baker OPEN: Tue to Sun L 12 to 2.30, Tue to Sat D 7 to 9 CLOSED: 25 Dec to 2 Jan, bank hols MEALS: alc (main courses £9 to £15). Set L £10.95 (2 courses), Set D Tue to Thur £10.95 (2 courses) SERVICE: not inc CARDS: Amex, Delta, MasterCard, Switch, Visa DETAILS: 45 seats. 20 seats outside. Private parties: 26 main room, 26 private room. Car park. Vegetarian meals. Children's helpings. No smoking in 1 dining room. Music

SHINFIELD Berkshire map 2

L'Ortolan

The Old Vicarage, Church Lane, Shinfield RG2 9BY
TEL: (0118) 988 3783 FAX: (0118) 988 5391 COOKING 7
off A33, S of M4 J11 COST £54–£131

The bar and dining-room of this old red-brick vicarage have undergone refurbishment and now sport, among other things, a teak floor, extravagant curtains, and smartly dressed tables with heavy cloths. The conservatory, we understand, is next on the list. John Burton-Race has always set himself the most challenging and demanding technical standards, his style characterised by complex cooking which, at its best, delivers clear and vivid flavours. He lists himself as the chef, although he may not have been able to give L'Ortolan his undivided attention over the past year, since he has been planning a new venture, backed by the Bass brewing group, to open a restaurant in London in late 1997.

The level of workmanship is undiminished, however, perhaps exemplified by an assiette of Japanese fish, consisting of raw salmon marinated in oil (with a dipping puddle of creamed wasabi), a 'juicy' fried scallop, lightly battered tuna tempura (cooked pink) on a sweet ginger syrup, and breadcrumbed langoustine on a bed of fine, cold noodles in soy, all arranged round a mound of well-dressed frisée. Another 'technically impressive' dish, that also tasted good, paired three pink quail breasts (each on a slice of roasted potato set on a truffled *jus*), with a straw potato basket containing three quail's eggs coated in batter and deep-fried 'but still squirtingly soft'.

Richness can build up during a meal, helped on the way by desserts: for example, layers of caramelised puff pastry with honey ice-cream, or a caramel mousse sandwiched between two praline biscuits, served with praline ice-cream in a tuile basket on a creamy caramel sauce. Cheeses are kept in perfect condition, at room temperature, and helpfully labelled. Meals begin with accomplished canapés and end with well-crafted petits fours, and bread and butter are first-rate.

Service – very French and lots of it – has varied during the year from 'uneasy' to relaxed. Prices are in the premier league, justifiable perhaps when the kitchen is firing on all cylinders, but the five-course no-choice Menu Gourmand (with, admittedly a glass of wine with each course), at £190 for two, prompts a question about value for money, even if first courses at around £28 on the *carte* don't. Wines are in the same league, with some high prices scattered throughout the hefty list. Classical France is still the forte, although a revamped New World section gathers in some interesting bins. The house selection of 20 predominantly French wines starting at £14 affords some relief for strained wallets.

CHEF/PROPRIETOR: John Burton-Race OPEN: Tue to Sun L 12.15 to 2.15, Tue to Sat D 7 to 10 CLOSED: 1 week early Jan MEALS: alc (main courses £32 to £35). Set L £29.50 to £39.50, Set D £39.50. Menu Gourmand £190 for 2 people. BYO £8.50 SERVICE: not inc CARDS: Amex, Delta, Diners, MasterCard, Switch, Visa DETAILS: 60 seats. Private parties: 40 main room, 30 private room. Car park. Vegetarian meals. Children's helpings. Music

SHOTLEY Suffolk map 6

Old Boot House

Main Road, Shotley IP9 1EY
TEL: (01473) 787755 COOKING 3
10m SE of Ipswich on B1456 COST £21–£38

The Old Boot is house and home to Ian and Pamela Chamberlain and they run the dining-room that way: 'We like to think of it as friends for dinner,' they tell us. The building was a pub in a former life, but since 1990 has proved its worth as a country restaurant, even if it is stuck out on a limb overlooking the Orwell estuary. Ian's cooking seems to be on the up, his menus are sensible in length, and he's not afraid to tackle unusual ingredients such as cuttlefish and gulls' eggs. The result is a repertoire that calls into play layered chicken and Mediterranean vegetable terrine, seafood gumbo with spicy sausage, venison faggots with bubble and squeak, and 'toasted' fillet of brill topped with a herb crust and served with a saffron and white wine sauce. Proceedings might conclude with a steamed whisky and marmalade pudding ('if only school dinners had been like that'), hot baked banana and praline strudel, or iced lemon and pastis parfait with fresh fig and honey. Pamela Chamberlain deals with front of house efficiently, often helped out by cheery waitresses.

There may be only 50 bins on the wine list, but between them they offer a great range of flavours, from a fresh and fruity Tarrango to a steely premier cru Chablis. Prices are appealingly modest too, starting with house wines at £7.95. CELLARMAN'S CHOICE: Vin de Pays de Côtes de Pérignan, Viognier 1996, Pech-Céleyran, £13.90; Santa Carolina Malbec 1996, San Fernando, Chile, £9.85.

CHEF: Ian Chamberlain PROPRIETORS: Ian and Pamela Chamberlain OPEN: Tue to Sun L 12 to 1.30, Tue to Sat D 7 to 9 (later by arrangement) MEALS: alc Tue to Sat (main courses L £7 to £9, D £9 to £15). Set L Sun £14.95 SERVICE: not inc CARDS: Delta, MasterCard, Switch, Visa DETAILS: 45 seats. Private parties: 45 main room. Car park. Children welcome. No smoking in dining-room. No music

SHURDINGTON Gloucestershire map 2

▲ *The Greenway* 🍷

Shurdington GL51 5UG
TEL: (01242) 862352 FAX: (01242) 862780 COOKING 4
on A46, 2½m S of Cheltenham COST £29–£51

It is easy for trippers to become blasé about old Cotswold mansions until they see one as delightful as this gabled Elizabethan manor-house in acres of mature gardens, with its share of antiques, flagstoned floors and log fires. Meals are served in a conservatory extension, and Peter Fairclough's sharp, modern menu takes good account of fish and vegetables, offering a creamy butter-bean soup with morel tortellini and tarragon oil to start, followed perhaps by red mullet with a ratatouille timbale. Among classic offerings of wild mushroom risotto, or roast Cotswold venison with apple and blackberry compote, are dishes for the more adventurous: pressed terrine of mackerel, potato and foie gras, for example, or a warm passion-fruit risotto with raspberry sorbet to finish. A high degree of workmanship is evident throughout, and dishes are complete in themselves, a welcome sign that the kitchen considers the overall balance.

Wines are as classic – and classy – as the location, concentrating on champagne, claret and burgundy, with some interesting German Rieslings, but some of the prices reflect the setting too. House white and red are both £13.50. CELLARMAN'S CHOICE: Montagny premier cru, La Grande Roche 1994, Louis Latour, £25; Rioja Reserva 904, Gran Reserva Tinto 1985, La Rioja Alta, £39.50.

CHEF: Peter Fairclough PROPRIETORS: David and Valerie White OPEN: Sun to Fri L 12.30 to 2, all week D 7.30 to 9.30 (8.30 Sun) MEALS: Set L Mon to Fri £17, Set L Sun £17.50, Set D £29.50 SERVICE: not inc, card slips closed CARDS: Amex, Diners, MasterCard, Switch, Visa DETAILS: 50 seats. 20 seats outside. Private parties: 64 main room, 12 and 24 private rooms. Car park. Vegetarian meals. Children's helpings. No children under 7. No cigars/pipes in dining-room. Wheelchair access (also WC). Music ACCOMMODATION: 19 rooms, all with bath/shower. TV. Phone. B&B £87.50 to £215. Rooms for disabled. No children under 7. Afternoon teas. Garden (*The Which? Hotel Guide*)

SNAPE Suffolk map 6

▲ *Crown Inn* £ NEW ENTRY

Main Street, Snape IP17 1SL COOKING 3
TEL: (01728) 688324 COST £20–£37

The Crown is a little gem, a well-preserved fifteenth-century inn with beams and brick floors, handily placed for both the Maltings concert-hall, base of the Aldeburgh Festival, and the Minsmere bird sanctuary. Not only that, but it also boasts what the owners reckon to be 'the finest double Suffolk settle in existence'. Choose from daily-changing blackboard menus, where the offerings may include griddled baby squid dressed with chilli and lemon, soft herring roes on tapénade toast with capers, or perhaps a main-course tartlet of red peppers, plum tomatoes, ricotta and pesto.

A dish of sliced pigeon breast with parsnip chips and bacon kicked off a spring dinner in encouraging fashion, and fillet of sea bass with beurre blanc turned out to be a fine piece of fish. The partnership of melted Stilton with fillet steak is handled sensitively – no over-pungency here – and puddings might take in apple and treacle tart, chocolate cake with rum custard, or home-made ice-cream. Service, at inspection, was on the relaxed side of casual. An Adnams-based wine list is more high-falutin than pub diners may be used to, but it does the cooking justice, which is the object of the exercise. Spanish house wines from Navarra and Rueda are £9.50.

CHEF: Diane Maylott PROPRIETORS: Paul and Diane Maylott OPEN: all week 12 to 2, 7 to 9.30 (earlier and later for pre- and post-concert D; booking essential) CLOSED: 25 Dec, 26 Dec D MEALS: alc (main courses £7 to £13) SERVICE: not inc CARDS: none DETAILS: 48 seats. 40 seats outside. Private parties: 20 main room. Car park. Vegetarian meals. No children under 14. No cigars/pipes in dining-room. Wheelchair access (also WC). No music ACCOMMODATION: 3 rooms, all with bath/shower. B&B £35 to £50. No children under 14. Garden

SOUTHALL Greater London map 3

Brilliant £

72–74 Western Road, Southall UB2 5DZ COOKING 3
TEL: (0181) 574 1928 FAX: (0181) 574 0276 COST £19–£31

'We find ourselves hardly considering any alternative Indian restaurant these days,' writes a regular, who is clearly addicted to this Southall institution. Even with the rather glitzy upstairs extension – complete with its grand chandeliers – the place gets busier and busier. Main-course curries are complex affairs, with 'tender' meat suffused with fresh and varied spices, vegetables are a 'delight', and the home-made pickles are not to be missed. Fish pakora, masala egg, and mixed bhajias with a 'remarkable' sambal sauce are just some of the great offerings to be had. Otherwise, lamb chops cooked slowly on the bone in an intense, dark sauce, chilli chicken, and masala fish (made with Kenyan tilapia) are worth noting. To drink, there is lassi as well as bottles of imported Tusker or Kingfisher beer and a handful of workaday wines. House French is £7.50. The Anand family also run Madhu's Brilliant at 29 South Road, Southall; Tel: (0181) 574 1897.

CHEF: D.K. Anand PROPRIETORS: K.K. and D.K. Anand OPEN: Tue to Fri L 12.15 to 2.30, Tue to Sun D 6.15 to 11.15 (11.30 Fri and Sat) CLOSED: L Christmas and bank hols, Aug MEALS: alc (main courses £5 to £8). Set L £10, Set D £12.50 SERVICE: 10%, card slips closed CARDS: Amex, Delta, Diners, MasterCard, Switch, Visa DETAILS: 150 seats. Private parties: 75 main room, 75 private room. Vegetarian meals. Children's helpings. No-smoking area. Wheelchair access (also WC). Music. Air-conditioned

Lahore Karahi & Tandoori £ NEW ENTRY

162–164 The Broadway, Southall UB2 1NN COOKING 1
TEL: (0181) 813 8669 FAX: (0181) 574 1630 COST £9–£24

This brightly coloured Asian eating-house is noisy, bustling and full of extended family groups eating together. Rudimentary service at inspection was less bright, but this was deemed forgivable for such food at such prices. More specialised than its name and long menu suggest, the kitchen excels at tandoori dishes, be it simple chicken or 'the best fish tikka I have ever had': moist, lightly cooked, and 'bursting with flavour'. They are best accompanied by superlative naan and roti breads. The food is prepared in full view behind a window looking into the kitchen and cooked in an authentic tandoor or on the charcoal grill. Mutter paneer and methi chicken have also been praised, and Lahore specialities include nihari (lamb leg pieces), and paya (lamb trotters). There is no wine list, but you can bring your own or drink mango shake or lassi.

CHEF: Mohammad Muslim PROPRIETORS: A. Mohammad and A. Rahman OPEN: all week 12 to 12 MEALS: alc (main courses £3 to £8) SERVICE: not inc, card slips closed CARDS: Amex, Delta, MasterCard, Switch, Visa DETAILS: 200 seats. Private parties: 120 main room, 300 private room. Car park. Vegetarian meals. Children welcome. Wheelchair access (also WC). Music

SOUTH MOLTON Devon map 1

▲ *Whitechapel Manor* **NEW ENTRY**

South Molton EX36 3EG COOKING 5
TEL: (01769) 573377 FAX: (01769) 573797 COST £44–£52

A listed Elizabethan manor-house on the edge of Exmoor in one of the most unsullied parts of Devon, Whitechapel saw a change of ownership in late 1996 and a new chef, Mathew Corner, who arrived in May 1997. 'The place has a lived-in feeling,' and an impressive Jacobean carved oak screen in the entrance hall, and visitors are soon made to feel at home.

Start, perhaps, with a salmon fish-cake, finely crumbed and full of roughly chopped onion and served with a sauce of mustard and lemon. Indeed, fish cookery is highly confident. Monkfish is spiced and sliced on to thick and glistening saffron risotto, while red mullet fillets appear on diced ratatouille, with segments of orange cutting the richness of a chive cream sauce. Meat dishes, such as a fillet of local beef, are also treated handsomely, perhaps with a sauce of foie gras and truffles with braised red cabbage to throw it into relief. Intensity of flavour is apparent too, in a trio of fruit sorbets zigzagged with a cassis coulis. Other desserts include thought-provoking combinations such as lavender ice with orange tart, or mango sorbet with white chocolate cheesecake. France and Australia dominate the wine list, the latter providing many good bottles, but mark-ups are pretty brisk. Prices start at £11.50.

CHEF: Mathew Corner PROPRIETORS: Margaret Aris and Charles Brown OPEN: all week 12 to 1.45, 7 to 8.45 MEALS: Set L and D £34 SERVICE: not inc, card slips closed CARDS: Delta, Diners, MasterCard, Switch, Visa DETAILS: 26 seats. Private parties: 22 main room, 10 private room. Car park. Children welcome. No smoking in dining-room. No music ACCOMMODATION: 11 rooms, all with bath/shower. TV. Phone. B&B £70 to £170. Children welcome. Baby facilities. Afternoon teas. Garden (*The Which? Hotel Guide*)

'I ordered a double espresso and, as so often happens, a small cup arrived with a tiny pool of coffee at the bottom of it. I get fed up of this practice, and asked the waiter, "Is this a double espresso? It is tiny." He smiled and said, "Sir, you should see the single espresso," and waltzed off.' (On eating in London)

SOUTHWATER West Sussex map 3

Cole's

Worthing Road, Southwater RH13 7BS COOKING 4
TEL: (01403) 730456 COST £23–£47

From the outside, Cole's looks less like a converted barn (which it is) and more like a cottage, set among other houses in a part of Southwater that is 'more suburb than rural-idyll'. Within, the high-ceilinged cream and maroon dining-room with its huge inglenook fireplace is the scene for Elizabeth Cole's cooking, which can be as simple as a salad of sesame-seeded goats' cheese with 'clear, fresh and sharp' flavours, or as refined as 'intelligently conceived and well-executed' roast duck with a sauce of orange and ginger.

Well-timed turbot is complemented by a leek and chive cream sauce, and a first-course terrine of crab and crayfish is 'very smooth and well flavoured'. Mascarpone and basil parfait with a bitter chocolate sauce is an off-beat dessert that succeeds in offering complexity and coherence; more down-to-earth is a spot-on rendition of sticky toffee pudding with toffee sauce and fine vanilla custard. Bread and coffee could be better, but good petits fours compensate. A few reasonable New World bottles supplement the mainly French wine list; French house wines are £10.95.

CHEF: Elizabeth Cole PROPRIETORS: the Cole family OPEN: Tue to Fri and Sun L 12 to 2, Tue to Sat D 7 to 9 CLOSED: 1 week winter, 2 weeks summer MEALS: alc (main courses £12 to £18). Set L £12.95 (2 courses) to £15 SERVICE: not inc CARDS: Amex, Delta, Diners, MasterCard, Visa DETAILS: 36 seats. Private parties: 26 main room, 10 private room. Car park. Vegetarian meals. Children's helpings. No smoking in dining-room. Wheelchair access (also WC). Music

SOUTHWOLD Suffolk map 6

▲ *The Crown*

90 High Street, Southwold IP18 6DP COOKING 4
TEL: (01502) 722275 FAX: (01502) 727263 COST £23–£34

The Crown has been dolled up a little over the years since its eighteenth-century beginnings as a coaching-inn. Classical columns form an almost tongue-in-cheek addition to the cream exterior, but it looks impressive none the less. For over a decade it has been the hotel and restaurant arm of Adnams, wine merchant and brewer of some repute. Eat either in the spacious and comfortable bar or in the plusher and more formal dining-room. The food is modern European in the least-startling sense, as demonstrated by warm duck leg confit dressed with honey and soy that started a spring lunch in style. This was followed by fillet of grilled mackerel with smoked salmon and spinach and a very delicate champagne butter sauce. English puddings, such as jam roly-poly, and lime and ginger syllabub typically round off a meal. Service – especially of wine – is supremely assured and knowledgeable.

The Crown's jewel – the wine list – is more like a treasure trove, with its huge range of greats from around the world. Each wine is concisely described to aid selection, and the sight of so many gems priced at around £10 will lend courage to those who may feel daunted at so much choice. House wines change every four to six weeks, with prices starting at about £8.20 a bottle, £1.65 a glass. CELLARMAN'S CHOICE: Pouilly-Fumé, Ch. de Tracy 1995, £15.20; Noceto Sangiovese/Cabernet 1994, Shenandoah Valley, California, £15.20.

CHEF: Simon Reynolds PROPRIETOR: Adnams Hotels OPEN: all week 12.30 to 1.30, 7.30 to 9.30 CLOSED: 1 week early Jan MEALS: Set L £13.50 (2 courses) to £16.25, Set D £18.50 (2 courses) to £21.50. BYO £5. Bar food available SERVICE: not inc, card slips closed CARDS: Amex, Delta, Diners, MasterCard, Switch, Visa DETAILS: 22 seats. 12 seats outside. Private parties: 22 main room, 20 private room. Car park. Vegetarian meals. Children's helpings. No smoking in dining-room. Wheelchair access (no WC). No music. Air-conditioned ACCOMMODATION: 12 rooms, all with bath/shower. TV. Phone. B&B £43 to £65. Children welcome. Baby facilities (*The Which? Hotel Guide*)

STADDLEBRIDGE North Yorkshire map 9

▲ *McCoy's*

The Cleveland Tontine, Staddlebridge DL6 3JB
TEL: (01609) 882671 FAX: (01609) 882660 COOKING 5
6m NE of Northallerton, at junction of A19 and A172 COST £33–£57

'This place is just uniquely fabulous,' began one supporter, happy to travel two and a half hours to get to it. It is family-run, idiosyncratic, 'special in every way', with an extremely relaxed demeanour and no end of agreeable clutter. The restaurant is only open three mealtimes a week, but the downstairs bistro serves the same food and is open all week. The style is reminiscent of a brasserie, although the McCoy brothers give the impression of having got there before everybody else. Virtually every item on the global shopping list is here: start perhaps with marinated oriental vegetables served with deep-fried ginger, coriander and lime dressing, and follow it with pot roast pigeon that comes with swede purée, Puy lentils, potato and pancetta rösti, deep-fried garlic, and foie gras sauce.

While there seems to be a lot going in some dishes, there is no feeling that the food is too elaborate, and indeed it is possible to eat a simple meal of six Irish oysters, chargrilled steak, and orange tart, although that may be difficult given all the other temptations. A list of daily specials and fish might include pea and ham risotto with mustard, and red mullet with a crust of olive and sun-dried tomato, while desserts have featured made-to-order black cherry and almond pithivier served with cherry-beer ice-cream, and the long-standing choc-o-block Stanley: a fondant sponge soaked in Tia Maria with a coffee-bean sauce.

Wines change roughly every quarter, but high-quality bins from both the Old and New Worlds seem to be a constant factor. Unfortunately, this is reflected in the prices, with very few bottles coming in under £20. House Chardonnay and Merlot are £12.50 a bottle, £2.30 a glass.

CHEF: Tom McCoy PROPRIETORS: the McCoy brothers OPEN: restaurant Thur to Sat D only 7 to 10; bistro all week L 12 to 2, D 7 to 9.30 CLOSED: 25 and 26 Dec, 1 Jan MEALS: alc (main courses £12.95 to £19.95). SERVICE: not inc CARDS: Amex, Diners, MasterCard, Switch, Visa DETAILS: 59 seats. Private parties: 50 main room, 30 private room. Car park. Vegetarian meals. Children welcome. Music. Air-conditioned ACCOMMODATION: 6 rooms, all with bath/shower. TV. Phone. Air-conditioned. B&B £79 to £99. Children welcome. Dogs welcome. Garden (*The Which? Hotel Guide*)

STAITHES North Yorkshire map 9

▲ *Endeavour* £

1 High Street, Staithes TS13 5BH COOKING **2**
TEL: (01947) 840825 COST £24–£44

Staithes is an endearing fishing village of lopsided cottages built around a rocky harbour where smugglers once hauled in their contraband. Captain Cook lived here at one time, and Lisa Chapman's tiny restaurant, which occupies one of those cottages, is named after his ship. The drill is a daily-changing blackboard menu for lunch and dinner, but always offering a good balance of meat and fish. The latter might include smoked halibut with lemon and pepper butter sauce, or a starter of risotto of Whitby cod with parsley cream. Crab and prawns play their part, as do one or two trendier touches, such as bresaola with shaved Parmesan and olive oil. Puddings offer food for thought in the shape of blackberry and marzipan gratin with crème fraîche; one can only wonder what Captain Cook would have made of courgette cake with Greek yoghurt as afters. The friendly informality of the approach is commended by readers. The modest wine list includes a few old favourites at unarguable prices, leading with house French – including a Pinot Noir from Corsica – at £8.45.

CHEF/PROPRIETOR: Lisa Chapman OPEN: Mon to Sat 12 to 2, 6.45 to 9 (later in summer), plus Sun bank hols and Sun in summer CLOSED: 25 and 26 Dec, weekdays Feb MEALS: alc (main courses £8.50 to £16) SERVICE: not inc CARDS: none DETAILS: 45 seats. Private parties: 30 main room, 12 and 18 private rooms. Vegetarian meals. Children welcome. No smoking in 1 dining-room. Music ACCOMMODATION: 3 rooms, 2 with bath/shower. TV. B&B £38 to £45 (double rooms). Children welcome. Dogs by arrangement

STANTON Suffolk map 6

Leaping Hare Cafe £

ENGLISH VINEYARD 1998 CAFE

Wyken Vineyards, Stanton IP31 2DW COOKING **2**
TEL: (01359) 250287 FAX: (01359) 250240 COST £24–£35

A reporter wandering around Wyken Vineyard found the Leaping Hare Café a 'stylish and peaceful' place to stop for carrot cake and coffee. Another who couldn't resist a gander thought the medieval barn and Sunday lunch both superb. Lucy Crabb brings a touch of urban chic to the cooking, so the smoked haddock fish-cakes come with cucumber salsa, and there's spiced loin of lamb with chickpeas, aubergine and coriander. Tuscan bean soup, or Caesar salad, might start things off, and the finishing line is reached with caramel cream pots and Russian teacakes, or seasonal strawberries and unpasteurised Jersey cream. Cornish Yarg and Gorgonzola might tempt cheese-lovers. All wines are the produce of the Wyken vineyard, prices starting at £8.50.

CHEF: Lucy Crabb PROPRIETORS: Kenneth and Carla Carlisle OPEN: Thu, Fri and Sun L 12 to 3, Thu to Sat D 7 to 9.30 CLOSED: Christmas to end Jan MEALS: alc (main courses £8 to £12.50) SERVICE: not inc, card slips closed CARDS: Delta, MasterCard, Switch, Visa DETAILS: 50 seats. 16 seats outside. Private parties: 50 main room. Car park. Vegetarian meals. Children's helpings. No smoking in dining-room. Wheelchair access (also WC). Music

STOKE HOLY CROSS Norfolk map 6

Wildebeest Arms £

Norwich Road, Stoke Holy Cross NR14 8QJ
TEL: (01508) 492497 FAX: (01603) 766403
from Norwich take A140 Ipswich road; directly after roundabout take the left turn signposted Stoke Holy Cross

COOKING 1
COST £20–£39

'The Beest' charges on. Such is demand that the restaurant is booked weeks ahead, especially at weekends, say the owners, who also tell us that major refurbishment is in the pipeline. Chef Eden Derrick draws on ideas from the Mediterranean and the Far East for a short menu that is built around local ingredients. Seafood from Lowestoft market might appear in the shape of curried mussel risotto with coriander and spring onions, or fillet of halibut on a cassoulet of butter-beans and chorizo. Duck is also a fixture, perhaps served on thyme mash with oyster mushrooms and red wine sauce, or turned into a sausage and accompanied by ginger-scented cabbage. Side orders include hand-cut chips with their skins on. Desserts might take in sticky toffee pudding, or passion-fruit and blackberry parfait. Most of the wines on the lively, modern list are supplied by Adnams. House wine is £8.95.

CHEFS: Eden Derrick and Paul Hatch PROPRIETORS: Henry Watt and Andrew Wilkins OPEN: all week 12 to 2 (12.30 to 2.30 Sun), 7 to 10 (9 Sun) CLOSED: 25 Dec MEALS: alc L Sun and D all week (main courses L £7 to £8, D £8.50 to £14). Set L Mon to Sat £12 SERVICE: not inc CARDS: Amex, Delta, Diners, MasterCard, Switch, Visa DETAILS: 70 seats. 70 seats outside. Private parties: 70 main room. Car park. Vegetarian meals. Children's helpings. No smoking area. Wheelchair access (no WC). Music

STOKESLEY North Yorkshire map 10

▲ *Chapters* £

27 High Street, Stokesley TS9 5AD
TEL: (01642) 711888 FAX: (01642) 713387

COOKING 4
COST £18–£47

'Homely' is how one reporter described the tone of this village restaurant on the banks of the River Leven. The three-storeyed building faces the square, with an 'active, busy bistro' at the front and a quieter, more relaxing dining-room at the back. Upbeat modern food is the style, with fish and fresh local produce subject to all kinds of culinary input, including a bowl of mussels, paella Valencia, and an unlikely but successful version of fish-cakes served with curried Malibu sauce. Chicken liver pâté comes enterprisingly with fig chutney, and a variation on Caesar salad had one reporter reaching for superlatives to describe the combined effect of olives, dried tomatoes, sardines, scallops, Parmesan and dressing. Materials include king prawns, duck breast, and best end of lamb, which the kitchen, in turn, partners with spicy Thai sauce, mushroom risotto, and a simple rosemary *jus*. 'The best crème brûlée', and a fine hot chocolate soufflé served with an orange and Cointreau ice-cream, add to the impression of 'excellent value for money', as do the 40-plus wines, mostly under £20, which make good use of the southern hemisphere. House Duboeuf is £9.50.

CHEFS: Richard West and Alan Thompson PROPRIETORS: Alan and Catherine Thompson OPEN: Mon to Sat 12 to 2, 6.30 to 9.30 CLOSED: 25 Dec, 1 Jan MEALS: alc (main courses £6 to £16.50). BYO £3 SERVICE: not inc CARDS: Amex, Delta, Diners, MasterCard, Switch, Visa DETAILS: 60 seats. Private parties: 60 main room. Car park. Vegetarian meals. Children's helpings. No smoking in 1 dining-room. Wheelchair access (no WC). Music ACCOMMODATION: 13 rooms, all with bath/shower. TV. Phone. B&B £40 to £63. Children welcome. Baby facilities. Dogs welcome. Garden (*The Which? Hotel Guide*)

STON EASTON Somerset map 2

▲ *Ston Easton Park*

Ston Easton BA3 4DF
TEL: (01761) 241631 FAX: (01761) 241377 COOKING **6**
on A37, 12m S of Bristol COST £26–£70

This is about as impeccable as a Palladian mansion gets. The grey (inside and out) may be overdone for some tastes, but *cognoscenti* find it elegant, praising the purist approach and lack of flounce. Amid the period furniture, portraits and antique prints, the one modern concession – plumbing – is welcomed. Above all, Ston Easton makes 'a wholly successful attempt to be customer-focused'. Service – for which, commendably, no charge is made or expected – sees that everything runs smoothly, and adds significantly to the enjoyment, as do the excellent and varied appetisers, such as smoked duck, or feta and chorizo tartlet.

Mark Harrington's cooking turns sound ingredients into simple and effective dishes on a seasonally changing *carte* and daily-changing set-price menu. The foundation is prime materials – fillet of turbot, saddle of rabbit, foie gras – which receive a generally mainstream treatment, producing grilled Dover sole, deep-fried scallops in tempura batter, or squab pigeon with Puy lentils. Freshness and accurate timing are hallmarks. Lamb is Welsh and invariably impressive, cooked pink, tasting as it should, and served perhaps with grilled vegetables. The kitchen appears more at ease in traditional mode than with, say, red onion and mango salsa (to accompany scallops), and the classical emphasis makes a success of the mostly cold desserts. The one hot one needs to be ordered in advance, and has included a first-rate banana clafoutis in a pastry tartlet.

The rather grand wine list concentrates on the classic regions and older vintages, and this is reflected in the prices. Those who do not wish to work their way through pages of fine French wines can choose from the 11 bottles, starting at £14.50, which introduce the list. The more adventurous may be rewarded by Penfolds Grange 1983 at £120. CELLARMAN'S CHOICE: St Hallett Chardonnay 1995, Barossa Valley, S. Australia, £19.50; Côtes de Castillon, Ch. Pitray 1990, £18.50.

CHEF: Mark Harrington PROPRIETORS: Peter and Christine Smedley OPEN: all week 12.30 to 2, 7.30 to 9.30 (10 Fri and Sat) MEALS: alc (main courses £10.50 to £25.50). Set L Mon to Sat £14 (2 courses) to £16, Set L Sun £26, Set D £39.50. BYO £12 SERVICE: none, card slips closed CARDS: Amex, Delta, Diners, MasterCard, Switch, Visa DETAILS: 45 seats. 20 seats outside. Private parties: 50 main room, 40 private room. Car park. Vegetarian meals. Babies and children over 8 welcome. Jacket and tie. No smoking in dining-room. Wheelchair access (also WC). No music ACCOMMODATION: 21 rooms, all with bath/shower. TV. Phone. Room only £135 to £390. Children welcome. Baby facilities. Dogs kennelled by arrangement. Afternoon teas. Garden (*The Which? Hotel Guide*)

STORRINGTON West Sussex map 3

▲ *Manleys* 🍷

Manleys Hill, Storrington RH20 4BT COOKING 5
TEL: (01903) 742331 FAX: (01903) 740649 COST £43–£62

In 1998 Karl Löderer celebrates 20 years at this comfortable Queen Anne house overlooking the South Downs. Two dining-rooms, a few beams, and a peach and green colour scheme are the setting for his traditional style. 'Time-warp cooking' one called it, who felt that Karl Löderer pays little attention to 'current trends of light healthy eating'. After two decades, and Salzburger Nockerln honorably excepted, his Austrian background seems to be disappearing under the weight of a more Anglo-French repertoire, including roast beef and Yorkshire pudding for Sunday lunch. But for those who crave traditional dishes, and appreciate traditional skills such as professional pastrywork, his food has much to recommend it.

Prime ingredients constitute the solid foundation of a menu that takes in substantial first-courses – boned and roast quail with foie gras purée and potato galette, perhaps – followed by duck confit, venison fillet with sweet-and-sour cherry sauce, or 'superb' hake fillet with a cheesy sauce. Silver domes are lifted, vegetables are many, and extras include first-rate amuse-bouche (a filo pastry basket of scallops, or fennel soup with Pernod) and 'irresistible' petits fours. Wines are predominantly from Burgundy and Bordeaux, bolstered by some fine German Rieslings. Support from the home country comes in the form of two Austrian domaine wines, bottled in the monastery cellars of Stift Klosterneuburg, and a luscious Ausbruch Weisser Burgunder. House French is £14.80. CELLARMAN'S CHOICE: Chablis premier cru Montmain 1994, Louis Michel, £26.75; Haut-Médoc, Ch. Villegeorge 1992, £25.

CHEF/PROPRIETOR: Karl Löderer OPEN: Tue to Sun L 12.15 to 1.45, Tue to Sat D 7.15 to 9.30 CLOSED: first 2 weeks Jan, bank hols (exc Good Friday) MEALS: Set L £15 (2 courses) to £19.60, Set L Sun £23.50, Set D £31.50. BYO £5 SERVICE: not inc CARDS: Amex, Delta, MasterCard, Switch, Visa DETAILS: 48 seats. Private parties: 28 main room, 12 and 22 private rooms. Car park. Vegetarian meals. Children's helpings. No cigars/pipes in dining-room. Wheelchair access (also WC). Music. Air-conditioned ACCOMMODATION: 1 room, with bath/shower. TV. Phone. B&B £50 to £95

Old Forge

6 Church Street, Storrington RH20 4LA COOKING 3
TEL: (01903) 743402 FAX: (01903) 742540 COST £22–£39

'Congenial and comfortable' is a fair description of this collection of fifteenth-century oak-beamed buildings in a small Downland village. Clive and Cathy Roberts have been here for a decade, managing to give their basic Anglo-French approach an individual twist without straying into exotica. Ambition and achievement are well matched. Menus include both a set-price lunch and dinner and an à la carte that also happens to be a set price. The difference is that while the former typically offers a choice of two items per course, the latter offers between four and six.

Fish is simply treated so as not to overwhelm the excellent raw materials – a lemon and parsley dressing for a 'gâteau' of salmon rillettes and gravlax, or a sharply flavoured butter for grilled Cornish skate – yet there is scope for imaginative treatment in stir-fried strips of beef fillet served around a steamed tomato and onion pudding, or a mousseline of oak-smoked duck with celeriac crisps. Desserts are treated seriously – iced armagnac parfait with a prune bavarois, or steamed black treacle sponge – as are the accompanying wines by the glass. The rest of the list takes particular delight in the southern hemisphere. House French, Australian and Spanish are £9.75 (£2.50 per large glass).

CHEF: Clive Roberts PROPRIETORS: Clive and Cathy Roberts OPEN: Wed to Fri and Sun L 12.30 to 1.30, Wed to Sat D 7.15 to 9 CLOSED: 2 weeks autumn, 3 weeks spring MEALS: Set L Wed to Fri £13 (2 courses) to £25, Set L Sun £16, Set D £16.50 (2 courses) to £25. BYO £5 SERVICE: not inc, card slips closed CARDS: Amex, Delta, Diners, MasterCard, Switch, Visa DETAILS: 36 seats. Private parties: 16 main room, 12 private room. Vegetarian meals. Children's helpings. No smoking while others eat. Wheelchair access (no WC). Music

STOW-ON-THE-WOLD Gloucestershire map 5

▲ *Wyck Hill House*

Burford Road, Stow-on-the-Wold GL54 1HY
TEL: (01451) 831936 FAX: (01451) 832243 COOKING **3**
on A424, 2m SE of Stow-on-the-Wold COST £27–£62

A balustraded entrance, mullioned windows, the imposing grandeur of honey-coloured stone: this is the full-on Cotswold package, sited somewhere between Stow and Burford. In the grand luxe of the dining-room, a mainstream style of country-house cooking is offered in the form of set-price menus that carry one or two supplements for the likes of fillet steak; they are not, however, entirely averse to incorporating the odd contemporary flourish. There may be a mille-feuille of smoked chicken, tomato and goats' cheese dressed in pesto, for example, but the centre of gravity remains very much in the vein of smoked salmon with cucumber and dill, or pork medaillions with caramelised apples on grain-mustard sauce. Treats to finish may include double chocolate brownies with Grand Marnier ice-cream, or crème brûlée with tropical fruits and a mango sorbet. New World wines represent better value than anything from the French regions, but choices all round are a bit run of the mill. House wines from California are £13.95.

CHEF: Ian Smith PROPRIETOR: Lyric Hotels OPEN: all week 12.30 to 2, 7 to 9.30 MEALS: Set L £10.95 (2 courses) to £14.95, Set D £32.50. BYO from £8 SERVICE: not inc, card slips closed CARDS: Amex, Delta, Diners, MasterCard, Switch, Visa DETAILS: 70 seats. 24 seats outside. Private parties: 80 main room, 10 to 40 private rooms. Car park. Vegetarian meals. Children's helpings. No smoking in dining-room. Music. Air-conditioned ACCOMMODATION: 30 rooms, all with bath/shower. TV. Phone. B&B £95 to £195. Children welcome. Baby facilities. Dogs welcome in bedrooms only. Afternoon teas. Garden

If you have access to the Internet, you can find The Good Food Guide *online at the Which? Online web site (http://www.which.net).*

STRETE Devon map 1

Laughing Monk

Blackawton Road, Strete TQ6 0RN
TEL: (01803) 770639 COOKING **2**
5m from Dartmouth on coast road to Kingsbridge COST £18–£36

Forget Friar Tuck. Although next to the church, this is a country restaurant housed in Strete's early-Victorian village school, with exposed-stone walls, a big fireplace and traditional settles for seating. If the repertoire remains familiar from one year to the next, this is because the Rothwells cook to please their customers, not to follow fashion, maintaining a consistent standard into the bargain. A generous menu might begin with mushrooms filled with pesto, or Avon mussels cooked in white wine and cream. Those two stalwarts of provincial cooking, alcohol and cream, appear in main courses too: pork with calvados, chicken with a leek and cream sauce, and fillet steak with a red wine sauce, for example. Puddings, 'perhaps the best bit of the meal', arrive on a trolley and might include cheesecake, apple meringue, and chocolate mousse on a crunchy biscuit base. 'Like a good wine, the Laughing Monk has matured rather than changed,' observed one reporter, speaking of which the list is varied, arranged by style, and sympathetically priced: most bottles are under £15, including house Chilean and French at £8.50.

CHEF: David Rothwell PROPRIETORS: David and Trudy Rothwell OPEN: Tue to Sat D only 7 to 9.30; also Sun L last Sun of month and Mon D June to Sept MEALS: alc (main courses £10 to £14). Set L Sun £11.95. BYO £2.50 SERVICE: not inc, card slips closed CARDS: Delta, MasterCard, Switch, Visa DETAILS: 50 seats. Private parties: 60 main room, 36 private room. Car park. Vegetarian meals. Children's helpings. Music

STUCKTON Hampshire map 2

▲ *Three Lions* 🍷 £✱

Stuckton Road, Stuckton SP6 2HF
TEL: (01425) 652489 FAX: (01425) 656144
½m SE of Fordingbridge, off A338 but not signposted
from it: take the turn just S of Fordingbridge and COOKING **7**
follow a sign down a narrow country lane COST £24–£46

Now into their third year in Stuckton, the Womersleys have 'obviously settled in at this pub-cum-restaurant' and their confidence shows, not least front-of-house, where Jane Womersley and her team combine efficiency with friendliness and easy charm. A high standard of cooking, allied to complete lack of pretence, is the distinguishing mark. Typical of the kitchen's output was one reporter's meal that began with ravioli of Jerusalem artichoke and truffle sauce, followed by lightly spiced saddle of venison with pears, and then lime parfait with passion-fruit sauce. Other pasta options have included cannelloni of fresh crab, and lasagne of wild mushrooms, while a fondness for meat and fruit pairings shows in roast duck with either figs in a port sauce or quince and pears.

The New Forest and the sea are not far away, which may help to explain why game figures prominently – perhaps simple roast partridge wrapped in bacon with a madeira sauce – and why fish is a strength: red mullet with saffron sauce, or sea bass with 'oriental juices'. Variety is provided by poultry and onion consommé, galette of smoked haddock, or cassolette of kidneys and livers, and there is good bread to mop up the sauces. If meals don't end with the lively zip of a fruity sorbet, they will probably comfort with a bread-and-butter pudding or a 'scrummy chocolate cake'. 'Not cheap, but good value' is how reporters view the *carte*. 'Roll on the day when they provide rooms,' wrote one who has since been overtaken by events.

The opportunity provided by the new accommodation will no doubt be seized by those who have previously gazed wistfully at the tempting wine list but have been the evening's designated driver. The Bonny Doon Malvasia from California (£22.50) is just one of some sunny New World wines that look particularly appealing. The house selection of 16 wines starts at £12.75, with nine being offered by the glass at £2.60 upwards. CELLARMAN'S CHOICE: Condrieu, Dom. du Chêne 1987, Marc Rouvière, £35.50; Parrots Hill Shiraz 1992, Barossa Valley, S. Australia, £18.25.

CHEF: Michael Womersley PROPRIETORS: Michael and Jayne Womersley OPEN: Tue to Sun L 12.15 to 2, Tue to Sat D 7.15 to 9.45 (10 Sat) CLOSED: last 2 weeks Jan, first week Feb MEALS: alc (main courses £10.50 to £16). Set L Tue to Fri £13.50 (2 courses) SERVICE: not inc CARDS: Delta, MasterCard, Switch, Visa DETAILS: 60 seats. 20 seats outside. Private parties: 60 main room. Car park. Vegetarian meals. Children's helpings. No smoking in dining-room. Wheelchair access (no WC). Music ACCOMMODATION: 3 rooms, all with bath/shower. TV. B&B £55 to £75. Rooms for disabled. Children welcome. Baby facilities. Garden

STURMINSTER NEWTON Dorset map 2

▲ *Plumber Manor*

Sturminster Newton DT10 2AF
TEL: (01258) 472507 FAX: (01258) 473370
A357 to Sturminster Newton, take first left to Hazelbury Bryan, on left-hand side after 2m

COOKING 4
COST £23–£42

The drive up to Plumber Manor, with its magnificent mullioned frontage, is lined with fine old chestnut trees, and a mature magnolia stands by the entrance. Inside, past generations captured in oils gaze down from the walls. Brian Prideaux-Brune's cooking may not be state-of-the-art trendy, but in these surroundings one would hardly expect it to be. It is couched in the form of fixed-price menus, with a gourmet option for high rollers. The regular menu offers as starters old favourites along the lines of avocado, prawns and melon marie-rose, or moules marinière, as well as items such as boned quail stuffed with wild rice and wrapped in filo. Rich main courses have included pork with prunes and brandy, and beef with Stilton mousse and a port sauce. Meals end with traditional English puddings, or cheese and biscuits. Service is relaxed but helpful and willing. Wines are strong in the major French regions, a little more perfunctory elsewhere, but there is a good handful from the New World. The house selection starts at £10.

CHEF: Brian Prideaux Bruno PROPRIETOR: Richard Prideaux-Brune OPEN: Sun L 12.30 to 2, all week D 7.30 to 9 CLOSED: Feb MEALS: Set L £17.50, Set D £17.50 (2 courses) to £30. BYO £7.50 SERVICE: net prices, card slips closed CARDS: Amex, Diners, MasterCard, Switch, Visa DETAILS: 65 seats. Private parties: 45 main room, 14 and 23 private rooms. Car park. Vegetarian meals. Children's helpings. Wheelchair access (also WC). No music ACCOMMODATION: 16 rooms, all with bath/shower. TV. Phone. B&B £65 to £130. Rooms for disabled. Children welcome. Baby facilities. Dogs welcome. Garden (*The Which? Hotel Guide*)

Sudbury Suffolk map 6

Red Onion Bistro £

57 Ballingdon Street, Sudbury CO10 6DA COOKING **2**
TEL: (01787) 376777 FAX: (01787) 883156 COST £13–£29

Keep prices low and quality high: such are the Ford family's admirable aims for their lively bistro. By turns the cooking is French or English, and at times might take a spin in Greece or Mexico. Highbrow mixes with lowbrow at lunch-time, when deep-fried squid tempura may be followed by fish and chips, chargrilled rump steak, or beefburger. Reporters have praised chicken liver salad with bacon and croûtons, and 'succulent' chicken on a bed of garlic served with 'delectable' vegetables. Crème brûlée is said to be 'excellent', and other puddings may run to apple and amaretti tart, or chocolate pot. Select your own wine from the largely bin-end-filled cellar, or from the short, frequently changing list. House wine is £6.95 a jug.

CHEFS: Jane Ford and Darren Boyles PROPRIETORS: Gerry and Jane Ford OPEN: Mon to Sat 12 to 2, 6.30 to 9.30 (10 Fri and Sat) CLOSED: 1 week after Christmas, bank hols MEALS: alc (main courses £5 to £10). Set L £5.75 (2 courses) to £7.50, Set D Mon to Thur £9.75 SERVICE: not inc, card slips closed CARDS: Delta, MasterCard, Switch, Visa DETAILS: 70 seats. 30 seats outside. Private parties: 24 main room. Car park. Vegetarian meals. Children's helpings. No cigars/pipes in dining-room. Wheelchair access (no WC). Music

SWAFFHAM Norfolk map 6

▲ *Strattons*

Stratton House, 4 Ash Close, Swaffham PE37 7NH COOKING **4**
TEL: (01760) 723845 FAX: (01760) 720458 COST £35–£41

Vanessa Scott's commitment to home cooking is a fiery beacon of conviction. 'A whole generation in this country has lost its food roots and doesn't know where or how to find them,' she writes. She would like us all to go back to baking our own bread and such but, before that renaissance dawns, is happy to play a part by offering her own contributions at this elegant Queen Anne restaurant-with-rooms in Swaffham's market square. Culinary ideas range from the tried-and-true, such as rillettes of local duck, to innovations such as a soup of red mullet and radicchio. Kedgeree is given a new spin with smoked eel and soft-boiled quails' eggs, and main courses may include poached pike with walnut mayonnaise, or roast pork leg with olive and pepper gravy and wild mushroom dumplings. Ice-creams are the pudding stars: from chestnut and rum to raspberry and rose-petal. Service adds to the overall feeling of homeliness.

The wine list is longer on explanatory notes, but there are some decent bottles in evidence. Prices start at £8.90.

CHEF: Vanessa Scott PROPRIETORS: Les and Vanessa Scott OPEN: all week D only 6.30 to 9 (Sun 7.30 for 8) CLOSED: 25 and 26 Dec MEALS: Set D £23.75 SERVICE: not inc, card slips closed CARDS: MasterCard, Switch, Visa DETAILS: 21 seats. 6 seats outside. Private parties: 10 main room. Car park. Vegetarian meals. Children's helpings. No smoking in dining-room. Music ACCOMMODATION: 7 rooms, all with bath/shower. TV. Phone. B&B £60 to £85. Deposit: £50. Children welcome. Baby facilities. Dogs welcome. Afternoon teas. Garden (*The Which? Hotel Guide*)

SWANAGE Dorset map 2

Galley

DORSET 1998 PLAIN COOKING

9 High Street, Swanage BH19 2LN COOKING 2
TEL: (01929) 427299 COST £25–£30

'Not much wrong with this little restaurant,' volunteered one reporter. It is close to the seafront, plainly decorated, 'a bit of a squeeze', with a set menu offering four choices per course. Nick Storer's approach is a personal one. He opened a decade ago simply because there wasn't a fish restaurant in the vicinity, then added game dishes and expanded the repertoire in accordance with his own tastes. 'I know that a grilled scallop in its shell is better than a scallop mousseline,' he writes, and serves them oven-baked with herb butter. Likewise, local crab and lobster are presented as simply as possible, cockles are served with hop shoots from the garden, and fish soup comes in a jug. There might also be duck, venison or calf's liver, and desserts have included 'pleasingly thick and bitter' blackcurrant sorbet. Portions can be generous. Service is efficient, even under pressure. Forty-plus wines embrace some crisp and fruity whites, all at fair prices. House Chilean is £8.50.

CHEF: Nick Storer PROPRIETORS: N.D. and M.G. Storer OPEN: all week D only 6.45 to 9.30 (10 Sat) CLOSED: 3 weeks Nov, 1 Jan to 14 Feb MEALS: Set D £18.50. BYO £5 SERVICE: not inc, card slips closed CARDS: Amex, Delta, Diners, MasterCard, Visa DETAILS: 34 seats. Private parties: 30 main room. Vegetarian meals. Children welcome. Wheelchair access (no WC). Music. Air-conditioned

TADCASTER North Yorkshire map 9

Singers £

16 Westgate, Tadcaster LS24 9AB COOKING 2
TEL: (01937) 835121 COST £23–£28

The musical theme, with sheet music on the walls, and tables named after well-known singers, is either 'a nice touch' or 'corny', according to taste, although when it comes to dividing the wine list into soprano and alto whites, and tenor, bass and baritone reds, it is difficult not to side with the corn merchants. Salads are a good way to begin – perhaps shredded duck with orange and celeriac – though potato and onion cake with smoked haddock, or a pastry tart of kidneys and bacon, provides stiff competition. Generally the cooking is straightforward, relying on pan-frying (calf's liver), roasting (salmon) and chargrilling (sirloin steak) for effect, and any doubts about the British tenor (forgive us) of the food will be dispelled by a glance at the puddings: sticky toffee, or plum and apple crumble with 'custard sauce'. Midweek diners might be tempted in by the two-course deal, and the vinous chorus (champagne soloist excepted) stays helpfully under £20. House Duboeuf is £8.25.

CHEFS: David Lockwood and Steven Ardern PROPRIETORS: Philip Taylor and Guy Vicari OPEN: Tue to Sat D only 6 to 9.30 CLOSED: 25 and 26 Dec, 1 week Feb, 1 week Aug MEALS: Set D Tue to Thur £12.50 (2 courses) to £15.50, Set D Fri and Sat £15.50 SERVICE: not inc, card slips closed CARDS: Delta, MasterCard, Switch, Visa DETAILS: 38 seats. Private parties: 38 main room. Children welcome. No smoking in dining-room. Wheelchair access (no WC). Music

TADWORTH Surrey map 3

Gemini

28 Station Approach, Tadworth KT20 5AH COOKING 2
TEL: (01737) 812179 COST £21–£48

The building Gemini occupies may once have been a tea-room, but these days it is a crisply decorated popular local restaurant, although extension at the back just as the *Guide* went to press may perhaps make it less 'snug' than it was. Robert Foster moves with the times, having once described his cooking as 'neo-classical French' and now as 'modern European'. In fact it travels even further afield, with hoisin vinaigrette and toasted sesame seeds accompanying duck confit, and halibut given a pan global treatment: tempura-fried, and served with Chilean scallops and a coriander Thai sauce. Ostrich and kangaroo might also make an appearance on the menus. Starters of smoked salmon parcel, and a 'mountain' of mussels and clams, pleased two reporters one Sunday lunch, and although the English roast beef that followed was less successful, 'good humour was restored by two splendid desserts': a coconut confection, and a duo of chocolate. Or there might be apples baked with mincemeat and cider in puff pastry served with cinnamon ice-cream. Service is 'attentive without being obsequious'. Forty-five considerately priced wines feature prime regions of France with representations from other countries. Seven house wines start at £8.95.

CHEF/PROPRIETOR: Robert Foster OPEN: Tue to Fri and Sun L 12 to 2.30, Tue to Sat D 7 to 9.30 CLOSED: 2 weeks Christmas MEALS: Set L £10.50 (2 courses) to £14.50, Set D Tue to Thur £20 (2 courses) to £24.50, Set D Fri and Sat £24.50. BYO £3.50 SERVICE: not inc CARDS: Amex, Delta, MasterCard, Switch, Visa DETAILS: 48 seats. Private parties: 38 main room. Vegetarian meals. Children's helpings L. No children under 12 at D. No cigars/pipes in dining-room. Wheelchair access (no WC). Music

TAPLOW Berkshire map 3

▲ *Cliveden, Terrace Restaurant*

Cliveden, Taplow SL6 0JF
TEL: (01628) 668561 FAX: (01628) 661837 COOKING 3
off A4, 2m N of Taplow on Cliveden Rd COST £40–£108

The entrance hall of this grandest of country houses has a 'time-warped charm', thanks to 'several hectares of tapestries', suits of armour, and massive oil paintings, including one of Nancy Astor by Sargent that hangs above the huge ornate fireplace. Settees, couches and chairs are arranged in hospitable groups, brass bowls are filled with mammoth flower displays, and the small studies and libraries where aperitifs are taken have handsome chairs, big chandeliers and book-lined shelves. The Terrace has what Waldo's (see entry below) doesn't: a magnificent view across formal gardens and box hedges to the Thames beyond.

In marked contrast to Waldo's, some of the dishes have an old-fashioned air about them – tournedos Rossini, chateaubriand for two, mixed grill, or Dover sole 'fried in lashings of butter' – although Irish rock oysters, Colchester natives, and a ballottine of foie gras with truffle dressing confirm that luxury is never far away. One visitor was buoyed by properly made mushroom risotto served with shreds of Reggiano Parmesan, but vegetables and cheeses have disappointed. Desserts might include hot chocolate sponge, or apple tart with prune and armagnac ice-cream. The Falstaffian wine list is par for the course in an establishment with lofty aspirations, and some of the mark-ups fly high indeed. Premium names, mostly from France, add weight to every page, although North America makes a notable contribution. Faced with such grandeur, it was disappointing for one experienced reporter to find wine service less than knowledgeable. CELLARMAN'S CHOICE: Niersteiner Oelberg Riesling Kabinett 1995, Rheinhessen, £25; Viña Ardanza Reserva 1989, La Rioja Alta, £30.

CHEF: Ron Maxfield PROPRIETOR: Cliveden plc OPEN: all week; 12.30 to 2.30, 7.30 to 9.30 MEALS: alc (main courses £14 to £29). Set L £26, Set D £38.50 SERVICE: net prices, card slips closed CARDS: Amex, Diners, MasterCard, Switch, Visa DETAILS: 65 seats. Private parties: 54 main room, 12 to 54 private rooms. Car park. Vegetarian meals. Children's helpings. Jacket and tie. No smoking in dining-room. Wheelchair access (also WC). No music ACCOMMODATION: 38 rooms, all with bath/shower. TV. Phone. Air-conditioned. Room only £230 to £410. Rooms for disabled. Children welcome. Baby facilities. Dogs welcome. Garden. Swimming-pool. Fishing

▲ *Cliveden, Waldo's*

Taplow SL6 0JF — COOKING **8**
TEL: (01628) 668561 FAX: (01628) 661837 — COST £63–£106

Drive round the Fountain of Love and scrunch up the gravel drive to where 'butlers' in frock coats greet visitors and valet-park the cars. Take a short trek along a corridor lined with busts of dignitaries, then down the stairs to a 'gentlemen's club' of a bar and the restaurant. It might seem odd to build a luxurious restaurant on the 'lower ground floor' when the house overlooks such beautiful English countryside, but the Terrace restaurant (see entry above) bags the view. Nevertheless, Waldo's is a room of 'warm serenity', with rich fabrics, well-upholstered chairs 'ready to embrace the most ample forms', and dozens of paintings and prints. 'It hums with seriousness.'

The option is between a set seven-course 'menu gourmande' at £75, and either three (£49) or four (£55) courses with very fair choice. At these prices, expect caviare, foie gras and truffles, especially among first courses. Ron Maxfield uses fine ingredients for his 'doggedly consistent' cooking. Dishes are well rehearsed, precisely planned and timed, and freshness is apparent in both tastes and textures: sweet, plump, chargrilled langoustines 'firm to the bite', or 'yielding but not soft' brill, served with trompette mushrooms in a 'silky smooth sauce' made from cooking juices. The food is well crafted – for example, a ballottine of foie gras with duck confit and truffle that was considered 'a dish of tremendous care and refinement' – and execution is both deft and decorative, as in crisp-skinned red mullet fillets, served with a potato and mullet brandade, that came with zig-zags of colourful tapénade, tomato and basil sauces looking 'like interference on a television screen'.

Desserts are a hedonistic 'tour de force', from warm chocolate fondant, or caramelised apple and filo tart, to hot mirabelle plum soufflé served with a 'glorious liquorice ice-cream'. Formally dressed staff are on the ball, although it seemed bizarre, when an inspector wished to know how some of the dishes were cooked, to be told it was 'the chef's secret'. Ancillaries such as appetisers, bread, and petits-fours are of a high standard, still or fizzy water is included in the price, and no service charge is either made or expected. The only extra is a £2.50 levy for the National Trust, owners of the house. Wines are the same as in the Terrace restaurant.

CHEF: Ron Maxfield PROPRIETOR: Cliveden plc OPEN: Tue to Sat D 7 to 10.30 MEALS: Set D £49 to £75 SERVICE: net prices, card slips closed CARDS: Amex, Diners, MasterCard, Switch, Visa DETAILS: 28 seats. Car park. Vegetarian meals. Children's helpings. Jacket and tie. No smoking in dining-room. Wheelchair access (also WC). Music. Air-conditioned ACCOMMODATION: See entry above for details

TAUNTON Somerset map 2

SOUTH-WEST 1998 STAR

▲ *Castle Hotel*

Castle Green, Taunton TA1 1NF COOKING 8
TEL: (01823) 272671 FAX: (01823) 336066 COST £29–£68

The wistaria-covered Castle wears its history lightly. It was a fortress nine centuries ago (the Norman garden is still there), and has been a hotel for three (centuries, that is), with a string of worthy visitors. But the town centre location gives even the smartly furnished dining-room an ordinary, lived-in feel, which endears it to all-comers. Castle-watchers have witnessed a few tweaks to prices and ingredients here and there as the Chapmans juggle with the delicate balance between value for customers and a healthy bottom line for the business, but a mark of their success has been that quality never suffers. They know their market, Phil Vickery delivers the goods with assurance, and the operation appears in perfect harmony with itself and its surroundings.

Perhaps the biggest attraction of the food is that it combines high quality with approachability. Nothing intimidates, yet no corners are cut. Some of the food may sound everyday fare – deep-fried cod with mushy peas, chips and tartare sauce, or chicken hash cake with spinach, poached egg and béarnaise sauce – but fine ingredients, real flavours and proper textures lift it all out of the ordinary. A strong British theme runs through, from salmon and sole fish-cakes to braised ox-tongue with mashed potato, and although the food may seem safe it is never boring. Indeed, the simplicity is deceptive. A humble slice of shoulder of lamb with thyme, garlic and seasonal vegetables makes just as vivid an impression as a more refined crab and saffron tart.

At lunch the *carte* offers generous choice and a fair range of prices – some dishes can be ordered either as a starter or as a main course – but the more expensive set-price menus are much the more exciting. Any restaurant with such proudly British credentials has to do a good line in puddings, and these range from an improvable steamed jam roll to lemon-curd tart, and baked egg-custard tart with nutmeg ice-cream. Incidentals such as bread are first-rate, and service is smooth and accomplished. Choose from the 'short' list of 33 wines mostly priced under £20, or from the 'full' list of around 300. French classics are in the majority here, but most other regions offer some modern classics of their own. Malt lovers may wish to save their drink ration for the end of the meal – 30 are available at £6.40 for a 50ml glass. There are 30 half-bottles, and Australian house wines are £11.50. CELLARMAN'S CHOICE: Rossj-Bass Chardonnay 1994, Gaja, Italy, £33.10; Rutherford Niebaum Coppola Rubicon 1986, Napa Valley, California, £34.80.

CHEF: Phil Vickery PROPRIETORS: the Chapman family OPEN: all week 12.30 to 2.30, 7.30 to 9 MEALS: alc L Mon to Sat (main courses £8.50 to £14.50). Set L £34 to £38.50, Set D £23 to £38.50 SERVICE: not inc, card slips closed CARDS: Amex, Diners, MasterCard, Switch, Visa DETAILS: 65 seats. Private parties: 110 main room, 10 to 25 private rooms. Car park. Children's helpings. No smoking in dining-room. Wheelchair access (also WC). Music ACCOMMODATION: 36 rooms, all with bath/shower. TV. Phone. B&B £80 to £195. Rooms for disabled. Children welcome. Baby facilities. Dogs welcome in bedrooms only. Afternoon teas. Garden

TAVISTOCK Devon map 1

▲ *Horn of Plenty*

Gulworthy, Tavistock PL19 8JD
TEL/FAX: (01822) 832528
3m W of Tavistock on A390, turn right at Gulworthy Cross

COOKING **6**
COST £27–£59

The 'pleasant country house in fine Devon countryside' is Georgian and sits high above the Tamar with views across folding fields. There is ample room to nurse a menu and aperitif before moving to the pink and green dining-rooms, one with a curved wooden ceiling faintly reminiscent of an old railway carriage. Lunch (considered good value) is a flexible two- or three-dish arrangement, and dinner offers a varied choice.

Peter Gorton's menu cheerfully picks up what it can from all over the world, including tempura of lemon sole, rabbit confit, and pan-fried saffron risotto cake, and materials are well chosen. For one reporter, a panaché of brill, mullet and sea bass with a chive-flecked beurre blanc 'demonstrated the joys of very fresh fish'. A characteristic depth of flavour infuses the food, not least robust game dishes such as medallions of venison with caramelised shallots and port sauce, and Italian themes are well handled: tomato consommé with spinach and pesto tortellini, for example, or garlic and rosemary polenta to accompany pink roast lamb with wild mushrooms.

Warm chocolate cake with a melted centre, or date pithiviers (with crème fraîche ice-cream and vanilla sauce) may be among desserts, and the 'intensely citric' lemon tart has been authoritatively praised. Elaine Gatehouse presides over a tightly run operation, the atmosphere is 'warm and welcoming', and the predominantly French wines are well chosen. Quality is high throughout, whether in classic regions or among the nine fairly priced house wines, all available at £2.50 a glass, including a local white.

CHEF: Peter Gorton PROPRIETORS: Elaine and Ian Gatehouse OPEN: Tue to Sun L 12 to 2, all week D 7 to 9 CLOSED: 25 and 26 Dec MEALS: Set L £10.50 (2 courses) to £17.50, Set D £29.50 SERVICE: not inc CARDS: Amex, MasterCard, Visa DETAILS: 50 seats. 20 seats outside. Private parties: 50 main room, 12 private room. Car park. Vegetarian meals. No children under 13. No smoking in dining-room. Wheelchair access (also WC). No music ACCOMMODATION: 7 rooms, all with bath/shower. TV. Phone. B&B £63 to £98. Rooms for disabled. No children under 13. Dogs welcome. Garden (*The Which? Hotel Guide*)

Neil's $*

27 King Street, Tavistock PL19 0DT — COOKING 3
TEL: (01822) 615550 — COST £25–£40

In 1998 Janet Neil celebrates ten years in this converted sixteenth-century farmhouse, where she has championed local materials and free-range meats, many from rare breeds. She has little truck with the contemporary repertoire, preferring instead to deal in such classic ideas as seafood chowder, chicken with tarragon, or a Swiss cheese soufflé with a creamy cheese sauce. Cream, butter and alcohol are the basis of much saucing, and some flavours may lack definition, but wild Tamar salmon surfaces in season, Tamworth pork is served with red cabbage, apples, cream and calvados, and Gressingham duck might appear with a green peppercorn sauce and leek purée. Cheeses are from Devon, as is the cream served with local soft fruits in summer. Fairly priced wines from around the world, and a dozen half-bottles, add to the appeal. House vin de pays is £8.95.

CHEF/PROPRIETOR: Janet Neil OPEN: Tue to Sat D only 7 to 9 CLOSED: 24 to 30 Dec MEALS: alc (main courses £12.50 to £14). Set D £17 SERVICE: not inc CARDS: Amex, MasterCard, Visa DETAILS: 20 seats. Private parties: 20 main room. Vegetarian meals. Children welcome. No smoking in dining-room. No music

TEFFONT EVIAS Wiltshire — map 2

▲ *Howard's House* $*

Teffont Evias SP3 5RJ
TEL: (01722) 716392 and 716821
FAX: (01722) 716820
off B3089, W of Dinton and 9½m W of Salisbury, signposted Chicksgrove — COOKING 3, COST £26–£40

The setting of this seventeenth-century dower house is so indelibly pastoral English, thought one reporter, that all it lacks are the strains of Vaughan Williams's 'Lark Ascending' hovering in the air. The criss-crossed paths through the gardens, a tinkling fountain, the croquet lawn, the view to a wooded hill beyond are what you leave the city for. It may look twee, was the verdict, 'but at least it's lived-in twee'. The dining-room is done out in soothing leafy green with comfortable bamboo-backed chairs and a Grecian urn overflowing with blooms.

A well-balanced first course of seared red mullet has been given a Chinese sauce of soy, ginger and five-spice powder, and a main course of whole poussin marinated in lemon and lime and with a scattering of fennel seeds comes juicily roasted. Rabbit casseroled with tomatoes, tarragon and garlic, or pork loin with apricots, rosemary and madeira may be alternative main courses. Dessert sorbets mobilise interesting flavours such as mango or rhubarb, or there is a squishy version of bread-and-butter pudding with plenty of calvados in it. Home-made bread is good. Service is generally competent, and wines are mostly French with some selected bins from the New World, though prices are a bit on the high side. Half a dozen house wines start at £9.95.

CHEF: Paul Firmin PROPRIETORS: Paul Firmin and Jonathan Ford OPEN: Sun L 12.30 to 2, all week D 7.30 to 9.30 MEALS: Set L Sun £18.50, Set D £22 (2 courses) to £25. BYO £6 SERVICE: not inc, card slips closed CARDS: Amex, Delta, Diners, MasterCard, Switch, Visa DETAILS: 30 seats. 10 seats outside. Private parties: 40 main room. Car park. Children's helpings. No smoking in dining-room. Wheelchair access (no WC). Music ACCOMMODATION: 9 rooms, all with bath/shower. TV. Phone. B&B £75 to £115. Children welcome. Dogs welcome. Afternoon teas. Garden (*The Which? Hotel Guide*)

TETBURY Gloucestershire map 2

▲ *Calcot Manor*

Tetbury GL8 8YJ
TEL: (01666) 890391 FAX: (01666) 890394 COOKING **2**
on junction of A4135 and A46, 3m W of Tetbury COST £24–£53

'Everything is pristine,' observed one reporter eyeing the car park, lawns and flower-beds around this beautifully renovated thirteenth-century farmhouse and its cluster of outbuildings. The main restaurant is set partly in a 'tasteful' conservatory with arresting colours, and partly in a dining-room with a seafood buffet on weekday lunch-times, while the global shopping bag supplies materials from tempura vegetables to smoked eel, from gnocchi to Thai herbs. Good bread and 'exceptional' pasta are locally made, the latter having appeared as garganelli with mussels, scallops, cockles and calamares in a sauce 'laced with cream and herbs' that smacked of the sea. At an inspection meal, however, it was felt that bolder flavours, and perhaps a keener sense of direction to the cooking, might have had more impact.

The modern style seems to have more success in the attached Gumstool Inn, serviced by the same kitchen, where similar brasserie food is served at lower prices. Both venues are helped by a two-tier pricing system, allowing many dishes to be taken in either smaller or larger portions. The Gumstool's wine list comprises two dozen well-travelled bins, arranged by style and priced from £8.50 a bottle, with several available by the glass. The conservatory's is a lengthier affair and mostly French, but a brief flirtation with the New World results in plenty of good drinking under £20. House French is £12. CELLARMAN'S CHOICE: Jurançon Sec 1992, Clos Lapeyre, £20; Côtes de Provence, Roches Noires 1993, Dom. de Curebeasse, £18.

CHEF: Michael Croft PROPRIETORS: Michael and Louisa Stone OPEN: all week 12 to 2, 7 to 9.30 MEALS: alc (main courses L £7 to £13, D £8.50 to £17). Set L £17, Set D £22 SERVICE: not inc, card slips closed CARDS: Amex, Delta, Diners, MasterCard, Switch, Visa DETAILS: 80 seats. Private parties: 80 main room, 16 and 70 private rooms. Car park. Vegetarian meals. Children's helpings. No smoking in 1 dining-room. Wheelchair access (also WC). No music ACCOMMODATION: 25 rooms, all with bath/shower. TV. Phone. B&B £95 to £145. Rooms for disabled. Children welcome. Baby facilities. Afternoon teas. Garden. Swimming-pool (*The Which? Hotel Guide*)

THORNBURY South Gloucestershire map 2

▲ *Thornbury Castle* 🍷 £✱

Castle Street, Thornbury BS12 1HH
TEL: (01454) 281182 FAX: (01454) 416188 COOKING 5
off B4061, at N end of town COST £30–£66

Driving in past the church and the castle's own vineyards (the results are served by the glass) and through an ancient gateway is 'a big thrill'. Thornbury was built in 1511, and embraces the historical theme enthusiastically, with open fires, wood panelling, heraldic shields and Old Master prints. Dinner offers either three courses with generous choice, or four with none at all beyond either cheese or dessert. The food may be straightforward, even simple, but it is all 'very much to the point', as our inspector found in a first course of seared scallops sitting on a sweetly intense tomato and onion 'fondue', topped with a mound of well-dressed rocket: 'all very fresh, just right for a starter.'

The kitchen is fond of wrapping (smoked salmon around Cornish crab), crushing (potatoes) and creaming (leeks, served with salmon), and makes good use of the herb garden. Raw materials are first-rate, presentation is colourful, and there are some 'excellent flavour and texture combinations', from 'supple and juicy' chunks of loin of new season's lamb (served with couscous and tomato-stuffed baby courgette), to sun-dried apricot parfait ('like a big bowl of solidified clotted cream') with honey sauce and ice cream. Formally dressed service strikes an individual note without becoming too familiar, although it has been criticised for its slow pace. The wine list contains some great burgundies and clarets that date back to 1916, so although you may blink at the prices, in some cases they are warranted. There is also plenty of reliable drinking to be had under £20, particularly from the New World, where bins are helpfully arranged by grape variety, and half-bottles have a good showing. House wines start at £12 with the Thornbury Castle Müller-Thurgau.

CHEF: Steven Black PROPRIETOR: Baron of Portlethen OPEN: all week 12 to 1.45, 7 to 9.30 (10 Sat) CLOSED: 3 days Jan MEALS: Set L £18.50, Set D £34.50 to £36. BYO £10 SERVICE: not inc, card slips closed CARDS: Amex, Delta, Diners, MasterCard, Switch, Visa DETAILS: 60 seats. Private parties: 28 main room, 14 private room. Car park. No children under 12. Jacket and tie at D. No smoking in dining-room. Wheelchair access (no WC). Music ACCOMMODATION: 18 rooms, all with bath/shower. TV. Phone. B&B £75 to £225. No children under 12. Afternoon teas. Garden (*The Which? Hotel Guide*)

▲ *means accommodation is available.*

THORNTON CLEVELEYS Lancashire map 8

Didier's £

Trunnah Road, Thornton Cleveleys FY5 4HF
TEL: (01253) 860619 FAX: (01253) 865350 COOKING 2
off A585, 3m N of Blackpool COST £14–£36

If you have memories of the Victorian House that this used to be, prepare to shed them now. In March 1997, the place reopened under the same ownership, but with a redesign that has transformed it from English nineteenth-century domicile to modern cross-Channel bistro. Soft greens and blues now lighten the décor and the food has lightened too: Caesar salad comes with chargrilled chicken breast and crunchy croûtons, while prawns are served in a salad dressed with black beans and cumin. Despite the Gallic décor, influences are pretty cosmopolitan. Main courses take in skewered lamb on couscous, grilled bratwurst with mustard and frites, and kangaroo rump with béarnaise, while desserts include Häagen-Dazs ice-creams as well as an attractively presented pear charlotte with raspberry coulis. Didier's is also a wine-bar, and the short but interesting list is happy to look outside France for ideas. Prices start at £6.95.

CHEF: Didier Guerin PROPRIETORS: Louise and Didier Guerin OPEN: all week 12 to 2, 6 to 10 MEALS: alc (main courses £6 to £11). Set L £6 (2 courses) to £8. BYO £5 SERVICE: not inc, card slips closed CARDS: Amex, MasterCard, Switch, Visa DETAILS: 65 seats. 30 seats outside. Private parties: 40 main room. Car park. Vegetarian meals. No children under 6. Music

TORQUAY Devon map 1

Table

135 Babbacombe Road, Torquay TQ1 3SR COOKING 4
TEL/FAX: (01803) 324292 COST £35–£42

The small converted shop unit, part of a late-nineteenth-century terrace on a winding road out of Torquay, may not be the most auspicious location for a restaurant, but the size makes it suitable for Julie Tuckett's single-minded solo enterprise. There are few distractions, so attention tends to focus on the short, sharp dinner menu (lunch is a lighter affair) that typically offers four starters and four main courses. Devon beef, Cornish or Somerset veal, and Exmoor venison are among the raw materials, and local seafood has proved its freshness in a salad of seared scallops, a rust-coloured crab-laden fish soup, and an 'absolutely natural' sea bass simply roasted.

Sauces might be knocked up at the last minute from *jus* plus a little alcohol and cream, depending on the circumstances: calvados and cider with guinea-fowl, or blackberry and juniper with Barbary duck. The house speciality dessert is an apricot soufflé made with brioche crumbs – 'a sort of queen of puddings with egg whites inside rather than on top' – or there might be chilled chocolate terrine with plum purée. The carefully chosen wine list holds many eye-catching bins, with the majority priced under £20. A dozen house wines from £10.85 a bottle offer a good range of styles and are also available by the glass in three helpful sizes: 125ml, 175ml and a whopping 250ml. Half-bottles are generous too.

CHEF/PROPRIETOR: Julie T. Tuckett OPEN: Tue to Fri L 12.15 to 1.45, all week D 7.30 to 9.30 CLOSED: Christmas, 2 weeks Feb, 2 weeks Mar, L May to Aug MEALS: Set L £8.50 (1 course) to £12.50 (2 courses), Set D £26.50 SERVICE: not inc, card slips closed CARDS: Amex, Diners, MasterCard, Switch, Visa DETAILS: 20 seats. Private parties: 20 main room. Children's helpings. No children under 10. No smoking while others eat. Wheelchair access (no WC). No music

---

TRUSHAM Devon map 1

▲ *Cridford Inn* £

Trusham TQ13 0NR
TEL: (01626) 853694
3m N of Chudleigh; from A38 take Teign Valley exit on to B3193, follow signs for Trusham; inn is signposted after 3m, at lower part of village

COOKING 1
COST £20–£38

The inn, dating from Saxon times, was rebuilt shortly after the Norman Conquest and still retains some medieval trappings, including the earliest example of a domestic window in Britain. Perhaps best considered as a pub rather than a restaurant, it nevertheless gets fish from Brixham, game from a nearby estate, and smokes its own salmon. Dishes are commendably simple – warm vichyssoise soup, game pie with a suet crust, and well-soaked summer pudding – and grilled plaice and lamb chops have been 'faultless' in execution, served with 'straightforward' vegetables. Cheeses, however, are 'a bit basic' given the wealth available in Devon. The dining-room is open only in the evening, but bar meals are served at lunch-time, when one reporter enjoyed chicken-liver pâté, 'first-class, abundant smoked eel', coffee and a pint of Dartmoor bitter for £10. A short, serviceable wine list offers a good selection by the glass. House French is £10.75.

CHEF: David Hesmondhalgh PROPRIETORS: David and Sally Hesmondhalgh OPEN: restaurant Tue to Sat D 7 to 8.45; bar/bistro all week 12.15 to 1.45, 7 to 8.45 CLOSED: 25 Dec MEALS: alc (main courses restaurant £5.50 to £13, bar/bistro £5 to £10.50). Set D £18.75 SERVICE: not inc, card slips closed CARDS: MasterCard, Visa DETAILS: 65 seats. 25 seats outside. Private parties: 18 main room. Car park. Vegetarian meals. Children welcome until 8.30pm in bar/bistro only. No smoking in restaurant. No music ACCOMMODATION: 4 rooms, all with bath/shower. TV. B&B £40 to £60. Deposit: £20. Dogs welcome in bedrooms and on a lead in bar only

---

TUNBRIDGE WELLS Kent map 3

Sankey's

39 Mount Ephraim, Tunbridge Wells TN4 8AA
TEL: (01892) 511422 FAX: (01892) 536097

COOKING 1
COST £28–£57

The appeal is 'good-quality fish and shellfish served in a jolly atmosphere' in this Victorian villa. Bright lighting and prints on the walls set the tone, and the menu offers 'traditional British seafood standards' such as grilled Dover sole, lobster, and dressed crab, with few frills beyond an occasional foray into paella or Portuguese cataplana (with clams, mussels and chorizo). The choice is between a *carte* with Loch Fyne oysters, fish soup, and skate wing with black butter, and (at dinner) a three-course set-price menu with four or five items at each stage. It is probably best to stick to the simpler dishes. A seafood platter costs £17.50, and there may be fillet steak or rack of lamb for a change. Finish with crème brûlée, lemon tart, or very thin chocolate roulade with raspberries. Forty-plus wines are well chosen and decently priced. House white is Domaine Virginie's Vin de Pays d'Oc Marsanne at £10.

CHEF: Kim Adams PROPRIETOR: Guy Sankey OPEN: Mon to Fri L 12 to 2, Mon to Sat D 7 to 10 CLOSED: Christmas, bank hols MEALS: alc (main courses £10 to £25). Set L £7.50 (2 courses), Set D £23.50. BYO by arrangement SERVICE: not inc CARDS: Amex, Delta, Diners, MasterCard, Switch, Visa DETAILS: 70 seats. Private parties: 24 main room, 12 to 24 private rooms. Vegetarian meals. Children's helpings. Wheelchair access (no WC). Music. Air-conditioned

Thackeray's House 🍷

85 London Road, Tunbridge Wells TN1 1EA
TEL: (01892) 511921 and 537559 — COOKING **6**
FAX: (01892) 511921 — COST £35–£68

This white-tiled seventeenth-century house at the edge of the common was once the home of the author of *Vanity Fair*. It is now Tunbridge's gastronomic flagship, thanks to the talents of chef-patron Bruce Wass, who has chalked up 13 years here. Drinks are taken in the pleasant first-floor bay-windowed sitting-room, among some endearingly worn furnishings.

The *carte* is supplemented by set-price menus, with the midweek three-course deal looking particularly good value. Duck liver terrine impresses for the textural variety it incorporates as well as the spoonful of sweet red onion marmalade served with it. Mussel risotto has been praised for its 'intense flavour of the sea', while a main course of duck breast and leg, slow-cooked for eight hours then crisped under the grill, comes with 'most unusual and enjoyable' wood mushrooms. Other main courses – 'first-class' fricassee of brill with scallops, for instance, or 'incredibly tender' lamb fillets with flageolets and garlic fritters – work equally well.

The signature dessert of toffee pudding with apricots, walnuts and ginger arrives with toffee sauce as 'sticky and rich' as previous reporters have found it, while passion-fruit cheesecake, and prune and armagnac ice-cream are among the alternatives. Petits fours include hard little chocolate balls full of runny truffle, candied orange peel and mini-meringues that shatter to the bite. Service is charming, attentive and informed. Although fine wines from France continue to dominate the huge list, the New World section has increased its appeal with the addition of some classy bottles from the USA, New Zealand and Western Australia. Italy and Spain provide sound support, while 60 half-bottles are a plus. House French is £11.90. CELLARMAN'S CHOICE: Coteaux du Languedoc, Mas Morties 1994, £22; Marsannay Les Estaces 1995, Alain Guyard, £24.50.

CHEF/PROPRIETOR: Bruce Wass OPEN: Tue to Sun L 12.30 to 2, Tue to Sat D 7 to 10 CLOSED: 5 days Christmas MEALS: alc D (main courses £14 to £20). Set L Tue to Sat £13 to £19.75 (both 2 courses), Set L Sun £23.50, Set D Tue to Thur £24.50, Set D Tue to Sat £45 SERVICE: not inc CARDS: Delta, MasterCard, Switch, Visa DETAILS: 50 seats. 40 seats outside. Private parties: 60 main room, 12 to 22 private rooms. Children's helpings. No cigars/pipes in dining-room. Wheelchair access (no WC). No music

TWICKENHAM Greater London map 3

McClements

2 Whitton Road, Twickenham TW1 1BJ COOKING 6
TEL: (0181) 744 9610 FAX: (01784) 242 956 COST £28–£53

A selection of art nouveau mirrors, the motif echoed in curlicues around the front window, lends distinction to John McClements's restaurant close to Twickenham station. Illumination levels at night may mean that people have to peer at each other, but those used to big bright brasseries may find that 'it makes a change'. What matters is that 'we had a warm welcome and service was good'. The attractive modern approach yields some interesting combinations: for example, tarte Tatin of scallops, or Yorkshire pudding and foie gras, or a salad containing lobster, quail and boudin of foie gras. Innovation is concentrated more in starters, while main courses lean towards the mainstream, including perhaps saddle of lamb with rosemary and grilled provençale vegetables, or ribeye steak with green peppercorns.

Seafood has been notably fresh – for example, 'firm' sea bass, perhaps crusted and served with diced peppers – and the food is characterised by high-quality ingredients and 'superb' presentation, according to one who ate smoked salmon on a potato galette with caviare, crab salad with a basil dressing, and lobster ravioli. A hot soufflé or rum baba may be among desserts. 'Faultless' is a plaudit that has turned up in more than one report, and service is very professional. We are unable to provide any information about wines, since the restaurant has chosen not to send us any details.

CHEF/PROPRIETOR: John McClements OPEN: Mon to Sat 12 to 2.30, 6.30 to 10.30 CLOSED: 27 to 30 Dec MEALS: alc (main courses £12 to £15). Set L £14 (2 courses), Set D £22 (2 courses) to £25, Set D Mon to Fri £23 (inc wine, minimum 2), Set L and D £38 (inc wine, minimum 2). BYO £2.50 SERVICE: 10%, card slips closed CARDS: Amex, MasterCard, Visa DETAILS: 40 seats. Private parties: 100 main room, 100 private room. Car park. Vegetarian meals. Children welcome. Wheelchair access (also WC). Music. Air-conditioned

UCKFIELD East Sussex map 3

▲ Horsted Place Hotel, Pugin Restaurant

Little Horsted, Uckfield TN22 5TS
TEL: (01825) 750581 FAX: (01825) 750459 COOKING 5
on A26, 2m S of Uckfield COST £26–£59

A certain Mr Pugin designed Horsted, and the present owners of what is now a top-flight country-house hotel with all the frills and furbelows have named the restaurant after him. Approach through mature woodland to a spectacular frontage. Deep enveloping sofas await inside, as do generous vistas from the tall bay windows of the dining-room where walls have been re-papered in dark red.

Allan Garth and his team cook in a modern hotel idiom, the soft-focus presentations often belying some pretty earthy treatments. A monkfish tail is bound up in Parma ham, seasoned with basil and set on a thick pea purée, while rabbit and venison go improbably well together in a slice of terrine served with richly buttery brioche. At inspection, well-judged baked cod on ratatouille had plenty of flavour, though chicken breast stuffed with langoustines was less successful. Vegetarians might eat a tartlet of spinach and mushrooms with caramelised red onions and a tomato butter sauce. Desserts have included 'excellently textured' mousse of coffee and chocolate in a tulip. Service is well drilled and professional. The wine list is very posh with some fine German classics and top-notch antipodeans, but mark-ups press hard. The house selection opens at £12.50 for Vin de Pays d'Oc Sauvignon and Merlot.

CHEF: Allan Garth PROPRIETOR: Granfel Holdings Ltd OPEN: all week 12 to 2, 7.30 to 9.30 MEALS: alc (main courses £18 to £19.50). Set L Mon to Sat £15.95, Set L Sun £16.95, Set D £28.50 SERVICE: not inc, card slips closed CARDS: Amex, Delta, Diners, MasterCard, Switch, Visa DETAILS: 40 seats. Private parties: 24 main room, 16 and 24 private rooms. Car park. Vegetarian meals. No children under 12. No smoking in dining-room. Music ACCOMMODATION: 17 rooms, all with bath/shower. TV. Phone. B&B £60 to £285. Rooms for disabled. No children under 12. Afternoon teas. Garden. Swimming-pool (*The Which? Hotel Guide*)

ULLSWATER Cumbria map 10

▲ *Sharrow Bay*

Ullswater CA10 2LZ
TEL: (01768) 486301 FAX: (01768) 486349
2m from Pooley Bridge on E side of lake, signposted Howtown and Martindale

COOKING 7
COST £44–£66

'No matter what one thinks about Sharrow when one is away, the moment one arrives, one is seduced by the whole atmosphere,' sighed a return visitor. Simply to call this country house on Ullswater's eastern shore an institution would be unfair to the achievement of Francis Coulson and Brian Sack. With 37 years in the *Guide* under its belt and still shining bright, this is the northern star of post-war English catering.

The evening drill impresses for its seamless professionalism, and for the ease with which it encourages diners to relax and enjoy. Nothing truly startling emerges from the kitchen, nor is there a sense of time-warp about the menus. A first course of whole boned quail wrapped in a cabbage leaf and served on a ragoût of wild mushrooms with roasted shallots and a port sauce was thought 'perfection' by one reporter. The wide range of starters is followed by a no-choice fish course – perhaps sole fillet stuffed with salmon mousseline and accompanied by a cardamom sauce – and then a fruit sorbet. Meaty main courses have included herb-crusted lamb with a tomato and thyme sauce, and medallion of local venison with tagliatelle, adorned with glazed apple, fried pimentos and chestnuts. Alcohol is a typical sauce ingredient, and accompanying vegetables are usually two sorts plus potatoes done two ways. Heritage desserts might include Regency syllabub with hearts of shortbread, or creamed rice with blackberries, or there may be a marzipan basket of marsala parfait topped with plum compote. 'Great British cheeses' follow.

If you've managed to digest all that overnight, get set for breakfast. 'This is the only place I know that can make proper scrambled eggs,' insists a perfectionist. Francis Coulson and Brian Sack keep watch over proceedings, dispensing courtesies with fluent ease as they have been since before the end of rationing. The wine list opens with a mouthwatering collection of 33 by the glass, including nine dessert wines, starting at £3. High quality is maintained throughout, not only in the French classic regions, but also in Germany, Austria and the New World. Mark-ups are reasonable at all levels and, surprisingly for a country house, over 100 bottles are offered under £20. House wines are £13.95. CELLARMAN'S CHOICE: Chablis Vaucoupin 1992, William Fèvre, £27.50; St-Joseph, Déschants 1994, Chapoutier, £21.50.

CHEFS: Johnnie Martin, Colin Akrigg and Philip Wilson PROPRIETORS: Francis Coulson and Brian Sack OPEN: all week 1 to 1.45, 8 to 8.45 CLOSED: end Nov to end Feb MEALS: Set L £32.25, Set D £42.75 SERVICE: none, card slips closed CARDS: MasterCard, Switch, Visa DETAILS: 65 seats. Private parties: 10 main room. Car park. No children under 13. Jacket and tie at D. No smoking in dining-room. Wheelchair access (also WC). No music. Air-conditioned ACCOMMODATION: 28 rooms, 24 with bath/shower. TV. Phone. D,B&B £93 to £340. No children under 13. Afternoon teas. Garden (*The Which? Hotel Guide*)

ULVERSTON Cumbria map 8

▲ *Bay Horse*

Canal Foot, Ulverston LA12 9EL
TEL: (01229) 583972 FAX: (01229) 580502
off A590; just before centre of Ulverston, follow signs to Canal Foot

COOKING 5
COST £24–£43

The approach is past Glaxo's not-exactly-inspiring chemical works, but 'when you get there the scenery changes spectacularly'. The Bay Horse is perched at the edge of the peaceful Leven Estuary, whose tidal meanderings cover vast expanses of sand. Co-owner John Tovey also runs Miller Howe in Windermere (see entry), and the hotel's informed but informal style is very much in the Lakeland tradition.

Pub meals are served in the small bar, but diners 'step into a different world' when they enter the large glassed-in verandah dining-room, with its crisp linen, butter-sculpted swans, and serious culinary intentions. Soups are particularly enjoyed: thick, dark cold gazpacho or 'piping hot' mushroom and marsala with croûtons. Alternatively there may be galantine of duck with Cumberland sauce. A main-course poached lemon sole filled with fresh crab and avocado, accompanied by a Noilly Prat and chive cream sauce, pleased one reporter, while another thought stuffed chicken breast with a soft cheese filling 'excellent'. Among well-reported desserts are Cape brandy pudding ('like a superior sticky toffee'), and lemon soufflé. Cheeses are in good condition, and strong aromatic coffee, with truffles, is complimentary. Service is both welcoming and accomplished.

The revamped list features wines full of individuality and character from forward-looking producers around the world. Prices are very reasonable, mostly staying below £20. A welcome innovation is the 'personal tasting', whereby customers are offered a glass each of six different wines throughout a meal for £15.

The Guide *always appreciates hearing about changes of chef or owner.*

CHEFS: Robert Lyons and Esther Jarvis PROPRIETORS: John Tovey and Robert Lyons OPEN: Tue to Sat L 12 to 1.30, all week D 7.30 for 8 (1 sitting) MEALS: alc (main courses £12 to £16). Set L £15.75. BYO £5. Bar L available Tue to Sun SERVICE: 10%, card slips closed CARDS: MasterCard, Visa DETAILS: 50 seats. Private parties: 50 main room. Car park. No children under 12. No smoking in dining-room. Wheelchair access (also WC). Music. Air-conditioned ACCOMMODATION: 7 rooms, all with bath/shower. TV. Phone. D,B&B £80 to £150. No children under 12. Dogs welcome in bedrooms only. Afternoon teas (*The Which? Hotel Guide*)

UPPER SLAUGHTER Gloucestershire map 5

▲ *Lords of the Manor*

Upper Slaughter, nr Bourton-on-the-Water GL54 2JD
TEL: (01451) 820243 FAX: (01451) 820696 COOKING **6**
turn W off A429, 3m S of Stow-on-the-Wold COST £35–£87

If the fundamentals have not changed – a mellow stone manor of gables and mullioned windows in eight acres of parkland with lake and secluded, mature gardens – things behind the scenes have. New owners Empire Ventures took over in 1997; they claim not to be planning any major changes, although a new chef is already in place. John Campbell's cooking fits the country-house hotel mould, and an inspection meal pointed to astute handling of fine raw materials. Some ideas are as simple as baked turbot with mashed peas and truffle dressing, while others are clever: for instance an impeccably executed rump of lamb in thyme *jus* with vegetable niçoise and wafer-thin aubergine crisps. First courses might include 'beautifully timed, nutty, roasted' scallops in a citrus beurre blanc, or terrine of duck and roasted shallots with a madeira jelly, and a meal for one reporter ended well with poached pear with cinnamon ice-cream on a biscuit Japonais. Alternatively, opt for 'hot strawberry Bakewell'.

Most dishes stay clear of the overwrought school of five-star hotel catering, being simply presented without extraneous garnishings, and attention is paid to extras such as nibbles, bread and petits fours. Wines are an interesting collection from around the globe, but high mark-ups have not pleased reporters, and that is before the addition of the obligatory 12.5% service charge. On the plus side, 15 wines are served by the glass (starting at £4.50). French house wines are £14.95 a bottle.

CHEF: John Campbell PROPRIETOR: Empire Ventures Ltd OPEN: all week 12.30 to 2 (2.30 Sun), 7 to 9.30 MEALS: alc (main courses £18.50 to £24.50). Set L £16.95 (2 courses) to £19.95, Set D £26.50 (2 courses) to £29.50 SERVICE: 12.5% CARDS: Amex, Delta, Diners, MasterCard, Switch, Visa DETAILS: 60 seats. 56 seats outside. Private parties: 60 main room, 30 private room. Car park. Children's helpings. No smoking in dining-room. Wheelchair access (also men's WC). No music ACCOMMODATION: 28 rooms, all with bath/shower. TV. Phone. B&B £90 to £245. Deposit: £50. Children welcome. Baby facilities. Afternoon teas. Garden (*The Which? Hotel Guide*)

'The caviare was such a minute portion that I could almost count the eggs. I gave my husband a generous taster (about eight eggs) and then took four of them back.'
(On eating in Somerset)

VIRGINSTOW Devon map 1

▲ *Percy's at Coombeshead*

Virginstow EX21 5EA
TEL: (01409) 211236 FAX: (01409) 211275
follow signs to Percy's at Coombeshead from Gridley corner on A388, or from B3218 at Metherell Cross junction

COOKING 5
COST £28–£42

As the *Guide* went to press the Bricknell-Webbs were debating whether or not to sell their far-flung North Harrow operation, listed in last year's edition. Certainly, the vegetables, salad leaves and herbs grown on their nearby farm have a much shorter journey to the kitchen here, and there is the added attraction of guest rooms in converted stabling. Bring walking-shoes, and don't startle the badgers.

Tina Bricknell-Webb is an ambitious chef. Her menus take note of far-off fashion as attentively as they follow the seasons. Thus chicken liver parfait comes with toasted sage bread and a chutney of marrow and onion, while a plate of grilled vegetables that incorporates courgettes, spring onions and tomatoes is adorned with stringy Taleggio cheese and a sherry vinaigrette. Main courses offer interesting fish preparations, such as mango, coriander and coconut cream sauce with wing of skate, or a chillied-up sweet pepper production for a fried fillet of tope (a rough-skinned and tasty species of shark). Organic Aberdeen Angus fillet with a mix of green and pink peppercorns is a favoured meat dish. At the end comes lavender crème brûlée, or caramelised pear tart with crème fraîche and cinnamon ice-cream. Tony Bricknell-Webb is an accomplished host and is more than happy to discuss the menu or indeed anything on the wine list. The latter is a compact but imaginative document that kicks off with South African house wines at £8.95.

CHEF: Tina Bricknell-Webb PROPRIETORS: Tony and Tina Bricknell-Webb OPEN: all week 12 to 2, 6.30 to 9.30 MEALS: Set L and D £15.50 (2 courses) to £19.50 SERVICE: not inc CARDS: Amex, Delta, Diners, MasterCard, Switch, Visa DETAILS: 46 seats. 30 seats outside. Private parties: 30 main room, 16 private room. Car park. Vegetarian meals. Children's helpings. No smoking in dining-room. Wheelchair access (also WC). Music ACCOMMODATION: 8 rooms, all with bath/shower. TV. B&B £34 to £80. Deposit: £50. Rooms for disabled. Children welcome. Dogs welcome. Garden (*The Which? Hotel Guide*)

WALKINGTON East Riding of Yorkshire map 9

▲ *Manor House*

Northlands, Newbold Road, Walkington HU17 8RT
TEL: (01482) 881645 FAX: (01482) 866501
off B1230 towards Beverley from Walkington

COOKING 3
COST £25–£44

This Victorian house sits in the rolling Yorkshire Wolds less than ten miles from Hull, surrounded by paddock and parkland. 'Difficult to find in the dark,' admitted one, but the effort is worthwhile; another reporter writes that 'the quality of the food and presentation was matched by the attentiveness of the staff and the warm welcome of the Baughs'.

Derek Baugh cooks a pair of fixed-price menus, one of three courses, the other of four plus coffee, the latter comprising more elaborate dishes and a choice of soup or sorbet for the second course. Fish-cakes are made with smoked haddock, prawns and egg and served on a Meaux mustard sabayon, while quail salad is dressed with strawberries. Main courses run from chargrilled cod with samphire and a saffron and ginger sauce, to pigeon with bubble and squeak sauced with Muscat wine and raisins. One reader was more than happy with a smooth-textured chocolate and hazelnut parfait for dessert, and there may also be lemon and passion-fruit bavarois, or bread-and-butter pudding. A small but carefully selected group of burgundies and some fine vintage clarets take pride of place on the wine list, while Spain and Australia provide some more affordable bins. House wines are £8.95.

CHEF: Derek Baugh PROPRIETORS: Derek and Lee Baugh OPEN: Mon to Sat D only 7 to 9.15 CLOSED: 25 and 26 Dec, bank hol Mons MEALS: Set D £16.50 and £28.50 SERVICE: not inc CARDS: Delta, MasterCard, Switch, Visa DETAILS: 55 seats. Private parties: 24 main room. Car park. Vegetarian meals. No children under 12. No cigars/pipes in dining-room. Music ACCOMMODATION: 7 rooms, all with bath/shower. TV. Phone. B&B £70 to £100. No children under 12. Dogs welcome by arrangement. Garden

WARE Hertfordshire map 3

Riverside Cafe

NEW ENTRY

The Priory, High Street, Ware SG12 9AL COOKING **5**
TEL: (01920) 486110 FAX: (01920) 486110 COST £20–£48

The fourteenth-century priory was saved from demolition at the time of the dissolution of the monasteries by becoming a private house. Now huge and handsome, as a result of extension and renovation over the generations, it accommodates (among other things) the district council chambers and the Riverside Café. A modern, light-filled room is 'done out in this year's colours – burnt orange and Mediterranean blues'.

Peter Brewer cooks modish, trans-global food that 'waves a big hello to the Mediterranean'. A starter of cappuccino of warm vichyssoise and smoked salmon is a very state-of-the-art frothed-up soup. Artful but not over-fussy presentation brings about juxtapositions such as vegetable spaghetti, straw potatoes and an orange and vanilla sauce with roasted brill. At inspection, a well-constructed salad of king scallops with langoustines and a red pepper sauce offered carefully considered flavours, and was followed by roast Barbary duck breast on 'creamy and luxurious' mushroom risotto with a juniper *jus*. Flavours are often at the subtle end of the spectrum, but rarely bland. Orange and lemon tart with a basket of 'sharp-tasting' matching sorbet makes a delicate but impressive dessert; alternatives might include mango Tatin with strawberry and peach compote. 'Young, attractive and professional' staff do their utmost to oblige. 'Hertfordshire should be pleased,' was the conclusion of one reporter. The wine list is as pleasingly inclusive as the food, and manages to offer most bins at less than £20. House Vin de Pays d'Oc is £9.

CHEF: Peter Brewer PROPRIETOR: Sally Hart OPEN: Wed to Sun L 12 to 3, Wed to Sat D 7 to 10 MEALS: alc (main courses L £6.50 to £11.50, D £9 to £17). Set L £8.50 (2 courses) SERVICE: not inc, card slips closed CARDS: Delta, MasterCard, Switch, Visa DETAILS: 70 seats. 12 seats outside. Private parties: 70 main room, 100 private room. Car park. Vegetarian meals. Children's helpings. No-smoking area. Wheelchair access (also WC). Music. Air-conditioned

WAREHAM Dorset map 2

▲ *Priory Hotel*

Church Green, Wareham BH20 4ND COOKING **5**
TEL: (01929) 551666 FAX: (01929) 554519 COST £25–£66

The name of the hotel reflects the building's origins as a Benedictine monastery in the sixteenth century. Its setting is thorough-going English pastoral: four manicured acres of green surround it, and the Frome flows by at the bottom of the lawn. Serious eating takes place in the cellar, which offers a more diverting backdrop for meals than most country houses can boast. Stephen Astley's approach is not to lull everybody into a dull sense of security, as can often be the case in this context, but to perk up interest.

Hot English mustard goes into watercress soup, and a salad of smoked salmon, crab and avocado is challengingly sharpened with horseradish as well as pink grapefruit. Thai seasonings of coconut milk, spring onions and lime light up a main course of baked snapper, while honey-roast duck appears with spiced pineapple. Lobster and crab are specialities in summer, and game comes from surrounding estates and the New Forest. 'Light and exquisite' bread-and-butter pudding can end things well; other desserts may include creamed rice-pudding with rhubarb compote, or raspberry mousse with minted passion-fruit coulis. Service is 'first-rate' and 'unassuming'.

A collection of fine vintage claret includes several from 1970 and a Ch. Montrose 1961, as well as some great burgundies. France still dominates, but the New World section has gained in interest with some exciting wines from California and Oregon. Prices throughout are fair, beginning with the Dom. Laroche house vins de pays at £10.50 a bottle, £3.50 a glass. CELLARMAN'S CHOICE: Wairau River Sauvignon Blanc 1995, Marlborough, New Zealand, £19.50; Canon-Fronsac, Ch. Lariveau 1990, £18.50.

CHEF: Stephen Astley PROPRIETORS: Stuart and John Turner OPEN: all week 12.30 to 2, 7.30 to 10 MEALS: alc (main courses £20 to £22.50). Set L Mon to Sat £13.95 (2 courses) to £15.95, Set L Sun £19.95, Set D Mon to Fri and Sun £26.50, Set D Sat £31.50 SERVICE: not inc, card slips closed CARDS: Amex, Delta, Diners, MasterCard, Switch, Visa DETAILS: 68 seats. 40 seats outside. Private parties: 44 main room, 24 and 44 private rooms. Car park. Vegetarian meals. Children's helpings. No children under 8. Wheelchair access (also WC). Music ACCOMMODATION: 19 rooms, all with bath/shower. TV. Phone. B&B £75 to £215. No children under 8. Afternoon teas. Garden. Fishing (*The Which? Hotel Guide*)

'The view . . . is of a petrol station, which is "just as well, as otherwise all the customers who didn't get the window seats might be offended".'
(On eating in Hereford & Worcester)

WARMINSTER Wiltshire map 2

▲ *Bishopstrow House*

Warminster BA12 9HH
TEL: (01985) 212312 FAX: (01985) 216769 COOKING 3
on B3414, SW of Warminster COST £26–£53

The ivy-clad Georgian house has been delightfully refurbished without being overly designed, and the effect is heightened by 'wonderfully extravagant' flower displays. Bishopstrow's health aspirations are evident not just in the health club but also on the menu, which draws attention to low-cholesterol and low-fat dishes. Some combine both 'virtues' – a salad of leaves (including spinach) with vegetables, or a tartlet of okra and tomatoes with a soft herb crumble – while others cock a snook at them: black pudding with apples and bashed mash, or sticky lemon and lime pudding with custard. Country-house flourishes are generally avoided in favour of a more down-to-earth approach that takes in fish-cakes with buttered spinach and parsley sauce, or braised shank of lamb with winter vegetables. Service is carried out by 'real human beings' in smart uniforms who talk to guests, as well they might in view of the 15 per cent 'optional' service charge. This is added to wines, too, some of them already heavily marked up. House wine starts at £13.50.

CHEF: Chris Suter PROPRIETORS: Simon Lowe, Andrew Leeman and Howard Malin OPEN: all week 12.30 to 2, 7.30 to 9 (9.30 Fri and Sat) MEALS: alc (main courses £10 to £15.50). Set L £14.50, Set D £29.50. Bar meals available all week L, Sun to Thur D SERVICE: 15% (optional) CARDS: Amex, Delta, Diners, MasterCard, Switch, Visa DETAILS: 70 seats. 25 seats outside. Private parties: 65 main room, 20 private room. Car park. Vegetarian meals. Children's helpings. No smoking in dining-room. Wheelchair access (also men's WC). Music ACCOMMODATION: 31 rooms, all with bath/shower. TV. Phone. D,B&B £85 to £140. Deposit: £100. Rooms for disabled. Children welcome. Baby facilities. Dogs welcome. Afternoon teas. Garden. Swimming-pool. Fishing (*The Which? Hotel Guide*)

WATERHOUSES Staffordshire map 5

▲ *Old Beams*

Leek Road, Waterhouses ST10 3HW
TEL: (01538) 308254 FAX: (01538) 308157 COOKING 6
on A523, 7m SE of Leek COST £29–£47

Last year's entry flagged up the Old Beams as having a new chef. In fact, Nigel Wallis was only putting his feet up for a while, and is now back in harness, as if the call of the stoves had proved too siren-like to ignore. The 'comforting and cossetting' atmosphere of the place, with its low-slung ceilings and conservatory extension, is much-liked by most, as is the 'attentive and friendly' service.

The cooking seems to stay alive in people's memories, and excites much praise, even down to bread, butter, olives and coffee. A late-summer lunch took in rich and vividly coloured tomato and fennel soup, a main-course tart of 'good, gamey' pigeon breast and creamed sweetbreads in a restrained stock reduction, and a wild strawberry parfait. Brill stuffed with salmon mousse in a lobster sauce was 'magnificent' for another luncher. At dinner, a fixed-price extravaganza brings on the likes of ham hock and foie gras terrine with madeira vinaigrette to start, followed by a sorbet, and then perhaps duck confit roasted in honey and lemon with a tarragon *jus*. Apricot clafoutis with amaretto ice-cream or lemon and cinnamon gratin with caramelised pear are alternatives to fine cheeses.

Mature bins from the Old World form the foundation of a carefully crafted wine list, which is given strong support by some choice bottles from the New World and topped off nicely by a generous collection of half-bottles. Although there is plenty of good drinking to be had around £20, if you are after a real bargain then look no further than the 1981 Ch. Pétrus at £365 a magnum. Five French house wines start at a more down-to-earth £13.90.

CHEF: Nigel Wallis PROPRIETORS: Nigel and Ann Wallis OPEN: Wed to Sun L 12 to 1.30, Tue to Sat D 7 to 9.30 MEALS: Set L £15.95 to £21, Set D £29 to £39.50 SERVICE: none, card slips closed CARDS: Amex, Delta, Diners, MasterCard, Switch, Visa DETAILS: 46 seats. 10 seats outside. Car park. No children under 6. No smoking in dining-room. Wheelchair access (also women's WC). No music ACCOMMODATION: 5 rooms, all with bath/shower. TV. Phone. B&B £65 to £95. Rooms for disabled. Baby facilities. Garden (*The Which? Hotel Guide*)

WATERMILLOCK Cumbria map 10

▲ *Rampsbeck Hotel*

Watermillock, Ullswater CA11 0LP
TEL: (01768) 486442 FAX: (01768) 486688 COOKING 6
on A592 Penrith to Windermere road COST £30–£58

In quite a number of country house hotels they not only take your money but leave you with an uneasy feeling that they are doing you a favour by having you to stay. This place could not be more different.' So began one enthusiastic endorsement of the relaxed and unpretentious approach at this white-painted house by the shores of Ullswater. Three things mark out the appeal of the food. First, ingredients are well sourced: lobster and sea bass from the Cumbrian coast, Herdwick lamb, Orkney beef, flour from Little Salkeld, and air-dried ham from Richard Woodall. Second, there is a willingness to play with flavour combinations, as in roast grouse with damsons, or a brave-sounding first course of poached peach with sauté foie gras and a passion-fruit dressing. Third, results are consistent and combinations work: even a dish of roasted calf's sweetbreads and lobster, served with a curried sabayon and balsamic rice.

Most of the food is more straightforward: grilled wild salmon with Cornish crab-cake and salsa, perhaps, or Barbary duck accompanied by meatballs made from the leg meat. Whatever their style, dishes are linked by Andrew McGeorge's sound judgement and sympathetic treatment. The taste of a fillet of beef for one reporter 'lasted almost as long as my aches and pains from the fells'. Desserts might include hot blackcurrant soufflé, or that rarity nowadays outside catering colleges, baked Alaska. Home-made bread is 'terrific' and includes a Cumberland sausage version. 'Prompt and friendly service' adds to the satisfaction. The wine list is friendly too, helpfully divided and sub-divided by style. So if a dry, medium-bodied, soft and fruity white is required, you are guided to an Australian Traminer/Riesling, or if a light, fresh red is preferred, there might be a choice between a Bardolino or a Maréchal Foch from Canada. House wines are from £10.25. CELLARMAN'S CHOICE: Verdicchio dei Castelli di

Jesi 1995, Casal di Serra, £13; Coteaux de Tricastin, Dom. Le Vieux Micocoulier 1990, £13.50.

CHEF: Andrew McGeorge PROPRIETORS: Mr and Mrs T.I. Gibb OPEN: all week 12 to 1.15 (booking essential Mon to Sat exc. for light lunch), 6.30 for 7 and 8 for 8.30 (2 sittings) CLOSED: Jan to mid-Feb MEALS: Set L £22, Set D £26 to £38.50. Light L available Mon to Sat SERVICE: not inc, card slips closed CARDS: MasterCard, Visa DETAILS: 40 seats. 20 seats outside. Private parties: 60 main room. Car park. Vegetarian meals. Children welcome. No smoking in dining-room. No music ACCOMMODATION: 21 rooms, all with bath/shower. TV. Phone. B&B £50 to £160. Deposit: £15. Children welcome. Dogs welcome in some rooms and must be kept on lead. Afternoon teas. Garden (*The Which? Hotel Guide*)

WATH-IN-NIDDERDALE North Yorkshire map 8

▲ *The Sportsman's Arms*

Wath-in-Nidderdale HG3 5PP
TEL: (01423) 711306 FAX: (01423) 712524
take B6156 or B6265 to Pateley Bridge, follow signs by village, 2m NW of Pateley Bridge

COOKING **4**
COST **£22–£51**

Not far from Harrogate, but a lure for Dales walkers too, Wath represents the gentler side of the North Yorkshire Moors. Birdlife crowds the nearby reservoir, and there are many abbeys and castles worth visiting in the area. The Sportsman's Arms is a seventeenth-century inn of golden stone, in which the Carters have been plying their trade for nigh on 20 years. Ray Carter's cooking keeps to established principles with nothing to jar the nerves. Fresh fish and seafood from the east coast is always offered, perhaps in the form of lobster feuilleté with orange and white wine sauce, but there are freshwater species nearer to hand, such as Nidderdale trout, which is smoked and paired with smoked salmon in a basil and cucumber salad. Meats are well-selected too: best end of local lamb is done with roasted garlic, tomato and spring onions, while sirloin steak comes peppered and sauced with Dijon mustard and mushrooms. Fruity desserts are the strong suit, and may encompass apricot tart, summer pudding or raspberry crème brûlée. Efficient service keeps things ticking over.

France provides most of the bins on the modestly priced list, offering eight attractive regional house wines at £9.95 as well as much finer fare, and there is plenty of good drinking to be had under £15. Wines by the glass vary from day to day. CELLARMAN'S CHOICE: Sancerre, Cuvée Prestige 1994, Dom. Lucien Crochet, £29.50; Cabernet Sauvignon de Martino 1996, Chile, £10.90.

CHEF: Ray Carter PROPRIETORS: Ray and Jane Carter OPEN: Sun L 12 to 2.30, Mon to Sat D 7 to 10 CLOSED: 25 Dec MEALS: alc (main courses L £8.50 to £15, D £12 to £18). Set L £15, Set D £21 SERVICE: not inc, card slips closed CARDS: MasterCard, Switch, Visa DETAILS: 60 seats. 50 seats outside. Private parties: 60 main room. Car park. Vegetarian meals. Children's helpings. No smoking in dining-room. Wheelchair access (also WC). Music ACCOMMODATION: 7 rooms, 2 with bath/shower. TV. B&B £40 to £65. Children welcome. Dogs welcome. Afternoon teas. Garden. Fishing (*The Which? Hotel Guide*)

The Guide *always appreciates hearing about changes of chef or owner.*

WELLS Somerset map 2

Ritcher's

5 Sadler Street, Wells BA5 2RR COOKING 2
TEL: (01749) 679085 COST £15–£31

In a quiet side-street in this pint-sized cathedral city, Ritcher's does its best to accommodate most types of customer, offering a first-floor restaurant, a bustly bistro downstairs and a courtyard for clement-weather occasions. Fixed-price menus at lunch and dinner might offer tomato and tarragon soup, smoked chicken parfait dressed with dill mustard, or rack of lamb on potato and onion rösti with a beaujolais *jus*. Fruit often features in starters, as was discovered by one reporter who began with kiwi and mango salad with raspberry vinegar and approved of the 'beautiful presentation and good dressing'. Less successful was a main course of salmon served with hot avocado, but the same fish poached and glazed with a thermidor sauce was 'cooked and served to complete perfection' for another . Finish, perhaps, with warm apple tart and whipped cream. A compact list of bistro-style wines is offered at friendly prices. House wines from Antonin Rodet are £7.95.

CHEF: Nicholas Hart PROPRIETORS: Nicholas Hart and Kate Ritcher OPEN: all week 12 to 2, 7 to 9 (6.30 to 9.45 in summer) CLOSED: 26 Dec, 1 Jan MEALS: Set L £5.50 (1 course) to £7.50, Set D £13.95 (2 courses) to £16.95 SERVICE: not inc, card slips closed CARDS: Delta, MasterCard, Switch, Visa DETAILS: 36 seats. 12 seats outside. Private parties: 26 main room. Children welcome. No cigars/pipes while others eat. Wheelchair access (no WC). Music

WELLS-NEXT-THE-SEA Norfolk map 6

Moorings 🍷 ✱

6 Freeman Street, Wells-next-the-Sea NR23 1BA COOKING 4
TEL: (01328) 710949 COST £29–£53

'We are still here,' write the Phillipses, who are aiming to retire from their small restaurant when the right moment presents itself. They have spent a dozen years in this seaside town – a cross between Cambridge and 'kiss-me-quick' Blackpool – attracting a loyal following of reporters who return because the Phillipses 'really care about good food'. Bernard – big, bearded and rosy-cheeked – squeezes behind the tiny bar where he fits 'like a whelk in a shell', while Carla moves in and out of the kitchen according to circumstance. The long and detailed menu reflects the abundance of Norfolk produce, offering a generous choice (20 starters are not unusual), dealing in local game and vegetables, but majoring in seafood: cockles with shallot vinaigrette, crab-cakes, half a lobster, or sea trout with threads of samphire.

Soups (crab, or smoked mussel) are well reported, and 'wholesome and copious vegetables' – usually half a dozen – might include hot beetroot in a creamy sauce, or 'cardiologically challenging' mashed potatoes in winter. Desserts divide into rich (chocolate mousse), frozen (coffee ice-cream), and fruity (apple tart), and wines into Old World classics (Château Gruaud Larose), New World favourites (Cloudy Bay) and Wine World stars (Château Musar). The list is strongest in France, with a particularly appealing Alsace selection, but offers plenty of good bins elsewhere. Prices are commendably low, with ten house wines starting at £8.50 a bottle, £1.80 a glass. CELLARMAN'S CHOICE: Hayshed Hill Sauvignon Blanc 1995, Margaret River, W. Australia, £14.50; Fleur de Carneros Pinot Noir 1995, Los Carneros, California, £15.50.

CHEF: Carla Phillips PROPRIETORS: Bernard and Carla Phillips OPEN: Fri to Mon L 12.30 to 1.45, Thu to Mon D 7.30 to 8.45 MEALS: Set L and D £11.50 (1 course) to £24. BYO £3.75 SERVICE: not inc CARDS: none DETAILS: 32 seats. Private parties: 32 main room. Vegetarian meals. Children's helpings. No smoking in dining-room. Wheelchair access (also WC). No music

WEMBLEY

Sakonis £ NEW ENTRY

119–121 Ealing Road, Wembley HA0 4BP COOKING 2
TEL: (0181) 903 9601 FAX: (0181) 903 7260 COST £7–£14

Vegetarian rules in this South Indian eating-house (and at its twin two doors away at 127–129 Ealing Road), where plastic flooring and tables amplify the chatter of happy family groups and prices are 'absurdly low'. The menu is divided into 'bites' (snacks) and 'eats' (larger dishes), plus a section of 'vegetarian Chinese cuisine (prepared Indian-style)' with such crossover dishes as 'Szechuan noodles topped with Szechuan rice topped with mixed vegetable curry'. Snacks such as aloo papdi chat, and bhel poori, are distinguished by 'fresh and accurate' spicing, and a reporter's uttapa (Indian pizza) was 'zinging with spicy flavour'. Vegetable biryani is attractively presented and 'nicely balanced, the vegetables retaining their texture'. 'Superb, light, creamy' shrikhand topped with pistachio nuts was, noted an experienced inspector, 'the best I have ever had', and fine home-made kulfi comes in custard-apple and other exotic-fruit flavours. Sakonis is unlicensed, but lassi is recommended. Another branch can be found at 114–116 Station Road, Edgware; Tel: (0181) 951 0058.

PROPRIETOR:Everfresh Ltd OPEN:all week 11 to 11 MEALS:alc (main courses £3 to £5) SERVICE:not inc, card slips closed CARDS:MasterCard, Switch, Visa DETAILS:330 seats. Private parties: 80 private room. Vegetarian meals. Children welcome. No smoking in dining-room. Wheelchair access (also WC). Music. Air-conditioned

WEST BAY Dorset map 2

Riverside £

West Bay DT6 4EZ
TEL/FAX: (01308) 422011 COOKING 2
off A35, 1m S of Bridport COST £21–£61

A no-frills seafood restaurant, sitting agreeably on a bank of the River Brit and overlooking a harbour, has been the Watsons' preoccupation for over 30 years. Proximity to the Channel means the freshest fish, such as beautifully flaking fried lemon sole and grilled brill with crisply fried spinach and plate-scrapingly good seaweed sauce. Looking further afield, the menu stretches to chargrilled tuna with sweetcorn relish. Skate with black butter and capers is done well, and a Greek salad has been thought one of the best anywhere. Simple desserts, such as strawberries and ice-cream, or seaside specialities like knickerbocker glory, will provide a sense of satiety. Service can be 'absolutely chaotic' when the crowds arrive but somehow muddles through. The 'carte des vins' offers an unexpectedly wide range at fair prices, with house French at £11.50 a litre.

CHEFS: Mike Mills and Nic Larcombe PROPRIETORS: Arthur and Janet Watson OPEN: Tue to Sun L 12 to 2.30, Tue to Sat D 6.30 to 9 (with variations possible in low season) CLOSED: 1 Dec to 1 Mar MEALS: alc (main courses £6 to £28) SERVICE: not inc, card slips closed CARDS: MasterCard, Switch, Visa DETAILS: 80 seats. 25 seats outside. Private parties: 90 main room. Vegetarian meals. Children's helpings. No cigars/pipes in dining-room. Wheelchair access (no WC). Music

WETHERSFIELD Essex map 6

Dicken's 🍷

The Green, Wethersfield CM7 4BS COOKING 5
TEL/FAX: (01371) 850723 COST £25–£42

The building dates back to the seventeenth century, and wears its half-timbering and minstrels' gallery well. The atmosphere within is relaxed, and John Dicken's cosmopolitan approach to food might bring Tuscan bean soup or crispy Peking duck salad, for example, before a venison, rabbit and hare pudding. This is not so much crossover cooking as a simple enthusiasm for variety. While it is perfectly possible to build a diverse meal of, say, crispy fried wun-tun with spicy mango relish, then grilled sea bass with provençale vegetables, finishing with blackberry and apple crumble, it is notable that individual dishes have a cohesion and integrity. Duck breast might be served with apple and cider sauce, or a tenderloin of lamb with roasted parsnips and lentils.

Despite such distinctive samplings as Mediterranean fish soup, or turkey tikka masala, flavours tend to be gentle rather than robust. One referred to the 'clean, restrained sauces', forgiving the kitchen's tendency to 'play down spiciness so as not to offend Middle Essex'. Maria Dicken is 'the perfect hostess' and there is genuine friendliness and helpfulness from the servers, though at busy times staggered bookings might help the kitchen to deliver accurately timed food at a more reasonable pace. Whatever else, there is no doubting the good value (especially on the fixed-price menu), even though bread is charged extra.

The wine list holds much of interest with plenty of upfront fruity flavours. Quality is high, prices are reasonable and the tasting notes are helpful. House wines begin at £8.25. CELLARMAN'S CHOICE: Frog's Leap Sauvignon Blanc 1994, Napa Valley, California, £20.95; Fleurie, Clos de la Roilette 1994, Coudert, £19.95.

CHEF/PROPRIETOR: John Dicken OPEN: Wed to Sun L 12.30 to 2, Wed to Sat D 7.30 to 9.30 CLOSED: bank hols MEALS: alc (main courses L £8 to £13.50, D £11.50 to £15). Set L £15, Set D Wed to Fri £17.50. BYO £6 SERVICE: not inc CARDS: Delta, MasterCard, Switch, Visa DETAILS: 60 seats. 12 seats outside. Private parties: 36 main room, 10 and 18 private rooms. Car park. Vegetarian meals. Children's helpings. Wheelchair access (also WC). Music

WHIMPLE Devon map 1

▲ *Woodhayes*

Whimple EX5 2TD
TEL: (01404) 822237 FAX: (01404) 822337 COOKING 4
off A30, 9m E of Exeter COST £33–£40

The pretty Georgian house comes with a rural setting and soothing pastel furnishings, but the real appeal for some is the 'charming' Rendle family. 'If one could bottle Katherine Rendle, one could make a fortune.' The dinners which she and Michael cook, offer no choice until dessert. A well-balanced spring menu started in refreshing mode with melon, mango and pink grapefruit in elderflower dressing, followed by a good herby mushroom soup, then monkfish with tomatoes, black olives and basil. Next came roast duck with apple, sage and red cabbage, with excellent potatoes and vegetables.

Desserts have included 'perfect' crème brûlée, and sponge pudding with macerated strawberries; home-made ice-creams are another possibility. Unpasteurised Cheddar and Stilton with grapes and walnuts are served before coffee with home-made sweets. A reporter who enjoyed afternoon tea, 'which arrives as you do', as well as dinner, also praised the 'wonderful' breakfast. More than 50 wines, largely French, are helpfully listed with alcohol content as well as vintage and producer. Around a dozen house wines all cost £11.50.

CHEFS: Katherine and Michael Rendle PROPRIETORS: Frank, Katherine and Michael Rendle OPEN: all week D only 7.30 for 8 (1 sitting); L by arrangement CLOSED: 4 days Christmas MEALS: Set D £27.50 SERVICE: net prices, card slips closed CARDS: Amex, Diners, MasterCard, Switch, Visa DETAILS: 16 seats. Car park. No children under 12. No smoking in dining-room. Music ACCOMMODATION: 6 rooms, all with bath/shower. TV. Phone. B&B £65 to £90. No children under 12. Afternoon teas. Garden (*The Which? Hotel Guide*)

WHITBY North Yorkshire map 9

Magpie Cafe £

14 Pier Road, Whitby YO21 3PU COOKING 3
TEL/FAX: (01947) 602058 COST £16–£35

A whitewashed eighteenth-century merchant's house overlooking Whitby harbour is where the Magpie has settled. What it offers is the freshest fish cooked to order and served as often as not with impeccably crisp chips. If you're feeling fancy, you might venture into the realms of salmon sauced with orange herb butter, or monkfish skewered with bacon, banana and tomato and served with spicy barbecue sauce, though the skewering and grilling may take half an hour. Otherwise, it's crab marie-rose, and battered cod, generously proportioned and served by 'homely, friendly, helpful and prompt' staff. For pudding-lovers, boozy banana cheesecake or treacle sponge might await. A list of seafood-friendly wines supplied by Bibendum Wines is available for those in the mood for more than a pot of tea. House wines are £6.95.

CHEF: Ian Robson PROPRIETORS: Sheila and Ian McKenzie, Ian Robson and Alison McKenzie-Robson OPEN: Nov to Easter 11.30 to 6.30 (9 Fri and Sat); Easter to end Oct all week 11.30 to 9 CLOSED: 24 and 25 Dec, Jan to mid-Feb MEALS: alc (main courses £4.50 to £16). Set L and D £8.95 to £13.95 SERVICE: not inc, card slips closed CARDS: Delta, MasterCard, Switch, Visa DETAILS: 100 seats. Private parties: 50 main room. Vegetarian meals. Children's helpings. No smoking in 1 dining-room. Music. Air-conditioned

WHITSTABLE Kent map 3

▲ *Whitstable Oyster Fishery Co*

Royal Native Oyster Stores, The Horsebridge,
Whitstable CT5 1BU COOKING 3
TEL: (01227) 276856 FAX: (01227) 770666 COST £28–£56

'The food is fresh, cooking is honest, the portions are generous and the prices fair' was one summing up of this brick-built Victorian oyster store on the seafront. The beach is a bonus for families. Shellfish are stored in tanks beneath the restaurant, there is a cinema upstairs, and the dining-room wears its bare boards, wobbly check-clothed tables and nautical bric à brac with a jaunty air. Those who crave simplicity are well rewarded. Rock oysters are £1 each, and salmon is smoked on the premises. The kitchen has gained in assurance without straying from its ideal of plain treatment, and delivers deep-fried local baby plaice, cod in beer batter, and grilled brill with hollandaise. Puddings are chalked on a board, and the short list of white wines is mostly French, beginning with Chardonnay and Muscadet at £9.95.

CHEFS: Nikki Billington and C. Williams PROPRIETOR: Whitstable Oyster Fishery Co OPEN: Tue to Sun (all week June to Sept) 12 to 2, Tue to Sat (all week June to Sept) 7 to 9 CLOSED: 24 to 26 Dec MEALS: alc (main courses £9 to £18) SERVICE: not inc CARDS: Amex, Delta, Diners, MasterCard, Visa DETAILS: 135 seats. 75 seats outside. Private parties: 100 main room, 100 private room. Car park. Children's helpings. Wheelchair access (also WC). Music ACCOMMODATION: 7 rooms, all with bath/shower. TV. Room only £40 to £80. Children welcome (*The Which? Hotel Guide*)

WILLITON Somerset map 2

▲ *White House*

Long Street, Williton TA4 4QW COOKING 6
TEL: (01984) 632306 and 632777 COST £40–£53

An architecturally simple Georgian town house in the centre of an appealing Somerset village, the White House is filled with an eclectic mix of antique and modern furnishings, with some original paintings and decorative ceramics adding lustre to the sense of civility. The Smiths remain closed for half the year rather than run themselves to a standstill, and the wisdom of working to such a rhythm is amply demonstrated by the fact that they have been in the business here for three decades.

Dinner is a four-course affair at a set price, beginning with soup of the evening (sorrel and potato, perhaps, or smoked haddock and yellow pepper) and concluding with a choice of pudding or a plate of English cheeses with home-made oatmeal biscuits. Sound culinary principles underpin the cooking, and twiddly garnishes are not allowed to intrude. Marinated salmon and mushrooms are put into a tartlet case and given a classical béarnaise sauce, while pickled herrings come in Scandinavian fashion with potato salad and a glass of iced aquavit. When it comes to main courses, a straightforward sauce vierge is sufficient for seared scallops, and cassis is the lubricant for magret of Barbary duck, the meat quickly sauté until just pink and then thinly sliced. Sablé aux fraises with strawberry sorbet, or almond meringue filled with apricot compote and cream are the kinds of puddings to expect.

In the introduction to his wine list Dick Smith pays tribute to his suppliers and thanks his wife Kay, who 'forces herself to taste everything', but he should step forward and take a bow himself for assembling so fine a collection at such reasonable prices. The New World selections and German Rieslings continue to impress, while Francophiles will not go away disappointed. House wines start at £10.50. CELLARMAN'S CHOICE: Wairau River Sauvignon 1996, Marlborough, New Zealand, £16; Côte de Nuits Villages, Clos de Chapeau 1992, Dom. de l'Arlot, £24.

CHEFS/PROPRIETORS: Dick and Kay Smith OPEN: all week D only 7.30 to 8.30 CLOSED: early Nov to mid-May MEALS: Set D £29.50 SERVICE: not inc CARDS: none DETAILS: 26 seats. Private parties: 8 main room. Car park. Children's helpings. No smoking in dining-room. Wheelchair access (no WC). No music ACCOMMODATION: 12 rooms, 9 with bath/shower. TV. Phone. B&B £33 to £90. Deposit: £25. Rooms for disabled. Children welcome. Baby facilities. Dogs welcome (*The Which? Hotel Guide*)

WILMINGTON East Sussex map 3

▲ *Crossways*

Lewes Road, Wilmington, nr Polegate BN26 5SG COOKING **2**
TEL: (01323) 482455 FAX: (01323) 487811 COST £35–£42

The white-painted, green-shuttered Georgian house is well sited for visitors: close to the South Downs Way, the 'Long Man of Wilmington' (a 226ft-high figure cut into the downland chalk), and the remains of a thirteenth-century Benedictine Priory, not to mention Glyndebourne. Dinner, five nights a week, consists of four courses (the second a soup) and the menu changes monthly to accommodate a few seasonal options, although smoked chicken, seafood pancake, duck or guinea-fowl might turn up almost any time.

David Stott and Juliet Anderson mix a broadly traditional approach with some unexpected twists; thus lamb might appear one month with a rosemary and redcurrant gravy, and another with peanuts in a mild curry sauce. Likewise, guinea-fowl has been served European-style with bacon, mushrooms and lentils, and also with a pickled ginger and mango sauce. Begin perhaps with salmon fish-cakes, or game terrine, finish with a home-made ice-cream or sorbet, and drink a fairly priced bottle from a modest list that starts with house Australian red and English white at £9.95.

All entries, including Round-ups, are fully indexed at the back of the Guide.

CHEFS: David Stott and Juliet Anderson PROPRIETORS: David Stott and Clive James OPEN: Tue to Sat D only 7.30 to 8.45 CLOSED: 24 Dec to 24 Jan MEALS: Set D £26.95 SERVICE: not inc, card slips closed CARDS: Amex, Delta, MasterCard, Switch, Visa DETAILS: 24 seats. Private parties: 6 main room. Car park. No children under 12. No smoking while others eat. Wheelchair access (no WC). Music ACCOMMODATION: 7 rooms, all with bath/shower. TV. Phone. B&B £46 to £75. No children under 12. Garden

WINCHCOMBE Gloucestershire map 5

▲ *Wesley House*

High Street, Winchcombe GL54 5LJ COOKING 5
TEL: (01242) 602366 FAX: (01242) 602405 COST £25–£47

The father of Methodism may or may not have stayed here in 1779, but the house bears his name with pride in any case. It is a half-timbered, pleasingly crooked-looking place that now boasts a terrace where one can sip a sherry and gaze at the North Cotswold Edge. The split-level dining-room is plush without being unduly lavish, and boasts a wrought-iron spiral staircase that leads to nowhere in particular.

The culinary tone is very much in the country-house mould, and there may be chicken liver parfait with onion 'confit' and toasted brioche to start, and perhaps steamed sole filled with scallop mousseline, or medallions of venison with dauphinois and a sauce of sloe-gin, to follow. Bar lunchers might be offered bourride with garlic bread, or a textbook club sandwich. Balsamic vinegar and tapénade have crept stealthily on to the menu of late, but the idiom remains essentially a familiar one to English palates. Soufflés such as passion-fruit, or pear with an apricot sauce, are well-reported desserts, while the Wesley House Selection offers a morsel of all the puddings. France and South Africa are the twin preoccupations of the wine list, but there are other good New World choices too. House wines start at £11.50, and most are offered by the glass.

CHEFS: Jonathan Lewis and James Lovatt PROPRIETORS: Matthew Brown and Jonathan Lewis OPEN: Mon to Sat 12 to 2, 7 to 9.30 (10 Sat) CLOSED: 12 Jan to 12 Feb MEALS: alc L (main courses £12 to £14.50). Set L £14.50, Set D £21 (2 courses) to £26. Bar L available. BYO £6 SERVICE: not inc CARDS: Amex, Delta, MasterCard, Switch, Visa DETAILS: 50 seats. 20 seats outside. Private parties: 60 main room. Children's helpings. No smoking in dining-room. Wheelchair access (no WC). Music ACCOMMODATION: 5 rooms, all with bath/shower. TV. Phone. D,B&B £72.50 to £130. Children welcome. Baby facilities. Afternoon teas (*The Which? Hotel Guide*)

WINCHESTER Hampshire map 2

▲ *Hotel du Vin & Bistro*

14 Southgate Street, Winchester SO23 9EF COOKING 5
TEL: (01962) 841414 FAX: (01962) 842458 COST £27–£45

Robin Hutson and Gerard Basset have a clear purpose – to serve colourful, distinctive food and first-rate wines in an informal atmosphere – and for the most part they seem to be achieving it. A second property in Tunbridge Wells has been purchased and was undergoing conversion as the *Guide* went to press, and there are plans to expand further the burgeoning empire. The building dates from 1715, makes a virtue of bare wooden floors and tables, and comes into its atmospheric own when packed, candelit and lively. 'The meal was fun and great value,' summed up one reporter after an array of dishes that included a 'huge portion' of bruschetta with Taleggio, field mushrooms and garlic butter, and a tarte Tatin of caramelised shallots with seared foie gras.

The food's centre of gravity is somewhere near the Mediterranean, but it picks up other ideas of no fixed abode, such as pan-fried scallops and black pudding with apple and celeriac mash and a parsley purée, or honey-roast confit of duck with a mango, mint and chilli salsa, and there simply isn't room for monotony. 'Choc-o-bloc Stanley' has come all the way down from McCoy's (see entry, Staddlebridge) and vies with sticky toffee pudding and creamy tiramisù for richness. Service has seemed to some 'tight-lipped' and 'officious', but Gerard Basset's wine service is 'genuinely enthusiastic and an absolute delight'.

The same could be said of his choice of wines. The main list is a cosmopolitan collection from some prestigious producers: Austria's Willi Opitz, to name but one. A shorter list offering around a dozen wines by the bottle or glass changes throughout the week to accommodate new wines or special promotions, or to allow a particular grape variety to partner the day's food. House wines are £9.95 a bottle (£2.60 a glass). CELLARMAN'S CHOICE: Cachagua Chardonnay 1993, Durney Vineyard, Carmel Valley, California, £19.20; Crozes-Hermitage 1994, Alain Graillot, £19.75.

CHEF: James Martin PROPRIETORS: Robin Hutson and Gerard Basset OPEN: all week 12 to 1.45, 7 to 9.30 MEALS: alc (main courses £10 to £15). Set L Sun £19.50 SERVICE: not inc, card slips closed CARDS: Amex, Delta, Diners, MasterCard, Switch, Visa DETAILS: 45 seats. Private parties: 48 private room. Car park. Vegetarian meals. Children welcome. Wheelchair access (no WC). No music ACCOMMODATION: 23 rooms, all with bath/shower. TV. Phone. Room only £75 to £150. Rooms for disabled. Children welcome. Garden (*The Which? Hotel Guide*)

Old Chesil Rectory £✱

1 Chesil Street, Winchester SO23 8HU — COOKING 4

TEL: (01962) 851555 FAX: (01962) 869704 — COST £30–£46

'Mr and Mrs Ruthven-Stuart have sensibly avoided the ministrations of the rampant interior decorator,' noted one couple who visited this untarnished fifteenth-century beamed house. Pictures by local artists line the walls, floors are wooden, windows leaded. Everything is immaculate. The kitchen now works to a changing fixed-priced menu of, at dinner, around six choices at each stage. A panaché of mixed fish has included scallops and a beurre blanc, and 'superbly cooked' medallions of venison and pigeon breasts have arrived with a 'perfectly glazed' bitter chocolate sauce. The high points for one reporter were a really delicate wild mushroom tartlet with a Parmesan tuile, and seared rib of beef with a potent bourguignonne-style sauce.

Raw materials are high-quality, thanks to top-notch local suppliers; flavours are intense, up-front and pungent; and saucing is good. Pastry-work has been approved – in an almond and pear tart served with cinnamon ice-cream – and syrup and orange sticky pudding has been endorsed. The wine list is wide-ranging, with a decent French selection and some vintage bin-ends. House wines start at £9.95.

CHEFS: Nicholas Ruthven-Stuart and Nicola Saunders PROPRIETORS: Nicholas and Christina Ruthven-Stuart OPEN: Tue to Sat 12 to 2, 7 to 9.30 (10 Fri and Sat) CLOSED: 2 weeks Christmas, 2 weeks summer MEALS: Set L £15 (2 courses) to £20, Set D £22.50 (2 courses) to £28 SERVICE: not inc; 10% for parties of 6 or more CARDS: Delta, Diners, MasterCard, Switch, Visa DETAILS: 60 seats. Private parties: 24 main room, 24 private room. Children welcome. No smoking in 1 dining-room. Wheelchair access (no WC). Music

▲ *Wykeham Arms* 🍷 £

75 Kingsgate Street, Winchester SO23 9PE — COOKING **2**
TEL: (01962) 853834 FAX: (01962) 854411 — COST £19–£40

'The décor is the work of a magpie – me!' writes Graeme Jameson of the heterogeneous ornamentation at this welcoming Winchester pub, where tankards hang from the beams and there are over 700 pictures to look at. Although elements of oriental and Mediterranean cookery are brought in to show that the kitchen's finger is on the pulse, a backbone of Old English heartiness bolsters the cooking as well. Venison and beef are casseroled together with juniper and thyme, and cuts of Aberdeen Angus are grilled as you wish. Similarly, for pudding there may be apple and kumquat fool, mincemeat crumble tart, or lemon posset. That Graeme Jameson has a passion for wine is apparent from the eager tasting notes that accompany the 100 bins on his cleverly chosen list. Wines vary with the seasons – more whites appearing in summer, reds making a comeback in winter – although Burgundy maintains a strong presence at all times. Prices are very reasonable, beginning with house French at £11.95, and 20 wines by the large glass (from £2.20) have proved extremely popular. CELLARMAN'S CHOICE: Beaujolais Blanc, Grand Clos de Loyse 1994, Ch. Des Jacques, £13.95; Marsannay 1994, Dom. Louis Jadot, £17.95.

CHEFS: Belinda Watson and Helen Brooks PROPRIETOR: Graeme Jameson OPEN: Mon to Sat 12 to 2.30, 6.30 to 9, Sun (lighter food only) 12.30 to 3.30, 6.30 to 8.30 CLOSED: 25 Dec MEALS: alc (main courses L £4 to £7, D £9 to £13) SERVICE: not inc, card slips closed CARDS: Amex, Delta, Diners, MasterCard, Switch, Visa DETAILS: 75 seats. 30 seats outside. Private parties: 8 main room. Car park. Vegetarian meals. No children under 14. No smoking in 1 dining-room. No music ACCOMMODATION: 7 rooms, all with bath/shower. TV. Phone. B&B £69.50 to £79.50. No children under 14. Dogs by arrangement. Afternoon teas. Garden (*The Which? Hotel Guide*)

WINDERMERE Cumbria — map 8

▲ *Gilpin Lodge* 🍷

Crook Road, Windermere LA23 3NE
TEL: (01539) 488818 FAX: (01539) 488058 — COOKING **4**
on B5284, 2m SE of Windermere — COST £25–£47

Refurbishment continues apace in this Victorian house, where the Cunliffes have notched up a decade. In 1996 the kitchens were re-done and a conservatory extension added to the dining-room, and in 1997 a new accommodation wing was opened. All this activity confirms the confidence with which the place is run. Decorated in William Morris style, with antiques and lots of flowers, the house feels relaxing, and service is just formal enough. As a hotel it covers everything from breakfast to packed lunches to afternoon teas, with a flexible lunchtime *carte* and serious four-course dinners.

The cooking is 'professional and dependable', and makes use of abundant local resources, including Windermere char, Flookburgh shrimps, Holker pheasants, Lakeland lamb and Waberthwaite hams. It might take in grilled goats'-cheese salad, oriental spiced chicken, or roast cod at lunch, but moves up a gear in the evening with a starter of smoked haddock, mash and poached egg with a champagne and chive sauce, followed perhaps by beef fillet with Parmesan polenta and salsa verde on a madeira sauce. The dextrous kitchen is able to turn out a home-made pork sausage to accompany woodpigeon, as well as a lime and coconut feuillantine of exotic fruits, made even more exotic by a passion-fruit cream and an orange and banana coulis. The wine list offers several interesting bins from the New World – and Italy – along with plenty of tried-and-trusted offerings from France. Mark-ups are reasonable too. Five house wines start at £11.50 and there is an encouraging number of half-bottles. CELLARMAN'S CHOICE: Elk Cove Pinot Gris 1994, Willamette Valley, Oregon, £20.75; Grant Burge Old Vine Shiraz 1994, Barossa Valley, S. Australia, £22.50.

CHEF: Chris Davies PROPRIETORS: John and Christine Cunliffe OPEN: all week 12 to 2.30, 6.45 to 8.45 MEALS: alc L Mon to Sat (main courses £7.50 to £12). Set L Sun £15.50, Set D £27.50 SERVICE: not inc CARDS: Amex, Delta, Diners, MasterCard, Switch, Visa DETAILS: 60 seats. 12 seats outside. Private parties: 24 main room, 14 and 24 private rooms. Car park. Vegetarian meals. No children under 7. No smoking in dining-room. Wheelchair access (no WC). Music ACCOMMODATION: 14 rooms, all with bath/shower. TV. Phone. B&B £75 to £140. Rooms for disabled. No children under 7. Afternoon teas. Garden (*The Which? Hotel Guide*)

▲ *Miller Howe* 🍷

Rayrigg Road, Windermere LA23 1EY
TEL: (01539) 442536 FAX: (01539) 445664
on A592, between Windermere and Bowness

COOKING 7
COST £26–£54

As settings go, the Lake District (one reporter thinks 'the world') has difficulty coming up with anything to match Miller Howe's view over Lake Windermere to Langdale Pikes and Bow Fell. Comfortable leather Chesterfields in the lounges, a cushioned conservatory and starched-linen dining-room combine to produce a 'traditional and elegant' feel. The dinner format never varies: sit down at 8 o'clock to four courses, plus an array of extras from canapés on the patio to first-rate bread to home-made truffles with coffee. There is no choice before dessert, which in theory gives the kitchen an easy time of it. But where some kitchens might relax at the prospect, this one fires up and produces a roller-coaster ride of 'brilliant' flavours and textures.

Indeed, our inspector had an attack of the 'brilliants' to describe much of his meal, from the materials themselves to the care taken over combinations. Salmon of 'wonderful quality' was 'perfectly seared' yet undercooked inside, and similar treatment produced just the right texture in a richly flavoured marinated guinea-fowl. Then come the accompaniments, the 'natural deep flavours' of a tomato and olive oil coulis for the salmon, and a prune and orange confit that could not have suited the guinea-fowl better. Finally come the vegetables, subject of much discourse over the years, but now that they are five instead of seven it is easier to make sense of the range of tastes: braised white cabbage with caraway, mange-tout, diced celeriac with fennel, grated beetroot with orange, and 'the best bubble and squeak you'll ever have'.

As if all that were not enough, desserts are generous in scope, from lemon cheesecake to tiramisù, from pannacotta with poached rhubarb to a dish of fresh berries set in sweet wine jelly. Reporters have nothing but praise for the staff, who are welcoming, professional, chatty, informative – especially when it comes to matching wine and food – and make visitors feel very much at ease. Overnighters relish breakfast, and packed lunchers marvel at the value and variety. Wines consist of a fairly short selection of good-quality classics, followed by nearly a hundred gems from the New World. Most hale from Australia, New Zealand and South Africa and fully deserve the enthusiastic – and helpful – tasting notes. House wines start at £15.50. CELLARMAN'S CHOICE: Manure Brook Chardonnay 1994, S.E. Australia, £21; Fleur du Cap Pinotage 1991, Stellenbosch, South Africa, £20.75.

CHEFS: Chris Blaydes and Sue Elliott PROPRIETOR: John Tovey OPEN: all week 12.30 to 1.30, 7.30 for 8 (1 sitting) CLOSED: early Dec to mid-Feb MEALS: Set L £16, Set D £32. BYO £8 SERVICE: 12.5% (optional), card slips closed CARDS: Amex, Diners, MasterCard, Visa DETAILS: 60 seats. 20 seats outside. Private parties: 36 main room, 36 private room. Car park. Vegetarian meals. No children under 8. No smoking in dining-room. Wheelchair access (no WC). Music. Air-conditioned ACCOMMODATION: 12 rooms, all with bath/shower. TV. Phone. D,B&B £95 to £250. No children under 8. Dogs welcome. Afternoon teas. Garden (*The Which? Hotel Guide*)

Miller Howe Café ⁂ [£]

Lakeland Plastics Ltd, Alexandra Buildings,
Station Precinct, Windermere LA23 1BQ — COOKING 1
TEL: (01539) 446732 FAX: (01524) 734502 — COST £18–£27

Changes to the Duttons' all-day café since last year include a new system of table allocation designed to cut down the queues: leave your name with the receptionist, have a browse around the shop, and wait until you are called. You now order at table rather than at the counter. In addition, the menu takes on a new format as we go to press, but the style (and many dishes) stays essentially the same: children still get their own mini-menu of macaroni cheese, baked potatoes or sandwiches, and the broad appeal remains. Soups, salads, filled baguettes, or smooth chicken liver parfait are among the 'light bites', with more substantial devilled kidneys, beef in beer, or baked Cumberland sausage laid on for serious lunchers. Indulgent sweets might include Bailey's Irish Cream mousse, and sticky toffee pudding, and an espresso machine has been installed to supplement the teas, home-made lemonade, fruit juices and French house wine at £8.95.

CHEFS: Ian Dutton and James Wood PROPRIETORS: Ian and Angela Dutton OPEN: all week 9 to 6 (5 Sat, 4 Sun) CLOSED: 25 Dec, 1 Jan MEALS: alc (main courses £6 to £7) SERVICE: not inc, card slips closed CARDS: Delta, MasterCard, Switch, Visa DETAILS: 50 seats. Private parties: 50 main room. Car park. Vegetarian meals. Children's helpings. No smoking in dining-room. Wheelchair access (also WC). Music. Air-conditioned

Roger's ✱

4 High Street, Windermere LA23 1AF — COOKING 4
TEL: (01539) 444954 — COST £24–£43

Now in their seventeenth year, the Pergl-Wilsons have built up a strong local following in their canopied and 'cosy' green restaurant at the top of the High Street. A French theme runs through the menu, from twice-baked Roquefort soufflé to 'cassoulet de Toulouse', but there is much else besides, including baked spinach gnocchi, game pie, and braised oxtail with basil dumplings. Good ingredients and sound judgement indicate a kitchen in safe hands. Timing in a dish of scallops served with Pernod on a bed of puréed leeks was just right for its reporter, and flavours are well-balanced. Vegetables are charged extra. Changes are rung with occasional oriental spicing, and with dessserts such as treacle tart with an almond crust, or chocolate marquise with a lemon sauce. Coffee comes with Kendal mint cake, and the pace of service can be a bit jerky, but it is 'pleasant and helpful'. A sound collection of wines is divided into groups by colour or style and then sub-divided by country or region. Prices are very reasonable, with plenty of bins under £15, and house Duboeuf is £9.90 per litre, £2 a glass.

CHEF: Roger Pergl-Wilson PROPRIETORS: Roger and Alena Pergl-Wilson OPEN: Mon to Sat D only 7 to 9.30 MEALS: alc (main courses £6.50 to £11). Set D Mon to Fri £16.50 SERVICE: not inc, card slips closed CARDS: Amex, Delta, Diners, MasterCard, Switch, Visa DETAILS: 40 seats. Private parties: 28 main room, 25 private room. Children's helpings. No smoking in dining-room. Wheelchair access (no WC). Music

WINKLEIGH Devon — map 1

Pophams ✱ £

Castle Street, Winkleigh EX19 8HQ — COOKING 5
TEL: (01837) 83767 — COST £19–£39

Monochrome photos, mostly of film stars of yesteryear, cover the green walls of this diminutive restaurant, which is open only for lunch. Melvyn Popham works away cheerfully in his open kitchen while chatting with guests, and Dennis Hawkes is only too pleased to expand on what is offered on the daily-changing blackboard menus.

The cooking focuses on using sound ingredients to allow fresh and clear flavours to shine through in, for example, leek and watercress soup, salad of feta cheese with orange and beetroot in a citrus dressing, or roast salmon in red pepper sauce. Onion tart gets raves from more than one reporter, and boned best end of lamb is coated with 'superb' mushroom pâté in puff pastry. A warm summertime salad might consist of chicken with asparagus served with a soya and sesame dressing. Home-made ice-creams – made with honey or Irish whiskey, perhaps – have been consistently endorsed by reporters. 'A very warm welcome, excellent cooking and splendid service' is how a regular sums it all up. Pophams is unlicensed but does not charge corkage for those who bring their own wine.

CHEF: Melvyn Popham PROPRIETORS: Dennis Hawkes and Melvyn Popham OPEN: Wed to Sat L only 11.30 to 4 CLOSED: Feb MEALS: alc (main courses £10 to £16). Unlicensed; BYO (no corkage) SERVICE: not inc, card slips closed CARDS: MasterCard, Visa DETAILS: 10 seats. Private parties: 10 main room. Vegetarian meals. No children under 14. No smoking in dining-room. Wheelchair access (no WC). Music. Air-conditioned

WINSFORD Somerset map 1

▲ *Savery's at Karslake House* NEW ENTRY

Halse Lane, Winsford TE24 7JE COOKING 5
TEL/FAX: (01643) 851242 COST £32–£38

John Savery and Patricia Carpenter have moved several exits down the M5 from their pretty village restaurant in Frampton-on-Severn to a 'beautiful but non-posh' country restaurant-with-rooms on Exmoor. The long, low building – part of which was originally a fifteenth-century malt-house – sits on a hillside overlooking the village of Winsford. A three-course set dinner menu is served in the spacious but homely dining-room and keeps to a sensible length. Although the cooking takes an occasionally adventurous turn, it concentrates mainly on unshowy combinations based on excellent ingredients from local suppliers. This results in plenty of game in winter and fish in summer.

Starters might include a terrine of pheasant with red onion and whisky marmalade, or marinated salmon with pickled quail's eggs. Recommended have been sea bass with a crispy skin ('caught by line at nearby Porlock Bay'), which has come with fresh prawns and a rich chive beurre blanc, and a casserole of 'succulent' venison with bacon and fried polenta, although its reporter felt the latter might have been better under, rather than on top of, the meat so as to absorb the sauce. Desserts tend towards the rich and boozy: dense rum-laced white chocolate ice cream with summer fruits, perhaps, or baked rice pudding with caramelised bananas and Drambuie. 'A really nice place' writes one reporter, with 'friendly and efficient service by Pat Carpenter and a charming and vivacious waitress'. Twenty-plus wines, selected by Wickhams of Bideford, are a varied, if mainly French, choice, and prices are friendly. House wines start at £9.75.

CHEF: John Savery PROPRIETORS: John Savery and Patricia Carpenter OPEN: Tue to Sat D only 7.15 to 9.15 MEALS: Set D £23.95 SERVICE: not inc, card slips closed CARDS: Delta, MasterCard, Switch, Visa DETAILS: 30 seats. Private parties: 35 main room. Car park. Vegetarian meals. No children under 14. No smoking in dining-room. Music ACCOMMODATION: 7 rooms, all with bath/shower. TV. D,B&B £49 to £64. Deposit: £25. No children under 15. Dogs welcome. Garden

WINTERINGHAM North Lincolnshire map 9

LINCOLNSHIRE 1998 BIG CHEESE

▲ *Winteringham Fields*

Winteringham DN15 9PF COOKING 8
TEL: (01724) 733096 FAX: (01724) 733898 COST £33–£84

The Schwabs have established a place of 'class, calm and comfort' in a village which is 'not a main tourist attraction'. The sixteenth-century house – a repository for Victoriana – has two drawing-rooms and a conservatory, with deep settees and colours, and a well-appointed, formal dining-room, as well as a new kitchen garden bravely attempting to grow figs, cherries, citrus fruits and peaches. 'Winteringham effortlessly achieves the balance between correctness, efficiency and an easy friendliness', thanks to the 'wonderful, attentive' Annie Schwab, and long-serving staff who are knowledgeable about the food and 'highly professional without being fussy'.

Germain Schwab's dedication to the job is exemplary. He never leaves the stoves, except for a quick tour of the dining-room after meals, and seems to be 'forever in a mildly experimental phase'. The food is 'eye-catchingly elegant', ingredients are 'impeccable', sauces 'brilliant'. Dishes indicate not only precision and skill (this is a very labour-intensive kitchen), but also the fidgety creativity at the heart of it: a 'sensational' ravioli, for instance, made from contrasting strips of plain and squid ink pasta, looking like a 'striped carrier bag or a giant humbug', stuffed with 'the freshest of crab,' served on a disc of horseradish mash, in a crab stock with pieces of lime. This may be 'fussy', but it is far from just gimmickry; taste remains the be-all and end-all. 'I have always felt that truffles were an over-rated delicacy,' confided one reporter, 'but here I got the flavour, and the point.' The conversion was brought about by a scoop of foie gras pâté rolled in finely chopped black truffles, on a mound of chopped marsala jelly.

Germain's grandparents used to produce milk and cheese in the Jura region of Switzerland, which may help to explain the 'memorable' and 'legendary' cheese trolley, offering most things from Cotherstone to Milleens, from Vacherin to properly served Tête de Moine. Another Swiss speciality restored the faith of one couple in chocolate desserts, this one a teardrop combining dark and light chocolates. The cooking's 'delicate brilliance' is also apparent in rice crème brûlée with rhubarb, and a 'fantastic' almond and apricot cake with mascarpone ice-cream. One or two questions surface: is there too much workmanship? Are prices high for the size of the portions? Could the set lunch be more exciting? But when level heads prevail, Winteringham is seen as 'a centre of excellence'.

The knowledgeable and helpful sommelier will provide guidance to the numerous wine regions covered in the extensive list, including Switzerland. Quality is high, as are a few of the prices, but there is a good choice under £20. Half a dozen house wines are £13. CELLARMAN'S CHOICE: Cape Mentelle Semillon/Sauvignon, Margaret River, W. Australia, £27; Valdepeñas Gran Reserva 1984, Señorio de Los Llanos, £20.70.

CHEF: Germain Schwab PROPRIETORS: Annie and Germain Schwab OPEN: Tue to Fri (Tue to Sat from Jan) L 12 to 1.30, Mon to Sat D 7.15 to 9.30 CLOSED: 2 weeks Christmas, first week Aug, bank hols MEALS: alc (main courses £25 to £26). Set L £16.50 (2 courses) to £20, Set D £29 to £46 SERVICE: not inc, card slips closed CARDS: Amex, Delta, MasterCard, Switch, Visa DETAILS: 46 seats. Private parties: 10 main room, 10 private room. Car park. Vegetarian meals. Children welcome. No smoking in dining-room. Wheelchair access (no WC) ACCOMMODATION: 7 rooms, all with bath/shower. TV. Phone. Room only £60 to £105. Rooms for disabled. No children under 8. Garden (*The Which? Hotel Guide*)

'The restaurant is 43 miles away from my house. If it was five miles away I might occasionally visit, if I had come home from work tired and bored and wanted to stay bored.' (On eating in South Yorkshire)

WITHERSLACK Cumbria map 8

▲ *Old Vicarage*

Church Road, Witherslack LA11 6RS
TEL: (01539) 552381 FAX: (01539) 552373
off A590, take first left in village to church

COOKING 4
COST £24–£45

Built of mellow golden-grey stone in the first decade of the last century, the Old Vicarage benefits from its tranquil Lake District setting. The garden is strewn with wild flowers, and there is hardly any traffic round about to scare the birdlife away. Witherslack venison, Waberthwaite pork and lamb from Grange-over-Sands play their part on the menus; looking further afield, Orkney beef and Loch Fyne seafood crop up too. Nothing is too elaborate. Starters, such as salmon ceviche with lime and dill, or a smoked Cumberland cheese soufflé with spinach sauce, are accompanied by a speciality bread made with molasses. Main-course choices are sensibly limited: a single fish option, which may be parsleyed sea bass with chive cream sauce, plus meat dishes of Gressingham duck with red berry compote, or fillet of beef with garlic confit, shallots and red wine. Guard's pudding, an English classic with damson and vanilla sauces, can be found alongside rhubarb and ginger crumble, and pear and cranberry sponge.

The wine list comes straight to the point with its selections from the world's key wine regions and positively waxes lyrical over Italy. Plans are afoot to complement an already impressive collection of half-bottles with an increased number of wines available by the glass. Alternatively try one of the quartet of local beers. House French starts at £13.50. CELLARMAN'S CHOICE: C.J. Pask Sauvignon Blanc 1996, Hawke's Bay, New Zealand, £18; Montefalco Rosso 1991, Paolo Bea, £23.

CHEF: Stanley Reeve PROPRIETORS: the Brown and Reeve families OPEN: Sun L 12.30 to 1.30, all week D 7 to 9 MEALS: Set L £15.50, Set D £27.50 SERVICE: not inc, card slips closed CARDS: Amex, Delta, MasterCard, Switch, Visa DETAILS: 36 seats. Private parties: 20 main room, 10 private room. Car park. Vegetarian meals. Children's helpings. No smoking in dining-room. Wheelchair access (no WC). Music ACCOMMODATION: 14 rooms, all with bath/shower. TV. Phone. B&B £59 to £138. Rooms for disabled. Children welcome. Baby facilities. Dogs welcome in bedrooms only and not left unattended. Afternoon teas. Garden (*The Which? Hotel Guide*)

WOBURN Bedfordshire map 6

Paris House

Woburn Park, Woburn MK17 9QP
TEL: (01525) 290692 FAX: (01525) 290471
on A4012, 1½m E of Woburn in Abbey grounds

COOKING 4
COST £34–£67

'A beautiful place in a magnificent setting,' summed up one visitor to this black and white timbered house just inside Woburn's deer park. In 1998 it is 120 years since the building made its appearance at the Paris Exhibition, and 15 since Peter Chandler rescued it from neglect. Perhaps it was a combination of the view and the 'mobile home' idea that made it feel 'like eating in somebody's summer house' for one reporter.

Lunch is three courses and coffee with no choice, while three-course dinners take in, perhaps, smoked haddock and poached egg florentine, rabbit and mushroom pie, and hot raspberry soufflé. Anglo-French is the predominant style, judging by Stilton and celery soup, potato galette with frogs' legs, and tarte Tatin. Occasional offal dishes make a welcome appearance, perhaps in the form of feuilleté of lamb tongues in tarragon, or veal kidneys in Meaux mustard. Service has not always been as tightly organised as it should be at these prices, and wines offer little of interest under £20, though house French is £12.

CHEF/PROPRIETOR: Peter Chandler OPEN: Tue to Sun L 12 to 2, Tue to Sat D 7 to 9.30 CLOSED: Feb MEALS: Set L £25, Set D £45 SERVICE: not inc, card slips closed CARDS: Amex, Delta, Diners, MasterCard, Switch, Visa DETAILS: 45 seats. 20 seats outside. Private parties: 48 main room, 16 private room. Car park. Vegetarian meals. Children's helpings. Music

WOODSTOCK Oxfordshire map 2

▲ *Feathers Hotel*

Market Street, Woodstock OX20 1SX COOKING 3
TEL: (01993) 812291 FAX: (01993) 813158 COST £31–£55

Visitors come to see Blenheim, a short walk away, and are impressed that the 'smart, comfortable, well-decorated and stylish' hotel has retained its character and not been 'themed' into a pastiche. Bar food runs to lamb and rosemary hotpot, or salmon and halibut fish-cake, while the yellow dining-room puts on a display of crab pancake roll with coriander and lemon grass, pesto soufflé with chorizo, or roast breast and confit leg of duckling with pulses, soy sauce and ginger. Desserts might take in warm poppy seed and orange pudding, or baked cheesecake with blackberries and pistachio. The 15 per cent 'optional' service charge, plus extra charges for vegetables and petits fours, has come in for criticism, along with high wine mark-ups: Antinori's Chianti Classico at nearly £25, for example. Look to Iberia, South Africa, South America and regional France for bottles under £20. House Duboeuf is £11.75.

CHEF: David Lewis PROPRIETORS: Simon Lowe, Howard Malin and Andrew Leeman OPEN: all week 12.30 to 2.15, 7.30 to 9.15 CLOSED: D 25 Dec MEALS: alc (main courses £14.50 to £18). Set L Mon to Sat £16.50 (2 courses) to £21, Set L Sun £19.50 SERVICE: 15% (optional), card slips closed CARDS: Amex, Delta, Diners, MasterCard, Switch, Visa DETAILS: 60 seats. 60 seats outside. Private parties: 60 main room, 25 private room. Vegetarian meals. Children's helpings. No smoking in dining-room ACCOMMODATION: 16 rooms, all with bath/shower. TV. Phone. B&B £88 to £105. Children welcome. Baby facilities. Dogs welcome. Afternoon teas. Garden (*The Which? Hotel Guide*)

'The duck looked glorious, lacquered a rich golden brown. The waiter drew on a pair of white cotton gloves and produced a towel. Had he produced a magic wand and turned the duck into a prince we could not have been more gobsmacked. He grabbed one leg in the towel and forced it into a splits movement. He then proceeded to carve chunks of meat and skin from one side of it, swivelled it around in a graceful pirouette, like a movement from "Duck Lake", and performed microsurgery on its other side.' (On eating in London)

WORCESTER **Hereford & Worcester** map 5

Brown's

24 Quay Street, Worcester WR1 2JJ COOKING 4
TEL: (01905) 26263 FAX: (01905) 25768 COST £24–£48

'Somebody who thinks big, and stark' probably converted this late-eighteenth-century grain mill into the slick restaurant it is today. It is helped by a Severn-side location, a 'custardy' colour scheme, original works of art, and 'fittingly well-heeled' customers. 'One has to admire Brown's for their consistency,' reckoned one reporter. 'They found a formula years ago and have stuck to it.' Soup and fish vary with the day, and the kitchen relies on short cooking times to grill calf's liver or fillet of Aberdeen Angus beef, and to roast duck or pheasant.

It succeeds partly because it keeps things simple – monkfish kebab with herb mayonnaise, or carré of lamb with pease pudding – and partly because materials, timing, textures and flavours are all well handled. Finish perhaps with lemon meringue, chocolate truffle, or apple and blackberry crumble. Nobody pretends that the set-price dinner (four courses plus coffee) is given away, but impressively good service is included. A largely French wine list is well off for half-bottles, although mark-ups can be high. House French or Australian is £11.50.

CHEFS: W.R. Tansley and L. Jones PROPRIETORS: W.R. and P.M Tansley OPEN: Tue to Fri and Sun L 12.30 to 1.45, Tue to Sat D 7.30 to 9.45 CLOSED: 24 Dec to 31 Dec MEALS: Set L Tue to Fri £18.50, Set L Sun £24.50, Set D £34.50 SERVICE: net prices, card slips closed CARDS: Amex, Delta, MasterCard, Switch, Visa DETAILS: 100 seats. Private parties: 80 main room. Vegetarian meals. No children under 8. No-smoking area. Wheelchair access (also WC). Music

WORFIELD **Shropshire** map 5

▲ *Old Vicarage Hotel*

Worfield WV15 5JZ
TEL: (01746) 716497 FAX: (01746) 716552 NEW CHEF
2m N of A545, 3m E of Bridgnorth COST £28–£55

A new chef arrived at this red-brick Edwardian vicarage just as the *Guide* went to press. John Williams left after eight years to set up a venture of his own, and Richard Arnold has come from Lake Country House (see entry, Llangammarch Wells, Wales). He brings sound technique, a seasonal awareness, and a flair for presentation to the Old Vicarage's classically British approach with its regional supply lines and penchant for home-smoking. Reports please. Meanwhile, the wine list continues to provide some high-quality bins at very reasonable prices. The selections from the Rhône, Germany and Spain in particular catch the eye, while in California, Grgich Hills and Gundlach Bundschu trip off the tongue. There are no house wines as such, but prices start at £13.50, and half-bottles number an impressive 75. CELLARMAN'S CHOICE: Côtes de Thongue, Condamine l'Eveque Viognier 1996, £17.50; Jim Barry Macrae Wood Shiraz 1993, Clare Valley, S. Australia, £19.50.

CHEF: Richard Arnold PROPRIETORS: Peter and Christine Iles OPEN: Sun L 12 to 1.45, Mon to Sat D 7 to 8.30 MEALS: Set L Sun £16.50, Set D £25 to £32.50 SERVICE: not inc CARDS: Amex, Diners, MasterCard, Visa DETAILS: 40 seats. Private parties: 40 main room, 16 private room. Car park. Vegetarian meals. Children's helpings. No smoking in dining-room. Wheelchair access (also WC). Music ACCOMMODATION: 14 rooms, all with bath/shower. TV. Phone. B&B £70 to £152.50. Deposit: £50. Rooms for disabled. Children welcome. Baby facilities. Dogs welcome. Not in public rooms. Garden (*The Which? Hotel Guide*)

WORLESTON Cheshire map 5

▲ *Rookery Hall*

Worleston CW5 6DQ
TEL: (01270) 610016 FAX: (01270) 626027 COOKING 4
on B5074, 2½m N of Nantwich COST £29–£61

The Hall was built in 1816 for a well-to-do local landowner, but was transformed some 50 years later from a straightforward Georgian mansion into an imitation château with a tower on one corner. It has 38 acres of Cheshire to itself, mainly wooded parkland, while opposite the front entrance a willow weeps over an ornamental lake. The dining-room has a formal but lived-in feel, the austerity of dark panelling relieved by candelight and the cosseting attentions of the staff.

Lunch and dinner are set-price affairs, the former three courses, the latter four, with coffee and petits fours included. David Alton's menus are very much country-house style: escalope of foie gras comes on a saffron brioche with a sauce of raisins, apples and Muscat wine, while roast loin of lamb has wild mushrooms, herb dumplings and creamed spinach in attendance. The menu-writing makes free with culinary metaphors. There may be a pithiviers of goats' cheese, carpaccio of monkfish or a tarte Tatin of leeks and shallots, not to mention a seafood soup called minestrone. Third course is a cheese selection that celebrates the best of Britain and Ireland in the company of some date and hazelnut bread, and then it's warm lemon tart, iced banana parfait or apple and cinnamon soufflé with calvados sauce to finish. The main wine list is supplemented by a lengthier volume of connoisseurs' stuff, but prices are high all round and the starting point is £17 a bottle. That said, a good selection is available by the glass from £3.50. If you're starting with a glass of champagne, though, you'll get Gosset Grande Réserve at £12.50 a measure.

CHEF: David Alton PROPRIETOR: Arcadian Hotels Ltd OPEN: all week 12 to 2, 7 to 9.45 MEALS: Set L £17.50, Set D £37.50 SERVICE: not inc CARDS: Amex, Delta, Diners, MasterCard, Switch, Visa DETAILS: 30 seats. Private parties: 66 main room, 12 to 66 private rooms. Car park. Vegetarian meals. Children's helpings. No smoking in dining-room. Wheelchair access (also WC). Music ACCOMMODATION: 45 rooms, all with bath/shower. TV. Phone. B&B £110 to £250. Rooms for disabled. Children welcome. Baby facilities. Dogs welcome in courtyard rooms by arrangement only. Afternoon teas. Garden. Fishing

---

'The three ravioli were like flattened green flying saucers, squashed rejects from a Spielberg film.' (On eating in Wiltshire)

WRIGHTINGTON Lancashire map 8

High Moor

High Moor Lane, Wrightington WN6 9QA
TEL: (01257) 252364 FAX: (01257) 255120
off A5209, between M6 J27 and Parbold, take Robin Hood Lane at crossroads W of Wrightington Hospital, then next left

COOKING 4
COST £20–£41

'It is some years since since I have visited High Moor, and how things have changed,' began one reporter, welcoming the successful makeover from what used to be a 'pretentious place' to a much more informal set-up. The white-painted building dates back to 1642, but modernisation has retained the stone floors, oak beams and log fires that make up its essential character. 'Down to earth' menus might include chargrilled rump steak, beef and real ale casserole, and rice pudding: 'nothing fancy', as one observer noted.

There is a little more to it than that, however, as the kitchen feels able to turn out not just deep-fried fish and chips with mushy peas, or braised boneless oxtail with bubble and squeak, but also a boudin of chicken and lamb sweetbreads, and smoked shoulder of lamb with rosemary and olive oil mash. Propping up sticky toffee pudding is another old favourite, knickerbocker glory. 'Absolutely marvellous' value is helped by over 15 wines by the glass which head up a good-quality list. House red and white from Alto Adige are £9.95.

CHEF: Darren Lynn PROPRIETORS: John Nelson and James Sines OPEN: all week 12 to 2, 5.30 to 10 (9.30 Sun) CLOSED: 26 Dec, 1 Jan MEALS: alc Mon to Sat (main courses L £5 to £14, D £6.50 to £14). Set L Mon to Sat and 'early doors' D Mon to Sat (5.30 to 7pm) £9.50 (2 courses) to £11.50. Bar L available Mon to Sat SERVICE: not inc CARDS: Amex, Delta, Diners, MasterCard, Switch, Visa DETAILS: 100 seats. Private parties: 100 main room. Car park. Vegetarian meals. Children's helpings. Wheelchair access (no WC). Music

WYE Kent map 3

▲ *Wife of Bath*

4 Upper Bridge Street, Wye TN25 5AW
TEL: (01233) 812540 and 812232
FAX: (01233) 813630
just off A28, Ashford to Canterbury road

COOKING 3
COST £21–£38

John Morgan's village restaurant-with-rooms is comfortable and pleasant, the food modern and crafted from good local ingredients. Robert Hymers cooks tried-and-tested Anglo-French combinations such as home-made pasta with mushrooms, garlic, Parma ham and Parmesan, or rack of lamb with ratatouille sauce. Occasionally restraint makes way for a more unusual partnership of tangy Sauternes jelly with guinea-fowl and bacon terrine, or rich roast duckling offset by limes and redcurrants. An inspector commended a light and fluffy steamed orange sponge with crème anglaise, as well as the general excellence of the fresh produce, the attractive presentation of dishes, and a determination to please that began with a warm welcome. As well as à la carte lunches, there is a cheap and cheerful two-course 'Pilgrim's' set menu, with alternative first- and main-course choices. The list of 60-plus wines is strongest in Australia, New Zealand and Chile, but there are some tempting clarets and burgundies. House selections start at £9.95.

CHEF: Robert Hymers PROPRIETOR: John Morgan OPEN: Tue to Sat 12 to 2.30, 7 to 10 CLOSED: 1 week early Jan MEALS: alc (main courses £11 to £14). Set L £8.75 (2 courses), Set D £22.75. BYO £5 SERVICE: not inc CARDS: Delta, Diners, MasterCard, Switch, Visa DETAILS: 55 seats. Private parties: 60 main room. Car park. Vegetarian meals. Children's helpings. No pipes in dining-room. Wheelchair access (also WC). No music ACCOMMODATION: 6 rooms, all with bath/shower. TV. Phone. B&B £40 to £70. Rooms for disabled. Children welcome. Garden (*The Which? Hotel Guide*)

YARM Stockton-on-Tees map 10

D.P. Chadwick's £

104 High Street, Yarm TS15 9AU COOKING 3
TEL: (01642) 788558 COST £21–£45

This double-fronted modern brasserie hiding under its awnings looks as though it could have been transplanted brick by brick from London's Fulham Road, and even the menu might have come with it. A starter of Italian meats and caponata, or peppered salmon fillet with wild mushrooms and chive velouté, keeps local folk abreast of metropolitan culinary chic. France rubs shoulders with Italy here just as it does on the map, so there is also grilled swordfish with provençale vegetables and pistou. If all that sounds a bit too Continental, then have the fish-cakes, made with smoked haddock and served with spinach and a tomato sauce. Expect to find your favourite puddings; there have been reports of a nifty tiramisù. Wines are an inspiring international collection, with a commendably wide range available by the glass. Prices open at around £10.

CHEF: David Brownless PROPRIETOR: D.P. Chadwick OPEN: Tue to Sat 11.30 to 5, 5.30 to 9.30 CLOSED: 1 week late Oct MEALS: alc (main courses L £5 to £9, D £6 to £13) SERVICE: not inc CARDS: Delta, MasterCard, Switch, Visa DETAILS: 65 seats. Vegetarian meals. Children's helpings. No smoking in 1 dining-room. Music

YARMOUTH Isle of Wight map 2

▲ *George Hotel*

Quay Street, Yarmouth PO41 0PE COOKING 6
TEL: (01983) 760331 FAX: (01983) 760425 COST £23–£49

The former governor's house dates from the seventeenth century and has been extensively, attractively and colourfully restored: a couple who stayed two nights were 'impressed by everything'. It maintains a 'quietly luxurious ambience' not typically associated with a seaside hotel, and offers two options for eating. The spacious brasserie with bright, butter-yellow walls, high ceiling, pine furniture, and large windows overlooks the lawns and gardens towards the Solent, and aims for a 'rustic' approach: braised pork shins flavoured with chilli and lemon grass in winter, perhaps, and baked crab and monkfish with a provençale crust in summer.

The more formal restaurant, in deep red with comfortably upholstered chairs, goes in for 'modern classical' food that might touch on a few luxuries along the way: foie gras, roast lobster with squid ink ravioli, and garnishes of caviare and truffle oil. It also has an appealingly innovative streak in, for example, a first course that combines roast pigeon breast with fried ox tongue on creamed celeriac, or a dish of cod poached in coconut milk with stir-fry vegetables. Overall, fish is well reported, from risotto with scallops and langoustine, to 'pristine-fresh' seared tuna in a niçoise salad, served with rich black olives, marinated anchovies and new potatoes with a good olive oil dressing.

The mix of familiar and more unusual items continues into desserts of, for example, chocolate fondant with pistachio ice-cream, and rice pudding flavoured with aniseed, served with a mango and pineapple crêpe. Appetisers of olives and mini-pizzas might be followed at table by a small ramekin of smoked haddock soup, and bread and petits-fours are up to scratch. The wine list, too, blends old favourites with enterprising newcomers, offering an enticing spread of styles and flavours from the Old and New Worlds grouped into price bands, and the mark-ups on the whole are very reasonable, starting with ten bins at £11.50 and finishing with a fine collection of classed growth clarets dating back to 1937. CELLARMAN'S CHOICE: Muscadet sur lie 1995, Chasseloir, £14.50; Errazuriz Merlot 1996, Maule, Chile, £11.50.

CHEF: Kevin Mangeolles PROPRIETORS: Jeremy and Amy Willcock, and John Illsley OPEN: restaurant Sun L 12 to 3, Tue to Sat D 7 to 10; brasserie all week 12 to 3, 7 to 10 MEALS: restaurant Set L £22.50, Set D £34.50; brasserie alc (main courses £7 to £12), Set L Mon to Fri £22.50. BYO £0 SERVICE: none, card slips closed CARDS: Amex, Delta, MasterCard, Switch, Visa DETAILS: 25 seats (restaurant), 45 seats, 60 seats outside (brasserie). Private parties: 20 main room (restaurant), 10 main room (brasserie), 20 private room. Vegetarian meals. Children's helpings. No children under 8 in restaurant. No music. Air-conditioned ACCOMMODATION: 16 rooms, all with bath/shower. TV. Phone. B&B £80 to £140. Children welcome. Afternoon teas. Garden (*The Which? Hotel Guide*)

YATTENDON Berkshire map 2

▲ *Royal Oak*

The Square, Yattendon RG18 0UG
TEL: (01635) 201325 FAX: (01635) 201926 COOKING 6
off B4009, 5m W of Pangbourne COST £27–£58

The red-brick inn on Yattendon's square is not quite an archetypal village pub. It may look convincingly rustic from without, luxuriantly clad in thick wistaria, but the dining-room would not be out of place in an intimate grand hotel and the guest rooms are appointed to the same high standard. In contrast to this, the front-of-house approach is warm and amiable. Simple, homely dishes such as gravad lax, faggots with bubble and squeak, or navarin of lamb with garlic mash are available in the bar.

The restaurant *carte*, however, enters another dimension entirely. Chargrilled scallops with a cinnamon velouté, or spiced duck with honey-glazed parsnips are the likely order of the day, and technique to back up the ambition is evident most of the time. An inspector was impressed by a first-course escabèche of red mullet with caramelised langoustines and tapénade croûtons; everything from the dressing on the accompanying leaves to the faultless judging of sweetness in the shellfish was spot-on. A sorbet – maybe apple, served in a glass of calvados – comes before the main course, which may be chargrilled beef fillet with red onion and a creamy Meaux mustard sauce, or noisette of lamb with wild mushrooms and couscous flecked with peppers, aubergine and courgette. For dessert, a rich old-fashioned blancmange is modishly garnished with caramelised figs, while an otherwise unremarkable red fruit sablé comes with a surprise element in the form of a scoop of garlic ice-cream. Prices are high for both food and wines, but there are some high-quality bottles. House French, however, is £9.75 per bottle, £2.05 the glass.

CHEF: Robbie Macrae PROPRIETOR: Regal Hotel Group OPEN: Tue to Fri and Sun L 12.30 to 2, Mon to Sat D 7.30 to 9.30 (10 Fri and Sat) MEALS: alc (main courses £15.50 to £22.50). Bar food available SERVICE: not inc CARDS: Amex, Delta, Diners, MasterCard, Switch, Visa DETAILS: 30 seats. 40 seats outside. Private parties: 25 main room, 10 private room. Car park. Vegetarian meals. Children's helpings. No smoking in dining-room. No music ACCOMMODATION: 5 rooms, all with bath/shower. TV. Phone. B&B £69 to £105. Children welcome. Baby facilities. Dogs welcome. Afternoon teas. Garden (*The Which? Hotel Guide*)

YORK North Yorkshire map 9

Melton's

7 Scarcroft Road, York YO2 1ND COOKING **5**
TEL: (01904) 634341 FAX: (01904) 635115 COST £18–£31

The Hjorts have livened up the décor with a new mural, a display of drinks and a collection of guide and recipe books, but theirs remains a supremely functional approach in which frills would be out of place. Menus change monthly, supplemented by daily additions. Tuesdays bring extra vegetarian items such as sea kale with hollandaise, or three-onion risotto with red wine and olives, while Thursdays bring more fish: escabèche of sardines with ginger, perhaps, or ragoût of skate wing with mussels and saffron. Ideas are generally simple, from mackerel kebabs with piccalilli to marinated roast leg of lamb with parsnip and potato mash, but the foundations include rare-breed pork, organic vegetables and herbs, and impressively wild mushrooms: 'not the usual shop sort'.

Desserts, which might include rhubarb baked Alaska with champagne syrup, can be very sweet. Even though service may be casual – one reporter's wine arrived already open – it is worth bearing in mind that Abbey Well water, coffee and service are included, and wine mark-ups are modest, all of which contribute to the general impression of good value. Because no more than £10 is added to any wine, the more expensive wines offer best value: the perfect excuse to try a bottle of Condrieu or St-Julien cru classé. Twenty single-malt whiskies end the list with a flourish. For those who wish to learn more about wine in a relaxed way, a series of informal tastings are held throughout the year. CELLARMAN'S CHOICE: St-Véran 'Les Chailloux' 1995, Dom. des Deux Roches, £14.70; Maranges premier cru, Clos des Loyères 'Vielles Vignes' 1993, Vincent Girardin, £20.60.

CHEFS: Michael Hjort and T.J. Drew PROPRIETORS: Michael and Lucy Hjort OPEN: Tue to Sun L 12 to 2, Mon to Sat D 5.30 to 10 CLOSED: 3 weeks from 24 Dec, 24 to 31 Aug MEALS: alc (main courses £10.50 to £15). Set L £15, Set D £14.50 (before 7.45pm) to £19.50 SERVICE: net prices, card slips closed CARDS: Delta, MasterCard, Switch, Visa DETAILS: 40 seats. Private parties: 30 main room, 16 private room. Vegetarian meals. Children's helpings. No smoking in 1 dining-room. Wheelchair access (no WC). Music

▲ *Middlethorpe Hall*

Bishopthorpe Road, York YO2 1QB COOKING 5
TEL: (01904) 641241 FAX: (01904) 620176 COST £21–£55

The house, built in 1699, is one of three in the *Guide* owned and maintained by Historic House Hotels (see Hartwell House, Aylesbury, and Bodysgallen Hall, Llandudno), which seems to have the knack of keeping these large period piles in good decorative order. It sits in 26 acres overlooking the racecourse, just a mile and a half from the city, sedate and stately on the outside, comfortable and chintzy on the inside, with two dining-rooms. Andrew Wood cooks two dinner menus, too, the 'gourmet' version being the repository for luxury ingredients from foie gras terrine via langoustine ravioli to fillet of beef with spinach and white truffles.

Lunch and the cheaper dinner menu are both plainer and less rich, although neither stints on either interest or workmanship, judging by a scallop and salmon sausage with dill risotto, Yorkshire lamb cassoulet, or a chicken liver and bacon salad with grilled new potatoes and poached egg. Desserts have plenty to offer, too, including steamed chocolate sponge, and mango and berry soufflé. The wine list is well-suited to the grandeur of its setting, with some very worthy examples from the classical French regions supported by some estimable New World offerings. As might be expected, prices are rather grand too, although some lower-priced bins can be found. Half a dozen house wines start at £12.50. CELLARMAN'S CHOICE: Mitchell Riesling 1995, Clare Valley, S. Australia, £19; Côteaux du Languedoc, Ch. Ricardelle 1994, La Clape, £17.75.

CHEF: Andrew Wood PROPRIETOR: Historic House Hotels OPEN: all week 12.30 (12 on race days) to 1.45, 7.30 to 9.45 CLOSED: 25 Dec (residents only) MEALS: Set L Mon to Sat £12.50, Set L Sun £14.50, Set D £26.95 to £36.95. BYO £7.50 SERVICE: net prices, card slips closed CARDS: Amex, Delta, MasterCard, Switch, Visa DETAILS: 50 seats. Private parties: 50 main room, 50 private room. Car park. Vegetarian meals. No children under 8. Jacket and tie at D. No smoking in dining-room. Wheelchair access (no WC). No music ACCOMMODATION: 30 rooms, all with bath/shower. TV. Phone. Room only £95 to £215. Deposit: 1 night's stay. Rooms for disabled. No children under 8. Afternoon teas. Garden (*The Which? Hotel Guide*)

Scotland

ABERDEEN Aberdeen map 11

Courtyard

1 Alford Lane, Aberdeen AB10 1YD — COOKING 2
TEL: (01224) 213795 FAX: (01224) 212961 — COST £21–£39

Both format and chef remain the same under new ownership. Downstairs is Martha's Vineyard, a cheerful bistro with a blackboard menu of smoked salmon, mushroom risotto, daily specials and a £4.95 deal of soup and a sandwich, while the quieter upstairs Courtyard dining-room goes in for black pudding and mash, halibut or tuna steaks, and chargrilled loin of venison. Straightforward ideas and techniques make for simple and approachable food: at one meal a 'decent, basic' smoked haddock soup, followed by chicken breast with lime and coriander, and plum and almond tart with whipped cream. Some dishes can be taken as either a first or a main course, which helps to keep the bill down, and the short, fairly priced wine list helps even more. House French is £9.50.

CHEF: Glen Lawson PROPRIETORS: N.R. and I. Findlay OPEN: Tue to Sat 12 to 2.30, 6.30 to 9.30 CLOSED: first week Jan MEALS: alc (main courses £7.50 to £14.50). Bistro menu SERVICE: not inc CARDS: Amex, MasterCard, Switch, Visa DETAILS: 80 seats. Private parties: 30 main room. Vegetarian meals. Children's helpings. No cigars/pipes in dining-room. Wheelchair access (also WC). Music

Faraday's

2–4 Kirk Brae, Cults, Aberdeen AB1 9SQ
TEL/FAX: (01224) 869666 — COOKING 1
on A93, 4m from city centre — COST £19–£51

John Inches has notched up a decade in this narrow Edwardian building, where he serves a varied menu with some Scottish overtones. Stornoway black pudding, ham and haddie, and pan-fried oatmeal haddock are as home-grown as can be, but there is also a strong emphasis on more exotic dishes such as provençale bourride of chicken, cassoulet of turkey, and curry dhansak of Scottish lamb with brinjals and pilau rice. Dinner is four courses mid-week, five on Friday and Saturday. British cheeses or a simple dish of fresh fruit are among the alternatives to crème caramel or blackcurrant and Pernod cheesecake. A carrot in the form of a five per cent reduction is offered for immediate forms of payment, and a stick of five per cent surcharge for the use of credit cards. By the time the *Guide* appears, accommodation may well be on offer. Most of the sixty-odd wines make it under a £20 ceiling, including half a dozen house wines from £11.90.

CHEFS: John Inches and Roger Ross PROPRIETOR: John Inches OPEN: Tue to Sat 12 to 2, 7 to 10 CLOSED: 26 Dec to 6 Jan MEALS: alc L (main courses £5 to £12.50). Set D Tue to Thur £19.95, Set D Fri and Sat £23.95. BYO £4.50 SERVICE: 10%, card slips closed CARDS: Amex, Delta, MasterCard, Switch, Visa DETAILS: 38 seats. Private parties: 38 main room. Car park. Vegetarian meals. Children's helpings. No smoking in dining-room until 2 L, 10 D. Wheelchair access (also WC). Music. Air-conditioned

Q Brasserie

NEW ENTRY

9 Alford Place, Aberdeen AB10 1YD COOKING **3**
TEL: (01224) 595001 FAX: (01224) 582245 COST £21–£50

The first-floor room of this former divinity college has the feel of a converted school hall, with leaded windows, and a bar where the staff and headmaster would have sat. Fabrics favour 'bruise-like' colours of red, blue, purple and black, modern paintings hang on the walls, and its 'Q' logo, although 'subtly different from' Quaglino's (see entry, London), is at any rate a sincere form of flattery. Contemporary brasserie favourites make much use of the pig, with black pudding, a terrine of pork knuckle, and braised trotters stuffed with sweetbreads and ceps. A foundation of good ingredients has included 'slightly bloody' pigeon breast on parsnip purée, and fine, moist curry-crusted cod fillets in a creamy sauce, while desserts have yielded dark chocolate sponge, spiced pear, and liquorice charlotte with roasted pineapple. A short but serviceable list of wines begins with house French at £10.95.

CHEF: Paul Whitecross PROPRIETORS: J. and S. Clarkson OPEN: Mon to Fri L 12 to 2, Mon to Sat D 7 to 10 (10.45 Fri and Sat) MEALS: alc (main courses L £4.50 to £8, D £10 to £15) SERVICE: not inc CARDS: Amex, Delta, MasterCard, Switch, Visa DETAILS: 119 seats. Private parties: 100 main room, 16 private room. Vegetarian meals. Children's helpings. Music

Silver Darling

Pocra Quay, North Pier, Aberdeen AB11 5DQ COOKING **4**
TEL: (01224) 576229 FAX: (01224) 791275 COST £25–£50

The approach is a long, lonely trek past boats and shipyards, but then all the industry suddenly disappears and the converted Customs House turns out to be in a delightful spot by the mouth of the Dee. Plants dangle over the beams of the small, chintzy, red-brick dining-room, and somebody's crochet work is draped over the lights. Evenings can be busy and peppered with snatches of oil-talk. Didier Dejean's main business is fish with a French accent, from a gratin of langoustines and wild mushrooms to a 'tartare' of scallops and sea trout, from grilled snapper with smoked bacon and mint to steamed halibut with lemon and butter sauce.

The food can be imaginative and sometimes elaborate, techniques are varied, but any given meal can see-saw from disappointing to outstanding. Among highlights have been lobster in saffron sauce with salmon ravioli, and generous chunks of roast monkfish served with whole roast garlic cloves in a clear fish stock. Cream sometimes features in savoury dishes, but comes into its own in desserts such as chocolate-flavoured pancake soufflé with vanilla Chantilly. Pastry could be improved, but the sorbets are good. Around thirty wines are, understandably, mostly French and white, including house wine at £9.50.

CHEF: Didier Dejean PROPRIETORS: Didier Dejean and Catherine Wood OPEN: Mon to Fri L 12 to 2, Mon to Sat D 7 to 10 CLOSED: 2 weeks Christmas to New Year MEALS: alc D (main courses £15.50 to £17). Set L £16.50 SERVICE: not inc CARDS: Amex, Delta, Diners, MasterCard, Switch, Visa DETAILS: 34 seats. Private parties: 30 main room. Children's helpings. Wheelchair access (also WC). Music

ABERFELDY Perthshire & Kinross map 11

▲ *Farleyer House*

Aberfeldy PH15 2JE
TEL: (01887) 820332 FAX: (01887) 829430
on B846, Aberfeldy to Kinloch Rannoch road, 1½m W of Weem

COOKING 5
COST £23–£50

Farleyer has done the sensible thing and responded to market forces. For a time it ran the swish Menzies dining-room in tandem with the bistro, but found the former sometimes struggling for numbers, while having to turn away custom from the bistro. There could not be a plainer demonstration of the eating public's weariness with formal and expensive country-house mannerisms, and its preference for something brighter, more casual, flexible and contemporary. A set menu still operates for those inclined to eat four courses, but the focus is now firmly on a wide ranging *carte* for the upgraded and extended bistro, which is now open all year. A sense of purpose has been restored.

The kitchen smokes and cures salmon, bakes bread, and takes advantage of organic pork, Perthshire lamb, and sea kale and wild garlic in season. Flavours emanate mostly from Scotland and the Mediterranean, producing a salad of smoked haddock, or a tartlet of onion marmalade with Gigha goats' cheese, rocket and Parmesan. Game, seafood and vegetable dishes contribute to a well-balanced menu, and among recommendations have been seared Skye scallops, roast turbot fillet, and filo-baked wood pigeon with barley risotto and cinnamon sauce. Iced coffee parfait with Glayva chantilly might appear at any season, while autumn has yielded a soup of strawberries, raspberries and blackberries with ice-cream. Sharp, intelligent service backs everything up. The wine list still reflects the old regime, with too little under £20 for the context, but eight wines are available by the glass, including house Moldovan Merlot and Chardonnay at £10.50 a bottle.

CHEF: Richard Lyth PROPRIETOR: Janice Reid OPEN: all week 12 to 2.30, 6 to 10 MEALS: alc (main courses £7 to £14.50). Set L and D £32. BYO £10 SERVICE: not inc CARDS: Amex, Delta, Diners, MasterCard, Switch, Visa DETAILS: 110 seats. 20 seats outside. Private parties: 60 main room, 30 and 40 private rooms. Car park. Vegetarian meals. Children's helpings. No smoking in 1 dining-room. Wheelchair access (also WC). Music ACCOMMODATION: 19 rooms, all with bath/shower. TV. Phone. D,B&B £110 to £220. Deposit: £95. Rooms for disabled. Children welcome. Baby facilities. Dogs welcome in kennels. Afternoon teas. Garden. Fishing (*The Which? Hotel Guide*)

ABERFOYLE Stirling map 11

Braeval

Aberfoyle FK8 3UY
TEL: (01877) 382711 FAX: (01877) 382400 COOKING 6
on A81, 1m SE of Aberfoyle COST £29–£52

This rough-stone rectangular building on the outskirts of Aberfoyle is home to Nick Nairn, the likeable, energetic TV chef who always seems to be bursting with ideas and enthusiasm. It consists of a single room with a slab floor, wooden beams and dexterously draped fabric at the windows. Although it is small, tables are sympathetically spaced and set with blue water jugs and glasses, linen is crisp, and there is 'no pomposity, no unnecessary flourishes'. Likes and dislikes are discussed when booking, otherwise there is no choice before dessert, and the four-course dinner usually begins with soup, followed by fish, then meat.

At its best the kitchen can hit the high spots with, for example, a huge bowl of fragrant, sweet-tasting, terracotta-coloured tomato soup with swirls of green pesto trailing across. Buying is evidently good, producing 'ozone-fresh' chargrilled halibut, with 'flesh-like mother of pearl', served with a niçoise salad. Organic beef has impressed for flavour and texture, served to acclaim with artichoke purée, wild mushrooms and a light, tarragon-flavoured *jus*. It may or may not have anything to do with Mr Nairn's soaraway televisual success, but output does appear to be variable. Our inspector found individual elements good in their own right, but not always combined to mutual advantage. Service has been judged so good that 'the young manageress should be cloned, to bring a little charm to some of the soulless London establishments', although another visitor begged to differ.

The wine list takes off with an eclectic group of 16 house wines priced between £14 and £20, then flies around the world's major wine regions, touching down briefly to pick up a few bins before moving on to the next exciting location. Every bottle deserves its seat on board the list, which offers a broad range of styles and vintages. CELLARMAN'S CHOICE: Bourgogne Blanc 1995, J-P. Fichet, £19.50; Devil's Lair Cabernet Sauvignon 1994, Margaret River, W. Australia, £22.50.

CHEF: Nick Nairn PROPRIETORS: Nick and Fiona Nairn OPEN: Thu to Sun L 12.30 to 1.30, Thu to Sat D 7.30 to 9.30 CLOSED: 1 and 2 Jan, 1 week in Feb, June and Nov MEALS: Set L Thu to Sat £18.50, Set L Sun £21.50, Set D £31.50 SERVICE: not inc, card slips closed CARDS: Delta, MasterCard, Switch, Visa DETAILS: 36 seats. Private parties: 36 main room. Car park. No children under 10. No cigars/pipes in dining-room. No smoking before coffee is served. Wheelchair access (also WC). No music

'It would all be a little gloomy if the staff were not so relaxed and welcoming. This came as something of a surprise after my telephone reservation had been dealt with by a person trained in the "Good-evening-my-name-is-Tracy-how-may-I-help-you" school of customer care.' (On eating in West Sussex)

ABOYNE Aberdeenshire map 11

▲ *White Cottage*

ABERDEENSHIRE 1998 ENTHUSIAST

NEW ENTRY

Dess, Aboyne AB34 5BP
TEL/FAX: (013398) 86265
on A93, 2½m E of Aboyne

COOKING 4
COST £22–£43

Despite the name, these two former estate workers' cottages beside the main road have had their original granite facing restored, and seem to come 'right out of a Hansel and Gretel fairy-story'. Meals are eaten either in the pine-floored dining-room – the spiral iron staircase in the centre is from a Glasgow tramcar – or in the conservatory that leads out into a pond garden complete with fountain and doves. The Mills ('a genuinely friendly couple') greet, serve and cook, and have laid down a foundation of good supplies. Fish comes from Aberdeen, fruit and vegetables from local organic market gardeners, and the kitchen garden chips in a few items.

Dishes are imbued with a contemporary feel, whether on the lunchtime *carte* (also available early evening) or the set-price menu: smoked Perthshire goats'-cheese and tarragon tartlet, for example, or a salad of pan-fried red fish with gazpacho sauce. Accurate timing makes the most of ingredients: briefly seared king scallops in a Pernod-flavoured butter sauce, and steamed noisettes of pink lamb served with a caul-wrapped thyme and chicken mousse. Portions are 'generous but not over-facing', and desserts have included lemon tart with Muscat sauce, and provençale prune and armagnac pie. Wines range from négociant burgundy to Chilean Cabernet Sauvignon, and five house wines, starting at £11.20, are also available by the glass.

CHEF: Laurie Mill PROPRIETORS: Laurie and Josephine Mill OPEN: Tue to Sun 11.30 to 3, 7 to 9; light meals served 6 to 7 CLOSED: 25, 26 and 27 Dec, 1 week Easter, 1 week summer MEALS: alc L (main courses £7 to £10). Set D £23 (2 courses) to £26.70 SERVICE: not inc CARDS: MasterCard, Switch, Visa DETAILS: 45 seats. 24 seats outside. Private parties: 45 main room, 25 private room. Car park. Children's helpings. No smoking in 1 dining-room. Wheelchair access (also WC). Music ACCOMMODATION: 1 room, with bath/shower. B&B £24 to £48. Children welcome. Garden

ACHILTIBUIE Highland map 11

▲ *Summer Isles Hotel*

Achiltibuie IV26 2YG
TEL: (01854) 622282 FAX: (01854) 622251
off A835 at Drumrunie, 10m N of Ullapool

COOKING 5
COST £40–£48

The remote Highland village of Achiltibuie is little more than a straggle of cottages, among which you will find Mark and Gerry Irvine's peaceful and civilised white Edwardian villa. Evenings might begin in the lounge with an oyster on a bed of seaweed, and proceed to the serenely decorated dining-room. Both share a spectacular view across the bay.

The five-course dinner menu (no choice except for puddings) is built around splendid local seafood. Starters of velvety mussel soup with coriander, or a filo parcel of langoustines with spinach and ginger, are matched with imaginative home-made breads – warm onion for the mussels, malted wholemeal for the langoustines – and might be followed by a Scottish blue cheese soufflé, or ravioli stuffed with crabmeat. Main courses are likely to be sophisticated showpieces – lobster with vermouth butter sauce, or woodpigeon with oyster mushrooms and red wine sauce – yet it's often the plainest dishes that please the most: a 'memorable, simple and exquisite' chargrilled turbot fillet, for example. An impressive selection of well-kept, mainly Scottish cheeses precedes pudding. From nursery stalwarts, such as steamed syrup pudding, to fudgy chocolate cake and lemon roulade, these are rapturously received. Service is friendly and informal. A light lunch menu offers platters of locally smoked salmon and shellfish, cured meats and Scottish cheeses.

Relaxing in the sitting-room with a pre-prandial drink in hand is a good way to study the splendid wine list, which offers French classics and some fine examples from Italy and the New World. Prices range from very low to very high, with fair mark-ups, and there is a good number of half-bottles, particularly in the dessert section. Wines to complement the day's starters are offered by the glass. CELLARMAN'S CHOICE: Rully Rabourcé 1994, Olivier Leflaive, £17.50; Marsannay Les Longeroies 1993, Dom. Bruno Claire, £17.50.

CHEF: Chris Firth-Bernard PROPRIETORS: Mark and Gerry Irvine OPEN: all week light L 12.30 to 2, D 8 (1 sitting) CLOSED: mid-Oct to Easter MEALS: Set D £34.50. Light L available. BYO £5 SERVICE: net prices, card slips closed CARDS: Delta, MasterCard, Switch, Visa DETAILS: 30 seats. Private parties: 8 main room. Car park. Children's helpings. No children under 6. No smoking in dining-room. No music ACCOMMODATION: 12 rooms, all with bath/shower. Phone. B&B £48 to £102. Deposit: £50. No children under 6. Dogs welcome in bedrooms only. Fishing (*The Which? Hotel Guide*)

ALEXANDRIA Dumbarton & Clydebank map 11

▲ *Cameron House Hotel, Georgian Room*

Loch Lomond, Alexandria G83 8QZ
TEL: (01389) 755565 FAX: (01389) 759522 NEW CHEF
off A82, ½m N of Balloch roundabout, 1m S of Arden COST £31–£88

Exceedingly grand in 'Scots baronial' mould, Cameron House has 'heaps of atmosphere and feels like a castle'. Great picture windows overlook Loch Lomond and the hills beyond, logs crackle in the grate, big flower arrangements adorn the tables, and comfortable chairs are set out in conversational groups. Despite the conference centre and timeshare options also on the site, it doesn't feel overly commercialised. In the summer of 1997, as the *Guide* went to press, Jeff Bland left and Peter Fleming replaced him from the ranks. Since the two have worked here together for five years the style is probably set to continue, but the changeover occurred too late for us to receive sufficient feedback, hence the lack of cooking mark.

If the food does remain as before, it promises a mix of the luxurious (truffle dumplings in a langoustine bisque, for example), the hearty (fillet of beef with oxtail ragoût) and the modern European (scallops with lime-scented risotto), followed by the unlikely-to-make-at-home (dark chocolate tear drop filled with white chocolate mousse, or iced banana parfait with caramelised bananas and a creole sauce). Some fine wines appear on the list (there are no house wines as

such), though mark-ups are a bit on the high side. Four wines by the glass are priced between £3 and £6. Reports please.

CHEF: Peter Fleming PROPRIETOR: De Vere Hotels OPEN: Mon to Fri L 12 to 1.45, all week D 7 to 9.45 CLOSED: 25 and 26 Dec MEALS: alc (main courses £21.50 to £29.50). Set L £15.95 (2 courses) to £18.50, Set D £37 to £45. BYO £15 SERVICE: not inc, card slips closed CARDS: Amex, Diners, MasterCard, Visa DETAILS: 45 seats. Private parties: 14 to 270 private rooms. Car park. Vegetarian meals. No children under 14. Jacket and tie. No smoking in dining-room. Music. Air-conditioned ACCOMMODATION: 98 rooms, all with bath/shower. TV. Phone. D&B £85 to £170. Deposit: £50. Rooms for disabled. Children welcome. Baby facilities. Afternoon teas. Garden. Swimming-pool. Fishing

ALYTH Perthshire & Kinross map 11

▲ *Drumnacree House*

St Ninians Road, Alyth PH11 8AP
TEL/FAX: (01828) 632194
turn off A926 Blairgowrie to Kirriemuir road to Alyth; take first left after Clydesdale Bank; hotel entrance is 300 metres on right

COOKING 4
COST £28–£37

The Culls call it a country-house hotel, citing a 1½-acre flower and vegetable garden in evidence, although the estate sits squarely within the boundaries of this small rural town. Antiques and a personal collection of exotic objects in the dining-room constitute the background for Allan Cull's 'modern international' cooking, which is a canny blend of regular and seasonal items. Arbroath smokie mousse, home-cured gravlax, and chargrilled Aberdeen Angus steaks appear regularly, while Scottish snails, asparagus, Tay salmon, and wild mushrooms flit in and out with the seasons.

Despite the international tag (covering spicy gumbos, dirty rice, and Chinese-style duck breast with sweet-and-sour cabbage), local resources are used to good effect. Pink loin of venison, for example, might be served on pearl barley risotto, and the garden is a rich source of unusual varieties, including excellent Pink Fir Apple potatoes, and salad leaves that might appear dressed in a Tuscan olive oil vinaigrette. Eleanor Cull oversees desserts, from steamed puddings to French apple tart, and raspberry cream. A functional list of around forty wines concentrates on Europe, beginning with house French at £9.50.

CHEF: Allan Cull PROPRIETORS: Allan and Eleanor Cull OPEN: Tue to Sat D only 7 to 9 (residents only Sun D and Mon D) CLOSED: 15 Dec to 30 Mar MEALS: Set D £18.50. BYO £5 SERVICE: not inc CARDS: Amex, MasterCard, Visa DETAILS: 50 seats. Private parties: 50 main room, 12 and 30 private rooms. Car park. Children's helpings. No smoking in dining-room. Wheelchair access (also women's WC). Music ACCOMMODATION: 6 rooms, all with bath/shower. TV. B&B £43.50 to £80. Deposit: £20. Children welcome. Dogs welcome. Garden

'Chicken and ham ballottine came studded with the occasional pistachio and was texturally as exciting as sucking on wallpaper paste with the occasional undissolved lump in it.'
(On eating in Hampshire)

ANSTRUTHER Fife map 11

Cellar

24 East Green, Anstruther KY10 3AA COOKING **6**
TEL: (01333) 310378 FAX: (01333) 312544 COST £25–£47

'I am enjoying working as much now as when we first opened,' writes Peter Jukes, who, in 1998, will have spent 15 years at his restaurant behind the Scottish Fisheries Museum. It has a small bar, a long dining-room and a feel for fish that is difficult to beat on the east coast. The repertoire evolves slowly. As Peter Jukes points out, return visitors come in search of their favourite dishes, so anything more than a gradual update would be counter-productive. Nevertheless, saucing now embraces oils and emulsions rather than cream, and vegetables are an integral part of the dish, but the essentially simple treatment of fish remains at the heart of the operation.

This approach produces local crab with mayonnaise, a quiche of lobster and smoked salmon, and an omelette of creamy smoked haddock. A year ago, as we write, reports showed a dip in enthusiasm, but this year has seen the return of 'superb' and 'excellent' in letters received by the *Guide*. One couple enjoyed a meal of crayfish bisque, roast monkfish on a courgette and pepper stew, and grilled halibut served with savoy cabbage, bacon, pine kernels and hollandaise. More staff are now on hand to polish up the service, and lunchtime openings have increased to five.

As one might expect, a classy range of whites from Burgundy and Alsace takes pride of place on the wine list, although die-hard red wine drinkers will find some fine clarets to keep them happy. Sommelier Gordon Armitage has introduced a selection of sherries from Lustau and Hidalgo which are available by the glass at £2.35; Hidalgo manzanilla would make a good accompaniment to the crayfish bisque. House wines are £12.50. CELLARMAN'S CHOICE: Chablis premier cru 'Montée de Tonnerre' 1990, Louis Michel, £25; Nederburg Edelrood Cabernet/Merlot 1992, Paarl, South Africa, £13.50.

CHEF/PROPRIETOR: Peter Jukes OPEN: Wed to Sun L 12.30 to 1.30, Mon to Sat D 7 to 9.30 CLOSED: 3 days Christmas MEALS: alc L (main courses £7 to £11.50). Set D £23.50 (2 courses) to £28.50 SERVICE: not inc, card slips closed CARDS: Amex, Delta, MasterCard, Switch, Visa DETAILS: 30 seats. Private parties: 32 main room. No children under 8. No smoking in dining-room. Music

ARCHIESTOWN Moray map 11

▲ *Archiestown Hotel* £ NEW ENTRY

Archiestown AB38 7QX COOKING **2**
TEL: (01340) 810218 FAX: (01340) 810239 COST £17–£42

Given the proximity of the River Spey, the village makes a natural base for both fishermen and distillery visitors, and there are apparently 15 golf courses within an hour's drive. The sturdy hotel stands at a crossroads, and meals – ordered from a blackboard in the bar – can be eaten either in the dining-room, or at bare wooden tables in the informal bistro. Lunch might be crab salad followed by a whole large plaice – 'rustic' portions are the norm – while dinner might revolve around a piece of monkfish roasted with peppercorns, coriander seeds, sea salt and herbs, or slices from a haunch of venison.

The main business is fish, and succeeds partly because supplies are very fresh, partly because the cooking remains simple. If there is shellfish, garlic will probably not be far away: be it in the mayonnaise for langoustines, or suffusing the juice that oozes from scallops baked in their shell with Parmesan cheese. Desserts, like the rest of the menu, assume a healthy appetite, and satisfy it with treacle pudding, rum and ginger syllabub, or a fine version of banoffi pie. Cheerful service from the proprietor is obliging without being fussy, and the short, reasonably priced wine list opens with house French at £10.

CHEF: Judith Bulger PROPRIETORS: Judith and Michael Bulger OPEN: all week 12.30 to 2, 6.30 to 8.30 CLOSED: 1 Oct to 9 Feb MEALS: alc (main courses £6.50 to £12.50) SERVICE: not inc, card slips closed CARDS: MasterCard, Visa DETAILS: 30 seats. 12 seats outside. Private parties: 20 main room, 14 private room. Car park. Children's helpings. No music ACCOMMODATION: 9 rooms, 7 with bath/shower. TV. Phone. B&B £32.50 to £80. Deposit: £10. Children welcome. Baby facilities. Dogs welcome. Afternoon teas. Garden

ARISAIG Highland map 11

▲ *Arisaig House* $\bigstar

Beasdale, by Arisaig PH39 4NR
TEL: (01687) 450622 FAX: (01687) 450626 COOKING 5
on A830, 3m E of Arisaig COST £27–£46

This refurbished grey-stone house on the road from Fort William to Mallaig presents a rather formal appearance, with an impressive fireplace, large staircase, antique furniture, panelling, and a 'wonderful view' from the terrace. Lunches might offer smoked salmon, Loch Moidart mussels marinière, or lambs' kidneys, but dinner is when Gary Robinson gets into gear with his modern, cosmopolitan, Franco-Scottish-style dishes. The menu changes daily, while sticking to a format of four courses, the second either soup or salad. For a supplement, Robinson incorporates a few luxuries – poached lobster, or terrine of duck foie gras with madeira truffle jelly – but the real interest lies in the combination of ideas and workmanship which produces, for example, a boudin of wild mushrooms with mustard dressing, or a honeyed aubergine and red pepper tian served with smoked duck and Parma ham.

Fish understandably features, with varied and appropriate treatments ranging from Mediterranean-style red mullet with basil and tapénade sauce to more northerly monkfish with celeriac purée and rösti. In like vein, guinea-fowl has been served with couscous, while roast pigeonneau has come with braised red cabbage. Occasionally a gamey dish such as roast saddle of hare with mustard sauce will ring the changes on more mainstream roast rack of lamb or Angus beef fillet, adding to the impression of a kitchen in search of distinctive flavours. Desserts are given just as much attention, judging by lemon mousse topped with pistachio crème brûlée, and pineapple tarte Tatin with prune and armagnac ice-cream. The wine list concentrates mainly on France, while the New World makes a late entrance in the form of two reds from South Africa and a Californian dessert Muscat. Four house wines are priced at £14.50.

CHEF: Gary Robinson PROPRIETORS: Ruth, John and Andrew Smither OPEN: all week 12.30 to 2, 7.30 to 8.30 CLOSED: Nov to end Mar MEALS: alc L (main courses £10). Set D £35 SERVICE: none, card slips closed CARDS: Amex, MasterCard, Switch, Visa DETAILS: 36 seats. 20 seats outside. Private parties: 10 main room. Car park. Vegetarian meals. No children under 10. No smoking in dining-room. No music ACCOMMODATION: 14 rooms, all with bath/shower. TV. Phone. B&B £65 to £240. Deposit: £50. No children under 10. Afternoon teas. Garden (*The Which? Hotel Guide*)

AUCHMITHIE Angus map 11

But 'n' Ben [£]

Auchmithie DD11 5SQ
TEL: (01241) 877223 COOKING 1
on coast, 3m NE of Arbroath, off A92 COST £14–£34

The village is a cul-de-sac above the red sandstone cliffs, and But 'n' Ben makes a handy break in a walker's day, providing 'sound food, in quantity, at very reasonable prices'. The two 'homely' cottages, knocked into one and white-washed, display paintings by local artists. Lunch typically offers crab salad, hot buttered Arbroath smokies (the local speciality), kedgeree, and perhaps a garlic mushroom pancake, while high tea is more like a re-run of lunch, with the addition of 'honest, homely baking' of tarts, scones, cakes and pies. Dinner is the more serious meal, with local lobster and giant prawns, pan-fried sole on the bone, and usually a big platter of shellfish with a bowl of salad, as well as game pie, venison, and a choice of steaks. Twenty basic wines (house French is £8) are outnumbered and outclassed by the single malt collection.

CHEFS: Margaret and Angus Horn PROPRIETORS: Martin, Iain and Angus Horn OPEN: Wed to Mon L 12 to 2.30, Mon and Wed to Sat D 7 to 9.30 CLOSED: 25 and 26 Dec, 1 and 2 Jan MEALS: alc (main courses £4.50 to £12.50). High tea available SERVICE: not inc, card slips closed CARDS: Delta, Diners, MasterCard, Switch, Visa DETAILS: 40 seats. Private parties: 40 main room. Car park. Vegetarian meals. Children's helpings. No smoking in dining-room. No music

---

AUCHTERARDER Perthshire & Kinross map 11

▲ *Auchterarder House*

Auchterarder PH3 1DZ COOKING 3
TEL: (01764) 663646 FAX: (01764) 662939 COST £28–£65

Kiernan Darnell remains at the stoves of this Scottish manor-house, sold by the Browns to Wren Hotels in the spring of 1997. The grand country-house style is reflected in its 17 acres of grounds, and in the spacious, lofty rooms with ornate ceilings and impressive woodwork. This is about as solid and reassuring as houses come this side of baronial, and dinner reinforces the sense of substantial scale. Scottish produce makes itself felt at every turn, from west-coast seafood soufflé to loin of Perthshire lamb, sometimes with an unusual flourish in the form of the gold leaf applied to a local game and wild mushroom consommé, or a warm terrine of cheese and potato layered with chorizo, wrapped in Ayrshire bacon and served with a sweet mustard dressing.

The 'Taste of Auchterarder House' dinner menu has featured guinea-fowl sausage, Shetland salmon, and a fruit sabayon with Drambuie, while other desserts might include fruit salsa, a chocolate and mint confection, or iced banana parfait. The traditional wine list focuses mainly on the classic regions of France, offering a good range of vintage clarets and burgundies, but if you switch your gaze to the New World you will see some classy bins there too. Spanish house wines are £12.50 a bottle, £3 a glass. CELLARMAN'S CHOICE: Pinot Grigio Collio 1991, Puiatti, £21.50; St-Julien, Ch. Léoville-Lascases 1985, £50.

CHEF: Kiernan Darnell PROPRIETOR: Wren Hotel Group OPEN: all week 12.30 to 2.30, 7 to 9.45 MEALS: Set L £18.50, Set D £37.50 to £42.50 SERVICE: not inc, card slips closed CARDS: Amex, Delta, Diners, MasterCard, Switch, Visa DETAILS: 100 seats. Private parties: 20 main room, 20 to 35 private rooms. Car park. Children's helpings. No children under 10. Jacket and tie. No smoking in dining-room. Wheelchair access (also WC). Music ACCOMMODATION: 15 rooms, all with bath/shower. TV. Phone. B&B £95 to £225. Rooms for disabled. No children under 10. Dogs welcome in bedrooms only. Afternoon teas. Garden

AYR South Ayrshire map 11

Fouter's Bistro

2A Academy Street, Ayr KA7 1HS COOKING 2
TEL: (01292) 261391 FAX: (01292) 619323 COST £20–£48

The Blacks have occupied the basement of this former bank opposite the town hall for a quarter of a century, setting the bistro tone by painting the walls white, stencilling a few stylised trees and baskets of fruit on top, and covering the wooden tables with red cloths. A friendly welcome, good value and generous portions endear it to locals and visitors alike. First-rate Scottish produce forms the foundation of the frequently changing menus, and it is the materials that shine through, not least 'superbly fresh' fish – salmon, hake, monk, mackerel and lemon sole are the sort of thing to expect – and chargrilled beef from local certified herds. The advice is to take these as plainly cooked as possible. Mussels and smoked salmon are from Loch Fyne, the latter perhaps served on toast with shrimps and horseradish cream. Desserts revel in cream and alcohol, from chocolate and brandy cheesecake to an iced soufflé with Grand Marnier, and cheeses are good. Wines start at £12.50 and stay mostly below £20.

CHEF: Laurie Black PROPRIETORS: Fran and Laurie Black OPEN: Tue to Sat 12 to 2, 6.15 to 10 CLOSED: 4 days Christmas, 4 days New Year MEALS: alc Tue to Sat L (main course £4 to £10), Tue to Fri D (main courses D £9 to £15.50). Set D Tue to Fri £11.50 (2 courses) to £21.50, Set D Sat £25. BYO £5 SERVICE: not inc CARDS: Amex, Delta, Diners, MasterCard, Switch, Visa DETAILS: 38 seats. Private parties: 20 main room. Vegetarian meals. Children's helpings. No pipes in dining-room. Music. Air-conditioned

The Guide *office can quickly spot when a restaurateur is encouraging customers to write recommending inclusion – and sadly, several restaurants have been doing this in 1997. Such reports do not further a restaurant's cause. Please tell us if a restaurateur invites you to write to the* Guide.

BALLATER Aberdeenshire map 11

▲ *Darroch Learg* 🍷

Braemar Road, Ballater AB35 5UX COOKING 4
TEL: (01339) 755443 FAX: (01339) 755252 COST £22–£44

This Victorian country residence overlooking the River Dee has been in the hands of the Franks family since 1961. Chef David Mutter cannot match this longevity, but his solidly British cooking has been endorsed by many reporters. Most visit on holiday and, appropriately, informality is the tone in the conservatory dining-room. In the kitchen the mandate for freshness and quality is met with home-made bread, pasta and petits fours, and industry is apparent throughout: in the risotto accompanying a first-course fillet of halibut, or in the braised oxtail and rösti that come with fillet of Aberdeen Angus beef. Salmon is home-smoked, and a varied selection of game and poultry adds interest: roast quail, breast of goose, pigeon in pastry, and breast of teal with a brioche dumpling. Desserts such as aniseed parfait, and ice-creams – cinnamon, mango and vanilla, for example – have come in for praise. Lunch is lighter and might take in goat's-cheese salad, ravioli of Loch Fyne crab, or cold roast sirloin. Service has ranged from slow to 'second to none'.

The well-annotated and kindly-priced wine list stretches to over 30 pages and features some excellent producers and vintages, particularly from Bordeaux. French classics take pride of place, but Italy is well represented and there is a canny selection from the New World. House wines start at £13.30 and nine wines are available by the glass from £3. CELLARMAN'S CHOICE: Puligny-Montrachet premier cru 'Les Garennes' 1994, Olivier Leflaive, £24.40; Haut-Médoc cru bourgeois, Ch. Liversan 1990, £19.10.

CHEF: David Mutter PROPRIETORS: the Franks family OPEN: all week 12.30 to 2, 7 to 8.30 (9 Fri and Sat) CLOSED: Christmas, 10 to 31 Jan MEALS: Set L Sun £14.75, Set D £24.75. Set L Mon to Sat by arrangement. Light L available Mon to Sat SERVICE: net prices, card slips closed CARDS: Amex, Delta, Diners, MasterCard, Switch, Visa DETAILS: 48 seats. Private parties: 48 main room. Car park. Children's helpings. No smoking in dining-room. No music ACCOMMODATION: 18 rooms, all with bath/shower. TV. Phone. Deposit: £50. Rooms for disabled. Children welcome. Baby facilities. Dogs welcome in bedrooms only. Afternoon teas. Garden (*The Which? Hotel Guide*)

▲ *Green Inn* 🍷

9 Victoria Road, Ballater AB35 5QQ COOKING 6
TEL/FAX: (01339) 755701 COST £20–£51

This comfortable restaurant-with-rooms has been run by the Purveses since 1990. The small dining-room is done in muted colours, enlivened with jovial pictures, and smart crockery sets the tone for Jeffrey Purves's even smarter cooking. Good use is made of local supply-lines in a culinary style that isn't afraid of elaborate refinement. Scrambled eggs laced with vodka and topped with caviare are served with chive-dressed smoked salmon. Onion soup comes with a mature-Cheddar soufflé. Flavours are carefully built up so as to maximise the impact of a dish: a roasted turbot fillet arrives with a brandade of smoked trout and a reduction of red wine and veal stock. A parfait made from Ovaltine brings a whole new meaning to the term 'nursery puddings'. One party who had previously found the Inn closed when visiting Ballater had their persistence rewarded by 'one of the best meals we have ever enjoyed'.

Inventiveness continues through to desserts such as mandarin soufflé with chocolate sauce, and crème brûlée with a compote of rhubarb. Service is both cheery and informative, and wines range from good to very good. The short selections from each region demonstrably earn their places, and prices are mostly restrained. Fine malts are accorded pride of place; the cask-strength specimens are certainly worth a look. House wines are £9.95. CELLARMAN'S CHOICE: Meursault, Clos du Cromins 1994, Olivier Leflaive, £24.50; Pomerol, Ch. Rouget 1990, £22.50.

CHEF: Jeffrey Purves PROPRIETORS: Jeffrey and Carol Purves OPEN: Sun L 12.30 to 1.45, all week D 7 to 9 CLOSED: 24 to 27 Dec MEALS: Set L £9.25 to £12.25, Set D £23 to £25.50 SERVICE: not inc CARDS: Amex, Delta, MasterCard, Visa DETAILS: 30 seats. Private parties: 36 main room. Vegetarian meals. Children's helpings. No smoking while others eat. Wheelchair access (not WC). Music. Air-conditioned ACCOMMODATION: 3 rooms, all with bath/shower. TV. D,B&B £60 to £99. Deposit: £20. Children welcome. Dogs welcome. Garden

BALQUHIDDER Stirling map 11

▲ *Monachyle Mhor*

Balquhidder, nr Lochearnhead FK19 8PQ COOKING 2
TEL: (01877) 384622 FAX: (01877) 384305 COST £23–£44

'Scenically stunning' was the verdict of one who surveyed the valley view from this converted farmhouse not far from Rob Roy's burial-place. Informality reigns but the place is well run by the Lewises. Son Tom does most of the cooking, reaching out to embrace the new with a dish of Mallaig scallops, ginger and spring onion served with squid-ink tagliatelle, or breasts of widgeon and mallard with Puy lentils and a bramble reduction. Game is a particular passion, venison with prunes and garlic cropping up in more than one report. Puddings keep up the creativity, as in a brown-bread ice-cream sauced with cinnamon and tea. A simple wine list briskly covers western Europe and Australasia at no-nonsense prices starting at £8.80.

CHEF: Tom Lewis PROPRIETORS: Jean, Rob and Tom Lewis OPEN: all week 12 to 2, 7 to 8.45 CLOSED: last 2 weeks Jan MEALS: alc L Mon to Sat (main courses £8 to £13.50). Set L Sun £16, Set D £19.50 to £23.50 SERVICE: not inc, card slips closed CARDS: MasterCard, Switch, Visa DETAILS: 32 seats. 20 seats outside. Private parties: 14 main room, 14 and 22 private rooms. Car park. Vegetarian meals. No children under 10. No smoking in dining-room. Wheelchair access (also WC). No music. Air-conditioned ACCOMMODATION: 10 rooms, all with bath/shower. Phone. B&B £29 to £37.50. No children under 10. Afternoon teas. Garden. Fishing (*The Which? Hotel Guide*)

'We discovered that the term "fresh" was used rather loosely here. When asked if the prawns were fresh rather than frozen, Mrs X said, "Yes; that is, they have been previously frozen."' (On eating in Yorkshire)

BLAIRGOWRIE Perthshire & Kinross map 11

▲ *Kinloch House* 🍷

by Blairgowrie, PH10 6SG
TEL: (01250) 884237 FAX: (01250) 884333 COOKING 4
on A923, 3m W of Blairgowrie towards Dunkeld COST £23–£42

The two-storeyed ivy-clad building is set back off the road up a short drive, with open log fires and a forest of oak panelling in the public rooms. An air of formality combined with friendly service, and a good selection of whiskies, indicates that the Shentalls take the business of hospitality seriously. Fruit and vegetables from their nineteenth-century walled garden will now replace many of the bought ones, which they find 'increasingly taste of nothing'. National credentials are given a high priority, with seasonal game – grouse, partridge, woodcock, hare, red and roe deer – never far from the pot.

Dinner is where the kitchen's energies and main resources are directed. It 'begins when you are asked to wear a tie', and offers a generous four-course menu (plus a no-choice Scottish one) with supplements for scallops, smoked salmon and fillet steak, among others. Highlights at an inspection meal indicate the kitchen's strengths: a properly made pike quenelle served with a creamy orange and vermouth sauce, and three good slices of dark pink venison liver in red wine sauce. One curious (and successful) dessert is a UFO-shaped pasta filled with citrus-flavoured sorbet. The seriously Francophile wine list includes a good spread of vintage clarets and some fine burgundies, with over 50 wines available by the half-bottle. The New World gets a look-in too, with the South Africans giving good value for money. Twelve French house wines start at £12.20.

CHEF: Bill McNicoll PROPRIETORS: David and Sarah Shentall OPEN: all week 12.30 to 2, 7 to 9.15 CLOSED: last 2 weeks Dec MEALS: alc L (main courses £8.50 to £9.50). Set L £15.95, Set D £28.90 SERVICE: none, card slips closed CARDS: Amex, Delta, Diners, MasterCard, Switch, Visa DETAILS: 55 seats. Private parties: 25 private room. Car park. Vegetarian meals. Children's helpings. No children under 7 at D. Jacket and tie. No smoking in dining-room. Wheelchair access (not WC). No music ACCOMMODATION: 21 rooms, all with bath/shower. TV. Phone. D,B&B £85 to £215. Rooms for disabled. Children welcome. Baby facilities. Dogs welcome by arrangement. Afternoon teas. Garden. Swimming-pool. Fishing (*The Which? Hotel Guide*)

BOWMORE Argyll & Bute map 11

▲ *Harbour Inn* £

ISLAND 1998 INN

NEW ENTRY

The Square, Bowmore, Isle of Islay PA43 7JR COOKING 4
TEL: (01496) 810330 FAX: (01496) 810990 COST £16–£41

It may be the peaty malt whiskies of Islay that lure you out here, but the Harbour Inn – in a small square near the sea but not in fact by a harbour – should not be missed either. Apart from offering a convivial saloon in which to sample the odd dram, as the *Guide* went to press, Scott and Wendy Chance were in the process of creating a comfortable and lavishly appointed restaurant-with-rooms. Portholes and bells add a nautical air, and there is an occasional singsong in the bar.

Good local ingredients are handled with respect and flair, as in 'deliciously crumbly and chunky' gamekeeper's terrine containing venison and hare, richly dressed with a curried mayonnaise and slices of melon. Lagavulin scallops may be stir-fried and sauced with ginger and cream, while meats may include well-timed roast best end of local lamb on ratatouille vegetables. If dark chocolate délice on coffee sauce, or 'light and buttery' apple and toffee sponge with good custard, doesn't spoil you, then the whisky fudge and rum truffles with coffee surely will. Lunch is less elaborate and less expensive. The range of wines offered is inclusive and inspiring, with virtually everything below £20. House Côtes du Roussillon is £8.90.

CHEF: Scott Chance PROPRIETORS: Scott and Wendy Chance OPEN: Mon to Sat 12 to 2, 7 to 9 CLOSED: 25 Dec, 1 Jan MEALS: alc (main courses L £5 to £8.50, D £9.50 to £15). BYO £3 SERVICE: not inc CARDS: MasterCard, Visa DETAILS: 44 seats. Private parties: 40 main room. Vegetarian meals. Children's helpings. Wheelchair access (also men's WC). No music ACCOMMODATION: 4 rooms, all with bath/shower. TV. Phone. B&B £32.50 to £55. Children welcome. Baby facilities. Dogs welcome. Afternoon teas. Garden

CAIRNDOW Argyll & Bute map 11

Loch Fyne Oyster Bar £ $*

Clachan Farm, Cairndow PA26 8BH
TEL: (01499) 600236 FAX: (01499) 600234 COOKING 3
on A83, at head of Loch Fyne COST £20–£62

If there is ever a classless society, it will be full of oyster bars like this. The whitewashed barn beside the loch sells reasonably priced seafood to all-comers at all times of day, with no set format or minimum spend. One couple aiming for lunch arrived at breakfast time 'by accident', and were unfazed by a simple meal of kippers and bread that they considered unbeatable for quality. John Noble and Andrew Lane founded the company 20 years ago, at a spot where the Gulf Stream provides ideal growing conditions for shellfish. Rock oysters are served all year round, natives from September to April, and they are best eaten as simply as possible, at most served with hot pork sausage, or baked with garlic and breadcrumbs. Freshness and good value (£8.90 a dozen) are hallmarks.

Salmon is the other mainstay, served fresh, cold-smoked (mild or strong), and hot-smoked (bradan rost) with a horseradish and whisky sauce. The buzzword this year is 'sustainability'. Numbers of wild salmon 'have slumped to critical levels and are now threatened with extinction', according to Andrew Lane, and he is concerned to ensure that the farmed salmon they use are not fed on a high-fat, growth-promoting diet, but on chemical-free fishmeal that is 'in harmony with the marine environment'. A blackboard lists daily specials, and fish and chips is for diehards. Service is good, and the twenty-five or so reasonably priced wines include a fair proportion by the glass and half bottle. Try the Gros Plant (£11.55 a bottle) with oysters.

CHEFS: Greta Cameron and Morag Keith PROPRIETOR: Loch Fyne Oysters Ltd OPEN: all week 9am to 9pm (5pm weekdays Nov to Mar) CLOSED: 25 and 26 Dec, 1 Jan MEALS: alc (main courses £5 to £8.50) SERVICE: not inc CARDS: Amex, Delta, Diners, MasterCard, Switch, Visa DETAILS: 80 seats. 20 seats outside. Private parties: 45 main room. Car park. Vegetarian meals. Children's helpings. No smoking in 1 dining-room. Wheelchair access (also WC). Music

CANONBIE Dumfries & Galloway map 11

▲ *Riverside Inn* 🍷 £

Canonbie DG14 0UX
TEL: (01387) 371295 and 371512 COOKING 3
off A7, just over the border COST £18–£35

For more than 20 years, Robert and Susan Phillips have been caring custodians of this seventeenth-century inn close to the River Esk and a few miles from the Scottish border. What stands out is their crusading commitment to local and seasonal produce, which means their larder is stocked with roe-deer fillet, Highland lamb, Kirkcudbright scallops, Aberdeen premier beef, free-range eggs and unpasteurised cheeses. They also bake an ever-improving range of breads (ciabatta, onion, Guinness and so on). Fixed-price menus served in the dining-room feature such things as potted guinea-fowl with peppercorns, chargrilled steaks, and roast cod with a Cheddar and red onion crust. Desserts are homely offerings along the lines of rhubarb crumble with 'real custard', rum and sultana crème caramel, and home-made Caledonian ice-cream. A traditional lunch is served on Sundays, and the inn has a deserved reputation for its bar meals – anything from 'enormous' haddock fillet in beer batter with 'damn fine' chips to beef hash with baked red cabbage.

Wines have been cleverly selected with an eye towards combining quality with interest and reasonable prices. House wines from the Côtes de St-Mont are £8.95 per bottle, £1.65 a glass. CELLARMAN'S CHOICE: Cape Mentelle Semillon/ Sauvignon 1996, Margaret River, W. Australia, £14.45; Brouilly, Ch. Thivin 1996, £14.65.

CHEFS/PROPRIETORS: Robert and Susan Phillips OPEN: Sun L 12.30 to 1.30, Tue to Sat D 7.30 to 8.30 CLOSED: 2 weeks Nov, 25 and 26 Dec, 1 and 2 Jan, 2 weeks Feb MEALS: Set L Sun £11.95, Set D £18.50 to £22.50; bar food available. BYO £5 SERVICE: not inc, card slips closed CARDS: MasterCard, Switch, Visa DETAILS: 36 seats. 16 seats outside. Private parties: 30 main room. Car park. Vegetarian meals. Children's helpings. No smoking in dining-room. No music. Air-conditioned ACCOMMODATION: 7 rooms, all with bath/shower. TV. B&B £55 to £85. Deposit: £20. Rooms for disabled. Children welcome. Dogs by arrangement. Garden

COLBOST Highland map 11

Three Chimneys 🍷

Colbost, by Dunvegan, Isle of Skye IV55 8ZT
TEL: (01470) 511258 FAX: (01470) 511358 COOKING 4
on B884, 4m W of Dunvegan COST £19–£63

At 50 miles from the Skye Bridge, this stone-walled former crofter's cottage is one of the more remote Highland addresses in the *Guide*. Those who make the trek through some of Scotland's most spectacular scenery come in search of the fresh seafood that is the kitchen's strength: plump Skye langoustines with a pot of garlic butter and home-baked bread, or the *pièce de résistance*, a grand seafood platter for two preceded by squat lobster bisque or hot crab croustades. A different vein is tapped in a savoury first-course 'cheesecake' of Dunsyre Blue served with lime and avocado crème fraîche. A trio of game with beetroot and blackcurrants offers comfort for robust appetites, while the long-standing signature dish is a large sirloin steak stuffed with smoked salmon. Regional pride continues with puddings such as cranachan made into a parfait and served with raspberry sauce, and hot marmalade sponge with Drambuie custard, or there is a fine Scottish cheeseboard. A reporter notes appreciatively that, however busy the hosts are, they always have time to talk.

Wines are an intelligent, wide-ranging selection with quality to the fore. Fine whites to match the seafood are plentiful, including an elegant Austrian trio from Heinrich. Over fifty bins are priced under £20, with the dozen house wines starting at £10.95. CELLARMAN'S CHOICE: Chinon Blanc, Ch. de Ligré 1992, £16.45; Dry River Estate Pinot Noir 1994, Neil McCallum, Martinborough, New Zealand, £34.45.

CHEF: Shirley Spear PROPRIETORS: Eddie and Shirley Spear OPEN: Mon to Sat 12.30 to 2.30, 7 to 9, plus D Easter Sun and Whit Sun CLOSED: Nov to Easter MEALS: alc (main courses L £5 to £25, D £16.75 to £25) SERVICE: not inc CARDS: MasterCard, Switch, Visa DETAILS: 30 seats. 8 seats outside. Private parties: 15 main room. Car park. Vegetarian meals. Children welcome. No children under 10 at D. No smoking in dining-room. Wheelchair access (not WC). Music

CUPAR Fife map 11

Ostlers Close 🍷

FIFE 1998 LOCAL RESOURCE STAR

25 Bonnygate, Cupar KY15 4BU COOKING 6

TEL: (01334) 655574 FAX: (01334) 654036 COST £24–£48

The 'friendly and informative' Grahams run a welcoming restaurant with a relaxed atmosphere. 'Yes, it is cramped,' write one couple who count it among their favourite places, but nobody minds. Menus change almost daily, for the benefit of both kitchen and customers. After 16 years 'it is important to keep ourselves motivated and moving on', confess the Grahams, as they weave old and new ideas around proudly Scottish materials. These provide impetus for the kitchen, from game and shellfish to locally grown vegetables (some of them organic) and their own garden herbs. Seafood and vegetable combinations might include Pittenweem langoustines with asparagus, or seared West Coast scallops with Glamis sea kale, typically served with a shellfish or champagne butter sauce. Game dishes might pair woodpigeon with butter-beans, or roe-deer with lentils, and be given a game or red wine sauce.

Does all the local produce make a difference? You bet. Seafood soup is 'exemplary', and breast of chicken with chanterelles is 'a reminder of what real chickens used to taste like'. Perhaps the kitchen's strongest passion is collecting mushrooms – St George's, pennybun, giant puffball – and using them with home-made pasta, in soups, or perhaps with a breast and confit leg of a free-range duck bred especially for them. Desserts are more static than the rest of the menu – one couple of regular visitors can reel them off by heart – but no less impressive for that. Trios are popular: the chocolate one comprises a tart, a mousse and a sorbet, while the meringue version includes hazelnut, strawberry pavlova, and an iced meringue cake.

The wine list spreads its favours evenly between the Old World and the New, providing plenty of variety and interest at reasonable prices. Chilean house wines start at £8.75 a bottle, £2 a glass. CELLARMAN'S CHOICE: Neil Ellis Sauvignon Blanc, Vineyard Selection 1996, Elgin, South Africa, £15.95; Charles Melton Nine Popes 1995, Barossa Valley, S. Australia, £17.50.

CHEF: James Graham PROPRIETORS: James and Amanda Graham OPEN: Tue to Sat 12.15 to 2, 7 to 9.30 CLOSED: 25 and 26 Dec, 1 Jan, 2 weeks spring MEALS: alc (main courses £9.50 to £17.50). BYO £5 SERVICE: not inc, card slips closed CARDS: Amex, Delta, MasterCard, Switch, Visa DETAILS: 26 seats. Private parties: 22 main room. Children's helpings. No smoking while others eat. No music

DALRY North Ayrshire map 11

Braidwoods

Drumastle Mill Cottage, by Dalry KA24 4LN
TEL: (01294) 833544 COOKING 5
1m off A737 on Dalry to Saltcoats road COST £24–£45

There are just seven tables – 'yours for the whole evening or lunch' – in this whitewashed conversion of two mill cottages. The 'comfortable and homely' feel is helped by Nicola Braidwood, who does a grand job out front advising, serving and generally charming the socks off reporters. There is no bar or lounge, so it is straight down to business with appetisers and a menu founded on Scottish ingredients, from Shetland salmon to roast loin of red deer. Dinner is typically a choice of three items per course, plus either a cream soup or Parmesan tart with basil dressing after the first.

Native produce is treated to a variety of interpretations, including wild mushroom risotto, or pan-fried scallops with ravioli of langoustine on a shellfish *jus*. Gressingham duck comes well recommended: perhaps a grilled breast and confit of the leg, with tarragon sauce and Puy lentils. 'We ran out of superlatives' is typical of the effect all this has, and the accolade embraces creamy desserts, from lemon and lime cream on a rhubarb compote to chilled, caramelised passion-fruit cream on a macedoine of fruit. The well-chosen wine list samples from ten countries, with a good range of styles and prices, beginning with house Saumur (red and white) at £11.95.

CHEF: Keith Braidwood PROPRIETORS: Keith and Nicola Braidwood OPEN: Wed to Sun L 12 to 1.45, Tue to Sat D 7 to 9 CLOSED: last week Sept, first week Oct, first 3 weeks Jan MEALS: Set L £14 to £16, Set D £25 to £28 SERVICE: not inc, card slips closed CARDS: Amex, Delta, MasterCard, Switch, Visa DETAILS: 24 seats. Private parties: 14 main room. Car park. No children under 12. No smoking in dining-room. No music

DERVAIG Argyll & Bute map 11

▲ *Druimard Country House*

Dervaig, Isle of Mull PA75 6QW
TEL: (01688) 400345 and 400291 COOKING 5
FAX: (01688) 400345 COST £29–£35

A dauntless reporter who travelled the eight miles of winding one-track road across Mull to reach Dervaig wrote that it 'really is outstanding and deserves that you drive it while there is still light to see'. At journey's end waits a comfortably furnished Victorian manse that the Hubbards open to guests in the season. Wendy Hubbard incorporates a light French touch into her modern Scottish cooking, serving duck breast on a bed of Puy lentils and lardons with a Sauternes sauce. Local salmon, lightly cooked and given a champagne and chive sauce, has been a masterpiece of timing, and local venison too is resonant with flavour, served perhaps on a mound of red cabbage and surrounded by a fine game reduction. Presentation is appreciated in desserts such as a ramekin of 'summer fudge fruit crumble' accompanied by tart raspberry coulis and sliced strawberries, or go for the simplicity of an intense pear sorbet. 'Caring and cheerful service that doesn't intrude' is exactly what is required. Wines confine themselves to two or three choices for most regions, with house Côtes de Duras at £8.95.

CHEF: Wendy Hubbard PROPRIETORS: Haydn and Wendy Hubbard OPEN: Mon to Sat D only 7 to 8.30 (L and Sun D residents only) CLOSED: Nov to Mar MEALS: Set D £21.95 SERVICE: not inc CARDS: MasterCard, Visa DETAILS: 32 seats. Private parties: 28 main room. Car park. Vegetarian meals. Children's helpings. No smoking in dining-room. Music ACCOMMODATION: 6 rooms, all with bath/shower. TV. Phone. D,B&B £69.50 to £150. Deposit: £50. Children welcome. Baby facilities. Dogs welcome in bedrooms only. Garden (*The Which? Hotel Guide*)

DRYBRIDGE Moray map 11

Old Monastery

Drybridge AB56 5JB
TEL/FAX: (01542) 832660
2½m S of Buckle, just over 2m S of junction of A98 and A942

COOKING 3
COST £26–£50

Built in 1904 as a holiday retreat for Benedictine monks from Fort Augustus Abbey, the building was converted by the Grays in 1987. Church windows remain in the high-ceilinged refectory, and a sense of repose still prevails, helped by the solitary location, impressive views over the Moray Firth, and the benign attentions of the owners. The style is country-cooking with one eye on Europe, and although deep-fried whitebait may not be cutting edge, there may also be mushroom and spring onion ravioli, or a starter of prawns in mayonnaise sandwiched between butter biscuits sprinkled with Parmesan. French onion is a typical soup, made from good beef stock, with soft caramelised onions in a rich brown liquid.

A variety of herbs, spices and fruit get an airing in main courses, producing plum, sultana and apricot chutney to accompany duck, or sweet-and-sour onions with guinea-fowl, while traditional partnerships might surface in the shape of venison medallions with redcurrant and port sauce. Vegetables and desserts are good, the latter involving some nifty footwork in the production of, for example, a sweet and crisp pastry tart filled with hazelnut paste, topped with chocolate icing and served with chocolate custard and ice-cream. Sharp-eyed service can make for speedy meals. A sensible selection of wines – many interesting, many affordable, and twenty of them in half-bottles – begins with four house wines under £12.

CHEF: Douglas Gray PROPRIETORS: Maureen and Douglas Gray OPEN: Tue to Sat 12.15 to 1.30 (1 Sat), 7 to 9.30 CLOSED: 2 weeks Nov, 25 and 26 Dec, 1 and 2 Jan, 3 weeks Jan MEALS: alc (main courses L £10 to £14.50, D £15 to £17.50) SERVICE: not inc, card slips closed CARDS: Amex, MasterCard, Switch, Visa DETAILS: 50 seats. Private parties: 50 main room. Car park. Children's helpings. No children under 8. No smoking in dining-room. Music

DUNKELD Perthshire & Kinross map 11

▲ *Kinnaird*

Kinnaird Estate, by Dunkeld PH8 0LB
TEL: (01796) 482440 FAX: (01796) 482289
from A9 2m N of Dunkeld, take B898, signposted Kinnaird, for 4½m

COOKING 4
COST £36–£63

The 9,000-acre estate, which includes a loch, has been in the Ward family for 70 years. In addition to the Edwardian house itself, there are eight well-appointed 'cottages' available for weekly rent, fishing on the Tay by arrangement, and all the golf, tennis and bird-watching you can handle. The house is late-eighteenth-century, with a spacious, airy, classically inclined dining-room, and wonderful views over unspoilt countryside.

John Webber embraces a 'modern British' approach in which shellfish, game and beef figure prominently. He uses flavours positively, providing a parsley and mint salsa for noisettes of lamb, or saffron mash and a spring onion butter sauce for seared fillet of cod. Anything from pasta to Thai spices might appear, alongside such traditional treatments as breast of pigeon with lentils and smoked bacon, yet at the same time his food is characterised by enterprising partnerships such as the pork and beetroot ravioli served with a terrine of duck cassoulet, or the ragoût of pig's trotter and morels that perches on a Scotch fillet steak.

Puddings favour traditional themes, in the form of dark chocolate marquise with coffee cream sauce, or baked egg custard tart with nutmeg ice-cream. Service is pleasant and friendly, and the wine list impresses with its range of vintage claret, lovely old burgundies, some fine wines from the Rhône and an excellent selection of producers from outside France. However, the quality is reflected in the prices: only a few bottles, such as the eleven country French, come in under £20, although over eighty half-bottles are offered. CELLARMAN'S CHOICE: De Loach Vineyards Fumé Blanc 1994, Russian River Valley, California, £27; St-Estèphe 1993, Frank Phélan, £25.

CHEF: John Webber PROPRIETOR: Constance Ward OPEN: all week 12.30 to 1.45, 7.15 to 9.30 CLOSED: Mon to Thur from 5 Jan to 1 Mar MEALS: Set L £19.50 (2 courses) to £24, Set D £39.50 SERVICE: not inc, card slips closed CARDS: Amex, MasterCard, Switch, Visa DETAILS: 35 seats. Private parties: 25 main room, 25 private room. Car park. Children's helpings. No children under 12. Jacket and tie. No smoking in dining-room. Wheelchair access (also WC). No music ACCOMMODATION: 9 rooms, all with bath/shower. TV. Phone. B&B £210 to £295. Rooms for disabled. No children under 12. Dogs welcome in heated kennels or drying room. Afternoon teas. Garden. Fishing (*The Which? Hotel Guide*)

DUNVEGAN Highland map 11

▲ *Harlosh House*

Dunvegan, Isle of Skye IV55 8ZG
TEL/FAX: (01470) 521367 COOKING 5
off A863, 3m S of Dunvegan COST £36–£43

The 250-year-old house is 'a delightful place to stay', combining enviable views of the Cuillin Hills with comfortable accommodation. The Elfords, who notch up a decade here in 1998, operate on a domestic scale, serving four-course dinners with no choice before dessert. Fish and vegetables are Peter Elford's entirely understandable preoccupation, although one who stayed for four nights began to yearn for meat by the end. A lightness of style is apparent, and dishes have an appealing directness and purpose about them, thanks to the kitchen's sense of balance. If there are few exotic flourishes, then that seems entirely appropriate in the circumstances.

The second-course soup – perhaps parsnip and apple, or cream of watercress – might follow a red pepper and smoked goats'-cheese tart, or asparagus risotto with local langoustine tails. Tastes and textures are considered, and main courses generally get straightforward treatment: pan-fried fillet of sea trout with summer vegetables and sorrel sauce, for example, or maybe roast monkfish with a confit of shallots, spinach and a rosemary beurre blanc. Proudly-native cheeses might include a ewes' milk from Cairnsmore, or Lanark Blue ('Scotland's Roquefort'), or there might be pear and almond pastries, or date pudding. 'Faultless and enjoyable' was one description of the food, and service is 'swift and pleasant'. Even though fish is the main business, the wine list does not ignore reds. Both colours offer interesting choices within a sensible price range, and house South African is £10.20.

CHEF: Peter Elford PROPRIETORS: Peter and Lindsey Elford OPEN: all week D only 7 to 8.30 CLOSED: Nov to Easter MEALS: Set D £26. BYO £6 SERVICE: not inc, card slips closed CARDS: MasterCard, Switch, Visa DETAILS: 18 seats. Car park. No smoking in dining-room. Music ACCOMMODATION: 6 rooms, all with bath/shower. B&B £35 to £95. Deposit: £50. Children welcome; high tea before 6.30pm. Baby facilities. Afternoon teas. Garden (*The Which? Hotel Guide*)

indicates that smoking is either banned altogether or that a dining-room is maintained for non-smokers. The symbol does not apply to restaurants that simply have no-smoking areas.

'Françoise, who is Parisian and has lived and worked in Paris for 50 years, thinks the food in Britain, generally, is of a much higher standard than anything you can get for the equivalent price in France. When I said, "But, Françoise, your rabbit is very dry, don't you think?" she said, "But rabbit is always dry. That's why you have the sauce." Obvious, really.' (On eating in the West Country)

EDINBURGH Edinburgh map 11

Atrium 🍷

10 Cambridge Street, Edinburgh EH1 2ED COOKING **6**
TEL: (0131) 228 8882 FAX: (0131) 228 8808 COST £20–£45

The shock of the new seems to be fading, as the idiosyncratic wire-sculpted, railway-sleepered setting is now considered to be 'restful and comfortable'. What has not changed is the feeling that Atrium, now in its fifth year, leads the Edinburgh field. Vitality is a key, as evident in a *carte* that keeps all on their toes by changing twice daily. Lunchtime 'snacks' might include beef stir-fry, and chocolate fudge cake, while the full menu offers a varied choice at each stage. It deals in brasserie classics, comfort foods, Mediterranean ideas, and gives a high priority to fish and vegetables: halibut with wild mushrooms, lemon sole with crab pasta, or a feta, courgette, artichoke and garlic crumble.

The commitment to prime ingredients is evident, and game is a favourite: wild duck with roast root vegetables, mallard with mash, and, for one reporter, pigeon that was 'full of flavour and very tender', and incidentally better than its leek, lentil and potato accompaniments. Otherwise the range runs from paesano sausage and mash to chocolate tart, from tomato soup to a dish of baked banana, sun-dried banana and cocoa sorbet. Loyal staff and a team spirit help to produce service that is 'quick, polite, helpful, knowledgeable'. The wide-ranging wine list holds much that catches the eye, with 13 sherries by the glass and a luscious selection of pudding wines vying for attention. CELLARMAN'S CHOICE: Blackwood Park Riesling 1994, Michelton, Victoria, Australia, £14.50; St-Emilion grand cru, Ch. Pipeau 1990, £29.50. As the *Guide* went to press, Andrew Radford was due to open the Blue Bar Café in the same building, serving casual dishes at lower prices.

CHEFS: Andrew Radford and Glyn Stevens PROPRIETOR: Andrew Radford OPEN: Mon to Fri L 12 to 2.30, Mon to Sat D 6 to 10.30 CLOSED: 10 days Christmas MEALS: alc (main courses L £5.50 to £9.50, D £12.50 to £16.50). Snack L available. Set L and D available for groups of 12 or more. BYO £3.50 SERVICE: not inc CARDS: Amex, Delta, MasterCard, Switch, Visa DETAILS: 70 seats. 20 seats outside. Private parties: 100 main room. Children's helpings. Wheelchair access (also WC). Music. Air-conditioned

Café St-Honoré

34 N.W. Thistle Street Lane, Edinburgh EH2 1EA COOKING **2**
TEL: (0131) 226 2211 COST £22–£45

On a dark and quiet street close to the city centre is where you will find the café; inside, wooden tables, mirrors and dark wood give it a homely air of French provincial domesticity. The menus are anything but provincial, however, as a starter of warm squid and bacon salad with smoked haddock, sage and pine-nuts would indicate. Earthy accompaniments to fish have included butter-beans, wild garlic and aïoli with turbot, while saddle of venison arrives, fashionably, with celeriac purée and deep-fried leeks. Desserts come in for praise: a 'not too sweet' chocolate and coffee mousse with white chocolate sauce, for example, and baked apple stuffed with raisins, banana, currants and nuts. Home-made bread and good coffee add the finishing touches, while the range of wines on the modern list provides plenty of satisfying drinking at reasonable prices. House wines start at £9.50.

CHEFS: Chris Colverson and Stephen Smyth PROPRIETORS: Chris Colverson and P.J. Mallet OPEN: Mon to Fri L 12 to 2.15, Mon to Sat D 7 to 10.30 (open all week during festival) CLOSED: 1 week Oct/Nov, 3 days Christmas, 2 weeks Easter MEALS: alc (main courses L £7 to £11.50, D £14.50 to £15.50) SERVICE: not inc; 10% for parties of 10 or more CARDS: Amex, Delta, Diners, MasterCard, Switch, Visa DETAILS: 40 seats. Private parties: 30 main room, 18 private room. Children's helpings. No smoking in dining-room. Wheelchair access (not WC). Music

Fishers Bistro £

NEW ENTRY

1 Shore, Leith, Edinburgh EH6 6QW — COOKING 1
TEL: (0131) 554 5666 — COST £21–£39

Painted white and blue, Fishers is one of a long row of restaurants that have transformed the Leith waterfront over the last fifteen years or so. Wooden tables and chairs denote an informal approach, the same food is served in both bar and dining-room, and anybody who can take advantage of the long opening hours will avoid the evening crush at weekends. A generous choice rolls over from day to day, putting fish centre stage – perhaps baked crab, pan-fried herring, seared tuna, or grilled lemon sole – and although some dishes consist of little more than side-by-side ingredients there has been praise for Arbroath smokie with chive cream, for spinach and goats' cheese in filo, and for a robust first course of clams in a red wine and tomato sauce, with good bread to mop it up. Desserts are less successful, but the wine list has some interesting bottles and stays mostly below £20. House Vin de Pays des Côtes de Gascogne is £8.15.

CHEFS: Mary Walker and Richard Hewat PROPRIETORS: Jake Millar and Graeme Lumsden OPEN: all week 12.15 to 10.30 CLOSED: 25 and 26 Dec, 1 Jan MEALS: alc (main courses £8 to £14) CARDS: Amex, Diners, MasterCard, Switch, Visa DETAILS: 46 seats. 23 seats outside. Private parties: 35 main room. Children welcome. Wheelchair access (not WC). No music

Haldanes

NEW ENTRY

39A Albany Street, Edinburgh EH1 3QY — COOKING 4
TEL: (0131) 556 8407 — COST £21–£52

Haldanes is in the basement of the Albany Hotel, a Georgian house some ten minutes' walk from Princes Street on the edge of the New Town. In view of the fact that George Kelso came from Ardsheal House at Kentallen, it is perhaps not surprising that the aim is to reproduce the feel of 'a country house in the city'. The tone is set by muted colours, a fake library for pre- and post-dinner drinks, and the sort of tablecloths, napkins, china and glassware that give an impression of opulence. Smoked salmon tartare, Cullen skink, and roast saddle of venison with lentils show where the kitchen is coming from, but the overall style is very much in contemporary mould.

Indeed, the Mediterranean is never far away, making itself felt in a red mullet salad with sauce vierge, or in the mix of pesto and herbs that might appear as a dressing on a gâteau of roasted vegetables and goats' cheese. Meats are 'perfectly cooked' and typically come with a little alcohol in the sauce: madeira with calf's liver, or red wine with beef fillet dressed in a mustard sabayon. Savoury courses have so far won more applause than desserts. Considered 'expensive for Edinburgh', Haldanes makes amends with a good-value set-price lunch. Despite the country-house gloss, there are plenty of wines under £20 on the international list, starting with house French and South African at £9.50, and a fair spread of half-bottles.

CHEF: George Kelso PROPRIETORS: Mr and Mrs George Kelso OPEN: Mon to Fri L 12 to 2.15, all week D 6 to 9.45 MEALS: alc D (main courses £14.50 to £19). Set L £9.95 (2 courses) to £13.95, Set D £21.50. Bar L available SERVICE: not inc CARDS: Amex, Delta, MasterCard, Switch, Visa DETAILS: 40 seats. Private parties: 40 main room. Children's helpings. No smoking in dining-room. Music. Air-conditioned

Kalpna [£]

2–3 St Patrick Square, Edinburgh EH8 9EZ — COOKING 1
TEL: (0131) 667 9890 — COST £11–£31

Kalpna – in the *Guide* now for 15 years – produces good value Gujarati and South Indian vegetarian dishes. Lunch is always a buffet, and choice of four thalis (one vegan) for under £10 is particularly useful for tight budgets. Otherwise perhaps start with bhel poori, utapa (pancakes topped with onion, tomatoes, chillies and coriander), or lentil-stuffed kachoris, before one of several main-course 'specialities' served with coriander and fresh cream: makhani sabzi (stir-fried vegetables in sweet-and-sour sauce) or mughal kufta (vegetable fritters with cheese curd in a hot spicy sauce). Desserts include carrot halva, and kulfi flavoured with saffron and pistachio. A short wine list aims to explode the myth that 'wines do not go well with Indian food'. See if you agree. House South African is £7.95.

CHEF: Ajay Bhartdwaj PROPRIETORS: Ajay Bhartdwaj and Kaushlandra Pandey OPEN: Mon to Fri L 12 to 2, Mon to Sat D 5.30 to 11 MEALS: alc (main courses £4 to £7.50). Set L £4.50, Set D Wed £8.95 SERVICE: 10%, card slips closed CARDS: Diners, Visa DETAILS: 65 seats. Private parties: 30 main room. Vegetarian meals. Children welcome. No smoking in dining-room. Wheelchair access (not WC). Music

Martins

70 Rose Street North Lane, Edinburgh EH2 3DX — COOKING 3
TEL: (0131) 225 3106 — COST £28–£54

The location – between Rose Street and George Street – may not be Edinburgh's most beguiling, but big windows (and a sunny day) help to light up the restfully green dining-room, and Martin Irons welcomes and chats amiably about the food. He plays the Scottish card in the form of game, shellfish and Cairngorm mushrooms so enthusiastically that some starters – lamb and game casserole with wild mushrooms, for example – seem like scaled-down versions of main courses, making them difficult to follow with anything but gamier and even more robust items: grilled breasts of widgeon, perhaps, or roast breast and stuffed leg of guinea-fowl. Alternatively, there is usually a soup (leek and blue cheese perhaps) to begin, and plenty of fish: tagliatelle with scallops, grilled red snapper, or sauté sea bass with samphire.

An inspector, lunching on steamed wolf fish (aka rock halibut) with Jerusalem artichoke and fennel, followed by pear and pistachio tart, felt that standards wavered and more consistency was needed. Among desserts, raspberry crème brûlée has impressed, and the cheeseboard, clearly a pride and joy, is stocked with unpasteurised Irish and Scottish cheeses. Wines are predominantly French, with the seven Rolly-Gassman estate-bottled Alsatians a continuing highlight. The small but perfectly formed Californian section also impresses. House wines start at £9.95. CELLARMAN'S CHOICE: Dry River Estate Chardonnay 1995, Martinborough, New Zealand, £30.25; Welgemeend Estate Cabernet Sauvignon, Louise Hofmeyer, Paarl, South Africa, £16.45.

CHEF: Forbes Stott PROPRIETORS: Martin and Gay Irons OPEN: Tue to Fri L 12 to 2, Tue to Sat D 7 to 10 CLOSED: 24 Dec to 21 Jan, 1 week May/June, 1 week Sept/Oct MEALS: alc (main courses £17 to £19.50). Set L £13.50 (2 courses) SERVICE: not inc; 10% for parties of 6 or more CARDS: Amex, Delta, Diners, MasterCard, Switch, Visa DETAILS: 48 seats. Private parties: 28 main room, 8 and 12 private rooms. No children under 8. No smoking in dining-room. No music

Shore £

3–4 Shore, Leith, Edinburgh EH6 6QW
TEL/FAX: (0131) 553 5080 — COOKING 2
off A199 on Firth of Forth, 2m E of city centre — COST £19–£34

'Unpretentious, jolly and efficient' is one reporter's view. 'A good place for fish' is another's, and the two are not mutually exclusive. Leith has been up and coming for some time, and restaurants are very much a part of the area's redevelopment. Shore occupies an eighteenth-century building overlooking the Water of Leith, and serves the same menu in both bar (with jazz or folk music twice a week) and more peaceful dining-room. Grilling is a popular way of dealing with the fish, be it sardines, lemon sole, salmon or tuna, while Cullen skink brings variety to first courses, and whole baked sea bass adds style to the mains. Local game appears in season, and widgeon has been served with red cabbage and blackberry gravy. One reporter's dishes varied from 'all right to very good', with chocolate mousse, and plum and lemon tarts, in the latter category. Thirty wines are fairly priced, the majority under £15, and around half a dozen are available by the glass, including house wine at £1.80.

CHEFS: Kevin O'Connor and Innes Gibson PROPRIETOR: Stuart Linsley OPEN: all week 12 to 2.30 (12.30 to 3 Sun), 6.30 to 10 CLOSED: 25 and 26 Dec, 1 and 2 Jan MEALS: alc (main courses £7.50 to £12). Set L Mon to Sat £6.95 (2 courses), Set L Sun £9.95 (2 courses) to £11.95 SERVICE: not inc CARDS: Amex, MasterCard, Visa DETAILS: 36 seats. 12 seats outside. Private parties: 36 main room. Vegetarian meals. Children's helpings. No smoking in dining-room. Wheelchair access (not WC). Music

Siam Erawan £

48 Howe Street, Edinburgh EH3 6TH — COOKING 1
TEL: (0131) 226 3675 — COST £14–£33

First-timers should note that the entrance to this basement Thai restaurant is in South-East Circus Place on the corner of Howe Street. Down the steps are arched caverns, whitewashed rough stone walls, some handsome ethnic artefacts and service that is friendly, cheerful and generally efficient. 'Flavours are clear and cooking is nicely judged,' summed up one visitor, although the consensus view is that some dishes give more pleasure than others. A mixed seafood starter, and four-stick chicken satay drew more fulsome praise than chicken and pork curries from one reporter, while another rated the tom yam kai soup highly for 'flavours and fragrance [that] came across loud and clear'. The batter for deep-fried tempura-style fish is crisp and clean, and the sweet chilli sauce gives it a lift. Claims to authenticity diminish with the banana fritter in a puddle of toffee sauce accompanied by 'a vast swirl of aerosol cream'. The wine list harbours a few good bottles among the usual clichés.

CHEF/PROPRIETOR: Miss W. Chinnapong OPEN: Mon to Sat L 12 to 2.30, all week D 6 to 11 CLOSED: 25 and 26 Dec, 1 and 2 Jan MEALS: alc (main courses £6 to £9). Set L £5.95 (2 courses) to £6.95, Set D £15.95 (2 courses) to £19.95 SERVICE: L not inc, D 10%, card slips closed CARDS: Delta, MasterCard, Switch, Visa DETAILS: 50 seats. Private parties: 30 main room, 13 private room. Vegetarian meals. Children welcome. Music

Silvio's £

54 Shore, Leith, Edinburgh EH6 6RA COOKING 1
TEL/FAX: (0131) 553 3557 COST £21–£37

Silvio's overlooks the Water of Leith near the docks, and impresses for friendly service and good value as well as for the food. The kitchen turns out a varied array of pasta, from ravioli (with a choice of meat or vegetable filling) to spaghetti with anchovy and hot sausage, or tagliatelle with rabbit stew. Calf's liver with sage, venison with juniper berries, and lamb with rosemary may not be cutting-edge Mediterranean, but the simplicity is welcome and the dishes work. Saltimbocca combines tender veal and thin ham in a sage butter sauce: 'a straightforward dish with a delicious flavour.' The chef's special dessert, a kind of frozen crème brûlée, seems the one to have: 'the crunchy caramel topping was particularly good'. Lunch is the busy time; dinner is more relaxed. Over forty vintages of Barolo (from varied producers) are the high point of a short list of mostly northern Italian wines. House wine is £9.20.

CHEF: Fabrizio Taroni PROPRIETOR: Silvio Praino OPEN: Mon to Sat 12 to 2, 6 to 10.30 CLOSED: 25 and 26 Dec, 1 and 2 Jan MEALS: alc (main courses £6.50 to £11.50). Set L £10.50 (2 courses) SERVICE: not inc CARDS: Amex, Delta, Diners, MasterCard, Switch, Visa DETAILS: 40 seats. Private parties: 40 main room. Vegetarian meals. Children's helpings. No smoking in dining-room. Wheelchair access (also WC). Music

Skippers NEW ENTRY

1A Dock Place, Leith, Edinburgh EH6 6UY COOKING 3
TEL: (0131) 554 1018 FAX: (0131) 553 5988 COST £21–£37

Skippers is a cheerfully cluttered pub conversion, the front a maze of close-packed tables, the back extension lighter and plastered with wine posters. Fish is the Kitchen's forte. Most dishes come with a sauce but still allow the main attraction star billing. Thus, a whole grilled Dover sole is gently buttery, carefully cooked and hearteningly proportioned, and not at all shouted down by its smoked salmon butter. Fish-cakes are the business, too, made with smoked haddock, light in texture but crisply coated. Other starters may include scallops marinated in lime and coriander, or potted crab of exemplary intensity, while meat-eaters may go on to roast guinea-fowl with apples in calvados. Puddings such as banoffi pie and chocolate pot are designed for swooning into, and coffee is good and strong. The wine list contents itself with offering a handful of bottles from each of the regions it covers, and choices are sound, particularly in the New World. House wines from Georges Duboeuf are £8.80.

CHEFS: Kerr Marrian, Neil Wright and Jennifer Corbett PROPRIETORS: Allan and Jennifer Corbett OPEN: Mon to Sat 12.30 to 2, 7 to 10 CLOSED: 25 and 26 Dec, 1 and 2 Jan, 1 week Mar, 2 weeks Sept MEALS: alc L (main courses £7 to £12). Set D £16.75 (2 courses) to £19.75 SERVICE: not inc CARDS: Amex, Delta, MasterCard, Switch, Visa DETAILS: 56 seats. 12 seats outside. Private parties: 24 main room. Vegetarian meals. Children welcome. No pipes in dining-room. Wheelchair access (also WC). Music

Valvona & Crolla Caffè Bar £

19 Elm Row, Edinburgh EH7 4AA — COOKING 3

TEL: (0131) 556 6066 FAX: (0131) 556 1668 — COST £19–£32

The opening of this simple daytime venue that runs from breakfast through to tea (and dinner too if you visit during the Festival) was an inspired move on the part of the Contini family, established for many years as among the best Italian wine merchants in the UK. What you see is what you get, in the sense that the kitchen cooks from what the shop sells, so the in-house spicy pork sausage turns up on a pizza with tomato and mozzarella, and lunches might end with a hunk of Pecorino or Gorgonzola, or the pannacotta that is laced with espresso. One reporter appreciated the Italian slant of putting canellini beans in a soup that resembled Cullen skink, and enjoyed an array of roasted vegetables whose juices were 'sopped up by a wedge of polenta'.

The shop's excellent-value list includes 600 of the best wines from the length and breadth of Italy; any bottle can be chosen with a corkage charge of only £2. For those in a hurry or wanting some guidance in making a choice, there is a regularly changing list of eight to ten specially selected wines, starting at £6.99 a bottle. CELLARMAN'S CHOICE: Pinot Grigio 1996, Le Veritière, Veneto, £6.99; Montepulciano d'Abruzzo 1995, Barone Cornacchia, £6.99.

CHEFS/PROPRIETORS: the Contini family OPEN: Mon to Sat 8 to 11, 11.30 to 4 (also D during Edinburgh Festival) CLOSED: 25 and 26 Dec, 1 and 2 Jan MEALS: alc L (main courses £6 to £8). Breakfast, light L and afternoon tea also available SERVICE: not inc, card slips closed CARDS: Amex, Delta, MasterCard, Switch, Visa DETAILS: 70 seats. 8 seats outside. Private parties: 70 main room, 70 and 50 private rooms. Vegetarian meals. Children's helpings. No smoking in dining-room. Wheelchair access (also WC). Music

Vintners Rooms

The Vaults, 87 Giles Street, Leith,
Edinburgh EH6 6BZ — COOKING 5

TEL: (0131) 554 6767 FAX: (0131) 467 7130 — COST £22–£51

Harveys (see entry, Bristol) is perhaps the only other restaurant that comes close to challenging these rooms for antiquity, and it is no coincidence. Both cities have been involved in the wine trade for centuries, and the Vintners Rooms have seen many bottles change hands. Indeed, quite a few are lined up behind the handsome bar, where good-value lunches are served. The dining-room is more formal – 'I was impressed by the cool elegance' – and serves a well-balanced, modern menu that might take in grilled goats' cheese on olive bread, grilled mackerel with rhubarb sauce, or loin of lamb with couscous.

Ingredients are attractively varied, from West Coast oysters and baked scallops to game in the form of hare with beetroot and port sauce, or roast wild boar with rosemary and orange. Sherry, port and madeira often find their way into sauces, and the kitchen takes its manufacturing role seriously: there are boudins white and black, and duck and pistachio terrine. The resulting textures and 'full flavours' – of scallops, guinea-fowl, and apricot tart for one reporter – ensure satisfaction: 'we left with a glow.' Cheeses are 'top-class' for range, quality and condition, and desserts might include a while-you-wait version of sticky toffee pudding, or cherry and almond tart.

Wines live up to the setting with an impressive array of predominantly French bins of good repute. Prices on the whole are fair, even for the older vintages, of which there are quite a few. House wines start at £10. CELLARMAN'S CHOICE: Sylvaner d'Alsace 1994, Hugel, £13; Etude Pinot Noir 1993, Carneros, California, £30.

CHEFS: A.T. Cumming and J. Baxter PROPRIETORS: A.T. and S.C. Cumming OPEN: Mon to Sat 12 to 2, 7 to 10.30 (later during Edinburgh Festival) CLOSED: 2 weeks Christmas and New Year MEALS: alc (main courses £14 to £18.50). Set L £10 (2 courses) to £13. BYO £5 SERVICE: not inc CARDS: Amex, MasterCard, Switch, Visa DETAILS: 66 seats. Private parties: 36 main room. Car park. Vegetarian meals. Children's helpings. No smoking in dining-room. Wheelchair access (not WC). No music

Winter Glen

EDINBURGH 1998 NEWCOMER

NEW ENTRY

3A1 Dundas Street, Edinburgh EH3 6QG — COOKING **4**
TEL: (0131) 477 7060 FAX: (0131) 624 7087 — COST £18–£36

It might equally well have been called Glen Winter, since this welcome addition to Edinburgh's already healthy restaurant scene is named after the owners. The approach, down a short flight of steps and through a narrow door, does not quite prepare first-time visitors for the huge, bare, stone-walled eating space complete with fireplace and garden view, but the avowed aim – to serve 'modern Scottish' food in relaxed surroundings – is transparently achieved. Reliance on Scottish produce probably explains the main-course emphasis on fish – typically two items out of four at lunch, or out of five at dinner – which has included seared salmon with basil and oregano mash, and well-timed cod served with lentils.

The foundation is good-quality ingredients treated simply yet interestingly, and served up at reasonable prices, with a range that covers baked polenta with goats' cheese, and braised beef with herb dumplings, by way of 'perfectly cooked' lambs' liver with 'a really great' onion gravy made from stock and red wine. Desserts are recited, perhaps banana with filo pastry and caramel sauce ('excellent saucing and deep, rich flavours') or hot chocolate cake. Service is 'just the right side of funny and entertaining', and wines are a short but cosmopolitan assortment starting with house French at £10.25.

CHEF: Graham Winter PROPRIETORS: Blair Glen and Graham Winter OPEN: Mon to Fri L 12 to 2, Mon to Sat D 6 to 10.30 CLOSED: 1 to 20 Jan MEALS: Set L £8.95 (2 courses) to £10.95, Set D £19.95 (2 courses) to £22.50 SERVICE: not inc CARDS: Amex, MasterCard, Visa DETAILS: 60 seats. Private parties: 60 main room, 10 and 30 private rooms. Car park. Children welcome. No children under 8 at D. Music. Air-conditioned

---

ERISKA Argyll & Bute map 11

▲ *Isle of Eriska*

Ledaig, Eriska PA37 1SD
TEL: (01631) 720371 FAX: (01631) 720531 NEW CHEF
off A828, 12m N of Oban COST £44–£52

The house of granite and sandstone was built in 1884, but the Buchanan-Smiths have been here for only twenty-five years. During the last five they have overseen the installation of an indoor leisure centre complete with swimming-pool and gymnasium, plus the construction of a nine-hole golf course, and refurbishment of the main house. As if that were not enough, they now have a new chef.

Robert McPherson used to cook at Darroch Learg (see entry, Ballater), where he had a distinguished track record, but we learned of his arrival too late to send an inspector, hence no cooking mark. The format is now a set-price dinner only, with quite a lot of courses. One example began with a choice of duckling salad or scallop risotto, followed by pea and mint soup or deep-fried calamari, then roast leg of lamb, breast of guinea-fowl, or skate wing. Dessert is followed by a savoury and then cheese. The classical French tilt of the wine list is balanced by a few more modest numbers from the southern hemisphere. House wines start at £7.90. Reports please.

CHEF: Robert McPherson PROPRIETORS: the Buchanan-Smith family OPEN: all week, D only 8 to 9 CLOSED: Jan MEALS: Set D £35 SERVICE: not inc, card slips closed CARDS: Amex, MasterCard, Switch, Visa DETAILS: 40 seats. Private parties: 40 main room. Car park. No children under 5. Jacket and tie. No smoking in dining-room. Wheelchair access (also WC). No music ACCOMMODATION: 17 rooms, all with bath/shower. TV. Phone. B&B £150 to £215. Deposit: £50. Rooms for disabled. Children welcome. Baby facilities. Garden. Swimming-pool. Fishing (*The Which? Hotel Guide*)

FORT WILLIAM Highland map 11

Crannog

Town Pier, Fort William PH33 7NG COOKING 1
TEL: (01397) 705589 FAX: (01397) 700134 COST £22–£43

The idea behind Crannog was to integrate the catching, curing and cooking of local seafood, a simple and laudable aim. This converted smokehouse down by the loch opened in 1989 and has adhered to the principle ever since. Simply furnished with wooden tables, white walls, and huge picture windows overlooking the loch, it offers langoustines ('a must') served cold with three mayonnaises, or hot with garlic butter, as well as potted crab, mussel soup, or skate wing with black butter. Daily specials are chalked up on a board. 'Simpler fare is more successful than more adventurous dishes,' claims a typical reporter, and success is down to the freshness of supplies: 'full of flavour, plenty of it'. Puddings are not central to the operation, but might include cranachan, that characteristically native combination of whipped cream, raspberries, oats and whisky. A short list of wines begins with house French white at £9.95.

CHEFS: Annie Mackinnon and Jon Macleod PROPRIETOR: Crannog Ltd OPEN: all week 12 to 2.30, 6 to 9.30 (9 in winter) CLOSED: 25, 26 and 31 Dec, 1 and 2 Jan MEALS: alc (main courses L £6.50 to £11.50, D £9.50 to £15) SERVICE: not inc CARDS: MasterCard, Switch, Visa DETAILS: 54 seats. Private parties: 50 main room. Children's helpings. No smoking in 1 dining-room. Wheelchair access (also WC). Music

▲ *Inverlochy Castle*

Torlundy, Fort William PH33 6SN
TEL: (01397) 702177 FAX: (01397) 702953 — COOKING 5
3m N of Fort William on A82 — COST £41–£69

If it were any bigger the castle might compete with the Albert Hall for size. It already shares something of the Victorian Gothic style, sits in a 500-acre estate, and counts Ben Nevis among the local peaks. 'It is hardly necessary to comment on the glorious entrance hall,' wrote one enthusiast, commenting anyway. Public rooms and bedrooms, already elegant and well furnished, are about to be upgraded, and despite its enormity Inverlochy doesn't intimidate. The dining-room is small, and although some of the staff may be short-term and unskilled, management is usually on hand to supervise and keep things running smoothly, in which context Michael Leonard is mentioned in dispatches.

At dinner (the main meal) a cake-stand of nibbles arrives in the lounge, along with a four-course menu which, for those used to the country-house norm, holds few surprises. There is some luxury, a lot of workmanship, and good use of native produce without banging the tartan drum: notably fresh seafood includes Loch Linnhe prawns, perhaps roasted and paired with a ravioli of scallops, while Scottish lamb has come with a gâteau of provençale vegetables. Interest and variety might be provided by rabbit (braised leg, roast loin), quail salad, oxtail, or perhaps duck confit layered with crispy potatoes, served with soused vegetables. Visual impact is strong, and chocolate usually features among desserts: in a rich hot tart, for instance, served now with orange sauce, now with roasted bananas and banana ice-cream.

The lofty wine list is in keeping with the surroundings, and if you intend to scale the peaks of the mature Bordeaux and burgundy ranges you'll need a head for high prices. A stroll through the foothills of Italy and the New World will exercise your wallet more gently. The house white and red from Justerini & Brooks are £15 each.

CHEF: Simon Haigh PROPRIETOR: Inverlochy Castle Ltd OPEN: all week 12.30 to 1.45, 7 to 9.30 CLOSED: mid-Jan to 1 Mar MEALS: Set L £23.50 (2 courses) to £27.50, Set D £45 SERVICE: not inc, card slips closed CARDS: Amex, Delta, MasterCard, Switch, Visa DETAILS: 34 seats. Private parties: 34 main room, 12 and 20 private rooms. Car park. Vegetarian meals. No children under 12. Jacket and tie. No smoking in dining-room. No music ACCOMMODATION: 17 rooms, all with bath/shower. TV. Phone. B&B £175 to £385. Children welcome (meals for under 12s in bedrooms only). Baby facilities. Afternoon teas. Garden. Fishing

GLASGOW Glasgow map 11

Buttery

652 Argyle Street, Glasgow G3 8UF — COOKING 4
TEL: (0141) 221 8188 FAX: (0141) 204 4639 — COST £22–£54

Unless you know the city-centre location, ask for directions first, recommended one visitor, since 'stopping to enquire in the dark is not always prudent' (city centres can be like that). A strong Victorian feel pervades, with swirling rococo plasterwork, portraits and chintzy curtains, but the effect is intimate and restful. Furnishings have been pillaged from Northumberland churches, with pews in the bar, and a very handsome lectern to support Stephen Johnson's largely traditional menu. First-course ideas show initiative, from vegetable kebab on turmeric couscous, to a herb choux pastry filled with lambs' sweetbreads, but dishes such as steamed chicken breast filled with Brie hark back to earlier days.

Vegetarians get a fair deal (ratatouille-filled ravioli served with a mild curry and raisin sauce, perhaps), but hunks of meat go down well in Glasgow too, not least gutsy beef fillet with a 'noble Old Scotland flavour', and a generous breast of duck with cabbage and bacon. Materials and timing are both well handled, and reduced pan juices give sauces their richness and flavour, although dishes may taste simpler than they sound. Accompanying vegetables could be improved, although there is nothing much wrong with desserts such as crème brûlée with a properly glazed top, served with tangy spring rhubarb to offset the creaminess. Service is humorous, correct, chatty and not in the least obsequious. Familiar and generally reliable French names constitute the backbone of the wine list, though other sections offer a bit more choice at under £20. House wine is £10.95.

CHEF: Stephen Johnson PROPRIETOR: Alloa Pubs & Restaurants Ltd OPEN: Mon to Fri L 12 to 2.30, Mon to Sat D 7 to 10.30 CLOSED: 25 and 26 Dec, 1 and 2 Jan MEALS: alc (main courses £14 to £15.50). Set L £12.85 (2 courses) to £14.85 SERVICE: 10% (optional), card slips closed CARDS: Amex, Delta, Diners, MasterCard, Switch, Visa DETAILS: 50 seats. Private parties: 10 private room. Car park. Vegetarian meals. Music. Air-conditioned

Café Gandolfi [£]

64 Albion Street, Glasgow G1 1NY — COOKING 2
TEL: (0141) 552 6813 — COST £16–£36

'I am baffled that there is nowhere in Ascot that comes near this,' mused a reporter from Berkshire, perhaps unaware of Glasgow's dynamism. Gandolfi scores with its all-day opening and dazzling décor, featuring heavy furniture by Scottish designer Tim Stead ('no chance of wobbly table or chair') and a 'flock of fish' etched in stained glass. It's cool, buzzy and laid back, and Scottish and French flags on the walls hint at the kitchen's stock-in-trade. Baked Arbroath smokies, Stornoway black pudding, and smoked venison are more patriotic than Caesar salad, gravlax, and duck breast with port and cherries, while the seasonal menu casts its net wider for Italian sausage cassoulet, and red kidney bean chilli with avocado and tomato salsa. Tarte au citron is a recommended dessert; otherwise try hot marmalade steamed pudding. Service is casual yet enthusiastic. Bottled beers and proper Martinis are alternatives to the sharp list of wines, almost all served by the glass. House wine is £10.50.

CHEFS: Margaret Clarence and Alasdair Braidwood PROPRIETOR: Seumas MacInnes OPEN: all week 9 (12 Sun) to 11.30 CLOSED: 25 and 26 Dec, 1 and 2 Jan MEALS: alc (main courses £5.50 to £12) SERVICE: not inc; 10% for parties of 6 or more CARDS: Delta, MasterCard, Switch, Visa DETAILS: 65 seats. Private parties: 25 main room. Vegetarian meals. Children's helpings. No children under 16 after 8.30. No smoking in 1 dining-room. Wheelchair access (not WC). Music

Killermont Polo Club

2022 Maryhill Road, nr Bearsden, Glasgow G20 0AB COOKING 2
TEL: (0141) 946 5412 COST £16–£41

'It's an unusual restaurant, and fun,' wrote one visitor. The converted manse functions as both a restaurant and a polo club, and if that sounds unusual, a note on the menu explains the relationship. Following in the tradition of the Maharaja of Jaipur and other notable sponsor-players, hospitality during a polo tournament was lavish, banquets the norm. The game may have declined in popularity since its heyday in the 1920s and 1930s, but Killermont still groups tandooris, curries and some old-fashioned Raj dishes variously into 'First Chukka' or the 'Jaipuri Clubhouse Celebration'. Despite prawn cocktail with marie-rose sauce, the emphasis remains firmly on the sub-continent in the form of tamarind-based chicken Cochin, lamb with ginger and coriander, or a three-dish thali. Vegetables are given serious attention, saucing is good, and 'crossover' dishes might include tandoori salmon, and 'nouveau' mango kulfi with daubs of coulis. Drink lassi.

CHEF: Balbir Farwaha PROPRIETORS: Kal Dhaliwal and Parmjit Dhaliwal OPEN: Mon to Sat L 12 to 1.45, all week D 5 to 10 CLOSED: 25 Dec, 1 Jan MEALS: alc (main courses £5 to £12). Set L £6.95 (2 courses) to £7.95 SERVICE: not inc, card slips closed CARDS: Amex, Delta, Diners, MasterCard, Switch, Visa DETAILS: 90 seats. Private parties: 90 main room, 24 to 42 private rooms. Vegetarian meals. Children welcome. No cigars/pipes in dining-room. Wheelchair access (also men's WC). Music

Mitchells £

157 North Street, Glasgow G3 7DA COOKING 1
TEL: (0141) 204 4312 FAX: (0141) 204 1818 COST £17–£39

For a dash of breezy informality, a good social mix, and some bright-sounding dishes, this branch of Mitchells is as good as anywhere in the city centre (see opposite for its sister restaurant). The food on offer reminded one reporter of 'a vivid piece of modern art', and the menu obligingly throws on colourful splashes of paint in the form of marinated scallops with a minted pea dressing, chargrilled chicken with lemon sauce, and light oriental fish-cakes that are crisp outside, moist within. To finish, there is marbled liqueur cake served with an orange and chocolate sauce. A short list of serviceable wines begins with house French at £9.50.

CHEFS: Scott Marshall and Chris Walsh PROPRIETORS: Angus and Veronica Boyd OPEN: Mon to Sat 12 to 3, 5 to 10 CLOSED: 25 Dec, 1 and 2 Jan, L bank hols MEALS: alc (main courses L £5 to £8, D £8 to £13). Set pre-theatre D £8.95 (2 courses) to £10.95 SERVICE: not inc CARDS: Amex, Delta, Diners, MasterCard, Switch, Visa DETAILS: 50 seats. Private parties: 50 main room, 30 private room. Vegetarian meals. Children's helpings. Wheelchair access (not WC). Music

Mitchells West End £

31–35 Ashton Lane, off Byres Road, Glasgow G12 8SJ — COOKING 1
TEL: (0141) 339 2220 FAX: (0141) 204 1818 — COST £17–£40

Both branches of Mitchells (see previous entry) aim for a casual approach, this one occupying a 'cramped' upstairs room near the university. The food is similar in each, with a short menu and a jazzy approach to flavours: potato and coriander cake with an apple and mustard seed relish, satay-style chicken in toasted pitta bread, or sauté strips of beef in chilli sauce in a tortilla shell. Sound ingredients are the foundation, fish has included steamed salmon and roast cod, and Scottish cheeses offer an alternative to lemon steamed pudding or cheesecake. Wines are the same too.

CHEF: Scott Baxter PROPRIETORS: Angus and Veronica Boyd OPEN: Mon to Sat D only 5.30 to 10.30 CLOSED: 25 Dec, 1 and 2 Jan MEALS: alc (main courses £7 to £13). BYO £2.95 SERVICE: not inc CARDS: Amex, Delta, Diners, MasterCard, Switch, Visa DETAILS: 34 seats. Private parties: 34 main room, 34 private room. Vegetarian meals. Children's helpings. No pipes in dining-room. Music. Air-conditioned

▲ *One Devonshire Gardens* £✱

1 Devonshire Gardens, Glasgow G12 0UX — COOKING 5
TEL: (0141) 339 2001 FAX: (0141) 337 1663 — COST £41–£70

In a tree-lined Victorian terrace which once housed the merchants and shipowners of Glasgow, the house lays out its solid bourgeois credentials from the porticoed front door through a wide hallway to spacious and comfortable rooms that are attractively carpeted, heavily decorated, subtly lit and filled with plants. Andrew Fairlie leads the Glasgow field with a beguiling repertoire and assured skill. Some classic French techniques are put at the service of modern ideas, and each dish has something distinctive to say for itself. Menus typically combine the heartiness of braised beef in red wine with the sunny outlook of roast red mullet salad, while the immediacy of grilled asparagus (with shaved Parmesan and a lemon and pepper aïoli) is balanced against a rather more studied roulade combining pheasant confit and foie gras.

Produce, much of it Scottish, is of the highest order, with poultry, game and fish in the ascendant, and appropriate treatment is the order of the day: braised lentils with maize-fed guinea-fowl, or a confit of endives and an orange butter sauce for seared spiced scallops. Lunch is a shade simpler than dinner, but is still likely to include asparagus soup, roast loin of organic pork, and dark chocolate fondant with vanilla ice and blackcurrant sauce. Among desserts, passion-fruit ravioli with coconut sorbet is as modish as they come, but there may also be tarte Tatin, and a version of pain perdu with caramelised bananas. Friendly and professional staff contribute to the sense of occasion without resorting to undue formality. Wines are extremely well chosen, from humble to aristocratic, with a good showing from America and Australia, but mark-ups are high. House wine is £18.

CHEF: Andrew Fairlie PROPRIETOR: Ken McCulloch OPEN: Sun to Fri L 12.15 to 2, all week D 7.15 to 10 CLOSED: D 25 Dec MEALS: Set L £25, Set D £40. BYO £12.50 SERVICE: not inc, card slips closed CARDS: Amex, Diners, MasterCard, Switch, Visa DETAILS: 38 seats. 12 seats outside. Private parties: 32 main room, 10 to 32 private rooms. Car park. Children's helpings. No smoking in dining-room. Music ACCOMMODATION: 27 rooms, all with bath/shower. TV. Phone. Room only £120 to £180. Children welcome. Baby facilities. Dogs welcome in bedrooms only. Afternoon teas. Garden (*The Which? Hotel Guide*)

La Parmigiana £

447 Great Western Road, Glasgow G12 8HH — COOKING 2
TEL: (0141) 334 0686 FAX: (0141) 332 3533 — COST £18–£49

Of a genre that has almost died out, La Parmigiana serves trattoria favourites from minestrone through spaghetti carbonara to zabaglione (made, incidentally, with 'egg yoke'). It survives because it does them well, and among reported successes are warm seafood salad, and simply grilled chicken and quail, both served with rosemary and lemon. Wine and tomatoes naturally play their part, in a starter of Loch Etive mussels or a main course of veal topped with Parma ham and mozzarella, while pasta is typically available as a first or main course, including ravioli filled with spinach and ricotta, and tagliolini with either porcini mushrooms or home-made pesto. For dessert, cantuccini biscuits come with a dipping glass of vin santo, and a coffee-and-liqueur-soaked sponge layered with mascarpone and chocolate is deliberately not called tiramisù. Good-quality Italian wines at generally fair prices begin with house wine at £9.60.

CHEF: Sandro Giovanazzi PROPRIETORS: Angelo and Sandro Giovanazzi OPEN: Mon to Sat 12 to 2.30, 6 to 11 CLOSED: 25 and 26 Dec, 1 and 2 Jan, bank hols MEALS: alc (main courses £6.50 to £16). Set L Mon to Fri £7.50 SERVICE: not inc CARDS: Amex, Diners, MasterCard, Switch, Visa DETAILS: 60 seats. Private parties: 60 main room. Vegetarian meals. Children's helpings. No pipes in dining-room. Music. Air-conditioned

Puppet Theatre $★

11 Ruthven Lane, Glasgow G12 9BG — COOKING 4
TEL: (0141) 339 8444 FAX: (0141) 339 7666 — COST £25–£53

There are four dining-rooms at this pleasingly eccentric West End venue: a Gaudi-esque conservatory, a mirror room hung with theatrical drapes, a candlelit altar room, and an oak room with a portrait of the boy David and 'a padded intimate booth for lovers'. After choosing the setting for your meal, there's Paul Rushforth's equally idiosyncratic cooking to contemplate. Evening fare might start with a soup of leeks, potato and smoked salmon, or a salad of roasted scallops with lime, chilli and coriander dressing, followed by parsley-crusted halibut with spinach, or saddle of venison with fondant potatoes and a chocolate enriched game sauce. Chocolate also turns up in a malted mousse with popcorn and a whisky sauce. Otherwise, pudding might be a mango and passion-fruit cheesecake. Service is 'full of Glasgow warmth and humour,' wrote one pair of reporters. A broad regional spread is in evidence on the wine list, and there are plenty of half-bottles. House French is £11.50.

CHEF: Paul Rushforth PROPRIETORS: Ron McCulloch and George Swanson OPEN: Tue to Fri and Sun L 12 to 2.30, Tue to Sun D 7 to 10.45 CLOSED: 25 and 26 Dec, 1 and 2 Jan MEALS: Set L £12.50 (2 courses) to £14.95, Set D £21.95 (2 courses) to £24.95 SERVICE: not inc CARDS: Amex, Delta, MasterCard, Switch, Visa DETAILS: 68 seats. Private parties: 26 main room, 10 to 26 private rooms. Car park. Vegetarian meals. Children welcome. No smoking in 1 dining-room. Music. Air-conditioned

Splash £ NEW ENTRY

Royal Concert Hall, 2 Sauchiehall Street,
Glasgow G2 3NY COOKING 1
TEL: (0141) 332 3163 FAX: (0141) 332 9238 COST £21–£37

Few people expected Antony Worrall-Thompson to lie dormant for long after leaving Simpson's of Cornhill and the London restaurants it operates, and here he is: consultant chef to this appropriately named, brightly coloured second-floor restaurant in the Royal Concert Hall. 'The menu is pure eclecticism, if eclecticism can be pure!' reckoned one visitor, and it certainly carries the trademark of its mentor in the A to Z range of dishes: caramelised onion tart, deep-fried chilli-salt squid, tea-smoked cod on wilted spinach, and 'flavoursome' duck with cherry sauce and wun-tuns on celeriac purée. Soups are good – intense tomato 'with real depth', and artichoke with truffle oil – although some of the promised flavourings and seasonings can be shy, and some dishes at inspection lacked necessary moisture. 'Little pavs' consists of a single pavlova with balsamic strawberries and mascarpone ice-cream, or there might be frozen espresso cake. Note the set-price meal served at lunch-time and before concerts. The wine list runs to 21 bottles, with house wines at £12.

CHEF: Michael Hughes PROPRIETOR: Letheby & Christopher Limited OPEN: all week 12 to 2.30, 5.30 to 9.30 CLOSED: 25 Dec MEALS: alc (main courses £7.50 to £11). Set L and Set D 5.30 to 7.30 £9.50 (2 courses) to £12.50 SERVICE: not inc, card slips closed CARDS: Amex, Delta, Diners, MasterCard, Switch, Visa DETAILS: 82 seats. Private parties: 80 main room, 100 and 400 private rooms. Vegetarian meals. Children's helpings. Wheelchair access (also WC). Music. Air-conditioned

Ubiquitous Chip

12 Ashton Lane, Glasgow G12 8SJ COOKING 4
TEL: (0141) 334 5007 FAX: (0141) 337 1302 COST £23–£64

The Chip is a treasured and long-standing entry in the *Guide*. A cobbled courtyard gives an 'outside' feeling even though it is completely indoors, and overhead greenery is 'beguiling and distracting'. The whole place takes its cue from the individual approach of Ronald Clydesdale, who summons up native produce and turns out haggis (venison or vegetarian) with neeps, clapshot (a mixture of potatoes, kail and swede) served with burnt onions, and Aberdeen

Angus fillet steak with stovies and wild mushrooms. Reports suggest that nuance is not the name of the game here.

The real appeal is the inventive approach: sometimes, though not always, with the feeling that a Scottish granny might be at the back of it. In this vein might be suet puddings (of mixed game, or lamb and kidney), or free-range Perthshire pork with yellow split-pea pudding. Novelty might appear in the form of shark with couscous and Chablis sauce. 'Avoid steamed puds and crumbles,' recommended one regular who has enjoyed brown-bread and sherry ice-cream with a 'delicious scrunch factor and proper rich sherry flavour'. Upstairs is a less-expensive alternative, and wines are great value whether you eat up or down: this is the place to celebrate with something out of the ordinary. The splendid main list is dominated by French and German classics, but there are also some impressive bottles from Australia, New Zealand and California. Half-bottles and magnums are liberally scattered throughout, and house red, white and rosé are £9.95 a bottle.

CHEF/PROPRIETOR: Ronald Clydesdale OPEN: all week 12 to 2.30, 5.30 to 11 CLOSED: 25 and 31 Dec, 1 and 2 Jan MEALS: Set L Mon to Sat £18.60 (2 courses) to £23.60, Set L Sun £16, Set D £26.60 (2 courses) to £31.60 SERVICE: not inc CARDS: Amex, Delta, Diners, MasterCard, Switch, Visa DETAILS: 150 seats. Private parties: 80 main room, 25 and 45 private rooms. Vegetarian meals. Children's helpings. Wheelchair access (also WC). No music

Yes

22 West Nile Street, Glasgow G1 2PW — COOKING 4

TEL: (0141) 221 8044 FAX: (0141) 248 9159 — COST £24–£55

Not (necessarily) the answer to a Scottish referendum on devolution, more a 'stylish, trendy place to be seen', Ferrier Richardson's restaurant is spacious, light, seemingly made of glass and chrome, and hung with good modern pictures. Iain McMaster has taken over the kitchen since last year, and continues in modern vein, trying to build a bridge to link the Mediterranean with the Pacific. He does it with the help of roast duck with Thai spices, and tuna teriyaki with noodles and shiitakes, but is careful not to neglect his own doorstep. Scotland provides much of the produce, from beef to a platter of west coast seafood, as well as some of the dishes: gâteau of haggis with neeps, tatties and a whisky sauce, for example.

A careful hand is capable of timing things well – prime seared scallops, for example – although it doesn't always. The kitchen seems to thrive on variety, particularly at dinner, which might see a starter of oriental vegetable, duck and tofu broth beside a plate of vodka-cured salmon and caviare with baked potato and soured cream. Desserts don't elicit much enthusiasm, but the flavoured breads do, among them sun-dried tomato and Parmesan. Service is attentive, the bar and brasserie offers more casual eating in the form of pasta or sandwiches, and the wine list is a short, concentrated, interesting selection at suitable prices. House French is £10.95.

CHEF: Iain McMaster PROPRIETOR: Ferrier Richardson OPEN: Mon to Sat 12 to 2.30, 7 to 11 CLOSED: 25 and 26 Dec, 1 and 2 Jan, bank hols MEALS: Set L £12.95 (2 courses) to £15.95, Set D £19.95 (2 courses) to £27.50 SERVICE: not inc CARDS: Amex, Diners, MasterCard, Switch, Visa DETAILS: 100 seats. Private parties: 100 main room, 20 private room. Vegetarian meals. Children's helpings. Music. Air-conditioned

GULLANE East Lothian map 11

▲ *Greywalls*

Muirfield, Gullane EH31 2EG
TEL: (01620) 842144 FAX: (01620) 842241 COOKING 5
on A198, at W end of Gullane COST £21–£54

In the Weaver family for forty years, Greywalls is an impressive house. The terrace overlooks Muirfield, and golfing memorabilia take up the theme inside, but this is not a formal place to eat, even if gentlemen are requested to wear jacket and tie. It is a good venue for 'an elegant light lunch' of perhaps soup, steamed lemon sole fillets, and praline ice-cream, while dinner is a more serious affair: four courses, the second a soup or sorbet.

Salmon appears in various forms, often on the same menu: smoked perhaps, pan-fried with sauce vierge, or made into rillettes with a tomato and saffron dressing. Luxuries, meanwhile, add a note of richness: foie gras might be paired with duck in a confit served with toasted brioche, or added to a sauce for roast breast of chicken. Traditional venison with red wine sauce indicates that Paul Baron is not geared for novelty, but he has a talent for consistency, which is much harder to achieve, and for which he deserves credit.

The Franco Scottish theme is as apparent among desserts as anywhere, in banana Tatin with caramel sauce and ice-cream, or in lemon tart with a blackcurrant sauce. The wine list adopts a traditional approach, leading with many classic French lines, featuring some top vintages thoughtfully stashed away over the years, and balancing it all with less-expensive bottles from elsewhere, including six house wines at £12. CELLARMAN'S CHOICE: Gavi di Gavi 1995, Villa Lanata, £19; Christa-Rolf Shiraz/Grenache 1996, Barossa Valley, S. Australia £18.50.

CHEF: Paul Baron PROPRIETORS: Giles and Ros Weaver OPEN: all week 12.30 to 1.45, 7.30 to 9.15 CLOSED: Nov to Mar MEALS: alc (main courses £8 to £12). Set L Mon to Sat £10 (2 courses) to £12.50, Set L Sun £20, Set D £33 SERVICE: not inc, card slips closed CARDS: Amex, Diners, MasterCard, Switch, Visa DETAILS: 50 seats. Private parties: 50 main room, 20 private room. Car park. Children welcome. Jacket and tie D and Sun L. No smoking in dining-room. No music ACCOMMODATION: 22 rooms, all with bath/shower. TV. Phone. B&B £95 to £185. Deposit: £100. Children welcome. Baby facilities. Dogs welcome by arrangement. Afternoon teas. Garden (*The Which? Hotel Guide*)

La Potinière

Main Street, Gullane EH31 2AA
TEL/FAX: (01620) 843214 COOKING 8
on A198, 4m SW of North Berwick COST £36–£43

'Pleasantly old-fashioned and genteel' is how this small, low-ceilinged dining-room with exposed timbers and heavy lace curtains struck one visitor. There is no choice; in fact, there is not even a menu. Lunch is four courses, dinner five, and you may not know what you are about to eat until you are eating it. 'It appears you have to accept some idiosyncracies,' summed up one reporter, apparently quite happy to do so.

After 23 years, 22 of them in the *Guide*, La Potinière is entitled to a few quirks. As one visitor observed, 'Still the same two people do all the work: worth commenting on as so many chefs now leave their restaurants to others while they promote books or appear on TV.' Most readers would say 'Amen' to that. Hilary Brown has evolved her own style and sticks to it, so although the menu varies daily, similar dishes recur. The advantage this bestows is that, although the style may be 'superficially homely', dishes are honed and polished. Our inspectors found that 'every dish we had was precisely cooked, and tasted as if great care had gone into the balancing of flavours'.

A sample meal serves to highlight the strengths. It began with a vivid tomato soup spiked with 'little bursts of minty flavour'. Next came crisply seared salmon fillet, timed so that the interior was 'moist and barely cooked'. A fruity, peppery extra virgin olive oil was used to make the sauce vierge. This demonstrates a guiding principle of the Browns: there are no superfluous ingredients or garnishes. The same was true of a breast of corn-fed chicken on a bed of cabbage and bacon. A serious salad comes as 'an unexpected treat' after the main course, followed by one excellent cheese, then perhaps richly flavoured, 'wonderfully quivering, barely set' pannacotta. Portions will satisfy even the very hungry, especially those who cannot resist the springy, light-textured walnut and raisin bread or French stick.

David Brown's service is unhurried, and he oversees the wines, although the list (like the menu) may not always be offered. South-west France is among the enthusiasms, and sixteen South African wines are new to the list. More bins (including vintage claret) are stored in the cellar, to appear as they reach maturity, although David Brown now considers the price of fine young Bordeaux to be so prohibitive that future mature stocks look uncertain. House French is £11.50.

CHEF: Hilary Brown PROPRIETORS: David and Hilary Brown OPEN: Mon, Tue, Thur and Sun L 1 (1 sitting), Fri and Sat D 8 (1 sitting) CLOSED: Oct, 25 and 26 Dec, 1 and 2 Jan, 1 week June MEALS: Set L £20, Set D £30 CARDS: none DETAILS: 30 seats. Private parties: 30 main room. Car park. Children welcome. No smoking in dining-room. Wheelchair access (not WC). No music

INVERNESS Highland map 11

▲ *Culloden House*

Inverness IV1 2NZ
TEL: (01463) 790461 FAX: (01463) 792181
from Inverness take A96 to Nairn, turn right after 1m, then left at Culloden House Avenue

COOKING 2
COST £28–£56

The house in its original and larger incarnation (it was rebuilt in 1788) was the headquarters of Bonnie Prince Charlie in the days leading up to the Battle of Culloden in 1746. Today, ivy-covered and sitting in 40 acres, it must have appealed immediately to its new American owners. Inside, tassels, large fireplaces and painted radiators are the decorative norm, and sitting in the lounge is like being 'inside a pink and white wedding cake'. Lunch is à la carte, dinner set-price, but the style is much the same at both, a rather traditional version of country-house, with an intermediate sorbet or soup (cream of tomato, apple and celery perhaps) and generous choice.

Alcohol, herbs and cream are favoured saucing ingredients – port and mint with venison, Noilly Prat and chive with salmon, for example – materials are sound, and the kitchen is careful to produce pink venison and 'nicely cooked' scallops. Desserts might include toffee and banana tart, or Heather Cream Liqueur parfait with a dark chocolate sauce. Service is 'pleasant' but needs sharpening up. Wines are extensive, predominantly French, but with a reasonable spread from other countries under £20. Half-bottles are plentiful, and house wine is £11 (red) or £13.75 (white).

CHEF: Michael Simpson PROPRIETOR: North American Country Inns OPEN: all week 12.30 to 2.30, 7 to 9 MEALS: alc L (main courses £9.50 to £13). Set D £35 SERVICE: not inc, card slips closed CARDS: Amex, Diners, MasterCard, Switch, Visa DETAILS: 60 seats. Private parties: 80 main room, 25 private room. Car park. Vegetarian meals. Children's helpings. No children under 10. Jacket and tie. No smoking in dining-room. No music ACCOMMODATION: 28 rooms, all with bath/shower. TV. Phone. B&B £130 to £240. Deposit: 100%. No children under 10. Dogs welcome by arrangement. Afternoon teas. Garden

▲ *Dunain Park*

Inverness IV3 6JN
TEL: (01463) 230512 FAX: (01463) 224532 COOKING 2
on A82, 1m from Inverness town boundary COST £36–£51

This Georgian former shooting-lodge five miles from Loch Ness has been run as a hotel for more than a dozen years. Ann Nicoll now opens the dining-room only for dinner, and takes her cue from a range of Scottish produce augmented by fruits, leaves, vegetables and herbs from the garden. Collops of venison might be pan-fried in oatmeal, and fillet of Shetland salmon has been baked in a sea-salt crust and served with a sauce of white port, lime and ginger.

A separate steak menu, using only beef from accredited Aberdeen Angus herds, lists ten ways with fillet or sirloin, from plain or peppered through whisky-flamed to red-wine-sauced. Desserts are from the buffet, and a serious and well-annotated wine list (house French is £11.50) makes contact with some very good bottles. If we gave awards for whisky, this would undoubtedly get one for its sheer range and depth, including single-cask bottlings from the Scotch Malt Whisky Society.

CHEF: Ann Nicoll PROPRIETORS: Ann and Edward Nicoll OPEN: all week D only 7 to 9 MEALS: alc (main courses £16) SERVICE: not inc, card slips closed CARDS: Amex, Delta, Diners, MasterCard, Switch, Visa DETAILS: 36 seats. Private parties: 12 main room, 12 private room. Car park. Vegetarian meals. Children's helpings. No smoking in dining-room. Wheelchair access (not WC). No music ACCOMMODATION: 14 rooms, all with bath/shower. TV. Phone. B&B £55 to £158. Deposit: £50. Rooms for disabled. Children welcome. Baby facilities. Dogs by arrangement (not in public rooms). Afternoon teas. Garden. Swimming-pool (*The Which? Hotel Guide*)

'Is it true chicken Kiev was invented by a dry cleaning firm?' (On eating in London)

KILLCHRENAN Argyll & Bute map 11

▲ *Taychreggan*

Kilchrenan PA35 1HQ
TEL: (01866) 833211 and 833366 NEW CHEF
FAX: (01866) 833244 COST £22–£44

The 'great sense of peace and tranquillity' in this 300-year-old drovers' inn, six miles down a single-track road on the edge of Loch Awe, is much appreciated. 'I have tried to analyse why this hotel is so special,' writes a reporter, coming up with 'a combination of position, atmosphere, friendliness and quality' as the answer. Certainly the cobbled courtyard and antique furnishings help, while modernisation has been carried out with a degree of flair. Martin Wallace has come up through the ranks, reaching the top slot too late for us to receive reports or send an inspector, which is why there is no cooking mark, but he continues the tradition of serving five-course dinners – the second a soup or sorbet, the last one cheese – and Scottish ingredients from Perthshire lamb to Grampian pork remain the foundation. Classic claret is the pride of the reasonably priced list, with vin de pays at £9.95. Reports please.

CHEF: Martin Wallace PROPRIETOR: Annie C. Paul OPEN: all week 12.30 to 2, 7.30 to 8.45 MEALS: Set L £15, Set D £28 SERVICE: not inc CARDS: Amex, Delta, MasterCard, Switch, Visa DETAILS: 45 seats. Private parties: 50 main room, 24 private room. Car park. Vegetarian meals. No children under 13. No smoking in dining-room. Wheelchair access (also WC). Music. Air-conditioned ACCOMMODATION: 20 rooms, all with bath/shower. Phone. D,B&B £75 to £190. Deposit: £50. No children under 13. Dogs by arrangement. Afternoon teas. Garden. Fishing

KILLIECRANKIE Perthshire & Kinross map 11

▲ *Killiecrankie Hotel*

Killiecrankie, by Pitlochry PH16 5LG
TEL: (01796) 473220 FAX: (01796) 472451 COOKING 3
off A9, 3m N of Pitlochry COST £37–£44

Killiecrankie, which owes its fame to the battle fought in 1689, is today little more than a scattering of houses near the Pass. It is doubtful if any modern-day vicar would build himself (or indeed herself) a house on this scale, as one did here in 1840. There is enough space for ten bedrooms, a wood-panelled bar, a relaxing sitting-room and a smartly appointed dining-room, where John Ramsay's four-course dinners offer the option of a cold main course (poached salmon salad, perhaps), in addition to three hot choices, and end with cheese. Mussels from Inverawe, scallops from Skye, and Gigha goats' cheese demonstrate the focus on materials, while home-made grouse sausage and home-preserved fruits point up the kitchen's industry. The style is varied enough to incorporate griddled bream with fennel and beurre blanc, spicy Indonesian meatballs, and a pot-roast shoulder of lamb stuffed with goose. A glass of sweet wine is recommended with dessert – perhaps warm fig tart with lemon-curd ice-cream, or chocolate whisky cake – and the fifty-plus wine list is a serviceable collection that begins in the French countryside at around £12.

CHEF: John Ramsay PROPRIETORS: Colin and Carole Anderson OPEN: all week D only 7 to 8.30 CLOSED: 10 days early Dec, Jan/Feb MEALS: Set D £28. Bar food available L and D SERVICE: not inc, card slips closed CARDS: Delta, MasterCard, Switch, Visa DETAILS: 34 seats. Private parties: 12 main room. Car park. Children's helpings. No children under 5. No smoking in dining-room. No music ACCOMMODATION: 10 rooms, all with bath/shower. TV. Phone. D,B&B £65 to £158. Deposit: £40. Children welcome; early supper for under-5s. Dogs welcome. Garden (*The Which? Hotel Guide*)

KINCLAVEN Perthshire & Kinross map 11

▲ *Ballathie House*

Kinclaven, by Stanley PH1 4QN
TEL: (01250) 883268 FAX: (01250) 883396 COOKING 5
off B9099, take right fork 1m N of Stanley COST £21–£48

High ceilings, ornate plasterwork, a marble fireplace and heavy curtains all testify to the Scottish baronialism of which this 1850 mansion is a prime example. It feels luxuriously spacious – helped by its location on a 1,500-acre estate beside the River Tay – and has 'not been spoiled by commercialism', something to which many hotels on the international circuit are prone. Kevin MacGillivray's food has a generous streak – chargrilled fillet of sea bass, for example, comes on a purée of potato and lobster – and although it may not take many risks it still incorporates plenty of variety.

Dinner is the main meal, and typically begins with a terrine (meaty chunks of Highland game with a pear and rosemary jelly for one reporter) or salad, or perhaps a platter of smoked seafood, and the standard of cooking fulfils expectations. At least it did for one visitor who enjoyed 'one of the best chicken dishes I have tasted', the plump, moist breast of the maize-fed bird served with an earthy woodland mushroom sauce. Restraint with cream and butter has produced some well-balanced dishes, 'slightly crisp' vegetables are served on the plate, and good bread and appetisers reinforce the view of a kitchen that takes the whole operation seriously.

Presentation is attractive, not least in desserts such as rum-poached pear in cinnamon syrup with butterscotch ice-cream. Service places napkins on knees but is sympathetic to individual customers, and the wine list combines traditional strengths with good variety at a fair range of prices. House Dalwood from Australia is £9.90.

CHEF: Kevin MacGillivray PROPRIETOR: Ballathie House Hotel Ltd OPEN: all week 12.30 to 2, 7 to 9 MEALS: alc L (main courses £5.50 to £7.50). Set D £26 to £29. BYO £10 SERVICE: not inc CARDS: Amex, Delta, Diners, MasterCard, Switch, Visa DETAILS: 90 seats. Private parties: 60 main room, 10 to 60 private rooms. Car park. Vegetarian meals. Children welcome. No smoking in dining-room. Wheelchair access (also WC). Music ACCOMMODATION: 30 rooms, all with bath/shower. TV. Phone. B&B £70 to £170. Rooms for disabled. Children welcome. Baby facilities. Dogs welcome in bedrooms only. Afternoon teas. Garden. Fishing

See the inside of the front cover for an explanation of the new 1 to 10 rating system for cooking standards.

KINGUSSIE Highland map 11

▲ *The Cross*

Tweed Mill Brae, Ardbroilach Road,
Kingussie PH21 1TC
TEL: (01540) 661166 FAX: (01540) 661080

COOKING 6
COST £45–£54

'What a civilised place this is,' summed up one reporter, while another considered that eating here is 'a great deal more than just a meal'. The overnight package begins with afternoon tea on arrival, and has good value written all over it. There is a room on the first floor for lolling about and reading the menu in, and a stone-walled whitewashed dining-room with lots of lazy space between tables. The pattern is first course, soup, fish, choice of main course, and cheese or a choice of dessert, where 'choice' usually means either A or B. In case all that sounds a lot, portions are well judged.

'I like the honesty of intent,' wrote one visitor, considering it a clear reflection of the people themselves. Ruth Hadley has the confidence to produce simple but satisfying food, and (understandably in view of the quality that Scotland provides) makes fish a focus. At one meal, 'wonderfully fresh, brilliantly tasty, translucent' scallops were served with no more than they needed: just a few spears of asparagus. At other times more industry will be apparent – scallops might be made into a sausage, or smoked haddock into a savoury custard – while main courses tend to be plain: venison with redcurrants and port, or pink lamb fillet flavoured with garlic and rosemary, served with ratatouille.

Desserts are as good as everything else: on one occasion 'an excellently poached pear', its stalk dipped in chocolate, with honey ice-cream and a thick chocolate fudge sauce. There are several ways of tackling the wine. First, half a dozen suggestions are listed on the back of the menu, picked out specifically to accompany the evening's dishes; nothing could be simpler than choosing one of these. Second, ask Tony Hadley himself. He is one of the most helpful, least intimidating wine waiters you could come across. Third, just browse through the list of some 400 wines which opens with a generous 67 half-bottles. Despite Tony Hadley's aversion to France's nuclear testing, a good range of French wines is still offered, now matched by some excellent contributions from the New World. Prices are reasonable, with over 60 bottles under £15.

CHEF: Ruth Hadley PROPRIETORS: Tony and Ruth Hadley OPEN: Wed to Mon D only 7 to 9 CLOSED: 1 to 26 Dec, 8 Jan to 28 Feb MEALS: Set D £35 SERVICE: not inc, card slips closed CARDS: Delta, MasterCard, Switch, Visa DETAILS: 28 seats. Private parties: 28 main room. Car park. No children under 12. No smoking in dining-room. Wheelchair access (also WC). No music ACCOMMODATION: 9 rooms, all with bath/shower. TV. D,B&B £85 to £190. Deposit: £50. No children under 12. Garden (*The Which? Hotel Guide*)

The 1999 Guide *will be published before Christmas 1998. Reports on meals are most welcome at any time of the year, but are particularly valuable in the spring (no later than June). Send them to* The Good Food Guide, *FREEPOST, 2 Marylebone Road, London NW1 1YN. Or email your report to guidereports@which.co.uk.*

KINLOCHMOIDART Highland map 11

Kinacarra ✱ [£]

Kinlochmoidart PH38 4ND
TEL: (01967) 431238 COOKING 4
on A861, at head of Loch Moidart COST £16–£36

The dining-room of this little stone building on the shore of Loch Moidart has been decorated in singular taste, the deer skulls and antlers perhaps a jolt to the system for townies. Against this backdrop, Frances MacLean's cooking seems designed to soothe. Mussels are gratinated under a coat of melted Brie, monkfish is baked in lemon and cream, and old-fashioned profiteroles may crop up for pudding. A couple who arrived on a bone-chillingly cold May lunch-time were soon revived by gutsy mushroom soup and a generous portion of briefly cooked scallops in garlic butter. Meringues make an accomplished dessert, cooked *à point* to retain some gooeyness inside and served with caramel sauce. Home-made ice-creams receive plaudits too. The keenly priced wine list, boldly, is exclusively non-European, with prices starting at £10 for a crisp South African Sauvignon.

CHEF: Frances MacLean PROPRIETORS: Angus and Frances MacLean OPEN: Tue to Sun 12 to 2, 7 to 8.30 CLOSED: end Oct to Easter MEALS: alc (main courses L £4 to £7, D £9 to £13.50) SERVICE: not inc CARDS: none DETAILS: 24 seats. 6 seats outside. Private parties: 24 main room. Car park. Vegetarian meals. Children's helpings. No smoking in dining-room. Wheelchair access (also WC). No music

KYLESKU Highland map 11

▲ *Kylesku Hotel* £ ✱

Kylesku IV27 4HW
TEL: (01971) 502231 FAX: (01971) 502313
on A894, at S side of old ferry crossing, by new bridge linking Ullapool and Kylestrome COOKING 1
COST £19–£35

The hotel overlooks the sea loch of Glencoul, in what Marcel Klein describes as 'the only unspoilt part of Europe'. There is certainly plenty of wildlife, good fishing and walking, splendid views, and abundant seafood to supply the kitchen. Langoustines with garlic mayonnaise, and pan-fried haddock with lemon butter are typical, while the all-purpose lobster sauce is applied to such diverse dishes as baked mussels in puff pastry, and grilled local salmon. Highland lamb, beef, and game in season are also likely to feature, plus chicken tikka with savoury rice by way of a change. The simplest dishes appear to work best, service might be more enthusiastic, and the predominantly French wine list runs the gamut from classed growth claret to house wine at £6.95.

▲ *means accommodation is available.*

CHEF/PROPRIETOR: Marcel Klein OPEN: all week 12 to 2, 6.30 to 9.45 CLOSED: 28 Oct to 1 Mar MEALS: alc (main courses £7.50 to £14). Set L and D £15 (2 courses) to £18. Bar meals available SERVICE: not inc, card slips closed CARDS: MasterCard, Switch, Visa DETAILS: 32 seats. Private parties: 20 main room. Car park. Children welcome. No smoking in dining-room. Wheelchair access (also WC). Music ACCOMMODATION: 8 rooms, all with bath/shower. TV. B&B £25 to £65. Deposit: £20. Children welcome. Baby facilities. Dogs welcome. Afternoon teas. Garden. Fishing

LINLITHGOW West Lothian map 11

▲ *Champany Inn*

WEST LOTHIAN 1998 BEEF CHAMPION

Champany, Linlithgow EH49 7LU
TEL: (01506) 834532 FAX: (01506) 834302 COOKING 7
2m NE of Linlithgow at junction of A904 and A803 COST £35–£77

The farm buildings date from the time of Mary Queen of Scots, and the dining-room is a simple, circular, stone-built, vaulted former mill with mahogany tables and antiques. One reporter sums up the appeal thus: 'Champany Inn is an enormously reassuring, utterly competent vindication of how a good chef can take great ingredients and enhance them rather than screw them up.' Clive Davidson works his magic on prime ingredients of Aberdeen Angus beef (displayed near the kitchen), on lobsters and Loch Gruinart oysters (in a seawater pool), and on vegetables and wild mushrooms filling a basket that is hawked round for inspection.

'There is a strong sense of pride and determination in everything they do,' from the materials themselves – beef is hung for three weeks in an ionised chill room – to the simple but dedicated preparation with unaffected sauce accompaniments: béarnaise with chateaubriand, or perhaps lemon butter with charcoal-grilled salmon. This is utterly plain food taken about as far as it can go, and nobody does it better. Prices may appear high, but the simple truth is that good food costs money. The chop and ale house, however, offers less-formal, less-expensive food, from home-made sausages, via more steaks, to hot waffles with maple syrup.

The hefty wine list is positively regal in its range of reds, from the expected grand cru burgundies to the surprising South Africans, while for oyster lovers there are some steely Chablis or a Sancerre. Spirits drinkers will delight in the selection of Hine Cognacs, the Armagnacs and over a hundred malt whiskies. CELLARMAN'S CHOICE: Bateleur Chardonnay 1995, De Wetshof, Robertson, South Africa, £25; Thelema Mountain Vineyards Merlot 1993, Stellenbosch, South Africa, £28.

CHEF: Clive Davidson PROPRIETORS: Clive and Anne Davidson OPEN: Mon to Fri L 12.30 to 2, Mon to Sat D 7 to 10 CLOSED: 25 and 26 Dec, 1 and 2 Jan MEALS: alc (main courses £14.50 to £27.50). Set L £15.75 (2 courses) SERVICE: 10%, card slips closed CARDS: Amex, Delta, Diners, MasterCard, Switch, Visa DETAILS: 60 seats. Private parties: 60 main room, 25 private room. Car park. Vegetarian meals. No children under 8. Wheelchair access (also WC). No music ACCOMMODATION: 16 rooms, all with bath/shower. TV. Phone. (No B&B prices available at time of going to press). Rooms for disabled. Children welcome. Garden

MILNGAVIE East Dumbartonshire map 11

Gingerhill [£]

1 Hillhead Street, Milngavie G62 8AF
TEL: (0141) 956 6515 COOKING 2
off A81, 4m N of Glasgow COST £10–£44

'Tucked away in a shopping precinct, but well worth seeking out' was one visitor's judgement on Carol Thomson's eight-year-old enterprise. It acts as a showcase for local artist Pam Carter's pictures, and accords a high priority to all-round enjoyment. 'Cheerfulness is the essence of this restaurant,' claimed one reporter, adding, 'do not go to admire delicately presented dishes, but take a good appetite and join in the fun'. Simplicity is the key, with Scottish seafood and chargrilled Aberdeen Angus steak sharing the limelight.

The acclaimed chowder might make a meal on its own, although since it is not unknown for evenings to last from 7.30 until after midnight, there is obviously plenty of time to take in other options: pan-fried langoustines, steamed Oban mussels, or seared halibut with coriander and lemon, for example. A few vegetable dishes constitute the only other main courses, and desserts do not seem to figure prominently. There is no licence, hence no wine list, but no corkage charge either, and mineral water is free.

CHEF: Heather Gorman PROPRIETOR: Carol Thomson OPEN: Mon to Sat L 11 to 3, Thu to Sat 7.30 (1 sitting) MEALS: alc (main courses L £4 to £8, D £8.50 to £18). Unlicensed, BYO (no corkage) SERVICE: not inc, card slips closed CARDS: MasterCard, Visa DETAILS: 26 seats. 14 seats outside. Private parties: 14 main room, 10 and 16 private rooms. Vegetarian meals. Children's helpings. No pipes/cigars in dining-room. Music

MOFFAT Dumfries & Galloway map 11

▲ *Well View*

Ballplay Road, Moffat DG10 9JU
TEL: (01683) 220184 FAX: (01683) 220088 COOKING 3
off A708 between Moffat and Selkirk COST £17–£38

The three-storeyed Victorian manse overlooks the town on one side and sheep galore on the other. Long drapes, 'sofas you could lose yourself in', and 'five long-haired Burmese cats in search of laps' populate the lounge. The Schuckardts go out of their way to be helpful, with John acting more like a butler than a waiter, and Janet preparing a no-choice menu that begins with canapés, throws in a sorbet halfway through, and delivers a plate of cheese before dessert.

Roast saddle of venison (cooked pink) provides a typical centrepiece, perhaps with a gin and juniper sauce. Before that there may have been carrot roulade, air-dried beef with a sweet red pepper chutney, or fillet of cod on a potato galette. Though the food may have the feel of 'something you could rustle up at home', it is well executed, and the change to a set meal format since last year seems to have given the kitchen a chance to shine. Finish perhaps with an orange mousse and ice-cream. The wide-ranging and fairly priced wine list patriotically includes a trio of white Scottish country wines at £10 a bottle. But if silver birch sap sounds a bit scary, the powerful red Rhônes, priced between £10.50 and £38, would be a good, traditional match for the venison. House wines are from £9 a bottle (£2 a glass).

CHEF: Janet Schuckardt PROPRIETORS: Janet and John Schuckardt OPEN: Sun to Fri L 12.15 to 1.15, all week D 6.30 to 8.30 CLOSED: 2 weeks Oct, 2 weeks Jan to Feb MEALS: Set L £12.50, Set D £27.50 SERVICE: none, card slips closed CARDS: Amex, Delta, MasterCard, Visa DETAILS: 24 seats. Private parties: 20 main room, 6 private room. Car park. No children under 6 at D. No smoking in dining-room. Wheelchair access (not WC). No music ACCOMMODATION: 6 rooms, all with bath/shower. TV. B&B £40 to £80. Deposit: £20. Children welcome. Baby facilities. Garden

MUIR OF ORD Highland map 11

▲ *Dower House*

Highfield, Muir of Ord IV6 7XN
TEL/FAX: (01463) 870090 COOKING 4
on A862, 1m N of Muir of Ord COST £40–£48

'Cosy' is a word that recurs to describe the interior of this seventeenth-century stone-built house, where the Aitchisons run a welcoming, relaxed regime in a friendly manner. Watered-silk curtains and 'genuinely interesting pictures' contribute to the dining-room's elegance, and four-course meals offer no choice before dessert. Robyn Aitchison applies a light hand to first courses of summer vegetable terrine, or salmon with tomato and basil vinaigrette, and the second course is soup, perhaps chicken with lemon and mint, or thick green lentil.

Soups and sauces use good stock, and herbs are from the garden, adding to the impression of integrity. Game and seafood are mainstays, main courses can be generous – five ovals of half-inch thick venison fillet on a base of rösti potato for example – and vegetables are served as an integral part of the dish. Cheese or dessert is the only choice: maybe cherry crêpes with chocolate sauce, or fresh apricot tart. France accounts for a substantial part of the wine list, but Spain and the New World chip in some interesting bottles, and half-bottles are plentiful. House Vin de Pays d'Oc is £13. CELLARMAN'S CHOICE: Michelton Marsanne Reserve 1992, Victoria, Australia, £17; Rust en Vrede Tinta Barocca 1994, Stellenbosch, South Africa, £16.

CHEF: Robyn Aitchison PROPRIETORS: Robyn and Mena Aitchison OPEN: all week D only 7.30 to 9; L by arrangement CLOSED: Christmas MEALS: Set D £30 SERVICE: not inc, card slips closed CARDS: MasterCard, Visa DETAILS: 25 seats. 6 seats outside. Private parties: 25 main room. Car park. Children's helpings. No children under 5 at D. No smoking in dining-room. Wheelchair access (also WC). No music ACCOMMODATION: 5 rooms, all with bath/shower. TV. Phone. B&B £45 to £120. Deposit: £50. Rooms for disabled. Children welcome. Baby facilities. Dogs welcome in bedrooms only. Garden (*The Which? Hotel Guide*)

'The tagliatelle adhered to the plate like superglue, and the mozzarella formed a rubbery slab on top. The mushrooms, which I picked out from the congealing mass, were fine, but it was a bit like pulling survivors out of the Blitz.' (On eating in the West Country)

NAIRN Highland map 11

▲ *Clifton House*

Viewfield Street, Nairn IV12 4HW
TEL: (01667) 453119 FAX: (01667) 452836 COOKING 4
W of town roundabout on A96 COST £26–£42

The Victorian house has been in the Macintyre family for over 65 years, and J. Gordon of that ilk has been cooking here since 1952, which must be something of a record. Good taste prevails, and the Macintyre collection of drawings and paintings is particularly impressive, adding distinction to a highly personal enterprise. Why the entirely French menu does not warrant a translation is anybody's guess, although to be fair the dishes are in French provincial mould. In any case, nobody should be surprised by a little eccentricity here.

Well-sourced materials include wild salmon, Skye shellfish, and beef from a 'closed' herd of pedigree highland cattle. Some dishes in the repertoire – pork kidneys 'Henri IV', for example – come round time and again, but are none the worse for being well practised. Seafood is a strong suit, and treatments are notable for their simplicity: some garlic with the monkfish, or a flavoured butter for scallops. Desserts do not appear to excite reporters, but one would have to be comatose – or teetotal – to remain unaroused by the sight of all the classics on the wine list. Vintage clarets cover four decades and mature burgundies abound. Despite such grandeur, around seventy-five perfectly drinkable bins are priced at £15 or less. CELLARMAN'S CHOICE: Sancerre, Dom. Claude Riffault 1995, £18; Margaux, Ch. du Tertre 1981, £34.

CHEFS: J. Gordon Macintyre and Charles Macintyre PROPRIETOR: J. Gordon Macintyre OPEN: all week 12.30 to 1, 7 to 9.30 CLOSED: Nov to March MEALS: alc (main courses £10 to £15) SERVICE: none, card slips closed CARDS: Amex, Delta, Diners, MasterCard, Visa DETAILS: 45 seats. Private parties: 50 main room, 12 private room. Car park. Vegetarian meals. No smoking in 1 dining-room. Children welcome. Music ACCOMMODATION: 12 rooms, all with bath/shower. B&B £54 to £100. Children welcome. Dogs welcome. Afternoon teas. Garden (*The Which? Hotel Guide*)

NEWTON STEWART Dumfries & Galloway map 11

▲ *Kirroughtree Hotel*

Newton Stewart DG8 6AN
TEL: (01671) 402141 FAX: (01671) 402425 COOKING 1
off A712, just outside Newton Stewart COST £20–£44

The large, ornate white house, set in eight acres of landscaped gardens, was built in 1719. An original fireplace in the lounge has been opened up, and rococo furnishings abound, including a staircase from which Burns used to recite his poems. Despite oatcake with smoked salmon, and cheeses from St Andrew's to Dunsyre Blue and local Cairnsmore made from ewes' milk, the food does not bang the Scottish drum too loudly. It might take in boudin blanc with an apple and calvados sauce, or artichoke heart filled with poached egg, and one reporter enjoyed a spring meal of 'full-flavoured' leek and potato soup, seared halibut steak scattered with coarse salt, and crème brûlée. Wines emphasise the traditional, and there is a good choice under £20 alongside some more prestigious bottles. House Vin de Pays d'Oc is £12.

CHEF: Ian Bennett PROPRIETOR: McMillan Hotel Ltd OPEN: all week 12 to 1.30, 7 to 9 CLOSED: 3 Jan to mid-Feb MEALS: alc L Mon to Sat (main courses £9.50 to £12.50). Set L Sun £12, Set D £27.50 SERVICE: not inc, card slips closed CARDS: Delta, MasterCard, Switch, Visa DETAILS: 50 seats. Private parties: 16 main room. Car park. Vegetarian meals. No children under 10. Jacket and tie. No smoking in dining-room. Music ACCOMMODATION: 17 rooms, all with bath/shower. TV. Phone. B&B £60 to £75. Deposit: £15. No children under 10. Dogs welcome. Afternoon teas. Garden

OBAN Argyll & Bute map 11

▲ *Heatherfield House* £

Albert Road, Oban PA34 5EJ — COOKING 3
TEL/FAX: (01631) 562681 — COST £23–£49

Old family photographs decorate the walls of this late-Victorian manse, which used to be a boarding-house before the Robertsons took over in 1991. Seafood is a strong suit, from simple grilled or baked fillets and steaks to spiced potted crab or sweet pickled trout salad. Salmon is smoked in-house over birch and applewood, and is a match for the best according to one visitor who ate it with a fat warm langoustine and a smoked scallop. Alasdair Robertson also smokes haddock, oysters and cheese, and grows herbs and salad leaves in the garden. Apart from fish there might be guinea-fowl in honey sauce, roast pork with apple sauce, or beef Stroganov, followed by first-rate rum and chocolate mousse, or baked lemon cheesecake. The round-the-world selection of wines includes some good producers and affordable bottles. House French is £9.95.

CHEF: Alasdair Robertson PROPRIETORS: Alasdair and Jane Robertson OPEN: all week 12.30 to 2, 7.30 to 10 (bookings only) MEALS: alc Mon to Sat L, all week D (main courses L £7 to £23.50, D £13 to £23.50). Set L Sun £12.50, Set D £16.50 (2 courses) to £22 SERVICE: not inc, card slips closed CARDS: MasterCard, Visa DETAILS: 30 seats. Private parties: 16 main room. Car park. Vegetarian meals. Children's helpings. No children under 5. No smoking in dining-room. Music ACCOMMODATION: 4 rooms, all with bath/shower. TV. D,B&B £51 to £87. Deposit: £30. Children welcome; high tea for under-5s. Baby facilities. Small dogs welcome in bedrooms only. Garden

▲ *Knipoch Hotel* £

Knipoch, by Oban PA34 4QT
TEL: (01852) 316251 FAX: (01852) 316249 — COOKING 3
on A816, 6m S of Oban — COST £39–£60

The mustard-yellow building, set back from the road, has a luxurious lounge with big leather armchairs and sofas to sink into, and a smaller dining-room with polished wooden tables. Knipoch is informally run, and service is 'clued up' and 'in easy control of things'. Staff may be helped by the unvarying pattern of dinner: a choice of either three or five courses. The main business may be either fish – halibut and Dover sole in champagne sauce, perhaps – or a meat such as boned and rolled shoulder of lamb with herbs in a dark and 'nicely concentrated' stock-based sauce.

In-house smoking is applied to salmon and to 'soft, moist' scallops that might be served before a meat main course, and might be preceded in turn by cock-a-leekie soup for those on five courses. After the main course may come a single cheese such as Bonchester or Tobermory, and dessert of strawberry tuile, or a pancake with ice-cream and whisky sauce. The sheer length of the wine list may seem at first daunting, but the quality on offer and the fair pricing will reassure. The range extends from classed-growth clarets to half-a-dozen Bulgarians priced under £10, and from fine German Rieslings to crisp New World whites. If you have a sweet tooth, don't miss the four Tokaji Aszús. House wines start at £11.50. CELLARMAN'S CHOICE: Concha y Toro Private Reserve Amelia 1995, Casablanca, Chile, £19.50; Valpolicella Ripasso 'Campo Fiorin' 1993, Masi, Veneto, £16.50.

CHEFS: Colin, Jenny and Kamma Craig PROPRIETORS: the Craig family OPEN: all week D only 7.30 to 9; L by arrangement CLOSED: mid-Nov to mid-Feb MEALS: Set D £29.50 to £39.50 SERVICE: not inc, card slips closed CARDS: Amex, Delta, Diners, MasterCard, Switch, Visa DETAILS: 44 seats. Private parties: 12 main room, 12 private room. Car park. Children's helpings. No smoking in dining-room. No music ACCOMMODATION: 16 rooms, all with bath/shower. TV. Phone. B&B £35 to £150. Children welcome. Baby facilities. Afternoon teas. Garden. Fishing

PEAT INN Fife map 11

▲ *Peat Inn*

Peat Inn KY15 5LH
TEL: (01334) 840206 FAX: (01334) 840530 COOKING 9
at junction of B940 and B941, 6m SW of St Andrews COST £28–£65

The Peat Inn wears well. 'We expected great things,' began one reporter, 'and it did not disappoint.' Smoke hangs in the lounge, giving the impression the log fire has probably never been allowed to go out in the twenty-five years the Wilsons have been here. The setting is not formal, yet it conveys the feel of a rather grand provincial restaurant, with high-backed chairs, crisp linen and starched napkins. The Wilsons' achievement has been to run a restaurant rooted in its environment, which has meant encouraging and developing local industry to the point where artisans supply herbs, salad ingredients, wild mushrooms, organic vegetables, honey, sea kale and the like.

Since the bulk of the produce is Scottish, it naturally involves a lot of fish, shellfish and venison, and since the Wilsons distance themselves from anything that might remotely be called fashionable, the repertoire retains its focus on proven successes. This gives a timeless quality to the food, and a sense of traditional culinary values, even if it does mean that similar dishes recur. First courses can sometimes seem like scaled-down main courses, but are no less enjoyable for that: generous ovals of pink venison liver, for example, topped with its kidney, on a soft, caramelised onion marmalade. Sauces for meat tend to be intense reductions, often with a dash of red wine, while the seafood side of the coin has produced a whole local lobster in a fennel-flavoured broth of vegetables and herbs. The only common theme among complaints refers to over salting.

Traditional desserts rely on sound technical accomplishment, in the form of caramelised apple on buttery puff pastry with caramel sauce and ice-cream, or a light but flavourful dark chocolate mousse. Meals might begin with warm cheese and onion tart, and generally end with an indulgent array of chocolate-laden petits fours. Staff are smartly dressed in black and white, and administer correct but obliging service with no fuss. Red wines are decanted when ordered, then brought to table for you to pour when you wish. David Wilson aims to offer wines from around the world which give pleasure and excite interest, and succeeds with this top-quality list. Reasonable mark-ups, and a generous selection of half-bottles, permit experimentation. CELLARMAN'S CHOICE: Auxey-Duresses 1993, Jean Pascal, £24; Margaux, Ch. Labégorce-Zédé 1989, £24.

CHEF: David Wilson PROPRIETORS: David and Patricia Wilson OPEN: Tue to Sat 12.30 for 1 (1 sitting), 7 to 9.30 CLOSED: 25 Dec, 1 Jan MEALS: alc D (main courses £16 to £19). Set L £18.50, Set D £28 to £42. BYO £7 SERVICE: not inc, card slips closed CARDS: Amex, Diners, MasterCard, Switch, Visa DETAILS: 48 seats. Private parties: 24 main room, 12 private room. Car park. Children's helpings. No smoking in dining-room. Wheelchair access (also WC). No music ACCOMMODATION: 8 rooms, all with bath/shower. TV. Phone. B&B £75 to £135. Rooms for disabled. Children welcome. Dogs welcome. Garden (*The Which? Hotel Guide*)

PEEBLES Borders map 11

▲ *Cringletie House*

Peebles EH45 8PL
TEL: (01721) 730233 FAX: (01721) 730244 COOKING 3
on A703, 2½m N of Peebles COST £23–£43

The sandstone house, built in 1861, is Scottish baronial with knobs on; or, to be more precise, turrets. Round about are 28 acres of grounds and a walled kitchen garden that supplies vegetables, herbs and fruit. One reporter, having admired the rows of beetroot, enjoyed a colourful soup made from them. Indeed, soups are generally interesting and good, ranging from carrot with honey and ginger, through chickpea and lime to sweetcorn and coriander. This constitutes the first of four courses at dinner (the main meal), and might be followed by smoked fish terrine with cucumber salad, or grilled goats'-cheese tartlet with spinach and mushrooms.

Timing is good, which does a lot for the textures of fish and meat, and among the recommendations are poached salmon with lemon balm sauce, and roast duckling with a blueberry and kirsch sauce. An old-fashioned air pervades desserts of lemon posset, baked almond pudding and Danish apple flan, while the fudge that comes with coffee is said to be addictive. Some reputable producers figure on the wide-ranging wine list, and there is good representation at under £20. House Duboeuf is £12.50 a litre.

CHEFS: Sheila McKellar and Paul Maguire PROPRIETORS: Aileen and Stanley Maguire OPEN: all week 1 to 1.45, 7.30 to 8.30 CLOSED: 2 Jan to mid-Mar MEALS: alc L Mon to Sat (main courses £6.50 to £7). Set L Sun £16.50, Set D £26.50 SERVICE: not inc, card slips closed CARDS: Amex, MasterCard, Switch, Visa DETAILS: 60 seats. Private parties: 30 main room, 30 private room. Car park. Vegetarian meals. Children's helpings. No smoking in dining-room. No music ACCOMMODATION: 13 rooms, all with bath/shower. TV. Phone. B&B £50 to £120. Children welcome. Baby facilities. Afternoon teas. Garden (*The Which? Hotel Guide*)

PERTH Perthshire & Kinross map 11

Let's Eat £

77–79 Kinnoull Street, Perth PH1 5EZ COOKING 3
TEL: (01738) 643377 FAX: (01738) 621464 COST £21–£40

'You know it will be good as soon as you walk in,' insists a reporter, citing 'smiling Shona' (Shona Drysdale, who runs the front of house) in evidence. People who knew Shona and Tony Heath when they were at the Courtyard (see entry, Aberdeen) seem happy to have followed them to this high-ceilinged Perth bistro situated in what, in pre-Victorian times, was the Theatre Royal. The name may be off-putting for some, but the reputation has already spread. Tony Heath's cooking is proudly contemporary, offering pigeon breast with avocado and toasted pine-nuts as a possible starter before moving on to brioche-crusted cod on creamy mash with aïoli, tapénade and extra virgin olive oil, or tagliatelle with roasted red peppers, shallots, tomato and Parmesan. Desserts are straight from the nursery, taking in sticky toffee pudding with butterscotch, blackberry and apple crumble, and their French cousin, crème brûlée. Service is crisply turned out and highly diligent, and the atmosphere is convivial. The wine list is a brisk international roll-call at realistic prices, the house selections starting with South Africans at £9.50.

CHEFS: Tony Heath, Lewis Pringle and Thomas Burns PROPRIETORS: Tony Heath and Shona Drysdale OPEN: Tue to Sat 12 to 2.15, 6.30 to 9.45 CLOSED: 25 and 26 Dec, 1 and 2 Jan, 2 weeks mid Jul MEALS: alc (main courses L £6.50 to £10, D £7 to £14) SERVICE: not inc, card slips closed CARDS: Amex, Delta, MasterCard, Switch, Visa DETAILS: 70 seats. Private parties: 70 main room. Vegetarian meals. Children's helpings. Wheelchair access (also WC). Music

Number Thirty Three

33 George Street, Perth PH1 5LA COOKING 1
TEL: (01738) 633771 COST £25–£45

Decorative sea shells give a clue that fish is the main business of this pink and grey art deco restaurant. In addition to the main dining room menu, light meals of gravad lax, grilled mussels with pesto, or deep-fried king prawns are always available in the Oyster Bar. Although treatments such as pan-fried lemon sole or goujons of plaice with tartare sauce 'can hardly be described as innovative', supplies are fresh, and fish is 'intelligently and respectfully handled'. Among non-fishy successes have been avocado soup, and chicken liver pâté. 'Sweets are a good feature', perhaps including raspberry cheesecake gâteau, or chocolate roulade with coconut cream and passion-fruit. Service is friendly and obliging. A new wine list was being planned as we went to press; house wine is £10.60, or £1.95 a glass.

CHEF: Mary Billinghurst PROPRIETORS: Gavin and Mary Billinghurst OPEN: Tue to Sat 12.30 to 2.30, 6.30 to 9.30 CLOSED: 25 and 26 Dec, 1 and 2 Jan, last 2 weeks Jan, first week Feb MEALS: alc (main courses £11 to £15). BYO £5 SERVICE: not inc CARDS: Amex, MasterCard, Visa DETAILS: 24 seats. Private parties: 24 main room. Children's helpings. No children under 5. No cigars in dining-room. Wheelchair access (not WC). Music

PORT APPIN Argyll & Bute map 11

▲ *Airds Hotel*

Port Appin PA38 4DF
TEL: (01631) 730236 FAX: (01631) 730535 COOKING 7
2m off A828, on E shore of Loch Linnhe COST £47–£56

The road down to Port Appin and the lochside leads nowhere else, so the sense of seclusion is powerful. Looking out over Loch Linnhe towards Lismore and the hills beyond, this white-stuccoed gable-windowed house provides a cocoon of warmth and comfort, as it has been doing under the Allens for two decades. It is customary to stay, and both menu and wine list are left in the room, the latter particularly needing time to study. Dinner runs to a simple format, starting with something to nibble over an aperitif in one of the colourful lounges, followed by a troop into the low-ceilinged dining-room at around 8pm. The pattern is four courses of high-quality country cooking from a rotating repertoire that manages to combine local produce, a few luxuries and some contemporary ideas.

Shellfish might appear in the form of crabmeat sausage, or sauté oysters with smoked salmon and champagne jelly, and first courses have turned up rich partnerships of foie gras and wild mushrooms in a gamey context: with roast loin of rabbit and tagliatelle, or with rare breast of pigeon. A soup generally follows, maybe 'glorious' cream of red pepper and fennel, in which there is a sense of a unified whole rather than of separate components. What helps to make Graeme Allen's cooking special is firstly its 'deceptively simple' style, indicating a high degree of skill applied across the board, from a 'wish-I-could-make-that' madeira sauce to an 'exquisite' warm chocolate and pear tart with 'beautiful pastry' and an orange sauce.

Then there is the composition of a dish, which generally includes just enough elements to excite interest, yet not too many to compete. 'I kept coming across diferent flavours as I ate my way through it,' wrote one reporter of a 'delightfully moist, extremely fresh-tasting' monkfish served with spinach, mussels and shelled squat lobsters in a tarragon-flavoured butter sauce. Given this achievement, the extra vegetables seem unnecessary, and 'more human' service would be welcome. Plentiful wines are of good pedigree with not a mongrel in sight. France has the strongest presence but the Italian collection is particularly impressive, featuring wines from the likes of Marchese Antinori, Gaja and Silvio Jermann, and the German Rieslings are appealing. Prices are kept within reason and there is a baker's dozen of house wines starting at £11.

CHEF: Graeme Allen PROPRIETORS: Eric and Betty Allen, and Graeme and Anne Allen OPEN: all week D only 8 (1 sitting) CLOSED: Jan MEALS: Set D £35. Light L available SERVICE: not inc, card slips closed CARDS: MasterCard, Switch, Visa DETAILS: 36 seats. Private parties: 36 main room. Car park. No children under 6. Children's helpings. No smoking in dining-room. No music ACCOMMODATION: 12 rooms, all with bath/shower. TV. Phone. B&B £81 to £206. Rooms for disabled. Children welcome; high teas for under-6s. Baby facilities. Afternoon teas. Garden (*The Which? Hotel Guide*)

See inside the front cover for an explanation of the symbols used at the tops of entries.

▲ *Pierhouse*

Port Appin PA38 4DE
TEL: (01631) 730302 FAX: (01631) 730400
off A828, on E shore of Loch Linnhe, opposite Lismore ferry

COOKING 4
COST £20–£47

'Outstandingly good locally sourced ingredients, perfectly cooked and served in an unfussy and unpretentious manner – this is the kind of place we like to eat at.' So enthused one regular visitor to the MacLeod family's hotel and restaurant, now into its second decade. All is tranquillity and friendliness inside the former ferryman's house, which looks out to Lismore Island and Port Appin light: 'one of the best views in Scotland.' The newly revamped restaurant area provides plenty of extra sea-view seats that allow diners to watch fishing-boats arriving with their dinner.

Seafood – simply cooked, with no unnecessary garnishings – is the great draw here and reporters compliment succulent Loch Awe smoked salmon, plump lobster in garlic butter, and 'perfect, moist' giant prawns. Copious seafood platters might include langoustine, half a lobster, scallops, Lismore oysters and mussels, while meat-eaters can opt for pan-fried saddle of venison, steaks or perhaps chicken with mango. Respectful treatment of vegetables makes them 'a positive pleasure to eat'. Around 60 wines on the wide-ranging and intelligent list are predominantly French. Six house wines start at £10.75 for a Sauvignon Blanc from Chile.

CHEF: Sheila MacLeod PROPRIETORS: the MacLeod family OPEN: all week 12 to 3, 6.30 to 9.30 CLOSED: 25 Dec MEALS: alc (main courses £6.50 to £17) SERVICE: not inc CARDS: MasterCard, Switch, Visa DETAILS: 70 seats. 24 seats outside. Car park. Vegetarian meals. Children's helpings before 7.30. No cigars/pipes in dining-room. Wheelchair access (also WC). Music ACCOMMODATION: 11 rooms, all with bath/shower. TV. Phone. B&B £70 to £80 (double rooms). Children welcome

PORTPATRICK Dumfries & Galloway map 11

▲ *Knockinaam Lodge*

Portpatrick DG9 9AD
TEL: (01776) 810471 FAX: (01776) 810435
off A77, 3m S of Portpatrick

COOKING 2
COST £36–£56

It is a lovely house in a wonderful spot, at the end of a long road, overlooking a quiet and picturesque inlet of the Irish Sea, with an elegant, dark wood-panelled bar and 'gracious' dining-room. Staff are friendly – napkins are laid on laps with a flourish – and multiple nibbles are delivered alongside an elaborately worded menu which promises lots of flavours: for example, turbot with lobster 'knuckles' and a carrot and vanilla emulsion.

Local seafood usually features, Galloway lamb might be served with a rosemary scented *jus*, and Highland venison has been wrapped in pastry, Wellington-style. A lot of work undoubtedly goes into producing elaborate dishes, some of which appear to be 'designed for the eye rather than the palate', in an inspector's view, although this is counterbalanced by general 'well-flavoured' comments from others. Big plates emphasise the modest portions.

Desserts have classic leanings, including tarte Tatin with roasted figs, and sticky toffee and date pudding. Bread is first-rate and can outshine the cheese. Predominantly European wines balance drinkable young bottles with some highly marked-up older ones. A dozen house wines range from £12 to £16.

CHEF: Tony Pierce PROPRIETORS: Michael Bricker and Pauline Ashworth OPEN: all week 12 to 2, 7 to 9.30 MEALS: Set L £25, Set D £35 SERVICE: not inc CARDS: Amex, Delta, Diners, MasterCard, Switch, Visa DETAILS: 32 seats. Private parties: 35 main room, 10 private room. Car park. Vegetarian meals. No children under 12. No smoking in dining-room. Wheelchair access (also WC). Music ACCOMMODATION: 10 rooms, all with bath/shower. TV. Phone. DB&B £90 to £240. Deposit: 50%. Children welcome; high tea for under-12s. Baby facilities. Dogs welcome in bedrooms only. Afternoon teas. Garden. Fishing (*The Which? Hotel Guide*)

ST MARGARET'S HOPE Orkney map 11

▲ *The Creel*

Front Road, St Margaret's Hope KW17 2SL
TEL: (01856) 831311
off A961, 13m S of Kirkwall, on South Ronaldsay island

COOKING **6**
COST £32–£39

The 'special magic' of these islands derives from a cocktail of huge, ever-changing skies, endless sea vistas, neolithic remains, and wildlife. But even without all that 'the food at the Creel is reason enough to travel to Orkney', according to one couple who could hardly tear themselves away after a week. Thirteen miles from Kirkwall over the Churchill barriers, the plain three-storey house sits at the water's edge, filled during the day with tantalising smells of stocks and 'irresistible' breads and beremeal bannocks. 'We have eaten at the Creel for three consecutive years and have witnessed a blossoming in Alan Craigie's confidence in the kitchen,' reckoned one pair of visitors, adding that enthusiasm, dedication and achievement all seem to escalate each time.

To start, Alan Craigie's fish soups, from Parton Bree (brown crab) to smoked haddock, are 'packed with flavour and body' and are now 'up there with the best'. His repertoire covers a wide range of dishes and there is a willingness to try new combinations of flavours, but where seafood is concerned it is often the simpler dishes that impress most. Among the delights have been memorably fine fresh crabs of different species presented as simply as possible with well-dressed leaves and mayonnaise, firm fleshed lobsters, and large, tender, seared scallops served intriguingly with garlic butter into which are stirred some coarsely mashed chickpeas to give a grainy-textured contrast to the silky smooth scallops.

As a change from seafood, wiry and strongly flavoured North Ronaldsay sheep might be pot roasted with chunks of swede and carrot. Puddings have ranged from clootie dumpling parfait with Orkney ice-cream to lemon pie. Breakfasts are a good reason to stay, but the food deserves better than the basic wine list. House wine is £8.

The Guide *always appreciates hearing about changes of chef or owner.*

CHEF: Alan Craigie PROPRIETORS: Alan and Joyce Craigie OPEN: Mar to Oct all week D only 7 to 9.30, Nov and Dec open weekends only CLOSED: Jan and Feb MEALS: alc (main courses £15) SERVICE: not inc, card slips closed CARDS: MasterCard, Visa DETAILS: 36 seats. Private parties: 36 main room. Car park. Children's helpings. No smoking in dining-room. Wheelchair access (also WC). No music ACCOMMODATION: 3 rooms, all with bath/shower. TV. B&B £35 to £60. Deposit: 10%. Children welcome. No dogs

SPEAN BRIDGE Highland map 11

▲ *Old Pines* £✱ NEW ENTRY

Spean Bridge PH34 4EG
TEL: (01397) 712324 FAX: (01397) 712433 COOKING 3
off A82, 1m N of Spean Bridge COST £28–£33

'Old' refers to the surrounding trees, not the Scandinavian-style chalet building on the road to Gairlochy, which is a mere 15 years old. Bill and Sukie Barber converted their home to a business in 1990, and there is still a strong family appeal about the place. Meals are friendly, communal, 'dinner party' affairs, and strangers often share tables in a space that serves as dining-room, afternoon tea-room, library (with 'a great messy collection' of books, magazines, maps and guides 'begging to be looked at'), and after-dinner coffee-lounge. The Barbers are nothing if not enthusiastic. Local ingredients are paramount: they smoke their own meat and seafood, rear hens and ducks for eggs, and are keen hunter-gatherers, collecting wild fruits and mushrooms in season.

The menu – four courses with little if any choice – is decided 'after we have shopped' but will almost certainly produce something fishy: perhaps a 'homely' dish of mussels, monkfish and squat lobsters in a soupy medium made from the liquor, or an 'utterly fresh, thoroughly moist' piece of salmon with a creamy sorrel sauce. Simplicity and honesty are key factors in the food's success, and venison and lamb are typical meat options: smoked loin of the latter might be served on a barley, leek and cep risotto, with kale, carrots and roasted onions. To finish, there may be a meringue with pears, a scoop of pear liqueur ice-cream, and a sauce of red wine, orange and cinnamon. There is no drinks licence, but no corkage charge either, and soft drinks are provided free of charge.

CHEF: Sukie Barber PROPRIETORS: Bill and Sukie Barber OPEN: Mon to Sat L by arrangement, all week D 7.30 (1 sitting, May to Sept Sun D residents only). Light meals available all day CLOSED: 2 weeks end Nov/early Dec MEALS: Set L £17.50 to £25, Set D £25. BYO (no corkage) SERVICE: not inc, card slips closed CARDS: Amex, Delta, MasterCard, Switch, Visa DETAILS: 30 seats. Private parties: 30 main room. Car park. Children's helpings. No smoking in dining-room. Wheelchair access (also WC). Music ACCOMMODATION: 8 rooms, all with bath/shower. D,B&B £60 to £120. Deposit: £20. Rooms for disabled. Children welcome. Baby facilities. Afternoon teas. Garden (*The Which? Hotel Guide*)

'The menu said, "Please ask for the flavour of today's soup." I did, but they weren't at all helpful; perhaps because I only asked after I'd finished it.'
(On eating in South Yorkshire)

STEIN Highland map 11

▲ *Lochbay* [£]

1–2 Macleod Terrace, Stein IV55 8GA COOKING 1
TEL: (01470) 592235 COST £17–£46

A 'stunningly beautiful bay' provides the setting for this pair of fishermen's cottages, with little more decoration than Artexed walls and rustic dark wood tables. Fish is naturally the business, the best of it plain and simple: local oysters in tip-top condition, lobster grilled or boiled, prawns from the loch, or flash-fried scallops with 'wonderful flavour'. One couple enjoyed 'the best fish soup we have had' and also appreciated the generous portion. Puddings include traditional clootie dumpling with cream, and service is speedy and enthusiastic. A modest list of fairly priced wines includes a trio from Scotland (silver birch, elderflower and blackberry), and house wine is £9.50 a litre.

CHEFS/PROPRIETORS: Peter and Margaret Greenhalgh OPEN: Sun to Fri (and Easter Sat) 12 to 3, 6 to 9 CLOSED: end Oct to Easter MEALS: alc (main courses £6 to £19.50) SERVICE: not inc, card slips closed CARDS: MasterCard, Visa DETAILS: 24 seats. 8 seats outside. Car park. Children's helpings. No smoking in dining-room. Music ACCOMMODATION: 2 rooms, both with bath/shower. TV. B&B £25 to £40. Children welcome. Baby facilities. Afternoon teas. Garden

STEWARTON East Ayrshire map 11

▲ *Chapeltoun House*

Irvine Road, Stewarton KA3 3ED
TEL: (01560) 482696 FAX: (01560) 485100 COOKING 4
on B769 towards Irvine, 2m from Stewarton COST £24–£41

The comfortable stone-and-pebbledash house, built at the turn of the century, is more solid than grand, built for living in rather than showing off, with log fires, leaded windows, and a mass of oak panelling. Conference trade doesn't detract from the pleasingly domestic scale, and service is personable. New owner/ partner Simon Dobson describes himself as 'host' and the food as 'Scottish/ cosmopolitan', which covers a gâteau of Arbroath smokies, salmon served with a dill and green peppercorn mousse and, for all we know, a boudin blanc with wild rice and onion gravy.

Tom O'Donnell can stuff a chicken breast with a wild mushroom and tarragon mousse without it seeming either gauche or flashy. Technical accomplishment, accurate timing and sound judgement are typical, and dishes are thoughtfully constructed. A guinea-fowl terrine with apricots, accompanied by salad and a well-judged chutney, impressed an inspector for its balance – 'interesting without being fussy' – while an apple and cinnamon sponge with vanilla custard displayed a light hand. All the food seems to lack is a bit more oomph and zing in the flavours. The wine list reflects most of the major regions and includes some impressive clarets and four vintages of Ch. Musar. Around thirty good-quality bins are priced under £15, and there are sixteen French and German half-bottles. CELLARMAN'S CHOICE: Nogales Estate Chardonnay 1996, Montes, Chile, £11.90; St-Aubin 1993, Dom. Henri Prudhon, £17.75.

CHEF: Tom O'Donnell PROPRIETORS: the Dobson family OPEN: all week 12 to 2.30, 7 to 9.30 MEALS: Set L £15.95, Set D £24.80. Bar L available. BYO £7.50 SERVICE: not inc CARDS: Amex, Delta, MasterCard, Switch, Visa DETAILS: 50 seats. 25 seats outside. Private parties: 40 main room, 20 to 55 private rooms. Car park. Vegetarian meals. Children's helpings. No smoking in dining-room. Music ACCOMMODATION: 8 rooms, all with bath/shower. TV. Phone. B&B £69 to £139. No children under 12. Dogs welcome in bedrooms only. Afternoon teas. Garden. Fishing

---

STONEHAVEN Aberdeenshire map 11

Tolbooth **NEW ENTRY**

Old Pier, Stonehaven AB3 2JU COOKING 3
TEL: (01569) 762287 COST £22–£39

The worn steps outside one of Stonehaven's oldest buildings lead to a single large room overlooking the harbour, with an ornamental fish tank at one end just in case there is any doubt about its preoccupation. Any restaurant sited 10 feet from the North Sea that didn't have a penchant for seafood would be considered more than just eccentric. As it is, 'we try to use as much locally landed fish as possible,' writes a perfectly normal Chris McCarrey, although more exotic species also find a home here.

Jean-François Meder is half-French, half-Dutch, and his assistant is all Australian, so no wonder we find baked fillets of red ocean perch with a ginger and basil crust, served with egg noodles and a satay sauce. From nearer home might come smoked haddock and crab (combined in ravioli), Orkney scallops, or a whole, 'palpably fresh' grilled plaice. Meals have begun with pigeon breast salad with chanterelles (they collect their own mushrooms) or roasted red pepper soup with zough relish (from Yemen), and ended with chocolate and Grand Marnier marquise. Flavours tend to be gentle, service cracks along, and sensibly priced wines make good use of the southern hemisphere. House French is £8.95.

CHEF: Jean-François Meder PROPRIETORS: Jean-François Meder and Chris McCarrey OPEN: Sun L 12 to 2.30, Tue to Sun D 6.30 to 9 (9.30 Fri and Sat) CLOSED: first 2 weeks Jan MEALS: alc D Tue to Sat (main courses £11 to £16.50). Set L Sun £13.95, Set D Sun £16.95 SERVICE: not inc CARDS: MasterCard, Visa DETAILS: 44 seats. Private parties: 40 main room. Vegetarian meals. Children's helpings. No children under 8. No cigars/pipes in dining-room. Music

---

STRONTIAN Highland map 11

▲ *Kilcamb Lodge* 🍷 £✶

Strontian PH36 4HY
TEL: (01967) 402257 FAX: (01967) 402041 COOKING 3
on A861, by N shore of Loch Sunart COST £33–£40

Abundant wildlife indicates just how isolated the setting is, overlooking the loch. Already refurbished to a high standard, the lodge is destined to benefit from a conservatory extension to make the most of the dining-room's enviable views. Reports indicated a rocky patch over the winter, then Neil Mellis from

Taychreggan (see entry, Kilchrenan) arrived as second chef and things took a turn for the better.

The deal is as before – four courses with a wee choice – perhaps starting with asparagus and monkfish on crisp, light puff pastry. Some familiar favourites turn up in the shape of roasted bacon-wrapped quail with apple and apricot stuffing, for example, and second-course soups (onion and thyme, or mushroom and madeira) remain of a high standard. Timing is good across the board, from baked Gigha goats' cheese (crisp outside, creamy in the centre) to meats such as pink and tender Highland lamb. Highlights among desserts have included glazed lemon soufflé tart, and a light vacherin with moist dark chocolate mousse. Wines offer a good range of styles and flavours, with some particularly interesting bins from the New World. A style guide helpfully follows the supermarket convention of numbering the whites 1 to 9 for dry-to-sweet and labelling the reds A to E for body. House wines start at £9.50. CELLARMAN'S CHOICE: Dry River Estate Sauvignon Blanc 1996, Martinborough, New Zealand, £21.50; Neil Ellis Pinotage 1995, Stellenbosch, South Africa, £12.50.

CHEFS: Peter Blakeway and Neil Mellis PROPRIETORS: the Blakeway family OPEN: all week D only 7.30 (1 sitting) CLOSED: late Nov to early Mar MEALS: Set D £25. Light L available SERVICE: not inc, card slips closed CARDS: Delta, MasterCard, Switch, Visa DETAILS: 26 seats. Private parties: 50 main room. Car park. Children's helpings. No children under 8. No smoking in dining-room. No music ACCOMMODATION: 11 rooms, all with bath/shower. TV. D,B&B £62 to £170. Deposit: £35. Children welcome; high tea for under-8s. Baby facilities. Dogs welcome by arrangement. Afternoon teas. Garden. Fishing (*The Which? Hotel Guide*)

SWINTON Borders map 11

▲ *Wheatsheaf Hotel*

Main Street, Swinton TD11 3JJ
TEL: (01890) 860257 FAX: (01890) 860257 COOKING **2**
on A6112, Coldstream to Duns road COST £19–£45

A stone-built edifice overlooking the village green, the Wheatsheaf offers a choice of eating, either in the conservatory extension or in a more formal small dining-room. The menus are extensive and the cooking energetically ambitious, although an inspector felt that the kitchen was being overstretched and that 'a more manageable-sized menu would benefit everyone'. However, a starter of pigeon breast on black pudding brings two good ingredients together well, while a bowl of parsnip and coriander soup gains aromatic intensity from its herb and sweetness from its root. Simple main courses such as langoustines with garlic butter and an expertly dressed salad impress more than the fiddly dishes that may take too long to prepare. Summer pudding with a blackcurrant coulis was just the ticket at a July lunch; colder weather may bring marmalade and sultana steamed pudding with vanilla and cardamom-flavoured custard. Wines are an enterprisingly international bunch, and there is a good spread of half-bottles. House wines are £9.50.

▲ *means accommodation is available.*

CHEFS: Alan Reid and John Keir PROPRIETORS: Alan and Julie Reid OPEN: Tue to Sun 12 to 2, 6.30 to 9.30 CLOSED: Last week Oct, last 2 weeks Feb, Sun D winter MEALS: alc (main courses L £4.50 to £15, D £8 to £16) SERVICE: not inc, card slips closed CARDS: MasterCard, Visa DETAILS: 48 seats. 24 seats outside. Private parties: 30 main room, 18 and 26 private rooms. Car park. Vegetarian meals. Children's helpings. No smoking in dining-room. Wheelchair access (also WC). No music ACCOMMODATION: 5 rooms, 4 with bath/shower. TV. B&B £32 to £68. Deposit: £20. Children welcome. Baby facilities. Dogs welcome by arrangement in bedrooms only. Garden (*The Which? Hotel Guide*)

TROON South Ayrshire map 11

▲ *Highgrove House*

Old Loans Road, Troon KA10 7HL COOKING 1
TEL: (01292) 312511 FAX: (01292) 318228 COST £19–£45

Built as a private house in the 1920s, Highgrove overlooks the Ayrshire coast and the Isle of Arran. The view is 'charming', and the comfortable interior is fitted out with tartan carpet and 'heavy festoonings of assorted objects', including brassware and deer heads. The menu works to a barely changing repertoire – in which 'chunky slabs' of the main ingredient are sauced with various combinations of wine, garlic, cheese and cream – and is the repository of some old favourites, from beef Stroganov to first-rate Cullen skink. The *carte* is generous, concentrating on shellfish and smoked fish to begin, and offering duckling with crayfish, and halibut with cheese sauce for mains. If the rich saucing and 'perky garnishes' are not up your street, consider plain grills of fillet or sirloin steak, or lamb cutlets. Pastry is reliable, shortbread is good, and 'above-average' desserts might include tiramisù, or apple and almond sponge with custard. Service seems to have taken a turn for the better. An attractive wine list tees off with Spanish-made Hugh Ryman house wines at £9.95.

CHEF: James Alison PROPRIETORS: William and Catherine Costley OPEN: all week 12 to 2.30, 6 to 9.30 MEALS: alc (main courses L £6 to £13.50, D £9.50 to £15). Set L £14.95, Set D Sun to Fri £22.50. Brasserie menu Sun to Fri D SERVICE: not inc, card slips closed CARDS: Amex, Delta, MasterCard, Switch, Visa DETAILS: 90 seats. Private parties: 40 main room, 18 and 40 private rooms. Car park. Vegetarian meals. Children's helpings. No cigars/pipes in dining room. Wheelchair access (also WC). Music ACCOMMODATION: 9 rooms, all with bath/shower. TV. Phone. B&B £65 to £85. Children welcome. Baby facilities. Afternoon teas. Garden

▲ *Lochgreen House*

Monktonhill Road, Southwood, Troon KA10 7EN COOKING 4
TEL: (01292) 313343 FAX: (01292) 318661 COST £27–£47

'Everything here is a joy,' enthused one visitor who swept up the drive through immaculate gardens then strolled into one of the many drawing-rooms and sank into a deep sofa. The house, built in 1905, is set in 30 acres near the Royal Troon Golf Course, and everything, from oak and cherry panelling to splendid furniture and pictures, feels as if it belongs. Native ingredients underpin the kitchen's integrity, which naturally involves a good spread of seafood. What makes a difference is the variety of modern treatments: salmon with pesto pasta, or poached sole and scallops in a Thai curry sauce, for example.

A generous menu makes this variety available at every meal-time, so it is possible to eat a lunch of red pepper and orange soup, followed by tagliatelle with wild mushrooms, and lemon posset, or a dinner of confit of duckling, then soup, then rack of lamb, and finally warm banana and walnut sponge with butterscotch sauce. Service is attentive – indeed 'meticulous' – and wines cover a lot of ground at a wide range of prices, calling in at some good producers along the way. House French is £13.50.

CHEF: William Costley PROPRIETORS: William and Catherine Costley OPEN: all week 12 to 2, 7 to 9 MEALS: alc L (main courses £8.50). Set L £17.95, Set D £28.50 SERVICE: not inc, card slips closed CARDS: Amex, Delta, MasterCard, Switch, Visa DETAILS: 90 seats. Private parties: 40 main room, 10 to 40 private rooms. Car park. Vegetarian meals. No smoking in dining-room. Wheelchair access (also WC). Music ACCOMMODATION: 15 rooms, all with bath/shower. TV. Phone. D,B&B £110 to £175. Rooms for disabled. Garden (*The Which? Hotel Guide*)

TURNBERRY South Ayrshire map 11

▲ *Turnberry Hotel, Turnberry Restaurant*

Turnberry KA26 9LT COOKING **6**
TEL: (01655) 331000 FAX: (01655) 331706 COST £36–£117

Built in 1906 as the world's first hotel and golf complex, Turnberry maintains something of an Edwardian air despite being 'embalmed in a concrete setting'. It began with a natural westward-facing advantage, looking out to Ailsa Craig, the Isle of Arran, and the Mull of Kintyre, and has added comfort, luxury and a health spa, all in the service of its two championship golf courses. The menu assumes that money is no object, and in return doesn't stint on luxuries from caviar to foie gras to lobster, but also makes good use of Ayrshire lamb, Galloway beef, Culzean bay prawns and the like. It can turn out a plainly grilled Dover sole, or chateaubriand with béarnaise sauce, but also slips into more contemporary mode with venison cutlet accompanied by celeriac mousse, poached pear, cranberries and a lavender game sauce.

Fillets and prime cuts are understandably the norm in this context, the Mediterranean is acknowledged (perhaps in the form of courgette, aubergine and a herby black olive dressing for charred bresaola), forest mushrooms abound, and the set-price dinner offers an old-fashioned carving trolley. Desserts (the cheapest course by far on the à la carte) go in for flavoured syrups – of thyme, for example, to accompany a bitter chocolate mousse – and often take an interesting turn, as in a strawberry and Cointreau gâteau served with grilled marzipan. The wine list is extensive, and quality varies, but prices are painfully high. House wines offer just 25p change from £20. Alternative eating places in the hotel include the Bay restaurant, Clubhouse and Ailsa Room snackery.

Report forms are at the back of the book; write a letter if you prefer; or email us at guidereports@which.co.uk.

CHEF: Stewart Cameron PROPRIETOR: Nitto World Ltd OPEN: Sun L 1 to 2.30, all week D 7.20 to 10 MEALS: alc D (main courses £24 to £33). Set L £23, Set D £45.50 SERVICE: not inc, card slips closed CARDS: Amex, Delta, Diners, MasterCard, Switch, Visa DETAILS: 180 seats. Private parties: 240 main room, 16 to 20 private rooms. Car park. Vegetarian meals. Children's helpings. Jacket and tie. No pipes in dining-room. Wheelchair access (also WC). Music ACCOMMODATION: 132 rooms, all with bath/shower. TV. Phone. B&B £120 to £275. Rooms for disabled. Children welcome. Baby facilities. Dogs welcome in bedrooms only. Afternoon teas. Garden. Swimming-pool (*The Which? Hotel Guide*)

TURRIFF Aberdeenshire map 11

▲ *Fife Arms*

NEW ENTRY

The Square, Turriff AB53 4AE COOKING **2**
TEL: (01888) 563124 FAX: (01888) 563798 COST £15–£38

This is essentially a pub in the process of renovation, and by the time the *Guide* appears the dining-room will probably be on the first floor. John Ferrier used to cook at the Bayview Hotel in Cullen, and takes his Taste of Scotland membership seriously, featuring Cullen skink, and haggis with neeps, tatties and a whisky sauce. He credits suppliers, aims for a broadly brasserie style, and makes fish and game something of a speciality, offering chargrilled venison, Deveron salmon, and west coast mussels with garlic bread. Choice is generous, and the blackboard gets red hot as dishes are changed daily.

An inspector who enjoyed a 'tempura style' trio of haddock, lemon sole and scampi served with tartare sauce, found the fish 'particularly fresh, carefully cooked'. A separate steak menu lists well-hung fillet and sirloin cooked all ways from 'Diane' to 'Mexican'. Vegetables are included, chips are good, portions are big, and there might be cheese or a version of sticky toffee pudding to follow. Two dozen wines from around the world offer a decent choice of varietals and styles at reasonable prices. House French is £9.15 for a litre-carafe.

CHEF: John Ferrier PROPRIETORS: D. and E. Pearson OPEN: all week 12 to 2, 7 to 9 (10 Sat) CLOSED: 25 Dec, 1 Jan MEALS: alc (main courses L £4.50 to £7, D £8 to £15.50) SERVICE: not inc, card slips closed CARDS: Delta, MasterCard, Visa DETAILS: 30 seats. Private parties: 22 main room, 75 private room. Car park. Children's helpings. No smoking in dining-room. Wheelchair access (not WC). Music ACCOMMODATION: 7 rooms, all with bath/shower. TV. B&B £35 to £48. Rooms for disabled. Children welcome. Dogs welcome in kennels by arrangement. Afternoon teas

UIG Western Isles map 11

▲ *Baile-na-Cille*

Timsgarry, Uig, Isle of Lewis HS2 9JD
TEL: (01851) 672242 FAX: (01851) 672241 COOKING **3**
B8011 to Uig, then right down track on to shore COST £29–£34

The setting is unbeatable. There are beaches galore, Atlantic rollers break on the sands, and the house – like 'the home of a warm, if slightly eccentric, couple' – is a combination of manse, stables and cow shed. It may not be sumptuous, but the point of coming here is to unwind and escape stress. The atmosphere is cheerful and good humoured, informality prevails, and there are no rules, apart from a prompt start to dinner at 7pm.

Likes, dislikes and special needs are discussed when booking, but the essence is a simple no-choice four-course meal centred around chicken, boned and stuffed with a pesto mix perhaps, or lamb with a redcurrant and rosemary sauce. Mixed vegetable soup might start things off, local salmon, trout and venison feature, and desserts have included chocolate mousse cake, and lemon roulade. The food may be no more ambitious than a good dinner party, but Joanna Gollin's cooking skills are much appreciated, and certainly missed when she is absent. Bread is freshly baked, and meals end with cheese and a big basket of fruit. Wines (from Robin Yapp) cost either £8.50 or £12.50. Pick up a bottle on your way into dinner, earlier if you want it chilling.

CHEF: Joanna Gollin PROPRIETORS: Richard and Joanna Gollin OPEN: all week D only 7 (1 sitting) MEALS: Set D £24. BYO (no corkage) SERVICE: net prices, card slips closed CARDS: MasterCard, Visa DETAILS: 24 seats. Private parties: 32 main room. Car park. Children's helpings. No smoking in dining-room. No music ACCOMMODATION: 9 rooms, 7 with bath/shower. B&B £25 to £78. Children welcome. Baby facilities. Dogs welcome. Afternoon teas. Garden (*The Which? Hotel Guide*)

ULLAPOOL Highland map 11

▲ *Altnaharrie Inn*

Ullapool IV26 2SS COOKING **10**
TEL: (01854) 633230 COST £75–£91

Anticipation sets in even before taking the short boat-trip across Loch Broom. The fear is that Altnaharrie will not live up to expectations, the excitement is that it might. The house itself is 'magical', with small, simply decorated rooms and a sense that an 'intelligent and tasteful' hand has arranged everything carefully but not fussily. There is no choice at dinner but, thanks to Gunn Eriksen's record-keeping, every time you visit there will be something different to eat. Whatever it is, it sounds astonishingly normal. This food doesn't try to impress, it just impresses, and scores for sheer inventiveness, skill, flair, stunning visual appeal and directness of flavour throughout.

First courses arrive in waves across the room, in one case a large piece of 'perfectly cooked' turbot with spinach and two different sauces, each studded with morels. This was followed by a lobster soup 'unlike any lobster soup anywhere else', with chunks of tail meat, the contents of a claw pulled out and displayed in a circle, topped with truffle shavings, on a pool of intense stock with wine and cheese. 'Easily the best dish I have ever tasted,' reckoned our inspector of this 'multi-layered' sensation.

By this point it should have dawned that this is not just a succession of dishes but a balanced meal that builds as it goes. There is a real sense of progress, perhaps to a tower of 'tender and wonderfully flavoursome' lamb on a pool of intense stock and wine sauce with chanterelles dotted about, and next to it another tower, of thinly sliced new potatoes with a perfectly pitched garlic flavour. Is this the climax of the meal? Judge for yourself. There follows an assortment of French, Scottish, Irish and Norwegian cheeses, recited not shown, but all at their peak, 'perfectly ripe, in the best condition', and then dessert.

Or rather, desserts. 'Gunn and Fred cruelly make you try all three': crumbly lemon and pistachio cheesecake; crisp apple slices with a caramel sauce, calvados ice-cream and a light filo pastry topping; and a tear-shaped chocolate mould decorated with edible flowers and combining 'the most intense chocolate flavour you could wish to experience' in the form of a mousse, the mould and ice-cream. There are petits fours for anybody with room left to eat them. Good value is a slippery concept at the best of times, but the view is that Altnaharrie's package is well worth the cost.

Classic French wines head up the high-quality list, and there is lots to tempt burgundy fans. The pricing policy is fairer than at a number of other top-scoring restaurants, although wines by the glass are expensive. Half-bottles are particularly generous in scope, and a dozen house wines start at £10.90 for Ch. de Gourgazaud, Minervois, 1990.

CHEF: Gunn Eriksen PROPRIETORS: Fred Brown and Gunn Eriksen OPEN: all week D only 8 (1 sitting) CLOSED: early Nov to Easter MEALS: Set D £70. Light L available for residents SERVICE: none, card slips closed CARDS: Delta, MasterCard, Switch, Visa DETAILS: 18 seats. Private parties: 16 main room. Car Park. No children under 8. No smoking in dining-room. No music ACCOMMODATION: 8 rooms, all with bath/shower. D,B&B £155 to £370. No children under 8. Dogs by arrangement. Garden (*The Which? Hotel Guide*)

WALLS Shetland map 11

▲ *Burrastow House*

Walls ZE2 9PB
TEL: (01595) 809307 FAX: (01595) 809213
at Walls drive to top of hill, turn left, then follow road for 2m to Burrastow

COOKING 3
COST £23–£44

Despite its splendid isolation on the west coast of Shetland, Burrastow is a vital and energetic enterprise that scores 'A1 for freshness and local produce'. The white-painted house dates from 1759, and Henry Anderton and Bo Simmons are prized for their unstuffy approach, genuine hospitality and warmth. Lunch is three courses, dinner four, and for a trial period there is an early-evening 'Taste of Shetland' menu for casual callers.

As for ingredients, one reporter's baked salmon fillet with ginger and coriander was a fine example of 'perfectly cooked fish which had been swimming only that morning in the clear, cold waters of the voe'. Some exotic flavours occasionally surface, as in aubergine with sweet potato and ginger curry, but one of Bo Simmons's strengths is her commendably restrained approach with seafood, as in sea trout with lemon grass, or turbot with saffron sauce. It is a style that is 'never abused by overcooking or saucing', according to one observer. Desserts have included chocolate tart and Caribbean bananas, home-baking turns up first-rate bread (and croissants for breakfast), and 'very fair prices' obtain. Organically produced French house wines are £9.25.

Dining-rooms where music, either live or recorded, is never played are signalled by No music *in the details at the end of an entry.*

CHEF: Bo Simmons PROPRIETORS: Bo Simmons and Henry Anderton OPEN: Tue to Sun L 12 to 2.30, Tue to Sat D 7.30 to 9 CLOSED: Christmas and New Year MEALS: Set L £15, Set D £28.50 (booking essential L and D). Light lunches available. 'Taste of Shetland' D at 6pm SERVICE: not inc, card slips closed CARDS: Delta, Diners, MasterCard, Switch, Visa DETAILS: 30 seats. Private parties: 16 main room, 30 private room. Car park. Vegetarian meals. Children's helpings. No smoking in dining-room. Wheelchair access (also WC). No music ACCOMMODATION: 5 rooms, all with bath/shower. D,B&B £60 to £160. Deposit: 10%. Rooms for disabled. Children welcome. Baby facilities. Dogs by arrangement. Afternoon teas. Garden. Fishing (*The Which? Hotel Guide*)

Wales

ABERDOVEY Gwynedd map 7

▲ *Penhelig Arms Hotel*

Aberdovey LL35 0LT
TEL: (01654) 767215 FAX: (01654) 767690
on A493 Tywyn to Machynlleth road, opposite Penhelig station

COOKING 2
COST £14–£43

Overlooking the picturesque harbour and the Dovey Estuary, the Penhelig Arms feels like a pub that has grown into the shoes of a restaurant, helped along by Robert Hughes's enthusiasm for wine. He now presides over a completely refurbished kitchen, offers a set two-course lunch as well as an à la carte, an extensive evening bar menu on top of the restaurant dinner menu, and has secured a good supply of fish, which makes the half-mile journey from its source six days out of seven.

Among the seafood offerings might be cod with creamed potatoes, or goujons of plaice with tartare sauce and chips. First courses in the restaurant can sound like bar meals – home-cured salmon, garlic mushrooms on tapénade toast – while main courses might run to chunks of tender pork with a celery and orange stuffing, or grilled lamb cutlets with tarragon béarnaise. Desserts are as straightforward as bread-and-butter pudding or tiramisù. Although the wine list continues to change on a regular basis, the generous prices remain a constant. France still dominates, but the range from South Africa, Chile and California has increased, and there is an exciting new Italian selection supplied by Bibendum. Robert Hughes will also gladly put together a case to take away with the option of returning and replacing any bins not to your liking. CELLARMAN'S CHOICE: Frog's Leap Sauvignon Blanc 1995, Napa Valley, California, £17.50; Bourgogne Passetoutgrain 1990, Henri Jayer, £14.50.

CHEF: Jane Howkins PROPRIETORS: Robert and Sally Hughes OPEN: all week 12 to 2, 7 to 9.30 CLOSED: 25 and 26 Dec MEALS: alc L and bar D (main courses £6 to £9). Set L Mon to Sat £7.50 (2 courses), Set L Sun £12.50, Set D £19 SERVICE: not inc, card slips closed CARDS: Delta, MasterCard, Switch, Visa DETAILS: 34 seats. Private parties: 18 main room. Car park. Vegetarian meals. Children's helpings. No smoking in dining-room. No music ACCOMMODATION: 10 rooms, all with bath/shower. TV. Phone. B&B £39 to £78. Deposit: £40. Children welcome. Dogs welcome. Afternoon teas (*The Which? Hotel Guide*)

denotes an outstanding wine cellar; *denotes a good wine list, worth travelling for.*

ABERSOCH Gwynedd map 7

▲ *Porth Tocyn Hotel*

Abersoch LL53 7BU
TEL: (01758) 713303 FAX: (01758) 713538
on minor road 2m S of Abersoch through hamlets of Sarn Bach and Bwlchtocyn
COOKING 4
COST £25–£44

Not content with celebrating forty years in the *Guide* last year, Porth Tocyn is now getting out the candles for its own half-century in 1998. Reporters come for the friendliness and tranquillity, and for the warm, relaxed atmosphere that surrounds meals, which is echoed in the Fletcher-Brewers' approach: 'We like to think of ourselves running a dinner party each evening.' The dining-room looks out across Cardigan Bay to Snowdonia, watercolours line the walls, and the regularly changing menu is open to ideas ranging from roast Welsh lamb, or grilled seafood kebabs with lobster cream sauce, to a baked herb butter pancake filled with smoked duck and berries.

The search for novelty brings occasional eccentricities such as chargrilled duck breast over peppered strawberries with a redcurrant and orange coulis, although the kitchen aims to appeal to a wide audience, according to Nick Fletcher-Brewer, and stays well clear of 'dishes involving pig's trotters or brains or other such oddities'. One couple, grateful for meals that were not over-sauced, found themselves 'surprised and delighted' to be enjoying their fifteenth successive dinner just as much as the first. A vegetarian main course is now standard, and puddings often look back to the nursery with butterscotch ice-cream, lemon and lime soufflé, or steamed chocolate sponge. Wines appeal to a variety of tastes and pockets, and don't take many risks. House vin de pays red is £9.95, white £10.85.

CHEFS: Louise Fletcher-Brewer and David Carney PROPRIETORS: the Fletcher-Brewer family
OPEN: Sun L 12.30 to 2, all week D 7.15 to 9.30 CLOSED: mid-Nov to week before Easter
MEALS: Set L Sun buffet £16.50, Set D £20.75 (2 courses) to £27.75. Light L Mon to Sat
SERVICE: not inc, card slips closed CARDS: MasterCard, Switch, Visa DETAILS: 50 seats. 30 seats outside. Private parties: 50 main room. Car park. Vegetarian meals. Children's helpings. No children under 7 at D. No smoking in dining-room. Wheelchair access (not WC). No music
ACCOMMODATION: 17 rooms, all with bath/shower. TV. Phone. B&B £45 to £108. Rooms for disabled. Children welcome. Baby facilities. Dogs welcome in bedrooms only. Afternoon teas. Garden. Swimming-pool (*The Which? Hotel Guide*)

▲ *Riverside Hotel*

Abersoch LL53 7HW
TEL: (01758) 712419 and 712818
FAX: (01758) 712671
on A499, 6m SW of Pwllheli
COOKING 1
COST £32–£39

Occupying a stretch of river past the tidal harbour, the beige-painted hotel – 'typical of a seaside resort' – caters for regulars in a simple, homely fashion. The dining-room overlooks the river, reeds and lawns, and the Bakewells continue to cook and serve a nightly three-course meal, much as they have for thirty years. Local ingredients, from Lleyn Peninsula lamb to fish to sausages, make a contribution, and from the Aga come casseroles such as beef and venison with apricots and chestnuts. Proceedings might begin with soup, or asparagus and bacon tartlet, and end with toffee apple tart and mascarpone cream, or Mars bar ice-cream. Wines on the forty-strong list are varied and sensibly priced. House Australian is £9.95.

CHEFS/PROPRIETORS: John and Wendy Bakewell OPEN: all week D only 7.30 to 9 CLOSED: 5 Nov to 1 Mar MEALS: Set D £24. Bar L available SERVICE: not inc, card slips closed CARDS: Amex, MasterCard, Switch, Visa DETAILS: 32 seats. Private parties: 32 main room. Car park. Children's helpings. No children under 6. Music ACCOMMODATION: 12 rooms, all with bath/shower. TV. Phone. DB&B £35 to £88. Deposit: £40. Children welcome. Baby facilities. Afternoon teas. Garden. Swimming-pool

---

BASSALEG Newport map 4

Junction 28 🍷 £✱ **NEW ENTRY**

Station Approach, Bassaleg NP1 9LD
TEL: (01633) 891891 FAX: (01633) 892326
from M4 J28 take A468 towards Caerphilly, turn right at Tredegar Arms and take first left

COOKING 2
COST £19–£49

Built on the site of Bassaleg railway station, Junction 28 may seem unprepossessing from the outside, but its 'watercolour prints, plates, and pots', warm pink colours and reasonably spacious seating – a railway carriage-shaped area has views of hills and river – make it a pleasant place in which to eat. Jon West's robust style has produced a black pudding in pastry with apple, onion and thyme, followed by 'really successful' pan-fried lamb's liver with pulses and light braised dumplings. His extensive *carte* is considerate to vegetarians, offering spinach and mushroom bhaji with tomato and rosemary sauce, for example, and diners arriving before 7pm can save money by taking the daily-changing 'Early Evening Flyer' menu. Iced vanilla parfait with caramelised brown bread was 'quite a treat', or the adventurous could end with grilled fruit and marshmallow kebabs with hot chocolate sauce and ice-cream.

The place is run without flourish or pretence, and service is informal but efficient. Wines are taken seriously, with a wide-ranging, 100-strong list that includes some well-known producers. Prices are reasonable, and plenty of bottles come under £12; house vins de pays are £8.95. CELLARMAN'S CHOICE: Mâcon Fuissé 1996, Dom. de Fussiacus, £13.50; Moulis 1981, Ch. Poujeaux, £23.95.

CHEF: Jon West PROPRIETORS: Richard Wallace and Jon West OPEN: all week L 12 to 2 (4 Sun), Mon to Sat D 5.30 to 9.30 MEALS: alc Mon to Sat (main courses £7 to £16). Set L Sun £8.95 (2 courses) to £10.95. Set D (5.30 to 7pm) £11.95 SERVICE: not inc CARDS: Delta, MasterCard, Switch, Visa DETAILS: 160 seats. Private parties: 50 main room, 14 and 50 private rooms. Car park. Vegetarian meals. Children welcome. No smoking in 1 dining-room. Wheelchair access (also WC). Music. Air-conditioned

---

▲ *means accommodation is available.*

BEAUMARIS Gwynedd map 7

▲ *Ye Olde Bulls Head*

Castle Street, Beaumaris LL58 8AP COOKING 3
TEL: (01248) 810329 FAX: (01248) 811294 COST £24–£46

To get a fix on the timescale of the Bull, think of Columbus in 1492 sailing the ocean blue, and in that year the building was already twenty years old. Nearby Beaumaris Castle, by comparison, was nearly two centuries old. No wonder the pub has a venerable edge to its wooden beams, uneven floors, and a staircase that twists and turns on its way up to the A-framed dining-room. The appeal is that it doesn't stray too far from its pubby roots – 'informality' and 'decent-sized portions' are among the attractions – and yet is able to produce grilled venison burger, turbot with Conwy samphire and laverbread, and hotpot of Llanrwst goat's cheese with gnocchi, leaks and cream.

Native ingredients are well to the fore, in the form of ribeye of Welsh Black beef, and roast loin of Welsh lamb, while rabbit, partridge and smoked pigeon breast add gamey variety. Desserts have included rich orange tart, and bara brith butter pudding with can y delin (a Welsh liqueur) ice-cream. The wines are as august as their surroundings, being of demonstrably high quality and good value throughout the range. Five house wines are £13.50 a bottle (£2.95 a glass). CELLARMAN'S CHOICE: Chablis Les Clos 1991, Dom. Gerard Duplessis, £29.95; Recioto della Valpolicella 1988, Monte Fontana, Tedeschi, £22.50.

CHEFS: Soames Whittingham and Keith Rothwell PROPRIETOR: Rothwell and Robertson Ltd OPEN: Sun L 12 to 1.30, all week D 7.30 to 9.30 CLOSED: 25 and 26 Dec, 1 Jan MEALS: alc (main courses £12 to £15.50). Set L Sun £14.95, Set D Mon to Fri £20.95. Bar L available Mon to Sat SERVICE: not inc CARDS: Amex, Delta, MasterCard, Switch, Visa DETAILS: 60 seats. Private parties: 60 main room. Car park. Vegetarian meals. Children's helpings. No children under 7 at D. No smoking in dining-room. No music ACCOMMODATION: 15 rooms, all with bath/shower. TV. Phone. B&B £47 to £79. Children welcome. Baby facilities (*The Which? Hotel Guide*)

BROAD HAVEN Pembrokeshire map 4

▲ *Druidstone* £

Druidstone Haven, nr Broad Haven SA62 3NE
TEL: (01437) 781221 FAX: (01437) 781133
from B4341 at Broad Haven turn right at sea; after 1¾m COOKING 3
turn left to Druidstone Haven; hotel is 400yds on left COST £16–£32

'A million miles from city life' goes Rod and Jane Bell's slogan. Indeed, their holiday hotel sits on a wonderfully remote clifftop overlooking St Bride's Bay, and if relaxation could be measured this would probably top the scale. The trade-off is that you're likely to find wellies and surfboards *en route* to reception, and a laid-back approach to housekeeping. The attitude to food is more committed. After 26 years, 'the cooking is as robust and confident as ever', writes a regular, who is particularly fond of the home-made wholemeal bread. Vegetarians should find more than a perfunctory choice, and praiseworthy dishes have included 'light, tangy' watercress and cream-cheese soufflé, and sea bass cooked in vine leaves with an orange and vermouth sauce. Strawberry cheesecake worked well at inspection. The wine list is short, with no half-bottles, but the choice is varied and house wine is only £1.20 a glass, or £7 a bottle.

CHEFS: Rod and Jane Bell, Jon Woodhouse and Donna Banner PROPRIETORS: Rod and Jane Bell OPEN: Sun L 1 to 2, Mon to Sat D 7.30 to 9.30 CLOSED: Mon to Thur 10 Nov to 12 Dec and 5 Jan to 6 Feb MEALS: alc (main courses £6 to £12). Bar food available SERVICE: not inc, card slips closed CARDS: Amex, Delta, MasterCard, Switch, Visa DETAILS: 40 seats. 20 seats outside. Private parties: 40 main room, 10 private room. Car park. Vegetarian meals. Children's helpings. No smoking in dining-room. Wheelchair access (also WC). No music ACCOMMODATION: 9 rooms. B&B £28 to £67. Deposit: £20. Rooms for disabled. Children welcome. Baby facilities. Dogs welcome. Afternoon teas. Garden (*The Which? Hotel Guide*)

CAPEL GARMON Conwy map 7

CONWY 1998 RETREAT

▲ *Tan-y-Foel*

Capel Garmon, nr Betws-y-Coed LL26 0RE
TEL: (01690) 710507 FAX: (01690) 710681
take turning marked Capel Garmon and Nebo from A470 about halfway between Betws-y-Coed and Llanrwst

COOKING **4**
COST £37–£49

Peace and tranquillity are a big draw at this manor-house a couple of miles from Betws-y-Coed overlooking the Conwy Valley. Parts of it date from the sixteenth century, acres of hillside surround it, footpath walks abound, and Snowdonia is on the doorstep. Given such healthy surroundings, it seems natural that Tan-y-Foel should be a totally non-smoking establishment. The decor may have a touch of Hollywood about it, but the personal ministrations of the Pitmans count for a lot. He serves, she cooks, and daily-changing three-course dinners can be extended to four by eating both cheese and dessert.

The choice of only two items at each stage allows the kitchen to concentrate its energies effectively. Main courses tend towards simple treatments – loin of Welsh lamb with lemon, garlic and mint, or roasted salmon fillet with mustard seed butter – while first courses provide an upbeat start: fresh mackerel pieces with Thai spices and plum sauce, for example, or cauliflower florets in batter with rouille dip. For one reporter, salmon sabayon was 'outstanding – I shall never forget it'. Fruit and cream are common dessert ingredients: hazelnut meringue with nectarines and whipped cream, or baked orange tart with crème fraîche. The wine list is varied, interesting, decently priced, and well-off for half-bottles. Mexican and French house wines start at £10.

CHEF: Janet Pitman PROPRIETOR: Peter and Janet Pitman OPEN: all week D only 7.30 to 8.30 (booking essential) CLOSED: Christmas MEALS: Set D £25 to £29 SERVICE: not inc, card slips closed CARDS: Amex, Delta, Diners, MasterCard, Switch, Visa DETAILS: 16 seats. Car park. No children under 7. No smoking in dining-room. No music ACCOMMODATION: 7 rooms, all with bath/shower. TV. Phone. D,B&B £90 to £200. Deposit: £50. No children under 7. Afternoon teas. Garden (*The Which? Hotel Guide*)

Card slips closed *in the details at the end of an entry indicates that the total on the slips of credit cards is closed when handed over for signature.*

CARDIFF Cardiff map 4

Armless Dragon £

97 Wyeverne Road, Cathays, Cardiff CF2 4BG COOKING 2
TEL: (01222) 382357 COST £15–£38

David Richards continues to cook a string of bistro favourites at this friendly cottage conversion near the university. At its liveliest the style embraces laverballs and mushrooms, crab soup with lemon grass, and soused mackerel with a mustard and yogurt sauce. Fish may be simply grilled, and chicken or fillet steak treated to a herb or garlic butter. Hunter's pie combines venison and pheasant with more domesticated lamb and beef, while vegetarian main courses have included stuffed pepper with couscous, and 'laverburger' as part of a vegan platter. Raspberry trifle, or lime and lemon syllabub might bring up the rear, and wines stay comfortably under £20 for the most part. House French is £7.90.

CHEF/PROPRIETOR: David Richards OPEN: Tue to Fri L 12 to 2.15, Tue to Sat D 7 to 10.30 CLOSED: 25 Dec MEALS: alc (main courses £9 to £14). Set L £7.50 (2 courses) to £9.50 SERVICE: not inc CARDS: Amex, Delta, Diners, MasterCard, Switch, Visa DETAILS: 45 seats. Private parties: 50 main room. Vegetarian meals. Children's helpings. No smoking in dining-room. Wheelchair access (not WC). Music

La Brasserie £

60 St Mary Street, Cardiff CF1 1FE COOKING 1
TEL: (01222) 372164 FAX: (01222) 668092 COST £22–£50

The same lively informality pervades all three Martinez restaurants (see Champers and Le Monde opposite), helped along by Muzak, sawdust and – in this 'French wine bar' set-up – all-day opening in summer, and a capacity crowd of 300-plus. Oysters, scallops with garlic butter, and frogs legs convey the jaunty bistro style. Main courses can be as plain as fillet steak, roast suckling pig, or a short selection of daily-changing fish at so much a pound – hake, sole, salmon or lobster – while roast duckling or game in season help to ring the changes. Wines change frequently, and typically start at £8.95 (£1.55 a glass) for Spanish red, white or rosé.

CHEFS: David Legg and Armando Volpi PROPRIETOR: Benigno Martinez OPEN: Mon to Sat 12 to 2.30, 7 to 12 CLOSED: 25 and 26 Dec MEALS: alc (main courses £7 to £19). Set L £5 (2 courses) SERVICE: not inc, card slips closed CARDS: Amex, Diners, MasterCard, Visa DETAILS: 300 seats. Private parties: 30 main room, 120 private room. Vegetarian meals. Children's helpings. Wheelchair access (also WC). Music. Air-conditioned

Le Cassoulet

5 Romilly Crescent, Canton, Cardiff CF1 9NP NEW CHEF
TEL/FAX: (01222) 221905 COST £31–£37

Andrew Reagen used to be a sous-chef in Gilbert and Claire Viader's small terraced restaurant, then went on workabout, and has returned as head chef, just too late for us to receive any feedback. He should, though, be familiar with the house speciality, cassoulet toulousain, a typically hearty dish containing duck, boudin blanc and haricot beans. As for the rest, we wait and see. Your reports are welcomed. The wine list remains the same, a 100 per cent Gallic affair with plenty of choice through the range. House wine is £9.95.

CHEF: Andrew Reagen PROPRIETORS: Gilbert and Claire Viader OPEN: Tue to Fri L 12 to 2, Tue to Sat D 7 to 10, post-theatre D by arrangement CLOSED: 2 weeks Christmas, Aug MEALS: Set L £15, Set D £26 SERVICE: not inc CARDS: Amex, Delta, Diners, MasterCard, Switch, Visa DETAILS: 40 seats. Vegetarian meals. Children's helpings. No music

Champers £

62 St Mary Street, Cardiff CF1 1FE — COOKING 1
TEL: (01222) 373363 FAX: (01222) 668092 — COST £22–£40

Calling itself a wine bar and 'Spanish bodega', this branch of the Martinez trio (see La Brasserie, opposite, and Le Monde, below) concentrates on a mix of simple seafood starters and main-course steaks. It is completely informal, with a display of ingredients awaiting simple chargrilling. Beyond straightforward fillet, rump or sirloin might be barbecued pork spare ribs, or chicken Mexicana (with chillies and tabasco), served with French fries, baked or new potatoes. Begin with a pint of shrimps (hot or cold), or oysters or dressed crab when available, and finish perhaps with Spanish cheese. One reporter wrote at length to complain of unsympathetic service. House wine starts at £8.95 (£1.60 a glass).

CHEFS: David Legg and Dinis Louis PROPRIETOR: Benigno Martinez OPEN: Mon to Sat L 12 to 2.30, all week D 7 to 12 CLOSED: 25 and 26 Dec MEALS: alc (main courses £6 to £17). Set L £5 (2 courses) SERVICE: not inc CARDS: Amex, Diners, MasterCard, Visa DETAILS: 180 seats. Private parties: 1 main room, 120 private room. Wheelchair access (also WC). Music

Le Monde £

60 St Mary Street, Cardiff CF1 1FE — COOKING 1
TEL: (01222) 387376 FAX: (01222) 668092 — COST £22–£48

Where Champers (see entry above) deals mostly in meat, Le Monde concentrates on fish in a similarly informal set-up. The choice is wide, including provençale fish soup, grilled sardines and deep-fried squid to begin, and sea bass baked in rock salt or whole lemon sole to follow. There is 'no apparent menu'; the cold display from which you select the fish is usually enough, and price is calculated on weight, from salmon at the bottom to crawfish tail at the top. There is meat for diehards, and a simple choice of either cheese or crêpes suzette to finish. House wine is £8.95 (£1.55 a glass).

CHEFS: David Legg and Chris Ruck PROPRIETOR: Benigno Martinez OPEN: Mon to Sat 12 to 2.30, 7 to 12 CLOSED: 25 and 26 Dec MEALS: alc (main courses £6 to £19) SERVICE: not inc, card slips closed CARDS: Amex, Diners, MasterCard, Visa DETAILS: 200 seats. Private parties: 90 to 120 private rooms. Vegetarian meals. Children's helpings at manager's discretion. Music. Air-conditioned

'My companion and I were shown to the famous cramped table in the corner by the window, where guests sit side by side as if they were on a train.' (On eating in London)

CLYTHA Monmouthshire map 2

▲ *Clytha Arms*

Clytha NP7 9BW
TEL/FAX: (01873) 840206
off old Abergavenny to Raglan road, S of A40, 5m E of Abergavenny

COOKING 4
COST £20–£41

The hotel is a whitewashed inn set back from the road in lawns that were once part of the estate of eighteenth-century Clytha Castle. You may sit on church pews in the bar to eat bacon, laverbread and cockles, or wild boar sausage with potato pancakes, or proceed to the more formal dining-room. The Cannings are proud of their supply lines of fish, which extend from Loch Fyne through West Wales to Cornwall, and offer beer-battered oysters with a Thai dipping sauce, and a bourride of hake, langoustines and mussels. A regular who had a pre-Christmas Sunday lunch of roast goose with sage and onion stuffing and a 'sauce involving kumquats' thought that it was all 'exceptional value for money'. Blackboard extras are always worth investigating, and main courses come with a profusion of vegetables. Nursery puddings, such as treacle sponge and custard, offer an alternative to more refined creations like iced Grand Marnier soufflé. One reporter found service exceptionally slow on a busy night. The predominantly French wine list starts with house French and Australian at £8.25 (£1.40 a glass).

CHEFS/PROPRIETORS: Andrew and Beverley Canning OPEN: Tue to Sun L 12.30 to 2.15, Tue to Sat D 7.30 to 9.30 CLOSED: 25 Dec MEALS: alc (main courses £8.50 to £13.50). Set L Sun £12.50. Bar food available. BYO £3.50 SERVICE: not inc, card slips closed CARDS: Delta, MasterCard, Switch, Visa DETAILS: 65 seats. Private parties: 45 main room, 20 private room. Car park. Vegetarian meals. Children's helpings. Wheelchair access (not WC). No music ACCOMMODATION: 3 rooms, all with bath/shower. TV. Room only £45 to £70. Children welcome. Garden

COLWYN BAY Conwy map 7

Café Niçoise

124 Abergele Road, Colwyn Bay LL29 7PS
TEL: (01492) 531555

COOKING 3
COST £20–£44

'A warmer and brighter environment' has been created by redecoration at this unassuming bistro that aims simply to bring a soupçon of France to North Wales. The cultural reference points extend to a 'menu touristique', on which sauté mushrooms with garlic and grain mustard, chicken breast with tarragon and green peppercorns, and crème brûlée with banana fly the flag. A regular visitor detailed a typical spring dinner that took in light-textured mussel and red pepper soup with pesto croûtons, cod with salsify and vanilla ('a delectable combination of flavours'), tender and tasty loin of Welsh lamb with rosemary and creamed leeks, and a 'richly satisfying but uncloying' chocolate tart with white chocolate sauce. What was on show, she felt, were 'the best ingredients used with flair and imagination'. Cheeses are Welsh and French, and the assiette du chef dessert selection, the restaurant tells us, has gained considerable local renown. Professional service keeps things running smoothly. A brisk international range of wines includes seven southern French house wines from £7.95.

CHEF: Carl Swift PROPRIETORS: Carl and Lynne Swift OPEN: Wed to Sat L 12 to 2, Mon to Sat D 7 to 10 CLOSED: 1 week Jan, 1 week June MEALS: alc (main courses £7 to £16). Set L £10.95 (2 courses) to £12.95, Set D Wed to Fri £10.95 (2 courses) to £12.95. BYO £3.95 SERVICE: not inc, card slips closed CARDS: Amex, Delta, MasterCard, Switch, Visa DETAILS: 32 seats. Private parties: 32 main room. Vegetarian meals. Children's helpings. No-smoking areas. Music

---

CREIGIAU Cardiff map 4

Caesar's Arms [£]

Cardiff Road, Creigiau CF4 8NN COOKING 1
TEL: (01222) 890486 FAX: (01222) 892176 COST £19–£46

'What you see is what you get' is a promise that has extra resonance when you can see before you choose, which is precisely the drill at this whitewashed pub with its large dining-room extension. Everything is on show in refrigerated counters, and fish is the pride and joy. A well-matched trio of Dover sole, halibut and salmon with a light Thai-inflected lemon grass sauce has been both attractively presented and faultlessly timed. Eastern overtones also characterise a starter of fish-cakes made with hake, delicately battered and served with a gentle curry sauce. Meat eaters are accommodated with the likes of pork kebab, or simply grilled Welsh lamb steak with a piquant tomato sauce. Puddings can be viewed too, and include Dutch apple pie, and citrus fruit cheesecake. Quantities throughout are large, and the sense of cheer is enhanced by staff who make sure everyone understands the system. House wines are £8.95.

CHEF: Earl Smikle PROPRIETOR: Steady Chance Ltd OPEN: all week L 12 to 2.30 (3 Sun), Mon to Sat D 7 to 10.30 CLOSED: 25 Dec MEALS: alc (main courses £5 to £17) SERVICE: not inc, card slips closed CARDS: Amex, Delta, Diners, MasterCard, Switch, Visa DETAILS: 100 seats. 60 seats outside. Private parties: 50 main room, 60 private room. Car park. Vegetarian meals. Children welcome. Wheelchair access (also WC). Music

---

CRICKHOWELL Powys map 4

▲ *Bear Hotel*

Crickhowell NP8 1BW COOKING 3
TEL: (01873) 810408 FAX: (01873) 811696 COST £26–£43

This old coaching-inn with its open fires and antiques has a 'real Middle Ages feel' about it. Menus go in for lavish descriptions – 'a warm gâteau of fresh crab and lightly sauté provençale vegetables finished with a mild ginger butter sauce', for example – and the style takes in both classical and provincial French ideas. An inspector praised 'ultra-fresh' scallops wrapped in Parma ham with a chive cream sauce, and 'very tender' venison with spinach and nutmeg mousse in a fine juniper-flavoured sauce. Desserts kept up the momentum with a 'chocoholic's delight' that combined a covered banana, a parfait, mousse, ice-cream and an amaretti studded slice. Staff are friendly and service is generally well paced, although one reporter found it disorganised. The wine list, arranged by style, leans heavily towards the New World and includes some tempting bottles. House French is £7.95.

CHEF: Darren Bridge PROPRIETORS: Stephen and Judy Hindmarsh OPEN: all week L 12 to 2, Mon to Sat D 7 to 9.30 CLOSED: 25 Dec MEALS: alc (main courses £10.50 to £17). Bar meals available. BYO £12 SERVICE: not inc CARDS: Amex, Delta, MasterCard, Switch, Visa DETAILS: 60 seats. 60 seats outside. Private parties: 60 main room, 30, 60 private rooms. Car park. Vegetarian meals. Children's helpings. No children under 6. No smoking in 1 dining-room. Wheelchair access (also WC). Music ACCOMMODATION: 36 rooms, all with bath/shower. TV. Phone. B&B £45 to £100. Rooms for disabled. Children welcome. Dogs welcome. Garden (*The Which? Hotel Guide*)

Nantyffin Cider Mill Inn £

Brecon Road, Crickhowell NP8 1SG
TEL/FAX: (01873) 810775 — COOKING 3
1½m W of Crickhowell at junction of A40 and A479 — COST £18–£38

The setting is as good as they come – a fifteenth-century inn beside the River Usk in the Brecon Beacons National Park – and the format is a sympathetic mix of casual eating off wooden tables in the bar, or choosing from the same menu in the bookable dining-room. Local supplies are accommodated. 'We cannot resist when people ring up offering so many different foods, from mushrooms to Usk salmon,' writes Sean Gerrard, and the repertoire has taken in cockles with laverbread, steamed venison pudding, and braised shank of lamb with olive oil mash. Despite its remoteness, modern touches might include 'oriental chicken' with Thai noodles, but for one reporter it was plain grilled lemon sole, and pan-fried breast of local pigeon that constituted the highlights of an autumn meal.

The package generally pleases – 'excellent ambience, first-class meal, friendly service', for example – although service has not always lived up to expectations. 'Downright unacceptable,' one regular reporter called it. Though it does not excuse such lapses, the other side of the story is a 'chronic shortage of qualified staff', which the proprietors, despite their best intentions, find equally frustrating, and to which, sadly, there would appear to be no immediate solution. The selection of international, fairly priced wines is helpfully arranged by style. A new list favouring easy drinking, inexpensive wines was being drawn up as we went to press. House wines start at £7.25.

CHEFS/PROPRIETORS: Sean Gerrard and Glyn Bridgeman OPEN: Tue to Sun 12 to 2.30, 6.30 to 10 (7 to 9 Sun) CLOSED: 2 weeks Jan, 1 week Nov MEALS: alc (main courses £7.50 to £14). Set L Sun £9.95 (2 courses) to £11.95. BYO £5 SERVICE: not inc, card slips closed CARDS: Amex, MasterCard, Switch, Visa DETAILS: 90 seats. 50 seats outside. Private parties: 65 main room. Car park. Vegetarian meals. Children's helpings. No cigars in dining-room. Wheelchair access (also WC). No music

£ *indicates that it is possible to have a three-course meal, including coffee, a half-bottle of house wine and service, at any time the restaurant is open (i.e. at dinner as well as at lunch, unless a place is open only for dinner), for £25 or less per person.*

DOLGELLAU Gwynedd map 7

Dylanwad Da

2 Ffos-y-Felin, Dolgellau LL40 1BS COOKING **2**
TEL: (01341) 422870 COST £22–£35

Sturdy fare still makes up the bulk of the offerings at this sunny bistro, but now the repertoire includes some dishes that are less challenging to the waistline: minted spring vegetable broth, hake with tomatoes and peppers, and pears baked with marsala and cinnamon, for example. 'Flavours are subtle and well-balanced,' noted a couple of reporters who enjoyed cucumber, pea and mint soup, Greek salad, vegetable puff pastry in red pepper sauce, and blackberry and apple pie. There has been praise, too, for the 'attentive but unpressured' service. Wines continue to be sold at bargain prices: only three of the 35 bins listed cost more than £15, and one of those is a Cloudy Bay Chardonnay at an appealing £17. Quality is impressive, and so is the range of styles. CELLARMAN'S CHOICE: Bordeaux Rosé, Ch. de Sours 1996, £11.80; Gigondas 1992, Dom. Raspail-Ay, £14.30.

CHEF/PROPRIETOR: Dylan Rowlands OPEN: Thu to Sat (all week Easter to Whitsun, Tue to Sun July to Sept) D only 7 to 9; L by arrangement (parties only) CLOSED: Feb MEALS: alc (main courses £8 to £12.50). BYO £5 SERVICE: not inc CARDS: none DETAILS: 30 seats. Private parties: 30 main room. Vegetarian meals. Children's helpings. No smoking in dining-room. Wheelchair access (not WC). Music

EGLWYSFACH Powys map 7

▲ *Ynyshir Hall*

Eglwysfach SY20 8TA
TEL: (01654) 781209 FAX: (01654) 781366 COOKING **6**
off A487, 6m SW of Machynlleth COST £30–£50

Ynyshir is a characterful Georgian house in eleven acres of landscaped grounds next door to a bird sanctuary. The blaze of rhododendrons outside is mirrored inside in owner Rob Reen's colourful pictures, evident throughout the elegant lounge and stylish dining-room. The bold style is reflected in the cooking of Chris Colmer, a Roux accolade-winner who spent some time at Troisgros in Roanne. Juxtapositions are novel but carefully thought through.

For an appetiser, there might be 'smooth, light' parsley soup with an oyster in it. Care in preparation is evident in a first course of steamed cod fillet with expertly made prawn wun-tuns and a red pepper fondue. Central ingredients are more daring than is often encountered in this kind of context – a trio of venison includes fillet, liver and braised heart, accompanied by a parsnip and truffle purée – and saucing is a cut above the country-house norm. At inspection, roast squab came with an unlikely sounding but apposite 'turnip-scented gravy' and a portion of swede and carrot dauphinoise. Hot griottine soufflé, or chocolate charlotte, might be among desserts, while the commendable platter of Welsh cheeses comes with a complimentary glass of port. Service is a model of considerate discretion.

The nearly 200-strong wine list has an exemplary range from Bordeaux and Burgundy, and displays imagination in the New World selection. Prices can be on the high side, with the dozen recommended house wines starting at £15, but lower-priced bins can be found, particularly in the Southern French selection. CELLARMAN'S CHOICE: Henschke Gewurztraminer 1996, Eden Valley, S. Australia, £19.80; Mountains Ridge Vineyards Cabernet Sauvignon 1994, Santa Cruz, California, £29.

CHEF: Chris Colmer PROPRIETORS: Joan and Rob Reen OPEN: all week 12.30 to 1.30, 7 to 8.30 MEALS: Set L £19.50, Set D £29.50 SERVICE: not inc, card slips closed CARDS: Amex, Delta, Diners, MasterCard, Switch, Visa DETAILS: 35 seats. Private parties: 30 main room, 16 private room. Car park. Vegetarian meals. No children under 9. No smoking in dining-room. Music ACCOMMODATION: 8 rooms, all with bath/shower. TV. Phone. B&B £75 to £160. Deposit: 20%. No children under 9. Dogs welcome by arrangement. Afternoon teas. Garden (*The Which? Hotel Guide*)

FISHGUARD Pembrokeshire map 4

▲ *Three Main Street*

3 Main Street, Fishguard SA65 9HG COOKING 4
TEL: (01348) 874275 COST £26–£40

Right at the heart of an old south-west Wales fishing harbour, this restaurant-with-rooms occupies a carefully restored Georgian town house. Marion Evans, co-owner and chef, states that the aim is to make diners feel that a table is theirs for the evening: a refreshing change for those used to the frenetic pace of big-city eating. Locally sourced produce is exploited to maximum effect on the varied menus in a culinary style that is up to date without attempting anything too outrageous. Baked fillet of smoked haddock under a Welsh rarebit crust might start things off, and be followed by roast loin of Welsh lamb with a minted port sauce. Local Black beef is presented as a sauté fillet crusted with Dijon mustard and herbs, while satisfying desserts might take in caramelised poached pear sablé with home-made ice-cream and a calvados sauce. Light lunches offer the likes of pasta cooked with tomato and pesto sauce, and hazelnut meringues with raspberry coulis and cream. The high-flying and cosmopolitan wine list includes a plentiful spread of half-bottles. House French is £9.75.

CHEF: Marion Evans PROPRIETORS: Marion Evans and Inez Ford OPEN: Tue to Sat D only 7 to 9 CLOSED: Tue in winter, Feb MEALS: alc (main courses £10 to £14.50). Light L available SERVICE: not inc CARDS: none DETAILS: 35 seats. Private parties: 22 main room, 12 private room. Vegetarian meals. Children's helpings. No smoking in dining-room. Wheelchair access (not WC). No music ACCOMMODATION: 3 rooms, all with bath/shower. B&B £35 to £60. Children welcome (*The Which? Hotel Guide*)

'One French waitress laid on the accent so thickly we thought she was probably from Westcliffe: "Très bien, you choose ze Mohhrgone, M'shuuh," she purred after my choice of a superior bottle of Beaujolais.' (On eating in Suffolk)

FORDEN Powys map 4

▲ *Edderton Hall* £

Forden SY21 8RZ
TEL: (01938) 580339 and 580410
FAX: (01938) 580452 COOKING **2**
off A490, 4m S of Welshpool COST £17–£32

This bow-fronted Georgian house looks out from its hilltop near Offa's Dyke across rolling countryside and the Severn Valley towards Powys Castle. It is a peaceful place, where Evelyn Hawksley plies her bright style of country cooking to an appreciative audience of reporters. Local materials play their part, including Welshpool ham (served as a starter with roast chicory mousse) and lamb, simply roasted and accompanied by a sauce using Welsh honey and mint from the garden; or it may come with elderflower fritters. Modest ingenuity is applied in the form of chicken smoked over rosemary, or one of many variations on a first-course tart, in which leeks and Shropshire blue cheese rest on a duxelles of leeks, mushrooms and thyme, the better to concentrate flavour. Pâtés and terrines come with home-made pickles and chutneys, breads are 'first-class', and traditional desserts might include gooseberry fool, or a wedge of steamed syrup pudding. Service is laid back. Some good producers and fair prices pepper the slightly uneven wine list, and house French is £8.50.

CHEF: Evelyn Hawksley PROPRIETORS: Evelyn and Warren Hawksley OPEN: all week 1 to 2.30 booking essential, 7.30 to 10 MEALS: Set L £12.95, Set D £10 to £19.95 SERVICE: not inc, card slips closed CARDS: MasterCard, Visa DETAILS: 40 seats. Private parties: 20 main room, 12 and 45 private rooms. Car park. Vegetarian meals. Children's helpings. Wheelchair access (also WC). No music ACCOMMODATION: 8 rooms, all with bath/shower. TV. Phone. B&B £22 to £80. Children welcome. Dogs welcome. Afternoon teas. Garden (*The Which? Hotel Guide*)

HARLECH Gwynedd map 7

▲ *Castle Cottage* £*

Pen Llech, Harlech LL46 2YL COOKING **1**
TEL/FAX: (01766) 780479 COST £19–£38

The décor in this oak-beamed dining-room hard by Harlech Castle is 'smart without being stuffy'. Staff are welcoming, and Glyn Roberts puts together a nightly menu of three courses that can range from eggs Harlech, and Cullen skink, through pork with prunes, or peppered steak, to lemon posset, and blackberry fool. Main courses usually include a vegetarian option (perhaps a strudel, or assorted ravioli), a fish dish (poached hake with a grain mustard beurre blanc, or locally caught sea bass) as well as pork with black-bean sauce, roast rack of lamb, or grilled duck breast with spiced plum sauce. 'Helpings are ample' and everything is nicely presented 'without being prissy'. The wine list contains 'a number of off-beat items: we were pleased with both a Welsh white and Uruguayan red'. House recommendations start at £9.50.

CHEF: Glyn Roberts PROPRIETORS: Jacqueline and Glyn Roberts OPEN: Sun L 12.30 to 2, all week D 7 to 9.30 (8.30 Mon to Fri in winter) CLOSED: 3 weeks Feb MEALS: Set L £12.50, Set D £17.95 (2 courses) to £19.95. BYO £5 SERVICE: not inc, card slips closed CARDS: Amex, Delta, MasterCard, Switch, Visa DETAILS: 45 seats. Private parties: 45 main room. Vegetarian meals. Children's helpings. No smoking in dining-room. Wheelchair access (not WC). Music ACCOMMODATION: 6 rooms, 4 with bath/shower. B&B £25 to £54. Deposit: £10. Children welcome. Baby facilities. Dogs welcome in bedrooms only (*The Which? Hotel Guide*)

HAY-ON-WYE Powys map 4

Nino's £ NEW ENTRY

The Pavement, Hay-on-Wye HR3 5BU COOKING **3**
TEL: (01497) 821932 FAX: (01497) 820706 COST £18–£41

The border town of Hay-on-Wye near the Black Mountains is famous for its book shops and annual literary festival, during which Nino's must be at its busiest. White walls and black furniture contribute to the clean, modern feel, and Rod Lewis applies an upbeat approach to native ideas and materials, making lively use of sharp flavours with pimento oil, balsamic dressing, coriander, chilli, and perhaps a port and plum chutney. A board of seafood specials balances the menu's meaty emphasis, and between them they might produce cawl (a traditional Welsh lamb broth), deep-fried Gower cockles with salsa and soured cream, or chargrilled rump of Herefordshire beef with Mediterranean vegetables and red pesto.

'Generally the food is tasty,' remarked an inspector whose meal included a rich ragoût of seafood, marinated chargrilled chicken, and two good desserts: lemon tart and cappuccino chocolate mousse. Service is skilled and meals are well paced. A small wine bar below offers a range of snacks and light meals for around £5. A list of some twenty wines includes eight by the glass or carafe, and house wines start at £8.25 a bottle.

CHEF: Rod Lewis PROPRIETORS: Mr and Mrs C.A. Letts OPEN: Wed to Sun 12 to 2, 7 to 9.30 (10 Sat) CLOSED: 25 and 26 Dec MEALS: alc D (main courses £8.50 to £14). Set L £8 (2 courses). Snack L and D menu available. BYO £5 SERVICE: not inc, card slips closed CARDS: Delta, MasterCard, Switch, Visa DETAILS: 26 seats. 9 seats outside. Private parties: 26 main room. Vegetarian meals. Children's helpings. Music

LLANARMON DYFFRYN CEIRIOG Wrexham map 7

▲ *West Arms* NEW ENTRY

Llanarmon Dyffryn Ceiriog LL20 7LD
TEL: (01691) 600665 FAX: (01691) 600622
off A5 Llangollen to Oswestry road at Chirk, then follow B4500 for 11m COOKING **2**
COST £21–£38

Halfway between Llangollen and Llanrhaeadr, in rolling Welsh-English border country, lies this 400-year-old inn, and the dark, hefty oak beams, slate-flagged floors and cavernous inglenook fireplaces look as if they have been there from the start. Thanks to sympathetic refurbishment, old and new coexist happily, and the place has been confidently run by Mavis Price for nearly a decade. Grant

Williams arrived in 1996 and has made an impression with his varied menus and straight-talking flavours.

Behind the sometimes florid descriptions are some modern dishes in typically British vein: steamed lemon sole with pickled samphire, rich-flavoured loin of lamb with onion chutney, or chargrilled fillet of beef with horseradish dumplings. The food remains commendably straightforward, and there has been praise for meat and fruit combinations such as pink, pan-fried pigeon breast with yellow plum sauce, and seared chicken breast with mango purée. A generous plate of vegetables prompted the view that 'portions are made for the Welsh side of the hills'. Homely desserts might include rhubarb crumble, or apricot muffin with a fruit compote, while cheeses are 'in A1 condition'. House wine is £8.75.

CHEF: Grant Williams PROPRIETOR: Mavis Price OPEN: Sun L 12.30 to 2, all week D 7.30 to 9.30 CLOSED: 25 Dec MEALS: Set L £14, Set D £24. Bar L available SERVICE: not inc CARDS: Delta, MasterCard, Switch, Visa DETAILS: 28 seats. 20 seats outside. Private parties: 28 main room, 60 private room. Car park. Vegetarian meals. Children's helpings. No smoking in dining-room. Wheelchair access (also WC). No music ACCOMMODATION: 12 rooms, all with bath/shower. TV. Phone. B&B £50 to £90. Deposit: £25. Rooms for disabled. Children welcome. Baby facilities. Dogs welcome. Afternoon teas. Garden (*The Which? Hotel Guide*)

LLANBERIS Gwynedd map 7

Y Bistro £✗

43–45 High Street, Llanberis LL55 4EU
TEL/FAX: (01286) 871278 COOKING 2
off A4086, at foot of Snowdon COST £31–£41

If you've just alighted from the Snowdon Mountain Railway, the Robertses' unshowy, warmly run bistro is probably the best place to get your bearings: it's only half a mile away. The interior may at first look somewhat unpromising, but the friendliness and the steady, unpretentious cooking are lures enough. Lamb ribs marinated in honey, rosemary and mint make a 'tender and delicious' starter, while main-course turkey escalope has come breadcrumbed, with a tomato sauce and roasted aubergine. Seafood may turn up as prawns and cockles bound in a crêpe with samphire, or as 'very good' salmon and haddock pâté wrapped in smoked salmon. Pork tenderloin, meanwhile, is divertingly cooked with grapes in Welsh white wine. Apple and blackberry pie has been among the more successful puddings. A good number of regions with a handful of wines from each are crammed on to the wine list, and prices are mostly reasonable. House wines are £8.50.

CHEFS: Nerys Roberts and Sion Llwyd Elis PROPRIETORS: Danny and Nerys Roberts OPEN: Mon to Sat and bank hol Sun D only 7.30 to 9.45 CLOSED: occasional days in winter MEALS: Set D £20 (2 courses) to £26.50 SERVICE: not inc, card slips closed CARDS: Delta, MasterCard, Switch, Visa DETAILS: 56 seats. Private parties: 44 main room, 8 and 20 private rooms. Vegetarian meals. Children welcome. No smoking in dining-room. Wheelchair access (not WC). Music

LLANDDEINIOLEN Gwynedd map 7

▲ *Ty'n Rhos*

Seion, Llanddeiniolen LL55 3AE
TEL: (01248) 670489 FAX: (01248) 670079
off B4366, 5m NE of Caernarfon on road signposted Seion

COOKING **6**
COST £31–£41

Calling itself 'a small hotel based on a farm', Ty'n Rhos looks across the Menai Strait to Anglesey, with Snowdonia as a backdrop. Despite the agricultural link, it is not knee-deep in muck, rather the opposite. The slate-roofed stone and whitewash building has carpets 'the shade of the hills', and strikes a good balance between comfort and formality. Evenings begin on sofas in the large lounge, 'where you munch offerings of pickled herring on toast, and mini pizza' while studying the four-course dinner menu whose price is determined by the main course.

The kitchen is a supporter of native ideas and local produce, and a fan of modern treatments, combining Welsh griddlecake and rosemary muffin with tomato and anchovy salsa, for example, or making a salmon and chive sausage to serve with creamed leeks and a lemon and gherkin butter sauce. Given the amount of industry, it is perhaps unsurprising that the food struck one reporter as 'elaborate', but good judgement is the order of the day, with a relatively light accompaniment of creamed fennel and a Pernod sauce for sea bass, and a weightier port and chicken pâté, plus black pudding flavoured potatoes, for fillet of beef. Welsh rarebit or a single wedge of the day's cheese follows dessert – of rhubarb cobbler, perhaps, or iced hazelnut parfait – and pleasant, relaxed service keeps everything on song. Wines are varied and sympathetically priced, the vast majority under £20, including six house wines at £8.50.

CHEFS: Carys Davies, Lynda Kettle and Ian Cashen PROPRIETORS: Nigel and Lynda Kettle OPEN: Sun L 12 to 1.45, Tue to Sat D 7 to 8.30 CLOSED: 23 to 30 Dec, 1 week Jan MEALS: Set L £14.95, Set D £23.50 to £26.50. BYO £5 SERVICE: not inc, card slips closed CARDS: Amex, Delta, MasterCard, Switch, Visa DETAILS: 35 seats. Private parties: 30 main room, 18 private room. Car park. Vegetarian meals. No children under 8. No smoking in dining-room. Wheelchair access (not WC). No music ACCOMMODATION: 14 rooms, all with bath/shower. TV. Phone. B&B £45 to £85. Deposit: £30. Rooms for disabled. No children under 8. Garden (*The Which? Hotel Guide*)

LLANDEGLA Denbighshire map 7

▲ *Bodidris Hall*

Llandegla LL11 3AL
TEL: (01978) 790434 FAX: (01978) 790335
on A5104 9m SE of Ruthin

COOKING **3**
COST £23–£46

The 'gem of a building', dating from the Crusades but rebuilt in Tudor times, plays on the historical theme with its heavy beams, huge open fireplace, and a knight in armour guarding the dining-room. Kevin Steel's food, though, is quite modern, and he spares no expense or effort. Sorbets and appetisers extend what is a basic three-course structure into four at lunch and six at dinner, and good ingredients form the foundation. Fish, for example, has impressed – in a scallop and monkfish salad, and a well-timed main course of seared tuna – although accompaniments have contributed to the impression of a kitchen that gives artistry an inflated priority. Caramelised calf's liver layered between thyme-flavoured rösti and served with a red wine sauce sounds good, though in fact it is a starter, while desserts (preceded by a dessert appetiser in the evening) go in for decorative spun sugar at the drop of a hat: on a pear poached in red wine, and on a 'rich and nutty' nougat pancake. Service may not be chatty, but it is well paced and assured, and a roving list of around 70 wines keeps prices reasonable. House wines start at £10.25.

CHEF: Kevin Steel PROPRIETOR: W.J. Farden OPEN: all week 12 to 2, 7 to 9.30 MEALS: Set L £16, Set D £27.50 SERVICE: not inc, card slips closed CARDS: Amex, Delta, Diners, MasterCard, Switch, Visa DETAILS: 50 seats. Private parties: 50 main room, 26 private room. Car park. Children's helpings. Jacket and tie. No smoking in dining-room. Music ACCOMMODATION: 9 rooms, all with bath/shower. TV. Phone. B&B £55 to £130. Deposit: £25. Children welcome. Baby facilities. Dogs welcome. Afternoon teas. Garden. Fishing

LLANDEILO Carmarthenshire map 4

▲ *Cawdor Arms Hotel*

NEW ENTRY

Rhosmaen Street, Llandeilo SA19 6EN COOKING 2

TEL: (01558) 823500 FAX: (01558) 822399 COST £23–£43

This Georgian coaching inn has been welcoming visitors for over 200 years, Sarah Siddons, Howard Hughes and Kenneth Clarke among them. It is a comfortable and sophisticated environment for the Welsh-infused but broadly based menu, which changes daily. Raw materials are good and if the cooking lacks sparkle, it is certainly proficient. A smooth duck terrine with rhubarb compote was 'competent and well-balanced' at inspection, and sauté calf's liver, charred on the outside, soft and pink inside and served with crisp bacon, has been praised by more than one reporter. Dessert might be a 'delicate and light' tropical fruit mousse with pear water ice and an intense raspberry coulis, or banana bread-and-butter pudding with a 'very sweet' crème anglaise. Service is 'prompt and fairly formal'. The short, moderately priced wine list is mostly French. House wine is £9.90.

CHEF: Rodney Peterson PROPRIETOR: Marc Williams OPEN: all week L 12 to 2, Mon to Sat D 7 to 9 CLOSED: first week Jan MEALS: alc (main courses £12.50 to £16.50). Set L Mon to Sat £8.50 (1 course) to £13.50, Set L Sun £15.50 SERVICE: not inc, card slips closed CARDS: Delta, MasterCard, Switch, Visa DETAILS: 70 seats. Private parties: 120 main room, 50 private room. Car park. Vegetarian meals. Children's helpings. No smoking in dining-room. Wheelchair access (also women's WC). Music ACCOMMODATION: 16 rooms, all with bath/shower. TV. Phone. B&B £55 to £65. Deposit: £25. Rooms for disabled. Children welcome. Baby facilities. Dogs welcome. Afternoon teas (*The Which? Hotel Guide*)

'In the centre of the plate was a lemon beautifully wrapped in muslin. The snag was that it was a second-hand lemon which had been squeezed dry by a previous customer and thus was juiceless.' (On eating in Essex)

LLANDEWI SKIRRID Monmouthshire map 4

Walnut Tree Inn

Llandewi Skirrid NP7 8AW
TEL: (01873) 852797 COOKING **8**
on B4521, 3m NE of Abergavenny COST £28–£61

'All the praise which has been lavished on Franco Taruschio is amazingly insufficient,' ran one tribute. He pre-dates the era of superchefs by some years, which may partly explain his modesty and lack of regard for the customary frills associated with high-scoring restaurants: although the outside always looks freshly painted, nobody comes here for the décor. The food's impact begins with the colours and smells as it arrives. Some diners even 'mmmm' enviously when dishes are presented at neighbouring tables. Quite by chance, as it happens, our inspector's main course arrived at the wrong table, but was then nonchalantly passed across a few minutes later when the mistake was discovered.

Pappardelle with just-roasted scallops and bright green pesto 'typifies the Walnut Tree at its Italian best', while a main course carré of lamb (with globe artichoke, peas and young broad beans) demonstrates not just 'impeccable raw materials and timing' but also the 'brilliant, gutsy clearness of accompanying flavours'. The all-important wild mushroom input has included pink roast breast of pigeon with white cabbage and chanterelles, and sea bass with porcini, but even a humble smoked haddock fish-cake with lobster bisque has been 'a revelation'. Food like this is capable of reconciling opposites: it is 'at the same time honest and complex, local and exotic, without pretension but with real class'.

Although first and main courses have evolved over the years, puddings remain much as they were a couple of decades ago. Ann Taruschio's mother, 'who must be in her 80s', knocks up a choice of twenty or more, from dolce Torinese to ricotta ice-cream with chocolate sauce, to a rich torte with three liqueurs and lots of amaretti biscuits. There are parts of the operation that some people don't like – crowds, tiny tables, smoking, the outside toilet and chaotic service – but, on the other hand, portions are generous, value for money can be 'astounding', and provision of the same food in both bistro and dining-room is enormously welcome. It all adds up to a highly individual restaurant that has captivated most reporters for well over 30 years.

The wine list opens with an impressive line-up of fine Italians, the range of styles providing plenty of choice to match the daily-changing menu, and the accompanying notes mean it is a good read as well as user-friendly. Francophiles and New World enthusiasts are also well served. Litres of house Italian are £12.

CHEF: Franco Taruschio PROPRIETORS: Franco and Ann Taruschio OPEN: Tue to Sat 12 to 3, 7 to 10.30 CLOSED: 5 days Christmas, 2 weeks Feb MEALS: alc (main courses £10 to £16) SERVICE: not inc CARDS: none DETAILS: 95 seats. 30 seats outside. Private parties: 46 main room. Car park. Vegetarian meals. Children's helpings. Wheelchair access (also WC). No music. Air-conditioned

All entries, including Round-ups, are fully indexed at the back of the Guide.

LLANDRILLO Denbighshire map 7

▲ *Tyddyn Llan*

Llandrillo LL21 0ST
TEL: (01490) 440264 FAX: (01490) 440414 COOKING 6
on B4401, 4½miles S of Corwen COST £24–£47

Grey stones might give the house a rustic appearance from outside, but all is ship-shape and comfortable within. A few classically inclined gestures, with cherubs here, antiques and china there, contribute to a sense of well manicured elegance. The Kindreds close for a couple of weeks every winter to redecorate, and this year the drive has been resurfaced and the car park attended to as well. A year on, Jason Hornbuckle continues to produce cosmopolitan food in a rural setting, using a seasonal menu for continuity, and a daily-changing one for spur-of-the-moment flexibility.

Seasonal dishes reflect the mood as much as materials – Brecon venison with wild mushroom duxelles and potted cabbage in autumn, or roast saddle of rabbit and braised leg in spring – and the frisson of excitement that this modern European style elicits from reporters would be just as notable in a city brasserie as beside the Dee. Boudin blanc with a ragoût of broad beans, or warm salt-cod sausage with seafood vinaigrette, gives an idea of the ambition: to package materials in a come-hither format. Likewise, mackerel and scallop kebab might be served with a spicy tomato relish, while the normally heavyweight meats are given a simple but effective lift: grilled rib eye of Welsh Black beef comes with parsley and potato gnocchi and caper sauce, and Welsh lamb might appear as a plate of rack, liver and kidney.

Welsh rarebit with anchovy, and Welsh cheeses, are regular savoury alternatives to desserts such as coconut-flavoured fried rice pudding, or spiced poached pear sandwiched between sablé biscuits and served with cassis mousse. The wine list favours the Old World but includes some fruity bins from the New. House wines start at £12.50.

CHEF: Jason Hornbuckle PROPRIETORS: Peter and Bridget Kindred CLOSED: 2 weeks Jan OPEN: Tue to Sun L 12.30 to 2, all week D 7 to 9.30 MEALS: Set L Tue to Sat £13 (2 courses) to £15, Set L Sun £15.50, Set D £25 to £27 SERVICE: not inc, card slips closed CARDS: Amex, Delta, Diners, MasterCard, Switch, Visa DETAILS: 60 seats, 16 seats outside. Private parties: 50 main room, 50 private room. Car park. Vegetarian meals. Children's helpings. No smoking in dining-room. Wheelchair access (also WC). Music ACCOMMODATION: 10 rooms, all with bath/shower. TV. Phone. B&B £64 to £110. Deposit: £25. Children welcome; early supper for under-8s. Baby facilities. Dogs welcome in bedrooms only. Afternoon teas. Garden. Fishing (*The Which? Hotel Guide*)

LLANDUDNO Conwy map 7

▲ *Bodysgallen Hall*

Llandudno LL30 1RS
TEL: (01492) 584466 FAX: (01492) 582519 COOKING 4
off A470, 2m SE of Llandudno COST £22–£50

The seventeenth-century house makes the most of its setting in 200 acres of gardens and parkland, with views of Conwy Castle and Snowdonia. Inside are dark wooden panels, old paintings and creaky stairs. 'If atmosphere was a commodity that could be bottled and marketed, Bodysgallen's would be an instant bestseller,' reckoned one visitor. Lunch and dinner menus normally offer around four or five choices per course, with a decent showing of fish, perhaps including skate wing with deep-fried vegetables, or pan-fried langoustines served with an onion and smoked bacon tart. Ideas are modern but generally familiar, in the vein of cod in a herb crust, while risotto and couscous appear among main-course accompaniments.

Although one reporter felt that 'the menu lacks variety for anyone staying longer than two nights', the repertoire does touch base with game (terrine of venison and pigeon), Welsh veal (with a honey and mead sauce), and vegetarian options such as wild mushroom pithiviers or laverbread noodles. Welsh rarebit is an understandable savoury alternative to desserts of pear and apple strudel with custard, or glazed lemon tart. 'Amateurish' service has some catching up to do in its role as an intermediary between customer and kitchen, and wine service does not seem to do justice to the list, although the wines themselves offer a good range of styles and flavours from around the world. A reasonable number of bottles come in under £15, but choice improves above this limit. House French is £11.75. CELLARMAN'S CHOICE: Bourgogne Chardonnay, Côtes d'Auxerre 1994, J. Felix, £16.50; Bordeaux Supérieur, Ch. Trocard 1993, £16.50.

CHEF: Mike Penny PROPRIETOR: Historic House Hotels OPEN: all week 12.30 to 1.45, 7.30 to 9.30 MEALS: Set L £12.50 (2 courses) to £13.50, Set D £27.50 (2 courses) to £36. BYO £5 SERVICE: net prices, card slips closed CARDS: Amex, Delta, MasterCard, Switch, Visa DETAILS: 60 seats. Private parties: 40 main room, 40 private room. Car park. Vegetarian meals. No children under 8. Jacket and tie. No smoking in dining-room. Wheelchair access (also WC). No music. Air-conditioned ACCOMMODATION: 35 rooms, all with bath/shower. TV. Phone. Room only £95 to £180. Rooms for disabled. No children under 8. Dogs welcome. Afternoon teas. Garden. Swimming-pool (*The Which? Hotel Guide*)

▲ *Martin's*

11 Mostyn Avenue, Craig-y-Don,
Llandudno LL30 1YS — COOKING 3
TEL: (01492) 870070 FAX: (01492) 876661 — COST £19–£47

This may not be the prettiest dining-room in Wales, with its stolid wheel-back chairs and busy wallpaper, but reports concur that it is definitely worth sticking around for Martin James's cooking. The ideas may be fairly simple, but execution is assured and the ingredients beyond reproach. Cauliflower soup with smoked ham and herb croûtons is 'rich, tasty and warming', and a sorbet sprinkled with frozen port crystals served with Ogen melon is a neat idea too. Main courses from the 'Bill of Fare' include baked salmon topped with prawn mousse on a white wine sauce, and loin of Welsh lamb stuffed with apricots. Game cookery is of a high order, as was found by the recipient of a saddle of carefully carved and succulent hare in a thickly reduced *jus* with bilberries. Custards and creams lend old-fashioned richness to the puddings, as do libations from the drinks cabinet, whether it be Cointreau in mandarin parfait or Tia Maria and Grand Marnier in two-tone chocolate mousse. Excellent freshly baked breads come in for praise. Service was 'slow' for one, 'charming' for another, and house Vin de Pays d'Oc is £8.50.

CHEF/PROPRIETOR: Martin James OPEN: Sun L 12 to 2, Tue to Sat D 5 to 9.30 CLOSED: first 2 weeks Jan MEALS: alc (main courses £10 to £15). Set L Sun £12.95, Set D pre-theatre 5 to 7 (reservations only) from £16.50. BYO £4 SERVICE: not inc, card slips closed CARDS: Amex, Delta, MasterCard, Switch, Visa DETAILS: 30 seats. 10 seats outside. Private parties: 30 main room. Vegetarian meals. No children under 12. No smoking in dining-room. Wheelchair access (not WC). Music ACCOMMODATION: 1 room, with bath/shower. TV. B&B £28 to £45. Deposit: £20

Richard's

7 Church Walks, Llandudno LL30 2HD — COOKING 2
TEL: (01492) 877924 and 875315 — COST £24–£39

Richard Hendey's cooking and warm welcome have made him many regular first-name customers and friends in this basement bistro a few hundred yards from the pier. They return for sea-fresh blackboard fish specials as well as the wide ranging printed menus. Roasted wing of skate with a crab sauce, and a chargrilled fillet of grey mullet with a white wine sauce were enjoyed by an inspector, and meat-eaters might opt for roast Welsh lamb, accompanied by its sauté kidneys, in a red wine and grain mustard gravy. Lemon tart with lemon ice-cream looks just about the lightest way to end things; otherwise plunge into chocolate truffle and praline terrine, or toffee apple cheesecake with caramel sauce. From time to time, Mr Hendey pops out to make sure all are enjoying themselves. An inspiringly international wine selection is arranged by price, the majority below £20. House wines start at £7.95.

CHEFS: Richard Hendey, Mark Roberts and John Crawford PROPRIETOR: Richard Hendey OPEN: all week D only 6 to 10 (pre- and post-theatre D by arrangement) MEALS: alc (main courses £11 to £13) SERVICE: net prices, card slips closed CARDS: Amex, Delta, MasterCard, Switch, Visa DETAILS: 50 seats. Private parties: 28 main room, 28 private room. Vegetarian meals. Children's helpings. Music

▲ *St Tudno Hotel* 🍷 *

Promenade, Llandudno LL30 2LP — COOKING 2
TEL: (01492) 874411 FAX: (01492) 860407 — COST £23–£58

The Liddell family, whose daughter Alice was the real-life model for the one who fell down the rabbit hole, stayed here on an Easter break in 1861, thus guaranteeing St Tudno's at least a footnote in history. Modern-day visitors to the terraced pink-faced hotel on the prom near the pier are greeted by traditional seaside décor, 'a happy band of smiling faces', and a feeling that 'brownie points for effort' are deserved on all fronts, not least for seafood. Seared smoked Conwy salmon, sea bass, or Great Orme lobster with saffron risotto might be among the offerings.

Alcohol lends zip to the saucing: vermouth flavoured for a spinach 'tortellino' of whizzed-up prawns and monkfish, and a strong, sweet madeira version for lamb cutlets. The penchant for garnishing reaches its height in desserts such as iced passion-fruit parfait; alternatively try the Welsh farmhouse cheeses. A high-quality, extensive selection of appealing bottles with, on the whole, fair prices begins with a quartet of French house wines at £9.50.

CELLARMAN'S CHOICE: Ca' del Solo Malvasia Bianca 1994, Bonny Doon, California, £17.50; Hamilton Russell Pinot Noir 1994, Walker Bay, South Africa, £22.50.

CHEFS: David Harding and Ian Watson PROPRIETORS: Martin and Janette Bland OPEN: all week 12.30 to 1.45, 7 to 9.30 (9 Sun) MEALS: Set L £16.50, Set D £22 (2 courses) to £29.50 SERVICE: not inc CARDS: Amex, Delta, Diners, MasterCard, Switch, Visa DETAILS: 55 seats. Private parties: 30 main room. Car park. Vegetarian meals. Children's helpings. No very young children at D. No smoking in dining-room. Wheelchair access (not WC). Music. Air-conditioned ACCOMMODATION: 20 rooms, all with bath/shower. TV. Phone. B&B £70 to £160. Deposit: £80. Children welcome. Baby facilities. Dogs by arrangement. Afternoon teas. Garden. Swimming-pool (*The Which? Hotel Guide*)

LLANFIHANGEL NANT MELAN Powys map 4

▲ *Red Lion Inn* ✻ [£]

Llanfihangel nant Melan, nr New Radnor LD8 2TN
TEL: (01544) 350220
on A44 Rhayader to Kington road, 3m W of New Radnor

COOKING 4
COST £13–£29

Anyone hurtling along the A44 may be aware of the Red Lion only as a roadside pub, but those who drop in for a bite find it to be rather more exalted. Amid the cosy old furniture and the plink of pool balls, Gareth Johns makes excellent use of British cheeses, meat from neighbourhood farms and locally grown vegetables. A thick slab of pheasant terrine, the marbled meat made vivid with pistachios, 'could have been from the best modern chef's repertoire'. Seared tuna is timed to the second, its strength of flavour enhanced by the freshness of a tomato and coriander salsa, while peppered duck – a signature dish – is roasted crisp, well rested and carved into tender slices accompanied by a subtly creamy sauce. A dark and white chocolate torte manages to be admirably light for all its richness, while bread-and-butter pudding is made with croissants. Gareth Johns is a talented chef who is clearly capable of rising well above the mundane demands of ordinary pub grub. To cap it all, prices seem reasonable to a fault, a policy that extends also to the modest wine list, where £4.95 is the starting point.

CHEF: Gareth Johns PROPRIETORS: Keith, Liz and Gareth Johns OPEN: all week 12 to 2, 6.45 to 9 (9.30 Sat) CLOSED: Tue Nov to May, 1 week mid-Nov, D 25 Dec, 26 Dec, 1 week Feb MEALS: alc (main courses £4.50 to £11) SERVICE: not inc, card slips closed CARDS: Delta, MasterCard, Visa DETAILS: 60 seats. 16 seats outside. Private parties: 20 main room. Car park. Vegetarian meals. Children's helpings. No smoking in 1 dining-room. No music ACCOMMODATION: 3 rooms, all with bath/shower. B&B £18 to £35. Children welcome. Baby facilities. Dogs welcome. Garden

[£] *means that it is possible to have a two-course lunch, including a glass of house wine, coffee and service, for £12 or less per person, at all lunch sessions, and for £25 or less for three courses at all times.*

LLANGAMMARCH WELLS **Powys** map 4

▲ *The Lake Country House*

Llangammarch Wells LD4 4BS
TEL: (01591) 620202 and 620474
FAX: (01591) 620457 NEW CHEF
off B483 at Garth, 6m W of Builth Wells COST £36–£43

As we go to press, Richard Arnold leaves for The Old Vicarage (see entry, Worfield, England) and Jeremy Medley – last listed in the *Guide* three years ago – comes to replace him. We had no time for feedback, but the inheritance is impressive: a spacious, well-appointed house standing in 50 acres, with a reputation for civilised living, a kitchen that uses organic produce, and a wine list that features 80 clarets ranging from plain Bordeaux to first growths. Selections from other regions, particularly Spain and Australia, have been astutely chosen, the opening page of house recommendations is well worth a look, and house French is £9.75.

CHEF: Jeremy Medley PROPRIETOR: Mr and Mrs J.P. Mifsud OPEN: all week 12.30 to 1.45, 7.30 to 9 MEALS: Set L £15.50, Set D £27.50 SERVICE: not inc CARDS: Amex, Delta, Diners, MasterCard, Switch, Visa DETAILS: 40 seats. Private parties: 85 main room. Car park. No children under 7 at D. Jacket and tie. No smoking in dining-room. Wheelchair access (also WC). No music ACCOMMODATION: 19 rooms, all with bath/shower. TV. Phone. B&B £75 to £180. Deposit: £40. Rooms for disabled. Children welcome. Baby facilities. Dogs welcome. Afternoon teas. Garden. Fishing (*The Which? Hotel Guide*)

LLANSANFFRAID GLAN CONWY **Conwy** map 7

▲ *Old Rectory*

Llanrwst Road, Llansanffraid Glan Conwy,
nr Conwy LL28 5LF
TEL: (01492) 580611 FAX: (01492) 584555 COOKING 6
on A470, ½m S of junction with A55 COST £37–£50

The Vaughans opened up their Regency home high on a hill facing Conwy Castle back in 1984, with self-taught Wendy doing the cooking and Michael front-of-house, and so the routine has continued. The garden is a picture, and this 'cultured Welsh household' boasts a panelled sitting-room with comfortable sofas, and 'some really interesting books' for those who stay. Visitors are in for a 'relaxed and genteel evening'. There is no choice until after the main course, but any special requirements are dealt with when booking, and everybody sits down at 8pm.

The foundation is as good as it is simple: main courses of duck, guinea-fowl, fillet of Welsh Black beef, or roast rack of mountain lamb, served pink where appropriate. At one typical spring dinner the lamb came in a mint and green peppercorn crust, with a tian of aubergine and a light, glossy brown gravy, the whole thing scoring high on composition, presentation and taste. Meals usually begin with fish, perhaps a roulade of salmon and brill with saffron risotto and chive sauce, or a platter of salmon parcels – poached, mousse and caviare – sharpened with a balsamic dressing.

The third course, for those who take it, might be a toss-up between Celtic cheeses, grilled Welsh goats' cheese, green salad or sorbet, and finally comes a choice of two puddings: raspberry tart, perhaps, or a rich-sounding assembly of coffee mousse, cream, sponge fingers dipped in rum, and chocolate 'coffee beans'. Fans of the Old World will be gladdened by the impressive array of fine French wines backed-up by some good bins from Spain and Italy. New World lovers may find this section a bit on the small side but the producers are of good repute. Prices are reasonable and half-bottles plentiful. CELLARMAN'S CHOICE: Rully 1993, Dom. Michel Briday, £19.90. Gran Sangre de Toro 1992, Torres, Penedès, £14.90.

CHEF: Wendy Vaughan PROPRIETORS: Michael and Wendy Vaughan OPEN: all week D only 7.30 for 8 (1 sitting) CLOSED: Dec and Jan MEALS: Set D £25 to £29.50 SERVICE: not inc, card slips closed CARDS: Amex, Delta, Diners, MasterCard, Switch, Visa DETAILS: 16 seats. Private parties: 12 main room. Car park. Children's helpings. No children under 5. No smoking in dining-room. No music ACCOMMODATION: 6 rooms, all with bath/shower. TV. Phone. D,B&B £109 to £199. Deposit: 20%. No children under 5. Dogs welcome. Garden (*The Which? Hotel Guide*)

LLANWDDYN Powys map 7

▲ *Lake Vyrnwy Hotel*

Lake Vyrnwy, Llanwddyn SY10 0LY
TEL: (01691) 870692 FAX: (01691) 870259 COOKING **2**
on B4393, at SE end of Lake Vyrnwy COST £23–£40

'A most convivial place to retire to after a day in the country,' reckoned one visitor to this late-nineteenth-century huntin', shootin' and fishin' lodge, where the combination of outdoor pursuits and indoor comfort is still a beguiling one. Views across the reservoir are suitably impressive, rooms are spacious, and the whole place feels warm and inviting. Dinner is the main meal – three courses with generous choice – and the menu goes into some detail about the origin of materials, cuts, cooking techniques and presentation, accurately conveying the impression that the kitchen is a busy one.

It makes sausages: of lamb and rosemary with apple, for example, to be served on creamed potato with a rich onion gravy. And that is just for starters. The main business has included Welsh Black beef, grilled salmon glazed with Welsh rarebit, and non-meat options such as aubergine moussaka, while desserts run from apple crumble tartlet with calvados mousseline and fudge sauce, to bread-and-butter pudding. An orthodox but well-spread wine list begins with house French at £9.85.

CHEF: Andrew Wood PROPRIETOR: Market Glen Ltd OPEN: all week 12.30 to 1.45, 7.30 to 9.15 MEALS: Set L £15.95, Set D £25.50. BYO £5.50 SERVICE: not inc, card slips closed CARDS: Amex, Diners, MasterCard, Switch, Visa DETAILS: 70 seats. Private parties: 120 main room, 20 and 40 private rooms. Car park. Vegetarian meals. Children's helpings. No smoking in dining-room. Wheelchair access (not WC). No music ACCOMMODATION: 35 rooms, all with bath/shower. TV. Phone. B&B £68 to £150. Children welcome. Baby facilities. Dogs welcome. Afternoon teas. Garden. Fishing (*The Which? Hotel Guide*)

LLANWRTYD WELLS **Powys** map 4

▲ *Carlton House*

Dolecoed Road, Llanwrtyd Wells LD5 4RA — COOKING **6**
TEL: (01591) 610248 FAX: (01591) 610242 — COST £29–£45

The style of this Edwardian house, filled with homely collectables from books to furniture, is 'comfortable' rather than luxurious, and everything is done 'with great taste'. The four-course no-choice format is welcomed by reporters, most of whom stay a few nights, and the difference between the normal and 'epicurean' options appears to be marginal: salmon instead of cod for the fish course, that sort of thing. The centrepiece may be unsurprising – roast Welsh lamb, pan-fried breast of chicken, peppered fillet of beef – but the treatment is invariably interesting. That chicken, for example, might come with lime, lemon grass, ginger, coriander and coconut cream, while watercress soup has been served with a Shropshire Blue crisp. These are soundly based ideas, no more exotic than smoked haddock with horseradish cream, perhaps, but they are distinguished by a sense of balance and by good ingredients.

The sourcing of raw materials is a passion, and much of the energy is directed locally, which ensures seasonality. For instance, Mary Ann Gilchrist has set up an enterprising arrangement with the local school which, unlike Carlton House, has a garden. She funds the purchase of seeds, which the children grow, and then buys a certain amount of the produce, which helps the school's finances. As a Private Finance Initiative it may be modest, but it does achieve the chef's aim: vegetables are grown organically, and are 'harvested, delivered and cooked on the same day'. No wonder lunch is not served, given all this activity, there probably isn't time. Another passion is hot sticky puddings – steamed syrup sponge with vanilla-flavoured custard – which take their turn with syllabub, chilled soufflé, or pavlova. Alan Gilchrist's wine service has been praised as meticulous. The wine list has been expanded to over 60 bottles, 27 of them new, including whites from Canada and New Zealand and reds from California. Prices remain very reasonable, and there is a good choice of half-bottles. Five house wines start at £9.95.

CHEF: Mary Ann Gilchrist PROPRIETORS: Alan and Mary Ann Gilchrist OPEN: Mon to Sat D only 7 to 8.30 CLOSED: Christmas MEALS: Set D £19.50 to £27.50 SERVICE: not inc, card slips closed CARDS: MasterCard, Visa DETAILS: 14 seats. Private parties: 12 main room. No children under 9. No smoking in dining-room. No music ACCOMMODATION: 7 rooms, all with bath/shower. TV. B&B £30 to £70. Deposit: £15. No children under 9. Dogs welcome in bedrooms only (*The Which? Hotel Guide*)

LLYSWEN **Powys** map 4

▲ *Griffin Inn* £

NEW ENTRY

Llyswen LD3 0UR — COOKING **1**
TEL: (01874) 754241 FAX: (01874) 754592 — COST £21–£44

Standing by the River Wye, the fifteenth-century whitewashed inn has practically disappeared behind its ivy cladding. Four generations of Stocktons are now involved in what is by most accounts an efficiently run food pub, although there may be delays at busy times. In the evening the same menu is served throughout, so either book a table in the dining-room, or squeeze in the bar where you can. The monthly-changing *carte* mostly keeps to the likes of ploughman's ('massive'), light chicken liver pâté ('full-flavoured and direct') and 'very good' fish pie. Chargrilling, meanwhile, is used to good effect on Welsh salmon with a basil and fine breadcrumb crust. Dessert might be alcoholic lemon crunch or an enjoyable if unorthodox strawberry meringue crème brûlée. Wines from all over are arranged partly by style, partly by whether they're Old World or New. House wine starts at £8.75.

CHEF: Richard Stockton PROPRIETORS: the Stockton family OPEN: Sun L 12 to 2, Mon to Sat D 7 to 9 CLOSED: 25 and 26 Dec MEALS: alc D (main courses £9 to £15). Set L Sun £14. Bar meals available Mon to Sat L SERVICE: not inc, card slips closed CARDS: Amex, Delta, Diners, MasterCard, Switch, Visa DETAILS: 70 seats. 16 seats outside. Private parties: 40 main room, 14 private room. Car park. Vegetarian meals. Children's helpings. No smoking in dining-room. Wheelchair access (not WC). Music ACCOMMODATION: 7 rooms, all with bath/shower. TV. Phone. B&B £40 to £80. Deposit: £20. Children welcome. Baby facilities. Dogs welcome. Garden. Fishing (*The Which? Hotel Guide*)

▲ *Llangoed Hall*

Llyswen LD3 0YP
TEL: (01874) 754525 FAX: (01874) 754545 COOKING 6
on A470, 2m NW of Llyswen COST £26–£63

This former Jacobean manor-house, redesigned by Clough Williams-Ellis in 1912, was recently given a further lease of life by Sir Bernard Ashley, widower of Laura Ashley. Inspired by the days of the great Edwardian country-house party, he has painstakingly created a discreetly luxurious hotel. It's a fairy-tale that even the Edwardians couldn't have bettered – achieved with the help of floor-to-ceiling Laura Ashley fabrics, of course, and Sir Bernard's personal art collection.

Staff appear seemingly from nowhere to usher diners into the comfortable lounge for pre-dinner canapés and a look at an imaginative menu that gives an occasional provençale spin to top-quality local meat, fish and game. In the modern idiom, hearty dishes like pot-roasted guinea-fowl with braised red cabbage are juxtaposed with more refined offerings such as chicken and foie gras mousse. Chef Ben Davies times his cooking to perfection and has a knack for balancing flavours and textures. Excellent olive oils are deployed to brilliant effect – drizzled over canapés, delicately coating the leaves of a green salad, or swirled into pan juices to create a sauce for roast Mediterranean vegetables and leg of Welsh lamb. Puddings tend towards lightness: a 'subtle and delicate' raspberry parfait, crisp apple tart, or savarin of poached fruits, for example. The country-house wine list is packed with classic wines at classic prices. The New World section has expanded again, but France is still the speciality. House wines start at £14 a bottle, £3.50 a glass.

▲ *means accommodation is available.*

CHEF: Ben Davies PROPRIETOR: Sir Bernard Ashley OPEN: all week 12.15 to 2, 7.15 to 9.30 MEALS: alc (main courses £14 to £19.50). Set L £14 (2 courses) to £17, Set D £29.50 SERVICE: not inc, card slips closed CARDS: Amex, Delta, Diners, MasterCard, Switch, Visa DETAILS: 40 seats. Private parties: 50 main room, 16 and 50 private rooms. Car park. Vegetarian meals. No children under 8. No smoking in dining-room. Wheelchair access (also WC). Music ACCOMMODATION: 23 rooms, all with bath/shower. TV. Phone. B&B £100 to £285. Deposit: £50. No children under 8. Dogs welcome. Afternoon teas. Garden. Fishing (*The Which? Hotel Guide*)

MATHRY Pembrokeshire map 4

Ann FitzGerald's Farmhouse Kitchen 🍷 £

Mabws Fawr, Mathry SA62 5JB
TEL: (01348) 831347 COOKING 3
off A487, 6m SW of Fishguard COST £16–£42

Some renovation has taken place at the FitzGeralds' thirteenth-century Pembrokeshire farmhouse since last year's *Guide*, and outbuildings have been converted into cottages. That said, the down-to-earth ambience is maintained, and all remains steady in the kitchen. The style might be described as Franco-Oriental for want of a less cumbersome label. That simply means that prawn and vegetable tempura, or curried crab and bean sprout pancake roll, may turn up among the moules marinière and the snails and garlic butter. A speciality is bumbu Bali: Indonesian spice-coated chicken breast with green pepper sauce. Less exotic fare is highly commended, though: a reader who dined in November found nothing to fault in leek and potato soup, roast duck, lemon tart, and fine Welsh cheeses. For those who like their dessert to come with a kick, there are bananas flamed in rum, or bread pudding with a whisky sabayon.

Over half of the 100-plus bottles on the impressive wine list hail from France but they are given strong competition from Italian and New World bins. Prices are reasonable, with a quartet of house wines priced at £9. CELLARMAN'S CHOICE: Cava Juvé y Camps 1992, Penedès, £16; Dolcetto d'Asti 1994, Bava, £15.

CHEFS/PROPRIETORS: Ann and Lionel FitzGerald OPEN: all week 12 to 2.30, 6 to 9.30 MEALS: alc (main courses L £5.50 to £14, D £10.50 to £14). Set L Mon to Sat £10, Set L Sun £14, Set D £17 to £21.50. BYO £4 SERVICE: not inc, card slips closed CARDS: MasterCard, Visa DETAILS: 40 seats. 16 seats outside. Private parties: 40 main room. Car park. Vegetarian meals. Children's helpings. No-smoking area. Wheelchair access (also WC). Music

NANTGAREDIG Carmarthenshire map 4

▲ *Four Seasons*

Cwmtwrch Farm Hotel, Nantgaredig SA32 7NY
TEL: (01267) 290238 FAX: (01267) 290808 COOKING 3
on B4310, 1m N of Nantgaredig COST £28–£37

'We are not trained chefs,' write Charlotte Pasetti and Maryann Wright, who run this small hotel just outside Carmarthen, 'so our cooking is simple, using good ingredients to offer quality and taste rather than elaborate techniques.' The philosophy is an admirable one, and translates into salmon with cucumber and dill, pork with mushrooms and mustard, or rack of local lamb with rosemary and garlic.

Despite the simplicity, the four-course fixed-price menu offers a broad choice. Starters might be a 'somewhat rich' dressed crab with herb mayonnaise, or smoked haddock tart with 'crunchy flaky pastry' and a tarragon sauce. An inspector's 'superbly tender, fiercely seared and very tasty' fillet steak was given a racy tang by melting horseradish butter, while apricot-stuffed duck was skilfully complemented by a Cointreau-flavoured *jus*. Chocolate terrine studded with smashed amaretti and flaked almonds has been praised, and fast-paced service delivers the goods on time. The wine list is usefully annotated and accessibly priced. House Bordeaux is £9.50.

CHEFS/PROPRIETORS: Charlotte Pasetti and Maryann Wright OPEN: Tue to Sat D only 7.30 to 9 CLOSED: Christmas MEALS: Set D £20 SERVICE: not inc CARDS: none DETAILS: 50 seats. 6 seats outside. Private parties: 50 main room. Car park. Vegetarian meals. Children's helpings. Wheelchair access (not WC). Music ACCOMMODATION: 5 rooms, all with bath/shower. TV. B&B £38 to £52. Deposit: £10. Rooms for disabled. Children welcome. Baby facilities. Dogs welcome. Garden. Swimming-pool

NEWPORT Pembrokeshire map 4

▲ *Cnapan* ✱ [£]

East Street, Newport SA42 0SY COOKING **2**
TEL: (01239) 820575 FAX: (01239) 820878 COST £15–£38

'It was a treat to eat honest food at very reasonable prices, served in a friendly way in a delightful, relaxed atmosphere.' Other reporters are similarly taken with the Lloyds' and Coopers' restaurant-with-rooms. The pink, listed building, in the Pembrokeshire Coast National Park, has the character and lived-in feel of a country auberge, with cooking to match. Its wholesome approach strikes a chord, vegetarians get more than a perfunctory choice, and local materials play their part.

The repertoire embraces simple Welsh beef fillet with garlic butter as well as more exotic duck breast marinated in ginger, chilli and soy sauce, and although technique may not be the strongest suit, an inspector enjoyed a first-course chowder with 'ample chunks of white fish', accurately cooked vegetables with his lamb cutlets, and a rich tiramisù for dessert. Thirty-plus wines come with notes and fair prices, mostly below £20. House red and white are £8.25.

CHEFS: Judith Cooper and Eluned Lloyd PROPRIETORS: John and Eluned Lloyd, and Michael and Judith Cooper OPEN: Mon and Wed to Sat 12 to 2, 6.45 to 8.45 Apr to end Oct; open only Sun L and Fri and Sat D in Nov, Dec and Mar CLOSED: 25 and 26 Dec, Jan and Feb MEALS: alc (main courses L £4.50 to £6, D £10.50 to £16) SERVICE: not inc, card slips closed CARDS: MasterCard, Visa DETAILS: 36 seats. 25 seats outside. Private parties: 36 main room. Car park. Vegetarian meals. Children's helpings. No smoking in dining-room. Music ACCOMMODATION: 5 rooms, all with bath/shower. TV. B&B £25 to £50. Deposit: £30. Children welcome. Baby facilities. Garden (*The Which? Hotel Guide*)

'The paintings looked like a cross between scene-of-crime photographs and the storyboard from The Saint.*'* (On eating in Bristol)

NORTHOP Flintshire map 7

▲ *Soughton Hall*

Northop CH7 6AB
TEL: (01352) 840811 FAX: (01352) 840382 COOKING 3
off A5119, 1m S of Northop COST £53–£77

Dating from the early eighteenth century, the former bishop's palace is approached along an impressive half-mile avenue of lime trees. It is grandly arrayed and furnished, with tapestries and antiques in the main house, where Michael Carney's three-course meals are served. It is not the first establishment in the *Guide*, however, to recognise the potential of a less-expensive alternative, and this year has duly opened a bistro-cum-pub in the stable block serving black pudding, smoked salmon, bangers and mash, cod and chips and real ales.

The main dining-room on the first floor, meanwhile, continues in more sedate vein with a swish à la carte offering warm lobster tart, and a parfait of foie gras and chicken livers served with grape chutney. Main courses centre on home-smoked fillet of beef or fish of the day, and desserts might include cheesecake, hot Grand Marnier soufflé, or an 'indulgence' of chocolate. Classy clarets and some fine burgundies head up the wine list, and the New World comes to the rescue of those with only £20 to spend. House red and white are £11.50.

CHEF: Michael Carney PROPRIETORS: John and Rosemary Rodenhurst OPEN: all week 12 to 3, 7 to 10 (9.30 Sun) MEALS: alc (main courses £20) SERVICE: not inc, card slips closed; 10% for parties of 10 or more CARDS: Amex, MasterCard, Switch, Visa DETAILS: 50 seats. Private parties: 50 main room, 20 and 120 private rooms. Car park. No music ACCOMMODATION: 13 rooms, all with bath/shower. TV. Phone. B&B £80 to £150. Deposit: 25%. Afternoon teas. Garden (*The Which? Hotel Guide*)

PEMBROKE Pembrokeshire map 4

Left Bank

NEW ENTRY

63 Main Street, Pembroke SA71 4DA COOKING 3
TEL: (01646) 622333 COST £19–£36

The Griffiths' French restaurant sits on the left bank of the River Cleddau, so why didn't they call it Rive Gauche? Perhaps because it also occupies a building that once housed a bank. Double entendre aside, the restaurant's intent is single-minded: to provide high-quality meals 'with a twist of originality'. The *carte* sticks to around half a dozen starters and main courses and is modish, with cappuccino-frothed soup, pithiviers of goats' cheese, and garnishings such as fricassee of mushrooms or spaghetti of vegetables. The hard-working kitchen bakes bread and makes its own pasta, and reports since the January 1997 opening are promising.

Dishes scoring well at inspection included a hearty fish soup, cannelloni filled with aubergine and tomatoes, and a 'jazzed-up' crème brûlée. 'It beats all the other locals hollow,' concluded one local reporter, the clinching factor being the attention paid to vegetables. Positive comments have come in, too, for the enthusiastic young staff and the colourful but uncluttered brasserie-style décor.

The wine list runs to around thirty-five well-chosen bottles, with prices to please. House French is £6.95.

CHEF: Andrew Griffith PROPRIETOR: Gareth Griffith OPEN: Tue to Sat (and Mon mid-July to end Sept) 12 to 2.30, 7 to 10 MEALS: alc D (main courses £10 to £14). Set L 11.95, Set D (for parties of 10 or more) £15.95. Light L available SERVICE: not inc, card slips closed CARDS: Delta, MasterCard, Switch, Visa DETAILS: 70 seats. Private parties: 35 main room. Vegetarian meals. Children's helpings. No smoking in dining-room. Wheelchair access (not WC). Music

PENMAENPOOL Gwynedd map 7

▲ *Penmaenuchaf Hall* 🍷 ⁵✱

Penmaenpool LL40 1YB
TEL/FAX: (01341) 422129 COOKING **6**
off A493, 2m W of Dolgellau COST £25–£55

The house is a Victorian mansion above the Mawddach estuary, built in 1860 as a sporting retreat by Bolton cotton magnate James Leigh Taylor, and run as a hotel since 1991. It makes a good base for visitors to Snowdonia and Cader Idris, and has 13 miles of river fishing to its name, not to mention a large estate. Inside, dark oak features in the impressive carved fireplace surround in the entrance hall, and in the dining-room's panelling, and the overall effect is 'stylish and individual'. So too is the food. Hugh Cocker cooks a modern version of the classic country-house repertoire, from leek and potato soup, via sirloin of Welsh Black beef with bordelaise sauce, to gâteau St Honoré with chocolate sauce.

Being only five miles from the coast helps fish supplies – local fishermen deliver bass, lobster and crab – and among the results might be mussel soup, or scallop mousseline with a caramelised shallot and bacon dressing. Interest is heightened with such additions as quince jelly (to chicken liver parfait) or tomato salsa and tapénade (to baked hake) and saucing tends to be in the form of a light flavoured *jus*, perhaps 'scented' with cinnamon tea to accompany pot-roast guinea-fowl. Chanterelles, boletus and hedgehog mushrooms are picked nearby, baking is of a high standard, and desserts have included a warm vanilla brioche flan with praline ice-cream.

The well-designed wine list offering a good range of styles from reputable producers has introductory maps of Burgundy and Bordeaux, a guide to claret vintages and helpful tastings notes for each wine. Ten house wines start at £10.95, while the trio of 'Wines of the Month' are well worth a look. CELLARMAN'S CHOICE: Pinot Grigio 1995, Trentino Azienda due Torri, £12.50; Kingsford Cabernet Sauvignon 1994, Napa Valley, California, £16.75.

CHEF: Hugh Cocker PROPRIETORS: Mark Watson and Lorraine Fielding OPEN: all week 12 to 2, 7 to 9.30 (9 Sun) CLOSED: 6 to 17 Jan MEALS: alc (main courses £15 to £18.50). Set L £12.95 (2 courses) to £14.95, Set D £25. BYO £6 SERVICE: not inc, card slips closed CARDS: Amex, Delta, Diners, MasterCard, Switch, Visa DETAILS: 30 seats. Private parties: 50 main room, 16 private room. Car park. Vegetarian meals. No children under 8. No smoking in dining-room. Wheelchair access (also WC). Music ACCOMMODATION: 14 rooms, all with bath/shower. TV. Phone. B&B £50 to £150. Deposit: £10. No children under 8. Baby facilities. Dogs welcome in gun room only. Afternoon teas. Garden. Fishing (*The Which? Hotel Guide*)

PONTFAEN Pembrokeshire map 4

▲ *Tregynon Country Farmhouse Hotel*

Gwaun Valley, Pontfaen SA65 9TU
TEL: (01239) 820531 FAX: (01239) 820808
at junction of B4313 and B4329, take B4313 towards Fishguard, then take first right, and first right again

COOKING 2
COST £26–£43

Tregynon is an isolated stone farmhouse – originally sixteenth-century – in the Pembrokeshire Coast National Park. It is geared to long-stay residents, and the menu rotates accordingly. Peter Heard describes it as a cartwheel with fifteen different spokes, designed so that no-one staying a fortnight repeats the same dish. Main courses might involve a choice between Preseli lamb cutlets, stuffed peppers, and skate wing with caper butter, while alternatives such as gammon steak smoked on the premises attract a supplement and need to be ordered in advance. Soup, or perhaps asparagus and cheese pancake, might start the ball rolling, and ice-creams might include chocolate chip and brandy, or banana and Bacardi. The extensively annotated list of forty-plus wines opens with house French at £10.25.

CHEFS: Peter and Jane Heard and Sian Davies PROPRIETORS: Peter and Jane Heard OPEN: all week D only 7.30 to 8.30 MEALS: Set D £17.95. BYO £5 SERVICE: not inc CARDS: Delta, MasterCard, Switch, Visa DETAILS: 28 seats. Private parties: 16 main room, 12 private room. Car park. Vegetarian meals. No young children. No smoking in dining-room. Music ACCOMMODATION: 0 rooms, all with bath/shower. TV. Phone. B&B £48 to £68. Deposit: 25%. Children welcome. Baby facilities. Afternoon teas. Garden (*The Which? Hotel Guide*)

PORTHGAIN Pembrokeshire map 4

Harbour Lights

Porthgain, nr St David's SA62 5BW
TEL: (01348) 831549
off A487 at Croesgoch, 4m W of Mathry

COOKING 4
COST £32–£38

Anne Marie Davies has added an arts and crafts gallery to the attractions of her stone cottage near the Pembrokeshire coastal path. Her small dining-room is made cheerful and homely with candle lighting, oak tables, colourful pictures and flowers everywhere. The cooking takes a homespun tack, using good, mostly local produce and keeps things simple but not dull.

The seafood-oriented set-price menu might offer crab with dill and lemon mayonnaise, seafood thermidor, or grilled Dover sole with herb butter. Organic sirloin steak is a permanent fixture, and vegetarians can expect a filo parcel of roasted vegetables with water chestnuts, hazelnuts and a basil and red pepper sauce, for example. Good banoffi pie is made with Jersey cream. Service is good-natured and the style is casual. Likewise, opening times can occasionally be relaxed, so check before going. Fifteen wines tap unusual, mostly regional vineyards of France, Italy and Spain and there is one from California. House French is £9.50.

CHEFS: Anne Marie Davies and Bernadette Lomax PROPRIETOR: Anne Marie Davies OPEN: Wed to Sat (and bank hol Sun) D only 6 to 9.30 (8.30 in winter) CLOSED: Christmas MEALS: Set D £19.50 (2 courses) to £22.50 SERVICE: not inc CARDS: Delta, MasterCard, Switch, Visa DETAILS: 35 seats. 20 seats outside. Car park. Vegetarian meals. Children's helpings. No smoking while others eat. Wheelchair access (not WC). Music

PORTMEIRION Gwynedd map 7

▲ *Hotel Portmeirion*

Portmeirion LL48 6ET
TEL: (01766) 770228 FAX: (01766) 771331 COOKING 3
off A487, signposted from Minffordd COST £21–£42

The hotel overlooks Cardigan Bay from its own private peninsula, and all the cottages and houses within the village form part of the hotel, surely one of the most individual in the British Isles. Sir Clough Williams Ellis incorporated so many architectural references that nothing should come as a surprise, from Indian drapes in the drawing-room to the semi-circular dining-room in which just about everything apart from the flowers is cream or white. Local produce is the foundation of a menu that considers itself a cross between Welsh and Mediterranean: in loin of lamb from the Lleyn peninsula served with roast garlic and thyme, for example.

Locally landed fish might appear in the form of cod with a mustard crust on Lyonnaise potatoes, and smoked salmon is considered 'excellent', served on its own, around a leek risotto, or in a sandwich as a bar snack. Vegetables are 'plain and fresh', desserts might contain a splash of alcohol – Baileys ice-cream and caramelised bananas, or prune and armagnac tart – and cheeses are Welsh farmhouse. Staff are 'a delight', although service can be slow. Anyone held prisoner here could select a different bottle from the wine list every night for over five months before running out, and a pleasurable experience it would prove too. Pricing is keen throughout (Edouard d'Enjie Brut house champagne is £23.50) and house wines start at £9.50. CELLARMAN'S CHOICE: Menetou-Salon, Le Petit Clos 1995, Jean-Max Roger, £15.50; Barolo 1990, Cordana, Prod. di Castiglione Falletto, £17.50.

CHEFS: Colin Pritchard and Billy Taylor PROPRIETOR: Portmeirion Ltd OPEN: Tue to Sun L 12.30 to 2, all week D 7 to 9.30 CLOSED: 11 Jan to 6 Feb MEALS: Set L Sun £14, Set L Tue to Sat £10.50 (2 courses) to £13.50, Set D £21.50 (2 courses) to £26.50 SERVICE: not inc, card slips closed CARDS: Amex, Delta, Diners, MasterCard, Switch, Visa DETAILS: 100 seats. 12 seats outside. Private parties: 100 main room, 12 and 30 private rooms. Car park. Vegetarian meals. Children's helpings. Children welcome before 7.30. No smoking in dining-room. No music ACCOMMODATION: 37 rooms, all with bath/shower. TV. Phone. Room only £110 to £175. Children welcome. Baby facilities. Garden. Swimming-pool (*The Which? Hotel Guide*)

'With the cheese came some walnut bread, which must have been two days old it was so stale, some rye bread also stale, and a curling stick of celery old enough to vote.'
(On eating in Berkshire)

PWLLGLOYW Powys map 4

Seland Newydd

NEW ENTRY

Pwllgloyw, nr Brecon LD3 9PY
TEL: (01874) 690282
on B4520 Brecon to Builth Wells road

COOKING 4
COST £18–£32

The combination of village pub and smart restaurant in a rural hideaway attracts all sorts, from 'ruddy-faced farmers' and the local cricket club to casual visitors and formally dressed folk out for a celebration. It consists of a stone-walled bar with a huge fireplace, a lounge with deep sofas arranged around low tables, and a warm pink dining-room, all 'in a different league' from the original Camden Arms pub which it was before the Harveys took over in 1996. 'We decided to start with soups,' declared one logical reporter, who was immediately drawn to the food's appeal by a rich seafood chowder, and a bowl of carrot and orange spiced up with ginger, a dash of honey, and a garnish of fresh coriander.

The balance of flavours and a sensitivity to textures marks out the kitchen's serious intent. A layered mousse of asparagus and tomato impressed an inspector with its delicacy and smoothness, while a 'glorious' herb risotto accompanied half a dozen fillets of megrim sole liberally strewn with mussels. The menu offers around six or seven choices per course, and desserts have included crème brûlée with black cherries, and a 'fully flavoured' white chocolate torte in a lake of dark chocolate sauce which had 'a surprising lightness'. On the short wine list, the rest of the world gets equal attention to New Zealand – the pub's name in Welsh recognises Freya Harvey's native country – and house French is £8.75.

CHEF: Maynard Harvey PROPRIETORS: Maynard and Freya Harvey OPEN: all week 12 to 2.30, 6.45 to 9 (9.30 Fri and Sat) MEALS: alc (main courses £10.50 to £13.50). Set L Sun £10.75 SERVICE: not inc, card slips closed CARDS: Delta, MasterCard, Switch, Visa DETAILS: 35 seats. 50 seats outside. Private parties: 36 main room. Car park. Children's helpings. No smoking in 1 dining-room. Wheelchair access (not WC). Music

PWLLHELI Gwynedd map 7

▲ *Plas Bodegroes*

Nefyn Road, Pwllheli LL53 5TH
TEL: (01758) 612363 FAX: (01758) 701247
on A497, 1m W of Pwllheli

COOKING 7
COST £30–£56

One reporter began by thanking goodness that the Chowns did not sell this 'stylish rural retreat', as was planned at one stage. There is no doubt that, in the dozen years they have been here, they have done as much as anyone for the image of Welsh food. Had they upped sticks completely and moved to Hole in the Wall (see entry, Bath), Wales would have been much the poorer. The delightful Georgian mansion, set in rolling green acres, complete with bluebells and beechwoods, now has an annexe with a couple of extra bedrooms, and 'this year the sitting-rooms are comfier and the dining-room is more elegant', with paintings and photographs all worth a second look. The five-course dinner meanwhile has been trimmed to a perfectly acceptable three under the aegis of new chef Shaun Mitchell.

Dinner for a springtime reporter began with an unannounced filo pastry parcel of spiced crab, before smoked haddock and scallop fish-cake, then chargrilled ribeye of Welsh beef with a 'rich and glossy' oxtail sauce that was 'quite the best'. Fine local materials remain at the heart of things, and herbs play a part in their transformation, turning up in cauliflower and thyme soup, or in the herb crust on a piece of halibut, and in the accompanying tarragon sauce. The food may not be particularly adventurous, but it carries the stamp of authority in its classical dealings with mushroom tartlet, duck liver parfait with onion and grape marmalade, or breast of Hereford duck with lentils, bacon and cabbage.

Fruit features prominently among desserts, from a gratin of exotic ones served with pineapple sorbet, to a heart-shaped cinnamon biscuit filled with apples and plums and served with an 'indescribably good' elderflower custard. The wine list opens with a good-value, food-friendly selection of 18 wines priced from £12, then moves on to a range of French classics which is balanced by some exciting bins from the New World. Alsace continues to be a speciality of the house and there are some great dessert wines. CELLARMAN'S CHOICE: Bordeaux, Ch. Beauregard Ducasse 1995, £26; Eyzaguirre Cabernet Sauvignon 1993, Chile, Cachapoal Valley, £15.

CHEF: Shaun Mitchell PROPRIETORS: Christopher and Gunna Chown OPEN: Sun L 12 to 2, Tue to Sun D 7 to 9.30 CLOSED: mid-Dec to Feb MEALS: Set L £18.50, Set D £29.50 SERVICE: not inc CARDS: Amex, Delta, MasterCard, Switch, Visa DETAILS: 40 seats. Private parties: 40 main room, 16 private room. Car park. Children welcome. No smoking in dining-room. Music ACCOMMODATION: 11 rooms, all with bath/shower. TV. Phone. D,B&B £70 to £200. Deposit: £50. Children welcome. Baby facilities. Garden

REYNOLDSTON Swansea map 4

▲ *Fairyhill*

Reynoldston SA3 1BS COOKING **4**

TEL: (01792) 390139 FAX: (01792) 391358 COST £24–£49

The Georgian house luxuriates in acres of parkland at the heart of the Gower Peninsula. The crunch of gravel, the 'manservant' (as one reporter put it) at the ready to welcome you, canapés in the serene drawing-room, and silver service at dinner add up to a textbook country-house hotel. In this case, however, one is unlikely to be overwhelmed, thanks to the easygoing staff and the fact that it isn't all that 'grand'. Fairyhill provides widely appealing lunches and dinners every day of the week, taps local producers for ingredients, and goes to some lengths to promote indigenous flavours: seared lamb with a 'cawl' sauce, to name one. The fruits of such hard work and dedication are mostly sound and, although some dishes have failed to excite, others excel: 'beautifully moist' lamb with kidneys and liver, for instance, and grilled turbot with garlic mashed potato, a basil oil dressing adding the 'extra dimension'. 'Divine' rhubarb syllabub with whisky makes an excellent dessert, and there may also be chocolate mousse with orange sauce.

Highlights on the wine list include eight vintages of Ch. Latour and five of Ch. Cissac, superb white burgundies from Jean-François Coche-Dury and ten bins from Australia's Henschke. Most of the world's major wine regions are covered (with the notable exception of Germany), plus there is the welcome inclusion of Wales. Prices have risen in the last year, sometimes steeply, so the highlighting of wines under £16 is helpful; house wines start at £12.50. CELLARMAN'S CHOICE: Pouilly-Fumé 'Les Loges' 1995, Dom. des Fines Caillottes, Jean Pabinot, £21.50; Tinto Pesquera 1993, Ribera del Duero, £24.50.

CHEF: Paul Davies PROPRIETORS: Paul Davies, Andrew Hetherington, and Jane and Peter Camm OPEN: all week 12.30 to 1.45, 7.30 to 9.15 CLOSED: 3 days Christmas, bank hols MEALS: Set L £11.50 (2 courses) to £14.50, Set D £24.50 (2 courses) to £29.50. BYO £6 SERVICE: not inc, card slips closed CARDS: Amex, Delta, MasterCard, Switch, Visa DETAILS: 60 seats. 20 seats outside. Private parties: 40 main room, 20 and 40 private rooms. Car park. Vegetarian meals. Children's helpings. No children under 8 at D. No smoking in dining-room. Wheelchair access (also WC). Music ACCOMMODATION: 8 rooms, all with bath/shower. TV. Phone. B&B £70 to £150. No children under 8. Dogs welcome. Garden (*The Which? Hotel Guide*)

ROSEBUSH Pembrokeshire map 4

Tate's at Tafarn Newydd ✱ [£]

Tafarn Newydd, Rosebush SA66 7RA
TEL: (01437) 532542 COOKING **2**
on B4313, 8m SE of Fishguard COST £17–£38

The Tafarn is a seventeenth-century coaching-inn once used by drovers on the Haverfordwest to Cardigan run. These days, Diana Richards caters for a different clientele: fans of real ales, folk music and crossover cooking that acknowledges no ethnic boundaries. She clearly has a good culinary library too: poulet au vinaigre, and guinea-fowl baked with 40 cloves of garlic bear the signatures of a couple of illustrious French masters. Other dishes may be characterised as Mediterranean with a Welsh accent: for example, local Rosebush goats' cheese on bruschetta with pine-nuts and basil, or Carmarthen ham with polenta and wild mushrooms. Puddings are from closer to home in the treacle tart and lemon posset vein. Despite being in the 'middle of nowhere', Tate's does manage to pull in the crowds. A couple of reports have mentioned unexpectedly cool service, which chimes oddly with the surroundings. The number of wines on offer has been greatly reduced, but it remains an eclectic and fairly priced selection. House wines are £9.50 a bottle, £1.65 a glass.

CHEF/PROPRIETOR: Diana Richards OPEN: Tue to Sun L 12 to 2.30, Tue to Sat D 7 to 9.30 CLOSED: 25 Dec MEALS: alc (main courses L £5 to £8, D £10.50 to £14). Set L Tue to Sat £5.50 (1 course) to £9.50, Set L Sun £5.75 (1 course) to £7.75. Bar meals available L and D all week SERVICE: not inc, card slips closed CARDS: MasterCard, Visa DETAILS: 50 seats. 25 seats outside. Private parties: 28 main room, 12 and 16 private rooms. Car park. Vegetarian meals. Children's helpings. No smoking in dining-room. Wheelchair access (also WC). Music

The Guide *is totally independent, accepts no free hospitality, and survives on the number of copies sold each year.*

ROSSETT Wrexham map 7

Churtons £

Machine House, Chester Road, Rossett LL12 0HW
TEL: (01244) 570163 FAX: (01244) 570099 COOKING 2
on B5445, off A483, between Chester and Wrexham COST £17–£37

Rossett is in border country, equidistant from Wrexham and Chester, and the Churton empire bestrides the national line (they have another wine bar in Tarporley, Cheshire). The formula is a blackboard menu in the context of a thriving wine outlet, although the cooking is not by any means formulaic. Salmon fillet marinated in lemon juice and chilli and then coated with a herb crust is baked and sauced with yoghurt and turmeric, or you could opt for Morecambe Bay potted shrimps, or steak au poivre. Fruity garnishes with meats, such as blackberries with a lamb leg steak, are a favourite with the kitchen, and to finish there is apple brown betty, or cherry and kirsch ice-cream. The wine list has some noteworthy producers among the predominantly French names, and a tempting run of vintage ports. The house selection starts at £8.50.

CHEFS: Ade Garratt, Jackie Lloyd, Louise MacDougall and Tracey Roberts PROPRIETORS: Nicholas and James Churton OPEN: Mon to Fri L 12 to 2.15, Mon to Sat D 7 to 10 CLOSED: 24 Dec to 3 Jan, bank hols MEALS: alc (main courses £5 to £15) SERVICE: not inc, card slips closed CARDS: Amex, Delta, MasterCard, Visa DETAILS: 55 seats. 16 seats outside. Private parties: 20 main room, 12 private room. Car park. Vegetarian meals. No children under 12. Wheelchair access (not WC). Music. Air-conditioned

ST DAVID'S Pembrokeshire map 4

Morgan's Brasserie

20 Nun Street, St David's SA62 6NT COOKING 4
TEL: (01437) 720508 COST £23–£38

Ceri and Elaine Morgan's small, 'relatively smartish' brasserie ambles merrily along despite comings and goings in the kitchen, but Ceri Morgan has now promoted himself to head chef. Enthusiastic reports imply no lack of confidence or flair under the new arrangement, and ingredients are top-notch. Fish is still the thing, and the *carte* is sensibly short, complemented by blackboard specials that might include 'simple and flavoursome' escalope of sea trout with Penclawdd cockle butter. Guests wanting meat might find locally raised lamb, or beef in the form of fillet steak Rossini, perhaps. Singled out for praise at inspection were mushroom and chestnut soup, tiger prawns in filo pastry with chilli and coconut mayonnaise, and Celtic crunch butterscotch ice-cream in an almond basket. 'A nice place with rather interesting artefacts on walls and in cabinets, and friendly service,' writes one reporter. Wines number around forty, with a bias towards France and Australia. House French and Italian are £8.75 a bottle.

CHEF: Ceri Morgan PROPRIETORS: Ceri and Elaine Morgan OPEN: Mon to Sat D only 6 to 9 CLOSED: Jan and Feb, and occasional days in winter MEALS: alc (main courses £9.50 to £14) SERVICE: not inc CARDS: Amex, MasterCard, Visa DETAILS: 36 seats. Private parties: 22 main room. Vegetarian meals. Children's helpings. No cigars/pipes in dining-room. Music

SWANSEA Swansea map 4

L'Amuse

2 Woodville Road, Mumbles, Swansea SA3 4AD COOKING **2**
TEL: (01792) 366006 COST £21–£33

'L'amuse gueule' kicks off proceedings in appropriate style in Kate Cole's street-corner bistro. This signature opener is a wonderfully gutsy terrine of liver and pork laced with raisins and 'booze' served with cornichons and toasted baguette. Regularly changing menus are in the bourgeois mould of pied de cochon with sauce gribiche, confit of duck Perigueux, and herb-crusted fillet of hake with beurre blanc, and the value for money is reckoned to be admirable. In recent months reporters have singled out for praise soup of sweet red peppers and mussels, and roast chump of lamb with caramelised shallots, garlic and rosemary. Superlatives have also been sprinkled liberally over desserts such as roast peaches with white chocolate and raspberry coulis, and 'exquisite' orange tart with chocolate and whisky ice-cream. Service is 'informed and knowledgeable'. House wine is £8.50.

CHEF/PROPRIETOR: Kate Cole OPEN: Tue to Sat 12 to 2.15, 6.30 to 9 CLOSED: Jan MEALS: Set L £6.45 (1 course) to £12.45, Set D £18.50 SERVICE: not inc CARDS: Delta, MasterCard, Visa DETAILS: 35 seats. Private parties: 50 main room. Children welcome. No music

La Braseria [£]

28 Wind Street, Swansea SA1 1DZ COOKING **1**
TEL: (01792) 469683 FAX: (01792) 470816 COST £20–£40

The atmosphere is as Spanish as wooden wine crates, terracotta jars and sawdust can make it, and the formula is both simple and successful. Great chunks of beef fillet or sirloin steak along with suckling pig or even ostrich are cooked as plain as can be, usually chargrilled, with no sauce to mess up the straightforward flavour. The same approach is applied to seafood from shark to gurnard, from halibut to lobster, as well as bass, snapper or (when available) bream cooked in rock salt. The price of fish is calculated according to weight. Start with any of two dozen items – moules marinière, beef satay, spare ribs, stuffed mushrooms – and finish perhaps with tiramisù. For value, consider the two-course lunch. House wines start at £9.25 (£1.60 a glass).

CHEF/PROPRIETOR: Manuel Tercero OPEN: Mon to Sat 12 to 2.30, 7 to 11.30 MEALS: alc (main courses £4 to £13.50). Set L £6.50 (2 courses) SERVICE: not inc, card slips closed CARDS: Amex, Delta, Diners, MasterCard, Switch, Visa DETAILS: 170 seats. Private parties: 100 main room. Children welcome. Wheelchair access (also WC). Music

Number One Wind Street 🍷

1 Wind Street, Swansea SA1 1DE COOKING **4**
TEL: (01792) 456996 COST £20–£34

'Still the best place to eat in Swansea,' reckoned one supporter, while a first-timer found it 'a splendid surprise'. After years here, the Taylors are building a new extension and refurbishing throughout, but still producing their particular style of Franco-Welsh food. Fish plays a central role, appearing in provençale fish soup with aïoli, or as grilled, roast or poached fillets: monk with prawn risotto, sea bass with laverbread sauce, or red mullet with pesto. Its freshness is appreciated, as is the sympathetic treatment: perhaps a 'delicate' terrine of lobster and shrimp with a cucumber sambal, or 'a stunning match' of sewin with sorrel and beurre blanc.

The first course is brought to table by Kate Taylor 'looking demure in white uniform with a Vermeer sort of headgear', and she might deliver a well-judged salad of smoked goose breast with a compote of celery and apple, and a walnut oil vinaigrette. Her 'accomplished cooking' might also produce roast quails with mushroom risotto, or a ragoût of wild boar with 'clever additions of apple and peach'. Vegetables are generous, and desserts might include coeur à la crème, or a mousse of dark and white chocolate. This is a relaxed, informal place with helpful, knowledgeable service and a modestly priced but interesting selection of wines – the sort that takes a keen eye to put together – beginning with house French at £8. CELLARMAN'S CHOICE: Allan Scott Sauvignon 1996, Marlborough, New Zealand, £16.75; Rioja Viña Bosconia 1989, Bod. Lopez de Heredia, £15.50.

CHEF: Kate Taylor PROPRIETORS: Peter Gillen and Kate Taylor OPEN: Tue to Sat 12 to 2.30, 7 to 9.30 CLOSED: 1 week Christmas, bank hol Mons MEALS: alc (main courses £9 to £13). Set L £9.50 (2 courses) to £11.95, Set D £17 (2 courses) to £21. BYO £5 SERVICE: not inc, card slips closed CARDS: Amex, MasterCard, Switch, Visa DETAILS: 50 seats. Private parties: 50 main room, 20 private room. Vegetarian meals. Children welcome. Wheelchair access (not WC). Music

TALSARNAU Gwynedd map 7

▲ *Maes-y-Neuadd*

Talsarnau LL47 6YA
TEL: (01766) 780200 FAX: (01766) 780211 COOKING 4
off B4573, 1m S of Talsarnau COST £19–£46

Relaxing isn't hard to do here. Harlech is within reach, there are plenty of walks in Snowdonia if the weather's fine, and reassuringly thick walls keep out the worst of the elements in winter. Menus offer anything from a one-course lunch to a five-course dinner, and a Franco-Welsh motif runs through the cooking, taking in terrine of hare with laverbread, sea bass with herbs and olive oil, and skate with capers and brown butter. Those who take the full five courses might begin with a salad (duck confit), or terrine (crab and lobster), then a soup (French onion) and fish course (smoked haddock omelette), before roast sirloin of Welsh beef with a red wine sauce. A Welsh lamb dish is offered every evening.

The Grand Finale, for those with the appetite, starts with cheese – perhaps Llanboidy, Merlin and Dunsyre Blue, served with carrot and herb bread – and proceeds to three desserts in succession: at one meal glazed rice-pudding, banana mousse with chocolate sauce, and a selection of ice-creams and sorbets. Desserts, according to one reporter, are 'what people talk about months later'. Service is young and enthusiastic, and wines are well spread, with some good producers in Alsace, Burgundy and the southern hemisphere. House French is £9.75.

CHEF: Peter Jackson PROPRIETORS: Olive and Malcolm Horsfall, and June and Michael Slatter OPEN: all week 12.15 to 1.45, 7 to 9 MEALS: Set L Mon to Sat £8.50 (1 course) to £12.75, Set L Sun £14.95, Set D £24 to £30 SERVICE: not inc, card slips closed CARDS: Amex, Delta, Diners, MasterCard, Switch, Visa DETAILS: 50 seats. Private parties: 50 main room, 12 private room. Car park. Vegetarian meals. Children's helpings. No children under 8 after 7. No smoking in dining-room. Wheelchair access (also WC). Music ACCOMMODATION: 16 rooms, all with bath/shower. TV. Phone. D,B&B £72 to £209. Deposit: £50. Rooms for disabled. Children welcome. Baby facilities. Dogs by arrangement. Afternoon teas. Garden (*The Which? Hotel Guide*)

TALYLLYN Gwynedd map 7

GWYNEDD 1998 PERFORMER

▲ *Minffordd Hotel*

Talyllyn LL36 9AJ
TEL: (01654) 761665 FAX: (01654) 761517 COOKING 5
at junction of A487 and B4405, 8m SW of Dolgellau COST £26–£31

This former seventeenth-century drovers' inn near Dolgellau has been transformed by its present owners into a small but perfectly formed country hotel. The interior is distinguished by 'striking spotlessness', as well as an eclectic taste in prints that ranges from Leonardo through Degas to a contemporary one of sheep in various moods. The format is a fixed-price dinner of four courses, with cheese following pudding in the British way, built around main-course alternatives of meat or fish. Gilding the lily is emphatically not Mark Warner's style, and what turns up on the plate is all the better for it. A simple twice-baked Cheddar soufflé, 'neat and skilfully made', comes garnished with an impeccably dressed salad of leaves and black olives. Oeuf en cocotte with asparagus, bortsch with sour cream, and melon with Carmarthen ham add up to an exercise in a different kind of nostalgia than is the norm these days.

Top-flight corn-fed chicken with lemon and thyme cream sauce is an essay in clean, clear flavours with all its elements in balance. Portmeirion lemon tart, with more than a touch of apple and cinnamon about it, is a pleasing way to finish, or choose from steamed sponge puddings or fresh fruit salads. Wines don't exert themselves much beyond a core selection of serviceable French bottles. The house quartet are all £8.45.

CHEF: Mark Warner PROPRIETORS: Mary McQuillan and Mark Warner OPEN: all week D only 7.30 for 8 (1 sitting) CLOSED: Jan and Feb MEALS: Set D £18.95. BYO £2.50 SERVICE: none, card slips closed CARDS: Delta, MasterCard, Visa DETAILS: 20 seats. Private parties: 20 main room. Car park. Children's helpings. No children under 5. No smoking in dining-room. No music ACCOMMODATION: 7 rooms, all with bath/shower. Phone. D,B&B £52.50 to £110. Deposit: 20%. No children under 3. Garden (*The Which? Hotel Guide*)

Restaurateurs justifiably resent no-shows. If you quote a credit card number when booking, you may be liable for the restaurant's lost profit margin if you don't turn up. Always phone to cancel.

THREE COCKS Powys map 4

▲ *Three Cocks Hotel*

Three Cocks LD3 0SL
TEL/FAX: (01497) 847215 COOKING 3
on A438, between Brecon and Hay-on-Wye COST £34–£55

This and another inn are practically all there is to the tiny hamlet. The nearby Black Mountains and Brecon Beacons National Park provide energetic diversion for walkers, and the Winstones offer welcome restoration in their fifteenth-century creeper-covered house with its cobbled yard, antiques, log fires and four-course dinners. 'Excellent quantity, brilliant value,' reckoned one reporter who had not come across such a good deal in months, and who enjoyed a meal of vegetable soup with home-made bread, skate with caper sauce, lamb en croûte with blue cheese, chocolate pudding, and coffee with Belgian chocolates.

Michael Winstone's repertoire does not vary much, but it spans a few disparate styles, allowing him to incorporate a warm salad of Scottish scallops alongside Ardennes ham with pickled onions, not to mention loin of Welsh lamb with tarragon sauce. He also uses his fair share of garlic. Service is quiet and efficient, and the place is 'anything but pretentious'. Drink Belgian beer, or a wine from the predominantly French list, which starts with house wine at £8.50.

CHEF: Michael Winstone PROPRIETOR: Mr and Mrs Michael Winstone OPEN: Wed to Mon D only 7 to 9 CLOSED: Dec and Jan MEALS: alc (main courses £16 to £19.50). Set D £26 SERVICE: net prices, card slips closed CARDS: MasterCard, Visa DETAILS: 30 seats. Private parties: 18 main room. Car park. Vegetarian meals. Children's helpings. No cigars/pipes in dining-room. Music ACCOMMODATION: 7 rooms, all with bath/shower. B&B £40 to £65. Children welcome. Baby facilities. Afternoon teas. Garden (*The Which? Hotel Guide*)

TREFRIW Conwy map 7

Chandler's 🍷 ✱ [£]

Trefriw LL27 0JH
TEL: (01492) 640991 COOKING 3
off B5106, NW of Llanrwst COST £14–£38

Adam and Penny Rattenbury are English expatriates who have been running this cheery little bistro in the Conwy Valley for a decade. An unpretentious atmosphere is created by simple willow-seated chairs, an absence of formality in the front-of-house approach and by the four-square domestic cooking that always includes a full vegetarian menu. Mushrooms stuffed with smoked bacon and garlic, beef fillet cooked in soured cream, and coffee meringues with hot fudge sauce will suit many folk down to the ground. At inspection, a main course of sauté lamb's liver in lemon butter sauce with garlic mash was a triumph, the liver thinly sliced and the vegetables both plentiful and accurately cooked. Sea bass is given the Chinese treatment, with spring onions, garlic, ginger and soy. Puddings have included an 'excellent' exotic fruit pavlova made with properly chewy meringue. Service is friendly but can be slow.

The wine list is simply arranged by colour and country, but a good forage will turn up many well-chosen treasures, including a nugget of Welsh gold from

Planteg, and they won't cost you a fortune. House wines from France, Australia and Chile are £8.95. CELLARMAN'S CHOICE: Ca'del Solo Malvasia Bianca 1996, Bonny Doon, California, £13.95; Rockford Dry County Grenache 1996, Barossa Valley, S. Australia, £15.

CHEFS/PROPRIETORS: Adam and Penny Rattenbury OPEN: Wed to Fri and Sun L 12 to 2, Thur to Sat D 7 to 9.30 CLOSED: 26 Dec to 1 Jan MEALS: alc (main courses L £4 to £7, D £8.50 to £13). Set L £7.50. BYO £5 SERVICE: not inc, card slips closed CARDS: MasterCard, Switch, Visa DETAILS: 24 seats. Private parties: 30 main room. Car park. Vegetarian meals. Children's helpings. No smoking in dining-room. Music

WELSH HOOK Pembrokeshire map 4

▲ *Stone Hall*

Welsh Hook, Wolf's Castle SA62 5NS
TEL: (01348) 840212 FAX: (01348) 840815
1½m off A40, between Letterston and Wolf's Castle, W of Welsh Hook

COOKING **2**
COST £26–£39

Heavy oak beams and slate floors hint at the manor-house's long history. It may be of modest dimensions, but the partially wood-panelled lounge dates from 1700, and the dining-room from 1400. Even the waitresses are dressed in seventeenth-century peasant costume. Despite that, it feels more like a French auberge, an impression strengthened by Martine Watson's repertoire of moules marinière, snails with garlic and parsley butter, duck confit, and tarte Tatin. Dinner is a choice between the quarterly-changing *carte* and a daily-changing set-price menu, raw materials come mainly from local suppliers, bread is baked and fish smoked on the premises, and cooking techniques are sound. The predominantly French wine list combines quality and value; house wine is £10.50.

CHEFS: Martine Watson and Jean-Yves Poujade PROPRIETORS: Alan and Martine Watson OPEN: all week D only 7 to 9.30 MEALS: alc (main courses £12 to £13.50). Set D £17 SERVICE: not inc CARDS: Amex, Diners, MasterCard, Visa DETAILS: 34 seats. Private parties: 45 main room, 20 private room. Car park. Vegetarian meals. Children's helpings. No cigars/pipes in dining-room. Wheelchair access (not WC). No music ACCOMMODATION: 5 rooms, all with bath/shower. TV. B&B £46 to £68. Deposit: £20. Children welcome. Baby facilities. Garden (*The Which? Hotel Guide*)

WHITEBROOK Monmouthshire map 2

▲ *The Crown at Whitebrook* 🍷 $✱

MONMOUTH 1998 STAR

Whitebrook NP5 4TX
TEL: (01600) 860254 FAX: (01600) 860607
5m S of Monmouth, between A466 and B4293

COOKING **5**
COST £25–£47

La Couronne à Blancruisseau one might expect the place to be called, given the strong French emphasis throughout. The ancient alehouse and one-time pub rightly dubs itself a restaurant-with-rooms and makes the most of views over delightful forested countryside. Sandra Bates aims to cook French food using quite a few local ingredients, although the precise provenance of either dishes or ingredients matters less than her food's proven ability to stand on its own merits. 'This was confident cooking,' summed up one reporter, 'with individual variations on classic dishes which were both inventive and successful.' Choice is generous and varied, with first courses offering perhaps a warm scallop mousse with nori seaweed and a chive beurre blanc, or a plate of lamb – liver, kidney and sausage – with onion marmalade and a mustard sauce.

Mrs Bates makes stocks, bread, pastry and ice-creams, and craves indulgence while meals are cooked to order, a necessary request in view of some of the workmanship: rack of lamb is served with a spinach and laverbread mousse, and breast of Gressingham duck comes with a pithiviers of its livers. Desserts are no less exacting, producing flamed pancakes, treacle and apple tart, and plum and almond strudel. Most effort seems to go into dinners, but good-value lunches sound promising, too, with smoked haddock fish-cake, Welsh goats'-cheese soufflé, or venison sausages cooked in puff pastry.

A strong French emphasis is also evident in the thoughtful selection of wines, with over a hundred bottles hailing from France. But the rest of the world has not been ignored: Spain and Australia make a good showing, and even Wales has a representative duo. Prices are reasonable and the house wines are £9.75 a bottle, £1.90 a glass. CELLARMAN'S CHOICE: Graves Blanc, Ch. de Seuil 1995, £16.95; Weinert Carrascal 1985, Bodegas Weinert, Argentina, £17.95.

CHEF: Sandra Bates PROPRIETORS: Rodger and Sandra Bates OPEN: Tue to Sun L 12 to 1.45, Mon to Sat D 7 to 9 (Sun D residents only) CLOSED: 25 and 26 Dec, 2 weeks Jan, 2 weeks Aug MEALS: Set L £15.95, Set D £26.95. BYO £5. Light L available SERVICE: not inc CARDS: Amex, Delta, Diners, MasterCard, Switch, Visa DETAILS: 32 seats. 24 seats outside. Private parties: 12 private room. Car park. Vegetarian meals. Children's helpings. No smoking in dining-room. No music ACCOMMODATION: 12 rooms, all with bath/shower. TV. Phone. D,B&B £65 to £130. Children welcome. Dogs welcome in bedrooms only. Garden

Isle of Man

▲ *Boncompte's/La Tasca*

Admiral House, Loch Promenade, Douglas IM1 2LX COOKING **3**
TEL: (01624) 629551 FAX: (01624) 675021 COST £23–£49

The Admiral House Hotel is home to two quite different styles of eating. In Boncompte's restaurant, fish from the local catch forms the centrepiece of the recognisably haute cuisine menus. Monkfish, lobster and sea bass all feature regularly, and the kitchen is happy to consider special requests for methods of preparation. Crab in filo with pink grapefruit salad may start a meal, and those who don't feel fishy may opt for honey-roasted Gressingham duck on rösti with blackcurrant sauce, or even ostrich medallions with oyster mushrooms in a brandied mustard sauce. Down in the basement, La Tasca has, the owners tell us, the island's only tapas bar. In addition to the usual nibbles of tortillas, croquetas and battered squid, a full-scale Spanish menu offers grilled sardines, paella, and zarzuela. Finish with ice-creams and sorbets. House wine is £10.50.

CHEFS: Jaime Boncompte, Todd Bignall and Jose Lustro PROPRIETOR: Michael Proffitt OPEN: Boncompte's Mon to Fri L 12.30 to 2, all week D 7.30 to 10, La Tasca Mon to Fri L 12 to 2.30, all week D 7 to 10 MEALS: Boncompte's alc (main courses £9.50 to £16.50). Set L £13; La Tasca alc (main courses £8 to £10.50). Tapas menu available 12 to 2, 6 to 7 SERVICE: not inc CARDS: Amex, Delta, MasterCard, Switch, Visa DETAILS: 65 seats. Private parties: 100 main room, 25 private room. Vegetarian meals. Children welcome. No cigars/pipes in dining-room. Wheelchair access (also WC). Music. Air-conditioned ACCOMMODATION: 12 rooms, all with bath/shower. TV. Phone. B&B £55 to £120. Children welcome. Afternoon teas

L'Expérience £

Summerhill, Douglas IM2 4PL
TEL: (01624) 623103 FAX: (01624) 626214 COOKING **2**
at the northern end of promenade COST £19–£34

The Quirks' long-established family restaurant is French through and through, to the extent that you may find yourself eating escargots à la bourguignonne to the sound of a live accordionist. The lunchtime *carte* specialises in open omelettes with a variety of toppings, and in the evening a choice of fixed-price menus is offered. The cooking is resolutely bistro-French – local queen scallops might be served sauté with leeks and garlic and a wine and butter sauce – except when it turns to Italy for grilled goats'-cheese salad with sun-dried tomatoes and toasted pine-nuts, or aubergine slices spread with pesto and topped with mozzarella.

Otherwise, steak Diane, poulet normande, or pork escalope in a sauce of three mustards hark nostalgically back to gastronomic days gone by, and the cheeses are entirely French. So – *quelle surprise* – are the wines, a straightforward, fairly priced selection, with everything except sparklers under £20. House vin de table is £9.50 a litre.

CHEF: Tony Quirk PROPRIETORS: Tony and Jill Quirk OPEN: Mon and Wed to Fri 12 to 2, 7 to 11 MEALS: alc (main courses £5.50 to £7). Set D £15.50 to £20.50 SERVICE: not inc CARDS: Amex, Diners, MasterCard, Switch, Visa DETAILS: 65 seats. 6 seats outside. Private parties: 65 main room. Vegetarian meals. Children's helpings. No cigars/pipes in dining-room. Wheelchair access (also WC). Music

Channel Islands

ST PIERRE DU BOIS Guernsey map 1

Café du Moulin ✱

Rue du Quanteraine, St Pierre du Bois GY7 9DP COOKING **2**
TEL: (01481) 65944 FAX: (01481) 65708 COST £21–£46

A good map and steady nerves are required to find the Café, which is only three miles from St Peter Port, and David and Gina Mann suggest phoning for directions if you find yourself going round in circles. Perseverance is rewarded with some imaginative bistro cooking along the lines of asparagus and pine-nut ravioli with hollandaise, or casseroled mixed fish with saffron butter. Occasionally the kitchen might venture beyond Anglo-French boundaries into Moroccan-style roast loin of lamb with harissa and couscous, or chargrilled Thai beef served with spiced rice and satay sauce. An assiette for chocaholics, sticky toffee pud, or good home-made ice-creams round things off. The sensibly priced wine list includes such goodies as Sancerre from Gitton and Mitchell's Peppertree Shiraz from Clare Valley, Australia. House wines are £9.

CHEF: David Mann PROPRIETORS: David and Gina Mann OPEN: Tue to Sun L 12.15 to 1.30, Tue to Sat D 7.15 to 9.30 (all week L and D July and Aug) MEALS: alc (main courses L £7 to £12, D £14). Set D Tue to Fri £17.95. Light L available. BYO £10 SERVICE: not inc CARDS: MasterCard, Switch, Visa DETAILS: 50 seats. 30 seats outside. Private parties: 50 main room. Car park. Vegetarian meals. Childrens' helpings. No children under 7 at D. No smoking in dining-room. Wheelchair access (no WC). Music

ST SAVIOUR Jersey map 1

▲ *Longueville Manor* ✱

St Saviour JE2 7WF COOKING **5**
TEL: (01534) 25501 FAX: (01534) 31613 COST £25–£58

An impressive entranceway under an ancient stone arch leads to one of the UK's most venerable country house-hotels, standing in 15 acres at the foot of a wooded valley. The original building dates back to the thirteenth century, while the interior marks the passing of the ages in its dark oak-panelled dining-room, some 300 years younger. Seasonal produce comes from the walled kitchen garden, and some of the not-so-seasonal stuff from the hothouses.

Andrew Baird is a busy chef. Not only are there vegetarians and children to formulate menus for, but the extensive *carte* is supplemented by a seven-course tasting menu with pre-selected wines. The style of cooking is strongly classical and not given to fashionability for its own sake, though there are ingredients to remind you that we are in the 1990s. Calves' sweetbreads are folded into a potato pancake with asparagus and pancetta, and the shellfish nage is scented with lemon grass. Main courses might include the house hotpot made with lamb, boulangère potatoes, garlic and rosemary, or an escalope of salmon with lobster risotto. Desserts aim to spoil by adding banana to the crème brûlée and red summer fruits to the pavlova, or by piling sorbets and ice-creams into an almond tuile basket. Staff ensure that no one is neglected. Wines are a magisterial collection of the great and the good, not to mention the antique. Some prices are very high, but there is plenty that is affordable, a more than adequate selection of halves, and house Vin de Pays d'Oc is £9.

CHEF: Andrew Baird PROPRIETORS: Malcolm Lewis and Susan Dufty OPEN: all week 12.30 to 2, 7.30 to 9.30 MEALS: alc (main courses £19 to £21.50). Set L £20, Set D £35. SERVICE: net prices, card slips closed CARDS: Amex, Delta, Diners, MasterCard, Switch, Visa DETAILS: 65 seats. 18 seats outside. Private parties: 65 main room, 16 to 65 private rooms. Car park. Vegetarian meals. Children's helpings. No smoking in 1 dining-room. Wheelchair access (no WC). No music ACCOMMODATION: 32 rooms, all with bath/shower. TV. Phone. B&B £137.50 to £225. Deposit: £100. Rooms for disabled. Children welcome. Dogs welcome in bedrooms only. Afternoon teas. Garden. Swimming-pool

Northern Ireland

BALLYCLARE Co Antrim map 16

Ginger Tree

29 Ballyrobert Road, Ballyclare BB9 9RY COOKING 4
TEL: (01232) 848176 COST £14–£43

'Well worth the effort of driving out there' is an inspector's conclusion about this unusual Japanese restaurant. One oddity is that number 29 Ballyrobert Road is still a farmhouse surrounded by a working farm with parking in the farmyard. The white and black dining-room, with a Japanese garden outside, is 'elegant in a minimalist way' with pleasing flower arrangements. At a lunchtime inspection three people enjoyed everything they ate. An appetiser of green beans in a 'subtle' sauce, garnished with sesame, was followed by miso soup, 'drunk with relish'. Main dishes were a generous 'light, crispy' tempura of prawns with sliced potato and green pepper; buta shogayaki (pork stir-fried with vegetables); and kabayaki (grilled, sauced Lough Neagh eel), which was 'meaty' and 'substantial'. Finish, perhaps surprisingly, with banoffi pudding. House wine is £9.50.

CHEFS/PROPRIETORS: Shotapo Obana and Elizabeth English OPEN: Mon to Fri L 12 to 2.30, Mon to Sat D 7 to 9 (9.30 Sat) CLOSED: 24 to 26 Dec, 12 and 13 July MEALS: alc (main courses £8.50 to £14). Set L £6.80 to £10.25, Set D £12.95 to £26.50 SERVICE: not inc CARDS: Amex, Delta, Diners, MasterCard, Visa DETAILS: 60 seats. Private parties: 80 main room, 25 private room. Car park. Vegetarian meals. Children's helpings. Wheelchair access (also WC). Music. Air-conditioned

BANGOR Co Down map 16

Shanks 🍷

The Blackwood, 150 Crawfordsburn Road,
Bangor BT19 1GB COOKING 6
TEL: (01247) 853313 FAX: (01247) 853785 COST £25–£46

'What a wonderful addition to Northern Ireland's restaurants,' began one report of this gem on the estate of the Dowager Marchioness of Dufferin and Ava. The golf course doesn't intrude, the Conran design and Hockney paintings give it a distinctly cosmopolitan air, and while the upstairs bar's wooden verandah is a good spot for a summer aperitif, the kitchen is fashionably open to view behind glass in the main (downstairs) dining-room. The place generates a sense of luxury and well-being, and considerable buzz. This is a restaurant 'not afraid to express itself'. Part of that expression is a relaxed approach – staff are generally young and pony-tailed – and part is the open-minded way in which good ingredients (some organic) are treated, whether in mainstream European fashion, or with Far Eastern overtones, or both: chicken and foie gras wun-tuns served with a ginger sauce and mango, for instance.

There is no shortage of meaty dishes, from home-made venison sausages to chargrilled loin of lamb with ratatouille and chilli polenta, but fish challenges for supremacy, with scallops in a grain mustard sauce served with black risotto, or salmon fillet, now crusted with tapénade, now with a powerful mix of pecans and chillies. The generally simple grilling of main ingredients is enlivened with bright attendant flavours such as rosemary cream, coriander butter, or truffle mayonnaise. Vegetarians get a fair deal, and the economical kitchen cannily turns a first course of wild mushroom and broccoli brioche with white truffle aïoli into an accompaniment to calf's liver for a meat eater's main course. After all the strong and individual flavours, fruit desserts are a good way to finish, although there is stiff competition from mango steamed pudding with lemon grass syrup and coconut ice-cream, or a warm pear and chocolate tart with pistachio custard.

The wine list ranges from Old World aristocrats, such as Burgundy's Georges Duboeuf and Joseph Drouhin, to New World adventurers in the guise of California's Robert Mondavi and Randall Grahm. The pricing is very reasonable, with plenty of bottles under £15 and house wines starting at £10.95. CELLARMAN'S CHOICE: Rocholi Sauvignon Blanc 1995, Sonoma, California, £16; Ca' del Solo Big House Red 1995, Bonny Doon, California, £14.75.

CHEF: Robbie Millar PROPRIETORS: Robbie and Shirley Millar OPEN: Tue to Fri and Sun L 12.30 to 2.30, Tue to Sat D 7 to 10 CLOSED: 25 and 26 Dec, 1 Jan MEALS: Set L £12.95 (2 courses) to £16.95, Set D £24.50 (2 courses) to £28.50. BYO £5 SERVICE: not inc; 10% for parties of 6 or more CARDS: Amex, Delta, MasterCard, Switch, Visa DETAILS: 85 seats. Private parties: 12 main room, 24 private room. Car park. Vegetarian meals. Children's helpings. No cigars/pipes in 1 dining-room. Music. Air-conditioned

BELFAST Co Antrim map 16

La Belle Epoque £

61–63 Dublin Road, Belfast BT2 7RS COOKING 3
TEL/FAX: (01232) 323244 COST £17–£36

In a smart area of the city centre, the dark green and cream restaurant has an easygoing style which, even when the place is not full, conveys the impression that everyone is having a good time. It is, of course, French, though the pressure to absorb 'international' members into the club – in avocado and chicory salad with sun-dried tomatoes and pine-nuts, for instance – seems to be growing. Elaborate presentation, repetitive garnishes, and the tendency to cut things into small bite-sized pieces irked one reporter, but dishes work well thanks to concentrated sauces and good use of herbs, fruits and spices. Tartare of salmon with capers and gherkin, duck with cherry sauce, and Cajun-style monkfish in ratatouille sauce all illustrate the kitchen's know-how. Crème brûlée with rhubarb has been less successful, or there may be fruit kebab 'that burst juicily into the mouth' served on a bed of pomegranate sauce. Service is unobtrusive and helpful, although the loud music may not be to everyone's taste. The mostly French wine list fails to include vintages and producers of many bottles, though prices are reasonable. House wines start at £8.75.

CHEF: Alain Rousse PROPRIETORS: J. Delbart, Alain Rousse and G. Sanchez OPEN: Mon to Fri L 12 to 5, Mon to Sat D 6 to 11 CLOSED: 25 and 26 dec, 9 to 14 July MEALS: alc (main courses L £4.50 to £7.50, D £7 to £11.50). Set L £5.95 to £10.95 (both 2 courses), Set D Mon to Thur £15 SERVICE: not inc CARDS: Amex, Diners, MasterCard, Switch, Visa DETAILS: 83 seats. Private parties: 20 main room. Vegetarian meals. Children welcome. Wheelchair access (also WC). Music

Deane's

NEW ENTRY

38–40 Howard Street, Belfast BT1 6PF — COOKING 7
TEL: (01232) 560000 FAX: (01232) 560001 — COST £23–£55

Michael Deane moved from his converted railway station in St Helen's Bay and opened up in this former fashion boutique in the thick of things in May 1997. Judging by the crowds, it was a wise move. The upstairs restaurant needs to be booked weeks in advance, and customers for the brasserie cheerfully hang around for an hour waiting for a table. Locals have obviously taken the place to their hearts, which is why it captures 'the mood and atmosphere of Belfast the cosmopolitan international city'.

This is some of the sharpest looking food around, grafting oriental spices and flavourings on to a range of European materials to produce a set of clearly defined dishes of verve and character. Virtually every one has a personal stamp to it. Kedgeree of squab comes with foie gras and curry oil, for instance, and a broth of harissa roast quail is served with lemon grass and glass noodles. A dashing sense of innovation lends vitality to traditional and classical ideas, but the result always seems both simple and appropriate, as in a combination of roast and brandade monkfish niçoise, or Thai-style duck with confit wun tun and chilli. Dishes typically home in on a trio of items, the zest coming from flavoured oils or a *jus*, and desserts are treated likewise: a citrus fruit brûlée with lemon grass ice-cream and physalis, perhaps, or roulade of chocolate with mango and vanilla.

Raymond McArdell does a similarly fine job in the brasserie, where his workplace is open to view amid the loud rock music, bustling waiters, hubbub of chatter and thick smoke. He serves generous pork steaks with leek and coppa risotto, 'exquisite' Thai-spiced salmon and chilli noodles with a lobster and coriander oil, and a trio of 'pungent' mango, passion-fruit and cassis sorbets. There is also a separate vegetarian menu, and around 20 serviceable wines mostly under £15. The restaurant's wine list is an appealing blend of Old and New World bottles with just the sort of bright flavours the food deserves. Sixteen house wines (six of them by the glass) start at £12.50.

CHEFS: Michael Deane and Raymond McArdell PROPRIETORS: Linda and Brian Smyth, and Michael Deane OPEN: restaurant Tue to Sat D only 7 to 9.45; brasserie Mon to Sat 12 to 3, 5 to 11 MEALS: restaurant Set D £27 (2 courses) to £33.50; brasserie alc (main courses £5 to £8.50) SERVICE: not inc; 10% for parties of 8 or more CARDS: Amex, Delta, MasterCard, Switch, Visa DETAILS: 40 seats (restaurant), 90 seats (brasserie). Private parties: 40 main room. Vegetarian meals. Children welcome. Music. Air-conditioned

Nick's Warehouse 🍷

35–39 Hill Street, Belfast BT1 2LB | COOKING 5
TEL: (01232) 439690 FAX: (01232) 230514 | COST £21–£36

Nick and Kathy Price's converted warehouse, divided into downstairs wine bar and upstairs restaurant, is 'well worth seeking out'. The brick walls and modern art add up to 1960s retro-style, but a more 1990s approach is taken to meals. 'The kitchen is serious!' wrote someone who ate in the restaurant, proving the point with starters of 'magnificent' moist crab-cakes with soy and chilli dressing, and excellent lentil and vegetable soup. A glossy red wine and thyme sauce perfectly suited succulent lamb chops, and similar respect for ingredients made duck with red cabbage and apple compote 'a joy'. Fish options may range from turbot with a marmalade of apricots, coriander and chillis, to fillet of hake with rocket pesto. Puddings – crème brûlée, and apple and raisin crumble, for example – keep up the standards. Interesting home-made breads, good, unadorned vegetables, and willing and knowledgeable service also come in for praise.

The short but appealing wine list has been put together with one eye on quality and both eyes on price. There are some real bargains to be found here, particularly on the page of fine wines. Eight house wines start at £7.35 a bottle, £1.85 a glass. CELLARMAN'S CHOICE: St-Véran 'Les Chailloux' 1995, Dom. des Deux Roches, £15.30; Ch. Clare Cabernet Sauvignon 1991, Wakefield, S. Australia, £11.35.

CHEFS: Nick Price and Simon McCance PROPRIETORS: Nick and Kathy Price OPEN: Mon to Fri L 12 to 2.30, Tue to Sat D 6 to 9 CLOSED: 25 and 26 Dec, Easter Mon and Tue, 12 July MEALS: alc L (main courses £8 to £13.50). Set D £16.95 (2 courses) to £19.95. Minimum £7.95 L SERVICE: not inc, card slips closed; 10% for parties of 6 or more CARDS: Amex, Delta, Diners, MasterCard, Switch, Visa DETAILS: 100 seats. Private parties: 50 main room. Vegetarian meals. Children's helpings in restaurant; no children under 12 in wine bar at L. Wheelchair access (also WC). Music. Air-conditioned

Roscoff 🍷 £✱

7 Lesley House, Shaftesbury Square, Belfast BT2 7DB | COOKING 7
TEL: (01232) 331532 FAX: (01232) 312093 | COST £27–£48

'I am told by all my Belfast friends that there is still nowhere else quite like this in the city,' wrote a reporter on her travels. 'It is still considered the height of fashion to dine here.' A gastronomic version of the Grand Tour could well begin, indeed, by heading west rather than towards the Continent. Ireland is crammed with fine places to eat and here is one of the finest. Paul Rankin has long since joined the legion of TV celebrity chefs, which adds to the allure, but there is enough infectious glamour anyway in a dining-room where starkness and brightness prevail.

Brightness is the tone set by the menus too, printed on sunflower-yellow paper: how about crispy fried skate with chilli jam and aïoli to awaken the tastebuds? This is a kitchen that gives the impression of having truly mastered the Italian techniques that it uses, rather than simply having bought a couple of recipe books and crossed its fingers. Risotto primavera thus becomes something 'truly memorable', a bright pea-green assemblage of seasonal asparagus, broad beans and peas, the rice 'cooked to glutinous perfection', the top finished with shaved Parmesan. The whole gamut of pasta, bruschetta and carpaccio comes into play, the last made with salmon which is dressed with lemon oil and herbs and garnished with avocado and tomato. Unusually, there isn't much in the way of offal, but fish has its say in chargrilled eel with Puy lentils, salsa verde and frites, or turbot roasted with tomatoes, olives and thyme. A main course of beef fillet at inspection was 'the sort of thing that makes you realise how a restaurant gains its excellent reputation'. It came with a bacon salad spiked with Roquefort.

Thoughtful flavour combinations inform desserts too: a mascarpone mousse is scented with lemon and accompanied by roast nectarines and amaretti, and a praline ice-cream comes with roast banana slices and a caramel sauce. If there are drawbacks, they extend to no more than the 'awed hush' of the atmosphere that seems odd in this sort of setting, and the occasional lapse in service. The relatively short wine list is full of interest, sharp on quality, and fair with prices, listing Hamilton Russell, Bonny Doon, Cloudy Bay and Ridge from the New World. House wines begin around £12.50 (£2 a glass). CELLARMAN'S CHOICE: Henschke Dry Riesling 1994, Eden Valley, S. Australia, £18; Côtes du Rhône Reserve 1994, Perrin, £14.

CHEF: Paul Rankin PROPRIETORS: Paul and Jeanne Rankin OPEN: Mon to Fri L 12.15 to 3.15, Mon to Sat D 6.30 to 10.15 CLOSED: 25 and 26 Dec, 1 Jan, 12 and 13 July MEALS: Set L £16.50, Set D £28.95 SERVICE: not inc CARDS: Amex, Diners, MasterCard, Switch, Visa DETAILS: 75 seats. Private parties: 75 main room. Vegetarian meals. Children's helpings. No smoking in 1 dining-room. Wheelchair access (also WC). Music. Air-conditioned

Strand £

12 Stranmillis Road, Belfast BT9 5AA — COOKING 1

TEL: (01232) 682266 FAX: (01232) 663189 — COST £16–£41

A straightforward bistro done in shades of purple in the student quarter of Belfast, the Strand serves good-quality ingredients in often interesting combinations, showing care in preparation without fussiness. A lot of deep-frying goes on for the nibbly first courses – mushrooms stuffed with chicken liver pâté and coated in breadcrumbs, plaice goujons, and smoked Cheddar tossed in oats, for example – while main courses go Continental for lamb souvlakia, Corsican cannelloni (filled with ratatouille and topped with cream cheese), and escalope of pork with a layer of Parma ham in a fresh tomato and basil salsa. Puddings have an inventive streak that brings on whisky-laced grape fool, and fresh fruit kebabs with mango and yoghurt sauce. The compact wine list offers mainstream drinking at manageable prices; house French is £7.95.

CHEF: Sean McConnell PROPRIETORS: Stephen McCombe and Frank Cullen OPEN: all week 12 to 11 (9.30 Sun) MEALS: alc (main courses £5 to £13.50). Set L Mon to Sat £6.95 (2 courses), Set L Sun £10.95, Set D £15.95 SERVICE: not inc, card slips closed CARDS: Amex, Diners, MasterCard, Switch, Visa DETAILS: 65 seats. 12 seats outside. Private parties: 25 main room, 10 private room. Vegetarian meals. Music. Air-conditioned

'I made the mistake, when booking, of asking for a vegetarian meal, which elicited the following extraordinary response: "Vegetarians are just difficult people. They don't do it out of principle, you know. They just do it to be awkward".'
(On eating in Hereford & Worcester)

LONDONDERRY Co Londonderry map 16

▲ *Beech Hill Country House, Ardmore Restaurant*

32 Ardmore Road, Londonderry BT47 3QP
TEL: (01504) 49279 FAX: (01504) 45366
turn off A6 Londonderry to Belfast road at Faughan Bridge and proceed to Ardmore chapel; hotel is opposite chapel

COOKING **5**
COST £23–£49

Two miles from the centre of Northern Ireland's second city, but sufficiently off the beaten track to feel entirely pastoral, Beech Hill was built in the early part of the eighteenth century for a family of English merchants. It has been sensitively converted, making much use of pastel shades, and the Ardmore Restaurant looks out on to waterfalls and ponds. Lunch is a four-course fixed-price deal while dinner offers the choice of five courses or à la carte, and there is a separate menu for vegetarians. Techniques bring novelty to familiar items, so that mussels are deep-fried and served with fondant potato and a 'tagliatelle' of carrot, and duck confit and shallots are fashioned into a mille-feuille and garnished with glazed beetroot. Champ scone accompanies grilled poussin in a rosemary *jus*, while the single fish option on the *carte* may be red snapper with deep-fried squid sauced with tomato and saffron. Artistry comes to the fore in desserts such as teardrop of chocolate truffle with a sauce of Irish cream liqueur, or in a pairing of rice pudding and mango with blackcurrant sorbet. A couple who stayed over commended the 'superb' breakfasts. New World wines head up a wide-ranging and fairly priced list. House wines start at £10.

CHEF: J. Nicholas PROPRIETOR: Seamus Donnelly OPEN: all week 12 to 2.30, 6 to 9.30 CLOSED: 24 and 25 Dec MEALS: alc D (main courses £14 to £17). Set L £15.95, Set D £21.95. Light snacks served 10am to 10pm SERVICE: not inc CARDS: Amex, MasterCard, Switch, Visa DETAILS: 45 seats. Private parties: 80 main room, 15 to 80 private rooms. Car park. Vegetarian meals. Children welcome. No smoking in dining-room. Music ACCOMMODATION: 17 rooms, all with bath/shower. TV. Phone. B&B £52.50 to £85. Rooms for disabled. Children welcome. Baby facilities. Afternoon teas. Garden

PORTRUSH Co Antrim map 16

Ramore 🍷 £

The Harbour, Portrush BT56 8BN
TEL: (01265) 824313

COOKING **4**
COST £23–£45

You must book well in advance at this restaurant, whose views of Victorian houses fronting the boat-filled harbour are only part of its appeal. In an open-plan area along one of the long walls, George McAlpin cooks an inventive *carte* that shows willingness to experiment with combinations of flavours. His skill in doing so is demonstrated in starters of smoked salmon and Caesar salad with pancetta and prawn croûtons, and Parma ham with truffled mushrooms, for example. 'Pink and succulent' Peking duckling is accompanied by artichokes, salsify, button onions, red wine *jus* and truffle mayonnaise, while fillet of spring lamb comes with goats'-cheese soufflé. A blackboard announces specials of the day – curried lentil soup, halibut, and an apple, raspberry and pear crumble, perhaps – while desserts could include pannacotta with a punch of red fruit and wine, or chocolate pizza with hot white chocolate sauce. The attractive layout and buzz of conversation in the light, airy room help 'turn just a meal into a proper outing'. Staff are polite, friendly and efficient.

Stylish wines from around the world embrace the best of modern and traditional winemaking. Prices are kept to a modest level, with house wines starting at £7.95. CELLARMAN'S CHOICE: Cape Mentelle Chardonnay 1994, Margaret River, W. Australia, £18.95; Meerlust Rubicon 1991, Stellenbosch, South Africa, £16.25.

CHEF: George McAlpin PROPRIETORS: George and Jane McAlpin OPEN: Tue to Sat D only 6.30 to 10.30 CLOSED: 24 to 26 Dec, 1 Jan MEALS: alc (main courses £8.50 to £13) SERVICE: not inc CARDS: Delta, MasterCard, Switch, Visa DETAILS: 75 seats. Private parties: 75 main room. Car park. Children welcome before 9pm. Wheelchair access (no WC). Music

Republic of Ireland

We have not given marks for cooking for the Republic of Ireland entries because of a shortage of reports; please do give us feedback should you visit. To telephone the Republic from mainland Britain, dial 00 353 followed by the number listed, but dropping the initial 0. Prices are quoted in Irish punts.

ADARE Co Limerick map 16

▲ *Adare Manor*

Adare

TEL: (061) 396566 FAX: (061) 396124 COST £36–£73

It would be hard to conceive of a more ostentatiously grand country-house operation than this. The Manor sits in 900 acres of County Limerick, its colossal Gothic façade fronting landscaped gardens, its interior nonchalantly mimicking Versailles. The view from the dining-room stretches across box-hedged lawns towards 18 holes' worth of golf course. It must be intimidating for any chef to try to match these surroundings, but Gerard Costello took on the challenge since the last edition of the *Guide* and produces pan-fried fillet of beef with leeks and shallots; loin of pork with braised red cabbage, caramelised apples and cider sabayon; and brill with a salad of peas and redcurrants. Desserts might include banana mousse with caramel sauce or coconut meringue nest with fresh berries and raspberry sorbet. House wines from the south of France are £19.

CHEF: Gerard Costello PROPRIETORS: Mr and Mrs Tom Kane OPEN: Sun L 12.30 to 2, all week D 7 to 9 MEALS: alc (main courses £17 to £24). Set L £21.50, Set D £32.50. BYO £10 SERVICE: 15%, card slips closed CARDS: Amex, Diners, MasterCard, Visa DETAILS: 75 seats. Private parties: 100 main room, 30 to 130 private rooms. Car park. Vegetarian meals. Children's helpings before 8pm. No children under 10. Jacket and tie. No-smoking area. Wheelchair access (also WC). Music. Air-conditioned ACCOMMODATION: 64 rooms, all with bath/shower. TV. Phone. Air-conditioned. Room only £215 to £350. Rooms for disabled. Children welcome. Afternoon teas. Garden. Swimming-pool. Fishing

AHAKISTA Co Cork map 16

Shiro

Ahakista

TEL: (027) 67030 FAX: (027) 67206 COST £51–£63

Ahakista lies almost as far west as you can get in Europe, but this Japanese dinner house (their own description) maintains the traditional elegance and hospitality of Mrs Kei Pilz's homeland. Werner Pilz greets and shows you to a table 'beautifully set with origami decorations'. A short menu in Western format begins with zensai appetisers and soup, followed by a choice of some seven main dishes including sushi, fish and vegetable tempura, steamed wild salmon with ginger and lemon, and 'exceptional' quail yakitori. Finish with home-made ice-cream. As for wine, 'We BYO'd.'

CHEF: Kei Pilz PROPRIETORS: Werner and Kei Pilz OPEN: all week D only 7 to 9.30 CLOSED: 23 to 25 Dec, 31 Dec, Jan and Feb MEALS: Set D £43. BYO £4 per person SERVICE: inc CARDS: Amex, Diners, MasterCard, Visa (5% surcharge) DETAILS: 20 seats. Private parties: 18 main room, 6 private room. Car park. Children's helpings. No children under 10. Jacket and tie. No smoking in 1 dining-room. Wheelchair access (no WC). Music. Air-conditioned

BALLINA Co Mayo map 16

▲ *Mount Falcon Castle* ✱

Ballina
TEL: (096) 70811 FAX: (096) 71517
on N26 between Foxford and Ballina COST £27–£33

Angling and game shooting are the principal leisure pursuits in the vicinity of this handsome grey-stone country house, run by the same family since 1932. Dinner is at eight o'clock sharp and everyone eats at a long antique table headed by the redoubtable Constance Aldridge, nearly 90 and still playing host as if it were all a new adventure. Homely food cooked on an Aga is the order of the day – cheese soufflés, carrot soup, roast beef with horseradish, profiteroles with chocolate sauce – and it is served against a background of garrulous informality. Wines are overwhelmingly French but well-selected, with house burgundy at £9.50.

CHEF: Denise Moyles PROPRIETORS: the Aldridge family OPEN: all week D only 8 (1 sitting) CLOSED: 23 to 26 Dec, Feb and March MEALS: Set D £20. BYO £5 SERVICE: not inc, card slips closed CARDS: Amex, Delta, Diners, MasterCard, Visa DETAILS: 30 seats. Private parties: 55 main room, 10 private room. Car park. Children's helpings. No smoking in dining-room. No music ACCOMMODATION: 10 rooms, all with bath/shower. Phone. B&B £45 to £98. Deposit required. Children welcome. Baby facilities. No dogs in public rooms. Afternoon teas. Garden. Fishing

BALLYDEHOB Co Cork map 16

Annie's

Main Street, Ballydehob
TEL: (028) 37292 COST £29–£37

Pre-dinner drinks come with a difference at Annie's roadside village restaurant: you have them in the pub over the road, taking the menus with you, and you'll be called across when the starters are nearly ready. That should tell you all you need to know about the scrupulously casual feel to the place. That said, there is nothing slapdash about the cooking, which takes in a salad of lambs' kidneys cooked in port, seafood soup with garlic bread, and fillets of brill and sole stuffed with crabmeat. Toffee, fudge and butterscotch are the pudding themes most in evidence, but there may also be apple and blackberry sponge, or strawberry shortcake. Each section on the wine list is limited to no more than three bottles, which are nearly always well chosen. House Côtes du Ventoux from Jaboulet is £11.50.

CHEFS/PROPRIETORS: Dano and Anne Barry OPEN: Tue to Sat D only 7 to 9.30 CLOSED: Oct to Nov. Phone to check opening during low season MEALS: alc (main courses £14). Set D £22 SERVICE: not inc CARDS: MasterCard, Visa DETAILS: 24 seats. Private parties: 26 main room. Children's helpings. No cigars/pipes in dining-room. Wheelchair access (no WC). Music

---

BALLYLICKEY Co Cork map 16

▲ *Ballylickey Manor*

Ballylickey, Bantry Bay
TEL: (027) 50071 FAX: (027) 50124 COST £32–£55

Built as a shooting-lodge some 300 years ago, the gleaming white manor-house lies among the inlets of Bantry Bay. The place may seem like a different world but, like many another drowsy Irish retreat, it exerts a powerful pull on visitors from more hectic faraway places. A good part of the spell is cast by Gilles Eynaud's highly polished French cooking. That means salmon mousse and avocado wrapped in smoked salmon, tournedos with béarnaise, and carré d'agneau persillé. The kitchen is not afraid to branch out, however, when the mood takes it, so there may also be monkfish with spaghetti and a créole tomato sauce. Délice au chocolat, and tarte au citron are classical ways to finish. The wine list furnishes pretty classic drinking too – all French – with prices starting at £13.

CHEF: Gilles Eynaud PROPRIETORS: Mr and Mrs Graves OPEN: all week 12.30 to 2, 7 to 9.30 CLOSED: Nov to Apr MEALS: alc (main courses £10 to £18). Set D £25 to £30 SERVICE: 10%, card slips closed CARDS: Amex, MasterCard, Visa DETAILS: 30 seats. 20 seats outside. Private parties: 40 main room, 15 private room. Car park. Vegetarian meals. Children's helpings. No children under 5. No smoking in dining-room. Music ACCOMMODATION: 11 rooms, all with bath/shower. TV. Phone. B&B £100 to £180. Deposit: 1 night's stay. Children welcome; high teas for under-5s. Baby facilities. Dogs by arrangement. Garden. Swimming-pool. Fishing

---

BALLYVAUGHAN Co Clare map 16

▲ *Gregans Castle* 

Ballyvaughan
TEL: (065) 77005 FAX: (065) 77111
on N67, 3½m S of Ballyvaughan COST £22–£73

In the middle of mountainous County Clare, in a strikingly beautiful region called the Burren, stands this low white building that was once an ancestral home and is now a hotel with all mod cons. Gary Masterson took over the kitchens in 1997, and maintains the highly accomplished standards of his predecessor in steamed local mussels with ginger, garlic and coconut cream, and panaché of Aran seafood cooked with tomatoes and herbs. Chinese technique creeps into a main course of Barbary duck breast with stir-fried noodles and a plum and honey sauce, and the show-off stuff comes at dessert stage, when a terrine of five fruits is matched with assorted coulis and a brandy-snap. Local cheeses are served with apple chutney.

The restaurant tells us that 'Quiet and well-behaved children under the firm supervision of their parents are very welcome'. The helpfully annotated wine list travels the world, picking up an interesting range of styles and varietals along the way, such as Fendant from Switzerland, Malbec from Argentina and Tinta Barocca from South Africa. Half a dozen house wines start at £14 a bottle, and are all available by the glass at £3.25. CELLARMAN'S CHOICE: Frog's Leap Carneros Chardonnay 1995, Napa Valley, California, £38; Meerlust Rubicon 1993, Stellenbosch, South Africa, £27.50.

CHEF: Gary Masterson PROPRIETORS: the Haden family OPEN: all week 12 to 3, 7 to 8.30 CLOSED: mid-Oct to late March MEALS: alc (main courses L £5.50 to £11, D £16 to £30). Set D £30 SERVICE: not inc, card slips closed CARDS: Amex, MasterCard, Visa DETAILS: 50 seats. Private parties: 90 main room. Car park. Vegetarian meals. Children's helpings. No smoking in 1 dining-room. Wheelchair access (also WC). Music ACCOMMODATION: 22 rooms, all with bath/shower. Phone. B&B £90 to £260. Rooms for disabled. Children welcome. Baby facilities. Dogs welcome in stable only. Afternoon teas. Garden

BLACKLION Co Cavan map 16

IRISH 1998 BISTRO

▲ *MacNean Bistro* NEW ENTRY

Blacklion
TEL: (072) 53022 FAX: (072) 53404
on N16, 10m W of Enniskillen COST £21–£51

'What a find!' exulted a reporter who stumbled over the border into County Cavan and discovered the Maguire family's comforting bistro and bar. Neven the chef is still in his early twenties, but is cooking at a level that one would expect to find in some grand metropolitan hotel. Organic ingredients, top-quality oils and elaborate spun-sugar creations are among its more obvious manifestations, and the menu delivers the likes of lobster raviolo with coconut sauce garlanded with nasturtiums and flowering thyme, but with the emphasis as much on flavour as on the visuals. After sorbet or salad, it's on to silver-domed main courses such as roast monkfish with spiced cabbage 'all very delicately done', and dressed with a truffle vinaigrette, or duck leg confit with a polenta cake, wun-tun and lemon thyme gravy. Desserts are where the fireworks really flare up, in double-decker cheesecake or gooseberry meringue, and the pastrywork in a classic tarte fine aux pommes with caramel ice-cream was exemplary. The rather perfunctory wine list opens with a slate of house selections from here and there, starting at £9.70.

CHEF: Neven Maguire PROPRIETORS: Vera and Joe Maguire OPEN: Sun L 12.30 to 3.30, Tue to Sun D 6 to 8.45 CLOSED: 25 to 27 Dec MEALS: alc (main courses £12 to £15). Set L £12, Set D £26 to £32 (Menu Prestige for whole table only). BYO £4 SERVICE: not inc CARDS: Visa DETAILS: 40 seats. Private parties: 40 main room, 14 private room. Car park. Vegetarian meals. Children's helpings. No smoking in dining-room. Music ACCOMMODATION: 10 rooms, all with bath/shower. TV. Phone. B&B £23 to £46. Deposit: £20. Children welcome. Baby facilities. Afternoon teas

'For the fish course [the waitress] told us with a smile that the halibut would be on a bed of "crapinata". "Sounds terrible," my husband said. She convulsed with merriment. . . . Later she returned to tell us it was caponata. "One of the chefs looked it up in a book," she explained.' (On eating in Scotland)

BRAY Co Wicklow map 16

Tree of Idleness

Seafront, Bray
TEL: (01) 2863498 COST £28–£51

Susan Courtellas has been at the helm of this popular seafront restaurant since 1979, and continues to chart a steady course. The thrust of the cooking is Mediterranean, with Greek-Cypriot dishes much in evidence. Traditional classics such as melitzanosalata, dolmades, souvlaki and roast suckling pig share the billing with squid ink ravioli filled with salmon and dill, or roast Wicklow venison with red wine sauce and cranberry confit. The dessert trolley is loaded with home-made baklava, ice-creams and fruit. A huge wine list is dominated by fine clarets dating back to 1945, and Burgundy and the Rhône are well represented too. The bulk of the list is sadly bereft of vintage information, but interest ranges from California's Opus One, via dessert and fortified wines from the Crimean Massandra Collection, to Greek and Cypriot house wines starting at £11.50.

CHEF: Ismail Basaran PROPRIETOR: Susan Courtellas OPEN: Tue to Sun D only 7.30 to 11 (10 Sun) CLOSED: 25 Dec, last 2 weeks Aug MEALS: alc (main courses £10 to £16.50). Set D £18.50 to £21 SERVICE: 10%, card slips closed CARDS: Amex, Diners, MasterCard, Visa DETAILS: 50 seats. Private parties. 25 main room. Vegetarian meals. Children welcome. No-smoking area. Wheelchair access (no WC). Music

CASHEL Co Tipperary map 16

Chez Hans 🍷

Moor Lane, Cashel
TEL: (062) 61177 COST £34–£51

It will soon be 30 years since Hans-Peter Matthiä left his native Germany to come and live in a converted church at the foot of Cashel Rock. If the ambience sounds strange or foreboding, fear not: the informality of service and the bubbly atmosphere at Chez Hans are infectious. 'Tender and succulent' chicken breast is stuffed with Cashel Blue cheese and leeks, green tagliatelle comes with smoked salmon and Parmesan, and roast duckling is enhanced with garlic, honey and thyme. 'Rich and delicious' walnut ice-cream with caramel sauce is a good way to finish. The Chez Hans wine list begins with 11 bottles under £12, including a spätlese from the proprietor's family vineyards in Germany. The list continues with a French selection of impressive provenance, moves on to Italy and Spain, then makes a flying visit to the New World. CELLARMAN'S CHOICE: Montagny premier cru 'Les Chagnots' 1995, Antonin Rodet, £17.50; Crozes-Hermitage 'Font Vignal' 1994, Caves St-Pierre, £14.50.

CHEF/PROPRIETOR: Hans-Peter Matthiä OPEN: Tue to Sat D only 6.30 to 10 CLOSED: 24 to 26 Dec, first 3 weeks Jan, Good Friday MEALS: alc (main courses £15.50 to £21). BYO £3 SERVICE: not inc CARDS: MasterCard, Visa DETAILS: 75 seats. Private parties: 90 main room. Car park. Vegetarian meals. Children's helpings. No-smoking area. Wheelchair access (also WC). Music. Air-conditioned

CASTLEBALDWIN Co Sligo map 16

▲ *Cromleach Lodge*

Ballindoon, Castlebaldwin
TEL: (071) 65155 FAX: (071) 65455 COST £37–£59

Cromleach sits on a hillside gazing over Lough Arrow to the mountains beyond. As if the views weren't enough to tempt visitors to stay, Moira Tighe offers residents a multi-course tasting menu that may take them from a paupiette of lemon sole filled with crabmeat and ginger through to a platter of assorted desserts. Other customers are equally well served, though, with the likes of baked turbot with an emulsified rosemary dressing, or loin of lamb crusted with garlic and herbs. Layered torte of banana and caramel with toffee sauce is an example from a pudding list headed 'Tonight's Delights'. A couple of pages of wines from around the world priced under £20 introduce the predominantly French list. The producers have been carefully chosen to combine reliability with interest. House Bordeaux is £12.95.

CHEF: Moira Tighe PROPRIETORS: Christy and Moira Tighe OPEN: all week D only 6.30 to 9 CLOSED: Nov to Jan MEALS: alc (main courses £17). Set D £35. Minimum £25 SERVICE: not inc, card slips closed CARDS: Amex, Diners, MasterCard, Visa DETAILS: 50 seats. Private parties: 25 main room, 4 to 25 private rooms. Car park. Children's helpings. No children under 7 after 7. No smoking in dining-room. Music ACCOMMODATION: 10 rooms, all with bath/shower. TV. Phone. B&B £59 to £138. Children welcome. Baby facilities. Dogs welcome in kennels. Garden. Fishing

CLONAKILTY Co Cork map 16

Dunworley Cottage

Butlerstown, Clonakilty
TEL: (023) 40314
signposted from Timoleague, south of Bandon COST £29–£40

Katherine Norén has a new chef this year at Dunworley, but the Scandinavian influence in the food lives on in the cured herring still offered as a starter. Enjoy the bounty of the seas in the selection from the day's catch that the menu calls Dunworley Ocean Plate, or opt for greater complexity in meat dishes such as fillets of chicken and pigeon with sweet-and-sour sauce and a warm tomato salad. Home-made ice-creams or a chocolate tart will fill the bill for pudding-eaters. The wine list flits briskly between hemispheres, leading with a choice of French and Italian house wines from £10.25.

CHEF: Alexander Flach PROPRIETOR: Katherine Norén OPEN: Wed to Sun 12.30 to 3, 7 to 9 (L in summer only; booking essential L and D all year) CLOSED: mid-Sept to mid-Mar (phone to check) MEALS: alc (main courses £12). Set D £22.50 SERVICE: 10% CARDS: Amex, Diners, MasterCard, Visa DETAILS: 50 seats. Private parties: 30 main room, 20 private room. Car park. Children's helpings. No children after 8pm. No smoking in 1 dining-room. Music. Air-conditioned

▲ *means accommodation is available.*

CORK Co Cork map 16

▲ *Arbutus Lodge* 

Montenotte
TEL: (021) 501237 FAX: (021) 502893 COST £23–£70

The Lodge is named after the arbutus tree that stands in the garden. It was once the residence of the Lord Mayor of Cork and retains an agreeable feeling of grandeur. For 35 years it has also been one of the landmarks on Ireland's gastronomic map, turning out spiced beef with home-made chutney, tripe and drisheen, traditional Irish stew, and rum-flavoured chocolate gâteau. The food has typically been modern yet rooted in Ireland, although shortly before the *Guide* went to press Helen Ward took over the kitchens, too late for us to discover whether any changes were planned, or how the cooking was received. Friendly service adds to people's enjoyment. The justly praised wine list combines modern wonders of the winemaking world with some venerable, not to say ancient, institutions – Château Margaux 1904, anyone? Mark-ups are kept to a very fair level and prices start with a Chilean Sauvignon at £9.95. CELLARMAN'S CHOICE: Morey-St-Denis 'Clos de Monts Luisants' 1992, Dom. Ponsot, £42.50; Eileen Hardy Reserve Shiraz 1993, McLaren Vale, S. Australia, £23.75.

CHEF: Helen Ward PROPRIETORS: the Ryan Family OPEN: Mon to Sat L and D 1 to 2, 7 to 9.30; bar menu 12.30 to 2.30 MEALS: alc (main courses £17 to £19.50). Set L £15.50, Set D £24.50 to £29.75 SERVICE: not inc CARDS: Amex, Diners, MasterCard, Visa DETAILS: 60 seats. Private parties: 12 main room, 25 to 100 private rooms. Car park. Vegetarian meals. Children's helpings. No cigars/pipes in dining-room. No music. Air-conditioned ACCOMMODATION: 20 rooms, all with bath/shower. TV. Phone. Air-conditioned. B&B £50 to £120. Children welcome. Baby facilities. Afternoon teas. Garden

Crawford Gallery Café £

Emmet Place, Cork
TEL: (021) 274415 COST £18–£28

A daytime café housed in what was originally part of Cork Custom House. The place is owned by Ballymaloe House (see entry, Shanagarry) and their speciality breads are always on offer. A new menu appears each week and fresh fish from the pier in Ballycotton is a strength. Otherwise expect open sandwiches, warm salads, lamb curry, or Mediterranean-style roast pork with tomato and chilli sauce. Desserts tend to be old-school favourites of Irish apple cake, rice pudding, and chocolate rum mousse. Afternoon teas are also put on for leg-weary shoppers. House French is £10.

CHEF: Chris O'Brien PROPRIETOR: Ballymaloe House OPEN: Mon to Sat L only 12 to 2.30 (3 Sat) CLOSED: 25 Dec to 2 Jan, bank hols MEALS: alc (main courses £7.50). Set L £10. BYO (no corkage) SERVICE: not inc CARDS: MasterCard, Visa DETAILS: 70 seats. Private parties: 00 main room, 150 private room. Vegetarian meals. Children's helpings. No-smoking area. Wheelchair access (no WC). Music

denotes an outstanding wine cellar; 𝐈 *denotes a good wine list, worth travelling for.*

DINGLE Co Kerry map 16

Beginish 🍷 $✱

Green Street, Dingle
TEL: (066) 51588 FAX: (066) 51591 COST £19–£44

The Moores' restaurant occupies a Georgian terraced house with an immaculately appointed dining-room where original paintings and antique plates adorn the walls. 'The fish dishes were excellent,' reports one correspondent, praise that should lift Pat Moore's heart because fish cookery is her chief vocation. Crab with spiced avocado and tomato, traditional fish chowder, and roast cod on sweet red peppers and potatoes scented with thyme are what to expect, though meat eaters are by no means neglected. Finish, perhaps, with a parfait of Baileys with raspberry coulis. The cosmopolitan wine list is strongest in its range of clarets and burgundies, although Spain and Australia throw up some interesting bins and there is a good choice of half-bottles. Nine house wines are priced at £12 a bottle, £3 a glass. CELLARMAN'S CHOICE: Muscadet de Sèvre et Maine sur lie, Ch. de la Cassemichère 1995, £13.50; Fleurie 1995, Joseph Drouhin, £18.50.

CHEF: Pat Moore PROPRIETORS: John and Pat Moore OPEN: Tue to Sun 12.30 to 2.15, 6 to 10 CLOSED: mid-Nov to mid-march MEALS: alc (main courses £9.50 to £14.50) SERVICE: not inc, card slips closed CARDS: Amex, MasterCard, Visa DETAILS: 52 seats. Private parties: 20 main room. Vegetarian meals. Children's helpings. No smoking in 1 dining-room. Wheelchair access (no WC). Music

▲ *Doyle's* 🍷 $✱

4 John Street, Dingle
TEL: (066) 51174 FAX: (066) 51816 COST £24–£45

A town-house restaurant with additional guest rooms in a cluster of little houses up the street, Doyle's is all about straight-down-the-line fish cookery with a light French accent. You may start simply with a plate of salmon smoked in-house, or more ambitiously with a seafood sausage on Puy lentils with honey mustard sauce. Lobster is sold by weight as a main course, or there may be garlicky mussels or crab claws in beurre blanc. Meringues and cheesecakes are the sorts of puddings to expect, and an Irish farmhouse cheese selection is always available. The wine list has been carefully chosen to marry well with seafood dishes and has a particularly fine selection of whites from Burgundy and the Loire Valley. Lovers of reds are not neglected, however, as a quick trawl reveals some robust Riojas and some classy clarets. House wines begin at £10.80 and, appropriately, include a Reichensteiner from Blackwater Valley in County Cork (£17), Ireland's sole commercial vineyard.

CHEF: Stella Doyle PROPRIETORS: John and Stella Doyle OPEN: Mon to Sat D only 6 to 9.30 CLOSED: mid-Nov to mid-Mar MEALS: alc (main courses £11.50 to £16). Set D £14.50. BYO £5 SERVICE: 10%, card slips closed CARDS: Diners, MasterCard, Visa DETAILS: 50 seats. Private parties: 30 main room. Vegetarian meals. Children's helpings. No smoking in 1 dining-room. Wheelchair access (also women's WC). No music ACCOMMODATION: 8 rooms, all with bath/shower. TV. Phone. B&B £45 to £68. Deposit: £45. Rooms for disabled. Children welcome

▲ *Half Door* £✱

3 John Street, Dingle
TEL: (066) 51600 and 51883 COST £20–£59

There is a certain stylishness in the low-ceilinged restaurant of stone and wood, and Denis O'Connor's cooking looks forward as well as back. Crisp monkfish medallions with tomato and basil sauce, and pasta gratin, share the bill with lobster thermidor and roast duckling with citrus. A pair who ate mustard-crusted plaice, and salmon en croûte with leek and wine sauce fulsomely praised the skills in evidence. Bailey's cheesecake is light and agreeably alcoholic, or you may prefer to finish with armagnac parfait served with marinated prunes. An enterprising wine list is strong on French classics but has some good New World bins as well. Fourteen house wines start at £12.50.

CHEF: Denis O'Connor PROPRIETORS: Denis and Teresa O'Connor OPEN: Mon to Fri L 12.30 to 2.15, Mon to Sat D 6 to 10 CLOSED: mid-Jan to mid-Mar MEALS: alc (main courses L £5 to £20, D £11.50 to £25) SERVICE: not inc CARDS: Amex, MasterCard, Visa DETAILS: 56 seats. Private parties: 18 main room. Children's helpings before 8pm. No smoking in 1 dining-room. Wheelchair access (no WC). Music. Air-conditioned ACCOMMODATION: 7 rooms, all with bath/shower. TV. Phone. B&B £25 to £50. Deposit. £20. Children welcome. Garden

DONEGAL Co Donegal map 16

▲ *Harvey's Point*

Lough Eske, Donegal
TEL: (073) 22208 FAX: (073) 22352 COST £21–£51

A little piece of Switzerland on the shores of Lough Eske is what Harvey's Point sets out to be, with the Blue Stack mountains standing in for the Alps. Marc Gysling's cooking is more haute cuisine French, though, offered in the form of prix-fixe menus at both lunch and dinner, with a soup or sorbet option preceding the main course in the evening. Local oysters in a shallot vinaigrette, and a version of Caesar salad are typical first courses. Then it might be a slice of salmon with spinach and a crab bisque sauce, but most of the main courses are meats along the simple but classical lines of chicken breast stuffed with wild mushrooms on a port sauce, or rack of lamb with potato cakes and a mint *jus*. Black chocolate cake with Sauternes sabayon makes a dramatic dessert. The predominantly French wine list lacks some burgundy producers' names, but begins with Côtes du Roussillon at £11.75.

CHEF: Marc Gysling PROPRIETOR: Jody Gysling OPEN: all week 12.30 to 2.30, 6.30 to 9.30 CLOSED: weekdays Nov to Mar MEALS: alc D (main courses £10.50 to £15). Set L £9.50 (2 courses) to £12.50, Set D £22.50 SERVICE: 10%, card slips closed CARDS: Amex, Diners, MasterCard, Visa DETAILS: 80 seats. Private parties: 30 main room, 60 and 300 private rooms. Car park. Vegetarian meals. No children under 10. Jacket and tie. Wheelchair access (also WC). Music. Air-conditioned ACCOMMODATION: 20 rooms, all with bath/shower. TV. Phone. B&B £55 to £99. Deposit: £30. Rooms for disabled. Dogs welcome. Afternoon teas. Garden. Fishing

See inside the front cover for an explanation of the symbols used at the tops of entries.

DOUGLAS Co Cork map 16

Lovetts 🍷

Churchyard Lane, off Well Road, Douglas
TEL: (021) 294909 and 293604 FAX: (021) 294024 COST £23–£50

This combined formal restaurant and brasserie is now run by the second generation of Lovetts. It is housed in a late-Georgian building set in its own impressive grounds and, as in much of Ireland, fish cookery is the kitchen's first love. Black sole is grilled on the bone and straightforwardly sauced with citrus butter. Gratinated mussels with garlic, fine beef carpaccio, and polenta with a Neapolitan sauce have all shown up well, even if the pace of service made the diners feel that they 'were all in training for the Irish Derby'. Medallions of venison with a potato and apricot cake and brandy sauce is an example of the grander fare on offer. Finish with coffee and almond meringue, or Irish farmhouse cheeses. An international list of fine wines in the restaurant is condensed to essentials for the brasserie. House wines are an Alsace Pinot Blanc and a Rioja at £12.75. CELLARMAN'S CHOICE: Aotea Sauvignon Blanc 1996, Gisborne, New Zealand, £15.75; Ch. Musar 1989, Gaston Hochar, £19.45.

CHEF: Marie Harding PROPRIETORS: Dermod and Margaret Lovett, and family OPEN: Mon to Fri L 12.30 to 2, Mon to Sat D 6.30 to 9.45 CLOSED: 24 to 30 Dec, bank hols MEALS: alc D (main courses £12.50 to £18). Set L £14.50, Set D £24 SERVICE: not inc, card slips closed CARDS: Amex, Diners, MasterCard, Visa DETAILS: 50 seats. Private parties: 50 main room, 24 and 50 private rooms. Car park. Vegetarian meals. Children welcome. No-smoking area. Wheelchair access (no WC). Music

DUBLIN Co Dublin map 16

▲ *The Clarence, Tea Room* NEW ENTRY

6–8 Wellington Quay, Dublin 2
TEL: (01) 670 7766 FAX: (01) 670 7800 COST £25–£55

Rock bands were once better known for trashing hotels than refurbishing them in the manner of Charles Rennie Mackintosh. Notwithstanding that, the Clarence reopened in 1996 after an extensive facelift under the ownership of internationally renowned supergroup U2. 'Young, attentive and extremely helpful' staff set the tone, and the cooking in the whimsically named Tea Room is by Michael Martin, a chef who has worked with the Roux brothers, Nico Ladenis and Pierre Koffman. The pedigree shows in a first course of sauté foie gras on caramelised peppered mango, and in a spice-crusted tian of crab with ginger cream and chilli oil. Confident creativity runs through the menu, delivering grilled yellowfin tuna with buttered bok choi, or fillet of new season's lamb with celeriac purée and a black olive *jus.* It is all subject to the most scrupulous technique, as shown at dessert stage by the show-stopping assiette gourmandise, but also by a Kirsch-infused crème brûlée with seasonal berries. Dublin has yet another new restaurant to be proud of. The enterprising wine list has many names to quicken the pulse, but prices soon escalate. House French is £10.

CHEF: Michael Martin PROPRIETOR: Brushfield Ltd OPEN: Mon to Fri L 12.30 to 2.20, all week D 6.30 to 10.20 (10 Sun) MEALS: alc (main courses £10 to £18.50). Set L £13.50 (2 courses) to £17 SERVICE: not inc CARDS: Amex, Diners, MasterCard, Visa DETAILS: 90 seats. Private parties: 90 main room. Vegetarian meals. Children welcome. No-smoking area. Wheelchair access (also WC). Music ACCOMMODATION: 50 rooms, all with bath/shower. TV. Phone. Room only £165 to £190. Deposit: 50%. Rooms for disabled. Children welcome. Baby facilities. Afternoon teas

Commons

Newman House, 85–86 St Stephen's Green, Dublin 2
TEL: (01) 475 2597 and 478 0530 FAX: (01) 478 0551 COST £32–£74

The setting must be one of the swishest in the city. Commons occupies Newman House, a fine Georgian town-house (complete with a south-facing terrace) that was the original home of University College. Now it exudes grandeur. Another new chef took up residence at the end of 1996, but the menu continues to deal in modern luxuries and re-workings of the classics. Mosaic of quail and vegetables is served with a black truffle dressing, salmon is dressed up with potato 'scales', asparagus tips and champagne mousseline, while veal sweetbreads are accompanied by hazelnut mash and Irish mead *jus*. There's also something advertised as 'squab cooked two ways with a pollen and birdseed galette, and black grape sauce'. Desserts might include 'excellent' warm glazed plum tart, or brown-bread parfait with red berry coulis. Wines, which are arranged by varietal or style, are mostly of a high quality with prices to match. Six French and Chilean house wines are £18.

CHEF: Sebastien Masi PROPRIETOR: Michael Fitzgerald OPEN: Mon to Fri L 12.30 to 2.15, Mon to Sat D 7 to 10.15 CLOSED: 1 week Christmas, bank hols MEALS: alc (main courses £18 to £22). Set L £20, Set D £35. BYO £7 SERVICE: not inc CARDS: Amex, Diners, MasterCard, Switch, Visa DETAILS: 60 seats. Private parties: 12 main room, 26 and 60 private rooms. Vegetarian meals. No-smoking area. Music. Air-conditioned

Le Coq Hardi

35 Pembroke Rd, Ballsbridge, Dublin 4
TEL: (01) 6689070 FAX: (01) 6689887 COST £31–£80

In 1997 the Howards celebrated two decades at their grand and elegant restaurant in leafy Ballsbridge. A flight of granite steps leads to smart Victorian interiors, and a style of entertaining often thought in danger of disappearing from cities. John Howard is still very much a hands-on chef, composing dishes such as grilled king scallops with bacon, potato cake and garlic cream, or steamed mussels with a sauce of muscadet and grated celery. Peppered ostrich steak now features, accompanied by wild mushrooms, red berries and a *jus* based on Hermitage wine, and meals might end with warm Jamieson tart served with whiskey custard and caramel ice-cream.

The lengthy wine list majors in vintage clarets – dating back to 1870 – mature burgundies and classy Rhônes. The stellar wines come with sky-high price-tags, but more affordable fare can be found in Alsace, Italy, Spain and the New World.

House wines start at £16. CELLARMAN'S CHOICE: Pinot Blanc d'Alsace 1995, Hugel, £16; St-Julien, Ch. Mazeris 1990, £32.

CHEFS: John Howard and James O'Sullivan PROPRIETORS: John and Catherine Howard OPEN: Mon to Fri L 12.30 to 2.30, Mon to Sat D 7 to 10.45 CLOSED: 2 weeks Christmas, 2 weeks Aug, bank hols MEALS: alc (main courses £17.50 to £24). Set L £19, Set D £34 SERVICE: 12.5%, card slips closed CARDS: Amex, Diners, MasterCard, Visa DETAILS: 50 seats. Private parties: 50 main room, 10 and 35 private rooms. Car park. Vegetarian meals. Children welcome. No-smoking area. No music. Air-conditioned

Eastern Tandoori

34–35 South William Street, Dublin 2
TEL: (01) 6710428 and 6710506 FAX: (01) 6779232 COST £14–£56

Reporters enjoy the ambience here, and colourfully dressed staff are keen as mustard, making sure nobody misses out on aperitifs, and watching tables like the proverbial hawk. 'Delightfully prepared' plain naan went well with lamb sag gosht with meat that 'melted in the mouth', and tandoori baked mackerel was 'cooked to perfection' – both were 'superbly spiced'. Less successful was tandoori tikka masala, perhaps forgivable in that it is not a particularly authentic dish anyway. Drink Indian beer at £2.50 or house French wine at £11.50 a bottle.

CHEFS: Henry Paul, Olli Ullah and A. Azad PROPRIETOR: Feroze Khan OPEN: Mon to Sat L 12 to 2.30, all week D 6 to 11.30 CLOSED: 25 and 26 Dec, Good Friday MEALS: alc (main courses £8 to £13.50). Set L £6.50, Set D £17.95 to £19.95 SERVICE: 12.5%, card slips closed CARDS: Amex, Diners, MasterCard, Switch, Visa DETAILS: 64 seats. Private parties: 80 main room. Car park. Vegetarian meals. Children's helpings. No-smoking area. Wheelchair access (no WC). Music. Air-conditioned

Ernie's

Mulberry Gardens, Dublin 4
TEL: (01) 2693300 FAX: (01) 2693260
off Morehampton Road COST £29–£64

The address suggests a leafy setting and, indeed, this family-run restaurant overlooks an enclosed garden complete with a fountain. Inside, the walls of the dining-room are covered with a private collection of more than 200 Irish paintings. There's also plenty to distract on the fixed-price menus, which follow the seasons as best they can. The modern world has its say with ravioli of veal with black olive and tarragon cream, and medallions of beef with tomato and Puy lentils, while grilled black pudding and potato cakes suggest a taste of the home country. Desserts might include date and walnut pudding or home-made banana and poppyseed ice-cream. The wines are predominantly French classics with just a few from other regions, although the list is fortified by the presence of 12 vintage ports. French house wines begin at £13.50.

The Guide *is totally independent, accepts no free hospitality, and survives on the number of copies sold each year.*

CHEF: Sandra Earl PROPRIETORS: the Evans family OPEN: Tue to Fri L 12.30 to 2, Tue to Sat D 7.30 to 10 CLOSED: 24 Dec to 1 Jan MEALS: alc (main courses £13 to £19). Set L £13.95, Set D £25 SERVICE: 12.5% CARDS: Amex, Diners, MasterCard, Visa DETAILS: 60 seats. Private parties: 70 main room. Vegetarian meals. Children's helpings. No-smoking area. No music. Air-conditioned

Les Frères Jacques

74 Dame Street, Dublin 2
TEL: (01) 6794555 FAX: (01) 6794725 COST £23–£60

As the name announces, this is an unambiguously French restaurant. Situated in the Temple Bar district, next to the Olympia Theatre, it uses the classic haute cuisine idiom to make the most of Irish produce. Sea trout comes in a parcel with a watercress cream sauce as a starter or with aïoli as a main, while a mignon of pork is accompanied by a tartlet of apple purée. A 'first-class treatment' of monkfish with cider won one new convert, and the herb, garlic and brown breads have also been lauded. Meals end with chocolate mille-feuille with espresso sauce. House wine – French – is £10.50.

CHEF: Nicolas Boutin PROPRIETORS: Jean-Jacques and Suzy Caillabet OPEN: Mon to Fri 12.30 to 2.30, 7.30 to 10.30 (11 Fri and Sat) CLOSED: 25 Dec, 1 Jan, bank hols MEALS: alc D (main courses £16.50 to £19). Set L £13.50, Set D £20 SERVICE: 12.5% (optional) CARDS: Amex, Diners, MasterCard, Visa DETAILS: 65 seats. Private parties: 40 main room, 16 and 40 private rooms. Car park. Children's helpings. No smoking in 1 dining-room. Music

Kapriol

45 Lower Camden Street, Dublin 2
TEL: (01) 475 1235 COST £32–£52

This old-stager changed hands in 1997, passing from its previous Italian owners to the stewardship of Ronan Flanagan. The kitchen is unaffected by the changes, however, and the menu of Italian stalwarts that has sustained Dubliners down the years is still going strong. Cream sauced pasta starters may seem old-fashioned, but are popular none the less, as are the spanking-fresh seafood dishes. The attachment to unabashed richness is such that turbot comes with prawns and a brandy cream sauce, while the *de rigueur* veal scallopini may be stuffed with chopped fillet steak, onions and garlic and casseroled in wine and tomatoes. Favourite desserts are promised too. The wine list is Italian with French additions, and kicks off with house wines from the Abruzzi at £11.

CHEF: Mary Hughes PROPRIETOR: Ronan Flanagan OPEN: Tue to Sat D only 7 to 12 MEALS: alc (main courses £12.50 to £17). BYO £5 SERVICE: 12.5% CARDS: Amex, Diners, MasterCard, Visa DETAILS: 32 seats. Private parties: 32 main room, 20 private room. Vegetarian meals. Children's helpings. No-smoking area. Wheelchair access (no WC). Music. Air-conditioned

indicates that there has been a change of chef since last year's Guide, *and the Editor has judged that the change is of sufficient interest to merit the reader's attention.*

Patrick Guilbaud

21 Upper Merrion Street, Dublin 2
TEL: (01) 6764192 FAX: (01) 6610052 COST £32–£90

Patrick Guilbaud moved house in September 1997 from his old premises behind the Bank of Ireland to this new address. His chef, Guillaume Lebrun, goes in for a style of French cooking that likes to show its flashy side. He gets results too. One correspondent was bowled over by a meal that progressed from foie gras with pears and dried fruits to poached sole in champagne sauce with caviare. With a half-bottle of Chablis and crème brûlée to finish, the experience – 'one to be savoured and lingered over' – was complete. More daring dishes have included a warm salad of caramelised rabbit livers with grilled potatoes and orange sauce, and roast Challans duck with honey, lemon, aniseed and soy. The proprietor writes that the wine list is too large to be sent in, so we are unable to comment.

CHEF: Guillaume Lebrun PROPRIETOR: Patrick Guilbaud OPEN: Tue to Sat 12.30 to 2, 7.30 to 10.15 CLOSED: first two weeks Jan MEALS: alc (main courses £21 to £30). Set L £22, Set D £38 to £65 SERVICE: net prices CARDS: Amex, Diners, MasterCard, Visa DETAILS: 85 seats. 20 seats outside. Private parties: 85 main room, 30 private room. Children welcome. No music. Air-conditioned

Roly's Bistro

7 Ballsbridge Terrace, Dublin 4
TEL: (01) 6682611 and 0623 FAX: (01) 6608535 COST £19–£40

A modern bistro in the Ballsbridge district, situated opposite the US embassy, Roly's offers up-to-the-minute international food done with panache. Chorizo, egg noodles and roast salsify is a starter that owes no allegiance to any individual cuisine, and the same may be said of potato and sweetcorn rissoles with chilli butter sauce. A pair of English visitors praised the succulence and clarity of flavour in a sole and crab terrine, as well as tender cutlets of organic lamb with minted ratatouille. For dessert, lime and pistachio ice-cream has made a successful accompaniment to crème brûlée. 'Efficient and friendly' service helps things along. The modest wine list is mainly French with token New World representatives, but ten house wines from all over the place come at £9.95.

CHEF: Colin O'Daly PROPRIETORS: Colin O'Daly, Roly Saul, John O'Sullivan and John Mulcahy OPEN: all week 12 to 3, 6 to 10 (10.30 Fri and Sat) CLOSED: 25 to 27 Dec, Good Friday MEALS: alc D (main courses £7.50 to £13). Set L £10.50. BYO £5 SERVICE: 10%, card slips closed CARDS: Amex, Diners, MasterCard, Visa DETAILS: 150 seats. Private parties: 12 main room. Vegetarian meals. Children's helpings. No children under 6. No-smoking area. Wheelchair access (also WC). Music. Air-conditioned

La Stampa

35 Dawson Street, Dublin 2
TEL: (01) 6778611 FAX: (01) 6773336 COST £20–£47

The high-ceilinged dining-room has been described as 'stunning' by reporters. Waiters wear spectacular waistcoats and provide extremely attentive service, while the cooking has typically taken a modern Franco-Italian line in tomato tart with black olives, spinach and ricotta tortellini, and rack of lamb with roasted garlic. As the *Guide* went to press, Michael Birmingham took over the kitchen from Paul Flynn, and we have had no feedback yet on whether the style and standards remain the same. Assuming it continues, the set lunch is good value. Italian house wine is £12.50 or £2.60 a glass.

CHEF: Michael Birmingham PROPRIETOR: Louis Murray OPEN: Mon to Fri L 12.30 to 2.15, all week D 6.30 to 11.15 (11.30 Fri and Sat) CLOSED: 25 Dec, Good Fri MEALS: alc (main courses £10 to £17). Set L £11.50 SERVICE: not inc; 10% for parties of 6 or more CARDS: Amex, Diners, MasterCard, Visa DETAILS: 200 seats. Private parties: 160 main room, 60 private room. Vegetarian meals. Children welcome. No pipes in dining room. Music. Air-conditioned

Thornton's

1 Portobello Road, Dublin 8
TEL: (01) 4549067 FAX: (01) 4539247 COST £30–£70

'A superior dining experience' is promised by Kevin Thornton at this relative youngster on the Dublin scene. In its tree-lined canalside setting, his restaurant has fired the imagination of a discerning city crowd with cooking of refinement and skill, and the whole operation exudes confidence. The style is largely classical French, as may be seen in a slice of foie gras sauté with scallops and salsify in a morel *jus* and served with warm brioche. Less Gallic inflections surface in a terrine of hare and ostrich with sesame seed vinaigrette, and game fans may go on to partridge with shallot tarte Tatin and celeriac mousse. Fish dishes may appeal to less hearty appetites: John Dory is steamed with baby fennel and served with a grape sauce.

The largely classical French list includes some fine dessert wines; sadly, the 1945 vintage Château d'Yquem at £1,600 is beyond the means of most, but the Château de Belle Rive 1978, Quarts de Chaume would provide sweet consolation to many at £32.50, or £6 a glass. Half-bottles are plentiful and house wines begin at £13.50. CELLARMAN'S CHOICE: Meursault 'Chevaliers' 1993, Dom. René Monier, £38; Aloxe-Corton 1992, Louis Latour, £37.

CHEF: Kevin Thornton PROPRIETORS: Kevin and Muriel Thornton OPEN: Fri L 12.15 to 2, Tue to Sat D 5 to 10.30 MEALS: alc (main courses £19 to £21). Set L £18.95, Set D £32. BYO £8 SERVICE: 10% CARDS: Amex, Diners, MasterCard, Visa DETAILS: 40 seats. Private parties: 30 main room, 14 private room. Car park. Vegetarian meals. Children's helpings. No smoking in 1 dining-room. Air-conditioned

DURRUS Co Cork map 16

Blairs Cove

Durrus, nr Bantry
TEL/FAX: (027) 61127
1½m out of Durrus on Barleycove to Goleen road COST £41–£48

The set-up is as follows: dinner revolves around a fixed-price deal, where you help yourself from a buffet for starters and sweets and order the centrepiece. To begin, you might find ceviche, home-made brawn, Westphalian ham, curried courgettes and much more; next are lively things like veal sweetbreads in a spinach pancake, steamed John Dory on a bed of wilted greens with white wine sauce, and confit of duck with five spices. As an alternative to dessert try the farmhouse cheeses. One Irish wine rears its head on the international list. House wines are £12. Accommodation is planned for spring 1998.

CHEFS/PROPRIETORS: Philippe and Sabine De Mey OPEN: Tue to Sat D only 7.30 to 9.30 CLOSED: 1 Nov to 17 Mar MEALS: Set D £27.50 SERVICE: not inc, card slips closed CARDS: Amex, Diners, MasterCard, Visa DETAILS: 35 seats. 45 seats outside. Private parties: 35 main room. Car park. Children's helpings. No cigars/pipes in dining-room. No-smoking area. Wheelchair access (no WC). Music

GOREY Co Wexford map 16

▲ *Marlfield House*

Courtown Road, Gorey
TEL: (055) 21124 FAX: (055) 21572 COST £26–£58

This magnificent mansion house, built around 1830 for the Earl of Courtown, is set in 14 hectares of gardens and woodland. Jason Matthiä, previously at his father's restaurant, Chez Hans (see entry, Cashel), took over in the kitchen in 1996. Fixed-price menus are the drill, and the cooking is broad-minded enough to take in smoked duckling risotto with Parmesan and pear; turbot with braised fennel, buttered spinach and a chive velouté; loin of lamb with provençale vegetables, olive oil mash and a rosemary *jus*; and crème brûlée with pistachio praline and dried apple. The wine list combines the traditional strengths of a classical French selection with a few interesting bottles from elsewhere. Six house wines are either £13 or £14.

CHEF: Jason Matthiä PROPRIETORS: Mary and Ray Bowe OPEN: Sun L 12.30 to 1.45, all week D 7.30 (7 Sat and Sun) to 9 (8 Sun) CLOSED: 17 Dec to 31 Jan MEALS: Set L £17.50, Set D £35.50. Light L available SERVICE: not inc, card slips closed CARDS: Amex, Diners, MasterCard, Visa DETAILS: 65 seats. Private parties: 20 main room, 20 and 30 private rooms. Car park. Vegetarian meals. Children's helpings. No children under 6 at D. Jacket and tie. No smoking in dining-room. Wheelchair access (also WC). No music. Air-conditioned ACCOMMODATION: 19 rooms, all with bath/shower. TV. Phone. B&B £95 to £450. Rooms for disabled. Children welcome. Baby facilities. Small dogs welcome by arrangement. Afternoon teas. Garden

HOWTH Co Dublin map 16

King Sitric

East Pier, Howth
TEL: (01) 8325235 and 6729 FAX: (01) 8392442 COST £20–£61

The MacManuses have big plans for the near future. They hope to add guest accommodation to their bayside restaurant, which has been serving immaculate fish cookery to the denizens of Howth and beyond for over 25 years. An adventurous vein runs through the menus, so that squid may be stir-fried with soy sauce and ginger, and wild salmon served as teriyaki accompanied by beetroot chips. One or two of the more novel ideas have not been a total success –

one reporter was not convinced that tomato ice-cream made an ideal accompaniment to marinated monkfish – but the nerve generally holds steady. Meals might end with something simple such as pears in red wine, or 'chocolate plate'. The majestic wine list has a fine array of classic French whites, as you might expect from a classy fish restaurant, but it also has a surprisingly good selection of vintage clarets and other reds. A glass of the sweet red Banyuls would be a good choice for anyone opting for the chocolate dessert. House French is £12 a bottle, £6.25 a half. CELLARMAN'S CHOICE: Chablis premier cru 'Vaillons' 1992, Droin, £30; Pomerol, Ch. Beauregard 1989, £32.

CHEF: Aidan MacManus PROPRIETORS: Aidan and Joan MacManus OPEN: Mon to Sat D only 6.30 to 10.30 CLOSED: 2 weeks Jan, bank hols MEALS: alc (main courses £12.50 to £21). Set D £19.50 (winter Mon to Thurs only) to £26. BYO £4. Light L available in Seafood bar in summer SERVICE: not inc CARDS: Amex, Diners, MasterCard, Visa DETAILS: 75 seats. Private parties: 45 main room, 16 and 20 private rooms. Vegetarian meals. Children's helpings. No smoking in 1 dining-room. Wheelchair access (also women's WC). Music

KANTURK Co Cork map 16

▲ *Assolas Country House*

Kanturk
TEL: (029) 50015 FAX: (029) 50795
signposted from N72, NE of Kanturk, 8m W of Mallow COST £37–£44

This handsome manor house clad in trim, leafy livery dates from the 1600s, and has been the family home of the Bourkes since the time of the Great War. It offers the genuine Irish pastoral experience, with a little river flowing past the immaculate gardens, and in Hazel Bourke a chef who knows how to get the best from her resources. Produce from the grounds yields a celery and lovage soup, while scallops from Kenmare Bay are fried and sauced with a beurre blanc. Although the touch is light, dishes can be robust when the climate dictates, so that monkfish stars in a red wine ragoût with parsnip purée and potato cakes, and home-made mint jelly is used to dress a roast loin of lamb with capers and thyme. Desserts are served from a trolley or there are Irish farmhouse cheeses to ponder. As one visitor reported, 'The food was all extremely good and reasonably priced.' The wine list confines itself to Western Europe, not forgetting Ireland itself, and leads commendably with Guigal's Côtes du Rhône in all three colours at £14.

CHEF: Hazel Bourke PROPRIETORS: the Bourke family OPEN: all week D only 7 to 8.30 CLOSED: 1 Nov to late March (except for residential groups) MEALS: Set D £30 SERVICE: none, card slips closed CARDS: Amex, Diners, MasterCard, Visa DETAILS: 30 seats. Private parties: 10 main room, 20 private room. Car park. Vegetarian meals. No cigars in dining-room. No music ACCOMMODATION: 9 rooms, all with bath/shower. Phone. B&B £62 to £160. Deposit: £100. Children welcome; high teas for under-8s. Baby facilities. Garden. Fishing

The Guide *relies on feedback from its readers. Especially welcome are reports on new restaurants appearing in the book for the first time. All letters to the* Guide *are acknowledged.*

KENMARE Co Kerry map 16

▲ *Park Hotel Kenmare*

Kenmare
TEL: (064) 41200 FAX: (064) 41402 COST £53–£97

The Park Hotel is a well-kept Victorian pile built of weathered grey stone, furnished throughout with an offbeat collection of curios. Offbeat might also describe the cooking of much-travelled chef Bruno Schmidt, who introduces challenging echoes of the Pacific Rim to the tranquil environs of Kerry. Codling lasagne with wun-tun 'sheet' and crab cream sauce might start you off before moving you on to a mille-feuille of squab with aubergine, caviare, bacon and wild mushrooms. Warm banana fritter with cinnamon ice-cream and ginger syrup is typical of dessert options. The huge but easy-to-follow wine list contains classics, from Bordeaux to Burgundy and beyond. From the New World, California is particularly well represented with a choice of over 40 wines, including four vintages of Opus One, but even Canada gets a look-in with Mission Hill Chardonnay. French house wines are £16.75. CELLARMAN'S CHOICE: Vernaccia di San Gimignano 1992, Ponte a Rondolino, £19.25; Gigondas 1990, Dom. Santa Duc, £27.

CHEF: Bruno Schmidt PROPRIETOR: Francis Brennan OPEN: all week D only 7 to 8.45 CLOSED: 31 Oct to 23 Dec, 2 Jan to mid-Apr MEALS: alc (main courses £20 to £23.50). Set D £39 SERVICE: not inc CARDS: Amex, Diners, MasterCard, Visa DETAILS: 80 seats. Private parties: 30 main room, 15 private room. Car park. Vegetarian meals. No children under 5. No smoking in 1 dining-room. Wheelchair access (also WC). Music ACCOMMODATION: 49 rooms, all with bath/shower. TV. Phone. B&B £118 to £302. Rooms for disabled. Children welcome. Baby facilities. Afternoon teas. Garden

▲ *Sheen Falls Lodge, La Cascade*

Kenmare
TEL: (064) 41600 FAX: (064) 41386
follow signs for Glengariff from Kenmare; hotel signposted after about ½m COST £54–£65

Local produce is high on the agenda at this de luxe hotel, sporting and leisure complex by the side of Kenmare Bay. Kerry lamb, fresh fish and organic vegetables are used for daily-changing menus that feature such things as warm oysters with fresh tagliarini, Noilly Prat and tarragon cream; roast fillet of monkfish with lardons on a toasted brioche with red pepper rouille; or loin of veal with braised leeks topped with guacamole and a ragoût of split-peas. Wild mushrooms are gathered from nearby woods, salmon is smoked in-house and served with avocado and tapénade toasts, while desserts range from iced nougat parfait with orange wafers and a seasonal fruit compote to pear tarte Tatin with calvados. The hefty wine list ranges from the sublime to the gorblimey, with a bottle of Ch. Pétrus 1983 at £600 perhaps falling into both categories. As a mere 5 per cent of the bottles cost under £20, this is not a list for the fainthearted, but the valorous can take their reward from what must rank as one of Ireland's finest wine collections. CELLARMAN'S CHOICE: Tokay Pinot Gris d'Alsace 1994, Ch. d'Orschwihr, £26; Chinon 'Les Granges' 1995, Dom. Bernard Baudry, £25.

CHEF: Fergus Moore PROPRIETOR: Bent Hoyer OPEN: all week D only 7.15 to 9.30 CLOSED: 3 weeks before Christmas, 5 weeks from 2 Jan MEALS: Set D £29 (2 courses) to £37.50 SERVICE: not inc, card slips closed CARDS: Amex, Diners, MasterCard, Visa DETAILS: 120 seats. Private parties: 120 main room, 18 private room. Car park. Vegetarian meals. Children's helpings. No cigars/pipes in dining-room. Wheelchair access (also WC). Music ACCOMMODATION: 60 rooms, all with bath/shower. TV. Phone. Room only £185 to £240. Deposit: £100. Rooms for disabled. Lift. Children welcome. Baby facilities. Afternoon teas. Garden. Swimming-pool. Fishing

KILKENNY Co Kilkenny map 16

▲ *Lacken House*

Dublin Road, Kilkenny
TEL: (056) 61085 FAX: (056) 62435 COST £33–£52

The McSweeneys' small restaurant and guesthouse in Kilkenny has long been a proud beacon of regionality, using local ingredients to create a style of cooking flagged as 'modern Irish' by the proprietors. Four-course menus with a choice of soup or sorbet before the main business are the drill. They may feature salmon and crabmeat fashioned into a cake and sauced boldly with ginger and coriander, or mushrooms sauté in garlic and cream to start. Then, after an intermediate course, it's on to seared scallops with bacon and chives, or pigeon in port with a venison sausage, for example. End with an unusual dessert such as caramelised pineapple and rice-pudding in rum sauce or a serving of Irish farmhouse cheeses. Wines feature some top-class producers and although prices can be steep at times, there is a reasonable selection under £20. House Côtes du Ventoux is £13.

CHEF: Eugene McSweeney PROPRIETORS: Eugene and Breda McSweeney OPEN: Tue to Sat D only 6.30 to 10.30 CLOSED: 1 week Jan MEALS: alc (main courses £12 to £18). Set D £23 SERVICE: not inc, card slips closed CARDS: Amex, Diners, MasterCard, Visa DETAILS: 30 seats. Private parties: 40 main room, 10 and 30 private rooms. Car park. Vegetarian meals. Children's helpings. No-smoking area. No music. Air-conditioned ACCOMMODATION: 9 rooms, all with bath/shower. TV. Phone. B&B £31 to £60. Deposit: £10. Children welcome. Garden

KINVARA Co Galway map 16

▲ *Merriman* **NEW ENTRY**

Kinvara
TEL: (091) 638222 FAX: (091) 637687 COST £26–£40

When Michael Clifford closed his original eponymous restaurant in Cork in the spring of 1997, he didn't waste any time between postings, but moved on to open this elegant new hotel in a tranquil fishing village on the shores of Galway Bay. It is named after a County Clare poet, and aims to celebrate the best of Ireland in other ways too: in 'pure Irish cooking using local produce'. The signature dish – a gâteau of Clonakilty black pudding – survives from Clifford's although a starter of roasted tomato and aubergine linguine with Parmesan shavings shows more cosmopolitan influences. Beef fillet with red wine sauce is garnished with a poached egg, or there may be wild salmon with champ and lemon butter. Desserts include strawberry choux puffs with white chocolate sauce – 'with which I could not find fault,' said a reporter – and spiced rhubarb with a honey muesli topping. The wide-ranging wine list starts at £9.50.

CHEF: Michael Clifford PROPRIETOR: Lowstrand Properties OPEN: all week D only 7 to 10 MEALS: alc (main courses £9.50 to £14). Bar snacks available 12 to 9.30 SERVICE: not inc CARDS: Amex, Diners, MasterCard, Visa DETAILS: 40 seats. 20 seats outside. Private parties: 60 main room, 45 private room. Car park. Vegetarian meals. Children's helpings. No smoking in 1 dining-room. Wheelchair access (also WC). Music ACCOMMODATION: 32 rooms, all with bath/shower. TV. Phone. B&B £45.50 to £70. Rooms for disabled. Children welcome. Baby facilities. Afternoon teas

LETTERFRACK Co Galway map 16

▲ *Rosleague Manor* $*

Letterfrack
TEL: (095) 41101 FAX: (095) 41168
on N59 to Westport, 7m NW of Clifden COST £24–£54

Some of the manor is Georgian, some 1970s-Georgian, but it all adds up to 'a beautiful house, furnished and decorated in impeccable taste', and with the wild winds of Connemara whistling around the doorstep too. As well as a *carte*, Nigel Rush offers a four-course dinner menu that may include smoked salmon stuffed with a mousse of smoked eel, followed by a soup such as chilled tomato and orange, then roast pork loin with apples, sage and calvados, rounded off with profiteroles ladled with dark chocolate sauce. As may be seen, the style is resolutely classical, and the depth achieved in most dishes fully justifies the approach. The wine list may be thought a little run-of-the-mill under the circumstances. House French is £11.50.

CHEF: Nigel Rush PROPRIETORS: Anne and Patrick Foyle OPEN: all week 1 to 2.30, 8 to 9.30 CLOSED: Nov to Easter MEALS: alc (main courses L £7 to £10.50, D £12 to £16.50). Set D £28 SERVICE: not inc, card slips closed CARDS: Amex, MasterCard, Visa DETAILS: 60 seats. Private parties: 50 main room. Car park. Vegetarian meals. Children's helpings. No smoking in dining-room. Wheelchair access (no WC). No music ACCOMMODATION: 20 rooms, all with bath/shower. Phone. B&B £40 to £120. Rooms for disabled. Children welcome. Dogs welcome in bedrooms only. Afternoon teas. Garden

MALLOW Co Cork map 16

▲ *Longueville House*

Mallow
TEL: (022) 47156 FAX: (022) 47459
3m W of Mallow on N72 Killarney road COST £40–£48

Grandeur without pomp is the keynote of this Georgian country mansion standing in 500 acres of park and woodland in the Blackwater valley. 'The hotel, and its Presidents' restaurant, are beautifully run,' wrote an enthusiastic reporter who also commended the attentive staff and owners. Chef William O'Callaghan bakes loin of Longueville lamb in a herb and potato crust, using vegetables and herbs from the garden, and serves home-smoked wild salmon with sauce gribiche. Main courses, although good, can seem elaborate, and reporters have been more generous in their praise for starters of terrine of asparagus, salmon and prawns with sorrel sauce, individual lobster and crab tartlet, and warm salad of chicken livers and Parma ham. 'Mouthwatering' desserts might include feuilleté of summer fruits with sabayon, or crème brûlée. House wine is £14.

CHEF: William O'Callaghan PROPRIETORS: the O'Callaghan family OPEN: all week D only 7 to 9 CLOSED: mid-Dec to mid-Feb MEALS: Set D £29 SERVICE: not inc, card slips closed CARDS: Amex, Diners, MasterCard, Visa DETAILS: 70 seats. Private parties: 40 main room, 16 private room. Car park. Vegetarian meals. Children's helpings. Wheelchair access (also WC). Music ACCOMMODATION: 21 rooms, all with bath/shower. TV. Phone. B&B £55 to £164. Deposit: 50%. Children welcome. Baby facilities. Afternoon teas. Garden. Fishing

MIDLETON Co Cork map 16

Farmgate

Coolbawn, Midleton
TEL/FAX: (021) 632771 COST £16-£31

Máróg O'Brien's restaurant in the centre of Ireland's southern coast makes the most of its position and builds its menu around seafood dishes both classical and modern. Traditionalists may go for grilled oysters with hollandaise, or moules marinière, while vanguardists will be delighted to see crab-cakes on red pepper coulis. A salad of spiced walnuts and Brie with a sherry vinaigrette also belongs to more recent culinary thinking. Meat main courses take in loin of lamb with rosemary *jus* or duck with sage and onion stuffing and apple sauce. The compact wine list has some good producers on it, but still no vintage information. House wines are £10.

CHEFS: Máróg O'Brien and David Doran PROPRIETOR: Máróg O'Brien OPEN: Mon to Sat L 12 to 4, Thur to Sat D 7.30 to 9.45 CLOSED: Christmas MEALS: alc (main courses £5 to £10) SERVICE: not inc, card slips closed CARDS: MasterCard, Visa DETAILS: 60 seats. 20 seats outside. Private parties: 20 main room, 20 private room. Vegetarian meals. Children's helpings. Wheelchair access (no WC). Music

MOYCULLEN Co Galway map 16

Drimcong House 🍷

Moycullen
TEL: (091) 555115 and 555585 FAX: (091) 555836
on Galway to Clifden road, 1m W of Moycullen COST £31–£56

Drimcong, dating from the seventeenth century, is set in 25 acres of woodland and lake. The kitchen's declared aim is to provide 'progressive cooking'. Thus menus may feature pan-fried seafood sausage with coconut and chilli sauce, grilled corn-fed chicken tagliatelle with green sauce, and hot rhubarb tart with rosemary ice-cream. Hotpot of mussels, dillisk (alias the edible seaweed, dulse) and smoked eel might be hard to find elsewhere. The three- to five-course set-price menus might revive a tired palate with a duet of black-and-white puddings with apple in puff pastry, or resurrect fond memories with roast loin of mutton with tomato, thyme and lovage. Some thought has gone into assembling the wine list, which numbers over 100 bins. Classical France takes precedence, but careful selections from the rest of Europe and the New World add variety and style. The house selection starts at £11.50.

CHEF: Gerry Galvin PROPRIETORS: Gerry and Marie Galvin OPEN: Tue to Sat D only 6.30 to 10.30 CLOSED: Christmas to Mar MEALS: alc (main courses £15 to £20). Set D £22 to £25 SERVICE: not inc CARDS: Amex, Diners, MasterCard, Visa DETAILS: 50 seats. Private parties: 50 main room, 10 to 30 private rooms. Car park. Vegetarian meals. Children's helpings. Wheelchair access (also WC). Music

NEWPORT Co Mayo map 16

▲ *Newport House*

Newport
TEL: (098) 41222 FAX: (098) 41613 COST £34–£40

A creeper-clad country mansion in the west of Mayo, Newport boasts immaculate Regency interiors, as well as exclusive salmon fishing rights in the river that flows nearby, so guests gathering for a pre-prandial sherry may well be telling tales of the one that got away. If it didn't get away, John Gavin may have hung it in the smokehouse and then used it to wrap up a terrine of avocado on a tomato coulis. Oysters may appear in season after such a first course, before a soup like carrot and coriander. Main courses may take in grilled John Dory with asparagus in a lemon and parsley butter, or duck breast with rillettes en croûte sauced with orange and damson. Irish farmhouse cheeses come next, by which time frozen lemon cream may be all the dessert you need. 'Our hosts were attentive and caring,' concludes a testimonial. Kieran and Thelka Thompson have put together a seriously good list of wines, offered at some impressively low prices. French classics claim the lion's share of attention – clarets dating back to 1961, Rhônes to 1978 – but Italy and particularly Australia make some notable additions. Four French house wines start at £11 a bottle, £2 a glass.

CHEF: John Gavin PROPRIETORS: Kieran and Thelka Thompson OPEN: all week 12.30 to 2, 7 to 9.30 CLOSED: 6 Oct to 18 Mar MEALS: Set D £30 SERVICE: none, card slips closed CARDS: Amex, Diners, MasterCard, Visa DETAILS: 38 seats. 40 seats outside. Private parties: 12 main room. Car park. Vegetarian meals. Children's helpings. No smoking in dining-room. Wheelchair access (also men's WC). No music ACCOMMODATION: 18 rooms, all with bath/shower. Phone. Room only £63 to £138. Rooms for disabled. Children welcome. Baby facilities. Dogs welcome. In courtyard bedrooms only. Afternoon teas. Garden. Fishing

OUGHTERARD Co Galway map 16

▲ *Currarevagh House*

Oughterard, Connemara
TEL: (091) 552312 and 552313 FAX: (091) 552731
4m NW of Oughterard on Hill of Doon Lakeshore road COST £28–£34

Despite the 150 acres it stands in, there is nothing unduly imposing in the way the Hodgsons run their Victorian family home. It is 'friendly and warm', according to one who stayed, and the sense of stopping over with particularly generous friends is emphasised by the format of dinner. One sitting is served with a no-choice menu handwritten on a card. A soup or salad usually precedes a fishy course such as turbot with tapénade, or curried crab, to get the ball rolling. Simple main course meats may be roast leg of lamb with mint sauce, or corned beef with parsley sauce and colcannon, while puddings have included lemon curd gâteau, and brown-bread ice-cream. It all ends with good Irish cheeses. France is the centre of attention for wines, the house selections opening with négociant burgundy at £8.80.

CHEF: June Hodgson PROPRIETORS: Harry and June Hodgson OPEN: all week D only 8pm (1 sitting) CLOSED: 20 Oct to 9 Aril MEALS: Set D £21 SERVICE: 10% CARDS: none DETAILS: 32 seats. Private parties: 10 main room. Car park. No smoking in dining-room. No music ACCOMMODATION: 15 rooms, all with bath/shower. Room only £47.50 to £100. Children by arrangement. Dogs welcome. Garden. Fishing

RATHMULLAN Co Donegal map 16

▲ *Rathmullan House*

Rathmullan
TEL: (074) 58188 FAX: (074) 58200 COST £22–£41

Donegal has some of the wildest countryside in Ireland, but Rathmullan surveys a peaceable enough scene, set a short way back from the sandy beaches of Lough Swilly. Kevin Murphy cooks in country-house mode, his palette enlivened with splashes of oriental colour. Thus do Mulroy Bay oysters find themselves in the company of a lime and chilli salsa, while crisp spring rolls contain duck meat and vegetables and come with a sweet chilli sauce. Soup, salad or sorbet precedes the main course at dinner, which may be grilled salmon on creamed leeks, or baked chicken breast filled with mushroom mousseline on a whiskey sauce. Chocolate truffle cake or Irish cheeses are available for those with space left to fill. The wine list is considerably more exciting in the New World than in Europe, though 'Connoisseurs' Corner' is worth a look. Half-bottles are abundant, and the house wines start at £9.50.

CHEF: Kevin Murphy PROPRIETORS: the Wheeler family OPEN: Sun L 1 to 2, all week D 7.30 to 8.45 CLOSED: Nov to mid-Mar MEALS: Buffet L Sun £14, Set D £25. Bar meals available SERVICE: 10%, card slips closed CARDS: Amex, Diners, MasterCard, Visa DETAILS: 70 seats. Private parties: 30 main room. Car park. Vegetarian meals. Children's helpings. No smoking in dining-room. No music ACCOMMODATION: 20 rooms, all with bath/shower. TV. Phone. B&B £40 to £125 plus 10% service. Deposit. £25. Children welcome. Baby facilities. Afternoon teas. Garden. Swimming-pool

SCHULL Co Cork map 16

▲ *Restaurant in Blue*

Gubbeen, Schull
TEL: (028) 28305
2m out of Schull on main Crookhaven road COST £33–£39

The name may make the place sound a little melancholy, but the reality will lift the spirits. It's a 'cosy haven in the foggy wetness of west Cork,' opines one in lyrical mood. Burvill Evans cooks creatively and elaborately, pulling off such tricks as a peppercorned boudin blanc of chicken and foie gras with duxelles. A vast plate of langoustines drew rhapsodic praise one evening, and the signature dish of duck with apricot and ginger sauce is 'succulent, with a crispy skin' and well supported by the chosen vegetables. There is now a choice of desserts, which may include iced meringue with fresh fruits and Bailey's, as well as excellent Irish cheeses. Some illustrious French names crop up on the broadly based wine list. A large slate of house wines opens at £10.50.

CHEF: Burvill Evans PROPRIETORS: Chris Crabtree and Burvill Evans OPEN: Wed to Sun D only, plus Tue D in high season, 7 to 9.45 CLOSED: Nov to Mar MEALS: Set D £24.50 SERVICE: not inc, card slips closed CARDS: Amex, Diners, MasterCard, Switch, Visa DETAILS: 50 seats. Private parties: 40 main room. Car park. Vegetarian meals. No children under 8. Wheelchair access (no WC). Music ACCOMMODATION: 2 rooms, both with bath/shower. B&B £25 to £45. Garden

SHANAGARRY Co Cork map 16

▲ *Ballymaloe House* $*

Shanagarry, nr Midleton
TEL: (021) 652531 FAX: (021) 652021
2m outside Cloyne on Ballycotton road COST £26–£51

It would not be too much of an exaggeration to say that this is where Irish gastronomy all began, when the Allens purchased this rambling old farmhouse just after the war. These days it is a thriving industry, boasting a cookery school, a working farm where much of the kitchen's produce is grown, and a comfortably domestic hotel and restaurant of great reliability. 'Modern, crisp and imaginative' were the epithets with which one British visitor summed up the cooking. Poached monkfish with red pepper sauce, turkey baked with tarragon served with Gujarati green beans, and peppered steak in a salad with Cashel Blue dressing certainly show that time has not stood still. The wine list blends predominantly traditional selections from France with a few modern contributions from New Zealand, California and Lebanon. House Duboeuf is £14.

CHEF: Rory O'Connell PROPRIETORS: Myrtle and Ivan Allen OPEN: Mon to Sat L 12.45 to 1.30, Sun L 1 (1 sitting), Mon to Sat D 7 to 9 CLOSED: 24 to 26 Dec MEALS: Set L Mon to Sat £16.50, Set L Sun £19.50, Set D £31.50. BYO £5 SERVICE: not inc, card slips closed CARDS: Amex, Diners, MasterCard, Visa DETAILS: 100 seats. Private parties: 30 main room, 10 to 30 private rooms. Car park. Vegetarian meals. Children's helpings L. No smoking in 1 dining-room. Wheelchair access (no WC). Music ACCOMMODATION: 32 rooms, all with bath/shower. Phone. B&B £80 to £140. Deposit: £30. Rooms for disabled. Children welcome. Baby facilities. Garden. Swimming-pool

'Yorkshire pudding was like a thick piece of burnt plastic filled with steam. It brought to mind Monet's recipe . . . . Apparently, he had a pudding in England once and was smitten for ever more. He used to put lots of eggs into his pudding and that is what this one needed. It was all air. And that air was burnt.' (On eating in the West Country)

WATERFORD Co Waterford map 16

Dwyers

8 Mary Street, Waterford
TEL: (051) 877478 FAX: (051) 871183 COST £22–£41

It is not the Dwyers' style to try to keep up with fashionable modes elsewhere: 'starched linen and polished glass are probably old-fashioned, but we prefer it that way,' they write. So do many who eat at their small, homely restaurant in Waterford town, although the approach is anything but starched. Martin Dwyer cooks a fixed-price, early-evening menu of three courses plus coffee alongside the *carte*. Bacon glazed with honey and mustard and bedded on cabbage and apple is one set-price offering; the *carte* goes in for baby leek and Kilmeaden cheese tartlet with walnut vinaigrette, and perhaps chargrilled salmon with chervil butter sauce to follow. Bailey's ice-cream may be found throughout Ireland, but here it crops up next to fresh peach, or there may be chocolate and praline roulade. The modest wine list is mainly French, with short excursions elsewhere, and starts at £10 for Montepulciano d'Abruzzo.

CHEF: Martin Dwyer PROPRIETORS: Martin and Sile Dwyer OPEN: Mon to Sat D only 6 to 10 CLOSED: Christmas, bank hols MEALS: alc (main courses £10.50 to £15.50). Set D 6 to 7.30 £15 SERVICE: not inc CARDS: Amex, Diners, MasterCard, Visa DETAILS: 32 seats. Private parties: 24 main room, 8 private room. Vegetarian meals. Children's helpings. No smoking in 1 dining-room. Wheelchair access (also WC). Music

WICKLOW Co Wicklow map 16

▲ *Old Rectory*

Wicklow
TEL: (0404) 67048 FAX: (0404) 69181 COST £35–£48

Look for the pale green sign as you enter Wicklow coming from Dublin, and behind stone walls in this sleepy harbour town lurks the rectory. It is 20 years since Paul and Linda Saunders launched it as a hotel and restaurant, and the intervening time has seen many exploratory byways opened up. Seasonal cookery courses and themed menus are offered regularly, the most celebrated of the latter being Linda Saunders's floral cuisine, when the cooking blooms with primroses and lavender. One reporter sang the praises of dishes that included roast quail stuffed with grapes in a wild berry sauce, and chocolate-stuffed figs in an aromatic floral syrup. Service is 'swift and attentive' and only the 'dubious Muzak' clouded the horizon. The wine list is as imaginative in scope as the food, with Spain featuring prominently, where those with a taste for mature red Rioja will be happy to forage. Prices start at £13.

CHEF: Linda Saunders PROPRIETORS: Paul and Linda Saunders OPEN: all week D only 8 (1 sitting) CLOSED: 1 Jan to end Feb MEALS: alc (main courses £16 to £18). Set D £28.50 SERVICE: net prices, card slips closed CARDS: Amex, MasterCard, Visa DETAILS: 20 seats. Private parties: 24 main room. Car park. Vegetarian meals. Children's helpings. No smoking in dining-room. Wheelchair access (no WC). Music ACCOMMODATION: 8 rooms, all with bath/shower. TV. Phone. B&B £48 to £96. Deposit: £30. Children welcome. Baby facilities. Garden

Round-ups

Looking for a suitable place to eat at can be a lottery, especially if you are travelling around the country with no set plans in mind. The Round-up section is intended to provide some interesting gastronomic possibilities, whether you find yourself in the West Country or the northern outposts of Scotland. Pubs are becoming increasingly valuable as sources of high-quality food, but the listings also include modest family-run enterprises in country towns, racy café/bars and ethnic restaurants in big cities, and a sprinkling of hotel dining-rooms in all parts of the land. Dip into this section and you are almost bound to find somewhere that suits your needs and your pocket. Entries are based on readers' recommendations supported by inspectors' reports. Sometimes a restaurant appears in the Round-up section instead of the main entries because seasonal closures or weekly openings limit their usefulness, or because there are changes in the air, or because positive feedback has been thin on the ground. Reports on these places are especially welcome, as they help to broaden our coverage of good eating places in Britain. Round-up entries (outside London) are arranged alphabetically by location within England, Scotland, Wales and the Channel Islands.

England

• **Aldeburgh** (Suffolk)
Café 152 152 High Street, (01728) 454152. A stone's throw from the sea, this 'upmarket seaside café' offers an eclectic modern menu of, for example, grilled goats' cheese with walnut dressing and beetroot crisps, Moroccan-style chicken with preserved lemons and couscous, and pan-fried monkfish with ginger and cracked peppercorns. A recommended dessert has been lime tart with papaya sauce.

• **Altrincham** (Greater Manchester)
Franc's 2 Goose Green, (0161) 941 3954. A handy pit-stop for shoppers and a useful venue for snacks and light bistro-style meals. The menu offers everything from 'butties' filled with steak and salad to beef and vegetable stew with mash and kidneys in mustard sauce. Apple tart is a typical sweet. There is a second branch in Chester (see Round-up entry).

• **Ambleside** (Cumbria)
Sheila's Cottage The Slack, (01539) 433079. People have been coming to the Greaveses' all-day tea-room and restaurant for over 30 years for cakes (Lakeland lemon bread), light lunches (leek tart with raclette cheese) and evening meals (Mediterranean fish soup, and Eden Valley lamb). A new chef is being sought as we go to press. Reports please.

• **Barham** (Kent)
Old Coach House Dover Road, (01227) 831218. The A2 may be the road to France, but there is no need to go over or under the water to find croustade of mushrooms, or steak persillade; Jean-Claude Rozard's small hotel sits off the south-bound carriageway. Daily specials are led by the seasons and might include lobster, turbot or carp, as well as local pheasant or wild duck. Vegetables are seasonal too and, along with fresh herbs, much is home-grown.

• **Barnard Castle** (Co Durham)
Market Place Teashop 29 Market Place, (01833) 690110. 'Good homely honest fare' is the attraction for shoppers and hikers in this unpretentious teashop with paintings on the walls and flowers on the tables. Home-baked cakes and scones come with morning coffee or afternoon teas, while light lunches generally include

some vegetarian options. Efficient, friendly service.

• **Baslow** (Derbyshire)

Cavendish Hotel, Garden Room Baslow, (01246) 582311. Delightful views over the Chatsworth Estate can be had from the conservatory extension to this upper-crust country hotel. Food is served throughout the day; expect anything from 'designer' sandwiches and French boudins to chargrilled ham and eggs, onion tart with wild mushroom and herb sauce or sweet chilli chicken with noodles.

• **Bath** (Bath & N.E. Somerset)

Circus 34 Brock Street, (01225) 318918. Intimate little restaurant on two floors, offering sound French cooking with a few forays into faraway lands. Hot chicken liver and bacon salad, and roast lamb with rosemary and redcurrant sauce sit alongside chicken stuffed with bananas, and crisp stir-fried duck with ginger-scented vinaigrette. Desserts tend to be rich confections.

Priory Hotel Weston Road, (01225) 331922. Civilised Georgian country hotel in secluded grounds a mile from the centre of Bath. Long-serving chef Michael Collom cooks a repertoire of classic and modern dishes: pickled artichoke hearts with crispy pancetta, sea bass on couscous with ratatouille, breast of duck with Cassis sauce, and raspberry soufflé show the style.

Toxique Fish 14 North Parade, (01225) 445983. Peter Jewkes and Helen Bartlett of Toxique, Melksham (see Main entry) have joined forces with Mitchell Tonks of Bath's fish market to produce this lively new venue. The décor is bright and bold, and each of the three eating areas has its own menu. Opt for wonderful shellfish, or try tuna with chilli, or hot-smoked salmon with spinach. A new chef was being sought as we went to press, so more reports please.

• **Beeston** (Nottinghamshire)

Brasserie 69 69 Chilwell Road, (0115) 925 9994. A touch of 'welcome sophistication' in an area not well endowed with decent eating places. The kitchen goes about its business with youthful optimism and the menu reads well. Warm chicken salad with balsamic dressing, sea bass in a nage of lime and olive oil, and pheasant in blackcurrant and wild mushroom sauce are typical offerings. Service is energetic and full of goodwill. Open evenings only Tues to Sat.

• **Berwick-upon-Tweed** (Northumberland)

Foxtons 26 Hide Hill, (01289) 303939. Elegant, Georgian-fronted café/bistro run by Master of Wine and chef David Foxton. Light meals might include parsnip and rocket quiche, hummus with tapénade toast, and warm salad of chicken livers, while more substantial offerings range from various pastas to grilled Mediterranean vegetables with goats' cheese. Redcurrant and passion-fruit cheesecake is a recommended sweet.

• **Beverley** (East Riding of Yorkshire)

Cerutti 2 Beverley Station, (01482) 866700. Rail travellers and others are regular visitors to this cheerful East Riding venue. The menu features plenty of East Coast seafood (crab cakes with lemon butter, monkfish au poivre) as well as warm chicken liver salad, Beverley sausage and mash, and duck breast with calvados sauce. The original Cerutti is a few miles away at 10 Nelson Street, Hull.

Wednesdays 8 Wednesday Market, (01482) 869727. Promising new venture set up by Wendy Rowley (ex-Angel Inn, Long Crendon). The décor is modest, staff are casual and the menu is bolstered by blackboard specials. Fish shows up well in the shape of, say, steamed halibut with stir-fried king prawns or monkfish with provençale-style vegetables. Warm salad of duck and bacon is a recommended starter, sticky toffee meringue makes a great finish.

• **Bibury** (Gloucestershire)

Swan Bibury, (01285) 740695. A new chef is guiding the kitchen in this ivy-clad hotel by a bridge over the Colne. In the Signet dining-room you can expect a menu that takes in warm salad of monkfish with pink grapefruit and sugarsnap peas, lamb rissole on herbed rice with sauté kidneys, and pineapple tarte Tatin with lavender ice-cream. The hotel will shortly start bottling its own water. More reports, please.

• **Birkenhead** (Merseyside)
Banks Bistro 5 Rose Mount, (0151) 670 0446. 'Free-range meat, poultry and eggs. We remain committed,' says a note on the menu at this friendly and highly atmospheric bistro. The menu goes on a world tour for Italian roasted peppers, Chinese spring rolls, Thai pork and sweetcorn fritters, and strips of fillet steak in Dijon mustard sauce.

• **Birmingham** (West Midlands)
San Carlo 4 Temple Street, (0121) 633 0251. The blackboard of up to a dozen daily fish specials steals the limelight in this buzzy city-centre venue: scallops, monkfish, tuna, shark and sea bass all put in regular appearances. Otherwise the menu deals largely in pizzas and pastas backed up by salads, grills and trattoria stalwarts such as fegato veneziana.

• **Blackmore End** (Essex)
Bull Blackmore End, (01371) 851037. Revamped Essex pub/restaurant run as a family affair by Christopher and Mary Bruce. Ambitious menus promise the likes of warm tiger prawns with Chinese noodles, collops of chicken with thyme rice, and duck breast with damsons and red wine sauce. Puddings tend to be old favourites like hot banana and toffee pancake. The wine list earns top marks.

• **Bottesford** (Leicestershire)
La Petite Maison 1 Market Street, (01949) 842375. Fixed-price lunches draw good reports from visitors to this pine-furnished bistro-style restaurant. Grilled salmon with lemon and chive butter sauce, and marinated barbecued chicken with peppered watercress salad have been well received, and daily specials are worth considering. The full menu hops between Thai chicken and tagliatelle verde with mushrooms and avocado.

• **Bradford** (West Yorkshire)
Bharat 502 Great Horton Road, (01274) 521200. Long-serving Indian restaurant with a touch more luxury than many of its neighbours. The kitchen majors in curry-house favourites, including chicken tikka, king prawn karahi, Bombay potatoes and mushroom bhajia – plus nan and rice. Good value.
Mumtaz Paan House 390 Great Horton Road, (01274) 571861. 'You are entering an alcohol-free zone,' says the sign. This lively Muslim restaurant offers mighty portions of good-value food: order curries and vegetable dishes by the pound or half-pound and eat them with good-quality nan and parathas.
Symposium 7 Albion Road, (01274) 616587. Much-liked 'food and wine bar' three miles from the city centre. Menus are listed on blackboards and the kitchen delivers appealing bistro cooking with a modern edge. Reporters have spoken highly of smoked haddock risotto, lamb fillet with bubble-and-squeak, and confit of duck with mustard mash. Chocolate fondue with marshmallows makes a good finish. The two-course 'early bird menu', which includes half a bottle of wine, is particularly good value.

• **Brighouse** (West Yorkshire)
Brook's 6–8 Bradford Road, (01484) 715284. The surroundings are 'a blend of village hall, jumble sale and modest antique shop' but Darrell Brook's likeable bistro succeeds in an understated kind of way. Judging by reports, the kitchen generally knows what it is doing and weekly menus promise such things as salt cod fish-cake with samphire salad, grilled kangaroo fillet with red wine and thyme sauce, and grilled sole with lemony beurre blanc. Finish with bread-and-butter pudding.

• **Brighton** (East Sussex)
Terre à Terre 7 Pool Valley, (01273) 729051. As we went to press this restaurant was about to move to larger premises at 71 East Street, Brighton, tel. (01273) 327561. No doubt the concept of high-quality vegetarian food from all corners of the globe will continue, and the kitchen will retain its loyality to organic produce, including organic wines. Reports please.

• **Bristol** (Bristol)
Red Snapper 1 Chandos Road, (0117) 973 7999. Up-and-coming neighbourhood restaurant in a converted shop, with minimalist décor and a keen approach to food. Decent supplies – especially of fish – define the repertoire, which might range from braised baby squid with grilled polenta to tiny helpings of poached figs with plum sauce and Greek yoghurt. Creditable wines, esoteric bottled beers.

• **Brockton** (Shropshire)
Feathers Brockton, (01746) 785202. You will find this particular Brockton on the B4378 between Ludlow and Much Wenlock. This up-beat pub offers secure bistro-style cooking, with a printed menu and blackboards promising the likes of crostini of three cheeses, crisp-roasted half-shoulder of lamb, and roulade of pork with sausagemeat and leek stuffing, perhaps followed by strawberry pavlova.

• **Burgh Le Marsh** (Lincolnshire)
Windmill 46 High Street, (01754) 810281. Bread is baked with flour from the adjoining mill, vegetables are creatively handled and coffee comes with home-made shortbread. Recent successes have included prawn and lobster mornay, stuffed chicken breast in mushroom sauce, and noisettes of lamb with brambles and mint. Crème brûlée is the favoured dessert and Sunday lunch has been praised.

• **Burley In Wharfedale** (West Yorkshire)
David Woolley's 78 Main Street, (01943) 864602. David Woolley's bonhomie and sense of local colour helps along the congenial mood in this popular neighbourhood restaurant. Fixed-price menus (Thursday to Saturday) are great value, otherwise the *carte* might feature chargrilled calf's liver with spinach and port wine jelly, saddle of lamb with Mediterranean vegetables, and poached pear in elderflower syrup.

• **Burnham Market** (Norfolk)
Hoste Arms The Green, (01328) 738777. Up-beat, greatly extended Georgian inn overlooking the green offering a family atmosphere, music, art exhibitions plus a forward-looking menu of pub food for the '90s. Fish gets top billing – local oysters, seared salmon with bok choi and tamarind oil, baked cod with lime and spring onion – but the kitchen also handles meat and game with deftness. Also an excellent wine list.

• **Burpham** (West Sussex)
Burpham Country Hotel Burpham, (01903) 882160. Once reputedly a hunting lodge for the Duke of Norfolk, now a pleasing family-run hotel in a fold of the South Downs. Fixed-price dinners are served in the Rösti Room, where the menu runs to hot smoked salmon parcels filled with broccoli mousse, and duck breast with pink peppercorn sauce, followed by a choice of puddings.

• **Bury St Edmunds** (Suffolk)
Ravenwood Hall Rougham Green, (01359) 270345. The country-house ambience continues to charm visitors to this historic hall in a delightful rural setting. The kitchen deals in a mix of classic and modern – 'excellent sirloin' suet pudding, crab-cakes and so forth, followed by crème brûlée, sticky toffee pudding, and ice-cream with interesting 'ginger bits'.

• **Bythorn** (Cambridgeshire)
White Hart Bythorn, (01832) 710226. Refurbished Victorian pub that is now firmly in the food stakes. Bar and restaurant menus offer a mixed bag of dishes ranging from minestrone soup, and Thai chicken to pear and Roquefort salad, or crispy Gressingham duck with pickled cabbage. A scallop mousse with 'bouncy pneumatic appeal' greatly impressed one reporter, as did the quality of the house wine.

• **Cambridge** (Cambridgeshire)
Cambridge Arts Theatre, The First Floor 6 St Edward's Passage, (01223) 578912. Stylish new restaurant on the first floor of the re-opened Cambridge Arts Theatre. Fixed-price menus (two or three courses) read well and early reports suggest the place is one to watch. Carrot and apricot soup, pheasant breasts on a croûton with

a purée of autumn fruits, and warm walnut and honey flan have been heartily endorsed. Wines are from Adnams.

• **CANTERBURY** (Kent)
Cafe des Amis du Mexique 95 St Dunstans Street, (01227) 464390. Huge portions of soundly cooked Tex-Mex food served in a laid-back setting of bare wood floors, orange walls and green partitions. The menu offers spiced-up favourites such as ceviche, fajitas, burritos and mole poblano (pork with a chocolate-flavoured sauce). Adjust the chilli levels to suit your palate and drink San Miguel beer.

• **CHAGFORD** (Devon)
22 Mill Street 22 Mill Street, (01647) 432244. Promising newcomer run by Duncan Walker (one-time sous-chef at nearby Gidleigh Park) and local girl Amanda Leaman. Their short fixed-price menus strike a modern note in grilled red mullet with warm potato and basil salad, grilled lamb stuffed with spiced aubergine, and bitter chocolate mousse with banana sorbet. More reports please.

• **CHEAM** (Surrey)
Bistro des Amis 22 Ewell Road, (0181) 643 8838. Neighbourhood bistro manned by friendly French staff and offering sound cooking of the old school. Starters such as cassolette de poissons and home-made pâté could be followed by tournedos and the like. The keen pricing policy extends to the modest wine list.

• **CHELTENHAM** (Gloucestershire)
Beaujolais 15 Rotunda Terrace, (01242) 525230. The billing may be 'Restaurant Français', but the menu promises dishes from far and wide. Expect warm salad of Cajun chicken with guacamole and tortilla, or Thai fish-cakes garnished with crispy spinach, alongside confit of duck with Puy lentils and mushrooms, or baked fillet of salmon with chargrilled fennel in a niçoise dressing.

• **CHESTER** (Cheshire)
Franc's 14A Cuppin Street, (01244) 317952. Excellent-value pre-theatre menus draw the crowds to this bustling, cosmopolitan bistro. The kitchen delivers a mixed bag of dishes ranging from Cullen skink and moules marinière to jambalaya, brochette of marinated lamb with cucumber salsa, and poached salmon with tomato sauce. Related to Franc's in Altrincham (see Round-up entry).

• **CHETTLE** (Dorset)
Castleman Hotel Chettle, (01258) 830051/830096. Edward Burke and Barbara Garnsworthy have converted this former dower house into a handsome hotel with an inviting country-house atmosphere. Recommended dishes from the menu have included salmon fish-cakes with spicy tomato ketchup, smoked haddock and Cheddar soufflé, and fillet of veal with mushrooms, tarragon and brandy. Sensibly priced wines.

• **CHIPPING NORTON** (Oxfordshire)
Morel's 2 Horsefair, (01608) 641075. Reporters have been known to drive '100 miles each way' for Sunday lunch in Fabrice and Rachel Morel's restaurant. But the main thrust is the Anglo-French dinner menu (with diversions), which promises such things as braised and stuffed pig's trotter with capers and gherkins, and medallions of kangaroo with a pepper sauce. Note the cheaper set-price dinner menu available from Tuesday to Thursday.

• **CHITTLEHAMHOLT** (Devon)
Highbullen Chittlehamholt, (01769) 540561. Country pursuits, glorious views over the Mole and Taw valleys and a personable family atmosphere explain why this imposing Victorian Gothic mansion attracts a loyal following. Three-course dinners might run to hotpot of prawns followed by navarin of lamb, with lemon-cream crunch to finish. Buffet breakfasts and the prospect of unlimited golf on the 18-hole course are a boon for residents.

• **CLACTON-ON-SEA** (Essex)
Wendle's 3 Rosemary Road, (01255) 426316. Fish and shellfish from near and faraway waters are the big sellers in this well-supported local restaurant in a quiet back street. Mussels in white wine sauce, monkfish tails with ginger and lime, and whole dorade pan-fried with lemon butter have all been enthusiastically

reported. Desserts such as triple chocolate layer gâteau have also hit the button.

• **Coggeshall** (Essex)
Baumann's Brasserie 4–6 Stoneham Street, (01376) 561453. Historic Essex timber-framed building housing a popular neighbourhood brasserie. A veritable gallery of fine art hangs on the walls, and the menu is printed on an A3-sized card. What you get is a mixed bag of dishes ranging from toad-in-the-hole, and grilled ham with red onion purée and parsley sauce, to seared sirloin of beef with porcini sauce, and Cajun-style chicken with curry cream sauce.

• **Colchester** (Essex)
North Hill Exchange Brasserie 19 North Hill. Offshoot of Baumann's Brasserie, Coggeshall (see entry above) housed in one of Colchester's best-known buildings. Weekday fixed-price lunches attract locals and shoppers, while the full menu moves into the realms of gratin of skate wing and leeks in Sancerre sauce, roast rump of lamb on flageolet beans, and passion-fruit tart with mango coulis. Promising wine list.

• **Colerne** (Wiltshire)
Lucknam Park Colerne, (01225) 742777. Majestic Palladian mansion set in 500 acres of parkland, six miles out of Bath. Sous-chef Paul Collins was promoted to number one as we went to press, but menus follow the luxurious style of his predecessor. Sauté of foie gras with caramelised peach and pickled ginger, fillet of turbot braised with madeira and clam essence, and mille-feuille of raspberries with champagne sabayon are examples. Reports please.

• **Corbridge** (Northumberland)
Valley Old Station House, (01434) 633434/633923. Possibly the only Indian restaurant in the land that is housed in an old railway station building. The owners arrange special deals, which means that customers can be brought from Newcastle by train. Expect a broadly based menu with a few fashionable flourishes.

• **Crick** (Northamptonshire)
Edwards of Crick The Wharf, (01788) 822517. Set in a converted wharf by the banks of the Grand Union Canal. Eat downstairs for snacks and light meals served throughout the day. English country cooking is the theme in the upstairs restaurant, where menus might advertise chicken Sahib or poacher's grill, followed by flummery or Debden chocolate pudding.

• **Crondall** (Hampshire)
Chesa Bowling Alley, (01252) 850328. Comfortable small modern restaurant using excellent ingredients and offering a good variety of dishes. Start with fillet of Dover sole and its mousseline on a bed of spinach followed by braised, boned and stuffed guinea-fowl, and finish with a sablé of pear with a wine sabayon, or a cinnamon parfait.

• **Cuddington** (Buckinghamshire)
Annie Bailey's Upper Church Street, (01844) 291215. More a restaurant than a pub, in a picturesque village popular with walkers. Blackboard menu described as 'different and exciting' offers the likes of king prawns with a lemon and thyme sauce, or Annie Bailey's hot salad with black pudding, smoked bacon and lentils for starters. Main dishes might include breast of duck, or couscous with leeks and shallots garnished with ratatouille. Daily desserts are displayed on the blackboard.

• **Cumnor** (Oxfordshire)
Vine Inn 11 Abingdon Road, (01865) 862567. Vine-draped village pub dating from 1743 and now an affluent, up-beat venue only 15 minutes' drive from Oxford. The kitchen moves with the times by offering pigeon breast and sun-dried tomato salad, tuna steak with pesto sauce and even the odd-sounding kangaroo with blueberry caramel. Decent real ales, reasonably priced wines.

• **Dartington** (Devon)
Cott Inn Dartington, nr Totnes, (01803) 863777. Ancient whitewashed Devon pub, built in 1320 and boasting one of the longest thatched roofs in the land. Evening meals are based around blackboard menus advertising colourful dishes of warm goats' cheese with cranberry sauce, gravlax, and casseroled

venison with red wine and juniper berries. Lunch is a hot and cold buffet.

● **DEAL** (Kent)

Boathouse Restaurant Royal Hotel, Beach Street, (01304) 375555. Historic seafront hotel poised on the edge of the English Channel. Local seafood dominates the monthly-changing menu – perhaps mussels in lobster sauce, line-caught halibut with chervil, or sea bass cooked with sea salt. Poultry in the shape of roast poussin with red wine gravy, satisfies the carnivores.

● **DENSHAW** (Greater Manchester)

Rams Head Ripponden Road, (01457) 874802. Four-hundred-year-old moorland pub, now conveniently two miles from the M62. Have anything from a pint of Timothy Taylor Landlord and a baguette to a three-course meal. Reporters have applauded smoked salmon terrine, a trio of beef, lamb and venison fillet with elderberry sauce, and steamed lobster with garlic. Sticky toffee pudding is a typical sweet.

● **DODDISCOMBSLEIGH** (Devon)

Nobody Inn Doddiscombsleigh, (01647) 252394. Gloriously atmospheric Devon inn renowned for its remarkable selection of more than 40 West-country farmhouse cheeses and its even more staggering list of over 800 wines – not to mention 200-plus whiskies along with beers and ciders. The kitchen is wholly committed to 'real food' and local produce, and the cooking has a big heart: expect anything from duck pie or butter-bean casserole to Arabian lamb with couscous.

● **DUNCTON** (West Sussex)

Cricketers Duncton, (01798) 342473. Two-storey farmhouse pub offering a good line in straightforward food based on decent ingredients. There's a refreshing simplicity about carrot and tarragon soup, whole grilled plaice, perfectly roasted partridge and apple pie. Fine real ales and creditable wines also feature.

● **EAST BUCKLAND** (Devon)

Lower Pitt East Buckland, (01598) 760243 Suzanne Lyons has been cooking in this converted sixteenth-century farmhouse for nigh on 20 years, and continues to base her dishes around well-chosen raw materials. Roast Trelough duck with sage and apple purée, and venison on spiced red cabbage with port and redcurrant sauce have drawn choruses of approval, as have 'substantial, sweet and highly enjoyable' puddings.

● **EAST STOKE** (Dorset)

Kemps East Stoke, Wareham, (01929) 462563. Converted Victorian rectory with hands-on owners and a pleasant conservatory dining-room. Home-made bread and 'superb vegetables' support a menu that offers the likes of chunky tartare of crab and smoked salmon, fillet of brill with lime butter, and confit of duckling with citrus sauce. To finish, try apple pie with loads of clotted cream. More reports, please.

● **ELTON** (Cambridgeshire)

Loch Fyne Oyster Bar The Old Dairy, (01832) 280298. Cambridgeshire relative of the original oyster bar set-up in Cairndow (see main entry, Scotland). Meals are served in the courtyard or in the lofty, pine-furnished dining-room. Expect anything from plates of oysters, or salmon marinated with dill and ginger, to queen scallops mornay. Some better-than-average wines provide back-up.

● **EXETER** (Devon)

La Chandelle 12 Lower North Street, (01392) 435953. Old-school French restaurant housed in an eighteenth-century building below the iron bridge on St David's Hill. Chef/patron Didier Croze pleases the crowds with hot goats'-cheese salad with garlic dressing, tender fillet of beef in green peppercorn sauce, and sea trout with herb and cream sauce. There's tarte Tatin, or chocolate mousse to finish.

● **FAWLEY** (Buckinghamshire)

Walnut Tree Fawley, (01491) 638360. One of the Chilterns' most civilised country pubs, hidden away in the beechwoods. Meals are served in the bar or the attractive conservatory dining-room, where menus promise such things as baked Brie stuffed with walnuts and celery, grilled lemon sole with caper butter, and chocolate truffle torte. Real ales, fairly priced wines.

● **Fletching** (East Sussex)
Griffin Inn Fletching, (01825) 722890. Tip-top family hospitality is the feature of this quintessential 400-year-old pub with spectacular views. Nigel Pullan and family keep real ales in fine condition, wines are worth delving into and a blackboard menu offers some splendid stuff. The kitchen ranges far and wide for Thai fish-cakes, polpette with tagliatelle, lamb shank on couscous, and tarte Tatin.

● **Forton** (Lancashire)
El Nido Whinney Brow Lane, (01524) 791254. A Spanish accent comes through strongly on the menu in this old stone building, offering choices such as mussels in saffron cream, or chicken breast in marsala sauce. In addition, there's a short selection of brasserie-style dishes including taco hotpot and vegetable tempura. Sunday lunch and an 'early bird' dinner (from 6 to 7pm) provide decent value for money.

● **Gedney Dyke** (Lincolnshire)
Chequers Main Street, (01406) 362666 Rob and Judith Marshall's Fenland pub/restaurant is regarded as one of the best in the region. Choose from the 'Just a Bite' snack menu or something more ambitious such as bang-bang chicken, lamb Shrewsbury or one of the fish specials (feuilleté of salmon and sole has been recommended). Puddings are star turns and the drinking is good.

● **Gillan** (Cornwall)
Tregildry Hotel Gillan, (01326) 231378. Modest, privately run hotel with 'a warm Mediterreanean feel' and an enviable location overlooking Gillan Creek. Daily menus feature tried-and-tested dishes, but are none the worse for that. Asparagus with 'correct' hollandaise sauce, chicken breast stuffed with herbs and leeks, and medallions of beef with peppercorn sauce have been endorsed of late.

● **Gosfield** (Essex)
Green Man The Street, (01787) 472746. Succulent soft roes, pork chops with dill sauce, and strawberry cheesecake are typically robust offerings in this hugely popular Essex country pub. The atmosphere is genuinely traditional, knowledgeable waitresses serve with plenty of smiles and Greene King beers are well kept. Useful wines, too.

● **Goudhurst** (Kent)
Hughenden The Plain, (01580) 211771. Nick and Sara Martin's delightful little cottage restaurant by the village pond is a real asset to the area. Fixed-price dinner menus feature starters of warm seafood salad with coriander, or mushroom brioche with caramelised peppers, followed by noisettes of lamb with red and green peppers, magret of duck with honey and cloves, and may finish with lemon and almond tart, or double chocolate marquise.

● **Grampound** (Cornwall)
Eastern Promise 1 Moor View, (01726) 883033. Promising family-run restaurant that provides some of the better Chinese cooking in the West Country. Szechuan dishes have been 'absolutely wonderful', according to reporters, and the crispy aromatic duck is a winner. Better-than-average wines, friendly service.

● **Great Yarmouth** (Norfolk)
Seafood Restaurant 85 North Quay, (01493) 856009. 'It has always been the best,' writes a regular who has been supporting this restaurant for more than a decade. Greek owners specialise in the freshest of fish cooked the old way in all sorts of guises. Turbot with herb butter, brill with port wine sauce and lobster Thermidor are typical offerings, and there are fine seafood platters, too. Staff are 'a great team'.

● **Grimsby** (N.E. Lincolnshire)
Leon's Family Fish Restaurant Alexandra Road, (01472) 356282. Leon Marklew set up this popular venue by the waterfront in 1985 and it is still going strong. The name says it all: fish and chips is the name of the game, families are eagerly encouraged and the place is perfect for a sit-down meal. Kick off with soup, finish with ice-cream or spotted dick.

• **Guildford** (Surrey)
The Gate 3 Milkhouse Gate, (01483) 576300. 'A joy,' enthused one reporter, after discovering honest, unpretentious cooking in the Surrey commuter belt. It's modest, it's cheap, but the owners are on 'the modern British wavelength'. A feuilleté of hummus and creamed parsnip with a pesto-based sauce has been rapturously received, otherwise look for ribeye steak with wild mushrooms and marsala, or roast cod with lentils and a tomato and cumin sauce.

• **Harrogate** (North Yorkshire)
Bettys 1 Parliament Street, (01423) 502746. Founded by young Swiss confectioner Frederick Belmont in 1919 and dedicated to the principle that everything should be 'fresh and dainty'. Patisserie is out of the top drawer as are breads and cakes. Savouries range from Alpine macaroni and rösti to Yorkshire rarebit and Masham sausages. Branches in Ilkley, Northallerton and York (see Round-up entries).
Garden Room Harlow Carr Botanical Gardens, Crag Lane, (01423) 505604. Admirable enterprise providing sustenance for visitors to Harlow Carr Botanical Gardens. Snacks and light lunches are served during the day, more ambitious dinners from Thursday to Saturday. Regular changing menus feature hot salmon and crab parcels, confit of duck with orange marmalade, and raspberry mousse. Sit on the patio when the sun shines and don't forget to browse in the gift shop.
Rick's Just for Starters 7 Bower Road, (01423) 502700. Rick Hodgson turns menu convention on its head in this easy-going pavement bistro. The cooking focuses on light dishes and starters, with just a few 'main courses' chalked on a board. Expect well-wrought ideas such as smoked haddock niçoise, sauté chicken livers in a filo pastry box, and grilled chorizo with pesto mash and red onion marmalade. Neat idea, great value.

• **Harvington** (Hereford & Worcester)
Mill at Harvington Anchor Lane, (01386) 870688. Phone for directions: this pretty Georgian house by the banks of the Avon is in a bucolic setting of sheep and apple orchards away-from-it-all. The kitchen puts its faith in well-tried country cooking based on seasonal ingredients. Warm bacon and potato salad, salmon in white wine sauce with local asparagus, and strawberry shortbread show the style. 'Lovingly annotated' wine list.

• **Hatch Beauchamp** (Somerset)
Nightingales Bath House Farm, West Hatch, (01823) 480806. Set in a clever conversion of farm buildings a few miles from Taunton, with an atmosphere that is cosy and inviting; the menu looks to the Mediterranean and the Far East for much of its inspiration. Herb risotto comes with scallops and roasted baby fennel, Thai chicken is served with lemon-grass sauce and spring rolls. Open only Friday and Saturday evenings and Sunday lunch, plus other times for groups of ten or more.

• **Hemel Hempstead** (Hertfordshire)
Gallery Restaurant Old Town Hall Arts Centre, (01442) 232416. 'An overgrown café' rather than a full-blown restaurant in a pleasant 'woody' room above the Old Town Hall theatre and arts complex. The blackboard menu is based on good fresh ingredients and prices are reasonable. Expect anything from snacks and baguettes to chicken schnitzel, salmon kedgeree, and French onion tart. Keen, friendly service.

• **Hexham** (Northumberland)
Black House Dipton Mill Road, (01434) 604744. Converted farm buildings on a hilltop overlooking the environs of Hexham. Opening times are limited (Friday and Saturday dinner, plus monthly Sunday lunch), but Hazel Pittock offers sound cooking with a noticeable French bias. Confit of Yorkshire duck has been 'just as it should be'; otherwise expect local asparagus with poached egg and hollandaise, and some 'stupendous' puddings.

• **Houghton Conquest** (Bedfordshire)
Knife & Cleaver The Grove, (01234) 740387. More of a restaurant-with-rooms

than a country pub, and worth noting in an area of few decent eating places. Menus in the conservatory restaurant feature particularly good oysters and ribeye steaks, as well as Chinese-style braised sea bass, loin of lamb with port and redcurrant sauce, and blackberry crème brûlée. Serious wines.

• **Hove** (East Sussex)
Quentin's 42 Western Road, (01273) 822734. Assured cooking, good value, and an increasingly ambitious monthly changing menu are the attractions here. Among the recommendations are breast of chicken 'embroidered' with smoked ham, glazed onions and tarragon sauce, stuffed guinea-fowl, and lamb cutlets with rösti, roasted vegetables and rosemary *jus*.

• **Ilkley** (West Yorkshire)
Bettys 34 The Grove, (01943) 608029. Bettys is a famous Yorkshire institution, with other branches in Harrogate, Northallerton and York (see Round-up entries). The same principles apply across the board: great value, exemplary baking, wondrous savouries, state-of-the-art facilities for children and families. Excellent teas, coffees and wines.

• **Ipswich** (Suffolk)
Il Punto Neptune Quay, (01473) 289748. The Italian name of this floating restaurant belies the fact that it is a 'mecca for French cooking'. Situated in Ipswich Docks it can deliver guinea-fowl in a celeriac sauce, slow-cooked shank of lamb in a rich red wine sauce, or grilled monkfish on glazed apple with a cider sauce. Effective French service.

• **Ivy Hatch** (Kent)
Plough High Cross Road, (01732) 810268. Country restaurant with a bar serving good-quality French food to the affluent denizens of Kent. Sit in the sophisticated conservatory and sample well-constructed dishes along the lines of goose rillettes and foie gras crostini, seafood terrine with lobster sauce, and pan-fried guinea-fowl with caramelised chestnuts.

• **Langtoft** (East Riding of Yorkshire)
Old Mill Mill Lane, (01377) 267284. Converted from an eighteenth-century farmhouse attached to a corn mill, this is now a family-run hotel in the rural reaches of the Yorkshire Wolds. Fish specials of grilled cod fillet with ginger and coriander crust are alternatives to, say, roast Deben duck with plum sauce, or spiced pork fillet with apples and calvados. Also bar meals from 7pm.

• **Lechlade** (Gloucestershire)
Rieunier's 6 Oak Street, (01367) 52587. Chef/patron René Rieunier aims high in his Cotswold restaurant. His *carte* includes some vivid ideas, such as a terrine of Parma ham, pork and vegetables with spiced water-melon relish, or roast rack of lamb with sweet potatoes and beetroot, plus a tomato and sherry sauce. Lunch also calls into play simpler offerings such as devilled kidneys with herb rice.

• **Leeds** (West Yorkshire)
Bibis Minerva House, 16 Greek Street, (0113) 243 0905. Blackboard specials get top marks in this lively pizzeria/all-in trattoria. Excellent grilled sea bass with creamy sauce, calf's liver and rack of lamb are the kind of dishes to expect, and the coffee is 'fine'. No bookings; packed out on Saturday nights.

La Grillade 31–33 East Parade, (0113) 245 9707. Long-serving, authentic French brasserie famed for its all-day snack menu, grills and 'le formule express' fixed-price deal. Tomato and basil salad, and cod basquaise with a rich sauce and proper pommes frites have pleased reporters. Excellent French bread, modestly priced house wine.

Marcell's 300 Harrogate Road, (0113) 236 9991. Unusually decorated new venue much patronised by the bright young things of Leeds. 'Orange walls, weird paintings, funny little chairs' belie the fact that serious cooking is going on here. Typical menu dishes are lobster ravioli with lobster bisque, confit of chicken and foie gras with orange emulsion, and fillet of rabbit with coriander *jus* and broad beans. Sunday opening is much appreciated. More reports, please.

Olive Tree 55 Rodley Lane, Rodley, (0113) 256 9283. Much-publicised Greek restaurant just outside Leeds. Expect dishes on the lines of kotopitakia (chicken pastries), keftedes (meatballs), finishing with their special dessert stafidhopitta (sultanas, orange liqueur and cinnamon in filo pastry). Vegetarians are catered for with several dishes including spanakopitta (oven-baked spinach, feta cheese, onions and dill encased in layers of filo pastry).

● **Leicester** (Leicestershire)

Welford Place 9 Welford Place, (0116) 247 0758. Recommended for its prime location bang in the city centre and for the fact that food is served all day. Proceedings kick off with breakfast (served till noon), otherwise choose between daily and seasonal menus. Sandwiches and snacks appear alongside fish-cakes with tartare sauce, smoked duck with roasted tomatoes, and sea bass with spinach and saffron butter sauce.

● **Lewdown** (Devon)

Lewtrenchard Manor Lewdown, (01566) 783256. 'Mildly eccentric' Jacobean manor house with magnificent views over Dartmoor and a plethora of antiques within. New chef Tim Rogers moved here from the Cornish Cottage Hotel, New Polzeath (see main entry), at the end of our inspection season and his menus promise a great deal. Honey-roast quail is sliced over a saffron and vegetable risotto, and confit of belly pork comes on a parsnip purée with a sage and shallot sauce. Reports please.

● **Little Addington** (Northamptonshire)

Bell High Street, (01933) 651700. Home-made tortellini of crab with chive butter sauce, medallions of pork with sauté black pudding, and baked salmon and squid ink noodles with warm lobster vinaigrette are typically ambitious offerings in this jazzed up pub/restaurant. One menu is served throughout, and wines of the month are worth considering.

● **Liverpool** (Merseyside)

Armadillo 31 Mathew Street, (0151) 236 4123. The 'new' Armadillo, across the road from its original venue in Liverpool's Cavern Quarter, has a neat, well-groomed appearance. Menus change every few weeks, and lunch and early supper are particularly good value. Crispy duck is served with steamed Chinese greens, baked sea bass receives a fennel confit, and roast spring lamb fillet is accompanied by tapénade-enriched *jus*.

Becher's Brook 29A Hope Street, (0151) 707 0005. Usefully placed for the city's cathedrals, cultural hot-spots and the university. The bare-walled dining-room is decked out with ethnic artwork and the menu shows plenty of ambition. Set lunches are well reported, and evening menus take in split-pea soup with maple-cured bacon and polenta, grilled Irish salmon with orange and fennel sauce, and butter tart on a spiced apple compote with calvados sauce.

Beluga Bar 24–40 Wood Street, (0151) 708 8896. Unlikely venue occupying a cellar in clubland, but serving splendid food at very fair prices. In a setting of bare brick walls and local artwork, you can sample some of the best duck confit in town, as well as king scallops in a creamy mustard and lentil sauce, Thai chicken, and perch fillets with braised leeks. But be warned: after about 9pm bouncers appear at the door and the place becomes a late-night 'young-set' bar.

Number Seven Café 7 Falkner Street, (0151) 709 9633. Students, families and theatregoers pile into this affordable asset to the locally regenerated cultural heartland of the city. Vegetarians do well here and the menu is a straight-down-the-line assortment of dishes at bargain-basement prices. Hummus, guacamole and mushroom risotto share the billing with Thai fish soup, spicy lamb meatballs and provençale cod with coriander dressing. Puddings are the nursery kind.

Shangri La Ashcroft Buildings, 37 Victoria Street, (0151) 255 0708. In the city centre rather than Chinatown, and worth knowing about if you need a break from business or shopping. Three-course dim-sum lunches are a good idea and the range encompasses everything from sui mai, steamed spare ribs and fried custard buns to 'novel and excellent' prawn and leek dumplings. The full menu is in the steamed lobster/aromatic crispy duck mould.

• **Longdon Green** (Staffordshire)
Red Lion Inn Longdon Green, (01543) 490250. Extended country pub on the village green, idyllically situated on the fringes of Cannock Chase. The floors are stripped wood, menus are on blackboards and dishes arrive on 'large white plates'. Tagliatelle with wild mushrooms, venison sausage with onion gravy, and braised oxtail have been noted, and desserts include good versions of cheesecake and treacle pudding.

• **Long Melford** (Suffolk)
Chimneys Hall Street, (01787) 379806. Warmly decorated, half-timbered building housing a much-liked restaurant with a congenial atmosphere. Reporters have endorsed filo parcels with prawns and feta cheese, 'superb' roast duckling with apples, calf's liver and bacon with onion sauce, and raspberry mousse. The wine list is regularly praised – although prices may seem a shade high.

• **Lower Oddington** (Gloucestershire)
Fox Inn Lower Oddington, (01451) 870555. Cleverly extended, civilised Cotswold pub with a flagstoned bar, eating areas all around and a walled garden. Much of the menu changes fortnightly and dishes are based on good raw materials. Expect perhaps Caesar salad, rack of English lamb with onion sauce, and kedgeree, and finish with chocolate roulade or hot walnut tart. Decent real ales, thoughtfully chosen wines.

• **Ludlow** (Shropshire)
Dinham Hall (01584) 876464. Family-run Georgian hotel within walking distance of Ludlow's historic castle. The kitchen works to fixed-price menus (have anything from two to five courses) and dishes are in the mould of smoked chicken salad, medley of sole and scallops in aromatic juices, and raspberry and vanilla parfait. Well-chosen wines.
Oaks 17 Corve Street, (01584) 872 325. Organic produce, wild foods and industrious domestic enterprise colour the menus in this enthusiastically supported Ludlow restaurant. Recommended dishes from Ken Adams's repertoire have included red mullet terrine, crab and salmon risotto, and wild duck on a bed of fresh figs. Al dente vegetables draw heaps of praise, as do desserts such as home-made mulberry ice-cream.

• **Lymington** (Hampshire)
The Old Bank House 68 High Street, (01590) 671128. Up-and-coming wine bar/restaurant offering good-value dishes based around local fish and seasonal New Forest produce. Reporters have applauded smoked chicken parcels, and timbale of crab with dill sauce, as well as warm salad of stir-fried scallops with mange-tout, and salmon fish-cakes on spinach. More reports, please.

• **Manchester** (Greater Manchester)
Beijing 48 Portland Street, (0161) 228 0893. Smart new venue providing a creditable Pekinese alternative to Manchester's Cantonese warhorses. Fried pork and vegetable dumplings, spring onion pancakes, and a mix of aubergines, green pepper and bean curd with minced prawn stuffing and black-bean sauce are typical of the menu. Fried rice and tea get the thumbs-up.
Brasserie St Pierre 57–63 Princess Street, (0161) 228 0231. Long-established Manchester fixture, attractively decorated, with bags of character and a menu of sound Anglo-French dishes. Reports have singled out lobster and crab risotto, goats' cheese with avocado mousse, and lamb's liver garnished with deep-fried herbs. To finish there might be pistachio brûlée or lemon parfait.
Café Istanbul 79–81 Bridge Street, (0161) 833 9942. Since 1980, owner Sacit Onur has been providing the citizens of Manchester and beyond with genuine Turkish cooking in modestly appealing

surroundings. The three-course set lunch remains outstanding value, and the menu offers two dozen hot and cold meze, kebabs, grills and long-cooked stews. Drinkable wines.

New Emperor 52–56 George Street, (0161) 228 2883. Recent addition to the ranks of Cantonese restaurants in Manchester's Chinatown. The setting is a pleasant ground-floor room with white walls and deep-pink cloths, and the menu reads well. Salt and chilli ribs and special chow mein with an 'omnium gatherum' of meat, fish and vegetables have pleased reporters. Generous portions, pretty good value for money.

Primavera 48 Beech Road, (0161) 862 9934. New owners have jazzed up the décor in this popular Manchester venue in a converted shop. The menu is up-to-the-minute brasserie, taking in crab in filo pastry with ginger and spring onions, guinea-fowl with aubergine purée, and loin of lamb with mash, red cabbage and shallot *jus*. Open evenings only.

Sanam 145–151 Wilmslow Rd, (0161) 224 1008/8824. 'A strong value-for-money performer' among Manchester's myriad Indian restaurants. Reliability is the kitchen's strength and the menu promises decent, vividly spiced curry-house favourites such as chicken tikka and king prawn karahi. Service is helpful, courteous and attentive. Unlicensed, but there is lassi to drink.

Victoria & Albert Hotel Water Street, (0161) 832 1188. The menu may raise a chuckle or two with its jokes and puns, but the kitchen takes its work seriously in this modern hotel by the banks of the Irwell. In the Sherlock Holmes Restaurant you can sample decent bread, plates of smoked salmon, chicken with noodles and baby turnips, and a trio of caramel desserts – not to mention Welsh rarebit.

• **MELLOR** (Greater Manchester)

Devonshire Arms Longhurst Lane, (0161) 427 2563. The setting is a dyed-in-the-wool North-Country pub built of stone, but the kitchen looks to the world's larder for inspiration. Expect anything from Polish sausage soup and heart-warming mussel chowder to stuffed peppers, shahi korma and Malaysian chicken. Chatty service, excellent value. Note that food is served only at lunch-times and on Monday evenings.

• **MERLEY** (Dorset)

Les Bouviers Oakley Hill, (01202) 889555. There is always plenty going on at James Coward's classily refurbished cottage restaurant: special events and day trips are just part of the package. The cooking speaks with a forthright French accent, offering dishes such as smoked chicken consommé, fillet of sea bass with fennel and Pastis butter sauce, and caramelised lemon tart.

• **MINCHINHAMPTON** (Gloucestershire)

Markey's Restaurant The Old Ram, Market Square, (01453) 882287. Ian and Ann Markey's eponymous restaurant was once the local pub but now provides sustenance of a different order for all comers. Start with, say, warm salad of pigeon, bacon and black pudding, move on to grilled salmon with asparagus and a tomato and tarragon sauce, and finish off with warm pear and almond tart.

• **MORPETH** (Northumberland)

Brasserie 59 Bridge Street, (01670) 516200. A favourite north-east address offering sound brasserie cooking. King prawns in filo pastry with lobster sauce is a perennial favourite, but the menu also promises crisp-skinned confit of duck with Grand Marnier sauce, roast fillet of salmon with béarnaise sauce, and loin of pork with creamy Dijon mustard sauce. Relaxed service.

• **NANCENOY** (Cornwall)

Trengilly Wartha Inn Nancenoy, (01326) 340332. A remote but entrancing setting, tip-top real ales and a serious wine list are just three of the attractions at this stylishly organised pub/restaurant with rooms. Eat in the bar or in the main restaurant, where fixed-price menus promise smoked pheasant salad, medallions of monkfish on vegetable 'linguine', and mango and raspberry parfait.

• **Newcastle upon Tyne** (Tyne & Wear)
Magpie Room St James's Park Stadium, (0191) 232 3408. A far cry from the days of a meat pie at half-time. Expect spiced king prawn tempura with ginger, cumin and coriander, or pepper-crusted sea bream with red pepper relish and watercress butter sauce. Finish with pear parfait with sweet apple crisps, while enjoying 'unrivalled' views of the pitch on one side and of Tyneside on the other.

• **Newent** (Gloucestershire)
Three Choirs Restaurant Newent, (01531) 890223. Views across the vineyard are a bonus at this popular restaurant attached to the winery. Lunch is served during the day, and dinner only on Friday and Saturday. The menu makes good reading – chargrilled summer vegetables with balsamic vinegar, breast of chicken with parsnip and horseradish mash, prune and Armagnac frangipane, for example.

• **Northallerton** (North Yorkshire)
Bettys 188 High Street, (01609) 775154. The most modest of a quartet of classic tea-rooms dotted around West and North Yorkshire. In addition to superb breads, cakes and pastries, reporters have enthused about parsnip and pear soup, warm croissants filled with smoked salmon and cream cheese, crisp röstis and pasta specials. Exemplary children's facilities.

• **North Bovey** (Devon)
Blackaller Hotel North Bovey, (01647) 440322. Honey from the hotel hives is just one of the treats at this converted seventeenth-century woollen mill hidden away by the banks of the River Bovey. Daily fixed-price dinner menus run to hot Stilton soufflé with red pepper sauce, poached plaice with a scallop and white wine sauce, and chocolate and raspberry roulade.

• **Norton** (Shropshire)
Hundred House Hotel Bridgnorth Road, (01952) 730353. Roadside hotel serving English and Continental dishes using local game, farm produce and the hotel's own herbs and fruit. Expect dishes such as Greek salad, or bruschetta, followed by steak and kidney pie, or Bridgnorth pork sausages with mash and onion gravy. Vegetarian dishes are also available.

• **Nottingham** (Nottinghamshire)
Café de Paris 2 Kings Walk, (0115) 947 3767. A particularly useful 'fuelling stop' for city-centre shoppers and those heading for the nearby theatre. The atmosphere is sunny and cheerful, and the kitchen deals in Franco-Italian 'bistro' cooking in the shape of grilled goats'-cheese salad, penne with smoked salmon and chives, rack of lamb with rosemary, and pork with wild mushrooms and sun-dried tomatoes.
Le Pub Français 9A Warser Gate, The Lace Market, (0115) 955 6060. Up-beat pub/wine bar/restaurant rolled into one. The décor might be described as 'period bistro', the mood is trendy, the atmosphere relaxed. Generous French cooking is the order of the day, and reporters have found plenty to enjoy in the shape of chicken terrine with leek sauce, salmon with light orange sauce, mignons of pork with sage, and crème brûlée.
Saagar 473 Mansfield Road, (0115) 962 2014/969 2860. Smartly decorated tandoori house with well-groomed staff and a distinctive menu of mainly Punjabi dishes. Specialities such as shajahani lamb and king prawn karahi are prepared from top-notch ingredients, and the repertoire also features a crop of baltis, Kashmiri kormas and Parsee dishes. Cobra lager suits the food.

• **Odiham** (Hampshire)
Grapevine 121 High Street, (01256) 701122. Neighbourhood French bistro with a sound local reputation for brisk service, fair prices and reliable cooking. Reporters have praised soups, chicken and ham terrine, steak au poivre with frites, and scallops with bacon. 'Very drinkable' house wine.

• **Orford** (Suffolk)
Butley-Orford Oysterage Market Hill, (01394) 450277. For more than three decades this long-established venue has served up 'the freshest/smokiest fish on

the east coast'. Butley Creek oysters, Irish smoked salmon, slip soles, gargantuan lobsters, crab salad and griddled prawns are just some of the delights on offer. Functional, canteen-style décor, great atmosphere and long queues during the season. Note: no credit cards.

• **Over Stratton** (Somerset)

New Farm Over Stratton, (01460) 240584. Jane and Crispin Bond's likeable village restaurant is in what was an old storage barn on the farm. It makes a pleasant, but unlikely, setting for cooking with a strong metropolitan undercurrent. Fixed-price monthly menus might feature tagliatelle with asparagus and oyster mushrooms, spiced Cajun chicken with roasted red peppers, or Chinese leaves stuffed with black beans on tomato sauce.

• **Oxford** (Oxfordshire)

Le Petit Blanc 71–72 Walton Street, (01865) 510700. A polished wooden 'squash court' floor and plastic-topped tables are the style in Raymond Blanc's brasserie, where a new chef was due to be appointed before the *Guide* appeared. Materials include Aberdeen Angus beef, Gloucester Old Spot pork and Oxford sausages (with parsleyed mash), but vegetarians get a fair deal too. Chips are good, and sorbets and ice-creams are from the Manoir (see main entry, Great Milton).

Restaurant Elizabeth 82 St Aldate's, (01865) 242230. Still running after all these years and still offering the kind of bourgeois French cooking that was all the range in the '60s. Here is a kitchen that deals in salmon quenelles with sauce Nantua, duck with orange, chateaubriand, and chocolate mousse. A great nostalgia trip, right down to the ancient clarets and bow-tie service.

• **Penkridge** (Staffordshire)

William Harding's House Mill Street, (01785) 712955. Occasional Victorian breakfasts and 'supper club' evenings are just two of the crowd-pullers in this sixteenth-century beamed house (once a stable block). Dinner is a drawn-out affair that could run as follows: mushroom filo parcels with garlic sauce, duck breast with blackberry and balsamic sauce, then dark chocolate parfait, plus 'British rural cheeses'. Only open for dinner from Tuesday to Saturday, and lunch on the first and last Sunday of the month. No children.

• **Pinner** (Greater London)

La Giralda 66–68 Pinner Green, (0181) 868 3429. Long-serving Continental restaurant offering creditable cooking with Spanish flourishes backed up by a stupendous Spanish wine list. Fabada (white beans with chorizo) and paella represent the *español* side of things; other dishes such as escalope of salmon and pan-fried trout are more broadly based. Swift, amicable service.

• **Plymouth** (Devon)

Ocean Palace 30A Western Parade, (01752) 660170. One of the better provincial Chinese restaurants in the West Country, 'an excellent place with charming, friendly service'. The cooking is a mix of Cantonese and Pekinese with a few novelties for good measure. Champagne pork cooked in sea salt, sizzling lemon sole with black-bean sauce, chilli chicken, and deep-fried shredded beef with carrots all feature on the menu.

• **Polperro** (Cornwall)

Kitchen The Coombes, (01503) 272780. Ian and Vanessa Bateson's minuscule cottage restaurant is a godsend for visitors to this tourist hot-spot. The kitchen works to a lively menu of cosmopolitan dishes along the lines of chargrilled hog's pudding with minted flageolet beans, blackened Cajun salmon, and Malaysian lamb with coconut and lime. Good choice for vegetarians.

• **Pool In Wharfedale** (West Yorkshire)

Monkman's Bistro Pool Bank, New Road, (0113) 284 1105. Large 'hustly bustly' modern bistro-with-bedrooms, decorated in bold primary colours and with an up-to-the-minute menu to match. Dishes change weekly and the kitchen draws on all the fashionable ingredients of the moment. Risotto of home-dried tomatoes, peas and saffron, charred salmon with ratatouille couscous and caviare, and banana and caramel pavlova are typical dishes. There's a mini-offshoot, called Monkman's Cookhouse, in Ilkley.

● **Portreath** (Cornwall)
Tabb's Tregea Terrace, (01209) 842488. Nigel and Melanie Tabb's converted granite forge is a pleasing local venue offering seasonal menus with an eclectic flavour. Expect dishes such as provençale egg soup, roast breast of duck with lemon honey and toasted sesame seeds, and fillet of venison on a potato and cumin cake; local fish specials are also worth noting. Once a year, the owners stage a splendid Victorian Sunday breakfast.

● **Powerstock** (Dorset)
Three Horseshoes Powerstock, (01308) 485328. Remote country inn famous for its atmospheric location not far from Eggardon Hill, and for landlord Pat Ferguson's passion for fish. The catch from the Weymouth boats might show up in pan-fried squid with chilli dressing, scallops with peach chutney, and shark steak with herbed hollandaise. Local real ales, 20 wines by the glass.

● **Ramsgill** (North Yorkshire)
Yorke Arms Ramsgill, (01423) 755243. The Nidderdale valley is now home to Frances and Gerald Atkins (previously featured in the *Guide* at Shaw's in London, and before that Farleyer House in Scotland). Very much a traditional inn, with 13 rooms, restaurant and bar. Wild salmon, grilled venison steak and summer pudding set the tone in the restaurant. Bar food might include open sandwiches, Thai spiced fish-cakes or freshly made pasta. Reports please.

● **Redmile** (Leicestershire)
Peacock Inn Main Street, (01949) 842554. Greatly extended traditional Shires inn with a dyed-in-the-wool locals' bar, elegantly furnished restaurant and a sunny new Garden Room with hand-painted murals. The food is in the French idiom with dips into the Med: seafood risotto, cassoulet, wild boar and game stew, home-made pastas, and vegetable couscous with pine kernels are typical. Well-kept beers, sound wines.

● **Reeth** (North Yorkshire)
Burgoyne Hotel Reeth, (01748) 884292. Local produce looms large on the menus at this stylishly fitted-out Dales hotel on the village green. Pheasant is roasted and served in traditional fashion with bread sauce and game chips, monkfish tails are cooked with lime and garlic sauce, and best-end of lamb is accompanied by redcurrant jelly. Good North Country cheeses to finish.

● **Richmond** (Surrey)
Petersham Hotel Nightingale Lane, (0181) 940 7471. Standing proud on Richmond Hill, this ornate Victorian edifice boasts some of the best Thameside views south of the river. Fish gets a good airing, otherwise the kitchen delivers anything from confit of duck with cumin-roasted carrots, and noisettes of lamb with madeira gravy, to wild mushroom and Parmesan risotto.

● **Rochdale** (Greater Manchester)
After Eight 2 Edenfield Road, (01706) 46432. Impressive old house with its own front garden and a noticeable home-from-home atmosphere. Recommended dishes from the varied menus have included Bury black pudding with mustard sauce, blackened red snapper with Caesar salad, stuffed loin of pork with cider gravy, and blackcurrant and marzipan tart. Friendly, personal service.

● **Romsey** (Hampshire)
Bertie's 80 The Hundred, (01794) 830708. Housed in a former women's workhouse, this lively venue takes as its theme P.G. Wodehouse's famous literary toff. The cooking promises 'culinary nostalgia with a modern twist': fish-cakes on chilli potato salad, individual toad-in-the-hole, fresh pasta, chump of lamb on pea and mint mash, and so on. Related to Hunters in New Alresford and Winchester (see main entries).

● **Saffron Walden** (Essex)
Old Hoops 15 King Street, (01799) 522813. Mid-week set lunches and dinners are 'incredible value' in this beamed first-floor restaurant that

reminded one visitor of 'a bistro on the left bank of Paris'. Recommendations have singled out tomato and mozzarella salad with pine kernels, poached fillet of sea bass with mushroom and herb sauce, and strawberry Romanoff. Sound wine list.

• **Salisbury** (Wiltshire)
Harpers 6–7 Ox Row, (01722) 333118. 'Real food is our speciality,' proclaims the menu in this long-serving upstairs restaurant overlooking the Market Square. Bargain-price lunches (have just a main dish or a three-course meal) attract shoppers, but the *carte* strikes a more modern note with specialities including salad of pan-fried scallops with an oriental ginger dressing.

• **Scarborough** (North Yorkshire)
Stephen Joseph Theatre, The Restaurant Westborough, (01723) 368463. Airy, art deco-style restaurant on the first-floor of the theatre (Alan Ayckbourn's home patch). An all-day menu, 'theatre specials', and an evening *carte* may take in anything from warm chicken liver salad and Welsh rarebit to hot-smoked duck breast with a compote of lentils and juniper *jus*. Also good for scones with 'wonderful' home-made jam. More reports, please.

• **Seaview** (Isle of Wight)
Seaview Hotel High Street, (01983) 612711. Birds, boats and sea breezes provide the atmosphere outside this popular Victorian hotel; inside, the décor strikes a nautical note. Local produce – especially fish – dictates both bar and restaurant menus. From the latter you might choose moules marinière, terrine of crab with a cheese crust, poached monkfish with queenies, or chargrilled entrecôte steak.

• **Sheffield** (South Yorkshire)
Greenhead House 84 Burncross Road, (0114) 246 9004. Neil and Anne Allen run their stone-built suburban residence as house and home, opening for dinner (Wednesday to Saturday) and now offering light lunches (Thursday and Friday) as well. The kitchen looks across the Channel for much of its inspiration and there are some good things on the monthly menu. Hot salmon mousse with a crab Thermidor sauce, cassoulet of seafood, and lemon meringues with raspberries and strawberry ice-cream have been enjoyed. Well-chosen cheeses, 'lovely' coffee.
Mediterranean 271 Sharrowvale Road, (0114) 266 1069. The name might suggest pesto and polenta, but there's much more on offer in this converted shop out of the city. Mussels are steamed in Thai fashion, oxtail is braised with belly pork and served with mashed potato, while zarzuela suggests España. Following the Spanish theme, tapas are also served at lunchtime and most evenings (5.30 to 7pm Tuesday to Friday).

• **Sherborne** (Dorset)
Pheasants 24 Greenhill, (01935) 815252. Andrew Overhill's homely restaurant-with-rooms is a perennial favourite with parents visiting children at the town's prestigious schools. Monthly theme nights are a feature, otherwise the kitchen delivers fixed-price menus made up of dishes such as chilled gazpacho, monkfish with saffron butter sauce, and triple chocolate terrine.

• **Sissinghurst** (Kent)
Rankins' Restaurant The Street, (01580) 713964. Worth knowing about if you are in this part of Kent and have been on the castle-and-garden-trail. Hugh and Leonora Rankin have been in residence at this weatherboarded shop since 1986 and still court their regulars. The kitchen pulls in ideas from everywhere: parsnip and Chinese five-spice soup, hot-smoked 'bradan rost' salmon with mustard dressing, gnocchi with tomato and basil sauce are typical.

• **Speen** (Buckinghamshire)
Old Plow Inn Flowers Bottom, (01494) 488300. Hidden away in the Chiltern beechwoods (phone for directions), this classic red-brick building has evolved from local pub into a full-blown bistro and restaurant. Wherever you eat, the

food is fashionably in tune with the times: typical dishes might include home-cured bresaola, crispy duck leg with beetroot chutney, and red plum sorbet with summer-fruit confit.

• **STALISFIELD GREEN** (Kent)
Plough Stalisfield Green, (01795) 890256. Creditable French bistro cooking in the unlikely setting of a great little country pub some way off the beaten track. The all-Gallic menu is a daily blackboard that offers the likes of onion soup, stuffed mussels, plates of charcuterie, confit of duck and tarte Tatin; ploughman's and sandwiches, too. Real ales from Kent, wines from France.

• **STEEPLE ASTON** (Oxfordshire)
Red Lion South Street, (01869) 340225. Colin and Margaret Mead have run this 300-year-old inn for more than 25 years and it is very much their pride and joy. Light lunches are served in the bar and on the terrace, more ambitious evening meals (Tuesday to Saturday) are offered in the restaurant. Margaret's cooking is honest and robust – hot Arbroath smokies, fillet of brill with hollandaise, duck with green peppercorn sauce and so on. First-rate wines.

• **STOCKLAND** (Devon)
Kings Arms Inn Stockland, (01404) 881361. Greatly extended 200-year-old thatched inn offering everything from lunchtime snacks in the Farmers' Bar to more elaborate meals in the Cotley Restaurant. Expect Scottish king scallops, medallions of venison, tournedos Rossini and gooseberry crunch gâteau. Good real ales, wines kept using the 'Verre de Vin' preservation system.

• **STOKE BRUERNE** (Northamptonshire)
Bruerne's Lock The Canalside, (01604) 863654. Well known in narrowboat circles as it stands next to the Canal Museum by a lock on the Grand Union Canal. Smoked haddock soup, sea trout, and pan-fried beef on a bed of onions and peppers have been endorsed, and the kitchen also gets to grips with blackened tuna with olive and avocado salsa, and baked gammon with parsley crumble. Praiseworthy wines.

• **STOKE-ON-TRENT** (Staffordshire)
Ria 61–67 Piccadilly, (01782) 264411. Since 1989 Charoon and Anong Sangpreechakul have offered a taste of Thailand in the Potteries. Their longish menu includes most accessible aspects of the cuisine from soups, salads and stir-fries to curries, rice and noodles. Also note the useful vegetarian section and the fruity exotica at the end – longans, palm seeds, rambutans and so on. Open evenings only.

• **STONOR** (Oxfordshire)
Stonor Arms Stonor, (01491) 638866. A new chef was due to arrive here as we went to press, but the format seems set to remain the same. One menu is served throughout this wistaria-covered, stone building and you can eat in the bar (a shrine to rowing), the dining-room, or the conservatory overlooking the well-tended garden. The food has a metropolitan accent, wines are well spread and affordable.

• **STRATFORD-UPON-AVON** (Warwickshire)
Opposition 13 Sheep Street, (01789) 269980. 'Useful pre-theatre watering-hole' that deals admirably with the rush before the show. Booking is advisable, the queues ever present. Reports have spoken favourably of mozzarella with tomatoes and olives, chargrilled chicken salad, a panaché of seafood with Basmati rice, and roasted vegetables with couscous.

Russons 8 Church Street, (01789) 268822. Tiny, beamed eating-house conveniently placed for the theatre. Menus and blackboards offer a mixed bag of dishes with a global accent, taking in black pudding with mustard sauce, Indonesian fish stew, guinea-fowl with red wine sauce and Cantonese stir-fried vegetables. Service is fast, but cheerful and obliging.

• **STRETTON** (Leicestershire)
Ram Jam Inn Great North Road, (01780) 410776. 'An oasis of calm and cleanliness . . . on the A1' and a great place for a refreshing pit-stop. An all-day menu – plus blackboard specials – offers

such things as smoked Whitby whiting on a bed of mash, sausages with onion marmalade and chips. Superb garlic bread, smartly turned-out staff.

• **Sudbury** (Suffolk)
Brasserie 47 47 Gainsborough Street, (01787) 374298. Formerly Mabey's Brasserie, but now owned by Fraser and Fiona Green. Little else seems set to change. The décor is jauntily nautical and the kitchen deals successfully with the likes of warm oyster mushroom and artichoke salad, teriyaki cod with buttered Chinese noodles, and lemon mousse with lime sauce.

• **Sutton Coldfield** (West Midlands)
La Truffe 65 Birmingham Road, (0121) 355 5836. Swish-looking neighbourhood restaurant set in a parade of shops. An atmosphere of laid-back confidence pervades the tasteful dining-room and the menu offers classic French cooking with a few modern flourishes. Lobster ravioli in cream and herb sauce, breast and confit leg of duck with Puy lentil sauce, and a duo of chocolate mousses have been recommended.

• **Sutton Gault** (Cambridgeshire)
Anchor Inn Sutton Gault, (01353) 778537. Seventeenth-century ferry inn on the New Bedford River, making good use of local and seasonal produce – Cromer crab, Denham Estate venison – and rare and unusual breeds, such as Gloucester Old Spot pork, and Castlemilk Morrit lamb. 'Excellent' farmhouse cheeses are recommended.

• **Tewkesbury** (Gloucestershire)
Le Bistrot André 78 Church Street, (01684) 290357. Cheery French bistro with a regularly changing blackboard menu of old-school Gallic favourites, backed up by a handful of patriotic wines. Expect classics such as moules marinière, coq au vin, cassoulet, rabbit with prunes, and medallions of beef Rossini.

• **Torquay** (Devon)
Mulberry Room 1 Scarborough Road, (01803) 213639. Fun, good value and discreetly personal service are the keys to the success of Lesley Cooper's idiosyncratic enterprise in a 'beautifully decorated front room'. Her cooking is straightforward, fish is 'cleverly flavoured' and the repertoire extends to pheasant soup, baked ham with cherries and mulberries, and ragoût of lamb. Interesting wines.

• **Tresco** (Isles of Scilly)
Island Hotel Tresco, (01720) 422883. Stunning maritime views and swaths of unspoilt landscape bring visitors to the Island of Flowers. Seafood in the shape of, say, home-cured gravlax or shellfish bisque has been given the thumbs-up, along with breast of turkey with wild mushrooms and thyme, and an exotic version of bread-and-butter pudding with banana and almonds.

• **Wansford** (Cambridgeshire)
Haycock Hotel Wansford, (01780) 782223. Impressive seventeenth-century honey-coloured stone edifice by the River Nene and just off the A1. The kitchen yo-yos between traditional roasts on silver trolleys and modern ideas such as seared scallops on grilled red pepper with lime vinaigrette, and calf's liver with olive oil mash. Wines are excellent value.

• **Warwick** (Warwickshire)
Findons 7 Old Square, (01926) 411755. Elegantly spacious restaurant set in part of a Georgian house furnished in domestic style with book-laden bookcases and more besides. The kitchen delivers sound Anglo-French cooking along the lines of king prawns with beetroot salad, scallops with sweet chicory and lemon sauce, and fillet of beef with tapénade. Comprehensive wine list.

• **Weybridge** (Surrey)
Colony 3 Balfour Road, (01932) 842766. Since 1984 the Pangs have been dispensing reliable Pekinese and Szechuan food to the citizens of Weybridge and beyond. Their 80-dish menu is sound provincial stuff: bang-bang chicken, braised chilli fish, sea-spiced shredded duck, and aromatic crispy lamb are the kinds of dishes to expect.

• **Weymouth** (Dorset)
Perry's 4 Trinity Road, (01305) 785799. A delightful restaurant overlooking

Weymouth harbour that convinces locals and visitors about the quality and worth of fresh seafood. Reporters have spoken fondly of crab fish-cakes with cheese sauce, moules marinière, and lemon sole with crisp fresh vegetables. Carnivores are also accommodated, and desserts such as crème brûlée have been praised.

● **WHITLEY BAY** (Tyne & Wear)

Le Provençale 183 Park View, (0191) 251 3567. Much favoured by reporters for its generous brand of French cooking 'ancienne et moderne'. Steaks loom large among the main courses along with coq au vin and loin of pork provençale; starters include salade niçoise and black pudding with mustard sauce, desserts range from tarte aux pommes to pears Belle Hélène.

● **WICKHAM** (Hampshire)

Old House The Square, (01329) 833049. Annie and Richard Skipwith have been custodians of this modest Georgian house since 1970 and the place continues to please. Regional French dishes dominate the weekly-changing menu: expect to find moules marinière, salmon fish-cakes with tomato sauce and more intricate ideas such as smoked duck breast with orange and lemon vinaigrette, cranberries and chestnuts. Rhubarb crème brûlée makes a good finish, and France rules on the wine list.

● **WILLINGTON** (Co Durham)

Stile 97 High Street, (01388) 746615 Nine miles outside Durham is Mike Boustred and Jenny James's informally run country restaurant. Monthly-changing menus offer ideas from 'ploughman's' soufflé of onions and Cheddar cheese to oriental strips of beef fillet. Regular themed evenings are popular, and wines are taken seriously here.

● **WINDERMERE** (Cumbria)

Holbeck Ghyll Holbeck Lane, (01539) 432375. Great views of Windermere and the mountains are a bonus at this converted Victorian hunting lodge. A new kitchen brigade is upping the level of cooking by several notches and the daily fixed-price menu deals in imaginative modern dishes. Air-dried pigeon with foie gras, green beans and cep oil, roast chump of Tunstall pork with parsnip and honey purée, and pineapple tarte Tatin give an idea of the style. More reports, please.

● **WOODSEAVES** (Staffordshire)

Old Parsonage High Offley, (01785) 284446. Pleasant country restaurant-with-rooms with an elegant conservatory overlooking the Staffordshire hills. Pigeon breasts on a bed of mushrooms and Caesar salad have been praised; seafood platter contains good, fresh ingredients, and well-reported sweets include light passion-fruit soufflé, and cinnamon mousse with spiced rhubarb. Pleasant, discreet service.

● **WOOLTON HILL** (Hampshire)

Hollington House Woolton Hill, (01635) 255100. Splendidly decorated Edwardian stone mansion set in 25 acres of mature woodland gardens. A new head chef was being sought as we went to press, but it is hoped that the cooking will remain on course. Australian owners John and Penny Guy will, no doubt, ensure that the cellar continues to house some real treasures from Down Under.

● **YORK** (North Yorkshire)

Bettys 6–8 St Helen's Square, (01904) 659142. Founder Frederick Belmont travelled on the maiden voyage of the Queen Mary in 1936 and modelled this famous tea-room on the interior of the liner. Like the other branches in Harrogate, Ikley and Northallerton, this place excels at pâtisserie, baking and savouries, as well as splendid teas and coffees. It is also great for families.

Grange Hotel Clifton, (01904) 644744. Impressive Regency hotel not far from the city centre and the Minster. The Ivy restaurant might offer salad of queen scallops with bacon, sauté lamb fillet with oyster mushrooms in grain mustard sauce, and almond tuile basket with summer berries and creme fraîche. Meals in the Brasserie and Seafood Bar have also been endorsed.

• **YOXFORD** (Suffolk)
Jacey's Charcoal Pit Blythburgh House, (01728) 77298. Billed as a 'Mediterranean restaurant with imagination', this is certainly a novel set-up. The location is a converted draper's shop and the cooking is based around chargrills and kebabs which are hung on special stands at the table. As a back-up there are some splendid pastas and a few 'pot' dishes including Armenian lamb.

Scotland

• **ALLOA** (Clackmannan)
Gean House Gean Park, Tullibody Road (01259) 219275. Grand country-house hotel in an 'ideal location' surrounded by beautiful gardens. The kitchen delivers good-value dishes including a trio of game with buttery herb vinaigrette, suprême of chicken stuffed with haggis in a whisky sauce, and bread-and-butter pudding.

• **ARDUAINE** (Argyll & Bute)
Loch Melfort Hotel Arduaine, (01852) 200233. Splendid views down the Sound of Jura are a plus point at this popular hotel next to Arduaine Gardens (National Trust). Eat light meals in the Chartroom Bar or try the full menu in the dining-room. Fresh fish and shellfish are the stars; also wild mushrooms in marsala cream, and guard of Scottish lamb with herb and green peppercorn crust.

• **BALLATER** (Aberdeenshire)
Balgonie Country House Braemar Place, (013397) 55482 A striking Edwardian mansion on the edge of the village, close to the River Dee. The kitchen's reputation hinges on its devotion to local produce – Angus beef, Orkney seafood, Highland game and more. A new chef was due to be appointed shortly after we went to press. Reports, please.

• **BIGGAR** (South Lanarkshire)
Culter Mill Coulter Village, (01899) 20950. Standing on the site of a twelfth-century grain mill (the original water wheel still stands in the beer garden). Local produce – including game from the Culter Allers estate and beef direct from the abbatoir – features strongly in the first-floor restaurant. Menus take in everything from wild mushroom risotto to chargrilled chicken breast with pasta.

• **CLYDEBANK**
(Dumbarton & Clydebank)
Beardmore Hotel, Symphony Room Beardmore Street, (0141) 951 6000. Part of the Clydebank private hospital complex. The mood is that of an international hotel, but Mossiman-trained chef James Murphy is capable of delivering a fabulous modern interpretation of cock-a-leekie soup, terrine of salmon with queen scallops, and fillet of halibut with fennel ravioli and squid ink vinaigrette. Open only for dinner on Friday and Saturday.

• **CRINAN** (Argyll & Bute)
Crinan Hotel Crinan, (01546) 830261. Be prepared for panoramic views, which are second to none from this hotel overlooking the harbour. Lock 16, recommended for its seafood dinners, is open only from May to about the middle of September (catches being very much dependent on the weather). The all-year Westward Restaurant offers dishes such as leek soup, a marinated herring platter, or French lemon tart. Vast wine list.

• **EDINBURGH** (Edinburgh)
Balmoral Hotel Princes Street, (0131) 556 2414. Chef Jeff Bland moved here in July 1997 after having made a name for himself at Cameron House Hotel in Alexandria (see main entry). His cooking is stylish and highly accomplished, moving into the realms of soused red mullet with tapénade croûton, roast loin of venison with beetroot sauce and garlic confit, and warm chocolate pudding with mascarpone sorbet. More reports, please.
Fitz Henry 19 Shore Place, (0131) 555 6625. Up-and-coming brasserie housed in a seventeenth-century warehouse with bare walls, brick floors and a slightly

'industrial feel'. The menu features ultra-modern dishes of lamb's sweetbreads with a sesame crust, garlic studded monkfish with aniseed sauce and spinach, and pan-fried pigeon breast with sweetcorn biscuits. Walnut, fig and apricot ice is a good sweet.

Howie's 208 Bruntsfield Place, (0131) 221 1777. Happy-go-lucky eating-house specialising in a lively mix of Scottish and French cooking. Local seafood is a strong suit, but also expect terrine of Highland game with plum salad, beef bourguignon and banoffi pie. There are branches at 63 Dalry Road and 75 St Leonard's Street, Edinburgh.

Pepe Vittorio 7 Victoria Street, (0131) 226 7267. Casual, cheery venue that operates as part of the ever-growing Pierre Victoire group of cut-price eateries. Décor is a cross between 'school lunch-room' and 'Euro caff'. 'Incredibly cheap' lunches feature open mushrooms in cream sauce, braised leg of lamb with tomato sauce, and 'boozy' tiramisu. Affordable wines.

Pierre Victoire 10 Victoria St, (0131) 225 1721. The first of many. Pierre Levicky has franchised the theme and the food, but this is where it all began. The décor is basic, the food no-nonsense and the value excellent. The daily-changing menu might include chicken liver gâteau, then casserole of beef with red wine, and red fruit pavlova. The service zips along.

● **Fairlie** (North Ayrshire)

Fins Fencefoot Farm, (01475) 568989. Converted farm building now functioning as an 'animated and homely' seafood restaurant with a deli/wine shop attached. Home-smoked and marinated fish line up alongside 'slinky sweet oysters', a duo of turbot and salmon with Chardonnay and squat lobster sauce, and pan-fried scallops with lime sauce. Finish with home-made ice-creams or Scottish cheeses.

● **Glasgow** (Glasgow)

Rogano 11 Exchange Place, (0141) 248 4055. Billed as 'Glasgow's oldest surviving restaurant' and famed for its sumptuous art deco restaurant modelled on the liner 'Queen Mary'. Seafood is the star turn, whether you opt for the dining-room, the bar or the basement café. The owners were seeking a new chef as we went to press.

● **Kelso** (Borders)

Sunlaws House Heiton, (01573) 450331. Grandiose Jacobean-style mansion owned by the Duke and Duchess of Roxburghe and lately renowned for its golf course and beauty clinic. Well-reported dinners run to wild mushroom risotto, steamed fillet of sea bass with ratatouille and red pepper essence, and chocolate marquise with pistachio custard.

● **Kilchrenan** (Argyll & Bute)

Ardanaiseig Hotel Kilchrenan, (01866) 833333. Impressive-looking quasi-baronial granite edifice up a single-track road, with horticulturally fascinating gardens and great views of Loch Awe. Expect tomato and basil soup, grilled sardines with lemon butter, monkfish coated in oatmeal with tarragon sauce, and a trio of iced parfaits.

● **Kinbuck** (Stirling)

Cromlix House Kinbuck, (01786) 822125. Breathtaking Edwardian mansion set amid a 3,000-acre estate with glorious views. Formal meals are served in the Red Room, the Green Room and the bright modern conservatory. Five-course dinners focus on luxuries like liver and foie gras pâté rolled in pistachios, marinated saddle of venison with pickled walnuts, and raspberry and passion-fruit délice. Serious wines.

● **Lochinver** (Highland)

Lochinver Larder Main Street, (01571) 844356. Riverside bistro with panoramic views of Lochinver Bay. Hill walkers pack in during the day for home-made pies, sandwiches and cakes. In the evening, the kitchen serves locally smoked salmon, chicken-liver pâté with oatcakes, and Scotch sirloin steaks with various sauces. A 'Heat Away' service is available for those wanting to eat at home.

● **Melrose** (Borders)

Burts Hotel Market Square, (01896) 822285. Family-run coaching-inn built in

1722 and still very much the hub of the town. Bar snacks are commendable as are more formal meals in the restaurant. Potted Borders ostrich is a wacky starter, otherwise expect dishes such as seared scallops on black pudding with Traquair Ale beurre blanc, and saddle of hare with pear and cinnamon mousse.

• **Moffat** (Dumfries & Galloway)
Beechwood Country House Hotel Harthope Place, (01683) 220210. Gracious Victorian country house set in 12 acres of beech trees overlooking the Annan valley. Weekly-changing dinner menus offer creditable hotel cooking that takes in Scotch salmon and dill mousse with lemon mayonnaise, roast saddle of venison with wild mushroom sauce, and chocolate Amaretto pear tart with blackcurrant purée.

• **Scarista** (Western Isles)
Scarista House Scarista, Isle of Harris, (01859) 550238. White-walled Georgian manse in a magical setting overlooking the Atlantic. The Callaghans use only home-grown and organic produce and supplies of fresh fish for their fixed-price dinner menus. A typical night's offering might be smoked haddock and whisky soup, skate in black butter, and miniature strawberry soufflés backed up by fruit and cheeses.

• **Spean Bridge** (Highland)
Old Station Station Road, (01397) 712535. Housed in what was the ticket office of a charming Victorian station, with décor to match. Menus follow the seasons and the kitchen makes good use of local produce for dishes of Mallaig scallops with saffron sauce, chargrilled venison with port and redcurrant *jus*, and warm bramble and almond tart with vanilla ice-cream. Open evenings only Tuesday to Sunday.

Wales

• **Aberaeron** (Ceredigion)
Hive on the Quay Cadwgan Place, (01545) 570445. As we went to press the Holgates told us that, lacking an evening chef of the quality required, they are now only offering lunch, and light meals from 3 to 7pm after which they will be closing. On offer will be soups, Welsh rarebit or lobster and crab salads. Tea, coffee, sandwiches and cakes are available all day.

• **Cardiff** (Cardiff)
De Courcey's Tyla Morris Ave, (01222) 892232. The three-course Sunday lunch might include tian of avocado and prawns, a choice of two roast joints, and steamed treacle pudding. In the evening 'house' and 'gourmet' menus are available, with a special French menu on Fridays.

Quayles 6–8 Romilly Crescent, (01222) 341264. Fresh ingredients and value for money make this a dependable venue in the Cardiff suburbs. Lunch and 'early bird' menus are the things to go for: expect ballottine of duck with onion confit, mixed seafood grill with sun-dried tomatoes and, of course, quail with a liver stuffing. Crème brûlèe is a decent sweet.

Riverside Cantonese 44 Tudor Street, (01222) 227333. Long-standing South Wales Cantonese restaurant and a good spot for cooked-to-order dim-sum. A long list includes such morsels as seafood dumpling with caviare, whelks in black-bean sauce, bean curd rolls in oyster sauce and pork rice balls. The rest of the menu is a familiar run through barbecued pork, grilled fish with seasonal greens, lemon chicken and the like.

• **Carmarthen** (Carmarthenshire)
Quayside Brasserie The Quay, (01267) 223000. Barn-like brasserie decorated with wine artefacts and local scenes, boasting a large terrace overlooking the Towy valley. Local lamb, beef, poultry and fish (including sewin) are given simple treatment: salad of scallops with ginger, steak on a bed of onions, délice of Carmarthen Bay fish with julienne of

leeks, for example. Good youthful service. More reports, please.

• **GLANWYDDEN** (Conwy)
Queen's Head Glanwydden, (01492) 546570. Neatly converted wheelwright's cottage that draws crowds from near and far, thanks to its civilised atmosphere, better-than-average pub wines and 'superior' bar food. Local mussels, Conwy crab, pot-roasted wild duck, and medallions of pork with Welsh mustard and cider sauce sound a patriotic note. First-rate puddings, too.

• **GRESFORD** (Wrexham)
Pant-yr-Ochain Old Wrexham Road, (01978) 853525. A great location in a wide open valley and quirkily eccentric décor (floor-to-ceiling bookcases, advertising posters and more) are plus points at this fine old building with a conservatory tacked on. The place functions as pub-cum-brasserie with a menu to match. Black pudding with bubble-and-squeak, baked cod topped with Welsh rarebit, and courgette and spring onion koftas on couscous are typical. Good beers.

• **LAMPHEY** (Pembrokeshire)
Dial Inn The Ridgeway, (01646) 672426. Formerly the Dower House to Lamphey Court, now a pub/restaurant with a big following. Bar and restaurant menus promise robust country cooking with a few Continental flourishes. Cawl, faggots and Glamorgan sausages line up alongside Welsh fillet of beef with chips, and herb-crusted best-end of lamb with chervil butter sauce.

• **LLANABER** (Gwynedd)
Llwyndu Farmhouse Llwyndu, (01341) 280144. Eminently affordable seventeenth-century farmhouse in an 'outstanding location' offering B&B as well as dinner for non-residents. Honest country cooking is the order of the day: fish-pie, superbly presented local salmon, chicken curry, and gooseberry and apple crumble are typical. Decent wines from Tanners.

• **LLANFYLLIN** (Powys)
Seeds 5 Penybryn Cottages, (01691) 648604. Cottagey restaurant run by a friendly husband-and-wife team and decorated with the theme of children's toys. Soups such as carrot and red pepper are 'outstanding' and the Welsh lamb is reckoned to be 'superb'. Other good dishes include grilled tuna with ratatouille, chicken breast in port and cream sauce, and treacle tart with home-made ice-cream.

• **LLANGOLLEN** (Denbighshire)
Gales 18 Bridge Street, (01978) 860089. Long-established wine and food bar (with accommodation) in a substantial eighteenth-century building. The daily menu features everything from soups, pâtés and cold smoked meats to more substantial specials of chilli chicken on rice, or pork casseroled in cider. Interesting wines.

• **LLANRHIDIAN** (Swansea)
Welcome to Town Llanrhidian, (01793) 390015. Modernised 'bistro-tavern' run by the family who used to be at Fanny's in Llandeilo. Local produce shows up well on the monthly menu: brioche buns are filled with laverbread, cockles and leeks, peppered fillet of spring lamb comes with mint sauce, and there is berry fruit crumble to finish. Jolly atmosphere, fair prices. More reports, please.

• **MOLD** (Flintshire)
Chez Colette 56 High Street, (01352) 759225. Colette and Jacques Duvauchelle offer the denizens of north Wales an authentic taste of French bistro cooking in their informal venue. Dishes are in the classic mould of pâté maison, lapin à la moutarde, steak au poivre, and saumon julienne de légumes. Fixed-price theatre deals are good value.

• **PORTHKERRY** (Vale of Glamorgan)
Egerton Grey Porthkerry, (01446) 711666. Peaceful Victorian rectory in seven acres of secluded gardens with lovely views, but still only a few minutes' drive from Cardiff Airport. Most dishes read elaborately on the menu, although it is the simpler offerings such as smoked haddock and salmon mousse with rocket salad, braised liver in wine sauce, and 'assorted desserts' that get most praise.

• **St George** (Conwy)
Kinmel Arms St George, (01745) 832207. Former coaching-inn with an increasingly serious attitude to food. Mid-week fixed-price menus are good value, while the *carte* promises such things as salad of monkfish with balsamic dressing, rabbit in filo pastry, pork loin stuffed with prunes and chocolate marquise. Home-baked bread, well-chosen wines.

• **Swansea** (Swansea)
Annie's 56 St Helen's Road, (01792) 655603. 'Consistently the most enjoyable eating-out in the area' is one verdict on Anne Gwilym's converted schoolhouse. Her fixed-price dinner menus are full of lively touches: mille-feuille of grilled asparagus with prosciutto and Parmesan, pot-roast lamb shank with sweet pepper couscous, and coconut and cardamom crème caramel with pineapple and lime sauce are typical.
Barrows 42 Newton Road, (01792) 361443. Variety is the watchword at this wine bar/restaurant overlooking Oystermouth Castle. Lunch and dinner menus change daily and may offer stir-fried duck with hoisin and plum sauce, Creole chicken breast topped with mango and Cajun-spiced fillet of sea bass with bell-pepper salsa.
P.A.'s Wine Bar 95 Newton Road, Mumbles, (01792) 367723. Pleasant modern wine bar offering a short menu of straightforward bistro-style dishes. Fish shows up well with crab and potato beignets, sea bass and cider beurre blanc, and salmon with hollandaise among the specialities. Crispy smoked duck and orange salad, and bread-and-butter pudding have also been endorsed.
Patricks 638 Mumbles Road, (01792) 360199. Chilled paw-paw, pineapple and lime soup, lamb shank with tomato and cinnamon sauce, and roast sea bass on leeks and bacon are typically eclectic choices from the menu in Patrick and Catherine Walsh's enthusiastically run restaurant. Also look for beans on toast 'Patrick's style'. Decent choice of reasonably priced wines.

Channel Islands

• **Gorey** (Jersey)
Jersey Pottery Restaurant Gorey, (01534) 851119. Pottery and restaurant complex arranged around a prettily maintained garden. Lunch in the conservatory-style dining-room always includes a fine showing of local seafood, as well as dishes such as roasted breast of duck with armagnac and black-pepper sauce, pan-fried fillet of beef with pearl barley risotto and white truffle-oil broth. Finish with summer fruit tart.

• **St Brelade** (Jersey)
Sea Crest Hotel Petit Port, (01534) 46353. The setting is one of the draws: overlooking La Pulente headland and a short stroll from the sands of St Ouen's Bay. Fresh fish is the star of the show on the French menu, and staff are keen on flambé dishes. Expect salmon with lobster sauce or grilled sole.

• **St Peter Port** (Guernsey)
Fregate St Peter Port, (01481) 724624. Long-established hotel with pretty views of the harbour and castle. The kitchen delivers old-style French cooking with the accent on fish. Stir-fried scallops with ginger, and poached turbot with hollandaise have been recommended alongside asparagus soup, and home-made profiteroles with hot chocolate sauce. Service cannot be faulted.

• **St Peter Port** (Guernsey)
Le Nautique Quay Steps, (01481) 721714. Old cellar restaurant with charming views of the harbour and yachts. Seafood shows up well (oysters in curry sauce with spinach have been singled out), otherwise the menu promises warm salad of calf's liver with asparagus, fillet of lamb with port and tarragon, and vanilla pudding with apricot sauce. Polished service.

The Good Food Club 1997

Many thanks to all the following people who contributed to this year's *Guide* . . .

Dr Sidney Abrahams
A.D. Abrams
Prof R.J. Adam
Ken Adams
Mr and Mrs R.W.G. Adams
Robert Adams
Mr and Mrs Adamson
Peter Adcock
Mr and Mrs Richard Adkin
Alan Adlington
Dino Adriano
Mr and Mrs Edward Album
Lawrence Alexander
Mr and Mrs M. Alexander
D.E. Allen
Julia Allen
I.C. Allen
Margaret Allen
Martin Allen
R. Allenby
R. Allwright
Sir Anthony Alment
John Amandini
Elizabeth Anderson
Gwen and Peter Andrews
D.A. Angless
Mr and Mrs R.L. Annesley
Mrs Cynthia Archer
K.G. Archer
P.F. Arden
C.R.F. Arkwright
Rev Michael Armitage
K.C. Armstrong
Paul Armstrong
Mrs H.G. Ashburn
Brian Ashby
K. Ashken
G.P. Ashton
Graham Ashton
David Askew
Mrs M. Aspinall
Dr P.L. Aston
D.M. Atkin
Chris Atkins
Mrs Wendy Atkins
Brian Atkinson
George Atkinson
Mrs J. Atkinson
Martin Attewell
Mr and Mrs Frank Attwood
Mrs M.J. Ausobsky
Freda Austin
Kate Austin
Mal Austin
Roger Austin
Mr and Mrs Walter Avery
Mrs Isabelle Avetoom
Michael Awty
Mr and Mrs B. Ayers
A.B. Gittins
Andrew Backhouse
Ms Wendy Bookhouse
Mr and Mrs R. Baggalley
Brian Bagnall
Jane and Martin Bailey
Ian Baillie
Martyn Bainbridge
A.A. Baker
D.A. Baker
Mr and Mrs I. Balaam
Tony Balacs
Klaus Baldus
George Baldwin
Dr I.C. Balfoor
Graham Balfry
B.E. Ball
Charlie Ballantyne
Gillian B. Smith
Brian Bamford
Mr and Mrs K. Banery
P. Banks
Andrew Bannister
Alan Bant
Sir Brian Barder
Jill Barker
John Barker
Stella Barnass
R.J. Barnes
Mr and Mrs R. Barnett
Mrs P. Baron
Geoff Barratt
Mr and Mrs J. Bartholomew
Mr and Mrs H.B. Bartlett
Matthew Bartlett
Tim Barton
Prof B.H. Bass
Mr and Mrs John Bateman
Robert Bates
Jeremy Bath
T. Battle
Mr and Mrs Michael Baws
Mrs C. Bayley
Conrad Bayliss
Tony and Theo Beamish
Sarah Beattie
F.R. Beckett
Mrs G. Beckett
Mr and Mrs J.W. Beckford
Mrs L. Beddoe
Mrs Anne Beddow
Prof and Mrs John Belchem
R.P. Bellamy
T. Bendhem
G. Bennet
J. Bennett
Prof John Bennett
Mr and Mrs R.G. Bennett
S. Bennett
Nicola Benman
Mrs Jane Bentham
Diane Bentley
William Bentsen
Bill Beresford
Mrs G. Berneck
David Berry
Mr and Mrs E. Berry
W.J. Best
Timothy Betts
Jeff Bidwell
J. Biggs
Mrs V.A. Bingham
Mr and Mrs Chris Birch
Sir Roger Birch
Malcolm Birkett
R.G. Birt
Mrs Judith Bishop
Mrs Rosemary Bishop
J.S. Black
Michael Black
Mrs Blackburn
Anne Blackburn
C.T. Blackburn
Roger Blackburn
M. Blackstaff
C. Blake
Timothy Blake
Mr and Mrs J.L Blakey
James Blandy
Mrs J.A. Blanks
Mrs H.B. Blazey
Edward Blincoe
Mrs M. Blogg
Peter Bloore
Mr and Mrs Bruce Blundell
Dr S.M. Blunden
Mr and Mrs K.G.R. Blythe
K.W. Bogle
J. Bolt
C.T. Bolton
Mrs Julia Bolwell
Clive Boosey
Alastair Booth
Yvonne Booth
C. Boothroyd
Martin and Elaine Borish
Mr and Mrs D. Borton
Canon M.A. Bourdeaux
Robin Bourne
Richard Bowden
A.J. Bowen
John Bowers
Mr and Mrs Peter Bowles
Miss E.R. Bowmer
Jonathan Boyce

P.J.R. Boyd
Jacqueline Boyle
J. Boynton
Mr and Mrs K.G. Bracey
Lawrence Brackstone
Drs David and Elsa Bradshaw
Nial Brannigan
Dr A.M. Braverman
Simon Brenner
Patricia Brent
Mr and Mrs M. Brentnall
Mrs J. Bridge
Rowena Bridge
Tom Bridge
Mr and Mrs J.M. Bridgeman
Mr and Mrs John Brierley
Jack Bright
David Brimble
G.T. Bristow
L.D. Brook
Dr Oliver Brooke
Mrs Jennifer Brooker
Douglas Brooks
G. Brooks
John Brooks
Mrs Kathleen Broom
Mrs V. Broom
Michael Brotherton
Agnes Brown
Andrew Brown
C.L. Brown
Dr and Mrs D.G. Brown
David Brown
F.E. Brown
Mr and Mrs H.N. Brown
Lynda Brown
Caroline Browne
Mrs Mary Bruce
Mr and Mrs S.G. Brunning
Mr and Mrs Max Bryan
Mr and Mrs Edgar Bryant
Mrs J.K. Bryant
Mr and Mrs John Bryant
M. Bryden
Jennifer Brzozowska
J.N.G. Buckeridge
Mrs Alexa Buckley
Jack Buckley
P.M.A. Buckman
Richard Bulger
Mrs Daphne Bullock
Richard Bunje
Chris Bunkell
Mr and Mrs Stephen Bunn
R.M. Burbeck
Mr and Mrs A.G.M. Burge
Bridget Burgess
Mrs Daphne Burgess
M.J. Burke
Mr and Mrs John Burns
M.H. Burr
H.R. Burrell
Mr and Mrs John Burridge
David Burrows
F. Burton
Mrs J.A. Burton
Rebecca Burton-Brown
Khan Busby
Mrs J. Bush
John Butler
Mike Butler
Mr and Mrs P.D. Butler
Mr and Mrs Paul Butler
J.G Butlin
D. Butterfield
Mr and Mrs J.M. Butterfield
David Caeder
Nicholas Caiger
Robert Caine
Mr and Mrs Donald Cammack
Mrs Betty Campbell
Steve Cant
Chris Cape
Mr and Mrs P.H. Carlisle
J.J. Carmody
Mrs Patricia Carr
Roger Carr
Shani Carr
Dr and Mrs D.H. Carroll
Dr John Carroll
Grant Carson
Andrew Carter
Dr J.M. Carter
John Carter
N. Carter
P.E. Carter
David Cartwright
Miss L.B. Cartwright
Robert Carty
Richard Cashmore
Penny Caslin
Cynthia Casperson
Ms S.C. Cassells
Mr and Mrs G. Castle
Mrs E. Catham
Mrs C.M. Cathcart
Dr R.E. Catlow
Dr Celia Caulcott
Ann Causton
J.A. Cave
Simon Cawkwell
George Cernoch
John Chadwick
Mrs Susan Chait
Tania Chalcroft
G. Challice
Mr and Mrs Richard Chamberlain
A.W.T. Chapman
Ronald Chapman
Miss S. Chappell
Mr and Mrs Barry Charles
Selina Charles
R. Chater
Peter Cheetham
Clive Chilcott
Prof Clair Chilvers
Ann Chiswick
P. Chklar
W.V. Church
Mrs Grace Ciappara
Dr and Mrs A. Clark
Mrs K. Clark
Mrs Patricia Clark
Philip Clark
Mrs S.M. Clark
T.G. Clark
Jane Clarke
Sheila Clarke
Kenneth Cleveland
Jennifer Clickner
E. Clifford White
A.H. Coates
H.M. Cockram
Lorna Cohen
Dr John Coker
Mr and Mrs Cole
Cecilia Cole
Mr and Mrs Roger Colebrook
Mr and Mrs G.G. Coleman
Roger Coles
W. Colfer
R.K. Collard
Mrs C.J. Collier
Mr and Mrs S.P. Collins
Robin Collomb
P.H. Coltman
Mrs Hannah Colton
John Colton
Sara Colville
Mrs S. Colvin
Susan Colvin
R.T. Combe
M. Comninos
Clara Connolly
Sean Connolly
David Conville
Miss H.M. Cooke
Mrs June Cooke
Tim Cooke
Mr and Mrs A.M. Cooper
John Cooper
Peter Cooper
Philip Cooper
Dr and Mrs J.C.W. Cope
Mrs O.A. Copsey
J. Corbluth
Tom Cordiner
Miss Gayle Cotgrove
Heather Couper
Stephen Court
I.D. Courtnage
H.L. Cowdy
Mrs Audrey Cox
Richard Coxon
J.L. Crammer
R.D. Cramond
Mark Cran
Jock Craven
Bernard Crean
Mr and Mrs Bruce Creed
Gordon Cresswell
Rosalind Cressy
Mr and Mrs Charles Croft
Tom Crompton
Helen Crookston
Dr David Croser
John and Judy Cross
Dr N.E. Cross
Rodney Cross
Simon Crouch
Mrs M. Cuncliffe
Emma Cundiff
N.P. Cutcliffe
Dr and Mrs S.R.D da Prato
Eric Dale
Theo Dampney
B. Daneshanof
Peter Danny
Miss Louise Darby

Wing Cdr R. Dauncey
David Davey
Mr and Mrs D.W.M. Davidson
Mr and Mrs R. Davidson
W.H. Davidson
C.H. Davies
D.D.G. Davies
Graham Davies
Dr I.H. Davies
Ms J. Davies
J.L. Davies
Martina Davies
Roger Davies
Andrew Davis
Brian Davis
Michael Davis
Dr and Mrs R.P.R. Dawber
Elizabeth Dawes
Julian Dawson
Mr and Mrs Keith Dawson
Anna Day-Lewis
Mr and Mrs F.C. de Paula
David de Saxe
Mr and Mrs J.I. de Villiers
Mr and Mrs Nigel Deacon
L.D.H. Dean
N.C. Dee
James Delahooke
Mr and Mrs A.E. Demby
Jonathan and Louise Denby
H.R. Denne
Sarah Denney
C. Derby
J.G. Derounian
Roger Desoutter
Mr and Mrs J.P. Deuchar
Sean Devlin
C. Divall
Derek Divine
Mr and Mrs J. Dixey
John Dixon
G.M. Dobbin
A. Docherty
M.H. Dods
Sarah Dodwell
Kay Donoghue
E.D. Dore
Mr and Mrs James Douglas
Bruce Douglas-Mann
Sidney Downs
Colin Dowse
Mrs Brenda Doyle
Danielle Drake
A. Drinkey
Capt Spencer Drummond
G.H.B. Dryland
A.B.K. Dubach
John Ducker
Richard Duggleby
Alexander Dunbar
Mrs A.D. Duncan
Rev J. Duncan
Ivor Dunkerton
A. Dunn
Mrs J.M. Dunster
Denis Durno
Clive Dutson
P.F. Dutton
Mrs P. Dyer
Sarah Dykes
John Earthy
Max Easterman
Dr and Mrs Lindsay Easton
Mr and Mrs John Eastwell
Mrs M.E. Eastwood
Mr and Mrs K. Eckott
Dr S. Eden
P.G. Edgington
Mrs M. Edward
Mrs Aileen Edwards
Malcolm Edwards
The Earl of Effingham
E. Eisenhandler
John Elder
Myra and Ray Elderfield
G. Elflett
Amanda Elithorn
Mrs C.M. Elkington
Dr A.J. Ellen
D. Ellery
Mr and Mrs J. Elliott
S. Elliott
Richard Ellis
H. Elmy
James Elvy
K. Emrys-Roberts
Prof Harry Emson
Prof and Mrs C.E. Engel
Dr D. Entwistle
C.G Erwin
A.J. Evans
C.D. Evans
Dr Carolyn Evans
J.L.D. Evans
Mr and Mrs Jeff Evans
M.E. Evans
P.D. Evans
Peter Evans
Dr R.G. Evans
R.W. Evans
Michael Evered
Mrs G. Everson
C.R. Exley
Mrs C. Exwood
Toni Ezekiel
John Fahy
Mr and Mrs Peter Fairley
Jed Falby
Caroline Faricliff
Ann Farrow
Mr R. Fausset
R.S. Fawssett
Roger Feakins
Catherine Feeny
Mr and Mrs C. Feingold
R. Felton
Adam Fenton
Jonathan Fenton
A.B.X. Fenwick
M.J. Ferguson
Anna Fergusson
Allen Ferns
M.C. Ferrier
Neville Filar
Leonida Fineberg
Dr N. Finer
T.R. Finlow
Mrs Jill Firth
Mrs A.L. Fisher
Mr and Mrs John Fisher
Mr and Mrs Paul Fisher
R.A. Fisk
Patricia Flack
F. Fleischer
Colin Fleming
J.G. Fleming
A.T.R. Fletcher
C.W Fletcher
Clare Fletcher
Mr and Mrs I.H.R. Flinter
D. Floyd-Douglass
Julie Flynn
Ms N. Foley
Sean Foley
A.Y. Fontes
David Foot
M.L.N. Forrest
Mrs P.L. Forrest
Peter Forrest
Anthony Forster
Mrs V. Fortnam-King
Mr and Mrs Roger Forward
Lady Foster
Gerald Foulkes
R.J.N. Fowler
Paul Fox
Mrs Angela Frank
Mrs P. Frankel
A.J. Franklin
Dr L.M. Franks
Dr M.L. Franks
Mrs Josephine Frantzis
C. Fraser
Mr and Mrs C. Fraser
Dr and Mrs P.J. Fray
Mrs Carole Freer
Mrs S. Fretwell
Anthony Froggatt
G.E. Frost
N.B. Fuller
Peter Fyson
John Gagg
J. Gale
Mrs J.R. Gale
Mrs L. Galloway
Mrs K. Garden
Mr and Mrs B. Garford
Michael Garrison
Mrs S. Gatta
J.D. Gelder
Mrs Christine Gerezdi
D. Gibbon
Mr and Mrs Austin Gibbons
J. Gibbs
Vernon Gibbs
Richard Gibson
Ken Gilbert
Tim Giles
Keith Gilham
Anthony Gill
Mr J. Gill
K.A. Gillies
D.A. Gilmour
Barbara Glastonbury
John Glaze
J. Gloster-Smith
R.J.N. Glover
Mrs Gillian Goddard
Kim Goddard
Mr and Mrs Ian Godfrey
Mr and Mrs Jim Godfrey
Mrs H. Goil
R. Goldstein
Tom Gondris

Norman Goodchild
D. Goodger
John Goodman
T. Goodwin
Ken Goody
Neil Gordon
M. Gordon-Russell
Paul Gordon-Saiger
Jillian Gore
Mr and Mrs A. Gough
M.B. Gowers
A.B. Goyder
Christopher Graham
Mr and Mrs John Graham
Brian Grant
Lavinia Grant-Ives
Mrs J. Granville
Mrs J. Graves
D.W. Gray
C.A. Green
James Green
C. Greenhow
N.D.A. Greenstone
Dr Arthur Greenwood
Fiona Greenwood
Jim Greenwood
Mr and Mrs K. Greenwood
Mrs S. Greetham
Conal Gregory
Mrs J. Gregory
Mr and Mrs Peter Gregory
John Gresty
R.F. Grieve
Alan Griffee
Charlotte Griffin
Edward Griffin
J.P. Griffin
J.R. Griffin
Miss S. Griffin
Brian Griffiths
Peter Griffiths
R.F.B Grimble
Mr and Mrs Jim Grimes
Nigel Grimshaw
N.M. Grimwood
A.D Grumley-Grennan
Mr and Mrs J.C. Guild
E. Gulliver Stephens
B.G. Gunary
T.M. Haines
B. Hall
Mr and Mrs B. Hall
Dr Bryan Hall
Gail Hall
P.J. Hall
W.J. Hallett
Mr and Mrs Michael Hallsworth
Tom Halsall
Malcolm Hamer
Kirstie Hamilton
Mrs M. Hampson-Moores
Jean Hancock
Mrs K.M. Hancott
Lisa Handley
Lorraine Handley
F.G. Hankins
Shaun Hannan
R.F. Hannay
Paul Hansell
Mr and Mrs John Hanson
Kenneth Hanson
P.L. Harbinson
D.J. Harding
Mrs G. Hargreaves
R.A. Hargreaves
Herman Harmelink
Tim Harper
Tracy Harper
E.C. Harrill
A.G. Harris
Clifford Harris
James Harris
John Harris
Raymond Harris
Mr Frank Harris-Jones
Nigel Harrison
P.B. Harrison
Mr and Mrs D.J. Harrold
Ms W. Hart
D.T. Harthog
Mr and Mrs E. Hartley
J.D. Hartley
Mrs E. Harvey
Dr Peter Harvey
Peter Harvey
Martin Hasseck
Stewart Haworth
Mrs Corinne Haynes
Mr and Mrs K.M. Hazelgrove
Mrs C.E. Hazlehurst
Peter Head
P.C. Heane
W.R. Heap
Canon N. Heavisides
D. Heeley
Mr and Mrs H.H. Hellin
Mr and Mrs Roger Hemingway
Prof and Mrs A.H. Henderson
N.F. Henshaw
Mr and Mrs S. Herbert
J.M. Herbertson
A. Heron
Victoria Herriott
Lord Herschell
Dr Andrew Herxheimer
Mr and Mrs Peter Heslop
Gad Heuman
Mrs M.J. Hewitt
James Hewlett
D.A Hickling
A. Hickman
Michael Hicks
Mr and Mrs Frank Higginson
A.W Higgs
F.R. Hilborne
A.W. Hill
G. Hill
G.W. Hill
H. Hill
J.M.M. Hill
Jane Hill
Mrs Jennifer Hill
P.L. Hill
Peter Hill
Wendy Hillary
Mr and Mrs D.W. Hills
L.M.M. Hinch
E. Hinds
Mr and Mrs R. Hinds
Mr and Mrs John Hirst
Mr and Mrs P.A. Hoare
Mrs U. Hofheinz
David Holbrook
C.D. Hollamby
J. Holland
Nick Hollis
Mr and Mrs David Holmes
Mr and Mrs R. Holmes
Mr and Mrs P. Holt
Neil Honeyman
Mrs I.P. Honeywood
Mr and Mrs Honour
Richard Hook
Tamsin Hooper
Derek Hopes
Mrs Susan Hopper
Mrs M. Horgan
Martha Horlock
Mr and Mrs R.H. Horncastle
Mrs Bev Hornsby
A.D.J. Horsler
Mrs R. Horton
Mr and Mrs Trevor Hoskins
Dr Keith Hotten
Mr and Mrs W.R. Hough
David House
Mr and Mrs Howard
Mrs Carolyn Howard-Johnston
Michael Howarth
D.P. Howell
Nicholas Howell
D.J. Howells
John Howells
G.A. Howes
Mrs Dianne Howlett
Tim Huband
Mr and Mrs P.N. Hubbard
Hazel Huckridge
Mr and Mrs David Hudd
Mr and Mrs C.H.F. Hudson
J.A. Hudson
J.M. Hudson
Mr and Mrs Max Hudson
Jennifer Huggett
Mr and Mrs C.R. Hughes
J. Hughes
P.H.O. Hughes
Tina Hulbert
Dr Tim Hunt
Rev J.W. Hunwicke
C.J. Hurd
R.A. Husain
D.G. Hussey
Mr and Mrs P.J. Hussey
Sir Michael Hutchison
T.J. Hypher
John Hyter
J. Ibbotson
Sarah Iceton
Yvonne Imfeld
P. Ingham
A.H. Ingram
Mark Ingram
Mr and Mrs C. Innes
Dr Sheila Innes
Wendy Insole
Alexandra Iron
I.C. Irvine

Mrs A. Irving
Prof P.G. Isaacson
Mrs C.A. Jackson
Mrs E.A. Jackson
Mrs H.C. Jackson
James McG. Jackson
Maggie Jackson
Eric and Lois Jaffé
Mr and Mrs R.A. James
B.G.W. Jamieson
Mr and Mrs R. Jamieson
M. Janson
Miss P.M. Jarvis
Antony Jay
Patrick Jefferson
Mrs G.P. Jeffreys
Mr and Mrs Jenkins
Paul Jerome
David Jervois
Mr and Mrs Nigel Jestico
Mr and Mrs Brian Jobson
B.M. Joce
J. John
Dr I.H.D. Johnston
R.M. Jolly
K. Jones
Arthur Jones
Mrs Audrey Jones
Colin Jones
Deborah Jones
Douglas Jones
Hilary Jones
Ian Jones
Lyndon Jones
M. Jones
Peter Jordan
Mr and Mrs Nathan Joseph
Alan Josey
Paul Joslin
Helen Joubert
Peter Jowitt
M.D. Joy
Mrs L. Judd
M.R Judd
Clare Judkins
Monica Kaplan
Lawrence Kaufman
Dr Leon Kaufman
Ann Kay
J.A. Kay
P.C. Kay
Roger Kay
Paul Keane
Hugh Kearney
K. Kearney
W.B. Keates
Dr and Mrs B.E. Keen
K.R. Keen
Christopher Kellett
A. Kellett-Long
Peter Kellner
Carys Kelly
Frances Kelly
Jenny Kelly
R.J. Kelsey
Mrs J.P. Kembery
Henry Kemp
Roger Kenber
Norman Kershaw
Rev Peter Kettle
Elizabeth Key
K. Khokhar
Susan Kidman
Charles Kiefer
J.H. Kilby
Ernest Kilner
John Kimble
Ms S. King
Mr and Mrs Michael Kirk
Stephen Kitchen
Mrs J. Klarfeld
Annie Klein
Mrs Sylvia Knapp
C. Kone
C.J. Koster
P. Krause
Jack Krelle
Mr and Mrs R. Krupinski
D.S. Kyle
Caroline Lamb
Angela Lambert
John Lancaster
Jan Lancucki
M.D. Lane
Maggie Langdon
Helen Lange
Mr and Mrs K. Lavender
Andy Lawman
E.M.C. Lawrence
Michael Lawrence
R.L.H. Lawrence
Norman Lazenby
Mr and Mrs David Le Fevre
J. Leadley
Alec Leggatt
C.L. Leighton
Malcolm Lennox
Richard Lent
David Leonard
P.L. Leonard
Dr Michael Lerner
Lucy Leslie
D.J. Lethem
Lionel Leventhal
Nicola Lewin
Clive Lewis
Dr David Lewis
Dr P.L. Lewis
Mr and Mrs V.M. Lewsey
Mr and Mrs L.S. Light
Mr and Mrs Freddy Lind
R.W. Lindo
E. Lindsay
Mrs S.A. Linington
Mr and Mrs D.R. Linnell
Mrs J.D. Lister
Dr Neil Livesey
Jan Ljunggren
Dr David Lloyd
James Lloyd
Mrs Lorna Lloyd
David Lloyd-Jacob
Mrs Brigitta Lock
Mrs Janet Lockett
Joan Lockley
D.R. Lockyear
Victoria Logue
K. London
Mr and Mrs Oliver Long
Deborah Lovelock Newman
Andrew Low
Mr and Mrs P.A. Lowater
C.P. Lowell
Anthony Lowther
M.H. Lynch
Mrs Heather Lynn
Ian Macbey
Joanna Macdonald
Mr and Mrs Miles MacEacharn
R.B. MacGeachy
J.B. MacGill
A.J. Macintosh
C.F. Mack
Edward Mack
R.D. Mackay
Peter Mackenzie-Williams
C.H.N. Mackey
Sharon Maclaren
Jean Macpherson
N. Macray
Simon Maddrell
Sean Magee
Dr B.A. Maguire
S.J. Maguire
Peter Mahaffey
Julian Maher
Peter Mair
Mrs Jayne Mallett
Mr and Mrs David Malyon
Adrian Mann
Prof R. Mansell Prothero
Judge Bernard Marder
Prof Marshall Marinker
Mr and Mrs R.L. Marks
Dr C. Markus
Leonard Marlow
Mrs Christine Marris
Mrs June Marsden
Ms Chris Marsh
Peter Marsh
Roger Marsh
Dr and Mrs Rosemary Marsh
W. Marsh
Mr and Mrs Dennis Marshall
John Marshall
R.F.D. Marshall
R.O. Marshall
A.S. Martin
Mr and Mrs G.D. Martin
Ian Martin
Roger and Joan Martin
Prof and Mrs H.T. Mason
Christopher Mason-Watts
Donald Massey
Ian May
Mr and Mrs D.G. McAdam
Andrew McAlpine
Mrs E.J. McBurney
A. McCarten
Mrs J.M. McCarthy
Dr and Mrs A.N McClean
Mrs Denise McColl
Dr and Mrs G. McDade
Catriona Mcdonald
Dr M. McEvoy
Prof and Dr I.D. McFarlane
Charles McFeeters
Colin and Lilian McGhee
Dr P. McGill
M. McGowan
Mrs May McIver

Mr and Mrs Maurice McKee
Mrs L. McKeown
Colin McKerrow
A.S. McKiddie
Mrs J. McLaren
G.W.H. McLaughlin
Ms A. McLean
Dr Irene McNicol
Mr and Mrs Archie McPherson
Mrs J.A. McQuade
Barry Meacham
Simon Melhuish
J.C. Mellers
Mrs Phyllis Mendoza
G.L. Menzies
Mr and Mrs J. Mercer
Marshall Meredith
D.V Merritt
Major J.B. Merritt
Mr and Mrs Arni Mertens
John Messer
Michael Meyer
Mrs M.P. Middleton
Barbara Millar
J.D Millard-Barnes
Mr Miller
Deborah Miller
Dr Eric Miller
H. Miller
T.W. Miller-Jones
Mrs K. Mills
H.G. Millward
Dr C. Milne
Amy Minden
K.S. Mingle
Celia Minoughan
R. Minshall
Donald Mitchell
Mr and Mrs K. Mivehall
A.M. Siriwardena
David Molecey
Dr J. Mollon
Dr V. Montegriffo
R.N. Montgomery
David Mooney
Mr and Mrs Colin Moore
E.A. Moore
Robert Moore
Mr and Mrs A.R. Moreton
Mrs Elizabeth Morgan
M.K. Morgan
R.C. Morgan
Dr W.T.W Morgan
Mr and Mrs Iain Morley
David Morrell
Mrs J. Morris
Janet Morris
Nick Morris
V.G.F. Morris
D. Morroll
Lady Belinda Morse
Mr and Mrs A. Moss
Brian Moss
David Moss
Keith Moss
Mrs Sheila Moulds
Dr Barbara Moyes
Mr and Mrs Matt Mulcahy
L. Mullan
Dominic Mullen
J.M.W. Mullens
Mr and Mrs William Mullins
A. Mumford
Mr and Mrs R.G. Muriel
Mr and Mrs A.M. Murphy
David Murray
G.R. Murray
Mr and Mrs P. Murray-Smith
Ms S. Myers
K. Nabeshima
Sara Nathan
Mr and Mrs B. Natton
Dr Malcolm Nattrass
Dr and Mrs A. Naylor
C.H. Naylor
B.W. Neill
Mr and Mrs Tim Nelson
Dr J.M. Newbery
Mr and Mrs Adrian Newell
Stephen Newell
Brian and Tessa Newman
Mr and Mrs Alan Nicholls
N.H. Nicholls
Mrs Jean Nicol
Roger Norman
P. Normanton
J.G. Norris
Mr and Mrs J. Norwell
Graham Norwood
Mrs R.H. Nugent
G.H. Nuttall
Gordon O'Brien
Gerard O'Donnell
P.N. O'Donoghue
Neal O'Leary
Jane and Kevin O'Mahoney
Sally O'Neil
Greg O'Reilly
Charles Oatwig-Thain
John Oddey
Dr C. Offord
Dr David Offox
G. Oglanby
R.A.L. Ogston
Prof Anthony Ogus
Dr Simon Old
Mrs Pauline Oram
R.I. Orchard
B.C. Osborn
R.M. Osborn
J. Osborn-Clarke
J.F. Osborne
Mr and Mrs R.E. Osborne
Tom Osborne
Mrs M.R. Osbourne
Mrs S. Oswell
B.T. Overall
Georgina Owens
Mrs Meriel Packman
Aidan Paddick
Dr S.D. Page
Stephen Page
Brian Palmer
A. Palureus
Mrs Susan Park
J.J. Parker
Margaret Parker
G.B. Parkin
Tim Parkinson
Dr Heather Parry
P. Parry
Miss Joy Passey
J.S. Patterson
Iain Patton
Nick Patton
Ms D. Paulson
Maria Pavlopoulos
Mrs C. Payne
Anthony Pearce
N.L. Pearce
Alex Pearson
John Pearson
Pam Peers
M. Romain Pellerin
Louise Pemberton
Pamela Pepper
Mr and Mrs C.S. Perkins
Neil and Alison Perkins
Mrs E. Perry
Mr and Mrs A. Peryer
A.J. Peters
Mrs C.S. Petherick-Brian
Mary-Anne Petit
Bruce Pettie
B.W.B. Pettifer
Ms D. Pheby
Drs Anne and Andrew Phellas
D.A. Philip
R.A. Phillips
Helen Pickering
Mr and Mrs Michael Pickersgill
Miss J.S. Pickles
Mrs Pidgeon
C.J. Pinney
Michael Pitel
Mr and Mrs C. Pitt
Hugh Pitt
Mr and Mrs J.B. Plant
P. Pleasance
Prof Peter Plesch
Dr and Mrs A.F. Polmear
Mrs A. Pompilis
Mr and Mrs R.J.M Pope
Lucy Portch
Dr Joanna Porter
R.H. Porter
Mrs Gillian Potts
Keith Poulter
Canon K. Povey
Joan Powell
Mr and Mrs S.G. Pratt
Dr R.J. Prescott
Mrs Jenny Preston
G.V. Price
Mr and Mrs John Price
Roger Price
Mr and Mrs D.E. Priestley
Mr D.J. Priestley
Edwin Prince
J.T. Prince
K. Prince
Richard Pritchard
G.O. Probert
Mrs Probett
Dr and Mrs J. Proctor
E. Punchard
Axel Queval
Mr and Mrs Peter Radcliffe
Ingrid Radford

K. Radley
Mrs Marian Rae
Aileen Raggatt
Mr and Mrs Luke Rainey
Dr and Mrs D.S. Rampton
J.M. Rampton
Duncan Rand
Tom Rand
A. Randall
Dr A.M. Rankin
Caroline Raphael
Dr and Mrs Len Ratoff
Peter Ratzer
Gerald Ratzin
Mrs K.E. Rawes
Michael Rawling
Mrs Mary Rayner
Mrs P.A. Read
Philip Reasbeck
Mr and Mrs Frank Redfern
Dr A.R. Reece
Jeffrey Reed
Mr and Mrs Andrew Reeves
Sir Patrick Reilly
Dr T.A. Reilly
Robin Reip
C. Reuben
John Reuter
Carolyn Reynier
Mr and Mrs C. Rhodes
Mrs R. Rhodes-Horrell
Ken Rice
J. Richards
J.M. Richards
O.H.W. Richards
C.J. Richardson
Carol Riddick
Michael Riddle
John Riddleston
Adam Riley
P.F.D Riley
L.I. Rimmer
Ann Ringle
Gordon Ringrose
J.T. Rissbrook
Mrs M. Robathan
Celia Robbins
Alan Roberts
Claire Roberts
Mrs R.N. Roberts
M.A.J. Robertson
Maureen Robertson
Mr and Mrs Stuart Robertson
Audrey Robinson
D.R. Robinson
Mrs E. Robinson
Mr and Mrs John Robinson
Mrs Philippa Robinson
Mrs Sheila Robinson
Stephen Robinson
J. Rochelle
Mrs Jackie Rochester
L. Roffey
Christopher Rogers
Mr and Mrs James Rogers
C.A.J. Rollason
Mrs Sylvia Rondel
Mr and Mrs B.G. Rose
Ian Rose
Mr and Mrs Jeffery Rose
Edward Rookill
C. Ross
Lt Col C. C.G. Ross
Mrs Cicely Ross
Graham Ross
P.W.A. Ross
A.W. Rossetto
D. Rounthwaite
Mrs Virginia Routh
J.E. Rowe
Michael Rowland
Mr and Mrs D. Rowlands
Prof David Rowley
Mrs Jill Rowley
I.J. Roxburgh
Mr and Mrs Ian Royle
C. Ruck
Peter Rudd
Simon Rudd-Clarke
Allan Rudolf
J.A. Rumble
Mrs L. Rushton
Andy Russell
Gordon Russell
Dr J.G.B. Russell
Mrs R. Russell
Mr and Mrs B. Rustchynskyj
Duncan Rutter
J.S. Rutter
R.S. Ryder
David Rymer
Mrs Shirley Sabin
Miss N. Sacchetti
Lady Sachs
L. Saffron
Mrs E.J. Salmon
Keith Salway
Stephen Sandham
Louise Sargent
Dr C. Saunders
Mrs Marjorie Saunders
Anne Savage
R.H. Sawyer
Paul Saxon
Julie Sayce
Sally Saysell
J. Scanlon
Mr and Mrs M.J. Schafer
Prof P.J. Scheuer
Michael Schofield
Ernst Schudel
K.H. Scollay
Esme Scott
Ms S. Scott
B.E. Scoullar
Richard Scrubb
Marc Seale
Dr Stephen Sebag-Montefiore
Leonard Seberry
A.J. Seeds
Gillian Seel
Peter Seglow
Mrs Alison Sennett
Mr and Mrs F. Seymour
C. Sharp
Dr and Mrs C.W. Sharp
Dr J.T.R. Sharrock
E.A. Sheard
Barbara Shepherd
Dr Martin Shepherd
Mrs Louise Sheppard
Nick Sheridan
Mrs D. Shevis
E. Shirras
A.G. Short
Mrs E.A. Short
T.M.K. Short
H. Sibley
Mr and Mrs J. Siderfin
Daniel Silverstone
Dr G. Silverstone
George Sim
Robert Simon
J.L. Simpole-Clarke
Andrew Simpson
Helen Simpson
Mr and Mrs J.A. Simpson
Mrs J. Sims
C.E. Siviter
Mr and Mrs Paul Skelton
Alan Skinner
Charles and Lucy Skipwith
D.A. Slade
H. Slim
Malcolm Slocombe
Dr A.J.M Slovak
N.S.L. Smart
Mr and Mrs A. Smith
F.H. Smith
Gillian B. Smith
Mrs Jane Smith
Kenneth Smith
Mr and Mrs N.L.V. Smith
Paul Smith
Mrs Selma Smith
T.A. Smith
V. Smith
Mrs J.C. Smye
Mr and Mrs W.R. Soley
Mr and Mrs Ronnie Somerville
David South
Wing Cdr R.M. Sparkes
Ian Sparks
Alan Spedding
N.B Spiers
Brian Spink
Mr and Mrs P.J. Spridgeon
Dr Mark Spring
Dr and Mrs W.B. Spry
Dr Mark Spurway
Ms L. Squire
Ms J.E. Squires
Mrs S.C. Stalker
Emma Stall
T.J. Stanford
David Stanley
Mr and Mrs Mike Staples
Mr Derek St.Clair-Stannard
John Stead
Mrs Caroline Steane
J.M. Steel
Graham Steer
C. Steiger
Mrs G.M. Stein
Rev and Mrs Peter Stell
R.L. Stephenson
Jayne Steven
Malcolm Stevens
Mr and Mrs P. Stevens

Adrian Stevenson
Dr Andrew Stevenson
Capt and Mrs J.S. Stewart
Robin Stewart
Judy Stimson
Mrs D. Stirling
R.M. Stobart
R.H. Stone
C.M.R. Stoneham
Mr and Mrs C.M. Stooke
J.S. Stooke
Mr and Mrs R. Storm
Heather Storr
J.C. Stott
R.T.D. Stott
Mary Stow
Mrs S. Stradling
B.F. Strange
B. Stratfield
J.W. Straw
Mr and Mrs Jason Streets
Tessa Stuart
Roger Summers
Ms J. Sundall
Mrs Simone Sussock
Dr George Sutton
A.M. Sutton-Scott-Tucker
Mrs Gail Swansan
Mrs A. Swatton
Mrs Erica Swift
Brenda Symes
A. Symon
G.D. Tan
Sir Saxon Tate
Dennis Tate
Mr and Mrs M. Tate
Dr Peter Tate
Dr and Mrs P.H. Tattersall
Mrs A.C. Taylor
A.M. Taylor
Chris Taylor
D.G. Taylor
George Taylor
J.D. Taylor
Jacqueline Taylor
Mrs Jean Taylor
S. Taylor
Mrs Wendy Taylor
Mrs E. Tench
Mr et Mme Jean-Francois Ternynck
Mr and Mrs E.A. Tetlow
Alan Thomas
Anthony Thomas
Mrs Jean Thomas
Clive Thompsett
Brian Thompson
Mr and Mrs D.S. Thompson
Mr and Mrs Jeff Thompson
R.M.A. Thompson
Dr Roger Thompson
Mr and Mrs Thomson
Alan Thomson
Dr Geoff Thorley
Mrs Susan Thornely
Dr A.G. Thornton
Mr and Mrs G.N. Thornton
Peter Throssell
M.A. Thurston
E.A. Thwaite
Graham Thwaites
Mr and Mrs Derek Tilsley
Dr T.W. Tinsley
H. Tint
B.A. Tizard
R. Tizard
Julian Tobin
Mrs Susan Todd
Alexander Tomlinson
Michael Tomlinson
Mrs Lesley Torkington
Drs E. and.J. Towner
R.P. Toye
Paul Treadaway
Norman Tree
Steve Trotman
Dr M.J.A. Trudgill
N. True
Nick Tsatsas
Beryl and Dick Tudhope
John Tulloch
L.K. Tune
Mr and Mrs Turner
Adrian Turner
B.W.B. Turner
Mr and Mrs G. Turner
Jane Turner
Patricia Turner
Stuart Turner
Curzon Tussaud
Jane Twelves
Gary Twynam
Elizabeth Tylor
Nicholas Underhill
Dr A. Ungar
R.W. Unwin
J. Vanderbilt-Sloane
P. Vanzieleghem
J. Varley
A. Vernon
Mark Vickers
Hon Mrs A.M. Viney
Fiona Vodden
Michael Wace
Keith Wailes
Dr T.E. Waine
Mrs A.M. Walden
R. Walden
Tom and Angela Walford
Mrs Sharon Walker
Mr and Mrs G. Walker-Dendle
Mrs H. Walker-Simmons
Andrew Wall
James Waller
W.J. Wallett
D.J. Wallington
Gentian Walls
Mrs J. Walsh
Dr Nigel Walsh
P.K. Walsh
Mrs V.M. Walsh
Peter Walshe
Oliver Walston
Mr and Mrs P.E. Walter
G. Walton
Mr and Mrs A. Ward
Mrs Clarissa Ward
Susie Ward
Ian Ward-Brown
A.J. Wardrop
Liz Warner
Michael Warren
Mrs P.M. Warrington
R.A. Wartnaby
Toshio Watanabe
Mr and Mrs J.S. Waters
Susan Watkin
Lady Watson
Richard Watson
E.K. Watts
Adrian Waynforth
A.J. Webb
Richard Webb
Marcia Webster
John Wedge
Mrs Barbara Weightman
Libby Weir-Breen
Michael Wellby
Barrie Wells
Marion Wells
A.M. West
J.F.M. West
M.J. West
Mrs Bethanne Westaway
Sarah Weston
David Whaley
Brian and Sue Wharton
Julie Wheat
Rev J.G. Wheeldon
Mr and Mrs John Wheeler
B. Whitaker
B. White
M.J. White
N.H. White
Paul White
J. Whitehead
K. Whitehead
R.J. Whitelam
Mrs Whiteley
Mrs Sandra Whitham
Mrs J.S. Whiting
Mr and Mrs M.C. Whiting
Mrs G.M. Whitley
Paul Whittard
Mr and Mrs Stephen Whittle
K. Widdowson
Giles Wigoder
Mr and Mrs D.C Wild
G. Wilding
M.J. Wilding
Keith Willcocks
P. Willer
Margaret Willes
Mrs Alma Williams
Prof Bernard Williams
C.J.N. Williams
I.G.K. Williams
J.A. Williams
Dr M.K. Williams
Mrs P. Williams
Capt R.G. Williams
Mr and Mrs R.W. Williams
Simon Williams
Stephen Williamson
Dr Bryan Wilson
Mr and Mrs Ian Wilson
Prof P.N. Wilson
R. Wilson
Mr and Mrs T. Wilson
M.L. Windsor
A.R. Winser
Mr and Mrs T. Withers

Mr and Mrs Mark Witherspoon
Dr A.G. Wolstenholme
Robert Wood
Mrs R.E Woodman
Mrs M. Woods
Mrs P.A. Woolley
Richard Wootton
Alan Worsdale
Mrs Kay Worsley-Cox
Nicholas Wraight
Dr D.E. Wray
Alan Wright
Mr and Mrs G.L. Wright
H.M. Wright
M. Wright
Mr and Mrs P. Wrightson
Mr and Mrs John Wyatt
K.C. Wyatt
Mrs Suzanne Wynn
Richard Yates
Mr and Mrs Douglas Young
A. Zannoni
Mr and Mrs Philip Zimmerman
Z.M.J. Zimnoch

Index of entries

Names in bold are main entries. Names in italics are Round-ups.

To the Editor *The Good Food Guide*
FREEPOST, 2 Marylebone Road, London NW1 1YN

Or send your report by electronic mail to: *guidereports@which.co.uk*

From my personal experience the following establishment should/should not be included in the *Guide* (please print in BLOCK CAPITALS):

____

____

Telephone______________________

I had lunch/dinner/stayed there on (date) ________________ 19___

I would rate this establishment _____ out of ten.

please continue overleaf

My meal for ____ people cost £ ____________ *attach bill where possible*

☐ Please tick if you would like more report forms

Reports received up to the end of **May 1998** will be used in the research of the 1999 edition.

I am not connected in any way with management or proprietors.
Name and address (BLOCK CAPITALS, please)

____

____

Signed ________________________________

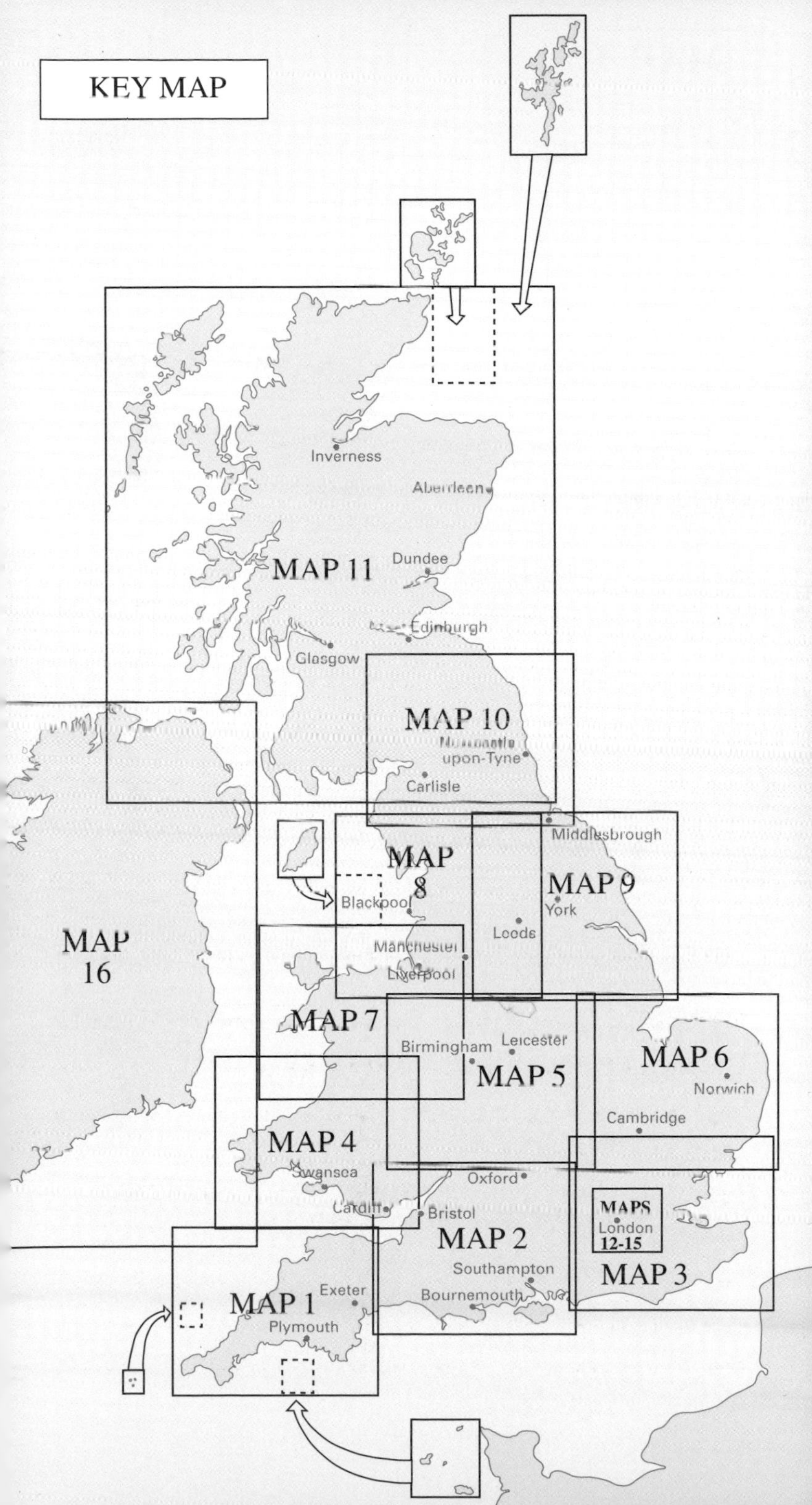
KEY MAP
MAP 11
Inverness
Aberdeen
Dundee
Edinburgh
Glasgow
MAP 10
upon-Tyne
Carlisle
Middlesbrough
MAP 8
MAP 9
York
Blackpool
Leeds
Manchester
Liverpool
MAP 16
MAP 7
Birmingham
Leicester
MAP 5
MAP 6
Norwich
Cambridge
MAP 4
Swansea
Cardiff
Oxford
Bristol
MAPS
London
12-15
MAP 2
Southampton
Bournemouth
MAP 3
Exeter
MAP 1
Plymouth

MAP 1

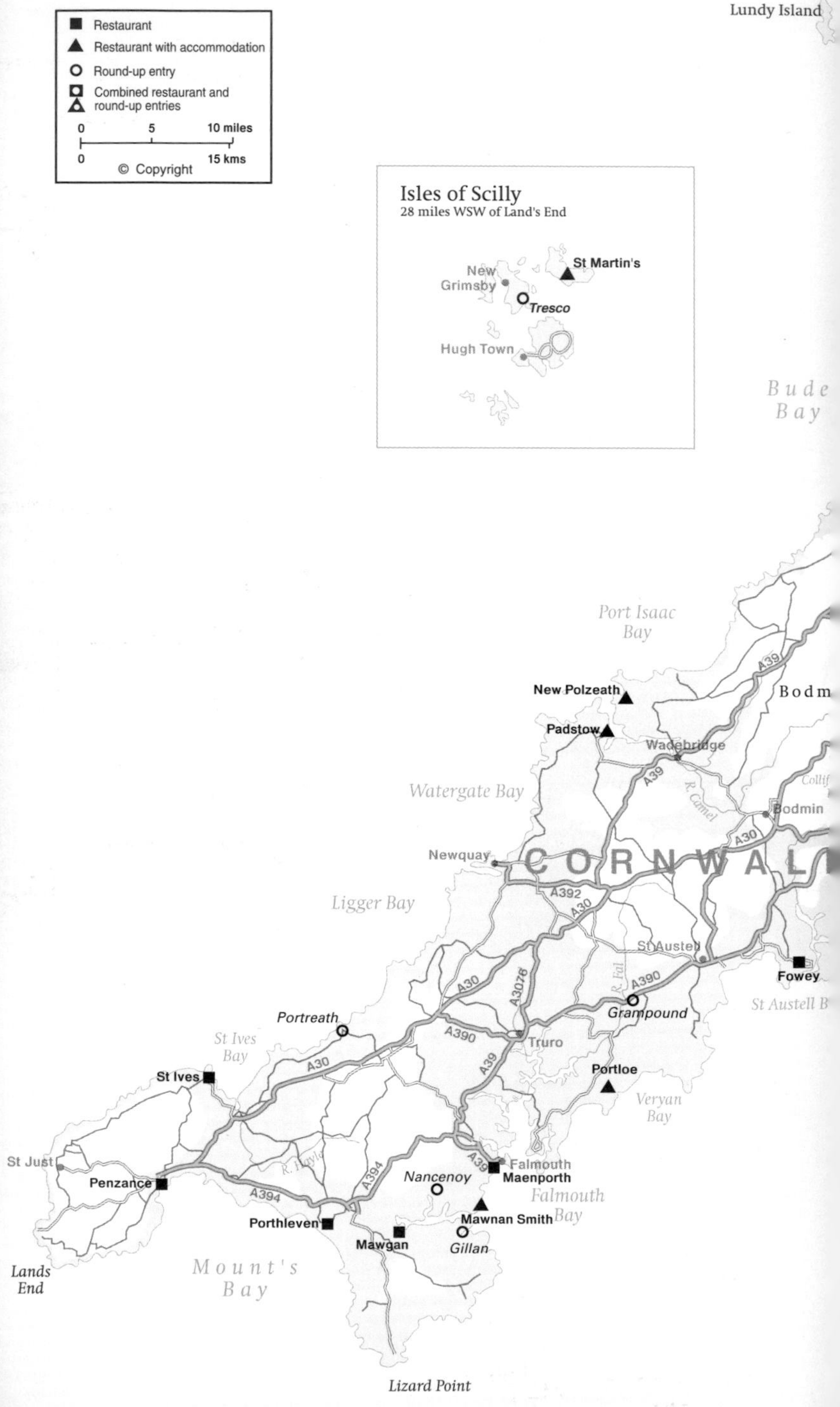

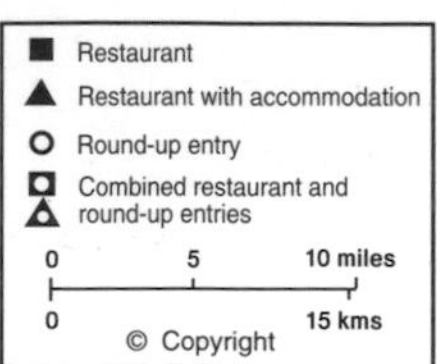

Lundy Island

Bude Bay

Port Isaac Bay

New Polzeath

Padstow

Wadebridge

Bodm

Watergate Bay

A39

R. Camel

Collif

Bodmin

A30

Newquay

CORNWAL

A392

Ligger Bay

A30

St Austell

Fowey

A3076

R. Fal

A390

Grampound

St Austell B

Portreath

A30

A390

St Ives Bay

Truro

A39

St Ives

Portloe

Veryan Bay

A30

St Just

R. Hayle

A39

Falmouth

Penzance

Maenporth

Nancenoy

A394

A394

Falmouth Bay

Porthleven

Mawnan Smith

Mawgan

Gillan

Lands End

Mount's Bay

Lizard Point

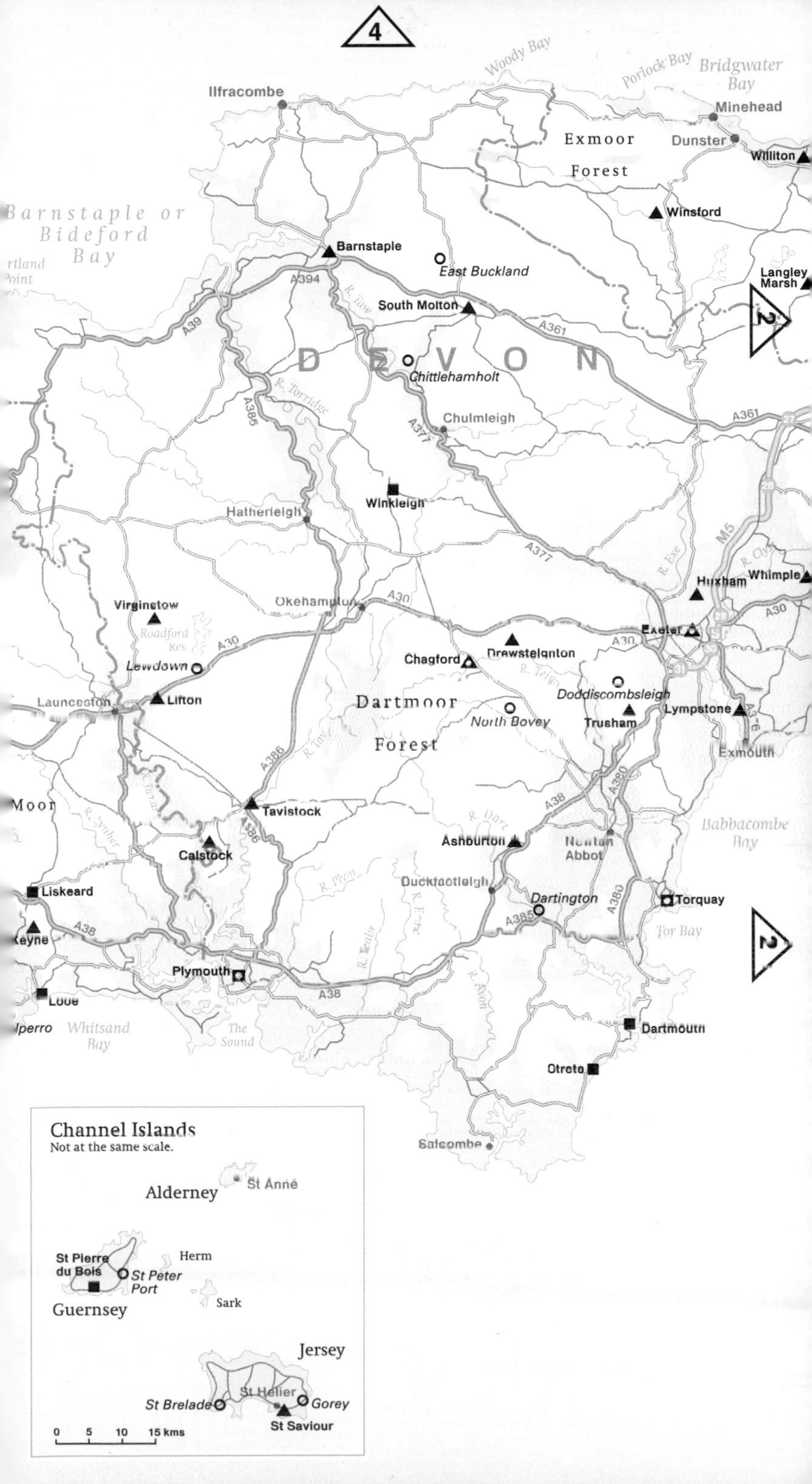
4
Woody Bay
Porlock Bay
Bridgwater Bay
Ilfracombe
Minehead
Exmoor
Dunster
Williton
Forest
Winsford
Barnstaple or Bideford Bay
Barnstaple
East Buckland
Langley Marsh
A394
South Molton
2
A39
A361
DEVON
Chittlehamholt
R. Torridge
A386
Chulmleigh
A377
A361
Winkleigh
Hatherleigh
A377
M5
Huxham
Whimple
Virginstow
Okehampton
A30
Roadford Res.
A30
Exeter
Chagford
Drewsteignton
A30
Lewdown
R. Teign
Doddiscombsleigh
Launceston
Lifton
Dartmoor
North Bovey
Trusham
Lympstone
Forest
Exmouth
A386
A38
A380
Moor
Tavistock
R. Dart
Babbacombe Bay
Calstock
Ashburton
Newton Abbot
Liskeard
Buckfastleigh
Dartington
Torquay
A385
A380
Tor Bay
2
A38
Plymouth
A38
Looe
Whitsand Bay
The Sound
Dartmouth
Salcombe
Channel Islands
Not at the same scale.
Alderney
St Anne
St Pierre du Bois
Herm
St Peter Port
Sark
Guernsey
Jersey
St Helier
St Brelade
Gorey
St Saviour
0 5 10 15 kms

Crickhowell
Llandewi Skirrid
Drybrook
Monmouth
GLOUCESTERSHIRE
Painswick
Clytha
Whitebrook
BLAENAU GWENT
Merthyr Tydfil
TORFAEN
Pontypool
MONMOUTHSHIRE
Minchinhampton
Nailsworth
Stroud
CAERPHILLY
R. Usk
Tetbury
Cotswolds
Thornbury
Bassaleg
NEWPORT
New Severn Crossing
SOUTH GLOUCESTERSHIRE
Creigiau
CARDIFF
Cardiff
Portishead
BRISTOL
Bristol
Castle Combe
VALE OF GLAMORGAN
Porthkerry
Mouth of the Severn
Colerne
N.W. SOMERSET
Bath
Hunstrete
Melksham
Weston-Super-Mare
Hinton Charterhouse
BATH & N.E. SOMERSET
Mendip Hills
R. Axe
Burnham-on-Sea
Ston Easton
Bridgwater Bay
Wells
Frome
R. Brue
Williton
Shepton Mallet
Warminster
Glastonbury
Bridgwater
Castle Cary
Bruton
R. Parrett
SOMERSET
Langley Marsh
Gillingham
Taunton
Hatch Beauchamp
Shaftesbury
Montacute
Sherborne
Yeovil
Sturminster Newton
Over Stratton
Barwick
Chard
Broadhembury
Evershot
Stockland
Corscombe
N. Dorset Downs
DORSET
Honiton
Beaminster
Whimple
Powerstock
Maiden Newton
R. Axe
R. Otter
West Bay
Lyme Bay
Dorchester
R. Piddle
R. Frome
Sidmouth
Restaurant
Restaurant with accommodation
Round-up entry
Combined restaurant and round-up entries
0 5 10 miles
0 15 kms
© Copyright
Weymouth
Weymouth Bay
Babbacombe Bay
Bill of Portland

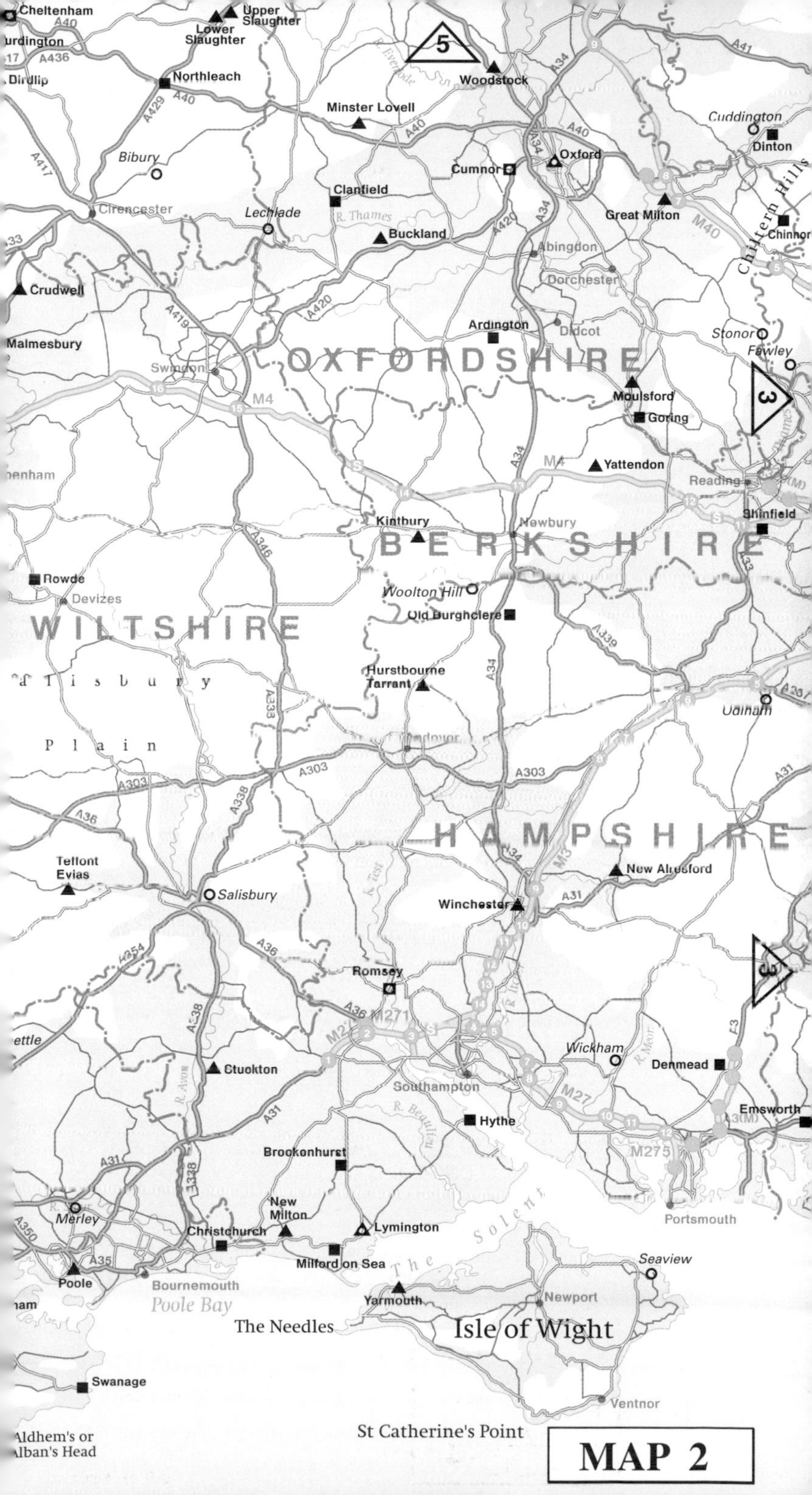

Cheltenham
Upper Slaughter
Lower Slaughter
Northleach
Woodstock
Minster Lovell
Cuddington
Dinton
Bibury
Oxford
Cumnor
Clanfield
Cirencester
Lechlade
R. Thames
Buckland
Great Milton
Chinnor
Chiltern Hills
Abingdon
Dorchester
Crudwell
Ardington
Didcot
Stonor
Malmesbury
Fawley
Swindon
OXFORDSHIRE
Moulsford
Goring
M4
Yattendon
Reading
Shinfield
Kintbury
Newbury
BERKSHIRE
Rowde
Devizes
Woolton Hill
Old Burghclere
WILTSHIRE
Hurstbourne Tarrant
Salisbury Plain
Odiham
HAMPSHIRE
Teffont Evias
New Alresford
Salisbury
Winchester
Romsey
Wickham
Denmead
Stuckton
Southampton
Hythe
Emsworth
Brockenhurst
M27
M275
Merley
New Milton
Lymington
Portsmouth
Christchurch
Milford on Sea
Seaview
Poole
Bournemouth
Poole Bay
Yarmouth
Newport
The Solent
The Needles
Isle of Wight
Swanage
Ventnor
St Catherine's Point
Aldhem's or Alban's Head
MAP 2

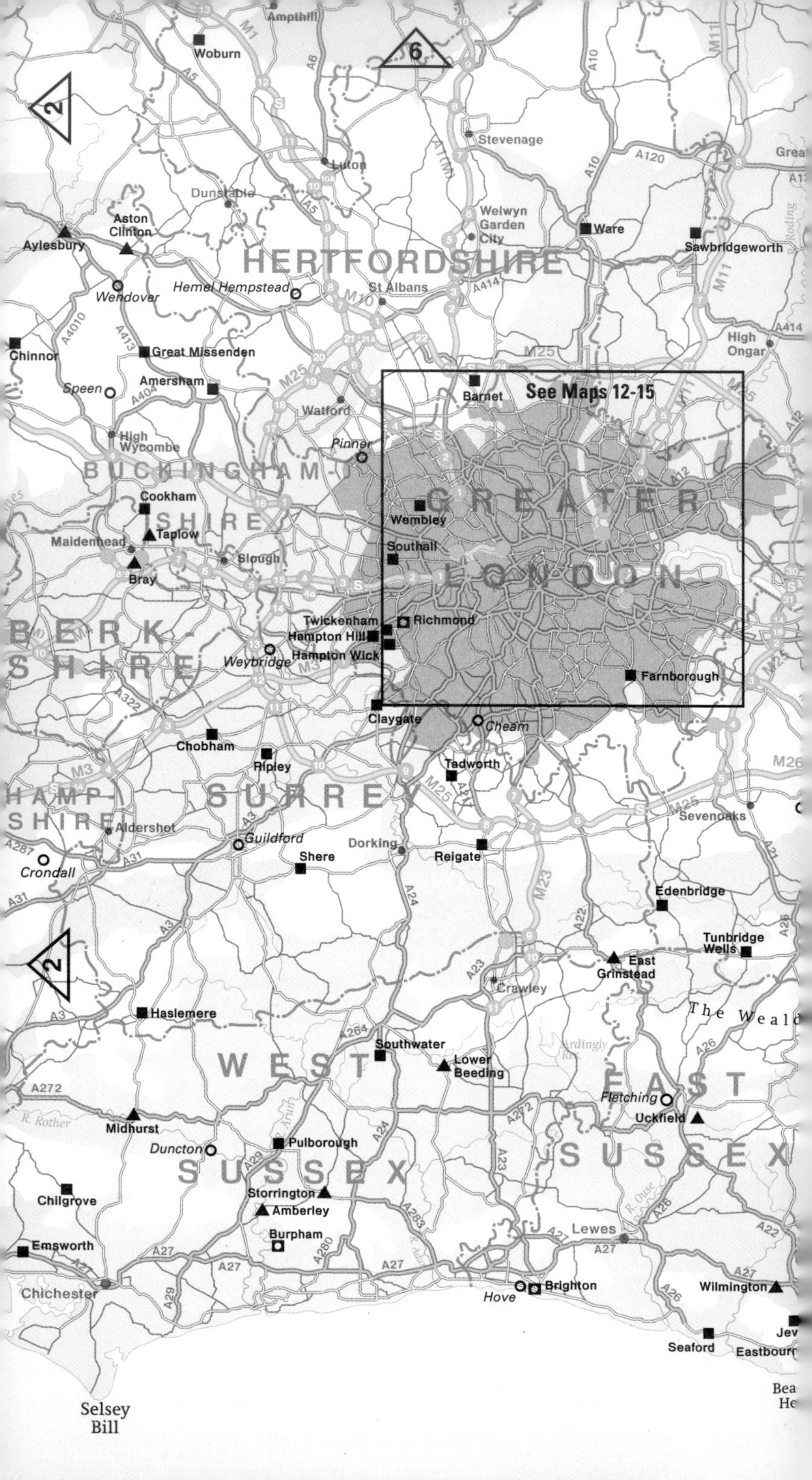

Ampthill
Woburn
6
2
Stevenage
Luton
Dunstable
Welwyn Garden City
Ware
Sawbridgeworth
Aston Clinton
Aylesbury
HERTFORDSHIRE
Wendover
Hemel Hempstead
St Albans
Chinnor
Great Missenden
High Ongar
Speen
Amersham
Barnet
See Maps 12-15
Watford
High Wycombe
Pinner
BUCKINGHAMSHIRE
Cookham
GREATER LONDON
Wembley
Taplow
Maidenhead
Southall
Slough
Bray
Twickenham
Richmond
Hampton Hill
Hampton Wick
BERKSHIRE
Weybridge
Farnborough
Claygate
Cheam
Chobham
Ripley
Tadworth
HAMPSHIRE
SURREY
Sevenoaks
Aldershot
Guildford
Dorking
Reigate
Crondall
Shere
Edenbridge
Tunbridge Wells
2
East Grinstead
Crawley
The Weald
Haslemere
Ardingly Res.
Southwater
Lower Beeding
WEST
EAST
Fletching
R. Rother
Midhurst
Uckfield
Duncton
Pulborough
SUSSEX
SUSSEX
Chilgrove
Storrington
Amberley
R. Ouse
Burpham
Lewes
Emsworth
Chichester
Brighton
Hove
Wilmington
Seaford
Selsey Bill

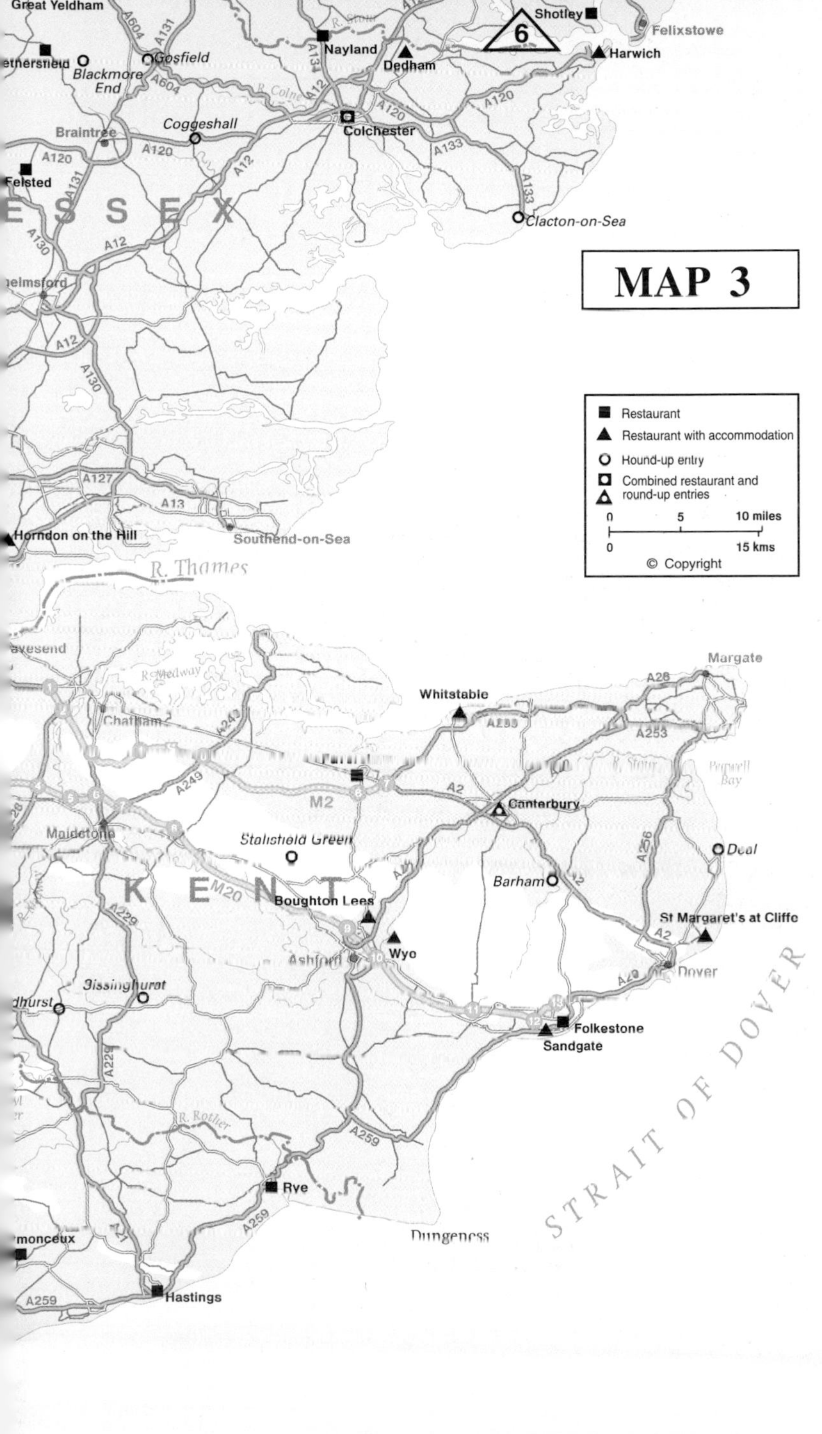
MAP 3
Restaurant
Restaurant with accommodation
Round-up entry
Combined restaurant and round-up entries
0
5
10 miles
0
15 kms
© Copyright
Great Yeldham
Gosfield
Blackmore End
Nayland
Dedham
Shotley
Felixstowe
Harwich
Coggeshall
Colchester
Braintree
Felsted
ESSEX
Clacton-on-Sea
Horndon on the Hill
Southend-on-Sea
R. Thames
Chatham
Maidstone
Margate
Whitstable
Canterbury
Pegwell Bay
Stalisfield Green
Deal
Barham
KENT
Boughton Lees
St Margaret's at Cliffe
Wye
Ashford
Dover
Biddenden
Folkestone
Sandgate
Rye
Dungeness
Hastings
STRAIT OF DOVER

MAP 4

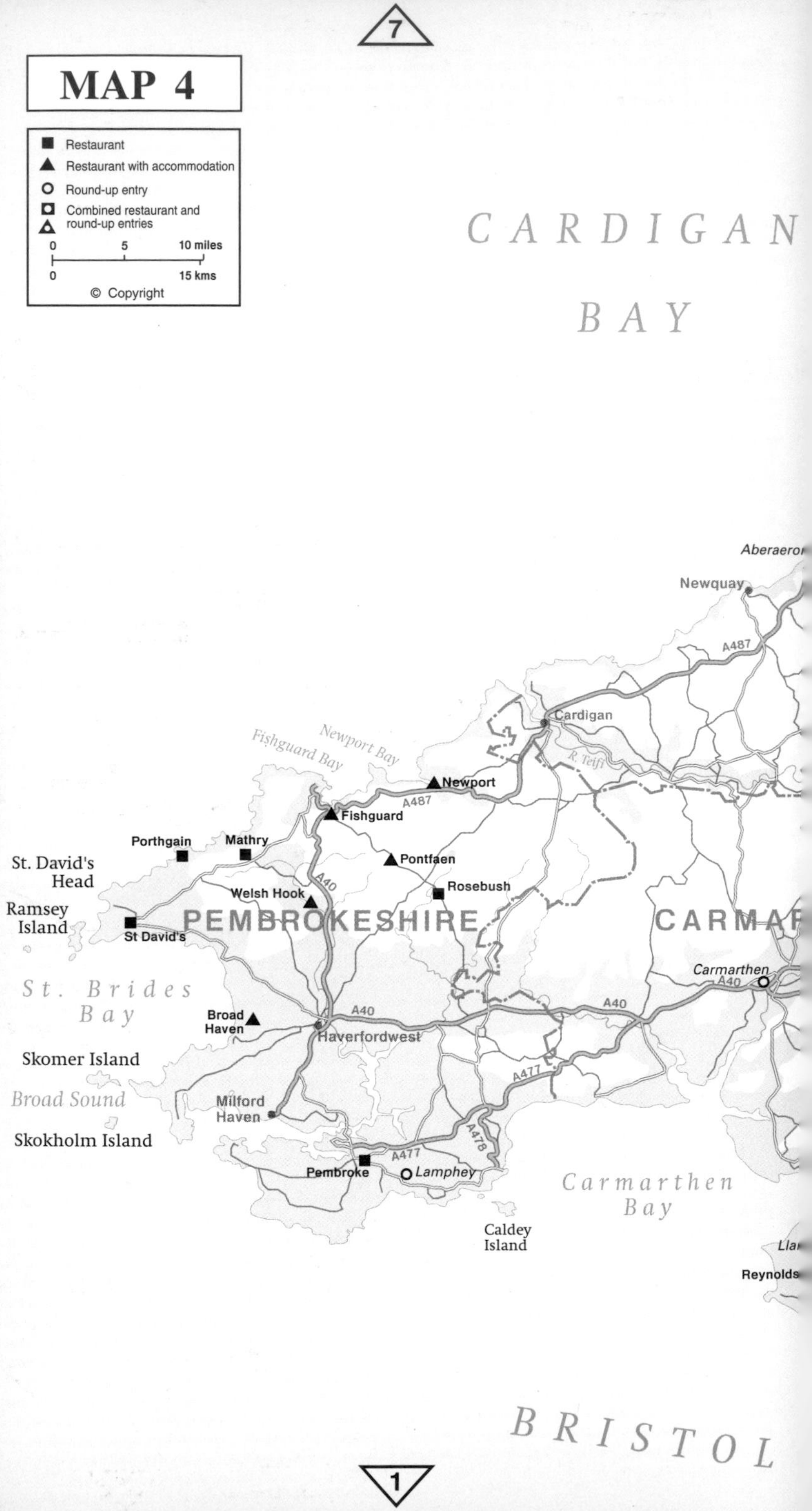

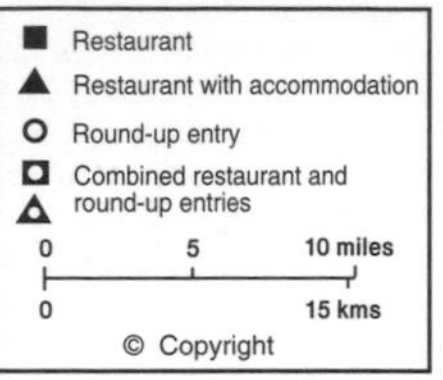

CARDIGAN
BAY

Aberaeron
Newquay
A487
Cardigan
R. Teifi
Fishguard Bay
Newport Bay
Newport
A487
Fishguard
Porthgain
Mathry
St. David's Head
Pontfaen
Rosebush
A40
Welsh Hook
Ramsey Island
St David's
PEMBROKESHIRE
CARMAR
Carmarthen
A40
St. Brides Bay
A40
Broad Haven
A40
Haverfordwest
Skomer Island
A477
Broad Sound
Milford Haven
Skokholm Island
A478
A477
Pembroke
Lamphey
Carmarthen Bay
Caldey Island
Lla
Reynolds

BRISTOL

Llanaber
Penmaenpool
Barmouth
Dolgellau
Cader Idris
893
7
Llanwddyn
Llanfyllin
Talyllyn
A470
A487
A458
A483
A489
Afon Dyfi
SHROPSHIRE
Aberdovey
Eglwysfach
Forden
Montgomery
Newtown
Cambrian Mountains
A44
Aberystwyth
Llangurig
5
A487
POWYS
Presteigne
CEREDIGION
Llandrindod Wells
Llanfihangel nant Melan
Kington
Lampeter
Llanwrtyd Wells
Llangammarch Wells
Builth Wells
A438
Hay-on-Wye
Llyswen
Three Cocks
Llandovery
A40
Pwllgloyw
A479
R. Usk
R. Monnow
Brecon
ENSHIRE
R. Tywi
Llandeilo
Nantgaredig
Brecon Beacons
Crickhowell
Llandewi Skirrid
A465
BLAENAU GWENT
Merthyr Tydfil
MERTHYR TYDFIL
CAERPHILLY
TORFAEN
NEATH PORT TALBOT
SWANSEA
Swansea
RHONDDA CYNON TAFF
Port Talbot
Swansea Bay
BRIDGEND
M4
Bassaleg
NEWPORT
Creigiau
CARDIFF
Cardiff
A48(M)
2
VALE OF GLAMORGAN
CHANNEL
Porthkerry
Mouth of the Severn

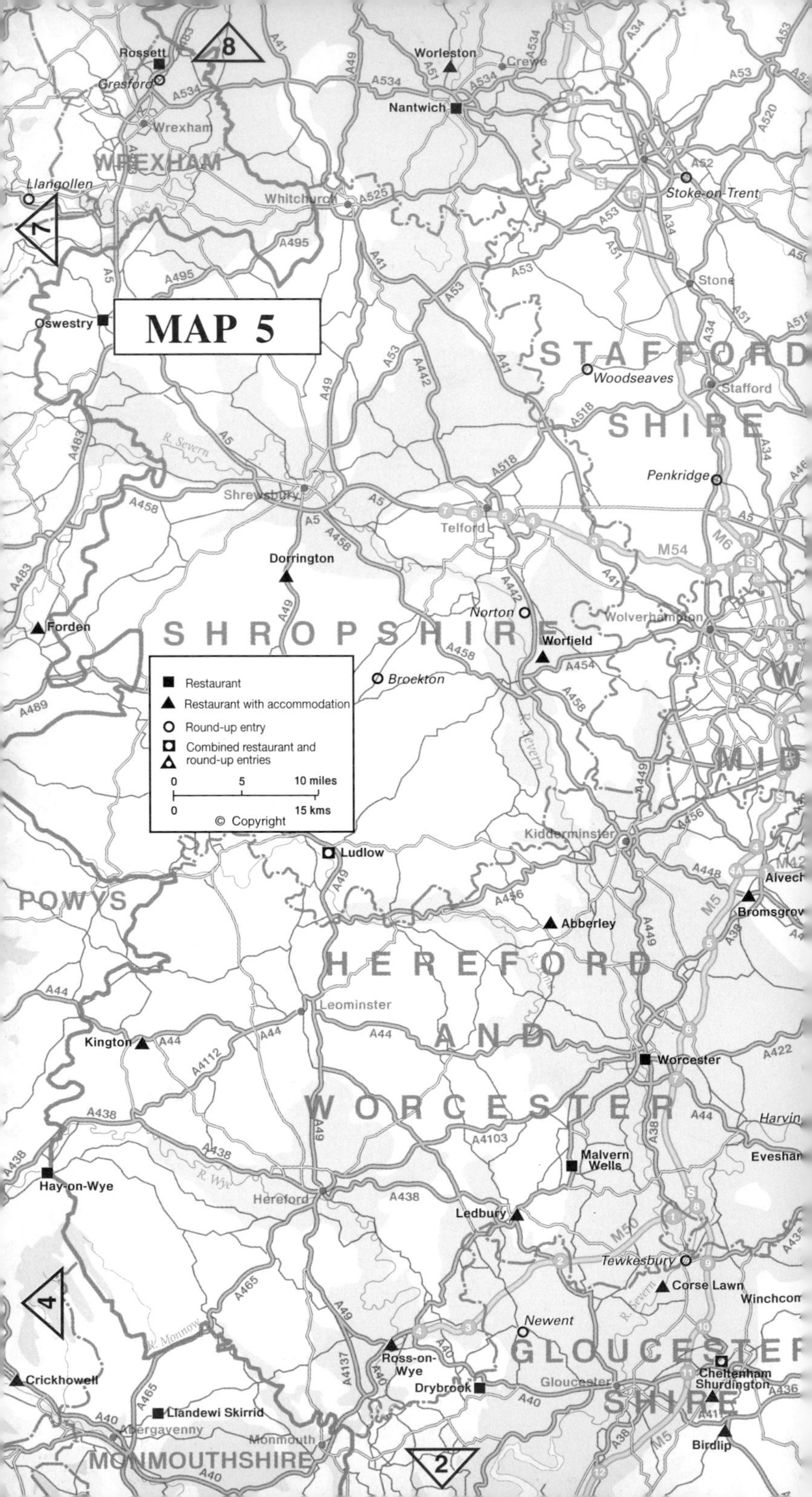
MAP 5
Restaurant
Restaurant with accommodation
Round-up entry
Combined restaurant and round-up entries
0 5 10 miles
0 15 kms
© Copyright
Rossett
Gresford
Wrexham
WREXHAM
Llangollen
Oswestry
Forden
Worleston
Crewe
Nantwich
Whitchurch
Stoke-on-Trent
Stone
STAFFORDSHIRE
Woodseaves
Stafford
Penkridge
Shrewsbury
Telford
Dorrington
SHROPSHIRE
Norton
Wolverhampton
Worfield
Brockton
Ludlow
Kidderminster
Alvech
Bromsgrov
Abberley
POWYS
HEREFORD AND WORCESTER
Leominster
Kington
Worcester
Harvin
Evesham
Malvern Wells
Hay-on-Wye
Hereford
Ledbury
Tewkesbury
Corse Lawn
Winchcom
Newent
GLOUCESTERSHIRE
Cheltenham
Shurdington
Birdlip
Gloucester
Ross-on-Wye
Drybrook
Crickhowell
Llandewi Skirrid
Abergavenny
Monmouth
MONMOUTHSHIRE
R. Dee
R. Severn
R. Wye
R. Monnow
R. Teme
8
7
4
2

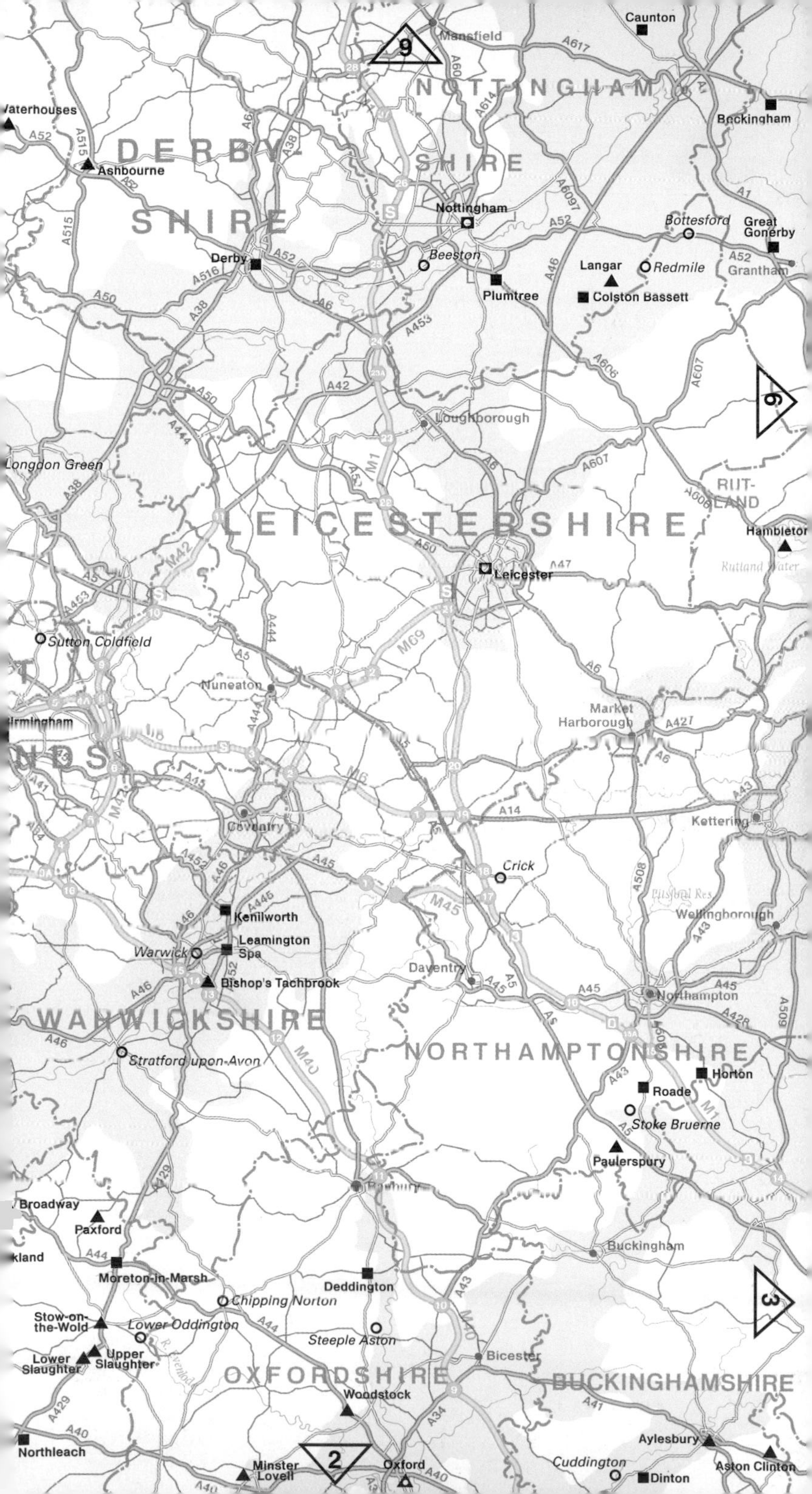

9
Mansfield
Caunton
NOTTINGHAM
SHIRE
Beckingham
Waterhouses
DERBY
SHIRE
Ashbourne
Nottingham
Bottesford
Great Gonerby
Derby
Beeston
Langar
Redmile
Grantham
Plumtree
Colston Bassett
6
Loughborough
Longdon Green
RUT-
LAND
LEICESTERSHIRE
Hambleton
Leicester
Rutland Water
Sutton Coldfield
Nuneaton
Market Harborough
Birmingham
Coventry
Kettering
Crick
Pitsford Res.
Wellingborough
Kenilworth
Leamington Spa
Warwick
Daventry
Bishop's Tachbrook
Northampton
WARWICKSHIRE
Stratford upon Avon
NORTHAMPTONSHIRE
Horton
Roade
Stoke Bruerne
Paulerspury
Banbury
Broadway
Paxford
Buckingham
Moreton-in-Marsh
Deddington
3
Chipping Norton
Stow-on-the-Wold
Lower Oddington
Steeple Aston
Upper Slaughter
Lower Slaughter
Bicester
OXFORDSHIRE
BUCKINGHAMSHIRE
Woodstock
Aylesbury
Northleach
2
Minster Lovell
Oxford
Cuddington
Dinton
Aston Clinton

Lincoln
Horncastle
9
A158
Burgh le Marsh
Skegness
LINCOLNSHIRE
Steeping R.
A46
A15
A52
Beckingham
A17
R. Witham
A16
Boston
The Wash.
Great Gonerby
Grantham
A52
A17
A1
5
R. Welland
Gedney Dyke
A151
Grimsby
King's Lynn
Stretton
RUTLAND
A606
Hambleton
Rutland Water
Stamford
A16
Wisbech
A1101
A47
A10
A134
Great Ouse
A1122
A6003
A47
A43
King's Cliffe
Wansford
Elton
Peterborough
R. Nene
A141
A605
A6116
A603
Littleport
A142
Kettering
Keyston
Bythorn
Sutton Gault
Ely
CAMBRIDGE-SHIRE
A14
A6
Little Addington
Huntingdon
Grafham Water
Wellingborough
A45
A509
R. Cam
Newmarket
A1
A428
Madingley
Cambridge
5
Little Shelford
A11
Bedford
BEDFORDSHIRE
Biggleswade
Melbourn
A505
A604
Saffron Walden
Houghton Conquest
ESSEX
M1
Woburn
A5
Wethersfield
Stevenage
3
Luton
A120

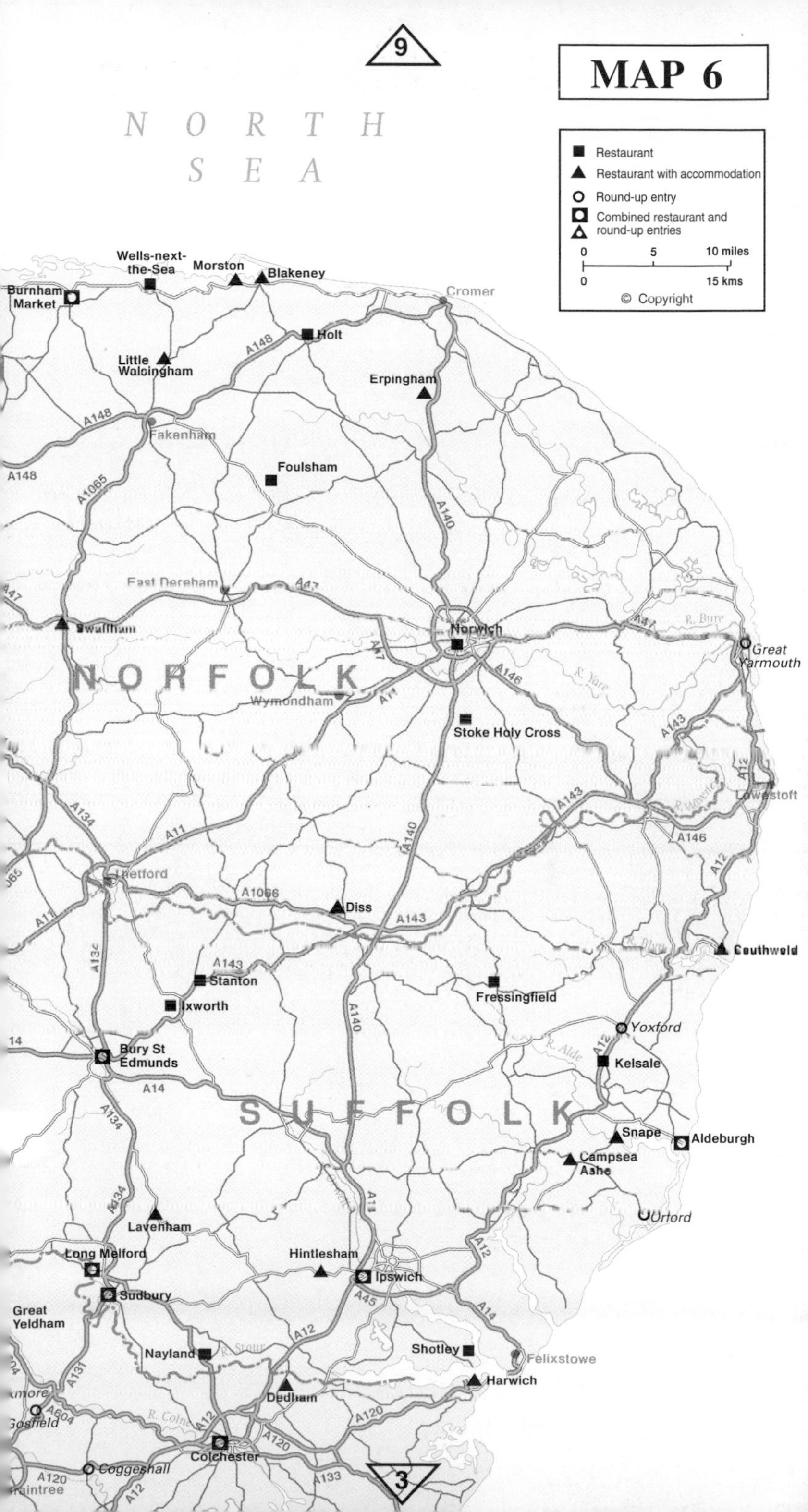
9
MAP 6
NORTH SEA
Restaurant
Restaurant with accommodation
Round-up entry
Combined restaurant and round-up entries
0 5 10 miles
0 15 kms
© Copyright
Wells-next-the-Sea
Morston
Blakeney
Burnham Market
Cromer
Holt
Little Walsingham
Erpingham
Fakenham
Foulsham
East Dereham
Swaffham
Norwich
Great Yarmouth
NORFOLK
Wymondham
Stoke Holy Cross
Lowestoft
Thetford
Diss
Southwold
Stanton
Ixworth
Fressingfield
Yoxford
Bury St Edmunds
Kelsale
SUFFOLK
Snape
Aldeburgh
Campsea Ashe
Orford
Lavenham
Long Melford
Hintlesham
Ipswich
Sudbury
Great Yeldham
Nayland
Shotley
Felixstowe
Harwich
Dedham
Gosfield
Colchester
Coggeshall
3

MAP 7

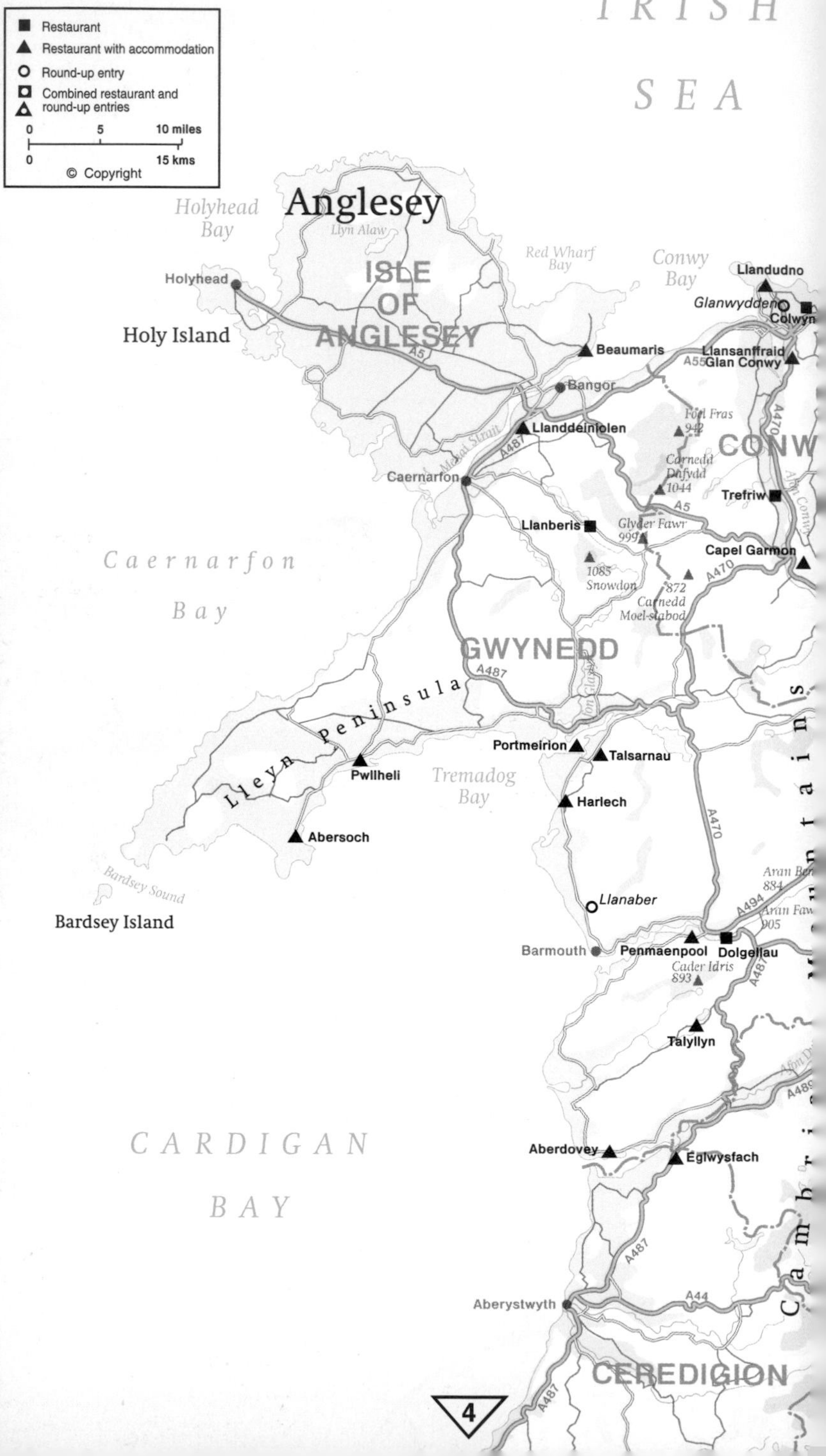

Restaurant
Restaurant with accommodation
Round-up entry
Combined restaurant and round-up entries
0 5 10 miles
0 15 kms
© Copyright
IRISH SEA
Anglesey
Holyhead Bay
Llyn Alaw
ISLE OF ANGLESEY
Holyhead
Holy Island
A5
Red Wharf Bay
Conwy Bay
Llandudno
Glanwydden
Colwyn
Beaumaris
Llansanffraid Glan Conwy
A55
Bangor
Foel Fras 942
Llanddeiniolen
Menai Strait
A487
CONWY
Caernarfon
Carnedd Dafydd 1044
Trefriw
A5
Llanberis
Glyder Fawr 999
Capel Garmon
A470
1085 Snowdon
872 Carnedd Moel-siabod
Caernarfon Bay
GWYNEDD
A487
Lleyn Peninsula
Portmeirion
Talsarnau
Pwllheli
Tremadog Bay
Harlech
A470
Abersoch
Bardsey Sound
Bardsey Island
Llanaber
A494
Barmouth
Penmaenpool
Dolgellau
Cader Idris 893
A487
Talyllyn
CARDIGAN BAY
Aberdovey
Eglwysfach
A487
Aberystwyth
A44
CEREDIGION
A487

4

8
Southport
Wrightington
Coppull Moor
Ormskirk
Skelmersdale
Wigan
Bolton
GTR
MANCHESTER
MERSEYSIDE
Wallasey
St Helens
Liverpool
Birkenhead
Warrington
8
Prestatyn
Rhyl
R. Mersey
St George
CHESHIRE
Mollington
Sandiway
Northop
Chester
FLINTSHIRE
Denbigh
Mold
DENBIGHSHIRE
Worleston
Crewe
Broxton
Llandegla
Gresford
Nantwich
Wrexham
WREXHAM
Whitchurch
Llangollen
Llandrillo
Llanarmon Dyffryn
Ceiriog
Oswestry
Bala
Lake
L. Vyrnwy
Llanfyllin
Llanwddyn
R. Severn
Shrewsbury
Dorrington
SHROPSHIRE
Forden
Norton
Brockton
Newtown
5
POWYS
Ludlow
5

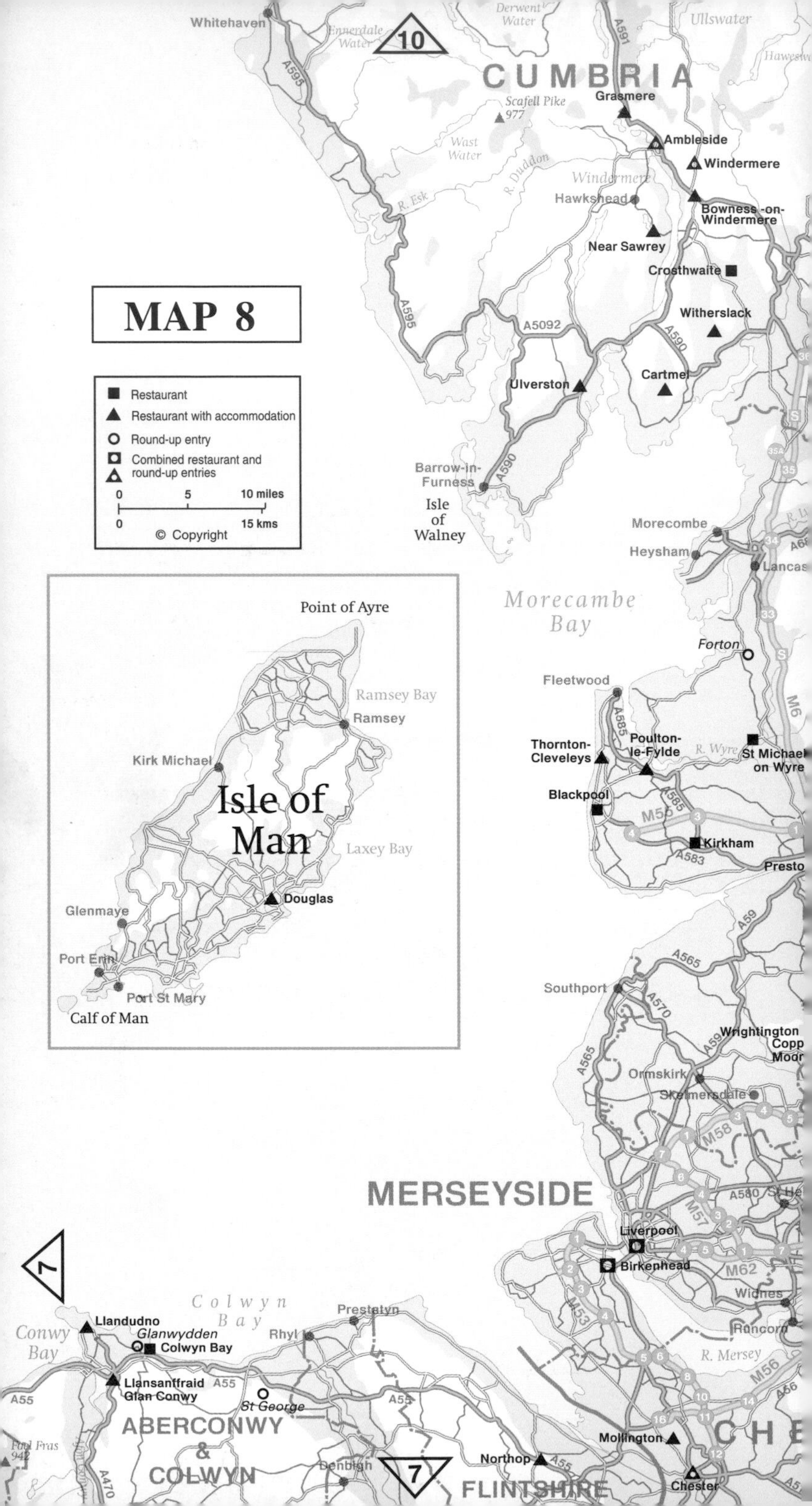

MAP 8
Restaurant
Restaurant with accommodation
Round-up entry
Combined restaurant and round-up entries
0 5 10 miles
0 15 kms
© Copyright
10
CUMBRIA
Whitehaven
Ennerdale Water
Derwent Water
Ullswater
Scafell Pike 977
Grasmere
Ambleside
Windermere
Wast Water
Hawkshead
Bowness-on-Windermere
Near Sawrey
Crosthwaite
Witherslack
Cartmel
Ulverston
Barrow-in-Furness
Isle of Walney
Morecambe
Heysham
Morecambe Bay
Forton
Fleetwood
Thornton-Cleveleys
Poulton-le-Fylde
St Michael on Wyre
Blackpool
Kirkham
Point of Ayre
Ramsey Bay
Ramsey
Kirk Michael
Isle of Man
Laxey Bay
Douglas
Glenmaye
Port Erin
Port St Mary
Calf of Man
Southport
Wrightington
Ormskirk
Skelmersdale
MERSEYSIDE
Liverpool
Birkenhead
Widnes
Runcorn
R. Mersey
Mollington
Chester
7
Colwyn Bay
Conwy Bay
Llandudno
Glanwydden
Colwyn Bay
Prestatyn
Rhyl
Llansanffraid Glan Conwy
St George
ABERCONWY & COLWYN
Denbigh
Northop
FLINTSHIRE
7

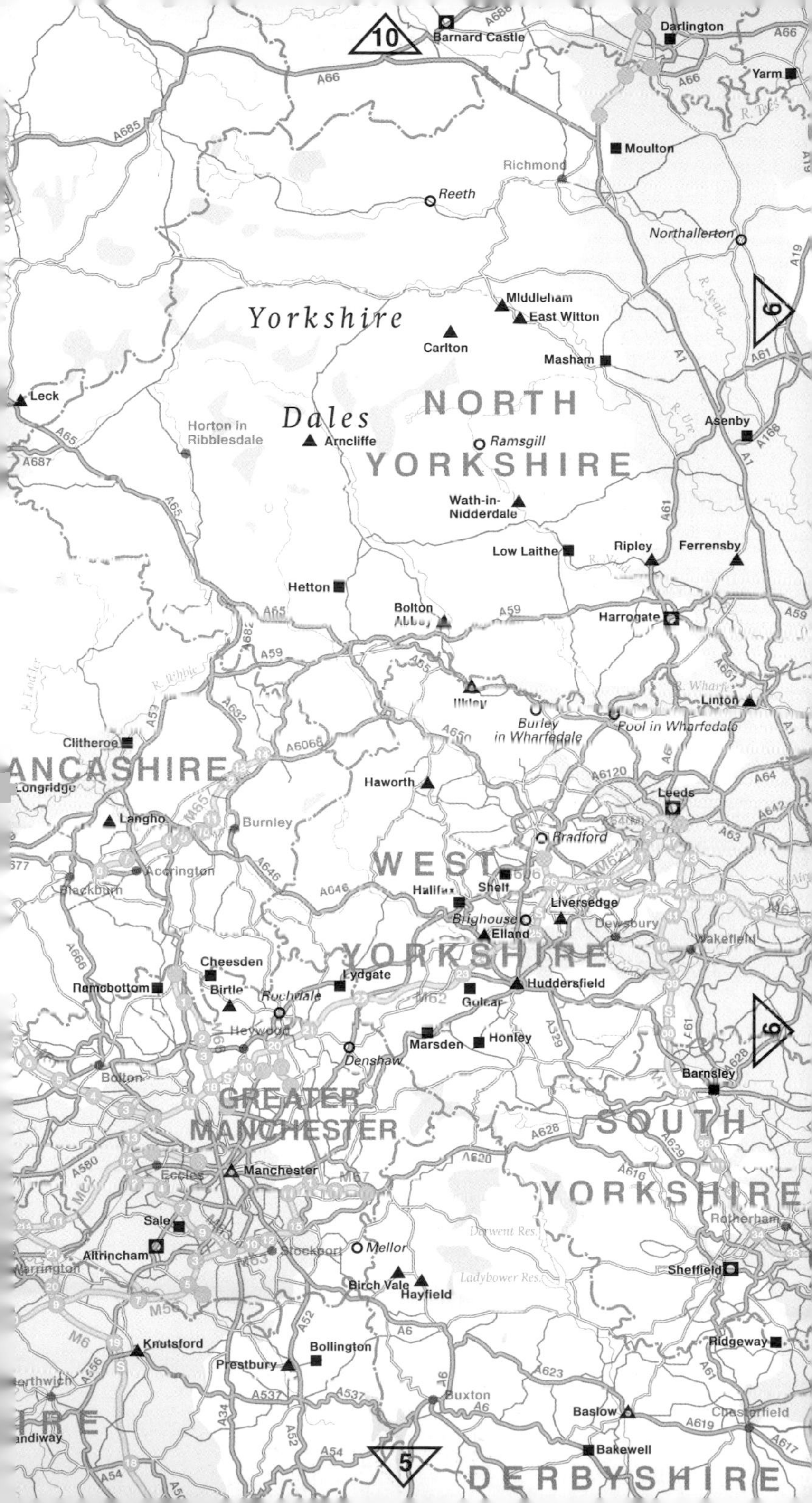

10
Barnard Castle
Darlington
Yarm
Moulton
Richmond
Reeth
Northallerton
6
Yorkshire
Dales
Middleham
East Witton
Carlton
Masham
Leck
NORTH
YORKSHIRE
Horton in Ribblesdale
Arncliffe
Ramsgill
Asenby
Wath-in-Nidderdale
Low Laithe
Ripley
Ferrensby
Hetton
Bolton Abbey
Harrogate
Ilkley
Burley in Wharfedale
Pool in Wharfedale
Linton
Clitheroe
LANCASHIRE
Longridge
Haworth
Leeds
Langho
Burnley
Bradford
Accrington
Blackburn
WEST
Shelf
Halifax
Liversedge
Brighouse
Dewsbury
Elland
Wakefield
YORKSHIRE
Cheesden
Ramsbottom
Birtle
Lydgate
Rochdale
Golcar
Huddersfield
Heywood
Marsden
Honley
Denshaw
Bolton
Barnsley
GREATER
MANCHESTER
SOUTH
Eccles
Manchester
YORKSHIRE
Sale
Rotherham
Altrincham
Stockport
Mellor
Warrington
Derwent Res.
Sheffield
Birch Vale
Hayfield
Ladybower Res.
Knutsford
Bollington
Ridgeway
Prestbury
Northwich
Buxton
Baslow
Chesterfield
Sandiway
Bakewell
5
DERBYSHIRE

Barnard Castle
Darlington
10
Stokesley
Moulton
Richmond
Reeth
Staddlebridge
North York Moors
Northallerton
Middleham
Carlton
East Witton
Masham
Thirsk
Harome
8
Asenby
Hovingham
Ramsgill
NORTH YORKSHIRE
Wath-in-Nidderdale
Low Laithe
Ripley
Ferrensby
Bolton Abbey
Harrogate
York
Ilkley
Burley in Wharfedale
Linton
Pool in Wharfedale
Tadcaster
Haworth
Saxton
WEST YORKSHIRE
Leeds
Bradford
Halifax
Shelf
Brighouse
Elland
Liversedge
Wakefield
Huddersfield
Golcar
Marsden
Honley
Barnsley
Epworth
8
SOUTH YORKSHIRE
Doncaster
Mexborough
Rotherham
Gainsborough
Birch Vale
Hayfield
Sheffield
NOTTINGHAMSHIRE
Ridgeway
Worksop
DERBYSHIRE
Buxton
Baslow
Chesterfield
Bakewell
5
Mansfield
Caunton

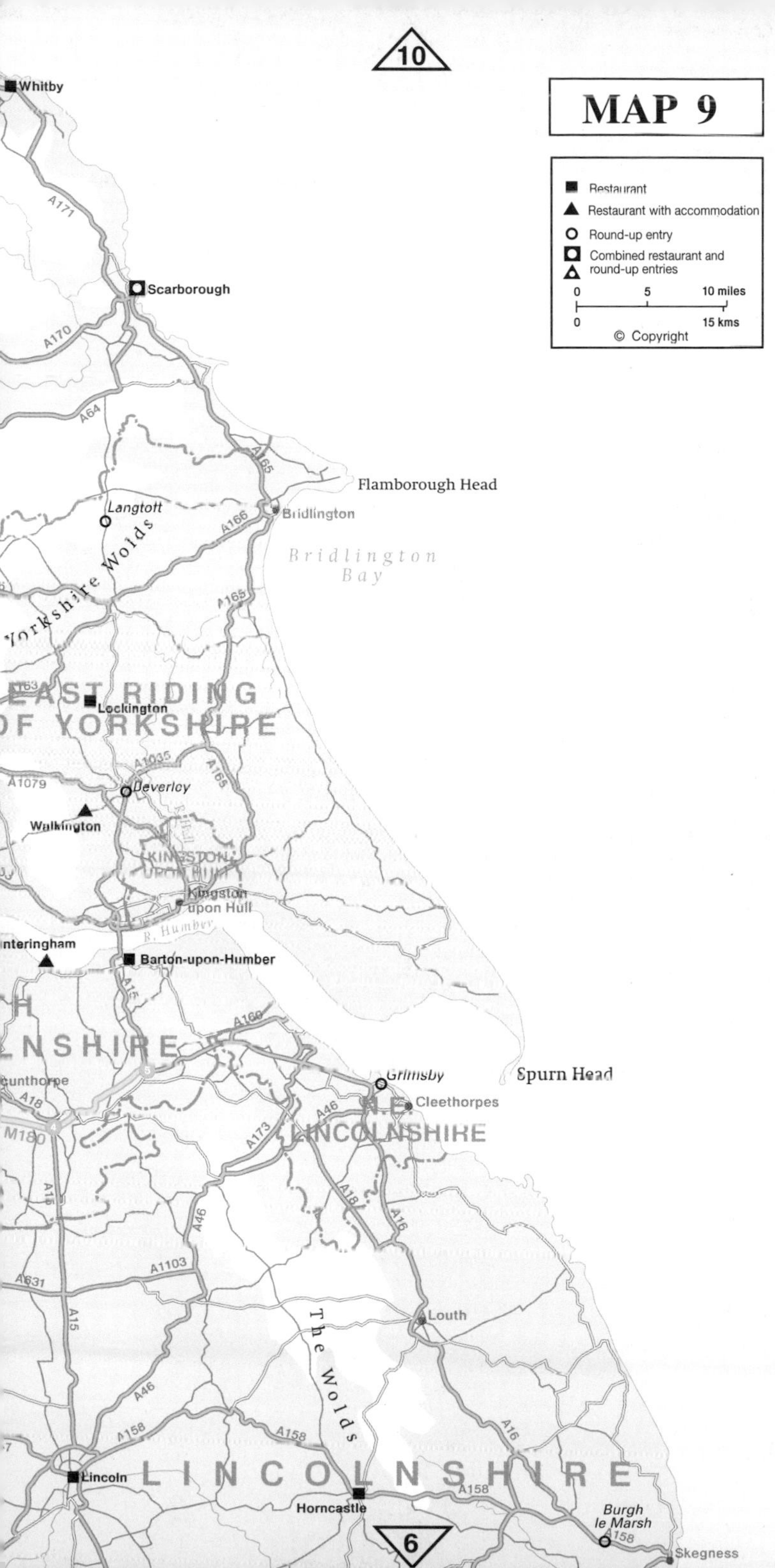
10
MAP 9
Restaurant
Restaurant with accommodation
Round-up entry
Combined restaurant and round-up entries
0 5 10 miles
0 15 kms
© Copyright
Whitby
A171
Scarborough
A170
A64
A165
Flamborough Head
Langtott
Bridlington
A166
Yorkshire Wolds
Bridlington Bay
A165
EAST RIDING OF YORKSHIRE
Lockington
A1035
A165
A1079
Beverley
Walkington
KINGSTON UPON HULL
Kingston upon Hull
R. Humber
Winteringham
Barton-upon-Humber
A15
A160
Scunthorpe
A18
M180
Grimsby
Spurn Head
Cleethorpes
N.E. LINCOLNSHIRE
A46
A173
A18
A16
A15
A46
A1103
A631
A15
Louth
The Wolds
A46
A158
A158
A16
LINCOLNSHIRE
Lincoln
Horncastle
A158
Burgh le Marsh
A158
Skegness
6

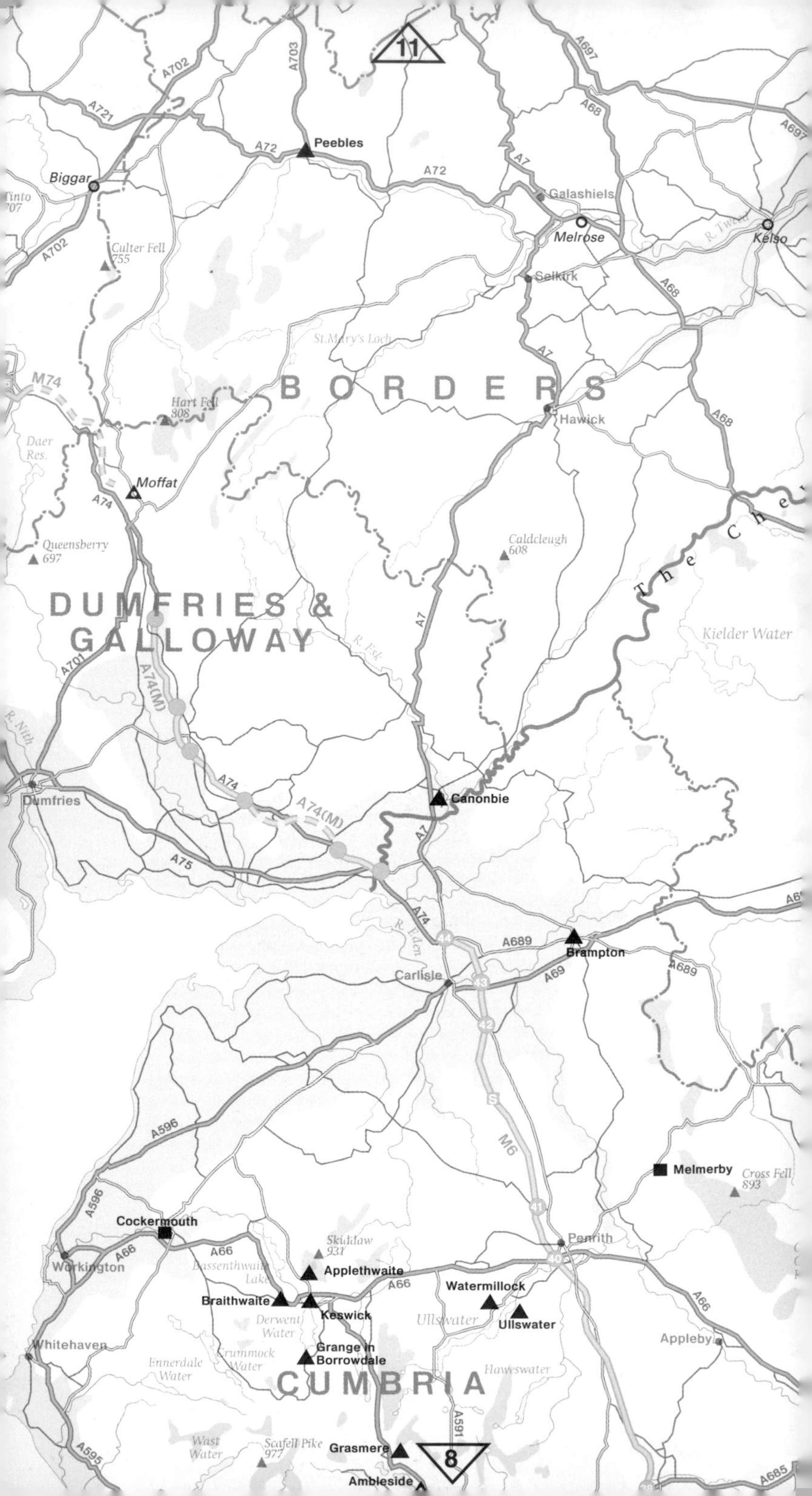

11
A702
A703
A697
A721
A72
Peebles
A68
A7
Biggar
Galashiels
Melrose
Kelso
R. Tweed
Culter Fell
755
Selkirk
St.Mary's Loch
A7
M74
BORDERS
Hart Fell
808
Hawick
Daer Res.
Moffat
A74
Queensberry
697
Caldcleugh
608
The Che
DUMFRIES & GALLOWAY
A7
Kielder Water
A701
A74(M)
R. Esk
R. Nith
A74
Canonbie
Dumfries
A74(M)
A75
A7
A74
R. Eden
44
A689
Brampton
Carlisle
43
A69
A689
42
A596
M6
Melmerby
Cross Fell
893
A596
41
Cockermouth
Skiddaw
931
Penrith
Workington
A66
A66
Bassenthwaite Lake
Applethwaite
40
Braithwaite
Keswick
A66
Watermillock
Ullswater
Ullswater
A66
Derwent Water
Whitehaven
Grange in Borrowdale
Appleby
Crummock Water
Ennerdale Water
Haweswater
CUMBRIA
A591
Wast Water
Scafell Pike
977
Grasmere
8
A595
Ambleside
A685

MAP 10
11
Restaurant
Restaurant with accommodation
Round-up entry
Combined restaurant and round-up entries
0 5 10 miles
0 16 kms
© Copyright
Berwick-upon-Tweed
Swinton
Holy Island
Farne Is.
The Cheviot 815
Alnwick
Alnmouth
NORTHUMBERLAND
Morpeth
Whitley Bay
Ponteland
Seaton Burn
Newcastle Upon Tyne
Corbridge
Hexham
Gateshead
East Boldon
TYNE & WEAR
Sunderland
Stanley
Chester-le-Street
Consett
Durham
Willington
DURHAM
Hartlepool
HARTLEPOOL
Tees Bay
Redcar
STOCKTON-ON-TEES
Middlesbrough
REDCAR
Romaldkirk
Barnard Castle
Darlington
Yarm
Stokesley
9

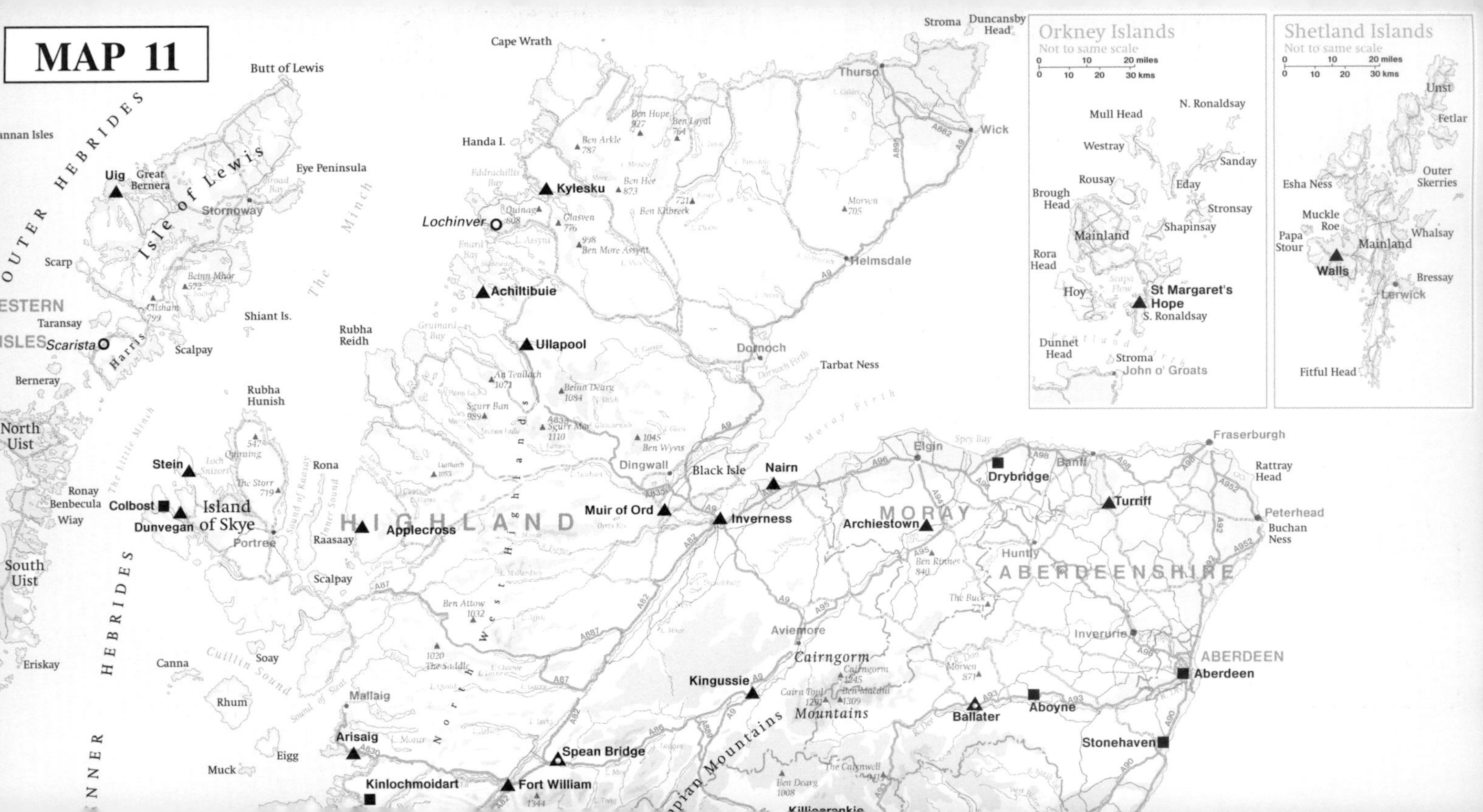
MAP 11
Orkney Islands
Not to same scale
Shetland Islands
Not to same scale
Uig
Stornoway
Isle of Lewis
Scarista
Harris
Stein
Colbost
Dunvegan
Island of Skye
Portree
Lochinver
Kylesku
Achiltibuie
Ullapool
Applecross
Muir of Ord
Inverness
Nairn
Archiestown
Drybridge
Turriff
Aberdeen
Aboyne
Ballater
Stonehaven
Kingussie
Spean Bridge
Fort William
Arisaig
Kinlochmoidart
Mallaig
St Margaret's Hope
Walls
Thurso
Wick
Helmsdale
Dornoch
Elgin
Huntly
Inverurie
Fraserburgh
Peterhead
Aviemore
HIGHLAND
MORAY
ABERDEENSHIRE
Cairngorm Mountains
OUTER HEBRIDES
WESTERN ISLES

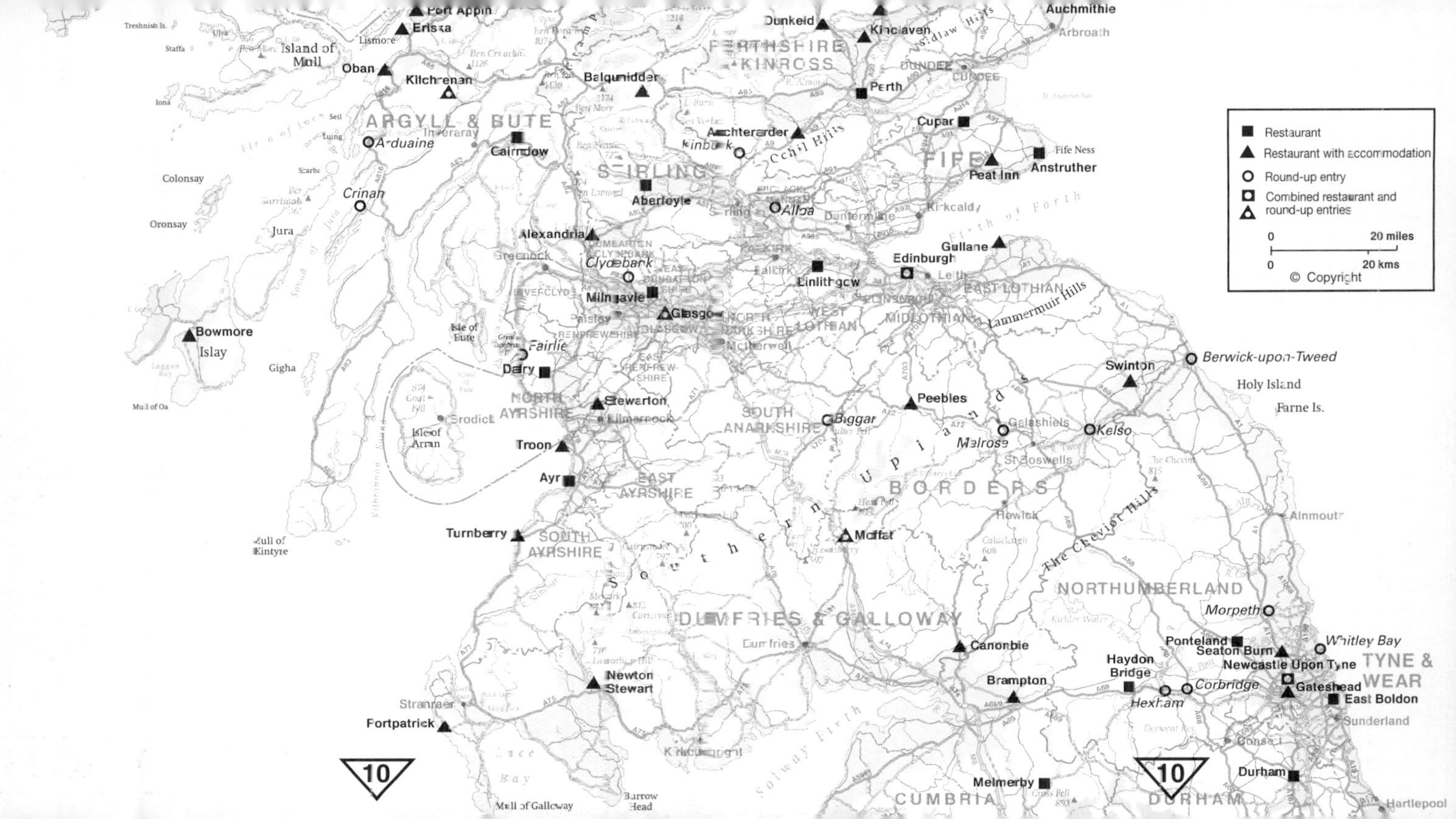
Restaurant
Restaurant with accommodation
Round-up entry
Combined restaurant and round-up entries
0
20 miles
0
20 kms
© Copyright
Port Appin
Eriska
Oban
Kilchrenan
Arduaine
Crinan
Cairndow
Balquhidder
Aberfoyle
Alexandria
Clydebank
Milngavie
Glasgow
Fairlie
Dalry
Stewarton
Troon
Ayr
Turnberry
Newton Stewart
Portpatrick
Bowmore
Islay
Dunkeld
Kinclaven
Perth
Auchterarder
Kinbuck
Alloa
Linlithgow
Edinburgh
Gullane
Cupar
Peat Inn
Anstruther
Auchmithie
Biggar
Peebles
Melrose
Kelso
Swinton
Berwick-upon-Tweed
Moffat
Canonbie
Brampton
Melmerby
Haydon Bridge
Hexham
Corbridge
Ponteland
Seaton Burn
Morpeth
Whitley Bay
Newcastle Upon Tyne
Gateshead
East Boldon
Durham
ARGYLL & BUTE
PERTHSHIRE KINROSS
STIRLING
FIFE
EAST LOTHIAN
MIDLOTHIAN
WEST LOTHIAN
SOUTH LANARKSHIRE
NORTH AYRSHIRE
EAST AYRSHIRE
SOUTH AYRSHIRE
DUMFRIES & GALLOWAY
BORDERS
NORTHUMBERLAND
TYNE & WEAR
DURHAM
CUMBRIA
Southern Uplands
Lammermuir Hills
The Cheviot Hills
Ochil Hills
Firth of Forth
Solway Firth
Holy Island
Farne Is.
Island of Mull
Colonsay
Oronsay
Jura
Gigha
Mull of Kintyre
Isle of Arran
Mull of Galloway
Barrow Head
10
10

Greater London

CHIGWELL
EDMONTON
Woodford
Hainault
REDBRIDGE
Walthamstow
WALTHAM FOREST
Rasa
Istanbul Iskembecisi
HACKNEY
ILFORD
Thai Garden
A102(M)
NEWHAM
Barking
BARKING & DAGENHAM
East Ham
TOWER HAMLETS
R. Thames
Poplar
Thamesmead
MPW
SOUTHWARK
Woolwich
Greenwich
Spread Eagle
GREENWICH
Thailand
Sun & Doves
Lewisham
LAMBETH
Thistells
Eltham
Dulwich
Catford
LEWISHAM
Sidcup
Crystal Palace
BROMLEY
Beckenham
Mantanah
BROMLEY
MAP 12
Restaurant
Restaurant with accommodation
Round-up entry
0 5km
0 4 miles
© Copyright

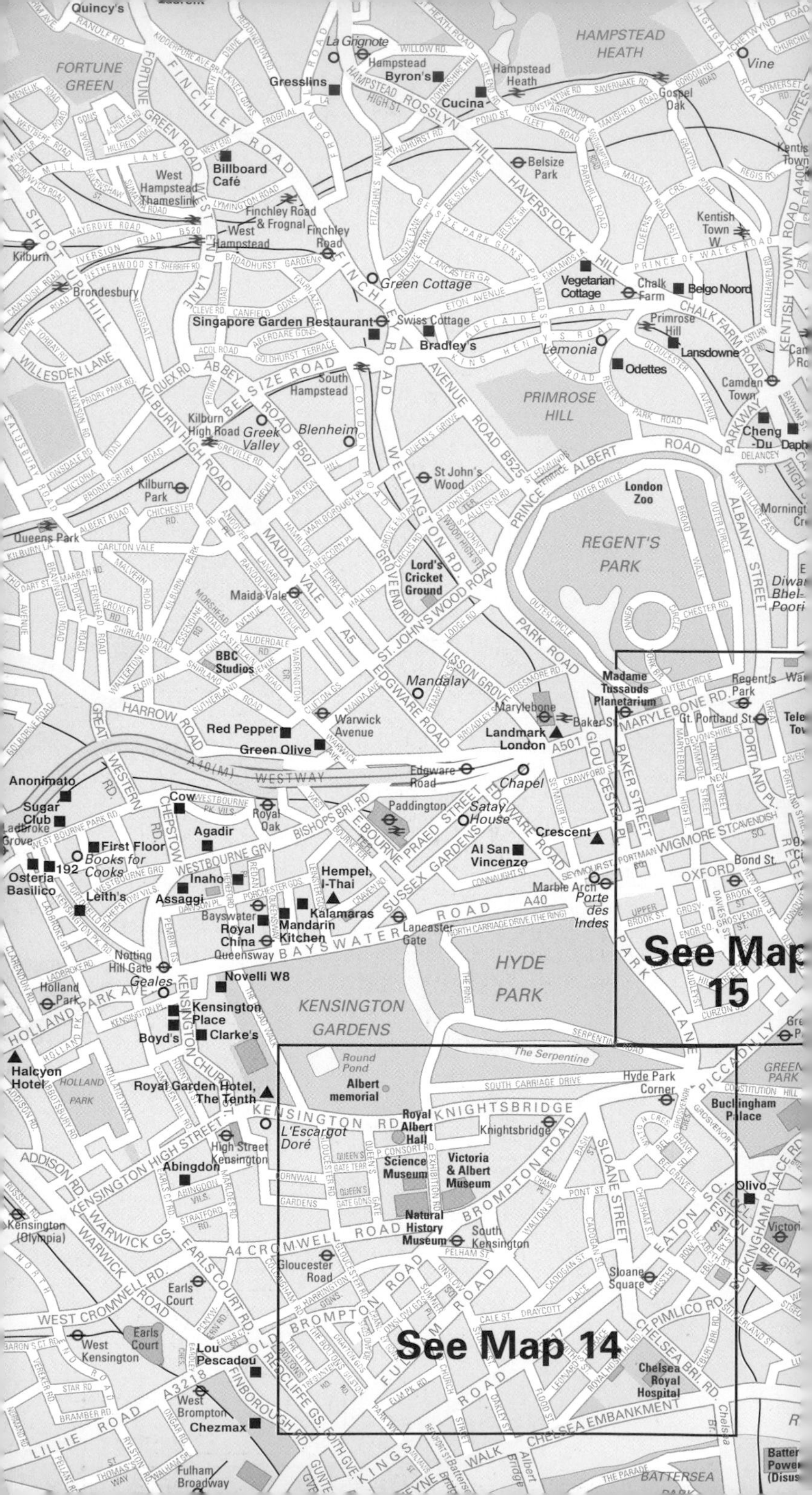

Quincy's
La Grignote
Hampstead
Byron's
Gresslins
Hampstead Heath
Cucina
HAMPSTEAD HEATH
Vine
Gospel Oak
FORTUNE GREEN
FINCHLEY ROAD
FORTUNE GREEN ROAD
Billboard Café
West Hampstead Thameslink
Finchley Road & Frognal
West Hampstead
Finchley Road
Belsize Park
HAVERSTOCK HILL
Kentish Town
Kentish Town W.
KENTISH TOWN ROAD
Kilburn
Brondesbury
Green Cottage
Vegetarian Cottage
Chalk Farm
Belgo Noord
CHALK FARM ROAD
Singapore Garden Restaurant
Swiss Cottage
Bradley's
Primrose Hill
Lansdowne
Lemonia
Odettes
WILLESDEN LANE
BELSIZE ROAD
South Hampstead
PRIMROSE HILL
Camden Town
PARKWAY
Cheng-Du
Kilburn High Road
Greek Valley
Blenheim
KILBURN HIGH ROAD
Kilburn Park
St John's Wood
PRINCE ALBERT ROAD
London Zoo
ALBANY STREET
Queens Park
REGENT'S PARK
MAIDA VALE
Lord's Cricket Ground
WELLINGTON RD.
AVENUE ROAD
ST. JOHN'S WOOD ROAD
Maida Vale
PARK ROAD
BBC Studios
Mandalay
EDGWARE ROAD
HARROW ROAD
Madame Tussauds Planetarium
Regent's Park
Marylebone
Baker St.
Landmark London
Great Portland St.
MARYLEBONE RD.
Red Pepper
Warwick Avenue
Green Olive
Anonimato
WESTWAY
Edgware Road
Chapel
Sugar Club
Cow
Royal Oak
Paddington
PRAED STREET
Satay House
BAKER STREET
PORTLAND PL.
Ladbroke Grove
Agadir
First Floor
Books for Cooks
Crescent
WIGMORE ST.
Osteria Basilico
192
WESTBOURNE GRV.
Al San Vincenzo
Bond St.
OXFORD
Leith's
Inaho
Assaggi
Hempel, I-Thai
Kalamaras
Bayswater
Royal China
Mandarin Kitchen
Marble Arch
Porte des Indes
Lancaster Gate
BAYSWATER ROAD
Queensway
Notting Hill Gate
Geales
Novelli W8
HYDE PARK
See Map 15
Holland Park
Kensington Place
KENSINGTON GARDENS
Boyd's
Clarke's
The Serpentine
Halcyon Hotel
HOLLAND PARK
Royal Garden Hotel, The Tenth
Round Pond
Albert memorial
Hyde Park Corner
GREEN PARK
Buckingham Palace
KENSINGTON RD.
KNIGHTSBRIDGE
Royal Albert Hall
Knightsbridge
L'Escargot Doré
PICCADILLY
High Street Kensington
Victoria & Albert Museum
Science Museum
KENSINGTON HIGH STREET
Abingdon
BROMPTON ROAD
SLOANE STREET
Olivo
Natural History Museum
South Kensington
Kensington (Olympia)
WARWICK GS.
CROMWELL ROAD
Gloucester Road
Victoria
Sloane Square
Earls Court
WEST CROMWELL RD.
PIMLICO RD.
Earls Court
West Kensington
See Map 14
Lou Pescadou
Chelsea Royal Hospital
West Brompton
CHELSEA EMBANKMENT
Chezmax
LILLIE ROAD
KINGS ROAD
Fulham Broadway
BATTERSEA
Battersea Power (Disus

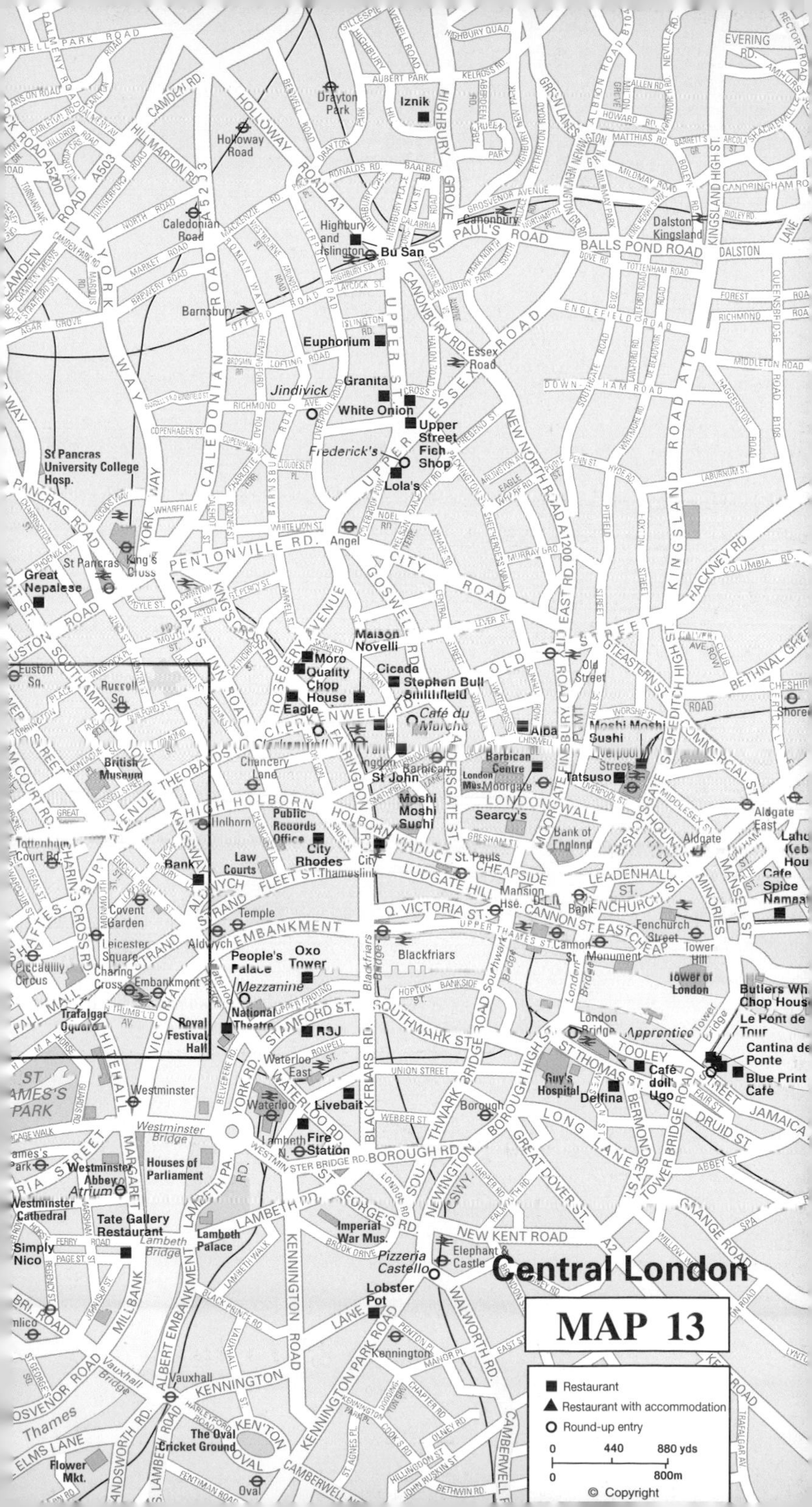
Central London
MAP 13
Restaurant
Restaurant with accommodation
Round-up entry
0 440 880 yds
0 800m
© Copyright
Iznik
Bu San
Euphorium
Granita
Jindivick
White Onion
Upper Street Fish Shop
Frederick's
Lola's
Great Nepalese
Maison Novelli
Moro
Quality Chop House
Cicada
Stephen Bull Smithfield
Eagle
Café du Marché
St John
Moshi Moshi Sushi
Alba
Tatsuso
Searcy's
City Rhodes
Bank
Oxo Tower
People's Palace
Mezzanine
RSJ
Livebait
Fire Station
Atrium
Tate Gallery Restaurant
Simply Nico
Pizzeria Castello
Lobster Pot
Apprentice
Café dell'Ugo
Delfina
Butlers Wharf Chop House
Le Pont de la Tour
Cantina del Ponte
Blue Print Café
Cafe Spice Namaste

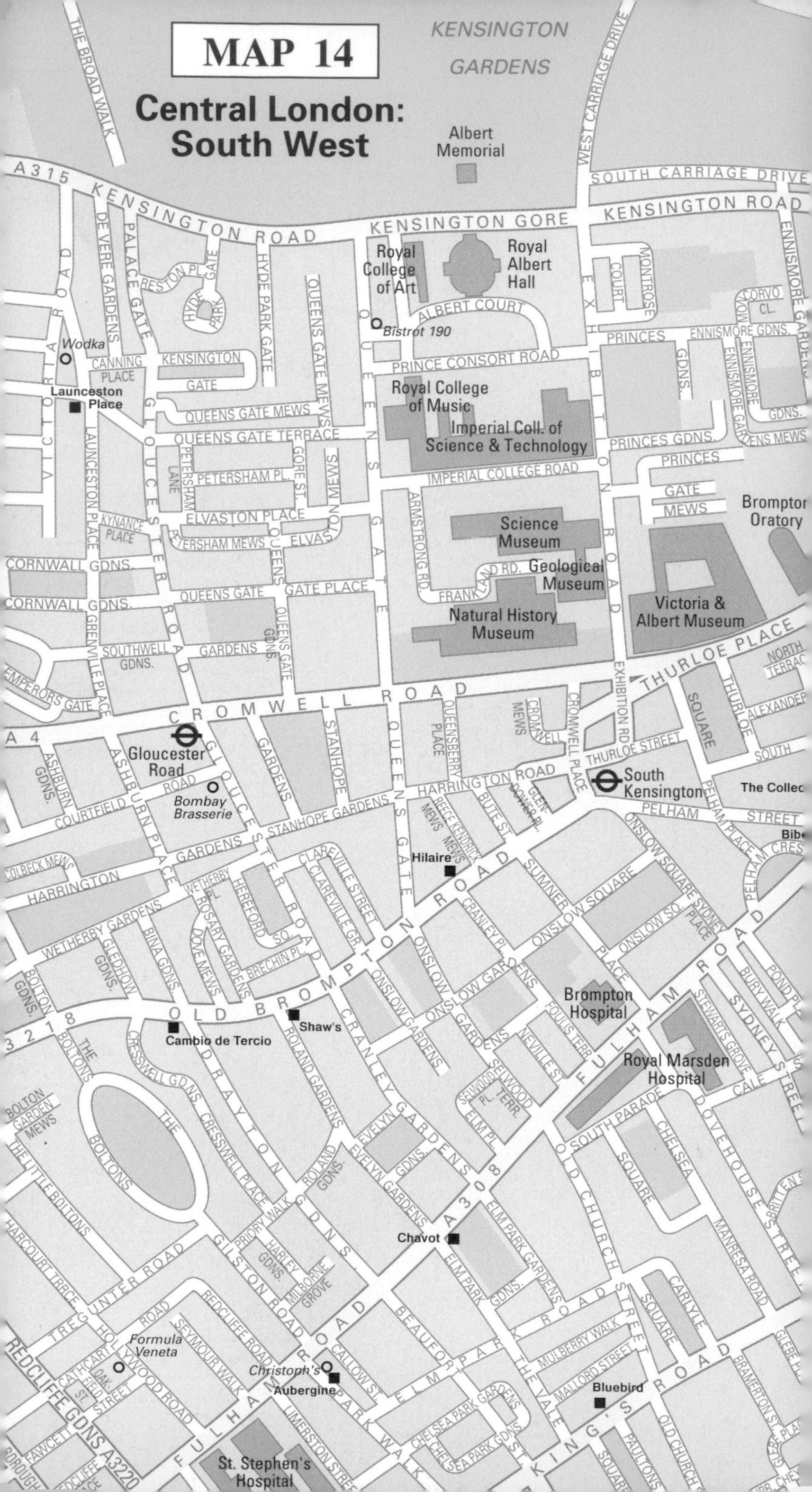
MAP 14
Central London: South West
KENSINGTON GARDENS
Albert Memorial
Royal College of Art
Royal Albert Hall
Bistrot 190
Wodka
Launceston Place
Royal College of Music
Imperial Coll. of Science & Technology
Science Museum
Geological Museum
Natural History Museum
Victoria & Albert Museum
Brompton Oratory
Gloucester Road
Bombay Brasserie
South Kensington
Hilaire
Brompton Hospital
Royal Marsden Hospital
Shaw's
Cambio de Tercio
Chavot
Formula Veneta
Christoph's
Aubergine
Bluebird
St. Stephen's Hospital
KENSINGTON ROAD
KENSINGTON GORE
CROMWELL ROAD
OLD BROMPTON ROAD
FULHAM ROAD
KING'S ROAD
QUEENS GATE
GLOUCESTER ROAD
EXHIBITION ROAD
PRINCE CONSORT ROAD
IMPERIAL COLLEGE ROAD
THURLOE PLACE
HARRINGTON ROAD
SOUTH CARRIAGE DRIVE
WEST CARRIAGE DRIVE

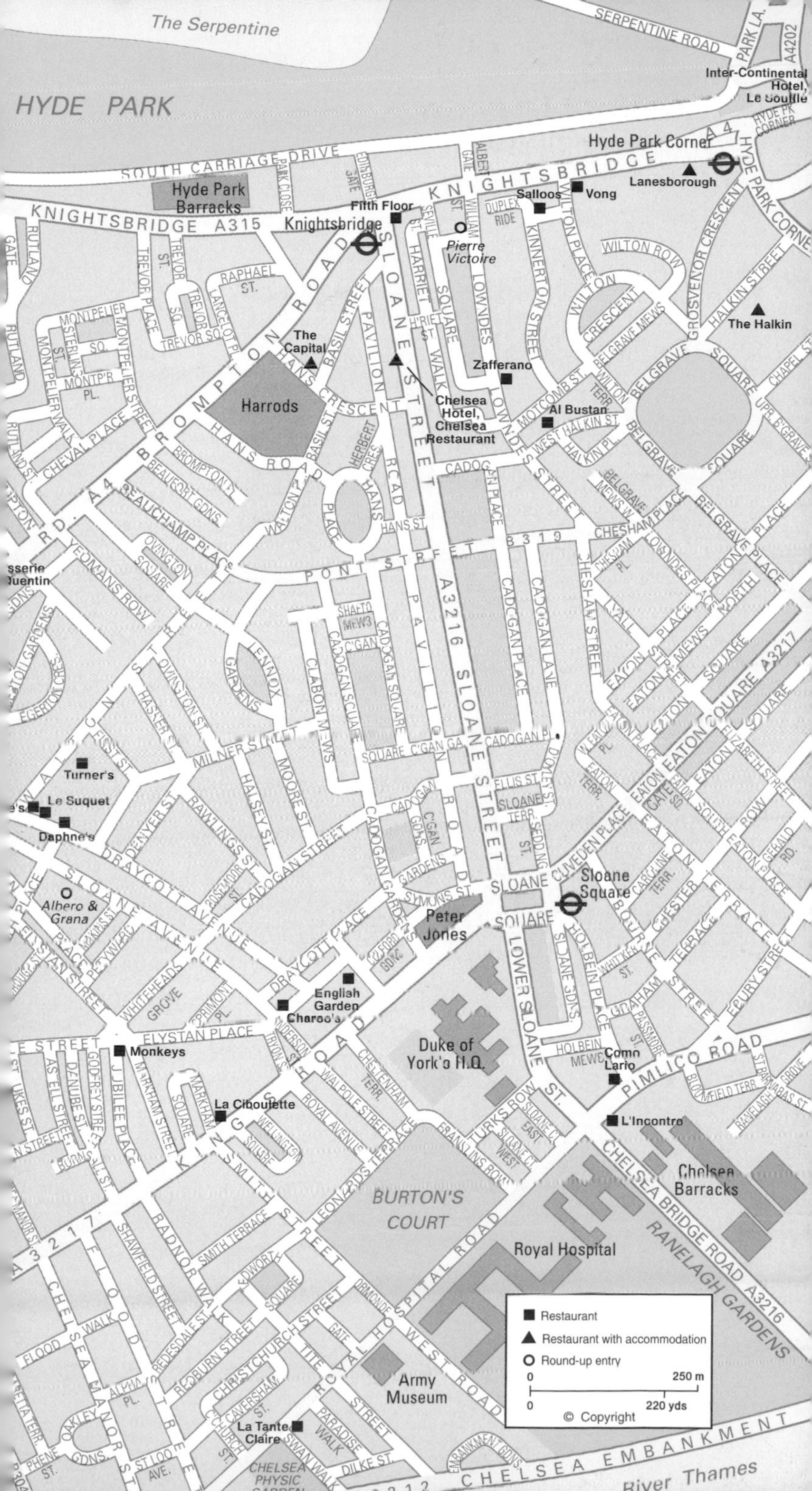

The Serpentine
HYDE PARK
SERPENTINE ROAD
PARK LA.
A4202
Inter-Continental Hotel, Le Soufflé
Hyde Park Corner
SOUTH CARRIAGE DRIVE
Hyde Park Barracks
KNIGHTSBRIDGE A315
KNIGHTSBRIDGE
Knightsbridge
Fifth Floor
Salloos
Vong
Lanesborough
Pierre Victoire
The Capital
Harrods
Chelsea Hotel, Chelsea Restaurant
Zafferano
Al Bustan
The Halkin
BROMPTON ROAD
SLOANE STREET
A3216
PONT STREET
B319
BELGRAVE SQUARE
EATON SQUARE
A3217
Turner's
Le Suquet
Daphne's
Albero & Grana
Sloane Square
Peter Jones
English Garden
Charco's
Monkeys
La Ciboulette
Duke of York's H.Q.
Como Lario
L'Incontro
Chelsea Barracks
PIMLICO ROAD
KING'S ROAD
BURTON'S COURT
Royal Hospital
ROYAL HOSPITAL ROAD
CHELSEA BRIDGE ROAD
RANELAGH GARDENS
Army Museum
La Tante Claire
CHELSEA PHYSIC GARDEN
CHELSEA EMBANKMENT
River Thames
Restaurant
Restaurant with accommodation
Round-up entry
0
250 m
0
220 yds
© Copyright

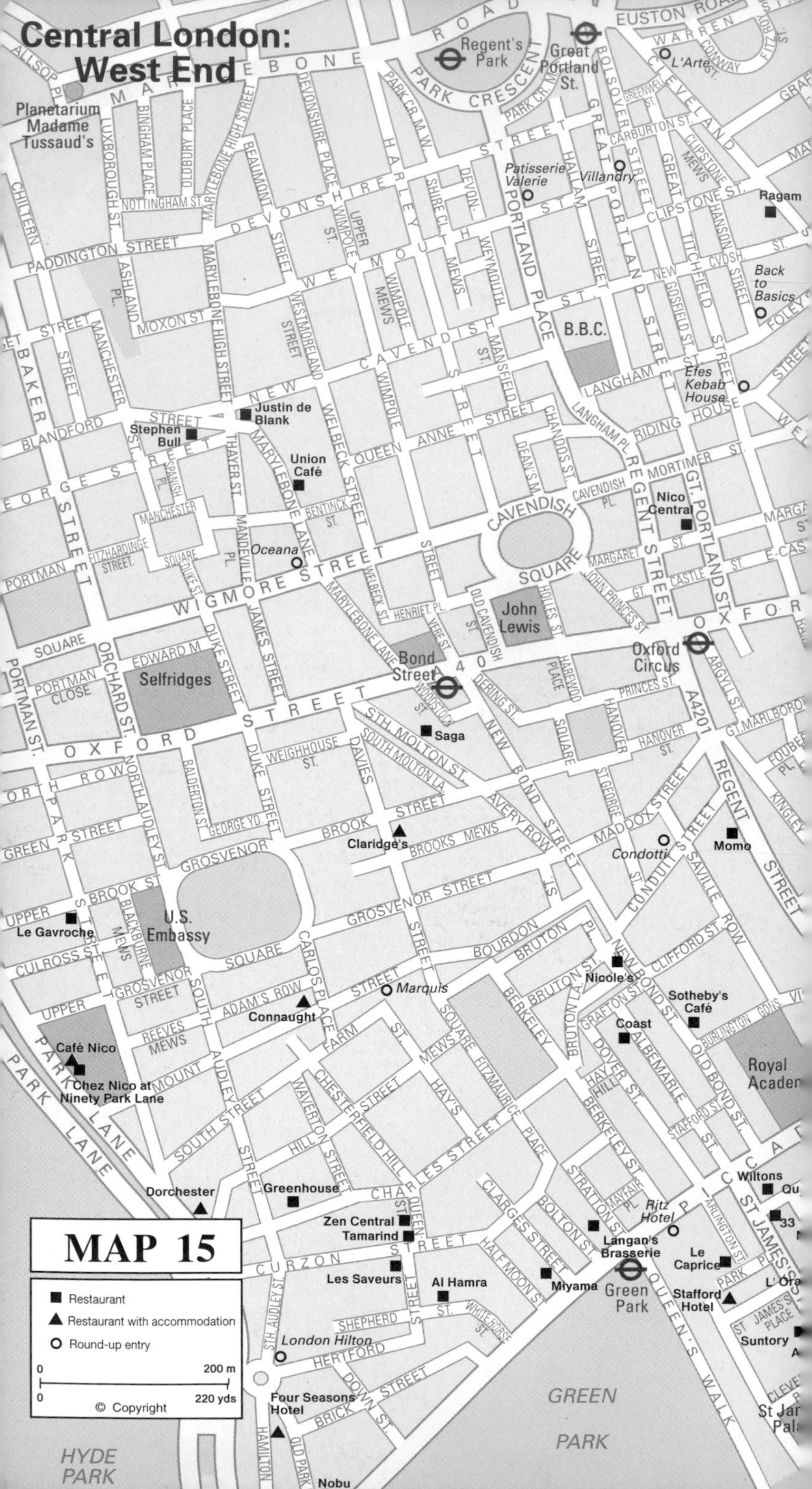

Central London: West End
MAP 15
Restaurant
Restaurant with accommodation
Round-up entry
0 200 m
0 220 yds
© Copyright
Planetarium
Madame Tussaud's
Regent's Park
Great Portland St.
L'Arte
Patisserie Valerie
Villandry
Ragam
Back to Basics
B.B.C.
Efes Kebab House
Justin de Blank
Stephen Bull
Union Café
Nico Central
Oceana
John Lewis
Oxford Circus
Bond Street
Selfridges
Saga
Claridge's
Condotti
Momo
Le Gavroche
U.S. Embassy
Nicole's
Marquis
Connaught
Sotheby's Café
Coast
Royal Academy
Café Nico
Chez Nico at Ninety Park Lane
Dorchester
Greenhouse
Zen Central
Tamarind
Les Saveurs
Al Hamra
Miyama
Langan's Brasserie
Ritz Hotel
Le Caprice
Wiltons
33
Stafford Hotel
Green Park
Suntory
London Hilton
Four Seasons Hotel
Nobu
HYDE PARK
GREEN PARK
OXFORD STREET
WIGMORE STREET
CAVENDISH SQUARE
REGENT STREET
PARK LANE
CURZON STREET
GROSVENOR SQUARE
BERKELEY SQUARE
NEW BOND STREET
BAKER STREET

Russell Square
National Childrens Hospital
University of London
British Museum
Goodge St.
Museum Street Café
Wagamama
Alfred
Tottenham Court Road
Pied-à-Terre
Bertorelli's
Chez Gérard
Interlude
Gay Hussar
Bistrot Soho
Au Jardin des Gourmets
Soho Soho
dell'Ugo
Vasco & Piero's Pavilion
Gopal's of Soho
Alastair Little
Mezzo
Bahn Thai
Sri Siam
Andrew Edmunds
French House Dining Room
Randall & Aubin
New World
Atelier
Gabriel
Melati
Golden Dragon
Poons
Mr. Kong
Fung Shing
Chuen Cheng Ku
Manzi's
Chung's
Atlantic Bar and Grill
Trocadero
Misato
Cork & Bottle
Leicester Square
Rentys
Piccadilly Circus
Criterion
Café Fish
Le Meridien, Oak Room Marco Pierre White
Mitsukoshi
Mon Plaisir
Neal Street Restaurant
Belgo Centraal
Poetry Society
Magno's
Bertorelli's
Covent Garden
COVENT GARDEN
Le Palais du Jardin
Ivy
Tokyo Diner
Saint
Stephen Bull
L'Estaminet
Sofra
Orso
Rules
Savoy
National Portrait Gallery
TRAFALGAR SQUARE
Nelson's Column
Charing Cross
Charing Cross Station
Embankment
Admiralty Arch
Ministry of Defence
Horse Guards Parade
Banqueting House
Marlborough House
ST JAMES'S PARK
River Thames
Square
GOWER ST.
BLOOMSBURY STREET
TOTTENHAM COURT ROAD A400
NEW OXFORD ST.
HIGH HOLBORN
ST GILES HIGH ST.
CHARING CROSS ROAD
SHAFTESBURY AVENUE
OLD COMPTON ST.
HAYMARKET A4
REGENT ST.
PALL MALL
PALL MALL EAST
COCKSPUR ST.
WHITEHALL A3212
THE STRAND
VICTORIA EMBANKMENT
NORTHUMBERLAND AV.
ST MARTINS LANE
LONG ACRE
SOUTHAMPTON ROW
RUSSELL SQUARE
BEDFORD SQUARE
GREAT RUSSELL STREET
THE MALL

MAP 16

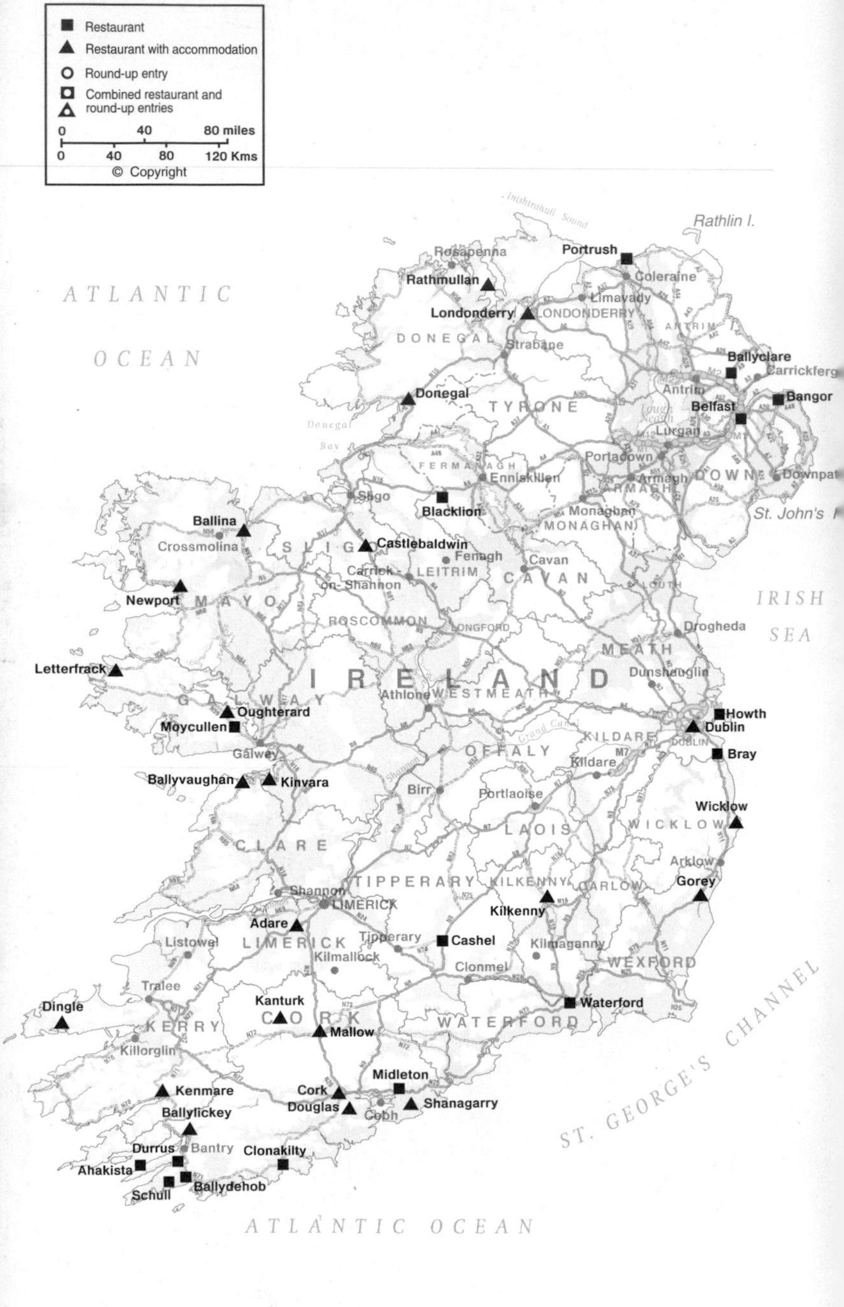

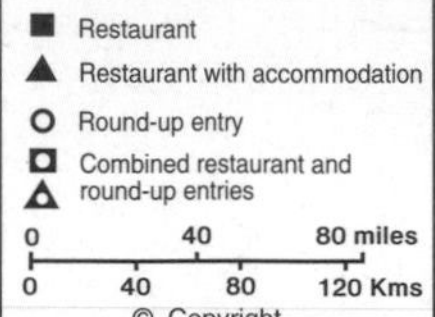

ATLANTIC OCEAN
Rathlin I.
Portrush
Rosapenna
Coleraine
Rathmullan
Limavady
Londonderry
LONDONDERRY
ANTRIM
DONEGAL
Strabane
Ballyclare
Carrickferg
Antrim
Donegal
TYRONE
Belfast
Bangor
Donegal Bay
Lurgan
Portadown
FERMANAGH
Enniskillen
Armagh
DOWN
Downpat
ARMAGH
Sligo
Blacklion
Monaghan
St. John's
Ballina
MONAGHAN
Crossmolina
SLIGO
Castlebaldwin
Fenagh
Carrick-on-Shannon
LEITRIM
Cavan
CAVAN
Newport
MAYO
LOUTH
IRISH SEA
ROSCOMMON
LONGFORD
Drogheda
MEATH
Letterfrack
IRELAND
Dunshaughlin
Athlone
WESTMEATH
GALWAY
Oughterard
Howth
Moycullen
Dublin
KILDARE
DUBLIN
Galway
OFFALY
Bray
Kildare
Ballyvaughan
Kinvara
Birr
Portlaoise
Wicklow
LAOIS
WICKLOW
CLARE
Arklow
TIPPERARY
KILKENNY
CARLOW
Gorey
Shannon
LIMERICK
Kilkenny
Adare
Tipperary
Cashel
Listowel
LIMERICK
Kilmaganny
Kilmallock
WEXFORD
Clonmel
Tralee
Kanturk
Waterford
Dingle
CORK
KERRY
Mallow
WATERFORD
ST. GEORGE'S CHANNEL
Killorglin
Midleton
Kenmare
Cork
Shanagarry
Douglas
Cobh
Ballylickey
Durrus
Bantry
Clonakilty
Ahakista
Schull
Ballydehob
ATLANTIC OCEAN